HUXFORD'S

OLD BOOK

VALUE GUIDE

**25,000 Listings of Old Books
with Current Values**

Thirteenth
Edition

COLLECTOR BOOKS

A Division of Schroeder Publishing Co., Inc.

The current values of this book should be used only as a guide. They are not intended to set prices, which vary from one section of the country to another. Auction prices as well as dealer prices vary and are affected by condition as well as demand. Neither the editor nor the publisher assumes responsibility for any losses that might be incurred as a result of consulting this guide.

On the Cover:

BLOND, Georges. *Beaver Valley,* Walt Disney's True Life Adventure. nd. NY. Simon & Schuster. 83p. pict bds. 4to. F. A8. $60.00

CABLE, George W. *Old Creole Days.* 1906. NY. Scribner. ils Albert Herter, photo gravures. lt green, gold decor cloth, teg. 8vo. 234 p. VG. A8. $40.00

ERSKINE, John. *Uncle Sam in the Eyes of His Family.* 1930. Bobbs Merrill. ltd 238/356. 8vo. 351 p. red cloth, gilt. teg. untrimmed. orig slipcase. F/NF. A8. $100.00

RAYNE, M.L. *Gems of Deportment.* Chicago. Tyler & Co. 414 p. ils. 8vo. brn cloth, embossed decor, slight wear. VG. A8. $40.00

VIERECK and ELDRIDGE. *My First Two Thousand Years.* 1929. NY. Macaulay. 8vo. 501 p. 1st. 12th ptg. missing fep. no dj. G. A8. $17.00

Books featured on cover courtesy of
AL-PAC
Lamar Kelley, Antiquarian Books
2625 E. Southern Ave., C-120
Tempe, AZ 85282
480-831-3121
fax 480-831-3193
alpac2625@aol.com

Please address all correspondence to:
Lisa Stroup, Editor
P.O. Box 9471
Paducah, KY 42002-9471
To become a part of our next edition, see page 397 for information.

Editor: Lisa Stroup
Cover Design: Beth Summers
Book Design: Holly C. Long

Searching for a Publisher?

We are always looking for people knowledgeable within their fields. If you feel there is a real need for a book on your collectible subject and have a large comprehensive collection, contact Collector Books.

COLLECTOR BOOKS
P.O. Box 3009
Paducah, KY 42002-3009

www.collectorbooks.com

Copyright © 2001 by Schroeder Publishing

Contents

Acknowledgments

I have only recently learned that the challenge in life is how to handle the rough spots with ease and dignity. Every experience takes you down a certain path, making you a whole person; luckily, many good people have crossed my path.

It takes a lot of people working together to make this book happen. I would especially like to thank the staff at Collector Books — Gail Ashburn, Holly Long, Laurie Swick, and Beth Summers. I owe a tremendous debt of thanks to Gail for her friendship and daily encouragement over the last few years. I am indeed fortunate enough to spend my working hours with friends.

Thanks to family for their support. To my father especially, for his sweet spirit and gentle guidance through every day of my life. To Palmer, for allowing me the time to work and complete so many projects. I love you so much. All I do, I do for you.

Special thanks to my friend, Lamar Kelley, who so unselfishly loaned his books for use in our cover photo and to Robert F. Lucas, who generously contributed articles to this 13th edition.

And finally, this book could never have been published without the encouragement of Bill Schroeder and Billy Schroeder. Your presence in my life has been more meaningful than you can ever imagine or I can ever express.

I would also like to take this opportunity to express our sincere gratitude and appreciation to each business who has contributed their time and knowledge to assist us in producing this new edition. We believe the credibility of our book is greatly enhanced through their efforts. Please see the codes in the Booksellers directory in the back of this book for their complete addresses and contact information. The Bookbuyers directory gives information concerning their specific genre interests.

A Tale of Two Sisters (A24)
A-Book-A-Brac Shop (A1)
Aard Books (A2)
Noreen Abbot Books (A3)
About Books (A4)
Ackley Books & Collectibles (A28)
Adelson Sports (A5)
AL-PAC, Lamar Kelley (A8)
American Botanist (A10)
An Uncommon Vision (A25)
Antiquarian Medical Books (A13)
Aplan Antiques & Art (A19)
David Armstrong, Bookseller (A26)
Aslan Books (A27)
Authors of the West (A18)
Avonlea Books Search Service (A7)
Beasley Books (B2)
Bella Luna Books (B3)
Between the Covers (B4)
Bicentennial Book Shop(B5)
Book & Tackle Shop (B14)
Book Treasures (B15)
Books Now & Then(B29)
Bromer Booksellers (B24)
Brooks Books (B26)
Chapel Hill Rare Books (C6)
Children's Book Adoption Agency (C8)
Steven Cieluch (C14)
Tom Davidson, Bookseller (D10)

Ursula Davidson (D1)
L. Clarice Davis (D2)
Dawson's Book Shop (D11)
Carol Docheff, Bookseller (D4)
Drusilla's Books (D6)
Eastside Books & Paper (E6)
Elder's Book Store (E4)
First Folio (F1)
Five Quail Books — West (F7)
Flo Silver Books (F3)
Fostoria Trading Post (F6)
John Gach Fine & Rare Books (G1)
Galerie De Boicourt
   Eva W. Boicourt (G2)
Grave Matters (G8)
Henry F. Hain III (H1)
Ken Hebenstreit, Bookseller (H11)
Susan Heller, Pages for Sages (H4)
Heritage Book Shop, Inc. (H5)
Jordan Gallery (J2)
Kenneth Karimole (K1)
Knollwood Books (K5)
Ken Lopez, Bookseller (L3)
Melvin Marcher, Bookseller (M4)
Paul Melzer Fine & Rare Books (M9)
Meyer Boswell Books, Inc. (M11)
Mordida Books (M15)
My Bookhouse (M20)
Brian McMillan, Books (M21)

McGee's First Varieties (M23)
Monroe Stahr Books (M25)
Nerman's Books (N1)
Norris Books (N4)
Nutmeg Books (N2)
Oak Knoll Books (O10)
October Farm (O3)
David L. O'Neal (O1)
Orpheus Books (O11)
K.C. & Jean C. Owings (O8)
Pacific Rim Books (P1)
Pandora's Books (P3)
R. Papinger, Baseball Books (P8)
Parmer Books (P4)
Parnassus Books (P5)
Kathleen Rais & Co. (R2)
Randall House, Pia Oliver (R3)
Jo Ann Reisler, Ltd. (R5)
Bill & Mimi Sachen (S1)
Stanley Schwartz (S3)
Second Harvest Books (S14)
Ellen Serxner (S13)
Snowy Egret Books (S15)
Thomas Books (T2)
Thorn Books (T10)
VERSEtility Books (V1)
Yesterday's Books (Y1)

Listing of Standard Abbreviations

#d . . . . .numbered
12mo . . . . .about 7" tall
16mo . . . . .6" to 7" tall
1st thus . . . .not 1st edition, but rather the 1st published
  in this particular format
24mo . . . . .5" to 6" tall
32mo . . . . .4" to 5" tall
48mo .less than 4" tall
4to .between 11" to 13" tall
64mo . . . . .about 3" tall
8vo . . . . .8" to 9" tall
aeg . . . . .all edge gilt
aka . . . . .also known as
ALS . . . . .autographed letter, signed
Am . . . . .American
AN . . . . .as new
AP . . . . . . .proof, advance proof, advance uncorrected
  proof, or galley
APVA Association for the Preservation of Virginia Antiquities
ARC . . . . advance reading or review copy
atlas folio . . . . .25"
b&w . . . . .black & white
BC, BCE . . . . .any book club edition
bdg . . . . .binding, bound
bds . . . . .boards
bfep . . . . .back free endpaper
bkplt . . . . .bookplate
bl . . . . .blue
blk . . . . .black
BOMC . . . . .Book of the Month Club
brd . . . . .boards
brn . . . . .brown, browning
bstp . . . . .blindstamp
c . . . . .copyright
ca . . . . .circa
cb . . . . .cardboard
cbdg . . . . .comb binding
chip . . . . .chipped
clip . . . . .clipped price
CMG . . . . .Coward McCann Geoghegan
dbl . . . . .double
decor . . . . .decoration, decorated
DIF . . . . .Donald I. Fine
dj . . . . .dust jacket
dk . . . . .dark
double elephant folio . . . . .larger than 25"
DSP . . . . .Duell Sloan Pearce
dtd . . . . .dated
E . . . . .east, eastern
ed . . . . .edition
edit . . . . .editor
elephant folio . . . . .23" or larger
emb .embossed, embossing
Eng .England, English

ep .end pages, endpapers
ERB . . . . .Edgar Rice Burroughs Inc.
ES . . . . .errata slip
ex lib . . . . .ex library copy
F . . . . .fine
facs . . . . .facsimile
fep . . . . .free endpaper
ffep .front free endpaper
fld . . . . .folding, folder
folio . . . . .13" or larger
fox . . . . .foxing, foxed
FSC . . . . .Farrar, Straus & Cudahy
FSG . . . . .Farrar, Straus & Giroux
FSY . . . . .Farrar, Straus & Young
ftspc . . . . .frontispiece
fwd . . . . .foreword
G . . . . .good
GPO . . . . .Government Printing Office
gr . . . . .green
gte . . . . .gilt top edge
HBJ . . . . .Harcourt Brace Jovanovich, Inc.
HBW . . . . .Harcourt Brace World
hc, hb . . . . .hard cover
hist . . . . .history
HRW . . . . .Holt Rinehart Winston
ils . . . . .illustrations, illustrated
imp . . . . .imprint, impression
inscr . . . . .inscribed
Inst . . . . .Institute
Internat .International
intl . . . . .initialed
intro . . . . .introduction
LEC . . . . .Limited Edition Club
lg . . . . .large
Lib . . . . .library
lt . . . . .light
ltd . . . . .limited
mc . . . . .multicolor
mfep . . . . .missing free endpaper
mini . . . . .miniature book
MIT . . . . .MA Institute of Technology
MOMA . . . . .Museum of Modern Art
mtd . . . . .mounted
MTI . . . . .movie tie-in
Mus . . . . .museum
N . . . . .north, northern
NAL . . . . .New American Library
Nat . . . . .national
nd . . . . .no date
ne . . . . .no edition given
NEL . . . . .New English Library
NF . . . . .near fine
NGS . . . . .National Geographic Society
np . . . . no place given, no publisher stated
NYGS . . . . .New York Graphic Society

obl	oblong
orig	original
OUP	Oxford University Press
o/w	otherwise
pb	paperback
pbo	paperback original
pc	piece
pict	pictorial
pl	plate, plates
poi	previous owner's inscription
p, pg	page, pages
Pr	press
pref	preface
pres	presentation
promo	promotion
prt	print, printing
ps	postscript
pub	publisher, publishing
rb	rebound
rem mk	remainder mark
repro	reproduction
rev	revised
rpl	replaced
rpr	repair
rpt	reprint
RS	review slip
rstr	restored
S	south, southern
S&S	Simon & Schuster
sans	none issued
sbdg	spiral binding
sc	softcover

SF	San Francisco, science fiction
sgn	signature, signed
slip	slip case or publisher's slip which is an inserted piece of paper — either promotional material or errata sheet
sltly	slightly
sm	small
sm 4to	about 10" tall, quarto
sm 8vo	7½" to 8" tall
soc.	society
sq	square
stp	stamp, stamped
supp	supplement
swrp	shrink wrap
TB	textbook
teg	top edge gilt
thus	see 1st thus
TLS	typed letter signed
trans	translated
TVTI	TV tie-in
U	University
unp	unpaged
UP	uncorrected proof
VG	very good
vol	volume
W	west, western
w/	with, indicates laid in material
wht	white
wrp	wrappers
xl	ex-library
yel	yellow

Books are keys to wisdom's treasure:
Books are gates to lands of pleasure:
Books are paths that upward lead:
Books are friends. Come, let us read.

Emilie Poulson
1835 – 1939

Introduction

This book has been compiled to help both buyers and sellers. Two questions that we are asked most frequently are "Can you tell me the value of my books?" and "Where can I sell them?" *Huxford's Old Book Value Guide* can answer both of these questions. Not only does this book place secondary market retail values (values that an interested party would be willing to pay to obtain possession of the book) on more than 25,000 old books, it also lists scores of buyers along with the type of material each is interested in purchasing. These prices are taken from dealers' selling lists that have been issued within the past year. Every listing is coded (A1, S7, etc.) before the price. This coding refers to a specific dealer's listing for that book. Their codes will be listed in the description line. Please refer to the section in the back of this book titled "Booksellers" for codes.

If you were to sell your books to a dealer, you should expect to receive no more than 50% of the values listed in this book, unless the dealer has a specific buyer in mind for some of your material. In many cases, a dealer will pay less than 50% of retail for a book to stock.

Do not ask a dealer to evaluate your old books unless you intend to sell them to him. Most antiquarian book dealers will appraise your books and ephemera for a fee that ranges from a low of $10.00 per hour to $50.00 per hour (or more). If you have an extensive library of rare books, the $50.00-an-hour figure would be money well spent (assuming, of course, the appraiser to be qualified and honest).

Unlike other price guides on the market which focus on the rare and very valuable books that many collectors will rarely encounter, *Huxford's Old Book Value Guide* places values on the more common holdings that many seem to accumulate. You will notice that the majority of the books listed are in the $10.00 to $50.00 range.

The format is very simple: listings are alphabetized first by the name of the author, translator, editor, or illustrator; if more than one book is listed for a particular author, each title is listed alphabetically under his or her name. When pseudonyms are known, names have been cross-referenced. (Please also see the section titled "Pseudonyms" for additional information.) Dust jackets or wrappers are noted when present, and sizes (when given) are approximate. Condition is usually noted as well. (If condition is not stated, it is assumed to be very good.) Dates within parentheses indicate the copyright page dates while dates without parentheses are dates found on the title pages and/or are the actual publication dates.

Fine condition refers to books that are in perfect, as-issued condition with no defects. Books in near-fine condition are perfect, but not as crisp as those graded fine. Near-fine condition books show only a little wear from reading (such as very small marks on binding), but they still have no major defects. Books rated very good may show wear but must have no tears on pages, binding, or dust jacket (if issued). A rating of good applies to an average used book that has all of its pages and yet may have small tears and other defects. The term reading copy (some dealers also use "poor") describes a book having major defects; however, its text must be complete. Ex-library books are always indicated as such; they may be found in any condition. This rule also applies to any book club edition. Some of our booksellers indicate intermediate grades with a + or ++, or VG-EX. We have endeavored to use the grade that best corresponded to the description of condition as given in each dealer's listing. If you want to check further on the condition of a specific book, please consult the bookseller indicated. Please note that the condition stated in the description is often for the book and then the dust jacket. (Dust jackets on many modern first editions may account for up to 80% of their value.)

In the back of the book we have listed buyers of books and book-related material. When you correspond with these dealers, be sure to enclose a self-addressed, stamped envelope if you want a reply. Please do not send lists of books for an appraisal. If you wish to sell your books, quote the price that you want or negotiate the price only on the items the buyer is interested in purchasing. When you list your books, do so by author, full title, publisher and place, date, and edition. Indicate condition, noting any defects on cover or contents.

When shipping your books, first wrap each book in paper such as brown kraft or a similar type of material. Never use newspaper for the inner wrap, since newsprint tends to rub off. (It may, however be used as a cushioning material within the outer carton.) Place your books in a sturdy corrugated box and use a good shipping tape to seal it. Tape reinforced with nylon string is preferable, as it will not tear. Books shipped by parcel post may be sent at a special fourth class book rate, which may be lower than regular parcel post zone rates.

> The following essays were contributed by Robert F. Lucas of Lucas Books. This basic information is intended to give an overview of the field to those just beginning the exciting hobby of book collecting.

Starting a Collection

You may have already started collecting books, but if you haven't, we have a few suggestions about collecting and we will even provide a few interesting topics/areas for you to consider.

Here are a few "suggestions" for successful book collecting.
- Collect an author or a subject that you enjoy
- Collect an author or a subject which is challenging
- Avoid collecting the most popular authors or subjects (unless favorites of yours)
- Collect within your means — do not try to collect very expensive books if you are on a limited budget
- Spend time learning which references/bibliographies pertain to your collecting area
- Purchase the reference tools appropriate to your collection and use them
- Do not collect primarily for monetary gain
- Learn the cornerstone or key items for which you should be searching
- Pay close attention to the condition of items for your collection
- When collecting books, also consider collecting related ephemera
- Experience various methods of purchasing books available to you — mail order catalogs, online catalogs, local bookshops, flea markets, etc.
- Learn which booksellers, ephemera dealers, antique dealers et al specialize in buying and selling items in your collecting area(s)
- Develop expertise in your chosen collecting area(s)
- Share your collection and knowledge of the area with others with similar interests
- Be determined to form the best possible collection within your means
- Most important — enjoy your collecting pursuits

It is difficult, if not impossible, and perhaps a little presumptuous and pompous, to suggest collecting areas for new book collectors to consider, but ... here are a few possibilities!

Authors

Instead of collecting the first editions of your favorite author (which is a great idea), start a collection of books and autographs and ephemera that relate to the family, friends, and acquaintances of the author — this is probably best done relative to a deceased author rather than a living author! Such a collection would be biographical/historical relative to the life of the author, i.e. books about the author's friends will probably contain many references and anecdotes about the author. This type of collection actually is a good companion to the collection of the works of the author.

If the author you have chosen to collect is very popular and the value of many first editions are sky-high, you could collect early printings (second or third printings) of the books which are expensive in the first printing or you could (in many instances) collect the same author's first printings in periodicals. Usually most such printings are less expensive than first printings of books and also somewhat difficult and challenging to find.

You could make a list of authors you consider important for various reasons and then attempt to collect the first appearance in print of each of the authors. This would be a very challenging collecting area, because many authors appear first in print in obscure high school yearbooks, small town newspapers, college literary magazines, and other obscure publications.

Books in Established Lists or Catalogs

Some collectors like to have a relatively finite goal and an established list of books for which to search. You could choose this collecting route and attempt to find as many items in a particular catalog or bibliography as possible. Some suggested "lists" are:

Carter, John & Percy H. Muir (editors). Printing and the Mind of Man. A Descriptive Catalogue Illustrating the Impact of Print on the Evolution of Western Civilization during Five Centuries. (London, Cassell & Company, 1967). Begun as an exhibit at the IPEX Exhibition of 1963 (International Printing Machinery and Allied Trades Exhibition) this catalog presents 424 of the most important books & other printings in the history of Western Civilization. Many of these works are so rare as to be essentially unobtainable, but others are available — other collectors have attempted to find as many of these works as possible — it is a lofty challenge.

(Grolier Club) One Hundred Influencial American Books Printed before 1900...Exhibition at The Grolier Club 1946. New York, The Grolier Club, 1947. Contains literary, political, historical, scientific, and other books considered to be influential. Many titles are rare and desirable and somewhat difficult to obtain — another major challenge.

Parsons, Nicholas. The Book of Literary Lists. A Collection of Annotated Lists, Statistics, and Anecdotes Concerning Books. New York, Facts on File Publications (1987). Many lists from which to choose — although some are as short as six books — include "The hundred books that most influenced Henry Miller," "The most popular fiction in Britain 1578 – 1930," "U.S. bestsellers 1895 – 1975," "Fifty works of English and American Literature we could do without," "Famous Banned Authors," etc.

Books Shunned by Other Collectors

If you consider yourself to be a contrarian and wish to pursue a collecting area in that light, you could consider collecting in one of the following areas:

Book of the Month Club editions — These and many other book club editions are printed in large quantities, usually on inexpensive, poor quality paper and bound in inexpensive bindings. For these reasons most collectors avoid the BOMC editions. You should have no trouble (in the US) finding BOMC books. You could easily wait for fine copies with fine dust jackets rather than add good or very good copies to your collection. The books would be very inexpensive and many of them classics. The collection may never have a high value in a monetary sense, but who knows?

Textbooks — Even relatively early textbooks from the 1830s to the 1900s are usually in very worn, abused condition and relatively available, until you start looking for them. You could limit your collection to nineteenth century math texts or English texts or spelling books or history texts, etc. Most textbooks are available at very reasonable prices because of the lack of general demand.

Bibles — The Bible is probably the most common book in America. It certainly was during the nineteenth century; virtually every Christian family household had a Bible, even if there were no other books in the house. The supply should be there and the demand is relatively low, thus the prices are very reasonable for most common Bibles. You could make the collection very challenging by collecting the first Bible printed/published in each major city and town in your country or state or region.

Telephone directories — Few collectors look for telephone directories and since most old directories were disposed of when a newer directory was issued, this could be a challenging area. You could make it even more interesting by determining when the first public telephones were used in your state or country and collect telephone directories from the first decade of use; they are probably very scarce or rare.

If you have a lot of shelf space for your book collection, you could collect encyclopedia sets. In general, booksellers find that there is not much of a market for old encyclopedias unless they concern a narrow subject area such as medicine, aeronautics, etc. You should be able to gather a mass of encyclopedias in short order.

Collecting Imprints by Specific Printers & Publishers

There are many very good bibliographies available which provide details on books from specific publishers, books printed in specific cities or towns, and books printed by specific printers. If there were printers present in your home town and enough books and pamphlets were printed, you could collect imprints from your "old stomping grounds."

The first items printed in each of the fifty states in the U.S. — A reference has been published which would be an excellent guide for such a collection: Thienens, Roger J. Pioneer Imprints from Fifty States. Washington, Library of Congress, 1971. Most of these items would be difficult to obtain and many would be expensive, but they would make a great collection.

There are many very good bibliographies listing local imprints. You could pick an interesting town or city and attempt to collect as many items listed in the bibliography as possible. One such example is McKeon, Newton Felch and Katharine Conover Cowles. Amherst, Massachusetts, Imprints 1825 – 1876. Amherst, Amherst College, 1946. There were more than 700 books, pamphlets, etc. printed in Amherst during this time span.

Another possible collection could be developed by searching for books published by a specific publishing house. An example is the high quality productions from the 1890s by Copeland & Day; the bibliography is Kraus, Joe W. Messrs. Copeland & Day 69 Cornhill, Boston 1893 – 1899. Philadelphia, George S. MacManus Co., 1979. This bibliography describes 108 publications.

In summary, there are so many different subject areas in which to collect books, you should have no problem finding a niche to fit your interests. Collect books that interest you and enjoy the hunt or search for items to add to your collection. Don't forget the importance of references — read as much as you can about your chosen collecting area. And if you haven't started collecting yet — it is time to get your feet wet!

Condition and Its Importance

"Condition is important to book collectors" is probably an understatement! When considering the addition of a book to your collection — you must consider condition of the book. A good adage to follow would be to "always choose the best condition copy that you can afford" with two important "ifs": if the copy is reasonably priced and if you cannot expect to find a better copy, then you must decide whether to settle for a copy in lesser condition.

If you decide to settle for a volume in less than desirable condition, it is normally with the hopes of upgrading when you have the opportunity to purchase a better copy. This is a personal decision; some collectors would prefer to not have a book in their collection if the condition does not meet their standards, and other collectors prefer to have a copy of the book even in lesser condition because they believe that it may be a long time before they have an opportunity to locate a very good or fine copy.

What constitutes a very good copy or a fine copy? Defining catagories of condition is a subjective business and applying the categories to rate a specific book is even more subjective. Over the years there have been attempts to establish what one might call a "uniform code" of definitions of condition which would be acceptable to all. However, due to the subjective nature such categories or ratings have been applied with considerable variation by very new booksellers versus those in the business for decades, by collectors of modern first editions versus collectors of local histories and genealogies, by a knowledgeable collector offering duplicates for sale versus someone who found a carton of dusty books in the attic — it is possible to define categories of condition, but difficult and really impossible to enforce a standard application of the categories.

Probably the best avenue to follow when describing the condition of a book is to list all of the obvious problems, defects, and signs of wear, and also to provide your impression of the overall condition. When reading book descriptions one should pay attention to the listed details of condition and to regard an overall condition term such as "good," "very good," or "fine" as the general impression of the bookseller, which may or may not coincide with your general impression of the same volume.

Often you may find the volume to be in better condition than you expected, other times in lesser condition. Virtually all booksellers want you to be pleased with the book(s) you purchase and hope that you remain a customer and for that reason prefer that you return the book(s) for a refund if you are not happy with the condition.

Most of us have seen descriptions of book condition which read like "scattered foxing, rubbing at corners and extremities of spine, weak hinge, otherwise very good condition" or "dust jacket with minor chips, rear free endpaper lacking, signature on title page but really much better con-

dition than it sounds." If you don't want a book with a weak hinge or a book with a missing endpaper, do not order the book. If the book is one for which you have been searching for ten years and this may be your only chance to purchase it, you probably should tolerate the damaged hinge or missing end paper. It is a personal decision.

Traditionally, book condition relates to the age of the book. A fine copy of a 1980 modern first edition is expected to be near perfect versus a fine copy of an 1840 traveler's guide to the western United States which will have very minor wear or perhaps very minor foxing or very minor soil or very minor rubbing on the covers — minor blemishes due to the expected handling of the book for approximately 160 years.

Some types of books are much more difficult to find in fine condition — those that normally receive considerable usage as opposed to being read once or a few times — cookbooks and children's books come to mind. If you collect eighteenth and nineteenth century cookbooks, you may have difficulty finding fine copies and may have to to settle for very good copies of the more common titles and good copies of the scarce or rare titles. And you will probably have to pay a premium should you have the opportunity to purchase a fine copy of a rare nineteenth century cookbook.

We will make an attempt to define some commonly used categories of condition for those of you who are new to book collecting to give you a general concept of what to expect when reading descriptions of condition. If you have been involved in book collecting or bookselling for some time, you will probably disagree with the definitions, having developed your own concepts over the years — we ask that you bear with us as we attempt these definitions.

Fine — If a twentieth century book, the condition should be almost like new with only very, very minor signs of use, no discernable wear or rubbing, no fading of the spine, no dogeared page corners, possibly lacking the fresh or crisp look of a brand new book and intact, nothing missing, no missing endpapers and if issued with a dust jacket, the dust jacket must be separately described. If an older book, nineteenth century or earlier, slightly more signs of usage are tolerated, but still a well-cared-for, fresh looking book with very minor rubbing , very minor fading of cloth or color of boards, but no cracked hinges, a few specks of foxing, nothing missing, no missing endpaper, half-title or spine labels. In both the twentieth century and the earlier book, there should not be any library markings (public or institutional), however there may be a bookplate from a private collector.

Very Good — A twentieth century book should show only minor rubbing at book extremities such as corners or spine, possibly very minor soil or very minor spots on covers, possibly a bumped corner, no fraying of spine extremities, no cracked hinges, no foxing, nothing missing, no missing endpapers, essentially just a little more evidence of use than a fine copy. If nineteenth century or earlier, minor rubbing of extremities is expected, no chipping (missing material) at top or bottom of spine, no signs of major fraying of cloth, no cracked hinges or cracked joints, possibly minor spots of soil or stain and occasional foxing is expected, nothing should be missing, no missing endpaper or half-title. A very good copy can be ex-library with library markings, but should be so described and with few exceptions the ex-library copy would not be a desirable book to add to your collection

Good — Either a twentieth century or an earlier book showing average use and wear, but not in need of a replacement binding, not all tattered and torn, not with moderate to heavy damp stain, basically still intact but worn, spine extremities can show minor chipping, corners can all be bumped, and (there is disagreement here) in the case of an earlier book a free endpaper, or other blank page such as a flyleaf, can be missing, a hinge can be cracked (the book should not be in need of recasing with the covers barely attached), there can be moderate to heavy foxing in earlier books, a good copy should be a book that has seen average/considerable use and is added to your collection because you care more about the content of the book than the condition or you hope someday to upgrade to a better copy of the same book

Fair — A book with much use and wear and multiple problems and/or defects and unless the book is very scarce or rare probably should not be added to your collection. A fair copy may exhibit moderate to heavy dampstain, excessive stain or foxing in the text, a very tattered cloth or very scuffed and rubbed leather binding with additional problems such as underlining in the text, lacking endpapers, both hinges cracked, heavy dogearring of page corners, in general only a step above a reading copy and not a desirable copy unless you value content much more than condition.

Binding copy — A copy in need of a replacement backstrip or spine or in need of recasing or reattachment of the original binding or recasing with a new binding; the book should be in very good condition otherwise, the cover is in

very good condition in the case of need for new backstrip and the text portion in clean, very good condition in both cases or the expense of rebinding is not warranted.

Reading copy — A copy in poor condition, practically synonymous with binding copy (when only the covers are excessively worn), but also used to describe a copy with excessive wear and/or abuse which does not warrant rebinding and is simply useful for the content it contains, sometimes referred to as a working copy.

Some booksellers choose to use intermediate categories such as "very good to fine" or "good to very good," when they believe that such categories are warranted. When a book is better than very good but not quite fine (in the case of a nineteenth century book perhaps a little too much rubbing on the cloth), we use the very good to fine designation. When a book is better than good condition, but is not quite very good (perhaps has moderate foxing or a small amount of very minor damp stain) we rate it as good to very good.

In summary, you should pay close attention to the listed details or specifics of wear and/or defects in a book description and you should realize that the overall rating of condition is the opinion of the bookseller or other individual writing the description. In most cases books are returnable for a refund when you believe they are not as described — and many booksellers allow the return of a book should you be dissatisfied with the condition for any reason. Read each bookseller's terms or policy statement prior to ordering to see if and when returns are allowed.

In general do not purchase books or pamphlets which are missing pages or portions of text, unless you have a personal reason for doing so — a book missing the top third of pages 102 – 103 will never have much value. And in general it is a poor idea to purchase odd volumes of a set, thinking that you will be able to find the missing volumes at a later date — it seldom happens.

As a beginning book collector, you should strive to collect books of very good or fine condition. There may be some bargains among the very worn books, but you should probably avoid the worn bargains unless you know the book is very scarce or rare.

Rarity and Scarcity

There are many rare books for which there is virtually no market, i.e., Arthur Deco's *Forty Years of My Poetry* which Art brought to a vanity publisher in 1965 and paid for the publication of 200 copies. Only Art's cousins are looking for a copy; even his local library has no interest in the book. To take this concept a step further, there are thousands of titles of older fiction, most of which went through only one printing and for which there is no interest, unless a scholar or bibliographer is studying that area of fiction. In general, there is a lack of demand for old textbooks, old Bibles, many self-help titles, long out-of-date technology handbooks, old encyclopedias, poetry by unknown poets, older fiction by unknown authors, and some local business histories; many of these books are either rare or scarce. In other words, not every rare book is valuable.

Another misconception is that every first edition is collectible and valuable. One has only to understand that every book has a first edition and only popular or successful titles have more than one printing to see that not every first edition is desirable. One could assemble an interesting (?) and fascinating (?) collection of esoteric, undesirable rare books for which there is little or no demand.

The concept of a rare book is easy to comprehend — it is a book which is seldom encountered and presumably exists in very small numbers. To define the term "rare book" is more difficult. I prefer to define it based on the frequency it is seen by the bibliographer, collector, or antiquarian bookseller who is searching for copies on a continual basis. A rare book is one encountered only occasionally by those working with and/or collecting books in the specifc genre. How frequently? That is the question that separates a rare book from a scarce book.

A book which is encountered about once every five years or less is a rare book (in the case of a specialized bookseller, in his/her stock, in the case of a collector, having a specific opportunity to purchase the book, in the case of a bibliographer, locating a "previously unrecorded" copy). A very scarce book might be encountered more frequently, but less often than once a year, perhaps once every two to four years. A scarce book is normally encountered approximately once a year by those actively seeking it. An uncommon book may be in the stock of a specialty bookseller four or five times a year, but is not always readily available as is a common book. Theoretically you should have no problem finding a fine copy of a common book at any time; an uncommon book may take a bit of searching.

These artificial standards provide you with at least some guide to understanding rarity and scarcity, but obviously are only a relative guide. A book you, as a collector, have the opportunity to purchase ten times per year obviously is neither rare nor is it scarce. When an antiquarian bookseller has five copies of a specific title for sale during any one year, it is neither a rare book nor is it scarce. There

can be exceptions to the rule. We once had an opportunity to buy three copies at one time of a rare whaling narrative from a collector who had been fortunate to be able to locate that many copies during a decade. During more than 25 years of bookselling, we have only had one other copy of that same title.

The Internet with its speedy international communications will probably make scarce and even rare titles more accessible and the frequency of encounter will increase, thus a book which might have been available for purchase only once every five years might be encountered once every three years! Another factor that occasionally has an effect on the level of scarcity is the "sudden" appearance of an accumulation or quantity of a previously rare or scarce book. This seems to happen most often with pamphlets and broadsides. A carton full of a previously scarce bicycle catalog or a Civil War regimental history or a stack of 200 broadsides announcing the formation of a company of gold miners in 1849 may be found in an attic and soon after one starts to see clean, crisp, fine copies of these scarce or even rare items appearing on the market. This type of occurrence obviously changes the status of the item, and although it may still be uncommon and still desirable in your collection, it is no longer scarce or rare.

When a scarce or rare item is offered for sale in fine condition at a price which seems too good to be true, you might inquire whether a large quantity of the item has appeared on the market. Even if that is the case, you probably should still purchase the item if it fits well into your collection and you like the price. Accumulations like these often disappear into collections in fast order and the item almost as suddenly again becomes much more difficult to obtain.

When you are just starting as a book collector, you do not have the luxury of one or two decades of experience as a collector and you must rely on antiquarian book catalogs, bibliographies, annual compilations of auction records, and national bibliographic card catalogs such as the pre-1956 National Union Catalogue or the British Museum Catalogue to assist you in determining the relative scarcity of a book.

Many bibliographies list locations (libraries) which hold particular titles. Sometimes the bibliographer, rather than attempting to locate every known copy, limits the locations to a few as examples of where to find the item. Even when the bibliographer attempts to locate every known copy, there will usually be many unreported copies not listed. Be careful when using bibliographies as a guide to scarcity and read the preface and/or introduction to determine the bibliographer's intent.

One can use a reference such as Milton Drake's *Almanacs of the United States* as a relative guide to scarcity. Drake lists 20 or 30 or even more locations for reasonably common almanacs, but when he locates only one copy, the almanac is probably very scarce and possibly rare. When he locates only three or four copies the almanac is probably scarce. Use bibliographies such as Drake as a guide to relative scarcity.

Wright Howes's *U.S.iana (1650 – 1950) A Selective Bibliography* makes no attempt to provide library locations for books, but does provide a value symbol for each item listed. The values associated with each symbol are now out-of-date, but the value symbols do have value as a measure of relative scarcity.

> a — mildly scarce, obtainable without much difficulty
> aa — quite scarce, obtainable only with some difficulty
> b — mildly rare, obtainable only with considerable difficulty
> c — quite rare, obtainable only with much difficulty
> d — very rare books, obtainable only with great difficulty
> dd — superlatively rare books, almost unobtainable

Personally we do not regard most "a" rating books as scarce, we would categorize many of them as uncommon or common, but most "aa" books are scarce and books with a rating of "b" or higher are usually rare books which are not easy to obtain.

Another way of determining relative scarcity is to use the annual compilations of book auction records such as *American Book Prices Current*. Because such compilations usually exclude common items, one has to be cautious about making extrapolations. If you look through the last ten years of auction records and find no copy of a particular title listed, it is probably either very common or rare. One would be better off to find one copy listed in the last ten years rather than no copies.

When at least one copy of a title is listed in virtually every year of the auction records, one can assume that it is neither very scarce nor rare. When a copy is listed only once every five years, the item is probably at least very scarce and possibly rare. If you find a listing only once every ten years, the book should probably be considered rare. If multiple copies of a book are listed every year, the book can still be considered scarce and desirable and is probably very much in demand or it wouldn't be consigned to auction so frequently. One must remember that most auction houses are not interested in offering common books, thus most titles found in the auction records are at least uncommon and probably scarce.

We find the pre-1956 imprints National Union Catalogue (NUC) valuable in determining relative scarcity. The NUC with its huge number of volumes often takes up a whole wall of book shelving in many libraries and is a compilation of the holdings of all reporting libraries (hundreds, if not thousands of libraries in the United States). Most large college and university libraries and most major city libraries have the NUC.

In general, when there are only one or two or three locations given for a particular item, the assumption can be made that the item is rare. When there are a reasonable number of holdings listed, from three to ten, the item is probably scarce (very scarce might be represented by four or five locations). When there are quite a number of locations, 11 to 20 locations, the item may be considered uncommon in most cases. When there are 20 to 30 or more locations, the item is probably common. We find that with certain areas such as children's books and cookbooks, the generalizations may not apply due to fewer holdings in these areas in most libraries, i.e., a common cookbook may have only ten locations listed. Please remember that we are making generalizations and that they are meant to be used only as a rough guide.

Antiquarian booksellers catalogs may also be used as a guide to scarcity, but be careful with your assumptions. Do not assume that because you did not find your favorite bird book listed in any of the ten ornithology catalogs you own, that the book is rare. In fact, the book may be so common or of so little demand that the natural history booksellers seldom catalog it.

Perhaps one of the best ways to use bookseller catalogs as a guide to scarcity is to rely on the expertise of the antiquarian bookseller and make note of items he or she lists as very scarce or rare. Obviously a decade or more in the business of selling antiquarian books provides the bookseller with the requisite experience for making knowledgeable judgements about scarcity (particularly in the specific speciality areas of that bookseller). Equally obvious would be that the experience found in catalog number 1 would not be the same as catalog number 20 from the same bookseller.

- A -

AARON, David. *State Scarlet.* 1987. Putnam. 1st ed. VG+/VG+ clip. N4. $15.00

AARON, Henry. *I Had a Hammer.* 1991. Harper Collins. 1st ed. F/F. P8. $75.00

AARONS, Jules. *Solar System Radio Astronomy.* 1965. NY. Plenum. 4to. 416p. xl. VG. K5. $25.00

ABBATE, Francesco. *Egyptian Art.* 1972. Octopus. 1st ed. 8vo. 158p. NF/dj. W1. $14.00

ABBEY, Edward. *Cactus Country.* 1973. Time Life. 1st ed. photos. F/sans. A18. $30.00

ABBEY, Edward. *Desert Solitaire.* 1968. McGraw Hill. 1st ed. author's 4th book. F/dj. S9. $650.00

ABBEY, Edward. *Fool's Progress.* 1988. Holt. 1st ed. M/M. A18. $30.00

ABBEY, Edward. *Hayduke Lives.* 1990. Little Brn. 1st ed. M/dj. A18. $25.00

ABBEY, Edward. *Monkey Wrench Gang.* 1985. Salt Lake City. 1st ed thus. F/F. C2. $75.00

ABBEY, Edward. *Monkey Wrench Gang.* 1990. Dream Garden. revised ils ed/1st prt. F/F. A18. $50.00

ABBEY, Edward. *Outlet.* 1905. Houghton Mifflin. 1st ed. ils E Boyd Smith. VG+. A18. $75.00

ABBEY, Edward. *Texas Matchmaker.* 1904. Houghton Mifflin. 1st ed. ils E Boyd Smith. VG+. A18. $60.00

ABBOT, Anthony. *About the Murder of the Clergyman's...* 1931. Covici Friede. 2nd. VG. P3. $20.00

ABBOT, Willis J. *Nations at War: A Current History.* 1914. NY. Syndicate. probable 1st ed. 366p. red cloth. VG/VG. B22. $25.00

ABBOTT, Austin. *Select Cases on the Examination of Witnesses.* 1894. NY. Diossy Law Book Co. sheep. working copy. M11. $50.00

ABBOTT, Austin. *Trial Evidence, Rules of Evidence Applicable...* 1900. NY. Baker Voorhis. orig sheep. reading copy. M11. $40.00

ABBOTT, Benjamin Vaughan. *Travelling Law-School & Famous Trials...* 1884. Chicago. Interstate. gilt brn cloth. M11. $125.00

ABBOTT, Bruce. *Sign of the Scorpion.* 1970. Grove. 1st ed. F/F. P3. $20.00

ABBOTT, I.A. *Laau Hawaii: Traditional Hawaiian Uses of Plants.* 1992. Bishop Mus. 4to. photos. 163p. F/pict wrp. B1. $36.00

ABBOTT, John. *Scimitar.* 1992. Crown. 1st ed. F/F. H11. $20.00

ABBOTT, John S.C. *George Washington; or, Life in America...* 1875. Dodd Mead. ils. xl. poor. B10. $12.00

ABBOTT, John S.C. *Napoleon at St Helena.* nd. Harper. G. P3. $85.00

ABBOTT, R.T. *Compendium of Land Shells.* 1989. Melbourne. Am Malacologists. 1st ed. 4to. 240p. F/F. B1. $50.00

ABBOTT, Shirley. *Womenfolks: Growing Up Down South.* 1983. Ticknor Fields. 1st ed. F/dj. B4. $45.00

ABBOTT, Twyman O. *Synopsis of the California Vehicle Act & Guide Book.* 1925. Sacramento. Division of Motor Vehicles. 77p. stapled wrp. M11. $15.00

ABBOTT, Winston. *Come Climb My Hill.* 1982. Inspiration. revised. ils Bette Eaton Bossen. VG/VG. B11. $8.50

ABBOTT, Winston. *Sing With the Wind.* 1982. Inspiration. sgn. ils/sgn BE Bossen. F/F. B11. $12.00

ABBOTT & DICKINSON. *Guide to Reading.* 1925. Doubleday Page. VG. P3. $13.00

ABDULLAH, Achmed. *Night Drums.* nd. AL Burt. VG/G. P3. $25.00

ABE, Kobo. *Ruined Map.* 1969. Knopf. 1st ed. VG/VG. P3. $25.00

ABEL, Kenneth. *Bait.* 1994. Delacorte. ARC. NF/wrp. M22. $15.00

ABEL-SMITH, Brian. *Hospitals 1800-1948: Study in Social Administration...* 1964. Cambridge. 1st ed. 415p. VG/dj. A13. $35.00

ABELLA, Alex. *Killing of the Saints.* 1991. Crown. 1st ed. F/F. A20. $20.00

ABERNETHY, John. *Hunterian Oration, for the Year 1819.* 1825. Hartford. 1st Am ed. extract. 40p. VG. A13. $40.00

ABRAHAMS, Peter. *Fury of Rachel Monette.* 1980. Macmillan. 1st ed. author's 1st book. NF/NF. H11. $40.00

ABRAHAMS, Peter. *Revolution #9.* 1992. Mysterious. 1st ed. F/F. A20. $18.00

ABRO, Ben. *July 14 Assassination.* 1963. Jonathan Cape. VG/VG. P3. $20.00

ACHEBE, Chinua. *Anthills of Savannah.* 1988. Anchor. 1st ed. F/F. M19. $17.50

ACHESON, Edward. *Grammarian's Funeral.* nd. Grosset Dunlap. VG. P3. $15.00

ACKER, Kathy. *My Mother: Demonology, a Novel.* 1993. Pantheon. 1st ed. F/NF. G10. $25.00

ACKER, Marian Francis. *Etchings of Old Mobile.* 1938. Mobile. Gill Prt. unp. F/G. B10. $20.00

ACKROYD, Peter. *Dickens.* 1991. Harper Collins. 1st ed. F/F. P3. $35.00

ACKROYD, Peter. *First Light.* 1989. London. 1st ed. sgn. F/NF. C2. $40.00

ACKROYD, Peter. *Great Fire of London.* 1982. Hamish Hamilton. 1st ed. author's 1st novel. F/F. C2. $200.00

ACKROYD, Peter. *Israel Under Babylon & Persia.* 1970. Oxford. 1st ed. 374p. VG/dj. W1. $18.00

ACKROYD, Peter. *TS Eliot: A Life.* 1984. Simon Schuster. 1st ed. rem mk. F/F. B35. $40.00

ACKWORTH, Robert C. *Dr Kildare Assigned to Trouble.* 1963. Whitman. TVTI. VG. P3. $10.00

ACOSTA, Jorge R. *El Palacio del Quetzalpapaloti.* 1964. Mexico. 1st ed. 85p. F3. $30.00

ADAM, Peter. *Art of the Third Reich.* 1992. Abrams. ils/pl. 332p. F/dj. A17. $30.00

ADAMCZEWSKI, Jan. *Nicolaus Copernicus & His Epoch.* ca 1965. Phil. Copernicus Soc of Am. 4to. 160p. VG/dj. K5. $30.00

ADAMIC, Louis. *House in Antigua.* 1937. Harper. 1st ed. ils. 300p. F3. $30.00

ADAMIC, Louis. *Robinson Jeffers.* 1938. Ward Ritchie. 1/250. VG+. S9. $60.00

ADAMS, Alice. *Families & Survivors.* 1974. Knopf. 1st ed. F/NF. B4. $65.00

ADAMS, Alice. *Mexico.* 1990. Prentice Hall. 1st ed. 216p. F3. $20.00

ADAMS, Alice. *To See You Again.* 1982. Knopf. 1st ed. F/NF. B4. $45.00

ADAMS, Andy. *Log of a Cowboy: A Narrative of Old Trail Days.* 1931. Houghton Mifflin. 1st ed thus. ils E Boyd Smith. F/VG. A18. $35.00

ADAMS, Andy. *Outlet.* 1905. Houghton Mifflin. 1st ed. ils E Boyd Smith. F. A18. $60.00

ADAMS, Andy. *Texas Matchmaker.* 1904. Houghton Mifflin. 1st ed. ils E Boyd Smith. F. A18. $75.00

ADAMS, Ansel. *Camera.* 1980. NYGS. 1st ed. 4to. F/NF. T10. $35.00

ADAMS, Ansel. *Letters & Images 1916-1984.* 1988. NYGS. 1st ed. 402p. F/dj. A17. $40.00

ADAMS, Bill. *Wind in the Topsails.* 1931. London. Harrap. 8vo. 163p. VG. T7. $30.00

ADAMS, Brian. *Flowering of the Pacific.* 1986. Sydney. Wm Collins. 1st ed. 4to. 16 pl. 194p. F/F. T10. $65.00

ADAMS, Charles. *Charles Adams' Mother Goose.* 1967. Windmill. ils. NF/VG. P2. $55.00

ADAMS, Charles Francis. *Autobiography.* 1920. Houghton Mifflin. 7th. 8vo. 224p. gilt blk cloth. VG. T10. $30.00

ADAMS, Charles Francis. *Railroads: Their Origin & Problems.* 1879. Putnam. 12mo. 216p. brick cloth. F. T10. $125.00

ADAMS, Charles True. *Contract Bridge Standardized.* 1929. Chicago. 2nd. 73p. VG. S1. $10.00

ADAMS, Clifton. *Hassle & the Medicine Man.* nd. BC. VG/G. P3. $5.00

ADAMS, Douglas. *Dirk Gently's Holistic Detective Age.* 1987. Simon Schuster. 1st ed. F/F. P3. $20.00

ADAMS, Douglas. *Hitchhiker's Guide to the Galaxy.* 1987. Heinemann. 3rd. VG/VG. P3. $20.00

ADAMS, Douglas. *Life, the Universe & Everything.* 1982. Harmony. 1st ed. F/F. P3. $20.00

ADAMS, Douglas. *Long Dark Tea-Time of the Soul.* 1989. Stoddart. 1st ed. VG/VG. P3. $20.00

ADAMS, Douglas. *Restaurant at the End of the Universe.* nd. Harmony. 4th. F/F. P3. $15.00

ADAMS, Douglas. *So Long, & Thanks for All the Fish.* 1985. Harmony. 1st ed. NF/NF. P3. $20.00

ADAMS, E.C.L. *Potee's Gal: A Drama of Negro Life Near Big Congaree Swamps.* 1929. Columbia. 1/250. 49p. maroon cloth. VG/VG. B11. $85.00

ADAMS, E.C.L. *Potee's Gal: A Drama of Negro Life Near Big Congaree Swamps.* 1929. Columbia. 1st ed. 1/250. sgn. red cloth. NF/NF. C2. $125.00

ADAMS, Eustace. *Andy Lane: Racing Around the World (#3).* 1928. Grosset Dunlap. 219p. lists 12 titles. VG/dj. M20. $25.00

ADAMS, Eustace. *Doomed Demons.* 1935. Grosset Dunlap. Air Combat Stories for Boys series. VG/poor. P12. $8.00

ADAMS, Frank. *Simple Simon.* nd. Dodge. 4to. pls/text on French-fold paper. VG. M5. $125.00

ADAMS, George I. *Gold Deposits of Alabama & Occurrences of Copper, Pyrite...* 1930. AL U. 1st ed. xl. VG. M8. $45.00

ADAMS, George Worthington. *Doctors in Blue.* 1985. Dayton, OH. 12mo. 237p. VG. T3. $20.00

ADAMS, H. *Golf Course Murder.* 1933. NY. Blk. VG/VG. B5. $27.50

ADAMS, Hanna. *Abridgement of History of New England for Use of Young...* 1805. Boston. B&J Homans. author's ed. 12mo. 186p. leather. poor. B36. $35.00

ADAMS, Harold. *Man Who Missed the Party.* 1989. Mysterious. 1st ed. sgn. F/F. P3. $25.00

ADAMS, Harold. *Naked Liar.* 1985. Mysterious. 1st ed. F/F. M23. $20.00

ADAMS, Henry. *Education of Henry Adams.* 1942. Merrymount. 12 orig etchings. gilt rust buckram. F/case. B14. $200.00

ADAMS, Herbert. *Mystery & Minette.* 1934. Lippincott. 1st ed. VG. P3. $35.00

ADAMS, Hugh. *Art of the Sixties.* 1978. Oxford. ils/biography. 80p. dj. D2. $25.00

ADAMS, James Truslow. *American.* 1943. Scribner. 1st ed. 8vo. 404p. F/NF. T10. $25.00

ADAMS, James Truslow. *Atlas of American History.* 1943. NY. 1st ed. 360p. buckram. G+. B18. $25.00

ADAMS, James Truslow. *Dictionary of American History.* 1940. Scribner. 6 vol. 2nd. 2625p. VG. A4. $245.00

ADAMS, James Truslow. *March of Democracy.* 1955. Scribner. 7 vol. VG. P12. $50.00

ADAMS, John. *Diary & Autobiography.* 1961. Cambridge, MA. 4 vol. 2nd. 8vo. F/djs. T10. $150.00

ADAMS, Katharine. *Gray Eyes.* 1934. Macmillan. 1st ed. 267p. VG+/dj. M20. $25.00

ADAMS, Leon. *Wines of America.* 1973. Houghton Mifflin. 1st ed. sgn. 465p. F/F. T10. $50.00

ADAMS, Mark H. *Bacteriophages.* 1959. NY. Interscience. ARC. sgn Salvadore Lurin. 8vo. ils. VG. B14. $75.00

ADAMS, Maryline P. *Merrie England, a Philatelic Celebration...* 1983. Poole. 1/101. sgn. 25 Frenchfold p. miniature. F. B24. $165.00

ADAMS, Nancy M. *Mountain Flowers of New Zealand.* 1965. Wellington. ils. VG/dj. B26. $22.50

ADAMS, Peter. *Clipper Ships: Done in Cork Models.* 1929. Dutton. VG/VG. A16. $17.50

ADAMS, Ramon F. *More Burs Under the Saddle: Books & Histories of West.* 1979. OK U. 1st ed. AN/dj. A18. $40.00

ADAMS, Ramon F. *Six-Guns & Saddle Leather.* 1982. 2491 books listed. hc. F. E1. $60.00

ADAMS, Randolph G. *Gateway to American History.* 1927. Boston. hc. VG. O7. $45.00

ADAMS, Richard. *Day Gone By.* 1990. Hutchinson. 1st ed. VG/VG. P3. $30.00

ADAMS, Richard. *Day Gone By.* 1991. Knopf. AP. 8vo. F/prt wrp. S9. $25.00

ADAMS, Richard. *Girl in a Swing.* 1980. Allen Lane. 1st ed. VG/VG. P3. $22.00

ADAMS, Richard. *Iron Wolf & Other Stories.* 1980. Allen Lane. 1st ed. F/F. P3. $25.00

ADAMS, Richard. *Plague Dogs.* 1977. Allen Lane. 1st ed. F/F. P3. $20.00

ADAMS, Richard. *Prehistoric Mesoamerica.* 1977. Little Brn. 1st ed. 370p. VG. F3. $25.00

ADAMS, Richard. *Shardik.* 1974. Simon Schuster. 1st ed. F/F. P3. $25.00

ADAMS, Richard. *Ship's Cat.* 1977. Knopf. 1st Am ed. ils Alan Aldridge. VG/VG. D1. $45.00

ADAMS, Richard. *Traveller.* 1988. Knopf. 1st ed. F/F. M23. $25.00

ADAMS, Richard. *Tyger Voyage.* 1976. Knopf. 1st Am ed. 30p. F/NF. T5. $25.00

ADAMS, Richard. *Watership Down.* 1974. Macmillan. 1st Am ed. NF/NF. B2. $65.00

ADAMS, Robert. *Nil: Episodes in Literary Conquest of Void...* 1966. Oxford. 255p. NF/VG. A4. $35.00

ADAMS, Sherman. *First-Hand Report: Story of Eisenhower Administration.* 1961. Harper. 1st ed. sgn. 481p. bl cloth. F/VG+. B22. $12.00

ADAMS, Susan. *Let's Play Cards.* 1981. Eng. G. S1. $3.00

ADAMS, Thomas R. *Non-Cartographical Maritime Works Published by Mount & Page.* 1985. London. VG/wrp. O7. $25.00

ADAMS, Thomas R. *Rare Americana: A Selection of One Hundred & One Books...* 1974. Providence. VG/wrp. O7. $45.00

ADAMS, Tom. *Agatha Christie & the Art of Her Crimes.* 1981. Everest House. 1st ed. NF/NF. P3. $35.00

ADAMS & ADAMS. *Smaller British Birds.* 1874. London. Bell. 1st ed. 4to. gr cloth. VG. T10. $125.00

ADAMS & CONNOR. *Poisonous Plants of New Zealand.* 1951. Wellington. 1st ed. inscr Connor. 39 pl. 141p. VG/wrp. B26. $22.50

ADAMS & HARBAUGH. *Favorite Torte & Cake Recipes.* 1951. Simon Schuster. 1st ed. sgns. 8vo. 164p. VG/G. B11. $10.00

ADAMS & LLOYD. *Meaning of Life.* 1984. Harmony. 1st Am ed. F/NF. T2. $12.00

ADAMS & LUNGWITZ. *Textbook of Horseshoeing.* 1966. Corvallis. facsimile of 1884 ed. VG/G. O3. $25.00

ADAMS & NEWHALL. *This Is the American Earth.* 1960. Sierra Club. 2nd. 89p. VG/dj. A17. $40.00

ADAMSON, David. *Ruins of Time.* 1975. Praeger. 1st ed. 272p. dj. F3. $30.00

ADAMSON, Joe. *Groucho, Harpo, Chico & Sometimes Zeppo.* 1973. NY. 1st ed. photos. 464p. F/dj. A17. $10.00

ADAMSON, Joy. *Born Free: A Lioness in Two Worlds.* 1960. NY. 1st ed. 220p. VG/dj. B14. $55.00

ADDAMS, Charles. *Addams & Evil.* nd. Simon Schuster. 8th. VG/VG. P3. $25.00

ADDAMS, Charles. *Dear Dead Days.* 1959. Putnam. 1st ed. 8vo. VG+/dj. M21. $30.00

ADDAMS, Charles. *World of Charles Addams.* 1991. Knopf. 1st ed. 4to. NF/dj. M21. $45.00

ADDEO & GARVIN. *Midnight Special: Legend of Leadbelly by...* 1971. Geis. 1st ed. F/NF. N3. $35.00

ADDISON, William. *English Fairs & Markets.* 1953. Batsford. 1st ed. ils Barbara Jones. VG/VG. M20. $40.00

ADE, George. *Doc' Horne.* 1899. 1st ed. ils McCutcheon. VG+. S13. $12.00

ADE, George. *Fables in Slang.* 1900. Herbert Stone. ils Clyde J Newman. G+. P12. $6.00

ADEN, Paul. *Hosta Book.* 1992 (1988). Portland. 2nd. 133p. sc. M. B26. $18.00

ADLEMAN, Melvin. *Sporting Time.* 1986. IL U. 1st ed. F/F. P8. $35.00

ADLEMAN, Robert H. *Annie Deane.* 1971. World. 1st ed. VG/VG. P3. $20.00

ADLEMAN & WALTON. *Rome Fell Today.* 1968. Boston. 1st ed. 336p. F/dj. A17. $10.00

ADLER, Bill. *Murder Game.* 1991. Carroll Graf. 1st ed. F/F. N4. $22.50

ADLER, Bill. *Murder in Manhattan.* 1986. Morrow. 1st ed. VG/VG. P3. $16.00

ADLER, Frederick Herbert. *Winds & Words.* 1947. Cleveland. Flozari/Pegasus. 8vo. 44p. G/wrp. B11. $10.00

ADLER, Renata. *Toward a Radical Middle: Fourteen Pieces of Reporting...* 1969. Random. 1st ed. 1F/F. B4. $65.00

ADLER, Warren. *Blood Ties.* 1979. Putnam. 1st ed. VG/VG. P3. $15.00

ADLER, Warren. *Casanova Embrace.* 1978. Putnam. 1st ed. NF/NF. P3. $13.00

ADLER & CHASTAIN. *Who Killed the Robins Family?* 1983. Morrow. 1st ed. xl. VG+/dj. N4. $12.50

ADMAS, Henry. *Democracy: An American Novel.* 1880. NY. 1st issue. NF. C6. $750.00

ADRIAN, E.D. *Basis of Sensation. The Action of Sense Organs.* 1928. Norton. 1st Am ed. 122p. VG. G1. $40.00

ADRIAN, E.D. *Physical Background of Perception.* 1947. Oxford. Clarendon. thin 8vo. 95p. VG. G1. $40.00

AESCHYLUS. *Oresteia.* 1961. LEC. 1st ed. 1/1500. ils/sgn Ayrton. F/case. C2. $100.00

AESOP. *Aesop for Children.* 1919. Rand McNally. 1st ed. ils Milo Winter. 112p. G. C14. $25.00

AESOP. *Aesop's Fables.* 1933. Viking. ils Boris Artzybasheff. F/VG. A20. $50.00

AESOP. *Aesop's Fables.* 1941. Heritage. 1st ed. ils Robert Lawson. 134p. VG+. P2. $45.00

AESOP. *Aesop's Fables.* 1982. Franklin Lib. aeg. leather spine. F. P3. $20.00

AESOP. *Aesop's Fables.* 1988. Jelly Bean. 1st ed. ils Charles Santore. 48p. F/F. P2. $25.00

AESOP. *Some of Aesop's Fables With Modern Instances.* 1983. Macmillan. 1st Am ed. ils Caldecott. VG. D1. $150.00

AFER, Publius Terentius. *Works...* 1822. Lincolns Inn Fields. Pickering. miniature. contemporary calf. F. T10. $100.00

AFRICANO, Lillian. *Businessman's Guide to the Middle East.* 1977. Harper Row. 1st ed. 8vo. 312p. NF/dj. W1. $20.00

AGASSIZ, Elizabeth Cary. *Louis Agassiz: His Life & Correspondence.* 1885. Boston. 2 vol. xl. VG. B14. $150.00

AGASSIZ & AGASSIZ. *Journey in Brazil.* 1868. Ticknor Field. 2nd. professionally rehinged. VG. A10. $125.00

AGEE, James. *Letters to Father Flye.* 1962. NY. 1st ed. inscr. NF/VG. C6. $350.00

AGEE & WALKER. *Let Us Now Praise Famous Men.* 1941. Houghton Mifflin. 1st ed. ils. reading copy. C2. $60.00

AGETON, Arthur A. *Naval Officer's Guide.* 1943. Whittlesey. 2nd. ils. 514p. G+. P12. $15.00

AGNEW, Spiro T. *Canfield Decision.* 1976. Playboy. 1st ed. rem mk. NF/VG. N4. $17.50

AHLSON, Hereward. *Thunderbolt & the Rebel Planet.* 1954. Lutterworth. 1st ed. VG/VG. P3. $15.00

AI. *Cruelty: Poems.* 1973. Houghton Mifflin. 1st ed. author's 1st book. sgn. NF/NF. C2. $75.00

AICHELE, Dietmar. *Was Bluht Denn Da?* 1973. Stuttgart. ils M Golte-Bechtle. 400p. VG/dj. B26. $20.00

AICKMAN, Robert. *Cold Hand in Mine.* 1975. Scribner. 1st ed. F/F. P3. $40.00

AICKMAN, Robert. *Painted Devils.* 1979. Scribner. 1st ed. NF/NF. P3. $30.00

AIKEN, Conrad. *Blue Voyage.* 1927. Scribner. 1st ed. F/VG. C2. $125.00

AIKEN, Joan. *Foul Matter.* 1983. Doubleday. 1st ed. VG/G. P3. $13.00

AIKEN, Joan. *Haunting of Lamb House.* 1993. St Martin. 1st Am ed. F/F. G10. $25.00

AIKMAN, Lonnelle. *Nature's Healing Arts: From Folk Medicine to Modern Drugs.* 1977. WA. 1st ed. 199p. VG. A13. $25.00

AIMONE, Alan C. *Military History: Biographical Guide.* 1987. West Point. VG/wrp. O7. $20.00

AINSLIE, Kathleen. *Catharine Susan & Me Goes Abroad.* ca 1909. London. Casteel. 1st ed. ils Kathleen Ainslie. VG. D1. $125.00

AINSWORTH, Ed. *California.* 1951. Los Angeles. House-Warven. 272p. VG/worn. P4. $15.00

AINSWORTH, Ed. *Maverick Mayor (Sam Yorty).* 1966. Doubleday. 1st ed. inscr Yorty. 8vo. F/F. T10. $45.00

AINSWORTH & AINSWORTH. *In the Shade of the Juniper Tree: A Life of Fray...* 1970. Doubleday. 1st ed. 8vo. 199p. gr cloth. NF. T10. $35.00

AIRD, Catherine. *Most Contagious Game.* 1967. Crime Club. VG/VG. P3. $15.00

AIRTH, Rennie. *Once a Spy.* 1981. Jonathan Cape. 1st ed. VG/VG. P3. $18.00

AJILVAQI, Geyata. *Wild Flowers of the Big Thicket.* 1979. College Station. photos/map/glossary. 360p. F/dj. B26. $22.50

AKINARI, Ueda. *Ugetsu Monogatari.* 1974. U British Columbia. F/F. P3. $30.00

AKINS, Zoe. *Old Maid.* 1935. Appleton. 1st ed. F/NF clip. B4. $350.00

AKSYONOV, Vassily. *Quest for an Island.* 1987. NY. 1st Am ed. sgn. F/NF. C2. $50.00

AKSYONOV, Vassily. *Say Cheese!* 1989. NY. 1st Am ed. sgn. F/NF. C2. $40.00

ALBA, Victor. *Horizon Concise History of Mexico.* 1973. American Heritage. 1st ed. 224p. dj. F3. $20.00

ALBAUGH, William A. *More Confederate Faces.* 1972. WA, DC. ABS Prt. 1st ed. 1/400. 233p. NF. M8. $175.00

ALBAUGH, William A. *Tyler, Texas, CSA.* 1958. Stackpole. photos. 235p. xl. VG/G. B10. $40.00

ALBEE, Edward. *Box & Quotations From Chairman Mao Tse-Tung.* 1969. NY. 1st ed. sgn. F/F. A11. $35.00

ALBEE, Edward. *Zoo Story, Death of Bessie Smith, The Sandbox.* 1960. 1st ed. MTI. VG/VG clip. S13. $30.00

ALBERT, Alpaeus H. *Record of American Uniform & Historical Buttons.* 1976. Bicentennial ed. 8vo. ils. 411p. VG. T3. $40.00

ALBERT, Herman W. *Odyssey of a Desert Prospector.* 1967. Norman. 1st ed. 12mo. 260p. F/F. T10. $25.00

ALBERT, Susan Wittig. *Witches' Bane.* 1993. Scribner. 1st ed. F/F. M23. $20.00

ALBERT, Virginia. *Peter Rabbit & Jimmy Chipmunk.* 1918. Saalfield. ils Fern Bisel Peat. unp. pict brd. VG. M20. $10.00

ALBION, Robert G. *Makers of Naval Policy 1798-1947.* 1980. Naval Inst. 737p. F. A17. $14.50

ALBION, Robert G. *Seaports South of Sahara.* 1959. NY. 1st ed. sgn. 316p. gilt bl cloth. F. H3. $75.00

ALBRAND, Martha. *Linden Affair.* 1956. Random. 1st ed. VG/VG. P3. $30.00

ALBRAND, Martha. *Manhattan North.* 1971. CMG. 1st ed. VG/VG. P3. $20.00

ALBRAND, Martha. *Mask of Alexander.* 1955. Random. 1st ed. VG/VG. P3. $20.00

ALBRAND, Martha. *Taste of Terror.* 1977. Putnam. 1st ed. NF/NF. P3. $20.00

ALBRIGHT & TAYLOR. *O Ranger!, a Book About the National Parks.* 1982. Stanford. 2nd. 8vo. VG. B17. $5.00

ALCOCK, Vivien. *Cuckoo Sister.* 1986. Delacorte. UP. 8vo. NF/wrp. C14. $8.00

ALCOHOLICS ANONYMOUS. *Alcoholics Anonymous Big Book.* 2nd ed/8th prt. F/poor. N3. $20.00

ALCOHOLICS ANONYMOUS. *Twelve Steps & Twelve Traditions.* 1953. stated 1st ed. F/F. H7. $100.00

ALCOHOLICS ANONYMOUS. *Twelve Steps & Twelve Traditions.* 1953. NY. 1st ed. F/poor. N3. $55.00

ALCORN, John S. *Jolly Rogers: History of 90th Bomber Group During WWII.* 1981. Temple City, CA. 1st ed. 212p. VG. A17. $40.00

ALCOTT, Louisa May. *Hidden Louisa May Alcott.* 1984. Avenel. VG/VG. P3. $15.00

ALCOTT, Louisa May. *Jo's Boys.* 1886. Boston. 1st ed. gilt brn cloth. VG. M5. $48.00

ALCOTT, Louisa May. *Little Men.* nd. Chicago. 357p. F/G. A17. $5.00

ALCOTT, Louisa May. *Little Men.* 1871. Boston. 1st Am ed/1st issue. VG. C6. $250.00

ALCOTT, Louisa May. *Little Women, Part 1.* 1879 (1868). Roberts. 12mo. gilt gr cloth. VG. M5. $55.00

ALCOTT, Louisa May. *Little Women.* 1912 (1868). Little Brn. 12mo. brn cloth. VG. M5. $25.00

ALCOTT, Louisa May. *Little Women.* 1922 (1915). Little Brn. ils JW Smith. 397p. VG. P2. $60.00

ALCOTT, Louisa May. *Little Women.* 1932. Garden City. ils Stein. VG. M5. $25.00

ALCOTT, Louisa May. *Little Women.* 1947. Grosset Dunlap. ils Louis Jambor. 546p. cloth. VG/dj. T5. $15.00

ALCOTT, Louisa May. *Louisa May Alcott: Her Life, Letters & Journals.* 1889. Roberts Bros. 1st ed. 404p. VG. P2. $100.00

ALCOTT, Louisa May. *Louisa's Wonder Book.* 1975. Central MI U. 8vo. F. B17. $10.00

ALCOTT, Louisa May. *Old-Fashioned Girl.* 1950. Little Brn. late rpt. VG/VG. B17. $6.50

ALCOTT, Louisa May. *Shawl Straps...Aunt Jo's Scrap Bag.* 1873 (1872). Roberts. 12mo. gilt royal bl cloth. VG. M5. $60.00

ALCOTT, Louisa May. *Under the Lilacs.* 1928. Little Brn. 1st ed. ils Marguerite Davis. F. M5. $38.00

ALDANOV, Mark. *For Thee the Best.* 1945. Scribner. 1st ed. VG/G. P3. $15.00

ALDELMAN. *Moving Pageant: A Selection of Essays.* 1977. np. 1/650. inscr. VG. A4. $85.00

ALDERMAN & KENNEDY. *Right to Privacy.* 1995. NY. Knopf. 1st ed. sgn. inscr Caroline Kennedy. dj. B14. $55.00

ALDERMAN & SMITH. *Library of Southern Literature.* 1923. Martin Hoyt. 642p. VG. B10. $35.00

ALDERSON, W.J.S. *Hints on Sailing Service Boats.* 1907. Portsmouth. G. A16. $20.00

ALDIN, Cecil. *Bunnyborough.* 1946. Eyre Spottiswode. 1st ed. 14 pl. VG+/G+. P2. $125.00

ALDIN, Cecil. *Cecil Aldin Book.* 1932. London. ils. VG. M17. $75.00

ALDIN, Cecil. *Ratcatcher to Scarlet.* 1932. London. Eyre Spottiswoode. binding copy. O3. $20.00

ALDIN, Cecil. *Romance of the Road.* 1928. London. Eyre Spottswode. 1st ed. folio. 10 mtd pl/fld map. VG. B14. $125.00

ALDIN, Cecil. *Time I Was Dead.* 1934. Scribner. 1st Am ed. VG. O3. $125.00

ALDING, Peter. *Man Condemned.* 1981. Walker. 1st ed. VG/VG. P3. $15.00

ALDIS, Dorothy. *Magic City, John & Jane at the World's Fair.* 1933. Minton Balch. 8vo. VG. B17. $7.50

ALDISS, Brian W. *Billion Year Spree.* 1973. Doubleday. 1st ed. F/F. P3. $40.00

ALDISS, Brian W. *Canopy of Time.* 1961. British SF BC. VG/torn. p3. $10.00

ALDISS, Brian W. *Dracula Unbound.* 1991. Harper Collins. 1st ed. F/F. P3. $19.00

ALDISS, Brian W. *Earthworks.* 1966. Doubleday. 1st ed. VG/VG. P3. $35.00

ALDISS, Brian W. *Helliconia Winter.* 1985. Jonathan Cape. 1st ed. F/F. P3. $30.00

ALDISS, Brian W. *Last Orders.* 1977. Jonathan Cape. 1st ed. F/F. P3. $28.00

ALDISS, Brian W. *Life in the West.* 1990. Caroll Graf. 1st ed. VG/G. P3. $15.00

ALDISS, Brian W. *New Arrivals, Old Encounters.* 1979. Jonathan Cape. 1st ed. F/F. P3. $25.00

ALDISS, Brian W. *Remembrance Day.* 1993. St Martin. 1st Am ed. F/NF. G10. $20.00

ALDISS, Brian W. *Report on Probability.* 1969. Doubleday. 1st ed. VG/VG. P3. $25.00

ALDISS, Brian W. *Rude Awakening.* 1978. Weidenfeld Nicolson. 1st ed. VG/VG. P3. $25.00

ALDISS, Brian W. *Ruins.* 1987. Hutchinson. 1st ed. F/F. P3. $15.00

ALDISS, Brian W. *Seasons in Flight.* 1984. Jonathan Cape. 1st ed. F/F. P3. $20.00

ALDISS, Brian W. *Soldier Erect.* 1971. CMG. 1st ed. VG/VG. P3. $35.00

ALDISS, Brian W. *Year Before Yesterday.* 1987. Watts. 1st ed. F/F. P3. $17.00

ALDISS & HARRISON. *Decade in the 1950s.* 1978. St Martin. 1st ed. NF/NF. P3. $20.00

ALDRED, Cyril. *Egyptians.* 1984. London. Thames Hudson. revised ed. 8vo. ils. 268p. VG. W1. $18.00

ALDRICH, T.B. *Stillwater Tragedy.* 1880. Houghton Mifflin. 1st ed. 324p. gilt bdg. VG. M20. $32.00

ALDRICH & SNYDER. *Florida Seashells.* 1936. Houghton Mifflin. 12mo. sgn Snyder. 11 pl. 126p. G. B11. $15.00

ALDRIDGE, Janet. *Meadow-Brook Girls on the Tennis Courts.* 1914. Altemus. 1st ed. 256p. VG+/ragged. M20. $25.00

ALDRIDGE, Richard. *Maine Lines.* 1970. Phil. 1st ed. 224p. F. A17. $10.00

ALDYNE, Nathan. *Cobalt.* 1982. St Martin. VG/VG. P3. $12.00

ALESHKOVSKY, Yuz. *Kangaroo.* 1986. FSG. 1st ed. author's 1st book in Eng. F. B35. $30.00

ALEXANDER. *Guide to Atlases: World, Regional, National, Thematic.* 1971. np. 671p. xl. VG. A4. $45.00

ALEXANDER, Archibald. *Biographical Sketches of the Founder & Principal Alumni...* 1851. Presbyterian Brd Pub. 279p. cloth. VG. M20. $32.00

ALEXANDER, David. *Most Men Don't Kill.* 1951. Random. 1st ed. VG/G. P3. $15.00

ALEXANDER, David. *Pennies From Hell.* 1960. Lippincott. 1st ed. VG/VG. P3. $25.00

ALEXANDER, Kent. *Heroes of the Wild West.* 1992. NY. Mallard. 1st pict. folio. NF/VG. R16. $45.00

ALEXANDER, Shana. *Nutcracker.* 1985. Doubleday. 1st ed. F/NF. H11. $20.00

ALEXANDER & JAY. *Federalist: Collection of Essays, Written in Favour...* 1983. Birmingham. Legal Classics Lib. facsimile. modern leather. M11. $75.00

ALEXANDER & SELESNICK. *History of Psychiatry: An Evaluation...* 1966. NY. 1st ed. 471p. A13. $30.00

ALEXIE, Sherman. *Lone Ranger & Tonto Fistfight in Heaven.* 1993. Atlantic Monthly. 1st ed. F/F. M23. $45.00

ALEXIE, Sherman. *Reservation Blues.* 1995. Atlantic Monthly. 1st ed. F/F. M23. $35.00

ALGER, Edwin. *Jacob Marlowe's Secret.* nd. AL Burt. decor brd. G. P3. $7.00

ALGER, Horatio. *Bertha's Christmas Vision. An Autumn Sheaf.* 1856. Boston. Brn Bazin. 1st ed. author's 1st book. red cloth. VG+. B24. $850.00

ALGREN, Nelson. *Chicago: City on the Make.* 1951. Garden City. 1st ed. inscr w/drawing of cat. F/NF. C2. $100.00

ALGREN, Nelson. *Galena Guide.* 1937. np. ils/23 photos. 79p. pict wrp. A4. $185.00

ALGREN, Nelson. *Man With the Golden Arm.* 1949. Doubleday. ltd ed. w/sgn leaf. F/NF. B2. $200.00

ALI, Tariq. *New Revolutionaries: Handbook of International Radical Left.* 1969. NY. Morrow. 1st ed. F/F. B4. $85.00

ALIBERT & BALOUET. *Extinct Species of the World.* 1990. NY. Barron. 192p. AN/dj. D8. $30.00

ALLAN, John B.; see Westlake, Donald E.

ALLAN, Mae. *Darwin & His Flowers.* 1977. NY. ils. VG+/dj. B26. $39.00

ALLAN, Mae. *Hookers of Kew, 1785-1911.* 1967. London. ils. 273p. VG/dj. B26. $80.00

ALLAN, Mae. *Plants That Changed Our Gardens.* 1974. Devon. Newton Abbot. ils. 208p. F/dj. B26. $29.00

ALLARD, Harry. *Tutti-Frutti Case: Starring the Four Doctors of Goodge.* 1975. Prentice Hall. 1st ed. 8vo. unp. NF. C14. $8.00

ALLARDYCE, Paula. *Adam's Rib.* 1963. Hodder Stoughton. 1st ed. F/F. B35. $30.00

ALLBEURY, Ted. *Alpha List.* 1979. General. 1st ed. VG/VG. P3. $20.00

ALLBEURY, Ted. *Children of Tender Years.* 1985. Beaufort. 1st ed. NF/NF. P3. $15.00

ALLBEURY, Ted. *Crossing.* 1987. Kent. NEL. 1st ed. F/F. T2. $30.00

ALLBEURY, Ted. *Omega-Minus.* 1975. Viking. 1st Am ed. F/F. T2. $15.00

ALLBEURY, Ted. *Pay Any Price.* 1983. Grande. 1st ed. VG/VG. P3. $20.00

ALLBEURY, Ted. *Snowball.* 1974. Lippincott. 1st ed. VG/G. P3. $20.00

ALLBEURY, Ted. *Wilderness of Mirrors.* 1988. Stoddart. 1st ed. F/F. P3. $20.00

ALLEGRETTO, Michael. *Suitor.* 1993. Simon Schuster. 1st ed. NF/NF. P3. $20.00

ALLEN. *NC Wyeth: Collected Paintings, Illustrations & Murals.* 1972. Bonanza. 4to. 335p. NF/VG. A4. $85.00

ALLEN, Betsy. *Clue in the Blue.* nd. Grosset Dunlap. VG/VG. P3. $10.00

ALLEN, C.D. *Classified List of Early American Bookplates.* 1894. Grollier. 1st ed. VG/wrp. B5. $90.00

ALLEN, Charles Warrenne. *Radiotherapy & Phototherapy...* 1904. Phil. 27 pl. 618p. red cloth. VG+. B14. $300.00

ALLEN, Dave. *Little Night Reading.* 1974. Schlesinger. 1st ed. F/F. P3. $20.00

ALLEN, David E. *Victorian Fern Craze.* 1969. London. ils/index/biblio. F. B26. $22.50

ALLEN, Edward. *Mustang Sally.* 1992. Norton. 1st ed. author's 2nd novel. AN/dj. M22. $15.00

ALLEN, Hervey. *Israfel: Life & Times of Edgar Allen Poe.* 1926. Doran. 2 vol. 1st ed. 8vo. gilt maroon cloth. F. T10. $75.00

ALLEN, Hugh. *Story of the Airship.* 1942. Akron. 1st ed. inscr. 74p. G/torn. B18. $37.50

ALLEN, James Lane. *Bride of the Mistletoe.* 1909. Macmillan. 1st ed. 109p. VG. B10. $20.00

ALLEN, James Lane. *Flute & Violin & Other Kentucky Tales.* 1910. Macmillan. 6th. 308p. VG. B10. $20.00

ALLEN, James Lane. *Kentucky Cardinal & Aftermath.* 1900. Macmillan. 1st ed thus. 276p. VG. B10/M5. $35.00

ALLEN, James Lane. *Reign of Law: Tale of the Kentucky Hemp Fields.* 1900. Macmillan. 1st ed/2nd state? ils Fenn/Earl. 385p. VG-. B10. $25.00

ALLEN, Jimmy. *Burden of a Secret.* 1995. Nashville. Moorings. 1st ed. sgn. F/F. M23. $35.00

ALLEN, L.J. *Trans Alaska Pipeline, the Beginning. Vol 1.* 1975. Seattle. Scribe. ils. 151p. NF/dj. D8. $30.00

ALLEN, Lee. *Cincinnati Reds.* 1948. Putnam. 1st ed. VG+. P8. $75.00

ALLEN, Mark. *Falconry in Arabia.* 1984. Orbis. tall 8vo. ils/map. VG. W1. $20.00

ALLEN, Maury. *Roger Maris: Man for All Seasons.* 1986. Donald Fine. 1st ed. photos. F/F. P8. $30.00

ALLEN, Paul H. *Rain Forests of Golfo Dulce.* 1986 (1956). Stanford. 2nd. 417p. M. B26. $55.00

ALLEN, Raymond. *Medical Education & the Changing Order.* 1946. NY. 1st ed. 142p. VG/dj. A13. $20.00

ALLEN, Steve. *Funny Men.* 1956. NY. 1st ed. pres. VG/VG. B5. $30.00

ALLEN, Steve. *Murder in Manhattan.* 1990. Zebra. 1st ed. F/F. P3. $19.00

ALLEN, Tim. *Don't Stand Too Close to a Naked Man.* 1994. Hyperion. 1st ed. F/F. H11. $25.00

ALLEN, Warner. *Uncounted Hour.* 1936. Constable. 1st ed. VG. P3. $30.00

ALLEN, Woody. *Getting Even.* 1971. Random. 1st ed. NF/F. M23. $45.00

ALLEN, Woody. *Play It Again, Sam.* 1969. Random. 1st ed. VG/G. P3. $30.00

ALLENDE, Isabel. *Eva Luna.* 1988. Knopf. 1st ed. author's 3rd book. F/F. H11. $40.00

ALLENDE, Isabel. *House of the Spirits.* 1985. Knopf. 1st ed. author's 1st book. NF/F. H11. $110.00

ALLENDE, Isabel. *Of Love & Shadows.* 1987. Knopf. 1st ed. F/F. M23. $30.00

ALLENDE, Isabel. *Stories of Eva Luna.* 1991. Athen. 1st ed. F/dj. H11. $30.00

ALLER, Lawrence H. *Astrophysics: Atmospheres of the Sun & Stars.* 1953. NY. Ronald Pr. 8vo. 412p. cloth. G. K5. $30.00

ALLINGHAM, Cedric. *Flying Saucers From Mars.* 1955. British BC. VG/fair. P3. $20.00

ALLINGHAM, Margery. *Cargo of Eagles.* 1968. Morrow. 1st ed. VG/VG. P3. $22.00

ALLINGHAM, Margery. *China Governess.* 1962. Doubleday. 1st ed. VG/G. P3. $30.00

ALLINGHAM, Margery. *Estate of the Beckoning Lady.* 1955. Doubleday. 1st ed. VG/VG. P3. $40.00

ALLINGHAM, Margery. *Gyrth Chalice Mystery.* 1931. Crime Club. 1st ed. VG. P3. $40.00

ALLISON, Annye Lewis. *Dogwood & Iris.* nd. np. sgn. VG. w/sgn Christmas card. B10. $12.00

ALLISON, Annye Lewis. *Foot-Path Way.* 1927. Whittet Sheperson. inscr. 74p. G. B10. $10.00

ALLISON, Dorothy. *Bastard Out of Carolina.* 1992. Dutton. 1st ed. F/F. A11. $100.00

ALLISON, Sam. *Wells Fargo & Danger Station.* 1958. Whitman. TVTI. NF. P3. $20.00

ALLISON, William. *Memories of Men & Horses.* 1924. NY. Brentano. 1st Am ed. xl. VG. O3. $35.00

ALLMENDINGER, Blake. *Cowboy: Representations of Labor in American Work Culture.* 1992. Oxford. 1st ed. ils. M/dj. A18. $32.50

ALLMOND, Marcus Blakey. *Estelle: Idyll of Old Virginia.* 1899. Louisville. self pub. 56p. G. B10. $35.00

ALLPORT, Gordon W. *Individual & His Religion: A Psychological Interpretation.* 1950. Macmillan. 8vo. pres. bl-gray cloth. G1. $45.00

ALLSOP, F.C. *Practical Electric Fitting Up of Buildings...* ca 1875. London. 12mo. ils/pl. 275p. gilt bl cloth. F. H3. $125.00

ALLYN, Doug. *Cheerio Killings.* 1989. NY. 1st ed. author's 1st book. F/F. H11. $35.00

ALLYN, Doug. *Motown Underground.* 1993. NY. 1st ed. NF/NF. H11. $20.00

ALMOND, Linda Stevens. *Peter Rabbit & Little White Rabbit.* 1935. Platt Munk. 16mo. VG. M5. $20.00

ALOU, Felipe. *My Life & Baseball.* 1967. World. 1st ed. sgn. VG+/VG+. P8. $65.00

ALSOP, Gulielma F. *April in the Branches.* 1947. Dutton. 1st ed. sgn. 8vo. 257p. VG/VG. B11. $15.00

ALTER, Dinsmore. *Lunar Atlas.* 1968. Dover. rpt. 4to. 174p. G. K5. $45.00

ALTER, Robert Edmond. *Shovel Nose & the Gator Grabbers.* 1963. Putnam. VG/VG. P3. $35.00

ALTERTON & CRAIG. *Edgar Allan Poe.* 1935. Am Book Co. 12mo. 563p. G. A17. $9.50

ALTIERS, J. *Spearheaders.* 1960. Indianapolis. 1st ed. ils. 318p. VG/VG. B5. $45.00

ALTMAN & MELBY. *Handbook of Laboratory Animal Science. Vol 1.* 1977. Cleveland. 2nd. 451p. 8vo. hc. F. B1. $40.00

ALTSHELER, Joseph A. *Horsemen of the Plains.* 1910. Grosset Dunlap. Thrushwood reissue. 390p. orange cloth VG/VG. T5. $22.00

ALVAREZ, Julia. *In the Time of Butterflies.* 1994. Algonquin. ARC. pres set of fld/gathered sheets. sgn. F/wrp. S9. $40.00

ALVERSON, Charles. *Fighting Back.* 1973. Bobbs Merrill. 1st ed. VG/VG. P3. $20.00

ALVERSON, Charles. *Not Sleeping, Just Dead.* 1977. Houghton Mifflin. F/F. P3. $13.00

AMADO, Jorge. *Gabriela. Clove & Cinnamon.* 1962. Knopf. 4th. 426p. dj. F3. $10.00

AMBEKDAR, B.R. *What Congress & Gandhi Have Done to the Untouchables.* 1945. Bombay. 1st ed. 368p. cloth. VG. A17. $15.00

AMBLER, Eric. *Care of Time.* 1981. FSG. 1st ed. VG/VG. M22/P3. $15.00

AMBLER, Eric. *Cause for Alarm.* 1940. Knopf. 1st ed. VG/G. P3. $15.00

AMBLER, Eric. *Dark Frontier.* 1990. Mysterious. 1st ed. F/F. P3. $19.00

AMBLER, Eric. *Dirty Story.* 1967. Bodley Head. 1st ed. VG/G. P3. $20.00

AMBLER, Eric. *Doctor Frigo.* 1974. Atheneum. 1st ed. VG/VG. P3. $20.00

AMBLER, Eric. *Intercom Conspiracy.* 1969. Atheneum. 1st ed. VG/VG. P3. $25.00

AMBLER, Eric. *Intrigue.* 1960. Knopf. VG/VG. P3. $20.00

AMBLER, Eric. *Kind of Anger.* 1964. Bodley Head. 1st ed. VG/G. P3. $30.00

AMBLER, Eric. *Passage of Arms.* 1960. Reprint Soc. VG/VG. P3. $8.00

AMBLER, Gifford. *Maxims of Marquis.* 1937. Eyre Spottiswood. 1st ed. ils. 111p. VG/VG. P2. $45.00

AMBROSE, Stephen E. *Eisenhower.* 1990. Simon Schuster. 1st ed. sgn. F/F. M23. $35.00

AMBROSE, Stephen E. *Undaunted Courage.* 1996. Simon Schuster. 1st ed. F/F. M23. $40.00

AMBROSIUS, Ernst. *Andrees Allgemeiner Hand Atlas.* 1914. Velhagen Klasing. lg folio. 24 maps. gr bdg. xl. F. O7. $350.00

AMERICAN STEAMSHIP COMPANY. *How to Make a Steamship Float.* 1985. MI. Harbor House. AN. A16. $10.95

AMES, Delano. *Body on Page One.* 1951. Hodder Stoughton. 1st ed. VG. P3. $20.00

AMES, Delano. *Murder, Maestro, Please.* 1952. Hodder Stoughton. VG. P3. $15.00

AMES, Fisher. *Practical Guide to Whist.* 1895. NY. 7th. 118p. VG. S1. $10.00

AMES, Jennifer. *Flight Into Fear.* 1954. Collins. 1st ed. VG/VG. P3. $20.00

AMHERST, Alicia. *History of Gardening in England.* 1969 (1896). Detroit. 2nd. ils. 405p. yel cloth. F. B26. $55.00

AMIRSADEGI, Hossein. *Twentieth-Century Iran.* 1977. NY. Holmes Meier. 1st ed. 8 pl/2 maps/tables. VG/torn. W1. $32.00

AMIS, Kingsley. *Alteration.* 1977. Viking. 1st ed. G/G. P3. $25.00

AMIS, Kingsley. *Colonel Sun.* England. 1st ed. VG/VG. M17. $22.50

AMIS, Kingsley. *Difficulties With Girls.* 1988. Summit. 1st ed. F/F. H11. $25.00

AMIS, Kingsley. *Egyptologists.* 1966. Random. 1st ed. VG/G. P3. $23.00

AMIS, Kingsley. *Girl, 20.* 1971. Jonathan Cape. 1st ed. VG/VG. P3. $20.00

AMIS, Kingsley. *I Want It Now.* 1968. Jonathan Cape. 1st ed. VG/VG. P3. $23.00

AMIS, Kingsley. *Jake's Thing.* 1978. Hutchinson. 1st ed. F/F. P3. $18.00

AMIS, Kingsley. *James Bond Dossier.* 1965. London. Cape. 1st ed. VG/VG. M19. $50.00

AMIS, Kingsley. *Memoirs.* 1991. Hutchinson. 1st ed. F/F. P3. $30.00

AMIS, Kingsley. *One Fat Englishman.* 1963. Gollancz. 1st ed. VG/VG. P3. $30.00

AMIS, Kingsley. *Russian Hide & Seek.* 1980. Hutchinson. 1st ed. VG/VG. P3. $20.00

AMIS, Kingsley. *Stanley & the Women.* 1984. Hutchinson. 1st ed. NF/NF. P3. $22.00

AMIS, Kingsley. *What Became of Jane Austen?* 1970. HBJ. 1st Am ed. F/NF. B4. $85.00

AMIS, Martin. *Dead Babies.* 1975. Knopf. 1st ed. NF/NF. P3. $75.00

AMIS, Martin. *London Fields.* 1989. London. 1st ed. sgn. F/F. A11. $70.00

AMIS, Martin. *Other People: A Mystery Story.* 1981. Viking. 1st Am ed. F/F. B2. $60.00

AMIS, Martin. *Rachel Papers.* 1974. Knopf. 1st ed. NF/NF. P3. $80.00

AMIS, Martin. *Time's Arrow.* 1991. London. 1st ed. sgn. F/F. A11. $55.00

AMIS, Martin. *Visiting Mr Nabokov & Other Excursions.* 1994. Harmony. 1st ed. F/F. B35. $20.00

AMMONS, A.R. *Six-Piece Suit*. 1978. Palaemon. 1/200. 6p. F/stiff wrp. B10. $35.00

AMORY, Cleveland. *Last Resorts*. 1952. Harper. 1st ed. sgn. 527p. VG/VG. B11. $30.00

AMOS, Alan. *Borderline Murder*. 1947. Crime Club. 1st ed. VG. P3. $12.00

AMOS, William. *Originals: An A-Z of Fiction's Real-Life Characters...* 1985. np. 40 photos. 634p. NF/NF. A4. $65.00

AMSBURY, Joe. *Bridge: Bidding Naturally*. 1979. London. 152p. VG. S1. $10.00

AMSBURY & PAYNE. *Bridge: TNT & Competitive Bidding*. 1981. London. 175p. VG/wrp. S1. $10.00

AMSDEN, Charles Avery. *Prehistoric Southwesterners From Basketmaker to Pueblo*. 1949. Los Angeles. Southwest Mus. 1st ed. ils/maps. 163p. F. T10. $75.00

AMUNDSEN, Bjorstad. *Kirkenesperda*. 1946 (1942). Oslo. fld chart/photos/maps. 464p. dj. A17. $35.00

AMUNDSEN & ELLSWORTH. *First Crossing of the Polar Sea*. 1928. Doubleday Doran. ils/fld map. 324p. VG. T7. $65.00

AN OBSERVOR. *Archangel American War With Russia*. 1924. Chicago. 1st ed. ils. 216p. VG. B5. $75.00

AN PHILIBIN; see Pollock, John Hackett.

ANATI, Emmanuel. *Camonica Valley*. 1961. Knopf. 1st Am ed. 8vo. ils. 262p. VG/dj. W1. $20.00

ANATI, Emmanuel. *Palestine Before the Hebrews*. 1963. Knopf. 1st ed. 8vo. 5 full-p maps. 453p. NF/dj. W1. $22.00

ANBUREY, Thomas. *Travels Through the Interior Parts of America*. 1923. Houghton Mifflin. 2 vol. 1/445. 1st Am ed. 8vo. T10. $225.00

AND, Metin. *Osmanli Senliklerinde Turk Sanatlari*. 1982. Ankara. Kultur ve Turism Bakanligi. 1st ed. VG/stiff wrp. W1. $45.00

ANDERSEN, Hans Christian. *Andersen's Fairy Tales*. 1932. McKay. 1st Am ed. ils Rackham. G+. B17. $80.00

ANDERSEN, Hans Christian. *Ausgewahlte Marchen Gerlach & Wiedling*. ca 1906. Wien Leipzig. ils H Steiner-Prag. VG. D1. $100.00

ANDERSEN, Hans Christian. *Die Kleine Seejungrau*. 1953. Elberfeld. Sulamith Wulfing Pub. ils Sulamith Wulfin. VG/wrp/dj. D1. $125.00

ANDERSEN, Hans Christian. *Emperor's New Clothes*. 1992. Atlantic Monthly. ils Karl Lagerfield. F/F case. P2. $45.00

ANDERSEN, Hans Christian. *Fairy Tales*. ca 1920s. Nelson. ils Honor Appleton. gilt bl cloth. VG. M5. $225.00

ANDERSEN, Hans Christian. *Fairy Tales*. 1924. Doran. 1st Am ed. ils Kay Nielsen. 280p. VG. D1. $650.00

ANDERSEN, Hans Christian. *Hans Andersen's Fairy Tales*. 1913. Eng. Boots the Chemists. ils WH Robinson. 320p. VG. D1. $250.00

ANDERSEN, Hans Christian. *Hans Christian Andersen's Fairy Tales*. nd. London. 1st ed. ils Jiri Trnka. F/torn. M5. $40.00

ANDERSEN, Hans Christian. *Little Fir Tree*. 1970. Harper Row. 1st ed. ils Nancy Burkert. 36p. F/NF. P2. $35.00

ANDERSEN, Hans Christian. *Little Mermaid*. 1939. Macmillan. 1st ed thus. ils Dorothy Lathrop. VG/torn. D1. $295.00

ANDERSEN, Hans Christian. *Nightingale*. 1984. Picture Book Studio. probable 1st ed. ils/sgn Zwerger. unp. glossy brd. F/F. T5. $55.00

ANDERSEN, Hans Christian. *Old Man Is Always Right*. 1940. Harper. stated 1st ed. ils Rojankovsky. VG. M5. $48.00

ANDERSEN, Hans Christian. *Snow Queen & Other Stories*. 1961. Golden. 1st Am ed. ils Andrienne Segur. 136p. NF. P2. $165.00

ANDERSEN, Hans Christian. *Snow Queen*. 1929. Dutton. ils Katherine Beverly/Elizabeth Ellender. VG. P2. $100.00

ANDERSEN, Hans Christian. *Snow Queen*. 1982. Dial. 1st ed. ils Susan Jeffes. gray cloth. F/VG. D1. $45.00

ANDERSEN, Hans Christian. *Stories From Hans Andersen*. nd. Nister. trans W Angeldorff. ils ES Hardy. aeg. cloth. VG. M5. $40.00

ANDERSEN, Hans Christian. *Wild Swan*. 1981. Dial. 1st ed. ils Susan Jeffers. F/VG. D1. $45.00

ANDERSEN, Johannes C. *Myths & Legends of the Polynesians*. 1986. Rutland. VG. O7. $25.00

ANDERSEN & WEI. *Action for the Defense: When the Enemy Opens the Bidding*. 1980. NY. 245p. VG/wrp. S1. $6.00

ANDERSEN & WEI. *Bidding Precisely: Volume 2*. 1976. NY. 159p. VG/wrp. S1. $5.00

ANDERSEN & WEI. *Profits From Preempts: Bidding Precisely Volume 3*. 1977. NY. 162p. VG/wrp. S1. $5.00

ANDERSON, Anne. *Bitter Green of the Willow*. 1967. Chilton. 1st ed. ils/6 pl. VG/worn. M5. $40.00

ANDERSON, Anne. *Nursery Zoo*. nd. Nelson. 48 pl. VG+. M5. $125.00

ANDERSON, Anne. *Old Old Fairy Tales*. nd. Nelson. 12 pl. 159p. G+. P2. $125.00

ANDERSON, Bernice. *Topsy Turvey's Pigtails*. 1937 (1930). Rand McNally. ils Bernice Friend. VG. P2. $75.00

ANDERSON, C.W. *Black, Bay & Chestnut*. 1939. NY. Macmillan. 2nd. obl 4to. VG/dj. T10. $25.00

ANDERSON, C.W. *Filly for Joan*. 1960. Macmillan. 1st ed. VG. O3. $25.00

ANDERSON, C.W. *Horse for Hurricane Hill*. 1957. Macmillan. 2nd. VG/VG. O3. $35.00

ANDERSON, C.W. *Horses Are Folks*. 1950. Harper Row. 15 full-p lithographs. G+. P2. $20.00

ANDERSON, C.W. *Lonesome Little Colt*. 1963. Macmillan. 4th. G+. O3. $25.00

ANDERSON, C.W. *Phantom, Son of the Gray Ghost*. 1969. Macmillan. 3rd. VG. O3. $15.00

ANDERSON, C.W. *Tomorrow's Champion*. 1946. Macmillan. ils. cloth. VG+. M5. $18.00

ANDERSON, C.W. *Tomorrow's Champion*. 1946. Macmillan. 1st ed. VG/G. P2. $32.00

ANDERSON, C.W. *Touch of Greatness*. 1945. NY. Macmillan. probable 1st ed. sm 4to. ils. pict cloth. F/VG+. C8. $85.00

ANDERSON, Charles Carter. *Fighting by Southern Federals*. 1912. NY. Neale. 1st ed. 408p. cloth. G+. M8. $85.00

ANDERSON, D. *Art of Written Forms. Theory & Practice of Calligraphy*. 1969. NY. 1st ed. ils/index. 358p. VG/VG. B5. $45.00

ANDERSON, Frank. *Birds of My Mind*. 1971. Spartenberg. Kitemaug. unp. VG/VG. B10. $15.00

ANDERSON, Frank. *Illustrated Treasury of Cultivated Flowers*. 1979. NY. Crown. folio. 50 full-p pl. AN/dj. A10. $45.00

ANDERSON, James Douglas. *Making the American Thoroughbred*. 1946. Nashville. Grainger Williams. 2nd. VG. O3. $68.00

ANDERSON, James. *Assault & Matrimony*. 1980. Muller. 1st ed. NF/NF. P3. $20.00

ANDERSON, Janice. *Marilyn Monroe*. 1983. Royce. VG/VG. P3. $25.00

ANDERSON, Jervis. *This Was Harlem*. 1982. NY. 1st ed. ils/photos/index. 390p. VG/VG. B5. $25.00

ANDERSON, John P. *Book of British Topography*. 1966. Amsterdam. TOT. rpt of 1881 London ed. AN. T7. $55.00

ANDERSON, John Quincy. *Campaigning With Parsons' Texas Cavalry Brigade...* 1967. Hill Jr College. 1st ed. 173p. F/NF. M8. $95.00

ANDERSON, Kenneth. *Black Panther of Sivanipalli.* 1960. Rand McNally. ils/photos. G. P12. $10.00

ANDERSON, Luther A. *How To Hunt a Whitetail Deer.* 1968. Funk Wagnall. photos. VG/G+. P12. $8.00

ANDERSON, Mabel Washbourne. *Life of General Stand Waite.* 1915. Pryor, OK. 1st ed. 58p. ES. VG/prt wrp. M8. $175.00

ANDERSON, Maxwell. *Storm Operation.* 1944. Anderson House. 1st ed. F/F. B4. $125.00

ANDERSON, Oma Carlyle. *I Hear the Lark Singing.* 1982. Brandon, FL. 1st ed. sgn. 90p. F/VG. B11. $10.00

ANDERSON, Per-Olow. *They Are Human Too...* 1957. Chicago. Regnery. ils. 191p. VG/tattered. W1. $28.00

ANDERSON, Poul. *Armis of Elfland.* 1994. Severn House. 1st hc ed. F/F. G10. $25.00

ANDERSON, Poul. *Avatar.* 1978. Berkley Putnam. 1st ed. F/F. P3. $20.00

ANDERSON, Poul. *Boat of a Million Years.* 1989. Tor. 1st ed. sgn. F/F. P3. $25.00

ANDERSON, Poul. *Harvest of Stars.* 1993. Tor. 1st ed. F/F. P3. $23.00

ANDERSON, Poul. *Infinite Voyage.* 1969. Crowell Collier. 1st ed. VG/VG. P3. $25.00

ANDERSON, Poul. *Kinship With the Stars.* 1993. Severn House. 1st Eng/1st hc ed. F/F. G10. $25.00

ANDERSON, Poul. *Let the Spacemen Beware!* 1969. London. Dennis Dobson. 1st hc ed. sgn. F/clip. T2. $35.00

ANDERSON, Poul. *Orion Shall Rise.* 1983. Timescape. 1st ed. F/F. P3. $17.00

ANDERSON, Poul. *Shield of Time.* 1990. Tor. 1st ed. AN/dj. M21. $15.00

ANDERSON, Poul. *Three Worlds to Conquer.* 1982. Sidgwick Jackson. F/F. P3. $22.00

ANDERSON, Poul. *Vault of the Ages.* 1967. HRW. 4th. VG/VG. P3. $30.00

ANDERSON, Robert E. *Story of Extinct Civilizations of the East.* 1904. Appleton. ils/maps. 213p. teg. VG. W1. $12.00

ANDERSON, Robert. *All Summer Long.* 1955. Samuel French. 1st ed. F/NF. B4. $125.00

ANDERSON, Roy. *White Star.* 1964. Prescott, Eng. Stephenson. 58 photos. 236p. VG/dj. T7. $35.00

ANDERSON, Sherwood. *New Testament.* 1927. NY. 1st ed. 1/250. sgn. NF/case. C2. $150.00

ANDERSON, Sherwood. *Sherwood Anderson's Memoirs.* 1942. Harcourt Brace. 1st ed. 507p. cloth. VG/dj. M20. $62.00

ANDERSON, Sherwood. *Sherwood Anderson's Notebook.* 1926. NY. 1st ed. inscr. NF/VG. C6. $150.00

ANDERSON, Sherwood. *Tar, a Midwest Childhood.* 1926. Boni Liveright. 1st ed. 346p. VG/dj. M20. $77.00

ANDERSON, Sherwood. *Windy McPherson's Son.* 1916. John Lane. 1st ed. author's 1st book. later bdg. NF. C2. $75.00

ANDERSON, William D. *Light Gymnastics: A Guide to Systematic Instruction...* 1893. NY. ils. 234p. pict cloth. VG. B14. $45.00

ANDERSON & ANDERSON. *Sailing Ship: Six Thousand Years of History.* 1926-27. NY/London. 20 pl. 211p. VG. T7. $45.00

ANDERSON & EKLUND. *Inheritors of Earth.* 1974. Chilton. 1st ed. VG/VG. P3. $20.00

ANDERSON & HUNTER. *Jack Ruby's Girls.* 1970. Atlanta. 1st ed. VG/VG. B5. $60.00

ANDERSON & MAY. *McCarthy: The Man, the Senator, the 'Ism.'* 1952. Beacon. 1st ed. NF/worn. B2. $25.00

ANDERTON, Philip. *Bridge in 20 Lessons.* 1961. London. 127p. VG. S1. $6.00

ANDREW, Christopher. *KGB: The Inside Story.* 1990. Hodder Stoughton. 1st ed. VG. P3. $35.00

ANDREW, Felicia; see Grant, Charles L.

ANDREW, T.G. *Twelve Wild Ducks: A Tale of the Norse.* 1859. Phil. 12mo. 31p. pebbled brn cloth. VG. H3. $175.00

ANDREWS, Allen. *Pig Plantagenet.* 1981. Viking. 1st ed. VG/G. P3. $15.00

ANDREWS, Arthur E. *Rags: Being an Explanation of Why They Are Used...* nd. Issued by 29 Rag Paper Mfgs. 4to. 30p w/samples. G. B14. $55.00

ANDREWS, Bart. *TV Addict's Nostalgia, Trivia & Quiz.* 1984. Greenwich. TVTI. VG/VG. P3. $15.00

ANDREWS, Charles M. *Colonial Period of American History.* Yale. 3 vol. later prt. bl cloth. VG. B30. $85.00

ANDREWS, Jean. *Peppers: Domesticated Capsicums.* 1984. Austin. 1st ed. ils. 170p. NF/dj. B26. $37.50

ANDREWS, Luman. *Catalogue of Flowering Plants & Ferns of Springfield, MA...* 1924. Springfield. ils/photos. 221p. wrp. B26. $22.00

ANDREWS, Nigel. *Horror Films.* 1985. Gallery. VG/VG. P3. $20.00

ANDREWS, Raymond. *Appalachee Red.* 1978. Dial. 1st ed. F/NF. B2. $40.00

ANDREWS, T.S. *World Sporting Annual Record Book.* 1928. Milwaukee. 320p. G/stiff wrp. A17. $22.50

ANDREWS, V.C. *Fallen Hearts.* 1988. Poseidon. 1st ed. VG/VG. P3. $20.00

ANDREWS, V.C. *Flowers in the Attic.* 1979. Simon Schuster. 1st ed. VG/VG. P3. $25.00

ANDREWS, Wayne. *American Gothic: Its Origins, Its Trials, Its Triumphs.* 1975. Random. 1st ed. 4to. 154p. T10. $25.00

ANDREWS & KARLINS. *Gomorrah.* 1974. Doubleday. 1st ed. NF/NF. P3. $13.00

ANGAS, W. Mack. *Rivalry on the Atlantic.* 1939. Lee Furman. G. A16. $40.00

ANGEL, Marie. *Beasts in Heraldry.* 1974. Stephen Greene. 1st ed. ils Marie Angel. unp. VG+/box. D1. $85.00

ANGELL, James Rowland. *Intro to Psychology.* 1918. Holt. 282p. dk gray cloth. G1. $40.00

ANGELL, Roger. *Baseball.* 1984. Abrams. 1st ed. photos Walter Ioos. F/F. P8. $45.00

ANGELL, Roger. *Late Innings: A Baseball Companion.* 1982. NY. S&S. 1st ed. VG/NF. R16. $30.00

ANGELL, Roger. *Day in the Life of Roger Angell.* 1970. 1st ed. VG/VG. C4. $40.00

ANGELL, Roger. *Summer Game.* 1972. Viking. 1st ed. VG+/VG. P8. $50.00

ANGELO, Valenti. *Golden Gate.* 1939. Viking/Jr Literary Guild. 8vo. 273p. ils cloth. VG+. C14. $8.00

ANGELO, Valenti. *Nino.* 1938. NY. 1st ed. ils. 244p. NF/worn. A17. $10.00

ANGELOU, Maya. *All God's Children Need Traveling Shoes.* 1986. Random. 1st ed. F/NF. B4. $65.00

ANGELOU, Maya. *And Still I Rise.* 1978. Random. 1st ed. F/F. B35. $40.00

ANGELOU, Maya. *Collapsing Universe.* 1983. Harper Row. 1st ed. F/F. M19. $17.50

ANGELOU, Maya. *Gather Together in My Name.* 1974. Random. 1st ed. sgn. rem mk. F/F clip. B4. $175.00

ANGELOU, Maya. *I Shall Not Be Moved.* 1990. Random. ARC/1st ed. inscr. RS. F/F. B4. $125.00

ANGELOU, Maya. *I Shall Not Be Moved.* 1990. Random. ARC/1st ed. RS. F/F. w/promo material. B4. $45.00

ANGELOU, Maya. *I Shall Not Be Moved.* 1990. Random. 1st ed. F/F. M19. $17.50

ANGELOU, Maya. *Oh Pray My Wings Are Gonna Fit Me Well*. 1975. Random. 1st ed. NF/F. B35. $50.00

ANGELOU, Maya. *Wouldn't Take Nothing for My Journey Now*. 1993. Random. 1st ed. inscr. AN/dj. B4. $85.00

ANGLE, Paul M. *American Reader: From Columbus to Today*. 1958. Chicago. VG. O7. $35.00

ANGLE, Paul M. *Portrait of Abraham Lincoln in Letters by His Oldest Son*. 1968. Chicago Hist Soc. 92p. VG+/dj. M20. $20.00

ANGLUND, Joan Walsh. *Childhood Is a Time of Innocence*. 1964. Harcourt. stated 1st ed. cloth. VG+/G. M5. $25.00

ANGLUND, Joan Walsh. *Christmas Is a Time of Giving*. 1961. Harcourt. 1st ed. ils. F/G. M5. $25.00

ANGLUND, Joan Walsh. *Do You Love Someone?* 1971. HBJ. 1st ed. 16mo. unp. ils cloth. NF/VG. C14. $15.00

ANGLUND, Joan Walsh. *In a Pumpkin Shell: A Mother Goose ABC*. 1960. Harcourt Brace. 1st ed. unp. VG. C14. $12.00

ANGLUND, Joan Walsh. *Joan Walsh Anglund Story Book*. 1978. Random. 7th. VG. B17. $7.50

ANGLUND, Joan Walsh. *Morning Is a Little Child*. 1969. Harcourt. sm 4to. F. M5. $25.00

ANGLUND, Joan Walsh. *Spring Is a New Beginning*. 1963. HBW. 1st ed. 16mo. unp. F/F. C14. $20.00

ANGLUND, Joan Walsh. *Teddy Bear Tales*. 1985. Random. 1st ed. 4to. F. M5. $18.00

ANGLUND, Joan Walsh. *What Color Is Love?* 1966. Harcourt. 1st ed. ils. F/VG+. M5. $30.00

ANIBARRO. *Intento de un Diccionario Biografico...* 1993. 1/1000. 4to. 628p. NF. A4. $125.00

ANNENBERG. *Type Foundries of America & Their Catalogs*. 1975. np. 4to. ils. 245p. F/VG. A4. $300.00

ANNIN, Robert Edwards. *Ocean Shipping*. 1920. Century. ils. 427p. gilt bl bdg. G+. P12. $10.00

ANNO, Mitsumasa. *Anno's Counting Book*. 1975. Crowell. 1st Am ed. ils. unp. F/VG. T5. $35.00

ANNO, Mitsumasa. *Dr Anno's Magical Midnight Circus*. 1972. Weatherhill. 1st ed. ils. 27p. F/NF. P2. $45.00

ANOBILE, Richard J. *Godfrey Daniels!* 1975. Crown. VG/VG. P3. $15.00

ANOBILE, Richard J. *Why a Duck?* nd. Darien. 8th. VG/VG. P3. $15.00

ANON. *Baby's Red Letter Days*. 1901. Syracuse, NY. Just's Food. ils JW Smith. VG. D1. $120.00

ANON. *Bicentennial Wagon Train Pilgrimage*. 1977. Kenosha. ltd ed. 1/2500. sgn pub. VG. O3. $45.00

ANON. *Bunny Cottontail*. (1910). Saalfield. ils. muslin. NF. D1. $60.00

ANON. *Bunty: The Book for Girls 1979*. 1978. London. DC Thomson. ils. 127p. VG+/clip. C14. $15.00

ANON. *Circus Fun*. 1946. Whitehall. ils Eiona. 4 moveables. NF/wrp. D1. $48.00

ANON. *Dame Crump & Her Pig*. 1900s. NY. McLoughlin. 4to. VG/gilt wrp. D1. $250.00

ANON. *Fairyland Tales & ABCs*. ca 1900. np. linen. VG/stiff wrp. M5. $45.00

ANON. *Fun Faces*. 1914. Chicago. Ideal. 6 die-cut faces. half cloth/pict brd. VG/torn box. D1. $300.00

ANON. *Half Hours in the Tiny World: Wonders of Insect Life*. 1882. London. 80 ils. 311p. Bickers bdg. A17. $30.00

ANON. *Indoor Polo*. 1931-32. Assn Am Offical Manual. VG. O3. $95.00

ANON. *Mountains & Mountain Climbing*. 1883. London. ils. 415p. gilt gr cloth. G. H3. $65.00

ANON. *Saddle & Song: A Collection of Verses...* 1905. Lippincott. 1st ed. G+. O3. $25.00

ANON. *Tall Book of Nursery Tales*. 1944. Harry Doehla. ils/moveables. VG. D1. $85.00

ANON. *Visit to the Tower*. ca 1820. York. J Kendrew. ils. 13p. NF/wrp. D1. $25.00

ANSAY, A. Manette. *Vinegar Hill*. 1994. Viking. 1st ed. sgn. F/F. M23. $45.00

ANSCOMBE, Roderick. *Secret Life of Laszlo, Count Dracula*. 1994. Hyperion. 1st ed. F/F. P3. $23.00

ANSHAW, Carol. *Aquamarine*. 1992. Houghton Mifflin. 1st ed. sgn. F/F. M23. $20.00

ANSTEY, F. *Vice Versa*. 1911. Smith Elder. 40th. VG. P3. $20.00

ANTEVS, Ernst. *Rainfall & Tree Growth in the Great Basin*. 1938. WA/NY. VG. O7. $20.00

ANTHOLOGY. *After the Darkness*. 1993. Baltimore. Maclay. 1st ed. 1/750. sgn all contributors. F/sans/case. T2. $50.00

ANTHOLOGY. *Antique Gems From the Greek & Latin*. 1901-1902. Phil. Barrie. 1/1000. 11 vol set. VG. A20. $350.00

ANTHOLOGY. *Battle Stations! Your Navy in Action*. 1946. NY. 402p. G. A17. $15.00

ANTHOLOGY. *Black Scenes*. 1971. Doubleday/Zenith. 1st ed. edit Alice Childress. F/VG clip. B4. $45.00

ANTHOLOGY. *Book of the Sixth World Fantasy Convention*. 1980. Underwood Miller. 1st ed. VG+. R10. $15.00

ANTHOLOGY. *Editor's Choice: Literature & Graphics From US Small Press*. 1980. np. 500p. VG. R10. $8.00

ANTHOLOGY. *Homes of American Authors*. 1853. Putnam. 1st ed/1st prt. aeg. marbled ep. emb morocco. F. B14. $250.00

ANTHOLOGY. *New Poems 1942*. 1942. Peter Pauper. 1st trade ed. NF/VG clip. B4. $85.00

ANTHOLOGY. *Pictorial History of the Second World War*. 1944-46. NY. VFW ed. 4 vol. VG. A17. $35.00

ANTHOLOGY. *Story Parade: A Collection of Modern Stories...* 1937. Winston. 8vo. 363p. pict ep. VG. T5. $20.00

ANTHOLOGY. *To Gwen With Love: Anthology Dedicated to Gwendolyn Brooks*. 1971. Chicago. Johnson. 1st ed. F/NF. B4. $85.00

ANTHONY, Evelyn. *Anne Boleyn*. 1986. Century. VG/VG. P3. $15.00

ANTHONY, Evelyn. *Avenue of the Dead*. 1981. Hutchinson. 1st ed. NF/NF. P3. $18.00

ANTHONY, Evelyn. *Charles the King*. 1987. Century. VG/VG. P3. $15.00

ANTHONY, Evelyn. *Scarlet Thread*. 1990. Harper Row. 1st ed. F/F. P3. $19.00

ANTHONY, Evelyn. *Voices on the Wind*. 1985. Hutchinson. 1st ed. NF/NF. P3. $18.00

ANTHONY, Florence. *Fate*. 1991. Boston. AP. VG. C4. $35.00

ANTHONY, Patricia. *Brother Termite*. 1993. HBJ. 1st ed. author's 2nd book. F/F. G10. $15.00

ANTHONY, Patricia. *Cold Allies*. 1993. HBJ. 1st ed. F/F. M23. $25.00

ANTHONY, Piers. *And Eternity*. 1990. Morrow. 1st ed. VG/VG. P3. $16.00

ANTHONY, Piers. *Demons Don't Dream*. 1993. Tor. 1st ed. F/F. P3. $20.00

ANTHONY, Piers. *Firefly*. 1990. Morrow. 1st ed. F/F. P3. $19.00

ANTHONY, Piers. *For Love of Evil*. 1988. Morrow. 1st ed. NF/NF. P3. $18.00

ANTHONY, Piers. *Fractal Mode*. 1992. Ace/Putnam. F/F. P3. $19.00

ANTHONY, Piers. *Isle of Woman*. 1993. Tor. 1st ed. NF/NF. P3. $24.00

ANTHONY, Piers. *Question Quest.* 1991. Morrow. 1st ed. F/F. P3. $20.00

ANTHONY, Piers. *Robot Adept.* 1988. Ace Putnam. 1st ed. NF/NF. P3. $17.00

ANTHONY, Piers. *Shade of the Tree.* 1986. Tor. 1st ed. F/F. P3. $16.00

ANTHONY, Piers. *Total Recall.* 1989. Morrow. 1st ed. NF/NF. P3. $20.00

ANTHONY, Piers. *Unicorn Point.* 1989. Ace Putnam. 1st ed. F/F. P3. $16.00

ANTON, Ferdinand. *Primitive Art.* 1979. Abrams. rem mk. F/dj. B18. $37.50

ANTONELLI, Lisa M. *Virginia: Commonwealth Comes of Age.* 1988. Windsor. 1st ed. ils. 470p. VG/VG. B10. $20.00

ANTONGINI, Tom. *D'Annunzio.* 1938. Boston. 1st Am ed. 583p. NF. A17. $15.00

APPLE, Max. *Free Agents.* 1984. 1st ed. F/F. C4. $35.00

APPLE, William. *Widowmakers.* 1994. Walker. 1st ed. F/F. M22. $15.00

APPLEBY, John. *Bad Summer.* 1958. Washburn. 1st ed. VG. P3. $10.00

APPLER, A.C. *Younger Brothers.* 1955. Frederick Fell. fwd Burton Rascoe. 245p. VG/dj. T10. $28.00

APPLETON, John Edward. *Beginner's Hand-Book of Chemistry.* 1888 (1884). NY. Chautauqua. 8vo. 256p. gilt cloth. G. K5. $50.00

APPLETON, Victor. *Desert of Mystery.* 1953. Children's Pr. 1st ed. VG/G. P3. $15.00

APPLETON, Victor. *Don Sturdy in the Port of Lost Ships (#6).* 1926. Grosset Dunlap. lists 11 titles. 214p. VG/dj. M20. $40.00

APPLETON, Victor. *Don Sturdy Lost in Glacier Bay (#13).* 1933. Grosset Dunlap. 204p. VG/dj. M20. $72.00

APPLETON, Victor. *Movie Boys at the Big Fair (#16).* 1926. Garden City. 214p. VG/pict wrp. M20. $32.00

APPLETON, Victor. *Moving Picture Boys on the Coast (#3).* 1913. Grosset Dunlap. lists 9 titles. 212p. VG/dj. M20. $25.00

APPLETON, Victor. *Tom Swift & His Electronic Retroscope (#14).* 1959. Grosset Dunlap. 1st ed. 184p. VG/dj. M20. $22.00

APPLETON, Victor. *Tom Swift & His House on Wheels (#32).* 1929. Grosset Dunlap. 1st ed. VG+. M21. $30.00

APPLETON, Victor. *Tom Swift & His Motor Boat.* nd. Keds premium ed. 92p. worn. M20. $275.00

APPLETON, Victor. *Tom Swift & His Television Detector.* 1938 (1933). Grosset Dunlap. 217p. brn brd. VG. B14. $35.00

APPLETON, Victor. *Tom Swift & the Captive Planetoid (#29).* 1967. Grosset Dunlap. lists to this title. 174p. VG+. M20. $20.00

APPLETON, Victor. *Tom Swift & the Caves of Nuclear Fire (#8).* 1956. Grosset Dunlap. 1st ed. 214p. VG/dj. M20. $22.00

APPLETON, Victor. *Tom Swift Among the Fire Fighters (#24).* 1921. Grosset Dunlap. lists to #30. 214p. VG/VG. M20. $55.00

APTHEKER, Herbert. *Negro in the Abolitionist Movement.* 1941. NY. Internat. 48 p. NF/wrp. R11. $14.00

AQUINAS, Thomas. *Basic Writings of...* 1945. NY. 2 vol. 1st ed. 8vo. gilt pict blk cloth. F/G case. H3. $150.00

ARBER, Edward. *First Three English Books on America.* 1971. NY. Kraus. rpt of 1885 ed. 408p. F3. $45.00

ARBUTHNOT, May Hill. *Children & Books.* 1957. Scott Foresman. TB. 684p. VG. M5. $25.00

ARCH, E.L. *Bridge to Yesterday.* 1963. Avalon. 1st ed. F/F. P3. $20.00

ARCHBOLD, Rick. *Hindenburg: An Illustrated History.* 1994. NY. ils. 229p. F/dj. A17. $35.00

ARCHER, Jeffrey. *First Among Equals.* 1984. Hodder Stoughton. 1st ed. F/F. P3. $20.00

ARCHER, Jeffrey. *Matter of Honor.* 1986. Linden. 1st Am ed. F/F. N4. $27.50

ARCHER, Jeffrey. *Shall We Tell the President.* 1977. Viking. 1st ed. VG/VG. P3. $20.00

ARCHER, Jeffrey. *Twist in the Tale.* 1988. Simon Schuster. 1st ed. NF/NF. P3. $20.00

ARCHIBALD, Norman. *Heaven High Hell Deep, 1917-1918.* 1935. NY. 350p. G. B18. $22.50

ARCINIEGAS, German. *Germans in the Conquest of America.* 1943. NY. VG. O7. $25.00

ARD, William; see Block, Lawrence.

ARDAI, Charles. *Great Tales of Madness & Macabre.* 1990. Galahad. F/F. P3. $15.00

ARDEN, William. *Mystery of the Dancing Devil.* 1976. Random. 1st ed. VG. P3. $12.00

ARDEN, William. *Mystery of the Laughing Shadow.* 1969. Random. VG. P3. $15.00

ARDIS. *Guide to Literature of Electrical & Electronics Engineering.* 1987. np. 697 annotated entries. 190p. VG. A4. $85.00

ARDIZZONE, Edward. *Little Tim & the Brave Sea Captain.* 1936. NY. 2nd. ils. fair/dj. M5. $25.00

ARDIZZONE, Edward. *Young Ardizzone: An Autobiographical Fragment.* 1970. NY. 1st ed. ils. F/VG. B17. $25.00

ARDOIN & FITZGERALD. *Callas: The Art & Life.* 1974. NY. 1st ed. VG/G. B5. $25.00

ARENSBERG, Ann. *Sister Wolf.* 1980. 1st ed. inscr. author's 1st book. VG+/VG+. S13. $20.00

AREVALO, Juan Jose. *Shark & the Sardines.* 1961. Lyle Stuart. 2nd. index. 256p. dj. F3. $10.00

ARLEN, Michael. *These Charming People.* 1924. Doran. 1st ed? VG. R10. $10.00

ARLINGTON & LEWISOHN. *In Search of Old Peking.* 1935. Peking. 1st ed. ils. 328p. pocket map. VG. B5. $95.00

ARMATAGE, George. *Horseowner & the Stableman's Companion.* 1892. London. 4th. 12mo. VG. O3. $25.00

ARMISTEAD, John. *Legacy of Vengeance.* 1994. NY. 1st ed. author's 1st book. F/F. H11. $30.00

ARMITAGE, Andrew. *Owen Sound: Steamboat Days.* 1981. Ontario. Boston Mills. G/wrp. A16. $7.50

ARMITAGE, Merle. *Accent on Life.* 1965. IA U. 52 photos. 386p. VG/VG. A4. $65.00

ARMITAGE, Merle. *Pagans, Conquistadores, Heroes & Martyrs.* 1960. Fresno. VG. O7. $55.00

ARMITAGE, Merle. *Stella Dysart of Ambrosia Lake.* 1959. DSP. 1st ed. 8vo. 160p. F/clip. T10. $65.00

ARMOUR, Robert A. *Douglas Southall Freeman: Reflections by His Daughter...* 1986. Richmond. 30p. VG. B10. $8.00

ARMSTRONG. *Nevada Printing History: A Bibliography of Imprints...* 1981. Reno. NV U. 16 pl. 441p. F/F. A4. $50.00

ARMSTRONG, Charlotte. *Black-Eyed Stranger.* 1952. Peter Davies. 1st ed. G. p3. $10.00

ARMSTRONG, Gregory. *The Dragon Has Come.* 1974. Harper. stated 1st ed. 238p. NF/NF. R11. $30.00

ARMSTRONG, Karen. *Gospel According to Woman.* 1986. Anchor/Doubleday. 1st ed. F/NF. B35. $65.00

ARMSTRONG, Margaret. *Blue Santo Murder Mystery.* 1941. Random. 1st ed. VG. P3. $30.00

ARMSTRONG, Margaret. *Man With No Face.* 1943. Tower. VG/torn. P3. $10.00

ARMSTRONG, Samuel. *Walt Disney's Lady.* 1954. Whitman. MTI. G. P3. $10.00

ARMSTRONG & CRAVEN. *200 Years of American Sculpture.* 1976. Whitney Mus Am Art. ils/pl. 336. cloth. dj. D2. $65.00

ARMSTRONG & LUDLOW. *Hampton & Its Students.* 1974. NY. 1st ed. ils. 256p. G. B5. $125.00

ARNASON, Eleanor. *Ring of Swords.* 1993. Tor. 1st ed. F/F. G10. $25.00

ARNASON, Eleanor. *Woman of the Iron People.* nd. BC. VG/VG. P3. $8.00

ARNESON, Ben Albert. *Elements of Constitutional Law.* 1928. NY. Harper. M11. $35.00

ARNOLD. *Concise History of Irish Art.* 1968. Praeger. F/F. D2. $20.00

ARNOLD, C.D. *Studies in Architecture at Home & Abroad.* 1888. np. photos. stiff wrp/ribbon ties. VG. M17. $20.00

ARNOLD, Edgar. *Young Refugee: Adventures of Two Lads From Virginia.* 1912. Hermitage. 305p. G. B10. $12.00

ARNOLD, Edwin. *Japonica.* 1891. NY. 1st Am ed. ils R Blum. cloth. VG. C2. $60.00

ARNOLD, Edwin. *Light of Asia.* 1926. London. 1st ed thus. ils Hamzeh Carr. NF/VG. C2. $50.00

ARNOLD, James. *All Drawn by Horses.* 1985. Newton Abbott. sm 4to. ils. VG. O3. $48.00

ARNOLD, Jean. *Prettybelle.* 1970. Dial. 1st ed. F/F. B35. $30.00

ARNOLD, Lloyd R. *High on the Wild With Hemingway.* 1969. Caldwell. 2nd. 343p. G/torn. B18. $17.50

ARNOLD & GUILLAUME. *Legacy of Islam.* 1952. London. Oxford. ils. 416p. VG. W1. $25.00

ARNOSKY, Jim. *Mouse Numbers & Letters.* 1982. HBJ. 5th. ils. unp. tan pict brd. VG+. T5. $12.00

ARNOW, Harriette Simpson. *Hunter's Horn.* 1949. 1st ed. author's 1st novel. VG/VG. C4. $75.00

ARNOW, Harriette Simpson. *Kentucky Trace: Novel of the American Revolution.* 1974. Knopf. 1st ed. F/F. B4. $45.00

ARNOW, Harriette Simpson. *Weedkiller's Daughter.* 1970. Knopf. 1st ed. F/NF. B4. $45.00

ARNTZEN & RAINWATER. *Guide to the Literature of Art History.* 1980. Am Lib Assn. 4to. 634p. F. A4. $80.00

ART INSTITUTE OF CHICAGO. *Radiance of Jade & the Clarity of Water. Korean Ceramics.* 1991. Chicago. 1st ed. photos. VG+. S13. $18.00

ARTAUD, Antonin. *Collected Works, Vol 3.* 1972. London. Calder Boyars. 1st ed. F/wrp. B2. $40.00

ARTHUR, Elizabeth. *Bad Guys.* 1986. Knopf. 1st ed. author's 3rd book. F/NF. B4. $65.00

ARUNDEL, Jocelyn. *Whitecap's Song.* 1982. NY. Whittlesey. 1st ed. ils Wesley Dennis. VG/G. O3. $30.00

ASBURY, E. *Horse Sense & Humor in Kentucky.* 1981. Lexington. 1st ed. w/author's sgn pasted in. VG/G. O3. $25.00

ASBURY, Herbert. *Sucker's Progress: An Informal History of Gambling...* 1938. Dodd Mead. 1st ed. 8vo. 493p. NF. B14. $50.00

ASH, Christopher. *Whaler's Eye.* 1962. Macmillan. 200 photos. 248p. VG/dj. T7. $28.00

ASH, Lee. *Serial Publications Containing Medical Classics.* 1961. New Haven. 1st ed. 147p. VG A13. $25.00

ASHBEE, C.R. *Socialism & Politics.* 1906. Campden. Essex House. 8vo. gilt quarter vellum. VG+. T10. $100.00

ASHBERRY, John. *Fairfield Porter.* 1982. NYGS. 1st ed. NF/NF. S13. $20.00

ASHBERRY, John. *Shadow Train: Poems.* 1981. Viking. ARC/1st ed. inscr/dtd 1981. RS. F/NF. C2. $150.00

ASHBROOK, H. *Murder of Cecily Thane.* 1930. Coward McCann. 1st ed. VG. P3. $25.00

ASHBROOK, H. *Murder of Steven Kester.* 1931. Coward McCann. VG. P3. $20.00

ASHBY, W. Ross. *Design for a Brain.* 1952. NY. John Wiley. 1st Am ed. 260p. VG/dj. G1. $65.00

ASHCROFT. *Ashcroft's Railway Directory for 1865...* 1865. NY. John W Amerman. 8vo. 182p. gilt emb cloth. G. B14. $150.00

ASHE, Geoffrey. *Discovery of King Arthur.* 1985. Debrett's Peerage. 1st ed. VG/VG. P3. $25.00

ASHE, Gordon; see Creasey, John.

ASHER, Benjamin. *American Builders Companion.* 1816. Boston. 3rd. ils/pl. 104p. full leather. G+. B5. $450.00

ASHFORD, Jeffrey. *Double Run.* 1973. Walker. 1st ed. VG/VG. P3. $20.00

ASHFORD, Jeffrey. *Honourable Detective.* 1988. St Martin. 1st ed. VG/VG. P3. $15.00

ASHFORD, Jeffrey. *Question of Principle.* 1986. St Martin. 1st ed. VG/VG. P3. $15.00

ASHLEY, Clifford W. *The Ashley Book of Knots.* 1953. NY. Doubleday. 1st ed. ils. 4to VG/djclip. R16. $45.00

ASHLEY, Franklin. *James Dickey: A Checklist.* 1972. Bruccoli Clark. 98p. VG. B10. $20.00

ASHLEY, Michael. *History of the SF Magazine 1926-1935.* 1974. NEL. 1st ed. F/F. P3. $35.00

ASHLEY & READ. *Thoroughbred: A Celebration of the Breed.* 1990. Simon Schuster. 1st ed. VG/VG. O3. $35.00

ASHMONT. *Dogs: Their Management & Treatment in Disease.* 1886. Boston. Thayer. 208p. VG. B14. $40.00

ASHTON, Dore. *Philip Guston.* 1960. Grove. Evergreen Gallery Book #10. ils. 63p. D2. $25.00

ASIMOV, GREENBERG & WAUGH. *7 Deadly Sins & Cardinal Virtues...* 1982. Bonanza. VG/VG. P3. $15.00

ASIMOV, Isaac. *Annotated Gulliver's Travels.* 1980. Potter. 1st ed. VG/VG. P3. $25.00

ASIMOV, Isaac. *Asimov's Galaxy.* 1989. Doubleday. 1st ed. F/F. P3. $18.00

ASIMOV, Isaac. *Asimov's Sherlockian Limericks.* 1978. NY. 1st ed. VG/VG. B5. $27.50

ASIMOV, Isaac. *Before the Golden Age.* 1974. Doubleday. 1st ed. VG/VG. P3. $25.00

ASIMOV, Isaac. *Choice of Catastrophes.* 1979. Simon Schuster. 1st ed. VG. P3. $23.00

ASIMOV, Isaac. *Counting the Eons.* 1984. Granada. 1st ed. VG/VG. P3. $20.00

ASIMOV, Isaac. *Exploring the Earth & the Cosmos.* 1982. Crown. 1st ed. VG. P3. $15.00

ASIMOV, Isaac. *Fantastic Voyage II: Destination Brain.* 1987. Doubleday. 1st ed. F/NF. N4. $22.50

ASIMOV, Isaac. *Far Ends of Time & Earth.* 1979. Doubleday. 1st ed. F/F. P3. $20.00

ASIMOV, Isaac. *Foundation & Earth.* 1986. Doubleday. 1st ed. F/F. P3. $20.00

ASIMOV, Isaac. *Foundation's Edge.* 1982. Doubleday. 1st ed. F/F. P3. $20.00

ASIMOV, Isaac. *I Asimov: A Memoir.* 1994. Doubleday. 1st ed. F/F. T2. $30.00

ASIMOV, Isaac. *Measure of the Universe.* 1983. Harper Row. 1st ed. F/F. M19. $17.50

ASIMOV, Isaac. *Nemesis.* 1989. Doubleday. 1st ed. F/F. M23. $20.00

ASIMOV, Isaac. *Opus 100.* 1969. Houghton Mifflin. 1st ed. VG/VG. P3. $50.00

ASIMOV, Isaac. *Opus 200.* 1979. Houghton Mifflin. 1st ed. NF/NF. P3. $20.00

ASIMOV, Isaac. *Our World in Space.* 1974. NYGS. 1st ed. F/VG. M19. $45.00

ASIMOV, Isaac. *Prelude to Foundation.* 1988. Doubleday. VG/VG. P3. $19.00

ASIMOV, Isaac. *Robots & Empire.* 1985. Doubleday. 1st ed. RS. F/F. P3. $20.00

ASIMOV, Isaac. *Robots of Dawn.* 1983. Doubleday. 1st ed. F/F. P3. $20.00

ASIMOV, Isaac. *Satellites in Outer Space.* 1966. Random. decor brd. VG. P3. $20.00

ASIMOV, Isaac. *Today & Tomorrow &...* 1973. Doubleday. 1st ed. VG/G. P3. $30.00

ASIMOV, Isaac. *World of Carbon.* 1958. Abelard. 1st ed. NF/torn. A15. $35.00

ASIMOV & GREENBERG. *Visions of Fantasy.* 1989. Doubleday. 1st ed. F/F. P3. $15.00

ASIMOV & SILVERBERG. *Ugly Little Boy.* 1992. Doubleday. 1st ed. F/F. P3. $23.00

ASINOF, E. *Eight Men Out.* 1963. NY. 1st ed. VG/VG. B5. $45.00

ASKINS, Charles. *American Shotgun.* 1910. NY. Outing. 1st ed. VG. H7. $50.00

ASMUS, Henry. *Farm Horseshoeing.* 1943. Ithaca. Cornell Bulletin #23. VG/wrp. O3. $15.00

ASPLER & PAPE. *Scorpion Sanction.* 1980. Viking. 1st ed. VG/VG. P3. $18.00

ASPRIN, Robert. *Bug Wars.* 1979. St Martin. 1st ed. VG/VG. P3. $20.00

ASTRUP, Elivind. *Lt Rober E Peary, USN's Journey Across Northern Greenland.* 1897. Phil. 8vo. photos. 560p. bl cloth. VG. B14. $55.00

ASWELL, James. *We Know Better.* 1927. Gordon Lewis. 1/500. bdg ils/sgn Don Miller. box. B10. $35.00

ATHELING, William. *Issue at Hand.* 1964. Advent. 1st ed. VG/VG. P3. $45.00

ATHERTON, Gertrude. *Ancestors.* 1907. Harper. 1st ed. NF. B4. $50.00

ATHERTON, Gertrude. *Dido: Queen of Hearts.* 1929. NY. Liveright. 1st ed. NF/VG+. B4. $85.00

ATHERTON, Gertrude. *House of Lee.* 1940. Appleton. inscr. NF. M19. $50.00

ATHERTON, Gertrude. *Rulers of Kings.* 1904. Harper. 1st ed. NF. B4. $75.00

ATHERTON, Gertrude. *Sophisticates.* 1931. Liveright. 1st ed. F/NF. B4. $75.00

ATKIN, Ronald. *Revolution!* 1970. John Day. 1st Am ed. 354p. dj. F3. $20.00

ATKINSON, Geoffroy. *La Literature Geographique de la Renaissance.* 1968. NY. VG. w/supplement. O7. $95.00

ATKINSON, Oriana. *Big Eyes.* 1949. NY. 1st ed. VG/VG. A17. $9.50

ATTANSIO, A.A. *Beast Marks.* 1984. Ziesing. 1st ed. sgn. F/F. P3. $45.00

ATTANSIO, A.A. *Hunting the Ghost Dancer.* 1991. Harper Collins. 1st ed. F/F. P3. $22.00

ATTANSIO, A.A. *In Other Worlds.* 1984. Morrow. 1st ed. VG/VG. P3. $20.00

ATTANSIO, A.A. *Wyvern.* 1988. Ticknor Fields. 1st ed. F/F. G10. $15.00

ATTWELL, Mabel Lucie. *Story Book.* ca 1920s. Whitman. 6 pl. G+. M5. $85.00

ATWOOD, Margaret. *Bluebeard's Egg.* 1983. McClelland Stewart. 1st ed. F/F. P3. $25.00

ATWOOD, Margaret. *Cat's Eye.* 1988. McClelland Stewart. 1st ed. 8vo. F/dj. S9. $75.00

ATWOOD, Margaret. *Cat's Eye.* 1989. Doubleday. 1st ed. NF/NF. P3. $20.00

ATWOOD, Margaret. *Dancing Girls & Other Stories.* 1977. McClelland Stewart. 1st ed. VG/VG. P3. $35.00

ATWOOD, Margaret. *Handmaid's Tale.* 1985. McClelland Stewart. 1st ed. VG/VG. P3. $30.00

ATWOOD, Margaret. *Procedures for Underground.* 1972. Atlantic/Little Brn. 1st Am ed. F/NF. M23. $25.00

ATWOOD, Margaret. *Robber Bride.* 1993. London. Bloomsbury. 1st ed. F/F. T2. $20.00

ATWOOD, Margaret. *Surfacing.* 1972. Tor. 1st ed. author's 2nd novel. sgn. F/NF. C6. $150.00

ATWOOD, Margaret. *Wilderness Tips.* 1991. NY. 1st ed. sgn. F/F. A9. $30.00

AUBIER & MORATH. *Fiesta in Pamplona.* 1956. London. 1st ed. folio. F/NF. B4. $125.00

AUCHINCLOSS, Louis. *Winthrop Covenant.* 1976. Houghton Mifflin. 1st ed. F/F. H11. $35.00

AUDEN, W.H. *Academic Graffiti.* nd. England. 1st ed. VG. M17. $20.00

AUDEN, W.H. *Collected Shorter Poems 1927-1957.* 1967. NY. 1st ed. sgn/corrected. F/F. C6. $175.00

AUDEN, W.H. *Enchafed Flood; or, Romantic Iconography of the Sea.* 1979. Charlottesville. VG. O7. $25.00

AUDEN, W.H. *Homage to Clio.* 1960. Random. 1st ed. F/VG. M19. $35.00

AUDEN & ISHERWOOD. *Ascent of F6: Tragedy in Two Acts.* 1936. London. Faber. 1st ed. F/NF. B24. $385.00

AUDEN & ISHERWOOD. *Journey to a War.* 1939. Random. 1st Am ed. NF/NF. C2. $75.00

AUDEN & PEARSON. *Poets of the English Language.* 1950. Viking. 1st Am ed. 5 vol. NF/NF. C2. $100.00

AUDOUZE, Jean. *Cambridge Atlas of Astronomy.* 1988. Cambridge. 350 color photos. F/dj. O7. $65.00

AUDUBON, Maria. *Audubon & His Journals.* Vol 2. 1898. London. John Nimmo. ils. 554p. VG. A4. $75.00

AUEL, Jean M. *Clan of the Cave Bear.* 1980. Crown. 1st ed. VG/G. P3. $25.00

AUEL, Jean M. *Clan of the Cave Bear.* 1980. NY. Crown. 1st ed. F/F. H11. $100.00

AUEL, Jean M. *Mammoth Hunters.* 1985. Crown. 1st ed. F/F. H11. $35.00

AUEL, Jean M. *Mammoth Hunters.* 1985. Crown. 1st ed. VG/VG. P3. $20.00

AUEL, Jean M. *Mammoth Hunters.* 1985. NY. Crown. ARC. NF. B4. $45.00

AUEL, Jean M. *Plains of Passage.* 1990. Crown. 1st ed. F/F. G6. $25.00

AUEL, Jean M. *Valley of Horses.* 1982. Crown. ARC. F/wrp. w/promo poster. M19. $85.00

AUEL, Jean M. *Valley of the Horses.* 1982. Crown. 1st ed. sgn. F/F. B35. $40.00

AUGUST, John. *Advance Agent.* 1944. Tower. 2nd. G/G. P3. $8.00

AULT, Phil. *Whistles Round the Bend.* 1982. Dodd Mead. VG/VG. A16. $10.00

AUNT LAURA; see Barrow, Frances Elizabeth.

AURNER, Nellie Slayton. *Caxton: Mirour of Fifteenth Century Letters.* 1926. Houghton Mifflin. 8vo. 16 pl. 304p. F/NF. T10. $45.00

AUSLANDER. *Unconquerables: Salutes to the Undying Spirit...* 1943. np. 59p. F/NF. A4. $25.00

AUSTEN, Jane. *Emma.* 1964. LEC. 1st ed. 1/1500. ils/sgn Kredel. F/case. C2. $100.00

AUSTEN, Jane. *Mansfield Park.* 1959. London. Folio Soc. Sangorski/Sutcliffe bdg. F. A4. $95.00

AUSTEN, Jane. *Pride & Prejudice.* 1951. Bombay. Jaico Books. 1st ed. NF/wrp. A11. $25.00

AUSTER, Paul. *Art of Hunger.* 1992. LA. 1st ed. sgn. F/F. A11. $55.00

AUSTER, Paul. *In the Country of Last Things.* 1987. Viking. 1st ed. F/F. M23. $20.00

AUSTER, Paul. *In the Country of Last Things.* 1987. Viking. 1st ed. VG/VG. P3. $16.00

AUSTIN, A.C. *Story of Diamonds.* 1941. Los Angeles. ils. bl cloth. VG. B14. $30.00

AUSTIN, Alicia. *Age of Dreams.* 1978. Donald Grant. 1st ed. VG/VG. P3. $35.00

AUSTIN, Aurelia. *Bright Feathers.* 1958. np. inscr. 59p. VG/VG. B11. $10.00

AUSTIN, David. *Heritage of the Rose.* 1988. Suffolk. ils. 445p. F/dj. B26. $60.00

AUSTIN, Doris Jean. *After the Garden.* 1987. NAL. 1st ed. F/F. B4. $35.00

AUSTIN, G.L. *Life & Times of Wendell Phillips.* 1884. Boston. 12mo. 431p. gilt brn cloth. T3. $29.00

AUSTIN, J.M. *Voice to the Married...Addressed to Husbands & Wives.* 1847. Boston. 16mo. 402p. emb brn cloth. G. T3. $32.00

AUSTIN, Jean. *Mexico in Your Pocket.* 1937. Doubleday. 1st ed. 140p. F3. $10.00

AUSTIN, Margot. *Churchmouse Stories.* 1956. Dutton. later reprint. VG. B17. $5.00

AUSTIN, Margot. *Trumpet.* 1943. Dutton. 1st ed. VG+/G. M5. $30.00

AUSTIN, Margot. *Very Young Mother Goose.* nd. Platt Munk. ils. 91p. G+. C14. $8.00

AUSTIN, Mary. *Cactus Thorn: A Novella.* 1988. NV U. 1st ed. fwd Melody Graulich. cloth. M/dj. A18. $30.00

AUSTIN, Mary. *Experiences Facing Death.* 1931. Bobbs Merrill. 1st ed. F. A18. $60.00

AUSTIN, William. *Peter Rugg: Missing Man.* 1948. Comet. 1st ed. F/sans. B4. $50.00

AVENI, Athony. *Empires of Time.* 1990. London. Tauris. 1st ed. ils. 371p. F3. $25.00

AVERA, Carl L. *Wind Swept Land.* 1964. San Antonio, TX. 1st ed. 89p. pict cloth. VG/VG. B18. $15.00

AVERILL, Esther. *Daniel Boone.* 1945. Harper. 1st ed. 4to. VG. M5. $42.00

AVERILL, Esther. *Voyages of Jacques Cartier.* 1937. Domino. 1st ed. ils Rojankovsky. F/dj. M5. $95.00

AVERILL, Naomi. *Whistling-Two-Teeth & the Forty-Nine Buffalos.* 1939. NY. ils. VG. M5. $45.00

AVIL, Christopher. *Strangers in Paradise.* 1976. Herbert Jenkins. 1st ed. F/F. P3. $20.00

AVNERY, Uri. *Israel Without Zionists: A Plea for Peace in Middle East.* 1968. Macmillan. 1st ed. sm 8vo. 215p. VG/dj. W1. $18.00

AWAD, Joseph. *Neon Distances.* 1980. Golden Quill. 80p. F/VG. B10. $7.00

AXFORD, Lavinne. *Index to the Poems of Ogden Nash.* 1972. Scarecrow. 139p. xl. F. B22. $5.00

AXTON, David; see Koontz, Dean R.

AYER, Frederick Jr. *Man in the Mirror.* 1965. Regnery. VG/VG. P3. $20.00

AYMAR, Gordon. *Yacht Racing Rules & Tactics.* 1962. Van Nostrand. VG/VG. A16. $9.00

AYRES. *British Folk Art.* 1977. Overlook. F/F. D2. $35.00

AYRES, Noreen. *World the Color of Salt.* 1992. Morrow. 1st ed. author's 1st book. F/F. H11. $30.00

AZIZ, Philippe. *Man in the Mirror.* 1965. Regnery. VG/VG. P3. $20.00

One of the silliest questions you can ask a book collector is, "Have you read all of these?" Of course he hasn't. Some books are bought to look at, not to read.

John Betjeman
1906 – 1984

– B –

BAADE, Fritz. *Race to the Year 2000.* 1963. Cresset. 1st ed. VG/VG. P3. $15.00

BABCOCK, Bernie. *Hallerloogy.* 1943. self pub. ils/photos. G+. P2. $65.00

BABCOCK, C. Merton. *Wisdom of the Koran.* 1966. Peter Pauper. 1st ed. 16mo. 62p. VG/dj. W1. $12.00

BABSON, Marian. *Murder, Murder, Little Star.* 1977. Collins Crime Club. 1st ed. VG/VG. P3. $20.00

BACH, Richard. *Bridge Across Forever.* 1984. Morrow. 1st ed. VG/VG. P3. $20.00

BACHMAN, Richard; see King, Stephen.

BACHMEYER, Arthur. *Hospital Trends & Developments 1940-46.* 1948. NY. 1st ed. 819p. A13. $75.00

BACON, Francis. *Cabala...Mysteries of State & Government...* 1691. London. Sawbridge. 3rd. contemporary calf. M11. $350.00

BACON, Peggy. *Good American Witch.* 1957. Franklin Watts. 1st ed. 222p. G+/G+. P2. $40.00

BACON, Peggy. *Mystery at East Hatchett.* 1939. Viking. 1st ed. ils. VG/G+. P2. $50.00

BADAWY, Alexander. *Architecture in Ancient Egypt & the Near East.* 1972. Cambridge/MIT. 2nd. ils/map. NF/dj. W1. $65.00

BADER, Barbara. *American Picture Books From Noah's Ark to the Beast Within.* 1976. Macmillan. 1st ed. VG/VG. P2. $95.00

BADSWORTH. *Principles of Bridge & Laws of the Game...* 1914. London/NY. New ed. 288p. VG. S1. $15.00

BAEDEKER, Karl. *Spain & Portugal.* 1913. Leipsic. VG. O7. $25.00

BAER, Helene G. *Heart Is Like Heaven: Life of Lydia Maria Child.* 1964. PA U. 1st ed. 339p. NF/dj. M20. $28.00

BAERS, Henri. *Les Tables Astronomiques de Louvain, 1528.* 1976. Brussels. Culture et Civililasion. 8vo. 90p. F/F. T10. $25.00

BAEZ, Carlos. *Las Lagrimas de Churun.* 1959. Caracas. Lipografia Londres. 1st ed. 8vo. 124p. VG. T10. $50.00

BAGBY, George. *Dead Wrong.* 1957. Doubleday. 1st ed. F/NF. M19. $25.00

BAGBY, George. *Old Virginia Gentleman & Other Sketches.* 1911. Scribner. 321p. VG. B10. $45.00

BAGBY, George. *Two in the Bush.* 1976. Crime Club. 1st ed. VG/VG. P3. $15.00

BAGLEY, Desmond. *Enemy.* 1978. Doubleday. 1st ed. VG/VG. P3. $18.00

BAGLEY, Desmond. *Flyaway.* 1979. Doubleday. 1st ed. VG/VG. P3. $18.00

BAGLEY, Desmond. *Juggernaut.* 1985. Collins. 1st ed. VG/VG. P3. $20.00

BAGLEY, Desmond. *Tightrope Men.* 1973. Collins. 1st ed. NF/NF. P3. $25.00

BAGLEY, Desmond. *Vivero Letter.* 1968. London. Collins. apparent 1st ed? 317p. gr brd. NF. B22. $4.00

BAGNOLD, Enid. *National Velvet.* 1935. Morrow. 1st ed. 303p. VG/G. P2. $35.00

BAGROW, Leo. *Die Geschichte der Kartographie.* 1951. Berlin. Safari-Verlag. ils. F/worn. O7. $125.00

BAGSTER, Samuel. *Management of Bees.* 1834. London. Bagster Pickering. 40 woodcuts. 244p. cloth. VG. A10. $350.00

BAHR, Edith Jane. *Nice Neighbourhood.* 1973. Collins Crime Club. 1st ed. VG/G. P3. $15.00

BAHTI, Tom. *Intro to Southwestern Indian Arts & Crafts.* 1966. Flagstaff. KC Pub. ils. 32p. F/thin wrp. T10. $10.00

BAIKIE, James. *History of Egypt From the Earliest Times...* 1929. London. Blk. 2 vol. 1st ed. 8vo. ils. VG. W1. $65.00

BAILEY, Alice Cooper. *Kimo, the Whistling Boy.* 1928. Volland. ils Holling. VG. K2. $80.00

BAILEY, C.S. *Lil' Hannibal.* 1938. Platt Munk. ils. VG. B5. $32.50

BAILEY, Carolyn Sherwin. *Finnigan II: His Nine Lives.* 1953. Viking. 1st ed. 95p. cloth. VG/dj. M20. $42.00

BAILEY, F.M. *Comprehensive Catalogue of Queensland Plants.* 1902. Brisbane. Cumming. 2nd. 8vo. ils/pl. 879p. VG. B1. $120.00

BAILEY, H.C. *Sullen Sky Mystery.* 1935. Crime Club. 1st ed. G. P3. $25.00

BAILEY, Harriet. *Nursing Mental Diseases.* 1929. 2nd. VG. K2. $10.00

BAILEY, J.O. *Pilgrims Through Time & Space.* 1947. Argus. 1st ed. VG/VG. P3. $50.00

BAILEY, J.O. *Poetry of Thomas Hardy: A Handbook & Commentary.* 1970. Chapel Hill. 1st ed. thick 8vo. 712p. NF/dj. C2. $45.00

BAILEY, Jean. *Cherokee Bill.* 1952. Abingdon/Cokesbury. ils Pers Crowell. VG/G. O3. $22.00

BAILEY, L.H. *Standard Cyclopedia of Horticulture.* 1939. NY. 3 vol. photos. 3639p. A17. $150.00

BAILEY, LAMB & MARKUN. *Pelican Tree & Other Panama Adventures.* 1953. North River. sgns. ils Beaudry. map ep. 96p. F/VG. B11. $50.00

BAILEY, Pearl. *Duey's Tale.* 1975. HBJ. 1st ed. inscr. F/F. B4. $40.00

BAILEY, Percival. *Intracranial Tumors.* 1933. Chicago. ils. 475p. NF. B14. $750.00

BAILEY & BAILEY. *Hortus Second.* 1959. Macmillan. 10th. 778p. cloth. VG. B1. $40.00

BAILEY & KNEBEL. *Convention.* 1964. Harper Row. VG/VG. P3. $18.00

BAILEY & KNEBEL. *Crossing in Berlin.* 1981. Doubleday. 1st ed. VG/VG. P3. $20.00

BAILY, Francis. *Journal of a Tour in Unsettled Parts of North America.* 1969. Carbondale. VG. O7. $35.00

BAIN, Donald. *War in Illinois: An Incredible True Story...* 1978. Prentice Hall. 1st ed. NF/NF. B35. $15.00

BAINBRIDGE, Beryl. *Bottle Factory Outing.* 1975. Braziller. 1st ed. F/F. B35. $20.00

BAINBRIDGE, Beryl. *Harriet Said.* 1972. Braziller. 1st ed. F/F. B35. $20.00

BAINBRIDGE, Henry C. *Peter Carl Faberge: Goldsmith & Jeweler.* 1949. London. 1st ed. 1/750. 126 pl. VG/dj. B14. $150.00

BAINBRIDGE. *Garbo.* 1971. HRW. 1st ed. VG/VG. D2. $35.00

BAKE, William A. *Blue Ridge.* 1977. Viking. photos/map ep. 112p. VG/G. B10. $15.00

BAKELESS, John. *Eyes of Discovery.* 1950. Phil. VG. O7. $55.00

BAKER, Betty. *Great Ghost Stories of the Old West.* nd. BC. VG. P3. $4.00

BAKER, Denys Val. *Family at Sea.* 1981. William Kimber. 1st ed. F/F. P3. $20.00

BAKER, Denys Val. *Mill in the Valley.* 1984. William Kimber. 1st ed. VG/VG. P3. $20.00

BAKER, Denys Val. *Waterwheel Turns.* 1982. William Kimber. 1st ed. VG/VG. P3. $20.00

BAKER, Denys Val. *When Cornish Skies Are Smiling.* 1984. William Kimber. 1st ed. VG/VG. P3. $20.00

BAKER, George. *New Sad Sack*. 1946. NY. 1st ed. VG/VG. B5. $25.00

BAKER, Kenneth. *Turbulent Years*. 1993. London. Faber. 1st ed. ils. 498p. F/F. T10. $50.00

BAKER, Kevin. *Sometimes You See It Coming*. 1993. NY. Crown 1st ed. author's 1st novel. NF/NF. R16. $40.00

BAKER, Marcus. *Geographic Dictionary of Alaska*. 1906. WA. VG. O7. $125.00

BAKER, Nicholson. *Mezzanine*. 1988. Weidenfield Nicolson. 1st ed. author's 1st book. F/F. B2. $125.00

BAKER, Nicholson. *Mezzanine*. 1989. London. Granta/Penguin. 1st ed. author's 1st novel. F/NF. A15. $30.00

BAKER, Nicholson. *Room Temperature*. 1990. Grove Weidenfeld. 1st ed. sgn. AN/dj. C2. $75.00

BAKER, Nicholson. *U & I*. 1991. Random. 1st ed. F/F. B2. $30.00

BAKER, Nicholson. *Vox*. 1992. Random. 1st ed. sgn. F/dj. C2. $60.00

BAKER, Richard M. *Death Stops the Rehearsal*. 1937. Scribner. 1st ed. VG/G. P3. $35.00

BAKER, Robert H. *Introducing the Constellations*. 1937. Viking. 1st ed. 8vo. 205p. cloth. G. K5. $10.00

BAKER, Roger. *Marilyn Monroe*. 1990. Portland. VG/VG. P3. $25.00

BAKER, Samuel. *Ismailia: A Narrative of Expedition to Central Africa...* 1875. NY. ils. 542p. G. B5. $70.00

BAKER, Scott. *Ancestral Hungers*. 1995. Tor. 1st ed. F/F. P3. $22.00

BAKER, Scott. *Night Child*. 1979. Berkley. 1st ed. AN/dj. M21. $25.00

BAKER, Susan. *My First Murder*. 1989. NY. 1st ed. author's 1st novel. F/F. H11. $25.00

BAKER & BAKER. *Water Elf & the Miller's Child*. 1928. Duffield. 1st ed. silhouettes. VG/G. M5. $75.00

BAKER & MURPHY. *Handbook of Marine Science*. 1981. Baca Raton. 8vo. hc. 223p. F. B1. $65.00

BAKKER, R.T. *Dinosaur Heresies*. 1986. Morrow. 481p. cloth. F/dj. D8. $36.00

BALCH, Glenn. *Little Hawk & the Free Horses*. 1957. Crowell. 1st ed. VG/G+. O3. $25.00

BALCHIN, Nigel. *Seen Dimly Before Dawn*. 1964. Reprint Soc. VG/VG. P3. $8.00

BALDACCI, David. *Absolute Power*. 1996. Warner. 1st ed. F/wrp. w/promo material. M22. $55.00

BALDWIN, Faith. *Arizona Star*. 1945. Farrar Rinehart. 1st ed. F/VG+ clip. B4. $65.00

BALDWIN, Faith. *Career by Proxy*. 1939. Farrar Rinehart. 1st ed. inscr. F/VG+ clip. B4. $125.00

BALDWIN, Faith. *Golden Shoestring*. 1949. Rinehart. 1st ed. F/VG+ clip. B4. $50.00

BALDWIN, Faith. *Something Special*. 1940. Farrar Rinehart. 1st ed. VG+/VG+. B4. $65.00

BALDWIN, Hanson W. *Sea Fights & Shipwrecks*. 1955. Garden City. VG. O7. $20.00

BALDWIN, J.L. *Laws of Short Whist Edited by Baldwin...* 1866. London. 111p. VG. S1. $25.00

BALDWIN, James. *Devil Finds Work*. 1976. Dial. 1st ed. F/F. H11. $55.00

BALDWIN, James. *Evidence of Things Not Seen*. 1985. Holt. 1st ed. F/F. H11. $30.00

BALDWIN, James. *Giovanni's Room*. 1956. NY. 1st ed. VG/VG. B5. $135.00

BALDWIN, James. *Going to Meet the Man*. 1965. Dial. 1st ed. F/NF. w/promo flyer. M19. $75.00

BALDWIN, James. *Nobody Knows My Name*. 1961. Dial. 1st ed. F/NF. B2. $45.00

BALDWIN, James Mark. *Development & Evolution Including Psychophysical Evolution*. 1902. Macmillan. 395p. panelled crimson cloth. xl. G1. $65.00

BALDWIN, James Mark. *Genetic Theory of Reality...* 1915. Knickerbocker. 335p. gr cloth. VG. G1. $75.00

BALDWIN, William. *Hard to Catch Mercy*. 1993. Algonquin. 1st ed. sgn. F/F. M23. $40.00

BALDWIN & MEAD. *Rap on Race*. 1972. London. Corgi. 1st ed. pb. 255p. reading copy. R11. $8.00

BALDWIN & STOTZ. *At Bat With the Little League*. 1952. Phil. Macrae. 1st ed. NF/VG+. B4. $65.00

BALET, Jan. *What Makes an Orchestra*. nd. NY. Oxford. 1st ed. 41p. VG. C14. $15.00

BALFOUR, Victoria. *Rock Wives*. 1986. NY. Beech Tree/Morrow. 1st ed. photos Harvey Wang. F/NF. B4. $45.00

BALFOUR. *Life of Robert Louis Stevenson*. 1908. np. 2 vol. ils. VG. A4. $25.00

BALL, Brian N. *Baker Street Boys*. 1983. British BC. 1st ed. VG/VG. P3. $20.00

BALL, John. *Cop Cade*. 1978. Crime Club. 1st ed. VG/VG. P3. $15.00

BALL, John. *Kiwi Target*. 1989. Carroll Graf. 1st ed. F/F. P3. $16.00

BALL, Robert S. *In Starry Realms*. 1908 (1892). London. Pitman. cheap ed. 371p. cloth. K5. $18.00

BALL & BREEN. *Murder California Style*. 1987. St Martin. 1st ed. F/F. P3. $18.00

BALL & HALBERT. *Creek War of 1813 & 1814*. 1895. Chicago. Donohue Henneberry. 1st ed. 4 pl/fld map. 331p. VG. M8. $350.00

BALLANTINE, Betty. *American Celebration: Art of Charles Wysocki*. 1985. Greenwich. 192p. NF/NF. M20. $30.00

BALLANTINE, Bill. *Clown Alley*. 1982. Boston. 1st ed. F/F. B5. $35.00

BALLANTINE, Henry Winthrop. *California Corporation Laws*. 1932. Los Angeles. Parker Stone Baird. orig buckram. M11. $100.00

BALLANTINE, Sheila. *Norma Jean the Termite Queen*. 1975. Doubleday. ARC. author's 1st novel. F/NF. B4. $50.00

BALLANTYNE, R.M. *Coral Island: Tale of the Pacific Ocean*. nd. London. red full leather. VG. B30. $50.00

BALLANTYNE, R.M. *Hudson Bay; or, Everyday Life in the Wilds of North America*. 1971. NY. VG. O7. $40.00

BALLARD, J.G. *Concrete Island*. 1974. FSG. 1st ed. NF/NF. P3. $30.00

BALLARD, J.G. *Hello America*. 1988. Carroll Graf. 1st ed. F/F. P3. $18.00

BALLARD, J.G. *High-Rise*. 1977. HRW. 1st Am ed. NF/VG+. R10. $20.00

BALLARD, J.G. *Kindness of Women*. 1991. FSG. 1st Am ed. NF/VG. M21. $10.00

BALLARD, J.G. *Memories of the Space Age*. 1988. Arkham. 1st ed. F/F. T2. $17.00

BALLARD, J.G. *Rushing to Paradise*. 1994. London. 1st ed. sgn. F/F. A11. $50.00

BALLARD, J.G. *Unlimited Dream Company*. 1979. HRW. 1st ed. VG/VG. P3. $25.00

BALLARD, J.G. *Venus Hunters*. 1986. Gollancz. 1st ed. F/F. P3. $20.00

BALLARD, J.G. *War Fever*. 1991. FSG. 1st Am ed. F/F. G10. $12.00

BALLARD, Robert D. *Explorer*. 1992. Turner. ils. F. B17. $15.00

BALLARD, Robert D. *Exploring the Titanic*. 1988. Ontario. Scholastic/Madison Pr. VG/VG. A16. $25.00

BALLIETT, Whitney. *Improvising*. 1977. Oxford. 1st ed. F/NF. B2. $30.00

BALLINGER, Bill S. *Bill S Ballinger Triptych.* nd. Sherbourne. 1st ed. VG/VG. P3. $20.00

BALLINGER, Bill S. *Wife of the Red-Haired Man.* 1957. Harper. 1st ed. VG/G. P3. $15.00

BALLINGER, W.A. *Rebellion.* 1967. Howard Baker. 1st ed. F/F. P3. $15.00

BALLS, W. Lawrence. *Egypt of the Egyptians.* 1920. London/Bath/NY. Pitman. 1st ed. 266p. VG. W1. $20.00

BALTZ, John. *Honorable Edward D Baker, US Senator From Oregon.* 1888. Lancaster, PA. 248p. VG. A4. $125.00

BAMBARA, Toni Cade. *Salt Eaters.* 1980. Random. 1st ed. rem mk. F/F. B4. $45.00

BANCROFT, Betsy Barber. *Wild Honeysuckle.* 1966. Birmingham. Banner. unp. VG. B10. $10.00

BANCROFT, George. *Martin Van Buren: To the End of His Career.* 1889. NY. 1st ed. 239p. VG. B18. $45.00

BANCROFT, Griffing. *Snowy: Story of an Egret.* 1970. McCall. 1st ed. sgn. VG/VG. B11. $10.00

BANCROFT, Hubert Howe. *Literary Industries, a Memoir.* 1891. np. 477p. VG. A4. $85.00

BANDELIER, Adolf F. *Delight Makers.* 1918. Dodd Mead. 2nd. preface Hodge. intro Lummis. gilt gold cloth. VG. B14. $60.00

BANG, Betsy. *Five Tales From Bengal, The Demons of Rajpur.* 1980. Greenwillow. 8vo. ils. F/VG. B17. $5.00

BANG, Molly. *Buried Moon & Other Stories.* 1977. Scribner. 1st ed. 63p. F/F. P2. $35.00

BANG, Molly. *One Fall Day.* 1994. Greenwillow. ARC. ils. RS. pict brd. AN/dj. C8. $30.00

BANG, Molly. *Paper Crane.* 1985. Greenwillow. 1st ed. ils. NF/VG. C8. $25.00

BANGDEL & FLEMING. *Birds of Nepal.* 1976. Kathmandu. 1st ed. sgns. VG/VG. B5. $30.00

BANGS, John Kendrick. *House-Boat on the Styx.* 1896. Harper. decor brd. VG. P3. $50.00

BANGS, John Kendrick. *House-Boat on the Styx.* 1902 (1896). Harper. rpt. gilt red cloth. G+. M21. $10.00

BANISTER, Margaret. *Tears Are for the Living.* 1963. Houghton Mifflin. 2nd. 506p. VG. B10. $10.00

BANKHEAD, Tallulah. *My Autogbiography.* 1952. Sears Readers Club. NF. D2. $9.00

BANKHEAD, Tallulah. *Tallulah: My Autobiography.* 1952. Harper. 1st ed. F/F. B4. $85.00

BANKS, Carolyn. *Dark Room.* 1980. Viking. 1st ed. 279p. VG/G+. B10. $15.00

BANKS, Iain M. *Complicity.* 1995. Talese/Doubleday. 1st Am ed. AN/dj. M22. $20.00

BANKS, Iain M. *Player of Games.* 1988. Macmillan. 1st ed. F/F. P3. $30.00

BANKS, Iain M. *Walking on Glass.* 1985. Macmillan. 1st ed. F/F. M21/P3. $30.00

BANKS, Russell. *Affliction.* 1989. Toronto. McClelland. 1st ed. F/F. H11. $20.00

BANKS, Russell. *Book of Jamaica.* 1980. Houghton Mifflin. 1st ed. sgn. F/NF. M23. $45.00

BANKS, Russell. *Continental Death.* 1985. Harper Row. 1st ed. sgn. F/NF. M23. $40.00

BANKS, Russell. *New World.* 1978. Urbana, IL. 1st ed. sgn. F/wrp. A11. $35.00

BANKS, Russell. *Searching for Survivors.* 1975. NY. 1st ed. sgn. NF/NF. C6. $40.00

BANKS, Russell. *Success Stories.* 1986. Harper Row. 1st ed. sgn. F/F. M23. $35.00

BANKS, Russell. *Sweet Hereafter.* 1991. Harper Collins. 1st ed. sgn. NF/F. M23. $25.00

BANKS & KENNY. *Looking at Sails.* 1979. Boston. Sail Books. ils Peter Campbell. 143p. VG. T7. $20.00

BANNERMAN, Helen. *Little Black Sambo Animated.* 1943. Duenewald. 8vo. ils/6 moveables. NF. T10. $600.00

BANNERMAN, Helen. *Little Black Sambo.* ca 1928. Saalfield. ils Florence White Williams. G. D1. $32.00

BANNERMAN, Helen. *Little Black Sambo.* nd. Whitman. Tell-A-Tale. ils Gladys Turley Michell. VG. C14. $30.00

BANNERMAN, Helen. *Little Black Sambo.* 1942. Saalfield. ils Ethel Hays. fair. M5. $65.00

BANNERMAN, Helen. *Little Black Sambo.* 1948. Simon Schuster. 1st ed thus. ils Gustaf Tenggren. VG. D1. $85.00

BANNERMAN, Helen. *Little Black Sambo.* 1961. Whitman. probable 1st ed. ils Rutherford. unp. G+. T5. $45.00

BANNERMAN, Helen. *Little Black Sambo/Red Hen/Peter Rabbit.* 1942. Saalfield. ils Ethel Hays. VG. D1. $185.00

BANNERMAN, Helen. *Story of Little Black Mingo.* 1902. Londons. Nisbet. ils Bannerman. VG/VG. D1. $225.00

BANNERMAN, Helen. *Story of Little Black Quasha.* 1908. London. Nisbet. ils Bannerman. yel cloth. VG/VG. D1. $225.00

BANNERMAN, Helen. *Story of Little Black Sambo.* nd. Harper Collins. rpt. ils. F/F. T2. $18.00

BANNERMAN, Helen. *Story of Little Black Sambo.* 1903. NY. Stokes. 1st Am ed/lg format. ils Bannerman. VG. D1. $850.00

BANNERMAN, Helen. *Story of Little Black Sambo.* 1959. Western Pub. probable 1st ed. ils Violet LaMont. pict brd. AN. T5. $45.00

BANNING, George Hugh. *In Mexican Waters.* 1925. Boston. Lauriat. 8vo. map/pl. 196p. teg. gilt bl cloth. F. T10. $65.00

BANNING & HUGH. *Six Horses.* (1930). Century. G. O3. $18.00

BANTOCK, Nick. *Sabine Trilogy: Griffin & Sabine...* 1991-93. San Francisco. Chronicle Books. 1st ed. 3 vol. F. C2. $175.00

BANVILLE, John. *Athena.* 1995. London. 1st ed. sgn. F/F. A11. $50.00

BANVILLE, John. *Doctor Copernicus.* 1976. Norton. 1st Am ed. F/NF. B4. $125.00

BARAKAT, Layyah A. *Message From Mt Lebanon.* (1912). Sunday School Times Co. 1st ed. 167p. bl cloth. VG+. B22. $4.50

BARBEAU, Marius. *Pathfinders in the North Pacific.* 1958. Caldwell/Toronto. pres. VG. O7. $75.00

BARBER, John. *Richard Brautigan: An Annotated Bibliography.* 1990. McFarland. 1st ed. sgn. gr cloth. F/sans. C2. $45.00

BARBER, Noel. *Sinister Twilight: Fall of Singapore 1942.* 1968. Houghton Mifflin. 2nd. 364p. F/dj. A17. $10.00

BARBER, Noel. *Sultans.* 1973. Simon Schuster. 1st ed. 304p. VG. W1. $18.00

BARBER, Noel. *Woman of Cairo.* 1984. Hodder Stoughton. 1st ed. 8vo. 592p. NF/dj. W1. $20.00

BARBER, Red. *Broadcasters.* 1970. Dial. 1st ed. sgn. 271p. VG/VG. B11. $55.00

BARBER, Red. *1947: When All Hell Broke Loose in Baseball.* 1982. Doubleday. 1st ed. VG+/G. P8. $40.00

BARBER, W. Charles. *Elmira College: The First 100 Years.* 1955. McGraw Hill. 1st ed. 16 pl. 8vo. F/VG. B11. $25.00

BARBICAN, James. *Confessions of a Rum Runner.* 1928. NY. 1st ed. 12mo. 310p. red stp blk cloth. VG. H3. $45.00

BARBIER, Dominique. *Dressage for the New Age.* 1990. NY. Prentice Hall. 1st ed. F/F. O3. $25.00

BARBOUR, Paul. *One Man's Family.* 1938. VG. K2. $8.00

BARBOUR, Ralph Henry. *Crimson Sweater.* 1933. Appleton Century Crofts. VG/VG. P12. $8.00

BARBOUR, Ralph Henry. *Joyce of the Jasmines.* 1911. 1st ed. ils Underwood/Holloway. VG+. S13. $16.00

BARBOUR, Ralph Henry. *Right End Emerson.* 1922. Grosset Dunlap. ils Leslie Crump. G+. P12. $8.00

BARCLAY, Bill; see Moorcock, Michael.

BARCUS, Frank. *Fresh-Water Fury.* 1960. Wayne State. 1st ed. maps/ils. VG/dj. A16. $50.00

BARENHOLZ, Edith F. *George Brown Toy Sketchbook.* 1971. Princeton. Pyne. 1st ed. ils George Brown. NF/case. D1. $125.00

BARETTI, Joseph. *Journey From London to Genoa Through England, Portugal...* 1970. Fontwell. VG. O7. $65.00

BARFIELD, Owen. *Owen Barfield on CS Lewis.* 1989. Wesleyan U. 1st Am ed. M/clip. A18. $20.00

BARHEL, Joan. *Death in California.* 1981. NY. 1st ed. F/F. A17. $8.00

BARICH, Bill. *Laughing in the Hills.* 1980. NY. 1st ed. inscr. F/VG+. A11. $60.00

BARJAVEL, Rene. *Immortals.* 1974. Morrow. 1st ed. VG/VG. P3. $20.00

BARKER, Cicely Mary. *Little Book of Old Rhymes.* 1976. London. Blackie. ils. unp. NF/F. C14. $10.00

BARKER, Clive. *Books of Blood V.* 1988. Scream. 1/333. sgn. ils/sgn Harry O Morris. F/sans/case. T2. $75.00

BARKER, Clive. *Cabal.* 1988. Poseidon. 1st ed. 1/750. sgn. F/sans/case. T2. $95.00

BARKER, Clive. *Damnation Game.* 1987. Putnam. 1st ed. author's 1st novel. F/F. H11. $40.00

BARKER, Clive. *Everville.* ARC. w/photo & promo kit. F/F. B30. $25.00

BARKER, Clive. *Great & Secret Show.* 1989. Harper Row. 1st ed. F/F. M21. $15.00

BARKER, Clive. *Imajica.* 1991. Harper Collins. 1st ed. VG/VG. P3. $23.00

BARKER, Clive. *In the Flesh: Tales of Terror.* 1986. Poseidon. 1st Am ed. F/F. T2. $25.00

BARKER, Clive. *Inhuman Condition: Tales of Terror.* 1986. Poseidon. 1st Am ed. F/F. T2. $25.00

BARKER, Clive. *Thief of Always.* 1992. Harper Collins. 1st ed. sgn. F/F. B35. $45.00

BARKER, Clive. *Weaveworld.* 1987. Poseidon. 1st ed. F/F. M19/R10. $17.50

BARKER, F. *Oliviers.* 1953. Phil. 1st ed. VG/G. B5. $35.00

BARKER, H.E. *Abraham Lincoln, His Life in Illinois...* 1940. NY. 1st ed. 64p. VG/dj. B18. $17.50

BARKER, John. *British in Boston Being the Diary of Lt John Barker...* 1924. Harvard. 1st ed. 73p. cloth. VG+. M8. $45.00

BARKER, Nicholas. *Printer & the Poet: An Account of Printing...* 1970. Cambridge. private prt. 1/500. 4to. 54p. NF. A4. $145.00

BARKER, Ralph. *Blockade Busters.* 1977. Norton. 1st ed. 224p. F/dj. B22. $5.00

BARKER, Samuel W. *Cast Up by the Sea.* 1869. Harper. ils. 419p. VG. T7. $50.00

BARKER, Shirley. *Swear by Apollo.* 1958. Ramdom. 1st ed. VG/VG. P3. $35.00

BARLOW, Roger. *Sandy Steele & Fire at Red Lake.* 1959. Simon Schuster. 1st ed. G+/G. P12. $7.00

BARLOW, Roger. *Sandy Steele Adventures.* 1959. Simon Schuster. 1st ed. G+/G. P12. $7.00

BARLOW, Ronald S. *How to Be Successful in the Antique Business.* 1985. 8vo. ils. 186p. G. T3. $10.00

BARLOW, Theodore. *Justice of Peace: A Treatise...* 1745. London. Lintot Knapton. folio. contemporary calf. M11. $450.00

BARNARD, George N. *Photographic Views of Sherman's Campaign.* Dover. facsimile of 1866 ed. ils. G. T3. $15.00

BARNARD, Robert. *Bodies.* 1986. Scribner. 1st ed. VG/VG. P3. $14.00

BARNARD, Robert. *Cherry Blossom Corpse.* 1987. Scribner. 1st ed. VG/VG. P3. $15.00

BARNARD, Robert. *Death & the Chaste Apprentice.* 1989. Scribner. 1st ed. sgn. F/F. T2. $18.00

BARNARD, Robert. *Death of a Literary Widow.* 1980. Scribner. 1st ed. F/F. H11. $30.00

BARNARD, Robert. *Death of a Perfect Mother.* 1981. Scribner. ARC. F/F. H11. $30.00

BARNARD, Robert. *Death of a Salesperson & Other Untimely Exits.* 1989. Scribner. 1st Am ed. sgn. F/F. T2. $17.00

BARNARD, Robert. *Political Suicide.* 1986. Scribner. 1st ed. sgn. F/F. T2. $18.00

BARNARD, Robert. *Talent to Deceive: Agatha Christie.* 1980. Dodd Mead. 1st ed. VG/VG. P3. $15.00

BARNERS, Parker T. *House Plants & How to Grow Them.* 1909. Doubleday Page. 1st ed. 12mo. 236p. red/blk stp gilt gr cloth. NF. T10. $50.00

BARNES, Djuna. *Book of Repulsive Women.* 1915. NY. Guido Bruno. 1st ed. author's 1st book. NF/yel wrp. B24. $950.00

BARNES, Djuna. *Vagaries Malicieux.* 1974. NY. Frank Hallman. 1/500. F/glassine. B2. $75.00

BARNES, Eva Salisbury. *Red-Letter Days.* 1908. Hot Springs. photos. 147p. VG. B10. $10.00

BARNES, Harper. *Blue Monday.* 1991. St Louis. Patrice. 1st ed. author's 1st novel. sgn. F/pict wrp. T2. $18.00

BARNES, John. *Kaleidoscope Century.* 1995. NY. Tor. 1st ed/1st prt. photo of ES. F/F. T2. $45.00

BARNES, John. *Man Who Pulled Down the Sky.* 1986. Congdon Weed. 1st ed. VG/VG. P3. $20.00

BARNES, John. *Mother of Storms.* 1994. Tor. 1st ed. F/F. G10. $27.50

BARNES, John. *Orbital Resonance.* 1991. Tor. 1st ed. F/F. G10. $25.00

BARNES, Josiah. *Green Mountain Travellers' Entertainment.* 1860. NY. 360p. G. A17. $10.00

BARNES, Linda. *Dead Heat.* 1984. St Martin. 1st ed. xl. dj. P3. $7.00

BARNES, Linda. *Snake Tattoo.* 1989. St Martin. 1st ed. VG/VG+. N4. $25.00

BARNES, Linda. *Trouble of Fools.* 1987. St Martin. 1st ed. F/F. C2. $75.00

BARNES, NIVEN & POURNELLE. *Legacy of Heorot.* 1987. Simon Schuster. 1st ed. rem mk. F/F. N4. $25.00

BARNES, Ruth. *I Hear America Singing.* 1937. Winston. ils Robert Lawson. VG. M5. $40.00

BARNES, Trevor. *Midsummer Night's Killing.* 1989. Morrow. 1st ed. author's 1st book. F/F. H11. $20.00

BARNES, Trevor. *Pound of Flesh.* 1991. Morrow. 1st Am ed. author's 2nd novel. F/NF. M22. $10.00

BARNETT. *Shipping Literature of the Great Lakes: A Catalogue...* 1992. MI State. ils. 194p. F. A4. $65.00

BARNEY, Libeus. *Letters of the Pike's Peak Gold Rush.* 1959. San Jose. Talisman. 1/975. F/NF. O7. $85.00

BARNEY, Maginel Wright. *Valley of God Almighty Joneses.* 1965. NY. 1st ed. VG/VG. B5. $45.00

BARON & CARVER. *Bud Stewart: Michigan's Legendary Lure Maker.* 1990. Marceline, MO. 1st ed. photos/pl. 227p. AN. A17. $75.00

BARONI, Aldo. *Yucatan.* 1937. Mexico. Ediciones Botas. 1st ed. 211p. F3. $20.00

BARR, Nevada. *Superior Death.* 1994. Putnam. 1st ed. F/F. M22/T2. $45.00

BARR, Nevada. *Track of the Cat.* 1993. Putnam. UP. author's 1st book. F/wrp. B5. $300.00

BARR, Nevada. *Track of the Cat.* 1993. Putnam. 1st ed. author's 1st mystery. F/F. T2. $125.00

BARR & CRANE. *O'Ruddy.* 1903. NY. 1st ed. NF. C6. $100.00

BARR & MALONEY. *Types of Mental Defectives.* 1920. Phil. 31 pl. 179p. red cloth. VG. B14. $225.00

BARRETT, John G. *Civil War in North Carolina.* 1975. Chapel Hill. 1st ed/2nd prt. 484p. cloth. NF/dj. M8. $35.00

BARRETT, John Paul. *Sea Stories: Harrowing Tales of Mystery...* 1987. Gaff. 1st ed. sgn. pict off-wht cloth. VG. B11. $25.00

BARRETT, Neal Jr. *Dead Dog Blues.* 1994. St Martin. 1st ed. F/F. T2. $23.00

BARRETT, Neal Jr. *Hereafter Gang.* 1991. Ziesing. 1st ed. F/F. P3/T2. $25.00

BARRIE, James M. *Farewell Miss Julie Logan.* 1932. Scribner. 1st ed. VG. P3. $20.00

BARRIE, James M. *Margaret Ogilvy by Her Son.* 1897. NY. 12mo. 207p. teg. gilt brd. VG+. C14. $12.00

BARRIE, James M. *Peter Pan & Wendy.* 1930 (1921). Scribner. ils ML Attwell. VG. M5. $65.00

BARRIE, James M. *Peter Pan.* 1987. Holt. 1st ed. ils Michael Hague. F/F. B17. $20.00

BARRIE, James M. *Plays of JM Barrie.* 1928. Lodnon. 1st ed. NF/NF. w/manuscript leaf from Half an Hour. C6. $250.00

BARRIE, James M. *Quality Street.* ca 1913. London. Hodder Stoughton. ils Hugh Thomson. 198p. gilt purple cloth. NF. T10. $275.00

BARRINGER, William E. *Lincoln's Rise to Power.* nd. np. 1st ed. 373p. VG/dj. B18. $25.00

BARRON, Greg. *Groundrush.* 1982. Random. 1st ed. rem mk. F/NF. B35. $20.00

BARROW, Frances Elizabeth. *Little Katy & Her Mother, by Aunt Laura.* 1863. Buffalo. 64p. lacks rear ep. B24. $95.00

BARROW, Frances Elizabeth. *Silver Medal, by Aunt Laura.* 1863. Buffalo. 64p. aeg. gilt pink cloth. NF. B24. $110.00

BARROWS, Marjorie. *Four Little Kittens.* 1957. Rand McNally. 1st ed. ils Harry Frees. F. M5. $12.00

BARROWS, Walter Bradford. *Michigan Bird Life.* 1912. MI Agriculture College. 70 full-p photos. 822p. wrp. A17. $50.00

BARRY, Iris. *DW Griffith: American Film Master.* 1940. MOMA Film Lib. 1st ed. VG+. B5/D2. $65.00

BARRY, James P. *Fate of the Lakes: Portrait of the Great Lakes.* 1972. Grand Rapids. Baker Book House. 1st ed. sgn. VG/VG. A16. $20.00

BARRY, Jerome. *Extreme License.* 1958. Crime Club. 1st ed. G/G. P3. $8.00

BARRY, Jerome. *Fall Guy.* 1960. Crime Club. 1st ed. VG/G. P3. $18.00

BARRYMORE, Ethel. *Memories.* 1955. Harper. 1st ed. inscr. NF/VG+. B4. $250.00

BARTH, John. *End of the Road.* 1958. Garden City. 1st ed. F/F. C2. $150.00

BARTHELME, Donald. *Great Days.* 1979. FSG. 1st ed. F/F. B35. $24.00

BARTHELME, Frederick. *Tracer.* 1985. Simon Schuster. 1st ed. F/F. B35. $24.00

BARTHELME, Frederick. *Two Against One.* 1988. Weidenfield Nicholson. 1st ed. F/F. A20. $17.00

BARTHOLOMEW, Ed. *Houston Story 1836-1865.* 1951. Frontier. 1st ed. sgn. VG. P12. $47.50

BARTHOLOMEW, Roberts. *Manual of Instructions for Enlisting & Discharging Soldiers.* 1864. Phil. 276p. gr cloth. VG. B14. $275.00

BARTLESS, James H. *Restricted Problem of Three Bodies.* 1964 & 1965. Copenhagen. Ejnar Munksgaard. xl. wrp. K5. $50.00

BARTLETT, Arthur. *Game-Legs.* 1928. Cupples Leon. 1st ed. VG/G. O3. $20.00

BARTLETT, D.W. *Heroes of the Indian Rebellion.* 1860. Follett Foster. 456p. cloth. VG. M20. $52.00

BARTLETT, Kim. *Finest Kind: Fishermen of Gloucester.* 1977. Norton. 1st ed. 8vo. 251p. VG/VG. B11. $25.00

BARTLETT, Mary. *Gentians.* 1981 (1975). Dorset. new revised ed. 21 pl. 144p. F/dj. B26. $22.50

BARTLETT, Robert A. *Log of Bob Bartlett: True Story of Forty Years...* 1932. Bl Ribbon. 352p. G/G. B11. $55.00

BARTLETT, W.H. *Jerusalem Revisited.* 1855. London. ils. 202p. 3-quarter leather. B5. $350.00

BARTLETT. *Nathaniel Tarn: A Descriptive Bibliography.* 1987. np. ils. 135p. F. A4. $135.00

BARTON, Clara. *Story of the Red Cross: Glimpses of Field Work.* 1904. Appleton. 1st ed. inscr/dtd 1904. 199p. tan cloth. VG. C6. $500.00

BARTON, F.P. *Barton Variation: The Only Certain Method of Slam Bidding.* 1935. London. 13th. 89p. VG. S1. $6.00

BARTON, Frederick. *El Cholo Feeling Passes.* 1985. Atlanta. Peachtree. 1st ed. author's 1st book. F/F. w/ephemera. H11. $40.00

BARTON, George A. *Archaeology & the Bible.* 1927. Am Sunday School Union. 5th. 127 pl. 481p. VG. W1. $65.00

BARTON, Mary. *Impressions of Mexico With Brush & Pen.* 1911. Methuen. 2nd. ils. 164p. G. F3. $20.00

BARTON, W. *JP Williamson: A Brother to the Sioux.* 1919. Revell. 1st ed. VG+/remnant. A15. $45.00

BARTON, William E. *Paternity of Abraham Lincoln...* 1920. NY. Doran. 1st ed. pres. 414p. VG. M8. $85.00

BARTON, William E. *Women Lincoln Loved.* 1927. London. 1st ed. ils. 284p. G+. B18. $37.50

BARTON & CAPOBIANCO. *Iris.* 1990. Doubleday. 1st ed. F/F. P3. $20.00

BARTRAM, George. *Job Abroad.* 1975. Macmillan. 1st ed. VG/VG. P3. $20.00

BARTRUM, Douglas. *Lilac & Laburnum.* 1959. London. ils/photos. 175p. cloth. VG. B26. $15.00

BARZUN, Jacques. *Catalogue of Crime.* 1971. Harper Row. 1st ed. xl. VG+/dj. N4. $30.00

BASCOM, Willard. *Crest of the Wave.* 1988. NY. xl. VG. O7. $10.00

BASCULE. *Advanced Auction Bridge (Royal Spades).* 1916. London. 2nd. 232p. VG. S1. $15.00

BASE, Graeme. *Eleventh Hour.* 1988. NY. 1st Am ed. NF/VG+. C8. $25.00

BASE, Graeme. *Sign of the Seahorse, a Tale of Greed & High Adventure...* 1992. NY. Abrams. 1st Am ed. 4to. F/F. C8. $25.00

BASKIN, Leonard. *Imps, Demons, Hobgoblins, Witches, Fairies & Elves.* 1984. NY. 1st ed. unp. VG+/dj. B18. $12.50

BASS, Rick. *Deer Pasture.* 1985. College Sta, TX. 1st ed. F/F clip. M23. $125.00

BASS, T.J. *Godwhale.* 1975. Eyre Methuen. 1st ed. NF/NF. P3. $40.00

BASSETT, John. *Medical Reports of John V Bassett, MD: The Alabama Student.* 1941. Springfield. 1st ed. 62p. A13. $60.00

BASSETT, Sara Ware. *Within the Harbor.* 1948. NY. 1st ed. VG/VG. A17. $8.50

BASTABLE, Bernard; see Barnard, Robert.

BASTIN, Bruce. *Crying for the Carolines.* 1971. London. Studio Vista. 1st ed. F/wrp. B2. $25.00

BASTOW, Thelma W. *If Only...Story of Henri Peney.* 1964. Dietz. ARC. 250p. VG/G. B10. $15.00

BATCHELOR, D. *Jack Johnson & His Times.* 1957. London. ils. 190p. VG/VG. B5. $45.00

BATCHELOR, John C. *Gordon Liddy Is My Muse.* 1990. Simon Schuster. 1st ed. F/F. A20. $14.00

BATCHELOR, John Calvin. *American Falls.* 1985. Norton. 1st ed. F/F. H11. $40.00

BATCHELOR & HOGG. *Naval Gun.* 1978. England. 1st ed. ils/photos. 142p. F/F. E1. $45.00

BATEMAN, Colin. *Divorcing Jack.* 1995. Arcade. 1st Am ed. author's 1st book. F/F. M23. $25.00

BATEMAN, Ed. *Horse Breaker!* 1947. Seattle. Wilson. 1st ed. photos. 110p. VG. O3. $35.00

BATES, Arthenia J. *Seeds Beneath the Snow.* 1969. NY. Greenwich. 1st ed. sgn. NF/VG. B4. $125.00

BATES, H.E. *Down the River.* 1937. Holt. ARC. ils Agnes Miller Parker. 141p. VG/dj. M20. $155.00

BATHE, Basil W. *Seven Centuries of Sea Travel: From Crusades to Cruises.* 1990. NY. Portland House. VG/dj. A16. $25.00

BATMAN, Richard. *Outer Coast.* 1985. NY. VG. O7. $15.00

BATTELL, Joseph. *Yankee Boy From Home.* 1864. NY. Miller. O3. $295.00

BATTEN, Jack. *Straight No Chaser.* 1989. Canada. Macmillan. 1st ed. F/F. P3. $20.00

BATTLE, Kemp Plummer. *Memories of an Old-Timer Tar Heel.* 1945. Chapel Hill. 1st ed. ils. 296p. VG/dj. B18. $22.50

BATTS, John Stuart. *British Manuscript Diaries of the 19th Century...* 1976. London. Centaur. M11. $35.00

BATTY, E.C. *Americans Before Columbus.* 1951. NY. 1st ed. VG/G. B5. $25.00

BAUCHER, F. *New Method of Horsemanship.* nd. NY. Jenkins. VG. O3. $65.00

BAUER, Margaret Jean. *Animal Babies.* 1949. Donohue. ils Jacob Bates Abbott. VG/G. B17. $10.00

BAUER, Steven. *Satyrday.* 1980. Berkley Putnam. 1st ed. NF/NF. P3. $15.00

BAUGHMAN, Robert W. *Kansas in Maps.* 1961. KS State Hist Soc. 90+ maps. F/worn. O7. $95.00

BAUM, L. Frank. *Aunt Jane's Nieces.* 1906. Reilly Lee. not 1st ed. as by Edith VanDyne. F/NF. A17. $10.00

BAUM, L. Frank. *Emerald City of Oz.* 1939. Rand McNally. G. P3. $10.00

BAUM, L. Frank. *Father Goose, His Book.* ca 1910. Donahue. 6th. ils WW Denslow. unp. VG/dj. D1. $385.00

BAUM, L. Frank. *Lost Princess of Oz.* 1941. Reilly Lee. NF/NF. P3. $100.00

BAUM, L. Frank. *Magic of Oz.* 1931. Reilly Lee. NF/NF. P3. $125.00

BAUM, L. Frank. *New Wizard of Oz.* (1899). Bobbs Merrill. 6th. 8 pl. 208p. VG/poor. P2. $75.00

BAUM, L. Frank. *New Wizard of Oz.* 1944. Bobbs Merrill. ils Evelyn Copelman. F. M19. $85.00

BAUM, L. Frank. *Ozma of Oz.* 1907. Reilly Lee. 1st ed/3rd state. ils JR Neill. tan cloth. VG. D1. $875.00

BAUM, L. Frank. *Tin Woodman of Oz.* 1937. Reilly Lee. NF/NF. P3. $120.00

BAUM, L. Frank. *Wizard of Oz.* 1939. Grosset Dunlap. abridged ed. ils Oskar Lebeck. F/VG. P3. $35.00

BAUM, L. Frank. *Wizard of Oz.* 1944. Bobbs Merrill. ils Evelyn Copelman. VG/dj. B30. $12.00

BAUM, L. Frank. *Wizard of Oz.* 1944. Saalfield. moveables Julian Wehr. sbdg. VG. D1. $200.00

BAUM, L. Frank. *Wizard of Oz.* 1991. Jelly Bean. 1st ed thus. ils Charles Santore. F/VG. B17. $8.50

BAUM, Vicki. *Headless Angel.* 1948. Doubleday. 1st ed. NF/NF. B4. $50.00

BAUMGARDT, Carola. *Johannes Kepler: Life & Letters.* 1951. NY. Philosophical Lib. 1st ed. 8vo. 209p. VG/G. K5. $30.00

BAUMGARTL, I. *Sea Gods.* 1937. Chicago. Kroch. 1st ed. ils Gertrude S Ruben. NF/dj. S9. $30.00

BAUSCH, Richard. *Violence.* 1992. Houghton Mifflin. 1st ed. F/F. M22. $25.00

BAUXBAUM, E.C. *Collector's Guide to the National Geographic Magazine.* 1956. Wilmington, DE. 1st ed. NF. H7. $25.00

BAVIER, Bob. *America's Cup Fever.* 1980. Ziff Davis. ils. 240p. VG/dj. T7. $20.00

BAXT, George. *Alfred Hitchcock Murder Case.* 1986. NY. 1st ed. F/F. H11. $20.00

BAXT, Geroge. *Neon Graveyard.* 1979. St Martin. 1st ed. VG/VG. P3. $30.00

BAXTER, Betty. *Supposin'.* 1931. Volland. A Sunny Book. 1st ed. sm 8vo. VG. M5. $60.00

BAXTER, Charles. *First Light.* 1987. Viking. 1st ed. F/F. M23. $20.00

BAXTER, Charles. *Relative Stranger.* 1990. Norton. 1st ed. F/F. M23. $20.00

BAXTER, Charles. *Shadow Play.* 1993. NY. Norton. ARC. sgn. F/decor wrp. S9. $75.00

BAXTER, John. *Kid.* 1981. Viking. 1st ed. F/F. B35. $15.00

BAXTER, Lorna. *Eggchild.* 1979. Dutton. 1st ed. VG/VG. P3. $18.00

BAXTER, Richard. *Guilty Women.* 1943. Quality Pr. 7th. NF/NF. P3. $9.00

BAYER, Oliver Weld. *Eye for an Eye.* 1946. Tower. VG/G. P3. $15.00

BAYER, William. *Blind Side.* 1989. Villard. 1st ed. F/F. H11. $35.00

BAYER, William. *Punish Me With Kisses.* 1980. Congdon Lattes. 1st ed. VG/VG. P3. $15.00

BAYER, William. *Punish Me With Kisses.* 1980. NY. Congdon. 1st ed. NF/NF. H11. $25.00

BAYER, William. *Switch.* 1984. Simon Schuster. 1st ed. F/NF. H11. $45.00

BAYLEY, Barrington J. *Rod of Light.* 1987. Arbor. 1st ed. F/F. P3. $16.00

BAYLEY & MAYNE. *Mouldy.* 1982. Knopf. 1st Am ed. ils Nicola Bayley. unp. M/M. D1. $45.00

BAYLEY & METCALFE. *Golden Calm.* 1980. NY. VG. O7. $20.00

BAYLISS, Marguerite F. *Yearbook of Show Horses.* 1936. NY. Blackwell. 2 vol. 4to. G. O3. $125.00

BAYLOR, Byrd. *Way to Start a Day.* 1978. Scribner. 1st ed. ils. NF/NF. C8. $35.00

BAYLOR, Don. *Don Baylor.* 1989. St Martin. 1st ed. inscr. F/F. P8. $55.00

BAYNE, Samuel G. *Pith of Astronomy...* 1898 (1896). Harper. 19 pl. 122p. ils cloth. K5. $35.00

BAYNES, Ernest. *Sprite: Story of a Red Fox.* 1938. Scribner. 1st Am ed. VG. O3. $25.00

BEACH, Bell. *Riding & Driving for Women.* 1912. Scribner. 1st ed in better bdg. VG. O3. $125.00

BEACH, Edward L. *Dust on the Sea.* 1972. Holt. 1st ed. F/NF. H11. $25.00

BEACH, Edward L. *Run Silent, Run Deep.* 1955. Holt. 1st ed. NF/NF. B4. $125.00

BEACH, Rex. *Ne'er-Do-Well.* 1911. NY. Harper. 1st ed. 8vo. ils HC Christy. gilt bl cloth. F. T10. $150.00

BEACH, S.A. *Apples of New York.* 1905. Albany. Lyon. 2 vol. pl. VG. H7. $140.00

BEACH, Sylvia. *Shakespeare & Company.* 1959. NY. 1st ed. VG/VG. B5. $35.00

BEADLE, J.H. *Western Wilds.* 1878. Cincinnati. lg map. 624p. marbled ep. half leather. fair. B18. $45.00

BEAGLE, Peter S. *Folk of the Air.* 1986. Ballantine. 1st ed. F/NF. G10. $20.00

BEAGLE, Peter S. *I See By My Outfit.* 1966. Muller. 1st Eng ed. F/F. M19. $75.00

BEAGLEHOLE, J.C. *Life of Captain James Cook.* 1974. Stranford. ils/fld map. 760p. F/dj. B26. $45.00

, George. *Stephen King Story: A Literary Profile.* 1991. Andrews McMeel. 1st ed. F/F. T2. $20.00

BEALE, Lionel S. *How to Work With the Microscope.* 1865. Phil. Lindsay Blakiston. 3rd. 8vo. gr cloth. F. B14. $75.00

BEALE, Lionel S. *Microscope: Its Application to Clinical Medicine.* 1854. London. ils. 303p. cloth. VG. B14. $125.00

BEALE, Marie. *Flight Into America's Past.* 1932. NY. Putnam. 1st ed. 286p. G. F3. $10.00

BEAMISH, Richard J. *Boy's Story of Lindbergh: The Lone Eagle.* 1928. Phil. Winston. 8vo. 288p. VG+. C14. $18.00

BEAN, L.L. *Hunting-Fishing-Camping.* 19444. LL Bean. photos/maps. blk stp red bdg. G. P12. $10.00

BEAR, Firman E. *Soils & Fertilizers.* 1953 (1924). NY. 4th. ils/maps. 420p. VG. B26. $15.00

BEAR, Greg. *Eon.* 1985. NY. Bluejay. 1st ed. F/F. M23. $75.00

BEAR, Greg. *Eternity.* 1988. Warner. 1st ed. F/F. P3. $17.00

BEAR, Greg. *Forge of God.* 1987. Tor. 1st ed. VG+/NF. M23. $35.00

BEAR, Greg. *Heads.* 1991. St Martin. 1st ed. F/F. M23. $15.00

BEAR, Greg. *Moving Mars.* 1993. NY. Tor. 1st ed. F/F. M23. $40.00

BEAR, Greg. *Psychlone.* 1990. Severn. 1st hc ed. author's 2nd book. F/F. G10. $30.00

BEAR, Greg. *Queen of Angels.* 1990. Warner. 1st trade ed (preceded by Easton ed). F/NF. G10. $15.00

BEAR, Greg. *Tangents.* 1989. Warner. 1st ed. F/F. M23. $30.00

BEAR, Greg. *Wind From the Burning Woman.* 1983. Sauk City. Arkham. 1st ed. 1/3046. F/F. T2. $85.00

BEARD, Henry. *Miss Piggy's Guide to Life.* 1981. Knopf. 1st ed. F/F. B17. $20.00

BEARDSLEY & GLASSCO. *Under the Hill.* 1959. Grove. 1st ed. ils. dj. A17. $9.50

BEARE, George. *Snake on the Grave.* 1974. Houghton Mifflin. 1st ed. VG/VG. P3. $15.00

BEASLEY, Conger. *Hidalgo's Beard.* 1979. Andrews McMeel. 1st ed. VG/VG. P3. $20.00

BEASLEY, H.M. *Beasley Contract Bridge System.* 1935. London. 128p. VG. S1. $8.00

BEASLEY, N. *Men-Working.* 1931. NY. 1st ed. ils/index. 296p. VG/VG. B5. $25.00

BEASLEY, Norman. *Freighters of Fortune.* 1930. Harper. G/dj. A16. $45.00

BEASTON, Bud. *Master Farrier.* 1975. Sperry. OK Farrier's College. sgn. 191p. VG/VG. O3. $25.00

BEATLEY, Janice C. *Vascular Plants of the NV Test Site & General S NV...* 1976. Springfield. photos. F. B26. $42.50

BEATON, Cecil. *Diaries 1955-1963.* 1976. 1st ed. NF/VG+. S13. $20.00

BEATON, Cecil. *Face of the World.* 1957. John Day. photos. 240p. NF. B14. $55.00

BEATON, M.C. *Death of a Hussy.* 1990. NY. 1st ed. F/NF. H11. $20.00

BEATON & TYNAN. *Persona Grata.* 1954. Putnam. 1st Am ed. F/NF. B4. $175.00

BEATTIE, Ann. *Distortions.* 1976. Doubleday. 1st ed. sgn. F/F. B35. $100.00

BEATTIE, Ann. *Falling in Place.* 1980. Random. 1st ed. sgn. author's 2nd novel. NF/F. B4. $75.00

BEATTIE, Ann. *Falling in Place.* 1980. Random. 2nd. VG/clip. B10. $25.00

BEATTIE, Ann. *Love Always.* 1985. Random. 1st ed. author's 3rd novel. F/F. B4. $45.00

BEATTIE, Ann. *Picturing Will.* 1989. Random. 1st ed. AN/dj. B4. $45.00

BEATTIE, Ann. *Where You'll Find Me.* 1986. NY. Linden. 1st ed. sgn. F/F. B4. $50.00

BEATTY, Bill. *Next Door to Paradise.* 1965. Melbourne. VG. O7. $20.00

BEATY, John. *Crossroads: Novel of the 20th-Century South.* 1956. Dallas. Wilkerson. VG/G. B10. $12.00

BEATY, John O. *Swords in the Dawn.* 1937. Longman Gr. 1st ed. ils Henry Pitz. 212p. map ep. F. C14. $12.00

BEATY, Josephine Powell. *Road to Jericho.* 1965. Dorrance. inscr pres. 154p. F/F. B10. $12.00

BEATY, Richard Edward. *Mountain Angels: Trials of the Mountaineers of Blue Ridge...* 1928. Front Royall. self pub. 125p. VG. B10. $25.00

BEAUCHAMP, Loren; see Silverberg, Robert.

BEAUMONT, Charles. *Shadow Play.* 1964. London. Panther. 1st ed. VG+. A11. $25.00

BECHET, Sidney. *Treat It Gentle.* 1960. Hill Wang. 1st ed. F/NF. B2. $65.00

BECHTEL, CRIBB & LAUNERT. *Manual of Cultivated Orchid Species.* 1981. Cambridge. 1st MIT ed. photos/drawings. 444p. F/dj. B26. $52.50

BECK, Ann. *History of the British Medical Administration of E Africa.* 1970. Cambridge. 1st ed. 271p. VG. A13. $30.00

BECK, Carl. *Roentgen Ray Diagnosis & Therapy.* 1904. NY. 1st ed. 460p. VG. B14. $225.00

BECK, K.K. *Murder in a Mummy Case.* 1986. Walker. 1st ed. author's 2nd book. rem mk. F/F. N4. $17.50

BECK, Richard. *Icelandic Lyrics.* 1930. Bjarnarson. Reykjavik. 1st ed. half leather. VG. A17. $30.00

BECK & ROTH. *Music in Prints.* 1965. NY Public Lib. 4to. 120p. F. A4. $85.00

BECKER, Stephen. *Chinese Bandit.* 1975. Random. 1st ed. VG/VG. P3. $25.00

BECKER, Stephen. *Dog Tags.* 1973. Random. 1st ed. VG/VG. P3. $25.00

BECKER, Stephen. *Last Mandarin.* 1979. Random. 1st ed. VG/VG. P3. $25.00

BECKER, Stephen. *When the War Is Over.* 1969. Random. 1st ed. VG/VG. P3. $25.00

BECKER. *Estelle Donheny Collection.* 1989. NY. Christie's. 4to. 134p. red cloth. F. A4. $85.00

BECKETT, Samuel. *How It Is.* 1964. London. 1/100. sgn. full vellum. C6. $350.00

BECKETT, Samuel. *Rockaby & Other Short Pieces.* 1981. Grove. 1st ed. F/F. B35. $22.00

BECKFORD, William. *Vathek.* 1928. John Day. 1st ed. 229p. NF/ragged dj/worn case. M20. $65.00

BECKMANN, Frank Harrison. *Dust of India.* 1937. Boston. 1st ed. 8vo. 300p. VG/G. B11. $25.00

BEDELL & CREHORE. *Alternating Currents: Analytical & Graphical Treatment...* 1893. NY. Johnston. 2nd. assn sgn. 8vo. 325p. gr cloth. VG. T10. $50.00

BEDFORD, Annie North. *Disneyland on the Air.* 1955. Mickey Mouse Club Book. TVTI. VG. P3. $20.00

BEDFORD, Annie North. *Susie's New Stove, the Little Chef's Cookbook.* nd. Little Golden. 1st/A ed. ils Corinne Malvern. VG. M5. $18.00

BEDFORD, Francis D. *Another Book of Verses for Children.* 1925. Macmillan. 1st rpt. 8vo. stp gray cloth. NF. M5. $65.00

BEDFORD, Sybille. *Aldous Huxley Vol 1: 1894-1939.* 1973. Chatto Windus. VG/VG. P3. $25.00

BEDNAR, Kamil. *Puppets & Fairy Tales.* 1958. Prague. ils/photos. 52p. VG/dj. A17. $20.00

BEEBE, Lucius. *Mansions on Wheels.* 1959. NY. 1st ed. VG/G. B5. $50.00

BEEBE, William. *Jungle Peace.* 1918. NY. 1st ed. inscr. NF. A9. $50.00

BEEBE, William. *Two Bird-Lovers in Mexico.* 1905. Houghton Mifflin. 1st ed/2nd issue. teg. VG. A20. $85.00

BEEBE & CLEGG. *American West.* 1955. Dutton. 1st ed. 4to. 412p. F/NF. T10. $65.00

BEEBE & CLEGG. *US West: The Saga of Wells Fargo.* 1949. Dutton. 1st ed. 8vo. 320p. red cloth. VG/dj. T10. $40.00

BEEBE & CLEGG. *When Beauty Rode the Rails.* 1962. NY. 1st ed. 222p. G+/torn. B18. $22.50

BEEBEE, Chris. *Hub.* 1987. MacDonald. F/F. P3. $22.00

BEECHER, Elizabeth. *Roy Rogers on the Double-R Ranch.* 1951. Simon Schuster. VG. P3. $15.00

BEECHER, Henry Ward. *Star Papers; or, Experiences of Art & Nature.* 1855. NY. JC Derby. 359p. aeg. gilt full leather. VG. A4. $45.00

BEECHER, Henry Ward. *Theodore Tilton Vs Henry Ward Beecher...* 1875. NY. McDivitt Campbell. 3 vol. VG. M11. $350.00

BEECHER, John. *Collected Poems 1924-1974.* 1975. Macmillan. inscr. VG/VG. w/sgn letter. M19. $45.00

BEEDING, Francis. *Death Walks in Eastrepps.* 1931. Mystery League. 1st ed. G. P3. $15.00

BEEMAN, Howard. *Veterinary Obstetrics & Zoo Technics.* 1932. Am Remount Assn. 131p. VG. O3. $45.00

BEER & BEER. *Vistas in Astonomy.* 1977. Oxford. Pergamon. 412p. VG. K5. $30.00

BEERBOHM, Max. *Christmas Garland, Woven by Max Beerbohm.* 1912. London. Heineman. 1st ed. gilt bl cloth. F. B24. $125.00

BEERBOHM, Max. *Happy Hypocrite. A Fairy Tale for Tired Men.* 1897. NY. Lane. 1st ed. sm 8vo. 53p. F/prt wrp. B24. $485.00

BEERBOHM, Max. *Letters to Reggie Turner.* 1965. np. photos/caricatures. 312p. F/VG. A4. $45.00

BEERBOHM, Max. *Mainly on the Air.* 1947. Knopf. 1st Am ed. 12mo. 142p. gilt blk cloth. F/NF. T10. $50.00

BEERBOHM, Max. *Peep Into the Past.* 1923. private prt. 1/300 on Japanese vellum. NF/rpr case. T10. $300.00

BEERBOHM, Max. *Rossetti & His Circle.* 1921. Heinemann. 1st ed. 23 mtd pl. gilt bl cloth. NF. T10. $125.00

BEERCROFT & HAYCRAFT. *Treasury of Great Mysteries. Vol 1 & 2.* nd. Nelson Doubleday. VG/VG. P3. $15.00

BEERY, Jesse. *Four Types of Disposition.* 1921. Pleasant Hill. VG/wrp. O3. $35.00

BEESLEY & HOSTETTER. *It's a Racket.* 1929. Chicago. 1st ed. photos. F/torn. A15. $75.00

BEETON, Isabella. *Book of Household Management.* 1892. np. ils. G. M17. $50.00

BEEZLEY, William. *Insurgent Governor.* 1973. Lincoln, NE. 1st ed. 195p. dj. F3. $15.00

BEGIN, Menachem. *Revolt Story of the Irgun.* 1951. NY. Schuman. 1st ed. 8vo. 386p. bl cloth. G. B14. $75.00

BEGLEY, Louis. *Man Who Was Late.* 1993. Knopf. 1st ed. F/F. M23. $20.00

BEHAN, Brendon. *Brendon Behan's New York.* nd. np. 1st ed. F/VG+. N3. $10.00

BEHAN & HOGARTH. *Brendan Behan's Island. An Irish Sketch-Book.* 1962. NY. Bernard Geis. 1st ed. sgns. F/F. A17. $135.00

BEHN, Harry. *All Kinds of Time.* 1950. Harcourt Brace. 1st ed. ils. F/VG+. P2. $35.00

BEHN, Noel. *Shadowboxer.* 1969. Simon Schuster. 1st ed. VG. P3. $12.00

BEHR, M. *Outlines of Universal History.* 1861. Boston. 8vo. 595p. quarter leather/blk brd. G. T3. $17.00

BEHRMAN. *Three Plays: Serena Blandish; Meteor; Second Man.* 1934. Farrar Rinehart. inscr/dtd 1939. cloth. NF. D2. $40.00

BEHRMAN, Cynthia F. *Victorian Myths of the Sea.* 1977. Athens. VG. O7. $20.00

BEITTEL, Will. *Santa Barbara's Street & Park Trees.* 1972. Santa Barbara. ils/5 maps. 94p. photo wrp. B26. $15.00

BELFRAGE, Cedric. *Let My People Go.* 1940. London. Gollancz. 319p. G. A17. $8.50

BELIAEV, Alexander. *Professor Dowell's Head.* 1980. Macmillan. 1st ed. VG/VG. P3. $15.00

BELILES, Mark A. *Thomas Jefferson's Abridgement of Words of Jesus...* 1993. self pub. 72p. VG. B10. $8.00

BELITT, Ben. *Five-Fold Mesh.* 1938. Knopf. 1st ed. 50p. VG. B10. $12.00

BELKNAP, Jeremy. *Foresters: An American Tale.* 1970. Gregg. 216p. VG. A17. $10.00

BELL, Bill. *Saxophone Boy.* 1980. Tundra. 1st ed. sgn. ils. 95p. VG+/dj. M20. $37.00

BELL, Charles G. *Sons for a New America.* 1966. Dunwoody, GA. 78p. VG. B10. $12.00

BELL, Clare. *Ratha's Creature.* 1983. Atheneum. 1st ed. F/F. P3. $11.00

BELL, Gertrude Lowthian. *Letters of...* 1927. London. Benn. 2 vol. 5th. 30 pl/2 maps. VG. W1. $65.00

BELL, Gordon B. *Golden Troubadour.* 1980. McGraw Hill. F/F. P3. $13.00

BELL, Joseph. *World Series Thrills.* 1962. Messner. later prt. VG/G. P8. $17.50

BELL, Josephine. *In the King's Absence.* 1973. Bles. 1st ed. F/F. P3. $20.00

BELL, Josephine. *New People of the Hollies.* 1961. Macmillan. 1st ed. VG/VG. P3. $25.00

BELL, Josephine. *Wilberforce Legacy.* 1969. Walker. 1st ed. VG/G. P3. $15.00

BELL, Josephine. *Wolf! Wolf! Wolf!* 1980. Walker. 1st ed. VG/VG. P3. $15.00

BELL, Larry. *Works From New Mexico.* 1989. Musee d'Art Contemporain. sgn. French/Eng text. ils/photos. 95p. stiff wrp. D2. $65.00

BELL, Madison Smartt. *Barking Man & Other Stories.* 1990. Ticknor. 1st ed. F/F. H11. $30.00

BELL, Madison Smartt. *Doctor Sleep.* 1991. HBJ. 1st ed. F/F. B4. $45.00

BELL, Madison Smartt. *Save Me, Joe Louis.* 1993. Harcourt Brace. NF/NF. A20. $20.00

BELL, Madison Smartt. *Straight Cut.* 1986. Ticknor. 1st ed. F/F. H11. $35.00

BELL, Madison Smartt. *Waiting for the End of the World.* 1985. Ticknor Fields. 1st ed. sgn. F/F. B35. $80.00

BELL, Madison Smartt. *Washington Square Ensemble.* 1983. Viking. 1st ed. F/F. B35. $80.00

BELL, Madison Smartt. *Year of Silence.* 1987. Tichnor Fields. 1st ed. 194p. VG/VG. B10. $35.00

BELL, Marvin. *Poems for Nathan & Saul.* 1966. Hillside. 1st ed. 1/350. NF/prt wrp. C2. $350.00

BELL, R.C. *Diaries From the Days of Sail.* 1974. NY. VG. O7. $25.00

BELL, Samuel D. *Justice & Sheriff, Practical Forms for Use of Justices...* 1843. Concord. G Parker Lyon. 1st ed. contemporary sheep. M11. $150.00

BELLADONNA & GAROZZO. *Percision & Superprecision Bidding.* 1975. NY. 237p. VG. S1. $20.00

BELLAH, James Warner. *Ward 20.* 1946. Doubleday. 1st ed. 160p. VG+/dj. M20. $35.00

BELLAIRS, George. *Intruder in the Dark.* 1966. John Gifford. 1st ed. VG/G. P3. $20.00

BELLAIRS, John. *Dark Secret of Weatherend.* 1984. Dial. 1st ed. VG/G. P3. $15.00

BELLAMY, David. *Queen's Hidden Garden.* 1984. Newton Abbott, Eng. ils. 224p. F/clip. B26. $32.50

BELLAMY, Edward. *Duke of Stockbridge.* 1901. NY. VG. O7. $20.00

BELLAMY, Edward. *Equality.* 1897. Appleton. 1st ed. NF. M22. $35.00

BELLAMY, Edward. *Looking Backward.* 1942. Modern Lib. 1st ed thus. VG. M21. $10.00

BELLI, Melvin M. *Blood Money.* 1956. NY. 1st ed. author's 1st book. F/F. A17. $15.00

BELLI, Melvin M. *My Life on Trail: An Autobiography.* 1976. Morrow. 1st ed. 5-line inscr/dtd 1976. 351p. F. P3. $125.00

BELLOC, H. *Bad Child's Book of Beasts.* nd. Duckworth. ils Basil Blackwood. 48p. VG. P2. $35.00

BELLOC, H. *Cruise of the Nona.* 1955. Newman. 347p. VG/dj. T7. $20.00

BELLOC, H. *Highway & Its Vehicles.* 1926. London. The Studio. 1/1250. 131 pl. VG. T10. $200.00

BELLOC, H. *More Beasts for Worse Children.* nd. Duckworth. 48p. VG. P2. $30.00

BELLOW, Saul. *Adventures of Augie March.* 1953. Viking. 1st ed/1st state. NF/VG+. M23. $115.00

BELLOW, Saul. *Dean's December.* 1982. NY. 1st trade ed. F/dj. A17. $10.00

BELLOW, Saul. *Him With His Foot in His Mouth.* 1984. NY. Harper. 1st ed. sgn. F/F. B2. $60.00

BELLOW, Saul. *Humboldt's Gift.* 1975. Viking. 1st ed. NF/VG. B35. $35.00

BELLOW, Saul. *More Die of Heartbreak.* 1987. NY. 1st ed. F/F. A17. $12.50

BELLOW, Saul. *Mr Sammler's Planet.* 1970. NY. 1st ed. sgn. VG+/VG. C6. $60.00

BELLOW, Saul. *Summations.* 1987. Bennington College. 1st ed. 1/1000. F/prt wrp. C2. $30.00

BELMONT, Bob; see Reynolds, Mack.

BELOTE & BELOTE. *Typhoon of Steel: Battle for Okinawa.* 1970. NY. BC. 384p. F/dj. A17. $7.50

BELT, Elmer. *Leonardo the Anatomist.* 1955. Lawrence. KS U. thin 12mo. ils. 76p. F/NF. T10. $50.00

BELTING, Natalia. *Summer's Coming In.* 1970. HRW. 1st ed. ils Adrienne Adams. 8vo. unp. VG/VG. T5. $30.00

BEMELMANS, Ludwig. *Castle No 9.* 1937. Viking. 1st ed. VG/fair. P2. $90.00

BEMELMANS, Ludwig. *Father, Dear Father.* 1953. Viking. 1st ed/deluxe issue. 1/151. F. w/sgn drawing. B24. $375.00

BEMELMANS, Ludwig. *Golden Basket.* 1936. Viking. 1st ed. ils. VG+/VG. C8. $200.00

BEMELMANS, Ludwig. *Madeline.* 1939. Simon Schuster. 1st ed. lacks ffep. ils. VG/VG. S13. $65.00

BEMELMANS, Ludwig. *Madeline.* 1939. Simon Schuster. 1st ed/1st issue. lg 4to. VG/G ist issue. M5. $225.00

BEMELMANS, Ludwig. *Madeline & the Bad Hat.* 1956. Viking. 1st ed. ils. VG/VG. D1. $225.00

BEMELMANS, Ludwig. *Madeline's Christmas.* 1985. Viking Kestrel. 1st ed. ils. F/F. P2. $50.00

BEMELMANS, Ludwig. *Madeline's Rescue.* 1953. London. Verschoyle. 1st probable UK ed. NF/VG. C8. $175.00

BEMELMANS, Ludwig. *Madeline's Rescue.* 1953 (1951). NY. Viking BC. ils. NF/F. C14. $15.00

BEMELMANS, Ludwig. *Sunshine.* 1950. Simon Schuster. 1st ed. ils. 42p. NF/NF. D1. $200.00

BEMMANN, Hans. *Stone & the Flute.* 1986. Viking. 1st ed. VG/VG. P3. $20.00

BENCHLEY, Nathaniel. *Monument.* 1966. McGraw Hill. 1st ed. VG/VG. P3. $20.00

BENCHLEY, Nathaniel. *Strange Disappearance of Arthur Cluck.* 1967. Harper Row. 1st ed. 8vo. F/VG+. M5. $25.00

BENCHLEY, Nathaniel. *Visitors.* 1965. McGraw. 1st ed. VG/VG. H11. $25.00

BENCHLEY, Peter. *Beast.* 1991. Random. 1st ed. F/F. B35. $20.00

BENCHLEY, Peter. *Deep.* 1976. Doubleday. 1st ed. 301p. VG/G+. P12. $12.50

BENCHLEY, Peter. *Island.* 1979. Doubleday. 1st ed. NF/NF. B35. $30.00

BENCHLEY, Peter. *Jaws.* 1974. Doubleday. 1st ed. F/VG+. B35. $75.00

BENDER, Roger James. *Hitler Albums: Mussolini's State Visit...* 1970. palo Alto. 1st ed. ils. 144p. leatherette. A17. $35.00

BENEDICT, Elizabeth. *Slow Dancing.* 1985. Knopf. 1st ed. 8vo. F/F. T10. $100.00

BENEDICT, Leonard. *Waifs of the Slums & Their Way Out.* 1907. NY. Revell. 1st ed. NF. B2. $50.00

BENEDICT, Pinckney. *Dogs of God.* 1994. NY. Doubleday. 1st ed. sgn. F/F. M23. $40.00

BENEDICT, Pinckney. *Town Smokes.* 1987. Princeton. Ontario Review. 1st ed. author's 1st book. sgn. F/wrp. C2. $100.00

BENESCH, Otto. *Artistic & Intellectual Trends From Rubens to Daumier...* 1969. np. ils. 176p. F. A4. $65.00

BENESCH, Otto. *Collected Writings. Vol I: Rembrandt.* 1970. London/NY. Phaidon. ils/notes. cloth. dj. D2. $60.00

BENET, Stephen Vincent. *John Brown's Body.* 1928. Doubleday Doran. 1st ed. sgn. 377p. VG. B11. $200.00

BENFORD, Gregory. *Across the Sea of Suns.* 1984. Timescape. 1st ed. F/F. P3. $18.00

BENFORD, Gregory. *Furious Gulf.* 1994. Bantam. 1st ed. NF/NF. P3. $23.00

BENFORD, Gregory. *Great Sky River.* 1987. Bantam. 1st ed. sgn bookplate. F/F. T2. $25.00

BENFORD, Gregory. *Jupiter Project.* 1975. Thomas Nelson. 1st ed. F/NF. M23. $40.00

BENFORD, Gregory. *Sailing Bright Eternity.* 1995. Bantam. 1st ed. AN/dj. M22. $20.00

BENFORD, Gregory. *Tides of Light.* 1989. Bantam. 1st ed. F/F. M21. $15.00

BENFORD, Gregory. *Timescape.* 1980. Simon Schuster. 1st ed. VG/G. P3. $30.00

BENFORD & CLARKE. *Beyond the Fall of Night.* 1990. Ace/Putnam. 1st ed. F/F. P3. $20.00

BENFORD & EKLUND. *If the Stars Are Gods.* 1977. Berkley. 1st ed. F/F. P3. $23.00

BENJAMIN, Paul; see Auster, Paul.

BENNETT. *How to Buy Photographs.* 1987. np. 150 photos. 159p. F/F. A4. $35.00

BENNET, Robert Ames. *Bowl of Baal.* 1975. Donald Grant. 1st hc ed. F/F. T2. $15.00

BENNETT, Arnold. *From the Log of the Velsa.* 1920. Chatto Windus. 1st ed. sgn. assoc copy. 209p. VG. B11. $75.00

BENNETT, Arnold. *Man From the North.* 1898. London/NY. 1st ed. author's 1st book. VG. C6. $150.00

BENNETT, Charles E. *Laudonniere & Fort Caroline: History & Documents.* 1964. Gainesville. sgn. 191 p. gilt bl brd. F. B11. $65.00

BENNETT, Dorothy. *Golden Encyclopedia.* 1946. NY. 1st ed. ils Cornelius DeWitt. 125p. G. A17. $15.00

BENNETT, Dwight. *Cheyenne Encounter.* 1976. Doubleday. 1st ed. VG/VG. P3. $12.00

BENNETT, E.D. *American Journeys.* 1975. Convent Station. VG/wrp. O7. $20.00

BENNETT, Geoffrey. *Death in the Dog Watches.* 1974. White Lion. VG/VG. P3. $15.00

BENNETT, J.M. *Local Matter.* 1985. Walker. 1st ed. F/F. M23. $20.00

BENNETT, James Gordon. *My Father's Geisha.* 1990. Delacorte. 1st ed. sgn. F/NF. M23. $30.00

BENNETT, James. *Overland to California: Journal of James Bennett...* 1987. Ye Galleon. 1st ed thus. F/sans. A18. $17.50

BENNETT, Rick. *King of a Small World.* 1995. Arcade. 1st ed. author's 1st novel. AN/dj. M22. $20.00

BENNETT, Rowena. *Runner for the King.* 1944. Chicago. apparent 1st ed. ils Fiore Mastri. F/torn. M5. $18.00

BENNETT, Rowena. *Songs From Around the Toadstool Table.* 1967. Follett. 1st ed. ils Betty Fraser. 61p. F/VG+. P2. $15.00

BENSON, Albert E. *History of the Massachusetts Horticultural Society.* 1929. Boston. 553p. cloth. VG. A10. $60.00

BENSON, L. *Book of Remarkable Trials & Notorious Characters...* 1871? London. Chatto Windus. gr cloth. M11. $175.00

BENSON, Lyman. *Treatise on the Northern American Ranunculi.* 1948. Nortre Dame. 264p. wrp. B26. $50.00

BENSON, Stella. *Kwan-Yin.* 1922. Grabhorn. 8vo. inscr Grabhorn/Benson. NF. T10. $100.00

BENSUSAN, S.L. *Morocco.* 1904. London. Blk. 1st ed. 74 pl. 231p. teg. xl. VG. W1. $35.00

BENT, A.C. *Life Histories of North America Diving Birds.* 1946. NY. 1st ed. VG/VG. B5. $27.50

BENTLEY, BURGIS & SLATER. *Dickens Index.* 1990. Oxford. VG/VG. P3. $45.00

BENTLEY, Gerald Eades. *Jacobean & Caroline Stage.* 1949-1956. Oxford. Clarendon. 5 vol. 1st ed. xl. F/dj. A17. $50.00

BENTLEY, KHOSLA & SECKLER. *Agroforestry in South Asia.* 1993. Internat Science Pub. 8vo. ils. brd. F/F. B1. $35.00

BENTON, Thomas Hart. *Artist in America.* 1937. McBride. 1st ed. VG/remnant. B5. $40.00

BENTON, Thomas Hart. *Thirty Years' View. Volume I.* 1854. NY. royal 8vo. 739p. brn cloth. T3. $12.00

BERCIU, Dumitru. *Romania.* 1967. Praeger. 1st ed. 8vo. 32 pl/10 maps/5 tables. VG/dj. W1. $22.00

BERDAN, Frances. *Aztecs of Central Mexico.* 1982. HRW. 1st ed. 195p. G. F3. $15.00

BERENDT, John. *Midnight in the Garden of Good & Evil.* 1994. Random. ARC. RS. AN/dj. B4. $250.00

BERENDT, John. *Midnight in the Garden of Good & Evil.* 1994. Random. 1st ed. F/clip. H11. $80.00

BERENSON, Bernard. *Arch of Constantine.* 1954. London. 1st ed. photos. VG+/VG. S13. $18.00

BERGER, Melvin. *Early Humans, a Prehistoric World.* 1988. Putnam. ils Michael Welply. rem mk. F. B17. $7.50

BERGER, Raoul. *Federalism, the Founder's Design.* 1987. OK U. M11. $35.00

BERGER, Suzanne. *These Rooms.* 1979. Penmaen. ltd ed. 1/200. sgn. F/F. V1. $35.00

BERGER, Thomas. *Changing the Past.* 1989. Little Brn. 1st ed. F/F. H11. $30.00

BERGER, Thomas. *Crazy in Berlin.* 1958. Scribner. 1st ed. author's 1st book. VG/dj. S9. $225.00

BERGER, Thomas. *Little Big Man.* 1964. Dial. 1st ed. sgn. F/NF. B24. $300.00

BERGER, Thomas. *Nowhere.* 1985. Delacorte. 1st ed. VG/VG. P3. $20.00

BERGER, Thomas. *Reinhart's Women.* 1981. Delacorte. 1st ed. F/NF. H11. $40.00

BERGER, Thomas. *Rhinehart in Berlin.* 1962. Scribner. 1st ed. F/NF. M19. $45.00

BERGER, Thomas. *Who Is Teddy Villanova?* 1977. Delacorte. 1st ed. NF/NF. P3. $25.00

BERGMAN, Ray. *Just Fishing.* 1932. Phil. 1st ed. VG/VG. B5. $50.00

BERGMAN, Tamar. *Boy From Over There.* 1988. Boston. Houghton Mifflin. 1st Am ed. 8vo. 180p. F/F. C14. $12.00

BERGSTEIN, Eleanor. *Advancing Paul Newman.* 1973. Viking. 1st ed. inscr. author's 1st novel. NF/VG. B4. $75.00

BERGSTEIN, Eleanor. *Ex-Lover.* 1989. Random. 1st ed. F/F. B4. $35.00

BERKE & WILSON. *Watch Out for the Weather.* 1951. NY. Viking. 8vo. 226p. G/dj. K5. $10.00

BERKELEY, Anthony. *Puzzle in Poison.* 1938. Crime Club. 1st ed. VG. P3. $45.00

BERKELEY, Sandra. *Coming Attractions.* 1971. Dutton. 1st ed. xl. F/VG. B4. $35.00

BERKOWITZ. *In Remembrance of Creation, Evolution of Art...* 1968. Brandeis U. 4to. pl. 300p. NF. A4. $150.00

BERKOWITZ, David Sandler. *From Ptolemy to the Moon: Progress in Art of Exploration...* 1965. Waltham. Brandeis. F. O7. $45.00

BERLANT, Jeffrey. *Profession & Molopoly: Study of Medicine in the US...* 1975. Los Angeles. 1st ed. 337p. dj. A13. $30.00

BERLANT & KAHLENBERG. *Navajo Blanket.* 1972. LA Co Mus of Art. 4to. ils. F/wrp. T10. $45.00

BERLINSKI, David. *Clean Sweep.* 1993. NY. 1st ed. author's 1st book. F/F. H11. $25.00

BERLITZ, Charles. *Atlantis: The Lost Continent Revealed.* 1984. Macmillan. 1st ed. VG. P3. $15.00

BERLITZ, Charles. *Bermuda Triangle.* 1974. Doubleday. 1st ed. NF/VG. H11. $20.00

BERLO, Janet. *Art of Pre-Hispanic Mesoamerica.* 1988. Boston. Hall. 1st ed. 272p. F3. $65.00

BERMAN, James Gabriel. *Uninvited.* 1995. Warner. 1st ed. author's 1st novel. AN/dj. M22. $15.00

BERNADAC. *Naked Puppets, Auschwitz.* 1978. np. 12 full-p photos. 308p. F. A4. $45.00

BERNAL, Ignacio. *Olmec World.* 1969. Berkeley. 1st ed. 273p. dj. F3. $60.00

BERNAL, Ignacio. *Tenochtitlan en una Isla.* 1959. Mexico. ils/lg fld map. 147p. VG. F3. $20.00

BERNARD, Claude. *Cahier Rouge of Claude Bernard.* 1967. Cambridge. 1st Eng trans. 120p. VG/dj. A13. $25.00

BERNARD, Claude. *Lecons sur la Physiologie et la Pahtologie du Systeme...* 1858. Paris. 2 vol. ils. contemporary blk sheep. VG. B14. $950.00

BERNARD, George Smith. *War Talks of Confederate Veterans.* 1892. Petersburg, VA. Fenn Owen. 1st ed. 2 fld maps. VG. M8. $175.00

BERNARD, Nelson T. *Wildflowers Along Forest & Mesa Trails.* 1984 (1957). Albuquerque. ils. 177p. sc. VG. B26. $12.50

BERNARD, William. *Jailbait: Story of Juvenile Delinquency.* 1949. Greenberg. 216p. VG. A17. $15.00

BERNATOVA, Eva. *Wonder Shoes.* 1990. FSG. 1st ed. sm 4to. 24p. F/NF. C14. $12.00

BERNAU, George. *Black Phoenix.* 1994. Warner. 1st ed. F/F. H11. $25.00

BERNAU, George. *Promises to Keep.* 1988. Warner. 1st ed. author's 1st book. rem mk. NF/F. H11. $15.00

BERNETT, Lincoln. *Treasure of Our Tongue.* 1964. Knopf. 1st ed. NF/F. B35. $28.00

BERNHARDT, P. *Wily Violets & Underground Orchids.* 1989. Morrow. 1st ed. photos/drawings. 255p. F/F. B1. $19.00

BERNHEIM, Bertram. *Story of the Johns Hopkins.* 1949. Surrey. Kingswood. 1st Eng ed. 274p. VG. A13. $35.00

BERNSTEIN, Burton. *Sinai: The Great & Terrible Wilderness.* 1979. Viking. 1st ed. 8vo. pl/map. 268p. NF/dj. W1. $18.00

BERNSTEIN & FEINBERG. *Cosmological Constants.* 1986. Columbia. 1st ed. VG/VG. K5. $23.00

BERRIE, BERRIE & EZE. *Tropical Plant Science.* 1987. Longman. 8vo. ils/phogos. 410p. pict new cloth. F. B1. $25.00

BERRISFORD, Judith. *Rhododendrons & Azaleas.* 1965. NY. ils/pl. 288p. F/dj. B26. $17.50

BERRY, Arthur. *Short History of Astronomy.* 1961 (1898). NY. Dover. pb. 440p. VG. K5. $10.00

BERRY, Carole. *Year of the Monkey.* 1988. St Martin. 1st ed. F/F. P3. $17.00

BERRY, Chester D. *Loss of the Sultana.* 1892. Lansing, MI. 1st ed. ils. 426p. G. B18. $150.00

BERRY, Don. *Moontrap.* 1962. Viking. 1st ed. F/F. A18. $50.00

BERRY, Erik. *Honey of the Nile.* 1938. Oxford. 1st ed thus. ils. 224p. VG. P2. $12.50

BERRY, Mike; see Malzberg, Barry.

BERRY, R.J.A. *Brain & Mind; or, The Nervous System of Man.* 1928. Macmillan. 8vo. 608p. xl. G1. $50.00

BERRY, Wendell. *Discovery of Kentucky.* 1991. Frankfort. 1st ed. 1/100. sgn/#d. F. C2. $60.00

BERRY, Wendell. *Farm.* 1993. Larkspur. sgn. VG/as issued. C4. $40.00

BERRY, Wendell. *Gift of the Good Land: Further Essays...* 1981. North Point. 1st ed. sgn. F/F. C2. $40.00

BERRY, Wendell. *Memory of Old Jack.* 1974. Harcourt. 1st ed. F/NF. C2. $125.00

BERRY, Wendell. *Nathan Coulter.* 1960. Boston. Houghton Mifflin. 1st ed. author's 1st book. NF/dj. S9. $150.00

BERRY, Wendell. *November Twenty-Six Nineteen Hundred Sixty-Three.* 1964. Braziller. ltd ed. sgn. F/case. C4. $175.00

BERRY, Wendell. *November Twenty-Six Nineteen Hundred Sixty-Three.* 1964. NY. ltd ed. sgn. ils/sgn Ben Shahn. F. C2. $150.00

BERRY, Wendell. *Recollected Essays 1965-1980.* 1981. North Point. 1st ed. sgn. F/F. C2. $40.00

BERRY, Wendell. *Sex, Economy, Freedom & Community.* 1993. NY. 1st ed. inscr. F/F. A11. $30.00

BERRY, Wendell. *There Is Singing Around Me.* 1976. Cold Mountain. 1st ed. 1/26 lettered. sgn. F. C2. $225.00

BERRY, Wendell. *Unsettling of America: Culture & Agriculture.* 1977. Sierra Club. sgn. F/VG. C6. $75.00

BERRY, Wendell. *Wild Birds.* 1986. Northpoint. 1st ed. F/F. M23. $20.00

BERRY & MASON. *Elements of Mineralogy.* 1968. Freeman. revised. 550p. VG. D8. $15.00

BERRY & MASON. *Mineralogy Concepts, Descriptions, Determinations.* 1959. San Francisco. Freeman. 630p. cloth. VG. D8. $25.00

BERRYMAN, John. *Berryman's Sonnets.* 1965. FSG. 1st ed. F/NF. C2. $50.00

BERRYMAN, John. *Delusions.* 1972. FSG. 1st ed. F/VG. H4. $30.00

BERRYMAN, John. *Dispossessed.* 1948. Wm Sloan. 1st ed. NF/dj. B24. $275.00

BERRYMAN, John. *Henry's Fate.* 1977. FSG. 1st ed. F/F. B4. $45.00

BERRYMAN, John. *Homage to Mistress Broadstreet.* 1956. FSC. 1st ed. F/NF clip. C2. $100.00

BERRYMAN, John. *Stephen Crane.* 1950. Wm Sloan. 1st ed. F/dj. B24. $250.00

BERTELSEN, Aage. *October 43.* 1955. London. Mus Pr. photos/map. 160p. VG/dj. A17. $10.00

BERTIN, Jack. *Brood of Helios.* 1966. Arcadia. 1st ed. VG/VG. P3. $13.00

BERTO, G. *Sky Is Red.* 1948. New Directions. 1st ed. F/VG. N3. $15.00

BERTO, G. *Works of God.* 1950. New Directions. 1st ed. VG/VG. M17. $17.50

BERTSCHE & SANDERS. *X Biedler: Vigilante.* 1969. Norman, OK. 3rd. 12mo. 164p. F/VG. T10. $35.00

BESKOW, Elsa. *Pelle's New Suit.* 1930. Platt Munk. unp. cloth. VG/dj. M20. $37.00

BESKOW, Elsa. *Vill Du Lasa.* 1937. Stockholm. Norstedt Soners. 1st reader in Swedish. 160p. VG. P2. $55.00

BESSIE, Alvah. *Inquisition in Eden.* 1965. Macmillan. 1st ed. F/F. B2. $45.00

BEST, Gerald M. *Ships & Narrow Gauge Rails.* 1981. San Diego. Howell North. 2nd. ils/fld map/index. F/dj. T10. $45.00

BESTER, Alfred. *Light Fantastic.* 1977. Gollancz. RS. VG/VG. P3. $25.00

BESTER, Alfred. *Star Light, Star Bright.* 1976. Berkley Putnam. 1st ed. NF/NF. P3. $20.00

BESTER, Alfred. *Stars in My Destination.* 1979. 1/3000. sgn. ils H Chaykin. F. M13. $30.00

BESTERMAN, Catherine. *Extraordinary Education of Johnny Lightfoot.* 1949. Bobbs Merrill. 1st ed. inscr. VG/VG. P2. $35.00

BESTERMAN, Theodore. *Art & Architecture: A Bibliography of Bibliographies.* 1971.. 230p. F. A4. $20.00

BESTERMAN, Theodore. *World Bibliography of Oriental Bibliographies.* 1975. np. revised. 4to. 349p. NF. A4. $65.00

BESTON, Henry. *Starlight Wonder Book.* 1923. Atlantic Monthly. 1st ed. ils Maurice Day. gilt bdg. VG. P2. $75.00

BESTON & COATSWORTH. *Chimney Farm Bedtime Stories.* 1977. HRW. 1st ed. ils Maurice Day. 78p. VG/G+. P2. $25.00

BESTOR, A. *Backwood Utopias.* 1959. Phil. 2nd. VG/VG. B5. $30.00

BETETA, Ramon. *Jarano.* 1970. Austin, TX. 1st ed. 163p. dj. F3. $20.00

BETHEL, L.C. *Compendium & Question Book of Parliamentary Law.* 1892. Columbus. self pub. 69p. prt stapled wrp. M11. $15.00

BETHELL, Nicholas. *War Hitler Won: Fall of Poland, September 1939.* 1973. NY. 1st Am ed. 472p. VG/tape rpr. A17. $15.00

BETTS, Doris. *Beasts of the Southern Wild & Other Stories.* 1973. NY. Harper. 1st ed. F/F. B4. $75.00

BETTS, Edwin M. *Thomas Jefferson's Garden Book, 1766-1824.* 1944. Am Philosophical Soc. 2nd. 704p. VG. B10. $45.00

BETTS, Tony. *Across the Board.* 1956. NY. Citadel. 1st ed. VG/VG. O3. $10.00

BEVAN & PHILLOT. *Mediaeval Geography: An Essay in Illustration of Hereford...* 1969. Amsterdam. Meridian. rpt of 1873 London ed. 3 maps. AN. O7. $55.00

BEVERIDGE, Albert Jeremiah. *Abraham Lincoln 1809-1858.* 1928. Houghton Mifflin. 2 vol. 1st ed. cloth. VG. M8. $45.00

BEWICK, Thomas. *My Life.* 1981. London. Folio Soc. 1st ed. 8vo. ils. F/case. T10. $50.00

BEYER, Harmann. *Analysis of Maya Hieroglyphs.* 1930. Brill Ltd. rpt. inscr. 20p. F3. $45.00

BEYER, William Gray. *Minions of the Moon.* 1950. Gnome. 1st ed. VG/VG. P3. $30.00

BIANCHINI, Francesco. *Complete Book of Fruits & Vegetables.* 1975. 1st ed. 4to. ils. VG. S13. $75.00

BIANCO & COLLISON. *Penny & the White Horse.* 1942. Messner. 4to. pict brd. VG. B17. $12.50

BIBBY, Geoffrey. *Looking for Dilmun.* 1969. Knopf. 1st ed. ils/maps. NF/dj. W1. $18.00

BIBLE. *Bible Alphabet.* ca 1890. np. 8vo. ils. VG/stiff wrp. A17. $12.50

BIBLE. *Bible in English; Common Prayer.* 1837. London. Bell. thick 12mo. fore-edge painting. full leather. T10. $450.00

BIBLE. *Biblia Hebraica.* 1838. Lipsiae. Ex Typis Caroli Tauchnitii. Stereotype ed. 1036p. VG. T10. $150.00

BIBLE. *Biblical Drawings With Illustrative Passages...* Dec 1951. Merrymount. 1/500. 100 drawings. 206p. Ruzicka bdg. VG. B14. $100.00

BIBLE. *Book of Psalms From Authorized King James Version.* 1960. LEC. 1/1500. ils/sgn Valenti Angelo. F/glassine/cloth chemise. B24. $225.00

BIBLE. *Book of Ruth.* 1947. LEC. ils/sgn Arthur Szyk. leather/pict brd. NF/gold case. B14. $200.00

BIBLE. *Book of the Prophet Isaiah in the King James Version.* 1979. LEC. 1/2000. sgn Chaim Gross/Franklin Littell. 121p. F/NF case. C2. $150.00

BIBLE. *First Bible.* 1934. Oxford. 1st ed. ils Helen Sewell. 109p. VG/G+. P2. $35.00

BIBLE. *Holy Bible: Containing the Old & New Testament & Apocrypha.* 1911. London. 3 vol. marbled ep. full leather. VG. B30. $125.00

BIBLE. *Nu Testament (in Fonetik Speling).* 1864. Sinsinati. G. V4. $65.00

BIBLE. *Second Chapter From the Gospel According to Saint Matthew.* np. nd. 1/100. ils/sgn Angelo. 10p. F/stiff wrp/dj. B24. $175.00

BIBLE. *Sermon on the Mount.* 1924. San Francisco. Grabhorn. 1/190. folio. 10p. F. B24. $325.00

BIBLE. *Sixth Chapter of St Matthew Containing the Lord's Prayer.* 1961. NY. Hammer Creek. 1/65. ils/sgn Valenti Angelo. 10p. F/stiff wrp. A4. $200.00

BIBLE. *Ten Commandments.* 1947. Winston. 1st ed (so stated). ils Arthur Szyk. gray cloth. VG. D1. $85.00

BICKEL, Alexander M. *Morality of Consent.* 1975. Yale. VG/dj. M11. $35.00

BICKNELL, A.J. *Bicknell's Public Buildings.* 1878. NY. 21 pl. VG. B5. $95.00

BIDDLE, A.J.D. *New Illustrated Do or Die.* 1944. WA. Leatherneck Assn. 108p. G. B18. $15.00

BIDDLE, George. *Tahitian Journal.* 1968. MN. 1st ed. F/NF. N3. $35.00

BIEBUYCK. *Tradition & Creativity in Tribal Art.* 1969. UCLA. F/VG. D2. $45.00

BIENEK, Horst. *Cell.* 1972. Unicorn. 2nd. 8vo. inscr/trans Ursula Mahlendorf. F/NF. S9. $45.00

BIERCE, Ambrose. *Shadow on the Dial & Other Essays.* 1909. San Francisco. Robertson. 1st ed. 249p. uncut. dj. A17. $175.00

BIERCE, Ambrose. *Tales of Soldiers & Civilians.* 1891. San Francisco. Steele. 1st ed. 300p. A bdg/gilt brn cloth. F/case/chemise. B24. $1,650.00

BIERRING, Walter. *History of Dept of Internal Medicine.* 1958. IA City. 1st ed. 116p. VG. A13. $20.00

BIGELOW, Edwin S. *Lowell on the Merrick: An Art Souvenir.* 1892. Lowell, MA. ils. unp. VG. B18. $35.00

BIGELOW, Henry J. *Orthopedic Surgery & Other Medical Papers.* 1900. Boston. 1st ed. 373p. A13. $100.00

BIGELOW, Henry J. *Rapid Lithotrity With Evacuation.* 1878. Boston. ils. 41p. blk cloth. NF. B14. $175.00

BIGELOW, Jacob. *Florula Bostoniensis: A Collection of Plants...* 1824. Boston. 2nd. 424p. modern bl cloth. B14. $150.00

BIGELOW, John. *Life & Public Services of John Charles Fremont.* 1856. NY. 1st ed. 12mo. 480p. olive cloth. G. T3. $55.00

BIGELOW, John. *Life of Benjamin Franklin Written by Himself.* 1879. Lippincott. 2 vol. 2nd. 8vo. gilt bl cloth. VG. T10. $45.00

BIGGERS, Earl Derr. *Black Camel.* 1929. Bobbs Merrill. early rpt. VG. M22. $15.00

BIGGERS, Earl Derr. *Charlie Chan Carries On.* 1930. Bobbs Merrill. 1st ed. G. P3. $20.00

BIGGLE, Lloyd. *This Darkening Universe.* 1977. Millington. VG/VG. P3. $30.00

BILGRAY & MARCUS. *Index to Jewish Festschriften.* 1970 (1935). NY. Kraus. rpt. 4to. cloth. VG. W1. $25.00

BILL & JOHNSON. *Horsemen Blue & Gray: A Pictorial History.* 1960. NY. 1st ed. photos. 236p. F/F. E1. $50.00

BILLARD, Jules B. *Ancient Egypt: Discovering Its Splendors.* 1978. NGS. 1st ed. 256p. NF/dj. W1. $45.00

BILLE-D MOT, Eleonore. *Age of Akhenaten.* 1966. McGraw Hill. 1st ed. 24 color pl. 200p. VG/dj. W1. $26.00

BILLINGS, C.K.G. *King & Queen.* 1921. private prt. O3. $45.00

BILLINGS, Donald E. *Guide to the Solar Corona.* 1966. NY. Academic. xl. VG. K5. $30.00

BILLINGS, John S. *Selected Papers of John Shaw Billings.* 1965. Chicago. 1st ed. 300p. VG. A13. $85.00

BILLINGS, M.P. *Structural Geology.* 1972. Prentice Hall. 606p. G. D8. $20.00

BILLINGTON, C. *Shrubs of Michigan.* 1977. Bloomfield Hills. Cranbrook Inst. 2nd/3rd prt. 339p. F/NF. B1. $27.50

BILLINGTON, Elizabeth T. *Randolph Caldecott Treasury.* 1978. Warne. 1st ed. 4to. 288p. NF/F. T5. $55.00

BILLINGTON, R.A. *Journal of Charlotte L Forten: Early Sea Island Teacher...* 1953. NY. 1st ed. 248p. VG/VG. B5. $35.00

BILLMAN. *Secret of the Stratemeyer Syndicate: Nancy Drew...* 1986. np. ils. 197p. F/F. A4. $65.00

BILYEU, Richard. *Tanelorn Archives.* 1981. Pandora. 1/250. sgn/#d. F. P3. $25.00

BINET, Alfred. *Les Revelations de l'Ecriture d'Apres...* 1906. Paris. Felix Alcan. ils. 260p. G1. $100.00

BINET & SIMON. *Intelligence of the Feeble-Minded.* 1916. Baltimore. Williams Wilkins. 1st Eng-language ed. 328p. VG. G1. $125.00

BINFORD, Lewis R. *In Pursuit of the Past: Decoding the Archeological Record.* 1983. Thames Hudson. 1st Am ed. 8vo. 256p. F/dj. T10. $50.00

BING & ROSENFELD. *Quality of Justice in the Lower Criminal Courts...* 1970. Boston. Lawyer's Commitee for Civil Rights Under Law. 149p. M11. $35.00

BINGAY, Malcolm W. *Detroit Is My Own Home Town.* 1946. Bobbs Merrill. 1st ed. sgn. G+. P12. $30.00

BINGHAM, Helen. *In Tamal Land.* 1906. San Francisco. Calkins. 1st ed. 8vo. 141p. NF. T10. $250.00

BINGHAM, Hiram. *Lost City of Incas.* 1962. NY. 1st ed. VG/VG. B5. $30.00

BINGHAM, Hiram. *Residence of Twenty-One Years in the Sandwich Islands.* 1848. Hartford. Huntington. 2nd. fld map. 616p. F. T7. $220.00

BINGHAM & HAWKEY. *Wild Card.* 1974. Stein Day. 1st ed. F/F. P3. $15.00

BINKLEY, Sue. *Clockwork Sparrow: Time, Clocks & Calendars...* 1990. Prentice Hall. 1st ed. F/NF. G10. $10.00

BINKS, C.J. *Pioneers of Tasmania's West Coast.* 1988. Hobart. VG. O7. $65.00

BINNS. *Introduction to Historical Bibliography.* 1953. London. ils. 383p. VG/worn. A4. $65.00

BINNS, Archie. *Roaring Land.* 1942. McBride. 1st ed. sgn. 284p. VG/VG. P3. $40.00

BINSTOCK, R.C. *Light of Home.* 1992. Atheneum. 1st ed. F/F. M23. $25.00

BIRCH, Franklin. *Pedigrees of Leading Winners 1912-1959.* 1960. London. VG. O3. $85.00

BIRCHMORE, Fred. *Around the World on a Bicycle.* 1939. Athens. 1st ed. photos. 345p. VG. B5. $40.00

BIRD, Isabella. *Hawaiian Archipelago, Six Months Among the Palm Groves...* 1881. np. ils. 318p. VG. A4. $85.00

BIRD, Joseph. *Protection Against Fire & Best Means of Putting Out...* 1873. NY. 278p. xl. gilt brn cloth. G. B14. $75.00

BIRD, Junius. *Excavations in Northern Chile.* 1943. NY. AMNH. ils/tables. F3. $45.00

BIRD, Sarah. *Virgin of the Rodeo.* 1993. NY. ARC/1st ed. RS. F/F. V4. $25.00

BIRD, Will R. *Two Jacks: Amazing Adventures of Major Jack M Veness...* 1955. Phil. 2nd. 209p. dj. A17. $9.50

BIRD & KLINGER. *Kosher Bridge.* 1992. London. 128p. VG/wrp. S1. $8.00

BIRDSALL, Ralph. *Story of Cooperstown.* 1925. NY. 433p. VG. B18. $22.50

BIRKERTS, Sven. *Electric Life: Essays on Modern Poetry.* 1989. Morrow. 1st ed. F/F. M23. $20.00

BIRRELL, Augustine. *Res Judicatae, Papers & Essays.* 1892. np. 308p. VG. A4. $25.00

BISHOP, Chris. *1400 Days: Civil War Day by Day.* 1990. folio. 256p. red cloth. F/dj. T3. $30.00

BISHOP, Claire Huchet. *Pancakes-Paris.* 1947. Viking/Jr Literary Guild. 1st ed thus. 8vo. ils Georges Schreiber. VG+/dj. M5. $22.00

BISHOP, Isabel. *Prints & Drawings 1925-1964.* 1964. NY. Shorwood. 8vo. pict brd. F/partial dj. B14. $55.00

BISHOP, Jim. *Day in the Life of President Johnson.* 1967. Random. 1st ed. 274p. bl cloth. F/F. B22. $4.50

BISHOP, Jim. *Day Lincoln Was Shot.* 1955. NY. 1st ed. ils. NF. B14. $45.00

BISHOP, Michael. *Blooded on Arachne.* 1982. Arkham. 1st ed. F/F. P3. $15.00

BISHOP, Michael. *Count Geiger's Blues.* 1992. Tor. 1st ed. F/NF. G10. $20.00

BISHOP, Michael. *One Winter in Eden.* 1984. Arkham. 1st ed. 1/3596. F/F. T2. $35.00

BISHOP, Michael. *Stolen Faces.* 1977. Harper Row. 1st ed. F/F. P3. $15.00

BISHOP, Michael. *Transfigurations.* 1980. Gollancz. 1st ed. VG/VG. P3. $20.00

BISSELL, Richard. *My Life on the Mississippi; or, Why I Am Not Mark Twain.* 1973. Boston. 1st ed. sgn. VG/VG. B5. $30.00

BISSON, Terry. *Bears Discover Fire.* 1993. Tor. 1st ed/1st issue. F/NF. G10. $25.00

BISSON & MCCONAUGHY. *Madame X.* nd. Grosset Dunlap. MTI. G. P3. $20.00

BITTING, Katherine. *Gastronomic Bibliography.* nd. np. rpt. 1/150. 8vo. F. A4. $95.00

BITTMAN, S. *Seeds: The Ultimate Guide to Growing Vegetables...* 1989. Bantam. 4to. 243p. F/F. B1. $40.00

BIXBY, William. *Hurricanes.* 1979. David McKay. xl. dj. K5. $7.00

BIXBY, William. *Seawatchers: Oceanographers in Action.* 1967. NY. VG. O7. $15.00

BJELKE & SHAPIRO. *Northern Light.* 1985. Potter. ils. 116p. VG/dj. T7. $30.00

BJORN, Thyra Ferre. *Home Has a Heart.* 1968. HRW. 1st ed. sgn. F/VG. B11. $25.00

BJORNSTAD, Edith. *Wings in Waiting: History of Iowa Methodist Hospital.* 1952. Des Moines. 1st ed. 238p. A13. $20.00

BLACK, Archibald. *Transport Aviation.* 1926. Chicago. 1st ed. 245p. G+. B18. $125.00

BLACK, Campbell. *Letters From the Dead.* 1985. Villard. 1st ed. NF/NF. P3. $16.00

BLACK, Gavin. *Golden Cockatrice.* 1975. Harper Row. 1st ed. VG/VG. P3. $20.00

BLACK, Gavin. *You Want to Die, Johnny?* 1966. Harper Row. 1st ed. VG/VG. P3. $20.00

BLACK, Jospeh. *Lectures on the Elements of Chemistry...* 1807. Phil. 2 vol. 1st Am ed. contemporary sheep. VG. B14. $600.00

BLACK, Lionel. *Flood.* 1971. Stein Day. VG/VG. P3. $13.00

BLACK, Lionel. *Life & Death of Peter Wade.* 1974. Stein Day. 1st ed. VG/VG. P3. $13.00

BLACK, Veronica. *Vow of Chastity.* 1992. NY. 1st ed. F/F. H11. $20.00

BLACK & LIPMAN. *American Folk Painting.* 1966. NY. rpt. 86 pl. 244p. F/dj. A17. $20.00

BLACK HAWK. *Autobiography of Ma-Ka-Tai-Me-She-Kia-Kiak, or Black Hawk.* 1882. Oquawka, IL. VG. A9. $100.00

BLACKBURN, Henry. *Randolph Caldecott: His Early Art Career.* 1886. NY. Routledge. 1st ed. 172 ils. NF/VG. D1. $150.00

BLACKBURN, John. *Bury Him Darkly.* 1970. Putnam. 1st ed. VG/VG. P3. $45.00

BLACKBURN, John. *Dead Man's Handle.* 1978. London. Cape. 1st ed. F/dj. M21. $45.00

BLACKBURN, John. *Devil Daddy.* 1972. London. Cape. 1st ed. VG/dj. M21. $50.00

BLACKBURN, John. *Gaunt Woman.* 1962. Mill Morrow. 1st ed. VG/VG. P3. $30.00

BLACKBURN, John. *Scent of New-Mown Hay.* 1958. Mill Morrow. 1st Am hc ed. VG+/dj. M21. $35.00

BLACKBURN, Paul. *In. On. Or About the Premises.* 1968. London. Cape Goliard. 1st ed. 1/100. sgn/#d. F/NF. C2. $175.00

BLACKBURN, William. *Love, Boy: Letters of Mac Hyman.* 1969. LSU. VG/VG. B10. $15.00

BLACKER, Irwin R. *Old West in Fiction.* 1961. Obolensky. 1st ed. F/chip. A18. $25.00

BLACKFORD, W.W. *War Years With Jeb Stuart.* 1945. NY. 1st ed. VG/G. B5. $45.00

BLACKMON, Anita. *Murder a la Richelieu.* 1937. Crime Club. 1st ed. VG. P3. $30.00

BLACKMORE, Howard L. *Guns & Rifles of the World.* 1965. Viking. 1st ed. 134p. VG+/dj. M20. $50.00

BLACKMORE, Jane. *Perilous Waters.* 1957. Collins. VG/VG. P3. $15.00

BLACKMUR, R.P. *From Jordan's Delight.* 1937. Arrow. 1st ed. NF/VG. B4. $150.00

BLACKSTOCK, Lee. *All Men Are Murderers.* 1958. Crime Club. 1st ed. VG/VG. P3. $15.00

BLACKSTONE, William. *Analysis of the Laws of England...* 1762. Oxford. Clarendon. M11. $650.00

BLACKSTONE, William. *Commentaries on the Laws of England...* 1790. Worcester. contemporary sheep. M11. $2,250.00

BLACKWELL, Alice Stone. *Songs of Russia Rendered Into English Verse.* 1906. Chicago. self pub. 62p. red cloth. VG. B14. $125.00

BLACKWELL, Leslie. *African Occasions, Reminiscences of 30 Years of Bar...* 1970. Westport. rpt of 1938 ed. 8vo. 287p. gilt red cloth. AN/sans. P4. $17.50

BLACKWOOD, A. *Prisoner in Fairyland.* 1913. np. NF. C6. $95.00

BLACKWOOD, Algernon. *Best Supernatural Tales of Blackwood.* 1973. Causeway. VG/VG. P3. $30.00

BLACKWOOD, Algernon. *Doll & One Other.* 1946. Arkham. 1st ed. F/VG. M19. $65.00

BLACKWOOD, Algernon. *Dudley & Gilderoy.* 1929. Dutton. 1st ed. VG/VG. P3. $75.00

BLACKWOOD, Algernon. *Education of Uncle Paul.* 1909. Macmillan Colonial Lib. VG. P3. $60.00

BLACKWOOD, Easley. *Complete Book of Opening Leads.* 1983. KY. 475p. VG. S1. $8.00

BLADES, John. *Small Game.* 1992. Henry Hold. 1st ed. author's first book. NF/NF. R16. $35.00

BLAGOWIDOW, George. *Last Train From Berlin.* 1977. Doubleday. 1st ed. VG/VG. P3. $13.00

BLAINE, John. *Magic Talisman.* 1989. Manuscript Pr. 1st ed. decor brd. VG. P3. $25.00

BLAINE, John. *Rick Brant: Egyptian Cat Mystery (#16).* 1961. Grosset Dunlap. 1st ed. 182p. Vg/dj. M20. $37.00

BLAIR, Claude. *Pistols of the World.* 1968. Viking. 205p. VG+/worn. M20. $50.00

BLAIR, Dierdre. *Anais Nin: A Biography.* 1995. NY. Putnam. 1st ed. 8vo. ils/index. 654p. F/dj. T10. $25.00

BLAIR, John M. *Control of Oil.* 1976. Pantheon. 1st ed. 8vo. ils/tables. 441p. NF/dj. W1. $25.00

BLAIR, Maria. *Mathew Fontaine Maury.* 1918. Whittet Shepperson. 1st ed. 13p. NF/wrp. M8. $37.50

BLAIR & SEYMOUR. *Seymour & Blair: Their Lives & Services.* 1868. NY. 12mo. 575p. brn cloth. T3. $15.00

BLAKE, E. Vale. *Arctic Experiences: Containing Capt George E Tyson...* 1874. NY. Harper. 1st ed. ils/map. 486p. VG. B14. $155.00

BLAKE, Forrester. *Johnny Christmas.* 1948. Morrow. 1st ed. map ep. F/VG. A18. $50.00

BLAKE, Michael. *Airman Mortensen.* 1991. Los Angeles. Seven Wolves. 1st ed. F/NF. H11. $25.00

BLAKE, Robert. *Disraeli's Grand Tour.* 1982. NY. VG. O7. $20.00

BLAKE, William. *Illustrations to the Divine Comedy of Dante.* 1922. London. 1st ed thus. 1/250. folio. loose as issued. C6. $320.00

BLAKE, William. *Land of Dreams.* 1928. Macmillan. 1st ed. ils Pamela Bianco. 42p. VG/G+. P2. $75.00

BLAKE, William. *Marriage of Heaven & Hell & a Song of Liberty.* 1911. NY. Dutton. 12mo. 79p. teg. paper brd/cloth spine. NF. T10. $40.00

BLAKE, William. *Song of Los.* 1975. Paris. Trianon. facsimile. 1/400. folio. half morocco. NF/case. C6. $200.00

BLAKE, William. *There Is No Natural Religion.* 1886. London. facsimile. 1/50. 12 sm engravings. C6. $325.00

BLAKEY, George C. *Gambler's Companion.* 1979. Paddington. 1st ed. NF/NF. P3. $20.00

BLANCHARD, Amy Ella. *Bonny Bairns.* 1888. Worthington. probable 1st ed. ils Ida Waugh. 48p. VG. D1. $325.00

BLANCHARD, Charles. *With Heaps O'Love.* 1925. Des Moines. Nichols Book & Travel. 12mo. 288p. gilt bl cloth. VG. B11. $25.00

BLANCHARD, Fessenden S. *Sailboat Classes of North America.* 1968. Doubleday. G/dj. A16. $20.00

BLANCHARD & WELLMAN. *Life & Times of Sir Archie 1805-1833.* 1958. Chapel Hill. 1st ed. VG/G. O3. $45.00

BLANCK. *Merle Johnson's American First Editions.* 1942. 4th/1st prt. 571p. VG. A4. $200.00

BLANCK. *Peter Parley to Penrod, a Bibliographical Description...* 1974. 159p. VG+. A4. $135.00

BLAND, Edward. *Discovery of New Brittaine.* 1966. Ann Arbor. xl. VG. O7. $20.00

BLAND, Henry Meade. *Day in the Hills.* 1926. San Francisco. private prt. 12mo. VG/stiff prt wrp. T10. $45.00

BLAND, Humphrey. *Treatise of Military Discipline.* 1759. London. Longman. 6 fld plans. old calf/rebacked. K1. $350.00

BLAND, William. *Forms of Ships and Boats.* 1917. London. Lockwood. ils. G. A16. $25.00

BLANDING, Don. *Vagabond's House.* 1943. Dodd Mead. inscr. 114p. F/VG. B11. $20.00

BLANK, Clair. *Beverly Gray on a Treasure Hunt.* (1938). Grosset Dunlap. 243p. gr bdg. VG/G. P2. $16.00

BLANK, Clair. *Beverly Gray's Adventure (#14).* 1944. Grosset Dunlap. 12mo. VG/VG. B17. $14.00

BLANK, Clair. *Beverly Gray's Assignment (#17).* 1947. Grosset Dunlap. 1st ed. lists to #16. 212p. VG/dj. M20. $20.00

BLANK, Clair. *Beverly Gray's Challenge (#15).* 1945. Grosset Dunlap. 1st ed. lists to #14. VG/worn. M20. $15.00

BLANK, Clair. *Beverly Gray's Discovery (#23).* 1953. Clover. lists 25 titles. 183p. VG. M20. $15.00

BLANK, Clair. *Beverly Gray's Quest (#12).* 1942. Grosset Dunlap. 1st ed. 220p. VG/dj. M20. $42.00

BLANK, Clair. *Beverly Gray's Secret (#21).* 1951. Grosset Dunlap. 1st ed. 212p. VG/dj. M20. $32.00

BLANK, Clair. *Beverly Gray's Vacation (#19).* 1949. Grosset Dunlap. 1st ed. lists to this title. 212p. VG+/dj. M20. $25.00

BLANKSTEN, George. *Ecuador: Constitutions & Caudillos.* 1951. Berkeley. index/biblio. 196p. F3. $25.00

BLANSHARD, Paul. *Religion & the Schools.* 1963. Boston. Beacon. M11. $35.00

BLANTON, Smiley. *Now or Never: The Promise of the Middle Years.* 1959. Prentice Hall. sgn. 273p. bl cloth. VG. G1. $50.00

BLATT & MURRY. *Origin of Sedimentary Rocks.* 1980. Prentice Hall. 2nd. 782p. NF. D8. $30.00

BLATTY, William Peter. *Legion.* 1983. Simon Schuster. 1st ed. NF/F. H11. $25.00

BLAUNER, Peter. *Slow Motion Riot.* 1991. Morrow. 1st ed. NF/NF. R16. $45.00

BLAUVELT, Anna. *Piece Bag Book.* 1927. Macmillan. 1st ed. ils. 96p. VG/G+. P2. $35.00

BLAYLOCK, James P. *Homunculus.* 1988. Morrigan. 1st ed. F/F. P3. $30.00

BLAYLOCK, James P. *Land of Dreams.* 1987. Arbor. 1st ed. inscr. F/F. T2. $35.00

BLAYLOCK, James P. *Last Coin.* 1988. NY. Ace. 1st trade ed. F/F. T2. $18.00

BLAYLOCK, James P. *Magic Spectacles.* 1991. Morrigan. 1st ed. F/F. P3. $30.00

BLAYLOCK, James P. *Paper Grail.* 1991. Ace. 1st ed. F/F. P3. $18.00

BLEECK, Oliver; see Thomas, Ross.

BLEGEN, T.C. *Norwegian Migration to America.* 1940. Northfield. 1st ed. ils. 655p. VG/VG. B5. $50.00

BLEGVAD & BLEGVAD. *One Is for the Sun.* 1968. HBW. 1st ed. ils. NF/G+. P2. $15.00

BLEVINS, Winfred. *Misadventures of Silk & Shakespeare.* 1985. Jameson. 1st ed. sgn. M/dj. A18. $15.00

BLICHFELDT, E.H. *Mexican Journey.* 1919 (1912). Chautaugua. 280p. VG. F3. $20.00

BLISH, James. *Cities in Flight.* 1970. Doubleday. 593p. F. M13. $35.00

BLISH, James. *Doctor Mirabilis.* 1971. Dodd Mead. 1st ed. NF/NF. P3. $75.00

BLISH, James. *Frozen Year.* 1957. Ballantine. 1st ed. VG/G. P3. $75.00

BLISH, James. *Jack of Eagles.* 1952. Greenberg. 1st ed. VG/VG. P3. $85.00

BLISH, James. *Star Trek Reader III.* 1977. Dutton. 1st ed. VG/VG. P3. $25.00

BLISS, Michael. *Discovery of Insulin.* 1982. Chicago. 1st ed. 304p. VG/dj. A13. $45.00

BLIVEN, Bruce Jr. *Battle for Manhattan.* 1956. NY. 1st ed. ils/map ep. 128p. VG/dj. B18. $20.00

BLOCH, Robert. *Bitter Ends.* 1987. Underwood Miller. 1st ed. NF. P3. $40.00

BLOCH, Robert. *Dead Beat.* 1960. Simon Schuster. 1st ed. 12mo. VG+. M21. $20.00

BLOCH, Robert. *Final Reckonings.* 1987. Underwood Miller. 1st ed. VG. P3. $40.00

BLOCH, Robert. *Night of the Ripper.* 1984. Doubleday. 1st ed. NF/VG. M22. $10.00

BLOCH, Robert. *Opener of the Way.* 1945. Arkham. 1st ed. author's 1st book. VG/VG. M19. $350.00

BLOCH, Robert. *Psycho House.* 1990. NY. 1st ed. 217p. AN/dj. A17. $7.50

BLOCH, Robert. *Screams: Three Novels of Suspense.* 1989. Underwood Miller. 1st ed thus. NF/VG. M22. $15.00

BLOCK, Eugene B. *Fabric of Guilt.* 1968. Doubleday. 1st ed. VG/VG. P3. $20.00

BLOCK, Francesca Lia. *Baby Be-Bop.* 1995. Harper Collins. 1st ed. sgn pub bookplate. F/dj. S9. $20.00

BLOCK, Herbert. *Straight Herblock.* 1964. Simon Schuster. 1st ed. ils. G+. P12. $6.00

BLOCK, Lawrence. *Ariel.* 1980. Arbor. 1st ed. inscr. F/NF. T2. $35.00

BLOCK, Lawrence. *Burglar Who Painted Like Mondrian.* 1983. Arbor. 1st ed. F/F. P3. $25.00

BLOCK, Lawrence. *Burglar Who Thought He Was Bogart.* 1995. Dutton. F/F. P3. $22.00

BLOCK, Lawrence. *Burglar Who Traded Ted Williams.* 1994. Dutton. sgn. F/F. A4. $35.00

BLOCK, Lawrence. *Dance at the Slaughterhouse.* 1991. Morrow. 1st ed. F/F. A20/T2. $25.00

BLOCK, Lawrence. *Devil Knows You're Dead.* 1990. 1st ed. inscr. F/F. M19. $35.00

BLOCK, Lawrence. *Into the Night.* 1987. Mysterious. 1st ed. sgn. F/F. T2. $20.00

BLOCK, Lawrence. *Private Party.* 1953. Rinehart. 1st ed. VG/VG. P3. $45.00

BLOCK, Lawrence. *Random Walk.* 1988. Tor. 1st ed. sgn. F/F. T2. $20.00

BLOCK, Lawrence. *Sins of the Fathers.* 1992. Dark Harvest. 1st hc ed. sgn. F/F. M19. $45.00

BLOCK, Lawrence. *Ticket to the Boneyard.* 1990. NY. Morrow. 1st ed. sgn. F/F. t2. $25.00

BLOCK, Lawrence. *Walk Among the Tombstones.* 1992. Morrow. 1st ed. sgn. F/F. T2. $25.00

BLOCK, Lawrence. *When the Sacred Ginmill Closes.* 1986. Arbor. UP/ARC. sgn. VG/wrp. M22. $45.00

BLOCK, Thomas H. *Airship Nine.* 1984. Putnam. 1st ed. VG/VG. P3. $17.00

BLOCK & KING. *Me Tanner, You Jane.* 1970. Macmillan. 1st ed. VG/VG. P3. $40.00

BLODGETT. *Photographs, a Collector's Guide.* 1979. np. 248p. F/VG. A4. $125.00

BLOM, Frans. *Conquest of Yucatan.* 1936. Houghton Mifflin. 1st ed. ils. 238p. F3. $20.00

BLOODGOOD, Lida Fleitmann. *Saddle of Queens.* 1959. London. Allen. 1st ed. VG/G. O3. $65.00

BLOODWORTH, Dennis. *Eye for the Dragon: Southeast Asia Observed, 1954-1970.* 1970. FSG. 1st ed. F/F. B35. $30.00

BLOOM, Amy. *Come to Me.* 1994. London. Macmillan. AP. author's 1st book. NF/wrp/proof dj. S9. $45.00

BLOOM, James D. *Left Letters: Culture Wars of Mike Gold & Joseph Freeman.* 1992. Columbia. 1st ed. F/F. B2. $30.00

BLOSSFELDT, Karl. *Karl Blossfeldt.* 1994. Koln. Benedikt Taschen. 1st ed. 8vo. F. S9. $35.00

BLOTNER, Joseph. *Faulkner: A Biography.* 1974. Random. 1st ed. 127p. VG/fair. B10. $15.00

BLOUNT, R. *About 3 Bricks Shy of a Load.* 1974. Boston. 1st ed. VG/VG. B5. $17.50

BLOUSTEIN, Edward J. *University & the Counterculture.* 1972. New Brunswick. Rutgers. 1st ed. inscr. F/F. B4. $50.00

BLUCK, Louise. *Proofs & Theories: Essays on Poetry.* 1994. Hopwell, NJ. Ecco. 1st ed. F/F. M23. $35.00

BLUM, Andre. *Les Origines du Livre a Gravures en France...* 1928. Paris. Van Oest. 4to. 78 pl. NF/self wrp. T10. $150.00

BLUM, Ann. *Picturing Nature, American 19th-Century Zoological Ils.* 1993. Princeton. 4to. 442p. F/F. A4. $60.00

BLUM, Daniel. *Pictorial History of the Silent Screen.* 1953. Grosset Dunlap. rpt. 4to. 334p. VG/VG. T10. $25.00

BLUMENTHAL, Joseph. *Art of the Printed Book, 1455-1955: Masterpieces...* 1978. Pierpont Morgan. 3rd. 125 pl. 192p. gilt blk cloth. F/dj. T10. $50.00

BLUMLEIN, Michael. *Brains of Rats.* 1990. Scream. 1st ed. 1/250. sgn/#d. F/F/case. T2. $65.00

BLUNDELL, Nigel. *World's Greatest Crooks & Conmen.* 1982. Octopus. 1st ed. F. P3. $13.00

BLUNK, Ira R. *Grouch Pills.* 1967. Dorrance. 1st ed. author's 1st book. NF/F. H11. $30.00

BLUNT, Wilfrid Scawen. *Secret History of the Englist Occupation of Egypt.* 1922. Knopf. 1st Am ed. 416p. VG. W1. $35.00

BLY, Robert. *Forty Poems Touching on Recent American History.* 1970. Beacon. 1st ed. sgn. F/NF. M19. $17.50

BLY, Robert. *Light Around the Body.* 1967. Harper Row. 1st ed. sgn. F/clip. B35. $100.00

BLY, Robert. *Loon.* 1977. Ox Head. 1/500. VG/hand-sewn wrp. C4. $40.00

BLY, Robert. *Loving a Woman in Two Worlds.* 1985. 1st ed. VG/VG. C4. $35.00

BLY, Robert. *Sibling Society.* 1996. Addison Wesley. 1st ed. inscr/drawing. F/F. B35. $55.00

BLYTHE, Legette. *Hear Me, Pilate!* 1961. Holt. 1st ed. VG/NF. H11. $30.00

BOARD, John. *From Point to Point.* nd. London. Johnson. 1st ed. VG/VG. O3. $45.00

BOARDMAN, John. *Oxford History of the Classical World.* 1988. Oxford. 3rd ed. F/F. P3. $30.00

BOARDMAN, Tom. *SF Stories.* 1979. Octopus. 1st ed. VG/VG. P3. $15.00

BOAS, Franz. *Handbook of American Indian Languages.* 1911. GPO. 2 vol. 8vo. xl. gilt olive cloth. T10. $100.00

BOASE, Wendy. *Sky's the Limit: Women Pioneers in Aviation.* 1979. NY. 1st ed. 223p. VG+/dj. B18. $25.00

BOCCACCIO, Giovanni. *Decameron.* 1930. LEC. 1/1500. ils/sgn TM Cleland. 2 vol. F/case. C2. $100.00

BOCH, Hal. *Pictorial History of Baseball* 1994. NY JG Press Folio. 208 pp. color. NF/NF. R16. $55.00

BODARD, Lucien. *Green Hell.* 1971. Dutton. 1st ed. 291p. dj. F3. $15.00

BODE. *New Mencken Letters.* 1977. np. 635p. F/VG. A4. $35.00

BODE, Vaughn. *Deadbone.* 1975. Northern Comfort Communications. 1st ed. VG/VG. P3. $100.00

BODENHEIM, Maxwell. *Replenishing Jessica.* 1925. Boni Liveright. 1st ed. F/NF. B2. $100.00

BODFISH, Hartson H. *Chasing the Bowhead.* 1936. Harvard. ils. 281p. teg. VG. T7. $110.00

BOELDEKE, Alfred. *With Graciela to the Head-Hunters.* 1948. McKay. 1st ed. ils/photos. 166p. F3. $15.00

BOESIGER & GIRSBERGER. *LeCorbusier 1910-1965.* 1967. photos. VG/VG. M17. $75.00

BOGAN, Louise. *Dark Summer.* 1929. Scribner. 1st ed. inscr/dtd 1936. F/VG+. B4. $650.00

BOGGS, Ralph. *Bibliography of Latin American Folklore.* 1940. Wilson. 1st ed. xl. F3. $25.00

BOGGS, Stanley. *Salvadoran Varieties of Wheeled Figurines.* 1973. Miami. 1st ed. 32p. wrp. F3. $20.00

BOGLE, Donald. *Brown Sugar: 80 Years of America's Black Female Superstars.* 1980. Harmony. 1st ed. 4to. 208p. F/NF. R11. $50.00

BOGLE, Donald. *Toms, Coons, Mullatos, Mammies & Books.* 1973. NY. 1st ed. VG/VG. B5. $20.00

BOHN, Dave. *Glacier Bay, the Land & Silence.* 1967. Sierra Club. folio. F/dj. T10. $50.00

BOK, Edward. *Americanization of Edward Bok.* 1922. Scribner. 1/1250. sgn. 15 pl. VG. B11. $50.00

BOK, Hannes. *Beauty & the Beasts.* 1978. De La Ree. 1st ed. NF/NF. P3. $45.00

BOLAND, Charles. *They All Discovered America.* 1961. Garden City. VG. O7. $35.00

BOLIN, C. *Narrative of the Life & Adventures of...* 1965. Palo Alto. VG. O7. $75.00

BOLITHO, William. *Twelve Against the Gods.* 1930. Simon Schuster. not 1st ed. 351p. bl cloth. NF/dj. B22. $4.50

BOLL, Heinrich. *Absent Without Leave.* 1965. McGraw Hill. 1st ed. VG/VG. A20. $22.00

BOLL, Heinrich. *Stories.* 1986. Knopf. 1st ed. rem mk. NF/NF. B35. $24.00

BOLOTIN & LAING. *Chicago World's Fair of 1893: The World Columbian Expo.* 1992. WA, DC. ils/photos. 166p. cloth. dj. D2. $35.00

BOLTON, Herbert E. *Coronado: Knight of Pueblos & Plains.* 1949. NY/Albuquerque. VG. O7. $25.00

BOLTON & COE. *American Samplers.* 1921. Boston. 1st ed. 125 pl. 416p. G. B5. $145.00

BOMBECK, Erma. *Aunt Erma's Cope Book.* 1979. McGraw Hill. VG/VG. P12. $6.00

BOMBECK, Erma. *Grass Is Always Greener Over the Septic Tank.* 1976. McGraw Hill. NF/VG. P12. $5.00

BOMMERSBACH, Jana. *Trunk Murderess: Winnie Ruth Judd.* 1992. Simon Schuster. 1st ed. sgn. F/F. T2. $25.00

BOND, Beverley W. Jr. *Civilization of the Old Northwest.* 1934. NY. 1st ed. 534p. G/tattered. B18. $37.50

BOND, Nelson. *Nightmares & Daydreams.* 1968. Arkham. 1st ed. VG/VG. P3. $40.00

BOND, Nelson. *State of Mind.* 1958. Samuel French. 76p. VG. B10. $15.00

BOND & YELLIN. *Pen Is Ours: A Listing of Writings...About African-American.* 1991. Oxford. ils/photos. 360p. F. A4. $40.00

BONDY, Louis. *Miniature Books: Their History From the Beginning...* 1981. ils. 227p. F/F. A4. $165.00

BONDY, Ruth. *Israelis, Profile of a People.* 1969. Funk Wagnall. 1st ed. inscr. 8vo. 320p. VG/dj. T10. $125.00

BONE, David W. *Capstan Bars.* 1931. Edinburgh. Porpoise. 1st ed. sgn. ils/sgn Freda Bone. teg. T7. $85.00

BONE, Neil. *Aurora: Sun-Earth Interactions.* 1991. NY. Horwood. 8vo. 156p. VG/wrp. K5. $15.00

BONER, Harold A. *Giant's Ladder: David H Moffat & His Railroad.* 1962. Kalmbach. 224p. NF/dj. M20. $42.00

BONFIGLIOLI, Kyril. *After You With the Pistol.* 1980. Crime Club. 1st ed. xl. dj. P3. $5.00

BONGE, Lyle. *Photographs of Lyle Bonge.* 1982. Jargon Soc. 1st ed. 4to. sgn Bonge/Williams. AN/dj. C2. $60.00

BONNARD, Andre. *Greek Civilization.* nd. np. 3 vol. 1st ed. photos. VG/VG/VG case. M17. $45.00

BONNER, M.G. *Baseball Rookies Who Made Good.* 1954. Knopf. later prt. G/clip. P8. $8.00

BONNER, Mary Graham. *Adventures in Puddle Muddle.* 1935. NY. 1st ed. ils Kolliker. VG/VG. B5. $45.00

BONNER, Mary Graham. *Magic Journeys.* 1928. Macaulay. ils Luxor Price. 286p. G. A17. $25.00

BONNER, Mary Graham. *365 Bedtime Stories.* 1987. Derrydale. 1st ed thus. 8vo. 302p. F/VG+. C14. $8.00

BONNER, Thomas. *William Faulkner: The William B Wisdom Collection...* 1980. Tulane. ils. 90p. VG. B10. $18.00

BONNETTE & ZUBAL. *Gritloaf Anthology.* 1978. Palaemon. 1/500. 44p. F. B10. $35.00

BONNEY, Richard. *Dorchester Old & New in the Old Bay Colony.* 1930. Dorchester. Tercentenary Committee. sgn. 79p. VG/wrp. B11. $20.00

BONNEY, Therese. *Europe's Children 1939-1943.* 1943. np. ltd ed. sgn. 62 full-p photos. F/stiff wrp/dj. S9. $125.00

BONSOR, N.R.P. *South Atlantic Seaway.* 1983. Jersey Channel Islands. Brookside Pub. VG/VG. A16. $25.00

BONTLY, Thomas. *Celestial Chess.* 1979. Harper Row. 1st ed. VG/VG. P3. $18.00

BOOKER, M. Keith. *Dystopian Impulse in Modern Literature.* 1994. Greenwood. F. P3. $50.00

BOOKMAN & POWERS. *March to Victory.* 1986. NY. 1st ed. 340p. dj. A17. $10.00

BOONZY, William. *Big Bill Blues: William Boonzy's Story.* 1955. London. Cassell. 1st ed. F/VG+. N3. $55.00

BOORMAN, John. *Emerald Forest Diary.* 1985. FSG. 1st ed. MTI. F/F. P3. $15.00

BOORSTIN, Daniel J. *Exploring Spirit.* 1976. NY. VG. O7. $15.00

BOOTH, Norman K. *Basic Elements of Landscape Design.* 1983. NY. 4th. ils. 315p. VG. B26. $25.00

BOOTHBY, Guy. *Pharos l'Egyptien.* ca 1910. Paris. La Vie Illustree. 1st ed. 188p. VG. W1. $20.00

BORAH, Woodrow. *Justice by Insurance.* 1983. Berkeley. 1st ed. 479p. dj. F3. $20.00

BORG, Scott. *Water Hazard.* 1995. Delacort. ARC. author's 1st novel. NF/wrp. M22. $30.00

BORGENICHT, Miriam. *Don't Look Back.* 1956. Doubleday. 1st ed. inscr. VG/VG. M22. $25.00

BORGENICHT, Miriam. *No Bail for Dalton.* 1974. Bobbs Merrill. 1st ed. VG/VG. P3. $18.00

BORING, Edwin. *History of Experimental Psychology.* 1929. NY. 1st ed. 699p. VG. A13. $45.00

BORLAND, Hal. *12 Moons of the Year.* 1979. NY. 1st ed. VG/VG. B5. $22.50

BORN. *American Landscape Painting.* 1948. Yale. cloth. NF. D2. $60.00

BOROWSKY, Marvin. *Queen's Knight.* 1955. NY. Random. 1st ed. 8vo. F/dj. T10. $75.00

BORRADAILE, L.W. *Animal & Its Environment.* 1922. London. 399p. red cloth. VG. B14. $125.00

BORTON, Elizabeth. *Pollyanna & the Secret Mission (#14).* 1951. Grosset Dunlap. 263p. VG/dj. M20. $20.00

BORTON, Elizabeth. *Pollyanna's Castle in Mexico (#7).* 1934. Page. 1st ed. 322p. red silk cloth. VG/dj. M20. $35.00

BORTON, Helen. *Jungle.* 1968. HBW. 1st ed. 13 double-p ils. G+. C14. $10.00

BOSCAWEN, William. *Treatise on Convictions on Penal Statues.* 1792. Dublin. 1st ed thus. contemporary calf. M11. $450.00

BOSE, Pradodh Chandra. *Introduction to Juristic Psychology.* 1917. Calcutta. Thacker Spink. 424p. ruled fuchsia cloth. G1. $50.00

BOSQUET, Alain. *Selected Poems.* 1972. OH U. 1st Am ed. F/NF clip. C2. $35.00

BOSSE. *Civil War Newspaper Maps: A Cartobibliography...* 1993. np. ils/2041 entries. 271p. F. A4. $75.00

BOSTON, John. *Ikenja.* 1977. Nigeria. F/F. D2. $70.00

BOSTON, Lucy. *Enemy at Green Knowe.* 1964. HBW. 6th. 156p. VG/VG. P2. $10.00

BOSWELL, H. *French Canada.* 1938. Viking. 1st ed. ils. beige cloth. NF/NF. D1. $75.00

BOSWELL, H. *French Canada: Pictures & Stories.* 1938. Viking. 1st ed. ils. NF. P2. $20.00

BOSWELL, Robert. *Crooked Hearts.* 1987. Knopf. 1st ed. author's 1st book. F/F. H11. $40.00

BOSWELL, Robert. *Dancing at the Movies.* 1986. IA City. 1st ed. author's 1st book. F/F. C2. $100.00

BOSWELL, Robert. *Mystery Ride.* 1993. Knopf. 1st ed. F/F. M23. $25.00

BOSWELL & FISHER. *Fenway Park Stadium Pop-Up Book.* 1992. Little Brn. 1st ed. M. P8. $25.00

BOTTING, Douglas. *Humbolt & the Cosmos.* 1973. NY. VG. O7. $20.00

BOTTING, Douglas. *Pirates*. 1978. Time Life. ils. 192p. gilt bdg. G+. P12. $12.00

BOTTOMS, David. *Any Cold Jordan*. 1987. Atlanta. Peachtree. 1st ed. author's 1st novel. NF/NF. H11. $35.00

BOTTOMS, David. *Easter Weekend*. 1990. Houghton Mifflin. 1st ed. F/F. H11. $25.00

BOUCHER, Anthony. *Best Detective Stories 19th*. 1964. Dutton. 1st ed. VG/VG. P3. $25.00

BOUCHER, Anthony. *Quintessence of Queen*. 1962. Random. 1st ed. VG/VG. P3. $40.00

BOUDINOT, Elias. *Elias Boudinot's Journey to Boston*. 1955. Princeton. VG. O7. $55.00

BOURDAIN, Anthony. *Bone in the Throat*. 1995. Villard. 1st ed. F/NF. H11. $25.00

BOURKE-WHITE, Margaret; see White, Margaret Bourke.

BOURNE, Peter. *Flames of Empire*. 1949. Putnam. 1st ed. VG/G. P3. $18.00

BOURNE, Peter. *Twilight of the Dragon*. 1954. Putnam. 1st ed. VG/VG. P3. $20.00

BOUTELL, Charles. *Heraldry: Historical & Popular*. 1864. London. ils 547p. 3-quarter leather. A9. $85.00

BOUTERWEK, Frederick. *History of Spanish & Portuguese Literature*. 1823. London. 2 vol. VG. O7. $100.00

BOUVIER, E.L. *Psychic Life of Insects*. 1922. Century. 1st Eng-language ed. trans LO Howard. VG. G1. $40.00

BOUVIER, John. *Law Dictionary & Concise Encyclopedia, Third Revision...* 1984. Buffalo. Hein. facsimile of 1914 ed. M11. $175.00

BOVA, Ben. *Cyberbrooks*. 1989. Tor. 1st ed. F/F. P3. $18.00

BOVA, Ben. *Dueling Machine*. 1969. HRW. 1st ed. sgn. F/NF. G10. $45.00

BOVA, Ben. *High Road*. 1981. Houghton Mifflin. 1st ed. VG. P3. $18.00

BOVA, Ben. *Kinsman Saga*. 1987. Tor. 1st ed. F/NF. M22. $15.00

BOVA, Ben. *Multiple Men*. 1976. Bobbs Merrill. 1st ed. NF/NF. P3. $25.00

BOVA, Ben. *Peacekeepers*. 1988. Tor. 1st ed. F/F. P3. $18.00

BOVA, Ben. *Winds of Altair*. 1973. Dutton. 1st ed. VG. P3. $13.00

BOVILL, E.W. *Niger Explored*. 1968. London. VG. O7. $55.00

BOVIS & HAGUES. *Les Oiseaux ABC*. 1945. Lyon. Agence Gutenberg. 4to. 24p. F/prt red wrp. B24. $250.00

BOWAN & DICKINSON. *Death Is Incidental*. 1937. Chicago. Willett. 1st ed. 111p. dj. F3. $20.00

BOWDEN. *Pop-Up Book for Christmas: A Treasury of Celebrations...* 1994. np. 4 double-p popups. F. A4. $35.00

BOWDITCH, Henry I. *Brief Memories of Louis & Some of His Contemporaries...* 1872. Boston. 37p. VG/prt wrp. B14. $75.00

BOWDITCH, Nathaniel. *American Practical Navigator, 1962*. 1966. np. corrected prt. A16. $35.00

BOWEN, Catherine Drinker. *Yankee From Olympus, Justice Holmes & His Family*. 1944. London. Benn. 1st Eng ed. VG/dj. M11. $45.00

BOWEN, Dana Thomas. *Memories of the Lakes*. 1946. FL. 1st ed. G/torn. A16. $22.50

BOWEN, Elizabeth. *House in Paris*. 1936. Knopf. 1st ed. VG/VG. P3. $20.00

BOWEN, John. *Scale Model Sailing Ships*. 1978. NY. Mayflower. ils. 192p. VG/dj. T7. $25.00

BOWEN, Robert O. *Weight of the Cross*. 1951. Knopf. 1st ed. NF/NF. B4. $45.00

BOWEN, Sidney R. *Dave Dawson at Singapore*. 1942. Saafield. VG. P12. $6.00

BOWEN, Sidney R. *Dave Dawson With the Air Corp*. 1942. Saalfield. G+. P12. $5.00

BOWEN, Sidney R. *Dave Dawson With the Pacific Fleet*. 1942. Saalfield. G+. P12. $5.00

BOWEN & JUX. *Afro-Arabian Geology*. 1987. London. Chapman Hall. ils. 295p. ils brd. F. B1. $42.50

BOWER, B.M. *Dark Horse: A Story of the Flying U*. 1931. Little Brn. 1st ed. F/clip. A18. $30.00

BOWERS, Claude G. *Beveridge & the Progressive Era*. 1932. Literary Guild. M11. $25.00

BOWERS, Claude G. *Thomas Jefferson*. 1945. Boston. 3 vol. 8vo. gilt red cloth. F/G case. H3. $90.00

BOWERS, Claude G. *Tragic Era: Revolution After Lincoln*. 1929. Houghton Mifflin. 1st ed. inscr pres. 567p. VG. B10. $45.00

BOWERS, Fredson. *Principles of Bibliographical Description*. 1949. Princeton. 522p. VG. A4. $185.00

BOWIE, Walter Russell. *Story of Jesus for Young People*. 1937. Scribner. 1st ed. 125p. G+. C14. $8.00

BOWKER, Richard. *Marlborough Street*. 1987. Doubleday. 1st ed. RS. F/F. P3. $18.00

BOWLBY, J. *Charles Darwin: A New Life*. 1990. Norton. 1st ed. 511p. F/dj. D8. $30.00

BOWLE, John. *Henry VIII: A Biography*. 1964. Little Brn. 1st Am ed. 316p. red cloth. VG+. B22. $5.50

BOWLES, Elisabeth Ann. *Good Beginning: First Decades of U of NC at Greensboro*. 1967. UNC. photos. 193p. VG/fair. B10. $15.00

BOWLES, Paul. *In Touch*. 1994. NY. 1/250. sgn. case. C4. $100.00

BOWLES, Samuel. *Across the Continent*. 1966. np. fld map. 42p. B18. $17.50

BOWLES & HAEBERLIN. *Yallah*. 1957. NY. 1st ed. VG/VG. B5. $50.00

BOWMAN, Dan M. III. *Giants of the Turf*. 1960. Lexington. 1st ed. VG/G. O3. $35.00

BOWMAN, Isaiah. *New World*. 1922. Yonkers. VG. O7. $35.00

BOWMAN & CARTEN. *Busy Bodies: The Busy ABC's*. 1959. Rand McNally. 1st ed. 8vo. unp. VG. C14. $9.00

BOWMAN & DICKINSON. *Westward From Rio*. 1936. Willett Clark. sgns. 100 woodblock prt. 351p. VG/VG. B11. $45.00

BOXER, Arabella. *Wind in the Willows Cookbook*. 1983. 1st ed. ils Shephard. NF/NF. S13. $25.00

BOYD, Blanche McCrary. *Mourning the Death of Magic*. 1977. Macmillan. 1st ed. author's 2nd novel. NF/dj. B4. $50.00

BOYD, David French. *Reminiscences of the War in Virigina*. 1989. Austin, TX. Jenkins. 1st ed. 37p. F/wrp. M8. $25.00

BOYD, Frank; see Kane, Frank.

BOYD, J. *Life of General William T Sherman*. 1891. np. 12mo. 608p. grn cloth. T3. $20.00

BOYD, James. *Long Hunt*. 1930. Scribner. 1st ed. 376p. VG. B10. $12.00

BOYD, James. *Marchin On*. 1927. Scribner. 1st ed. 426p. VG. B10. $25.00

BOYD, James. *Marching On*. 1927. Scribner. sgn. 426p. VG/dj. M20. $32.00

BOYD, John. *Girl With the Jade Green Eyes*. 1978. Viking. 1st ed. VG/VG. P3. $25.00

BOYD, Louise A. *Coast of Northeast Greenland With Hydrographic Studies...* 1948. Am Geographical Soc. 7 maps/5 panoramas. F/case. O7. $55.00

BOYD, Malcolm. *Runner*. 1974. Waco. Word. 1st ed. sgn. 203p. F/VG. B11. $15.00

BOYD, Marion. *Murder in the Stacks*. 1934. Lee Shepard. 1st ed. author's 2nd novel. VG. M22. $25.00

BOYD & PEDERSEN. *Folk Games of Denmark & Sweden for School...* 1915. Chicago. ils/songs/music. 58p. wrp. A17. $15.00

BOYER, Dwight. *Ghost Ships of the Great Lakes.* 1968. Dodd Mead. VG/dj. A16. $20.00

BOYER, Dwight. *Great Stories of the Great Lakes.* 1966. Dodd Mead. 2nd prt. VG/dj. A16. $15.00

BOYER, Dwight. *Ships & Men of the Great Lakes.* 1977. Dodd Mead. VG/VG. A16. $30.00

BOYER, Dwight. *Strange Adventures of the Great Lakes.* 1974. Dodd Mead. VG/VG. A16. $20.00

BOYER, Dwight. *True Tales of the Great Lakes.* 1971. Dodd Mead. VG/VG. A16. $20.00

BOYKIN, Edward. *Between Wind & Water.* 1966. NY. Norton. 1st ed. 207p. VG/dj. T7. $25.00

BOYLAN, Grace. *Kids of Many Colors.* 1901. Jamieson Higgins. ils Ike Morgan. 157p. VG. P2. $135.00

BOYLE, Kay. *Avalanche.* 1944. Simon Schuster. 1st ed. NF/VG. B4. $60.00

BOYLE, Kay. *Generation Without Farewell.* 1960. Knopf. 1st ed. F/F. B4. $50.00

BOYLE, Kay. *Pinky in Persia.* 1968. Crowell Collier. 1st ed. sgn. ils Lilian Obligado. rem mk. F/NF. B4. $150.00

BOYLE, Kay. *Words That Must Somehow Be Said.* 1984. London. 1st ed. sgn. F/F. A11. $35.00

BOYLE, Kay. *Year Before Last.* 1932. Harrison Smith. 1st ed. VG+/dj. B4. $100.00

BOYLE, T. Coraghessan. *Budding Prospects.* 1984. Viking. 1st ed. F/F. H11. $60.00

BOYLE, T. Coraghessan. *Descent of Man.* 1979. Little Brn. 1st ed. author's 1st book. F/F. S9. $550.00

BOYLE, T. Coraghessan. *Descent of Man.* 1979. Little Brn. 1st ed. author's 1st book. rem mk. NF/NF. A15. $125.00

BOYLE, T. Coraghessan. *East Is East.* 1990. Viking. 1st ed. F/F. H11. $35.00

BOYLE, T. Coraghessan. *East Is East.* 1990. Viking. 1st ed. sgn. F/F. C2. $50.00

BOYLE, T. Coraghessan. *If the River Was Whiskey.* 1989. Viking. 1st ed. sgn. F/F. H11. $55.00

BOYLE, T. Coraghessan. *Road to Wellville.* 1993. Viking. 1st ed. AN/dj. B4. $45.00

BOYLE, T. Coraghessan. *World's End.* 1987. NY. 1st ed. sgn. F/F. C2. $60.00

BOYLE, Thomas. *Only the Dead Know.* 1985. Stoddart. 1st ed. F/F. P3. $15.00

BOYLSTON, Helen Dore. *Sue Barton, Rural Nurse (#4).* 1939. Little Brn. 4th. 254p. VG+/worn. M20. $60.00

BOYLSTON, Helen Dore. *Sue Barton, Student Nurse (#1).* 1936. Little Brn. 244p. VG/dj. M20. $40.00

BOYS & SMITH. *Poisonous Amphibians & Reptiles.* 1959. Springfield. Thomas. inscr/dtd Boys. 149p. VG/dj. A10. $45.00

BRACHER, Karl Dietrich. *German Dictatorship: Origins, Structure & Consequences...* 1971. London. 1st ed. 553p. VG/dj. A17. $20.00

BRACKEN, Dorothy. *Rodeo.* 1949. Steck. ils Elizabeth Rice. VG. P2. $30.00

BRACKMAN, Arnold C. *Search for the Gold of the Tutankhamen.* 1976. Mason Charter. 1st ed. 8vo. 197p. VG/dj. W1. $16.00

BRADBURN, John. *Breeding & Driving the Trotter.* 1906. Boston. Am Horse Breeder. 1st ed. VG. O3. $45.00

BRADBURY, Edward P.; see Moorcock, Michael.

BRADBURY, Ray. *Dandelion Wine.* 1957. Doubleday. 1st ed. inscr. NF/VG. B4. $650.00

BRADBURY, Ray. *Dark Carnival.* 1947. Arkham. 1st ed. author's 1st book. sgn. blk cloth. F/dj. B24. $750.00

BRADBURY, Ray. *Death Is a Lonely Business.* 1985. Knopf. 1st ed. NF/NF. P3. $25.00

BRADBURY, Ray. *Golden Apples of the Sun.* 1953. NY. 1st ed. 12mo. brn cloth. F/G. H3. $225.00

BRADBURY, Ray. *Graveyard for Lunatics.* 1990. Knopf. 1st ed. F/F. G10. $15.00

BRADBURY, Ray. *Machineries of Joy.* 1964. Doubleday. 1st ed. inscr/dtd 1982. F/F. C2. $200.00

BRADBURY, Ray. *Martian Chronicles.* 1950. Doubleday. 1st ed. F/F. B24. $650.00

BRADBURY, Ray. *Medicine for Melancholy.* 1959. Doubleday. 1st ed. inscr/dtd 1982. F/clip. C2. $200.00

BRADBURY, Ray. *Star of Danger.* 1993. Severn. 1st ed. F/F. G10. $15.00

BRADBURY, Ray. *Stories of Ray Bradbury.* 1980. NY. 1st ed. inscr. F/F. C2. $100.00

BRADBURY, Ray. *Toynbee Convector.* 1988. Knopf. 1st ed. F/F. P3. $18.00

BRADEN, James A. *Trail of the Seneca.* 1907. Saalfield. ils RB Vosburgh. G+/G. P12. $10.00

BRADFORD, Beulah Harth. *Gems of Wisdom.* 1986. NY. Vantage. 1st ed. F/VG. B4. $45.00

BRADFORD, E. *Story of Mary Rose: Henry VIII's Flagship.* 1982. 1st ed. photos. NF/NF. S13. $16.00

BRADFORD, E. *Wall of Empire.* 1966. S Brunswick. VG. O7. $25.00

BRADFORD, Ernie. *Cleopatra.* 1972. HBJ. 1st ed. 279p. VG/dj. W1. $25.00

BRADFORD, Richard. *Red Sky at Morning.* 1968. Lippincott. 1st ed. author's 1st book. NF/NF. H11. $30.00

BRADFORD, Roark. *John Henry: A Play.* 1939. NY. 1st ed. F/F. C2. $50.00

BRADFORD, Roark. *Ol' King David an' the Philistine Boys.* 1930. Harper. 1st ed. 227p. ils AB Walker. VG/G. B10. $50.00

BRADFORD, Roark. *Ol' Man Adam & His Chillun.* 1928. NY. 1st ed. VG. B5. $45.00

BRADFORD, Roark. *This Side of Jordan.* 1929. Harper. 1st ed. 8vo. VG/dj. S9. $35.00

BRADLEY, John. *Best There Ever Was.* 1990. Atlantic. 1st ed. F/dj. H11. $30.00

BRADLEY, John. *Ils History of the Third Reich.* 1978. NY. photos. 256p. G. A17. $15.00

BRADLEY, Marion Zimmer. *House Between the Worlds.* 1980. Doubleday. ARC. sgn. F/F. M19. $45.00

BRADLEY, Marion Zimmer. *Mists of Avalon.* 1982. Knopf. 1st ed. inscr. 8vo. VG/F. T10. $300.00

BRADLEY, Mary Hastings. *Trailing the Tiger.* 1929. Appleton. 1st ed. sgn. 8vo. 246p. VG. B11. $35.00

BRADLEY, Muriel. *Murder in Montana.* 1950. NY. 1st ed. VG/VG. B5. $25.00

BRADLEY, Van Allen. *Gold in Your Attic.* 1958. NY. Fleet. 2nd. 8vo. VG+/dj. S9. $45.00

BRADLEY & PACKER. *Checklist of Rare Vascular Plants in Alberta.* 1984. Edmonton. Alberta Culture. 4to. 112p. wrp. B1. $15.00

BRADSHAW, Gillian. *Beacon at Alexandria.* 1986. Houghton Mifflin. 1st ed/1st prt. 8vo. 376p. F/F. T10. $25.00

BRADT & GIACCONI. *X- & Gamma-Ray Astronomy...* 1973. Dordrecht, Holland. 4to. 323p. xl. dj. K5. $30.00

BRADY, John. *Unholy Ground.* 1989. Canada. Collins. 1st ed. VG/VG. P3. $20.00

BRADY, Leo. *Edge of Doom.* 1949. Dutton. 1st ed. VG/G. P3. $13.00

BRADY, Ryder. *Instar.* 1976. Doubleday. F/F. P3. $13.00

BRADY & GARDNER. *Original Photographs Taken on Battlefields...* 1907. Hartford. 126p. professionally recased. VG. B18. $225.00

BRADZIL, Rudolf. *Climatic Change: In Historical & Instrumental Periods.* 1990. Masaryk. 8vo. 362p. VG/dj. K5. $12.00

BRAIN, Russell. *Galatea or the Future of Darwinism.* (1927). London. Kegan Paul. 16mo. 95p. bl cloth/paper labels. G1. $35.00

BRAIN, Russell. *Nature of Experience. The Riddell Memorial Lectures...* 1959. London. Oxford. 12mo. VG/clip. G1. $35.00

BRAIN & POLLOCK. *Bangwa Funerary Sculpture.* 1971. Toronto. F/F. D2. $90.00

BRAMBLE, Forbes. *Strange Case of Deacon Brodie.* 1975. Hamish Hamilton. 1st ed. F/F. P3. $20.00

BRAMELD, Theodore. *Japan: Culture, Education & Change in Two Communities.* 1968. HRW. dedication to/sgn Matsuura. 316p. VG. B11. $15.00

BRANCH, Douglas. *Cowboy & His Interpreters.* 1926. Appleton Century. 1st ed. 8vo. 278p. prt cloth. T10. $250.00

BRAND, Christianna. *Death in High Heels.* 1954. Scribner. 1st ed. VG/G. P3. $30.00

BRAND, Christianna. *Naughty Children.* 1963. Dutton. 1st ed. ils Ardizzone. 314p. VG/VG. P2. $25.00

BRAND, Max. *Best Western Stories Vol 2.* 1985. Dodd Mead. 1st ed. VG/VG. P3. $14.00

BRAND, Max. *Man From the Wilderness.* nd. Dodd Mead. 1st ed. F/F. P3. $15.00

BRAND, Millen. *Outward Room.* 1937. NY. 1st ed. author's 1st book. F/NF. A17. $15.00

BRANDAE, Ambrosis Fernandes. *Dialogues of the Great Things of Brazil.* 1987. NM U. 1st ed. ils. 385p. dj. F3. $20.00

BRANDER, Bruce. *River Nile.* 1966. NGS. 1st ed. 1 fld map. NF/dj. W1. $16.00

BRANDON, Jay. *Fade the Heat.* 1990. Pocket. 1st ed. author's 1st novel. AN/dj. M22. $40.00

BRANDON, S.G.F. *Ancient Empires (Milestones of History).* 1970. Newsweek. 2nd. 160p. VG/dj. W1. $20.00

BRANDT, Tom; see Dewey, Thomas B.

BRANLEY, Franklyn. *Lodestar Rocket Ship to Mars.* 1951. Crowell. 1st ed. VG/VG. P3. $18.00

BRANSON & TARR. *Introduction to Geology.* 1941. McGraw Hill. 2nd. 482p. VG. D8. $30.00

BRASHLER, William. *Josh Gibson.* 1978. Harper Row. 1st ed. F/VG+. P8. $110.00

BRASOL, Boris. *Elements of Crime.* 1931. Oxford. 2nd. ruled bl cloth. VG/dj. G1. $50.00

BRASSEY, A. *Sunshine & Storm in the East.* 1880. London. 1st ed. 2 maps. inscr author's husband. VG. A15. $75.00

BRASSEY, Mrs. *Voyage in the Sunbeam: Our Home on the Ocean...* 1881. Chicago. Belford Clarke. G+. A16. $50.00

BRAUDE, William G. *Pesikta Rabbati: Discourses for Feasts, Fasts...* 1968. Yale. 2 vol. Yale Judaica series. 8vo. cloth. VG/dj. W1. $65.00

BRAUN, Lilian Jackson. *Cat Who Sniffed Glue.* 1988. Putnam. 1st ed. VG/VG. P3. $18.00

BRAUN, Lilian Jackson. *Cat Who Went Into the Closet.* 1993. Putnam. 1st ed. F/F. P3. $20.00

BRAUNLICH, Tom. *Pente Strategy.* 1984. NY. 132p. VG/wrp. S1. $5.00

BRAUTIGAN, Richard. *Abortion: An Historical Romance 1966.* nd. Simon Schuster. VG/VG. P3. $20.00

BRAUTIGAN, Richard. *Dreaming of Babylon.* 1977. Delacorte. 1st ed. F/NF. T2. $35.00

BRAUTIGAN, Richard. *Dreaming of Babylon.* 1977. Delacorte. 1st ed. NF/NF. P3. $30.00

BRAUTIGAN, Richard. *Hawkline Monster.* 1974. NY. 1st ed. sgn. F/F. A11. $225.00

BRAUTIGAN, Richard. *Revenge of the Lawn.* 1971. Simon Schuster. 1st ed. F/NF. B2. $100.00

BRAUTIGAN, Richard. *Trout Fishing in America/The Pill Versus Springhill Mine...* 1969. Delacorte. 1st collected ed. NF. M19. $50.00

BRAUTIGAN, Richard. *Willard & His Bowling Trophies.* 1975. Simon Schuster. 1st ed. F/F. H11. $40.00

BRAWLEY, Benjamin. *Early Negro American Writers.* 1935. UNC. 1st ed. VG/VG. C6. $200.00

BRAY, Martha Coleman. *Joseph Nicollet & His Map.* 1980. Phil. Am Philosophical Soc. fld map. F/dj. O7. $45.00

BRAY, Wayne. *Common Law Zone in Panama.* 1977. San Juan. 1st ed. sgn. 150p. dj. F3. $20.00

BRAY & CARLTON. *Herreshoff of Bristol.* 1989. Brooklin, ME. Wooden Boat. 250+ photos. 241p. VG/dj. T7. $45.00

BRAYMER, Marjorie. *Atlantis: The Biography of a Legend.* 1983. Atheneum. 1st ed. VG/VG. P3. $20.00

BRAYNARD, Frank. *Search for the Tall Ships.* 1977. NY. Operation Ship. sgn. xl. VG/VG. B11. $18.00

BRAYNARD, Frank. *Tall Ships.* 1976. Sabine. portfolio. F. A16. $100.00

BRAZEAU, Peter. *Parts of a World Remembered.* 1983. Random. 1st ed. F/dj. V1. $20.00

BREASTED, James Henry. *History of Egypt From Earliest Times to Persian Conquest.* 1905. Scribner. 1st ed. 634p. gilt cloth. VG. W1. $65.00

BREASTED, James Henry. *History of the Ancient Egyptians.* 1908. Scribner. 2nd. sm 8vo. 469p. VG. W1. $18.00

BREAUX, Daisy. *Autobiography of a Chameleon.* 1930. Washington, DC. Potomac. ltd ed. sgn. 407p. VG/VG. B11. $50.00

BREBNER, John B. *Explorers of North America.* 1933. NY. VG. O7. $85.00

BRECHT, Bertolt. *Threepenny Opera.* 1982. LEC. 1/2000. intro/sgn Eric Bentley. ils/sgn Jack Levine. F/case. C2. $125.00

BRECKENRIDGE, Sean. *Yuppie Scum.* 1993. NY. 1st ed. author's 1st book. F/F. H11. $25.00

BREDIUS, Abraham. *Rembrandt: Complete Edition of the Paintings.* 1969. London. Phaidon. 3rd. 636p. cloth. dj. D2. $60.00

BREED, Clara E. *Turning the Pages.* 1983. Friends of San Diego Public Lib. 1st ed. NF/NF. B19. $25.00

BREED, W.J. *Age of Dinosaurs in North Arizona.* 1968. Flagstaff. Mus of N AZ. sgn. ils/pl. 45p. F/wrp. D8. $8.00

BREEN, Jon L. *Listen for the Click.* 1983. NY. Walker. 1st ed. F/NF. H11. $30.00

BREEN & COATES. *Pacific National Exhibition.* 1982. Vancouver. VG. O7. $20.00

BREHME, Hugo. *Mexico: Una Nacion Persistente.* 1995. Hugo Breheme. 1st ed. 1/3000. 154p. wrp. F3. $25.00

BREITENBACK, Josef. *Josef Breitenback.* 1985. NY. Temple Rock. 1st ed. 4to. F/wrp. S9. $60.00

BRENAMAN, J.N. *History of Virginia Conventions With Constitution of VA...* 1902. JL Hill. leatherette. G+. B10. $45.00

BRENNAN, Joseph Payne. *Chronicles of Lucius Leffing.* 1977. Donald Grant. 1st ed. F/F. T2. $40.00

BRENNAN, Joseph Payne. *Creep to Death.* 1981. Donald Grant. 1st ed. 1/750. sgn. ils/sgn Robert Lavoie. F/dj. T2. $45.00

BRENNAN, Joseph Payne. *Look Back on Laurel Hills.* 1989. Minneapolis. Jwindz Pub. 1st ed. F/prt wrp. T2. $12.00

BRENNAN, Joseph Payne. *Shapes of Midnight.* 1980. Berkley. 1st ed. VG/NF. R10. $5.00

BRENNAN, Joseph Payne. *Stories of Darkness & Dread.* 1973. Arkham. 1st ed. 1/4138. F/NF. T2. $45.00

BRENNAN, Joseph Payne. *60 Selected Poems.* 1985. Establishment Pr. 1st ed. F/F. R10. $5.00

BRENNER, Wendy. *Large Animals in Everyday Life.* 1996. Athens, GA. 1st ed. sgn. F/F. M23. $40.00

BRENNERT, Alan. *Her Pilgrim Soul.* 1990. Tor. 1st ed. F/F. G10. $25.00

BRENT, Joseph L. *Lugo Case.* 1926. New Orleans. 84p. VG. M8. $850.00

BRENT, Madeleine. *Capricorn Stone.* 1980. BC Associates. VG/VG. P3. $10.00

BRENT, P. *Charles Darwin: A Man of Enlarged Curiosity.* 1981. NY. Harper Row. 1st ed. 536p. F/chip. D8. $21.00

BRESLAUER & FOLTER. *Bibliography: Its History & Development.* 1984. Grollier. 1/600. ils. 224p. F. A4. $125.00

BRESLER, Fenton. *Mystery of Georges Simenon.* 1983. Beaufort. 1st ed. F/F. P3. $19.00

BRESLIN, Howard. *Silver Oar.* 1954. Crowell. 1st ed. VG/VG. P3. $15.00

BRESLIN, Jimmy. *Can't Anyone Here Play This Game?* 1963. Viking. 1st ed. VG+/VG. P8. $40.00

BRESLIN, Jimmy. *How Good Guys Finally Won.* sgn. VG/VG. K2. $60.00

BRESSON, Henri Cartier. *Face of Asia.* 1972. NY. Viking. 1st ed. 4to. NF/dj. S9. $90.00

BRETT, Simon. *Comedian Dies.* 1979. Scribner. 1st ed. VG/VG. P3. $15.00

BRETT, Simon. *Reconstructed Corpse.* 1994. Scribner. 1st Am ed. rem mk. F/F. N4. $15.00

BRETT, Simon. *Shock to the System.* 1985. Scribner. 1st ed. NF/NF. P3. $14.00

BRETT, Simon. *So Much Blood.* 1976. Scribner. 1st Am ed. VG/VG. N4. $17.50

BRETZ, J. Harlen. *Grand Coulee.* 1932. NY. VG. O7. $85.00

BREWER, David J. *Crowned Masterpieces of Literature.* 1908. Kaiser Pub. 10 vol. ils. 3-quarter leather. G+. P12. $85.00

BREWER, Sydney. *Do-It-Yourself Astronomy.* 1988. Edinburgh. 8vo. 137p. VG. K5. $7.00

BREWER. *Literature of Geography: A Guide to Its Organization...* 1978. np. 2nd. 264p. F/F. A4. $65.00

BREWERTON, George Douglas. *Fitz Poodle at Newport.* 1869. Cambridge. 1st ed. cloth. A17. $15.00

BREYER & POLMAR. *Guide to the Soviet Navy.* 1977. Annapolis. ils/drawings. 610p. F. A17. $25.00

BREYTENBACH, Breyten. *Sinking Ship Blues.* 1977. Toronto. Oasis. 1st Eng-language ed. F/decor wrp. C2. $125.00

BREZHNEV, Leonid I. *Leonid I Brezhnev: Pages From His Life.* 1978. Simon Schuster. 1st ed. 320p. F/dj. B22. $5.50

BRIAN, Denis. *Genius Talk: Conversations With Novel Scientists...* 1995. NY. Plenum. 8vo. ils. 428p. F/F. K5. $23.00

BRICE, Marshall Moore. *Daughter of the Stars.* 1973. McClure. sgn. 309p. xl. dj flaps missing. G. B10. $8.00

BRICKER, Charles. *Landmarks of Mapmaking: An Illustrated Survey...* 1968. Amsterdam. folio. 276p. F/VG. A4. $175.00

BRICKER, Charles. *Landmarks of Mapmaking: Ils Survey of Maps & Mapmakers.* 1989. Ware. Wordsworth. 10 fld maps/350+ ils. AN/dj. O7. $75.00

BRICKMAN, Richard P. *Bringing Down the House.* 1972. Scribner. 1st ed. author's 2nd book. F/NF. H11. $25.00

BRIDGMAN, Betty. *Lullaby for Eggs.* 1955. Macmillan. 1st ed. ils EO Jones. VG/G+. P2. $32.00

BRIDGWATER & GLOAG. *History of Cast Iron in Architecture.* 1948. London. 1st ed. 4to. 395p. F. T10. $150.00

BRIDWEL, Rodger. *Fidelio: My Voyage to a Distant Shore.* 1986. Dutton. 227p. VG/dj. T7. $20.00

BRIGGS, Lloyd Cabot. *Tribes of the Sahara.* 1960. Cambridge. Harvard. 1st ed. ils. 295p. NF/dj. W1. $45.00

BRIGGS, Philip. *Escape From Gravity.* 1955. Lutterworth. 1st ed. VG/VG. P3. $15.00

BRIGGS, Philip. *Silent Planet.* 1957. Lutterworth. 1st ed. VG/torn. P3. $15.00

BRIGGS, Walter. *Without Noise of Arms: 1776 Dominguez-Escalante Search...* 1976. Flagstaff. Northland. ils/15 maps. F/dj. O7. $75.00

BRIGHAM, C. *History & Bibliography of American Newspapers 1690-1820.* 1947. Worcester, MA. Am Antiquarian Soc. 2 vol. 8vo. xl. VG. T3. $95.00

BRIGHAM, Carl C. *Study of Error: Summary & Evaluation of Methods...* 1932. NY. College Entrance Examination Brd. 4to. xl. VG. G1. $40.00

BRIGHAM, Clarence. *50 Years of Collecting Americana for Lib Am Antiquarian Soc.* 1958. np. 1/1000. 185p. F/VG. A4. $75.00

BRIM, Charles. *Medicine in the Bible, the Pentatuch, Torah.* 1936. NY. 1st ed. 384p. A13. $130.00

BRIN, David. *Earth.* 1990. Bantam. 1st trade ed. F/F. M21. $20.00

BRIN, David. *Postman.* 1985. Bantam. 1st ed. F/F. H11/P3. $25.00

BRIN, David. *River of Time.* 1986. Dark Harvest. 1st ed. 1/400. sgns. F/F/case. T2. $85.00

BRINISTOOL, E.A. *Fighting Indian Warriors.* 1953. Stackpole. ARC. 353p. cloth. RS. VG/dj. M20. $52.00

BRINK, Carol. *Highly Trained Dogs of Professor Petit.* 1953. Macmillan. 1st ed. 139p. F/VG. P2. $35.00

BRINK, Carol. *Lad With a Whistle.* 1943 (1941). Macmillan. 3rd. 8vo. 235p. VG/G. T5. $25.00

BRINK, Carol. *Stopover.* 1951. Macmillan. 1st ed. sgn. 245p. VG/G. P2. $30.00

BRINKNER, Richard M. *Intellectual Functions of the Frontal Lobes.* 1936. Macmillan. pres. 10 pl. 354p. VG. G1. $75.00

BRINNIN, John Malcolm. *Beau Voyage: Life Aboard the Last Great Ships.* 1981. Dorset. VG/VG. A16. $58.00

BRINNIN, John Malcolm. *Sorrows of Cold Stone.* 1951. Dodd Mead. 1st ed. 109p. VG/dj. M20. $47.00

BRINNIN, John Malcolm. *Sway of Grand Saloon: A Social History of North Atlantic.* 1971. Delacorte. 1st ed. VG/VG. A16. $40.00

BRISE, Marshall Moore. *Vagaries in Verse.* 1977. McClure. inscr. 88p. G. B10. $8.00

BRISTOL, George. *Salute Me! The Dilemas of a Second Lieutenant.* 1943. NY. Dial. 1st ed. 172p. VG/chip. A17. $6.50

BRISTOL, Helen O. *Let the Blackbird Sing.* 1952. Exposition. 1st ed. F/VG+. B4. $50.00

BRITE, Poppy Z. *Drawing Blood.* 1993. Delacorte. 1st ed. F/F. H11. $35.00

BRITE, Poppy Z. *Lost Souls.* 1992. Delacorte/Abyss. 1st ed. author's 1st novel. sgn. F/F. T2. $45.00

BRITT, Albert. *Toward the Western Ocean.* 1963. Barre. VG. O7. $30.00

BRITTIN & WATSON. *International Law for Seagoing Officers, Second Edition.* 1961. US Naval Inst. NF/dj. M11. $35.00

BRITTON, Nathaniel L. *Flora of Bermuda.* 1918. NY. 1st ed. 585p. VG. B26. $95.00

BRITTON, William Everett. *Cases on the Law of Bills & Notes.* 1951. Chicago. Callaghan. worn. M11. $20.00

BROCK, Lynn. *Slip Carriage Mystery.* 1928. Harper. 1st ed. VG. P3. $35.00

BROCK, Rose; see Hansen, Joseph.

BROCK & BUDD. *Farming Once Upon a Time: An Illustrated History...* 1996. Concord. 1st ed. 159p. cloth. M. M20. $25.00

BROCKELMANN, Carl. *History of the Islamic Peoples.* 1947. Putnam. 1st ed. 8vo. 8 maps. VG. W1. $25.00

BROCKETT, L.P. *Woman's Work in the Civil War: A Record of Heroism...* 1867. Phil. Zeigler. 8vo. cloth. T10. $150.00

BROCKMAN, James. *Genesis.* 1924. Soho. Nonesuch. 1/375. lg 8vo. 28p on handmade. blk morocco. box. B24. $1,750.00

BRODER, Patricia Janis. *Hopi Painting: World of the Hopis.* 1979. NY. Brandywine. stated 1st ed. 4to. 319p. F/NF. T10. $75.00

BRODERICK, J.C. *Biographical Memoir of Archibald MacLeish.* nd. Am Phil Soc. F/prt wrp. V1. $25.00

BRODEUR, Paul. *Stunt Man.* 1970. Athen. 1st ed. F/NF. H11. $45.00

BRODIE. *Devil Drives: Life of Sir Richard Burton.* 1967. np. ils. 390p. VG/dj. A4. $35.00

BRODKEY, Harold. *Runaway Soul.* 1992. FSG. 1st ed. F/F. A20. $20.00

BRODRICK, A. Houghton. *Animals in Archaeology.* 1972. NY. Praeger. 1st Am ed. ils/index. F/dj. T10. $25.00

BRODRICK, Alan. *Prehistoric Painting.* 1948. London. Avalon. ils/pl. 38p. F3. $20.00

BRODSKY & HAMLIN. *William Faulkner: A Perspective From Brodsky Collection.* 1979. SE MO St Prt Service. 1/2500. unp. VG. B10. $25.00

BRODY, J.J. *Anazazi & Pueblo Painting.* 1991. NM U. 1st ed. 191p. F/dj. T10. $50.00

BROHL, Ted. *In a Fine Frenzy Rolling.* 1992. Vantage. 1st ed. sgn. F/F. P3. $20.00

BROIDY, Thomas Gately. *Rogue's Isles.* 1995. St Martin. 1st ed. F/F. M23. $35.00

BROMFIELD, Louis. *Modern Hero.* 1932. Stokes. 1st ed. 1/250. sgn. red/wht cloth. NF/dj/case. B24. $200.00

BROMFIELD, Louis. *Mr Smith.* 1951. Harper. 1st ed. VG/VG. P3. $29.00

BROMFIELD, Louis. *Out of the Earth.* 1948. Harper. 1st ed. 305p. VG/dj. M20. $30.00

BROMFIELD, Louis. *Strange Case of Miss Annie Spragg.* 1928. Stokes. ARC. sgn. F. M19. $65.00

BROMFIELD, Louis. *Wild Is the River.* 1941. Harper. 1st ed. inscr. cloth. VG/dj. B24. $100.00

BROMFIELD, Louis. *World We Live In.* 1944. Harper. 1st ed. VG/VG. M19. $35.00

BROMFIELD, Louis. *24 Hours.* 1930. NY. ltd ed. 1/500. sgn. VG/VG/VG box. B5. $95.00

BROMHALL, Winifred. *Chipmunk That Went to Church.* 1952. Knopf. 1st ed. 8vo. VG/G. B17. $12.50

BRONOWSKI, J. *Ascent of Man.* (1973). Little Brn. 8vo. ils/photos. 448p. rust cloth. F. B22. $6.50

BRONTE, Charlotte. *Professor: A Tale by Currer Bell.* 1857. Harper. 1st Am ed. 330p. VG. A4. $345.00

BRONTE, Charlotte. *Shirley: A Tale by Currer Bell, Author of Jane Eyre.* 1850. Harper. 572p. lacks ffep. VG. A4. $695.00

BROOK, Lynn. *Slip-Carriage Mystery: Colonel Gore's Fourth Case.* 1928. Harper. 1st Am ed. VG/VG. B4. $65.00

BROOKE, Keith. *Keepers of the Peace.* 1990. Gollancz. 1st ed. F/F. P3. $20.00

BROOKES, John. *Room Outside.* 1970 (1969). NY. ils/photos/plans. 192p. VG+/dj. B26. $20.00

BROOKES, Owen. *Gatherer.* 1982. Holt. 1st ed. F/F. H11. $35.00

BROOKES, Owen. *Gatherer.* 1982. HRW. 1st ed. VG/VG. P3. $20.00

BROOKES, Owen. *Inheritance.* 1980. Hutchinson. 1st ed. NF/NF. P3. $25.00

BROOKES, R. *General Gazetteer; or, Compendious Geographical Dictionary.* 1812. London. Ribington. 8 maps. VG+. O7. $195.00

BROOKS, C.E.P. *Evolution of a Climate.* 1925 (1922). NY. Coleman. 2nd. 8vo. 173p. G/tattered. K5. $21.00

BROOKS, Charles Walker. *Rhymes of a Southerner.* 1936. Dietz. 1st ed. inscr. 143p. VG/G. B10. $12.00

BROOKS, Gwendolyn. *Bean Eaters.* 1960. Harper. 1st ed. F/F. B4. $375.00

BROOKS, Gwendolyn. *Maud Martha.* 1953. Harper. 1st ed. F/VG+. B4. $250.00

BROOKS, Gwendolyn. *Very Young Poets.* 1983. Chicago. Brooks. 1st ed. sgn. F/stapled wrp. B4. $75.00

BROOKS, Lester. *Behind Japan's Surrender.* 1968. NY. 1st ed. 428p. F/F. A17. $12.50

BROOKS, Mary E. *King for Portugal.* 1964. Madson. VG. O7. $20.00

BROOKS, Noah. *First Across the Continent.* 1901. Scribner. 1st ed. 8vo. 24 pl/fld map. ribbed gr cloth. F. T10. $150.00

BROOKS, Terry. *Black Unicorn.* 1987. Del Rey. 1st ed. F/F. P3. $20.00

BROOKS, Terry. *Magic Kingdom for Sale! Sold!* 1988. 1st ed. F/NF. M19. $45.00

BROOKS, Terry. *Wizard at Large.* 1988. Del Rey. 1st ed. NF/NF. P3. $20.00

BROSBT & PRATT. *United States Mineral Resources, Geological Survey...* 1973. GPO. 722p. cloth. F. D8. $24.00

BROSSARD, Chandler. *Bold Saboteurs.* 1953. NY. 1st ed. author's 2nd book. F/NF. A15. $50.00

BROTHERS GRIMM; see Grimm & Grimm.

BROTHERUS, V.F. *Contributions to the Bryological Flora of NW Himalaya.* 1978 (1898). Dehra Dun. rpt. 4to. 46p. VG. B26. $15.00

BROTZ, H. *Black Jews of Harlem.* 1964. NY. 1st ed. 144p. VG. B5. $35.00

BROUGHTON, Jack. *Going Downtown.* 1988. NY. 1st ed. 300p. VG/dj. B18. $20.00

BROWER, Brock. *Late Great Creature.* 1972. Atheneum. 1st ed. sgn. F/clip. B11. $30.00

BROWN, Alan. *Audrey Hepburn's Neck.* 1996. NY. Pocket. 1st ed. author's 1st book. rem mk. F/F. H11. $35.00

BROWN, Alexander Crosby. *Mariners' Museum: A History & Guide.* 1950. Newport News. Mariners' Mus. 264p. VG. T7. $65.00

BROWN, Alexander Crosby. *Sea-Lingo: Notes on the Language of Mariners...* 1980. Mariners Mus. 40p. VG/stiff wrp. B10. $10.00

BROWN, Annora. *Old Man's Garden.* 1954. Toronto. 1st ed. ils. VG+/dj. B26. $24.00

BROWN, Bob. *Readies for Bob Brown's Machine.* 1931. Roving Eye. 1st ed. 1/300. rpr torn p. NF/prt wrp. B24. $850.00

BROWN, Charles H. *Insurrection at Magellan.* 1854. Boston. VG. O7. $55.00

BROWN, Christy. *Down All the Days.* 1970. Stein Day. 1st ed. author's 2nd book. NF/NF. H11. $20.00

BROWN, Christy. *My Left Foot.* 1st Am ed. NF/NF. B30. $50.00

BROWN, Clair A. *Vegetation of the Outer Banks of NC.* 1959. Baton Rouge. ils. VG. B26. $42.50

BROWN, Dale. *Hammerheads.* 1990. Donald Fine. 1st ed. NF/F. N4. $25.00

BROWN, Dale. *Night of the Hawk.* 1992. Donald Fine. 1st ed. NF/NF. N4. $20.00

BROWN, Dee. *Bury My Heart at Wounded Knee.* 1971. HRW. F/NF. T10. $10.00

BROWN, Dee. *Fetterman Massacre.* 1972. Barrie Jenkins. 1st ed. F/F. P3. $20.00

BROWN, Dee. *Fort Phil Kearney.* 1962. Putnam. 1st ed. 8vo. map ep. F/dj. T10. $35.00

BROWN, Dee. *They Went Thataway.* 1960. Putnam. 1st ed. ils Robert Galster. F/VG+. A18. $35.00

BROWN, Dee. *Westerners.* 1974. Holt. BC? 288p. brn brd. AN/dj. B22. $6.00

BROWN, Douglas; see Gibson, Walter.

BROWN, Earle B. *Modern Optics.* 1965. Reinhold. 8vo. 645p. VG/laid on. K5. $45.00

BROWN, Edward. *Wadsworth Memorial...* 1875. Wadsworth. 232p. G. B18. $125.00

BROWN, Frederic. *Screaming Mimi.* 1949. Dutton. 1st ed. 12mo. yel brd. F. T10. $275.00

BROWN, Fredric. *And the Gods Laughed: A Collection of SF & Fantasy.* 1987. Phantasia. 1st ed. 1/475. sgn Brown/Mack Reynolds. F/F/case. T2. $45.00

BROWN, Fredric. *Before She Kills.* 1984. Denis McMillan. 1st ed. 1/350. intro/sgn WF Nolen. F/F. T2. $100.00

BROWN, Fredric. *Gibbering Night.* 1991. Denis McMillan. 1st ed. 1/425. intro/sgn Joe Lansdale. F/F. t2. $50.00

BROWN, Fredric. *Happy Ending.* 1990. Missoula. McMillan. 1st ed. 1/450. F/F. T2. $50.00

BROWN, Fredric. *Homicide Sanitarium.* 1984. San Antonio. McMillan. 1st ed. 1/300. intro/sgn Bill Pronzini. F/F. T2. $125.00

BROWN, Fredric. *Lights in the Sky Are Stars.* 1953. Dutton. BC. VG/G. M22. $15.00

BROWN, Fredric. *Mrs Murphy's Underpants.* 1965. Boardman. 1st ed. VG. P3. $150.00

BROWN, Fredric. *Office.* 1958. Dutton. 1st ed. VG/tape rpr. P3. $250.00

BROWN, Fredric. *Paradox Lost & Twelve Other Great SF Stories.* 1975. London. Hale. 1st Eng ed. F/NF. T2. $15.00

BROWN, Fredric. *Pickled Punks.* 1991. Macmillan. F/F. P3. $35.00

BROWN, Fredric. *Red Is the Hue of Hell.* 1986. Miami Beach. McMillan. 1st ed. 1/400. intro/sgn Walt Sheldon. F/F. T2. $75.00

BROWN, Fredric. *The Best of Fredric Brown.* 1976. Doubleday. BC. VG/dj. M21. $10.00

BROWN, George E. *Pruning of Trees, Shrubs & Conifers.* 1995 (1972). Portland. ils/photos. 354p. M/dj. B26. $30.00

BROWN, George. *New & Complete English Letter-Writer; or, Whole Art...* 1775. London. A Hogg. 12mo. 216p+8p ads. aeg. F. B14. $250.00

BROWN, Hanbury. *Man & the Stars.* 1978. Oxford. ils/photos. 185. VG/VG. K5. $25.00

BROWN, Harrison. *Bibliography on Meteorites.* 1953. Chicago. 1st ed. xl. K5. $75.00

BROWN, Henry Collins. *In the Golden Nineties.* 1928. Valentine's Manual Inc. photos. G+. P12. $15.00

BROWN, Irving. *Gypsy Fires in America: Narrative of Life...* 1924. Harper. 1st ed. photos. 244p. cloth. NF. B14. $95.00

BROWN, John Gregory. *Decorations in a Ruined Cemetery.* 1994. Houghton Mifflin. 1st ed. F/F. M23. $35.00

BROWN, John K. *Baldwin Locomotive Works.* 1995. Johns Hopkins. 1st ed. 8vo. 328p. F/dj. T10. $45.00

BROWN, John Mason. *Many a Watchful Night.* 1944. NY. 219p. VG. A17. $7.50

BROWN, John. *Bridge With Dora.* 1965. London. 172p. VG/VG. S1. $10.00

BROWN, John. *Horae Subsecivae. Rab & His Friends & Other Papers.* 1862. Leipzig. 340p. half leather. VG. A13. $30.00

BROWN, John. *Rab & His Friends & Marjorie Fleming.* 1876. Boston. Osgood. 12mo. 93p. emb gr cloth. NF. T10. $65.00

BROWN, L. Carl. *Tunisia of Ahmad Bey, 1837-1855.* 1974. Princeton. 1st ed. ils/maps. 409p. NF/dj. W1. $25.00

BROWN, Larry. *Dirty Work.* 1989. Algonquin. 1st ed. F/F. H11/M23. $40.00

BROWN, Larry. *Facing the Music.* 1988. Algonquin. 1st ed. sgn. F/F. A11/C6. $65.00

BROWN, Larry. *Joe.* 1991. Chapel Hill. 1st ed. sgn. F/F. C2. $30.00

BROWN, Lloyd A. *British Maps of the American Revolution: A Guide...* 1936. Ann Arbor. 1/2000. F/NF wrp. O7. $30.00

BROWN, Lloyd A. *Jean Domenique Cassini & His World Map of 1696.* 1941. Ann Arbor. MI U. 236p. xl. F. O7. $150.00

BROWN, Lloyd A. *Story of Maps.* 1949. Little Brn. 2nd. 4to. ils. 397p. VG/VG. A4. $60.00

BROWN, Marcia. *Dick Whittington & His Cat.* 1950. Scribner/Weekly Reader. 4to. ils. unp. VG. C14. $14.00

BROWN, Margaret Wise. *Baby Animals.* 1989. Random. 1st ed. rem mk. VG/VG. B17. $12.50

BROWN, Margaret Wise. *Little Island.* 1946. Doubleday. early ed. as by Golden MacDonald. VG. M5. $30.00

BROWN, Margaret Wise. *Little Pig's Picnic & Other Stories.* 1939. Boston. DC Heath. ils Disney Studio. 8vo. 102p. VG. M8. $35.00

BROWN, Margaret Wise. *Red Light, Green Light.* 1944. Doubleday Doran. Jr Literary Guild. 1st ed. ils Weisgard. unp. VG. T5. $30.00

BROWN, Margaret Wise. *Runaway Bunny.* 1942. Hale. 8vo. lib bdg. M5. $10.00

BROWN, Margaret Wise. *Two Little Trains.* 1949. NY. Wm R Scott. 1st ed. ils Jean Charlot. unp. xl. G+. T5. $30.00

BROWN, Mark. *Game Face.* 1992. Woodbridge. Ox Bow. 1st ed. author's 1st book. F/F. H11. $40.00

BROWN, Mary. *Unlikely Ones.* 1986. McGraw Hill. 1st ed. F/F. P3. $16.00

BROWN, Merle E. *Poems as Act.* 1970. Wayne State. 1st ed. assn copy. F/NF. V1. $20.00

BROWN, O. Phelps. *Complete Herbalist; or, People Their Own Physicians.* 1867. Jersey City. hand-color pl. 407p. VG. B5. $60.00

BROWN, Paul. *Piper's Pony: The Story of Patchwork.* 1935. Scribner. 1st ed. ils. VG+. C8. $100.00

BROWN, Paul. *Sparkie & Puff Ball.* (1954). Scribner. ils. VG/VG. P2. $35.00

BROWN, Paul. *Ups & Downs.* 1936. Scribner. 1/750. sgn. VG. O3. $325.00

BROWN, R. Haig. *Fisherman's Spring.* 1951. NY. 1st ed. VG/VG. B5. $55.00

BROWN, R.A. *Horse Brasses: Their History & Origin.* 1952. Lewes. 64p. VG/G. O3. $25.00

BROWN, Richard. *Voyage of the Iceberg.* 1982. NY. Beaufort. 1st Am ed. VG/VG. A16. $25.00

BROWN, Rick. *Annotated Index of American Newspaper Editions...* 1992. NCSA. 8vo. 45p. VG. T3. $5.00

BROWN, Rita Mae. *Dolley.* 1994. Bantam. 1st ed. sgn. AN/dj. B4. $45.00

BROWN, Rita Mae. *High Hearts.* 1986. Bantam. 1st ed. 464p. VG/fair. B10. $15.00

BROWN, Rita Mae. *In Her Day.* 1976. Plainfield, VT. Daughters Inc. 1st ed. author's 4th book. NF/wrp. B4. $65.00

BROWN, Rita Mae. *Rest in Pieces.* 1992. Bantam. 1st ed. F/F. H11. $25.00

BROWN, Rita Mae. *Songs to a Handsome Woman.* 1973. Diana. 2nd. 39p. VG. B10. $75.00

BROWN, Rita Mae. *Sudden Death.* 1983. Bantam. 1st ed. 241p. VG/G. B10. $15.00

BROWN, Rita Mae. *Venus Envy.* 1993. Bantam. 1st ed. F/NF. B4. $35.00

BROWN, Rosellen. *Before & After.* 1992. FSG. 1st ed. F/F. H11/T2. $30.00

BROWN, Rosellen. *Cora Fry.* 1977. Norton. 1st ed. F/NF. B4. $50.00

BROWN, Rosellen. *Some Deaths in the Delta.* 1970. MA U. 1st ed. author's 1st book. F/NF. M19. $62.50

BROWN, Rosellen. *Tender Mercies.* 1978. Knopf. AP. NF. M19. $45.00

BROWN, Slater. *Ethan Allen & the Green Mountain Boys.* 1956. Random. Landmark Book. BC. 8vo. 184p. beige cloth. G/G. T5. $12.00

BROWN, Slater. *Spaceward Bound.* 1955. Prentice Hall. VG. P3. $15.00

BROWN, T. *Lectures on the Philosophy of the Human Mind.* 1836. Boston. 8vo. 538p. leather. xl. T3. $12.00

BROWN, Tom. *Tracker.* 1978. Englewood Cliffs. 1st ed. VG/VG. B5. $35.00

BROWN, William H. *Hand on My Shoulder.* 1962. Vantage. 1st ed. NF/NF. B35. $25.00

BROWN, William Moseley. *From These Beginnings: Life Story of Remmie LeRoy Arnold.* 1953. McClure. 1st ed. inscr Arnold. photos. 634p. VG. B10. $25.00

BROWN, William Robinson. *Horse of the Desert.* 1929. Derrydale. 4to. O3. $325.00

BROWN & BUCKINGHAM. *National Field Trials.* 1955. Harrisburg. ltd ed. sgns. leather. VG. B5. $150.00

BROWN & CONTENTO. *SF in Print: 1985.* 1986. Locus. VG. P3. $60.00

BROWN & LOVELL. *Exploration of Space by Radio.* 1957. London. Chapman Hall. 1st prt. xl. VG. K5. $24.00

BROWN & PHILLIPS. *Pre-Columbian Shell Engravings From the Craig Mound...* 1975-1982. Peabody Mus. 6 vol. ltd ed. folio. 360p. map ep. F/sans. T10. $450.00

BROWN & SCHMIDT. *Fighting Indians of the West.* nd. Bonanza. rpt. photos/biblio/index. 362p. NF/G. E1. $45.00

BROWN & SCHMIDT. *Fighting Indians of the West.* 1948. NY. 1st ed. 362p. VG+. E1. $75.00

BROWN & SNIFFEN. *James & John Bard: Painters of Steamboat Portraits.* 1970. Dodd Mead. ils. 272p. VG/dj. T7. $30.00

BROWN & VAN THIEL. *Rembrandt: The Master & His Workshop.* 1991. Yale/Nat Gallery. 288p. F/case. A17. $75.00

BROWNE, G. Waldo. *Young Gunbearer.* 1925. Page. new ed. ils Meynell. 334p. pict cloth. G. A17. $8.00

BROWNE, Georgiana. *Water Babies' Circus & Other Stories.* 1940. Boston. DC Heath. ils Disney Studio. 78p. VG. T5. $30.00

BROWNE, Gerald A. *Hazzard.* 1973. Arbor. VG/VG. P3. $13.00

BROWNE, Harry. *How to Find Freedom in an Unfree World.* 1973. NY. 1st ed. VG/VG. B5. $35.00

BROWNE, Howard. *Scotch on the Rocks.* 1991. St Martin. 1st ed. NF/NF. P3. $15.00

BROWNE, J. Ross. *Crusoe's Island.* 1867. NY. VG. O7. $75.00

BROWNE, Roland A. *Rose-Lover's Guide.* 1974. NY. photos/drawings. 235p. VG+/dj. B26. $17.50

BROWNE, Thomas. *Religio Medici, Hydriotaphia, & the Letter to a Friend.* 1869. London. 196p. VG. A13. $75.00

BROWNE, Thomas. *Religio Medici.* 1939. LEC. 1/1500. sgn. 4to. 113p. marbled brd/cloth spine. F. B11. $65.00

BROWNE, Thomas. *Works of Sir Thomas Browne.* 1928. London. 6 vol. 1st ed thus. 8vo. F. C2. $100.00

BROWNELL, Elizabeth. *Really Babies.* 1908. Rand McNally. 1st ed. 4to. fair. M5. $25.00

BROWNELL, W.C. *Tributes & Appreciations (Edith Wharton).* 1929. Scribner. 98p. VG. A4. $135.00

BROWNING, Elizabeth Barrett. *Correspondence of...& Benjamin Robert Haydon 1842-1845.* 1972. Harvard. 200p. F/F. A4. $55.00

BROWNING, Elizabeth Barrett. *Elizabeth Barrett Browning: Letters to Her Sister...* 1929. London. John Murray. 1st ed. 8vo. 344p. F/NF. C2. $35.00

BROWNING, Elizabeth Barrett. *Essays on the Greek Christian Poets & English Poets.* 1863. James Miller. 1st Am ed. VG. M19. $65.00

BROWNING, Elizabeth Barrett. *Letters to Mrs David Ogilvy.* 1974. np. ils. 220p. F/NF. A4. $35.00

BROWNING, Robert. *Agememnon of Aeschylus.* 1877. London. Smith Elder. 1st ed. VG. M19. $125.00

BROWNING, Robert. *Pied Piper of Hamelin.* 1934. London. Harrap. 1st ed. 1/410. ils/sgn Rackham. 45p. F/vellum wrp. B24. $750.00

BROWNSTEIN, Michael. *Highway to the Sky.* 1969. Columbia. 1st ed. F/NF. C2. $50.00

BRUCCOLI, Matthew. *Chandler Before Marlowe.* 1973. Columbia, SC. 1st trade ed. sgn. F/F. A11. $45.00

BRUCCOLI, Matthew. *F Scott Fitzgerald: A Descriptive Bibliography.* 1987. Pittsburgh. 1st revised ed. F. C6. $50.00

BRUCCOLI, Matthew. *Supplement to F Scott Fitzgerald Descriptive Bibliography.* 1980. np. ils. 234p. F. A4. $55.00

BRUCE, Errol. *Cape Horn to Port.* 1978. NY. McKay. ils. 175p. VG/dj. T7. $22.00

BRUCE, H.A.B. *Riddle of Personality.* 1908. NY. Moffat Yard. 12mo. prt panelled gr cloth. VG. G1. $35.00

BRUCE, Janet. *Kansas City Monarchs.* 1986. KS U. 1st ed. F/VG+. P8. $65.00

BRUCE, Jean. *Deep Freeze.* 1963. Cassell. 1st ed. VG. P3. $12.00

BRUCE, Lenny. *How to Talk Dirty & Influence People.* 1965. Playboy. 1st ed. photos. VG/dj. S9. $30.00

BRUCE, R. *National Road.* 1916. Clinton, NY. 1st ed. sgn. 94p. VG. B5. $65.00

BRUCKER, Gene. *Giovanni & Lusanna.* 1986. Berkeley. sgn. VG. O7. $30.00

BRUETON, Diana. *Many Moons: Myth & Magic, Fact & Fantasy...* 1991. Prentice Hall. 1st pb prt. 256p. K5. $15.00

BRUETTE, William. *American Duck, Goose & Brant Shooting.* 1929. NY. 1st ed. 415p. VG. B5. $60.00

BRUMBAUGH, Florence. *Donald Duck & His Nephews.* 1940. Boston. DC Heath. 1st ed. sm 8vo. Disney ils ep. 66p. ils cloth. H4. $60.00

BRUNA, Dick. *B Is for Bear.* 1977. London. Methuen. 12mo. unp. VG. C14. $7.00

BRUNDAGE, Burr C. *Empire of the Inca.* 1963. Norman. VG. O7. $25.00

BRUNDAGE, F. *Adventures of Jack.* 1921. Stecher. ils. VG/stiff wrp. M5. $55.00

BRUNDAGE, F. *Robin Hood.* nd. Saalfield. 12mo. VG-. B17. $7.50

BRUNEL, George. *Fun With Magic: Amusing Experiments in Physics...* 1901. NY. ils. 175p. cloth. G. A17. $10.00

BRUNHOUSE, Robert. *Frans Blom, Maya Explorer.* 1976. Albuquerque. 1st ed. 291p. dj. F3. $35.00

BRUNHOUSE, Robert. *In Search of the Maya.* 1973. NM U. 1st ed. 243p. dj. F3. $30.00

BRUNNER, John. *Crucible of Time.* 1983. Del Rey. 1st ed. xl. VG/VG. N4. $10.00

BRUNO, Anthony. *Bad Luck.* 1990. Delacorte. 1st ed. VG/VG. P3. $19.00

BRUNSON, H. *Oilman Who Didn't Want to Become a Millionaire...* 1955. Exposition. 1st ed. inscr. 84p. cloth. F/chip. D8. $12.00

BRUNT, David. *Weather Study.* 1948 (1942). London. Nelson. 8vo. 215p. G/dj. K5. $12.00

BRUSH, Peter. *Hunter Chaser.* 1948. Hutchinson. G+. O3. $15.00

BRUSSEL, I.R. *Bibliography of Writings of James Branch Cabell.* 1932. Century. revised ed. 126p. VG/G-. B10. $35.00

BRUST, Steven. *Agyar.* 1993. Tor. 1st ed. F/F. G10. $10.00

BRUST, Steven. *Phoenix Guards.* 1991. Tor. F/NF. G10. $10.00

BRUYN, G.W. *Centennial Bibliography of Huntington's Chorea 1872-1972.* 1974. Louvain. 1st ed. 314p. VG/wrp. A13. $40.00

BRY, Charlene. *World of Plants: MO Botanical Garden.* 1989. NY. ils. 191p. F/dj. B26. $32.50

BRYAN, C.D.B. *National Air & Space Museum.* 1979. NY. VG. O7. $35.00

BRYAN, C.D.B. *National Geographic Society: 100 Years of Adventure...* 1987. Abrams. 406 ils. 484p. VG/dj. D8. $25.00

BRYAN, C.W. *From NY to the Hills & Homes of Berkshire.* 1881. Great Barrington. VG/rpr wrp. O7. $35.00

BRYAN, Christopher. *Night of the Wolf.* 1983. Harper Row. 1st ed. VG/VG. P3. $15.00

BRYAN, George S. *Edison: The Man & His Work.* 1926. NY. 350p. red cloth. VG. B14. $50.00

BRYAN, Mike. *Baseball Lives.* 1989. Pantheon. 1st ed. F/F. P8. $10.00

BRYAN, William Alanson. *Natural History of Hawaii.* 1915. Honolulu. Hawaiian Gazette. 117 full-p pl. 596p. xl. VG. T10. $100.00

BRYANT, Billy. *Children of Ol' Man River.* 1936. NY. 1st ed. VG/VG. V4. $85.00

BRYANT, Edward. *Fetish.* 1991. Axolotl. 1/300. sgn. AN/dj. M21. $35.00

BRYANT, Sara Cone. *Epamindas & His Auntie.* 1938. Houghton Mifflin. ils Inez Hogan. VG. M5. $45.00

BRYANT, William Cullen. *Family Library of Poetry & Song.* 1880. NY. Fords Horard Hulbert. Memorial ed. lg 8vo. 1065p. aeg. pict cloth. VG. T10. $50.00

BRYNER, B.G. *Abraham Lincoln in Peoria, IL.* 1926. Peoria. 2nd. 1/1000. 304p. VG. B5. $70.00

BUBER, Martin. *Tales of the Hasidim: The Early Masters.* 1947. NY. Schocken. 1st ed. 8vo. trans Olga Marx. 335p. VG/VG. H4. $45.00

BUCHAN, John. *History of the First World War.* 1991. Scotland. Lochar. abridged/intro Victor Neuburg. 192p. F/dj. B18. $25.00

BUCHAN, John. *House of the Four Winds.* 1935. Hodder Stoughton. 1st ed. VG. P3. $30.00

BUCHAN, John. *Island of Sheep.* 1936. Hodder Stoughton. 1st ed. VG. P3. $35.00

BUCHAN, John. *Memory Hold the Door.* 1940. Musson. 1st ed. VG. P3. $30.00

BUCHAN, John. *Sick Heart River.* 1941. Musson. 1st ed. VG. P3. $20.00

BUCHANAN, Edna. *Contents Under Pressure.* 1992. Hyperion. ARC/1st ed. VG/VG. N4. $35.00

BUCHANAN, Edna. *Contents Under Pressure.* 1992. Hyperion. 1st ed. sgn. B stp on bottom edges. F/F. H11. $45.00

BUCHANAN, Edna. *Nobody Lives Forever.* 1990. Random. 1st ed. author's 1st novel. rem mk. F/F. H11. $35.00

BUCHANAN, Edna. *Nobody Lives Forever.* 1990. Random. 1st ed. VG/VG. P3. $18.00

BUCHANAN, Lamont. *Kentucky Derby Story.* 1953. Dutton. 1st ed. VG/G. O3. $20.00

BUCHANAN, Marie. *Dark Backward.* 1975. Hart Davis MacGibbon. 1st ed. VG/VG. P3. $20.00

BUCHANAN, Marie. *Morgana.* 1977. Doubleday. 1st ed. VG/VG. P3. $15.00

BUCHANAN. *Treasure of Auchinleck, Story of Boswell Papers.* 1974. np. ils. 390p. F/VG. A4. $65.00

BUCHARD, Peter. *River Queen.* 1957. Macmillan. 1st ed. 40p. F/VG. C14. $15.00

BUCHHEIM, Lothar-Gunther. *Boat.* 1975. Knopf. 1st ed. F/NF. H11. $35.00

BUCK, Frank. *Bring 'Em Back Alive.* 1930. NY. 1st ed. VG/G. B5. $47.50

BUCK, Pearl S. *China: Past & Present...* 1972. John Day. 1st ed. photos. F/clip. S9. $40.00

BUCK, Pearl S. *Essay on Myself.* 1966. NY. 1st ed. 1/1000. VG. B5. $35.00

BUCK, Pearl S. *Fighting Angel.* 1936. Reynal Hitchcock. 1st ed. NF/VG. B4. $125.00

BUCK, Pearl S. *House of Earth.* 1935. Reynal Hitchcock. 1st ed. NF/VG. B4. $125.00

BUCK, Pearl S. *Stories for Little Children.* 1940. John Day. 1st ed. Ils Weda Yap. VG/VG. C8. $100.00

BUCK, Pearl S. *Water Buffalo Children.* 1943. NY. John Day. 1st ed. ils WA Smith. pict cloth. G/G+. C8. $35.00

BUCK, Pearl S. *Young Revolutionist.* 1932. Friendship. 1st ed. ils. 182p. F/dj. B14. $95.00

BUCK, Peter H. *Vikings of the Sunrise.* 1938. NY. VG. O7. $30.00

BUCK, Peter. *Coming of the Maori.* 1966. Wellington. VG. O7. $65.00

BUCKERIDGE, Anthony. *Stories for Boys.* 1957. Faber. 1st ed. VG/VG. P3. $25.00

BUCKERIDGE, J. *Lincoln's Choice.* 1956. Harrisburg. 1st ed. VG/VG. B5. $65.00

BUCKINGHAM, Bruce. *Boiled Alive.* 1957. Michael Joseph. 1st ed. VG/VG. P3. $30.00

BUCKINGHAM, Nash. *De Shootinest Gent'man.* 1941. NY. 1st trade ed. ils. F/clip. A17. $75.00

BUCKLAND, Raymond. *Ancient & Modern Witchcraft.* nd. Castle. VG. P3. $8.00

BUCKLEY, Arabella B. *Fairy-Land of Science.* 1888 (1878). Lippincott. ils. 244p. G. K5. $13.00

BUCKLEY, William F. *Excerpts From an Address to Conservative Party of NY.* 1964. WA, DC. ltd 1st ed. 1/200. inscr. NF/sans. A11. $65.00

BUCKLEY, William F. *Mongoose, RIP.* 1987. Random. 1st ed. F/F. P3. $20.00

BUCKLEY, William F. *Saving the Queen.* 1976. Doubleday. 1st ed. author's 1st novel. NF/NF. H11. $30.00

BUCKLEY, William F. *Temptation of Wilfred Malachey.* 1985. Workman Pub. 1st ed. 8vo. 45p. F/F. C14. $18.00

BUCKLEY, William F. *Who's on First.* 1980. Doubleday. 1st ed. VG/VG. P3. $20.00

BUCKWALD, Ann. *Seems Like Yesterday.* 1980. Putnam. photos. VG/VG. P12. $5.00

BUD, Robert. *Science Versus Practice: Chemistry in Victorian Britain.* 1984. Manchester. 1st ed. 236p. VG. A13. $20.00

BUDAY, George. *History of the Christmas Card.* 1964. London. Spring Books. 8vo. ils/pl. red brd. F/dj. B24. $25.00

BUDGE, E.A. Wallis. *Osiris & the Egyptian Resurrection.* 1973. Dover. 2 vol. 1st ed thus. VG/stiff wrp. W1. $18.00

BUDGE, E.A. Wallis. *Tutankhamen. Amenish, Atenism & Egyptian Monotheism.* ca 1975. NY. Bell. rpt of 1928 ed. 8vo. ils. F/dj. W1. $18.00

BUECHER, Thomas S. *Norman Rockwell: Artist & Illustrator.* 1970. Abrams. 328p. VG+/dj. M20. $125.00

BUEL & DACUS. *Tour of St Louis.* 1878. St Louis. 1st ed. NF. A15. $75.00

BUELL, John. *Playground*. 1976. FSG. 1st ed. VG/VG. P3. $20.00

BUELL, John. *Shrewsdale Exit*. 1972. FSG. 1st ed. VG/VG. P3. $23.00

BUFF, Mary Marsh. *Dancing Cloud*. 1945. NY. Viking. 3rd prt. ils. 80p. VG/tattered. D1. $32.00

BUFF & BUFF. *Big Tree*. 1946. Viking. 1st ed. ils. F/VG. P2. $75.00

BUFF & BUFF. *Magic Maize*. 1953. Houghton Mifflin. 1st ed. ils. 76p. cloth. VG/dj. M20. $32.00

BUFFETT, Jimmy. *Where Is Joe Merchant?* 1992. Harcourt. 1st ed. author's 1st novel. NF/NF clip. M22. $20.00

BUFFIER, Claude. *Geographie Universelle*. 1759. Paris. Giffart. 18 fld maps. 442p. VG. B14. $850.00

BUHRER & ISENBART. *Imperial Horse*. 1986. Knopf. 1st Am ed. F/F. O3. $125.00

BUJOLD, Lois McMaster. *Mirror Dance*. 1994. Baen. 1st ed. F/F. M23. $30.00

BUKIET, Melvin J. *Sandman's Dust*. 1985. Arbor. 1st ed. F/NF. G10. $10.00

BUKOWSKI, Charles. *Crucifix in a Deathhand*. 1965. New Orleans. 1st ed. 1/3100. sgn. F/wrp/orig band. w/sgn letter. C2. $250.00

BUKOWSKI, Charles. *In the Shadow of the Rose*. 1991. Blk Sparrow. 1/750. sgn/#d. F/plain turquoise dj. S9. $175.00

BUKOWSKI, Charles. *Living on Luck. Selected Letters 1960s-1970s. Volume 2*. 1995. Blk Sparrow. 1/200. F/acetate dj. S9. $300.00

BUKOWSKI, Charles. *Longshot Poems for Broke Players*. 1962. 7 Poets. 1/200. author's 2nd book. F/stiff beige wrp. B24. $850.00

BUKOWSKI, Charles. *Love Poem*. 1979. Blk Sparrow. 1/26. sgn/lettered. handbound decor brd. F/F. S9. $200.00

BUKOWSKI, Charles. *One for the Old Boy*. 1984. Santa Barbara. 1st ed. 1/226. sgn. AN. A4. $125.00

BUKOWSKI, Charles. *Poems Written Before Jumping Out of an 8-Story Window*. nd. Berkley. Litmus. F/wrp. B2. $200.00

BUKOWSKI, Charles. *Shakespeare Never Did This*. 1995. Blk Sparrow. 1st ed thus. 1/326. F/dj. S9. $65.00

BUKOWSKI, Charles. *War All the Time*. 1984. Blk Sparrow. 1st ed. 1/500 hc trade copies. F/acetate dj. T10. $100.00

BUKOWSKI, Charles. *You Kissed Lilly*. 1978. Blk Sparrow. 1st ed. 1/75. sgn. F. B24. $285.00

BULEY, R. Carlyle. *Old Northwest: Pioneer Period 1815-1840*. 1951. IN U. 2 vol. 2nd. maps/pl. VG. A17. $40.00

BULFINCH. *Book of Myths: Selections From Bulfinch's Age of Fables*. 1942. Macmillan. 1st ed. ils Sewell. VG+/VG. C8. $65.00

BULFINCH. *Book of Myths: Selections From Bulfinch's Age of Fables*. 1953 (1942). Macmillan. 4th. ils Helen Sewell. 8vo. 128p. VG/torn. T5. $20.00

BULGAKOV, Mikhail. *Master & Margarita*. 1967. Grove. 1st ed. trans Mirra Ginsburg. NF/NF. B2. $25.00

BULGAKOV, Mikhail. *Master & Margarita*. 1967. Harper Row. 1st ed. VG/VG. P3. $30.00

BULL, Rene. *Arabian Nights*. 1917. Dodd Mead. 8 mc pl. 98 b&w ils. NF. A20. $50.00

BULL & COLEMAN. *Northwest Books, First Supplement...1942-1947*. 1949. np. 276p. VG. A4. $45.00

BULLA, Clyde Robert. *Donkey Cart*. 1946. Crowell. 1st ed. ils Lois Lenski. xl. M5. $35.00

BULLARD, E. John. *Mary Cassatt: Oils & Pastels*. 1972. Watson Guptill. orig ed. 32 pl. 87p. cloth. D2. $45.00

BULLEN, Frank T. *Men of the Merchant Service*. 1900. NY/London. 331p. T7. $45.00

BULLEN, K.E. *Introduction to the Theory of Seismology*. 1965. Cambridge. 3rd. 381p. F/torn. D8. $21.00

BULLER, Francis. *Introduction to the Law Relative to Trials at Nisi Prius...* 1806. NY. Riley. modern half crimson morocco. xl. M11. $225.00

BULLETT, Gerald. *Walt Whitman: A Study & Selection*. 1925. Phil. 1/780. NF/VG. C6. $55.00

BULLOCK, Alan. *Hitler: A Study in Tyranny*. 1962. NY. revised ed. 848p. fair. A17. $6.00

BULWER-LYTTON, Edward. *Athens: Its Rise & Fall*. 1843. Tauchnitz. G. P3. $40.00

BUNCH & COLE. *Warrior's Tale*. 1994. Ballantine. 1st ed. F/F. w/pub letter. G10. $12.00

BUNDY, Walter E. *Jesus & the First Three Gospels*. 1955. Cambridge. Harvard. 1st ed. sgn. 598p. F/G. B11. $50.00

BUNDY & STIMSON. *On Active Service in Peace & War, Vol 1*. 1948. Harper. 1st ed. sgn Stimson. VG/worn. B11. $15.00

BUNKER, M.N. *What Handwriting Tells You About Yourself...* 1951. Cleveland. World. sgn. 240p. VG/G. B11. $6.00

BUNN, Harriet. *Johann Sebastian Bach*. 1942. ils Rafaello Busoni. VG. B30. $10.00

BUNN, Thomas. *Closing Costs*. 1990. Holt. 1st ed. F/F. P3. $10.00

BUNNELL, L.H. *Discovery of the Yosemite & the Indian War of 1851...* 1911. LA. Gerlicher. 4th. ils/map. VG. H7. $75.00

BUNTING, Basil. *Collected Poems*. 1985. Mt Kisco, NY. 1st Am ed. sgn J Williams. w/sgn leaflett. F. A11. $150.00

BUNYAN, John. *Pilgrim's Progress*. 1942. Heritage. ils. case. A17. $17.50

BURBANK, Luther. *Harvest of the Years*. 1927. Boston. ils. 296p. VG/VG. B5. $22.50

BURCHAM, L.T. *California Range Land*. 1957. Sacramento. ils/photos/tables. 261p. B26. $30.00

BURDEN, Hamilton T. *Nuremberg Party Rallies 1923-39*. 1967. NY. photos. 206p. VG. A17. $22.50

BURGERS, Thornton. *Burgers' Book of Nature*. 1965. Boston. 1st ed. VG/VG. B5. $50.00

BURGESS, Anthony. *Any Old Iron*. 1989. London. 1st ed. sgn. F/F. C2. $75.00

BURGESS, Anthony. *End of the World News*. 1983. McGraw Hill. 1st ed. F/F. P3. $20.00

BURGESS, Anthony. *Ernest Hemingway & His World*. 1978. London. Thames Hudson. 1st ed. thin 4to. F/dj. C2. $75.00

BURGESS, Anthony. *Ernest Hemingway & His World*. 1978. Scribner. 1st ed. F/F. B2. $30.00

BURGESS, Anthony. *Kingdom of the Wicked*. 1985. Arbor. 1st ed. VG/VG. P3. $20.00

BURGESS, Anthony. *Napoleon Symphony*. 1974. NY. 1st Am ed. sgn. F/F. C2. $60.00

BURGESS, Anthony. *Pianoplayers*. 1986. Hutchinson. 1st ed. F/F. P3. $18.00

BURGESS, Anthony. *1985*. 1978. Little Brn. 1st ed. VG/VG. P3. $18.00

BURGESS, Gelett. *Why Be a Goop?* 1924. Stokes. 1st ed. ils. 159p. VG. P2. $110.00

BURGESS, Lorraine. *Garden Art*. 1981. NY. Walker. 1st ed. ils. 187p. F/F. T10. $15.00

BURGESS, Thornton W. *Adventures of Bob White*. 1919. Little Brn. 1st ed. ils Harrison Cady. VG. P2. $75.00

BURGESS, Thornton W. *Adventures of Buster Bear*. (1919). Little Brn. ils Harrison Cady. gray cloth. VG. M5. $30.00

BURGESS, Thornton W. *Adventures of Buster Bear*. 1964. Canada. Little Brn. decor brd. VG. P3. $8.00

BURGESS, Thornton W. *Adventures of Jimmy Skunk*. 1937. Little Brn. F/G. M5. $45.00

BURGESS, Thornton W. *Adventures of Peter Cottontail*. nd. McClelland Stewart. VG/G. P3. $12.00

BURGESS, Thornton W. *Burgess Bird Book for Children*. Oct 1919. Boston. Little Brn. 1st ed. 351p. F. B14. $65.00

BURGESS, Thornton W. *Burgess Seashore Book for Children*. 1946 (1929). Little Brn. ils Southwick/Sutton. VG/G. P2. $45.00

BURGESS, Thornton W. *Crooked Little Path*. nd. Bonanza. later rpt. ils Harrison Cady. VG/VG. B17. $10.00

BURGESS, Thornton W. *How Peter Cottontail Got His Name*. 1957. Wonder. ils Phoebe Erickson. VG. M5. $15.00

BURGESS, Thornton W. *Littlest Christmas Tree*. 1954. Wonder. ils Hauge. VG. M5. $30.00

BURGESS, Thornton W. *Mother West Wind Why Stories*. 1915. Little Brn. 1st ed. ils Harrison Cady. 230p. VG. P2. $110.00

BURGESS, Thornton W. *Old Mother West Wind, Golden Anniversary Ed*. 1960. Little Brn. ils Harrison Cady. 10th prt. VG/VG. B17. $8.50

BURGESS, Thornton W. *While the Story-Log Burns*. 1938. Little Brn. 1st ed. ils Lemuel Palmer. 195p. VG/VG. D1. $150.00

BURGHEIM, Fanny Louise. *First Circus*. 1930. Platt Munk. ils. 30p. emb brd. A17. $10.00

BURKE, Alan Dennis. *Driven to Murder*. 1986. Atlantic Monthly. 1st ed. F/F. P3. $16.00

BURKE, James Lee. *Burning Angel*. 1995. Hyperion. 1st ed. F/F. M19. $25.00

BURKE, James Lee. *Convict*. 1985. Baton Rouge. 1st ed. inscr. hc. NF. B4. $250.00

BURKE, James Lee. *Dixie City Jam*. 1994. Hyperion. 1st ed. F/F. A20/H11. $25.00

BURKE, James Lee. *In the Electric Mist With Confederate Dead*. 1993. Hyperion. 1st ed. F/F. H11. $35.00

BURKE, James Lee. *Stained White Radiance*. 1992. Hyperion. 1st ed. F/F. H11. $35.00

BURKE, Jan. *Goodnight, Irene*. 1993. Simon Schuster. 1st ed. sgn. F/F. T2. $40.00

BURKE, Martyn. *Commissar's Report*. 1984. Houghton Mifflin. 1st ed. NF/NF. H11. $20.00

BURKE, Pauline Wilcox. *Emily Donelson of Tennessee*. 1941. Garrett Massie. 2 vol. ils. box. B10. $45.00

BURKERT, Nancy Ekholm. *Valentine & Orson*. 1989. FSG. 1st ed. unp. NF/dj. M20. $27.00

BURKHARDT. *Concise Dictionary of American Biography*. 1990. np. 4th. 1549p. F/F. A4. $95.00

BURKHOLZ & IRVING. *Death Freak*. 1978. Summit. 1st ed. VG/VG. P3. $15.00

BURKHOLZ & IRVING. *Thirty-Eighth Floor*. 1965. McGraw Hill. 1st ed. VG/VG. P3. $20.00

BURLAND, Cottie. *People of the Ancient Americas*. 1970. London. Hamilyn. 1st ed. 159p. dj. F3. $20.00

BURLEIGH, Anne H. *John Adams*. nd. Arlington. 437p. bl cloth. F/VG. B22. $5.00

BURLEY, W.J. *Charles & Elizabeth*. 1981. Walker. 1st ed. NF/NF. P3. $13.00

BURLEY, W.J. *Wycliffe & the Tangled Web*. 1989. Crime Club. 1st ed. VG/VG. P3. $16.00

BURLINGAME, Roger. *Of Making Many Books*. 1946. Scribner. 1st ed. 8vo. 347p. gilt beige cloth. NF. T10. $35.00

BURLINGHAM, Gertrude S. *Study of the Lactariae of the United States*. 1908. NY. ils/photos. wrp. B26. $20.00

BURMAN, Ben Lucien. *Blow a Wild Bugle for Catfish Bend*. 1967. Taplinger. ils Alice Cady. VG/VG. B10. $15.00

BURMAN, Ben Lucien. *Owl Hoots Twice at Cafish Bend*. 1961. Taplinger. 1st ed. ils Alice Caddy. VG/VG. B10. $25.00

BURNETT, Constance Buel. *Shoemaker's Son: Life of Hans Christian Andersen*. 1941. Random/JLG. 1st ed thus. 313p. VG. P2. $12.50

BURNETT, Frances Hodgson. *Little Lord Fauntleroy*. 1936. NY. ils. 236p. VG/tape rpr. A17. $10.00

BURNETT, Frances Hodgson. *Little Princess*. 1905. Scribner. 1st ed thus. lg 8vo. teg. VG. M5. $90.00

BURNETT, Frances Hodgson. *Little Princess*. 1963. Lippincott. 1st ed. ils/sgn Tasha Tudor. VG/G+. P2. $85.00

BURNETT, Frances Hodgson. *Little Princess*. 1965. Lippincott. 8vo. ils Tasha Tudor. F/F. B17. $12.50

BURNETT, Frances Hodgson. *Making of a Marchioness*. 1901. NY. 1st ed. F/VG+. C6. $225.00

BURNETT, Frances Hodgson. *Secret Garden*. 1911. Stokes. 1st ed. 1 pl missing. fair. M5. $35.00

BURNETT, Frances Hodgson. *Secret Garden*. 1962. ils Tasha Tudor. NF/NF. S13. $25.00

BURNETT, Frances Hodgson. *Spring Cleaning As Told by Queen Crosspatch*. 1973. England. Tom Stacey. rpt. 12mo. 86p. gilt bdg. NF/VG. T5. $35.00

BURNETT, Frances Hodgson. *Two Little Pilgrims' Progress*. 1895. Scribner. 1st ed. 191p. bl cloth. VG. M20. $57.00

BURNETT, Francis Hodgson. *Once Upon a Time Stories, Jingles, Rhymes*. 1915. Cupples Leon. 8vo. 92p. fair. C14. $8.00

BURNETT, Hallie. *Brain Pickers*. 1957. Messner. 1st ed. VG+/VG. B4. $85.00

BURNETT, Virgil. *Towers at the Edge of the World*. 1980. St Martin. 1st ed. F/F. P3. $15.00

BURNETT, W.R. *Dark Hazard*. 1933. Harper. 1st ed. VG. P3. $25.00

BURNETT, W.R. *Goodhues of Sinking Creek*. nd. np 1st ed. ils JJ Lankes. NF/NF. A11. $60.00

BURNETT, W.R. *Iron Man*. 1930. Lincoln MacVeagh. 1st ed. VG+. M22/P3. $30.00

BURNETT, W.R. *Little Caesar*. 1929. Dial. 1st ed. author's 1st novel. VG. M22. $45.00

BURNETT. *Autobiography of the Working Class...1790-1900*. 1984. NY. 1028 entries. 501p. NF. A4. $65.00

BURNHAM, Frederick Russell. *Scouting on Two Continents*. 1934. Los Angeles. Ivan Deach. sgn. 370p. gilt bl cloth. VG. T10. $50.00

BURNHAM, Sophy. *Art Crowd*. 1973. McKay. 395p. cloth. dj. D2. $25.00

BURNINGHAM, John. *Mr Grumpy's Motor Car*. 1976. Crowell. 1st Am ed. ils. F/F. P2. $28.00

BURNINGHAM, John. *Seasons*. 1971. Bobbs Merrill. 1st Am ed. VG/VG. B35. $7.50

BURNINGHAM, John. *Where's Julius?* 1986. Crown. stated 1st ed. 4to. ils. unp. VG+/VG clip. C14. $10.00

BURNS, E. Bradford. *Perspectives of Brazillian History*. 1967. Columbia. 1st ed. 235p. dj. F3. $15.00

BURNS, Elizabeth. *Late Liz*. 1968. NY. sgn. VG/VG. B5. $25.00

BURNS, George. *I Love Her That's Why*. 1955. NY. 1st ed. VG/VG. B5. $30.00

BURNS, Olive Ann. *Cold Sassy Tree*. 1984. Ticknor Fields. 1st ed. F/NF. B2. $150.00

BURNS, Rex. *Alvarez Journal*. 1975. Harper Row. 1st ed. VG/VG. P3. $20.00

BURNS, Tex; see L'Amour, Louis.

BURNS, Walter Noble. *Saga of Billy the Kid*. 1926. Doubleday. 8vo. 322p. reading copy. T10. $25.00

BURNS. *Herbert Hoover: Bibliography of His Times & Presidency*. 1991. np. ils. 290p. F. A4. $70.00

BURNSIDE, H.M. *Noel*. nd. Raphael Tuck. inscr. G/wrp. B18. $17.50

BURR, Fearing. *Field & Garden Vegetables of America*. 1994. Chillicothe, IL. Am Botanist. rpt. 664p. M. A10. $35.00

BURROUGHS, Edgar Rice. *At the Earth's Core*. 1962. Canaveral. 1st ed. VG/VG. P3. $50.00

BURROUGHS, Edgar Rice. *Beasts of Tarzan.* 1916. AL Burt. ils J Allen St John. 337p. VG/dj. M20. $47.00

BURROUGHS, Edgar Rice. *Cave Girl.* 1925. Chicago. McClurg. 1st ed. F/NF. C2. $1,750.00

BURROUGHS, Edgar Rice. *Deputy Sheriff of Comanche County.* 1940. Tarzana. ERB. 1st ed. F/1st issue dj. B24. $650.00

BURROUGHS, Edgar Rice. *ERB Library of Illustration Vol 1.* 1976. Russ Cochran. 1st ed. F. P3. $200.00

BURROUGHS, Edgar Rice. *Fighting Man of Mars.* 1933. John Lane/Bodley Head. 2nd. VG. P3. $40.00

BURROUGHS, Edgar Rice. *Girl From Hollywood.* 1923. Macaulay. 1st ed. VG. P3. $55.00

BURROUGHS, Edgar Rice. *Jungle Girl.* 1933. Odhams. 1st ed. VG/G. P3. $75.00

BURROUGHS, Edgar Rice. *Land That Time Forgot.* nd. Doubleday. hc. 249p. F. M13. $20.00

BURROUGHS, Edgar Rice. *Mucker.* 1963. Canaveral. 1st ed. VG/VG. P3. $75.00

BURROUGHS, Edgar Rice. *Pirates of Venus.* 1962. Canaveral. NF/NF. P3. $60.00

BURROUGHS, Edgar Rice. *Return of Tarzan.* 1927. Grosset Dunlap. VG/G. P3. $75.00

BURROUGHS, Edgar Rice. *Savage Pellucidar.* 1963. Canaveral. 1st ed. G/G. P3. $40.00

BURROUGHS, Edgar Rice. *Son of Tarzan.* 1917. Grosset Dunlap. ils St John. 394p. VG/dj. M20. $52.00

BURROUGHS, Edgar Rice. *Son of Tarzan.* 1927. Grosset Dunlap. VG/G. P3. $50.00

BURROUGHS, Edgar Rice. *Tanar of Pellucidar.* 1962. Canaveral. NF/NF. P3. $50.00

BURROUGHS, Edgar Rice. *Tarzan & the Ant Men.* 1924. Grosset Dunlap. 346p. VG+/dj. M20. $52.00

BURROUGHS, Edgar Rice. *Tarzan & the Golden Lion.* 1923. Chicago. 1st ed. NF. C2. $75.00

BURROUGHS, Edgar Rice. *Tarzan & the Jewels of Opar.* 1919. McClurg. 2nd ed. VG. P3. $90.00

BURROUGHS, Edgar Rice. *Tarzan & the Lost Empire.* 1929. ERB. 313p. cloth. VG+/dj. M20. $77.00

BURROUGHS, Edgar Rice. *Tarzan & the Lost Empire.* 1932. Cassell. 2nd. VG. P3. $35.00

BURROUGHS, Edgar Rice. *Tarzan at the Earth's Core.* 1962. Canaveral. NF/NF. P3. $50.00

BURROUGHS, Edgar Rice. *Tarzan's Quest.* 1936. ERB. early rpt. F/F. M19. $125.00

BURROUGHS, Edgar Rice. *Tarzan the Avenger.* 1939. Dell/ERB. 192p. VG. B14. $125.00

BURROUGHS, Edgar Rice. *Tarzan the Magnificent.* 1948. Burroughs. F/F. P3. $75.00

BURROUGHS, Edgar Rice. *Tarzan the Untamed.* 1920. Canada. McClelland Stewart. 1st ed. G. P3. $125.00

BURROUGHS, Edgar Rice. *Tarzan the Untamed.* 1920. Chicago. McClurg. 1st ed. NF. C2. $75.00

BURROUGHS, Edgar Rice. *War Chief.* 1978. Gregg. 1st ed. VG/VG. P3. $40.00

BURROUGHS, Edgar Rice. *Warlord of Mars.* 1919. McClurg. 1st ed. G. P3. $75.00

BURROUGHS, Harry E. *Tale of a Vanished Land.* 1930. Houghton Mifflin. 1/1000. sgn. 336p. VG. B11. $40.00

BURROUGHS, John. *Squirrels & Other Fur-Bearers.* 1901. Boston/NY. Houghton Mifflin. sm 8vo. 149p. cloth. VG. H4. $35.00

BURROUGHS, John. *Writings of...* 1904. NY. 15 vol. marbled brd/brn half leather. F. B30. $235.00

BURROUGHS, Margaret T.G. *What Shall I Tell My Children Who Are Black.* 1968. Chicago. MAAH Pr. 2nd. inscr. NF/stapled wrp. B4. $45.00

BURROUGHS, Polly. *Zeb: A Celebrated Schooner Life.* 1972. Riverside, CT. Chatham. 4to. ils. 160p. VG/dj. T7. $35.00

BURROUGHS, Raleigh. *Horses, Burroughs & Other Animals.* 1977. Barnes. pres. F/F. w/sgn letter. O3. $65.00

BURROUGHS, W.J. *Weather Cycles: Real or Imaginary?* 1992. Cambridge. 4to. 201p. VG/VG. K5. $20.00

BURROUGHS, William Jr. *Map From Hell.* 1978. Red Ozier. rolled w/band. F. V1. $25.00

BURROUGHS, William S. *Cobble Stone Gardens.* 1976. Cherry Valley. 1st ed. 1/50. sgn. hc. NF. B4. $350.00

BURROUGHS, William S. *Dead Star.* 1969. San Francisco. Nova Broadcast. 1st ed. 1/2000. sgn. F/prt wrp. S9. $100.00

BURROUGHS, William S. *Exterminator!* 1973. Viking. 1st ed. F/F. M19. $75.00

BURROUGHS, William S. *Last Words of Dutch Schultz.* 1975. Viking. 1st ed. F/F. H11. $55.00

BURROUGHS, William S. *Nova Express.* 1964. NY. 1st ed. F/F. C6. $40.00

BURROUGHS, William S. *Soft Machine.* 1968. London. Calder Boyars. 2nd Eng ed. F/NF. B2. $50.00

BURROUGHS, William S. *Ticket That Exploded.* 1967. Grove. 1st Am ed. F/NF. B2. $65.00

BURST, Steven. *Gypsy.* 1992. Tor. 1st ed. F/F. P3. $19.00

BURST, Steven. *Phoenix Guards.* 1991. Tor. 1st ed. F/F. P3. $20.00

BURSTEIN & CRIMP. *Many Lives of Elton John.* 1992. Birch Lane. 1st ed. F/F. P3. $20.00

BURT & LEASOR. *One That Got Away.* 1956. Collins. 1st ed. VG/VG. P3. $15.00

BURTON, Mary Kerr. *Serenity & Other Poems.* 1975. Reynolds. 32p. VG. B10. $12.00

BURTON, Miles. *Hardway Diamonds.* 1930. Mystery League. 1st ed. VG. P3. $20.00

BURTON, William. *History & Description of English Porcelain.* 1902. Cassell. 1/1200. 8vo. 24 pl. 196p. gilt gr cloth. xl. T10. $100.00

BURTON, Yvonne. *Grady Country, Georgia.* 1981. Danielsville, GA. Heritage. 2nd. inscr. 357p. gilt brd. F. B11. $40.00

BUSBEY, Hamilton. *Recollections of Men & Horses.* 1907. Dodd Mead. 1st ed. lacks ffep. O3. $35.00

BUSBEY, Hamilton. *Trotting & the Pacing Horse in America.* 1904. Macmillan. 1st ed. O3. $45.00

BUSBY, F.M. *Long View.* 1976. Berkley Putnam. 1st ed. F/F. P3. $18.00

BUSBY, Roger. *Main Line Kill.* 1968. Walker. 1st ed. VG/VG. P3. $12.00

BUSBY, Roger. *New Face in Hell.* 1976. Collins Crime Club. 1st ed. VG/VG. P3. $20.00

BUSBY, Roger. *Snow Man.* 1987. Collins Crime Club. 1st ed. VG/G. P3. $15.00

BUSCEMA & LEE. *How to Draw Comics the Marvel Way.* 1978. hc. ils. 160p. F. M13. $23.00

BUSCH, Francis X. *Enemies of the State.* 1954. Bobbs Merrill. crimson brd. G. M11. $45.00

BUSCH, Frederick. *Closing Arguments.* 1991. Ticknor Fields. 1st ed. AN/dj. M22. $25.00

BUSCH, Frederick. *I Wanted a Year Without Fall.* 1971. London. 1st/only ed. F/NF. A11. $70.00

BUSCH, Wilhelm. *Max & Moritz.* 1925. Braun Schneider. pict brd. VG. M5. $35.00

BUSCH, Wilhelm. *Max und Moritz.* 1925. Munchen. Braun Schneider. ils. VG. M5. $22.00

BUSH, Caroll D. *Nut Growers Handbook: A Practical Guide...* 1941. NY. photos/drawings. 189p. B26. $25.00

BUSH, Christopher. *Dead Man's Music.* 1937. Heinemann. VG. P3. $20.00

BUSHNELL, Belle. *John Arrowsmith: Planter.* 1910 (1909). Torch. inscr. ils. 115p. G+. B10. $25.00

BUSHONG, Millard K. *Old Jube: A Biography of General Jubal A Early.* 1988 (1955). Wht Mane. 4th. 343p. AN. B10. $25.00

BUSS, Irven. *Wisconsin Pheasant Population.* 1943. Madison, WI. Conservation Dept. 318p. VG. A10. $45.00

BUTENKO, R.G. *Plant Cell Culture.* 1985. Moscow. MIR Pub. 207p. VG/wrp. B1. $22.00

BUTLER, Benjamin. *Butler's Book.* 1892. Boston. st ed. thick 8vo. ils. 1154p. G. T3. $40.00

BUTLER, Charles Henry. *Century at the Bar of the Supreme Court of United States.* 1942. putnam. G/worn. M11. $50.00

BUTLER, Constance. *Illyria, Lady.* 1935. Boston. Houghton Mifflin. 1st ed. NF/VG+. B4. $65.00

BUTLER, Ellis Parker. *Confessions of a Daddy.* 1907. Century. 1st ed. ils Fanny Cory. VG+. M5. $48.00

BUTLER, Gerald. *Kiss the Blood Off My Hands.* 1946. Farrar Rinehart. 1st ed. VG/G. P3. $20.00

BUTLER, Gwendoline. *Albion Walk.* 1982. CMG. 1st ed. VG/VG. P3. $20.00

BUTLER, Gwendoline. *Coffin in Malta.* 1965. Walker. 1st ed. VG/VG. P3. $30.00

BUTLER, Gwendoline. *Coffin on the Water.* 1986. St Martin. 1st ed. VG/VG. P3. $20.00

BUTLER, Gwendoline. *Red Staircase.* 1979. CMG. 1st ed. VG/VG. P3. $20.00

BUTLER, Margaret Manor. *Lakewood Story.* 1949. Stratford. 1st ed. sgn. 263p. VG. M20. $22.00

BUTLER, Octavia E. *Adulthood Rites.* 1988. Warner. 1st ed. F/F. B4. $45.00

BUTLER, Octavia E. *Blood Child.* 1995. 4 Walls 8 Windows. 1st ed. F/F. M23. $20.00

BUTLER, Octavia E. *Imago.* 1989. Warner. 1st ed. F/F. P3. $20.00

BUTLER, Octavia E. *Kindred.* 1979. Doubleday. 1st ed. F/NF. M23. $75.00

BUTLER, Octavia E. *Mind of My Mind.* 1977. Doubleday. 1st ed. xl. VG+/VG+. M23. $60.00

BUTLER, Octavia E. *Patternmaster.* 1976. Doubleday. 1st ed. VG+/VG. M23. $75.00

BUTLER, Octavia E. *Survivor.* 1978. Doubleday. 1st ed. F/VG+. M23. $65.00

BUTLER, Octavia E. *Wild Seed.* 1980. Doubleday. 1st ed. F/F. M23. $125.00

BUTLER, Robert Olen. *Alleys of Eden.* 1981. NY. 1st ed. F/F. A11. $65.00

BUTLER, Robert Olen. *Sun Dogs.* 1982. NY. 1st ed. author's 2nd novel. F/F. A11. $50.00

BUTLER, Robert Olen. *They Whisper.* 1994. Holt. 1st ed. sgn. F/F. B4. $50.00

BUTLER, Robert Olen. *Wabash.* 1987. Knopf. 1st ed. F/F. H11. $35.00

BUTLER, Samuel. *Erewhon.* 1901. LEC. 1/1500. ils/sgn Rockwell Kent. 8vo. striped bl/wht cloth. VG. B11. $100.00

BUTLER, Samuel. *Geographia Classica.* 1831. Phil. VG. O7. $35.00

BUTLER, Samuel. *Hudibras.* 1744. Cambridge. 2 vol. 1st 8vo ed. ils Hogarth. 19th-C morocco. VG. C6. $275.00

BUTLER, Samuel. *Way of All Flesh.* 1903. London. 1st ed. VG. C6. $195.00

BUTLER, William E. *Soviet Union & the Law of the Sea.* 1971. Baltimore. VG. O7. $15.00

BUTTERWORTH, Michael. *Virgin on the Rocks.* 1985. Crime Club. 1st ed. NF/NF. P3. $13.00

BUTTERWORTH, W.E. *Air Evac.* 1967. Norton. 1st ed. NF/clip. B4. $150.00

BYARS, Betsy. *After the Goat Man.* 1974. Viking. 1st ed. ils Ronald Himler. NF/VG+. P2. $20.00

BYATT, A.S. *Djinn in the Nightingale's Eye.* 1994. London. 1st ed. sgn. F/F. A11. $45.00

BYERS, Horace Robert. *Elements of Cloud Physics.* 1973 (1965). Chicago. 2nd. 8vo. 191p. VG/dj. K5. $20.00

BYNNER, W. *Caravan.* 1925. NY. 1st ed. inscr. NF. A15. $45.00

BYNNER, Witter. *Journey With Genius.* 1951. NY. John Day. 1st ed. NF/dj. H4. $40.00

BYRD, Richard E. *Alone.* 1938. NY. Putnam. 1st ed. sgn. VG. H4. $25.00

BYRD, Richard E. *Big Aviation Book for Boys.* 1929. Springfield, MA. 285p. F/dj. A17. $25.00

BYRD, Richard E. *Discovery: Story of Second Byrd Antarctic Expedition.* 1935. Putnam. 1st ed. sgn. ils/2 maps. 405p. VG. T7. $50.00

BYRD, Richard E. *Skyward.* 1928. NY. 1st ed. 359p. G+. B18. $22.50

BYRNE, Robert. *Tunnel.* 1977. Detective BC. VG. P3. $8.00

BYRON, Lord. *Childe Harold's Pilgrimage.* 1892. ils Nims/Knight. NF/G. M19. $85.00

– C –

CABELL, James Branch. *Letter of...* 1975. OK U. 1st. NF/dj. M2. $25.00

CABELL, James Branch. *Music Behind the Moon.* 1926. NY. John Day. 1/3000. ils Leon Underwood. VG. T10. $75.00

CABELL, James Branch. *Preface to the Past.* 1936. McBride. VG/dj. M2. $35.00

CABELL, James Branch. *Silver Stallion.* 1926. McBride. 1st. G. P3. $30.00

CABELL, James Branch. *Silver Stallion.* 1926. McBride. 1st. 358p. cloth. VG. M20. $45.00

CABELL, James Branch. *Something About Eve.* 1927. McBride. 1st. VG/VG. P3. $75.00

CABELL, James Branch. *Way of Ecben.* 1929. NY. McBride. 1st. NF. P3. $35.00

CABLE & FRENCH. *Gobi Desert.* 1950. Westminster. Readers Union. ils. 305+p. VG. A25. $16.00

CABOT, Calvin. *Year of Regeneration: 1933.* 1932. Harper. F/dj. M2. $25.00

CABRERA, Luis. *Tragic Bomb.* 1964. Mexico. 49x37mm. Eng text. 39p. gilt full tan leather. F. B24. $65.00

CADBURY, Henry J. *George Fox's Book of Miracles.* 1948. Cambridge. 162p. VG/dj. V3. $60.00

CADE, Leland P. *Well, I Guess I Was Lucky.* 1992. Cade. 1st. 243p. as new. J2. $45.00

CADIGAN, Pat. *Mindplayers.* 1988. London. 1st. F/dj. M2. $25.00

CADOGAN, Mary. *Women With Wings.* 1992. London. 1st. 280p. F/dj. B18. $25.00

CADUTO, M.J. *Pond & Brook: Guide to Nature Study...* 1985. Prentice Hall. 276p. rem mk. dj. B1. $14.50

CADY, Annie Cole. *History of Ohio in Words of One Syllable.* 1888. NY. 208p. G. B18. $25.00

CADY, Edwin H. *John Woolman: Mind of the Quaker Saint.* 1966. NY. WA Square Pr. 182p. G. V3. $15.00

CADY, Harrison. *Caleb Cottontail.* 1921. Houghton Mifflin. 1st. 8vo. orange-yel pict cloth. R5. $175.00

CADY, Jack. *Singleton.* 1981. Seattle, WA. Madrona. 1st. author's 4th book. NF/dj. M21. $25.00

CADY, Jack. *Well.* 1980. Arbor. 1st. NF/dj. M21. $45.00

CADY, John H. *Arizona's Yesterday.* 1916. private prt. 1st. sgn. ils. 120p. F. B19. $40.00

CADZOW, Donald A. *Achaeological Studies of Susquehannock Indians of PA.* 1936. Harrisburg. 1st. 8vo. ils/pl/maps. VG. H1. $40.00

CAESAR, Julius. *Ancient State Authoritie & Proceedings of Court of Requests.* 1975 (1597). London. edit/intro LM Hill. M11. $85.00

CAESAR, Sid. *Where Have I Been?* 1982. Crown. sgn. photos. VG+. C9. $40.00

CAGNEY, Peter. *Grave for Madam.* 1961. Herbert Jenkins. 1st. VG/G. P3. $18.00

CAHAN, Richard, and Jacobs, Mark. *The Game That Was.* 1996. Chicago. Contemporary Books. cm 4to. 246 pp. pict. rem. VG+/sc. R16. $25.00

CAHILL, James. *Hills Beyond a River.* 1976. NY/Tokyo. Weatherhill. 1st. ils. 198p. F/dj. W3. $85.00

CAHILL, Tim. *Road Fever.* 1991. Random. 1st. sgn. F/F. B3. $45.00

CAIANELLO, E.R. *Physics of Cognitive Processes.* 1987. NY. World Scientific. 463p. prt gr laminated brd. G1. $75.00

CAIDIN, Martin. *Devil Take All.* 1966. Dutton. 1st. NF/VG. N4. $15.00

CAIDIN, Martin. *Rendezvous in Space, Story of Projects Mercury...* 1962. NY. 1st. ils. VG/dj. B18. $20.00

CAILLE, Augustus. *Differential Diagnosis & Treatment of Disease.* 1906. NY. 1st. ils. 867p. half leather. A13. $100.00

CAILLET. *Manual Bibliographique des Sciences, Psychiques ou Occultes.* nd. 3 vol. 1/100. rpt. 11648 entries. F. A4. $175.00

CAIN, James M. *Baby in the Icebox & Other Short Fiction.* 1981. Holt. 1st. F/VG. B3. $30.00

CAIN, James M. *Baby in the Icebox & Other Short Fiction.* 1981. HRW. 1st. F/F. M15. $45.00

CAIN, James M. *Cloud Nine.* 1984. Mysterious. 1st. VG/VG. P3. $18.00

CAIN, James M. *Galatea.* 1953. Knopf. 1st. NF/NF. M15/M22. $45.00

CAIN, James M. *Institute.* 1976. Mason Charter. 1st. F/NF. M19. $35.00

CAIN, James M. *Love's Lovely Counterfeit.* 1942. Knopf. 1st. VG. P3. $100.00

CAIN, James M. *Moth.* 1948. Knopf. F/F. M22. $45.00

CAIN, James M. *Postman Always Rings Twice.* 1934. Knopf. 3rd. NF. M22. $15.00

CAIN, James M. *Rainbow's End.* 1975. Mason/Charter. 1st. inscr/dtd 1975. F/NF. R14. $150.00

CAIN, James M. *Serenade.* 1937. Knopf. VG/G+. M22. $90.00

CAIN, James M. *Serenade.* 1937. Knopf. 1st. VG. P3. $35.00

CAIN, Paul. *Fast One.* 1978. S IL U. 1st thus. VG/VG. M22. $60.00

CAIN, Paul. *Seven Slayers.* 1987. Los Angeles. Blood & Guts. 1st hc. sgn. F/F. T2. $25.00

CAIN & SHARP. *Bryophytic Unions of Certain Forest Types...* 1938. Notre Dame. rpt. G/wrp. B1. $14.00

CAIRD, G.B. *Revelation of St John the Divine.* 1966. Harper. 316p. VG/dj. B29. $11.50

CAIRNS, Bob. *Pen Men: Baseball's Greatest Bullpen Stories...* 1992. St Martin. 1st. F/F. T12. $25.00

CAJORI, F. *Sir Isaac Newton's Mathematical Principles...* 1947. Berkeley, CA. 680p. cloth. F. D8. $20.00

CALAHAN, H.A. *Ship's Husband: Guide to Yachtsmen in Care of Their Craft.* 1937. NY. 1st. 323p. VG. A17. $15.00

CALBE & FRENCH. *Gobi Desert.* 1944. Macmillan. ils/fld map. 302p. VG. W3. $38.00

CALDECOTT, Andrew. *Fires Burn Blue.* 1948. London. 1st. VG/dj. M2. $35.00

CALDWELL, E. *Fairy Ship.* ca 1890. London. Marcus Ward. ltd. sq 12mo. pict wrp. R5. $75.00

CALDWELL, Erskine. *Gulf Coast Stories.* 1956. Little Brn. 1st. F/NF. D10. $35.00

CALDWELL, Erskine. *Molly Cottontail.* 1958. Little Brn. stated 1st. sm 4to. VG/dj. M5. $75.00

CALDWELL, Erskine. *Sure Hand of God.* 1947. DSP. 1st. F/NF. D10. $40.00

CALDWELL, George W. *Ghost Stories of the California Missions & Rhymes...* 1939. Hollywood, CA. 1st. NF/G+. O4. $15.00

CALDWELL, Taylor. *Pillar of Iron.* 1965. Doubleday. 1st. 649p. VG/G. W2. $40.00

CALDWELL, Taylor. *There Was a Time.* 1947. Scribner. 1st. VG/VG. P3. $25.00

CALHOUN, Alfred R. *Lost in the Canyon.* 1888. NY. AL Burt. 8vo. 267p. gr cloth. G+. F7. $30.00

CALHOUN, Frances Boyd. *Miss Minerva & William Green Hill.* 1911 (1909). Reilly Britton. 212p. pict cloth. VG. M20. $20.00

CALHOUN, Mary. *Katie John.* 1960. Harper. possible 1st prt. 8vo. 134p. gr cloth. xl. G. T5. $22.00

CALHOUN & McCAFFERY. *Flower Mother.* 1972. Morrow. 1st. sm 4to. unp. NF/dj. C14. $14.00

CALISHER, Hortense. *Journal From Ellipsia.* 1965. Little Brn. 1st. NF/dj. B35. $20.00

CALISHER, Hortense. *Kissing Cousins.* 1988. Weidenfeld Nicholson. 1st. NF/dj. B35. $12.00

CALISHER, Hortense. *Tale for the Mirror.* 1962. Little Brn. 1st. NF/dj. B35. $18.00

CALLAHAN & O'HANLON. *Christianity Divided: Protestant & Roman Catholic...* 1961. Sheed Ward. 335p. G/dj. B29. $6.50

CALLAN, John F. *Military Laws of the United States 1776-1858...* nd. np. 8vo. 484p. full leather. VG. K7. $75.00

CALLAWAY, Lew L. *Montana's Righteous Hangmen: Vigilantes in Action.* 1973. Norman. 1st. inscr edit. F/NF. T11. $65.00

CALLOWAY, Cab. *Of Minnie the Moocher & Me.* 1976. Crowell. 1st. F/NF. B2. $35.00

CALNAN, Denis. *Knights in Durance.* 1966. Malta. 1st. 32 pl. VG/dj. K3. $20.00

CALVAN & HIRSHBERG. *Gardening for All Seasons.* 1893. Andover, MA. Brick House. 309p. VG. A10. $35.00

CALVERT, George H. *Charlotte Von Stein: A Memoir.* 1877. Boston. Lee Shepard. 1st. ils. 280p. teg. VG+. A25. $25.00

CALVERTON, V.F. *Man Inside.* 1936. Scribner. 1st. Vg/dj. M2. $35.00

CALVIN, Jack. *Sitka.* 1936. Arrowhead. 1st. 40p+photos. G/wrp. A17. $25.00

CALVIN, Ross. *River of the Sun: Stories of the Storied Gila.* 1946. ils. VG/partial. M17. $25.00

CALVIN, William H. *How the Shaman Stole the Moon.* 1991. NY. Bantam. 1st. 223p. M/wrp. K3. $13.00

CAM, Helen. *Law-Finders & Law-Makers in Medieval England...* 1962. London. Merlin. maroon cloth. M11. $65.00

CAM, Helen. *Selected Historical Essays of FW Maitland.* 1957. Cambridge. G/dj. M11. $85.00

CAMERON, Eleanor. *Room Made of Windows.* 1971. Little Brn. 1st. 271p. NF/VG+. P2. $30.00

CAMERON, Eleanor. *Spell Is Cast.* 1964. Atlantic Monthly. 1st. 271p. VG/G. P2. $35.00

CAMERON, Peter. *One Way or Another.* 1986. Harper Row. 1st. sgn. F/F. R13. $45.00

CAMERON, Polly. *Child's Book of Nonsense.* 1960. NY. Coward McCann. 1st. 32p. F/dj. D4. $35.00

CAMERON, Thomas W.M. *Internal Parasites of Domestic Animals.* 1934. London. Blk. 1st. VG. O3. $35.00

CAMM, F.J. *Watches: Adjustment & Repair.* nd. Brooklyn. Chemical Pub. 166p. dj. K3. $18.00

CAMP, Charles L. *Desert Rats.* 1866. Berkeley. Bancroft Lib. Friends Bancroft Lib #14. 55p. gilt red cloth. F. K7. $30.00

CAMP, John; see Sandford, John.

CAMP, Raymond R. *All Seasons Afield With Rod & Gun.* 1939. Whittlesey. 1st. sgn. 352p. VG. B11. $50.00

CAMP, Samuel G. *Art of Fishing.* 1911. NY. Outing. 1st. 177p. VG. H7. $25.00

CAMP, Walter. *Custer in '76.* 1976. Bringham Young U. 1st. 303p. VG/VG. J2. $95.00

CAMP, William Martin. *San Francisco.* 1947. Doubleday. 1st. VG/G. O4. $15.00

CAMP & WAGNER. *Plains & the Rockies.* 1937. Grabhorn. 1/600. 308p. VG. A4. $175.00

CAMPANA, Michele. *Oriental Carpets.* 1969. London. Hamlyn. 1st Eng language prt. 12mo. 66 mc pl. as new/dj. H1. $12.50

CAMPANELLA, Roy. *It's Good to Be Alive.* 1959. Boston. 1st. VG/dj. B5. $20.00

CAMPBELL, A.B. *When I Was in Patagonia.* (1953). London. Christopher Johnson. 1st. 202p. F3. $15.00

CAMPBELL, Alice. *Click of the Gate.* 1931. Farrar Rhinehart. 1st. F/dj. M15. $75.00

CAMPBELL, Bruce. *Ken Holt: Mystery of Sultan's Scimitar (#18).* 1963. Grosset Dunlap. 1st. 177p. last title in series. VG. M20. $350.00

CAMPBELL, Craig S. *Water in Landscape Architecture.* 1978. NY. ils. 128p. F/dj. B26. $17.50

CAMPBELL, Elizabeth. *Encyclopedia of World Cookery.* 1968. London. Hamlyn. G/dj. A16. $15.00

CAMPBELL, Harlan. *Monkey on a Chain.* 1973. NY. Doubleday. 1st. author's first book. NF/NF. R16. $35.00

CAMPBELL, H.J. *Beyond the Visible.* 1952. Hamish Hamilton. 1st. VG/VG. P3. $25.00

CAMPBELL, John Lord. *Lives of the Chief Justices of England.* 1894. Long Island. Ed Thompson. 3 vol (of 5). M11. $85.00

CAMPBELL, John W. *Analog 8.* 1971. Doubleday. 1st. VG/VG. P3. $18.00

CAMPBELL, John W. *Best of...* nd. SF BC. F/dj. M2. $15.00

CAMPBELL, John W. *Black Star Passes.* 1953. Fantasy. 1st. F/dj. M2. $125.00

CAMPBELL, John W. *Cloak of Aesir.* 1952. Shasta. 1st. VG/VG. P3. $75.00

CAMPBELL, John W. *Cloak of Aesir.* 1976 (1952). Hyperion. rpt. F. M2. $35.00

CAMPBELL, John W. *Incredible Planet.* 1949. Fantasy. 1st. F/dj. M2. $100.00

CAMPBELL, John W. *Mightiest Machine.* 1947. Hadley. 1st. VG/VG. P3. $250.00

CAMPBELL, John W. *Moon Is Hell.* 1951. Fantasy. 1st. sgn/#d. F/NF. P3. $200.00

CAMPBELL, Julie. *Rin Tin Tin's Rinty.* 1954. Whitman. Authorized ed. VG. W2. $30.00

CAMPBELL, Karen. *Wheel of Fortune.* 1973. Bobbs Merrill. 1st. VG/VG. P3. $15.00

CAMPBELL, Maria. *Halfbreed.* 1973. Saturday Review. 1st. F/NF. L3. $45.00

CAMPBELL, Mary Mason. *New England Butt'ry Shelf Almanac.* 1970. World. 1st. ils Tasha Tudor. 302p. cloth. VG+/dj. M20. $55.00

CAMPBELL, Mary Mason. *New England Butt'ry Shelf Cookbook.* 1968. World. 1st. ils/sgn Tasha Tudor. 192p. VG/dj. M20. $125.00

CAMPBELL, R. Wright. *Killer of Kings.* 1979. Bobbs Merrill. 1st. NF/dj. M25. $35.00

CAMPBELL, R. Wright. *Malloy's Subway.* 1981. NY. Atheneum. 1st. F/dj. M15. $45.00

CAMPBELL, Ramsey. *Ancient Images.* 1989. Scribner. 1st Am. NF/VG+. M21. $15.00

CAMPBELL, Ramsey. *Dark Companions.* 1982. Macmillan. 1st. F/F. P3. $60.00

CAMPBELL, Ramsey. *Dark Feasts.* 1987. London. 1st. F/dj. M2. $30.00

CAMPBELL, Ramsey. *Fantasy Readers Guide to Ramsey Campbell.* 1980. Cosmos/Borgo. 62p. NF/sans. R10. $15.00

CAMPBELL, Ramsey. *Incarnate.* 1983. Macmillan. 1st. F/NF. N4. $40.00

CAMPBELL, Ramsey. *Inhabitant of the Lake.* 1964. Arkham. 1st. inscr. F/dj. M2. $185.00

CAMPBELL, Ramsey. *Parasite.* 1980. Macmillan. 1st. F/dj. M2. $30.00

CAMPBELL, Robert. *Alice in La-La Land.* 1987. Poseidon. 1st. VG/VG. P3. $17.00

CAMPBELL, Robert. *In a Pig's Eye*. 1991. Pocket. 1st. as new/dj. N4. $20.00

CAMPBELL, Robert. *In La-La Land We Trust*. 1986. Mysterious. 1st. F/F. M25. $35.00

CAMPBELL, Robert. *Nibbled to Death by Ducks*. 1989. Pocket. 1st. F/F. P3. $18.00

CAMPBELL, Ruth. *Small Fry & the Winged Horse*. 1927. Volland. later. ils Gustaf Tenggren. NF/G. M5. $85.00

CAMPBELL, Sam. *Beloved Rascals*. 1957. Bobbs Merrill. 1st. sgn. VG. B11. $25.00

CAMPBELL, Thoma s J. *Jesuits 1534-1921*. 1921. Encyclopedia Pr. 937p. gilt cloth. A17. $25.00

CAMPBELL, Thomas. *Life of Mrs Siddons*. 1972. NY. Blom. 378p. wrp. A17. $12.50

CAMPEN, Richard N. *Architecture of the Western Reserve, 1800-1900*. 1971. Cleveland. 1st. 260p. VG+/dj. B18. $75.00

CAMPION, Lynn. *Training & Showing the Cutting Horse*. 1990. Prentice Hall. 1st. F/F. O3. $19.00

CAMPION & PULLINGER. *Piano*. 1994. NY. Miramax/Hyperion. 1st. F/F. B4. $50.00

CAMPOLO, Tony. *How to Rescue the Earth Without Worshiping Nature*. 1992. Nelson. 1st. sgn. VG/dj. B29. $8.50

CAMUS, Albert. *Happy Death*. 1972. Knopf. 1st. trans Richard Howard. F/dj. Q1. $60.00

CAMUS, Albert. *Outsider*. 1946. London. Hamish Hamilton. 1st Eng trans. author's 1st book. F/dj. Q1. $400.00

CANCIAN, Frank. *Change & Uncertainty in Peasant Economy*. 1972. Stanford. 1st. 208p. dj. F3. $20.00

CANFIELD, Cook. *Lucky Terrell: Secret Mission (#3)*. 1943. Grosset Dunlap. 210p. cloth. VG+/dj (lists to #2). M20. $16.00

CANFIELD, Cook. *Lucky Terrell: Springboard to Tokyo (#5)*. 1943. Grosset Dunlap. 210p. VG/dj (lists to #6). M20. $20.00

CANIFF, W. *History of the Province of Ontario*. 1872. Toronto. 672p. new cloth. NF. M4. $30.00

CANIN, Ethan. *Blue River*. 1991. Houghton Mifflin. 1st. author's 2nd novel. VG/VG. L1. $35.00

CANIN, Ethan. *Emperor of the Air*. 1988. Houghton Mifflin. 1st. author's 1st book. F/dj. A24. $75.00

CANNADINE, David. *Pleasure of the Past*. 1989. NY. 1st. dj. T9. $16.00

CANNE & BROWNE. *Treasury of Scripture Knowledge*. 1982. MacDonald. VG. B29. $9.50

CANNING, John. *50 Great Horror Stories*. 1971. Bell. 1st. F/dj. M2. $18.00

CANNING, Victor. *Dragon Tree*. 1958. Sloane. 1st. NF/NF. P3. $45.00

CANNING, Victor. *Mr Finchley Goes to Paris*. 1938. Carrick Evans. 1st. VG/fair. P3. $25.00

CANNING, Victor. *Rainbird Pattern*. 1972. Morrow. 1st Am. NF/VG. M22. $15.00

CANNON, Curt; see Hunter, Evan.

CANNON & GRIFFITHS. *Oxford Illustrated History of British Monarchy*. 1988. ils. VG/VG. M17. $30.00

CANTINE, Marguerite. *Beggar T Bear*. 1981. Cantine Kilpatrick. photos. 62p. F/wrp. H1. $17.50

CANTWELL, R. *Alexander Wilson: Naturalist & Pioneer*. 1961. 1st. VG/VG. M17. $35.00

CANTY, Kevin. *Stranger in This World*. 1994. Doubleday. 1st. F/F. R14. $35.00

CANTY, Thomas. *Monster at Christmas*. 1985. Donald Grant. 1st. 1/1050. sgn. F/dj. M2. $30.00

CAPE, Tony. *Cambridge Theorem*. 1990. Doubleday. 1st. NF/NF. P3. $20.00

CAPEK, Abe. *Chinese Stone Pictures*. 1962. London. Spring. ils. gilt cloth. F/F/case. W3. $65.00

CAPEK, Karel. *Absolute at Large*. 1974 (1927). Hyperion. rpt. F. M2. $25.00

CAPON, Edward. *Chinese Painting*. 1979. NY. Phaidon/Dutton. ils. F/wrp. W3. $32.00

CAPOTE, Truman. *Answered Prayers: Unfinished Novel*. 1987. Random. 1st. NF. T12. $15.00

CAPOTE, Truman. *Dogs Bark*. 1973. Random. 1st. F/dj. Q1. $60.00

CAPOTE, Truman. *Grass Harp*. 1951. Random. 1st. 2nd issue bdg (fine-grained beige cloth). F/clip. Q1. $100.00

CAPOTE, Truman. *Grove Day*. 1969. NY. 1st. fwd James Michener. VG/VG. B5. $40.00

CAPOTE, Truman. *In Cold Blood*. 1965. Random. 1st. F/F. Q1. $75.00

CAPOTE, Truman. *In Cold Blood*. 1965. Random. 1st. F/VG. M19. $25.00

CAPOTE, Truman. *Other Voices, Other Rooms*. 1948. Random. 1st. author's 1st book. VG+/G. D10. $175.00

CAPOTE, Truman. *Thanksgiving Visitor*. 1967. NY. 1st. F/box. B5. $35.00

CAPPER, Mary. *Memoir of..., Late of Birmingham, England, a Minister...* nd. Phil. Assn Friends Diffusion Religious & Useful Knowledge. V3. $16.00

CAPPON, Lester J. *History of Expedition Under Command of Capts Lewis & Clark*. 1970. NY. Columbia. as new/stiff wrp. O7. $25.00

CAPPS, Benjamin. *Great Chiefs*. 1980. Time Life. 4th. A19. $20.00

CAPPS, Benjamin. *Indians*. 1975. Time Life. A19. $20.00

CAPPS, Benjamin. *Warren Wagon Train Raid, the First Complete Account...* 1974. Dial. 1st. 304p. VG/VG. J2. $70.00

CAPPS, Benjamin. *Woman of the People*. 1966. DSP. 1st. F/VG+. B4. $25.00

CAPUTO, Philip. *Horn of Africa*. 1980. HRW. 1/250. sgn. F/acetate dj/case. R14. $100.00

CARAS, Roger A. *North American Mammals*. 1967. NY. ils/pl. 577p. VG. S15. $12.00

CARAS, Roger A. *Panther*. 1969. Little Brn. 1st. sgn. VG/VG. B11. $40.00

CARD, Orson Scott. *Abyss*. 1989. London. Legend/Century. 1st hc. F/F. M21. $35.00

CARD, Orson Scott. *Lost Boys*. 1992. Harper Collins. 1st. F/F. N4. $30.00

CARD, Orson Scott. *Prentice Alvin*. 1989. Tor. 1st. sgn. F/F. M23. $45.00

CARD, Orson Scott. *Red Prophet*. 1988. Tor. 1st. sgn. F/F. M23. $50.00

CARD, Orson Scott. *Songmaster*. 1980. NY. Dial. 1st. rem mk. NF/VG+. M23. $100.00

CARD, Orson Scott. *Speaker for the Dead*. 1986. NY. Tor. 1st. sgn. xl. VG/NF. M23. $75.00

CARELL, Paul. *Scorched Earth*. 1966. Boston. 1st. VG/VG. B5. $75.00

CAREY, Arthur A. *Memoirs of a Murder Man*. 1930. Doubleday Doran. 1st. VG. P3. $20.00

CAREY, Mary. *Gremlins Storybook*. 1984. Golden. 1st. as new. T12. $16.00

CAREY, Peter. *Fat Man in History & Other Stories*. 1980. Random. 1st Am. F/NF. M25. $45.00

CAREY, Peter. *Illywhacker*. 1985. Harper Row. 1st. F/F. M19. $25.00

CAREY, Peter. *Oscar & Lucinda*. 1988. Harper Row. ARC. sgn. F/wrp. B3. $40.00

CAREY, Peter. *Unusual Life of Tristan Smith*. 1995. Knopf. 1st. sgn. F/dj. Q1. $45.00

CAREY, Rosa Nouchette. *Our Bessie*. ca 1900. AL Burt. 1st thus. ils. 343p. VG+. A25. $12.00

CARFAX, Catherine. *Silence With Voices*. 1969. Macmillan. 1st. VG/VG. P3. $20.00

CARGILL, Morris. *Ian Fleming Introduces Jamaica.* 1965. Andre Deutsch. 1st. VG/G. P3. $30.00

CARIGAN, William. *Staves for Louisville.* 1981. Lexington. Juniper. 1st. inscr. F/F. B11. $55.00

CARKEET, David. *Greatest Slump of All Time.* 1984. Harper Row. 1st. F/F. M25. $35.00

CARLETON, Mark A. *Small Grains.* 1920. Macmillan. 699p. VG. A10. $28.00

CARLEY, K. *Minnesota in the Civil War.* 1961. Minneapolis. 1st. ils/maps. 168p. F/dj. M4. $20.00

CARLISLE, D.T. *Belvidere Hounds.* 1935. Derrydale. 1st. G. O3. $75.00

CARLISLE & STYRON. *Modern Russian Poetry.* 1972. Viking. 1st. 210p. cloth. F/F. D4. $35.00

CARLSON, E.A. *Genes, Radiation & Society. Life & Work of HJ Muller.* 1981. Cornell. 1st. ils. 457p. VG. K3. $15.00

CARLSON, Ed. *Look Back Once in Awhile.* 1981. Phoenix, AZ. self pub. sgn. A19. $20.00

CARLSON, John Roy. *Plotters.* 1946. Dutton. 1st. F/VG. B2. $30.00

CARLSON, Natalie Savage. *Family Under the Bridge.* (1958). Harper Row. 8vo. ils Garth Williams. 97p. G+. T5. $25.00

CARLSON, Raymond. *Flowering Cactus.* 1954. NY. ils/photos. 96p. VG/dj. B26. $20.00

CARLSON, Ron. *News of the World.* 1987. Norton. 1st. F/F. H11. $45.00

CARLSON, Victor I. *Matisse as a Draughtsman.* 1971. Baltimore Mus Art. 191p. 83 full-p pl. G. A17. $20.00

CARLSON, William. *Sunrise West.* 1981. Doubleday. 1st. F/dj. M2. $12.00

CARLTON, Charles. *Court of the Orphans.* 1974. Leicester. G. M11. $45.00

CARLYON, Richard. *Dark Lord of Pengersick.* 1980. FSG. 1st. F/F. P3. $15.00

CARMEL, Herman. *Black Days, White Nights.* 1984. Hippocrene. 323p. VG/dj. S3. $25.00

CARMER, Carl. *Susquehanna.* 1955. Rinehart. 2nd. sm 8vo. 493p. F/G. H1. $22.50

CARMICHAEL, Harry; see Creasey, John.

CARNEGIE, Andrew. *American Four-in-Hand in Britain.* 1884. NY. ils. 338p. G. B18. $35.00

CARNEGIE, D. *Among the Matabele.* 1970 (1894). Negro U. rpt. 128p. VG. W1. $25.00

CARNELL, John. *New Writings in Science Fiction 15.* 1969. Dennis Dobson. 1st. VG/VG. P3. $30.00

CARNER, Gary. *Jazz Performers: An Annotated Bibliography...* 1990. Westport. Greenwood. 1st. 364p. F/sans. B2. $50.00

CARNOT, S. *Reflections on the Motive Power of Heat.* 1943. NY. Am Soc Mechanical Engineers. 107p. box. K3. $30.00

CAROLL, HARGROVE & LUMMIS. *Women of the Cloth: A New Opportunity for the Churches.* 1983. Harper Row. 276p. F/dj. B14. $35.00

CARPENTER, Edward. *From Adam's Peak to Elephanta: Sketches in Ceylon & India.* (1910). London. Swan. new revised. ils/photos. 370p. VG. M12. $30.00

CARPENTER, Edwin H. *Printers & Publishers in Southern California 1850-1876.* 1964. La Siesta. 1st. inscr. ils/index. 48p. F. B19. $60.00

CARPENTER, F.B. *Six Months at the White House.* 1866. NY. 1st. F. O8. $32.50

CARPENTER, Frances. *Holiday in Washington.* 1958. Knopf. 1st. sgn. 207p. VG/dj. M20. $20.00

CARPENTER, Frances. *People From the Sky.* 1972. Doubleday. 1st. ils. 107p. F/dj. W3. $46.00

CARPENTER, Frank G. *Cairo to Kisumu: Egypt, the Sudan, Kenya Colony.* 1925. Doubleday Page. 96 pl/2 fld maps. 313p. teg. G. W1. $12.00

CARPENTER, Humphrey. *Tolkien: A Biography.* 1977. Houghton Mifflin. 1st. VG/VG. P3. $20.00

CARPENTER, Iris. *No Woman's World.* 1946. Houghton Mifflin. 1st. 378p. VG. A25. $28.00

CARPENTER, R.A. *Assessing Tropical Forest Lands.* 1981. Dublin. Tycooly Internat'l. 1st. 337p. dj. B1. $30.00

CARPENTER, William B. *Microscopes & Its Revelations.* 1881. London. Churchill. 6th. 882p. VG. K3. $60.00

CARPENTER & GROSSBERG. *Neutral Networks for Vision & Image Processing.* 1992. Cambridge, MA. MIT. lg 8vo. 467p. prt stiff wrp. G1. $40.00

CARPENTER & NASMYTH. *Moon: Considered As a Planet, a World, A Satellite.* 1874. London. John Murray. 408p. VG/VG. K5. $400.00

CARPENTER. *History of American Schoolbooks.* 1963. PA U. 322p. VG/VG. A4. $165.00

CARPENTIER, Alejo. *Kingdom of This World.* 1957. Knopf. 1st. NF/dj. M25. $150.00

CARR, Archie. *Handbook of Turtles.* 1983 (1952). Cornell. 9th. 542p. F. S15. $40.00

CARR, Caleb. *Alienist.* 1994. Random. 1st. F/F. B4. $100.00

CARR, Caleb. *Casing the Promised Land.* 1980. Harper Row. 1st. sm stp B on half title. F/NF. L3. $150.00

CARR, Charles. *Colonists of Space.* 1954. Ward Lock. VG/VG. P3. $20.00

CARR, Frank G.G. *Sailing Barges.* 1931. London. Hodder Stoughton. 1st. 68 pl. 328p. T7. $85.00

CARR, Jayge. *Treasure in the Heart of the Maze.* 1985. Doubleday. 1st. F/dj. M2. $15.00

CARR, John Dickson. *Bride of Newgate.* 1950. Harper. 1st. VG/G. P3. $25.00

CARR, John Dickson. *Captain Cut-Throat.* 1955. Harper. 1st. F/F. P3. $80.00

CARR, John Dickson. *He Wouldn't Kill Patience.* 1944. Morrow. 1st. NF/dj. M15. $250.00

CARR, John Dickson. *Scandal at High Chimneys.* 1959. Hamish Hamilton. 1st. NF/NF. P3. $35.00

CARR, Robert Spencer. *Beyond Infinity.* 1951. Fantasy. 1/350. sgn/#d. F/dj. M2. $100.00

CARR, SAUNDERS & STOM. *Geology of the Terrestrial Planets.* 1984. NASA SP-469. 317p. G. D8. $25.00

CARR, Terry. *Infinite Arena.* 1977. Thomas Nelson. 1st. VG/VG. P3. $18.00

CARR, Terry. *Universe 13.* 1983. Doubleday. 1st. F/F. P3. $25.00

CARR, Terry. *Year's Finest Fantasy.* 1979. Berkley Putnam. 1st. F/F. P3. $20.00

CARR, William H. *Desert Parade.* 1947. NY. 1st. ils. map ep. VG/rpr. B26. $15.00

CARR & CARR. *Fox-Hunting.* 1982. Oxford. 1st. F/F. O3. $10.00

CARRASCO, David. *To Change Place.* 1991. Niwot. CO U. 1st. 254p. dj. F3. $30.00

CARREL, Alexis. *Voyage to Lourdes.* 1950. NY. 1st. 52p. cloth. G. B5. $25.00

CARRICK, Valery. *Valery Carrick's Picture Folk-Tales.* 1928. Stokes. ils. 90p. VG/tattered dj. D1. $85.00

CARRIER, Jim. *Down the Colorado.* 1989. Rinehart. 8vo. 141p. stiff wrp. F7. $17.50

CARRIER, Robert. *Connoisseur's Cookbook.* 1954. Hanover. 1st Am. VG/G. B10. $35.00

CARRIER, Robert. *Cooking for You.* 1973. Viking. 1st. 4to. mc photos. dj. A16. $17.50

CARRIER, Robert. *Great Dishes of the World.* 1964. Random. 1st Am. photos. 297p. VG/fair. B10. $25.00

CARRIGHAR, Sally. *Wild Heritage.* 1965. Houghton Mifflin. dj. A19. $20.00

CARRILLO, Leo. *California I Love.* 1961. Englewood Cliffs. Prentice Hall. 1st. 8vo. 280p. half cloth. F/VG. T10. $35.00

CARRINGTON, Grant. *Time's Fool.* 1981. Doubleday. 1st. F/F. P3. $13.00

CARROLL, Alice. *Complete Guide to Modern Knitting & Crocheting.* 1943. NY. Wise. 1st. ils/photos. 310p. VG+. A25. $18.00

CARROLL, James. *Supply of Heroes.* 1986. Dutton. ne. F/F. W2. $20.00

CARROLL, John. *Benteen-Golden Letters on Custer & His Last Battle.* 1974. Liveright. 1st ltd. 1/27. sgn. 312p. VG. J2. $875.00

CARROLL, John. *Custer Trail, a Narrative of the Line of March of Troops...* 1983. Clark. 1/350. sgn. map/photos. 148p. VG. J2. $135.00

CARROLL, John. *Two Battles of the Little Big Horn.* 1974. Liveright. 1/1000. sgn. 214p. w/fld painting by Bjorklund. as new/case. J2. $275.00

CARROLL, Jonathan. *Land of Laughs.* 1980. 1st. author's 1st book. F/NF. M19. $45.00

CARROLL, Kay. *Han Solo's Rescue.* 1983. Random Pop-Up Book. F. P3. $10.00

CARROLL, Lewis. *Adventures in Wonderland.* 1932. Lippincott. reduced format ed. ils Gertrude Kay/John Tenniel. cloth. R5. $100.00

CARROLL, Lewis. *Alice in Wonderland, Through the Looking-Glass & Other...* 1929. London. ils Carroll. 335p. VG. B18. $25.00

CARROLL, Lewis. *Alice in Wonderland.* (1945). Grosset Dunlap. animated Julian Wehr/4 movables. VG/dj. D1. $475.00

CARROLL, Lewis. *Alice in Wonderland.* ca 1915. London. Blackie. ils Frank Adams. 12mo. top edge gr. gr cloth. R5. $100.00

CARROLL, Lewis. *Alice in Wonderland.* ca 1950. London. Juvenile Prod. ils AA Nash/24 mc pl. 4to. dj. R5. $125.00

CARROLL, Lewis. *Alice in Wonderland.* 1921. London. Raphael Tuck. 1st thus. ils AL Bowley. gr cloth/pict label. R5. $125.00

CARROLL, Lewis. *Alice in Wonderland.* 1934. Rand McNally. ils. VG. P3. $20.00

CARROLL, Lewis. *Alice in Wonderland.* 1969. London. Dean. 1st thus. ils/retold Rene Cloke. 4to. pict brd. unused. R5. $150.00

CARROLL, Lewis. *Alice's Adventures in Wonderland.* 1908. London. Thomas Nelson. 1st. ils Harry Rountree. 4to. teg. bl cloth. F. R5. $150.00

CARROLL, Lewis. *Alice's Adventures in Wonderland.* 1919. London. Humphrey Milford. ils AE Jackson. 8vo. teg. gr pict cloth. R5. $200.00

CARROLL, Lewis. *Alice's Adventures in Wonderland.* 1922. London. Ward Lock. ils MW Tarrant. 8vo. gray cloth. dj. R5. $200.00

CARROLL, Lewis. *Alice's Adventures in Wonderland.* 1945. London. Arthur Barron. 1st. ils Harry Riley. 12mo. gray cloth. dj. R5. $150.00

CARROLL, Lewis. *Alice's Adventures in Wonderland/Through the Looking Glass.* 1993. London. Folio Soc. 8th. 2 vol. gilt red cloth. F/case. T10. $60.00

CARROLL, Lewis. *Hunting of the Snark.* 1970. NY. Watts. 1st Am. 48p. NF/dj. D4. $55.00

CARROLL, Lewis. *Philosopher's Alice.* 1974. St Martin. intro Heath. xl. VG. N1. $12.00

CARROLL, Lewis. *Pig-Tale.* 1975. Little Brn. 1st thus. 30p. VG+/dj. M20. $25.00

CARROLL, Lewis. *Useful & Instructive Poetry.* 1954. Macmillan. 1st. F/F. D4. $45.00

CARROLL, Lewis. *Walt Disney's Alice in Wonderland.* 1951. Whitman. Cozy Corner series. ils Walt Disney Studio. VG. M5. $25.00

CARROLL, Paul. *Poem in Its Skin.* 1968. Follett. 1st. F/NF. V1. $25.00

CARROLL & CARROLL. *Danny & the Poi Pup.* 1965. Walck. 1st. F/VG. M5. $22.00

CARROLL & COLEMAN. *New Singing Time: Book of Songs for Little Children.* 1950. John Day. 1st. sm 4to. 32p. tan cloth. NF. C14. $14.00

CARROLL & DIPPIE. *Bards of the Little Big Horn.* 1978. Guidon. 1st. 1/350. sgn/ils Dave Powell. 344p. VG. J2. $115.00

CARROLL & GARDNER. *More Annotated Alice.* 1990. Random. 1st. 4to. 400p. F/dj. T10. $50.00

CARRUTH, Hayden. *For You — Poems.* 1970. New Directions. 1st. sgn. F/F. R14. $60.00

CARRUTH, Vance. *Teton Sketches of Summer.* 1969. Johnson Pub. 1st. sgn. 30p. VG/torn. J2. $35.00

CARRYL, Charles. *Admiral's Caravan.* 1892. Century. 1st. ils Reginald Birch. VG. M5. $95.00

CARSON, Gerald. *Social History of Bourbon.* 1963. NY. 1st. ils. 280p. VG/dj. B18. $17.50

CARSON, James. *Saddle Boys in the Grand Canyon.* 1913. Cupples Leon. 12mo. VG. F7. $37.50

CARSON, John F. *Boys Who Vanished.* 1959. DSP. 1st. 212p. cloth. VG/dj. M20. $15.00

CARSON, Mina. *Settlement Folk.* 1990. Chicago. 1st. as new/dj. V4. $20.00

CARSON, Rachel. *Edge of the Sea.* 1956. Houghton Mifflin. 1st. NF/VG. M19. $25.00

CARSON, Rachel. *Sea Around Us.* 1951. Oxford. 1st. gr pict brd. NF/NF later state. M24. $100.00

CARSON, Rachel. *Silent Spring.* 1962. Houghton Mifflin. 1st. F/NF. Q1. $150.00

CARSON, Rachel. *Under the Sea-Wind: A Naturalist's Picture of Ocean Life.* 1952. NY. Oxford. revised. 314p. VG/dj. A25. $18.00

CARSON, Robin. *Dawn of Time.* 1957. Holt. 1st. VG/worn. M2. $18.00

CARTER, Angela. *Fireworks.* 1981. Harper Row. 1st Am. F/NF. A24. $25.00

CARTER, Angela. *Love.* 1971. Hart Davis. 1st. VG/VG. P3. $50.00

CARTER, Angela. *Nights at the Circus.* 1985. Viking. 1st. F/NF. A24. $25.00

CARTER, Angela. *Shadow Dance.* 1966. Heinemann. 1st. VG/VG. P3. $100.00

CARTER, Clarence Edwin. *Territorial Papers of the US, Territory of Michigan 1805-37.* 1942-1945. GPO. 3 vol. D11. $100.00

CARTER, G.S. *General Zoology of the Invertebrates.* 1948. London. Sidgwick Jackson. 3rd. 13 pl. clip dj. B1. $35.00

CARTER, Henry. *Methodist Heritage.* 1951. Abingdon-Cokesbury. 246p. VG/dj. B29. $9.00

CARTER, Howard. *Tomb of Tutankhamen.* 1972. NY. Excalibur. 1st Am. 238p. NF/dj. W1. $22.00

CARTER, Jared. *Work for the Night Is Coming.* 1980. Macmillan. 1st. assn copy. F/dj. V1. $25.00

CARTER, Jimmy. *Always a Reckoning.* 1995. Times Books. 1st. sgn. F/F. S13. $55.00

CARTER, Jimmy. *Blood of Abraham: Insights to the Middle East.* 1985. Houghton Mifflin. 1st. sgn. VG/VG. A23. $75.00

CARTER, Jimmy. *Living Faith.* 1996. Times Books. 1st. sgn. F/F. A23. $75.00

CARTER, Jimmy. *Outdoor Journal.* 1988. Bantam. 1st. VG/VG. A23. $75.00

CARTER, Jimmy. *Talking Peace: A Vision for the Next Generation.* 1993. Dutton. 1st. sgn. VG/VG. A23. $75.00

CARTER, Jimmy. *Turning Point.* 1992. Times Books. 1st. sgn. F/F. A23. $75.00

CARTER, Lin. *Dreams From R'lyeh.* 1975. Arkham. 1st. F/dj. T2. $35.00

CARTER, Lin. *Invisible Death.* 1975. Doubleday. 1st. F/F. P3. $15.00

CARTER, Lin. *Man Who Loved Mars.* 1973. Wht Lion. hc. VG/G. P3. $17.00

CARTER, Lin. *Valley Where Time Stood Still.* 1974. Doubleday. 1st. NF/NF. P3. $20.00

CARTER, Lin. *Volcano Ogre.* 1976. Doubleday. 1st. F/F. M2/P3. $15.00

CARTER, M. *Isabella Stewart Gardner & Fenway Court.* 1972. photos. VG/VG. M17. $20.00

CARTER, Paul. *Road to Botany Bay.* 1988. NY. Knopf. 1st Am. 384p. half cloth. as new/dj. P4. $23.00

CARTER, Samuel. *Final Fortress.* 1980. 354p. O8. $12.50

CARTER, Youngman. *Mr Campion's Quarry.* 1971. Morrow. 1st. VG/VG. P3. $18.00

CARTIER, Ed. *Known & the Unknown.* 1977. De La Ree. NF/NF. P3. $35.00

CARTIER, John O. *Getting the Most Out of Modern Wildfowling.* 1974. NY. 396p. dj. A17. $15.00

CARTIN, Hazel. *Elijah.* 1980. St Martin. 1st. inscr. F/NF clip. L3. $75.00

CARTWRIGHT, H. Mills. *Photogravure: A TB on the Machine & Hand-Prt Processes.* 1930. Boston. 142p. A17. $12.50

CARUS, Titus Lucretius. *Of the Nature of Things.* 1957. LEC. 1st thus. 1/1500. ils/sgn Paul Landacre. F/remnant glassine/case. Q1. $125.00

CARUTHERS, William. *Loafing Along Death Valley Trails.* 1951. Death Valley Pub. 1st. VG/sans. O4. $15.00

CARVEL, John L. *Stephen of Linthouse.* 1950. Glasgow. Stephen & Sons. ils 311p. torn dj. T7. $50.00

CARVER, Jeffrey A. *Infinity Link.* 1984. Bluejay. 1st. sgn. F/F. P3. $25.00

CARVER, Jeffrey A. *Rapture Effect.* 1987. Tor. 1st. RS. F/F. P3. $20.00

CARVER, Raymond. *Carver Country: World of Raymond Carver.* 1990. Scribner. 1st. F/torn. A18. $35.00

CARVER, Raymond. *My Crow.* 1984. Ewert. 1/150. ils Thomas Berwick. F/wrp. V1. $30.00

CARVER, Raymond. *New Path to the Waterfall.* 1989. Atlantic Monthly. 1st. ils Tess Gallagher. F/NF. B3. $50.00

CARVER, Raymond. *Put Yourself in My Shoes.* 1974. Capra. 1st trade. sgn. F/wrp. B2. $300.00

CARVER, Raymond. *River.* 1986. Concord, NH. 1/26. sgn. w/sgn broadside by John Jagel. F. V1. $250.00

CARVER, Raymond. *Ultramarine.* 1986. Random. 1st. sgn. F/F. D10. $175.00

CARVER, Raymond. *What We Talk About When We Talk About Love.* 1981. Knopf. 1st. F/dj. B4/Q1. $200.00

CARVER, Raymond. *Where I'm Calling From: New & Selected Stories.* 1988. Atlantic Monthly. 1st. F/dj. A18. $40.00

CARVER, Raymond. *Where Water Comes Together With Other Water.* 1985. Random. 1st. NF/dj. D10. $75.00

CARVIC, Heron. *Miss Seeton Sings.* 1973. Harper Row. VG. P3. $22.00

CARVIC, Heron. *Picture Miss Seeton.* 1968. Geoffrey Bles. 1st. VG/G. P3. $25.00

CARY, Diana Serra. *Hollywood Posse: Story of a Gallant Band of Horsemen...* 1975. Houghton Mifflin. 1st. 268p. VG/VG. J2. $75.00

CARY, Gillie. *Uncle Jerry's Platform & Other Christmas Stories.* 1895. Boston. 1st. lg 12mo. VG. C8. $60.00

CARY, Joyce. *Cock Jarvis.* 1974. London. Michael Joseph. true 1st. author's last/unfinished novel. F/F. D10. $50.00

CARY, Joyce. *Prisoner of Grace.* 1952. Michael Joseph. 1st. 398p. VG+/dj. M20. $38.00

CARYLE, Thomas. *Oliver Cromwell's Letters & Speeches.* 1871. Chapman Hall. 5 vol. 8vo. decor brn cloth. VG. B22. $15.00

CASAL, U. *Some Notes on the Sakazuki.* 1940. Tokyo. Asiatic Soc Japan. rpt. 186p. VG/wrp. W3. $135.00

CASE, David. *Third Grave.* 1981. Arkham. 1st. F/dj. M2. $25.00

CASE, Shirley J. *Origins of Christian Supernaturalism.* 1946. Chicago. 239p. VG/torn. B29. $7.00

CASEY, John. *American Romance.* 1977. Atheneum. 1st. VG/dj. A20. $25.00

CASEY, John. *Spartina.* 1989. Knopf. 1st. inscr. F/F. D10. $85.00

CASEY, John. *Testimony & Demeanor.* 1979. Knopf. 1st. F/F. B3. $75.00

CASEY, Robert J. *Baghdad & Points East.* ca 1930. London. Hutchinson. 8vo. 16 pl. xl. VG. W1. $24.00

CASEY, Robert J. *Black Hills.* 1949. Bobbs Merrill. map. VG. A19. $55.00

CASEY, Robert J. *Easter Island: Home of the Scornful Gods.* 1931. Bobbs Merrill. 8vo. 43 photos. 337p. bl cloth. P4. $36.00

CASEY, Robert J. *Torpedo Junction: With the Pacific Fleet From Pearl Harbor.* 1942. Indianapolis. 1st. photos/map. 423p. VG/G. S16. $27.50

CASHIN, Hershel V. *Under Fire With the 10th Calvary.* 1970. NY. Bellwether. rpt. 361p. F/VG+. B4. $65.00

CASHMAN, A.W. *Vice-Regal Cowboy.* 1957. Edmonton. 1st prt. inscr. 199p. P4. $35.00

CASIMER & VAN VLECK. *Cherwell-Simon Memorial Lectures 1961 & 1962.* 1962. London. Oliver Boyd. 1st. VG. K3. $20.00

CASPARY, Vera. *Weeping & the Laughter.* 1950. Little Brn. 1st. VG/VG. P3. $35.00

CASS, Bevan. *History of the Sixth Marine Division.* 1948. WA, DC. 1st. ils/maps/ awards. 262p. VG. S16. $95.00

CASSANDRA, Knye; see Disch, Thomas.

CASSERLY, Gordon. *Elephant God.* 1921. Putnam. 1st. VG. M2. $15.00

CASSIDAY, Bruce. *Floater.* 1960. Abelard Schuman. VG/VG. P3. $20.00

CASSIDY, S.M. *Elements of Practical Coal Mining.* 1973. NY. Soc Mining Engineers Am Inst Mining. 614p. cloth. NF/dj. D8. $35.00

CASSILL, R.V. *Eagle on the Coin.* 1950. 1st. author's 1st book. F/VG. M19. $35.00

CASSIN, J. *Illustrations of California, Texas, Oregon...* 1991 (1856). Austin. TX Hist Assn. 1/250. facsimile. 8vo. 298p. half leather. F/F case. M12. $150.00

CASSIRER, Ernst. *Substance & Function & Einstein's Theory of Relativity.* 1923. Open Court. 8vo. 465p. G/tattered. K5. $25.00

CASSON, Herbert N. *History of the Telephone.* 1910. McClurg. 1st. ils. 8vo. 315p. VG. K3. $20.00

CASSON, Lionel. *Ancient Egypt.* 1978. NY. Time. 11th. 191p. VG. W1. $10.00

CASSON, Lionel. *Ancient Mariners: Seafarers & Sea Fighters...* 1968. Macmillan. 286p. VG/dj. P4. $30.00

CASTANEDA, Carlos. *Fire From Within.* 1984. S&S. 1st. F/dj. B4. $45.00

CASTANEDA, Carlos. *Tales of Power.* (1974). S&S. 1st. 207p. VG/dj. F3. $20.00

CASTANEDA, Pedro. *Journey of Coronado.* 1966. Readex Microprint. rpt. 8vo. F. F7. $30.00

CASTLE, Frederick. *Gilbert Green: The Real Right Way to Dress for Spring...* 1986. McPherson. 1st. F/VG+. A20. $20.00

CASTLE, Jeffery Lloyd. *Satelite E One.* 1954. Eyre Spottiswoode. VG/G. P3. $10.00

CASTLE, Lewis. *Cactaceous Plants: Their History & Culture.* 1974 (1884). Annapolis. ils. 94p. B26. $15.00

CASTLE & CASTLE. *Our Sentimental Garden.* 1914. Phil. Lippincott. 1st Am. ils Chas Robinson. 4to. gilt gr cloth. dj. R5. $275.00

CASTRO, Michael. *Interpreting the Indian.* 1983. Albuquerque. NM U. 1st. F/dj. L3. $50.00

CASWELL, J.E. *Arctic Frontiers. United States Explorations in Far North.* 1956. Norman, OK. 1st. photos/maps. 232p. F/dj. M4. $20.00

CATANZARO, Angela. *Italian Desserts & Antipasto.* 1958. NY. Liveright. VG/dj. A16. $15.00

CATHER, Willa. *April Twilights.* 1923. NY. Knopf. 1st trade. quarter gr cloth/patterned brd. F/sans. M24. $100.00

CATHER, Willa. *December Night: Scene From Willa Cather's Novel...* 1933. Knopf. 1st. ils. fancy brd. F/NF. A18. $40.00

CATHER, Willa. *Lucy Gayheart.* 1935. Knopf. 1st. 1/25000. F/NF. M24. $100.00

CATHER, Willa. *Obscure Destinies.* 1932. Knopf. 1st. gr cloth. F/VG clip (lowered before pub). M24. $100.00

CATHER, Willa. *Sapphira & the Slave Girl.* 1940. Knopf. ARC. F/F. D10. $175.00

CATHER, Willa. *Sapphira & the Slave Girl.* 1940. Knopf. 1st. F/NF. M24. $75.00

CATHER, Willa. *Shadows on the Rock.* 1931. Knopf. 1st. NF/VG. M23. $75.00

CATICH, Edward M. *Eric Gill, His Social & Artistic Roots.* 1964. IA City. Prairie Pr. 1st. M/dj. B24. $100.00

CATLIN, George. *Breath of Life; or, Mal-Respiration & Its Effects...* 1872. NY. John Wiley. 8vo. 76p. cloth. M1. $150.00

CATLIN, George. *Catlin's North American Indian Portfolio.* 1970. Chicago. Sage. 1/1000. facsimile 1844 London. stiff portfolio. B24. $500.00

CATLIN, George. *North American Indians: Being Letters & Notes...* 1926. Edinburgh. Jonn Grant. 2 vol. ils/fld map. maroon T-grain cloth. F. K7. $950.00

CATTELL, Ann. *Mind Juggler & Other Ghost Stories.* 1966. Exposition. 1st. VG/VG. P3. $15.00

CATTELL, Henry. *Post-Mortem Pathology: A Manual...* 1903. Phil. 1st. ils. 372p. A13. $100.00

CATTON, Bruce. *Glory Road: Bloody Route From Fredericksburg to Gettysburg.* 1952. Doubleday. 1st. 416p. cloth. NF/dj. M8. $35.00

CATTON, Bruce. *Mr Lincoln's Army.* 1951. Doubleday. 1st. 372p. VG/dj. O8. $21.50

CATTON, Bruce. *Reflections on the Civil War.* 1981. NY. 1st. ils John Geyser. F/dj. M4. $30.00

CATTON, Bruce. *Waiting for the Morning Train: An American Boyhood.* 1972. Doubleday. 1/250. sgn/#d. F/sans/case. Q1. $75.00

CAUDILL, Rebecca. *Come Along!* 1969. HRW. 1st. 32p. F/F. D4. $25.00

CAUFFMAN, Stanley. *Witchfinders.* 1934. Penn. 1st. VG. M2. $22.00

CAUMERY. *Becassine Voyage.* 1923 (1921). Paris. Gautier. Semaine de Suzette. ils Pinchon. VG. M5. $90.00

CAUNITZ, William J. *Exceptional Clearance.* 1991. Crown. 1st. F/F. N4. $20.00

CAUNITZ, William J. *One Police Plaza.* 1984. Crown. 1st. author's 1st book. F/F. H11. $50.00

CAUNITZ, William J. *Suspects.* 1986. NY. Crown. 1st. F/F. R14. $25.00

CAUSLEY, Charles. *Early in the Morning.* 1986. Viking. 1st. ils Michael Foreman/ music Anthony Castro. F/F. D4. $30.00

CAVALLO, A.S. *Tapestries of Europe & of Colonial Peru in Mus of Fine Arts.* 1967. Boston. 2 vol. ils. VG/VG case. M17. $25.00

CAVANNA, Betty. *Accent on April.* (1960). Morrow. BC. 8vo. 188p. bl brd. G+/dj. T5. $14.00

CAVANNA, Betty. *Boy Next Door.* 1956. Morrow. 1st. 253p. VG/dj. M20. $30.00

CAVANNA, Betty. *Passport to Romance.* 1955. Morrow. 1st. 249p. VG/dj. M20. $15.00

CAVANNA, Betty. *Pick of the Litter.* (1952). Phil. Westminster. 8vo. 222p. brn cloth. VG. T5. $15.00

CAVANNA, Betty. *Puppy Stakes.* 1948. Phil. Westminster. 1st. ils. G. O3. $18.00

CAVE, Emma. *Blood Bond.* 1979. Harper Row. 1st. F/F. P3. $25.00

CAVE, Henry. *Golden Tips: Descriptive of Ceylon & Its Great Tea Industry.* 1904. London. Cassell. 3rd. photos. teg. 476p. VG. W3. $185.00

CAVE, Hugh. *Cross on the Drum.* 1959. Doubleday. VG. M2. $12.00

CAVE, Hugh. *Long Were the Nights: Saga of PT Squadron X in Solomons.* 1943. NY. sgn pres. map/roster. 220p. VG/VG. S16. $45.00

CAVERLY, Carol. *All the Old Lions.* 1994. Aurora, CO. Write Way. 1st. sgn. F/F. B3. $35.00

CAWEIN, Madison. *Myth & Romance.* 1899. NY/London. 1st. 12mo. cloth. M1. $200.00

CAWTHORN & MOORCOCK. *Fantasy: 100 Best Books.* 1988. Carroll Graf. 1st Am. F/F. R10. $10.00

CAYTON & MITCHELL. *Black Workers & the New Unions.* 1939. Chapel Hill. 1st. inscr. 473p. NF/VG. B4. $200.00

CAZALET-KEIR, Thelma. *Homage to PG Wodehouse.* 1973. Barrie Jenkins. 1st. VG/VG. P3. $25.00

CECIL, David. *Two Quiet Lives.* 1948. London. 1st. VG/dj. T9. $20.00

CECIL, Henry. *Brief to Counsel.* 1958. Michael Joseph. 1st. VG. P3. $20.00

CECIL, Henry. *Unlawful Occasions.* 1962. London. Michael Joseph. 1st. F/NF. M22. $25.00

CEDERGREN, H.R. *Seepage, Drainage & Flow Nets.* 1967. John Wiley. 489p. F/dj. D8. $25.00

CELY, Michael. *Canada Calling.* nd. Frederick Warne. 240p. VG/ragged. M20. $17.50

CENDRARS, Blaise. *Shadow.* 1982. Scribner. 1st. 4to. VG+/NF. P2. $95.00

CERAM, C.W. *Gods, Graves & Scholars.* 1953. Knopf. 415p. G. B29. $9.00

CERAM, C.W. *Hands on the Past. Pioneer Archaeologists Tell Their Story.* 1966. Knopf. 1st. 31 pl. 434p. VG/dj. W1. $15.00

CERF, Bennett. *Favorite One Act Plays.* 1958. Doubleday. dj. A19. $20.00

CERF, Leon. *Letters of Napoleon to Josephine.* (1928). Paris. 12mo. French text. ils. 188p. 3-quarter leather. H3. $50.00

CERNY & NOVAK. *Tales of the Uncanny.* 1976. Hamlyn. 1st. VG/G. P3. $15.00

CERVANTES. *Don Quixote.* 1906. 2 vol. ils Gustave Dore. VG. M17. $45.00

CH'ANG, Lo-huang. *Ming-Hsien Mo-Chi.* 1971. Shanghai. Commercial Pr. 2 vol. VG/bl wrp. W3. $65.00

CHABER, M.E. *Acid Nightmare.* 1967. HRW. 1st. VG/VG. P3. $22.00

CHABER, M.E. *Green Grow the Graves.* 1970. HRW. 1st. F/F. P3. $15.00

CHABER, M.E. *Wanted: Dead Men.* 1965. HRW. 1st. VG/VG. P3. $18.00

CHABON, Michael. *Model World.* 1991. Morrow. 1st. author's 2nd book. F/F. B4. $45.00

CHABON, Michael. *Mysteries of Pittsburgh.* 1988. Morrow. 1st. author's 1st novel. F/F. D10. $50.00

CHABON, Michael. *Mysteries of Pittsburgh.* 1988. Morrow. 1st. NF/dj. A20. $30.00

CHADWICK, Douglas. *Fate of the Elephant.* 1993. Viking. 1st. 492p. F. S15. $10.00

CHADWICK, Lester. *Baseball Joe Around the World (#8).* 1918. Cupples Leon. 246p. cloth. VG/dj (lists to #14). M20. $37.50

CHAFER, Lewis Sperry. *Kingdom in History & Prophecy.* 1943. Dunham. 167p. VG/torn. B29. $6.50

CHAFETZ, Henry. *Legend of Befana.* 1958. Houghton Mifflin. 1st possible ed. 8vo. F/F. C8. $17.50

CHAHINIAN, B. Juan. *Sansevieria Trifasciata Varieties.* 1986. Reseda, CA. photos. 109p. F/dj. B26. $17.50

CHAILLEY, Jacques. *40,000 Years of Music: Man in Search of Music.* 1964. FSG. 1st Am. 229p. VG/dj. M20. $22.00

CHAIS, Pamela. *Final Cut.* 1981. S&S. 1st. F/dj. M25. $25.00

CHALFONT, Lord. *Waterloo.* 1979. Knopf. 1st Am. 239p. VG/dj. M20. $30.00

CHALK, Ocania. *Black College Sport.* 1976. Dodd Mead. 1st. photos. F/VG. P8. $30.00

CHALKER, Jack L. *Demons at Rainbow Bridge.* 1989. Ace. 1st. F/F. P3. $18.00

CHALMERS, Audrey. *Fancy Be Good.* 1941. Viking. 1st. 8vo. VG+/dj. M5. $20.00

CHALMERS, Mary. *Throw a Kiss, Harry.* 1958. Harper. probable 1st. 12mo. 32p. VG/VG. P2. $50.00

CHALMERS, Stephen. *Affair of the Gallows Tree.* 1930. Crime Club. 1st. VG. P3. $30.00

CHALMERS, Thomas. *On the Power, Wisdom & Goodness of God...* 1853. London. Bohn. later ed. rebound/red label. VG. K3. $30.00

CHAMALES, Tom. *Never So Few.* 1957. NY. 1st. VG/VG. B5. $35.00

CHAMBERLAIN, Allen. *Beacon Hill: Its Ancient Pastures & Early Mansions.* 1925. photos. VG. M17. $30.00

CHAMBERLAIN, Charles. *Methods in Plant Histology.* 1928. Chicago. 4th. 349p. dj. A10. $28.00

CHAMBERLAIN, Hope Summerell. *Old Days in Chapel Hill Being Life & Letters CP Spencer.* 1926. Chapel Hill. 1st. 325p. cloth. NF. M8. $45.00

CHAMBERLAIN, Joseph W. *Physics of the Aurora & Airglow.* 1961. Academic. 8vo. 704p. VG/dj. K5. $60.00

CHAMBERLAIN, Samuel. *Bouquet de France.* 1960. NY. Gourmet. G+. A16. $20.00

CHAMBERLAIN, Samuel. *British Bouquet.* 1973. Gourmet. G+. A16. $25.00

CHAMBERLAIN, Sarah. *Bremen Town Musicians. A Grimm Fairy Tale.* 1978. Chamberlain. 1/120. sgn. 10 wood engravings. Gray Parrot bdg. F. B24. $300.00

CHAMBERLAIN & SHAW. *Wilt.* 1973. Macmillan. 1st. VG/G+. P8. $15.00

CHAMBERLIN, F. *Private Character of Queen Elizabeth.* 1922. NY. ils. VG. M17. $17.50

CHAMBERLIN, Harry D. *Training Hunters, Jumpers & Hacks.* 1969. NY. Van Nostrand Reinhold. later rpt. VG/G. O3. $25.00

CHAMBERLIN & HOFFMAN. *Checklist of the Millipeds of North America.* 1958. Smithsonian. 236p. wrp. B1. $18.50

CHAMBERS, Dana. *Death Against Venus.* 1946. Dial. VG/VG. P3. $23.00

CHAMBERS, G.F. *Story of the Solar System.* 1905 (1895). NY. Appleton. ils. 188p. cloth. G. K5. $12.00

CHAMBERS, G.F. *Story of the Weather.* 1897. London. George Newnes. 232p. G. K5. $18.00

CHAMBERS, Robert E.S. *John Tom Alligator & Others.* 1937. Dutton. 1st. VG/dj. M2. $12.00

CHAMBERS, Robert W. *In Search of the Unknown.* 1974 (1904). Hyperion. rpt. F. M2. $30.00

CHAMBERS, Robert W. *Slayer of Souls.* 1920. Doran. 1st. VG/facsimile mc Canon dj. M2. $45.00

CHAMBERS, Robert W. *Streets of Ascalon.* 1912. Appleton. 1st. VG. P3. $25.00

CHAMBERS, Whitman. *Invasion!* 1943. Dutton. 1st. VG. P3. $20.00

CHAMBERS & SONNICHSEN. *San Agustin: First Cathedral Church in Arizona.* 1974. AZ Historical Soc. 1st. 1/100. inscr/sgns. ils/notes. 56p. F/F case. B19. $110.00

CHAN, Sucheng. *This Bittersweet Soil: Chinese in California Agriculuture...* 1986. Berkeley. 8vo. ils. burgundy cloth. F/dj. R3. $40.00

CHANDLER, A. Bertram. *Bring Back Yesterday.* 1981. Allison Busby. 1st. F/F. P3. $20.00

CHANDLER, Ann C. *Pan the Piper & Other Marvelous Tales.* 1923. Harper. 1st. ils. 234p. gilt bl cloth. VG. D1. $40.00

CHANDLER, David. *Campaigns of Napoleon.* 1966. 1st. ils/maps. VG/VG. M17. $50.00

CHANDLER, Edna Walker. *Cowboy Sam & Big Bill.* 1960. Chicago. Benefic. ils Jack Merryweather. xl. VG. C8. $15.00

CHANDLER, Edna Walker. *Cowboy Sam & Freckles.* 1960. Chicago. Benefic. ils Merryweather. xl. G. C8. $12.50

CHANDLER, Edna Walker. *Cowboy Sam & the Fair.* 1953. Chicago. Berkley-Cardy. lg 12mo. VG. C8. $15.00

CHANDLER, Edna Walker. *Cowboy Sam & the Rodeo.* 1959. Chicago. Benefic. 8vo. VG. C8. $15.00

CHANDLER, Raymond. *High Window.* 1942. Knopf. 1st. xl. VG. P3. $125.00

CHANDLER, Raymond. *Lady in the Lake.* 1944. London. Hamish Hamilton. 1st. G. M22. $45.00

CHANDLER, Raymond. *Long Goodbye.* 1953. London. Hamish Hamilton. true 1st. VG. M22. $60.00

CHANDLER, Raymond. *Midnight Raymond Chandler.* 1971. Houghton Mifflin. 1st. VG. M22. $15.00

CHANDLER, Raymond. *Playback.* 1958. London. Hamish Hamilton. 1st. NF/VG. M15. $100.00

CHANDLER, Raymond. *Playback.* 1958. Thriller BC. VG/G. P3. $15.00

CHANDLER, Raymond. *Red Wind.* 1946. World. 1st. VG. M22. $15.00

CHANDLER, Raymond. *Spanish Blood.* 1946. World. 1st. VG. M22. $15.00

CHANDLER & PARKER. *Poodle Springs.* 1989. Putnam. 1st. F/F. M22. $15.00

CHANEY, Jack. *Foolish Questions, Yellowstone Best.* 1924. Woodruff. 3rd. 104p. VG/wrp. J2. $165.00

CHANG, Garma. *Hundred Thousand Songs of Milarepa.* 1962. U Books. 1st. 2 vol. ils/index. F/VG box. W3. $125.00

CHANG, Kwang-chih. *Archeology of Ancient China.* 1963. Yale. 1st. 346p. F/VG. W3. $75.00

CHANG, Kwang-chih. *Shang Civilization.* 1980. Yale. 1st. ils/charts/tables. 417p. F. W3. $68.00

CHANG & SHEFTS. *Manual of Spoken Tibetan.* 1964. WA U. 286p. NF. W3. $72.00

CHANIN & CHANIN. *This Land These Voices: A Different View of AZ History...* 1977. Northland. 1st. ils/index. 266p. F/NF. B19. $50.00

CHANNING, Steven. *Crisis of Fear.* 1972. 315p. O8. $7.50

CHANNING, W.E. *Thoreau: Poet-Naturalist.* 1873. Boston. Roberts Bros. 1st. 1/1500. gilt gr cloth. M24. $100.00

CHANSLOR, Roy. *Ballad of Cat Ballou.* 1956. Little Brn. 1st. F/F. B4. $175.00

CHANSLOR, Roy. *Johnny Guitar.* 1953. NY. S&S. 1st. F/F. B4. $200.00

CHANTER, Charlotte. *Ferny Combes.* 1856. London. Lovell Reeve. 2nd. 16mo. A22. $85.00

CHAO, Yuen-ren. *Aspects of Chinese Socio-Linguistics.* 1976. Stanford. 1st. F/F. W3. $52.00

CHAPDELAINE, Perry A. *Laughing Terran.* 1977. London. Hale. 1st. sgn. F/VG. B11. $35.00

CHAPEL, Charles Edward. *Art of Shooting.* 1960. Barnes. 409p. dj. A17. $15.00

CHAPEL, Charles Edward. *Guns of the Old West, the Definitive Book on Firearms...* 1961. Coward McCann. 1st. VG/dj. J2. $65.00

CHAPELLE, Howard I. *History of American Sailing Ships.* (1935). NY. Norton. later prt. 400p. VG/worn. P4. $35.00

CHAPELLE, Howard I. *History of the American Sailing Navy: Ships & Developement.* (1949). Bonanza. later prt. 558p. VG/worn. P4. $40.00

CHAPIN, Howard Millar. *Tartar: Armed Sloop of the Colony of Rhode Island...* 1922. Providence. Soc of Colonial Wars. 7 pl. 67p. T7. $50.00

CHAPIN, James Henry. *From Japan to Granada.* 1889. Putnam. 1st. inscr. 12mo. gr cloth. G. B11. $25.00

CHAPIN & CHAPIN. *Stories of Pioneer Days; or, Advance Guard of Civilization.* 1894. Oriental Pub. 1st. VG. M19. $35.00

CHAPLIN, Charles. *My Autobiography.* 1966. London. 545p. F/dj. A17. $25.00

CHAPLIN, Ralph. *Somewhat Barbaric.* 1944. Seattle. McCaffrey Dogwood. 1st. inscr. F/NF. B2. $125.00

CHAPMAN, Allen. *Radio Boys at Mountain Pass (#4).* 1922. Grosset Dunlap. 218p+ads. VG/dj (lists to #5). M20. $35.00

CHAPMAN, Allen. *Radio Boys at Ocean Point.* 1922. NY. VG/G. B5. $17.50

CHAPMAN, Allen. *Radio Boys to the Rescue (#13).* 1930. Grosset Dunlap. 1st. 220p. last title in series. VG/dj (lists to #12). $150.00

CHAPMAN, Allen. *Radio Boys With the Iceberg Patrol (#7).* 1924. Grosset Dunlap. 218p. cloth. VG/dj (lists to #11). M20. $45.00

CHAPMAN, Charles. *Piloting Seamanship & Small Boat Handling.* 1968-69. NY. 664p. 4to. F. A17. $17.50

CHAPMAN, Clark R. *Planets of Rock & Ice: From Mercury to Moons of Saturn.* 1982. Scribner. 1st. F/dj. M2. $15.00

CHAPMAN, Frank. *Life in an Air Castle.* 1938. Appleton. 1st. 250p. xl. F3. $20.00

CHAPMAN, Frank M. *Handbook of Birds of Eastern North America.* 1966. NY. rpt (2nd). ils. 581p. VG. S15. $15.00

CHAPMAN, John Jay. *Treason & Death of Benedict Arnold.* 1910. Moffat Yard. 1st. 76p. brd/paper label. M1. $75.00

CHAPMAN, John Jay. *Two Greek Plays.* 1928. Houghton Mifflin. 1st. 12mo. 118p. salmon brd. dj. M1. $85.00

CHAPMAN, Lee; see Bradley, Marion Zimmer.

CHAPMAN, Paul H. *Spirit Runestones: A Study of Linguistics.* 1994. SF. Epigraphic Soc. 60p. F/prt wrp. P4. $22.50

CHAPMAN, Robert D. *Universe at Ultraviolet Wave Lengths...* 1981. NASA. 823p. VG/wrp. K5. $40.00

CHAPMAN & PRATT. *Methods of Analysis for Soils, Plants & Waters.* 1982. Berkeley. rpt. ils. new cloth. B1. $22.50

CHAPPELE, F.J. *Heather Garden.* 1952. London. ils. 180p. VG/torn. B26. $25.00

CHAPPELL, Fred. *Inkling.* 1965. HBW. 1st. author's 2nd book. F/NF. B3. $100.00

CHAPPELL, Fred. *More Shapes Than One.* 1991. St Martin. 1st. sgn. F/F. R13. $45.00

CHAPUT, Don. *Virgil Earp, Western Peace Officer.* 1994. Affiliated Writers of Am. 1st. photos/maps. 255p. as new. J2. $39.00

CHAPUT, W.J. *Dead in the Water.* 1991. St Martin. 1st. VG/VG. P3. $16.00

CHARBONNEAU, Louis. *Way Out.* 1966. Barrie Rockliff. 1st. VG/VG. P3. $25.00

CHARCOT, Jean Martin. *Clinical Lectures on Senile & Chronic Diseases.* 1881. New Sydenham Soc. 1st Eng. 6 pl. 308p. emb brn cloth. G1. $250.00

CHARDIN, John. *Sir John Chardin's Travels in Persia.* 1927. London. Argonaut. 1/975. ils. as new/unopened. O7. $225.00

CHARGAFF, Erwin. *Heraclitean Fire.* 1978. Rockefeller U. 1st. 252p. xl. VG. K3. $15.00

CHARLES, R.H. *Apocrypha & Pseudepigrapha of Old Testament in English.* 1963. Oxford. 2 vol. NF/dj. W3. $625.00

CHARLES, Robert H. *Roundabout Turn.* 1930. London. Warne. unp. cloth. G+/VG+. D4. $35.00

CHARLES, V.K. *Introduction to Mushroom Hunting.* 1974. Dover. 48p. VG/stiff wrp. B1. $12.50

CHARLESWORTH, J.K. *Historical Geology of Ireland.* 1963. London. Oliver Boyd Ltd. 565p. VG/dj. D8. $30.00

CHARLIP, Remy. *Arm in Arm: Collection of Connections, Endless Tales...* nd (1969). Parents Magazine. probable 1st. sm 4to. unp. NF/G+. C14. $17.00

CHARLIP & MOORE. *Hooray for Me!* 1975. NY. Parents. 1st. ils Vera Williams. F. C8. $20.00

CHARLOT, Jean. *Charlot Murals in Georgia.* 1945. Athens. 1st. VG/VG. B5. $65.00

CHARRIERE, Henri. *Papillon.* 1970. Morrow. 1st Am. NF/NF. M22. $15.00

CHARTERIS, Leslie. *Enter the Saint.* nd. Detective Story Club. NF/G. P3. $30.00

CHARTERIS, Leslie. *Saint Goes West.* 1942. Canada. Musson. VG/G. P3. $25.00

CHARTERIS, Leslie. *Saint on the Spanish Main.* 1955. Doubleday Crime Club. 1st. NF/rpr. M15. $65.00

CHARTERIS, Leslie. *Saint Sees It Through.* 1947. Canada. Musson. VG/G. P3. $20.00

CHARTERIS, Leslie. *Saint Vs Scotland Yard.* 1953. Doubleday. VG/VG. P3. $25.00

CHARTERIS, Leslie. *Senor Saint.* 1959. Hodder Stoughton. 1st. VG/VG. P3. $35.00

CHARTERIS, Leslie. *Vendetta for the Saint.* 1964. Crime Club. 1st. F/NF. M19. $25.00

CHARTERS, Ann. *Kerouac.* 1973. Straight Arrow. 1st. VG/VG. P3. $40.00

CHARYN, Jerome. *Darlin' Bill.* 1980. Arbor. 1st. F/F. T11. $30.00

CHARYN, Jerome. *Isaac Quartet.* 1984. Zomba. 1st. F/F. P3. $30.00

CHARYN, Jerome. *Once Upon a Droshky.* 1964. McGraw Hill. 1st. sgn. author's 1st book. F/F. L3. $150.00

CHARYN, Jerome. *Pinocchio Nose.* 1983. Arbor. 1st. F/NF. T12. $20.00

CHARYN, Jerome. *Seventh Babe.* 1979. Arbor. 1st. author's 13th book. F/F. T11. $40.00

CHASE, James Hadley. *Figure It Out for Yourself.* nd. Robert Hale. VG/G. P3. $20.00

CHASE, James Hadley. *Twelve Chinks & a Woman.* nd. Jarrolds. VG. P3. $25.00

CHASE, Pearl. *Cacti & Other Succulents.* 1930. Santa Barbara. 107p. sc. B26. $21.00

CHASE, Richard. *Old Songs & Singing Games.* 1938. Chapel Hill. 42p. VG+/wrp. D4. $35.00

CHASE, W.H. *Pioneers of Alaska.* 1951. KS City. sgn. ils/photos. 203p. F. M4. $30.00

CHASE, William C. *Front Line General: Command of Wm C Chase...* 1974. Houston. Gulf Pub. 1st. sgn. F/F. A23. $32.00

CHASTAIN, Thomas. *Pandora's Box.* 1974. Mason Lipscomb. 1st. VG/VG. P3. $20.00

CHATHAM, Russell. *Angler's Coast.* 1976. Doubleday. 1st. author's 1st book. F/VG clip. B3. $100.00

CHATTERTON, E. Keble. *Down Channel in the Vivette.* 1910. London. ils. G+. M17. $15.00

CHATTERTON, E. Keble. *English Seamen & the Colonization of America.* 1930. London. 1st. 326p. G. B18. $22.50

CHATTERTON, E. Keble. *Fore & Aft Craft & Their Story.* 1922-27. Phil/London. ils/plans. 347p. T7. $70.00

CHATTERTON, E. Keble. *On the High Seas.* 1929. London. Philip Allan. 16 half-tone pl/32 plans. 319p. gilt bl cloth. P4. $30.00

CHATTERTON, E. Keble. *Ship-Models.* 1923. London. The Studio. 1/1000. 142 pl. gilt bdg. P4. $225.00

CHATTERTON, E. Keble. *Windjammers & Shellbacks: Strange True Stories of the Sea.* 1926. London. Fisher Unwin. 254p. bl cloth. P4. $65.00

CHATTERTON, Fenimore C. *Yesterday's Wyoming.* 1957. Powder River. dj. A19. $100.00

CHATWIN, Bruce. *In Patagonia.* 1978. Summit. 1st Am. author's 1st book. F/F. D10. $125.00

CHATWIN, Bruce. *On the Black Hill.* 1983. Viking. 1st Am. author's 3rd book. F/F. D10. $50.00

CHATWIN, Bruce. *Songlines.* 1987. Viking. 1st. F/dj. A24. $35.00

CHATWIN, Bruce. *Utz.* 1988. Viking. 1st. F/F. H11. $25.00

CHATWIN, Bruce. *Viceroy of Ouidah.* 1980. Summit. 1st. F/F. H11. $65.00

CHAUCER, Geoffrey. *Tales From Chaucer, Canterbury Tales by Geoffrey Chauncer...* 1947. Heritage Pr. ils Szyk. tall 8vo. 182p. F. H1. $55.00

CHAVOOR & DAVIDSON. *50-Meter Jungle.* 1973. Coward McCann. 1st. VG/VG. P8. $20.00

CHAYEFSKY, Paddy. *Altered States.* 1978. Harper Row. 1st. NF/NF. M22. $20.00

CHEADLE & MILTON. *North-West Passage by Land: Being Narrative of Expedition...* nd. London. Cassell Petter Galpin. 394p. gilt gr cloth. P4. $55.00

CHEATLE & CUTLER. *Tumors of the Breast: Their Pathology, Symptoms, Diagnosis.* 1931. Phil. 1st Am. 596p. A13. $150.00

CHEESMAN, Evelyn. *Islands Near the Sun: Off the Beaten Track...* 1927. London. Witherby. 1st. ils. 304p. VG/VG. S25. $50.00

CHEETHAM, Anthony. *Science Against Man.* 1971. MacDonald. 1st. VG/VG. P3. $28.00

CHEEVER, John. *Wapshot Chronicle.* 1957. NY. Harper. 1st. author's 3rd book. F/NF. L3. $200.00

CHEEVER, John. *Wapshot Scandal.* 1964. Harper. 1st. assn copy. cloth. F/F. M24. $300.00

CHEEVER, John. *Way Some People Live.* 1943. Random. 1st. 1/2750. author's 1st book. G. L3. $400.00

CHEKHOV & MOSER. *Kashtanka.* 1991. Putnam. 1st. F/NF. C14. $17.00

CHENAK, Susan. *Smithereens.* 1995. Doubleday. 1st. sgn. F/F. A23. $34.00

CHENAULT, John Cabell. *Old Cane Springs.* 1937. Louisville, KY. 2nd. 257p. G. B18. $45.00

CHENEVIX-TRENCH, Charles. *History of Horsemanship.* 1970. Doubleday. 1st Am. VG/VG. O3. $45.00

CHENEY, E. *Farm Woodlot, a Handbook of Forestry for the Farmer.* 1926 (1914). xl. VG. E6. $25.00

CHENEY, Margaret. *Tesla: Man Out of Time.* 1981. Dorset. 320p. F/dj. K3. $15.00

CHENEY, Warren. *Yosemite Illustrated in Colors.* (1890). SF. HS Crocker. ils WH Hansen/Carl Dahlgren (13 full-p pl). rebound. R3. $750.00

CHENG, Chen-to. *Great Heritage of Chinese Art, Illustrated.* nd. np. 2 vol. 12 sets ils pl. emb gilt bdg. F/F. W3. $425.00

CHENG, Chu-yuan. *Scientific & Engineering Manpower in Communist China...* 1965. National Science Found. 588p. VG/stiff wrp. W3. $95.00

CHERF, John Frank. *Studies in the Text Tradition of St Jerome's 'Vitae Patrum.'* 1943. Urbana, IL. 1st. thick 4to. 566p. VG. T10. $75.00

CHERNIN, Kim. *Obsession.* 1981. Harper Row. 1st. author's 1st book. F/NF. M19. $25.00

CHERNIN, Milton. *Convict Road Work in California.* 1929. Los Angeles. 4to. typed dissertation. gilt bl lib cloth. NF. R3. $75.00

CHERRY, Kelly. *My Life & Dr Joyce Brothers.* 1990. Algonquin. 1st. F/F. B35. $15.00

CHERRY-GARRARD, Apsley. *Worst Journey in the World.* 1994. London. Picador. 4 maps. 607p. NF/dj. P4. $40.00

CHERRYH, C.J. *Chanur's Venture.* 1984. Phantasia. 1st. sgn. F/dj. M2. $30.00

CHERRYH, C.J. *Chernevog.* 1991. Methuen. 1st. F/F. P3. $25.00

CHERRYH, C.J. *Glass & Amber.* 1987. NESFA. 1st. F/dj. M2. $15.00

CHERRYH, C.J. *Kif Strike Back.* 1985. Phantasia. 1st. F/F. P3. $25.00

CHERRYH, C.J. *Rusalka.* 1989. Easton. 1st. sgn. leather. F/sans/swrp. P3. $100.00

CHESBRO, George C. *Second Horseman Out of Eden.* 1989. Atheneum. 1st. F/F. N4. $35.00

CHESBRO, George C. *Shadow of a Broken Man.* 1977. S&S. 1st. NF/dj. M25. $35.00

CHESBRO, George C. *Shadow of a Broken Man.* 1977. S&S. 1st. VG/VG. P3. $30.00

CHESEBROUGH, Caroline. *Foe in the Household.* 1871. Boston. Osgood. 1st. author's 8th/final book. gilt terra-cotta cloth. F. M24. $100.00

CHESELDEN, William. *Anatomy of the Human Body.* 1806. Boston. 2nd Am. 352p. half leather. A13. $400.00

CHESHIRE, Giff. *Stronghold.* 1963. Doubleday. 1st. F/NF clip. B4. $65.00

CHESLER, Ellen. *Woman of Valor: Margaret Sanger & Birth Control Movement.* 1992. S&S. 2nd. VG/VG. B4. $35.00

CHESMAN & JOAN. *Guide to Women's Publishing.* 1978. Paradise, CA. Dustbooks. 1st. sc. VG+. A25. $20.00

CHESNUTT, Charles W. *Colonel's Dream.* 1905. Doubleday Page. 1st thus. 1st. 1st state bdg (name misspelled). VG. M24. $1,500.00

CHESNUTT, Charles W. *Conjure Tales.* 1975. London. Collins. 1st thus. 1st. ils Ross/ Romano. 8vo. NF/VG. C8. $17.50

CHESNUTT, Charles W. *Conjure Woman.* 1899. Boston. 1st thus. 1st trade. 229p. pict cloth. VG. B18. $225.00

CHESNUTT, Charles W. *House Behind the Cedars.* 1900. Houghton Mifflin. 1st. author's 4th book. silver/gilt stp gr pict cloth. VG. M24. $275.00

CHESS & GOREY. *Fletcher & Zenobia.* 1967. Meredith. 1st. ils Victoria Chess. 12mo. VG/VG. P2. $25.00

CHESTERTON, G.K. *Annotated Innocence of Father Brown.* 1987. Oxford. 1st. F. M2. $20.00

CHESTERTON, G.K. *Collected Poems of GK Chesterton.* 1927. Great Britain. Cecil Palmer. 1st. G+. M23. $25.00

CHESTERTON, G.K. *Gloria in Profundis.* nd. 1/350. ils Eric Gill. yel brd. VG+. S13. $20.00

CHESTERTON, G.K. *Heretics.* 1960. London. VG. M2. $12.00

CHESTERTON, G.K. *Man Who Was Thursday.* 1908. Bristol/London. 1st. G-. M23. $50.00

CHESTERTON, G.K. *Paradoxes of Mr Pond.* 1945. 1st Am. F/NF. M19. $45.00

CHESTERTON, G.K. *St Francis of Assisi.* 1926. London. 1st. VG/dj. T9. $75.00

CHETWODE, Penelope. *Two Middle-Aged Ladies in Adalusia.* 1963. London. John Murray. 3rd. photos. VG/VG. A25. $18.00

CHETWYND-HAYES, R. *Quiver of Ghosts.* 1984. Wm Kimber. 1st. F/F. P3. $25.00

CHEUNG, D. *Isle Full of Noises.* 1987. Columbia. 1st. 257p. F. W3. $38.00

CHEUSE, Alan. *Grandmother's Club.* 1986. Peregrine Smith. 1st. F/F. A20. $20.00

CHEVALIER, Haakon. *Last Voyage of the Schooner Rosamond.* 1970. London. Deutsch. 248p. dj. T7. $35.00

CHEVALIER, Haakon. *Oppenheimer, The Story of a Friendship.* 1965. NY. 1st. xl. VG. K3. $15.00

CHEVALIER, Maurice. *Mome a Cheveux Blancs.* 1969. Paris. inscr. 280p. F/dj. B14. $60.00

CHEVIGNY, Hector. *Lost Empire: Life & Adventures of Nikolai Petrovich Rezanov.* 1937. Macmillan. 1st. 8vo. 356p. gray cloth. P4. $65.00

CHEW, Peter. *Kentucky Derby: The First 100 Years.* 1974. Houghton Mifflin. 1st. 4to. VG. O3. $45.00

CHEYNEY, Peter. *Curiosity of Etienne MacGregor.* 1952. 1st Eng. NF/VG. M19. $25.00

CHEYNEY, Peter. *Dames Don't Care!* nd. Coward McCann. 2nd Am imp. 250p. cloth. VG/dj. M20. $35.00

CHEYNEY, Peter. *Dark Bahama.* 1950. Collins. VG/VG. P3. $15.00

CHEYNEY, Peter. *Uneasy Terms.* 1947. Dodd Mead. 1st. VG/G. P3. $25.00

CHI, Wen-shun. *Readings in Chinese Communist Documents.* 1963. CA U. 478p. F. W3. $45.00

CHI & SERVICE. *Chinese-English Dictionary of Contemporary Usage.* 1977. CA U. 484p. F/F. W3. $135.00

CHIANG, Yee. *Chinese Calligraphy: An Introduction...* 1955. Harvard. 230p. VG/dj. W3. $52.00

CHIANG & WOLF. *Indians of North & South America: Supplement.* 1988. Scarecrow. 8vo. 3542 works described. F. T10. $50.00

CHICKERING, Carol. *Flowers of Guatemala.* 1973. Norman, OK. 128p. VG. A10. $25.00

CHIDAMIAN, Claude. *Book of Cacti & Other Succulents.* 1958. Garden City. BC. 243p. VG/dj. B26. $12.50

CHIDESTER, Otis. *Brand Book 1 of the Tucson Corral of the Westerners...* 1967. Tucson. Corral of Westerners. 1st. ils. 204p. F/sans. B19. $65.00

CHIDSEY, Donald Barr. *Captain Adam.* 1953. Crown. 1st. VG/VG. P3. $20.00

CHIKAMATSU, Shigenori. *Stories From a Tearoom Window.* 1982. Tuttle. ils. 191p. F/dj. W3. $38.00

CHILD, Frank. *Colonial Witch.* 1897. Baker Taylor. VG. M2. $75.00

CHILD, Georgie Boynton. *Efficient Kitchen.* 1914. McBride Nast. G. A16. $25.00

CHILD, Julia. *Julia Child & Company.* 1978. Knopf. 1st. 243p. B10. $10.00

CHILD, Julia. *Mastering the Art of French Cooking.* 1950. Knopf. BC. ils. 622p. VG/fair. B10. $15.00

CHILD, Julia. *Mastering the Art of French Cooking.* 1966 (1961). Knopf. 13th. 684p. VG/G. B10. $15.00

CHILD, Theodore. *Spanish-American Republics.* 1891. Harper. 1st. 444p. xl. F3. $25.00

CHILD STUDY ASSN. OF AMERICA. *Read Me More Stories.* (1951). NY. Crowell. 8vo. ils Barbara Cooney. 166p. G. T5. $18.00

CHILDE, Harold. *Child's Book of Abridged Wisdom.* 1905. SF. Elder/Tomoye. ils. gr cloth spine. VG. B14. $60.00

CHILDERS & RUSSO. *Nightshades & Health.* 1977. Somerville. Horticultural Pub. 189p. xl. B1. $16.50

CHILL, Abraham. *Mizvot: Commandments & Their Rationale.* 1974. Jerusalem. Keter. 508p. VG/dj. S3. $34.00

CHILLS, Marquis W. *This Is Democracy: Collective Bargaining in Scandinavia.* 1938. Yale. 1st. VG. V4. $22.50

CHIN, S.S. *Missile Configuration Design.* 1961. McGraw Hill. 8vo. 279p. VG/dj. K5. $45.00

CHINIQUY, Charles. *Fifty Years in the Church of Rome.* 1960. Baker. 597p. G. B29. $20.00

CHINNOCK & HEATH. *Ferns & Fern Allies of New Zealand.* 1974. Wellington. Reed. 8vo. cloth. VG/dj. A22. $15.00

CHIPAULT, Antoine Maxime. *Travaux de Neurologie Chirugicle.* 1896. Paris. Vigot Freres. 352p+208 woodcuts. contemporary bdg. xl. G1. $100.00

CHIPMAN, Frank W. *Romance of Old Sandwich Glass.* 1932. Sandwich Pub. 158p. VG. M20. $35.00

CHIPMAN, William Pendleton. *Roy Gilbert's Search: Tale of the Great Lakes.* 1889. AL Burt. 277p. bl cloth. VG. M20. $16.00

CHIRENJE, J. Mutero. *History of Northern Botswana 1850-1910.* 1977. Rutherford, NJ. Farleigh Dickinson. 1st. 8vo. ils. NF/dj. W1. $25.00

CHITTENDEN, Alfred K. *Red Gum.* 1905. WA, DC. ils/fld map. 56p. tan wrp. B26. $15.00

CHITTENDEN, H.M. *History of Early Steamboat Navigation on Missouri River.* 1962 (1903). Minneapolis. 2 vol in 1. 1/1500. F/dj. M4. $55.00

CHITTENDEN, H.M. *History of the American Fur Trade of the Far West.* 1954. Academic. 2 vol. VG/dj. J2. $195.00

CHITTENDEN, L.E. *Personal Reminiscences 1840-1890.* 1893. NY. 434p. O8. $12.50

CHITTENDEN & COLSON. *Children's Letters: A Collection...* 1905. NY. sm 8vo. gilt wine cloth. VG. M5. $85.00

CHITTENDEN & SYNGE. *RHS Dictionary of Gardening.* 1977. Oxford. Clarendon. 2nd. 4 vol+supplement. xl. F. A10. $300.00

CHIVERS, T.H. *Nacoochee; or, Beautiful Star, With Other Poems.* 1837. NY. WE Dean. 1st. 12mo. 143p. reddish-brn cloth. M1. $425.00

CHOI, Susan. *The Foreign Student.* 1998. NY. Harper. sgn 1st. F/F. M23. $35.00

CHOLMELEY & MELLAND. *Through the Heart of Africa: Being an Account...* 1912. Houghton Mifflin. 1st. ils/fld map. 305p. teg. VG+. H7. $125.00

CHOPIN, Kate. *Bayou Folk.* 1894. Houghton Mifflin. 1st. 1/1000. gilt gr sateen cloth. G. M24. $125.00

CHOPPING, Richard. *Fly.* 1965. FSG. 1st. author's 1st book. NF/F. H11. $40.00

CHORAO, Kay. *Lester's Overnight.* 1977. Dutton. 1st. lg 8vo. unp. F/VG. C14. $17.00

CHORIS, Louis. *San Francisco One Hundred Years Ago.* 1913. SF. Robertson. ils/drawings. 20p. F/dj. K7. $45.00

CHOW & COLLISON. *Gin Chow's First Annual Almanac.* 1932. Los Angeles. Wetzel. 2nd. 12mo. ils. red/blk/tan brd. F. R3. $20.00

CHRISTENSEN, Edwin O. *Index of American Design.* 1950. Macmillan. 1st. 229p. VG. A8. $26.50

CHRISTIANSEN, Harry. *Lake Shore Electric, Interurban Days 1893-1938.* 1963. Cleveland. photos. unp. VG/wrp. M20. $20.00

CHRISTIE, Agatha. *Agatha Christie Hour.* 1982. Collins. 1st. VG/VG. P3. $20.00

CHRISTIE, Agatha. *And Then There Were None.* 1945. Grosset Dunlap. photoplay ed. VG/VG. M22. $30.00

CHRISTIE, Agatha. *By the Pricking of My Thumbs.* 1968. Dodd Mead. 1st. VG/G. P3. $25.00

CHRISTIE, Agatha. *Caribbean Mystery.* 1964. Collins. 1st. NF/dj. M25. $25.00

CHRISTIE, Agatha. *Elephants Can Remember.* 1972. Collins. 1st. F/NF. M25. $25.00

CHRISTIE, Agatha. *Hercule Poirot: Clocks.* 1963. Dodd Mead. 1st Am. 276p. VG/dj. M20. $25.00

CHRISTIE, Agatha. *Miss Marple: In Mirror Cracked/Nemesis/Body in Library...* 1983. NY. Avenel. 3rd. F/F. T12. $25.00

CHRISTIE, Agatha. *Passenger to Frankfurt.* 1970. London. Collins. Crime Club. 1st. F/dj. Q1. $75.00

CHRISTIE, Agatha. *Postern of Fate.* 1973. Dodd Mead. 1st. VG/VG. P3. $25.00

CHRISTIE, Agatha. *Sleeping Murder.* 1976. Collins Crime Club. 1st. NF/NF. P3. $20.00

CHRISTIE, Agatha. *Third Girl.* 1966. London. Collins Crime Club. 1st. F/NF. N4. $50.00

CHRISTIE, Agatha. *Triple Threat.* 1943. Dodd Mead. omnibus ed. F/NF. M15. $150.00

CHRISTOPHER, John. *Little People.* 1966. S&S. 1st. VG/dj. M2. $15.00

CHRISTOPHER, John. *Pendulum.* 1968. S&S. 1st. VG/VG. P3. $15.00

CHRISTOPHER, John. *Ragged Edge.* 1965. S&S. 1st. VG/dj. M2. $25.00

CHRISTOPHER, John. *Scent of White Poppies.* 1959. 1st. NF/VG. M19. $25.00

CHRISTY, Howard Chandler. *Our Girls.* 1907. NY. 1st. VG. B5. $95.00

CHRISTY, Thomas. *Thomas Christy's Road Across the Plains...* 1969. Denver. Rosenstock. 1st. 94 maps. F. M4. $40.00

CHUBIN, Barry. *Feet of a Snake.* 1984. Arbor. 1st. VG/VG. P3. $18.00

CHUKOVSKY, Kornei. *Telephone.* 1977. Delacorte. 1st Am. 48p. F/F. D4. $45.00

CHUNG, Kyung-cho. *New Korea.* 1962. NY. ils. 274p. VG/dj. W3. $32.00

CHURCH, Peggy Pond. *Wind's Trail: Early Life of Mary Austin.* 1990. Mus of NM Pr. 1st. F/dj. A18. $20.00

CHURCH & PETERSON. *Nervous & Mental Diseases.* 1904. Phil. Saunders. 4th revised/2nd prt. 922p+ads. VG. G1. $50.00

CHURCHILL, Fleetwood. *On the Theory & Practice of Midwifery.* 1946. Phil. 2nd Am. 525p. full leather. A13. $200.00

CHURCHILL, Winston S. *Blood, Sweat & Tears.* 1941. NY. 1st Am. VG. M17. $20.00

CHURCHILL, Winston S. *London to Ladysmith Via Pretoria.* 1900. NY. 1st Am. VG. M17. $250.00

CHURCHILL, Winston S. *Marlborough: His Life & Times.* 1933. NY. 6 vol. 1st Am. VG. M17. $350.00

CHURCHILL, Winston S. *Secret Session Speeches.* UK. 1st. VG. M17. $30.00

CHURCHILL, Winston S. *Unrelenting Struggle.* 1942. NY. 1st Am. VG/G+. M17. $50.00

CHUTE, Carolyn. *Beans.* 1985. Chatto Windus/Hogarth. 1st Eng. author's 1st book. F/1st issue dj. R13. $60.00

CHUTE, Carolyn. *Beans.* 1985. Chatto Windus/Hogarth. 1st Eng. rem mk. F/F. R14. $35.00

CHUTE, Carolyn. *Letourneau's Used Auto Parts.* 1988. Ticknor Fields. 1st. sgn. F/F. B3. $45.00

CIARDI, John. *Alphabestiary.* 1966. Lippincott. 1st. 56p. cloth. F/VG. D4. $75.00

CIARDI, John. *Monster Den; or, Look What Happened at My House — And to It.* 1966. Lippincott. ils Edward Gorey. 64p. VG+/dj. D4. $45.00

CIARDI, John. *You Know Who.* 1964. Lippincott. 1st. 63p. VG/dj. M20. $50.00

CIARDI, John. *You Read to Me, I'll Read to You.* 1962. Phil. Lippincott. 1st. 64p. F/dj. D4. $75.00

CIMENT, Jill. *Small Claims.* 1986. NY. 1st. author's 1st book. NF/dj. R13. $25.00

CINTRON, Lola. *Goddess of the Bullring...Story of Conchita Cintron.* (1960). Bobbs Merrill. 1st. 349p. dj. F3. $25.00

CIPOLLA, Carlo M. *Clocks & Culture 1300-1700.* 1967. Walker. 1st. 8vo. 192p. ils. VG/dj. K3. $20.00

CISNEROS, Sandra. *Woman Hollering Creek.* 1991. Random. 1st. F/F. B3. $75.00

CIST, Henry M. *Army of the Cumberland.* 1882. NY. 1st. 289p. F. O8. $21.50

CLAGETT, Marshall. *Critical Problems in History of Science.* 1959. Madison, WI. 8vo. 547p. wrp. K3. $10.00

CLAIR, Maxine. *Coping With Gravity.* 1988. WA Writer's Pub. 1st. author's 1st book. F/wrp. A24. $75.00

CLAIRE, Mabel. *Crowley Milner's Cookbook.* 1932. NY. Greenberg. fair. A16. $20.00

CLAMPITT, John W. *Echoes From the Rocky Mountains.* 1889. ils. 671p. O8. $55.00

CLANCY, Tom. *Cardinal of the Kremlin.* 1988. Putnam. 1st. F/F. H11. $35.00

CLANCY, Tom. *Cardinal of the Kremlin.* 1988. Putnam. 1st. VG/VG. P3. $25.00

CLANCY, Tom. *Clear & Present Danger.* 1989. Putnam. 1st. NF/NF. P3. $40.00

CLANCY, Tom. *Red Storm Rising.* 1986. Putnam. 1st. F/F. D10. $50.00

CLANCY, Tom. *Red Storm Rising.* 1986. Putnam. 1st. sgn. F/F. A23. $90.00

CLANCY, Tom. *Sum of All Fears.* 1991. Harper Collins. 1st Eng. F/dj. Q1. $60.00

CLANCY, Tom. *Sum of All Fears.* 1991. Putnam. 1/600. sgn/#d. F/sans. M15. $225.00

CLANCY, Tom. *Sum of All Fears.* 1991. Putnam. 1st. NF/NF. P3. $25.00

CLANCY, Tom. *Without Remorse.* 1993. Putnam. 1st. sgn. F/F. A23. $75.00

CLARE, John. *Dwellers in the Wood.* 1967. Macmillan. ARC/1st. 43p. F/F. D4. $35.00

CLARK. *Children's Annual: A History & Collector's Guide.* 1988. London. 4to. 160p. F/NF. A4. $95.00

CLARK, Ann Nolan. *Bear Cub.* 1965. Viking. 1st. 62p. F/F. D4. $45.00

CLARK, Ann Nolan. *Blue Canyon Horse.* 1954. Viking. 1st. tall 8vo. F/VG. M5. $85.00

CLARK, Ann Nolan. *Magic Money.* 1950. Viking. 1st. 121p. VG/VG. P2. $80.00

CLARK, Ann Nolan. *Secret of the Andes.* 1953 (1952). Viking. 3rd. 8vo. 130p. VG/G+. T5. $25.00

CLARK, Ann Nolan. *Tia Maria's Garden.* 1966 (1963). NY. Viking. 3rd. ils Ezra Jack Keats. xl. VG/NF. C8. $15.00

CLARK, Anna Morris. *Sylvia of the Hills.* 1936. Custer, SD. Chronicle Shop. box. A19. $45.00

CLARK, B.F. *How Many Miles From St Jo?* 1929. SF. private prt. sm 8vo. marbled brd/maroon cloth. VG. O4. $45.00

CLARK, Badger. *Sun & Saddle Leather.* 1920. Boston. Gorham. A19. $35.00

CLARK, Curt; see Westlake, Donald E.

CLARK, Dorothy. *Little Joe.* 1940. Lee Shepard. 1st. ils Leonard Weisgard. VG+/G. P2. $50.00

CLARK, Douglas. *Big Grouse.* 1986. Gollancz. 1st. NF/NF. P3. $25.00

CLARK, Douglas. *Sick to Death.* 1971. Stein Day. 1st. VG/VG. P3. $20.00

CLARK, E. E. *Poetry: An Interpretation of Life.* 1935. Farrar Rhinehart. 1st. 584p. VG. W2. $30.00

CLARK, Eleanor. *Oysters of Locmariaquer.* 1964. Pantheon. 1st. 203p. F/VG. H1. $25.00

CLARK, Ellery H. *Red Sox Fever.* 1979. Hicksville. Exposition. inscr to Bob Watson. G/G. A23. $30.00

CLARK, Francis E. *In Christ's Own Country.* 1914. Grosset Dunlap. 1st. 8vo. 25 pl. VG. W1. $12.00

CLARK, H.H. *Lost in Pompeii.* 1883. Lothrop Lee Shepard. 1st. VG. M2. $30.00

CLARK, Mary Higgins. *All Around Town.* 1992. S&S. 1st. sgn. F/F. A23. $25.00

CLARK, Mary Higgins. *Cradle Will Fall.* 1980. S&S. 1st. F/F. T12. $25.00

CLARK, Mary Higgins. *Cry in the Night.* 1982. S&S. 1st. F/clip. P3. $20.00

CLARK, Mary Higgins. *Loves Music, Loves to Dance.* 1991. S&S. 1st. sgn. F/F. A23. $25.00

CLARK, Mary Higgins. *Stranger Is Watching.* 1977. S&S. 1st. F/F. M15. $50.00

CLARK, Mary Higgins. *While My Pretty One Sleeps.* 1989. S&S. 1st. sgn. F/F. A23. $30.00

CLARK, Mary Higgins. *While My Pretty One Sleeps.* 1989. S&S. 1st. F/F. H11. $25.00

CLARK, Ronald W. *Einstein, the Life & Times.* 1984. Abrams. lg 4to. VG+/dj. K3. $20.00

CLARK, Ronald W. *JBS: The Life & Work of JBS Haldane.* 1969. Coward McCann. 1st Am. ils. 326p. VG/dj. K3. $15.00

CLARK, Sterling B.F. *How Many Miles From St Jo?* 1988. Ye Galleon. 1st thus. F/sans. A18. $17.50

CLARK, Walter Van Tilborg. *Grove Day.* 1969. NY. 1st. VG/VG. B5. $45.00

CLARK, Walter Van Tilborg. *Watchful Gods.* 1950. NY. 1st. VG/G. B5. $40.00

CLARK, William. *Field Notes of Captain William Clark.* 1964. Yale. sgn. 335p. NF/dj. O7. $275.00

CLARK & LE GETTE. *Echo in My Soul.* 1962. Dutton. 1st. 243p. NF/VG. B4. $85.00

CLARK & STARN. *Geological Evolution of North America.* 1960. Ronald Pr. 1st. ils/figures, 434p. VG. D8. $15.00

CLARKE, Anna. *Legacy of Evil.* 1976. Collins Crime Club. 1st. VG/VG. P3. $20.00

CLARKE, Arthur C. *Deep Range.* 1957. Harcourt. 1st. F/dj. M2. $200.00

CLARKE, Arthur C. *Exploration of Space.* 1951. Harper. 1st. author's 3rd book. VG/VG. M19. $50.00

CLARKE, Arthur C. *Fall of Moondust.* 1961. Harcourt Brace. 1st. NF/VG. M19. $50.00

CLARKE, Arthur C. *Fountains of Paradise.* 1979. HBJ. 1st. VG/VG. P3. $25.00

CLARKE, Arthur C. *Ghost From the Grand Banks.* 1990. Bantam. 1st. F/F. P3. $20.00

CLARKE, Arthur C. *Imperial Earth.* 1975. London. 1st. F/dj. M2. $55.00

CLARKE, Arthur C. *Other Side of the Sky.* 1957. Harcourt Brace. 1st. VG/dj. M2. $100.00

CLARKE, Arthur C. *Promise of Space.* 1968. Harper. sgn. F/dj. M2. $40.00

CLARKE, Arthur C. *Reach for Tomorrow.* 1970. HBW. 1st. VG/VG. P3. $20.00

CLARKE, Arthur C. *Songs of Distant Earth.* 1986. Del Rey. 1/500. sgn/#d. F/case. M2. $85.00

CLARKE, Arthur C. *Songs of Distant Earth.* 1986. Del Rey. 1st. NF/VG+. N4. $20.00

CLARKE, Arthur C. *Songs of Distant Earth.* 1986. Del Rey. 1st. 256p. NF/clip. M20. $25.00

CLARKE, Arthur C. *2010: Odyssey Two.* 1982. Del Rey. 1st. F/dj. M2. $25.00

CLARKE, Covington. *For Valor.* 1928. Chicago. 264p. VG. B18. $25.00

CLARKE, Covington. *Mystery Flight of the Q2.* 1932. Reilly Lee. 270p. cloth. VG/dj. M20. $25.00

CLARKE, Donald Henderson. *That Mrs Renney.* 1937. Vanguard. 1st. F/NF. M19. $25.00

CLARKE, John Henrik. *Harlem, USA.* 1964. Seven Seas. ne. VG/wrp. M25. $45.00

CLARKE, Sara. *Lord Will Love Thee.* 1959. 1st. ils Tasha Tudor. VG+. S13. $25.00

CLARKE, T.E.B. *Murder at Buckingham Palace.* 1981. Hale. 1st. VG/VG. P3. $20.00

CLARKE, Walter E. *Alaska.* 1910. Boston. 207p. gilt cloth. F. A17. $30.00

CLARKE & LEE. *Cradle.* 1988. Warner. 1st. F/dj. M2. $20.00

CLARKE & LEE. *Garden of Rama.* 1991. Bantam. 1st Am. rem mk. NF/dj. M21. $10.00

CLARKE & LEE. *Rama II.* 1989. Bantam. 1st. F/F. N4. $25.00

CLARKSON, Henry E. *Yachtsman's A-Z.* 1979. Arco. 1st. 160p. F/F. W2. $20.00

CLARKSON, Rosetta E. *Herbs: Their Culture & Uses.* 1951. Macmillan. 10th. 226p. VG. A10. $20.00

CLARKSON, Rosetta E. *Magic Gardens.* 1939. Macmillan. 1st. 8vo. cloth. VG. A22. $30.00

CLARKSON, Thomas. *Memoirs of the Private & Public Life of William Penn.* 1813. London. Longman. 2 vol. 1st. thick 8vo. modern bdg. F. H13. $365.00

CLAUDE, Blair. *Pistols of the World.* 1968. Viking. 205p. cloth. VG+/dj. M20. $50.00

CLAUDINE. *Flight of the Animals.* 1971. NY. Parents. 1st. ils Claudine. F. C8. $15.00

CLAUSEN, Jens. *Stages in the Evolution of Plant Species.* 1951. Ithaca. Cornell. 206p. VG. A10. $24.00

CLAVELL, James. *King Rat, a Novel.* 1962. 1st. author's 1st book. NF/VG. A4. $200.00

CLAVELL, James. *Noble House.* 1981. Delacorte. 1st. F/NF. H11. $35.00

CLAVELL, James. *Shogun.* 1983. Delacorte. 1st. NF/F. H11. $45.00

CLAVELL, James. *Whirlwind.* 1986. Morrow. 1st. NF/NF. P3/T12. $35.00

CLAVER, Scott. *Under the Lash.* 1954. London. 1st. ils. 288p. G. B18. $15.00

CLAY, Catherine Lee. *Season of Love.* 1968. Atheneum. 1st. inscr. F/dj. T10. $45.00

CLAY & HUBBARD. *Trees for Hawaiian Gardens.* 1962. Honolulu. inscr. photos. 101p. sc. B26. $22.50

CLAYMORE, Tod. *Appointment in New Orleans.* 1950. Cassell. 1st. VG/G. P3. $30.00

CLAYTON, Edward T. *Negro Politician: His Success & Failure.* 1964. Chicago. Johnson. 1st. F/NF. B4. $85.00

CLEARY, Beverly. *Ramona & Her Mother.* 1979. Morrow. 1st. 208p. VG/VG. P2. $25.00

CLEARY, Jon. *Beufort Sisters.* 1979. Collins. 1st. VG/VG. P3. $23.00

CLEARY, Jon. *Fall of an Eagle.* 1964. Morrow. 1st. VG/G. P3. $25.00

CLEARY, Jon. *Faraway Drums.* 1982. Morrow. 1st. VG/VG. P3. $20.00

CLEARY, Jon. *Liberators.* 1971. Morrow. 1st. VG/VG. P3. $25.00

CLEARY, Jon. *Man's Estate.* 1972. Collins. 1st. VG/VG. P3. $20.00

CLEARY, Jon. *Very Private War.* 1980. Collins. 1st. NF/NF. P3. $25.00

CLEAVER & RODMAN. *Horace Pippin: The Artist as a Black American.* 1972. Doubleday. 1st. NF/dj. M25. $50.00

CLEEVE, Brian. *Death of a Painted Lady.* 1962. Hammond Hammond. 1st. VG/VG. P3. $25.00

CLELAND, Hugh. *George Washington in the Ohio Valley.* 1955. Pittsburgh. 1st. 405p. as new/dj. H1. $32.00

CLELAND, Robert Glass. *Cattle on a Thousand Hills.* 1941. Huntington Lib. 1st. VG. O4. $40.00

CLELAND, Robert Glass. *Irvine Ranch of Orange Country.* 1952. San Marino. Huntington Lib. 1st. VG/sans. O4. $25.00

CLELAND, Robert Glass. *Irvine Ranch.* 1966. San Marino. 2nd. NF/VG. O4. $15.00

CLEMENS, Samuel L. *Adventures of Huckleberry Finn.* 1912. Harper. new ed from new pl. 405p. VG. W2. $900.00

CLEMENS, Samuel L. *Adventures of Tom Sawyer.* 1879. Hartford. Am Pub. early rpt. gilt bl cloth/recased. M24. $100.00

CLEMENS, Samuel L. *Adventures of Tom Sawyer.* 1879. Toronto. Rose-Belford. 1st thus. sewn self-wrp. M24. $650.00

CLEMENS, Samuel L. *Adventures of Tom Sawyer.* 1920. Grosset Dunlap. Prt in USA. ne. 292p. G. W2. $500.00

CLEMENS, Samuel L. *Christian Science.* 1907. Harper. 1st. VG. M19. $35.00

CLEMENS, Samuel L. *Dog's Tale.* 1904. Harper. 1st. red pict cloth. VG. M24. $60.00

CLEMENS, Samuel L. *Editorial Wild Oats.* 1905. Harper. 1st. pink cloth. VG. M24. $60.00

CLEMENS, Samuel L. *Eve's Diary.* 1906. NY. Harper. 1st. red pict cloth. VG. M24. $65.00

CLEMENS, Samuel L. *Extract From Captain Stormfield's Visit to Heaven.* 1909. NY. 1st. VG. B5. $30.00

CLEMENS, Samuel L. *Extracts From Adam's Diary.* 1904. Harper. 1st. ils. 89p. pict cloth. G+. B18. $35.00

CLEMENS, Samuel L. *Following the Equator.* 1897. Hartford. Am Pub. 1st/single imp. teg. 3-quarter maroon morocco. M24. $300.00

CLEMENS, Samuel L. *Gilded Age.* 1873. Hartford/Chicago. 1st/early state+1st state ads. gilt blk cloth. M24. $350.00

CLEMENS, Samuel L. *Letters From the Sandwich Islands.* 1937. Grabhorn. 1st. 1/550. dk bl cloth. F. M24. $350.00

CLEMENS, Samuel L. *Life on the Mississippi.* 1883. Boston. Osgood. 1st Am/2nd state (points p441/443). NF. Q1. $600.00

CLEMENS, Samuel L. *Mark Twain's Letter to the California Pioneers.* 1911. Oakland. DeWitt Snelling. 1st/1st issue. F/prt wrp. M24. $125.00

CLEMENS, Samuel L. *Mark Twain's Letters.* (1917). Harper. 1st trade. 2 vol. teg. gilt red cloth. M24. $100.00

CLEMENS, Samuel L. *Mark Twain's Sketches, New & Old.* 1875. Hartford. Am Pub. 1st/2nd. aeg. gilt bl cloth/recased. VG. M24. $85.00

CLEMENS, Samuel L. *Personal Recollections of Joan of Arc.* 1896. London. Chatto Windus. 1st. teg. pict bl cloth. NF. M24. $200.00

CLEMENS, Samuel L. *Prince & the Pauper.* 1937. Winston. 1st thus. ils Lawson. gilt red cloth. VG. M5. $45.00

CLEMENS, Samuel L. *Roughing It.* 1872. Hartford. Am Pub. 1st/1st issue. gilt 3-quarter brn morocco. M24. $1,000.00

CLEMENS, Samuel L. *Stolen White Elephant.* 1882. Chatto Windus. 1st/1st prt. 8vo. G. T10. $185.00

CLEMENS, Samuel L. *Tramp Abroad.* 1880. Hartford. Am Pub. 1st/1st state sheets/state A portrait ftspc. M24. $450.00

CLEMENS, Will. *Ken of Kipling.* 1899. NY. New Amsterdam Book. 1st. gilt orange cloth. M24. $100.00

CLEMENT, Hal. *Mission of Gravity.* 1954. Doubleday. 1st. F/F. P3. $225.00

CLEMENT, Hal. *Mission of Gravity.* 1954. Doubleday. 1st. sgn. VG/dj. M2. $225.00

CLEMENT, Hal. *Needle.* 1950. Doubleday. 1st. VG/VG. P3. $60.00

CLEMENTE & LINDSLEY. *Aggression & Defense: Neural Mechanisms & Social Patterns.* 1967. Berkeley. 4to. 361p. wht/red cloth. VG/dj. G1. $40.00

CLEMENTS, F.E. *Minnesota Plant Studies I-III.* 1909-10. tall 8vo. VG/wrp. A22. $50.00

CLEMENTS, F.E. *Plant Succession & Indicators.* 1928. Wilson. ils/pl/figures. 453p. cloth. VG. A22. $65.00

CLERKE, Agnes M. *Familiar Studies in Homer.* 1892. London. Longman Gr. 8vo. 302p. xl. K5. $45.00

CLERKE, Agnes M. *Problems in Astrophysics.* 1903. London. Black. 1st/only. 567p. G. K5. $90.00

CLEVELAND, Anne. *It's Better With Your Shoes Off.* 1958. Rutland. Tuttle. 4th. ils. 94p. VG+. A25. $15.00

CLIFFORD, A.G. *Conquest of North Africa.* 1943. MA. 1st. 450p. VG. S16. $25.00

CLIFFORD, Francis. *Amigo, Amigo.* 1973. CMG. 1st. F/NF. H11. $25.00

CLIFFORD, Francis. *Amigo, Amigo.* 1973. CMG. 1st. VG/VG. P3. $20.00

CLIFFORD, Francis. *Battle Is Fought to Be Won.* 1961. Coward. 1st. F/NF. H11. $35.00

CLIFFORD, Francis. *Wild Justice.* 1972. CMG. 1st. VG/VG. P3. $25.00

CLIFFORD, Hugh. *Further Side of Silence.* 1916. Doubleday. 1st. F. M2. $50.00

CLIFTON, James. *Prairie People (Potawatomi, 1665-1965).* 1977. KS U. 1st. NF/NF. A20. $30.00

CLIFTON, Lucille. *Everett Anderson's Christmas Coming.* 1971. Holt Rinehart. 1st. sm 4to. F/F. C8. $25.00

CLIFTON, Lucille. *Good Woman.* 1969-80. BOA Ed. 1st. sgn/dtd 1997. F/dj. V1. $45.00

CLIFTON, Lucille. *My Friend Jacob.* 1980. Dutton. 1st. F/F. C8. $35.00

CLIFTON, Lucille. *Some of the Days of Everett Anderson.* 1970. HRW. 1st. ils Evaline Ness. F/F. B4. $100.00

CLIFTON, Mark. *Eight Keys to Eden.* 1960. Doubleday. 1st. VG/VG. P3. $40.00

CLIFTON, Oliver Lee. *Camp Fire Boys in Muskrat Swamp (#2).* 1923. Barse Hopkins. lists 3 titles. VG/G. M20. $35.00

CLIFTON, V. *Book of Talbot.* 1933. NY. 1st. ils/fld maps. 439p. VG/dj. B5. $45.00

CLINE, Isaac Monroe. *Storms, Floods & Sunshine.* 1945. New Orleans. Pelican. 1st. sgn. 290p. VG/G. B11. $35.00

CLINE, John. *Forever Beat.* 1990. Dutton. 1st. VG/VG. P3. $20.00

CLINE, Platt. *They Came to the Mountain.* 1976. N AZ U. 1st. ils/index. 364p. NF/NF. B19. $35.00

CLINE, Platt. *They Came to the Mountain.* 1986. Flagstaff. 4th. 8vo. blk cloth. F/F. F7. $25.00

CLINTON, Catherine. *Plantation Mistress.* 1982. Pantheon. 1st. 331p. VG/dj. M20. $22.00

CLISE, Michelle Durkson. *Ophelia's Voyage to Japan.* 1986. Potter. 1st. 4to. F/dj. M5. $65.00

CLIVE, William. *Tune That They Play.* 1973. Macmillan. 1st. VG/VG. P3. $15.00

CLOUD, P. *Cosmos, Earth & Man: A Short History of the Universe.* 1978. Yale. 372p. F. D8. $25.00

CLOUSTON, J. Storer. *Man From the Clouds.* 1919. Doran. 1st. VG. M2. $25.00

CLUTE, Nelson. *Our Ferns in Their Haunts.* 1901. Stokes. 332p. VG. A10. $48.00

CLUTESI, George. *Potlatch.* 1969. Sydney, BC. Gray's. 1st. ils. F/NF. L3. $85.00

CLYNE, Densey. *Australian Ground Orchids.* 1970. Melbourne. ils/photos. 112p. sc. VG. B26. $27.50

COAD. *New Jersey in Travelers' Accounts 1524-1971, Descriptive...* 1972. 633 entries. 221p. F. A4. $75.00

COATES, Walter John. *Land of Allen & Other Verse.* 1928. N Montpelier. Recluse. inscr assn copy. F. B11. $75.00

COATES & TUPPER. *Vermont Verse.* 1931. Brattleboro. Stephen Daye. sgn assn copy. gray cloth. VG. B11. $18.00

COATS, Alice. *Plant Hunters.* 1969. McGraw Hill. 400p. VG/dj. A10. $48.00

COATS, Alice. *Travels of Maurice.* 1939. London. ils. Vg/G+. M17. $20.00

COATSWORTH, Elizabeth. *Cat Who Went to Heaven.* 1930. Macmillan. 1st. ils Lynd Ward. 57p. cloth. VG+/dj. M20. $325.00

COATSWORTH, Elizabeth. *Children Come Running.* 1960. Golden Pr/Western Pub. 1st. 8vo. VG+/VG+. C8. $15.00

COATSWORTH, Elizabeth. *Door to the North.* (1950). Winston. Land of the Free series. 1st. brn bdg. F/VG+. N1. $10.00

COATSWORTH, Elizabeth. *Down Half the World.* 1968. Macmillan. 1st. 98p. F/F. D4. $35.00

COATSWORTH, Elizabeth. *Mouse Chorus.* 1955. pantheon. 1st. ils Geneive Vaughn-Jackson. VG+/VG. P2. $35.00

COATSWORTH, Elizabeth. *Princess & the Lion.* 1963. Pantheon. 1st. 78p. NF/VG. P3. $35.00

COATSWORTH, Elizabeth. *Trudy & the Tree House.* 1944. Macmillan. 1st. 114p. VG/G. P2. $25.00

COBB, Irvin S. *Cobb's Bill of Fare.* 1913. NY. Doran. 1st. ils Peter Newell/James Preston. pict brd. F/dj. M24. $125.00

COBB, Irvin S. *Roughing It Deluxe.* 1914. NY. Doran. 1st. 12mo. 219p. gray cloth. VG. F7. $30.00

COBBETT, William. *American Gardener.* ca 1830s. Claremont, NH. 16mo. 230p. A22. $125.00

COBLEIGH, Rolfe. *Handy Farm Devices & How to Make Them.* 1912. Orange Judd. 288p. VG. A10. $50.00

COBLENTZ, Stanton A. *After 12,000 Years.* 1950. Fantasy. 1st. F/dj. M2. $20.00

COBLENTZ, Stanton A. *Decline of Man.* 1925. Minton Balch. 1st. VG. M2. $35.00

COBLENTZ, Stanton A. *Sunken World.* 1948. Fantasy. 1st. sgn. F/dj. M2. $50.00

COBLENTZ, Stanton A. *Under Triple Suns.* 1955. Fantasy. 1/300. sgn/#d. F/M. M2. $160.00

COBLENTZ, Stanton A. *Villains & Vigilantes: Story of James King...* 1957. NY. Yoseloff. rpt. VG/G+. O4. $15.00

COBLENTZ, Stanton A. *When the Birds Fly South.* 1945. Wings. 1st. F/NF. M2. $50.00

COBLENTZ, Stanton A. *Winds of Chaos.* 1942. Wings. 1st. inscr. NF/G. M19. $25.00

COBURN, Andrew. *Sweetheart.* 1985. Secker Warburg. 1st. VG/VG. P3. $20.00

COBURN, Walt. *Barbwire.* 1931. Chicago. AL Burt. dj. A19. $30.00

COBURN, Walt. *Pioneer Cattleman in Montana, The Story of Circle C Ranch.* 1968. Norman, OK. 1st. sgn. 338p. VG/dj. J2. $145.00

COCHRAN, Johnnie. *Journey to Justice.* 1996. Ballantine. 1st. sgn bookplate. F/F. A23. $50.00

COCHRAN, Keith. *American West Historical Chronology.* 1992. Cochran. photos. 464p. dj. A19. $35.00

COCHRAN, Mike. *And Deliver Us From Evil.* 1989. TX Monthly. 1st. 213p. F/F. W2. $20.00

COCHRAN, Robert. *Vance Randolph, an Ozark Life.* 1985. U IL. 1st. VG/VG. V4. $15.00

COCKBURN, J.S. *Crime in England 1550-1800.* 1977. London. Methuen. 11 essays. M11. $45.00

COCKCROFT, G.L. *Index to the Weird Fiction Magazines.* 1975. Arno. 1st hc. VG. M2. $50.00

CODDINGTON, Edwin. *Gettysburg Campaign.* 1968. NY. 1st. VG/dj. B5. $50.00

CODMAN, C.R. *Drive.* 1957. MA. 1st. ils. 335p. VG/VG. S16. $30.00

CODMAN, C.R. *Years & Years: Some Vintage Years in French Wines.* 1932. private prt. inscr. 25p. stapled bdg. G+. B10. $65.00

CODRESCU, Andrei. *Craving for Swan.* 1986. Columbus. OH State. 1st. sgn. NF/NF. B4. $85.00

CODRESCU, Andrei. *History of the Growth of Heaven.* 1973. Braziller. 1st. photo Tom Veitch. F/NF. V1. $30.00

CODRINGTON, Robert. *Ten Books of Quintus Curtius Rufus...* 1652. London. Alsop. 1st this trans. sm 4to. 303p. modern bdg. C6. $350.00

COE, Michael D. *Maya.* (1986). Thames Hudson. 3rd. 190p. wrp. F3. $15.00

COE, Michael D. *Mexico.* 1977. Praeger. 2nd. 216p. NF/VG. W2. $15.00

COE, Tucker. *Don't Lie to Me.* 1972. Random. 1st. 181p. NF/NF. W2. $10.00

COELHO, Paul. *Valkyries: An Encounter With Angels.* 1992. Harper Collins. 1st. F/F. B3. $25.00

COETZEE, J.M. *Age of Iron.* 1990. Random. 1st. sgn. author's 7th book. F/F. D10. $35.00

COETZEE, J.M. *From the Heart of the Country.* 1977. Harper Row. 1st Am. sgn. author's 2nd novel. F/F. D10. $75.00

COETZEE, J.M. *Life & Times of Michael K.* 1984. NY. Viking. 1st Am. sgn. F/F. D10. $50.00

COETZEE, J.M. *Life & Times of Michael K.* 1984. Viking. 1st. F/NF. M23. $20.00

COFFEEN, J.A. *Seismic Exploration Fundamentals.* 1978. Tulsa, OK. Petroleum Pub. 277p. VG/dj. D8. $30.00

COFFEY, Brian; see Koontz, Dean R.

COFFEY, D.J. *Dolphins, Whales & Porpoises.* 1977. NY. 223p. VG/VG. S15. $15.00

COFFEY, Timothy. *History & Folklore of North American Wildflowers.* nd. Facts on File. 356p. dj. A10. $32.00

COFFIN, Charles Carleton. *Our New Way Round the World.* 1869. Boston. Osgood. 524p. VG. W1. $35.00

COFFIN, Charles Carleton. *Redeeming the Republic.* 1890. NY. ils. 478p. O8. $14.50

COFFIN, Margaret. *American Country Tinware 1700-1900.* 1968. photos. NF/VG. S13. $18.00

COFFMAN, Virginia. *From Satan, With Love.* 1983. Piatkus. F/F. P3. $15.00

COGGER & SWEIFEL. *Reptiles & Amphibians.* 1992. Smithmark. 1st. F/F. B1. $40.00

COGGESHALL, George. *History of American Privateers.* 1861 (1856). aeg. half leather/raised bands. VG. E6. $175.00

COGGINS & PRATT. *Rockets, Satellites & Space Travel.* 1958. Random. 2nd. 4to. 64p. VG. K5. $12.00

COGNIAT, Raymond. *XXth Century Drawings & Watercolors.* nd. NY. Crown. trans from French by Anne Ross. ils/list of artists. dj. D2. $75.00

COGSWELL, H.L. *Water Birds of California.* 1977. Berkeley. 399p. F/F. B1. $30.00

COHAN, George. *Broadway Jones.* 1913. Dillingham. 1st. F/NF. B4. $350.00

COHANE, Tim. *Great College Football Coaches of the Twenties & Thirties.* 1973. Arlington. 1st. photos. VG/dj. P8. $20.00

COHEN, Bernard. *Sociocultural Changes in American Jewish Life...* 1972. Fairleigh Dickinson. 282p. VG/dj. S3. $20.00

COHEN, Herman. *History of the English Bar & Attornatus to 1450.* 1967. London. Wildy & Sons Ltd. facsimile. cloth. M11. $125.00

COHEN, I. Bernard. *Newtonian Revolution...* 1980. Cambridge. inscr. 404p. VG/dj. K5. $45.00

COHEN, I. Bernard. *Some Early Tools of American Science.* 1950. Cambridge, MA. 1st. 8vo. 201p. VG. K3. $35.00

COHEN, Octavius Roy. *Bullet for My Love.* 1950. Macmillan. 1st. VG/dj. M25. $45.00

COHEN, Octavius Roy. *Eric Peters, Pullman Porter.* 1930. Appleton. 1st. 12mo. VG+/G. C8. $75.00

COHEN, Robert. *Organ Builder.* 1988. Harper. 1st. F/NF. R13. $35.00

COHEN, Sam. *Truth About the Neutron Bomb.* 1983. NY. 1st. F/dj. K3. $10.00

COHEN, Stanley. *Man in the Crowd.* 1981. Random. 1st. VG+/dj. P8. $10.00

COHEN, Stanley. *Park.* 1977. Putnam. 1st. F/F. P3. $15.00

COHEN & SMOLAN. *Day in the Life of America.* 1986. Collins. 272p. cloth. dj. D2. $65.00

COHN, Isadore. *Rudolph Matas: Biography of One Great Pioneers in Surgery.* 1960. Garden City. 1st. 431p. A13. $30.00

COHN, Norma. *Little People in a Big Country.* 1945. Oxford. 1st. sm 12mo. F/VG. M5. $45.00

COHN, Roy. *How to Fight for Your Rights & Win.* 1981. S&S. 1st. F/F. A20. $30.00

COHON, Samuel S. *Essays in Jewish Theology.* 1987. HUC Pr. 366p. VG/dj. S3. $25.00

COKER, Elizabeth Boatwright. *Bees.* 1968. Dutton. 1st. sgn. VG/VG. B11. $40.00

COKER, ELizabeth Boatwright. *India Allan.* 1953. Dutton. 1st. VG/G. P3. $15.00

COLACELLO, Bob. *Holy Terror: Andy Warhol Close Up.* 1990. Harper Collins. 1st. F/F. P3. $23.00

COLBERG, Nancy. *Wallace Stegner: Descriptive Bibliography.* 1990. Confluence. 1st. M/sans. A18. $50.00

COLBERT, E.H. *Age of Reptiles.* 1965. Norton. ils/drawings. 228p. F/NF. D8. $25.00

COLBERT, E.H. *Fosssil Hunter's Notebook.* 1980. Dutton. dj. A19. $25.00

COLBERT, E.H. *Men & Dinosaurs: Search in Field & Laboratory...* 1968. Dutton. 1st. ils. 283p. VG/dj. D8. $20.00

COLBERT, E.H. *Wandering Lands & Animals.* 1973. NY. Dutton. 1st. ils. 323p. NF/dj. D8. $22.00

COLBRY, Vera L. *Diagnostic Characteristics of Fruits & Florets...* 1957. WA, DC. ils. 24p. wrp. B26. $10.00

COLBY. *Children's Book Field.* 1952. 246p. VG. A4. $45.00

COLBY, C.B. *Moon Exploration.* 1970. Coward McCann. 4to. 48p. xl. K5. $10.00

COLCHIE, Thomas. *Hammock Beneath the Mangoes.* 1991. Dutton. 1st. F/dj. M2. $30.00

COLE, Adrian. *Place Among the Fallen.* 1987. Arbor. 1st. NF/NF. P3. $20.00

COLE, Burt. *Quick.* 1989. Morrow. 1st. NF/NF. P3. $20.00

COLE, Duane. *Vagabond Club.* 1967. Ken Cook Pub. 1st. sgn pres. 183p. VG/dj. B5. $30.00

COLE, G.D.H. *Last Will & Testament.* 1985. Collins Crime Club. VG/VG. P3. $15.00

COLE, H. *Heraldry: Decoration & Floral Forms.* 1988. ils. VG/VG. M17. $15.00

COLE, Helen R. *100 Years in Thatcher, 1883-1983.* 1983. Thatcher. 1st. ils. 384p. F. B19. $75.00

COLE, Maria. *Nat King Cole: An Intimate Biography.* 1971. Morrow. 1st. F/F. M25. $35.00

COLE, S.W. *American Fruit Book.* 1866. Orange Judd. 276p. cloth. VG. A10. $30.00

COLE, S.W. *Soil Management for Conservation & Production.* 1962. NY. Wiley. 527p. dj. A10. $20.00

COLE, W.R. *Checklist of Science Fiction Anthologies.* 1964. Cole. 1st. F/F. P3. $100.00

COLE, William. *Book of Animal Poems.* 1973. Viking. ARC/1st. 288p. F/F. D4. $35.00

COLE, William. *Book of Nature Poems.* 1969. Viking. 1st. ils RA Parker. F/NF. D4. $35.00

COLE, William. *Oh What Nonsense!* 1966. Viking. 1st. 80p. F/NF. D4. $45.00

COLEMAN, Ken. *So You Want to Be a Sportscaster.* 1973. Hawthorn. 1st. photos. VG+/dj. P8. $25.00

COLEMAN, McAlister. *Eugene V Debs: Man Unafraid.* 1930. Greenberg. 1st. VG/VG. V4. $50.00

COLEMAN, Satis N. *Book of Bells.* 1938. NY. 177p. xl. A17. $45.00

COLERIDGE, S.T. *Phantasmion.* 1874. Roberts Bros. G. M2. $150.00

COLERIDGE, S.T. *Poems.* 1848. NY/Boston. CS Francis. 1st thus. intro HT Tuckerman. full blk morocco. M24. $275.00

COLES, Manning. *All That Glitters.* 1954. Doubleday/Crime Club. 1st. VG+/dj. M20. $35.00

COLES, Manning. *Dangerous by Nature.* 1950. Doubleday. 1st. VG/VG. N4. $30.00

COLES, Manning. *Drink to Yesterday.* 1944. Canada. Musson. VG/VG. P3. $30.00

COLES, Manning. *Without Lawful Authority.* 1944. Canada. Musson. 1st. VG/G+. P3. $20.00

COLES, P. Catherine. *King's Command.* (1958). Victory Pr. bl bdg. VG/fair. N1. $8.50

COLETTA, Paolo. *Annotated Bibliography of US Marine Corps History.* 1986. Lanham. 1st. 417p. VG. S16. $45.00

COLETTE. *Cat.* 1936. Farrar Rhinehart. 1st. NF/NF. B4. $85.00

COLETTE. *Chats.* 1945. Lausanne. 1st. photos. natural linen. F/VG+. A11. $135.00

COLLEDGE & DITTMAR. *British Warships, 1914-1919.* 1972. London. Ian Allan. 150 photos. dj. T7. $35.00

COLLEDGE & LENTON. *Warships of World War II.* 1964. London. Ian Allan. 425 photos. 638p. dj. T7. $40.00

COLLETT, Marjorie. *Elizabeth in Toyland.* 1925. Harrap. 1st. ils Tarrant. 12mo. beige brd. pict dj. R5. $150.00

COLLIDGE, Mary Roberts. *Chinese Immigration: American Public Problems.* 1909. NY. Holt. thick 8vo. gilt bl cloth. F. R3. $125.00

COLLIE & FRASER. *George Borrow: A Bibliographical Study.* 1984. 1/750. 23 pl. 239p. F/VG. A4. $125.00

COLLIER, John. *Fancies & Goodnights.* 1951. Doubleday. 1st. F/dj. M2. $100.00

COLLIER, John. *Green Thoughts.* 1932. London. 1/550. sgn/#d. VG. M2. $125.00

COLLIER, John. *His Monkey Wife.* 1931. Appleton. 1st. VG. P3. $35.00

COLLIER, Peter. *Kennedy's: An American Drama.* 1984. Summit. 1st. sgn. VG/VG. A23. $32.00

COLLIER, Richard. *House Called Memory.* 1961. Dutton. 1st. VG/VG. P3. $15.00

COLLIER, S. *Mount Desert: Most Beautiful Island in the World.* 1952. photos. VG. M17. $30.00

COLLIER, V.W.F. *Dogs of China & Japan in Nature & Art.* 1921. London. Heinemann. ils. 207p. remnant rear xl pocket. VG. W3. $95.00

COLLIER & EATON. *Roland, the Warrior.* (1934). Harcourt Brace. ils Frank Schoonover. G+. B15. $45.00

COLLIER. *Collier's Photographic History of World War II.* 1945. NY. 800+ photos/map ep. gilt/red stp brn cloth. VG. K7. $50.00

COLLING, Susan. *Frogmorton.* 1956. Knopf. 1st Am. 148p. gr cloth/red spine. VG/torn. T5. $30.00

COLLINGWOOD, W.G. *Life & Works of John Ruskin.* 1893. Houghton Mifflin. 2 vol. 1st. 8vo. aeg. dk red ribbed cloth. H13. $95.00

COLLINS, A. Frederick. *Amateur Mechanic.* 1919 (1918). Appleton. 8vo. 208p. G. K5. $20.00

COLLINS, Clella R. *Army Woman's Handbook.* 1942. Whittlesey. revised. 239p. VG+. A25. $32.00

COLLINS, Erroll. *Mariners of Space.* 1949. London. VG. M2. $15.00

COLLINS, Freda. *Shrove-tide Fair.* 1960. Faith Pr. 1st. F/F. N1. $4.00

COLLINS, G.B. *Wildcats & Shamrocks.* 1977. Mennonite Pr. 2nd. inscr. VG/dj. D8. $12.00

COLLINS, Gary. *Magnificent Mind.* 1985. World. 262p. VG/dj. B29. $8.00

COLLINS, Gilbert. *Valley of Eyes Unseen.* 1924. McBride. 1st Am. VG. M2. $37.00

COLLINS, Hunt; see Hunter, Evan.

COLLINS, Jackie. *Lady Boss.* 1990. S&S. 1st. NF/F. T12. $20.00

COLLINS, Larry. *Maze.* 1989. S&S. 1st. VG/VG. P3. $20.00

COLLINS, Mary. *Sister of Cain.* 1943. Scribner. 1st. VG. P3. $20.00

COLLINS, Michael; see Lynds, Dennis.

COLLINS, Nancy. *Midnight Blue: Sonia Blue Collection.* 1995. Stone Mtn. 1st collection. VG+/dj. M21. $20.00

COLLINS, Paul. *Alien Worlds.* 1979. Void Pub. 1st. NF/NF. P3. $30.00

COLLINS, Randall. *Case of the Philosophers' Ring.* 1980. Harvester. 1st. VG/VG. P3. $30.00

COLLINS, Richard L. *Thunderstorms & Airplanes.* 1982. Delacorte. 1st. 8vo. 280p. VG/dj. K5. $15.00

COLLINS, Wilkie. *Man & Wife.* 1870. NY. Harper. 1st Am. gilt purple cloth. M24. $75.00

COLLINS, Wilkie. *Moonstone.* 1959. NY. LEC. 1st thus. 1/1500. ils/sgn Andre Dignimont. F/dj/case. Q1. $100.00

COLLINS, Wilkie. *Queen of Hearts.* 1859. NY. Harper. 1st Am. gilt brick-brn pebbled cloth. F. M24. $375.00

COLLINS & ERIKSSON. *Anne of Green Gable's Treasury.* 1991. Viking. 1st. 243p. F/dj. T10. $35.00

COLLINS & LAPIERRE. *Fifth Horseman.* 1980. S&S. 1st. NF/NF. M22. $15.00

COLLIS, Louise. *Soldier in Paradise: Life of Capt John Stedman 1744-97.* (1966). Harcourt Brace. 1st Am. 231p. F3. $20.00

COLLIS, Maurice. *Grand Peregrination.* 1959. London. Faber. 2nd. cloth. VG/dj. M20. $20.00

COLLODI, Carlo. *Adventures of Pinocchio.* nd. NY. Macmillan. 3rd. ils Attilio Mussino. 404p. dk bl cloth. VG. D1. $225.00

COLLODI, Carlo. *Adventures of Pinocchio.* 1939. London. Collins. 1st thus. ils AH Watson. 8vo. red textured cloth. dj. R5. $135.00

COLLODI, Carlo. *Pinocchio's Adventures in Wonderland.* 1898. Boston. Jordan Marsh. 1st Am. 12mo. M5. $275.00

COLLODI, Carlo. *Pinocchio.* (1932). Garden City. ils Petersham. G. B15. $40.00

COLLODI, Carlo. *Pinocchio.* 1904. Ginn. full-p mc pl. gilt cloth/mc pl. VG. M5. $75.00

COLLODI, Carlo. *Pinocchio.* 1904. Ginn. Once Upon A Time series. 12mo. gilt gr cloth. M5. $55.00

COLLODI, Carlo. *Pinocchio.* 1919. Dent Dutton. 2nd. thick 8vo. VG. M5. $110.00

COLLODI, Carlo. *Pinocchio.* 1933. Blue Ribbon. ils Harold Lentz/4 popups. 96p. VG+. D1. $650.00

COLLODI, Carlo. *Walt Disney's Pinocchio. A Giant Golden Punch-Out.* 1962. England. Purnell. adapted from movie. lg 4to. unpunched. R5. $150.00

COLMAN, Miss. *Bijou Alphabet.* 1846. Phil. 12mo. 111p. gilt cloth. VG. B14. $100.00

COLMONT, Marie. *Le Roi Chat.* 1944. Flammarion. 1st. ils Andre Paul. sq 12mo. VG+. M5. $65.00

COLNETT, James. *Voyage to the South Atlantic & Round Cape Horn...* 1968. Amsterdam. rpt. fld maps/charts. 179p. P4. $110.00

COLOMBO, John Robert. *Not to Be Taken at Night.* 1981. Lester Denys. F/NF. P3. $20.00

COLTMAN, Paul. *Tog the Ribber; or, Granny's Tale.* 1985. London. Deutsch. 1st. 29p. F/F. D4. $25.00

COLTMAN, Paul. *Witch Watch.* 1989. FSG. 1st. unp. VG/dj. M20. $20.00

COLTON, James; see Hansen, Joseph.

COLTON, Walter. *Three Years in California.* 1850. NY. Barnes. 456p. red cloth. VG. K7. $175.00

COLTON, Walter. *Three Years in California.* 1886. Boston. Cleaves Macdonald. 12mo. 456p. gilt cloth. VG. T10. $75.00

COLUM, Padraic. *Collected Poems.* 1953. NY. Devin-Adair. 1st thus. sgn. F/VG. B4. $85.00

COLUM, Padraic. *Six Who Were Left in a Shoe.* 1923. Chicago. Volland. ils Dugald Stewart Walker. 40p. NF. A4. $65.00

COLUM, Padraic. *Voyager, Legends & History of Atlantic Discoveries.* 1925. Macmillan. 1st. ils Winfred Jones. 188p. VG/worn. D1. $50.00

COLVILLE, Jessie. *Kentucky Woman's Handy Cookbook.* 1912. self pub. VG. E6. $45.00

COLWIN, Laurie. *Passion & Affect.* 1974. NY. Viking. 1st. author's 1st book. NF/VG. L3. $50.00

COMANCHO, El. *Old Timer's Tale.* 1929. Canterbury. 1st. pl. 114p. VG. J2. $95.00

COMBE, William. *Three Tours of Dr Syntax...* 1823. London. Ackerman. 3 vol. 1st thus. 78 hand-colored aquatints. Birdsall bdg. H13. $1,295.00

COMLY, John. *Epistle, or Salutation in Gospel Love...* 1832. Phil. J Richards. 1st. 36p. V3. $25.00

COMLY & COMLY. *Friends' Miscellany: Being Collection of Essays...* 1833-1835. Phil. J Richards. 2nd. 6 vol. full leather. V3. $185.00

COMMAGER. *St Nicholas Anthology.* (1948). Random. 3rd. ils. VG. B15. $40.00

COMMAGER, Henry Steele. *Blue & the Gray.* 1950. Indianapolis. 2 vol. 1st. VG/dj. B5. $125.00

COMMANDER SCOTT. *Romance of the Highways of California.* 1945. Pasadena. Commander Scott Prod. 1st ltd/sgn. G+/poor. O4. $20.00

COMPERTZ, M. *Corn From Egypt: Beginning of Agriculture...* 1928. 87p. xl. VG. E6. $15.00

COMPTON, Arthur Holly. *Cosmos of Arthur Holly Compton.* 1967. Knopf. 1st. VG/dj. K3. $20.00

COMPTON, D.G. *Windows.* 1979. Berkley Putnam. 1st. VG/VG. P3. $13.00

COMPTON, R.R. *Manual of Field Geology.* 1962. John Wiley. 378p. G. D8. $12.00

COMPTON-BURNETT, I. *First & the Last.* 1971. Knopf. 1st Am. F/NF. B4. $50.00

COMSTOCK, J.L. *Elements of Chemistry.* 1850. Pratt Woodford. 32nd ed from the 54th. 422p. full leather. G+. H1. $35.00

COMSTOCK, Sarah. *Moon Is Made of Green Cheese.* 1929. Doubleday. 1st. VG. M2. $12.00

CON, J. *American Orders & Societies & Their Decorations.* 1917. Phil. ils. VG. E6. $125.00

CONANT, Charles A. *History of Modern Banks of Issue.* 1896. Putnam. 1st. 8vo. 595p. teg. gilt brn cloth. VG. T10. $75.00

CONCHA, Joseph L. *Lonely Deer.* 1969. Taos Pueblo Council. 1st. sgn. NF/wrp. L3. $250.00

CONCIDINE, J. Francis. *Singing Rails.* 1934. Blk Cat. 1st. 1/300. unp. VG. D4. $45.00

CONDIT & TURNBLADH. *Hold High the Torch: History of 4th Marines.* 1989. Nashville. rpt. maps/biblio/index. 458p. VG. S16. $40.00

CONDON, Richard. *Ecstasy Business.* 1967. Dial. 1st. VG/VG. M22. $20.00

CONDON, Richard. *Infirmity of Mirrors.* 1964. Random. 1st. F/NF. H11. $30.00

CONDON, Richard. *Prizzi's Honor.* 1982. Coward. 1st. F/NF. H11. $35.00

CONDON, Richard. *Trembling Upon Rome.* 1983. Michael Joseph. 1st. F/F. P3. $25.00

CONDON, Richard. *Vertical Smile.* 1971. Dial. 1st. VG/VG. P3. $25.00

CONEY, Michael G. *Celestial Steam Locomotive.* 1983. Houghton Mifflin. 1st. F/dj. M2. $15.00

CONEY, Michael G. *Fang the Gnome.* 1988. NAL. 1st/1st prt. 8vo. 345p. F/F. T10. $75.00

CONEY, Michael G. *Gods of the Greataway.* 1984. Houghton Mifflin. 1st. VG/VG. P3. $16.00

CONGER, A. *Rise of US Grant.* 1931. 390p. xl. F. O8. $18.50

CONGREVE, William. *Way of the World & Love for Love.* 1929. Dodd Mead. 1st. ils John Kettelwell. NF. M19. $45.00

CONKLIN, Groff. *Omnibus of Science Fiction.* 1952. Crown. 1st. F/dj. M2. $37.00

CONKLIN, Groff. *Science Fiction in Mutation.* 1955. Vanguard. 1st. VG/dj. P3. $35.00

CONKLIN, Groff. *Treasury of Science Fiction.* 1948. Crown. 1st. VG/NF. M2. $30.00

CONLEY, Robert J. *Back to Malachi.* 1986. Doubleday. 1st. inscr. F/F. L3. $125.00

CONLEY, Robert J. *Saga of Henry Starr.* 1989. Doubleday. 1st. F/NF. L3. $65.00

CONNELL, Evan S. *Mrs Bridge.* 1960. London. Heinemann. 1st Eng. F/VG+ clip. B4. $225.00

CONNELL, Evans. *Anatomy Lesson.* 1957. 1st. sgn. F/VG. M19. $85.00

CONNELL, Will. *In Pictures: A Hollywood Satire.* 1937. NY. TJ Maloney. 106p. wrp/sbdg/cb case. D11. $500.00

CONNELLY, Marc. *Souvenir From Qam.* 1965. Holt. 1st. F/F. H11. $30.00

CONNELLY, Michael. *Black Echo.* 1992. Little Brn. ARC. F/F. D10. $50.00

CONNELLY, Michael. *Black Ice.* 1993. Little Brn. 1st. sgn. F/F. A23. $40.00

CONNELLY & KAUFMAN. *Beggar on Horseback.* 1924. Boni Liveright. 1st. F/NF. B4. $300.00

CONNINGTON, J.J. *No Past Is Dead.* 1942. Little Brn. 1st Am. Vg/dj. M15. $50.00

CONNOLLY, Cyril. *Condemned Playground, Essays.* 1945. London. 1st. VG. T9. $20.00

CONNOLLY. *Children's Modern First Editions, Their Value...* 1988. ils. 335p. F/F. A4. $165.00

CONNOR, Ralph. *Foreigner: A Tale of Saskatchewan.* 1909. Hodder Stoughton. dj. A19. $20.00

CONRAD, Barnaby. *How to Fight a Bull.* 1968. Doubleday. 1st. 224p. dj. F3. $20.00

CONRAD, Barnaby. *La Fiesta Brava.* 1953. Houghton Mifflin. later prt. photos. VG. P8. $20.00

CONRAD, Earl. *Invention of the Negro.* 1966. NY. Ericksson. 1st. NF/VG. B4. $45.00

CONRAD, Henry S. *How to Know the Mosses & Liverworts.* 1956. Dubuque. revised 2nd. Picture-Keyed Nature series. F. B26. $17.50

CONRAD, Joseph. *Almayer's Folly.* 1895. London. Fisher Unwin. 1st/1st issue. author's 1st book. teg. gilt gr cloth. M24. $1,650.00

CONRAD, Joseph. *Conrad Argosy.* 1942. Doubleday Doran. 4to. 713p. T7. $40.00

CONRAD, Joseph. *Dover Patrol, a Tribute.* 1922. Canterbury. Prt for Private Circulation/ 1st. 1/75. NF/prt wrp. M24. $375.00

CONRAD, Joseph. *Lord Jim: A Tale.* 1959. LEC. 1st thus. 1/1500. ils/sgn Lynd Ward. F/NF case. Q1. $150.00

CONRAD, Joseph. *Marcel Proust, an English Tribute.* 1923. Chatto Windus. 1st/lg paper issue. 1/150. quarter parchment. uncut. M24. $250.00

CONRAD, Joseph. *Outcast of the Islands.* 1896. Appleton. 1st Am. 3-quarter maroon roan. teg. pub bdg. M24. $600.00

CONRAD, Joseph. *Secret Agent.* 1907. Harper. 1st Am. 372p. gilt bl bdg. G+. H1. $40.00

CONRAD, Joseph. *Secret Agent: A Drama in Three Acts.* 1923. London. 1/1000. sgn/#d. NF/VG. A11. $400.00

CONRAD, Joseph. *Some Reminiscences.* 1912. London. Eveleigh Nash. 1st. 1/1000. gilt bl cloth. F. M24. $225.00

CONRAD, Joseph. *Suspense: A Napoleonic Novel.* 1925. Doubleday. 1st. 1/377. gilt cream brd/bl trim. inner & outer dj/case. B24. $250.00

CONRAD, Joseph. *Tremolino.* 1942. NY. Duschnes. 1st separate. ils/sgn EA Wilson. F/case. B24. $150.00

CONRAD, Joseph. *Victory.* 1921. Modern Lib. ne. G. W2. $250.00

CONRAD & DEMAREST. *Religion & Empire.* (1984). Cambridge. 1st. 2656p. reading copy. F3. $10.00

CONRAD & PATTERSON. *Scottsboro Boy.* 1950. Doubleday. 1st. G/dj. M25. $35.00

CONRAN, Shirley. *Savages.* 1987. S&S. 1st. F/F. T12. $25.00

CONRAN, Terence. *Vegetable Book.* 1976. Crescent. VG/dj. A16. $6.00

CONROY, Frank. *Midair.* 1985. Dutton. 1st. NF/F. H11. $25.00

CONROY, Frank. *Stop-Time.* 1967. Viking. 1st. F/F. B4. $150.00

CONROY, Pat. *Great Santini.* 1976. Houghton Mifflin. 1st. sgn. F/NF. B4. $300.00

CONROY, Pat. *Lords of Discipline.* 1980. Houghton Mifflin. 1st. author's 4th novel. F/NF. D10. $85.00

CONROY, Pat. *Lords of Discipline.* 1980. Houghton Mifflin. 1st. sgn. F/F. B4/Q1. $200.00

CONROY, Pat. *Prince of Tides.* 1986. Houghton Mifflin. 1st. inscr. F/dj. Q1. $75.00

CONROY, Pat. *Prince of Tides.* 1986. Houghton Mifflin. 1st. NF/NF. A24/T11. $35.00

CONSIDINE, Bob. *Toots.* 1969. NY. inscr Toots Shor. 214p. VG. B14. $45.00

CONSIDINE, Shaun. *Barbra Streisand: Woman, Myth, Music.* 1985. Delacorte. 1st. photos. 335p. VG/G. A25. $10.00

CONSTANTINE, K.C. *Man Who Liked Slow Tomatoes.* 1982. Godine. 1st. NF/NF. M22. $75.00

CONSTANTINE, K.C. *Upon Some Midnight's Clear.* 1985. Godine. 1st. NF/NF. M22. $25.00

CONWELL, Russell H. *Magnolia Journey: A Union Veteran Revisits...* 1974. AL U. 1st. 190p. cloth. VG/dj. M20. $25.00

CONYBEARE & HOWSON. *Life & Epistles of St Paul.* 1893. Longman Gr. 850p. fair. B29. $11.00

CONYBEARE & HOWSON. *Life & Epistles of St Paul.* 1980. Eerdmans. 850p. VG/dj. B29. $13.00

COOK, A.H. *Physics of the Earth & Planets.* 1973. Wiley. 8vo. 316p. VG/VG. K5. $20.00

COOK, Allyn Austin. *Diseases of Tropical & Subtropical Fruits & Nuts.* 1975. Hafner. 8vo. 317p. xl. A22. $22.00

COOK, Canfield. *Lucky Terrell: Lost Squadron (#4).* 1943. Grosset Dunlap. 1st. lists to this title. 216p. VG/dj. M20. $22.50

COOK, Canfield. *Lucky Terrell: Secret Mission (#3).* 1943. Grosset Dunlap. 1st. lists 2 titles. 210p. VG/dj. M20. $20.00

COOK, Canfield. *Lucky Terrell: Springboard to Tokyo (#5).* 1943. Grosset Dunlap. 210p. cloth. VG/rpr. M20. $20.00

COOK, Canfield. *Lucky Terrell: Wings Over Japan (#6).* 1944. Grosset Dunlap. 1st. lists 5 titles. VG/dj. M20. $25.00

COOK, Frederick A. *To the Top of the Continent: Discovery, Exploration...* 1996. Hurleyville. 1/200. 19th Anniversary ed. 312p. P4. $50.00

COOK, Harold J. *Tales of the 04 Ranch.* 1968. U NE. 1st. 221p. VG/VG. J2. $90.00

COOK, James. *Explorations of Capt James Cook in the Pacific...* nd (1955). Heritage. 292p. gilt bdg. VG/poor case. P4. $45.00

COOK, Marc. *Wilderness Cure.* 1881. NY. 153p. pict cloth. VG. B14. $95.00

COOK, Robin. *Brain.* 1981. Putnam. 1st. VG/VG. P3. $25.00

COOK, Robin. *Coma.* 1977. Little Brn. 1st. NF/clip. M22. $20.00

COOK, Robin. *Coma.* 1977. Little Brn. 1st. NF/NF. M19. $45.00

COOK, Robin. *Fever.* 1982. Putnam. 1st. sgn. NF/NF. M19. $25.00

COOK, Robin. *Mindbend.* 1985. Putnam. 1st. VG/VG. P3. $15.00

COOK, Robin. *Private Parts in Public Places.* 1969. Atheneum. 1st. VG/VG. P3. $40.00

COOK, Robin. *Sphinx.* 1979. Putnam. 1st. VG/VG. P3. $23.00

COOK, Thomas H. *Night Secrets.* 1990. Putnam. 1st. F/F. P3. $20.00

COOK, Thomas H. *Orchids.* 1982. Houghton Mifflin. 1st. F/F. T2. $45.00

COOK, Warren L. *Flood Tide of Empire: Spain & Pacific Northwest 1543-1819.* 1973. New Haven. Yale. Yale W Am series 24. 4to. 620p. F. O7. $35.00

COOK-LYNN, Elizabeth. *Badger Said This.* 1977. NY. Vantage. 1st. author's 1st book. NF/VG. L3. $350.00

COOK-LYNN, Elizabeth. *Power of Horses & Other Stories.* 1990. NY. Arcade/Little Brn. AP. wrp. R13. $30.00

COOKE, Alistair. *America.* 1974. Knopf. dj. A19. $25.00

COOKE, Alistair. *Americans: Fifty Letters From America.* 1979. London. 1st. VG/dj. T9. $20.00

COOKE, Alistair. *Patient Has the Floor.* 1986. Knopf. 1st trade. F/F. B35. $16.00

COOKE, D.E. *Firebird.* 1939. Winston. 1st. ils. red cloth. VG. M5. $45.00

COOKE, David C. *Best Detective Stories of the Year 1950.* 1950. Dutton. 1st. VG/G+. P3. $20.00

COOKE, David C. *My Best Murder Story.* 1955. Merlin. 1st. VG+/G. N4. $20.00

COOKE, Donald. *For Conspicuous Gallantry: Winners of Medal of Honor.* 1966. Maplewood. ils/roster/index. 93p. VG/VG. S16. $15.00

COOKE, G. Walter. *Death Is the End.* 1965. Geoffrey Bles. 1st. VG/VG. P3. $18.00

COOKE & MCQUEEN. *Girls of Silver Spur Ranch.* ca 1950. Chicago. Goldsmith. 1st. unp. VG/dj. A25. $20.00

COOL, Joyce. *Kidnapping of Courtney Van Allen & What's-Her-Name.* (1982). Knopf. 8vo. 175p. VG. T5. $18.00

COOLIDGE, Calvin. *Extracts From the Autobiography of...* 1930. Kingsport, TN. 21x15mm. 129p. aeg. full bl leather. B24. $150.00

COOLIDGE, Olivia. *George Bernard Shaw.* 1968. Houghton Mifflin. 1st. VG/dj. V4. $20.00

COOLIDGE, Olivia. *Greek Myths.* (1949). Houghton Mifflin. 8vo. 244p. VG. T5. $20.00

COOLIDGE, Susan. *What Katy Did.* (1936). Little Brn. ils Ralph Pallen Coleman. 271p. VG/dj. T5. $17.00

COOMBS, Charles. *Andy Burnett on Trial.* 1958. Whitman. TVTI. VG. P3. $15.00

COOMBS, Charles. *Maverick.* 1959. Whitman. TVTI. VG. P3. $15.00

COOMBS, Patricia. *Molly Mullett.* 1975. Lee Shepard. 1st. sm 4to. unp. brn cloth. F/NF. T5. $25.00

COON, Carleton S. *Living Races of Man.* 1965. Knopf. 1st. NF/VG. A20. $15.00

COON, Carleton S. *Seven Caves: Archaeological Explorations in Middle East.* 1957. Knopf. 1st. 8vo. 31 pl. VG. W1. $18.00

COONEY, Barbara. *Chanticleer & the Fox.* 1958. Crowell. 1st. Caldecott Medal. VG+/VG. P2. $125.00

COONEY, Barbara. *Courtship, Merry Marriage & Feast of Cock Robin.* 1965. Scribner. 1st. 32p. cloth. F/VG. D4. $35.00

COONTS, Stephen. *Flight of the Intruder.* 1986. Naval Inst. 1st. author's 1st book. F/F. N4. $35.00

COONTS, Stephen. *Minotaur.* 1989. Doubleday. 1st. NF/NF. P3. $20.00

COOPER, Basil. *Great White Space.* 1975. St Martin. 1st Am. F/dj. M2. $85.00

COOPER, Basil. *House of the Wolf.* 1983. Saulk City. Arkham. 1st. ils/sgn Stephen Fabian. VG. B11. $50.00

COOPER, Dennis. *Wrong.* 1980. Knopf. 1st. F/F. B35. $15.00

COOPER, Douglas. *Great Private Collections.* 1961. 1st. lg 4to. ils. NF/VG. S13. $18.00

COOPER, Edmund. *Prisoner of Fire.* 1974. Walker. 1st. F/dj. M2. $12.00

COOPER, Irving S. *Cerebellum, Epilepsy & Behavior.* 1974. NY. Plenum. 401p. brn cloth. G1. $50.00

COOPER, James Fenimore. *Last of the Mohicans.* 1919. Scribner. 1st. ils NC Wyeth. VG. M17. $85.00

COOPER, James Fenimore. *Last of the Mohicans.* 1977. Franklin Lib. ils NC Wyeth. aeg. F. A18. $50.00

COOPER, James Fenimore. *Pathfinder.* 1965. LEC. into Robert E Spiller. Ils Richard Powers. F/case. A18. $60.00

COOPER, James Fenimore. *Prairie, a Tale, by the Author of the Spy, the Pilot...* 1827. London. Henry Colburn. 1st. 3 vol. 12mo. contemporary polished calf. M1. $350.00

COOPER, James Fenimore. *Wing-And-Wing; or, Le Feu-Follet, a Tale.* 1842. Lee Blanchard. 1st. 2 vol. unusual variant pub bdg. M24. $450.00

COOPER, Merian C. *Grass.* 1925. Putnam. 2nd. inscr. VG/dj. B4. $450.00

COOPER, Nelle Grant. *Australians All. Bush Folk in Rhyme.* 1934. Australia. Angus Robertson. 1st. ils Dorothy Wall. 30p. pict brd. R5. $200.00

COOPER, Susan Rogers. *Funny as a Dead Relative.* 1994. St Martin. 1st. sgn. F/F. A23. $42.00

COOPER, Susan Rogers. *Gray King.* 1975. Atheneum. 1st. Newbery Medal. ils Michael Heslop. 208p. NF/VG+. P2. $145.00

COOPER, Susan Rogers. *Gray King.* 1975. NY. Atheneum. 1st. ils Michael Heslop. 8vo. 208p. gray-gr cloth. VG/VG. R5. $110.00

COOPER, Susan Rogers. *Houston in the Rear View Mirror.* 1990. St Martin. 1st. sgn. author's 2nd book. NF/F. A24. $90.00

COOPER, Susan Rogers. *One, Two, What Did Daddy Do?* 1992. St Martin. 1st. sgn. F/F. A23. $42.00

COOPER, Susan Rogers. *Other People's Houses.* 1990. St Martin. 1st. sgn. author's 3rd book. F/NF. A24. $55.00

COOPER, Susan Rogers. *Seaward.* 1983. Atheneum. 1st. 167p. NF/NF. P2. $35.00

COOPER, Will. *Death Has a Thousand Doors.* 1976. Bobbs Merrill. 1st. VG/VG. P3. $15.00

COOPER & GASKELL. *North Sea Oil: The Great Gamble.* 1966. Bobbs Merrill. 179p. VG/dj. T11. $14.00

COOPER & RATNER. *Many Hands Cooking.* 1974. Crowell/Unicef. 1st. ils Tony Chen. VG. M5. $20.00

COOPER & TRAVERS. *Surgical Essays.* 1821. Phil. 1st Am. 409p. A13. $300.00

COOPER & TREAT. *Man O'War.* 1950. photos. G. M17. $30.00

COOTE, Stephen. *Byron, the Making of a Myth.* 1988. London. 1st. as new. T9. $16.00

COOVER, Robert. *Origin of the Brunists.* 1966. Putnam. 1st. author's 1st book. F/dj. D10. $165.00

COOVER, Robert. *Pricksongs & Descants.* 1969. Dutton. 1st. author's 3rd book. F/NF. D10. $70.00

COOVER, Robert. *Public Burning.* 1977. Viking. 1st. F/F. A20. $25.00

COPE, Myron. *Broken Cigars.* 1968. Prentice Hall. 1st. VG/G+. P8. $25.00

COPE, Zachary. *Clinical Researches in Acute Abdominal Disease.* 1925. London. 1st. 148p. A13. $150.00

COPELAND, Bonnie. *Lady of Moray.* 1979. Atheneum. 1st. 313p. F/NF. W2. $25.00

COPELAND, Richard. *No Face in a Mirror.* 1980. Macmillan. 1st. VG/VG. P3. $15.00

COPEMAN, Edward. *Report of Cerebral Affections of Infancy...* 1995 (1873). NY. Classics Neurology/Neurosurgery Lib. facsimile. G1. $65.00

COPP, DeWitt S. *Forged in Fire.* 1982. Garden City, NY. 1st. 521p. quarter cloth. VG/dj. B18. $19.50

COPPARD, A.E. *Collected Tales of...* 1951. Knopf. VG/dj. M2. $30.00

COPPARD, A.E. *Nixey's Harlequin.* 1932. Knopf. 1st Am. VG. M2. $25.00

COPPEE, Henry. *Grant & His Campaigns.* 1866. NY. ils/maps. G. M17. $20.00

COPPEL, Alfred. *Apocalypse Bridge.* 1981. HRW. 1st. sgn. F/F. T12. $25.00

COPPEL, Alfred. *Apocalypse Brigade.* 1981. HRW. 1st. VG/VG. P3. $15.00

COPPEL, Alfred. *Dragon.* 1977. HBJ. 1st. VG/VG. P3. $15.00

COPPER, Basil. *From Evil's Pillow.* 1973. Arkham. 1st. F/dj. M2/M19. $25.00

COPPER, Basil. *Necropolis.* 1980. Arkham. 1st. F/dj. M2. $100.00

COPPER, Edmund. *All Fools' Day.* 1966. Hodder Stoughton. 1st. VG/VG. P3. $20.00

COPPER, Edmund. *Transit.* 1964. Faber. 1st. VG/VG. P3. $30.00

COPPIN, Glorgio. *Bears: Art, Legend, History.* 1993. Boston. 112p. F/F. S15. $8.00

COPWAY, George. *Kah-Ge-Ga-Gah-Bowh. Running Sketches of Men & Places...* 1851. NY. JC Riker. 1st. author's 3rd/last book. G. L3. $375.00

COQUIA, Jorge R. *Legal Status of the Church of the Philippines.* 1950. WA. Catholic U of Am Pr. 224p. F. P1. $20.00

CORBETT, A. *Poultry Yard & Market.* 1877. Orange Judd. 96p. gilt bdg. VG. A l 0. $30.00

CORBETT, Bertha L. *Sun-Bonnet Babies.* 1900. Minneapolis. 1st. sq 8vo. pale gr pict brd. R5. $200.00

CORBETT, Helen. *Helen Corbett Cooks for Company.* 1974. Houghton Mifflin. 1t. dj. A16. $10.00

CORBETT, Helen. *Helen Corbett's Cookbook.* 1962. Houghton Mifflin. VG/partial. A16. $8.00

CORBETT, James. *Death Pool.* 1936. Herbert Jenkins. 1st. VG/VG. P3. $75.00

CORBETT, James. *Merrivale Mystery.* 1931. Mystery League. 1st. NF. P3. $20.00

CORBETT, James. *Roar of the Crowd.* 1925. Garden City. VG/VG. B5. $40.00

CORBETT, Scott. *Hairy Horror Trick.* 1969. Little Brn. 1st. 8vo. F/VG+. C8. $17.50

CORBETT & CORBETT. *Pot Shots From a Grosse Ile Kitchen Cookbook.* 1947. Harper. 1st. G. A16. $12.00

CORDAN, Wolfgang. *Secret of the Forest.* 1963. London. Gollancz. 1st. 163p. F3. $25.00

CORDELL, Alexander. *Fire People.* 1972. Hodder Stoughton. 1st. VG/VG. P3. $15.00

CORDELL, Alexander. *Rape of the Fair Country.* 1959. Doubleday. VG/VG. P3. $10.00

CORDELL, L.S. *Prehistory of the Southwest.* 1984. Orlando. Academic. 50 maps/photos/drawings. 490p. VG/wrp. M12. $30.00

CORDER, Eric. *Murder, My Love.* 1973. Playboy. 1st. VG/G+. P3. $12.00

CORELLI, Marie. *Secret Power.* 1961. London. VG/dj. M2. $15.00

CORELLI, Marie. *Young Diana.* 1918. Doran. 1st. F/NF. M2. $50.00

COREVON, Henry. *Fleurs des Champ et des Bois des Haies et des Murs.* 1911. Geneva. Albert Kundig. 8vo. VG. A22. $65.00

CORK, Barry. *Dead Ball.* 1989. Scribner. 1st. F/F. P8. $12.50

CORLE, Edwin. *Gila: River of the Southwest.* 1951. Rinehart. 1st. ils/map/bibliography. 402p. VG+. B19. $30.00

CORLE, Edwin. *Listen, Bright Angel.* 1946. DSP. 1st. 8vo. 312p. brn cloth. VG/VG. F7. $35.00

CORLE, Edwin. *Story of the Grand Canyon.* nd. London. Sampson Low. 8vo. 312p. VG+/G+. F7. $35.00

CORLEY, Edwin. *Farewell, My Slightly Tarnished Hero.* 1971. Dodd Mead. 1st. VG/dj. M25. $35.00

CORLISS, Philip G. *Hemerocallis.* 1951. SF. self pub. 1/1000. 8vo. red cloth. NF. A22. $35.00

CORLISS, William R. *Moon & the Planets.* 1985. Glen Arm, MD. Sourcebook Project. 4to. 377p. VG. K5. $30.00

CORLISS, William R. *Propulsion Systems for Space Flight.* 1960. McGraw Hill. 1st. lg 8vo. 300p. VG. K5. $60.00

CORLISS, William R. *Radioisotopic Power Generation.* 1964. Englewood Cliffs. 8vo. 304p. VG/dj. K5. $60.00

CORNELIUS, Mrs. *Young Housekeeper's Friend.* Brn Taggard Chase. facsimile 1859 revised ed. 254p. B10. $12.00

CORNELL, John J. *Essays on the View of Friends...* 1884. Friends Book Assn. 2nd. 95p. V3. $12.00

CORNELL, Ralph D. *Conspicuous California Plants.* 1938. Pasadena. 1st. 1/1500. inscr. 192p. VG. B26. $65.00

CORNER, George. *Anatomy.* 1930. NY. 1st. 82p. A13. $60.00

CORNEY, Peter. *Voyages in Northern Pacific. Narratives...Trading Voyages...* 1965. Fairfield. Ye Galleon. rpt. 8vo. 238p. tan cloth. P4. $75.00

CORNEY, Peter. *Voyages in the Northern Pacific.* 1896. Honolulu. Thos G Thrum. 1st separate. 3-quarter leather/raised bands. P4. $600.00

CORNFORD, L. Cope. *Lord High Admiral & Others.* 1915. London. VG. M2. $35.00

CORNING, James Leonard. *Treatise on Headache & Neuralgia...* 1894. NY. EB Treat. 3rd enlarged. 12mo. pebbled mauve cloth. G. G1. $50.00

CORNISH & DIXON. *Chickory: Young Voices From the Black Ghetto.* 1969. NY. Assn Pr. 1st. xl. NF/VG. B4. $45.00

CORNSWEET, Tom N. *Visual Perception.* 1970. Academic. 3rd. tall 8vo. 475p. blk cloth. G1. $65.00

CORNWELL, Bernard. *Killer's Wake.* 1989. Putnam. 1st. NF/NF. P3. $20.00

CORNWELL, Bernard. *Sharpe's Devil.* 1992. Harper Collins. 1st. sgn. F/dj. Q1. $60.00

CORNWELL, Bernard. *Sharpe's Eagle.* 1981. NY. Viking. 1st Am. F/F. M23. $50.00

CORNWELL, Bernard. *Sharpe's Honour.* 1985. Viking. 1st Am. F/dj. T11. $65.00

CORNWELL, Bernard. *Sharpe's Regiment.* 1986. London. Collins. 1st. sgn. F/dj. Q1. $250.00

CORNWELL, Bernard. *Wildtrack.* 1988. Putnam. 1st. NF/F. T12. $30.00

CORNWELL, Patricia D. *All That Remains.* 1992. Scribner. 1st. F/F. M22. $35.00

CORNWELL, Patricia D. *Body of Evidence.* 1991. Scribner. 1st. F/NF. A20. $85.00

CORNWELL, Patricia D. *Cruel & Unusual.* 1993. Scribner. 1st. NF/dj. Q1. $40.00

CORNWELL, Patricia D. *Postmortem.* 1990. Scribner. 1st. blk cloth. NF/dj. D10. $600.00

CORRAL, Jesus C. *Caro Amigo: Autobiography of Jesus C Corral.* 1984. Westernlore. 1st. sgn. 238p. F/VG+. B19. $50.00

CORREDOR-MATHEOS, Jose. *Miro's Posters.* 1987. Barcelona. Poligrafa. 119 pl. 269p. dj. D2. $150.00

CORRELL, D.S. *Potato & Its Wild Relatives.* 1962. TX Research Found. 606p. cloth. dj. B1. $45.00

CORREVON, Henry. *Rock Gardens & Alpine Plants.* 1930. NY. ils/pl. 544p. VG. B26. $25.00

CORRIGAN, J.D. *Working With the Microscope.* 1971. McGraw Hill. 418p. F. D8. $15.00

CORRIN & CORRIN. *Pied Piper of Hamelin.* 1988. London. Faber. 1st. ils/sgn Errol LeCain. pict brd. dj. R5. $175.00

CORROTHERS, James D. *Black Cat Club.* 1902. NY. ils JK Bryans. 264p. pict cloth. B18. $45.00

CORROZET, Gilles. *Le Thresor des Histoires de France.* 1615. Paris. Jean Corrozet. 8vo. title device. calf. R12. $325.00

CORTWRIGHT, Edgar. *Exploring Space With a Camera.* 1968. NASA. F. M2. $15.00

CORVO, Baron. *Without Prejudice.* 1963. London. Allen Lane. 1st. 1/600. F/salmon dj. Q1. $250.00

CORY, Charles B. *Birds of Illinois & Wisconsin.* 1909. Field Mus Natural Hist. ils. 764p. VG. S15. $55.00

CORY, David. *Little Jack Rabbit & the Big Brown Bear.* 1921. Grosset Dunlap. 128p. cloth. VG/dj. M20. $12.50

CORY, Desmond. *Bennett.* 1977. Crime Club. 1st. VG/VG. P3. $15.00

CORY, Fanny. *Fanny Cory Mother Goose.* 1917. Bobbs Merrill. 12 mc full-p pl. 4to. cloth. R5. $300.00

CORY, H.T. *Imperial Valley & the Salton Sink.* 1915. SF. John J Newgegin. ils/fld maps/plans. gilt stp cloth. D11. $150.00

COSBY, Bill. *Fatherhood.* 1986. Doubleday. 1st. F/F. W2. $30.00

COSELL, Howard. *Cosell.* 1973. Playboy. 1st. sgn. VG/G. B11. $18.00

COSTAIN, Thomas B. *Below the Salt.* 1957. Doubleday. 1st. VG/VG. P3. $35.00

COSTAIN, Thomas B. *High Towers.* 1949. Doubleday. 1st. VG/VG. P3. $15.00

COSTAIN, Thomas B. *Silver Chalice.* 1952. Doubleday. 1st. inscr. VG. T12. $18.00

COTE, Phyllis. *Rabbit-Go-Lucky.* 1944. Doubleday Doran. 1st. 175p. VG/dj. M20. $15.00

COTT. *Pipers at the Gates of Dawn: Wisdom Children's Literature.* 1983. ils. 351p. NF/F. A4. $75.00

COTTER, Clay. *Mystery & Adventure Stories: Hidden Peril (#8).* 1939. Cupples Leon. 204p. cloth. VG+/dj. M20. $10.00

COTTON, Charles. *Poetical Works...* 1734. London. 34d. half leather/brd. A15. $25.00

COTTON, Robert. *Exact Abridgement of Records in Tower of London...* 1657. London. early tree calf/rebacked. G. M11. $650.00

COTTRELL, Edwin A. *Pasadena Social Agencies Survey.* 1940. Pasadena. 378p+4p ES. wrp/cloth spine (as issued). D11. $40.00

COTTRILL, GREENBERG & WAUGH. *Science Fiction & Fantasy Series & Sequels.* 1986. Garland. 1st. F. P3. $45.00

COUCH, Houston B. *Disease of Turfgrasses.* 1962. Rheinhold. 289p. NF/dj. A22. $25.00

COULTER, E. Merton. *South During Reconstruction 1865-1877.* 1947. LSU. later prt. 426p. cloth. NF/NF. M8. $25.00

COULTER, E. Merton. *Travels in the Confederate States.* nd. Broadfoot. facsimile 1st. 289p. index. F. A17. $30.00

COUNSELMAN, Mary Elizabeth. *Half in Shadow.* 1978. Arkham. 1st. F/dj. Q1. $30.00

COUNTER, S. Allen. *North Pole Legacy: Black, White & Eskimo.* 1991. Amherst. 8vo. 222p. blk cloth. P4. $45.00

COUPER, Greta Elena. *American Sculptor on Grand Tour...William Couper.* 1988. LA. Tre Cavalli. ils/photos/footnotes. 157p. dj. D2. $45.00

COUPPEY, Madeleine. *Rumor of the Forest.* 1947. Scribner. 1st. VG/VG. A4. $15.00

COURLANDER & SAKO. *Heart of the Ngoni: Heroes of African Kingdom of Segu.* 1982. NY. Crown. 1st. 178p. VG. W1. $18.00

COURTNEY, W. *Farmers' & Mechanics' Manual.* 1868. revised. ils. 505p. G+. E6. $95.00

COURTRIGHT, G. *Tropicals.* 1988. Timber. 155p. B1. $38.00

COUSINS, Geoffrey. *Golfers at Law.* 1959. Knopf. 1st. VG/VG. P8. $30.00

COUSTEAU, Jacques, and Richards, Mose. *Jacques Cousteau's Amazon Journey.* 1984. NY. Harry Abrams Pub. 4to. color pict. 236p. NF/NF. R16. $75.00

COUSY & LINN. *Last Loud Roar.* 1964. Prentice Hall. 1st. photos Robert Riger. VG/G+. P8. $30.00

COUTANT, F. *ABC of Goat-Keeping.* 1946. photos. sc. G+. E6. $12.00

COVARRUBIAS, M. *Eagle, Jaguar & Serpent.* 1954. NY. 1st. dj. F3. $125.00

COVARRUBIAS, M. *Indian Art of Mexico & Central America.* 1957. NY. 1st. VG/G. B5. $65.00

COVINGTON, Vicki. *Bird of Paradise.* 1990. S&S. 1st. sgn. F/F. B3. $45.00

COVINGTON, Vicki. *Gathering Home.* 1988. S&S. 1st. author's 1st book. F/F. B3. $60.00

COVVIN & PRUIT. *Energy Resources of the Denver Basin.* 1978. Rocky Mtn Assn Geol. 272p. 10 pocket maps. F. D8. $30.00

COWAN, James. *Daybreak, a Romance of an Old World.* 1896. Richmond. 1st. VG. M2. $50.00

COWAN, James. *Maori Folk-Tales of Port Hills.* 1923. Auckland. Whitcombe Tombes. 73p. gray wrp. P4. $50.00

COWAN, L. *Wit of the Jews.* 1970. VG/VG. E6. $8.00

COWAN, May. *Inverewe: Garden in the NW Highlands.* 1964. London. ils/photos/ map/plan. 152p. VG/dj. B26. $15.00

COWAN, Paul. *Orphan in History: Retrieving a Jewish Legacy.* 1982. Doubleday. 246p. VG/dj. S3. $24.00

COWAN, Robert G. *Ranchos of California.* 1977. Los Angeles. rpt. VG. H1. $20.00

COWAN, Sam. *Sergeant York.* 1928. NY. 1st. sgn Alvin York. VG/torn. S16. $450.00

COWAN. *Bibliography of History of California, 1510-1930.* 1964 (1933). 4 vol in 1. rpt. w/supp. VG. A4. $295.00

COWARD, Noel. *Play Parade.* 1933. NY. 1st. VG. T9. $20.00

COWARD, Noel. *Pretty Polly & Other Stories.* 1965. Doubleday. 1st Am. 8vo. NF/clip. T10. $40.00

COWARD, Noel. *Pretty Polly & Other Stories.* 1965. Doubleday. 1st. sgn. F/dj. Q1. $250.00

COWDRY, E.V. *Special Cytology: Form & Functions of Cell in Health...* 1828. NY. 1st. 2 vol. 1348p. A13. $150.00

COWLEY, Cecil. *Schiwikkard of Natal & Old Transvaal.* 1974. Cape Town. Struik. 1st. 8vo. ils Paul Wiles. VG/dj. W1. $12.00

COWLEY, John D. *Bibliography of Abridgments, Digests, Dictionaries...* 1979 (1932). Holmes Beach. Wm Gaunt. facsimile. M11. $85.00

COWLEY, Stewart. *Spacewreck: Ghostships & Derelicts.* 1979. Exeter. 1st. F/dj. M2. $15.00

COWPER, Richard. *Breakthrough.* 1967. London. Dennis Dobson. 1st. F/F. T2. $30.00

COWPER, Richard. *Clone.* 1972. London. Gollancz. 1st. F/F. T2. $45.00

COWPER, Richard. *Clone.* 1973. Doubleday. 1st. F/F. P3. $20.00

COWPER, Richard. *Custodians & Other Stories.* 1972. London. Gollancz. 1st. F/clip. T2. $30.00

COWPER, Richard. *Dream of Kinship.* 1981. London. Gollancz. 1st. F/F. T2. $25.00

COWPER, Richard. *Kuldesak.* 1972. Doubleday. 1st Am. F/NF. T2. $20.00

COWPER, Richard. *Profundis.* 1979. London. Gollancz. 1st. F/F. T2. $40.00

COWPER, Richard. *Shades of Darkness.* 1986. Salisbury, Wilts. Kerosina Books. 1st. F/F. T2. $25.00

COWPER, Richard. *Tapestry of Time.* 1982. London. Gollancz. 1st. F/F. T2. $25.00

COWPER, Richard. *Twilight of Briareus.* 1974. Day. 1st Am. F/dj. M2. $35.00

COWPER, Richard. *Web of the Magi.* 1980. London. 1st. F/dj. M2/T2. $40.00

COWPER, William. *Poems, of William Cowper, of the Inner Temple, Esq.* 1823. Boston. Bedlington. 3 vol. leather. VG. M20. $40.00

COWPER, William. *Task, a Poem in Six Books.* 1787. Phil. Thos Dobson. 1st Am. 12mo. 218p. contemporary calf/red label. H13. $295.00

COWPER, William. *Task.* 1856. NY. Robert Carter. ils Birket Foster. 263p. aeg. bl cloth. NF. B24. $100.00

COX, A.E. *Potato: A Practical & Scientific Guide.* 1967. London. Collingridge. 176p. dj. A10. $38.00

COX, Betty J. *New Sexuality.* 1969. NY. Medical Pr of NY. 1st. ils. 256p. VG/tattered. A25. $8.00

COX, E. H. *Plant Hunting in China.* 1945. London. 1st. ils/maps. 230p. VG/dj. W3. $95.00

COX, Erle. *Missing Angel.* 1947. Australia. 1st. VG. M2. $35.00

COX, Isaac. *Annals of Trinity County.* 1940. Eugene, OR. Nash. 1/350. 4to. 265p. NF/NF. T10. $250.00

COX, J. Charles. *Pulpits, Lecterns & Organs in English Churches.* 1915. London. 8vo. ils. 228p. xl. VG. B14. $45.00

COX, J. Charles. *Royal Forests of England.* 1905. London. Methuen. red cloth. VG. M11. $65.00

COX, Jacob D. *Atlanta.* 1882. NY. 274p. O8. $21.50

COX, Jacob D. *Franklin & Nashville: The March to the Sea.* 1882. NY. 1st. 265p. O8. $23.50

COX, James. *My Native Land.* 1903. ils. 400p. O8. $18.50

COX, Palmer. *Another Brownie Book.* 1890. Century. 1st. pict brd. R5. $275.00

COX, Palmer. *Brownies at Home.* 1893. NY. Century. 1st. 4to. 144p. pict brd. R5. $250.00

COX, Palmer. *Frolic on Wheels.* 1895. Hubbard. 4to. VG. M5. $110.00

COX, Samuel S. *Three Decades of Federal Legislation 1855 to 1885.* 1885. Providence. Reid. 726p. brn cloth. VG+. M20. $50.00

COX, Thomas R. *Park Builders: History of State Parks in Pacific Northwest.* 1988. WA U. 248p. F/F. S15. $15.00

COX, Wally. *Mr Peepers: A Sort of Novel.* 1955. S&S. 1st. NF/VG. B4. $85.00

COX & FUJII. *Three Treasures: Myths of Old Japan.* 1964. Harper. ils. 256p. pict wht cloth. F. W3. $38.00

COX & STOIKO. *Spacepower: What It Means to You.* 1958. Winston. 1st. F/VG. M2. $17.00

COXE, George Harmon. *Butcher, Baker, Murder-Maker.* 1954. Knopf. 1st. VG. P3. $25.00

COXE, George Harmon. *Double Identity.* 1970. Knopf. 1st. NF/NF. N4. $25.00

COXE, George Harmon. *Fenner.* 1971. Knopf. 1st. NF/NF. P3. $15.00

COXE, George Harmon. *Impetuous Mistress.* 1958. Knopf. 1st. VG/VG. N4. $25.00

COXE, George Harmon. *Inside Man.* 1974. Knopf. 1st. VG/VG. P3. $18.00

COXE, George Harmon. *Mrs Murdock Takes a Case.* 1941. Knopf. 1st. VG/NF. M19. $35.00

COXE, George Harmon. *Ring of Truth.* 1966. Knopf. 1st. 176p. VG/dj. M20. $15.00

COXE, George Harmon. *Silent Witness.* 1973. Knopf. 1st. VG/VG. P3. $20.00

COYLE, William. *Ohio Authors & Their Books, 1796-1950.* 1962. World. ARC/1st. 741p. VG/dj. M20. $50.00

COYNE, John. *Hobgoblin.* 1981. Putnam. 1st. F/dj. M2. $25.00

COYNE, John. *Piercing.* 1979. Putnam. 1st. inscr. F/dj. M2. $40.00

CRABBE, George. *Borough: A Poem, in Twenty-Four Letters.* 1820. London. Murray. 8vo. 347p. detailed fore-edge painting. red morocco. F. B24. $950.00

CRACE, Jim. *Continent.* 1986. Harper Row. 1st. NF/F. M11. $25.00

CRADDOCK, Harry. *Savoy Cocktail Book.* 1934. S&S. 287p. B10. $35.00

CRADDOCK, LOVELESS & VIERIMA. *Antarctic Geoscience.* 1982. Madison. 1st. 1172p. bl cloth. M/dj. P4. $65.00

CRAIG, David. *Albion Case.* 1975. Macmillan. 1st. VG/VG. P3. $20.00

CRAIG, Gordon. *Henry Irving.* 1930. ils. VG. M17. $15.00

CRAIG, Helen. *Angelena on Stage.* 1986. Clarkson Potter. 1st. ils Katherine Holabird. F. C8. $25.00

CRAIG, John A. *Judging Live Stock.* 1906. Austin. self pub. 193p. photos. cloth. NF. A10. $10.00

CRAIG, Robert T. *Mammillaria Handbook With Descriptions...* 1945. Pasadena. 1st. 390p. VG+. B26. $75.00

CRAINE & REINDORP. *Chronicles of Michoacan.* 1970. OK U. 1st. 259p. cloth. dj. D11. $35.00

CRAIS, Robert. *Freefall.* 1993. Bantam. 1st. sgn. F/F. A23. $42.00

CRAIS, Robert. *Lullaby Town.* 1992. Bantam. 1st. sgn. F/dj. D10. $175.00

CRAIS, Robert. *Stalking the Angel.* 1989. Bantam. 1st. F/F. M15. $45.00

CRAIS, Robert. *Stalking the Angel.* 1989. NY. Bantam. 1st. sgn. F/F. D10. $85.00

CRAM, Mildred. *Promise.* 1949. Knopf. 1st. VG/VG. P3. $30.00

CRAM, Ralph Adams. *Impressions of Japanese Architecture & Allied Arts.* 1905. NY. Baker Taylor. 1st. 227p. NF. W3. $165.00

CRAMER, Maurice. *Phoenix in East Hadley.* 1941. Houghton Mifflin. 1st. NF/dj. M2. $30.00

CRAMOND, Mike. *Killing Bears.* 1982. Outdoor Life. 2nd. 312p. VG/VG. S15. $15.00

CRAMP, Arthur J. *Nostrums & Quackery, Vol 2.* 1921. Chicago. AMA. 8vo. 832p. gilt dk gr cloth. H1. $37.50

CRAMPTON, C. Gregory. *Ghosts of Glen Canyon.* 1988. St George. 2nd. 4to. 135p. VG+/stiff wrp. F7. $25.00

CRAMPTON, C. Gregory. *Sharlot Hall on the Arizona Strip.* 1975. Flagstaff. 1st. 8vo. gr cloth. VG+. F7. $35.00

CRAMPTON, C. Gregory. *Standing Up Country: Canyon Lands of Utah & Arizona.* 1964. Knopf. 1st. ils. 191p. NF/VG+. B19. $60.00

CRAMPTON, J. *Falling Stars.* nd (ca 1866). London. Macintosh. xl. K5. $35.00

CRAN, Marion. *Garden of Experience.* ca 1920s. Herbert Jenkins. 6th. 8vo. 316p. VG. A22. $25.00

CRAN, Marion. *Gardens of Character.* 1939. Herbert Jenkins. 1st. 8vo. 284p. G. A22. $30.00

CRAN, Marion. *Story of My Ruin.* 1924. London. Herbert Jenkins. 1st. 8vo. 320p. G. A22. $25.00

CRANE, Aimee. *Marines at War.* 1943. NY. ils. 182p. S16. $28.50

CRANE, Clinton H. *Clinton Crane's Yachting Memories.* 1952. Van Nostrand. ils. 216p. T7. $35.00

CRANE, Frances. *Coral Princess Murders.* 1954. Random. 1st. 235p. cloth. VG+/dj. M20. $30.00

CRANE, J. *Fiddler Crabs of the World.* 1975. Princeton. 50 pl. cloth. dj. B1. $75.00

CRANE, Joan. *Willa Cather: A Bibliography.* 1982. NE U. 440p. F/F. A4. $45.00

CRANE, Laura Dent. *Automobile Girls at Chicago (#4).* 1912. Altemus. lists 6 titles. VG/ragged. M20. $20.00

CRANE, Laura Dent. *Automobile Girls at Palm Beach (#5).* 1913. Altemus. lists 6 titles. VG/ragged. M20. $20.00

CRANE, Leo. *Indians of the Enchanted Desert.* 1925. Little Brn. 1st. 8vo. 32 pl/fld map. pict bl cloth. VG. T10. $75.00

CRANE, Stephen. *Whilomville Stories.* 1900. NY. Harper. 1st. ils Peter Newell. gilt gr cloth. NF. M24. $165.00

CRANE, T. *Architectural Construction: Choice of Structural Design.* 1947. NY. Wiley. 1st. ils/index. 414p. VG/dj. B5. $20.00

CRANE, Walter. *Beatrice Crane: Her Book.* 1983. Toronto. Osborne Collection. facsimile. 12mo. gilt blk cloth. VG. D1. $45.00

CRANE, Walter. *Masque of Days.* 1901. London. Cassell. 1st. 44p. NF/dj. B24. $350.00

CRANE, Walter. *Princess Belle Etoile.* ca 1900. John Lane. 4to. stiff wrp. M5. $75.00

CRANE, Walter. *Sing a Song of Sixpence.* ca 1900. John Lane. reissue. 8 pl. VG. M5. $65.00

CRANE & DRESSES. *Masque of Days.* 1901. London. Cassell. 1st. 4to. unp. VG. D1. $325.00

CRANSTON, Edwin. *Izumi Shikibu Diary: Romance of the Heian Court.* 1969. Harvard. 1st. notes/bibliography. 332p. NF/NF. W3. $67.00

CRASE, Douglas. *Revisionist.* 1981. Little Brn. 1st. assn copy. F/F. V1. $15.00

CRAVEN, Avery O. *Soil Exhaustion as a Factor in Agricultural History...* 1965. Gloucester. Smith. rpt. 179p. VG. A10. $25.00

CRAVEN, J.B. *Doctor Robet Fludd: English Rosicrucian.* nd. Occult Research. 1/300. VG. M17. $25.00

CRAVEN, J.H. *Chiropractic Orthopedy.* 1922. Davenport. 2nd. ils. 399p. VG. B5. $45.00

CRAVEN, Thomas. *Treasury of American Prints.* 1939. S&S. 100 b&w pl. sbdg. D2. $65.00

CRAVENS, Gwyneth. *Speed of Light.* 1979. S&S. 1st. F/dj. M2. $17.00

CRAWFORD, F. Marion. *Adam Johnstone's Son.* 1896. Macmillan. 1st. VG. M2. $25.00

CRAWFORD, F. Marion. *Lady of Rome.* 1906. Macmillan. 1st. VG. M2. $25.00

CRAWFORD, F. Marion. *Saracinesca.* 1893. Macmillan. VG. M2. $25.00

CRAWFORD, F. Marion. *Zoroaster.* 1885. Macmillan. 1st Am. VG. M2. $50.00

CRAWFORD, Isabel. *Kiowa.* 1915. NY. Revell. G. A19. $75.00

CRAWFORD, M.H. *Methods & Theories of Anthropoligical Genetics.* (1973). Albuquerque. 1st. 509p. dj. F3. $15.00

CRAWFORD, Samuel. *Kansas in the Sixties.* 1911. McClurg. 1st. 438p. VG. J2. $285.00

CRAWLEY, Rayburn. *Chattering Gods.* 1931. Harper. 1st. G. M2. $17.00

CREASEY, John. *Alibi.* 1971. Scribner. 1st. VG/VG. P3. $15.00

CREASEY, John. *As Merry as Hell.* 1973. Hodder Stoughton. 1st. VG/VG. P3. $18.00

CREASEY, John. *Baron & the Chinese Puzzle.* 1966. Scribner. 1st. VG/VG. P3. $20.00

CREASEY, John. *Croaker.* 1973. HRW. 1st. VG/VG. P3. $15.00

CREASEY, John. *Dissemblers.* 1967. Scribner. 1st. F/F. H11. $30.00

CREASEY, John. *Executioners.* 1967. Scribner. 1st. NF/NF. N4. $20.00

CREASEY, John. *Gallows Are Waiting.* 1973. David McKay. 1st. VG/VG. P3. $20.00

CREASEY, John. *Gideon's Staff.* 1959. Harper. 1st. VG/NF. M19. $25.00

CREASEY, John. *Hang the Little Man.* 1963. Hodder Stoughton. 1st. NF/NF. P3. $25.00

CREASEY, John. *Inspector West Alone.* 1975. Scribner. 1st. VG/VG. P3. $15.00

CREASEY, John. *Lame Dog Murder.* 1972. Cleveland. World. 1st. F/F. H11. $25.00

CREASEY, John. *Make-Up for the Toff.* 1956. Walker. 1st. 189p. VG/dj. M20. $15.00

CREASEY, John. *Most Deadly Hate.* 1974. Dutton. 1st. VG/VG. P3. $18.00

CREASEY, John. *Sly as a Serpent.* 1967. Macmillan. 1st. 183p. cloth. VG/dj. M20. $12.00

CREASEY, John. *So Young to Burn.* 1968. Scribner. 1st. VG/VG. P3. $15.00

CREASEY, John. *Take a Body.* 1972. Cleveland. World. 1st. F/F. H11. $25.00

CREASEY, John. *Theft of Magna Carta.* 1973. Scribner. 1st. VG/VG. P3. $15.00

CREASEY, John. *Toff Proceeds.* 1968. Walker. 1st. F/F. P3. $15.00

CREASY, R. *Complete Book of Edible Landscaping.* 1983. Sierra Club. 3rd. 379p. dj. A10. $30.00

CREDLE, Ellis. *Flop-Eared Hound.* 1938. Oxford. 3rd. ils Chas Townsend. VG/VG. P2. $75.00

CREEL, H.G. *Studies in Early Chinese Culture.* 1938. Baltimore. 1st. 266p. F. W3. $125.00

CREELEY, Robert. *Charm.* 1971. Calder Boyars. 1st Eng. F/F. M19. $25.00

CREELEY, Robert. *Thanks.* 1977. Deerfield/Gallery. 1/250. sgn/#d. F/F. B2. $75.00

CREMER, Jan. *I Jan Cremer.* 1965. 1st. VG/VG. S13. $35.00

CRESPELLE, Jean-Paul. *Fauves.* 1962. NYGS. 100 b&w pl. 351p. dj. D2. $150.00

CRESSON, W.P. *Francis Dana.* 1930. Dial. 1st. 397p. VG/clip. M24. $20.00

CRESSWELL, Helen. *Bagthorpes Abroad.* 1984. London. Faber. 1st. ils Jill Bennett. 186p. xl. VG. T5. $25.00

CRESWICK, Alice M. *Red Book of Fruit Jars No 3.* 1978. Collector Books. ils. 224p. lib bdg w/orig ils cover. xl. H1. $45.00

CREWS, Donald. *Light.* 1981. Bodley Head. 1st. sm 4to. NF. C8. $25.00

CREWS, Donald. *Ten Black Dots Redesigned & Revised.* 1986. Greenwillow. 1st. ils. F/NF. C8. $25.00

CREWS, Harry. *All We Need of Hell.* 1987. Harper Row. 1st. F/F. M23. $50.00

CREWS, Harry. *Childhood: The Biography of a Place.* 1978. Harper Row. 1st. F/dj. Q1. $150.00

CREWS, Harry. *Karate Is a Thing of the Spirit.* 1972. Secker Warburg. 1st. F/NF. B3. $125.00

CREWS, Harry. *Scarlover.* 1992. Poseidon. 1st. sgn. F/F. B11/R13. $55.00

CRICHTON, Michael. *Andromeda Strain.* 1969. Knopf. 1st. F/F. D10. $200.00

CRICHTON, Michael. *Congo.* 1980. Knopf. 1st. author's 5th novel. F/F. D10. $50.00

CRICHTON, Michael. *Disclosure.* 1993. Knopf. 1st. sgn. F/F. A23. $50.00

CRICHTON, Michael. *Eaters of the Dead.* 1976. NY. Viking. 1st. author's 4th novel. F/clip. D10. $50.00

CRICHTON, Michael. *Electronic Life.* 1983. Knopf. 1st. NF/NF. T11. $40.00

CRICHTON, Michael. *Electronic Life.* 1983. Knopf. 1st. sgn. F/F. A23. $75.00

CRICHTON, Michael. *Five Patients.* 1970. Knopf. 1st. VG/VG. S13. $20.00

CRICHTON, Michael. *Great Train Robbery.* 1975. Knopf. 1st. NF/NF. A24. $40.00

CRICHTON, Michael. *Jurassic Park.* 1990. Knopf. 1st. F/F. D10. $50.00

CRICHTON, Michael. *Jurassic Park.* 1990. Knopf. 1st. NF/NF. M19. $35.00

CRICHTON, Michael. *Lost World.* 1995. Knopf. 1st. inscr. F/F. A23. $50.00

CRICHTON, Michael. *Odds On.* 1966. NAL. 1st. author's 1st book. F/wrp. Q1. $150.00

CRICHTON, Michael. *Rising Sun.* 1992. Knopf. 1st. sgn. F/F. A23. $45.00

CRICHTON, Michael. *Sphere.* 1987. Knopf. 1st. F/dj. B3/D10. $40.00

CRICHTON, Michael. *Terminal Man.* 1972. Knopf. 1st. NF/NF. B3/P3. $60.00

CRICHTON, Michael. *Travels.* 1988. Knopf. 1st. F/F. B35. $35.00

CRICK, Francis. *What Mad Pursuit.* 1988. Basic Books. 8vo. ils. NF/dj. K3. $10.00

CRIDER, Bill. *Galveston Gunman.* 1988. Evans. 1st. VG/VG. P3. $15.00

CRILE & LOWER. *Surgical Shock & Shockless Operation Through Anoci-Assoc.* 1921. Phil. 272p. A13. $100.00

CRIPPEN, David. *Two Sides of the River.* 1976. Nashville. Abingdon. 1st probable. obl sm 4to. as new/dj. C8. $25.00

CRIPPEN, T.G. *Christmas & Christmas Lore.* 1923. London. Blackie. ils. 221p. G-. B18. $30.00

CRIPPS, Richard S. *Critical & Exegetical Commentary on Book of Amos.* 1955. SPCK. 365p. G/torn. B29. $10.00

CRIPPS, Wilfred Joseph. *Old English Plate.* 1967. London. Spring Books. rpt of 1926 11th. 8vo. ils. 540p. F/VG. H1. $22.50

CRISLER, Lois. *Arctic Wild.* 1958. Harper. 1st. 301p. VG/G. W2. $30.00

CRISP, Frank. *Medieval Gardens.* 1924. London. Lane. 2 vol. A10. $150.00

CRISP, N.J. *Brink.* 1982. Viking. 1st. F/F. P3. $15.00

CRISP, N.J. *London Deal.* 1978. St Martin. 1st. VG/VG. P3. $18.00

CRISP, William. *Compleat Agent.* 1984. Macmillan. 1st. F/F. P3. $15.00

CRISPIN, Edmund. *Best of Science Fiction Three.* 1958. London. F/dj. M2. $20.00

CRISPIN, William Frost. *Bibliographical & Historical Sketch of Capt Wm Crispin...* 1901. Akron. ils. 144p. fair. B18. $22.50

CRISPIN & NORTON. *Gryphon's Eyrie.* 1984. NY. Tor. 1st. sgn. VG/VG. B11. $45.00

CRISTABEL. *Mortal Immortals.* 1971. Walker. 1st. VG/G+. P3. $20.00

CRITCHFIELD & LITTLE. *Geographic Distribution of Pines of the World.* 1966. USDA. 97p. wrp. B1. $28.50

CROCKETT, Lucy Herndon. *Kings Without Castles.* 1957. Rand McNally. 1st. sgn. VG/VG. B11. $18.00

CROCKETT, S.R. *Black Douglas.* 1899. Doubleday. 1st Am. VG. M2. $35.00

CROCKETT, S.R. *Flower o'the Corn.* 1902. London. 1st. VG. M2. $20.00

CROCOMBE & CROCOMBE. *Works of Ta'Unga. Records of a Polynesian Traveller...* 1968. Canberra. Australian Nat U. 1st. ils. 164p. P4. $45.00

CROFT, Terrell. *Library of Practical Electricity.* 1924. NY. 8 vol. 4th. limp cloth. A17. $30.00

CROFT-COOKE, Rupert. *Exotic Food.* 1971. NY. Herder. G/dj. A16. $20.00

CROFTON, Algernon. *Goat's Hoof.* 1928. Covici Friede. 1st. F. w/pub brochure. M2. $25.00

CROFTS, Freeman Wills. *Purple Sickle Murders.* 1929. Harper. 1st Am. G. N4. $25.00

CROFTS, Freeman Wills. *Tragedy in the Hollow.* 1939. Dodd Mead. 1st. VG. P3. $35.00

CROFUT, William. *Moon on the One Hand.* 1975. Atheneum. 1st. 80p. F/NF. D4. $45.00

CROLL, James. *Climate & Time, in Their Geological Relations.* 1893. NY. Appleton. 8vo. 577p. K5. $85.00

CROLY, George. *May Fair. In Four Cantos.* 1827. London. Ainsworth. 1st. 8vo. 194p. Riviere bdg. H13. $295.00

CROLY, George. *Salathiel.* nd. Funk Wagnall. NF. M2. $25.00

CROLY, George. *Tarry Thou Till I Come; or, Salathiel, the Wandering Jew.* 1901. Funk Wagnall. 1st. 8vo. 17 pl. 588p. VG. W1. $15.00

CROMARTIE, Countess. *Temple of the Winds.* 1925. London. 1st. VG. M2. $15.00

CROMBIE, Deborah. *Share in Death.* 1993. Scribner. 1st. author's 1st mystery. F/NF. A24. $40.00

CROMIE, Robert. *From the Cliffs of Croaghaun.* 1904. Saalfield. 1st. VG. M2. $27.00

CRONIN, Leonard. *Key Guide to Australian Palms, Ferns & Allies.* 1989. NSW. ils. 192p. as new/dj. B26. $20.00

CRONIN, Michael. *Night of the Party.* 1958. Ives Washburn. 1st. VG/VG. P3. $13.00

CRONKITE, Walter. *Reporter's Life.* 1996. Knopf. 1st. sgn bookplate. F/F. A23. $46.00

CRONLEY, Jay. *Quick Change.* 1981. Doubleday. 1st. VG/VG. M22. $35.00

CRONQUIST, Arthur. *Evolution & Classification of Flowering Plants.* 1968. Boston. ils. 396p. B26. $30.00

CRONQUIST, Arthur. *Intermountain Flora.* 1986. NY Botanical Garden. rpt. 270p. B1. $37.50

CRONQUIST & GLEASON. *Natural Geography of Plants.* 1964. Columbia. 420p. B1. $65.00

CROOKES, Marguerite. *New Zealand Ferns.* 1963. Whitcombe Tombs. 6th. 8vo. cloth. VG/dj. A22. $40.00

CROSBY, Bing. *Call Me Lucky.* 1953. S&S. 1st. VG/clip. A20. $40.00

CROSBY, Edward. *Radiana.* 1906. Ivy. 1st. VG. M2. $40.00

CROSBY, Ernest. *Captain Jinks, Hero.* 1902. Funk Wagnall. 1st. 393p. VG. M20. $20.00

CROSBY, John. *Company of Friends.* 1977. Stein Day. 1st. VG/VG. P3. $13.00

CROSLAND, Margaret. *Colette: Difficulty of Loving.* 1973. Bobbs Merrill. 1st Am. photos. VG/dj. A25. $18.00

CROSLAND, Margaret. *Madame Colette: A Provincial in Paris.* 1953. London. Peter Own. 1st. photos. 22p. VG/dj. A25. $18.00

CROSS, Amanda; see Heilbrun, Carolyn G.

CROSS, Helen Reid. *Simple Simon.* 1908. London. Chatto Windus. Dumpy Books. 24 full-p pl. 95p. brn cloth. R5. $200.00

CROSS, John Kier. *Angry Planet.* 1946. Coward McCann. NF/dj. M2. $25.00

CROSS, John Kier. *Best Black Magic Stories.* 1960. London. 1st. F/dj. M2. $30.00

CROSS, Melinda. *Bloomsbury Needlepoint: From Tapestries at Charleston...* 1992. ils. VG/VG. M17. $25.00

CROSS & PARKIN. *Captain Gray in the Pacific Northwest.* 1987. Bend, OR. Maverick. 2nd. sgn. VG/VG. B11. $25.00

CROSSEN, Kendell Foster. *Adventures in Tomorrow.* 1950. Greenberg. VG/VG. P3. $40.00

CROSSEN, Kendell Foster. *Future Tense.* 1952. Greenberg. 1st. NF/VG. P3. $45.00

CROTHER, Ruth. *Manly Manners.* 1946. Encee Pub. ils Ethel Hays. 115p. VG+/G. P2. $35.00

CROUCH, D.E. *Carl Rungius: Complete Prints.* 1989. Missoula. ils/figures. 203p. F/dj. M4. $55.00

CROUCH, Tom D. *Eagle Aloft: Two Centuries of the Balloon in America.* 1983. Smithsonian. thick 8vo. 770p. F/dj. T10. $60.00

CROWDER, Herbert. *Ambush at Osirak.* 1988. Presidio. 1st. F/NF. W2. $25.00

CROWDER, William. *Naturalist at the Seashore.* 1928. NY. 384p. VG. S15. $25.00

CROWE, Earle. *Men of El Tejon: Empire in the Tehachapis.* 1957. Ward Ritchie. 1st. NF/VG. O4. $25.00

CROWE, Jack. *Hopalong Cassidy Lends a Helping Hand.* 1950. John Martin's House. Bonnie Book. pict brd. VG+. M20. $40.00

CROWE, John; see Lynds, Dennis.

CROWE, Samuel. *Halsted of Johns Hopkins: Man & His Men.* 1957. Springfield. 1st. 247p. A13. $75.00

CROWE & CROWE. *Heaven, Hell & Salt Water.* 1955-57. London. Hart Davis. Mariners Lib 35. photos/maps. 221p. dj. T7. $24.00

CROWELL, Ann. *Hogan for the Bluebird.* 1969. NY. Scribner. 1st/Weekly Reader BC. VG. L3. $30.00

CROWELL, Pers. *First Horseman.* 1948. Whittlesey. 1st. obl 4to. VG/fair. O3. $30.00

CROWELL, Pers. *What Can a Horse Do That You Can't Do?* 1954. Whittlesey. 1st. 27p. G. O3. $20.00

CROWEN, T. *American Lady's Cookbook.* 1861 (1847). 15th thousand. VG. E6. $125.00

CROWLEY, John. *Deep.* 1977. London. NEL. 1st. author's 1st book. F/F. L3. $150.00

CROWLEY, John. *Engine Summer.* 1979. Doubleday. 1st. F/F. M2. $125.00

CROWLEY, John. *Love & Sleep.* 1994. Bantam. 1st. F/F clip. B4. $45.00

CROWNINSHIELD, Ethel. *For You: Stories, Songs, Rhythm & Dramatization.* nd (1956). Boston, MA. Boston Music Co. 8vo. 35p. VG. C14. $10.00

CROWNSHIELD, Mrs. Schuyler. *Lattitude 19 Degrees.* 1898. Appleton. 1st. VG. M2. $30.00

CROWTHER, Charles. *Steamboat Bill.* nd. London. pre WWII ed. ils Chas Crowther. NF. C8. $95.00

CROWTHER, Samuel. *Romance & Rise of the American Tropics.* 1929. Doubleday. 1st. 390p. F3. $15.00

CROZIER, M.J. *Landslides, Causes, Consequences & Environment.* 1986. np. 252p. xl. F/dj. D8. $20.00

CRUIKSHANK, George. *Jack & the Beanstalk From the George Cruikshank Fairy Lib.* 1854. London. David Bogue. 1st/1st issue. 12mo. prt paper wrp. R5. $350.00

CRUM, H. *Focus on Peatlands & Peat Moses.* 1988. Ann Arbor. 306p. F. B1. $50.00

CRUMBO, Kim. *River Runner's Guide to the History of the Grand Canyon.* 1988. Boulder, CO. 3rd. sm 8vo. 61p. VG/pict wrp. F7. $12.00

CRUMLEY, James. *Last Good Kiss.* 1978. Random. 1st. author's 3rd book. F/F. D10. $85.00

CRUMLEY, James. *Last Good Kiss.* 1978. Random. 1st. NF/VG+. M22. $50.00

CRUMLEY, James. *Mexican Tree Duck.* 1993. Mysterious 1st. sgn. F/F. D10. $40.00

CRUMLEY, James. *Mexican Tree Duck.* 1993. Mysterious. 1st. F/dj. M23. $25.00

CRUMLEY, James. *One to Count Cadence.* 1969. Random. 1st. author's 1st book. rem mk. F/NF. H11. $260.00

CRUMLEY, James. *Pigeon Shoot.* 1987. Neville. 1st. 1/350. sgn. F/sans. M15. $125.00

CRUMLEY, James. *Wrong Case.* 1975. Random. 1st. author's 1st mystery. G/VG. M22. $250.00

CRUMMELL, Alex. *Relations & Duties of Free Colored Men in America...* 1861. Hartford. 1st. 8vo. 54p. prt wrp. M1. $450.00

CRUMP, Irving. *Boy's Book of Mounted Police.* 1917. Dodd Mead. sgn/dtd 1917. 297p. cloth. VG. M20. $75.00

CRUMP, Irving. *Boys Book of Airmen.* 1927. Dodd Mead. 278p. VG+/dj. M20. $35.00

CRUMP, J. *Chinese Theatre in the Days of Kublai Khan.* 1980. AZ U. 1st. ils. 429p. F/NF. W3. $62.00

CRUSE, Amy. *Englishman & His Books in the Early 19th Century.* nd. NY. Crowell. 8vo. 311p. VG/dj. K3. $35.00

CRUSO, Solomon. *Last of the Jews & the Japs.* 1933. Lefkowitz. 1st. VG. M2. $75.00

CRUSO, Solomon. *Messiah on the Horizon.* 1940. Audobon. 1st. F/dj. M2. $45.00

CRUTCH & GREENE. *Lewis Carroll Handbook, Being a New Version...* 1979. revised. 12 pl. F/F. A4. $165.00

CSONKA, Larry. *Always on the Run.* 1973. Random. 1st. VG/dj. P8. $15.00

CUBIERES-PALMEZEAUX. *Le Calendrier Republicain, Poeme.* 1799. Paris. Merigot Chemin. 8vo. disbound. R12. $85.00

CUBITT, G. *Portraits of the African Wild.* 1986. Chartwell. ils/200+ mc photos. 208p. brd. VG. M12. $25.00

CUDDIHY, John Murray. *Ordeal of Civility: Freud, Marx, Levi-Strauss...* 1974. Basic. 272p. VG/dj. S3. $25.00

CULINARY ARTS INSTITUTE. *Pennsylvania Dutch Cook Book.* 1936. Culinary Arts Pr. VG/wood covers. A16. $15.00

CULLEN, Countee. *Color.* 1925. Harper. 1st. author's 1st book. 3-pc cover. VG. M25. $200.00

CULLEN, Countee. *One Way to Heaven.* 1932. Harper. 1st. cloth. VG. M25. $75.00

CULLEN, Thomas S. *Early Medicine in Maryland.* 1927. Baltimore. ils. 15p. brd. K3. $15.00

CULLMAN & GRONER. *Encyclopedia of Cacti.* 1987. Portland. ils. M/dj. B26. $55.00

CULLMANN, Oscar. *Christology of the New Testament.* 1963. Westminster. revised. 331p. VG/dj. B29. $13.00

CULLUM, Albert. *You Think Just Because You're Big You're Right.* 1976. Harlin Quist. obl 8vo. F/F. C8. $37.50

CULPAN, Maurice. *Minister of Injustice.* 1966. Walker. 1st. VG/VG. P3. $10.00

CULVER, Francis Barnum. *Blooded Horses of Colonial Days.* 1922. Baltimore. self pub. 1st. VG. O3. $65.00

CULVER, Timothy; see Westlake, Donald E.

CUMBERLAND, Charles. *Mexican Revolution.* 1972. Austin, TX. 1st. 449p. dj. F3. $20.00

CUMMING, Primrose. *Ben: Story of a Cart Horse.* 1940. Dutton. 1st Am. VG. O3. $25.00

CUMMING, W.P. *Exploration of North America 1630-1776.* 1974. NY. 400 pl/5 maps. 272p. VG+/dj. B26. $75.00

CUMMINGS, D. Duane. *William Robinson Leigh, Western Artist.* 1980. Norman. OK U. 1st. sm 4to. VG/VG. O3. $65.00

CUMMINGS, E.E. *One Times One.* 1944. NY. Henry Holt. 1st. gray cloth. dj. M24. $100.00

CUMMINGS, E.E. *Six Nonlectures.* 1954. Harvard. 2nd prt. sgn/dtd. w/poem & drawing on Christmas card. B35. $75.00

CUMMINGS, Ray. *Insect Invasion.* 1967. Avalon. 1st. RS. F/dj. M2. $40.00

CUNARD STEAMSHIP COMPANY. *Royal Mail Steamships.* nd (1893). Liverpool. Cunard. 5 fld charts/maps. 82p. T7. $95.00

CUNNINGHAM, E.V. *Case of Kidnapped Angel.* 1982. Delacorte. 1st. F/NF. M25. $25.00

CUNNINGHAM, Frank. *Sky Master, the Story of Donald Douglas.* 1943. Phil. 1st. 321p. G/dj. B18. $65.00

CUNNINGHAM, J. Morgan; see Westlake, Donald E.

CUNNINGHAM, Jere. *Abyss.* 1981. Wyndham. 1st. VG/VG. P3. $20.00

CUNNINGHAM, Michael. *Flesh & Blood.* 1995. FSG. 1st. author's 2nd novel. F/F. B3. $25.00

CUNNINGHAM, W. *Christianity & Social Questions.* 1910. Scribner. 232p. VG. B29. $7.50

CUNY, Hilaire. *Man & His Theories (Einstein).* 1965. NY. Erikson. 1st Am. ils. VG/dj. K3. $15.00

CURCIO, Vincent. *Suicide Blond, the Life of Gloria Grahame.* 1989. Morrow. 37 photos. cloth. NF/dj. C9. $30.00

CURIE, Eve. *Journey Among the Warriors.* 1943. NY. sgn/dtd 1943. 501p. VG. S16. $25.00

CURIE, Marie. *Pierre Curie.* 1926. Macmillan. 2nd. ils. VG-. K3. $35.00

CURRAN, Bob. *Violence Game.* 1966. Macmillan. 1st. photos. F/VG+. P8. $35.00

CURRAN, Terrie. *All Booked Up.* 1987. Dodd Mead. 1st. NF/NF. P3. $16.00

CURREY, L.W. *Science Fiction & Fantasy Authors.* 1979. GK Hall. VG/sans. P3. $75.00

CURRIE, Barton. *Fishers of Books.* 1931. 1st. VG/G. K3. $20.00

CURRIE, Ellen. *Available Light.* 1986. Summit. 1st. F/NF. M23. $40.00

CURRIE & MCHUGH. *Officer 666.* 1912. AL Burt. VG. M2. $12.00

CURRIER & TILTON. *Bibliography of Oliver Wendell Holmes.* 1953. NY. 1st. gilt brn cloth. F. M24. $65.00

CURRINGTON, O.J. *Breath-Out.* 1978. Andre Deutsch. 1st. VG/VG. P3. $18.00

CURRY, Jane. *Miss Sniff.* 1945. Whitman. Fuzzy Wuzzy Book. pict brd. VG/dj. M20. $25.00

CURRY, Larry. *American West: Painters From Catlin to Russell.* 1972. Viking. 1st. 132 pl. F/clip. A14. $40.00

CURRY, W.L. *Ohio, the Buckeye State.* 1915. Columbus. 64p. decor wrp. B18. $15.00

CURTIES, Henry. *Out of the Shadows.* 1911. Greening. decor brd. VG. P3. $35.00

CURTIS, Anna L. *Stories of the Underground Railroad.* 1941. Island Workshop Pr Co-op. 1st. sgn. F/NF. B4. $85.00

CURTIS, Charles. *Orchids: Their Description & Cultivation.* 1950. London. Putnam. 1st. 274p. dj. A10. $125.00

CURTIS, George William. *Equal Rights for All.* 1967. Rochester. 8vo. stitched. R12. $60.00

CURTIS, Jack. *Glory.* 1988. Dutton. 1st. VG/VG. P3. $25.00

CURTIS, M.M. *Book of Snuff & Snuff Boxes With 119 Rare & Unusual...* 1935. NY. 1st. 119 photos. 137p. F. M4. $35.00

CURTIS, Mary. *Stories in Trees.* 1925. Chicago. Lyons. 224p. VG. A10. $25.00

CURTIS, Wardon. *Strange Adventures of Mr Middleton.* 1903. Stone. 1st. G+. M2. $30.00

CURTISS, Ursula. *Noonday Devil.* 1953. Eyre Spottiswoode. 1st. VG/VG. P3. $25.00

CURWOOD, James O. *Baree, Son of Kazan.* nd. Grossett. G+. M2. $20.00

CURWOOD, James O. *Country Beyond.* 1922. Cosmopolitan. 1st. ils Walt Louderback. VG+/dj. A18. $50.00

CURZON, Clare. *Three-Core Lead.* 1988. Collins Crime Club. 1st. F/F. P3. $20.00

CURZON OF KEDLESTON, Marquess. *Tales of Travel.* 1923. Hodder Stoughton. 1st. 27 tipped-in pl. 344p. VG. W1. $50.00

CUSHING, Harvey. *Consecratio Medici & Other Papers.* 1928. Boston. 1st/1st prt. 276p. A13. $150.00

CUSHING, Harvey. *Medical Career & Other Papers.* 1940. Boston. 1st. 302p. A13. $100.00

CUSHING, Harvey. *Pituitary Body & Its Disorders.* 1912. Phil. 1st/1st prt. 341p. A13. $600.00

CUSHING, Harvey. *Pituitary Body & Its Disorders: Clinical States...* 1988 (1912). Birmingham. Classics Neurology/ Neurosurgy Lib. facsimile. G1. $100.00

CUSHION, John P. *Animals in Pottery & Porcelain.* 1974. Crown. 1st. VG/G. O3. $35.00

CUSHMAN, Dan. *Brothers in Kickapoo.* 1962. McGraw Hill. 1st. F/NF. M25. $35.00

CUSHMAN, J.A. *Foraminifera.* 1948. Harvard. 4th. 478p. VG. D8. $30.00

CUSSLER, Clive. *Dragon.* 1990. S&S. 1st. F/F. T2. $20.00

CUSSLER, Clive. *Flood Tide.* 1997. NY. S&S. 1st. sign. NF/NF. R16. $40.00

CUSSLER, Clive. *Inca Gold.* 1994. S&S. 1st. F/F. T2. $25.00

CUSSLER, Clive. *Raise the Titanic!* 1976. Viking. 1st. F/NF. B2/B3/M15. $65.00

CUSSLER, Clive. *Sahara.* 1992. S&S. 1st. F/F. T2. $35.00

CUSSLER, Clive. *Treasure.* 1988. S&S. 1st. F/F. H11/T2. $25.00

CUSSLER, Clive. *Vixen O3.* 1978. Viking. 1st. F/dj. P3/T2. $35.00

CUSTER, Elizabeth. *Boots & Saddles.* 1885. 1st. 312p. O8. $37.50

CUT-CAVENDISH. *Complete Bridge Player.* 1905. London. 232p. VG. S1. $20.00

CUTAK, Ladislaus. *Cactus Guide.* 1956. Princeton. ils. VG/dj. B26. $15.00

CUTLER, Carl C. *Queens of Western Ocean: Story of America's Mail...Lines.* 1961. ils. VG/VG. M17. $25.00

CUTLER, Thomas. *Surgeon's Practical Guide in Dressing...* 1838. Phil. Barrington Haswell. 1st Am. 16mo. 208p. cloth. M1. $250.00

CUTLER. *Sir James M Barrie: A Bibliography...* 1968. 1st. 254p. F. A4. $35.00

– D –

D'AMATO, Brian. *Beauty*. 1992. Delacorte. 1st ed. F/F. G10/H11. $20.00

D'AMBROSIO, Charles. *Point*. 1995. Little Brn. 1st ed. F/F. M23. $40.00

D'AULAIRE & D'AULAIRE. *Abraham Lincoln*. 1937. Doubleday. later rpt. VG. B17. $6.00

D'AULAIRE & D'AULAIRE. *Magic Meadow*. 1958. Doubleday. 1st ed. ils. 55p. VG/VG. D1. $60.00

D'AULAIRE & D'AULAIRE. *Sidsel Longskirt*. 1935. Winston. 1st ed thus. 124p. VG/VG. P2. $35.00

D'AULAIRE & PARIN. *Animals Everywhere*. 1940. Doubleday. 1st ed. sm 4to. VG. C8. $150.00

D'AULAIRE & PARIN. *Columbus*. 1955. Doubleday. 1st ed. lg 4to. VG/dj. M5. $65.00

DABBS, James McBride. *Southern Heritage*. 1932. UNC. 1st ed. 456p. VG. B10. $20.00

DABNEY, Betty Page. *Ancient Bond*. 1954. Dietz. ils Elizabeth Richmond. 47p. VG/VG. B10. $8.00

DABNEY, Virginius. *Don Miff, As Told by His Friend John Bouche Wacker*. 1890. Lippincott. 492p. VG. B10. $15.00

DACEY, Philip. *Gerald Manlry Hopkins Meets Walt Whitman in Heaven*. 1982. Penmaen. ltd ed. 1/75. sgn/#d. F/sans. V1. $75.00

DADD, George. *American Reformed Horse Book*. 1883. Orange Judd. VG. O3. $45.00

DAGMAR, Peter. *Alien Skies*. 1967. Arcadia. VG/VG. P3. $15.00

DAHL, Roald. *Charlie & the Great Glass Elevator*. 1972. Knopf. 1st ed. ils Schidelman. 163p. VG/VG. D1. $45.00

DAHL, Roald. *Danny the Champion of the World*. 1975. Knopf. 1st ed. ils Jill Bennett. F/NF. P2. $35.00

DAHL, Roald. *Going Solo*. 1st ed. VG/VG. M17. $22.50

DAHL, Roald. *Kiss Kiss*. 1960. Knopf. 1st ed. VG/VG. M22. $35.00

DAHL, Roald. *Roald Dahl Omnibus*. 1986. Dorset. 11th. F/F. P3. $15.00

DAHL, Roald. *Switch Bitch*. 1974. Knopf. 1st ed. F/F. M21. $35.00

DAHL, Roald. *Two Fables*. 1987. FSG. 1st ed. F/F. P3. $13.00

DAHL & KEHOE. *Young Judy*. 1975. NY. Mason Charter. 1st ed. inscr pres both authors. xl. T10. $50.00

DAIKEN, Leslie. *Children's Games, Throughout the Year*. 1949. Batsford Ltd. 1st ed. 8vo. 216p. red cloth. VG/G+. T5. $85.00

DAIKEN, Leslie. *Children's Toys Throughout the Ages*. 1965 (1963). Spring. revised ed. 8vo. ils. NF/G. M5. $15.00

DAILEY, Abraham H. *Mollie Fancher, the Brooklyn Enigma...* 1894. Brooklyn, NY. 6 pl. 262p. VG. G1. $100.00

DAILEY, Janet. *Glory Game*. 1985. Poseidon. 1st ed. sgn. rem mk. F/F. B35. $35.00

DALBY, Richard. *Horror for Christmas*. 1992. Michael O'Mara. 1st ed. F/F. P3. $28.00

DALBY, Richard. *Mistletoe & Mayhem*. 1993. Castle. F/F. P3. $15.00

DALBY, Richard. *Mystery for Christmas*. 1990. Gallery. VG/VG. P3. $13.00

DALE, Henry. *Harveian Oration on Some Epochs in Medical Research*. 1935. London. 1st ed. 35p. VG. A13. $25.00

DALE, T.F. *Polo Past & Present*. 1905. London. Scribner/Country Life. 1st ed. G+. O3. $85.00

DALE, T.F. *Riding & Polo Ponies*. 1902. London. Lawrence & Bullen. 1st ed. VG. O3. $125.00

DALEY, Brian. *Han Solo at Star's End*. 1979. Del Rey. 1st ed. VG/VG. P3. $15.00

DALEY, Robert. *Dangerous Edge*. 1983. Simon Schuster. 1st ed. NF/NF. P3. $25.00

DALEY, Robert. *Fast One*. 1978. Crown. 1st ed. VG/VG. P3. $20.00

DALEY, Robert. *Hands of a Stranger*. 1985. Simon Schuster. 1st ed. F/F. H11. $25.00

DALEY, Robert. *Hands of a Stranger*. 1985. Simon Schuster. 1st ed. VG/VG. P3. $20.00

DALEY, Robert. *Man With a Gun*. 1988. Hutchinson. 1st ed. NF/NF. P3. $22.00

DALEY, Robert. *Strong Wind Red as Blood*. 1975. Harper. 1st ed. VG/VG. p3. $18.00

DALEY, Robert. *Target Blue*. 1973. Delacorte. 1st ed. VG. P3. $25.00

DALEY, Robert. *To Kill a Cop*. 1976. Crown. 1st ed. VG/VG. P3. $20.00

DALEY, Robert. *Treasure*. 1977. Random. 1st ed. 341p. dj. F3. $15.00

DALEY, Robert. *Wall of Brass*. 1994. Little Brn. 1st ed. F/F. P3. $23.00

DALEY, Robert. *Year of the Dragon*. 1981. Simon Schuster. 1st ed. F/F. H11. $25.00

DALGLIESH, Alice. *Bears of Hemlock Mountain*. 1952. Scribner. 3rd. ils Helen Sewell. unp. VG+. C14. $8.00

DALGLIESH, Alice. *Courage of Sarah Noble*. 1954. Scribner. 1st ed. ils Leonard Weisgard. 54p. VG/VG. P2. $35.00

DALGLIESH, Alice. *Smiths & Rusty*. 1936. Scribner. 1st ed. sgn. 118p. VG/VG. P2. $40.00

DALI, Salvador. *Jerusalem Bible*. 1970. Doubleday. 32 full-p pl. 1200+p. aeg. leatherette. box. D2. $200.00

DALLAS, Sandra. *Buster Midnight's Cafe*. 1990. Random. 1st ed. F/F. M23. $25.00

DALMAS, Herbert. *Exit Screaming*. 1966. Walker. 1st ed. hc. VG/VG. P3. $18.00

DALRYMPLE, Dyron. *Hunting Across North America*. 1970. Outdoor Life/Harper Row. ils/photos. G. P12. $6.00

DALTON, John C. *Treatise on Human Physiology*. 1971. Phil. 8vo. 728p. full leather. w/32p catalog. VG. T3. $50.00

DALTON, W. *Bridge Abridged or Practical Bridge*. 1908. London. 8th. 215p. VG. S1. $8.00

DALTON, W. *Bridge at a Glance*. 1904. London. 2nd. 100p. VG. S1. $8.00

DALY, Carroll John. *Hidden Hand*. nd. Grosset Dunlap. hc. VG/VG. P3. $35.00

DALY, Carroll John. *Snarl of the Beast*. 1981. Gregg. 1st ed. F/F. P3. $25.00

DALY, Conor. *Local Knowledge*. 1995. Kensington. 1st ed. F/F. M23. $35.00

DALY, Louise Haskell. *Alexander Cheves Haskell: Portrait of a Man*. 1934. Norwood, MA. Plimpton. 1st ed. 1/300. 224p. VG. M8. $450.00

DAME, William Meade. *From the Rapidan to Richmond & the Spotsylvania Campaign*. 1920. Baltimore. Gr Lucas. 1st ed. 213p. cloth. NF. M8. $150.00

DAMIANI, B. Petri. *Opera Omnia. Primun Quidem Studio et Labore...* 1623. Lugduni. Landri. folio. 784p. VG. W1. $125.00

DAMM & LEHMANN. *Meyers Kleiner Weltatlas*. 1935. Leipzig. Bibliographisches Institut. 34 double-p maps. F. O7. $65.00

DANA, Charles A. *Recollections of the Civil War*. 1898. NY. 1st ed. 296p. VG. B18. $65.00

DANA, James D. *New Text-Book of Geology.* 1883 (1863). NY. Ivison Blakeman Taylor. 4th. 412p. G. K5. $20.00

DANA, Richard Henry. *Two Years Before the Mast.* 1947. NY. Aldus Printers. ils/sgn Mueller. ship's canvas brds. VG/case. T10. $115.00

DANA & FORD. *Dana's Textbook of Mineralogy.* 1922. NY. John Wiley. 3rd. 720p. VG. D8. $25.00

DANBY, Mary. *65 Great Tales of the Supernatural.* 1979. Octopus. 1st ed. F/F. P3. $20.00

DANCER, Rex. *Bad Girl Blues.* 1994. Simon Schuster. 1st ed. author's 1st book. F/F. H11. $25.00

DANDRIDGE, Dorothy. *Everything & Nothing.* 1957. NY. 1st ed. VG/VG. B5. $30.00

DANE, Clemence. *Arrogant History of White Ben.* 1939. Literary Guild. VG/VG. P3. $20.00

DANE, Clemence. *Babyons.* 1934. Doubleday Doran. rpt. VG/G+. M21. $30.00

DANE, Clemence. *Flower Girls.* 1955. Norton. 1st ed. VG. P3. $10.00

DANEON, Emile. *Tides of Time.* 1952. Ballantine. VG/G. P3. $30.00

DANFORTH, Keyes. *Boyhood Reminiscences.* 1895. NY. VG. O7. $35.00

DANIELS, Jonathan. *Devil's Backbone.* 1962. McGraw Hill. 8vo. 278p. F/dj. B5/T10. $25.00

DANIELS, Jonathan. *New South Creed: Study in Southern Mythmaking.* 1970. Knopf. 1st ed. 298p. VG/VG. B10. $10.00

DANIELS, Les. *Black Castle.* 1978. Scribner. 1st ed. NF/NF. P3. $25.00

DANIELS, Les. *Comix.* 1971. Outerbridge Dientsfrey. VG/VG. P3. $30.00

DANIELS, Les. *Silver Skull.* 1979. Scribner. 1st ed. VG/VG. P3. $30.00

DANIELSEN, Robert J. *Book One: Relay Precision: The One Heart Relay.* 1977. Hackensack. 84p. pb. NF. S1. $10.00

DANIELSSON, B. *Raroia: Happy Island of the South Seas.* 1953. Rand McNally. 55 ils. 304p. T7. $18.00

DANN, Jack. *Immortal: Short Novels of the Transhuman Future.* 1978. Harper Row. AN/wrp. M21. $15.00

DANN, Jack. *Starhiker.* 1977. Harper Row. 1st ed. F/F. P3. $25.00

DANSEREAU, Pierre. *Biogeography.* 1957. NY. 128 ils/39 tables/glossary/biblio. 394p. VG/dj. B26. $45.00

DANTICAT, Edwidge. *Breath, Eyes, Memory.* 1994. NY. Soho. 1st ed. author's 1st book. F/clip. H11. $35.00

DANTICAT, Edwidge. *Breath, Eyes, Memory.* 1994. Soho. 1st ed. author's 1st book. F/F. M23. $50.00

DARBY, J.N. *Murder in the House With Blue Eyes.* 1939. Bobbs Merrill. 1st ed. VG/VG. P3. $35.00

DARK & UNDERWOOD. *When in Doubt, Fire the Manager.* 1980. Dutton. 1st ed. VG+/VG. P8. $30.00

DARLING, Ester Birdsall. *Baldy of Nome.* 1923. Phil., Penn. 1st ed. ils Hattie Longstreet. sm 4to. 301p. NF. H4. $20.00

DARLING, Jay N. *As Dink Saw Hoover.* 1954. Ames, IA. inscr. 8vo. 139p. F. B11. $50.00

DARLINGTON, W.M. *Gist's Journals.* 1893. Pittsburgh. 1st ed. NF. A15. $225.00

DARLINGTON & HOWGEGO. *Printed Maps of London Circa 1553-1850.* 1964. London. Philip. 1st ed. 20 ils. F/rpr dj. O7. $75.00

DARLOW & MOULE. *Historical Catalogue of Printed Editions of Holy Scripture.* nd. np. 4 vol. rpt of 1903-1911 ed. F. A4. $200.00

DARNELL & LURIA. *Virologia Generale.* 1970. Bologna. 1st Italian ed. 8vo. ils. F/dj. B14. $50.00

DARNTON & DANIEL. *Revolution in Print: Press in France 1775-1800.* 1989s. CA U. 2nd. 351p. F/wrp. A17. $15.00

DARRACOTT, Joseph. *England's Constable: Life & Letters of John Constable.* 1985. London. Folio Soc. 1st ed. 8vo. ils. beige cloth. F/case. T10. $35.00

DARRAH, W.C. *Cartes Des Visite in 19th-Century Photography.* 1981. Gettysburg. 1st ed. F/F. B5. $80.00

DARRAH, W.C. *Cartes des Visite in 19th-Century Photography.* 1981. Gettysburg. 4to. 221p. red cloth. VG/dj. T3. $40.00

DARRAH, W.C. *Stereo Views.* 1964. Gettysburg, PA. 8vo. 255p. bl cloth. VG. T3. $40.00

DARRAH, W.C. *World of Stereographs.* 1977. Gettysburg. 4to. 246p. gr cloth. F/dj. T3. $35.00

DARROW, Clarence S. *Farmington.* 1904. Chicago. 1st ed. VG. B5. $35.00

DARROW, Clarence S. *Persian Pearl & Other Essays.* 1902. Chicago. Ricketts. 2nd. NF. B2. $85.00

DARROW, Clarence S. *Resist Not Evil.* 1903. Charles H Kerr. 1st ed. sgn. NF/sans. B4. $1,250.00

DARROW, George M. *Strawberry.* 1966. HRW. 1st ed. ils. 447p. F/dj. T10. $50.00

DARTON, John. *Neanderthal.* 1996. NY. Random House. 1st. author's 1st book. NF/NF. R16. $35.00

DARTON, N.H. *Geology & Underground Waters of South Dakota.* 1909. GPO. 14 pl/7 figures/lg fld map. 156p. new cloth. F. T10. $75.00

DARTON. *Children's Books in England: Five Centuries of Social Life.* 1958. Cambridge. 2nd. ils. 385p. F. A4. $75.00

DARVAS, Robert. *Right Through the Pack.* 1957. London. 2nd. 220p. VG/dj. S1. $15.00

DARVAS & LUKACS. *Spotlight on Card Play.* 1960. NY. 160p. VG. S1. $9.00

DARWIN, Charles. *Expression of the Emotions in Man & Animals.* 1872. London. John Murray. 1st ed/1st issue. NF. B2. $500.00

DARWIN, Charles. *Formation of Vegetable Mould.* 1882. NY. 1st Am ed. G+. M17. $50.00

DARWIN, Charles. *Insectivorous Plants.* 1875. Appleton. 1st Am ed. 12mo. VG. G1. $85.00

DARWIN, Charles. *Life & Letters of Charles Darwin...* 1888. London. John Murray. 3 vol. 3rd revised ed/2nd prt. G1. $150.00

DARWIN, Charles. *Monograph on the Subject of Sub-Class Cirripedia...* 1851-1854. London. Ray Soc. 2 vol. 1st ed. 40 pl. bl cloth. NF. C6. $1,200.00

DARWIN, Charles. *Origin of Species by Means of Natural Selection.* nd. NY. AL Burt. rpt from 6th London ed. 538p. VG. D8. $10.00

DARWIN, Charles. *Structure & Distribution of Coral Reefs.* 1897. NY. 3rd. 344p. half leather. NF. A13. $45.00

DARWIN, Charles. *Variation of Animals & Plants Under Domestication.* 1868. London. John Murray. 2 vol. 1st ed/2nd issue. ES. gr cloth. NF. C6. $750.00

DARWIN, Erasmus. *Zoomania or the Laws of Organic Life. Vol 1, Part 2.* 1797. Phil. 486p. full leather. VG. B5. $250.00

DARWIN, Francis. *Life & Letters of Charles Darwin.* 1959. NY. 2 vol. fwd GG Simpson. box. B26. $40.00

DARWIN, Francis. *More Letters of Charles Darwin.* 1903. NY. 2 vol. ils. xl. G. V4. $60.00

DASHIELL, Margaret. *Spanish Moss & English Myrtle.* 1930. Stratford. ils. 46p. G+. B10. $15.00

DASKAM, Josephine. *Memoirs of a Baby.* 1904. Harper. 1st ed. ils Fanny Cory. VG+. M5. $65.00

DASTRUP. *Field Artillery History & Sourcebook.* 1994. np. 232p. F. A4. $70.00

DAUBER. *Show Book of Nursery Rhymes.* 1945. Capitol. shaped book. spiral red metal. VG. D1. $50.00

DAUBS, Edwin H. *Monograph of Lemnaceae.* 1965. Urbana. 21 pl/map. 118p. F. B26. $25.00

DAUDET, Alphonse. *Recollections of a Literary Man.* 1889. London. Routledge. ils. 268p. VG. A4. $85.00

DAUGHERTY, James. *Daniel Boone.* 1939. Viking. 1st ed. VG+/partial. C8. $95.00

DAUGHERTY, James. *Of Courage Undaunted: Across the Continent With Lewis...* 1951. NY. 1st ed. ils. 168p. F. A17. $15.00

DAUM & WILLIAMSON. *American Petroleum Industry 1859-1899...* 1959. NW U. 864p. VG/torn. D8. $15.00

DAUMAS, E. *Horses of the Sahara.* 1863. London. Allen. 1st ed. trans James Hutton. VG+. O3. $225.00

DAUMAS, E. *Horses of the Sahara.* 1968. Austin, TX. ils. 256p. VG/VG. B5. $32.50

DAVENPORT, Basil. *SF Novel.* 1959. Advent. 1st ed. F/F. P3. $40.00

DAVENPORT, Basil. *13 Ways to Dispose of a Body.* 1966. Dodd Mead. VG/torn. P3. $13.00

DAVENPORT, Basil. *13 Ways to Kill a Man.* 1966. Faber. 1st ed. NF/NF. P3. $18.00

DAVENPORT, C. *Foot & Shoeing.* 1958. London. 1st prt. 55p. O3. $10.00

DAVENPORT, Horace. *Doctor Dock: Teaching & Learning Medicine...* 1987. New Brunswick, NJ. 1st ed. 342p. dj. A13. $30.00

DAVID, Elizabeth. *French Country Cooking.* (1951). Horizon. 1st Am ed. F/NF clip. B4. $150.00

DAVID, Lavinia R. *Buttonwood Island.* 1943. Doubleday. ils Paul Brown. cloth. VG. M5. $15.00

DAVID & MCKAY. *Blessings of Liberty, an Enduring Constitution...* 1989. Random. VG/dj. M11. $45.00

DAVIDSON, Avram. *Best of Avram Davidson...* 1979. Doubleday. 1st ed. VG/VG. P3. $20.00

DAVIDSON, Avram. *Redward Edward Papers.* 1978. Doubleday. 1st ed. VG/VG. P3. $20.00

DAVIDSON, Bill. *Cut Off.* 1972. Stein Day. 1st ed. VG/VG. P3. $15.00

DAVIDSON, Donald. *Lee in the Mountains & Other Poems.* 1938. Houghton Mifflin. 1st ed. 137p. VG/G. B10. $125.00

DAVIDSON, Donald. *Long Street Poems.* 1961. Vanderbilt. 1st ed. 92p. VG/box. B10. $75.00

DAVIDSON, Eugene. *Making of Adolf Hitler.* 1977. NY. 1st prt. 408p. A17. $12.50

DAVIDSON, Eugene. *Trial of the Germans: Account of 22 Defendants...* 1969. NY. 4th. 636p. VG/worn. A17. $18.50

DAVIDSON, Harold G. *Edward Borein, Cowboy Artist: Life & Works of JE Borein...* 1974. Doubleday. 1st trade ed. 4to. 189p. VG/dj. T10. $75.00

DAVIDSON, Lionel. *Long Way to Shiloh.* 1966. Gollancz. 2nd. VG/VG. P3. $15.00

DAVIDSON, Lionel. *Sun Chemist.* 1976. Knopf. 1st ed. VG/VG. P3. $25.00

DAVIDSON, Martin. *Stars & the Mind.* 1947. London. Scientific BC. ils/photos. 210p. cloth. G. K5. $12.00

DAVIE, Donald. *Poet as Sculptor (Ezra Pound).* 1965. London. 1st ed. assn copy. F/NF. V1. $45.00

DAVIES, Arthur Ernest. *Moral Life: A Study in Genetic Ethics.* 1909. Baltimore. Review Pub. 187p. bl cloth/paper labels. G1. $40.00

DAVIES, Arthur L. *Death Plays a Duet.* 1977. Exposition. 1st ed. VG/VG. P3. $10.00

DAVIES, David Stuart. *Holmes of the Movies.* 1978. Bramhall. 1st ed. VG/VG. P3. $15.00

DAVIES, Frederick. *Death of a Hit-Man.* 1982. St Martin. 1st ed. xl. dj. P3. $5.00

DAVIES, John. *Phrenology: Fad & Science, a 19th-Century American Crusade.* 1971. Hamden, CT. 1st ed. 203p. VG. A13. $50.00

DAVIES, Kenneth. *Ionospheric Radio Propagation.* 1965. Nat Bureau Standards. Monograph 80. 8vo. 470p. VG. K5. $25.00

DAVIES, L.P. *Land of Leys.* 1979. Doubleday. 1st Am ed. NF/NF. N4. $25.00

DAVIES, L.P. *Shadow Before.* 1970. Doubleday. BC. VG/G. N4. $8.00

DAVIES, Mary Carolyn. *Joy Toy Man of Joy Toy Town.* ca 1930. np ils Queen Holden. unp. VG/dj. M20. $77.00

DAVIES, Nigel. *Aztec Empire.* 1987. OK U. 1st ed. 342p. dj. F3. $35.00

DAVIES, Nigel. *Tolec Heritage.* 1980. OK U. 1st ed. 401p. dj. F3. $30.00

DAVIES, Paul. *Last Three Minutes.* 1994. Harper Collins. 1st ed. F/F. B35. $18.00

DAVIES, Pete. *Dollarville.* 1989. Random. 1st ed. F/F. P3. $18.00

DAVIES, Robertson. *Feast of Stephen.* 1970. Toronto/Montreal. 1st ed. F/VG+. A11. $150.00

DAVIES, Robertson. *What's Bred in the Bone.* 1986. Viking. 5th. F/F. P3. $18.00

DAVIES, William H. *True Travelers.* 1923. Harcourt Brace. 1st probable ed. ils Wm Nicholson. F/VG. C8. $120.00

DAVIS, A.M. *Illustrated Atlas of Berks Country.* 1876. 100 maps w/business directory. complete. loose. S13. $375.00

DAVIS, Berrie. *Fourth Day of Fear.* 1973. Putnam. 1st ed. VG/VG. P3. $13.00

DAVIS, Burke. *Billy Mitchell Affair.* 1967. Random. 1st ed. sgn. 8vo. 373p. VG/VG. B11. $50.00

DAVIS, Burke. *Civil War: Strange & Interesting Facts.* 1982. NY. 8vo. ils. 249p. blk cloth. F/dj. T3. $20.00

DAVIS, Burke. *Dwelling Places.* 1980. Scribner. 1st ed. sgn. VG/VG. B11. $25.00

DAVIS, Burke. *Roberta E Lee.* 1956. Winston-Salem, NC. Blair. 1st ed. inscr. ils John Opper. VG/VG. B11. $45.00

DAVIS, Charles G. *Ships of the Past.* 1929. Marine Research Soc. 1st ed. ils. 170p. VG. w/sgn letter & brochure. M20. $100.00

DAVIS, Charles J. *California Salt-Water Fishing.* (1949). NY. 1st ed. F/G+. N3. $15.00

DAVIS, Dorothy Salisbury. *Death in the Life.* 1976. Scribner. 1st ed. VG/VG. P3. $18.00

DAVIS, Dorothy Salisbury. *God Speed the Night.* 1968. Scribner. 1st ed. VG/G. P3. $18.00

DAVIS, Dorothy Salisbury. *Where the Dark Streets Go.* 1969. Scribner. 1st ed. F/F. H11. $25.00

DAVIS, E. Adams. *On the Night Wind's Telling.* 1946. Norman, OK. 1st ed. 276p. dj. F3. $30.00

DAVIS, Grania. *Moonbird.* 1986. Doubleday. 1st ed. rem mk. F/NF. G10. $15.00

DAVIS, H.L. *Honey in the Horn.* 1977. Franklin Lib. ils. full leather. A17. $25.00

DAVIS, H.L. *Kettle of Fire.* 1959. Morrow. 1st ed. M/dj. A18. $20.00

DAVIS, Harriet Eager. *Elmira: Girl Who Loved Edgar Allan Poe.* 1966. Houghton Mifflin. 1st ed. VG/dj. M21/P3. $20.00

DAVIS, J. Madison. *Murder of Frau Shutz.* 1988. NY. Walker. 1st ed. author's 1st book. F/F. H11. $30.00

DAVIS, Janet S. *Completely Cowed.* 1969. Phil. Chilton. 1st ed. author's 1st novel. F. B4. $75.00

DAVIS, John Gordon. *Taller Than Trees.* 1975. Doubleday. 1st ed. F/F. P3. $15.00

DAVIS, Kathryn. *Girl Who Trod on a Loaf.* 1993. Knopf. 1st ed. F/F. H11. $25.00

DAVIS, Kathryn. *Labrador.* 1988. FSG. 1st ed. author's 1st book. F/clip. H11. $40.00

DAVIS, Keith. *Desire Charnay.* 1981. NM U. 1st ed. 4to. 212p. dj. F3. $45.00

DAVIS, Kenneth C. *Don't Know Much About Geography.* 1992. NY. VG. O7. $20.00

DAVIS, Lavinia R. *Melody Muttonbone & Sam.* 1947. Doubleday. 1st ed. ils Paul Brown. 244p. F/VG. P2. $25.00

DAVIS, Lavinia R. *Roger & the Fox.* 1947. Doubleday. sgn. ils Hildegard Woodward. VG. P2. $25.00

DAVIS, Lavinia R. *Threat of Dragons.* 1948. Crime Club. G. P3. $7.00

DAVIS, Lindsey. *Silver Pigs.* 1989. Crown. 1st ed. NF/NF. M23. $20.00

DAVIS, Mac. *Lore & Legends of Baseball.* 1953. Lantern. 1st ed. ils. VG/G+. P8. $15.00

DAVIS, Margo. *Antique Black.* 1973. San Francisco. Scrimshaw. 1st ed. photos. F/dj. S9. $125.00

DAVIS, Marguerite. *Told Under the Blue Umbrella: New Stories for New Children.* 1934. Macmillan. 4th. 161p. VG. C14. $5.00

DAVIS, Mary Lee. *Uncle Sam's Attic.* 1930. Boston. WA Wilde. 8vo. 402p. VG. P4. $25.00

DAVIS, Mildred. *Strange Corner.* 1967. Crime Club. 1st ed. VG/VG. P3. $20.00

DAVIS, Mildred. *They Buried a Man.* nd. BC. VG/VG. P3. $8.00

DAVIS, Richard Beale. *Literature & Society in Early Virginia, 1608-1840.* 1973. LSU. 332p. VG/VG. B10. $35.00

DAVIS, Richard Harding. *Gallagher.* 1906. Scribner. VG. P3. $10.00

DAVIS, Richard Harding. *Rulers of the Mediterranean.* 1894. NY. Harper. 8vo. ils. VG. W1. $24.00

DAVIS, Richard Harding. *West From a Car Window.* 1892. Harper. 1st ed. ils Remington. bl cloth. NF. T10. $150.00

DAVIS, Richard. *Encyclopedia of Horror.* 1981. Octopus. 1st ed. VG. P3. $20.00

DAVIS, Richard. *Space 3.* 1976. Abelard. 1st ed. VG/VG. P3. $22.00

DAVIS, Robertson. *Manticore.* 1972. Viking. 1st Am ed. F/NF. B2. $45.00

DAVIS, Thulani. *1959.* 1992. Grove Weidenfeld. ARC. author's 1st novel. F/wrp. B4. $45.00

DAVIS, Thulani. *1959.* 1992. Grove Weidenfeld. 1st ed. F/F. M23. $20.00

DAVIS, William C. *Image of War, 1861-1865; Vol II: Guns of '62.* 1982. Garden City. 4to. 460p. F/NF. T3. $30.00

DAVIS, William C. *Rebels & Yankees: Commanders of the Civil War.* 1990. NY. folio. 256p. F/F. T3. $30.00

DAVIS, William M. *Coral Reef Problem.* 1928. NY. VG. O7. $55.00

DAVIS, William M. *Lesser Antilles.* 1920. NY. VG. O7. $35.00

DAVIS, William M. *Nimrod of the Sea; or, American Whaleman.* 1926. Boston. Lariat. 8vo. 406p. partially unopened. NF. T10. $125.00

DAVIS, William M. *Nimrod of the Sea; or, American Whaleman.* 1972. Quincy, MA. Christopher Pub. rpt. 405p. VG/dj. T7. $35.00

DAVIS, William Stearns. *Short History of the Near East.* 1922. Macmillan. 13 maps. 408p. VG. W1. $18.00

DAVIS & PEDLER. *Dynostar Menace.* 1975. Scribner. 1st ed. F/F. P3. $10.00

DAVIS & PEDLER. *Mutant 59.* nd. BC. VG/VG. P3. $8.00

DAVIS & WATKINS. *Children's Theatre.* 1960. NY. 416p. VG/VG. A17. $5.00

DAVY, Kenneth L. *Let's Learn Bridge.* 1946. London. 47p. stiff brd. VG. S1. $5.00

DAWE, Carlton. *Life Cartridge.* 1937. Ward Lock. 1st ed. xl. VG. P3. $20.00

DAWKINS, Cecil. *Quiet Enemy.* 1963. Atheneum. 1st ed. author's 1st book. NF/NF. B35. $30.00

DAWKINS, W. Boyd. *Early Man in Britain.* 1880. London. Macmillan. 1st ed. ils. 537p. teg. decor cloth. VG. T10. $125.00

DAWS & SHEEHAN. *Hawaiians.* 1970. Sydney. VG. O7. $75.00

DAWSON, Carol. *Body of Knowledge.* 1994. Algonquin. 1st ed. sgn. F/F. M23. $30.00

DAWSON, David Laing. *Last Rights.* 1990. Canada. Macmillan. 1st ed. NF/NF. P3. $20.00

DAWSON, James. *Hell Gate.* 1971. McKay. VG/VG. P3. $10.00

DAWSON, Joseph Martin. *Brooks Takes the Long Look.* 1931. Waco, TX. Baylor. sgn. VG. B11. $20.00

DAWSON, Muriel. *Happy Hours Picture Book.* nd. Raphael Tuck. 8vo. 16 glossy p. VG. M5. $65.00

DAWSON, Muriel. *My Book of Nursery Rhymes.* nd. Raphael Tuck. 4to. 16 glossy p. VG/stiff wrp. M5. $75.00

DAWSON, Muriel. *Nursery Rhymes for Children.* 1940. Lowe. ils Muriel Dawson. 20p. F. M5. $60.00

DAWSON, Percy. *Soviet Samples: Diary of an American Physiologist.* 1938. Ann Arbor. 1st ed. 568p. wrp. A13. $30.00

DAWSON, Raymond. *Chinese Experience.* 1978. NY. VG. O7. $20.00

DAWSON & FOSTER. *Seashore Plants of California.* 1982. Berkeley. 12mo. ils/pl. VG/VG. B1. $26.50

DAY, Alexandra. *Paddy's Pay-Day.* 1989. Viking Kestrel. 1st ed. 4to. F/F. B17. $9.00

DAY, Beth. *Little Professor of Piney Woods.* 1955. Messner. 1st ed. inscr. 192p. VG/VG. B11. $100.00

DAY, Clarence. *Life With Father.* 1947. Sun Dial. MTI. VG/VG. P3. $20.00

DAY, David. *Tolkien Bestiary.* 1979. Ballantine. 1st ed. VG/VG. P3. $25.00

DAY, Dianne. *Strange Files of Fremont Jones.* 1995. Doubleday. 1st ed. F/F. M23. $75.00

DAY, Gene. *Future Day.* 1979. Flying Buttress. 1st ed. decor brd. VG. P3. $15.00

DAY, Gina. *Tell No Tales.* 1967. Hart Davis. 1st ed. F/F. P3. $15.00

DAY & LEE. *Castles.* 1984. Bantam. 1st ed. hc. F/F. P3. $25.00

DAY & MOSELEY. *Chan Chan: Andean Desert City.* 1992. Jahrhundert, Germany. ils. 183p. wrp. F3. $45.00

DAYAN, Yael. *Dust.* 1963. World. 12mo. 190p. cloth. VG. W1. $16.00

DAYTON, Fred Erving. *Steamboat Days.* 1925. Stokes. ils John Wolcott Adams. G. B16. $60.00

DAZEY, Charles. *In Old Kentucky.* 1937. Detroit. Blue Ox. 147p. VG/stiff wrp. B10. $35.00

DE ALARCON, Pedro Antonio. *Three-Cornered Hat.* 1959. LEC. 1st ed. 1/1500. ils/sgn Duvoisin. 155p. F/case. C2. $50.00

DE ALMEIDA. *Ocupacao Portuguesa em Africa na Epoca Contemporanea.* 1936. Lisboa. inscr. VG/wrp. O7. $35.00

DE ANDREA, William L. *Killed in the Ratings.* 1978. HBJ. 1st ed. author's 1st book. F/F. H11. $45.00

DE ANGELI, Marguerite. *Black Fox of Lorne.* 1956. Doubleday. 1st ed. 8vo. VG. C14. $15.00

DE ANGELI, Marguerite. *Jared's Island.* 1947. Doubleday. 1st ed. ils. 95p. VG/poor. C14. $15.00

DE ANGELI, Marguerite. *Petite Suzanne.* 1937. Doubleday/Jr Literary Guild. ils. VG. M5. $25.00

DE ANGELI, Marguerite. *Turkey for Christmas.* 1949. Westminster. 1st ed. unp. VG/dj. M20/P2. $50.00

DE ANGELI & DE ANGELI. *Empty Barn.* 1946. Westminster. ils. VG/VG. P2. $35.00

DE AYALA, Juan. *Letter to Ferdinand & Isabella.* 1965. NM U. ltd ed. 1/750. 90p. F3. $45.00

DE BALZAC, Honore. *Eugenie Grandet.* 1960. London. 4to. ils Rene ben Sussan. beige cloth/leather decor. F/case. T10. $60.00

DE BEAUVOIR, Simone. *Les Belles Images.* 1968. Collins. 2nd ed. hc. NF/NF. P3. $15.00

DE BENHAM, Frank. *Discovery & Exploration: An Atlas-History...* 1960. np. ils. 272p. VG/VG. A4. $45.00

DE BENOUVILLE, Guillain. *Unknown Warriors.* 1949. Simon Schuster. 1st ed. 372p. VG. A17. $9.50

DE BERG, Jeanne. *Women's Rites.* nd. BC. VG/VG. P3. $8.00

DE BERNIERES, Louis. *Corelli's Mandolin.* 1994. Pantheon. ARC. 8vo. F/wrp. S9. $35.00

DE BERNIERES, Louis. *War of Don Emmanuel's Nether Parts.* 1992. NY. Morrow. 1st ed. author's 1st book. NF/F. M23. $20.00

DE BESAULT, Lawrence. *President Trujillo: His Life & the Dominican Republic.* 1941. Santiago. El Diario. 3rd. inscr to US Ambassador. VG/G. B11. $65.00

DE BOSSCHERE, Jean. *Marthe & the Madmen.* 1928. Covici Friede. 1st ed. author's 1st novel. F/NF. B35. $75.00

DE BOSSHERE, J. *Folk Tales of Flanders.* 1918. Dodd Mead. 1st Am ed. 4to. 179p. teg. gr cloth. VG. D1. $275.00

DE BRUNHOFF, Jean. *Babar the King.* 1935. Smith Haas. 1st Am ed. folio. 47p. VG. D1. $750.00

DE BRUNHOFF, Jean. *Historie de Barbar le Petit Elephant.* 1931. Paris. Jardin de Modes. 1st ed. sm folio. 48p. F. B24. $550.00

DE BRUNHOFF, Jean. *Le Roi Babar.* 1933. Jardin Des Modes. 1st ed. ils. 48p. VG-. P2. $275.00

DE BRUNHOFF, Jean. *Travels of Babar.* 1934. Random. 1st ed thus? 8vo. ils. VG/G. M5. $65.00

DE BRUNHOFF, Laurent. *Babar & That Rascal Arthur.* 1948. Methuen. 1st ed. 48p. VG-. P2. $215.00

DE BRUNHOFF, Laurent. *Babar's Mystery.* 1978. Random. 2nd. unp. NF. C14. $12.00

DE BRUNHOFF, Laurent. *Barbar's Bookmobile.* 1974. Random. 1st Am ed. ils. VG/VG box. P2. $35.00

DE BURY, Richard. *Philobibon.* 1888. Kegan Paul Trench. 12mo. 259p. teg. brn buckram. VG. T10. $70.00

DE BUSTAMANTE, Antonio S. *World Court.* 1925. Macmillan. VG/defective. M11. $65.00

DE CALLATAY, Vincent. *Atlas of the Sky.* 1958. Macmillan. trans Harold Spencer Jones. xl. K5. $18.00

DE CAMP, Catherine Crook. *Creatures of the Cosmos.* 1977. Westminster. 1st ed. VG/G. P3. $20.00

DE CAMP, L. Sprague. *Conan Grimoire.* 1972. Mirage. 1st ed. sng. VG/VG. P3. $65.00

DE CAMP, L. Sprague. *Conan Swordbook.* 1969. Mirage. 1st ed. sgn. VG. P3. $65.00

DE CAMP, L. Sprague. *Continent Makers.* 1953. Twayne. VG. P3. $25.00

DE CAMP, L. Sprague. *Energy & Power.* 1962. Golden. hc. NF. P3. $15.00

DE CAMP, L. Sprague. *Golden Wind.* 1969. Doubleday. 1st ed. hc. xl. dj. P3. $20.00

DE CAMP, L. Sprague. *Honorable Barbarian.* 1989. Del Rey. 1st ed. F/F. P3. $17.00

DE CAMP, L. Sprague. *Lest Darkness Fall.* 1949. Prime. 1st ed. NF/VG. M19. $50.00

DE CAMP, L. Sprague. *Literary Swordsmen & Sorcerers.* 1976. Arkham. 1st ed. F/F. P3. $20.00

DE CAMP, L. Sprague. *Tales Beyond Time.* 1973. GK Hall Lg Prt. xl. dj. G. P3. $10.00

DE CAMP, L. Sprague. *Unbeheaded King.* 1983. Del Rey. 1st ed. F/F. P3. $18.00

DE CAMP, L. Sprague. *Undesired Princess.* 1951. Fpci. 1st ed. VG/VG. P3. $75.00

DE CAMP, L. Sprague. *Wheels of If.* 1948. Shasta. 1st ed. VG/VG. P3. $150.00

DE CAMP & DE CAMP. *Dark Valley.* 1983. Bluejay. 1/1000. sgns/#d. F/F/case. P3. $80.00

DE CAMP & DE CAMP. *Footprints on Sand.* 1981. Advent. 1st ed. F/F. P3. $20.00

DE CAMP & NYBERG. *Return of Conan.* 1957. Gnome. 1st ed. VG/VG. P3. $90.00

DE CAMP & PRATT. *Castle of Iron.* 1950. Gnome. 1st ed. VG/G. P3. $75.00

DE CASTANEDA, Pedro. *Journey of Coronado.* 1990. Golden. VG. O7. $20.00

DE CASTELLANE, Comte. *Souvenirs of Military Life in Algeria.* 1886. Remington. 2 vol. 1st ed. VG. W1. $150.00

DE CASTRO, D. Joao. *Journal of Action Upon the Coast of Spain.* 1968. Amsterdam/NY. VG. O7. $75.00

DE CASTRO, D. Joao. *Le Routier de Dom Joan de Castro...* 1936. Paris. Librairie Orientaliste Paul Geuthner. F/prt wrp. O7. $300.00

DE CERVANTES, Miguel. *History of Don Quixote.* 1923. Doran. 1st Am ed thus. ils Jean DeBosschere. 311p. G+. P2. $75.00

DE CHANCIE, John. *Magicnet.* 1993. Baltimore. Borderlands. 1st ed. 1/350. sgn. F/F. T2. $18.00

DE CHATELAIN, Madame. *Blind Fisherman & His Three Sons.* ca 1860. Wm Tegg. 4to. 25p. VG. T10. $150.00

DE CHIRICO, Giorgio. *Hebdomeros.* 1966. Four Seasons Book Soc. 1st Eng-language ed. 1/500. F/NF. B2. $100.00

DE COY, Robert H. *Nigger Bible.* 1967. Holloway. 3rd. pb. 299p. VG+. P11. $20.00

DE DILLMONT, T.H. *Encyclopedia of Needlework.* ca 1940s. np. 1087 ils/pl. 813p. VG. B5. $55.00

DE FELITTA, Frank. *Entity.* 1978. Putnam. 1st ed. G/G. P3. $13.00

DE FOE, Daniel. *Life & Adventures of Robinson Crusoe.* 1914. Chicago/NY. Rand McNally. ils Milo Winter. 382p. gr pebble cloth. F. H4. $75.00

DE FOE, Daniel. *Life & Surprising Adventures of Robinson Crusoe, Mariner.* 1930. LEC. 1/1500. 8vo. ils/sgn EA Wilson. 385p. gr cloth. F/case. B24. $200.00

DE FOREST, J.W. *Miss Ravenel's Conversion.* 1867. NY. 1st ed. VG. A9. $100.00

DE FRANCESCO, Grete. *Power of the Charlatan.* 1939. New Haven. 1st ed. 288p. VG. A13. $60.00

DE GALBA, Marti Joan. *Tirant Lo Blanc.* 1984. Schocken. UP/1st Eng-language ed. F. B35. $25.00

DE GAMA, Jose Basilio. *Uruguay.* 1982. Berkeley. 1st ed. index/biblio. 264p. dj. F3. $25.00

DE GANS, Raymonde. *Tutankhamen.* 1978. Geneva. Ferni. 1st ed. 4to. ils. quarter morocco. VG. W1. $45.00

DE GAULE, Charles. *Call to Honour 1940-1942.* 1955. London. 1st Eng ed. 2 vol. VG/dj. B18. $25.00

DE GINGINS-LASSARAZ, F. *Natural History of the Lavenders.* 1967. Boston. NE Herb Soc. xl. VG. A10. $50.00

DE GRAZIA, Diane. *Correggio & His Legacy: 16th-Century Italian Drawings.* 1984. Nat Gallery of Art. ils/pl. 415p. D2. $65.00

DE GRAZIA, Edward. *Girls Lean Back Everywhere.* 1992. Random. M11. $27.50

DE GUERIN, Basil C. *Man With Three Eyes.* 1955. Children's Pr. 1st ed. decor brd. VG. P3. $15.00

DE HARSANYI, Zsolt. *Star-Gazer.* 1939. Putnam. 1st ed. 8vo. 572p. dj. K5. $12.00

DE HARTE, William C. *Observations on Military Law & the Constitution...* 1869. NY. Appleton. contemporary sheep. M11. $250.00

DE HEJIA & PAL. *From Merchants to Emperors.* 1986. Cornell/Pierpont Morgan. F. D2. $40.00

DE HOLGUIN, Beatrice. *Tales of Palm Beach.* 1968. NY. Vantage. 1st ed. sgn. 8vo. 181p. VG/G. B11. $40.00

DE JARNETTE, Eva Magruder. *Out on a Scurdgeon & Other Negro Stories in Dialect.* 1928. JW Burke. 52p. VG. B10. $20.00

DE JODE, Gerard. *Speculum Orbis Terrarum.* 1965. Amsterdam. Theatrvm Oribs Terrarvm. facsimile. AN/dj. O7. $325.00

DE JONG, Meindert. *Almost All-White Rabbit Cat.* 1972. Macmillan. 1st ed. ils H Vestal. 113p. VG/VG. P2. $30.00

DE JONG, Meindert. *Bells of the Harbor.* 1941. Harper. 1st ed. ils Kurt Wiese. 289p. NF/VG. P2. $50.00

DE JONG, Meindert. *Dirk's Dog, Bellow.* 1939. Harper. 1st ed. ils Kurt Wiese. VG/G. P2. $45.00

DE JONG, Meindert. *Journey From Peppermint Street.* 1968. Harper Row. ils Emily McCully. 242p. VG+/VG. T5. $25.00

DE JONG, Meindert. *Singing Hill.* 1962. Harper Row. 1st ed. ils Sendak. VG+/G. P2. $85.00

DE KNIGHT, Freda. *Date With a Dish. A Cookbook of American Negro Recipes.* 1948. NY. 1st ed. 426p. VG. B5. $25.00

DE LA FONTAINE. *Fables de la Fontaine.* 1981. Boston. Alphabet Pr. 1st ed. ils Marie Angel. AN/case. D1. $85.00

DE LA MARE, Walter. *At First Sight.* 1928. Crosby Gaige. 1st ed. 1/650. sgn. VG. S9. $45.00

DE LA MARE, Walter. *Ding Dong Bell.* 1924. London. 1st ed. F/F. C2. $65.00

DE LA MARE, Walter. *Down-Adown-Derry.* 1922. London. Constable. 1st ed. ils Dorothy Lathrop. teg. gilt bl cloth. VG. T5. $90.00

DE LA MARE, Walter. *Mr Bumps & His Monkey.* 1942. Chicago. Winston. 1st ed. ils Dorothy Lathrop. 67p. VG/VG. D1. $120.00

DE LA MARE, Walter. *Peacock Pie: Book of Rhymes.* 1913. London. 1st ed. F/dj. C2. $75.00

DE LA MARE, Walter. *Songs of Childhood.* 1916. Longman Gr. 2nd. 16mo. gr cloth. F. C2. $45.00

DE LA MARE, Walter. *Stuff & Nonsense & So On.* 1927. London. 1st ed. ils Bold. VG/dj. C2. $65.00

DE LA MARTINE. *Past, Present & Future of the Republic.* 1850. NY. 12mo. 163p. blk cloth. xl. T3. $12.00

DE LA MOTTE FOUQUE. *Undine.* 1909. Doubleday Page. 1st Am ed. ils Rackham. gr brd. VG. B17. $125.00

DE LA NEZIENE. *Tot au Cirque.* ca 1920. Paris. Hachette. ils. VG. D1. $95.00

DE LA REE, Gerry. *Art of the Fantastic.* 1978. De La Ree. 1st ed. NF/NF. P3. $50.00

DE LA REE, Gerry. *Second Book of Virgil Finlay.* 1978. De La Ree. 1st ed. 1/1300. NF/NF. P3. $40.00

DE LA REE, Gerry. *Sixth Book of Virgil Finlay.* 1980. De La Ree. 1/1300. NF/NF. P3. $35.00

DE LA ROCHE, Mazo. *Renny's Daughter.* 1951. Little Brn. 1st ed. VG/G. P3. $18.00

DE LA TORRE, Lillian. *Detections of Dr Sam Johnson.* 1960. Crime Club. 1st ed. VG/VG. P3. $30.00

DE LA TORRE, Lillian. *Dr Sam: Johnson, Detector.* 1946. KNopf. 12mo. 257p. VG/dj. T10. $60.00

DE LANOYE, Ferdinand. *Ramses le Grand ou l'Egypt il y a 3300 Ans.* 1872. Paris. Hachette. 2nd. sm 8vo. ils. 326p. xl. VG. W1. $20.00

DE LILLO, Don. *Americana.* 1971. Houghton Mifflin. 1st ed. author's 1st book. F/F. C2. $350.00

DE LILLO, Don. *Great Jones Street.* 1973. Houghton Mifflin. 1st ed. F/VG. H11. $85.00

DE LILLO, Don. *Libra.* 1988. Viking. 1st ed. F/F. P3. $20.00

DE LILLO, Don. *Names.* 1982. Knopf. UP. F/prt wrp. C2. $75.00

DE LILLO, Don. *Ratner's Star.* 1976. NY. 1st ed. F/F. C6. $50.00

DE LILLO, Don. *White Noise.* 1985. Viking. 1st ed. rem mk. F/NF. H11. $40.00

DE LINT, Charles. *Dreams Underfoot.* 1993. Tor. 1st ed. sgn. F/F. P3. $30.00

DE LINT, Charles. *Ghost of Wind & Shadow.* 1991. Axolotl Special Ed. 1st ed. sgn. F/F. P3. $45.00

DE LINT, Charles. *Ivory & the Horn.* 1995. Tor. 1st ed. F/F. P3. $22.00

DE LINT, Charles. *Memory & Dream.* 1994. NY. Tor. 1st ed. sgn. F/F. M23. $45.00

DE LINT, Charles. *Our Lady of the Harbor.* 1991. Axolotl Special Ed. 1st ed. sgn. F/F. P3. $45.00

DE LINT, Charles. *Wild Wood.* 1994. Bantam. 1st ed. F/F. P3. $20.00

DE LONG, George W. *Voyage of the Jeannette.* 1883. Boston. 1st ed. 2 vol. G+. B18. $125.00

DE LONGCHAMPS, Joanne. *Wishing Album.* 1970. Nashville. Vanderbilt. 1st ed. NF/NF. B4. $65.00

DE LORIA, Vine. *God Is Red.* 1973. NY. 1st ed. VG/VG. B5. $30.00

DE MARINIS, Rick. *Lovely Monster.* 1975. NY. 1st ed. author's 1st book. F/F. A11. $40.00

DE MARINIS, Rick. *Scimitar.* 1977. Dutton. 1st ed. VG/VG. P3. $25.00

DE MARINIS, Rick. *Year of the Zinc Penny.* 1989. Norton. 1st ed. VG/VG. P3. $18.00

DE MAUPASSANT, Guy. *Dark Side of Guy DeMaupassant.* 1989. Carroll Graf. 1st ed. F/F. T2. $20.00

DE MAUPASSANT, Guy. *Mont Oriel.* nd. St Dunstan Soc. hc. VG. P3. $15.00

DE MEDINA, Pedro. *Navigator's Universe.* 1972. Chicago. facsimile. 224p. dj. K5. $45.00

DE MILLE, Agnes. *Lizzie Borden: A Dance of Death.* 1968. Atlantic/Little Brn. 1st ed. AN/dj. B4. $100.00

DE MILLE, Nelson. *Charm School.* 1988. Warner. 1st ed. NF/NF. N4. $30.00

DE MONVEL, M. Boutet. *Nos Enfants par Anatole France.* (1900). Paris. Librarie Hachette. early prt. folio. NF. B4. $85.00

DE MORGAN, Augustus. *Essay on Probabilities on Their Application to Life...* 1838. Longman Brn Gr. 1st ed. 12mo. 306p. full bl calf. T10. $300.00

DE MOUSTIER, C.A. *Theatre...CA DeMoustier.* 1803. French text. marbled ep. aeg. full leather. VG. S13. $20.00

DE MUSSET, Paul. *Mr Wind & Madam Rain.* 1864. Harper. 1st Am ed. gilt bl cloth. VG. M5. $125.00

DE ONIS, Harriet. *Golden Land.* 1948. Knopf. 1st ed. 395p. dj. F3. $15.00

DE PAOLA, Tomie. *Songs of the Fog Maiden.* 1979. Holiday House. 1st ed. ils. NF/G+. P2. $28.00

DE PORTOLA, Gaspar. *Diary.* 1909. Berkeley. 1st ed. 8vo. 59p. T10. $50.00

DE PROROK, Byron. *Dead Men Do Tell Tales.* 1942. Creative Age. 1st ed. 8vo. 328p. VG. W1. $18.00

DE QUILLE, Dan. *Big Bonanza.* 1959. Knopf. 5th. 8vo. 440p. F/NF. T10. $35.00

DE RACHEWILTZ, Boris. *Black Eros: Sexual Customs of Africa.* 1964. NY. VG+. N3. $25.00

DE RIAZ, Yvan A. *Book of Knives.* 1981. Crown. 1000+ photos. 170p. cloth. dj. D2. $50.00

DE RICCI. *English Collectors of Books & Manuscripts 1530-1930...* 1960. IN U. ils. 212p. NF/VG. A4. $60.00

DE RICO, Ulderico. *Rainbow Goblins.* 1978 (1977). Warner. 1st Am prt. 4to. VG+. C8. $65.00

DE SAINT-EXUPERY, Antoine. *Little Prince.* nd. HBW. rpt. 8vo. VG/VG. B17. $6.50

DE SAINT-EXUPERY, Antoine. *Night Flight.* 1932. NY/London. Century. 1st Am ed. 198p. cloth. G. B18. $20.00

DE SAINT-EXUPERY, Antoine. *Wind, Sand & Stars.* 1939. Reynal Hitchcock. 1st Am trade ed. ils Cosgrave. VG+/dj. B14. $55.00

DE SAINT-EXUPERY, Antoine. *Wind, Sand & Stars.* 1939. Reynal Hitchcock. 1st ed. VG/VG. H4. $20.00

DE SEGONZAC, Andre. *Dunoyer de Segonzac: Dessins 1900-1970.* 1970. Geneva. Pierre Cailler. ils. 455p. cloth. dj. D2. $200.00

DE SEGUR, Madame. *Happy Surprises.* 1929. Whitman. ils Eleanore Mineah Hubbard. trans Julia Olcott. VG. M5. $30.00

DE SEGUR, Madame. *Memoirs of a Donkey.* 1924. Macmillan. 1st Am ed. Little Library. 12mo. 238p. VG. T10. $125.00

DE SEVERSKY, Alexander P. *Victory Through Air Power.* 1942. NY. 354p. dj. A17. $10.00

DE SUZE, J.A. *Little Folks Trinidad.* ca 1930. np. 8th. photos/maps. 170p. VG. A17. $10.00

DE TERRA, Helmut. *Humboldt.* 1955. NY. VG. O7. $35.00

DE TOCQUEVILLE, Alexis. *Democracy in America.* 1945. 2 vol. 1st ed thus. NF/VG. S13. $45.00

DE TROYES, Cretien. *Complete Romances of Chretien DeTroyes.* 1993. IN U. VG/VG. P3. $35.00

DE VAUCOULEURS, Gerald. *Physics of the Planet Mars.* 1954. London. Faber. 365p. G/dj. K5. $100.00

DE VIEL & MICHAELS. *How to Play Canasta.* 1949. NY. 32p. VG/wrp. S1. $3.00

DE VINNE, T.L. *Invention of Printing.* 1878. np. 2nd. 144 ils. 557p. VG. A4. $235.00

DE VOS, L. *Atlas of Sponge Morphology.* 1991. Smithsonian. 4to. ils. 117p. cloth. F. B1. $27.00

DE VOTO, Bernard. *Across the Wide Missouri.* 1947. Houghton Mifflin. later prt. 8vo. ils. 483p. map ep. S13/T10. $45.00

DE VRIES, Hugo. *Intracellular Pangeneis Including a Paper on Fertilization.* 1910. Chicago. 1st Eng trans. 270p. A13. $100.00

DE VRIES, Peter. *But Who Wakes the Bugler?* 1940. Boston. 1st ed. author's 1st book. ils Charles Addams. VG. A17. $35.00

DE WAAL, R. *World Bibliography of Sherlock Holmes & Dr Watson.* 1974. NY. ils. 526p. red br. F/F. H3. $50.00

DE WARVILLE, Brissot. *New Travels in United States of North America.* 1919. Bowling Gr, OH. CS Van Tassel. 544p. cloth. M20. $32.00

DE WITT & ERICKSON. *Littlest Reindeer.* c 1946. Children's Pr. probable 1st ed. 8vo. unp. VG. C14. $8.00

DEADERICK, Barron. *Forrest: Wizard of the Saddle.* 1960. Memphis. SC Toof. pb. F. B30. $45.00

DEAK. *Picturing America 1497-1899: Prints, Maps & Drawings...* 1988. Princeton. 2 vol. 4to. 1029 ils. VG/VG. A4. $335.00

DEAN, Amber. *Dead Man's Float.* 1970. Putnam. 1st ed. VG/VG. P3. $20.00

DEAN, Amber. *Foggy Foggy Dew.* 1947. NY. DDCC. 1st ed. NF/NF. H11. $20.00

DEAN, Amber. *Snipe Hunt.* 1949. Unicorn Mystery BC. VG. P3. $15.00

DEAN, Amber. *Wrap It Up.* 1946. Crime Club. 1st ed. VG/fair. P3. $20.00

DEAN, Bashford. *Helmets & Body Armor in Modern Warfare.* 1977. Tuckahoe. ltd ed. 1/1000. 325p. VG/dj. B18. $125.00

DEAN, Graham M. *Agent Nine Solves His First Case.* 1935. Chicago. 1st ed. VG/dj. A17. $9.50

DEAN, J.S. *ABC of the Electric Car.* 1925. E Pittsburgh. Westinghouse Electric Co. 2nd. ils. 83p. VG. B18. $22.50

DEAN, Robert George. *Affair at Lover's Leap.* 1953. Crime Club. 1st ed. G/G. P3. $18.00

DEAN, Spencer. *Dishonor Among Thieves.* 1958. Detective BC. G/G. P3. $7.00

DEAN, Spencer. *Murder After a Fashion.* 1960. Crime Club. 1st ed. xl. VG/VG. P10. $10.00

DEANDREA, William L. *Five O'Clock Lightning.* 1982. St Martin. 1st ed. F/F. T2. $20.00

DEANDREA, William L. *Killed in the Ratings.* 1978. HBJ. 1st ed. author's 1st novel. F/F. T2. $30.00

DEANDREA, William L. *Killed on the Rocks.* 1990. Mysterious. 1st ed. F/F. P3. $18.00

DEANE, Norman; see Creasey, John.

DEANS, Samuel. *New England Farmer.* 1822. Boston. Wells Lilly. 3rd. 532p. full leather. VG. A10. $135.00

DEARBORN, George V.N. *Moto-Sensory Development: Observations on First 3 Years...* 1920. Baltimore. Warwick. 12mo. 215p. gray cloth. xl. VG. G1. $50.00

DEARMAN, H.B. *Not the Critic: Novel of Psychiatry & the Law.* 1965. Wingate. 1st ed. 400p. VG/G+. B10. $15.00

DEBO, Angie. *Geronimo: The Man, His Time, His Place.* 1977. Norman, OK. 2nd. 8vo. 480p. F/dj. T10. $25.00

DEBUS, Allen. *Science, Medicine & Society in the Renaissance...* 1972. NY. 2 vol. 1st ed. VG. A13. $50.00

DECKER, J.S. *As Orquideas e sue Cultura.* 1956. Sao Paulo. 2nd. ils. 123p. pict brd. B26. $30.00

DECKER, Peter. *Beyond a Big Mountain.* 1959. Hastings. 1st ed. inscr. ils Nick Eggenhofer. F/F. A18. $35.00

DECKER & DECKER. *Volcanoes.* 1981. San Francisco. Freeman. 1st ed. 244p. F. D8. $22.00

DECKER & HAMMOND. *Christian Mother Goose Book.* Feb 1980. Grand Junction, CO. Christian Mother Goose Book Co. 3rd. 111p. VG+. C14. $12.00

DEE, Jonathan. *Liberty Campaign.* 1993. Doubleday. 1st ed. author's 2nd novel. F/F. M22. $30.00

DEEPING, Warwick. *Old Pybus.* 1930. Cassell. 8th. VG. P3. $10.00

DEERING, John Richard. *Lee & His Cause; or, The Why & How of the War...* 1907. NY/WA. Neale. 1st ed. 2 pl. 183p. cloth. VG. M8. $175.00

DEGGE, Simon. *Parson's Counsellor, With the Law of Tithes or Tithing...* 1695. London. Atkins. 5th. modern reverse calf. M11. $450.00

DEIGHTON, Len. *Battle of Britain.* 1980. Clarke Irwin. F/F. P3. $25.00

DEIGHTON, Len. *Berlin Game.* 1983. Hutchinson. 1st ed. F/F. P3. $18.00

DEIGHTON, Len. *Berlin Game.* 1984. Knopf. 1st Am ed. F/NF. N4. $22.50

DEIGHTON, Len. *Billion Dollar Brain.* 1968. London. Cape. 1st ed. NF/NF clip. M22. $65.00

DEIGHTON, Len. *Blitzkrieg.* 1979. Jonathan Cape. 1st ed. VG. P3. $20.00

DEIGHTON, Len. *Catch a Falling Spy.* 1976. Detective BC. VG. P3. $8.00

DEIGHTON, Len. *Close-Up.* 1972. Clarke Irwin. 1st ed. VG/G. P3. $25.00

DEIGHTON, Len. *Expensive Place to Die.* 1967. Jonathan Cape. 1st ed. VG/G. P3. $35.00

DEIGHTON, Len. *Funeral in Berlin.* 1965. Putnam. 1st ed. author's 2nd book. F/dj. H11/M19. $45.00

DEIGHTON, Len. *London Match.* 1985. Knopf. 1st ed. F/F. P3. $18.00

DEIGHTON, Len. *Mamista.* 1991. Harper Collins. 1st Am ed. F/F. N4. $25.00

DEIGHTON, Len. *Mamista.* 1991. London. Century. 1st ed. F/F. P3. $25.00

DEIGHTON, Len. *Mexico Set.* 1985. Knopf. 1st ed. VG/VG. P3. $17.00

DEIGHTON, Len. *Spy Hook.* 1988. Hutchinson. 1st ed. F/F. P3. $20.00

DEIGHTON, Len. *Spy Hook.* 1988. Knopf. 1st Am ed. F/F. N4. $25.00

DEIGHTON, Len. *Spy Sinker.* 1990. Harper Collins. 1st Am ed. F/F. N4. $25.00

DEIGHTON, Len. *Spy Sinker.* 1990. Hutchinson. 1st ed. F/F. P3. $25.00

DEIGHTON, Len. *Spy Story.* 1974. HBJ. 1st ed. VG/VG. P3. $20.00

DEIGHTON, Len. *SS-GB.* 1978. Jonathan Cape. 1st ed. VG/VG. P3. $25.00

DEIGHTON, Len. *SS-GB.* 1979. Knopf. 1st Am ed. F/VG. N4. $25.00

DEIGHTON, Len. *Violent Ward.* 1993. Harper Collins. 1st Am ed. F/F. N4. $25.00

DEIGHTON, Len. *Winter.* 1987. Knopf. 1st ed. VG+/VG+. A20. $17.00

DEIGHTON, Len. *Xpd.* 1981. Knopf. 1st ed. F/F. P3. $20.00

DEILITZSCH, Franz. *System der Biblischen Pshychologie.* 1861. Leipzig. Dorffling. 2nd. 500p. VG. G1. $100.00

DEKAN, Jan. *Moravia Magna: The Great Moravian Empire, Its Art & Times.* 1981. Control Data Arts. 1st Am ed. 166p. cloth. VG+/dj. M20. $22.00

DEKKER, Carl. *Woman in Marble.* 1972. Bobbs Merrill. 1st ed. VG/VG. P3. $20.00

DEL REY, Lester. *Badge of Infamy.* 1976. Dobson. 1st ed. VG/VG. P3. $20.00

DEL REY, Lester. *Best SF Stories of the Year.* 1972. Dutton. 1st ed. VG/VG. P3. $20.00

DEL REY, Lester. *Cave of Spears.* 1957. Knopf. 1st ed. VG. P3. $20.00

DEL REY, Lester. *Moon of Mutiny.* 1961. HRW. 1st ed. xl. dj. G. P3. $15.00

DEL REY, Lester. *Moon of Mutiny.* 1979. Gregg. 1st ed. F/F. P3. $20.00

DEL REY, Lester. *Rocket From Infinity.* 1966. HRW. 1st ed. NF/NF. P3. $30.00

DEL REY, Lester. *Step to the Stars.* 1954. Winston. 1st ed. VG/VG. P3. $25.00

DEL REY, Lester. *Year After Tomorrow.* 1954. Winston. 1st ed. VG. P3. $20.00

DEL VECCHIO, Giorgio. *Man & Nature, Selected Essays.* 1969. Notre Dame. M11. $35.00

DEL VECCHIO, John M. *13th Valley.* 1982. Bantam. 1st ed. author's 1st book. F/F. H11. $45.00

DELACROIX, Eugene. *Album de Croquis.* 1961. Paris. Quatre Chemins. 2 vol. 1/500. ils. quarter leather/cloth. D2. $180.00

DELAFIELD, R. *Report on the Art of War in Europe.* 1861. WA. Geo W Bowman. House ed. 41 pl/fld maps/plans. emb blk cloth. G. T10. $200.00

DELAMBRE, Jean-Baptiste. *Astronomie.* 1814. Paris. Courcier. 1st ed. 3 vol. VG. K5. $600.00

DELANEY & TOBIN. *Dictionary of Catholic Biography.* 1961. 4to. 1259p. VG. A4. $150.00

DELANO, Alonzo. *Life on the Plains & Among the Diggings.* 1966. Ann Arbor. U Microfilms. facsimile of 1854 ed. silvered bl cloth. NF. T10. $35.00

DELANY, Samuel R. *Atlantis: Three Tales.* 1995. Seattle. Incunabula. inscr. F/F. w/sgn typed letter. B2. $85.00

DELANY, Samuel R. *Bridge of Lost Desire.* 1987. Arbor. 1st ed. rem mk. F/NF. G10. $15.00

DELANY, Samuel R. *Nebula Winners Thirteen.* 1980. Harper Row. 1st ed. VG/VG. P3. $25.00

DELANY, Samuel R. *Stars in My Pocket Like Grains of Sand.* 1984. Bantam. 1st ed. NF/NF. P3. $18.00

DELANY & DELANY. *Having Our Say: The Delany Sisters' First 100 Years.* 1993. NY. Kodansha. UP. F/wrp. B4. $45.00

DELAUNAY, Charles. *New Hot Discography.* 1948. NY. Criterion. 1st ed. VG. B2. $75.00

DELEHANTY, Elizabeth. *Arise From Sleep.* 1942. NY. 1st ed. author's 1st novel. F/F. A17. $9.50

DELEHANTY, Elizabeth. *Arise From Sleep.* 1942. Viking. 1st ed. inscr. author's 1st novel. F/NF. B4. $50.00

DELISLE, Guillaume. *Atlante Novissimo Che Contiene Tutte le Parti del Mondo.* 1740-1750. Venice. 2 vol. 1st ed. 78 double-p maps. half vellum. C6. $9,000.00

DELL, Floyd. *Love in the Machine Age.* 1930. NY. Farrar. 1st ed. NF/G. B2. $75.00

DELLBRIDGE, John. *Unfit to Plead.* 1949. Hurst Blackett. 1st ed. VG/G. P3. $18.00

DELMAS, D.M. *Speeches & Addresses.* 1901. San Francisco. Robertson. 8vo. 363p. brn cloth/leather label. T10. $60.00

DELVING, Michael. *China Expert.* 1976. Scribner. 1st ed. NF/NF. P3. $25.00

DELVING, Michael. *Smiling the Boy Fell Dead.* 1967. MacDonald. 1st ed. VG/VG. P3. $30.00

DEMAREST, Arthur. *Archaeology of Santa Leticia...* 1986. Tulane. 4to. 272p. F3. $45.00

DEMAREST, Phyllis Gordon. *Angelic City.* 1961. London. Hutchinson. 1st ed. 8vo. bl cloth. F/VG. T10. $25.00

DEMARIS, Ovid. *Last Mafioso.* 1981. Time. 4th. hc. VG. P3. $15.00

DEMESSE, Lucien. *Quest for the Babingas.* 1958. London. Adventurers Club. 8vo. 187p. VG/VG. P4. $15.00

DEMIJOHN, Thomas; see Disch, Thomas M.

DEMILLE, Nelson. *Spencerville.* 1994. Warner. 1st ed. NF/NF. P3. $24.00

DEMING, Richard. *Famous Investigators.* 1963. Whitman. VG. P3. $6.00

DEMING. *James Joyce: Critical Heritage, Vol I & II...1941.* 1986. 2 vol. 821p. F/F. A4. $45.00

DEMOOR, Jean. *Die Anormalen Kinder und Ihre Behandlung in Haus und Schule.* 1901. Oskar Bonde. 292p. modern blk linen. VG. G1. $85.00

DENBY, Edwin. *Mediterranean Cities: Sonnets by Edwin Denby.* 1956. NY. Wittenborn. inscr. photos Rudolph Burckhardt. F/dj. C2. $250.00

DENDY, Walter C. *Philosophy of Mystery.* 1845. Harper. 442p. Victorian cloth. G1. $50.00

DENE, Shafto. *Trail Blazing in the Skies.* 1943. Akron. 1st ed. 34p photo section+78p text. VG/torn. B18. $22.50

DENEVI, D. *Earthquakes.* 1977. Celestial Arts. 1st ed. 230p. F/dj. D8. $15.00

DENEVI, Marco. *Secret Ceremony.* 1961. Time. ltd ed. F/NF case. B35. $30.00

DENHAM, Bertie. *Foxhunt.* 1988. St Martin. 1st Am ed. F/F. O3. $15.00

DENING, Greg. *Mr Bligh's Bad Language.* 1992. Cambridge. 1st Am ed. 8vo. 445p. F/dj. T10. $35.00

DENISON, E.E. *Play of Auction Hands.* 1922. Boston. 284p. VG. S1. $10.00

DENKER, Henry. *Experiment.* 1976. Simon Schuster. 1st ed. F/F. P3. $10.00

DENNIS, Morgan. *Morgan Dennis Dog Book, With Some Special Cats.* 1946. NY. 1st ed. 4to. 68p. NF/G+. C14. $20.00

DENNIS, Patrick. *Around the World With Auntie Mame.* 1958. Harcourt Brace. 1st ed. F/F. B35. $26.00

DENNIS, Patrick. *Little Me.* 1961. Dutton. 3rd. VG/VG. D2. $15.00

DENSLOW, W.W. *Denslow's Picture Book Treasury.* 1990. Arcade. 1st ed. rem mk. F/F. B17. $9.00

DENSLOW, W.W. *Denslow's Three Bears.* 1903. G/wrp. M17. $35.00

DENSLOW, W.W. *Dillingham's Magic Picture Book, Series 1.* 1908. Dillingham. 4to. NF/pict wrp. D1. $200.00

DENT, Lester. *Dead at the Take-Off.* 1946. Detective BC. VG/VG. P3. $18.00

DENTINGER, Jane. *Death Mask.* 1988. Scribner. 1st ed. NF/NF. N4. $20.00

DENTON, Clara J. *Daisy Dells, Rhymes & Verses.* 1927. Whitman. Just Right Book. ils Garnett Cheney. gr cloth. G+. T5. $35.00

DEPERO, Fortunato. *Fortunato Depero.* 1970. Luglio-Sett. ils. 305p. xl. D2. $95.00

DERBYSHIRE, John. *Seeing Calvin Coolidge in a Dream.* 1996. St Martin. 1st ed. author's 1st novel. F/F. M23. $40.00

DERLETH, August. *Beachheads in Space.* 1952. Pelligrini Cudahy. 1st ed. VG. P3. $20.00

DERLETH, August. *Bright Journey.* 1940. Scribner. sgn. 8vo. 424p. map ep. G. B11. $50.00

DERLETH, August. *Casebook of Solar Pons.* 1965. Mycroft Moran. 1st ed. xl. dj. R10. $10.00

DERLETH, August. *Chronicles of Solar Pons.* 1973. Mycroft Moran. 1st ed. 1/4176. F/F. T2. $15.00

DERLETH, August. *Dwellers in Darkness.* 1976. Arkham. 1st ed. 1/3926. F/F. T2. $35.00

DERLETH, August. *Harrigan's File.* 1975. Arkham. 1st ed. F/F. P3. $20.00

DERLETH, August. *Mischief in the Lane.* 1944. Scribner. 1st ed. G/G. N4. $65.00

DERLETH, August. *Mr Fairlie's Final Journey.* 1968. Mycroft Moran. 1st ed. F/F. P3. $40.00

DERLETH, August. *New Poetry Out of Wisconsin.* 1969. Stanton Lee. 1st ed. F/F. P3. $50.00

DERLETH, August. *Night Side.* 1947. Rinehart. 1st ed. VG/VG. P3. $65.00

DERLETH, August. *Outer Side of the Moon.* 1949. Pelligrini Cudahy. 2nd. VG. P3. $18.00

DERLETH, August. *Sleep No More.* 1944. Farrar Rinehart. 1st ed. F/VG. M19. $65.00

DERLETH, August. *Solar Pons Omnibus.* 1982. Arkham. 2 vol. 1st ed thus. 1/3031. F/sans/case. T2. $40.00

DERLETH, August. *Thirty Years of Arkham House.* 1970. Arkham. 1st ed. VG/VG. P3. $60.00

DERLETH, August. *Walden West.* 1961. NY. 1st ed. pres. VG/VG. B5. $35.00

DERLETH, August. *When Evil Wakes.* 1963. Souvenir. 1st ed. sgn. VG/VG. P3. $75.00

DERLETH, August. *Wind in the Elms. Poems by August Derleth.* 1941. Phil. Ritten. 1st ed. 1/25. sgn. tan linen. F/clear Lucite dj. B24. $325.00

DERLETH, August. *Writing Fiction.* 1971. Greenwood. rpt of 1946 ed. F. R10. $15.00

DERLETH & SCHORER. *Colonel Markesan & Less Pleasant People.* 1966. Arkham. 1st ed. NF/NF. P3. $40.00

DERRY, Joseph T. *Confederate Military History: Georgia.* 1976. Syracuse, NY. Bl & Gray. rpt of 1899 ed. 460p. F/NF. M8. $20.00

DERSHOWITZ, Alan M. *Advocate's Devil.* 1994. Warner. 1st ed. F/F. N4. $25.00

DERSHOWITZ, Alan M. *Contrary to Popular Opinion.* 1992. 1st ed. F/F. K2. $20.00

DERSHOWITZ, Alan M. *Reversal of Fortune.* 1986. Random. 1st ed. F/F. A20. $10.00

DESAULT, P.J. *Treatise on Fractures, Luxations & Other Affections...* 1805. Phil. pl. 412p. tree calf. VG. B14. $145.00

DESCURET, Jean Baptiste Felix. *La Medecine des Passions...* 1844. Liege. J-G Lardinois. 3rd. 476p. G. G1. $125.00

DESMOND, Adrian. *Archetypes & Ancestors: Palaeontology in Victorian London.* 1982. Chicago. 1st ed. 287p. dj. A13. $25.00

DESMOND, Alice Curtis. *Far Horizons.* 1931. McBride. 1st ed. sgn. 8vo. bl cloth. G. B11. $25.00

DESMOND, Hugh. *Terror Walks by Night.* 1945. Wright Brn. VG/G. P3. $20.00

DESMOND & MOORE. *Darwin.* 1992. Warner. 1st ed. F/F. M23. $35.00

DEUCHER & WHEELER. *Curtain Calls for Franz Schubert: A Musical Play.* 1941. Dutton. 1st ed. 103p. VG+. C14. $10.00

DEUCHER & WHEELER. *Sebastian Bach: Boy From Thuringia.* 1937. Dutton. 1st ed. 8vo. 126p. VG+. C14. $10.00

DEUEL, Leo. *Conquistadors Without Swords.* 1967. St Martin. 1st ed. 647p. cranberry cloth. NF. B22. $7.00

DEUTSCH, Babette. *Honey Out of the Rock.* 1925. Appleton. 1st ed. inscr to author Leon Feuchtwanger. NF. B4. $85.00

DEUTSCH, H. *Huey Long Murder Case.* 1963. Garden City. 1st ed. VG/VG. B5. $22.50

DEUTSCH, Harold C. *Conspiracy Against Hitler in the Twilight War.* 1968. Minneapolis. 1st ed. 394p. VG. B18. $22.50

DEUTSCH, Otto. *Music Publishers' Numbers: A Selection of 40 Dated Lists...* 1946. 30p. VG/wrp. A4. $45.00

DEUTSCHER, Isaac. *Stalin: A Political Biography.* 1949. NY/London. 1st ed. 600p. silvered red cloth. F/VG. H3. $50.00

DEUTSCHMAN, Deborah. *Signals.* 1978. Seaview. 1st ed. sgn. F/F. B4. $45.00

DEUTSCHMAN, Deborah. *Signals.* 1978. Seaview. 1st ed. VG/VG. P3. $15.00

DEVERDUN, Alfred Louis. *True Mexico: Mexico-Tenochtitlan.* 1938. Winasha, WI. private prt. sgn. 303p. bl brd. B11. $65.00

DEVEREUX, W.B. *Position & Team Play in Polo.* 1914. Brooks Bros. 1st ed. O3. $35.00

DEVLIN, R.M. *Plant Physiology.* 1975. Van Nostrand. 3rd. 8vo. ils. brd. B1. $32.00

DEVON, Gary. *Lost.* 1986. Knopf. 1st ed. VG/VG. P3. $18.00

DEW, Thomas. *Digest of the Laws, Customs, Manners & Institutions...* 1853. Appleton Century. 1st ed. contemporary tree calf. rebacked. M11. $150.00

DEWAR, John. *Dewar Manuscripts, Vol 1: Scottish West Higland Folk Tales.* 1963. Glasgow. 1st ed. ils. 397p. VG/VG. B5. $65.00

DEWDNEY, Selwyn. *Wind Without Rain.* 1946. Copp Clark. hc. VG. P3. $8.00

DEWEY, Evelyn. *Behavior Development in Infants...* 1935. Columbia. 321p. thatched red buckram. VG/dj. G1. $50.00

DEWEY, Frank L. *Thomas Jefferson, Lawyer.* 1986. VA U. 1st ed. sgn. 184p. F/F. B10. $20.00

DEWEY, John. *Psychology.* 1896. Am Book Co. 3rd. 427p. pebbled mauve cloth. VG. G1. $50.00

DEWEY, Thomas B. *Case of the Chased & the Unchaste.* nd. BC. VG/VG. P3. $8.00

DEWEY, Thomas B. *How Hard to Kill.* 1962. Simon Schuster. 1st ed. G/G. P3. $20.00

DEWHURST, Eileen. *House That Jack Built.* 1984. Crime Club. 1st ed. VG/VG. P3. $15.00

DEXTER, Colin. *Jewel That Was Ours.* 1992. Crown. 1st ed. F/F. P3. $20.00

DEXTER, Colin. *Wench Is Dead.* 1989. St Martin. 1st ed. F/F. P3. $16.00

DEXTER, Elisha. *Narrative of Wreck & Loss of Whaling Brig Wm & Joseph...* 1988. Ye Galleon. facsimile of 2nd of 1848. ils. T7. $30.00

DEXTER, John ; see Bradley, Marion Zimmer.

DEXTER, Pete. *Brotherly Love.* 1991. Random. 1st ed. sgn. F/F. H11. $45.00

DEXTER, Pete. *Paperboy.* 1995. Random. 1st ed. F/F. H11. $25.00

DEXTER, Pete. *Paris Trout.* 1988. Random. 1st ed. F/F. H11. $45.00

DEXTER, Will. *This Is Magic.* nd. Bell. 2nd. hc. VG. P3. $5.00

DI CHIARA, Robert. *Dick & the Devil.* 1989. NY. Tor. 1st ed. F/F. H11. $20.00

DI CLERICO & PAVELEC. *Jersey Game.* 1991. Rutgers. 1st ed. F/F. P8. $15.00

DI MAGGIO, Dom. *Real Grass, Real Heroes.* 1991. Zebra. 1st ed. photos. F/F. P8. $15.00

DI MAGGIO, Joe. *Di Maggio Album.* 1989. Putnam. 1/700. 2 vol. sgn. 4to. full leather. AN/cloth case/shipping carton. B4. $975.00

DIAMOND, Edwin. *Behind the Times.* 1993. Villard. 1st ed. sgn. rem mk. F/F. B35. $30.00

DIAZ DEL CASTILLO, Bernal. *Discovery & Conquest of Mexico 1517-1521.* 1933. London. Routledge. 8vo. ils/maps/plans. gilt red cloth. VG. T10. $45.00

DIAZ DEL CASTILLO, Bernal. *Discovery & Conquest of Mexico 1517-1521.* 1953. Mexico. 383p. leather. F3. $35.00

DIBBLE, Sheldon. *Voice From Abroad; or, Thoughts on Missions...* 1844. Lahainaluna. Pr of Mission Seminary. 1st ed. 12mo. 132p. VG. C6. $350.00

DIBDIN, Michael. *Cabal.* 1993. Doubleday. 1st ed. sgn. F/F. T2. $20.00

DIBDIN, Michael. *Dirty Tricks.* 1991. Summit. 1st Am ed. sgn. F/F. T2. $20.00

DIBDIN, Michael. *Dying of the Light.* 1993. London. Faber. 1st ed. sgn. F/F. T2. $20.00

DIBDIN, Michael. *Last Sherlock Holmes Story.* 1978. Pantheon. 1st ed. F/F. P3. $25.00

DIBDIN, Michael. *Ratking.* 1989. Bantam. ARC/1st ed. sgn. F/F. w/promo material. T2. $25.00

DIBDIN, Michael. *Vendetta.* 1991. Doubleday. 1st Am ed. AN/F. N4. $27.50

DIBDIN, Thomas F. *Bibliomania.* 1876. London. VG. O7. $175.00

DIBNER, Bern. *Atlantic Cable.* 1959. Norwalk. VG/wrp. O7. $35.00

DIBNER & RETI. *Leonardo da Vinci: Technologist.* 1969. Norwalk. 96p. brd. D2. $45.00

DICE, Lee R. *Natural Communities.* 1952. Ann Arbor. 1st ed. ils. 547p. VG+/dj. B26. $52.50

DICHTER & SHAPIRO. *Handbook of American Sheet Music, 1768-1889.* 1977. 8vo. 76 full-p ils. 297p. G. T3. $10.00

DICK, Philip K. *Beyond Lies the Wub.* 1988. Gollancz. 1st ed. F/F. P3. $25.00

DICK, Philip K. *Broken Bubble.* 1988. Arbor/Morrow. 1st ed. F/F. T2. $25.00

DICK, Philip K. *Divine Invasion.* 1981. Timescape. 1st ed. rem mk. F/F. G10. $30.00

DICK, Philip K. *Father-Thing.* 1989. Gollancz. 1st ed. F/F. P3. $25.00

DICK, Philip K. *Galactic Pot-Healer.* 1969. Berkley. 1st ed. F/VG. M19. $75.00

DICK, Philip K. *Golden Man.* 1980. SF BC. 1st hc ed. F/NF. T2. $15.00

DICK, Philip K. *Mary & the Giant.* 1988. Gollancz. 1st ed. F/F. P3. $25.00

DICK, Philip K. *Nick & the Glimmung.* 1988. Gollancz. 1st ed. F/F. P3. $30.00

DICK, Philip K. *Our Friends From Frolix 8.* nd. Ace. BC. NF/G. R10. $4.00

DICK, Philip K. *Radio Free Albemuth.* 1985. Arbor. UP. F/wrp/proof dj. C2. $60.00

DICK, Philip K. *Radio Free Albemuth.* 1985. Arbor. 1st ed. F/F. P3. $20.00

DICK, Philip K. *Transmigration of Timothy Archer.* 1982. Timescape. 1st ed. xl. dj. P3. $10.00

DICK, Steven J. *Plurality of Worlds.* 1982. Cambridge. 1st prt. xl. dj. K5. $25.00

DICK, Trella Lamson. *Tornado's Big Year.* 1956. Follett. 8vo. VG/VG. B17. $7.50

DICK, William B. *Dick's Games of Patience; or, Solitaire With Cards...* 1883. NY. Dick Fitzgerald. 33 full-p tableaux. 143p. brick cloth. VG. T10. $350.00

DICK & JANE READER. *Dick & Jane.* 1936. Scott Foresman. sc. VG+. G6. $250.00

DICK & JANE READER. *Elson Basic Reader. Dick & Jane.* 1936 (1930). Scott Foresman. 12mo. 40p. VG/wrp. D1. $85.00

DICK & JANE READER. *Elson Gray Basic Readers — Pre-Primer.* 1930. Scott Foresman. orig ed. 12mo. VG+/wrp. C8. $125.00

DICK & JANE READER. *Fun Wherever We Are.* 1962. Scott Foresman. sc. VG. G6. $70.00

DICK & JANE READER. *Fun With Dick & Jane.* 1946-47. Scott Foresman. hc. VG. G6. $125.00

DICK & JANE READER. *Fun With Our Family.* 1962. Scott Foresman. sc. VG. G6. $70.00

DICK & JANE READER. *Happy Days With Our Friends.* 1948. Scott Foresman. Teacher ed. 95p. cloth. VG. M20. $45.00

DICK & JANE READER. *Little Friends.* 1930. Elson Basic Reader. 4 heavy cutouts in portfolio. uncut. w/primer offer. M20. $200.00

DICK & JANE READER. *More Dick & Jane Stories.* 1934. Scott Foresman. sc. VG+. G6. $250.00

DICK & JANE READER. *Our New Friends.* 1946. Scott Foresman. 2nd reader for 1st grade. VG+. M5. $60.00

DICK & JANE READER. *Sally, Dick & Jane.* 1962. Scott Foresman. sc. VG. G6. $70.00

DICK & JANE READER. *We Come & Go.* 1940. Scott Foresman. 12mo. mk copy sold direct to public. VG/wrp. C8. $60.00

DICK & NELSON. *Ganymede Takeover.* 1988. Severn. 1st hc ed. F/F. G10. $25.00

DICK & ROBINSON. *Golden Age of the Great Passenger Airships...* 1987. WA. 2nd. 226p. VG/dj. B18. $37.50

DICKASON. *Daring Young Men: Story of American Pre-Raphaelites.* 1970. Bloomington. VG. D2. $25.00

DICKENS, Charles. *American Notes for General Circulation.* 1975. LEC. 1/1500. ils/sgn Raymond Houlihan. 272p. F/case. C2. $60.00

DICKENS, Charles. *Annotated Christmas Carol.* 1976. NY. 1st ed. 182p. VG/dj. A17. $25.00

DICKENS, Charles. *Barnaby Rudge.* 1987. Folio Soc. VG. P3. $30.00

DICKENS, Charles. *Bleak House.* 1853. Harper. 2 vol. 1st Am ed. VG. M19. $250.00

DICKENS, Charles. *Charles Dickens 1825-1870: His Portraits & Signatures.* nd. ils. F/wrp. A4. $35.00

DICKENS, Charles. *Chimes.* 1931. LEC. 1/1500. ils/sgn Rackham. 129p. F/case. B24. $475.00

DICKENS, Charles. *Christmas Carol in Four Staves.* 1979. private prt. ils Charles Dougherty. gilt red brd. F. M5. $25.00

DICKENS, Charles. *Christmas Carol.* nd. Lippincott. early ed. 8vo. ils Rackham. gr prt cloth. VG. T10. $25.00

DICKENS, Charles. *Christmas Carol.* 1990. Stewart Tabori & Chang. 1st ed. F/F. P3. $30.00

DICKENS, Charles. *Christmas Carol: A Changing Picture & Lift-the-Flap Book.* 1989. np. 18 flaps/4 changing picture wheels. 30p. F. A4. $40.00

DICKENS, Charles. *Christmas Stories.* nd. Doubleday Jr Classics. hc. VG/VG. P3. $12.00

DICKENS, Charles. *David Copperfield.* 1983. Folio Soc. hc. VG. P3. $30.00

DICKENS, Charles. *Dickens' Children.* 1912. Scribner. 1st ed. ils JW Smith. unp. VG. D1. $125.00

DICKENS, Charles. *Dickens Digest.* 1943. Whittlesey. VG. P3. $23.00

DICKENS, Charles. *Great Expectations.* 1987. Oxford. F/F. P3. $11.00

DICKENS, Charles. *Hard Times.* 1966. LEC. 1st ed. ils/sgn Charles Raymond. 279p. F/case. C2. $75.00

DICKENS, Charles. *Hard Times.* 1987. Oxford. F/F. P3. $11.00

DICKENS, Charles. *Haunted Man & the Ghost's Bargain.* 1848. Bradley Evans. 1st ed. 188p. cloth/rebacked spine. VG. M19. $125.00

DICKENS, Charles. *Life & Adventures of Nicholas Nickleby...* 1838-1839. London. Chapman Hall. 20 8vo parts in 19. 1st issue. morocco box. B24. $3,250.00

DICKENS, Charles. *Little Dorrit.* 1857. London. 1st book ed. contemporary half calf. VG. C6. $200.00

DICKENS, Charles. *Oliver Twist.* 1984. Folio Soc. VG. P3. $30.00

DICKENS, Charles. *Posthumous Papers of the Pickwick Club.* 1887. London. Chapman Hall. 2 vol. 1/8 on Japan vellum. sgn prt/pub/edit. F/box. B24. $3,000.00

DICKENS, Charles. *Posthumous Papers of the Pickwick Club.* 1933. Oxford. 1/1500. ils/sgn John Austen. gilt buckram. F/dj/case. T10. $200.00

DICKENSON, W.H. *Treatise on Albuminuria.* 1881. NY. Wood. 1st Am ed. 11 pl. VG. H7. $50.00

DICKEY, James. *Alnilam.* 1987. Doubleday. 1st ed. F/F. M23. $25.00

DICKEY, James. *Deliverance.* 1970. Houghton Mifflin. 1st prt. VG+/VG+. P10. $55.00

DICKEY, James. *Eye-Beaters, Blood, Victory, Madness, Buckhead & Mercy.* 1970. Doubleday. 1st trade ed. F/NF. B4. $100.00

DICKEY, James. *Tucky the Hunter.* 1978. Crown. 1st ed. ils Marie Angel. unp. AN. D1. $35.00

DICKEY & PENNER. *Soil Survey of Osage County Kansas.* 1985. USDA. 100p+50p maps. VG. D8. $5.00

DICKINSON, Emily. *Brighter Garden.* 1990. Philomel/Putnam. 1st prt. 4to. ils Tash Tudor. F/F. C8. $75.00

DICKINSON, Emily. *Complete Poems of Emily Dickinson.* 1960. Little Brn. 1st ed. F/NF. C2. $75.00

DICKINSON, Emily. *Five Poems.* 1989. London. 1/50. 12mo. 10p. tissue guards. F/emb stiff wrp. B24. $150.00

DICKINSON, Emily. *Poems. Second Series.* 1891. Boston. 1st ed. VG. C6. $1,000.00

DICKINSON, LAIRD & MAXWELL. *Voices From the Southwest.* 1976. Northland. ltd 1st ed. sgn Lawrence Clark Powell. 159p. F/case. B19. $100.00

DICKINSON, LAIRD & MAXWELL. *Voices From the Southwest.* 1976. Northland. 1st trade ed. F/F. B19. $30.00

DICKINSON, Peter. *Annerton Pit.* 1977. Atlantic/Little Brn. 1st ed. F/F. P3. $23.00

DICKINSON, Peter. *Blue Hawk.* 1976. Little Brn. 1st ed. VG/VG. P3. $20.00

DICKINSON, Peter. *City of Gold.* 1980. Pantheon. 1st ed. VG/VG. P3. $18.00

DICKINSON, Peter. *Devil's Children.* 1986. Delacorte. 1st ed. VG/VG. P3. $15.00

DICKINSON, Peter. *Flight of Dragons.* 1979. Harper Row. 1st ed. VG/VG. P3. $25.00

DICKINSON, Peter. *Lizard in the Cup.* 1972. Harper Row. 1st ed. VG/VG. P3. $20.00

DICKINSON, Peter. *Merlin Dreams.* 1988. Delacorte. 1st ed. 4to. F/F. B17. $14.00

DICKINSON, Peter. *Old English Peep Show.* 1969. Harper Row. 1st ed. VG/VG. P3. $20.00

DICKINSON, Peter. *Play Dead.* 1992. Mysterious. 1st Am ed. rem mk. F/F. N4. $15.00

DICKINSON, Peter. *Poison Oracle.* 1974. Pantheon. VG/VG. P3. $18.00

DICKINSON, Peter. *Sinful Stones.* 1974. Harper Row. 1st Am ed. F/NF. T2. $15.00

DICKMAN, William J. *Around the Potomac: Verses About Places & People I Love.* 1968. Newell-Cole. unp. VG. B10. $12.00

DICKSON, Carter; see Carr, John Dickson.

DICKSON, Gordon R. *Alien Art.* 1973. Dutton. 1st ed. F/F. P3. $25.00

DICKSON, Gordon R. *Alien Art.* 1973. Dutton. 1st ed. F/G+. M19. $17.50

DICKSON, Gordon R. *Dickson!* 1984. Nesfa. F/F. P3. $15.00

DICKSON, Gordon R. *Dragon & the Djinn.* 1996. NY. Ace. 1st ed. 8vo. AN/dj. T10. $25.00

DICKSON, Gordon R. *Dragon at War.* 1992. Ace. 1st ed. F/F. P3. $19.00

DICKSON, Gordon R. *Final Encyclopedia.* 1984. Tor. 1st ed. F/F. P3. $20.00

DICKSON, Gordon R. *Forever Man.* 1986. Ace. 1st ed. NF/NF. P3. $20.00

DICKSON, Gordon R. *In Iron Years.* 1980. Doubleday. 1st ed. rem mk. F/NF. G10. $10.00

DICKSON, Gordon R. *Mutants.* 1970. Macmillan. 1st ed. VG/VG. P3. $20.00

DICKSON, Gordon R. *R-Master.* 1973. Lippincott. 1st ed. VG/VG. P3. $25.00

DICKSON, Gordon R. *Star Road.* 1975. Robert Hale. 1st ed. VG/VG. P3. $15.00

DICKSON, Gordon R. *Wolf & Iron.* 1990. Tor. 1st ed. F/F. P3. $19.00

DICKSON, Gordon R. *Wolfing.* nd. BC. VG/VG. P3. $8.00

DICKSON, Grierson. *Traitors' Market.* 1936. Hutchinson. 1st ed. G. P3. $20.00

DICKSON, Harris. *Old-Fashioned Senator: Story-Biography of John S Williams.* 1925. Stokes. photos. 204p. VG. B10. $35.00

DICKSON & MCALEER. *Unit Pride.* 1981. Doubleday. 1st ed. F/NF. B4. $100.00

DICKSTEIN & DWORETSKY. *Horology Americana.* 1972. NY. private prt. ltd ed. sgns. 212p. F/VG. B11. $65.00

DIDEROT, Denis. *Rameau's Nephew & Other Works.* 1926. London. Chapman Hall. 1st ed thus. 1/1000. VG. A17. $15.00

DIDION, Joan. *After Henry.* 1992. Simon Schuster. 1st ed. F/F. B35. $24.00

DIDION, Joan. *Book of Common Prayer.* 1977. Simon Schuster. 1st ed. sgn. F/dj. B4. $125.00

DIDION, Joan. *Democracy.* 1984. Simon Schuster. 1st ed. rem mk. F/NF. G10. $15.00

DIDION, Joan. *Miami.* 1987. Simon Schuster. UP. F/wrp. B4. $45.00

DIDION, Joan. *Play It as It Lays.* 1970. FSG. 1st ed. F/VG+. A20. $17.00

DIDION, Joan. *Salvador.* 1983. Simon Schuster. 1st ed. 108p. dj. F3. $10.00

DIEHL, Charles. *Theodora: Empress of Byzantium.* 1972. NY. Unger. 204p. VG/dj. W1. $18.00

DIEHL, William. *Chameleon.* 1981. Random. 1st ed. F/NF. H11. $30.00

DIEHL, William. *Chameleon.* 1981. Random. 1st ed. NF/VG. M19. $20.00

DIEHL, William. *Sharky's Machine.* 1978. Delacorte. 1st ed. F/F. H11. $70.00

DIEHL, William. *27.* 1990. Villard. 1st ed. NF/NF. P3. $20.00

DIETRICH, Otto. *Hitler.* 1955. Chicago. 277p. VG/tape rpr. A17. $10.00

DIETZ, Lena. *History & Modern Nursing.* 1967. Phil. 2nd. 381p. VG. A13. $35.00

DIEZ, Ernst. *Die Kunst der Islamischen Volker.* ca 1915. Berlin. Athenaion. 199p. VG/dj. W1. $40.00

DIKTY, T.E. *Best SF Stories & Novels Ninth.* nd. BC. VG/VG. P3. $10.00

DILL, Alonzo Thomas. *George Wythe: Teacher of Liberty.* 1979. VA Independence Bicentennial Comm. 101p. VG. B10. $35.00

DILLARD, Annie. *American Childhood.* 1987. Harper Row. 1/250. sgn. F/NF case. S9. $150.00

DILLARD, Annie. *American Childhood.* 1987. Harper Row. 1st ed. F/NF. M23. $20.00

DILLARD, Annie. *Living.* 1992. Harper Collins. 1st ed. F/dj. A18. $25.00

DILLARD, Annie. *Living.* 1992. Harper Collins. 1st ed. sgn. F/F. B2. $35.00

DILLARD, Annie. *Living.* 1992. Harper Collins. 1st ltd ed. 1/300. sgn. F/case. A18/S19. from $100 to $125.00

DILLARD, Annie. *Pilgrim at Tinker Creek.* 1974. Harper. 1st ed. 271p. VG/dj. M20. $42.00

DILLARD, Annie. *Writing Life.* 1989. Harper Row. 1st ed. F/F. M23. $20.00

DILLARD, J. Hardy. *From News Stand to Cyrano.* 1935. Stratford. 46p. G/G. B10. $6.00

DILLARD, J.M. *Star Trek Generations.* 1994. Pocket. 1st ed. hc. VG/VG. P3. $20.00

DILLARD, R.H.W. *Sounder Few: Essays From the Hollins Critic.* 1971. GA U. VG/VG. B10. $12.00

DILLARD, R.H.W. *1st Man on the Sun.* 1983. LSU. 1st ed. AN/dj. G10. $10.00

DILLEY, Arthur U. *Oriental Rugs & Carpets.* 1959. Phil. 75 pl/7 maps. F/dj. A17. $40.00

DILLISTONE, F.W. *Jesus Christ and His Cross.* 1952. Westminster. G. B29. $4.00

DILLON, R. *Siskiyou Trail.* 1975. NY. 1st ed. Am Trail series. VG/VG. B5. $45.00

DIMAND, M.S. *Handbook of Muhammadan Art.* 1947. NY. Hartsdale. 2nd. ils. VG. W1. $35.00

DIMAND, M.S. *Indian Miniatures.* nd. NY. Crown. 28p. VG/wrp. W1. $20.00

DIMENT, Adam. *Bang Bang Birds.* 1968. Dutton. 1st ed. xl. dj. P3. $6.00

DIMENT, Adam. *Dolly, Dolly Spy.* 1967. Dutton. 1st ed. F/F. P3. $15.00

DIMITRY & HARRELL. *Confederate Military History: Louisiana & Arkansas.* 1976. Bl & Gray. rpt of 1899 ed. cloth. F/NF. M8. $20.00

DIMONA, Joseph. *To the Eagle's Nest.* 1980. Morrow. 1st ed. VG/VG. P3. $15.00

DINESEN, Isak. *Anecdotes of Destiny.* 1958. Random. 1st ed. NF/G. M19. $35.00

DINESEN, Isak. *Out of Africa.* 1938. Random. 1st Am ed. F/F. B4. $450.00

DINESEN, Isak. *Seven Gothic Tales.* 1934. Smith Haas. 1st ed. VG/G. P3. $60.00

DINESEN, Isak. *Winter's Tales.* 1942. NY. 1st ed. VG-. A17. $10.00

DINWIDDIE, Emily A. *Songs in the Evening.* 1911. Sherman. 1st ed. 79p. teg. VG. B10. $10.00

DIPPER, Alan. *Golden Virgin.* 1973. Walker. 1st ed. VG/VG. P3. $20.00

DIPPIE, Brian. *Looking at Russell.* 1987. Ft Worth. Amon Carter Mus. 1st ed. 8vo. 144p. beige cloth. F/F. T10. $25.00

DIRINGER & REGENSBURGER. *Alphabet: A Key to the History of Mankind.* 1968. 2 vol. 3rd. 4to. F/VG case. A4. $250.00

DIRLAM, H.K. *John Chapman by Occupation a Gatherer & Planter...* 1965. Mansfield, OH. Richland Co Hist Soc. 79p. VG. A10. $45.00

DISCH, Thomas M. *Bad Moon Rising.* 1973. Harper Row. 1st ed. VG/VG. P3. $28.00

DISCH, Thomas M. *Black Alice.* nd. BC. VG/VG. P3. $10.00

DISCH, Thomas M. *Businessman: Tale of Terror.* 1984. Harper Row. 1st ed. F/NF. G10. $20.00

DISCH, Thomas M. *Getting Into Death.* 1976. Knopf. 1st ed. F/F. M19. $25.00

DISCH, Thomas M. *Getting Into Death.* 1976. NY. 1st Am ed. inscr. F. A11. $35.00

DISCH, Thomas M. *MD: A Horror Story.* 1991. Knopf. 1st ed. VG/VG. P3. $15.00

DISCH, Thomas M. *On Wings of Song.* 1979. St Martin. 1st ed. xl. dj. P3. $8.00

DISCH, Thomas M. *Torturing Mr Amberwell.* 1985. Cheap Street. 1/124. sgn. ils/sgn Judy King-Rieniets. F/dj/case. S9. $125.00

DISERENS, Charles M. *Influence of Music on Behavior.* 1926. Princeton. 224p. prt beige cloth. VG. G1. $45.00

DISNEY, Doris Miles. *Chandler Policy.* 1971. Putnam. 1st ed. VG/VG. P3. $20.00

DISNEY, Doris Miles. *Departure of Mr Gaudette.* 1964. Crime Club. 1st ed. VG/VG. P3. $30.00

DISNEY, Doris Miles. *Last Straw.* 1954. Crime Club. 1st ed. VG/VG. P3. $25.00

DISNEY, Doris Miles. *Three's a Crowd.* 1971. Crime Club. 1st ed. VG/VG. P3. $20.00

DISNEY, Dorothy Cameron. *Hangman's Tree.* 1949. Random. 1st ed. VG/fair. P3. $10.00

DISNEY STUDIOS. *Adventures of Mickey Mouse, Book 1.* 1931. McKay. 1st ed. ils. pict label/cloth. G. A17. $400.00

DISNEY STUDIOS. *Adventures of Mickey Mouse, Book 2.* 1932. McKay. 8vo. pict brd. VG. D1. $400.00

DISNEY STUDIOS. *Baby Weems.* 1941. Doubleday Doran. 8vo. unp. ils bl cloth. VG. C14. $12.00

DISNEY STUDIOS. *Big Bad Wolf & Little Red Riding Hood.* 1934. Bl Ribbon. 1st ed. ils. VG/dj. D1. $450.00

DISNEY STUDIOS. *Bunty.* 1935. Whitman. popups. 28p. VG. D1. $85.00

DISNEY STUDIOS. *Donald Duck & His Nephews.* 1940. DC Heath. sm 8vo. VG+. C8. $65.00

DISNEY STUDIOS. *Donald Duck & the Hidden Gold.* 1951. Simon Schuster. 12mo. VG. B17. $12.00

DISNEY STUDIOS. *Donald Duck in Bringing Up Father.* 1948. Whitman. ils. VG. M5. $22.00

DISNEY STUDIOS. *Donald Duck in Bringing Up the Boys.* 1948. Whitman. 12mo. pict brd. VG. M5. $10.00

DISNEY STUDIOS. *Elmer Elephant.* 1938. Whitman. unp. VG/pict wrp. M20. $77.00

DISNEY STUDIOS. *Ferdinand the Bull.* 1938. Whitman. 12p. VG. M5. $25.00

DISNEY STUDIOS. *Jolly Jump-Ups See the Circus.* 1944. McLoughlin. 6 popups. VG. D1. $185.00

DISNEY STUDIOS. *Mickey Mouse & the Bat Bandit.* 1935. Whitman. Big Little Book. 427p. VG. B14. $125.00

DISNEY STUDIOS. *Mickey Mouse Goes Fishing.* 1936. Whitman. stand-out Mickey at center. 29p. NF. B24. $300.00

DISNEY STUDIOS. *Mickey Never Fails.* 1939. DC Heath. sm 8vo. VG+. C8. $65.00

DISNEY STUDIOS. *Nutcracker Suite From Walt Disney's Fantasia.* 1940. Little Brn. 1st ed. 4to. ils. 6 piano arrangements. F/dj. T10. $250.00

DISNEY STUDIOS. *Peculiar Penguins.* 1934. McKay. from Silly Symphony. 8vo. 45p. cloth/pict label. F. B24. $485.00

DISNEY STUDIOS. *Pop-Up Mickey Mouse.* 1933. Bl Ribbon. 1st ed. thin 8vo. 3 popups. NF. T10. $650.00

DISNEY STUDIOS. *Pop-Up Minnie Mouse.* 1933. Bl Ribbon. 1st ed. 8vo. 3 popups. pict brd. VG. T10. $700.00

DISNEY STUDIOS. *Sketchbook.* 1993. Old Strubridge, CT. Applewood Books. 1st Am trade ed. 4to. F/dj. T10. $30.00

DISNEY STUDIOS. *Snow White & the Seven Dwarfs.* 1979. ils. VG/VG. M17. $40.00

DISNEY STUDIOS. *Thumper.* 1942. Grosset Dunlap. VG+/VG. P2. $35.00

DISNEY STUDIOS. *Uncle Scrooge McDuck: His Life & Times.* 1981. Millbrae, CA. 1/500. gilt leatherette w/onlay. AN. B24. $275.00

DISNEY STUDIOS. *Walt Disney's Circus.* 1944. Simon Schuster. 1st ed. 8vo. unp. VG+/VG+. D1. $225.00

DISNEY STUDIOS. *Walt Disney's Mickey Mouse Cookbook.* 1975. Golden/Western. sm 4to. VG. C8. $35.00

DISSTON, Harry. *Riding Rhymes for Young Riders.* 1951. NY. Bond Wheelwright. 1st ed. pres. VG. O3. $58.00

DIVER, Maud. *Siege Perilous & Other Stories.* 1924. Houghton Mifflin. 1st ed. F/NF. A17. $10.00

DIXIE, Marmaduke. *Beauties of Bridge.* 1938. London. 64p. VG. S1. $15.00

DIXON, Franklin W. *Castaways of the Stratosphere.* nd. Grosset Dunlap. hc. VG/VG. P3. $30.00

DIXON, Franklin W. *Hardy Boys: El Misterio del Junco Chino (#39).* 1963. Editorial Acme. 188p. VG+/dj. M20. $45.00

DIXON, Franklin W. *Hardy Boys: Figure in Hiding (#16).* 1937. Grosset Dunlap. 1st ed. 212p. VG/dj. M20. $110.00

DIXON, Franklin W. *Hardy Boys: Flickering Torch Mystery (#22).* 1943. Grosset Dunlap. 1st ed. 212p. cloth. VG/dj. M20. $130.00

DIXON, Franklin W. *Hardy Boys: Footprints Under the Window (#12).* 1941 (1933). Grosset Dunlap. 218p. VG/dj. M20. $117.00

DIXON, Franklin W. *Hardy Boys: Hooded Hawk Mystery (#34).* 1954. Grosset Dunlap. 1st ed. 212p. VG/dj. M20. $20.00

DIXON, Franklin W. *Hardy Boys: Mystery of Cabin Island (#8).* 1929. Grosset Dunlap. lists 20 titles. 214p. VG/dj. M20. $125.00

DIXON, Franklin W. *Hardy Boys: Mystery of Cabin Island (#8).* 1932 (1929). Grosset Dunlap. 1932B ed. 214p. VG+/dj. M20. $130.00

DIXON, Franklin W. *Hardy Boys: Mystery of the Chinese Junk (#39).* 1960. Grosset Dunlap. 1st ed. 184p. VG+/dj. M20. $40.00

DIXON, Franklin W. *Hardy Boys: Secret of the Caves (#7).* 1929. Grosset Dunlap. lists 20 titles. 210p. brn cloth. VG+/wht spine dj. M20. $150.00

DIXON, Franklin W. *Hardy Boys: Secret of the Lost Tunnel (#29).* 1950. Grosset Dunlap. 1st ed. 210p. VG/dj. M20. $20.00

DIXON, Franklin W. *Hardy Boys: Secret of Wildcat Swamp (#31).* 1952. Grosset Dunlap. 1st ed. 212p. VG/dj. M20. $20.00

DIXON, Franklin W. *Hardy Boys: Short-Wave Mystery (#24).* 1945. Grosset Dunlap. 3rd. 217p. VG/dj. M20. $200.00

DIXON, Franklin W. *Hardy Boys: The Hidden Harbor Mystery (#14).* 1935. Grosset Dunlap. G+. P12. $4.00

DIXON, Franklin W. *Hardy Boys: The Hidden Harbor Mystery (#14).* 1935. Grosset Dunlap. lists 18 titles. 219p. VG/dj. M20. $75.00

DIXON, Franklin W. *Hardy Boys: The House on the Cliff.* 1927. Grosset Dunlap. ils Walter Rogers. G+. P12. $5.00

DIXON, Joseph S. *Wildlife Portfolio of the Western National Parks.* 1942. GPO. 1st ed. 4to. 121p. xl. VG. T10. $50.00

DIXON, Norman F. *On the Psychology of Military Incompetence.* (1986). NY. Basic. 1st Am ed. 448p. tan cloth. VG/dj. G1. $50.00

DIXON, Roger. *Noah II.* 1975. Harwood Smart. F/F. P3. $15.00

DIXON, T. *Black Hood.* 1924. Grosset. ils. VG/dj. B5. $25.00

DIXON, T. *Clansman.* 1905. NY. 1st ed. MTI. VG/VG. B5. $45.00

DIXON, T. *Foolish Virgin.* 1915. NY. 1st ed. VG/VG. B5. $40.00

DIXON, Thomas Jr. *Life Worth Living: A Personal Experience.* 1905. Doubleday Page. 1st ed. sgn. 32pl. teg. gr brd. G. B11. $45.00

DIXON, William Hepworth. *Holy Land.* 1869. Lippincott/Chapman Hall. ils. 418p. xl. G. W1. $24.00

DIXON, William Scarth. *Men, Horses & Hunting.* nd. Payson. 1st Am ed. VG/fair. O3. $45.00

DOANE, Francis. *Radio: Devices & Communications.* 1927. Internat Lib of Tech. 200p. gr cloth/red buckram spine. VG. B22. $6.00

DOANE, Michael. *City of Light.* 1992. Knopf. 1st ed. F/F. H11. $20.00

DOANE, Pelagie. *Child's Book of Prayers.* 1947. Catholic Man. 4to. ils. VG/G+. B17. $12.50

DOANE, Pelagie. *Small Child's Bible.* 1946. Oxford. 4to. ils. VG-. B17. $8.50

DOBBINS, Paul H. *Death Trap.* 1951. Phoenix. 1st ed. VG/G. P3. $15.00

DOBBS, Fred C. *Golden Age of BC.* 1976. Gage. 1st ed. VG/VG. P3. $15.00

DOBBS, Rose. *More Once Upon a Time Stories.* 1961. Random. 1st ed. 8vo. ils Flavia Gag. VG+/G. M5. $30.00

DOBIE, J. Frank. *Ben Lilly Legend.* 1952. London. Hammond. 1st ed. 8vo. F/VG. T10. $65.00

DOBIE, J. Frank. *Carl Sandburg & St Peter at the Gate.* 1966. Encino. 1/750. F/NF case. B35. $70.00

DOBIE, J. Frank. *I'll Tell You a Tale.* 1960. Little Brn. 2nd. inscr/dtd 1961. ils Carlton Mead. F/F. T10. $250.00

DOBIE, J. Frank. *Longhorns.* 1949. Little Brn. inscr. 388p. VG. B11. $50.00

DOBIE, J. Frank. *Rattlesnakes.* nd. London. Hammond. 1st ed. 8vo. NF/NF. T10. $50.00

DOBIE, J. Frank. *Some Part of Myself.* 1967. Little Brn. 1st ed. 8vo. F/F. T10. $45.00

DOBIE, J. Frank. *Tales of Old-Time Texas.* 1955. Little Brn. 12th. 8vo. F/F. T10. $25.00

DOBIE, J. Frank. *Texan in England.* 1945. Boston. 1st ed. VG/VG. B5. $35.00

DOBREE, Bonamy. *Unacknowledged Legislator.* 1942. Allen Unwin. 1st ed. hc. VG. P3. $20.00

DOBSON, Austin. *Four French Women.* 1890. London. Chatto Windus. 1st ed/lg paper issue. sgn. 207p. VG. T10. $250.00

DOBSON, Austin. *Old Kennsington Place & Other Papers.* 1910. London. inscr/dtd 1910. NF. C6. $85.00

DOBSON, Mrs. *Life of Petrarch.* 1803. London. 5th ed. 2 vol. 8 copper pl. full leather. VG. B18. $125.00

DOBYNS, Stephen. *Boat Off the Coast.* 1987. Viking. 1st ed. VG/VG. P3. $18.00

DOBYNS, Stephen. *Saratoga Snapper.* 1986. Viking. 1st ed. F/F. P3. $16.00

DOCTOR X; see Nourse, Alan.

DOCTOROW, E.L. *Book of Daniel.* 1971. Random. 1st ed. rem mk. NF/F. M22. $40.00

DOCTOROW, E.L. *Ragtime.* 1976. London. 1st ed. inscr. F/NF. A11. $60.00

DODD, Edward. *Polynesian Seafarring. Volume III: Ring of Fire.* 1972. Dodd Mead. ils/photos/maps. 192p. VG/dj. T7. $40.00

DODGE, Bertha S. *It Started in Eden.* 1979. NY. ils. 288p. VG. B26. $22.00

DODGE, David. *Plunder of the Sun.* 1950. Michael Joseph. G/torn. P3. $10.00

DODGE, David. *20,000 Leagues Behind the 8 Ball.* 1951. Random. 1st ed. VG/G. P3. $25.00

DODGE, Ernest S. *Beyond the Capes.* 1971. Little Brn. 1st ed. sgn. 8vo. 429p. VG/VG. B11. $35.00

DODGE, Jim. *Fup.* 1st ed. author's 1st book. F/F. B30. $20.00

DODGE, Louis. *Sandman's Forest.* 1918. Scribner. 1st ed. ils Paul Branson. 283p. G+. P2. $30.00

DODGE, Louis. *Sandman's Mountain.* 1920. Scribner. 1st ed. ils Paul Bransom. 278p. VG. T5. $45.00

DODGE, Mary Mapes. *Mary Anne.* 1983. Lothrop Lee. 1st thus. 8vo. VG/VG. B17. $6.50

DODWELL, Christina. *Traveller on Horseback in Eastern Turkey & Iran.* 1989. NY. Walker. 1st am ed. maps. 191p. NF/dj. W1. $18.00

DOE, John. *Bridge Manual Illustrated.* 1902. London. 4th. 122p. VG. S1. $15.00

DOEBEL, Gunter. *Johannes Kepler.* 1983. Verlag Styria. German text. 256p. dj. K5. $30.00

DOENITZ, Admiral. *Memoirs: Ten Years Twenty Days.* 1959. Cleveland. 1st ed. VG/VG. B5. $35.00

DOERFLINGER, William. *Shanty Men & Shanty Boys.* 1951. NY. 1st ed. ils 374p. VG/VG. B5. $45.00

DOERNER, Klaus. *Madmen Bourgeois: A Social History of Insanity...* 1981. Oxford. 1st Eng trans. 361p. VG/dj. A13. $45.00

DOERR, Harriet. *Consider This, Senora.* 1993. Harcourt. 1st ed. sgn. F/clip. H11. $40.00

DOHAN, Mary Helen. *Mr Roosevelt's Steamboat.* 1981. Dodd Mead. VG/VG. A16. $17.50

DOHERTY, James L. *Race & Education in Richmond.* ca 1972. self pub. 1st ed. 162p. VG-. B10. $35.00

DOIG, Ivan. *Dancing at the Rascal Fair.* 1987. Atheneum. 1st ed. VG/VG. B5. $40.00

DOIG, Ivan. *English Creek.* 1984. Atheneum. 1st ed. sgn. AN/dj. A18. $80.00

DOIG, Ivan. *Heart Earth.* 1993. Atheneum. 1st ed. sgn. F/F. M19. $30.00

DOIG, Ivan. *History of the Pacific Northwest Forest & Range...* 1977. Forest Service. 1st ed. sgn. F/stapled wrp. B4. $250.00

DOIG, Ivan. *Ride With Me, Mariah Montana.* 1990. Atheneum. 1st ed. F/F. A18. $30.00

DOIG, Ivan. *Sea Runners.* 1982. Atheneum. ARC. RS. NF/NF. A18. $30.00

DOIG, Ivan. *This House of Sky: Landscapes of a Western Mind.* 1978. HBJ. 1st ed. NF/VG. M19. $125.00

DOIG, Ivan. *Winter Brothers: A Season at the Edge of America.* 1980. HBJ. 1st ed. VG/VG. B5. $45.00

DOLE & GORDAN. *Maine of the Sea & Pines.* 1928. Boston. 1st ed. 2 fld maps/50 pl. VG. B5. $47.50

DOLINER, Roy. *Sandra Rifkin's Jewels.* 1966. NAL. 1st ed. VG/VG. P3. $20.00

DOLLAR, Robert. *Memoirs of Robert Dollar.* 1925. np. A16. $62.00

DOLLARD, John. *Frustration & Aggression.* 1939. Oxford. 209p. red cloth. G1. $35.00

DOLLARD, John. *Victory Over Fear.* (1942). Reynal Hitchcock. inscr. 12mo. 213p. gray cloth. G1. $75.00

DOLLING, Richard. *Critical Care.* 1991. Morrow. 1st ed. author's 1st book. NF/F. M23. $25.00

DOLMETSCH, Carl R. *Smart Set.* 1966. Dial. 1st ed. sgn. 262p. VG/VG. B11. $75.00

DOMATILLA, John. *Last Crime.* 1981. Atheneum. 1st ed. VG/VG. P3. $20.00

DOMBROWSKI, John. *Area Handbook for Guatemala.* 1970. GPO. 1st ed. 361p. xl. F3. $10.00

DOMINIC, R.B. *Murder, Sunny Side Up.* 1968. Abelard Schuman. 1st ed. VG/VG. P3. $25.00

DOMINIC, R.B. *Unexpected Developments.* 1984. St Martin. 1st ed. VG/VG. P3. $20.00

DOMVILLE & DUNBAR. *Flora of Ulster County, NY.* 1970. New Paltz, NY. map. 136p. sc. B26. $17.50

DONAHEY, William. *Teenie Weenie Neighbors.* 1945. Whittlesey. 2nd. ils. F/VG+. M5. $125.00

DONALD, Henry. *Happy Story of Wallace the Engine.* 1955. Nelson. 1st ed. ils Gilbert Dunlop. 94p. VG/G. P2. $20.00

DONALDSON, Frances. *PG Wodehouse: The Authorized Biography.* 1982. Weidenfeld Nicolson. 1st ed. F/F. P3. $25.00

DONALDSON, Frances. *Yours, Plum. Letters of PG Wodehouse.* 1983. London. 231p. F/F. A4. $25.00

DONALDSON, Henry Herbert. *Growth of the Brain.* 1895. London. Walter Scott/Scribner. 374p. xl. VG. G1. $65.00

DONALDSON, Peter. *Life of Sir William Wallace, Governor General of Scotland...* 1841. Rochester. 132p. G. B18. $22.50

DONALDSON, Stephen R. *Daughter of Regals.* 1984. Del Rey. 1st ed. F/F. P3. $15.00

DONALDSON, Stephen R. *Forbidden Knowledge.* 1991. Bantam. 1st ed. VG/VG. P3. $20.00

DONALDSON, Stephen R. *Gliden-Fire.* 1981. Underwood Miller. 1st ed. xl. dj. P3. $10.00

DONALDSON, Stephen R. *Lord Foul's Bane.* nd. HRW. 4th. VG/VG. P3. $15.00

DONALDSON, Stephen R. *Mirror of Her Dreams.* 1986. Ballantine. 1st ed. F/NF. H11. $35.00

DONALDSON, Stephen R. *One Tree.* 1982. Del Rey. 1st ed. VG/VG. P3. $20.00

DONALDSON, Stephen R. *White Gold Wielder.* 1983. Del Rey. 1st ed. F/F. P3. $20.00

DONAVAN, John. *Case of the Violet Smoke.* 1940. Mystery House. VG. P3. $20.00

DONER, Mary Frances. *Salvager.* 1958. Minneapolis. Ross Haines. 1st ed. G/poor. A16. $30.00

DONKERSLOOT, Marike. *World on Paper: Cartography in Amsterdam in 17th Century.* 1967. Amsterdam Historisch Mus. ils. F/wrp. O7. $45.00

DONLEAVY, J.P. *Beastly Beatitudes of Balthazar B.* 1968. np. 1st ed. F/VG. M19. $22.50

DONLEAVY, J.P. *Fairy Tales of New York.* 1961. Random. 1st ed. F/NF. M19. $22.50

DONLEAVY, J.P. *Leila.* Franklin Lib. 1st ed. sgn. VG. M17. $30.00

DONLEY, Michael. *Atlas of California.* 1979. Pacific Book Center. folio. maps. 175p. F/dj. O7. $75.00

DONNE, John. *Letters to Several Persons of Honour.* 1868. NY. 12mo. ils. 464p. brn cloth. G. T3. $17.00

DONNEL, C.P. *Murder-Go-Round.* 1945. McKay. VG. P3. $15.00

DONNELLY, Elfie. *Offbeat Friends.* 1982. Crown. 1st Am ed. 8vo. 119p. NF/clip. C14. $12.00

DONNELLY, Ignatius. *Great Cryptogram.* 1988. Chicago. 2nd. ils. 998p. G. B5. $65.00

DONNELLY, Joe. *Stone.* 1990. Barrie Jenkins. 1st ed. F/F. P3. $30.00

DONNISON, T.E. *Old Fairy Tales Told Anew.* ca 1901. London. Tuck. 4to. F/self wrp. B24. $150.00

DONOVAN, Robert J. *Assassins.* 1955. Harper. 1st ed. NF/NF. B35. $25.00

DONOVAN, Robert J. *Eisenhower: The Inside Story.* 1956. Harper. 1st ed. 423p. bl cloth. VG/fair. B22. $5.50

DONY, John G. *Flora of Bedfordshire.* 1953. Lutton. 1st ed. 24 photos/ils. map. 532p. VG/dj. B26. $45.00

DOOLEY, Sallie May. *Dem Good Ole Times.* 1916. Doubleday Page. ils Suzanne Gutherz. 150p. G+. B10. $45.00

DOOLING, Richard. *Critical Care.* 1987. Holt. 1st ed. F/F. M23. $25.00

DOOLITTLE, Hilda. *Hymen, by HD.* 1921. NY. Holt. 1st ed. author's 2nd book. NF/gr prt wrp. B24. $350.00

DOOLITTLE, Hilda. *Palimpsest.* 1926. Houghton Mifflin. 1st Am ed. 1/700 from French sheets. VG/NF. B4. $350.00

DOOLITTLE, Jerome. *Body Scissors.* 1990. Pocket. 1st ed. NF/NF. P3. $18.00

DOOLITTLE, Jerome. *Half Nelson.* 1994. Pocket. 1st ed. VG/VG. P3. $20.00

DOOLITTLE, Jerome. *Strangle Hold.* 1991. Pocket. hc. F/F. P3. $20.00

DORE, Gustave. *La Fontaine's Fables.* ca 1880. Cassell. NF. M19. $200.00

DORF, Fran. *Flight.* 1992. Dutton. 1st ed. F/NF. H11. $20.00

DORF, P. *Liberty Hyde Bailey.* 1956. Ithaca. 1st ed. VG/VG. B5. $25.00

DORIN, Patrick C. *Lake Superior Iron Ore Railroads.* 1969. Seattle. Superior. 1st ed. G/G. A16. $27.50

DORLING, Taprell. *Sea Escapes & Adventures.* 1927. Stokes. 15 pl/5 maps. 286p. VG. T7. $24.00

DORMAN, John Frederick. *Farish Family of Virginia & Its Forebears.* 1967. private prt. ils. 168p. VG. B10. $45.00

DORRIS, Michael. *Yellow Raft in Blue Water.* 1987. Holt. 1st ed. author's 1st book. F/F. A15/M19/M23. $25.00

DORRIS & ERDRICH. *Crown of Columbus.* 1991. Harper Collins. 1st ed. sgns. F/F. M19. $25.00

DORSON, Richard M. *America Begins: Early American Writing.* 1950. Pantheon. 26 pl. 438p. A17. $15.00

DORST, Jean. *Migrations of Birds.* 1963. Houghton Mifflin. 1st Am ed. 476p. F. B22. $16.00

DOS PASSOS, John. *USA. Trilogy.* 1930-1936. NY/London. Harper. 3 vol. 1st ed. 8vo. VG/dj. S9. $950.00

DOS PASSOS & SHAY. *Down Cape Cod.* 1947. Nat Travel Club. ils. VG. P12. $7.00

DOSS, James D. *Shaman Laughs.* 1995. St Martin. 1st ed. F/F. M23. $30.00

DOSTOEVSKY, Fyodor. *Brothers Karamazov.* 1990. North Point. 2nd. F/F. P3. $30.00

DOSTOEVSKY, Fyodor. *Crime & Punishment.* 1992. Knopf. 1st ed. F/F. P3. $25.00

DOTEN, Dana. *Art of Bundling.* 1938. Countryman/Farrar Rinehart. 1st ed. 190p. VG/dj. M20. $30.00

DOTY, Robert M. *American Folk Art in Ohio Collections.* 1976. Dodd Mead. VG/dj. D2. $20.00

DOUCETTE, E. *Fisherman's Guide to Maine.* 1951. Random. 1st ed. VG. H7. $20.00

DOUDS, William S. *Thy Kingdom Come — Why Not Now?* 1940. NY. Beaver. sgn. 12mo. 287p. fair/G. B11. $12.50

DOUGHTY, Paul. *Huaylas: An Andrean District in Search of Progress.* 1968. Ithaca. Cornell. 1st ed. 284p. dj. F3. $20.00

DOUGLAS, Arthur. *Last Rights.* 1986. St Martin. 1st ed. F/F. P3. $15.00

DOUGLAS, Carole Nelson. *Pussyfoot.* 1993. Tor. 1st ed. NF/NF. P3. $15.00

DOUGLAS, David C. *Norman Achievement: 1050-1100.* 1969. Berkeley. 1st ed. 271p. NF/dj. M20. $18.00

DOUGLAS, Ellen. *Can't Quit You, Baby.* 1988. Atheneum. 2nd. sgn. F/F. B11. $15.00

DOUGLAS, Jack. *Shams.* 1899. Thompson Thomas. G. P12. $8.00

DOUGLAS, James Postell. *Douglas's Texas Battery, CSA.* 1966. Smith County Hist Soc. 1st ed. 238p. F/NF. M8. $45.00

DOUGLAS, M. *Frozen North.* nd. Boston. De Wolfe Fiske. ils/map. 176p. VG. D1. $35.00

DOUGLAS, Marjorie Stoneman. *Everglades.* 1947. NY. Rivers of Am series. VG/G+. B5. $45.00

DOUGLAS, Norman. *Angel of Manfredonia.* 1929. San Francisco. Windsor. 1/225. sgn. marbled brd/cloth spine. NF. T10. $150.00

DOUGLAS, Norman. *Birds & Beasts of the Greek Anthology.* 1927. Florence. private prt. 1/500. sgn. 219p. VG/dj. T10. $250.00

DOUGLAS, William O. *Democracy's Manifesto.* 1962. Garden City. 1st ed. F/VG. N3. $10.00

DOUGLAS, William O. *My Wilderness, the Pacific West.* 1960. Doubleday. inscr. G/dj. M11. $125.00

DOUGLAS, William O. *Strange Lands & Friendly People.* 1951. Harper. 8vo. half cloth. VG. P4. $15.00

DOUGLASS, Ben. *History of Wayne County, Ohio.* 1878. Indianapolis. 1st ed. 868p. G. B18. $145.00

DOVE, Rita. *Darker Face of the Earth: A Verse Play in Fourteen Scenes.* 1994. Brownsville, OR. Story Line. 1/224. sgn. AN. B4. $85.00

DOVE, Rita. *Fifth Sunday.* 1985. Lexington. 1st ed. F/wrp. B4. $150.00

DOVE, Rita. *Mother Love.* 1995. Norton. 1st ed. sgn. F/F. B35. $65.00

DOVE, Rita. *Selected Poems.* 1993. Pantheon. 1st ed. F/F. B4. $65.00

DOW, Greorge Francis. *Slave Ships & Slaving.* 1927. Marine Research Soc. 1st ed. 349p. VG+/dj. M20. $255.00

DOW. *Anthology & Bibliography of Niagara Falls. Vol II.* 1921. np. ils. VG. A4. $30.00

DOWD, J.H. *Childhood.* 1935. Scribner. 1st ed. ils. VG/partial. M5. $65.00

DOWDEN, Anne Ophelia T. *Look at the Flower.* 1963. NY. ils. F/dj. B26. $17.50

DOWDEN & THOMSON. *Roses.* 1965. NY. ils Dowden. 42p. VG. B26. $11.00

DOWER, William. *Early Annals of Kokstad & Griqualand East.* 1978. Pietermaritzburg. Natal. 8vo. 192p. xl. VG. W1. $20.00

DOWLING, Edith Bannister. *Patchwork of Poems About SC.* 1970. Beaufort. Peacock. sgn. 47p. VG. B10. $8.00

DOWNES, Olin. *Olin Downes on Music. A Selection of His Writings...* 1957. NY. 1st prt. 473p. blk/bl bdg. F/VG clip. H3. $50.00

DOWNEY, Bill. *Tom Bass: Black Horseman.* 1975. St Louis. Saddle & Bridle Inc. 8vo. inscr. red cloth. F/dj. T10. $100.00

DOWNEY, Fairfax. *Cats of Destiny.* 1950. Scribner. 1st ed. 170p. VG/G. P2. $28.00

DOWNEY, Fairfax. *Dog of War.* 1943. Dodd Mead. 1st ed. VG/G. O3. $38.00

DOWNEY, Fairfax. *Guns at Gettysburg.* 1958. NY. 1st ed. VG/VG. B5. $32.50

DOWNEY, Fairfax. *Shining Filly.* 1954. Scribner. 1st/A ed. VG/G. O3. $25.00

DOWNEY, Fairfax. *Storming of the Gateway, Chattanooga, 1863.* 1960. McKay. 1st ed. 303p. cloth. NF/NF. M8. $50.00

DOWNING, A.J. *Fruits & Fruit Trees of America.* 1849. NY. 9th. VG. V4. $175.00

DOWNS & PFINGSTEN. *Salamanders of Ohio.* 1989. Columbus. 8vo. ils/photos/pl. pict wrp. B1. $28.00

DOYLE, Arthur Conan. *Adventures of Sherlock Holmes.* 1892. NY. Harper. 1st Am ed/later state. 8vo. gilt pict cloth. VG. T10. $250.00

DOYLE, Arthur Conan. *Book of Sherlock Holmes.* (1950). World/Rainbow Classics. 8vo. ils. 320p. VG+/G. C14. $6.00

DOYLE, Arthur Conan. *Case-Book of Sherlock Holmes.* 1927. London. John Murray. 1st ed in reddish-pink cloth. VG. C2. $225.00

DOYLE, Arthur Conan. *Croxley Master & Other Tales of the Ring & the Camp.* 1919. NY. 1st ed thus/1st issue. VG/VG. C6. $85.00

DOYLE, Arthur Conan. *Exploits of Brigadier Gerard.* 1896. Appleton. 1st ed. F. M19. $50.00

DOYLE, Arthur Conan. *Hound of the Baskervilles.* 1985. San Francisco. 1/400. photos/sgn Michael Kenna. 204p. AN/case. w/poster. B24. $400.00

DOYLE, Arthur Conan. *Man From Archangel & Other Tales of Adventure.* 1919. NY. 12mo. orange cloth. G. A17. $20.00

DOYLE, Arthur Conan. *Memories & Adventures.* 1924. Boston. 1st Am ed. VG. B5. $50.00

DOYLE, Arthur Conan. *Return of Sherlock Holmes.* 1987. Mysterious. 1st ed thus. ils FD Steele. F. A17. $20.00

DOYLE, Arthur Conan. *Rodney Stone.* 1896. NY. 1st Am ed. F/rare dj/case. C2. $500.00

DOYLE, Arthur Conan. *Sir Nigel.* 1906. McClure Phillips. 1st ed. VG. P3. $85.00

DOYLE, Arthur Conan. *Tragedy of the Korosko.* 1898. London. VG. C6. $65.00

DOYLE, Arthur Conan. *Vital Message.* 1919. Doran. 1st ed. VG. P3. $60.00

DOYLE, Arthur Conan. *Vital Message.* 1919. Hodder Stoughton. G. P3. $45.00

DOYLE, Arthur Conan. *White Company.* 1939. John Murray. 65th. VG. P3. $15.00

DOYLE, James E. *Chronicle of England: BC 55...AD 1485.* 1864. London. Longman Gr. 1st ed. ils Edmund Evans. gilt cloth. VG. T10. $450.00

DOYLE, Richard. *Jack the Giant Killer.* 1888. Eyre Spottiswoode. 4to. 48p. w/rare pub leaf. F. B24. $575.00

DOYLE, Roddy. *Paddy Clarke Ha Ha Ha.* 1994. Viking. 1st Am ed. F/F. T2. $45.00

DOYLE & MACDONALD. *Knight's Wyrd.* 1992. HBJ. 1st ed. F/F. P3. $17.00

DOYLE & MCDIARMID. *Baker Street Dozen.* 1987. Congdon Weed. F/F. P3. $20.00

DOZOIS, Gardner. *Goedesic Dreams: Best Short Fiction of Gardner Dozois.* 1991. St Martin. 1st ed. F/F. G10. $25.00

DR. SEUSS; see Geisel, Theodor.

DRABBLE. *Oxford Companion to English Literature, Fifth Edition.* 1985. np. 1167p. NF/NF. A4. $45.00

DRACO, F. *Devil's Church.* 1961. Rinehart. 1st ed. VG/VG. P3. $30.00

DRAGO, Harry Sinclair. *Canal Days in America.* 1972. Bramhall. 311p. VG/dj. M20. $32.00

DRAGO, Harry Sinclair. *Outlaws on Horseback.* 1964. Dodd Mead. 1st trade ed. 8vo. ils. F/NF. T10. $50.00

DRAKE, Lauren. *Getting the Most Out of a Powerboat.* 1953. Norton. 1st ed. VG/dj. A16. $17.50

DRAKE, W. Raymond. *Gods & Spacemen Throughout History.* 1975. Renery. VG. P3. $15.00

DRAYTON & SIZER. *Heads & Faces: How to Study Them...* 1888. NY. Fowler. 199p. Victorial bdg. NF. T10. $150.00

DREADSTONE, Carl; see Campbell, Ramsey.

DREISER, Theodore. *American Tragedy.* 1925. Boni Liveright. 2 vol. F. B2. $75.00

DREISER, Theodore. *American Tragedy.* 1925. Boni Liveright. 2 vol. 1st ed. 1/55 (795 total). sgn pres. w/pub card. F/case. B24. $950.00

DREISER, Theodore. *Bulwark.* 1946. Doubleday. 1st ed. F/F. B35. $30.00

DREISER, Theodore. *Sister Carrie.* 1917. Boni Liveright. 3rd (1st Boni). F/VG+. B4. $650.00

DREISER, Theodore. *Sister Carrie.* 1939. LEC. 1/1500. ils/sgn Reginald Marsh. 387p. F/NF case. C2. $250.00

DREISER, Theodore. *Traveler at Forty.* 1913. NY. 1st ed. 526p. G. A17. $25.00

DREPPARD. *American Pioneer Arts & Artists.* 1942. np. fwd Rockwell Kent. cloth. NF/VG. D2. $45.00

DRESSES, Elia. *Masque of Days.* 1901. London. Cassell. 1st ed. ils Walter Crane. VG. D1. $325.00

DREVER, James. *Instinct in Man: A Contribution to Psychology of Education.* 1917. Cambridge. 281p. ruled russet cloth. G1. $40.00

DREWRY, Carleton. *To Love That Well.* 1975. Barnes. VG/G. B10. $15.00

DREYER & SAXON. *Friends of Joe Gilmore.* 1948. Hastings. ils. VG+/dj. P4. $22.50

DRIGGS & JACKSON. *Westward America.* 1942. NY. Am Pioneer Trails Assoc. inscr/sgns. 40 mc pl. G. B11. $75.00

DRINKER, Cecil K. *Not So Long Ago: A Chronicle of Medicine & Doctors...* 1937. NY. 183p. bl cloth. dj. B14. $95.00

DRINKWATER, John. *American Vignettes 1860-1865.* 1931. Houghton Mifflin. 1/385. sgn. VG. T10. $125.00

DRUHOT, George Stanley. *American Topographer: Working Years of GS Druhot...* 1985. Rancho Cordova. Landmark. ils. map ep. F/rpr dj. O7. $45.00

DRUMMOND, D.H. *Montreal in Halftone.* ca 1910. Montreal. Clarke. obl 4to. photos. cloth. VG. T10. $50.00

DRUMMOND, Henry. *Tropical Africa.* 1891. Scribner. 4th ed. 228p. purple cloth. G. B22. $8.00

DRUMMOND, Ivor. *Frog in the Moonflower.* 1972. Macmillan. 1st ed. F/F. P3. $23.00

DRUMMOND, Walter; see Silverberg, Robert.

DRURY, Allen. *Preserve & Protect.* 1968. Doubleday. VG/VG. P3. $13.00

DRURY. *Diaries & Letters of Henry H Spalding & Asa Bowen Smith...* 1958. Arthur H Clark. ils. 379p. VG. A4. $125.00

DRUZHKOV, Yuri. *Adventures of Pencil & Screwbolt.* 1973. Moscow. Progress Pub. 1st ed. 128p. VG. A17. $10.00

DRYBROUGH, T.B. *Polo.* 1898. London. Vinton. 1st ed. VG. O3. $95.00

DRYDEN, John. *Of Dramatic Poetry: An Essay, 1668.* 1928. London. 1/580. 4to. marbled brd/linen spine. VG+. A11. $225.00

DRYDEN, John. *Poetical Works of...* 1855. Edinburgh. James Nichol. 1st standard ed. 2 vol. bl morocco. F. C2. $150.00

DRYER, J.L.E. *Tycho Brahe: Picture of Scientific Life.* 1890. Edinburgh. Blk. 1st ed. rebound. VG. K5. $250.00

DU BOIS, Theodora. *Fowl Play.* 1951. Detective BC. VG. P3. $8.00

DU BOIS, William Pene. *Bear Circus.* nd. Viking/Weekly Reader. possible 1st ed. ils. 48p. G+. C14. $11.00

DU BOIS, William Pene. *Bear Circus.* 1971. Viking. 1st ed. ils. F/VG. P2. $45.00

DU BOIS, William Pene. *Gentleman Bear.* 1985. FSG. 1st ed. 78p. VG+/dj. M20. $15.00

DU BOIS, William Pene. *Otto at Sea.* 1936. Viking. 1st ed. ils. unp. G. D1. $125.00

DU BOIS, William Pene. *Otto in Africa.* c 1961. NY. 1st ed. ils. 39p. VG+. C14. $30.00

DU BOIS, William Pene. *21 Balloons.* 1947. Viking BC. VG/VG. B17. $4.00

DU BOSE, John Witherspoon. *General Joseph Wheeler & the Army of Tennessee.* 1912. NY. Neale. 1st ed. 476p. cloth. NF. M8. $450.00

DU HAYS, Charles. *Percheron Horse.* 1886. Baltimore. ltd ed. 4to. trans WT Walters. VG/tissue dj. O3. $695.00

DU MAURIER, Daphne. *Breaking Point.* 1959. Doubleday. 1st ed. VG/VG. P3. $30.00

DU MAURIER, Daphne. *Echoes From the Macabre.* 1977. Doubleday. 1st ed. VG/VG. P3. $18.00

DU MAURIER, Daphne. *My Cousin Rachel.* 1952. Canada. Longman Gr. 1st ed. VG/G. P3. $18.00

DU MAURIER, Daphne. *My Cousin Rachel.* 1952. Doubleday. 1st Am ed. 348p. VG/dj. M20. $22.00

DU MAURIER, Daphne. *Parasites.* 1949. Canada. Ryerson. 1st ed. VG/VG. P3. $20.00

DU MAURIER, Daphne. *Rendezvous & Other Stories.* 1972. Gollancz. 1st ed. VG/VG. P3. $25.00

DU MAURIER, Daphne. *Scapegoat.* 1957. Doubleday. 1st ed. VG/VG. P3. $30.00

DU MAURIER, George. *Martian.* 1897. Harper. hc. VG. P3. $75.00

DU PONT, H.A. *Early Generations of the Du Pont & Allied Families.* 1923. np. 2 vol. VG. M17. $40.00

DU PONT, Victor M. *Journey to France & Spain.* 1961. Ithaca. VG. O7. $30.00

DU PUY, William Atherton. *Nation's Forests.* 1938. Macmillan. 1st ed. ils. VG. P12. $20.00

DU VAL, H.C. *Bridge Rules in Rhyme.* 1902. NY. 7p. G. S1. $8.00

DUANE, Diane. *Spider-Man: The Venom Factor.* 1994. Putnam. 1st ed. hc. F/F. P3. $20.00

DUBOIS, Gaylord. *Long Rider & Treasure Vanished Men.* nd. Whitman. VG. P3. $10.00

DUBOIS, Jules. *Operation America.* 1963. Walker. sgn. 8vo. 361p. VG/VG. B11. $25.00

DUBOIS, W.E.B. *Black Folk Then & Now.* 1940. NY. xl. G. B5. $35.00

DUBUS, Andre. *Bluesman.* 1993. Boston. Faber. 1st ed. F/F. T2. $25.00

DUBUS, Andre. *Finding a Girl in America: Ten Stories & a Novella.* 1980. Boston. Godine. 1st ed. inscr/dtd 1986. F/F. C2. $60.00

DUBUS, Andre. *Land Where My Fathers Died.* 1984. 1/200. sgn. F. C4. $100.00

DUBUS, Andre. *Lieutenant.* 1967. Dial. 1st ed. author's 1st book. inscr. NF/NF. C2. $175.00

DUBUS, Andre. *Selected Stories.* 1988. Boston. Godine. 1st ed. sgn. F/F. C2. $50.00

DUBUS, Andre. *Separate Flights: A Novella & Seven Short Stories.* 1975. Godine. 1st ed. inscr/dtd 1986. F/F. C2. $75.00

DUCKWORTH, C.L.D. *Clyde River & Other Steamers.* 1937. Glasgow. Brn, Son & Ferguson. G. A16. $65.00

DUDA & LUBOS. *Minerals of the World.* 1989. Arch Cape. 4to. 520p. F/F. B1. $65.00

DUDLEY, Carrie. *My Peek-a-Boo Show Book.* 1928. Volland. 1st ed. ils C Dudley. VG. D1. $325.00

DUDLEY & DUDLEY. *Glory & the Grandeur: Teacher's Notes on Richmond...* 1976. private prt. maps. 84p. VG/wrp. B10. $12.00

DUDNIK, Robert M. *Anatomy of a Personal Injury Law Suit...* 1969. Boston. Am Trial Lawyers Assn. bl cloth. M11. $20.00

DUERDEN. *Invisible Present: African Art & Literature.* 1975. Harper Row. F/F. D2. $30.00

DUERRENMATT, Friedrich. *Pledge.* 1959. Knopf. 1st ed. F/F. B35. $45.00

DUFF, Beldon. *Ask No Questions!* nd. Grosset Dunlap. VG/VG. P3. $25.00

DUFFIELD, Anne. *Stamboul Love.* 1934. Knopf. 1st ed. VG. P3. $15.00

DUFFIELD, J.W. *Rapid Boys Under the Sea.* 1923. NY. 1st ed. VG/VG. B5. $20.00

DUFFIELD, Samuel W. *English Hymns: Their Authors & History.* 1888. NY. 3rd. 675p. gilt cloth. A17. $20.00

DUFFY, James. *Murder for Lunch.* 1986. Simon Schuster. 1st ed. F/F. P3. $15.00

DUFFY, James. *Murder Saves Face.* 1991. Simon Schuster. 1st ed. inscr/sgn pen & real names. F/F. M22. $25.00

DUFFY, James. *Murders & Acquisitions.* 1988. Simon Schuster. 1st ed. F/F. P3. $17.00

DUGDALE, William. *Short View of the Late Troubles in England...* 1681. Oxford. Moses Pitt. sm folio. 971p. full calf. T10. $750.00

DUGGAR, Benjamin M. *Plant Physiology.* 1922 (1911). NY. Rural TB series. ils. 516p. B26. $15.00

DUGMORE, A. Radclyffe. *Romance of the New-foundland Caribou.* 1913. Lippincott. 186p. ils/maps. VG. A10. $50.00

DUGMORE, A. Radclyffe. *Wild Life & the Camera.* 1912. Heinemann. 1st ed. 8vo. 332p. bl cloth. VG. B11. $75.00

DUGUID, Julian. *Green Hell: Adventures in Mysterious Jungles of E Bolivia.* 1931. NY. Century. 1st ed. photos. 339p. F3. $20.00

DUKE, Donald. *Water Trails West.* 1978. Doubleday. 1st ed. VG/VG. P3. $20.00

DUKE, R.T.W. *In My Library & Other Poems.* 1927. Michie. 64p. G. B10. $15.00

DUKE OF SAINT-SIMON. *Memoirs of Louis XIV, Vol 1.* nd. Collier. VG. P3. $15.00

DULAC, Edmond. *Sinbad the Sailor & Other Stories.* 1914. 1st ed. 23 pl. VG+. S13. $275.00

DULAC, Edmund. *Edmund Dulac's Fairy Book.* nd (1916). Hodder Stoughton. 1st ed. 170p. VG. P2. $250.00

DULL, Paul S. *Battle History of Imperial Japanese Navy.* 1978. Naval Inst. 433p. VG. A17. $10.00

DULLES, Allen. *Great Spy Stories.* 1948. Castle. 2nd. VG/VG. P3. $15.00

DULLES, Foster. *American Red Cross, a History.* 1950. NY. 1st ed. 544p. VG. A13. $35.00

DULLES, Foster. *Lowered Boats.* 1933. NY. 1st ed. ils. 292p. VG. B5. $40.00

DUMAS, Alexandre. *Black Tulip.* nd. Collins. hc. VG/G. P3. $15.00

DUMAS, Alexandre. *Camille.* 1955. NY. 1/1500. ils/sgn Bernard Lamotte. F/case. T10. $75.00

DUMAS, Alexandre. *Chevalier d'Harmental.* 1899. Little Brn. VG. P3. $20.00

DUMAS, Alexandre. *Chicot the Jester.* 1956. Collins Classics. hc. VG/G. P3. $15.00

DUMAS, Alexandre. *Count of Monte-Cristo.* 1901. NY. 2 vol. 12mo. teg. half red leather. VG. H3. $50.00

DUMAS, Alexandre. *Edmund Dantes.* 1911. Leslie-Judge. VG. P3. $30.00

DUMAS, Alexandre. *Queen's Necklace.* nd. Collins. hc. leather. F. P3. $20.00

DUMAS, Claudine; see Malzberg, Barry.

DUMAYNE, Frederick. *Reminiscences of Frederick Dumayne.* 1945. Aberdeen. private prt. 52p. VG. M8. $85.00

DUMBAULD, Edward. *Life & Legal Writings of Hugo Grotius.* 1968. Norman, OK. G/dj. M11. $35.00

DUNBAR, Alexander. *Treatise on the Diseases Incident to the Horse...* 1871. Wilmington. James Webb. 1st ed. G. O3. $75.00

DUNBAR, Paul Laurence. *Candle-Lightin' Time.* 1901. Dodd Mead. 1st ed. photos. gilt cloth. F/dj. B24. $750.00

DUNBAR, Paul Laurence. *Joggin' Erlong.* 1906. Dodd Mead. photos. orig red calico/photo label. F. C6. $300.00

DUNBAR, Paul Laurence. *Poems of Cabin & Field.* 1900. Dodd Mead. ils Alice Morse. NF. M19. $150.00

DUNBAR, Paul Laurence. *Uncalled.* 1898. Dodd Mead. 1st ed. author's 1st novel. 255p. B bdg. fair. B10. $75.00

DUNBAR, Sophie. *Behind Eclaire's Doors.* 1993. NY. 1st ed. author's 1st book. F/F. H11. $25.00

DUNBAR, Tony. *Crooked Man.* 1994. Putnam. 1st ed. F/F. P3. $22.00

DUNBAR & RODGERS. *Principles of Stratigraphy.* 1957. NY. John Wiley. 356p. VG. D8. $20.00

DUNCAN, Dave. *Cursed.* 1995. Ballantine. 1st ed. RS. F/NF. G10. $12.00

DUNCAN, Dave. *Upland Outlaws.* 1993. Ballantine. 1st ed. F/F. G10. $12.00

DUNCAN, David. *Another Tree in Eden.* 1956. Heinemann. 1st ed. NF/NF. P3. $40.00

DUNCAN, Francis. *Dangerous Mr X.* 1939. Herbert Jenkins. 1st ed. VG. P3. $35.00

DUNCAN, Kunigunde. *Tether: Una Gray's Story.* 1953. Boston. Page. 1st imp. 394p. F/dj. A17. $10.00

DUNCAN, Louis. *Medical Men in the American Revolution.* 1970. NY. 414p. VG. A13. $100.00

DUNCAN, Robert L. *China Dawn.* 1988. Delacorte. 1st ed. VG/VG. P3. $20.00

DUNCAN, Robert L. *Temple Dogs.* 1977. Morrow. 1st ed. VG/VG. P3. $18.00

DUNCAN, Shirley. *Two Wheels to Adventure.* 1957. London. 1st ed. sgn. 8vo. 222p. gr cloth. VG. B11. $25.00

DUNCAN, T. Bentley. *Atlantic Islands.* 1972. Chicago. VG. O7. $25.00

DUNKIN, Edwin. *Midnight Sky.* ca 1869. Religious Tract Soc. ils/charts. 326p. K5. $150.00

DUNLAP, Knight. *Religion: Its Function in Human Life...* 1946. McGraw Hill. 362p. emb red cloth. NF. G1. $65.00

DUNLAP, Orrin E. *Advertising by Radio.* 1929. NBC. ARC/1st ed. 186p. bl cloth. F. B14. $55.00

DUNLAP, Susan. *Death & Taxes.* 1992. Delacorte. 2nd. F/F. P3. $18.00

DUNLAP, Susan. *Karma.* nd. Severn. 1st Eng hc ed. F/F. M19. $45.00

DUNN, Dorothy. *Murder's Web.* 1950. Harper. sgn. VG/VG. P3. $30.00

DUNN, J. Allan. *Boru: The Story of an Irish Wolfhound.* nd. Grosset Dunlap. VG/G. P3. $12.00

DUNN, Katherine. *Attic.* 1970. Harper. 1st ed. author's 1st book. F/F. B4. $275.00

DUNN, L.C. *Genetics in the 20th Century: Essays...* 1951. NY. 1st ed. 634p. NF. B14. $45.00

DUNNE, John Gregory. *Dutch Shea, Jr.* 1982. NY. Linden. 1st ed. rem mk. F/F. H11. $20.00

DUNNE, John Gregory. *Harp.* 1989. Simon Schuster. F/F. A20. $12.00

DUNNE, John Gregory. *Playland.* Franklin Lib. 1st ed thus. sgn. VG. M17. $30.00

DUNNE, Peter Masten. *Pioneer Black Robes on the West Coast.* 1940. Berkeley. 1st ed. 8vo. 286p. gilt red cloth. F. T10. $100.00

DUNNETT, Dorothy. *Dolly & the Nanny Bird.* 1982. Knopf. 1st ed. VG/VG. P3. $18.00

DUNNETT, Dorothy. *King Hereafter.* 1982. Michael Joseph. 1st ed. NF/NF. P3. $27.00

DUNNETT, Dorothy. *Photogenic Soprano.* 1968. Houghton Mifflin. 1st ed. VG/VG. P3. $30.00

DUNNING, H.W. *Today on the Nile.* 1905. Pott. 1st ed. 17 pl/1 fld map. 270p. VG. W1. $12.00

DUNNING, John. *Booked to Die.* 1992. Scribner. 1st ed. sgn. xl. VG/F. A20. $85.00

DUNNING, John. *Bookman's Wake.* 1995. NY. 1st ed. sgn. F/F. B5. $75.00

DUNNING, John. *Tune in Yesterday.* 1976. Hall. 1st ed. VG/VG. B5. $100.00

DUNSANY, Lord. *Alexander & Three Small Plays.* 1926. Putnam. 1st ed. VG. P3. $40.00

DUNSANY, Lord. *Ghosts of the Heaviside.* 1980. Owlswick. F/F. P3. $20.00

DUNSANY, Lord. *Mr Jorkens Remembers Africa.* 1934. Heinemann. 1st ed. VG. P3. $125.00

DUNSANY, Lord. *Sword of Welleran.* nd. Boston. Luce. ils. VG. B5. $55.00

DUPLAIX, Georges. *Gaston & Josephine.* 1936. Harper. 1st ed. ils. 48p. G. D1. $85.00

DUPLAIX, Georges. *Gaston & Josephine.* 1948. Simon Schuster. 1st ed thus. ils Rojankovsky. VG. D1. $37.50

DUPLAIX, Georges. *Merry Shipwreck.* 1942. Harper. 1st ed. ils Tibor Gergeley. VG+. P2. $42.00

DUPREY, Jacques. *Voyage aux Origines Francaises de L'Uruguay.* 1952. Montevideo. VG/wrp. O7. $75.00

DUPREY, Kenneth. *Old Houses on Nantucket.* 1965. NY. Architectural Pub. 2nd. VG/VG. B5. $55.00

DURAND, Loup. *Daddy.* 1988. Villard. 1st ed. F/F. H11. $30.00

DURAND, Loup. *Jaguar.* 1990. Villard. 1st ed. F/F. H11. $25.00

DURANT & DURANT. *Pictorial History of American Ships.* 1953. NY. Barnes. G/dj. A16. $38.00

DURBIN. *Observations in Europe, Principally in France...* 1844. NY. vol 2 only. 12mo. 312p. xl. G. T3. $15.00

DURDEN, Charles. *Fifth Law of Hawkins.* 1990. St Martin. 1st ed. NF/NF. P3. $20.00

DURHAM, Victor G. *Submarine Boys, for the Flag.* 1910. Altemus. ils. G+. P12. $5.00

DURHAM, Victor G. *Submarine Boys on Duty.* 1909. Saafield. 1st ed. ils. G+/G+. P12. $10.00

DURIE, Alistair. *Weird Tales.* 1979. Jupiter. 1st ed. NF/worn. R10. $20.00

DURRELL, Gerald. *Talking Parcel.* 1974. London. Collins. 1st ed. 8vo. 190p. F/F. T5. $30.00

DURRELL, Lawrence. *Clea.* 1960. London. Faber. 1st ed. red cloth. F/F. B24. $100.00

DURRELL, Lawrence. *Dark Labyrinth.* 1962. Dutton. 1st ed. F/F. M19. $45.00

DURRELL, Lawrence. *Nunquam.* 1970. London. 1st ed. sgn. F/F. C6. $100.00

DURRELL, Lawrence. *Quinx.* 1985. Viking. 1st ed. F/F. A20. $14.00

DURSO, Joseph. *Amazing.* 1970. Houghton Mifflin. 1st ed. VG/G. P8. $15.00

DURSO, Joseph. *Casey.* 1967. Prentice Hall. 1st ed. VG/VG. P8. $25.00

DURST, Paul. *Florentine Table.* 1980. Scribner. 1st ed. F/F. P3. $20.00

DUTHIE, Eric. *Mystery & Adventure Stories for Girls.* 1962. Odhams. 1st ed. hc. VG/VG. P3. $25.00

DUTOURD, Jean. *Dog's Head.* 1951. John Lehmann. 1st ed. VG/VG. P3. $40.00

DUTTON, Benjamin. *Navigation & Nautical Astronomy.* 1942. US Naval Inst. ils/graphs. gilt bl bdg. VG. P12. $8.00

DUVOISIN, Roger. *And There Was America.* 1938. Knopf. 1st ed. 75p. gray cloth. G+. T5. $25.00

DUVOISIN, Roger. *Donkey-Donkey.* 1933. Whitman. 1st ed. 8vo. VG. M5. $45.00

DUVOISIN, Roger. *Lonely Veronica.* nd. Knopf. sm 4to. unp. NF. C14. $10.00

DUYCKINCK & DUYCKINCK. *Cyclopaedia of American Literature.* 1855. NY. 2 vol. VG. O7. $125.00

DWIGHT, Allan. *To the Walls of Cartagena.* 1967. Colonial Williamsburg. ils Leonard Vosburgh. 161p. VG. B10. $12.00

DWIGHT, Theodore. *History of Connecticut From First Settlement to Present...* 1859. NY. 450p. VG. B14. $75.00

DWIGHT, Timothy. *Travels in New England & New York.* 1969. Harvard. 4 vol. VG/VG case. M17. $50.00

DWYER, Deanna; see Koontz, Dean R.

DWYER, K.R.; see Koontz, Dean R.

DWYER, MASON & MURDOCH. *New Perspectives on Politics...of Early Modern Scotland.* nd. Edinburgh. John Donald. 8vo. 329p. F/NF. P4. $20.00

DYER. *Pompeii: Its History, Buildings & Antiquities...* 1871. np. ils/fld maps. VG. A4. $35.00

DYERS, William E. *Dyers Story.* 1944. NY. 1st ed. VG/VG. B5. $22.50

DYJAK & WILKINS. *Bertha's Garden.* 1995. Houghton Mifflin. 1st ed. 12mo. unp. F/F. C14. $12.00

DYKES, Jeff C. *Western High Spots: Reading & Collecting Guides.* 1977. Northland. 1st ed. inscr. F/F. A18. $75.00

DYKES, Jeff. *Fifty Great Western Illustrators.* 1975. Northland. 1st collector's ed. 1/200. sgn. M/case. A18. $200.00

DYKES, Robert. *Amateur Cinematographer's Handbook on Movie Making.* 1931. Boston. 111p. red cloth. VG. B5. $100.00

DYKSTRA, Lenny. *Nails.* 1987. Garden City. 1st ed. VG/VG. B5. $25.00

DYLAN, Thomas. *Adventures in the Skin Trade & Other Stories.* 1955. New Directions. 1st ed. 275p. VG/dj. M20. $62.00

DYLAN, Thomas. *Quite Early One Morning.* 1954. New Directions. 1st ed. 239p. VG/dj. M20. $42.00

DYSON, Freeman. *Infinite in All Directions.* 1988. Harper Row. 8vo. 321p. F/F. K5. $15.00

DYSON, John. *South Sea Dream: Adventure in Paradise.* 1982. Little Brn. photos. 243p. VG/dj. T7. $22.00

DYSON. *Pictures to Print: The 19th-Century Engraving Trade.* 1984. 4to. ils. 234p. VG/VG. A4. $65.00

DZIEMIANOWICZ & WEINBERG. *Famous Fantastic Mysteries.* 1991. Gramercy. 1st ed. F/F. P3. $20.00

Like the old miner on the Mother Lode, the antiquarian bookseller never abandons the hope of striking a rich deposit. a nugget of gold, while hidden in the earth is worthless until found by the miner, and to the finder goes the reward. Rare and unusual books are worthless while hiding in the dust of an attic, or gathering mould in the basement. Not until they are rescued from oblivion by an informed bibliophile do they eventually find a worthy repository.

Harold C. Holmes
1878 – 1965

– E –

EAGAN, Lesley. *In the Death of a Man.* 1970. Harper. 1st. VG/dj. G8. $17.50

EAMES, G.T. *Horse to Remember.* 1947. Messner. 1st. ils Paul Brn. VG/dj. A21. $50.00

EAMES, H. *Winners Lose All: Dr Cook & Theft of North Pole.* 1973. Boston. photos/map. 346p. NF/dj. M4. $20.00

EARHART, Amelia. *Last Flight.* Nov 1937. NY. 8vo. 229p. map ep. gilt red cloth. VG. B14. $75.00

EARHART, Amelia. *20 Hours, 40 Minutes: Our Flight in Friendship.* 1928. Grosset Dunlap. rpt. ils. 314p. VG. B18. $32.50

EARL, Guy Chaffee. *Indian Legends & Songs.* 1980. np. 1/500. 79p. NF/sans. B19. $25.00

EARL, John Prescott. *School Team in Camp.* 1909. Penn. 1st. VG. P8. $45.00

EARL, Stephen. *Hills of the Boasting Woman.* 1963. London. Readers Union. ils/biblio. 160p. dj. F3. $15.00

EARLE, Olive. *Lampshades: How to Make Them.* 1921. Dodd Mead. 1st. tall 8vo. 102p. bl cloth. B20. $85.00

EARLEY, Tony. *Here We Are in Paradise.* 1994. Little Brn. 1st. author's 1st book. F/dj. R14. $35.00

EARLY, Gerald. *Daughters: On Family & Fatherhood.* 1994. Addison Wesley. 1st. F/dj. R14. $25.00

EARLY, Jack. *Creative Kind of Killer.* 1984. Franklin Watts. 1st. F/dj. A23. $32.00

EAST, Ben. *Danger!* 1970. Outdoor Life/Dutton. 1st. ils Tom Beecham. VG/dj. M20. $25.00

EAST, Charles. *Civil War Diary of Sarah Morgan.* 1991. Athens, GA. U GA. 1st. F/dj. A14. $25.00

EASTBURN, Robert. *Dangers & Sufferings of Robert Eastburn.* 1904. Cleveland. Burroughs. 1/27 on Imperial Japanese vellum. 76p. B18. $150.00

EASTLAKE, William. *Bamboo Bed.* 1971. NY. Zebra. 1st. VG/wrp. R11. $17.00

EASTLAKE, William. *Castle Keep.* 1965. NY. S&S. 1st. VG/dj. L1. $50.00

EASTLAKE, William. *Child's Garden of Verses for the Revolution.* 1970. NY. Grove. 1st. VG/dj. B30/R11. $30.00

EASTLAKE, William. *Dancers in the Scalp House.* 1975. Viking. 1st. F/NF clip. B3. $75.00

EASTMAN, Charles. *Soul of the Indian.* 1911. Boston. 1st. 170p. VG. B18. $45.00

EASTMAN, E.R. *Not With Dreams.* 1954. NY. Greenberg. 1st. sgn bookplate. NF/VG. T11. $10.00

EASTMAN, E.R. *Walking the Broad Highway.* 1956. Chicago. Am Agriculturist. 211p. VG. A10. $18.00

EASTMAN, P.D. *Cat in the Hat Beginner Book Dictionary.* 1964. Random. F/sans. T12. $25.00

EASTON, MOTTRAM & PARTRIDGE. *Three Personal Records of War.* 1929. London. 1/100. sgns. T9. $85.00

EASTWOOD, Alice. *Handbook of the Trees of California.* 1905. SF. 57 pl. 86p. new buckram. rare. B26. $120.00

EATON, Mary. *Cook & Housekeeper's Complete & Universal Dictionary...* 1823 (1822). ils. 493p. half leather/marbled brd. E6. $250.00

EAUCLAIRE, Sally. *Cat in Photography.* 1990. Boston. photos. VG/dj. M17. $15.00

EAVENSON, Howard N. *Coal Through the Ages.* 1935. NY. AIME. 1st. sm 8vo. 123p. gilt red cloth. VG+. B20. $25.00

EBAN, Eleanor F. *War in the Cradle of the World. Mesopotamia.* 1918. London. Hodder Stoughton. ils/pl. 312p. cloth. G. Q2. $46.50

EBERHART, A.G. *Everything About Dogs.* 1902. Camp Dennison, OH. Eberhart Kennels. stated 2nd. 8vo. 282p. purple cloth. B20. $35.00

EBERHART, Mignon G. *Bayou Road.* 1979. NY. Random. 1st. F/F. H11. $20.00

EBERHART, Mignon G. *Danger Money.* 1974. Random. F/NF. N4. $25.00

EBERHART, Mignon G. *Nine O'Clock Tide.* 1977. Random. 1st. F/F. H11. $20.00

EBERHART, Richard. *Collected Poems 1930-1976.* 1976. NY. Oxford. 1st. inscr/dtd 1984. VG/dj. R14. $75.00

EBERLE, Irmengarde. *Picture Stories for Children (A Rebus).* 1984. Delacorte. 1st thus. 98p. F/NF. C14. $20.00

EBERSOLE, Barbara. *Fletcher Martin.* 1954. Gainesville, FL. 1st. 4to. 51p. F/VG+. B20. $60.00

EBIN, David. *Drug Experience.* 1961. Orion. 1st. VG/dj. R8. $40.00

EBSEN, Buddy. *Other Side of Oz.* 1993. Newport Beach. Donovan. 285p. VG/dj. C5. $15.00

EBY & FLEMING. *Case of the Malevolent Twin.* 1946. Dutton. 1st. G+. G8. $12.50

ECCLES, Marjorie. *Cast a Cold Eye.* 1988. NY. Crime Club. 1st. F/F. H11. $40.00

ECHEVERRIAL & WILKIE. *French Image of America, a Chronological...Bibliography...* 1994. 1601 entries. NF. A4. $160.00

ECK, Joe. *Elements of Garden Design.* 1996. NY. Holt. 1st. ils/index. 164p. F/dj. H10. $17.50

ECKBO, Garrett. *Landscape for Living.* 1950. NY. 1st. photos/plans. 262p. VG/dj. B26. $40.00

ECKBO, Garrett. *Urban Landscape Design.* 1964. McGraw Hill. 4to. ils. gr cloth. VG. F1. $35.00

ECKENRODE, H.J. *Jefferson Davis: President of the South.* 1923. Macmillan. 1st. 371p. G+. B10. $25.00

ECKENRODE, Hamilton James. *George B McClellan, the Man Who Saved the Union.* 1941. Chapel Hill. U NC. 1st. 296p. cloth. VG. M8. $45.00

ECKER, Alexander. *Cebral Convolutions of Man Represented...* 1873. NY. Appleton. 1st Am. 87p. cloth. G7. $150.00

ECKERT, Allan W. *Dreaming Tree.* 1968. Little Brn. 1st. decor cloth. F/NF. T11. $75.00

ECKERT, Allan W. *Great Auk.* 1963. Little Brn. 1st. NF/VG. T11. $75.00

ECKERT, Allan W. *Incident at Hawk's Hill.* 1971. Little Brn. rpt. sgn. VG/G. B17. $22.50

ECKERT, Allan W. *Johnny Logan, Shawnee Spy.* 1983. Little Brn. 1st. NF/dj. T11. $70.00

ECKERT, Allan W. *Owls of North America (North of Mexico).* 1974. Doubleday. 1/250. sgn author/aritst. 278p. F/case. B20. $300.00

ECKERT, Allan W. *Sorrow in Our Heart: Life of Tecumseh.* 1992. NY. 1st. F/dj. T11. $40.00

ECKERT, Allan W. *Twilight of Empire.* 1988. Little Brn. 1st. Winning of Am #6. rem mk. NF/dj. T11. $40.00

ECKERT, Allan W. *Wild Season.* 1967. Little Brn. ils Karl Karalus. 244p. F/NF. D4. $30.00

ECKERT, Allan W. *Wilderness Empire.* 1980. Little Brn. 1st. inscr. G/dj. V4. $40.00

ECKSTEIN, Gustav. *Body Has a Head.* 1970. NY. 1st. 799p. dj. A13. $20.00

ECKSTEIN, Gustav. *Everyday Miracle.* 1965. Harper Row. ils Kevin McIntyre. 146p. F/NF. D4. $25.00

ECKSTEIN, Yechiel. *What Christians Should Know About Jews & Judaism.* 1984. Word. 336p. VG/dj. B29. $11.00

ECO, Umberto. *Foucault's Pendulum.* 1989. HBJ. 1st Am. F/dj. N4. $30.00

ECO, Umberto. *Postcript to the Name of the Rose.* 1984. HBJ. 1st. F/dj. M21/T12. $30.00

ECO, Umberto. *Search for the Perfect Language.* 1995. Oxford/Cambridge. VG+/dj. M17. $17.50

EDDICOTT, Wendell. *Adventures With Rod & Harpoon Along Florida Keys.* 1925. Stokes. ils. NF. B14. $75.00

EDDINGS, David. *Diamond Throne.* 1989. Del Rey/Ballantine. 1st. NF/clip. A14. $28.00

EDDINGS, David. *Queen of Sorcery.* 1983. London. Century. 1st hc. Belgariad #2. NF/dj. A14. $175.00

EDDINGS, David. *Ruby Knight.* 1991. Del Rey/Ballantine. 1st. Elenium #2. NF/dj. A14. $17.50

EDDINGS, David. *Sorceress of Darshiva.* 1989. Ballantine. 1st. F/F. B3. $20.00

EDDINGTON, A.S. *Nature of the Physical World.* 1929 (1928). Cambridge. 4th. 361p. cloth. G. K5. $25.00

EDDY, Clyde. *Down the World's Most Dangerous River.* 1929. Stokes. photos. 293p. VG/dj. F7. $210.00

EDDY, Daniel C. *Europe: Its Scenes & Society.* 1859. Bradley Dayton. 11th. S17. $10.00

EDDY, John A. *New Sun: Solar Results From Skylab.* 1979. NASA. SP-402. 4to. 198p. VG. K5. $35.00

EDDY, Mary Baker. *Christ & Christmas.* 1897. Christian Science Pub. 12mo. 59p. aeg. limp leather/ribbon marker. H4. $175.00

EDDY, Mary Baker. *Retrospection & Introspection.* 1899. Boston. 15th thousand. 130p. aeg. VG. B14. $35.00

EDDY, Mary Baker. *What Christmas Means to Me & Other Christmas Messages.* 1949. Boston. 50p. gr cloth. AN/dj. B14. $25.00

EDE, Charles. *Art of the Book.* 1951. London. The Studio. 4to. ils. gilt gr cloth. F/dj. F1. $80.00

EDEL, Leon. *James Joyce: The Last Journey.* (1947). NY. Gotham Book Mart. 1st. quarter bl cloth/prt brd. NF. M24. $65.00

EDEL & RAY. *Henry James & HG Wells: Record of Their Friendship...* 1958. Urbana, IL. ARC. 8vo. 272p. RS. F/worn. H4. $20.00

EDELMAN, Bernard. *Ownership of the Image, Elements for Marxist Theory of Law.* 1979. Routledge/Kegan Paul. M11. $45.00

EDERER, Bernard Francis. *Birch Coulie.* 1957. Exposition. G. w/sgn letter. A19. $30.00

EDGERTON, Clyde. *Floatplane Notebooks.* 1988. London. Viking. ARC. F/F. B3. $15.00

EDGERTON, Clyde. *In Memory of Junior.* 1992. Algonquin. 1st. sgn. NF/dj. B30. $22.00

EDGERTON, Clyde. *Raney.* 1985. Chapel Hill. 1st. author's 1st book. inscr/dtd 1985. F/dj. L3. $500.00

EDGERTON, Clyde. *Redeye.* 1995. Chapel Hill. 1st. sgn. F/dj. B20. $35.00

EDGERTON, Clyde. *Walking Across Egypt.* 1986. Algonquin. 1st. sgn. F/F. B3. $75.00

EDGERTON, Clyde. *Where Trouble Sleeps.* 1997. Algonquin. 1st. F/dj. M23. $25.00

EDGERTON, Jesse. *New Quakerism.* 1900. Columbiana, OH. Wilbur Union. 12mo. 12p. wrp. V3. $12.00

EDGERTON, Leslie H. *Death of Tarpons.* 1996. Denton, TX. 1st. author's 1st book. F/F. H11. $40.00

EDIE, George. *Art of English Shooting.* 1993. SF. Arion. 1st thus. 1/250. gilt quarter brn morocco. F/case. M24. $100.00

EDINBOROUGH, Arnold. *Festivals of Canada.* 1981. Lester/Orpen Dennys. 1st. VG/dj. P3. $20.00

EDINGER, William. *Samuel Johnson & Poetic Style.* 1977. Chicago. 1st. VG/dj. H13. $45.00

EDLIN, Herbert L. *Know Your Broadleaves.* 1973 (1968). London. 166 pl. 143p. sc. B26. $12.50

EDMINSTER, Frank C. *American Game Birds of Field & Forest.* 1954. NY. Scribner. 1st. VG/clip. H4. $35.00

EDMINSTER, Frank C. *Ruffled Grouse.* 1947. Macmillan. G/dj. A19. $30.00

EDMONDS, Harry. *Secret Voyage.* 1946. Mac Donald. VG. P3. $10.00

EDMONDS, Walter. *Beaver Valley.* 1971. Little Brn. 1st. ils Leslie Morrill. VG/dj. T11. $55.00

EDMONDS, Walter. *Chad Hanna.* (1940). Little Brn. 1st. NF/VG. T11. $50.00

EDMONDS, Walter. *Drums Along the Mohawk.* (1936). Little Brn. 64th prt. gilt cloth. F/dj. T11. $45.00

EDMONDS, Walter. *Drums Along the Mohawk.* 1936. Little Brn. 1st. NF/VG 1st state. B3. $110.00

EDMONDS, Walter. *In the Hands of the Senecas.* 1947. Little Brn. 1st. NF/dj. T11. $55.00

EDMONDS, Walter. *Three Stalwarts.* 1962. Little Brn. 1st thus. NF/clip. T11. $40.00

EDMONDS & MIMURA. *Paramount Pictures & People Who Made Them.* 1980. San Diego. AS Barnes. 1st. 4to. 272p. VG/dj. B11. $15.00

EDMONSON, Munro. *Ancient Furniture of the Itzas: Book of Chilam Balm...* 1982. Austin. U TX. 1st. 220p. dj. F3. $50.00

EDSON, Newell W. *Choosing a Home Partner.* 1926. NY. Assoc Pr. 1st. VG+. A25. $20.00

EDWARD, Oliver. *Talking of Books.* 1957. London. Heinemann. 1st. 8vo. 306p. F/dj. O10. $15.00

EDWARDES & MASTERS. *Cradle of Erotica.* 1966. NY. 1st. VG/dj. B5. $25.00

EDWARDS, A. Cecil. *Persian Carpet: Survey of Carpet-Weaving Industry of Persia.* 1975. London. Duckworth. 4th. 384p. NF/dj. W1. $90.00

EDWARDS, A. Herbage. *Paris Through the Attic.* 1922 (1918). Dutton. 4th. 12mo. VG/dj. A2. $20.00

EDWARDS, Anne. *Early Reagan: Rise to Power.* 1987. Morrow. 1st. F/VG. T12. $100.00

EDWARDS, Bill. *Millersburg, the Queen of Carnival Glass.* (1982). Collector Books. 8vo. 132p. VG/glossy wrp. H1. $30.00

EDWARDS, Clayton. *Treasury of Heroes & Heroines: Record of High Endurance...* 1920. Hampton. ils Choate/Cooke. VG. M19. $25.00

EDWARDS, Corwin D. *Price Discrimination Law, a Review of Experience.* 1959. Brookings Inst. private xl. M11. $35.00

EDWARDS, E.I. *Desert Voices: Descriptive Bibliography.* 1958. LA. Westernlore. 1st. 1/500. VG/dj. O4. $75.00

EDWARDS, Harry Stillwell. *Eneas Africanus.* 1930. Dallas. BC of TX. 1st. 1/300. batik brd/label. F/NF box. M24. $100.00

EDWARDS, I.E.S. *Tutanchamum Das Grab und Seine Schatze.* 1977. 4to. German text. 256p. VG/dj. B11. $18.00

EDWARDS, Isabel M. *Glove Making.* (1946). NY/Chicago. Pitman. later prt. 12mo. 90p. VG. H4. $25.00

EDWARDS, John O. *Peroxide Reaction Mechanisms.* 1962. NY. Interscience. 8vo. 245p. VG/dj. K5. $60.00

EDWARDS, Jonathan. *Great Christian Doctrine of Original Sin Defended...* 1761. London. Re-Prt for G Keith/J Johnson. 1st Eng. 8vo. VG. O1. $400.00

EDWARDS, Jonathan. *Life of Rev David Brainerd... nd.* NY. Am Tract Soc. Evangelical Family Lib #7. half leather. H10. $35.00

EDWARDS, Leo. *Jerry Todd, Editor-In-Grief.* (1930). Grosset Dunlap. VG/dj. H4. $60.00

EDWARDS, Leo. *Jerry Todd & the Bob-Tailed Elephant.* (1929). Grosset Dunlap. later ed of 3rd format. sm 8vo. 235p. pict ep. NF/dj. H1. $20.00

EDWARDS, Leo. *Jerry Todd & the Purring Egg.* 1926. Grosset Dunlap. 1st. sm 8vo. 213p. red cloth. G/dj. H1. $18.00

EDWARDS, Leo. *Jerry Todd: Buffalo Bill Bath Tub.* (1937). Grosset Dunlap. 1st of 3rd format. sm 8vo. 232p. pict ep. F/VG. H1. $25.00

EDWARDS, Leo. *Jerry Todd's Cuckoo Camp.* 1940. Grosset Dunlap. 1st of 3rd format. sm 8vo. 216p. VG. H1. $25.00

EDWARDS, Leo. *Jerry Todd's Poodle Parlor.* 1938. Grosset Dunlap. VG/dj. H4. $85.00

EDWARDS, Leo. *Poppy Ott: Poppy Ott's Pedigreed Pickles.* 1927. Grosset Dunlap. 1st. 243p. sm 8vo. red cloth. H1. $12.00

EDWARDS, Leo. *Poppy Ott: The Monkey's Paw.* 1938. Grosset Dunlap. 1st. sm 8vo. 214p. red cloth. VG/G. H1. $30.00

EDWARDS, Lionel. *Huntsmen Past & Present.* 1929. London. Eyre Spottiswoode. 1st. sm 4to. VG/G. O3. $125.00

EDWARDS, Peter. *Blood Brothers: How Canada's Most Powerful Mafia...* 1990. Toronto. Key Porter. 1st. inscr/sgn. NF/VG. A26. $35.00

EDWARDS, R.B. *Reason & Religion: Introduction to Philosophy of Religion.* 1972. HBJ. 386p. G. B29. $11.00

EDWARDS & TERRY. *Governor's Mansion of the Palmetto State.* 1978. Columbia. 1st. inscr/dtd 1978. G/VG. V4. $17.50

EDWARDS & ZANETTA. *Stardust: David Bowie Story.* (1986). McGraw Hill. 8vo. photos. 433p. F/NF. H4. $10.00

EDWARDS-YEARWOOD, Grace. *In the Shadow of the Peacock.* 1988. McGraw Hill. 1st. F/F. D10. $40.00

EEKELAAR & KATZ. *Marriage & Cohabitation in Contemporary Societies.* 1980. Toronto. Butterworth. 1st. VG. B27. $12.00

EELLS & O'DAY. *High Times Hard Times.* 1981. Putnam. 1st. F/F. B2. $45.00

EFFINGER, George Alec. *What Entropy Means to Me.* 1972. Doubleday. 1st. NF/NF. P3. $15.00

EGAMI, Tomo. *Typical Japanese Cooking.* 1959. Tokyo. Shibata. 1st. ils. VG. N2. $10.00

EGAN, Ferol. *Sand in a Whirlwind.* 1972. Doubleday. F/dj. A19. $40.00

EGEJURU, Phanuel Akubueze. *Towards African Literary Independence: A Dialogue...* 1980. Westport. Greenwood. 1st. 173p. R11. $17.00

EGERTON, Thomas. *Speech of the Lord Chancellor of England...* 1609. London. later blk morocco. M11. $650.00

EGGLESTON, William. *Democratic Forest.* 1989. Doubleday. 1st Am. F/dj. C9. $90.00

EGGLESTON & SEELYE. *Tecumseh & the Shawnee Prophet.* 1878. Dodd Mead. 1st. lg map. 332p. gilt cloth. D11. $60.00

EGLOFF, Fred. *El Paso Lawman.* ltd. ils/biblio/index. 141p. AN/dj. E1. $17.00

EHLE, John. *Last One Home.* 1984. Harper. 1st. NF/dj. S13. $10.00

EHRENBURG, Ilya. *Thaw.* 1955. Chicago. Regnery. 1st. 8vo. G/dj. B11. $15.00

EHRENFELD & MACK. *Chamelon Variant.* 1980. NY. Dial. 1st. F/F. H11. $25.00

EHRENFIELD, David. *Beginning Again: People & Nature in the New Millenium.* 1993. OUP. 216p. AN. S15. $6.00

EHRENSTEIN & REED. *Rock on Film.* 1982. NY. Delilah. 75 photos. VG/wrp. C9. $36.00

EHRLICH, Gretel. *Arctic Heart: A Poem Cycle.* 1992. Santa Barbara. Capra. 1st. sgn. F. O11. $25.00

EHRLICH, Gretel. *Drinking Dry Clouds.* 1991. Santa Barbara. Capra. 1st. F/wrp. R14. $25.00

EHRLICH, Gretel. *Islands, the Universe, Home.* 1991. Viking. 1st. sgn. F/dj. O11. $40.00

EHRLICH, Gretel. *Match to the Heart.* 1994. Pantheon. ARC. sgn. F/wrp/NF case. B4. $65.00

EHRLICH, Louise. *Baptism of Desire: Poems.* 1989. Harper Row. 1st. sgn. F/dj. O11. $35.00

EHRLICH & EHRLICH. *Population, Resources & Environment.* 1970. Freeman. 1st. 383p. VG. S15. $10.00

EHRLICHMAN, John. *Witness to Power.* 1982. S&S. 1st. f/dj. W2. $30.00

EICHLER, Alfred. *Death of an Ad Man.* 1954. Abelard-Schuman. VG/dj. P3. $15.00

EICKELMAN, Dale F. *Middle East: Anthropological Approach.* 1981. NJ. Prentice Hall. inscr. ils/figures. 336p. G/wrp. Q2. $15.00

EICKHOFF, Randy Lee. *Fourth Horseman.* 1998. NY. Tom Doherty Assoc. 1st. gilt blk bdg. F/dj. T11. $22.00

EIFERT, Virginia. *Delta Queen: Story of a Steamboat.* 1960. Dodd Mead. 1st. 242p. F/dj. B18. $22.50

EINSTEIN, Charles. *Willie Mays: Coast to Coast Giant.* 1963. Putnam. 1st. photos. VG. P8. $20.00

EISELEY, Loren. *Fox at the Wood's Edge.* 1990. NY. Holt. 1st. 517p. gray cloth. F/dj. T11. $45.00

EISELEY, Loren. *Innocent Assassins.* 1973. Scribner. 1st. ils Laszlo Kubinyi. NF/NF. B3. $35.00

EISELEY, Loren. *Night Country.* 1971. Scribner. 1st. VG/dj. M19. $17.50

EISEN, Gustavus A. *Portraits of Washington.* 1932. Hamilton. vol 1 only. 323p. VG. B10. $85.00

EISENHOWER, Dwight D. *At Ease: Stories I Tell to Friends.* 1967. Doubleday. ne. sm 4to. 400p. NF/VG. W2. $40.00

EISENHOWER, Dwight D. *Crusade in Europe.* 1948. Doubleday. 1st. 559p. F/dj. H1. $20.00

EISENSTADT, Jill. *Kiss Out.* 1991. Knopf. 1st. NF/F. R14. $25.00

EISENSTAEDT, Alfred. *Eisenstaedt's Guide to Photography.* 1978. Viking. VG/dj. S5. $16.00

EISENSTAEDT, Alfred. *Eisenstaedt's Guide to Photography.* 1978. Viking. 1st. ils. F/VG. P12. $25.00

EISENSTEIN, Phyllis. *Born to Exile.* 1978. Arkham. VG/blocked price. L1. $35.00

EISLER, Steven. *Space Wars, Worlds & Weapons.* 1979. Crescent. F/dj. P3. $6.00

EITELJORG, Harrison. *Treasures of the American West.* 1981. Balance House. 172p. VG/dj. J2. $65.00

ELDER, Art. *Blue Streak & Doctor Medusa.* nd. Whitman. VG. P3. $13.00

ELDER, W. *Biography of Elisha Kent Kane.* 1858. Phil. 4 pl. 416p. new cloth. M4. $60.00

ELDERFIELD, John. *Matisse in the Collection of the Museum of Modern Art.* 1978. MOMA. ils/fld ils. gilt linen cloth. F/VG. F1. $35.00

ELDRIDGE, Charlotte. *Godey Lady Doll.* 1953. Hastings. 1st. ils. VG+/G. M5. $12.00

ELFLANDSSON, Galad. *Black Wolf.* 1979. Grant. 1st. 1/1000. VG/G+. L1. $45.00

ELFONT, Edna A. *Roar of Thunder, Whisper of Wind: Portrait of MI Waterfalls.* 1993 (1984). E Lansing, MI. Thunder Bay. 4to. F/wrp. A2. $12.00

ELIOT, Charles W. *American Historical Documents 1000-1904.* 1969. Harvard Classics. 62nd. VG. P3. $20.00

ELIOT, Charles W. *Harvard Classics Five Foot Shelf of Books Vol 38...* nd (1910). NY. Collier. 418p. NF. C14. $15.00

ELIOT, George. *Adam Bede.* 1859. NY. Harper. 1st Am. gilt brn cloth. M24. $100.00

ELIOT, George. *Felix Holt: The Radical.* 1883. John B Alden. fair. P3. $12.00

ELIOT, Jane. *History of the Western Railroads.* 1995. Crescent. photos. AN. J2. $35.00

ELIOT, Porter. *In Wilderness Is the Preservation of the World.* 1962. Sierra Club. 107p. VG/dj. A10. $25.00

ELIOT, T.S. *Cocktail Party.* 1950. HBW. 189p. VG. C5. $12.50

ELIOT, T.S. *Cocktail Party.* 1950. Harcourt Brace. 1st. F/NF. L3. $85.00

ELIOT, T.S. *Confidential Clerk.* 1954. Harcourt Brace. 1st Am. NF/VG. L3. $45.00

ELIOT, T.S. *Confidential Clerk.* 1954. London. Faber. 1st issue. NF/1st issue. L3. $125.00

ELIOT, T.S. *Cultivation of Christmas Trees.* 1956. London. Faber. 1st. 1/10140. F/prt wrp/envelope. M24. $50.00

ELIOT, T.S. *Cultivation of Christmas Trees.* 1956. NY. Farrar Straus. 1st Am. 1/3pict brd. F. M24. $35.00

ELIOT, T.S. *Elder Statesman.* 1959. London. Faber. 1st. F/dj. L3. $75.00

ELIOT, T.S. *Ezra Pound: His Metric & Poetry.* 1917. Knopf. 1st. 1/1000. author's 2nd book. gilt pk brd. M24. $300.00

ELIOT, T.S. *Homage to John Dryden.* 1924. London. Hogarth. 1st. 1/2000. NF/prt wrp. M24. $125.00

ELIOT, T.S. *Literature of Politics.* 1955. London. Conservative Political Centre. 1st. 1/6160. F/prt wrp. M24. $65.00

ELIOT, T.S. *Little Gidding.* 1942. London. Faber. 1st. NF/hand-sewn brn wrp. Q1. $150.00

ELIOT, T.S. *Poems 1909-1925.* nd. NY/Chicago. 1st Am. VG. M17. $35.00

ELIOT, T.S. *What Is a Classic?* 1945. London. Faber. 1st. F/prt wrp. M24. $200.00

ELIOT, Willard A. *Forest Trees of the Pacific Coast.* 1948 (1938). NY. revised. 565p. B26. $32.50

ELKIN, Stanley. *Mrs Ted Bliss.* 1995. NY. Hyperion. 1/1500. sgn. author's final novel. maroon cloth. F/sans. A24. $70.00

ELKINS, Aaron. *Icy Clutches.* 1990. Mysterious. 1st. F/dj. M19. $15.00

ELKINS, Aaron. *Murder in the Queen's Armies.* 1985. Walker. 1st. inscr/dtd 1988. F/dj. A24. $200.00

ELKINS, Aaron. *Old Bones.* 1987. Mysterious. 1st. F/dj. M15. $95.00

ELKINS, Aaron. *Old Bones.* 1987. Mysterious. 1st. NF/dj. A14. $70.00

ELLER, E.M. *Chesapeake Bay in the American Revolution.* 1981. Century. 1st. ils. 600p. F/dj. M4. $40.00

ELLIN, Stanley. *Dark Fantasitic.* (1983). Mysterious. 1/250. sgn. blk-lettered blk cloth. F/box. R3. $60.00

ELLIN, Stanley. *Luxembourg Run.* 1977. Random. 1st. VG/dj. N4. $20.00

ELLIN, Stanley. *Specialty of the House & Other Stories.* 1979. Mysterious. 1st. 1/250. sgn/#d. F/NF. A24. $85.00

ELLINGTON & DANCE. *Duke Ellington in Person: An Intimate Memoir...* 1978. Houghton Mifflin. 1st. 8vo. 236p. F/NF. B20. $45.00

ELLIOT, E.D. *Training Gun Dogs to Retrieve.* 1952. NY. Field & Stream Outdoor series. 1st. VG/dj. M17. $15.00

ELLIOT, William. *Coming to Terms With Life.* 1944. John Knox. sgn. 142p. G. B29. $13.50

ELLIOTT, Eugene Clinton. *History of Variety: Vaudeville in Seattle...to 1914.* 1944. Seattle. 1/500. 85p. F/stiff brn wrp. B20. $65.00

ELLIOTT, Francis Perry. *Haunted Pajamas.* 1911. Bobbs Merrill. 1st. G. W2. $20.00

ELLIOTT, Franklin R. *Elliott's Fruit Book; or, American Fruit Grower's Guide...* 1858. NY. Moore. ils/index. 503p. fair. H10. $65.00

ELLIOTT, James. *Cold Cold Heart.* 1994. Delacorte. 1st. F/F. H11. $25.00

ELLIOTT, James. *Transport to Disaster.* 1962. NY. 1st. VG/dj. B5. $20.00

ELLIOTT, Lawrence. *Daniel Boone: Long Hunter.* 1977. London. Allen Unwin. 1st. 242p. VG/dj. B18. $15.00

ELLIOTT & HOBBS. *Gasoline Automobile.* 1915. NY/London. 1st. 8vo. gr cloth. F. B14. $55.00

ELLIS, A.F. *Adventuring in the Coral Seas.* 1937. Sydney. 2nd. photos. 264p. VG. M12. $50.00

ELLIS, Bret Easton. *Less Than Zero.* 1985. S&S. 1st. author's 1st novel. F/dj. R14. $75.00

ELLIS, Carleton. *Chemistry of Synthetic Resins. Vol II.* 1935. Reinhold. tall 8vo. VG. H1. $16.00

ELLIS, Constance Dimock. *Magnificent Enterprise: A Chronicle of Vassar College.* 1961. Poughkeepsie. Vassar. 1st. ils. 138p. VG+. A25. $30.00

ELLIS, Edward S. *Dewey & Other Naval Commanders.* 1900. 1st. 15 muc pl. VG. E6. $25.00

ELLIS, Edward S. *Life & Times of Col Daniel Boone.* 1884. Porter Coats. Alta ed. 269+16p pub book list. decor brd. VG. B36. $35.00

ELLIS, Edward S. *Path in the Ravine.* 1895. Phil. Coates. 319p. G. G11. $15.00

ELLIS, Edward S. *Young Scout: Story of a West Point Lieutenant.* 1895. NY. 275p. pict cloth. E1. $40.00

ELLIS, Frederick D. *Tragedy of the Lusitania.* 1915. np. ils. 320p. VG. B18. $22.50

ELLIS, Jerry. *Bareback! One Man's Journey Along Pony Express Trail.* 1993. Delacorte. 1st. F/dj. O3. $25.00

ELLIS, Jerry. *Walking the Trail: One Man's Journey Along Cherokee Trail.* 1991. Delacorte. 1st. VG/dj. N2. $10.00

ELLIS, John B. *Sights & Secrets of the National Capital.* 1869. US Pub Co. ils. 512p. VG. B10. $20.00

ELLIS, John Tracy. *Catholic Bishops: A Memoir.* 1983. Wilmington, DE. Michael Glazier. 1st. 182p. VG/dj. N2. $10.00

ELLIS, Mel. *Eagle to the Wind.* 1978. HRW. 1st. F/dj. P2. $12.50

ELLIS, Norman. *Instrumentation & Arranging for Radio & Dance Orchestra.* 1937. Schirmer. 193p. G. S5. $35.00

ELLIS, SEEBOHM & SYKES. *At Home With Books: How Booklovers Live With...Libraries.* 1995. NY. Carol Southern. 1st/later prt. 248p. F/dj. O10. $50.00

ELLIS, William T. *Billy Sunday: Man & His Message.* 1914. U Book/Bible House. Authorized ed. 8vo. 451p. dk bl cloth. VG. S17. $10.00

ELLIS, William. *Journal of William Ellis: Narrative of Tour of Hawaii...* 1963 (1825). rpt. ils/fld map. F. M4. $20.00

ELLIS & KELLER. *History of the German People.* 1916. 15 vol. 1/1500. leather. VG. A4. $95.00

ELLISON, Douglas. *David Lant: The Vanished Outlaw.* 1988. Aberdeen, SD. Midstates. sgn. F/dj. A19. $45.00

ELLISON, Harlan. *Again, Dangerous Visions.* nd. BC. VG/dj. S18. $8.00

ELLISON, Harlan. *Angry Candy.* 1988. Houghton Mifflin. 1st. F/dj. M25. $25.00

ELLISON, Harlan. *Deathbird Stories.* 1975. Harper. 1st. inscr. NF/F. S18. $55.00

ELLISON, Harlan. *Mefisto in Onyx.* 1993. Ziesing. 1/1000. sgn. ils/sgn Frank Miller. NF/case. M19. $60.00

ELLISON, Harlan. *Shatterday.* 1980. Houghton Mifflin. 1st. F/VG. M19. $45.00

ELLISON, Harlan. *Stalking the Nightmare.* 1982. Phantasia. 1st. 1/700. sgn. VG/case. L1. $175.00

ELLISON, James Whitfield. *Summer After the War.* 1972. Dodd Mead. 1st. F/price blocked. R11. $35.00

ELLISON, Mary. *Support for Secession: Lancashire & American Civil War.* 1972. Chicago. 259p. NF/dj. M10. $15.00

ELLISON, Rhoda Coleman. *Check List of Alabama Imprints 1807-1870.* 1946. U AL. 1st. 151p. NF/stiff prt wrp. M8. $45.00

ELLISON, Virginia H. *Pooh Party Book*. 1971. Dutton. 1st. ils Shepard. cloth. F/dj. B27. $55.00

ELLISON, Viriginia H. *Pooh Cookbook*. nd (c1969). Dutton. ils EH Shepard. 120p. VG. C14. $14.00

ELLISON & PRICE. *Life & Adventures in CA of Don Agustin Janssens 1834-1856*. 1953. Huntington Lib. sgn Price. 165p. dj. P4. $30.00

ELLROY, James. *Big Nowhere*. 1988. Mysterious. 1st. VG/dj. G8. $17.50

ELLROY, James. *My Dark Places*. 1996. Knopf. ARC/1st. sgn. NF/F. w/review material. B30. $50.00

ELLROY, James. *Suicide Hill*. 1986. Mysterious. 1st. inscr. F/dj. M15. $100.00

ELLROY, James. *White Jazz*. 1992. Knopf. 1st. NF/dj. G8. $25.00

ELLROY, James. *White Jazz*. 1992. Knopf. 1st. sgn. F/dj. R14. $45.00

ELLSBERG, Edward. *Hell on Ice: Saga of the Jeanette*. 1938. Dodd Mead. 1st. 8vo. 42p. bl cloth. G. P4. $30.00

ELLSWORTH, J. Lewis. *57th Annual Report Massachusetts State Board of Agriculture*. 1910. Boston. Wright. 357p+257p. VG. A10. $15.00

ELLSWORTH, Lincoln. *Beyond Horizons*. 1983. NY. BC. ils. 403p. VG/dj. B18. $45.00

ELLSWORTH, Lyman R. *Guys on Ice*. 1952. NY. McKay. later prt. 8vo. 277p. P4. $25.00

ELLSWORTH, M.S. *Mormon Odyssey: Story of Ida Hunt Udall, Plural Wife*. 1992. IL U. 1st. 296p. F/dj. M4. $20.00

ELLWANGER, H.B. *Rose: A Treatise on Cultivation, History, Family...* 1908 (1882). NY. revised. 310p. gilt bdg. B26. $30.00

ELLWOOD, Thomas. *History of Life of Thomas Ellwood...* 1855. Manchester. John Harrison. 6th. 12mo. 307p. G+. V3. $35.00

ELMAN, Robert. *Atlantic Flyway*. 1972. NY. 250 photos. 200 p. F/dj. A17. $35.00

ELMORE, James Buchanan. *Twenty-Five Years in Jackville*. 1904. Alamo, IN. self pub. ils. 215p. G. B18. $27.50

ELMSLIE, Kenward. *Girl Machine*. 1971. Angel Hair. 1st. 1/500. sgn. F/stapled wrp. L3. $45.00

ELMSLIE, Kenward. *I Trust the Wrong People*. 1966. NY. Chappell. 1st. inscr. NF. L3. $35.00

ELON, AMOS. *Timetable*. 1980. Doubleday. VG/dj. P3. $15.00

ELOSEGI, Joseba. *Quiero Morir por Algo*. 1977. Barcelona. Plaza Janes. 1st. VG/clip. N2. $10.00

ELSHTAIN & TOBIAS. *Women, Militarism & War*. 1990. Rowman Littlefield. 1st. F. R8. $15.00

ELSON, Marilyn. *Duffy on the Farm*. 1984. Golden. 1st A ed. folio. VG. M5. $12.00

ELSTER, John. *Local Justice in America*. 1995. NY. Russell Sage. 1st. VG/dj. N2. $12.50

ELVERSON, Virginia T. *Cooking Legacy*. 1975. NY. Walker. G/dj. A16. $15.00

ELY, David. *Mr Nicholas*. 1974. Putnam. 1st. rem mk. F/NF. B2. $25.00

ELY, Lawrence D. *Space Science for the Layman*. 1967. Springfield, IL. Chas C Thomas. ils. 200p. dj. xl. K5. $20.00

ELY, Scott. *Starlight*. 1987. NY. Weidenfeld Nickolson. 1st. F/F. H11/R11. $30.00

EMERICK, Richard G. *Man of the Canyon: Old Indian Remembers His Life*. 1992. Northern Lights. 8vo. 170p. dj. F7. $22.50

EMERSON, Alice B. *Ruth Fielding at Briarwood Hall*. 1913. NY. Cupples Leon. 1st. ils. 204p. VG+. A25. $20.00

EMERSON, Dorothy. *Among the Mescalero Apaches: Story of Father Albert Braum*. 1973. Tucson, AZ. ils. 224p. NF/NF. B19. $25.00

EMERSON, Earl. *Yellow Dog Party*. 1991. Morrow. 1st. F/F. H11/N4. $25.00

EMERSON, Edwin Jr. *History of the 19th Century: Year by Year, Vol I*. ca 1900. VG/sans. S18. $5.00

EMERSON, Elizabeth H. *Walter C Woodward: Friend on the Frontier, a Biography*. 1952. np. 12mo. 316p. xl. V3. $15.00

EMERSON, Jill; see Block, Lawrence.

EMERSON, L.O. *Golden Wreath: Choice Collection of Favorite Melodies...* 1956. Boston. Oliver Ditson. 240p. G. C5. $12.50

EMERSON, Ralph Waldo. *Essays of Ralph Waldo Emerson*. 1924. LEC. 1/1500. prt/sgn John Henry Nash. cloth. VG. F1. $65.00

EMERSON, Ralph Waldo. *Essays*. 1906. Hammersmith. Doves. 1/25 on vellum. sm 4to. 311p. F/case. H5. $4,000.00

EMERSON, Ralph Waldo. *Friendship*. 1939. Worcester. St Onge. mini. 1/950. aeg. Sangorski/Sutcliffe bl bdg (scarce). B24. $575.00

EMERSON, Ralph Waldo. *Napoleon*. ca 1920. Cincinnati/NY. Jennings Graham/Eaton Mains. 12mo. 45p. cloth. VG. W1. $10.00

EMERSON, Ralph Waldo. *Nature: Addresses & Lectures*. 1849. Boston/Cambridge. James Munroe. 1st/A bdg (no priority). gilt blk cloth. M24. $375.00

EMERSON, Ralph Waldo. *Representative Men*. 1850. Boston. Phillips Sampson. 1st/1st prt/1st bdg. gilt blk cloth. NF. M24. $400.00

EMERSON, Ralph Waldo. *Western Journey With Mr Emerson*. 1884. Little Brn. 1st. sm 4to. NF/dj. J3. $600.00

EMERTON, Norma. *Scientific Reinterpretation of Form*. 1984. Ithaca. 1st. 318p. A13. $25.00

EMERY, R.G. *High Inside*. 1948. MacRae Smith. later prt. VG/dj. P8. $65.00

EMME, Eugene M. *Aeronautics & Astronautics...* 1961. NASA. 8vo. 240p. gilt cloth. VG. K5. $25.00

EMMETT, Chris. *Texas Camel Tales*. 1932. San Antonio. Naylor. 1st. sgn. 8vo. 275p. VG/dj. w/pre-pub subscriber list. B11. $875.00

EMPSON, William. *Seven Types of Ambiguity*. 1930. London. 1st. dj. T9. $85.00

EMRICH, Duncan. *It's an Old Wild West Custom*. 1949. Vanguard. 1st. Am Customs series. NF/G. T11. $20.00

ENDE, Michael. *Never Ending Story*. 1983. Doubleday. 1st. ils. red/gr prt. VG/dj. B5. $50.00

ENDORE, Guy. *Werewolf in Paris*. 1933. Grosset Dunlap. G. L1. $50.00

ENG, Steve. *Jimmy Buffett*. 1996. St Martin. 1st. F/dj. T11. $25.00

ENGDAHL, Sylvia Louise. *Planet-Girded Suns: Man's View of Other Solar Systems*. 1974. Atheneum. 1st. NF/VG. O4. $15.00

ENGEBRETSON, Pat. *History of Butte County, South Dakota, 1988*. 1989. Dallas, TX. Curtis Media. F. A19. $125.00

ENGEL, Alan. *Variant*. 1988. DIF. 1st. F/NF. M21. $15.00

ENGEL, George. *Fainting: Physiological & Psychological Considerations*. 1950. Springfield, IL. Chas Thomas. 1st. 141p. NF. C14. $18.00

ENGELMAN & JOY. *Two Hundred Years of Military Medicine*. 1975. Ft Detrick. 1st. 56p. wrp. A13. $15.00

ENGER, L.L. *Sinner's League*. 1994. Penzler (S&S). 1st. F/dj. P8. $15.00

ENGERS, Joe. *Great Book of Wildfowl Decoys*. 1990. Thunder Bay. folio. 300 photos. 320p. F/VG. A4. $55.00

ENGLE, Paul. *Golden Child*. 1962. Dutton. 1st. ils. cloth. VG. B27. $45.00

ENGLE, William H. *State of the Accounts of the County Lieutenants...1777-1789*. 1896. PA. CM Busch. 3 vol. teg. half leather/marbled brd. B18. $125.00

ENGLEBERT, Omer. *Last of the Conquistadors: Junipero Serra.* 1956. NY. Harcourt Brace. 1st. trans from French. VG. O4. $15.00

ENGLISH, Barbara. *War for a Persian Lady.* 1971. Houghton Mifflin. VG/dj. M20. $22.00

ENGLISH, John. *Kindergarten Soldier-Military Thought of Lawrence of Arabia.* 1985. Toronto. Royal Canadian Military Inst. yearbook. NF/wrp. M7. $22.50

ENNIS, Michael. *Duchess of Milan.* 1992. NY. Viking. 1st. NF/NF. H11. $15.00

ENRIGHT, D.J. *Ill at Ease: Writers on Ailments.* 1989. London. 365p. A13. $30.00

ENROTH, Ronald. *Churches That Abuse.* 1992. Zondervan. 231p. VG/dj. B29. $8.00

ENSIGN, Georgianne. *Great Beginnings: Opening Lines of Great Novels.* 1993. 256p. F/F. A4. $25.00

ENSIGN, Georgianne. *Great Endings: Closing Lines of Great Novels.* 1995. ils. 276p. F/F. A4. $25.00

ENYEART, James L. *Jerry N Uelsmann: Twenty-Five Years, a Retrospective.* 1982. NYGS. 1st. photos. VG/dj. M17. $50.00

EPHRON, Nora. *Scribble Scribble.* 1978. Knopf. 1st. NF/dj. A24. $25.00

EPLING, Carl. *Californian Salvias.* 1938. St Louis. ils. VG/wrp. B26. $42.50

EPPLE, Anne Orth. *Field Guide to Plants of Arizona.* 1995. Mesa. ils. 347p. sc. AN. B26. $25.00

EPPS, John. *Life of John Walker, MD.* 1832. London. Whittaker Treacher. 342p. quarter roan/marbled brd. G7. $135.00

EPSTEIN, Daniel Mark. *No Vacancies in Hell.* 1973. NY. Liveright. ARC/1st. inscr/dtd 1977. F/NF. L3. $40.00

EPSTEIN, Daniel Mark. *Young Men's Gold.* 1978. Woodstock. Overlook. 1st. inscr. F/dj. L3. $45.00

EPSTEIN & VALENTINO. *Those Lips, Those Eyes.* 1992. NY. Birch Lane. unp. VG/dj. C5. $15.00

ERDOES, Richard. *Picture History of Rome.* 1965. Macmillan. 1st. ils. 60p. cloth. F/torn. D4. $35.00

ERDOES & ORTIZ. *American Indian Myths & Legends.* 1984. Pantheon. NF/wrp. B9. $15.00

ERDRICH, Louise. *Antelope Wife.* 1998. Harper Flamingo. ARC/UP. F. B30. $25.00

ERDRICH, Louise. *Baptism of Desire.* 1989. Harper Row. 1st. sgn. F/F. D10. $50.00

ERDRICH, Louise. *Beet Queen.* 1986. NY. Holt. 1st. sgn. F/F. D10/R14. $50.00

ERDRICH, Louise. *Beet Queen.* 1986. NY. Holt. 1st. F/F. H11/M25. $25.00

ERDRICH, Louise. *Blue Jay's Dance.* 1995. Harper Collins. 1st. sgn. F/dj. R14. $40.00

ERDRICH, Louise. *Jacklight.* 1984. HRW. 1st. sgn. F/wrp. D10. $195.00

ERDRICH, Louise. *Love Medicine.* 1984. HRW. 1st. F/NF. D10. $125.00

ERDRICH, Louise. *Tales of Burning Love.* 1996. Harper Collins. ARC. F/wrp. R14. $40.00

ERDRICH, Louise. *Tracks.* 1988. Holt. 1st. 226p. F/NF. B19. $10.00

ERDRICH, Louise. *Tracks.* 1988. NY. Holt. ARC. sgn. F/F. D10. $50.00

ERENS, Patricia. *Films of Shirley MacLane.* 1978. NY. AS Barnes. 202p. VG/dj. D4. $35.00

ERHARDT, Walter. *Hemerocallis.* 1992. Portland. photos. 160p. AN/dj. B26. $30.00

ERHLICH & ERHLICH. *Population, Resources, Environment: Issues in Human Ecology.* 1970. WH Freeman. 1st. 383p. VG. S15. $10.00

ERICKSON, Erik H. *Gandhi's Truth: On the Origins of Militant Nonviolence.* 1969. Norton. 1st. VG/clip. N2. $10.00

ERICKSON, Steve. *Arc d'X.* 1993. Poseidon. 1st. sgn. F/dj. R14. $45.00

ERICKSON, Steve. *Days Between Stations.* 1985. Poseidon. 1st. sgn. rem mk. F/dj. R14. $75.00

ERICSON, Eric E. *Guide to Colored Steuben Glass 1903-1933. Book 2.* 1965. self pub. 1st. 10 pl. 162p. stiff wrp. H1. $28.00

ERNSBERGER, George. *Mountain King.* 1978. Morrow. 1st. F/F. H11. $45.00

ERSHOFF, Peter. *Little Magic Horse.* 1942. Macmillan. 1st thus. ils Vera Bock. VG/G. P2. $35.00

ERSKINE, Jim. *Bert & Susie's Messy Tale.* 1979. Crown. 1st. 24mo. unp. F/NF. C14. $14.00

ERSKINE, John. *Helen Retires: An Opera in Three Acts.* 1934. Bobbs Merrill. 1st. 8vo. 107p. VG/dj. B20. $40.00

ERSKINE, Margaret. *Dead by Now.* 1953. Crime Club. 1st Am. VG/G. G8. $25.00

ERSKINE, Payne. *Harper & the King's Horse.* 1905. Chicago. Bl Sky Pr. 1/500. ils SK Smith. gilt maroon cloth. F1. $100.00

ERVIN, Keith. *Fragile Majesty.* 1989. Seattle. 272p. VG. S15. $7.50

ESAREY, Logan. *Indiana Home.* 1954. Bloomington. IU. 1/1550. ils Franklin Booth/Bruce Rogers. F/VG case. F1. $50.00

ESBACH, Lloyd Arthur. *Tyrant of Time.* 1955. Fantasy. 1st. Donald Grant bdg. F/dj. P3. $20.00

ESCOFFIER, A. *Escoffier Cook Book.* 1941. Crown. BC. G/dj. A16. $12.00

ESCOFFIER, A. *Kochkunst Fuhrer: Le Guide Culinaire, Deutsche...* 1904. Frankfurt. 806p. emb leather. VG. E6. $225.00

ESCOFFIER, A. *L'Aire-Memoire Culinaire.* 1919. Paris. 360p. G+. E6. $50.00

ESDAILE, Arundell. *Autolycus' Pack & Other Light Wares...* 1940. London. Grafton. 1st. H13. $65.00

ESHBACH, Lloyd Arthur. *Over My Shoulder: Reflections on a Science Fiction Era.* 1983. Oswald Train. 1st. sgn. NF/dj. P3. $30.00

ESIN, Emel. *Mecca the Blessed: Madinah the Radiant.* 1963. NY. Crown. 1st. 4to. 222p. VG. W1. $50.00

ESKELUNG, Karl. *Vagabond Fever: A Gay Journey in Land of Andes.* 1954. Chicago. Rand McNally. 1st. 240p. dj. F3. $15.00

ESKENAZI, Gerald. *Lip.* 1993. Morrow. 1st. F/VG+. P8. $20.00

ESPY, Hilda. *Another World: Central America.* 1970. Viking. 1st. 311p. dj. F3. $15.00

ESQUIVEL, Laura. *Like Water for Chocolate.* 1992. Doubleday. 1st Am. F/dj. O11. $65.00

ESSOE & LEE. *Cecil B DeMille: Man & His Pictures.* 1970. NY. Castle. rpt. ils. VG/dj. C9. $25.00

ESTERGREEN, M. Morgan. *Kit Carson: Portrait in Courage.* 1962. OK U. 1st. ils. 320p. D11. $50.00

ESTLEMAN, Loren D. *City of Widows.* 1991. NY. Forge. 1st. F/dj. A23. $32.00

ESTLEMAN, Loren D. *Kill Zone.* 1984. Mysterious. 1st. F/NF. M23. $30.00

ESTLEMAN, Loren D. *Lady Yesterday.* 1987. Houghton Mifflin. 1st. F/F. B3. $25.00

ESZTERHAS, Joe. *Nark!* 1974. Straight Arrow. 1st. NF/VG. M19. $25.00

ESZTERHAS & ROBERTS. *Thirteen Seconds: Confrontation at Kent State.* 1970. Dodd Mead. sgns. 308p. VG/dj. B18. $27.50

ETCHECOPAR & HUE. *Birds of North Africa From Canary Islands to Red Sea.* 1967. Edinburgh. 1st Eng-language. ils/24 mc pl. 612p. cloth. NF/dj. C12. $85.00

ETCHISON, Dennis. *California Gothic.* 1995. Dreamhaven. 1st ltd. 1/750. sgn. ils JK Potter. AN/dj. S18. $39.00

ETCHISON, Dennis. *Cutting Edge.* 1986. Doubleday. 1st. F/NF. S18. $25.00

ETCHISON, Dennis. *Shadow Man.* 1993. Dell. 1st. sgn. F/dj. S18. $30.00

ETHERIDGE, Kenneth. *Viola, Furgy, Bobbi & Me.* 1989. Holiday House. 1st. F/VG. P8. $12.50

ETS, Marie Hall. *Mister Penny.* 1935. Viking. 1st. obl 12mo. 48p. VG. D1. $150.00

ETTENBERG, Eugene M. *Type for Books & Advertising.* 1947. Van Nostrand. 1st. 4to. 160p. cloth. F/NF. O10. $35.00

ETTLESON, Abraham. *Lewis Carroll's Through the Looking Glass Decoded.* 1966. NY. Philosophical Lib. 84p. F/VG. A4. $125.00

EUBANK, H. Ragland. *Authentic Guide Book of Historic Northern Neck of Virginia.* 1934. Whittet Shepperson. ils/map. 108p. G+. B10. $25.00

EUBANK, Keith. *Summit at Teheran: Untold Story.* 1985. Morrow. 1st. sm 4to. 528p. NF/F. W2. $45.00

EUNSON, Robert. *Pearl King: Story of Fabulous Mikimoto.* 1955. NY. Greenberg. 1st. 8vo. 243p. VG+/dj. B20. $20.00

EURIPEDES. *Alcestis.* 1930. London. 1/260. trans/sgn Aldington. T9. $45.00

EVAN, Joe. *Biographical Dictionary of Rocky Mountain Naturalists.* 1981. Utrecht. 253p. cloth. AN. A10. $50.00

EVANOFF, Vlad. *Hunting Secrets of the Experts.* 1964. NY. photos. 251p. F/dj. A17. $12.50

EVANOVICH, Janet. *One for the Money.* 1994. Scribner. 1st. sgn. F/dj. M15. $100.00

EVANS, E.P. *Criminal Prosecution & Capital Punishment of Animals.* 1906. London. Heinemann. later cloth. VG. M11. $250.00

EVANS, Edna. *Tales From the Grand Canyon, Some True, Some Tall.* 1985. Northland. stiff pict wrp. F7. $13.00

EVANS, Eli N. *Judah P Benjamin: Jewish Confederate.* 1988. Free/Macmillan. 1st. NF/dj. A14. $28.00

EVANS, Eli N. *Provincials: Personal History of Jew in the South.* 1973. Atheneum. 2nd. 369p. VG/G. B10. $35.00

EVANS, Emory G. *Thomas Nelson & the Revolution in Virginia.* (1978). Bicentennial Comm. 57p. wrp. B10. $15.00

EVANS, Henry. *Botanical Prints.* 1977. SF. ils/pl/linocuts. VG/tattered. B26. $32.50

EVANS, J. Warren. *Horse.* 1977. WH Freeman. 1st. tall 8vo. 766p. F. H1. $12.00

EVANS, Joan. *Flowering of the Middle Ages.* 1966. McGraw Hill. 1st. ils/index. VG/dj. B5. $37.50

EVANS, Lawton B. *Trail Blazers: Pioneers of the Northwest.* 1925. Springfield. Milton Bradley. 1st. NF/VG. T11. $35.00

EVANS, Richard. *McEnroe: Rage for Perfection.* 1982. S&S. 1st. photos. 192p. NF/VG. S14. $8.00

EVANS, Walker. *Walker Evans.* 1971. NY. MOMA. sq 4to. ils. 189p. VG/dj. F1. $25.00

EVANS, William Bacon. *Jonathan Evans & His Time 1759-1839...* 1959. Boston. Christopher. 1st. 192p. VG. V3. $25.00

EVANS & EVANS. *Piety Promoted in Collection of Dying Sayings...Quakers...* 1854. Phil. Friends Book Store. new/completed ed. 4 vol. leather. V3. $125.00

EVELYN, John. *Memoirs for My Grand-Son.* 1926. Bloomsbury. Nonesuch. 1st thus. 1/1250. emb limp vellum. F/tissue dj/box. M24. $85.00

EVENSON, Brian. *Altmann's Tongue.* 1994. Knopf. AP. author's 1st book. NF/prt wrp. S9. $25.00

EVEREST, Allan S. *Rum Across the Border: Prohibition Era in Northern NY.* 1976. Syracuse. 1st. photos. VG/dj. M17. $15.00

EVERETT, Edward. *Life of George Washington.* 1860. Sheldon. 348p. VG. B10. $35.00

EVERETT, M. *Natural History of Owls.* 1977. London. photos. 156p. F/VG. M12. $20.00

EVERETT, Percival. *Suder.* 1983. Viking. 1st. F/VG. P8. $25.00

EVERETT, Percival. *Walk Me to the Distance.* 1985. Ticknor Fields. 1st. sgn. F/dj. R11. $50.00

EVERETT, Percival. *Zulus.* 1990. Sag Harbor. Permanent. 1st. F/dj. R14. $40.00

EVERETT, William. *Double Play.* 1874 (1870). Lee Shepard. VG. P8. $225.00

EVERS, Crabbe. *Duffy House: Fear in Fenway (#4).* 1993. NY. Morrow. 1st. F/F. H11. $20.00

EVERS, Crabbe. *Duffy House: Tigers Burning (#5).* 1994. Morrow. 1st. F/dj. P8. $15.00

EVERSON, David. *Suicide Squeeze.* 1991. St Martin. 1st. F/dj. P8. $12.50

EVERSON, William. *Hollywood Bedlam.* 1994. NY. Carol. 253p. VG/wrp. C5. $12.50

EVERSON, William. *Masks of Drought.* 1980. Blk Sparrow. 1/500. 92p. F. F1. $45.00

EVERSON, William. *Novum Psalterium Pii XII.* 1955. LA. Everson. 1/20 (48 total). maroon gilt cloth. w/ephemera. F/case. B24. $5,000.00

EVERSON, William. *Residual Years.* 1948. New Directions. 1st/expanded. VG/G. L3. $65.00

EWAN, Joseph. *Synopsis of the North American Species of Delphinium.* 1945. Boulder. ils/photos. 190p. B26. $50.00

EWEING, Juliana Horatia. *Story of a Short Life.* ca 1910. Little Brn. sm 8vo. 130p+ads. pict cloth. NF. B20. $25.00

EWELL, Alice Maude. *Virginia Scene; or, Life in Old Prince.* (1931). JP Bell. ils. 228p. VG. B10. $65.00

EWERS, John C. *Artists of the Old West.* 1965. Garden City. 1st. ils. 240p. E1. $75.00

EWING & EWING. *Ewing Genealogy With Cognate Branches.* (1919). np. 185p. G. S5. $75.00

EXLEY, Frederick. *Fan's Notes.* 1968. Harper. 1st. NF/dj. B4. $275.00

EXMAN, Eugene. *House of Harper, One Hundred Fifty Years of Publishing.* 1967. Harper Row. 1st. 8vo. 236p. F/dj. O1. $25.00

EYLES, Allen. *Cary Grant Film Album.* 1971. London. Ian Allen. 1st. VG/sans. C9. $30.00

EYLES, Desmond. *Doulton Lambeth Wares.* 1975. London. Hutchinson. 1st. 4to. 179p. gilt bl cloth. VG/dj. H1. $125.00

FABRE, D.G. *Beyond the River of the Dead.* (1963). London. Travel BC. 191p. F3. $15.00

FACKENHEIM, Emil L. *Quest for Past & Future: Essays in Jewish Theology.* 1968. IU. 336p. VG/G+. S3. $22.00

FACKLER, Elizabeth. *Arson.* 1984. Dodd Mead. 1st. author's 1st novel. F/F. T2. $20.00

FACKLER, Elizabeth. *Barbed Wire.* 1986. St Martin. 1st. F/F. T2. $15.00

FADIMAN, Clifton. *Joys of Wine.* 1975. Abrams. lg 4to. 449p. F/torn. T10. $75.00

FAIR, A.A.; see Gardner, Erle Stanley.

FAIR, Charles M. *Dying Self.* 1969. Middletown, CT. Wesleyan U. 240p. gray cloth. VG/dj. G1. $25.00

FAIR, Charles M. *Physical Foundations of the Psyche.* 1963. Wesleyan U. 287p. gr cloth. G1. $25.00

FAIRBAIRN, Henry. *Defence of William Penn, From Charges Contained...* 1849. Phil. Rakestraw. 1st. 38p. V3. $20.00

FAIRBAIRN, Roger; see Carr, John Dickson.

FAIRCHILD, David. *Garden Islands of the Great East.* 1943. Scribner. 1st. 8vo. 239p. F. A22. $30.00

FAIRLEIGH, Runa. *Old-Fashioned Mystery.* 1983. Denys. 1st. VG/dj. M2. $20.00

FAIRMONT, Ethel. *Rhymes for Kindly Children.* 1927. Volland. 46th. 8vo. ils brd. R5. $125.00

FAKHRY, Ahmed. *Pyramids.* 1969. Chicago. 1st. ils/maps. VG/dj. W1. $10.00

FALK, Edwin A. *Fighting Bob Evans.* 1931. ils. VG. M17. $17.50

FALK, K. George. *Chemistry of Enzyme Actions.* 1924. NY. Chemical Catalog Co. 249p. cloth. A10. $8.00

FALKNER, J. Meade. *Last Stradivarius.* 1896. Appleton. 1st. VG. M2. $75.00

FALL, Bernard B. *Hell in a Very Small Place: Siege of Dien Bien Phu.* 1967. Phil. ils/photos/maps. 515p. G. B18. $22.50

FALL, Thomas. *Ordeal of Running Standing.* 1970. NY. McCall. 1st. F/VG clip. L3. $50.00

FALLOWELL, Duncan. *Drug Tales.* 1979. Hamish Hamilton. 1st. F/F. P3. $20.00

FALLOWS & TRUITT. *Know Thyself, a Word at the Right Time.* 1911. SA Mulliken. salesman's copy. full leather. G-. B18. $22.50

FALS-BORDA, Orlando. *Peasant Society in the Columbian Andes.* 1962. Gainesville. 1st. 377p. dj. F3. $15.00

FALWELL, Jerry. *Aflame for God.* 1979. Nashville. Nelson. 2nd. inscr. A23. $32.00

FANNER, Janet. *Cubical City: With an Afterword by the Author.* 1974. Carbondale. S IL U. Lost American Fiction series. 1st thus. F/clip. Q1. $40.00

FANNIN, Cole. *Leave It to Beaver.* 1962. Whitman. TVTI. VG. P3. $15.00

FANNIN, Cole. *Rin Tin Tin & the Ghost Wagon Train.* 1958. Whitman. TVTI. VG. P3. $10.00

FANNIN, Cole. *Sea Hunt.* 1960. Whitman. TVTI. F. P3. $20.00

FANNING, Edmund. *Voyages & Discoveries in South Seas 1792-1832.* 1924. Salem. Marine Research Soc. 32 pl. 355p. P4. $135.00

FANNING, L.M. *Our Oil Resources.* 1945. NY. McGraw Hill. 331p. NF. D8. $10.00

FANTE, John. *Brotherhood of the Grape.* 1977. Houghton. 1st. F/NF. M25. $45.00

FANTE, John. *Dreams From Bunker Hill.* 1982. Blk Sparrow. 1st. F/dj. M25. $45.00

FARAGO, L. *Game of Foxes.* 1971 (1971). 696p. F/G+. E6. $13.00

FARAGO, Ladislas. *Abyssinia on the Eve.* 1935. Putnam. 4th. 8vo. ils/map ep. 286p. VG. W1. $22.00

FARBER, Eduard. *Nobel Prize Winners in Chemistry 1901-1950.* 1953. NY. Henry Schumann. 1st. ils. 291p. xl. dj. K3. $15.00

FARBER, Norma. *How Does It Feel to Be Old?* 1979. Dutton. 1st. ils TS Hyman. 34p. NF/worn. D4. $40.00

FARBER, Seymour. *Cytologic Diagnosis of Lung Cancer.* 1950. Springfield. 1st. sgn. 4to. 59p. A13. $50.00

FARHI, Moris. *Last of Days.* 1983. Crown. 1st. VG/VG. P3. $18.00

FARINA, Richard. *Been Down So Long It Looks Like Up to Me.* 1966. Random. 1st. author's 1st book. F/NF. M25. $100.00

FARINA, Richard. *Long Time Coming & Long Time Gone.* 1969. Random. 1st. F/dj. Q1. $50.00

FARIS, John T. *Old Churches & Meeting Houses in & Around Philadelphia.* 1926. Lippincott. 1st. 261p. VG. V3. $24.00

FARIS, John T. *Old Roads Out of Philadelphia.* 1917. Lippincott. VG. O3. $35.00

FARJEON, Eleanor. *Cherrystones.* nd (1942). Lippincott. 1st Am. sm 8vo. 61p. VG+/G+. C14. $25.00

FARJEON, Eleanor. *Children's Bells.* 1960. NY. Walck. 1st Am. ils Peggy Fortum. 212p. coth. NF/dj. D4. $45.00

FARJEON, Eleanor. *Gipsy & Ginger.* 1920. London. Dent. 1st. 151p. VG. P2. $55.00

FARJEON, Eleanor. *Martin Pippin in the Apple Orchard.* 1922 (1921). Stokes. 1st Am. 8vo. gr cloth. VG/G+. T5. $60.00

FARJEON, Eleanor. *Then There Were Three.* 1965. Lippincott. 174p. cloth. F/dj. D4. $40.00

FARJEON & FARJEON. *Kings & Queens.* nd (1932). London/NY. Gollancz/Dutton. 1st. 79p. VG/dj. D4. $75.00

FARLEY, Jim. *Jim Farley's Story: The Roosevelt Years.* (1948). McGraw. 3rd. inscr. 388p. VG/fair. B22. $9.00

FARLEY, Walter. *Black Stallion & Satan.* 1949. RAndom. 1st. VG/G. O3. $58.00

FARLEY, Walter. *Black Stallion's Courage.* 1956. Random. 1st. VG/VG. O3. $45.00

FARLEY, Walter. *Black Stallion's Filly.* 1952. Random. 1st. 309p. VG/dj. M20. $30.00

FARLEY, Walter. *Island Stallion Races.* 1955. Random. 1st. 256p. VG/dj. M20. $22.50

FARMER, Bernard J. *Gentle Art of Book Collecting.* 1950. Thorsons. 1st. VG/G. P3. $25.00

FARMER, E.J. *Resources of the Rocky Mountains...* 1883. Cleveland. 196p. VG. B18. $30.00

FARMER, Fannie Merritt. *Boston Cooking-School Cook Book.* 1924. Little Brn. fair. A16. $12.00

FARMER, Philip Jose. *Dark Is the Sun.* 1979. Del Rey. 1st. F/F. P3. $20.00

FARMER, Philip Jose. *Dayworld Rebel.* 1987. Putnam. 1st. F/F. H11. $20.00

FARMER, Philip Jose. *Flesh.* 1968. Doubleday. 1st. sgn. F/F. M2. $325.00

FARMER, Philip Jose. *Lord Tyger.* 1970. Doubleday. 1st. sgn. NF/dj. M2. $150.00

FARMER, Philip Jose. *Love Song*. 1983. McMillan. 1st. 1/500. sgn. F/F. M2/P3. $85.00

FARMER, Philip Jose. *Magic Labyrinth*. 1980. Berkley. 1st. F/F. M2. $13.00

FARMER, Philip Jose. *Night of Light*. 1975. Garland. 1st hc. F/sans. M2. $60.00

FARMER, Philip Jose. *Unreasoning Mask*. 1981. Putnam. 1st. VG/VG. P3. $20.00

FARNHAM, Eilza A. *Woman & Her Era*. 1864. NY. AJ Davis. 1st. gilt blk cloth. M24. $250.00

FARNOL, Jeffery. *Shadow*. 1929. Little Brn. 1st Am. VG. M2. $27.00

FARR, Finis. *Margaret Mitchell of Atlanta*. 1965. Morrow. 1st. 244p. cloth. VG/dj. M20. $50.00

FARR, John; see Webb, Jack.

FARR, Robert. *Electronic Criminals*. 1975. McGraw Hill. 1st. VG/VG. P3. $15.00

FARRAR, Frederick M. *Fred Farrar's Type Book*. 1927. Harper. 1st. ils. VG/dj. K3. $20.00

FARRAR, Mrs. John. *Recollections of Seventy Years*. 1866. Ticknor Fields. 331p. V3. $12.00

FARRARS, E.X. *Neck in a Noose*. 1943. Doubleday Crime Club. 1st Am. F/VG. M15. $45.00

FARRELL, James T. *Brand New Life*. 1968. Doubleday. 1st. F/VG+. A24. $30.00

FARRELL, James T. *Fate of Writing in America*. 1946. New Directions. 1st. inscr. NF/stapled wrp. B4. $125.00

FARRELL, James T. *Gas-House McGinty*. 1933. Vanguard. 1st. NF/dj. Q1. $450.00

FARRELL, James T. *Guillotine Party & Other Stories*. 1935. Vanguard. 1st. VG/dj. M22. $140.00

FARRELL, James T. *Lonely for the Future*. 1966. Doubleday. 1st. 263p. G. W2. $15.00

FARRELL, James T. *Note on Literary Criticism*. 1937. Vanguard. 1st. F/NF. B2. $75.00

FARRELL & KOCH. *Talking to the Sun*. 1985. HRW/Metro Mus Art. 1st. 112p. F/F. D4. $30.00

FARRIER, Denis. *Country Vet*. 1973. NY. Taplinger. 1st Am. VG/G. O3. $15.00

FARRIS, John. *Fury*. 1976. Playboy. 1st. VG/fair. P3. $20.00

FARRIS, John. *Sacrifice*. nd (1994). Forge. UP. sgn. F/prt wrp. M22. $65.00

FARRIS, John. *Scare Tactics*. 1988. Tor. 1st. VG/VG. P3. $18.00

FARRIS, John. *Sharp Practice*. 1974. S&S. 1st. 286p. half red cloth/gray brd. F/dj. H1. $28.00

FARRIS, John. *Uninvited*. 1982. Delacorte. 1st. F/F. M21. $25.00

FARSHLER, Earl R. *Riding & Training*. 1959. Van Nostrand. 2nd. 340p. VG/clip. M20. $15.00

FARWELL, George. *Mask of Asia: Philippines Today*. 1967. NY. Praeger. sm 4to. 227p. as new/VG. P1. $8.00

FASSET, Norman C. *Sping Flora of Wisconsin*. 1938. Madison. 12mo. VG. A22. $10.00

FASSETT & OGDEN. *Manual of Aquatic Plants*. (1957). Madison. revised ed. ils/figures. 405p. cloth. VG/VG. M12. $25.00

FAST, Howard. *Max*. 1982. Houghton Mifflin. 1st. F/F. B35. $18.00

FAST, Howard. *Outsider*. 1984. Houghton Mifflin. 1st. VG/VG. P3. $15.00

FAST, Howard. *Pledge*. 1988. Houghton Mifflin. 1st. 324p. F/F. W2. $35.00

FAST, Howard. *Spartacus*. 1951. NY. self pub. 1st. sgn. F/VG. B4. $250.00

FAST, Jonathan. *Mortal Gods*. 1978. Harper Row. 1st. F/F. P3. $15.00

FAST, Julius. *Model for Murder*. 1956. Rinehart. 1st. F/dj. M15. $45.00

FATOUT, Paul. *Mark Twain in Virginia City*. 1964. IU. 1st/1st prt. cream cloth. NF/dj. M24. $30.00

FATOUT, Paul. *Meadow Lake Gold Town*. 1969. Bloomington. IU. 1st. 8vo. 178p. gilt brn cloth. as new/dj. K7. $40.00

FAULCONER & KEYS. *Foundations of Anesthesiology*. 1965. Springfield. 1st. 2 vol. A13. $250.00

FAULK, John Henry. *Fear on Trial: Story of His Six-Year Battle...* 1964. S&S. 1st. F/F. V4. $20.00

FAULK, Odie B. *Arizona: Short History*. 1970. OK U. 1st. ils/bibliography. 265p. F/NF. B19. $20.00

FAULK, Odie B. *Land of Many Frontiers*. 1968. Oxford. 1st. 8vo. brn cloth. dj. F7. $35.00

FAULK, Odie B. *Tombstone, Myth & Reality*. 1972. Oxford. 1st. 242p. VG. J2. $69.00

FAULKNER, David. *The Short Season*. 1986. NY Times. 1st. iNF/NF R16. $40.00

FAULKNER, Georgene. *Old English Nursery Tales*. 1916. Chicago. 1st. ils Milo Winter. 8vo. blk cloth/label. R5. $125.00

FAULKNER, William. *Afternoon of a Cow*. 1991. Windover. 1/200. 1st separate appearance. F/wrp. B2. $75.00

FAULKNER, William. *Big Woods*. 1955. NY. 1st. VG/VG. B5. $125.00

FAULKNER, William. *Faulkner & Race*. 1987. Jackson, MS. 1st. edit Fowler/Abadie. F/F. B3. $25.00

FAULKNER, William. *Light in August*. 1932. Smith Haas. 1st. 480p. cloth. VG/dj/glassine dj cover. M20. $750.00

FAULKNER, William. *Mansion*. (1959). Random. 1st/1st prt. gilt bl cloth. F/F. M24. $150.00

FAULKNER, William. *Marble Faun/Green Bough*. 1965. Random. 1st thus. F/VG clip. B4. $65.00

FAULKNER, William. *Mirrors of Chartres Street*. 1953. Minneapolis. Faulkner Studies. 1st. 1/1000. F/dj. B24. $325.00

FAULKNER, William. *Miss Zilphia Gant*. 1932. Dallas. BC of Texas. 1st. 1/300. gilt rust cloth. F. M24. $2,250.00

FAULKNER, William. *New Orleans Sketches*. 1958. Rutgers. 1st Am. gilt quarter maroon cloth. F/dj. M24. $100.00

FAULKNER, William. *Reivers*. 1962. Random. 1st. F/VG+. T11. $50.00

FAULKNER, William. *Sanctuary*. 1931. Cape/Smith. 1st/1st prt. gray/magenta brd. M24. $200.00

FAULKNER, William. *Selected Letters...Edited by Joseph Blotner*. 1976. Franklin Lib. 1st. intro Albert Erskine. full leather. F. B4. $150.00

FAULKNER, William. *Spotted Horses*. 1989. U of SC. 1st separate of 600 deluxe. ils/sgn Saunders. F/case. A24. $195.00

FAULKNER, William. *Stallion Road*. 1989. MS U. 1st. F/dj. A24. $30.00

FAULKNER, William. *Town*. 1957. Random. 1st. F/G. M19. $45.00

FAUST, Frederick S. *Notebooks & Poems of Max Brand*. 1957. Dodd Mead. 1/750. #d. F/box. M2. $75.00

FAUST, Fredrick S. *Futitives' Fire*. 1991. Putnam. 1st. F/F. P3. $19.00

FAUST, Fredrick S. *On the Trail of Four*. 1967. Dodd Mead. rpt. F/NF. M15. $35.00

FAUST, Fredrick S. *Thunderer*. 1933. Derrydale. VG. O3. $85.00

FAUST, Ron. *Tombs of Blue Ice*. 1974. Bobbs Merrill. 1st. VG/VG. P3. $20.00

FAUSTER, Carl U. *Libby Glass Since 1918*. 1979. Len Beach Pr. 4to. 1300+ pieces ils on 71 mc pl. 415p. as new/dj. H1. $300.00

FAVOR, E.H. *Fruit-Growers Guide-Book*. 1911. St Joseph MO Fruit Grower. 285p. cloth. VG. A10. $20.00

FAVOUR, Alpheus H. *Old Bill Williams, Mountain Man.* 1936. NC C. Southwestern Century #30. 229p. VG/dj. J2. $175.00

FAWAD, D. *Victory Denied: Rise of Air Power & Defeat of Germany 1920.* 1987. 1st Am. F/VG. E6. $12.00

FAWCETT, Clara Hallard. *Dolls: A Guide for Collectors.* 1947. NY. Linquist. 1st. sgn. 194p. VG. B11. $45.00

FAWCETT, Clara Hallard. *Paper Dolls: A Guide to Costume.* 1951. HL Lindquist. 1st probable. lg 8vo. VG+. C8. $50.00

FAWCETT, E. Douglas. *Hartmann the Anarchist.* 1893. Arnold. 1st. VG. P3. $200.00

FAWCETT, P.H. *Lost Trails, Lost Cities.* 1953. NY. 1st Am. 332p. VG. B18. $17.50

FAX, Elton C. *Through Black Eyes: Journeys of a Black Artist...* 1974. Dodd Mead. 1st. 203p. F/NF. B4. $100.00

FAY, Charles Edey. *Mary Celeste: Odyssey of an Abandoned Ship.* 1942. Salem. Peabody Mus. ltd (not abridged). 1/1000. VG. O7. $150.00

FEATHERS, Davis L. *Camellia.* 1978. Columbia, SC. 8vo. 476p. cloth. VG/dj. A22. $30.00

FEATHERSTONHAUGH, G.W. *Canoe Voyage Up the Minnay Sotor.* 1970. MN Hist Soc. facsimile 1847 ed. cloth/case. A17. $25.00

FEELEY, Pat. *Best Friend.* 1977. Dutton. 1st. F/F. P3. $20.00

FEIBLEMAN, Peter S. *Charlie Boy.* 1980. Little Brn. 1st. VG/VG. P3. $15.00

FEID, Richard. *Upper Ottawa Valley to 1855: A Collection of Documents.* 1990. Toronto. Champlain Soc. 354p. gilt red cloth. F. P4. $95.00

FEIERBERG, M.Z. *Whither? And Other Stories.* 1972-73. JPS. 240p. VG/dj. S3. $23.00

FEIFER, George. *Tennozan: Battle of Okinawa & the Atomic Bomb.* 1992. nY. photos/ map/index. 622p. VG/VG. S16. $27.50

FEIFER. *Great Comic Book Heroes.* 1965. 1st. ils. 189p. F/dj. M13. $38.00

FEIFFER, Jules. *Carnal Knowledge.* 1971. NY. 1st. inscr. F/NF clip. A11. $80.00

FEIGENBAUM, Edward A. *Fifth Generation.* 1983. Addison-Wesley. 1st. 275p. NF/NF. W2. $25.00

FEIKEMA, Feike; see Manfred, Frederick.

FEINBLATT, Henry. *Transfusion of Blood.* 1926. NY. 1st. 137p. A13. $60.00

FEINGOLD, Henry L. *Zion in America: Jewish Experience in Colonial Times...* 1974. Twayne. 357p. VG/G+. S3. $21.00

FEIS, Herbert. *Japan Subdued.* 1961. VG/dj. K3. $20.00

FEIST, Raymond. *Silverthorn.* 1985. Doubleday. 1st. F/dj. M2. $35.00

FEJES, Claire. *People of the Noatak.* 1966. Knopf. 1st. inscr. 8vo. 368p. F/dj. P4. $45.00

FELDBORG, A.A. *Tour of Zealand.* 1807. Phil. Bartram Reynolds. 1st. 16mo. 131p. contemporary calf. M1. $200.00

FELDMAN, Anette. *Handmade Lace & Patterns.* 1975. NY. Harper Row. 1st. 4to. 208p. F/dj. T10. $75.00

FELDMAN & HATA. *Josephus, Judaism & Christianity.* 1987. Wayne State. 1st. 448p. F/dj. W3. $48.00

FELICE, Cynthia. *Downtime.* 1985. Bluejay. 1st. F/F. P3. $20.00

FELLER, Bob. *How to Pitch.* 1948. NY. 1st. VG/fair. B5. $20.00

FELLER, John Quentin. *Dorflinger: America's Finest Glass, 1852-1921* 1988. Antique Publications. 550+ photos. 374p. as new/dj. H1. $85.00

FELLINI, Frederico. *La Dolce Vita.* 1961. Ballantine. 1st. wrp. A17. $15.00

FELSKI, Elsa. *Blumen-Fibel.* 1959. Berlin. FA Herbig. 2 vol. 8vo. cloth. VG/djs/case. A22. $65.00

FELSKI, Elsa. *Book of Wild Flowes.* 1956. Yoseloff. 1st Am. 8vo. 160 full-p pl. VG/dj. A22. $35.00

FELTOE, Charles. *Memorials of John Flint South...1841-63.* 1884. London. 1st. 216p. A13. $45.00

FENELON. *Selections From Writings of Fenelon...By a Lady.* 1829. Boston. Hilliard Gray Little. 283p. gr leather. G. V3. $35.00

FENN, George Manville. *Seven Frozen Sailors.* 1896. New Amsterdam Book Co. 1st. VG. M2. $40.00

FENNER, Phyllis R. *Cowboys, Cowboys, Cowboys.* 1950. Franklin Watts. dj. A19. $15.00

FENTON, Robert W. *Big Swingers.* 1967. Prentice Hall. VG/VG. P3. $50.00

FENTON & FENTON. *Rock Book.* 1950. Doubleday. 357p. cloth. NF. D8. $20.00

FENWICK, Robert W. *Red Fenwick's West.* 1956. Denver. Sage Books. sgn. dj. A19. $30.00

FERBER, Edna. *Giant.* 1952. Doubleday. 1st. sgn. F/F. B4. $275.00

FERBER, Edna. *No Room at the Inn.* 1941. Doubleday. 1st. F. B4. $85.00

FERBER, Edna. *Showboat.* 1926. Doubleday Page. 1st. 1/201. sgn/#d. white Japanese vellum. F. B4. $600.00

FERBER, Nat. *One Happy Jew.* 1934. 1st. VG. E6. $20.00

FERDON, Edwin N. *Early Observations of Marquesan Culture 1595-1813.* 1993. Tucson/London. 1st. 184p. burgundy cloth. P4. $40.00

FERDON, Edwin N. *Early Tonga: As the Explorers Saw It: 1616-1810.* 1987. Tucson. 8vo. 339p. VG. P4. $40.00

FERE, Charles. *Les Epilepsies et les Epileptiques.* 1890. Paris. Gailliere. heavy 8vo. photos/ils. 636p. contemporary bdg. G1. $650.00

FERGUSON, Blanche E. *Countee Cullen & the Negro Renaissance.* 1966. Dodd Mead. 1st. NF/dj. M25. $35.00

FERGUSON, David L. *Cleopatra's Barge: Crowninshield Story.* 1976. Little Brn. 1st. 293p. cloth. VG/dj. M20. $22.00

FERGUSON, Delancey. *Mark Twain, Man & Legend.* 1943. Bobbs Merrill. 1st. gilt red cloth. F/dj. M24. $85.00

FERGUSON, Helen. *Julia & the Bazooka.* 1970. Knopf. 1st. F/F. B35. $45.00

FERGUSON, James. *Astronomy Explained Upon Sir Isaac Newton's Principles.* 1817. Phil. Abraham Small. 2 vol. enlarged. rebacked. K5. $150.00

FERGUSON, John C. *Survey of Chinese Art.* 1940. Shanghai. Commercial Pr. 200+ pl. 153p. VG/dj. W3. $65.00

FERGUSSON, Bruce. *Shadow of His Wings.* 1987. Arbor. 1st. F/F. P3. $17.00

FERGUSSON, Harvey. *Wolf Song.* 1927. Knopf. 1st. 1/100. sgn/#d. F/glassine dj. A18. $300.00

FERLANTTE, William J. *Flora of the Trinity Alps of Northern California.* 1974. Berkeley. 8vo. 206p. cloth. F. A22. $30.00

FERLINGHETTI, Lawrence. *Coney Island of the Mind.* 1968. New Directions. 1st. cloth. F/case. B2. $45.00

FERLINGHETTI, Lawrence. *Secret Meaning of Things.* 1969. New Directions. 1st. sgn. NF/NF. R14. $35.00

FERLINGHETTI & PETERS. *Literary San Francisco: A Pictorial History...* 1980. Harper Row. 1st. F/F. A18. $35.00

FERMAN, Edward L. *Best From Fantasy & Science Fiction 17th Series.* 1968. Doubleday. 1st. NF/dj. M2. $20.00

FERMAN, Edward L. *Best From Fantasy & Science Fiction: 40th Anniversary...* 1989. St Martin. 1st. F/F. P3. $20.00

FERMI, Laura. *Atoms in the Family. My Life With Enrico Fermi.* 1969. Chicago. ils. 8vo. 267p. wrp. K3. $9.00

FERMI, Laura. *Atoms of the World.* 1957. Chicago. 1st. VG/VG. A20. $20.00

FERNALD & PATTON. *Water Resources Atlas of Florida.* 1984. FL State. 291p. D8. $35.00

FERRARS, Elizabeth X. *Alibi for a Witch.* 1952. Crime Club. 1st. VG. P3. $20.00

FERRARS, Elizabeth X. *Decayed Gentlewoman.* 1963. Crime Club. 1st. F/NF. P3. $35.00

FERRARS, Elizabeth X. *Murder Too Many.* 1989. Doubleday. 1st. F/F. P3. $16.00

FERRARS, Elizabeth X. *Thinner Than Water.* 1982. Doubleday. 1st. VG/VG. P3. $15.00

FERRERO, Guglielmo. *Characters & Events of Roman History, From Ceasar to Nero...* 1922. Putnam/Knickerbocker. 8vo. 275p. VG. W1. $12.00

FERRIER, David. *Functions of the Brain.* 1886. Putnam. 2nd Am. 137 woodcuts. emb Victorian cloth. VG. G1. $475.00

FERRIS, Helen. *Love's Enchantment.* 1944. Doubleday. 1st. inscr. 120p. NF/dj. D4. $30.00

FERRIS, W.A. *Life in the Rocky Mountains, a Diary of Wanderings...* 1940. Old West Pub. 1st. ils/maps. 365p. VG. J2. $475.00

FERSON & FERSON. *Yesterday's Milk Glass Today.* 1987. self pub. 2nd. ils. 188p. w/separate 4p price guide. as new. H1. $90.00

FESBACH, Norma D. *Early Schooling in England & Israel.* 1973. McGraw Hill. 127p. VG. S3. $21.00

FESSENDEN, Thomas Green. *Terrible Tractoration!! A Poetical Petition...* 1804. NY. Stansbury. 16mo. 192p. ES. disbound. M1. $175.00

FETRIDGE, W.P. *Paris Commune.* 1871. Harper. 1st. gilt bl cloth. NF. B2. $150.00

FICOWSKI, Jerzy. *Sister of the Birds & Other Gypsy Tales.* 1976. Abingdon. 1st Am. ils Chas Mikolaycak. VG+/G+. P2. $20.00

FIELD, Eugene. *Love Affairs of a Bibliomaniac.* 1896. Scribner. 1st. VG. K3. $30.00

FIELD, Eugene. *Lullaby-Land.* 1897. Scribner. 1st. ils Chas Robinson. 231p. teg. gr cloth. R5. $175.00

FIELD, Eugene. *Poems of Childhood.* ca 1922 (1904). Scribner. later prt. ils Parrish/8 mc pl. 199p. VG. D4. $75.00

FIELD, Eugene. *Poems of Childhood.* 1904. Scribner. 1st. ils Maxfield Parrish/8 full-p pl. 199p. VG. D1. $175.00

FIELD, Eugene. *Sugar Plum Tree & Other Verses.* 1930. Saalfield. ils FB Peat. pink spine. VG. B15. $65.00

FIELD, Eugene. *Writings in Prose & Verse.* 1896-1901. Scribner. 1st. 12 vol. 1/100. 12mo. teg. uncut. M1. $375.00

FIELD, Henry M. *History of the Atlantic Telegraph.* 1866. Scribner. 1st. ils. 364p. VG. K3. $55.00

FIELD, Henry M. *Old Spain & New Spain.* 1888. Scribner. 1st. 8vo. 303p. gilt gr cloth. T10. $100.00

FIELD, Kate. *Drama of Glass.* ca 1895. Libby Glass Co. 16mo. ils. 46p. gilt decor brd. G. H1. $50.00

FIELD, Michael. *Culinary Classics & Improvisations.* 1968. Knopf. 2nd. ils Mozelle Thompson. VG/dj. A16. $10.00

FIELD, Rachel. *Christmas Time.* 1941. Macmillan. probable 1st. 16mo. F/VG+. M5. $25.00

FIELD, Rachel. *General Store.* 1988. Little Brn. 1st. ils Giles Laroche. F/F. C8. $25.00

FIELD, William B.O. *John Leach on My Shelves.* 1970 (1930). rpt. ils. F. K3. $25.00

FIELDER, Mildred. *Guide to Black Hills Ghost Mines.* 1972. Aberdeen, SD. N Plains. photos. dj. A19. $35.00

FIELDER, Mildred. *Railroads of the Black Hills.* 1960. NY. Bonanza. dj. A19. $45.00

FIELDER, Mildred. *Treasure of Homestake Gold.* 1970. Aberdeen, SD. N Plains. dj. A19. $35.00

FIELDING, A. *Eames-Erskine Case.* 1925. Knopf. 1st. NF/G. M19. $25.00

FIELDING, Henry. *Joseph Andrews.* 1939. Random. VG/VG. P3. $20.00

FIELDING, Howard. *Straight Crooks.* 1927. Chelsea House. 1st. VG. P3. $25.00

FIELDS, Annie. *How to Help the Poor.* 1884. Boston. Houghton Mifflin. 1st. gray-gr prt wrp. M24. $85.00

FIELDS, James T. *Boston Book.* 1850. Ticknor Reed Fields. 1st. gilt blk cloth. M24. $100.00

FIERZ & WEISSKOPF. *Theoretical Physics in the 20th Century.* 1960. NY. Interscience. 1st. VG/dj. K3. $35.00

FIFTOOT, C.H.S. *English Law & Its Background.* 1932. London. BEll. bl cloth. M11. $65.00

FIFTOOT, C.H.S. *Frederic William Maitland, a Life.* 1971. Harvard. M11. $45.00

FIGUIER, Louis. *Ocean World, Being a Description of the Sea...* 1869. Appleton. revised/enlarged ed. 8vo. 615p. rebound leather. H1. $40.00

FILLIS, James. *Breaking & Riding.* 1977. London. Allen. rpt. VG/VG. O3. $20.00

FINCH, C. *Of Muppets & Men.* 1981. NY. 1st. VG/VG. B5. $40.00

FINCH, Henry. *Law; or, A Discovrse Therof, in Foure Bookes.* 1627. London. Societie of Stationers. 12mo. calf. R12. $500.00

FINCH, Simon. *Slave Island.* 1983. Souvenir. 1st. VG/VG. P3. $15.00

FINDLATER, Richard. *Emlyn Williams.* 1956. Macmillan. 112p. dj. A17. $12.50

FINDLATER, Richard. *Grimaldi, King of Clowns.* 1955. MacGibbon Kee. 1st. 240p. cloth. VG/dj. M20. $20.00

FINDLEY, Ferguson. *Waterfront.* 1951. DSP. 1st. VG. P3. $15.00

FINDLEY, Francine. *Treeless Eden.* 1934. NY. King. 1st. VG/clip. B4. $85.00

FINDLEY, James S. *Bats: A Community Perspective.* 1993. Cambridge. 167p. F/F. S15. $17.00

FINEBERG, S. Andhil. *Rosenberg Case: Fact & Fiction.* 1953. Oceana Pub. 1st. VG/VG. V4. $20.00

FINGER, Charles J. *Spreading Stain.* 1927. Doubleday. 1st. NF. M2. $37.00

FINGER & HALDEMAN-JULIUS. *Oscar Wilde in Outline.* 1923. Girard, KS. Haldeman-Julius. 1st. Little Bl Book 442. VG+. A25. $10.00

FINLAY, Virgil. *Astrology Sketch Book.* 1975. Donald Grant. 1st. VG/dj. P3. $25.00

FINLEY, J.P. *Report of the Tornadoes of May 29 & 30, 1879...* 1881. WA, DC. US War Dept. xl. K5. $95.00

FINLEY, James B. *Autobiography of Rev James B Finley...* 1861. Cincinnati. later prt. 455p. half leather. VG-. B18. $45.00

FINLEY, Martha. *Elise at Home (#22).* 1897. Dodd Mead. 295p. cloth w/pansy design. lists to #27. M20. $15.00

FINN, Sidney B. *Clinical Pedodontics.* 1962. Phil. Saunders. 2nd. photos. VG+. A25. $15.00

FINNEY, Charles G. *Unholy City.* 1927. Vanguard. 1st. VG. M2. $22.00

FINNEY, Jack. *Assault on a Queen.* 1960. Eyre Spottiswoode. 1st. VG/dj. M2. $50.00

FINNEY, Jack. *Forgotten News.* 1983. Doubleday. 1st. NF/dj. M2. $20.00

FINNEY, Jack. *Night People.* 1977. Doubleday. 1st. F/dj. M2. $35.00

FINNEY, Jack. *Time & Again.* 1970. S&S. stated 1st. NF/NF. M22. $10.00

FINNIE, Richard. *Lure of the North.* 1940. Phil. 56 photos. A17. $25.00

FINSTAD, Suzanne. *Sleeping With the Devil.* 1991. Morrow. 1st. 382p. F/F. W2. $30.00

FIRBANK, Ronald. *Extravaganzas.* 1935. Coward McCann. 1st Am. F/dj. Q1. $125.00

FIRBANK, Ronald. *Odette: A Fairy Tale for Weary People.* 1916. London. Grant Richards. 1st separate ils ed. VG. Q1. $200.00

FIRBANK, Ronald. *Princess Zoubaroff: A Comedy.* 1920. London. Grant Richards. 1st. 1/513. NF/dj. Q1. $600.00

FIRSOFF, V.A. *Ski Track on the Battlefield.* 1943. photos. VG/VG. M17. $25.00

FIRTH, Anthony. *Tall, Balding, Thirty-Five.* 1967. Harper Row. 1st. F/NF. H11. $20.00

FIRTH, M.J. *Native Orchids of Tasmania.* 1965. Devonport, Tasmania. ils/drawings/ index. 90p. F/dj. B26. $32.50

FISCHER, Bruno. *More Deaths Than One.* 1947. Ziff-Davis. 1st. NF/VG. B4. $250.00

FISCHER, Bruno. *Quoth the Raven.* 1944. Crime Club. 1st. VG. P3. $25.00

FISCHER, Martin H. *Nephritis.* 1912. NY. 1st. 203p. A17. $15.00

FISCHER, Tibor. *Art of Eating.* 1954. World. 1st. F/VG. B3. $75.00

FISCHER, Tibor. *Dubious Honors.* 1988. Northpoint. 1st. F/F. B3. $35.00

FISCHLER, Stan. *Hockey's Great Rivalries.* 1974. Random. 1st. G+. P8. $6.00

FISH, John Perry. *Unfinished Voyages.* 1989. Lower Cape Pub. 1st. ils. 299p. dj. T7. $40.00

FISHER, Aileen. *In the Woods in the Meadow in the Sky.* 1965. Scribner. 1st. ils Margot Tomes. 64p. F/F. D4. $45.00

FISHER, Carrie. *Postcards From the Edge.* 1987. S&S. 1st. inscr. F/F. B4. $125.00

FISHER, Clay. *Yellowstone Kelly.* 1957. Houghton Mifflin. 1st. F/VG+. B4. $175.00

FISHER, H.A.L. *Collected Papers of Frederic William Maitland...* 1911. Cambridge. 3 vol. orig cloth. M11. $350.00

FISHER, Harrison. *American Belles.* 1911. Dodd Mead. 1st. 16 full-p mtd mc pl. folio. teg. rose brd/label. R5. $800.00

FISHER, John. *Reform & Insurrection in Bourbon New Granada & Peru.* 1990. LSU. 1st. 356p. dj. F3. $20.00

FISHER, L.H. *Territorial Governors of Oklahoma.* 1975. OK Hist Soc. 1st. inscr. photos. 150p. F. M4. $30.00

FISHER, M.F.K. *Boss Dog: A Story.* 1991. SF. Northpoint. 1st trade. F/NF. R13. $20.00

FISHER, M.F.K. *Gastronomical Me.* 1948. World. 1st thus. 295p. VG/G. H1. $15.00

FISHER, M.F.K. *Map of Another Town.* 1964. Boston. 1st. VG/VG. B5. $45.00

FISHER, M.F.K. *With Bold Knife & Fork.* 1969. NY. 1st. VG/VG. B5. $45.00

FISHER, Marjorie. *Food & Flowers for Informal Entertaining.* 1965. Hearthside. G/dj. A16. $10.00

FISHER, Paul R. *Hawks of Fellheath.* 1980. Atheneum. 1st. VG/dj. P3. $18.00

FISHER, Robert Lewis. *Odyssey of Tobacco.* 1939. Litchfield, CT. Prospect. 1st. 8vo. 93p. G. T10. $45.00

FISHER, Robert Moore. *How About the Weather?* 1951. NY. Harper. 1st. 8vo. 186p. G/dj. K5. $10.00

FISHER, Rudolph. *Conjure-Man Dies.* 1971. NY. Arno/NY Times. 1st thus. 316p. F/NF. B4. $85.00

FISHER, Steve. *Big Dream.* 1970. Doubleday. 1st. NF/dj. M25. $35.00

FISHER, Steve. *Destroyer.* 1941. Appleton. 1st. NF/VG. B4. $475.00

FISHER, Steve. *Giveaway.* 1954. Random. 1st. F/VG. B4. $100.00

FISHER, Sydney George. *True William Penn.* 1900. Lippincott. 392p. V3. $12.50

FISHER, Vardis. *Adam & the Serpent.* 1947. Vanguard. 1st. VG. M2. $20.00

FISHER, Vardis. *Children of God.* 1939. Harper. 1st. VG/VG. P3. $45.00

FISHER, Vardis. *City of Illusion.* 1941. Harper. 1st. VG. P3. $45.00

FISHER, Vardis. *Golden Rooms.* 1944. NY. 1st. VG/VG. B5. $35.00

FISHER, Vardis. *Idaho: A Guide in Word & Picture.* 1937. Caxton. 1st. F. A18. $200.00

FISHER, Vardis. *Mountain Man.* 1965. NY. 1st. VG/VG. B5. $35.00

FISHER, Vardis. *No Villain Need Be.* 1936. Caxton. 1st. F/dj. A18. $75.00

FISHER, Vardis. *Orphans in Gethsemane: A Novel of the Past in the Present.* 1960. Swallow. 1st. 1/200. sgn. VG/dj. A18. $250.00

FISHER, Vardis. *Pemmican: A Novel of the Hudson Bay Company.* 1956. Doubleday. 1st. F/dj. Q1. $50.00

FISHER, Vardis. *Toilers of the Hills.* 1928. Houghton Mifflin. 1st. NF/dj. A18. $80.00

FISHER, W.S. *Revision of the North American Species of Buprestid Beetles.* 1928. Smithsonian. 347p. NF. S15. $18.00

FISHER & FISHER. *Shackleton & the Antarctic.* 1958. Boston. ils/maps/photos. F/G. M4. $25.00

FISHER & HOLMES. *Gold Rushes & Mining Camps of the Early American West.* 1968. Caxton. 1st. inscr/sgns. F/dj. A18. $125.00

FISKE, Dorsey. *Bound to Murder.* 1987. St Martin. 1st. NF/NF. P3. $18.00

FISKE & LUMMIS. *Charles F Lummis: Man & His West.* 1975. Norman, OK. 1/200. sgn. F/F. O4. $65.00

FITCH, Florence Mary. *Book About God.* July 1956. Lee Shepard. 4th. sm 4to. unp. NF/VG clip. C14. $12.00

FITZ, Grancel. *North American Head Hunting.* 1957. NY. Oxford. 1st. 188p. F/F. H7. $30.00

FITZ & ODLUM. *Lady Sourdough.* 1941. NY. 1st. VG/VG. B5. $25.00

FITZGERALD, Edward. *Rubaiyat of Omar Khayyam.* 1878. Boston. Osgood. 1st Am. gilt terra-cotta decor cloth. F. M24. $250.00

FITZGERALD, F. Scott. *Afternoon of an Author.* 1957. Princeton. 1st. 1/1500. F/clip. Q1. $175.00

FITZGERALD, F. Scott. *Great Gatsby.* 1925. Scribner. 1st/1st prt (points on p60/119/205/211). F. Q1. $1,000.00

FITZGERALD, F. Scott. *Great Gatsby.* 1974. Franklin Lib. 1st thus/ltd. aeg. full leather. F. Q1. $75.00

FITZGERALD, F. Scott. *Pat Hobby Stories.* 1962. Scribner. 1st. NF/dj. M25. $60.00

FITZGERALD, F. Scott. *Tales of the Jazz Age.* 1922. 1st/3rd issue. VG. S13. $30.00

FITZGERALD, F. Scott. *This Side of Paradise.* 1920. Scribner. 1st. 1/3000. inscr/dtd 1920. author's 1st book. NF. L3. $7,500.00

FITZGERALD, Joe. *Championship Feeling.* 1975. Scribner. 1st. photos. F/F. P8. $35.00

FITZGERALD, John D. *Great Brain.* 1967. Dial. 1st. ils Mercer Mayer. 175p. NF/VG. P2. $25.00

FITZGERALD, John D. *More Adventures of Great Brain.* 1969. NY. Dial. 1st. 142p. VG/worn. M20. $22.50

FITZGERALD, Kevin. *Quiet Under the Sun.* 1954. Little Brn. 1st. VG/VG. P3. $20.00

FITZGERALD, Michael. *Universal Pictures: Panoramic History in Words.* 1977. New Rochelle. 766p. dj. A17. $20.00

FITZGERALD, Percy. *Sheridans.* nd (1937). NY. Atheneum. 2 vol. 8vo. tan cloth. H13. $125.00

FITZGERALD, Robert. *In the Rose of Time: Poems 1931-1956.* 1956. New Directions. 1st. F/dj. Q1. $75.00

FITZHUGH, Louise. *Long Secret.* 1965. Harper. sm 8vo. VG/VG. C8. $20.00

FITZHUGH, Percy Keese. *Roy Blakely: Lost, Strayed or Stolen (#7).* 1921. Grosset Dunlap. 207p+ads. VG/dj (lists 11 titles). M20. $25.00

FITZLYON, Kyril. *Before the Revolution: Russia & Its People Under the Czar...* 1978. Overlook. 1st. VG/dj. V4. $25.00

FITZPATRICK, Wendy. *Practical Sailing.* 1979. Mayflower. 1st Am ed. F/F. W2. $25.00

FITZSIMONS, Bernard. *Illustrated Encyclopedia of Weapons & Warfare.* 1977. NY. 24 vol. photos. VG. S16. $140.00

FLACH, Frederic F. *Fridericus.* 1980. Lippincott Crowell. 1st. VG/dj. P3. $13.00

FLACK, Marjorie. *Angus & the Cat.* 1931. Doubleday Doran. 1st. VG. P2. $65.00

FLACK, Marjorie. *Walter the Lazy Mouse.* 1937. Doubleday Doran. 1st. 4to. VG/VG. P2. $90.00

FLAGG, Fannie. *Fried Green Tomatoes at the Whistle Stop Cafe.* 1987. Random. 1st. F/F. T11. $95.00

FLAMMARION, Camille. *Atmosphere.* 1873. Harper. 4to. 453p. gilt cloth. K5. $125.00

FLAMMARION, Camille. *Mysterious Psychic Forces.* 1907. Small Maynard. 1st. VG. M2. $75.00

FLAMMARION, Camille. *Popular Astronomy: A General Description of the Heavens.* 1931. NY. Appleton. new imp/revised, 698p. K5. $80.00

FLANAGAN, E.M. *Corregidor: Rock Force Assault, 1945.* 1988. SF. Presidio. sm 4to. 331p. M/F. P1. $14.00

FLANAGAN, Edward Jr. *Angels: History of the 11th Airborne Division 1943-1946.* 1948. WA, DC. 1st. photos/maps. 176p. VG. S16. $125.00

FLANAGAN, Thomas. *Tenants of Time.* 1988. Dutton. 1st. F/F. T12. $25.00

FLAUBERT, Gustave. *Salambo.* 1931. Golden Cockrel. 1/500. ils R Gibbings. VG. T9. $100.00

FLAVELL, Geoffrey. *Oesophagus.* 1963. London. 1st. 168p. A13. $50.00

FLAVELL, M. Kay. *George Grosz: A Biography.* 1988. Yale. 1st. F/dj. V4. $45.00

FLEET, Simon. *Clocks: Pleasures & Treasures.* 1961. NY. Putnam. 1st. 8vo. 128p. pict cloth. VG/box. K3. $15.00

FLEETWOOD, Hugh. *Beast.* 1978. Hamish Hamilton. 1st. VG/dj. P3. $20.00

FLEETWOOD, Hugh. *Painter of Flowers.* 1972. Viking. 1st. VG/VG. P3. $22.00

FLEISCHMAN, Harry. *Norman Thomas: A Biography.* 1964. Norton. 2nd. VG/G. V4. $40.00

FLEISCHMAN, J. *Art of Blending & Compounding Liquors & Wines.* 1885. 1st. VG. E6. $45.00

FLEISCHMAN, Sid. *Chancy & the Grand Rascal.* 1966. Atlantic/Little Brn. 8vo. 179p. VG. T5. $15.00

FLEITMANN, Lida L. *Horse in Art: From Primitive Times to the Present.* 1931. London. Medici Soc. 1st. VG/G. O3. $95.00

FLEMING, Alice. *America Is Not All Traffic Lights.* 1976. Little Brn. 1st. 68p. cloth. F/NF. D4. $30.00

FLEMING, Alice. *Hosannah the Home Run!* 1972. Little Brn. ARC/1st. 68p. F/F. D4. $35.00

FLEMING, Archibald Lang. *Archibald the Arctic.* 1956. Appleton Century Crofts. 1st. 8vo. 399p. F/dj. T10. $25.00

FLEMING, Berry. *Lucinderella.* 1967. NY. John Day. 1st. F/F. T12. $30.00

FLEMING, Denise. *Barnyard Banter.* 1994. Holt. 1st. unp. F. C14. $14.00

FLEMING, Ian. *Bonded Fleming.* 1965. Viking. 1st. NF/NF. M19. $50.00

FLEMING, Ian. *Casino Royale.* 1954. NY. Macmillan. 1st Am. F/NF. M15. $800.00

FLEMING, Ian. *Chitty Chitty...* 1964. Random. 1st. 8vo. gilt red cloth. F/NF. R5. $275.00

FLEMING, Ian. *Diamond Smugglers.* 1957. London. Cape. 1st. F/F. M15. $250.00

FLEMING, Ian. *For Your Eyes Only.* 1960. London. Jonathan Cape. 1st. F/NF. M15. $350.00

FLEMING, Ian. *Goldfinger.* 1959. London. Cape. 1st. F/dj. M15. $650.00

FLEMING, Ian. *Live & Let Die.* 1954. London. Cape. 1st. F/clip. M15. $3,750.00

FLEMING, Ian. *Man With the Golden Gun.* 1965. London. Cape. 1st/1st imp. F/dj. M15. $100.00

FLEMING, Ian. *Man With the Golden Gun.* 1965. NAL. 1st Am. VG/G. M22. $20.00

FLEMING, Ian. *Octopussy & the Living Daylights.* 1966. London. Cape. F/F. M15. $45.00

FLEMING, Ian. *Octopussy.* 1965. NAL. 1st Am. F/NF. M2. $30.00

FLEMING, Ian. *On Her Majesty's Secret Service.* 1963. NAL. 1st Am. F/NF. M22. $60.00

FLEMING, Ian. *Spy Who Loved Me.* 1962. London. Cape. 1st. F/F. M15. $175.00

FLEMING, Ian. *You Only Live Twice.* 1964. London. Cape. 1st. F/dj. M15. $125.00

FLEMING, Ian. *You Only Live Twice.* 1964. NAL. 1st. VG/dj. P3. $35.00

FLEMING, Joan. *Good & the Bad.* 1953. Crime Club. 1st. NF/VG. P3. $25.00

FLEMING, Joan. *In the Red.* 1961. Ives Washburn. 1st. author's 5th novel. VG/VG. M22. $15.00

FLEMING, Joan. *Malice Matrimonial.* 1959. Ives Washburn. 1st. NF/NF. P3. $25.00

FLEMING, Joan. *Nothing Is the Number When You Die.* 1965. London. Collins. 1st. NF/VG. M22. $15.00

FLEMING, Joan. *Too Late! Too Late! the Maiden Cried.* 1975. Putnam. 1st. VG/VG. P3. $20.00

FLEMING, Joan. *You Won't Let Me Finish.* 1973. Collins Crime Club. 1st. VG/dj. P3. $20.00

FLEMING, Peter. *Flying Visit.* 1940. London. 1st. ils David Low. VG/dj. S13. $35.00

FLEMING. *Sinclair Lewis: A Reference Guide.* 1980. 240p. VG. A4. $45.00

FLETCHER, Colin. *Man Who Walked Through Time.* 1968. Knopf. 4th. 8vo. 239p. dj. F7. $20.00

FLETCHER, David. *Raffles.* 1977. Putnam. 1st. F/F. P3. $15.00

FLETCHER, Inglis. *Cormorant's Brood.* 1959. Lippincott. 1st. VG/dj. P3. $15.00

FLETCHER, Inglis. *Roanoke Hundred.* 1948. Bobbs Merrill. 1st. sgn. gilt bl cloth. B11. $50.00

FLETCHER, N.H. *Physics of Rainclouds.* 1962. Cambridge. 1st. 8vo. 396p. VG/dj. K5. $40.00

FLETCHER, R.A. *Steam-Ships.* 1910. London. Sidgwick Jackson. ils. 421p. rebacked. T7. $85.00

FLETCHER, Robert Samuel. *History of Oberlin College From Its Foundation...* 1943. Oberlin, OH. 2 vol. sgn. F. B4. $175.00

FLETCHER, S. *Strawberry in North America.* 1917. np. 1st. xl. VG. E6. $20.00

FLETCHER, Stevenson Whitcomb. *Pennsylvania Agriculture & Country Life 1640-1840.* 1950. PA Hist & Mus Comm. 8vo. 605p. rebound buckram. VG. H1. $25.00

FLEW, R. Newton. *Jesus & His Church.* 1949. Epworth. 192p. G. B29. $13.50

FLICK, Art. *Master Fly-Tying Guide.* 1972. NY. 207p. dj. A17. $35.00

FLINT, C. *Milch Cows & Dairy Farming.* 1867 (1858). ils. VG. E6. $20.00

FLINT, L. *Practical Treatise on Grasses & Forage Plants.* 1858 (1857). ils. VG. E6. $50.00

FLINT, Timothy. *Recollections of Last Ten Years in Valley of Mississippi.* 1968. S IL U. 1st. 337p. VG/clip. M20. $40.00

FLINT & NORTH. *Tiger Bridge.* 1970. NY. 1st. 191p. VG/dj. S1. $10.00

FLINT & RIMINGTON. *Grand Slam: International Bridge Tournament...* 1983. Eng. 1st. 174p. F/dj. S1. $12.00

FLOHERTY, J.J. *High, Wide & Deep.* 1952. Phil/Lippincott. ils/photos/pict ep. 154p. cloth. F/VG+. M12. $15.00

FLOOD, Charles Bracelen. *Lee, the Last Years.* 1981. Boston. later prt. cloth. F/F. M8. $25.00

FLOOD, Charles. *Hitler: Path to Power.* 1969. Boston. 1st. photos/notes/biblio/index. 686p. VG/VG. S16. $22.50

FLOOD, John Henry. *Rare Historical Document Biography of Wyatt Earp...* 1926. np. 1st. maps. 258p. as new. J2. $165.00

FLOOK, Maria. *Family Night.* 1993. Pantheon. ARC. author's 1st novel. RS. NF/dj. R13. $35.00

FLORA, Fletcher. *Irrepressible Peccadilo.* 1962. Macmillan. 1st. VG/dj. P3. $20.00

FLORA, Snowden D. *Tornadoes of the United States.* 1953. Norman, OK. 1st. 194p. G/dj. K5. $20.00

FLORENTIN, Eddie. *Battle of the Falaise Gap.* 1965. Hawthorn. 1st. 362p. cloth. VG/ragged. M20. $15.00

FLORES, Ivan. *Assemblers & Bal.* 1971. Prentice Hall. 1st. 420p. dj. A17. $15.00

FLORESCU, Radu. *In Search of Frankenstein.* 1975. NYGS. 1st. VG/VG. P3. $20.00

FLORIN, Lambert. *Western Wagon Wheels, a Pictorial Memorial...* 1970. Bonanza. rpt. 185p. VG/VG. O3. $35.00

FLORIS, Maria. *Bakery Cakes & Simple Confectionary.* 1968. Bonanza. G/dj. A16. $20.00

FLORNEY, Bertram. *World of the Inca.* (1956). Vanguard. 1st. 212p. dj. F3. $20.00

FLORY, Jane. *Faraway Dream.* 1968. Houghton Mifflin. 2nd. 8vo. 219p. gold cloth. VG/dj. T5. $22.00

FLOURNOY, Theodora. *From India to the Planet Mars.* 1900. Harper. 1st Am. G. M2. $35.00

FLOWER, John. *Moonlight Serenade: A Biodiscography of Glenn Miller Band.* 1972. NY. 1st. ils/photos. VG/VG. B5. $35.00

FLOWER, Pat. *Crisscross.* 1976. Collins Crime Club. 1st. F/F. P3. $13.00

FLOWER, William Henry. *Diagrams of the Nerves of the Human Body...* 1872. London. Churchill. 2nd. 6 double-p lithos. emb brn cloth. G. G1. $150.00

FLOWERS, A.R. *De Monjo Blues.* 1985. Dutton. 1st. F/F. B2. $60.00

FLOWERS & FLOWERS. *Finches: Their Care & Breeding.* nd. Reseda. Bird Haven. 8vo. ils/drawings. 80+p. pict brd. VG. M12. $37.50

FLOYD, Olive. *Doctora in Mexico: Life of Dr Katherine Neel Dale.* 1944. Putnam. 1st. 270p. VG+. A25. $30.00

FLUGUM, Charles T. *Birding From a Tractor Seat.* 1973. St Paul. 435p. NF/VG. S15. $18.00

FLYMAN, Rose. *51 New Nursery Rhymes.* 1932. Doubleday Doran. 1st stated. ils Dorothy Burroughes. VG. B15. $85.00

FLYNN, Lucine Hansz. *Antique & Deadly.* 1988. Walker. 1st. F/F. H11. $20.00

FLYNT, Candace. *Mother Love.* 1987. Random. 1st. inscr. F/F. R13. $35.00

FLYNT, Candace. *Sins of Omission.* 1984. Random. 1st. inscr. F/dj. R13. $35.00

FOCK, H. *Fast Fighting Boats 1870-1945: Their Design...* 1978. Naval Inst. 304p. F/dj. A17. $45.00

FODOR, Laszlo. *Argentina.* 1941. Hastings. 1st. 23p. dj. F3. $15.00

FODOR, M.W. *Revolution Is On.* 1940. Houghton Mifflin. 1st. sgn. NF. B2. $30.00

FOGG, H.G. Witham. *Coloured Leaved & Berried Plants, Shrubs & Trees.* 1972. GBC. ils/drawings. VG/dj. B26. $19.00

FOHRER, Stellin. *Introduction to Old Testament.* 1978. Abingdon. trans David Green. 540p. VG/torn. B29. $15.00

FOLDES, Francis F. *Narcotics & Narcotic Antagonists.* 1964. Springfield. Charles Thomas. 1st. F/F. B2. $50.00

FOLEY, James. *Songs of Schooldays.* 1906. Doubleday. 1st. 12mo. VG. M5. $35.00

FOLEY, Martha. *Best American Short Stories.* 1965. MacGibbon Kee. 1st. VG/dj. P3. $20.00

FOLEY, Rae. *Last Gamble.* 1956. Dodd Mead. 1st. VG/dj. P3. $29.00

FOLEY, Rae. *Trust a Woman?* 1973. Dodd Mead. 1st. VG/VG. P3. $15.00

FOLLETT, Helen. *Third Class Ticket to Heaven: A Black Forest Adventure.* 1938. Phil. Winston. 1st. ils Floethe. VG. A25. $15.00

FOLLETT, Ken. *Key to Rebecca.* 1980. Morrow. 1st. F/F. H11. $40.00

FOLLETT, Ken. *Man From Saint Petersburg.* 1986. Morrow. 1st Am. sgn. F/F. R14. $60.00

FOLLETT, Ken. *On Wings of Eagles.* 1983. Morrow. 1st. 444p. VG/torn. W1. $20.00

FOLLETT, Ken. *Pillars of the Earth.* 1989. NY. Morrow. 1st. F/F. T12. $30.00

FOLLETT, Ken. *Triple.* 1979. NY. Arbor. 1st. F/F. H11. $40.00

FONDA, Jane. *Jane Fonda's Workout Book.* 1981. S&S. 1st. sgn. F/NF. W2. $30.00

FONER, Philip. *Jack London. American Rebel.* 1947. Citadel. 1st. NF/NF. B2. $30.00

FONTANA, John M. *Mankind's Greatest Invention...* 1964. NY. Fontana. ils. 8vo. 112p. xl. K3. $20.00

FONTANINI, Giusto. *Biblioteca Dell'Eloquenza Italiana.* 1753. Venice. Giambatista Pasquali. 2 vol. VG. T10. $450.00

FOOTE, Horton. *Courtship, Valentine's Day, 1918.* 1987. Grove. 1st. sgn. F/dj. A24. $35.00

FOOTE, Horton. *Harrison, Texas.* 1956. Harcourt Brace. 1st. sgn. author's 1st book. F/NF. A24. $125.00

FOOTE, Horton. *Roots in a Parched Ground, Convicts, Lilly Dale...* 1988. Grove. 1st. sgn. F/dj. A24. $40.00

FOOTE, John Taintor. *Look of Eagles.* 1916. Appleton. 1st. VG/dj. H7. $35.00

FOOTE, Sam. *Dramatic Works of...* ca 1795. London. 4 vol. leather. VG. A15. $100.00

FOOTE. *American Imprints Inventory No 19, Bibliography...* 1942. 4to. 597p. VG. A4. $165.00

FOOTNER, Hulbert. *Rivers of the Eastern Shore, Seventeen Maryland Rivers.* 1944. Farrar Rhinehart. 4th. sm 8vo. 375p. F/G. H1. $16.00

FORBES, Alexander. *Radio Gunner.* 1924. Houghton Mifflin. 1st. VG. M2. $25.00

FORBES, Allan. *Sport in Norfolk Country.* 1938. Houghton Mifflin. 1/665. sgn/#d. VG. O3. $95.00

FORBES, Colin. *Target Five.* 1973. Collins. 1st. VG/VG. P3. $18.00

FORBES, Colin. *Year of the Golden Ape.* 1974. Dutton. 1st. NF/NF. P3. $20.00

FORBES, Edgar Allen. *Leslie's Photographic Review of the Great War.* 1920. Leslie-Judge. G+. P3. $40.00

FORBES, Eric G. *Gersham Lectures of John Flamsteed.* 1975. London. Mansell. 8vo. 479p. F. K5. $55.00

FORBES, Graham B. *Boys of Columbia High in Winter Sports (#7).* 1915. Grosset Dunlap. 1st. 236p. VG/dj (lists to this title). M20. $40.00

FORBES, Hugh. *Extracts From the Manual for the Patriotic Volunteer...* 1857. NY. Tinson. 1st. 16mo. 198p. prt wrp. M1. $1,750.00

FORBES, Jack D. *Apache, Navaho & Spaniard.* 1971. Norman. 3rd. 8vo. VG/stiff wrp. F7. $8.00

FORBES, Jack D. *Native Americans of California & Nevada.* 1969. Healdsburg. Naturegraph pub. 8vo. 200p. F/wrp. K7. $15.00

FORBES, Robert B. *Personal Reminiscences.* 1970. NY. Lib Eds. facsimile of 2nd 1882 ed. ils. 412p. T7. $40.00

FORBES, Rosita. *Secret of the Sahara: Kufara.* 1921. Doran. 1st Am. ils. 356p. VG. A25. $38.00

FORBES, Stanton. *Deadly Kind of Lonely.* 1971. Crime Club. 1st. VG/VG. P3. $20.00

FORBES, Stanton. *Terror Touches Me.* 1966. Collins Crime Club. 1st. VG/dj. P3. $15.00

FORBES, Thomas A. *Guide to Better Archery.* (1955). Harrisburg. 1st. 307p. F/VG. H7. $25.00

FORBIS, William. *Cowboys.* 1974. Time-Life. leather. A19. $20.00

FORBUSH, Bliss. *Elias Hicks: Quaker Liberal.* 1956. Columbia. 1st. sgn. 355p. VG/dj. V3. $25.00

FORBUSH, Edward H. *Birds of Massachusetts & Other New England States, Vol I.* 1925. MA Dept Agriculture. 481p. VG. B1. $75.00

FORBUSH, Edward H. *Birds of Massachusetts & Other New England States.* 1925-27. Boston. 3 vol. 1st. 4to. ils. NF. C6. $250.00

FORBUSH, Edward H. *History of Game Birds, Wild-Fowl & Shore-Birds of MA...* 1912. Boston. 1st. 4to. 622p. F. C6. $125.00

FORCE, M.F. *From Ft Henry to Corinth (Mississippi)...* 1881. 204p. O8. $21.50

FORD, Betty. *Betty: A Glad Awakening.* 1987. Doubleday. 1st. sgn. VG/VG. A23. $50.00

FORD, Corey. *Short Cut to Tokyo.* 1934. NY. 1st. VG/G. B5. $35.00

FORD, E.B. *Butterflies.* 1957. London. 3rd. ils/maps. 368p. VG. S15. $25.00

FORD, Florence. *Shadow on the House.* 1974. Hamish Hamilton. 1st. VG/VG. P3. $20.00

FORD, Madox. *Communist.* 1987. Babcock Koontz. 1st. 1/200. sgn. F/gr Roma wrp. Q1. $75.00

FORD, Madox. *Independence Day.* 1995. Knopf. 1st. sgn. F/dj. Q1. $75.00

FORD, Madox. *Portraits of My Life.* 1937. Houghton Mifflin. 1st. F/dj. Q1. $75.00

FORD, Gerald. *Humor & the Presidency.* 1987. Arbor. 1st. sgn. F/F. A23. $90.00

FORD, Gerald. *Portrait of the Assassin.* 1965. S&S. 1st. sgn. G/G. A23. $90.00

FORD, Gerald. *Time to Heal.* 1979. Harper Row. 1st. sgn. F/F. A23. $125.00

FORD, Grace Horney. *Button Collector's History.* 1943. Springfield, MA. sgn. 238p. VG/dj. M20. $40.00

FORD, Hilary; see Silverberg, Robert.

FORD, James L. *Hypnotic Tales.* 1891. Keppler Schwarzmann. 1st. VG. M2. $40.00

FORD, James. *Comparison of Formative Cultures in the Americas.* 1969. Smithsonian. 1st. 4to. 211p. F3. $45.00

FORD, John M. *Dragon Waiting.* 1983. Timescape. 1st. F/dj. M2. $65.00

FORD, Leslie. *Woman in Black.* 1947. Scribner. 1st. VG/G. N4. $25.00

FORD, Marilyn C. *Wildflowers of Mount Shasta: Lone Giant of the Cascades.* 1981. Klamath Falls. ils/photos/maps. 72p. F/dj. B26. $65.00

FORD, Richard. *Piece of My Heart.* 1987. London. Harvill. 1st. sgn. F/F. T2. $85.00

FORD, Richard. *Rock Springs.* 1988. London. Collins Harvill. 1st. sgn. F/F. T2. $55.00

FORD, Richard. *Sportswriter.* 1996. Knopf. 1st Am hc. sgn. F/F. D10. $50.00

FORD, Richard. *Ultimate Good Luck.* 1989. London. Collins Harvill. 1st. sgn. F/F. T2. $65.00

FORD, Richard. *Wildlife.* 1990. Atlantic Monthly. 1/200. sgn. M/case/swrp. B4. $200.00

FORD, Richard. *Wildlife.* 1990. Atlantic Monthly. 1st. sgn. F/F. A23/D10. $50.00

FORD, Tirey L. *Dawn & the Dons: Romance of Monterey.* 1926. San Francisco. 1st. ils/pict label. VG. O4. $25.00

FORD & MARTIN. *Musical Fantasies of L Frank Baum.* 1969. 1/1000. sgn/#d. F. A4. $95.00

FORD. *Bibliotheca Hamiltoniana: List of Books Written...* 1969 (1886). rpt. 165p. F. A4. $45.00

FORDHAM, Mary Weston. *Magnolia Leaves.* 1897. Charleston, SC. Walker Evans Cogswell. 1st. intro BT Washington. NF. B4. $450.00

FOREMAN, Grant. *Last Trek of the Indians.* 1946. Chicago. 1st. 8 fld maps. 382p. pict cloth. D11. $30.00

FOREMAN, Grant. *Pathfinder in the Southwest: Itinerary of Lt AW Whipple...* 1941. OK U. 1st. 7 full-p ils. cloth. dj. D11. $40.00

FOREMAN, L.L. *Farewell to Texas.* 1964. Doubleday. 1st. F/F. B4. $75.00

FORESTER, C.S. *Age of Fighting Sail, Story of the Naval War of 1812.* 1956. NY. 1st. 284p. G+/dj. B18. $27.50

FORESTER, C.S. *Barbary Pirates.* 1953. Random. 1st. ils Charles Mazoujian. red cloth. F/NF. T11. $125.00

FORESTER, C.S. *Captain From Connecticut.* 1942. Clipper Books. VG/dj. P3. $30.00

FORESTER, C.S. *Commodore Hornblower.* 1945. 1st Am. VG/VG. M17. $45.00

FORESTER, C.S. *General.* 1936. Little Brn. 1st. VG. P3. $35.00

FORESTER, C.S. *Hornblower & the Hotspur.* 1962. Michael Joseph. 1st. 286p. VG/dj. M20. $70.00

FORESTER, C.S. *Josephine, Napoleon's Empress.* 1925. London. Methuen. 1st. 1/2000. gr cloth. G+. T11. $250.00

FORESTER, C.S. *Long Before Forty.* 1967. Little Brn. 1st. F/NF. B2. $30.00

FORESTER, C.S. *Lord Hornblower.* 1946. Little Brn. 1st. VG. P3. $25.00

FORESTER, C.S. *Lord Nelson.* 1929. Bobbs Merrill. 1st Am. F/NF. T11. $400.00

FORESTER, C.S. *Louis XIV: King of France & Navarre.* 1928. Dodd Mead. 1st Am. 1/1700. VG+. T11. $175.00

FORESTER, C.S. *Lt Hornblower.* 1952. Little Brn. 1st Am. 306p. cloth. VG/dj. M20. $30.00

FORESTER, C.S. *Nightmare.* 1954. Michael Joseph. 1st. VG/VG. P3. $35.00

FORESTER, C.S. *Sky & the Forest.* 1948. Michael Joseph. 1st. VG/VG. P3/S13. $20.00

FORESTER, C.S. *To the Indies.* 1940. Canada. Saunders. 1st. VG. P3. $30.00

FORESTER, Frank. *Warwick Woodlands.* 1990. Derrydale. 1/2500. aeg. gilt leather. F. A17. $25.00

FORMAN, George. *By George.* 1995. Villard. 1st. sgn. F/F. A23. $50.00

FORMAN, H. Buxton. *Books of William Morris.* 1969. Frnklin. 224p. cloth. A17. $25.00

FORRER, Eric. *From the Nets of a Salmon Fisherman.* 1973. NY. 1st. 158p. wrp. A17. $7.50

FORREST, D.W. *Francis Galton: Life & Work of a Victorian Genius.* 1974. Taplinger. 1st. ils. 340p. VG/dj. K3. $15.00

FORRESTER, Glenn. *Falls of Niagara.* 1928. NY. 1st. ils/27 maps. 155p. VG. B5. $35.00

FORSTER, E.M. *Battersea Rise.* 1955. Harcourt Brace. 1st. decor brd/label. F. M24. $65.00

FORSTER, E.M. *Hill of Devi.* 1953. London. 1st. VG/dj. T9. $45.00

FORSTER, E.M. *Pharos & Pharillon.* 1923. Richmond. Hogarth. 1st. assn copy. VG. T9. $125.00

FORSTER, E.M. *Virginia Woolf.* 1942. Cambridge. 1st. 1/5000. F/prt wrp. M24. $100.00

FORSYTH, Frederick. *Day of the Jackal.* 1971. Viking. 1st. NF/dj. D10. $75.00

FORSYTH, Frederick. *Dogs of War.* 1974. Viking. 1st. VG/VG. M22. $15.00

FORSYTH, Frederick. *Fourth Protocol.* 1984. Hutchinson. 1st. F/dj. A24. $45.00

FORSYTH, Frederick. *Negotiator.* 1989. Bantam. 1st Am. NF/VG+. N4. $17.50

FORSYTH, Frederick. *Odessa File.* 1972. Viking. 1st Am. F/F. M15. $50.00

FORT, Charles. *Lo!* 1931. Kendall. 1st. VG. M2. $50.00

FORT, Charles. *Outcast Manufacturers.* 1909. Dodge. 1st. VG+. M2. $75.00

FORTESCUE, John. *Governance of England: Otherwise Called the Difference...* 1926. London. Oxford. 2nd imp. M11. $125.00

FORTIER, Y.O. *Geology of North-Central Part of Arctic Archipelago...* 1963. Geol Survey Canada Memoir 320. 671p. VG/torn box. D8. $25.00

FORTMAN, Edmund J. *Everlasting Life: Towards a Theology of the Future Life.* 1986. Alba House. 369p. G/wrp. B29. $7.50

FORTUINE, Robert. *Chills & Fever: Health & Disease in Early History of Alaska.* 1989. np. 1st. inscr. 8vo. 393p. gray cloth. NF/dj. P4. $45.00

FORTUNE, Dion. *Moon Magic.* 1972. Weiser. NF/dj. M2. $12.00

FORTUNE, T. Thomas. *Black & White: Land, Labor & Politics in the South.* 1884. NY. Fords Howard Hulbert. 1st. 310p. coth. VG. B4. $600.00

FOSTER, Alan Dean. *Day of the Dissonance.* 1984. Phantasia. 1st. 1/375. sgn/#d. F/F. P3. $40.00

FOSTER, Alan Dean. *Icerigger.* 1976. London. 1st. F/dj. M2. $45.00

FOSTER, Alan Dean. *Moment of the Magician.* 1984. Phantasia. 1/375. sgn/#d. F/dj/case. P3. $40.00

FOSTER, Alan Dean. *Star Wars.* 1976. NY. Del Rey BC. ghostwriter/sgn Alan Dean Foster. F/NF. A11. $275.00

FOSTER, Alan Dean. *To the Vanishing Point.* 1988. Warner. 1st. NF/NF. P3. $16.00

FOSTER, Charles H.W. *Eastern Yacht Club Ditty Box, 1870-1900.* 1932. Norwood, MA. Plimpton. 317p. T7. $65.00

FOSTER, Genevieve. *Abraham Lincoln's World.* 1944. Scribner 1st/A ed. sgn. 347p. cloth. VG+/clip. M20. $75.00

FOSTER, Genevieve. *Augustus Caesar's World.* 1947. Scribner. 1st/A ed. 4to. 330p. VG. T5. $40.00

FOSTER, Genevieve. *Year of the Flying Machine, 1903.* 1977. NY. 1st. 96p. half cloth. VG/dj. B18. $12.50

FOSTER, Hal. *Prince Valiant in the New World.* 1956. Hastings. VG/VG. P3. $35.00

FOSTER, M.S. *Causes of Spatial & Temporal Patterns...* 1988. CA Academy of Sci. 45p. pict wrp. B1. $15.00

FOSTER, Michael. *Claude Bernard.* 1899. NY. 1st. 245p. A13. $60.00

FOSTER, Mulford B. *Brazil: Orchid of the Tropics.* 1946 (1945). NY. 2nd. ils/photos. dj. B26. $46.00

FOSTER, Pearl Byrd. *Classic American Cooking.* 1983. S&S. G/dj. A16. $15.00

FOSTER, R.F. *Moat House Mystery.* 1930. MacAulay. G+. P3. $20.00

FOSTER, R.F. *Practical Poker.* 1905. Brentano. 1st. 253p. pict cloth. VG. J2. $125.00

FOSTER, Robert V. *Systematic Theology.* 1898. Cumberland Presb. 868p. xl. VG. B29. $11.00

FOSTER & GIFFORD. *Comparative Morphology of Vascular Plants.* 1974. Freeman. 2nd. ils. 751p. VG+. S15. $11.00

FOUQUE, DeLaMotte. *Undine.* (1909). London. 1st. ils Rackham/15 tipped-in pl. cloth. VG. S13. $150.00

FOURNIER, Pierre Simon. *Manuel Typographique.* 1764-1766. Paris. Fournier. 2 vol. 8vo. fld/double-p pl. aeg. full brn morocco. R12. $7,500.00

FOWLER, Christopher. *Rune.* 1991. Ballantine. 1st. author's 2nd novel. F/F. M22. $30.00

FOWLER, Connie May. *Sugar Cage.* 1992. Putnam. 1st. sgn. F/F. R13. $50.00

FOWLER, Guy. *Dawn Patrol.* 1930. Grosset Dunlap. MTI. 241p. VG+/dj. B18. $25.00

FOWLER, John M. *Fallout: Study of Superbombs, Strontium 90 & Survival.* 1960. NY. 2nd. 235p. F/dj. A17. $15.00

FOWLER, Karen Joy. *Sara Canary.* 1991. NY. Holt. 1st. sgn/dtd 1991. author's 1st novel. F/F. M23. $50.00

FOWLER, Manley B. *Prophecy; or, Love & Friendship...* 1821. NY. Murden Thomson. 1st. 18mo. 34p. M1. $150.00

FOWLER & WRIGHT. *Moving Frontier.* 1972. np. Great Explorers series. 348p. VG+/torn. B18. $22.50

FOWLES, John. *Brief History of Lyme.* 1981. Lyme Regis. Friends of the Mus. sgn. F/stapled wrp. B4. $125.00

FOWLES, John. *Collector.* 1963. London. Cape. 1st issue (no blurbs on dj). VG/dj. A24. $375.00

FOWLES, John. *Daniel Martin.* 1977. Jonathan Cape. 1st Eng. NF/VG. M19. $25.00

FOWLES, John. *Ebony Tower.* 1974. London. Cape. VG/clip. A24. $45.00

FOWLES, John. *Enigma.* 1987. Helsinki. Eurographica. 1st. 1/350. sgn. F/F. B4. $150.00

FOWLES, John. *Magus.* 1966. London. Cape. 1st. NF/dj. A24. $150.00

FOWLES, John. *Mantissa.* 1982. Little Brn. 1st. F/F. P3. $20.00

FOWLES, John. *Poems.* 1973. Ecco. 1st. NF/NF. M19. $35.00

FOWLES, John. *Swan Song of the European Wild.* 1965. Venture. 1st. NF. B3. $20.00

FOX, Frances L. *San Jose's Luis Maria Peralta & His Adobe.* 1975. San Jose. Smith-McKay. sgn. 92p. orange cloth. as new/dj. K7. $35.00

FOX, Frances Margaret. *Little Bear's Adventures.* 1923. Rand McNally. 1st. ils Frances Beem. bl cloth/mc pl. VG. M5. $75.00

FOX, George Henry. *Photographic Ils of Skin Diseases.* 1880. NY. 48 pl. 102p. brn cloth. B14. $375.00

FOX, George. *Amok.* 1978. S&S. 1st. VG/VG. P3. $15.00

FOX, George. *Concerning Persecution in All Ages to This Day.* 1682. London. John Bringhurst. 1st. V3. $140.00

FOX, George. *Gospel Truth Demonstrated in Collection Doctrinal Books.* 1706. London. Sowle. 1090p. full leather. V3. $185.00

FOX, George. *Journal or Historical Account of Life, Travels, Sufferings.* 1832. Phil. Kimber Sharpless. 672p. worn leather. V3. $50.00

FOX, George. *Warlord's Hill.* 1982. Times Books. 1st. VG+/VG+. N4. $17.50

FOX, Helen Morgenthau. *Patio Gardens.* 1929. NY. ils/fld plans. 228p. yel/bl cloth. VG. B26. $72.50

FOX, James M. *Iron Virgin.* 1951. Little Brn. 1st. VG/dj. M25. $45.00

FOX, James M. *Shroud for Mr Bundy.* 1952. Little Brn. 1st. VG. P3. $15.00

FOX, John Jr. *Little Shepherd of Kingdom Come.* 1931. Scribner. 1st. ils NC Wyeth/14 full-p pl. 322p. VG. D1. $200.00

FOX, Larry. *New England Patriots.* 1979. Atheneum. 1st. photos. VG+/dj. P8. $25.00

FOX, Norman A. *Arizona Stranger.* 1973. Collins. VG/VG. P3. $12.00

FOXE, Arthur N. *Plague: Laennec (1782-1826)...* 1947. NY. Hobson. 122p. VG. K3. $25.00

FOXON, David. *Libertine Literature in England 1660-1745.* 1965. NY. U Books. 70p+13 pl. F. A17. $17.50

FOXX, Jack; see Pronzini, Bill.

FRACKELTON & SEELY. *Sagebrush Dentist, Old WY in Days of Buffalo Bill...* 1947. Trails End. 1st revised. 258p. VG/dj. J2. $175.00

FRADKIN, Philip L. *River No More.* 1981. Knopf. 1st. 8vo. 360p. bl/blk cloth. VG+. F7. $35.00

FRAIGNEAU, Andre. *Jean Cocteau on the Film, a Conversation Recorded.* 1954. Roy Pub. ils. VG+/dj. C9. $75.00

FRANCATELLI, C. *Modern Cook; a Practical Guide to Culinary Art.* 1846 (1880). lg 8vo. 80p of menus. VG. E6. $75.00

FRANCE, Anatole. *Filles et Garcons. Scenes de la Ville et des Champs.* nd. Paris. Librairie Hachett. ils DeMonvel. 24p. pict brd. R5. $100.00

FRANCE, Anatole. *Golden Tales of Anatole France.* 1927. Dodd Mead. 1st. ils LA Patterson. F. M19. $45.00

FRANCIS, Dick. *Blood Sport.* 1967. London. Michael Joseph. 1st. NF/dj. Q1. $350.00

FRANCIS, Dick. *Bolt.* 1986. Michael Joseph. 1st. F/F. M25. $35.00

FRANCIS, Dick. *Bonecrack.* 1972. Harper. 1st Am. NF/NF. N4. $60.00

FRANCIS, Dick. *Break In.* 1986. Michael Joseph. 1st. VG/VG. P3. $18.00

FRANCIS, Dick. *Danger.* 1983. Putnam. 1st. VG/VG. P3. $20.00

FRANCIS, Dick. *Dead Cert.* 1989. NY. Armchair Detective. 1/26 lettered. sgn. F/case. M15. $150.00

FRANCIS, Dick. *Driving Force.* 1992. London. Michael Joseph. true 1st. sgn. F/dj. D10. $40.00

FRANCIS, Dick. *Edge.* 1988. London. Michael Joseph. true 1st. sgn. NF/NF. D10. $45.00

FRANCIS, Dick. *Edge.* 1988. NY. Putnam. 1st Am. F/F. T12. $45.00

FRANCIS, Dick. *For Kicks.* 1965. London. Michael Joseph. 1st. NF/dj. Q1. $1,000.00

FRANCIS, Dick. *High Stakes.* 1975. Harper. 1st Am. VG/VG. M22. $30.00

FRANCIS, Dick. *Hot Money.* 1987. Michael Joseph. 1st. F/F. B3/Q1. $60.00

FRANCIS, Dick. *In the Frame.* 1976. Harper Row. 1st Am. 8vo. F/NF. T10. $45.00

FRANCIS, Dick. *Jockey's Life.* 1986. Putnam. later prt. F/VG. P8. $25.00

FRANCIS, Dick. *Knockdown.* 1974. Harper. 1st. VG/G. M19. $35.00

FRANCIS, Dick. *Nerve.* 1964. London. Michael Joseph. 1st. F/NF. M15. $850.00

FRANCIS, Dick. *Proof.* 1984. London. Michael Joseph. 1st. F/F. M15/T12. $75.00

FRANCIS, Dick. *Rat Race.* 1971. Harper Row. 1st. F/VG. M19. $35.00

FRANCIS, Dick. *Risk.* 1977. London. Michael Joseph. 1st. F/F. M15. $75.00

FRANCIS, Dick. *Slay-Ride.* 1973. Michael Joseph. 1st. NF/dj. M25. $50.00

FRANCIS, Dick. *Smokescreen.* 1973. Harper Row. 1st. VG/VG. P3. $35.00

FRANCIS, Dick. *Sport of Queens.* 1969. Harper Row. 1st Am. F/F. M15. $250.00

FRANCIS, Dick. *Straight.* 1989. London. Michael Joseph. true 1st. sgn. F/dj. D10. $45.00

FRANCIS, Dick. *Trial Run.* 1978. London. Michael Joseph. 1st. NF/NF. T12. $85.00

FRANCIS, Dick. *Twice Shy.* 1981. Michael Joseph. 1st. NF/NF. P3. $30.00

FRANCIS, Philip W. *Remarkable Adventures of Little Boy Pip.* 1907. SF. Paul Elder. 1st. ils Merle Johnson. 4to. pict brd. dj. R5. $300.00

FRANCIS, Richard H. *Whispering Gallery.* 1984. Norton. 1st. VG/VG. P3. $15.00

FRANCK, Harry. *Vagabonding Down the Andes.* 1917. NY. Century. 1st. 612p. teg. F3. $20.00

FRANCL, Joseph. *Overland Journey of Joseph Francl, First Bohemian...* 1968. SF. Wm Wreden. 1/540. ils. 59p. pict brd. D11. $60.00

FRANCOIS, Yves. *Citz Paradigm.* 1975. Doubleday. 1st. F/dj. M2/P3. $15.00

FRANCOISE. *Fanchette & Jeannot.* 1937. Grosset Dunlap. ils. VG. P2. $50.00

FRANCOISE. *Springtime for Jeanne-Marie.* 1955. Scribner. 1st/A. 4to. VG+/dj. M5. $25.00

FRANCOISE. *Story of Colette.* 1940. Scribner. 1st/A. VG/G. M5. $110.00

FRANCOME & MACGREGOR. *Eavesdropper.* 1986. London. MacDonald. 1st. sgn. author's 1st novel. F/dj. M25. $60.00

FRANGSMYR, Tore. *Linnaeus: The Man & His Work.* 1983. Berkeley. ils. 203p. F/dj. B26. $29.00

FRANK, Alan. *Galactic Aliens.* 1979. Chartwell. 1st. F/F. M2. $12.00

FRANK, Alan. *Horror Movies.* 1974. Octopus. 1st. VG/VG. P3. $20.00

FRANK, Anne. *Anne Frank: The Diary of a Young Girl.* 1952. Doubleday Doran. 1st Am. 285p. VG/G+. P2. $250.00

FRANK, Benis. *Brief History of the 3rd Marines.* 1968. WA. maps/notes. sc. VG. S16. $25.00

FRANK, Bruno Z. *Man Called Cervantes.* 1935. Viking. 1st. F/F. M19. $25.00

FRANK, C.W. *Anatomy of a Waterfowl.* 1982. Gretna. Pelican. ils/mc pl/lg fld mc pl. 297p. cloth. NF. M12. $37.50

FRANK, Gerold. *Boston Strangler.* 1967. Jonathan Cape. 1st. VG/fair. P3. $18.00

FRANK, Niklas. *In the Shadow of the Reich.* 1991. Knopf. 371p. VG/dj. S3. $25.00

FRANK, Pat. *Forbidden Area.* 1956. Lippincott. 1st. inscr. VG/VG. B11. $65.00

FRANK, Pat. *Mr Adam.* 1946. Lippincott. 13th prt. 252p. G. W2. $10.00

FRANKAU, Pamela. *Pen to Paper: A Novelist's Notebook.* 1961. London. 1st. inscr. VG/dj. T9. $30.00

FRANKE, Herbert. *Zone Null.* 1974. Seabury. 1st. F/dj. M2. $25.00

FRANKLIN, G.C. *Wild Animals of the Five River Country.* (1947). Houghton Mifflin. ils MO Abbott. 271p. cloth. NF/VG+. M12. $15.00

FRANKLIN, H. Bruce. *Future Perfect.* 1968. Oxford. F/dj. M2. $20.00

FRANKLIN, John Hope. *Racial Equality in America.* 1976. Chicago. 1st. inscr. 113p. F/NF. B4. $150.00

FRANKLIN, John. *Narrative of 2nd Expedition to Shores of Plar Sea.* 1969 (1829). NY. Greenwood. facsimile. 4to. 6 fld maps. 320p. T7. $90.00

FRANKLIN, K.J. *Monograph on Veins.* 1937. Springfield. 1st. 410p. A13. $75.00

FRANKLIN, Stephen. *Knowledge Park.* 1972. Toronto. 1st. F/F. T12. $95.00

FRANKLYN, Irwin R. *Flight: An Epic of the Air.* 1929. Grosset Dunlap. photoplay ed. 245p. VG+/dj. B18. $25.00

FRANKLYN, Robert Alan. *Developing Bosom Beauty.* 1959. Frederick Fell. 1st. ils. 141p. VG+. A25. $18.00

FRANKS, K.A. *Early Oklahoma Oil: Photographic History 1859-1936.* 1981. TX A&M. 1st. 325 photos. F/dj. M4. $30.00

FRANKS, K.A. *Oklahoma Petroleum Industry.* 1980. OK U. 1st. 150 photos. F/dj. M4. $25.00

FRANZEN, Jonathan. *Twenty-Seventh City.* 1988. FSG. ARC. author's 1st book. NF/wrp. A24. $25.00

FRANZEN, Jonathan. *Twenty-Seventh City.* 1988. FSG. 1st. F/NF. P3. $20.00

FRANZEN, Jonathan. *Twenty-Seventh City.* 1988. FSG. 1st. sgn. author's 1st book. F/F. D10. $50.00

FRASER, Antonia. *Quiet as a Nun.* 1977. Viking. 1st. VG/VG. P3. $18.00

FRASER, Antonia. *Your Royal Hostage.* 1987. Weidenfeld Nicolson. 1st. VG/VG. P3. $19.00

FRASER, C.L. *Pirates.* 1922. 1st. ils. VG+. S13. $45.00

FRASER, Claud Lovat. *Book of Simple Toys.* 1982. Bryn Mawr. 1st thus. 8vo. red textured cloth/label. R5. $100.00

FRASER, Colin. *Harry Ferguson: Inventor & Pioneer.* 1972. London. Murray. 294p. dj. A10. $35.00

FRASER, Donald. *Autobiography of an African Retold in Biographical Form...* 1970 (1925). Negro U. rpt. VG. W1. $25.00

FRASER, George MacDonald. *Flashman.* 1969. London. Jenkins. 1st Eng. F/NF clip. T11. $125.00

FRASER, George MacDonald. *Flashman.* 1969. World. 1st Am. F/clip. Q1. $150.00

FRASER, George MacDonald. *Flashman & the Dragon.* 1986 (1985). Knopf. 1st Am. 320p. NF/dj. M20. $55.00

FRASER, George MacDonald. *Flashman & the Mountain of Light.* 1990. London. Collins. true 1st. F/clip. D10. $45.00

FRASER, George MacDonald. *Flashman & the Redskins.* 1982. Knopf. 1st. F/dj. Q1. $50.00

FRASER, George MacDonald. *Flashman in the Great Game.* 1975. Knopf. 1st Am. F/NF. Q1. $60.00

FRASER, George MacDonald. *Flashman in the Great Game.* 1975. London. Barrie Jenkins. true 1st. F/clip. D10. $50.00

FRASER, George MacDonald. *Flashman's Lady.* 1978. Knopf. 1st Am. F/dj. M15/Q1. $50.00

FRASER, George MacDonald. *General Danced at Dawn.* 1970. London. Barrie Jenkins. 1st. F/F. B4. $150.00

FRASER, George MacDonald. *McAusland in the Rough.* 1974. Knopf. 1st Am. F/dj. B4/Q1. $100.00

FRASER, George MacDonald. *Mr American.* 1980. S&S. 1st. rem mk. F/dj. Q1. $50.00

FRASER, George MacDonald. *Pyrates.* 1983. Collins. 1st. F/F. P3. $35.00

FRASER, George MacDonald. *Pyrates.* 1984. Knopf. 1st. F/F. P3. $30.00

FRASER, George MacDonald. *Royal Flash.* 1970. Knopf. 1st Am. F/NF. Q1. $150.00

FRASER, George MacDonald. *Steel Bonnets.* 1972. VG. M17. $30.00

FRASER, Kathleen. *Stilts, Somersaults & Headstands: Game Poems...* 1968. Atheneum. 1st. 37p. F/F. D4. $35.00

FRASER, Kathleen. *Stilts, Somersaults & Headstands: Game Poems...* 1968. Atheneum. 1st. 8vo. 37p. VG/VG clip. C14. $15.00

FRASER, R. *Once Round the Sun, Story of International Geophysical Year.* 1957. Macmillan. 160p. xl. G/dj. D8. $12.50

FRASER, Samuel. *Potato.* 1915. NY. Orange Judd. 185p. VG. A10. $22.00

FRASER, Samuel. *Strawberry: Culture, Harvesting, Marketing.* 1926. ils. xl. E6. $15.00

FRASSANITO, William A. *Grant & Lee: Virginia Campaigns 1864-1865.* 1983. Scribner. 1st. 442p. VG/dj. M20. $40.00

FRAYLING, Christopher *Vampyre: A Bedside Companion.* 1978. Scribner. 1st Am. F/F Gorey ils. B2. $45.00

FRAYN, Michael. *Landing on the Sun.* 1991. Viking. 1st. F/F. P3. $22.00

FRAYNE, Trent. *Mad Men of Hockey.* 1974. Dodd Mead. 1st. F/VG. P8. $30.00

FRAZAR, Douglas. *Perserverance Island.* 1899. Lee Shepard. VG. M2. $40.00

FRAZEE, Steve. *Sky Block.* 1953. Rinehart. 1st. F/F. B4. $125.00

FRAZER, Deryk. *Reptiles & Amphibians in Britain.* 1989 (1983). London. New Naturalist series. 254p. F/F. S15. $25.00

FRAZER, J.G. *Golden Bough.* 1951. Macmillan. G+. P3. $20.00

FRAZIER, E. Franklin. *Negro Family in the United States.* 1939. Chicago. 1st. charts/tables. 686p. VG. B4. $100.00

FRAZIER, Ian. *Dating Your Mom.* 1986. FSG. 1st. author's 1st book. F/F. M23. $30.00

FRAZIER, Ian. *Nobody Better, Better Than Nobody.* 1987. NY. FSG. 1st. F/NF. M23. $20.00

FRAZIER, Robert Caine; see Creasey, John.

FRAZIER & JARES. *Clyde.* 1970. HRW. 1st. photos. F/VG. P8. $30.00

FRAZIER & OFFEN. *Walt Frazier.* 1988. Times. 1st. sgn Frazier. F/F. P8. $50.00

FREDE, Richard. *Secret Circus.* 1967. Random. 1st. VG/VG. P3. $25.00

FREDERICKS, J. Paget. *Miss Pert's Christmas Tree.* 1929. Macmillan. 1st. lg 4to. VG. M5. $65.00

FREDERICS, Diana. *Diana, a Strange Autobiography.* 1939. NY. Dial. 1st. flexible gray cloth. F/dj. M24. $400.00

FREDMAN, John. *False Joanna.* 1970. Bobbs Merrill. F/F. P3. $15.00

FREE, John B. *Insect Pollination of Crops.* 1970. NY. Academic. 544p. VG/dj. A10. $35.00

FREEBORN, Brian. *Good Luck Mister Cain.* 1976. St Martin. 1st. VG/G+. P3. $12.00

FREEHAND, Julianna. *Seafaring Legacy: Photographs, Diaries, Letters...1859-1908.* 1981. Random. 1st. 209p. NF/NF. P4. $38.00

FREELAND, Humphrey. *Fountain of Youth.* 1866. London. 1st. VG. M2. $100.00

FREELING, Nicolas. *Tsing-Boum.* 1969. Harper Row. 1st. VG/VG. P3. $20.00

FREELING, Nicolas. *Wolfnight.* 1982. Pantheon. 1st. F/VG. P3. $15.00

FREEMAN, Bud. *You Don't Look Like a Musician.* 1974. Detroit. Balamp. 1st. F/F. B2. $50.00

FREEMAN, Don. *Seal & the Slick.* 1974. Viking. 1st. obl 4to. F/VG+. P2. $55.00

FREEMAN, Don. *Space Witch.* 1959. Viking. 1st. 48p. VG/G+. P2. $135.00

FREEMAN, Douglas Southall. *Lee's Lieutenants.* 1946. 3 vol. ils. VG. M17. $150.00

FREEMAN, Douglas Southall. *Robert E Lee: A Biography.* 1934. Scribner. 4 vol. 1st. sgn. gilt red cloth. VG. M20. $230.00

FREEMAN, Douglas Southall. *South to Posterity: An Intro to Writing Confederate Hist.* 1983. Broadfoot. facsimile 1951 Scribner. F/F. A17. $30.00

FREEMAN, Estelle B. *Their Sisters' Keepers: Women's Prison Reform in America.* 1981. MI U. 1st. VG/VG. V4. $17.50

FREEMAN, Ira M. *Look-It Up Book of Space.* 1969. Random. 4to. 129p. G. K5. $13.00

FREEMAN, James Dillet. *Once Upon a Christmas.* 1978. Unity. 1st. 173p. NF. W2. $20.00

FREEMAN, Joseph. *Long Pursuit.* 1947. Rinehart. 1st. VG/VG. B4. $85.00

FREEMAN, Lois M. *Betty Crocker's Parties for Children.* 1964. Golden/Western. 2nd. ils Martin. VG+. C8. $17.50

FREEMAN, Margaret B. *Story of the Three Kings.* 1955. MOMA. woodcuts. VG. M17. $25.00

FREEMAN, R. Austin. *Dr Thorndyke Omnibus.* 1933. Dodd Mead. later prt. VG+. N4. $30.00

FREEMAN, R. Austin. *Dr Thorndyke's Crime File.* 1941. Dodd Mead. 1st. G. N4. $45.00

FREEMAN, R. Austin. *John Thorndyke's Cases.* 1909. London. Chatto Windus. 1st. pict cloth. F. M15. $800.00

FREEMAN, R. Austin. *Mr Pottermack's Oversight.* 1930. Dodd Mead. 1st. F/NF. M15. $175.00

FREEMAN, R. Austin. *Silent Witness.* 1915. Winston. 1st. VG. M22. $65.00

FREEMAN, R. Austin. *Stoneware Monkey.* 1938. Hodder Stoughton. 1st. G+. P3. $35.00

FREEMAN, Walter Jackson. *Neuropathology: Anatomical Foundation of Nervous Diseases.* 1933. Phil. Saunders. 349p. panelled bl-gr cloth. VG. G1. $75.00

FREEMAN & PITCAIRN. *Adventures of Romney Pringle.* 1968. Train. 1st. xl. VG/VG+. N4. $25.00

FREEMANTLE, Anne. *Protestant Mystics.* 1964. Weidenfeld Nicolson. 1st. VG. A20. $25.00

FREEMANTLE, Brian. *Blind Run.* 1986. Bantam. 1st. VG/VG. P3. $16.00

FREEMANTLE, Brian. *November Man.* 1976. London. Cape. 1st. F/dj. M15. $75.00

FREEMANTLE, Brian. *O'Farrell's Law.* 1990. Tor. 1st. NF/NF. P3. $18.00

FREEMANTLE, Brian. *Run Around.* 1989. Bantam. 1st. F/F. P3. $17.00

FREID, Jacob. *Judaism & Community: New Directions in Jewish Social Work.* 1968. Yoseloff. 22 articles. 248p. VG/dj. S3. $23.00

FREIDEL, Frank. *Over There, Story of America's 1st Great Overseas Crusade.* 1964. Bramhall. 1st. 300+ photos. 385p. gr cloth. VG/dj. K7. $45.00

FREIDENREICH, Harriet Pass. *Jews of Yugoslavia: Quest for Community.* 1979. JPS. 323p. VG/dj. S3. $40.00

FRENCH, Albert. *Holly.* 1995. Viking. 1st. F/F. R13. $35.00

FRENCH, Joseph Lewis. *Great Ghost Stories.* 1918. Dodd Mead. 1st. VG. M2. $40.00

FRENCH, Marilyn. *Bleeding Heart.* 1980. Summit. 1st. F/F. T12. $12.50

FRENCH & KENNEDY. *Niels Bohr. A Centenary Volume.* 1985. Cambridge, MA. Harvard. ils. VG/dj. K3. $30.00

FRENEAU, Phillip. *Some Account of Capture of the Ship Aurora.* 1899. NY. Mansfield Wessels. 49p. VG. T7. $50.00

FRERE, Thomas. *Hoyle's Games With a Brief History of Playing Cards.* 1857. Boston. Improved ed. 356p. VG. S1. $30.00

FRESHNEY, R.I. *Animal Cell Culture, a Practical Approach.* 1986. IRL PR. 248p. pict brd. F. B1. $35.00

FREUD, Sigmund. *Collected Papers.* 1950. London. Hogarth. 5 vol. 5th & 6th imp. F/dj. H1. $125.00

FREUD, Sigmund. *Psychopathology of Everyday Life.* 1914. NY. 1st authorized. trans VG. M17. $250.00

FREYER, Fredric. *Black Black Hearse.* 1955. St Martin. 1st. VG/G+. P3. $25.00

FRICKE. *Wizard of Oz: Official 50th Anniversary Pictorial History.* 1989. 400 photos. 255p. F/F. A4. $85.00

FRIED, Henry B. *Watch Repairer's Manual.* 1949. Van Nostrand. 1st. ils. VG/dj. K3. $20.00

FRIED, John J. *Life Along the San Andreas Fault.* 1973. Saturday Review. 1st. sgn. NF/NF. O4. $15.00

FRIEDBERG, Gertrude. *Revolving Boy.* 1966. Gollancz. 1st. NF/NF. P3. $45.00

FRIEDEBERG, S. *Joshua: Annotated Hebrew Text With Introduction...* 1913. London. Heinemann. 245p. G+/poor. S3. $24.00

FRIEDENWALD, Harry. *Jews & Medicine, Essays.* 1944-1946. Baltimore. 1st. 2 vol. 817p. A13. $250.00

FRIEDHOFF, Richard Mark. *Visualization: Second Computer Revolution.* 1989. Abrams. 1st. F/dj. M2. $20.00

FRIEDLANDER, Saul. *Prelude to Downfall: Hitler & the United States 1939-41.* 1967. Knopf. 1st Am. 328p. VG/dj. M20. $10.00

FRIEDMAN, Bruce Jay. *Dick.* 1970. Knopf. 1st. sgn. VG/VG. R14. $35.00

FRIEDMAN, Bruce Jay. *Let's Hear It for a Beautiful Guy.* 1984. DIF. 1st. F/F. A20. $25.00

FRIEDMAN, Bruce Jay. *Let's Hear It for a Beautiful Guy.* 1984. DIF. 1st. NF/NF. P3. $20.00

FRIEDMAN, H. *Sun & Earth.* 1986. Scientific Am Books. ils/pl. 251p. F/dj. D8. $12.00

FRIEDMAN, Herbert. *Parasitic Weaverbirds.* 1960. WA. 15 pl. 196p. VG. S15. $28.00

FRIEDMAN, Jake. *Jake Friedman's Common Sense Candy Teacher.* 1915 (1911). w/supp by Wm Kennedy. VG. E6. $75.00

FRIEDMAN, Kinky. *Case of Lone Star.* 1987. NY. Morrow. 1st. sgn. author's 2nd book. NF/F. A24. $60.00

FRIEDMAN, Kinky. *Frequent Flier.* 1989. Morrow. 1st. F/F. M19. $25.00

FRIEDMAN, Kinky. *God Bless John Wayne.* 1995. S&S. 1st. sgn. F/F. A23. $40.00

FRIEDMAN, Kinky. *Greenwich Killing Time.* 1986. Morrow. 1st. inscr/dtd 1986. author's 1st book. F/NF. A24. $85.00

FRIEDMAN, Kinky. *When the Cat's Away.* 1988. Morrow. 1st. sgn. F/F. A23. $40.00

FRIEDMAN, M. *Jewish Life in Philadelphia 1830-1940.* 1983. ils. VG/VG. E6. $15.00

FRIEDMAN, Mickey. *Temporary Ghost.* 1989. Viking. 1st. VG/VG. P3. $18.00

FRIEDMAN, Norman. *US Aircraft Carriers: Illustrated Design History.* 1983. Annapolis. photos/drawings/notes. 427p. VG/VG. S16. $30.00

FRIEDMAN, Philip. *Roads to Extinction: Essays on the Holocaust.* 1980. JPS. 24 essays. 610p. VG/dj. S3. $39.00

FRIEDMANN, Marion. *I Will Still Be Moved: Reports From South Africa.* 1963. Quadrangle. later prt. NF/dj. M25. $25.00

FRIEDRICH, Otto. *Going Crazy.* 1976. S&S. 1st. F/F. B35. $20.00

FRIEL, Arthur O. *Mountains of Mystery.* 1954. Harper. 1st. G+. P3. $50.00

FRIEND, Esther. *Topsy Turvey & Tin Clown.* 1934 (1932). pict brd. VG+. S13. $25.00

FRIENDLY, A. *Beaufort of the Admiralty: Life of Sir Francis Beaufort...* 1977. ils. VG/VG. M17. $20.00

FRIER, Jane Eayre. *Mary Frances Housekeeper.* 1914. Phil. Winston. 1st. VG. B5. $175.00

FRIES, R. *Empire in Pine: Story of Lumbering in Wisconsin 1830-1930.* 1951. Madison. 1st. 285p. VG/G. B5. $35.00

FRINK, Maurice. *When Grass Was King.* 1956. CO U. 1st. ils/pl. 465p. VG/VG. J2. $315.00

FRISCH, Ephraim. *Historical Survey of Jewish Philanthropy...* 1969. Cooper Sq. 196p. VG+. S3. $24.00

FRISON-ROCHE, R. *Lost Trail of the Sahara.* 1952. Prentice Hall. 1st Am. trans Paul Bowles. F/dj. Q1. $75.00

FRITZ, Jean. *China Homecoming.* 1985. Putnam. 1st. sgn. VG/VG. B11. $25.00

FRITZ, Jean. *Homesick.* 1982. Putnam. 2nd. sgn. VG/VG. B11. $25.00

FRITZ, Samuel. *Journal of Travels & Labours of Father Samuel Fritz.* 1992. London. Hakluyt Soc. 2nd series. 164p. P4. $135.00

FRITZSCH, H. *Quarks, the Stuff of Matter.* 1983. Basic Books. 1st Eng. F/dj. D8. $15.00

FRODERSTROM, H. *Genus Sedum.* 1930-35. Goteborg. English text in 4 parts as 1. brn buckram. NF. B26. $195.00

FROSSARD, Jean. *Guide to Basic Dressage.* 1978. London. Pelham Horsemaster series. prt. VG/VG. O3. $15.00

FROST, Frances. *American Caravan.* 1944. Whittlesey. 1st. 4to. VG/G. P2. $20.00

FROST, Frances. *Christmas in the Woods.* 1942. Harper. stated 1st. ils Aldren Watson. F/VG. M5. $22.00

FROST, John. *Indian Wars of the United States.* 1859. NY. CM Saxton. 300p. gilt brn cloth. VG. K7. $125.00

FROST, John. *Thrilling Incidents of the Wars of the United States.* 1853. NY. Robert Sears. 8vo. 600p. brn brd. G. K7. $65.00

FROST, Kent. *My Canyon Lands.* 1971. Abelard-Schuman. sgn. 8vo. orange cloth. NF/VG+. F7. $30.00

FROST, Lawrence A. *Custer Album.* 1964. Seattle. Superior. 1st. A19. $50.00

FROST, Lawrence A. *General Custer's Libbie.* 1976. Seattle, WA. Superior. dj. A19. $45.00

FROST, Richard H. *Mooney Case: San Francisco Preparedness Day Bombing of 1916.* 1968. Stanford. 1st. VG/VG. V4. $35.00

FROST, Robert. *Accidentally on Purpose.* 1960. NY. HRW. 1st. F/wrp. Q1. $35.00

FROST, Robert. *Birches.* 1988. NY. Holt. 1st. 32p. F/F. D4. $30.00

FROST, Robert. *Boy's Will.* 1915. NY. 1st Am/1st state/1st bdg. bl silk. VG. w/ephemera. A11. $225.00

FROST, Robert. *Complete Poems.* 1949. NY. Henry Holt. 1st. 1/500. sgn. gilt cream cloth. F/NF box. M24. $550.00

FROST, Robert. *In the Clearing.* 1962. HRW. 1st. F/F. B35. $45.00

FROST, Robert. *Letters of Robert Frost to Louis Untermeyer.* 1963. Holt Rinehart. 1st. F/clip. Q1. $40.00

FROST, Robert. *Neither Out Far Nor in Deep: A Poem.* 1935. Holt. 1st. F/wrp. Q1. $125.00

FROST, Robert. *Poetry.* 1971. Barre, MA. Imp Soc. 1/1950. 2 vol. 8vo. sgn Rudolph Ruzicka. F/case. B24. $225.00

FROST, Robert. *You Come Too: Favorite Poems for Young Readers.* 1959. NY. Holt. 1st. 94p. F/dj. D4. $45.00

FROUD, Brian. *Goblins.* 1983. Macmillan. 1st Am. popup. VG+. P2. $35.00

FRY, J. *Combat Soldier.* 1968. DC. sgn. ils/maps. VG/G. S16. $35.00

FRY, Rosalie. *Wind Call.* 1955. Dutton. 1st. VG/G. M5. $65.00

FRYATT. *Horn Book Sampler on Children's Books & Reading...* 1969. 261p. F/F. A4. $35.00

FRYE, D.E. *12th Virginia Cavalry.* 1988. Lynchburg. 1st ltd. 1/1000. sgn. 188p. F/dj. M4. $40.00

FRYER, J.E. *Mary Frances Housekeeper: Adventures Among the Doll People.* 1914. Phil. 1st. all paper dolls present. VG. B5. $190.00

FRYER, J.E. *Mary Frances Knitting & Crocheting Books...* (1918). Winston. ils JA Boyer. VG. B15. $130.00

FRYER, J.E. *Mary Francis First Aid Book.* 1916. Phil. Winston. 1st. 8vo. bl cloth/pict label. dj. R5. $285.00

FU, Li-Kuo. *China Plant Red Data Book. Rare & Endangered Plants Vol I.* 1992. Beijing. 1st. ils/photos. 741p. as new/dj. B26. $195.00

FUCHIDA & OKUMIYA. *Midway: Battle That Doomed Japan.* 1955. ils. VG/G+. M17. $25.00

FUENTES, Carlos. *Buried Mirror.* 1992. Houghton Mifflin. 1st. 4to. 399p. F3. $30.00

FUENTES, Carlos. *Burnt Water.* 1980. FSG. 1st Am. sgn. F/F. D10. $50.00

FUENTES, Carlos. *Christopher Unborn.* 1989. FSG. 1st. F/F. A20. $20.00

FUENTES, Carlos. *Hydra Head.* 1978. FSG. 1st Am. sgn. F/F. D10. $50.00

FUENTES, Carlos. *Terra Nostra.* 1976. FSG. 1st. F/dj. A24. $50.00

FUENTES, Norberto. *Hemingway in Cuba.* 1984. Secaucus. Lyle Stuart. 1st. photos. F/F. D10. $50.00

FUERTES, Louis Agassiz. *Louis Agassiz Fuertes & the Singular Beauty of Birds.* 1971. NY. 1st. ils/edit Frederick G Marcham. 220p. NF/dj. S15. $95.00

FUJIKAWA, Gyo. *Child's Book of Poems.* nd (1969). Grosset Dunlap. 125p. VG+. C14. $20.00

FUJIKAWA, Gyo. *Mother Goose.* 1968. NY. early or 1st. 125p. VG. M5. $35.00

FULFORD, Margaret *Cladoniae of Eastern Kentucky.* 1938. Cincinnati. 8vo. stiff wrp. VG. A22. $17.00

FULGHUM, Robert. *It Was on Fire When I Lay Down on It.* 1989. Villard. 1st. 218p. F/dj. H1. $18.00

FULLER, Andrew. *Grape Culturist.* 1865 (1864). ils. VG. E6. $40.00

FULLER, Andrew. *Practical Forestry.* 1908. Orange Judd. 299p. VG. A10. $28.00

FULLER, Andrew. *Small Fruit Culturist.* 1867. 1st. ils. VG. E6. $35.00

FULLER, Bucky. *Tetrascroll: Goldilocks & the Three Bears.* 1982. FSG. 1st. F/F. A20. $25.00

FULLER, Jean Overton. *Double Webs.* 1958. Putnam. 1st. 256p. VG/dj. M20. $12.00

FULLER, Mabel Louise. *In Poppy Land.* 1890. ils. G+. M17. $15.00

FULLER, Roy. *Fantasy & Fugue.* 1954. London. Derek Verschoyle. 1st. F/dj. M15. $80.00

FULLERTON, Hugh S. *Jimmy Kirkland & the Plot for the Pennant.* 1915. Winston. 341p. G+/ragged. M20. $50.00

FULLERTON, Hugh S. *Jimmy Kirkland of the Shasta Boys Team.* 1915. Winston. 270p. cloth. VG. M20. $30.00

FULOP-MILLER, Rene. *Triumph Over Pain.* 1938. Bobbs Merrill. 1st. sm 4to. 438p. G+. H1. $8.50

FULTON, James. *Peach Culture.* 1870. Orange Judd. 190p. beveled brd. A10. $35.00

FULTON, John F. *Functional Localization in Relation to Frontal Lobotomy.* 1949. NY. Oxford. 1st Am. 140p. red cloth. VG. G1. $75.00

FULTON, John F. *Harvey Cushing: A Biography.* 1991. NY. Classics Neurology/Neurosurgery Lib. facsimile. G1. $75.00

FUMENTO, Rocco. *Tree of Dark Reflection.* 1962. NY. Knopf. 1st. F/dj. Q1. $50.00

FUNK, Michael. *Ruckenmarks-Entzundung.* 1832. Bamberg. Dresch. 3rd. 12mo. contemporary drab yel brd. G1. $125.00

FUNT, Allen. *Eavesdropper at Large: Adventures in Human Nature...* 1952. Vanguard. 1st. F/VG clip. B4. $85.00

FURBAY, James R. *Along Life's Trail: One Quaker's Experiences...* 1978. Dublin, IN. 157p. VG. V3. $14.00

FURCHTOTT, Ernest. *Pharmacological & Biophysical Agents & Behavior.* 1971. Academic. 402p. tan cloth. VG/dj. G1. $35.00

FURLONG, Charles Wellington. *Gateway to the Sahara.* 1914. Scribner. 2nd. ils/maps. 306p. VG. W1. $18.00

FURNIVALL, Frederick J. *Fifty Earliest English Wills in Court of Probate, London...* 1964 (1882). London. Oxford. facsimile. M11. $50.00

– G –

G.W.P.; see Pettes, G.W.

GABORIAU, Emile. *Champdoce Mystery.* 1913. Scribner. hc. VG. P3. $15.00

GABRIELI, Francesco. *Arabs: A Compact History.* 1963. Hawthorn. 1st ed. 8vo. ils. 216p. VG/dj. W1. $12.00

GADD & PHILIP. *Dickens Dictionary.* 1989. Crescent. F/dj. P3. $10.00

GADDIS, Vincent. *Native American Myths & Mysteries.* 1991. Borderland Sciences. revised ed. 183p. wrp. F3. $10.00

GADDIS, William. *Carpenter's Gothic.* 1985. Viking. 1st ed. F/F. H11. $35.00

GADDIS, William. *Frolic of His Own.* 1994. Poseidon. 1st ed. rem mk. F/F. H11. $30.00

GAG, Wanda. *Growing Pains.* 1946. NY. 1st ed. VG/VG. B5. $75.00

GAGE, Nicholas. *Mafia, USA.* 1972. Playboy. 1st ed. NF/G. R10. $10.00

GAGE, Simon Henry. *Microscope.* 1947 (1908). NY. Comstock. 17th. ils. 617p. xl. K5. $30.00

GAGE, Thomas. *English-American.* 1946. Guatemala City. VG. O7. $45.00

GAGE, Wilson. *Big Blue Island.* 1966. World. 3rd. ils Glen Rounds. 121p. NF/VG clip. C14. $6.00

GAGNON, Maurice. *Inner Ring.* 1985. Collins Crime Club. 1st ed. VG/VG. P3. $18.00

GAINES, Charles. *Stay Hungry.* 1972. Doubleday. 1st ed. author's 1st book. F/VG. M19. $35.00

GAINHAM, Sarah. *Appointment in Vienna.* 1958. Dutton. 1st ed. VG/VG. P3. $15.00

GAINHAM, Sarah. *Private Worlds.* 1971. HRW. 1st ed. VG/VG. P3. $15.00

GALBRAITH, John S. *Crown & Charter.* 1974. Berkeley. VG. O7. $35.00

GALDONE, Paul. *Cat Goes Fiddle-i-fee.* 1985. Clarion. 2nd. ils. unp. F/NF. C14. $10.00

GALE, Gloria. *Calendar Model.* 1957. NY. 1st ed. photos. 254p. NF/VG. N3. $45.00

GALE, Zona. *Birth.* 1937. Appleton Century. 1st ed. sgn. F/F. B4. $75.00

GALE, Zona. *Frank Miller of Mission Inn.* 1938. NY. 1st ed. VG/VG. B5. $25.00

GALEWITZ & WINSLOW. *Fontaine Fox's Toonerville Trolley.* 1972. Scribner. ils. VG/G. P12. $8.00

GALILEO. *Dialogue on the Great World Systems.* 1957 (1953). Chicago. 2nd. sm 4to. 506p. VG. K5. $35.00

GALILEO. *Dialogues Concerning Two New Sciences.* 1914. NY. 300p. cloth/brd. VG. B14. $200.00

GALLAGHER, Stephen. *Boat House.* 1991. NEL. 1st ed. F/F. P3. $28.00

GALLAGHER, Stephen. *Chimera.* 1982. NY. 1st ed. author's 1st book. F/F. H11. $200.00

GALLAGHER, Stephen. *Down River.* 1989. NEL. 1st ed. sgn. F/F. P3. $30.00

GALLAGHER, Stephen. *Follower.* 1991. NEL. 2nd. F/F. P3. $20.00

GALLAGHER, Stephen. *Oktober.* 1989. Tor. 1st ed. NF/F. H11. $25.00

GALLAGHER, Stephen. *Valley of Lights.* 1987. London. NEL. 1st ed. sgn. F/F. T2. $50.00

GALLAGHER. *Jules Verne: A Primary & Secondary Bibliography.* 1980. np. 387p. NF. A4. $65.00

GALLAND, Adolf. *First & the Last: Rise & Fall of German Fighter Forces...* 1954. NY. 1st ed. ils. 368p. G. B18. $50.00

GALLANT, Marvis. *Other Paris.* 1956. Boston. 1st ed. author's 1st book. F/NF. C2. $60.00

GALLANT, Mavis. *Overhead in a Balloon: Twelve Stories of Paris.* 1985. Random. 1st ed. F/F. B4. $65.00

GALLANT, Roy A. *Fires in the Sky.* 1978. NY. 4 Winds. 1st ed. xl. dj. K5. $6.00

GALLENKAMP, Charles. *Maya: The Riddle & Rediscovery of a Lost Civilization.* 1985. NY. Viking. 3rd. 235p. AN/dj. P4. $23.00

GALLICO, Paul. *Abandoned.* 1950. Knopf. 1st ed. VG/VG. P3. $25.00

GALLICO, Paul. *Further Confessions of a Storywriter.* 1961. NY. 1st ed. VG/VG. B5. $30.00

GALLICO, Paul. *Golf Is a Friendly Game.* 1942. NY. 1st ed. VG. B5. $35.00

GALLICO, Paul. *Hand of Mary Constable.* 1954. Heinemann. 1st ed. VG/VG. P3. $20.00

GALLICO, Paul. *Hurricane Story.* 1960. Doubleday. 1st ed. 165p. VG/dj. B18. $25.00

GALLICO, Paul. *Lou Gehrig: Pride of the Yankees.* 1942. Grosset Dunlap. VG/G+. P8. $35.00

GALLICO, Paul. *Love, Let Me Not Hunger.* 1963. Doubleday. 1st ed. VG/G. P3. $15.00

GALLICO, Paul. *Ludmila: Story of Liechtenstein.* 1960. Liechtenstein. Vaduz. 4th. ils. 53p. F/VG. C14. $8.00

GALLICO, Paul. *Man Who Was Magic.* 1966. NY. 1st ed. VG/VG. A17. $7.50

GALLICO, Paul. *Mrs 'Arris Goes to Moscow.* (1974). Delacorte. 1st Am ed. 214p. F/VG. C14. $7.00

GALLICO, Paul. *Mrs 'Arris Goes to Paris.* 1958. Doubleday. VG/G. P3. $15.00

GALLICO, Paul. *Poseidon Adventure.* 1969. Coward. 1st ed. F/NF. H11. $50.00

GALLICO, Paul. *Snow Goose.* 1948. Michael Joseph. 4th. ils Peter Scott. G+. B17. $5.00

GALLISON, Kate. *Death Tape.* 1987. Little Brn. 1st ed. VG/VG. P3. $15.00

GALLIX. *Letters to a Friend: Correspondence...TH White & LJ Potts.* 1982. np. 280p. NF/NF. A4. $55.00

GALSWORTHY, John. *On Forsythe Change.* 1930. Scribner. 1st ed. 285p. lavender cloth. xl. VG. B22. $5.00

GALT, Alexander S. *Cassell's Popular Science.* 1903 & 1904. London. Cassell. 2 vol. ils. VG. K5. $100.00

GALTON, Francis. *Hereditary Genius: An Inquiry Into Its Laws...* 1892. London. 2nd. 379p. VG. A13. $100.00

GAMOW, George. *Atomic Energy in Cosmic & Human Life.* 1946. NY. Macmillan. 1st ed. inscr. 8vo. 3 pl. red cloth. VG. T10. $75.00

GAMOW, George. *One, Two, Three...Infinity.* 1947. Viking. 1st ed. 8vo. 340p. G/dj. K5. $60.00

GANDHI, M.K. *Delhi Diary.* 1948. Ahmedabad. Navajivan. 1st ed. 406p. dj. A17. $25.00

GANDOLFI, Simon. *France-Security.* 1981. Blond Briggs. 1st ed. F/F. P3. $15.00

GANN, Ernest K. *Aviator.* nd. Arbor. 2nd. VG/VG. P3. $13.00

GANN, Ernest K. *Flying Circus.* 1974. NY. 1st ed. 224p. VG/dj. B18. $12.50

GANN, Thomas. *Ancient Cities & Modern Tribes.* 1926. Scribner. 1st ed. 256p. F3. $45.00

GANN, Thomas. *Discoveries & Adventures in Central America.* 1929. Scribner. 1st ed. 261p. NF. F3. $60.00

GANN, Thomas. *Glories of the Maya.* 1938. London. Duckworth. 1st ed. ils/index. 279p. VG. F3. $40.00

GANN, Thomas. *In an Unknown Land.* 1924. Scribner. 1st ed. 263p. F3. $45.00

GANN, W.D. *Tunnel Thru the Air.* 1927. Financial Guardian. 1st ed. VG. P3. $40.00

GANN & THOMPSON. *History of the Maya.* 1931. Scribner. 1st ed. 264p. VG+. F3. $45.00

GANNETT, Samuel S. *Geographic Tables & Formulas.* 1918. WA. 4th. VG. O7. $40.00

GANSBERG & GANSBERG. *Direct Encounters.* 1980. NY. Walker. 2nd. sgns. 8vo. 179p. VG/VG. B11. $25.00

GANTHER, MARTIN & SPALLHOLZ. *Selenium in Biology & Medicine.* 1981. Westport. AVI Pub. 8vo. 573p. cloth. F. B1. $68.00

GARCEAU, J. *Dear Mr G.* 1961. Boston. 1st ed. VG/VG. B5. $40.00

GARCIA, Christina. *Dreaming in Cuban.* 1992. Knopf. 1st ed. F/NF. B2. $65.00

GARCIA, Elise. *Guatemala in Six Tours.* 1976. Guatemala. 1st ed. 12mo. 102p. wrp. F3. $10.00

GARCIA, L. Pericot. *Balearic Islands.* 1973. WA, DC. Praeger. 1st Am ed. 184p. VG/dj. W1. $20.00

GARDINER, Dorothy. *Great Betrayal.* 1949. Doubleday. 1st ed. VG/VG. P3. $20.00

GARDINER, W. *Music of Nature.* 1837. Boston. 8vo. 505p. blk cloth. VG. T3. $30.00

GARDNER, Alexander. *Photographic Sketch Book of the Civil War.* nd. Dover. facsimile of 1866 ed. 224p. VG. T3. $12.00

GARDNER, Asa Bird. *Battles of Gravelly Run, Dinwiddle Courthouse & Five Forks.* 1881. Chicago. 1st ed. 126p. prt wrp bdg into cloth. M8. $85.00

GARDNER, Brian. *Allenby.* 1965. London. 1st ed. 314p. xl. VG. W1. $20.00

GARDNER, Craig Shaw. *Dragon Walking.* 1995. Ace. 1st ed. F/F. G10. $10.00

GARDNER, Eldon. *History of Biology.* 1965. Minneapolis. 2nd. 376p. VG. A13. $17.50

GARDNER, Elsie B. *Maxie at Brinksome Hall.* 1934. Cupples Leon. VG. P3. $15.00

GARDNER, Erle Stanley. *Case of the Amorous Aunt.* 1963. Morrow. 1st ed. NF/VG. B4. $35.00

GARDNER, Erle Stanley. *Case of the Borrowed Brunette.* 1946. Morrow. 1st ed. F/NF. H11. $65.00

GARDNER, Erle Stanley. *Case of the Counterfeit Eye.* 1947. Triangle. hc. VG/VG. P3. $15.00

GARDNER, Erle Stanley. *Case of the Fabulous Fake.* 1969. Morrow. 1st ed. NF/dj. H11. $25.00

GARDNER, Erle Stanley. *Case of the Grinning Gorilla.* 1952. Morrow. 1st ed. F/NF. H11. $45.00

GARDNER, Erle Stanley. *Case of the Lucky Loser.* 1957. Morrow. 1st ed. VG/VG. H11. $20.00

GARDNER, Erle Stanley. *Case of the One-Eyed Witness.* 1950. Morrow. 1st ed. VG/fair. H11. $25.00

GARDNER, Erle Stanley. *Case of the Stuttering Bishop.* 1946. Tower. hc. VG/VG. P3. $20.00

GARDNER, Erle Stanley. *Case of the Velvet Claws.* 1945. Triangle. 4th. VG/VG. P3. $18.00

GARDNER, Erle Stanley. *Court of Last Resort.* 1952. Wm Sloane. 1st ed. NF/G. M19. $35.00

GARDNER, Erle Stanley. *Cut Thin to Win.* 1965. Morrow. 1st ed. NF/F. H11. $35.00

GARDNER, Erle Stanley. *DA Breaks a Seal.* 1946. Morrow. 1st ed. F/F. H11. $70.00

GARDNER, Erle Stanley. *Kept Women Can't Quit.* 1960. Morrow. 1st ed. VG/VG. P3. $30.00

GARDNER, Ethel. *Soarings.* 1990. Cherokee. 1st ed. sgn. 8vo. 120p. F/wrp. B11. $8.50

GARDNER, John. *Amber Nine.* 1966. Viking. 1st ed. F/NF. M19. $45.00

GARDNER, John. *Corner Men.* 1974. Michael Joseph. 1st ed. F/F. P3. $25.00

GARDNER, John. *Every Night's a Bullfight.* 1971. Michael Joseph. 1st ed. NF/VG. M19. $17.50

GARDNER, John. *For Special Services.* 1982. Coward McCann. 1st ed. F/F. P3. $18.00

GARDNER, John. *For Special Services.* 1982. Jonathan Cape. 1st ed. VG/VG. P3. $25.00

GARDNER, John. *Icebreaker.* 1983. Jonathan Cape. 1st ed. F/F. P3. $25.00

GARDNER, John. *King of the Hummingbirds.* 1977. Knopf. decor brd. NF. P3. $18.00

GARDNER, John. *King's Indian.* 1974. Knopf. 1st ed. rem mk. F/F. H4. $30.00

GARDNER, John. *Last Trump.* 1980. McGraw Hill. 1st ed. VG/VG. P3. $15.00

GARDNER, John. *License Renewed.* 1981. Jonathan Cape. 1st ed. VG/VG. P3. $18.00

GARDNER, John. *Liquidator.* 1965. Viking. 1st ed. hc. VG/VG. P3. $20.00

GARDNER, John. *Madrigal.* 1968. Viking. 1st ed. VG/VG. P3. $23.00

GARDNER, John. *Maestro.* 1993. Otto Penzler. 1st ed. F/F. P3. $23.00

GARDNER, John. *Micklesson's Ghosts.* 1982. Knopf. 1st ed. VG/VG. A20. $12.00

GARDNER, John. *No Deals, Mr Bond.* 1987. Putnam. 1st ed. VG/VG. P3. $14.00

GARDNER, John. *Nobody Lives Forever.* 1986. London. Cape. 1st ed. F/NF. M19. $45.00

GARDNER, John. *Nostradamus Traitor.* 1979. Doubleday. UP/1st Am ed. NF/tall wrp. B4. $75.00

GARDNER, John. *October Light.* 1976. Knopf. 1st ed. VG/G. P3. $20.00

GARDNER, John. *Quiet Dogs.* 1982. Hodder Stoughton. 1st ed. NF/NF. P3. $20.00

GARDNER, John. *Role of Honour.* 1984. Jonathan Cape. 1st ed. F/F. P3. $25.00

GARDNER, John. *Scorpius.* 1988. Putnam. 1st ed. VG/VG. P3. $13.00

GARDNER, John. *Secret Houses.* 1987. Putnam. 1st ed. VG/VG. P3. $19.00

GARDNER, John. *Stillness & Shadows.* 1986. NY. 1st ed. F/F. A17. $12.50

GARDNER, John. *Win, Lose or Die.* 1989. Putnam. 1st ed. VG/VG. P3. $14.00

GARDNER, John. *Wreckage of Agathon.* 1970. NY. 1st ed. author's 2nd book. F/dj. B5/C6. $75.00

GARDNER, Leonard. *Fat City.* 1969. FSG. 1st ed. author's 1st novel. VG/VG. M22. $50.00

GARDNER, Martin. *Logic Machines & Diagrams.* 1958. McGraw Hill. 8vo. 157p. VG. K5. $25.00

GARDNER, Martin. *Scientific American Book of Mathematical Puzzles...* 1959. NY. Simon Schuster. ils. 178p. G/dj. K5. $15.00

GARDNER, Miriam; see Bradley, Marion Zimmer.

GARDNER, Robert E. *Small Arms Makers.* 1863. NY. 4to. 378p. gray cloth. VG. T3. $24.00

GARFIELD, Brian. *Crime of My Life.* nd. Walker. 1st ed. xl. dj. P3. $7.00

GARFIELD, Brian. *Death Sentence.* 1975. Evans. 1st ed. VG/VG. P3. $30.00

GARFIELD, Brian. *Deep Cover.* 1971. Delacorte. 1st ed. G/G. P3. $15.00

GARFIELD, Brian. *Kolchak's Gold.* 1973. McKay. 1st ed. F/F. H11. $30.00

GARFIELD, Brian. *Lawbringers.* 1962. Macmillan. 1st ed. NF/NF. P3. $40.00

GARFIELD, Brian. *Paladin.* 1980. Macmillan. 1st ed. NF/NF. P3. $20.00

GARFIELD, Brian. *Recoil*. 1977. Morrow. 1st ed. VG/VG. P3. $40.00

GARFIELD, Brian. *What of Terry Conniston?* 1971. World. 1st ed. VG/VG. P3. $20.00

GARFIELD, Brian. *Wild Times*. 1978. Simon Schuster. 1st ed. VG/VG. P3. $15.00

GARFIELD, Leon. *Fair's Fair*. 1983. Doubleday. stated 1st ed. ils. unp. NF/VG+. C14. $22.00

GARIEPY, Louis. *Saw-Ge-Mah: Medicine Man*. 1950. Northland. 1st ed. sgn. 12mo. 326p. G/worn. B11. $35.00

GARIS, Cleo F. *Arden Blake & the Orchard Secret (#1)*. 1934. AL Burt. 250p. VG/dj. M20. $24.00

GARIS, Howard R. *Buddy & His Chums*. 1930. NY. VG. A17. $6.00

GARIS, Howard R. *Rick & Ruddy Afloat*. 1922. Springfield. 1st ed. ils King. 262p. VG. A17. $7.50

GARIS, Howard R. *Rick & Ruddy in Camp*. 1921. Springfield. 1st ed. ils Milo Winter. 254p. G. A17. $7.00

GARIS, Howard R. *Tom Cardiff in the Big Top (#2)*. 1927. Milton Bradley. ils WB King. 256p. VG/dj. M20. $62.00

GARIS, Howard R. *Uncle Wiggily & the Barber*. 1939. Platt Munk. ils George Carlson. 12p. VG+. M5. $10.00

GARIS, Howard R. *Uncle Wiggily's Story Book*. 1939. Platt Munk. lg 8vo. ils Lang Campbell. red brd. VG/worn. M5. $45.00

GARIS, Lilian. *Dragon of the Hills*. nd. Grosset Dunlap. VG. P3. $15.00

GARIS, Roger. *My Father Was Uncle Wiggily*. 1966. McGraw Hill. 1st ed. 217p. VG/dj. M20. $27.00

GARLAKE. *Great Zimbabwe*. 1973. Stein Day. F/VG. D2. $50.00

GARLAND, Hamlin. *Back-Trailers From the Middle Border*. 1928. NY. 1st ed. ils Constance Garland. gilt cloth. VG. A17. $15.00

GARLAND, Hamlin. *Mystery of Buried Crosses*. 1939. NY. 1st ed. photos. 352p. VG/VG. B5. $90.00

GARLAND, Joseph E. *Experiment in Medicine. The 1st 20 Years of Pratt Clinic...* 1960. Riverside. 107p. inscr John F Sullivan. bl cloth. VG. B14. $55.00

GARLAND, Phyl. *Sound of Soul*. 1969. Regnery. 1st ed. inscr. NF/NF. B2. $50.00

GARLAND. *Bibliography of Writings of Sir James Matthew Barrie*. 1928. London. 1/520. ils. 146p. NF. A4. $135.00

GARLAND. *Boy Life on the Prairie*. 1899. Macmillan. 1st ed. F. A18. $75.00

GARLICK, T. *Treatise on Artifical Propagation of Fish*. 1857. Cleveland. ils/maps. 142p. xl. G. B5. $40.00

GARNER. *World of Edwardiana*. 1974. Hamlyn. F/F. D2. $40.00

GARNER, Alan. *Bag of Moonshine*. 1986. Delacorte. 1st Am ed. 8vo. ils. F/F. T10. $50.00

GARNER, Alan. *Red Shift*. 1973. Macmillan. 1st ed. VG/fair. p3. $13.00

GARNER, Elvira. *Ezekiel*. 1937. Holt. 1st ed. unp. NF. C14. $25.00

GARNER, Elvira. *Ezekiel Travels*. 1938. Holt. 1st ed. unp. VG. M20. $60.00

GARNER, Elvira. *Way Down in Tennessee*. 1941. Messner. 1st ed. ils. VG/VG. P2. $50.00

GARNER, William. *Ditto, Brother Rat!* 1972. Collins. 1st ed. hc. VG/VG. P3. $20.00

GARNER, William. *Think Big, Think Dirty*. 1983. St Martin. 1st ed. VG/VG. P3. $16.00

GARNETT. *Letters From John Galsworthy 1900-1932*. 1934. np. 1/3000. pres. 255p. VG. A4. $60.00

GAROZZO & YALLOUZE. *Blue Club*. 1971 (1970). London. VG. S1. $20.00

GARRETT, George. *Evening Performance*. 1985. Doubleday. 1st ed. 518p. VG/VG. B10. $20.00

GARRETT, George. *Luck's Shining Child: Miscellany of Poems & Verses*. 1981. Palaemon. 1st ed. 1/300. sgn. blk cloth. VG. B10. $75.00

GARRETT, George. *Magic Striptease*. 1973. Doubleday. 1st ed. sgn. 272p. VG/VG. B10. $45.00

GARRETT, George. *Welcome to the Medicine Show: Postcards/Flashcards...* 1978. Palaemon. 1/300. sgn. 27p. VG. B10. $75.00

GARRISON, Jim. *Star Spangled Contract*. 1976. McGraw Hill. 1st ed. F/F. P3. $18.00

GARRISON, Karl C. *Psychology of Adolescence*. 1934. Prentice Hall. pub copy. panelled dk gr cloth. G1. $35.00

GARRISON, Webb. *Strange Facts About Death*. 1978. Abingdon. 1st ed. VG/VG. P3. $13.00

GARROTT, Hal. *Snythergen*. 1923. NY. 1st ed. ils Dugald Walker. VG+. M5. $50.00

GARTON, Ray. *Crucifax Autumn*. 1988. Dark Havest. 1st ed. pub copy. sgn Garton/ils Bob Eggleton. F/F/case. T2. $65.00

GARTON, Ray. *Live Girls*. 1987. London. Macdonald. 1st Eng/1st hc ed. AN/dj. B4. $250.00

GARTON, Ray. *Lot Lizards*. 1991. Shingletown. Zeising. 1st ed. F/F. T2. $22.00

GARTRAM, John. *Travels in Pennsylvania & Canada*. 1966. Ann Arbor. VG. O7. $20.00

GARVE, Andrew. *Ascent of D-13*. 1969. Thriller BC. VG/VG. P3. $8.00

GARVE, Andrew. *Cuckoo Line Affair*. 1953. Collins Crime Club. 1st ed. VG/VG. P3. $40.00

GARVE, Andrew. *Hide & Go Seek*. 1966. Harper Row. 1st ed. VG/VG. P3. $25.00

GARVEY, Ruth. *Who Dealt? 100 Guideposts to Bridge Bidding*. nd. St Louis. lg format. 24p. VG. S1. $10.00

GARY, Jim. *King of the Royal Mounted*. 1940s. France. Jim Gary dailies. French text. 240p. M13. $35.00

GASCOIGNE, Bamber. *World Theatre*. 1968. Boston. Little Brn. xl. F/VG. D2. $40.00

GASH, Joe. *Newspaper Murders*. 1985. HRW. 1st ed. VG/VG. P3. $15.00

GASH, Joe. *Priestly Murders*. 1984. HRW. 1st ed. F/F. P3. $15.00

GASH, Jonathan. *Firefly Gadroon*. 1982. St Martin. 1st ed. F/F. P3. $35.00

GASH, Jonathan. *Grail Tree*. 1979. Harper. 1st Am ed. 3rd in Lovejoy series. VG/VG. M22. $20.00

GASH, Jonathan. *Great California Game*. 1991. St Martin. 1st ed. VG/G. P3. $15.00

GASH, Jonathan. *Sleepers of Erin*. 1983. Dutton. 1st ed. F/F. P3. $35.00

GASH, Jonathan. *Spend Game*. 1981. Ticknor Fields. 1st ed. F/F. P3. $60.00

GASH, Jonathan. *Tartan Sell*. 1986. St Martin. 1st ed. F/F. P3. $25.00

GASH & LINGENFELTER. *Newspapers of Nevada: A History & Bibliography 1854-1979*. nd. NV U. 4to. 13 vintage photos. 337p. F/F. A4. $45.00

GASK, Arthur. *Crime Upon Crime*. nd. Roy. hc. VG/G. P3. $18.00

GASK, Arthur. *Silent Dead*. 1950. Herbert Jenkins. 1st ed. VG. P3. $25.00

GASKELL. *New Introduction to Bibliography*. 1978. np. 141 ils. 438p. VG/VG. A4. $85.00

GASS, William H. *In the Heart of the Country AOS*. 1968. NY. 1st ed. author's 2nd book. inscr. F/F. A11. $75.00

GASS, William H. *Omensetter's Luck*. 1966. NAL. 1st ed. author's 1st book. NF/NF. B2. $150.00

GASS, William H. *Willie Masters' Lonesome Wife*. 1968. Evanston. TriQuarterly. inscr. NF/wrp. B2. $75.00

GATENBY, Rosemary. *Deadly Relations*. nd. BC. VG/VG. P3. $8.00

GATENBY, Rosemary. *Fugitive Affair*. 1976. Dodd Mead. 1st ed. VG/VG. P3. $15.00

GATES, Doris. *Blue Willow*. 1956 (1940). Viking. 11th. 8vo. 172p. bl cloth. VG/G. T5. $28.00

GATES, Josephine S. *Live Dolls' Busy Days*. Sept 1907. Bobbs Merrill. 1st ed. ils Virginia Keep. 105p. VG+. P2. $110.00

GATES, Josephine S. *More About Live Dolls*. 1903. Franklin. 1st ed. ils V Keep. VG. D1. $100.00

GATES, Josephine S. *Sunshine Annie*. 1910. Bobbs Merrill. ils Fanny Cory. 148p. red cloth. VG. D1. $135.00

GATES, Susa Young. *Life Story of Brigham Young. By One of His Daughters*. 1930. NY. 1st ed. 388p. gilt blk cloth. VG. H3. $50.00

GATTY & POST. *Around the World in 8 Days*. 1931. NY. 1st ed. sgns. G. V4. $250.00

GAUBA, K.L. *Battles at the Bar*. 1956. Bombay. Tirpathi Ltd. M11. $65.00

GAUCH, Frederick Augustus. *Psychology; or, View of the Human Soul*. 1841. Dodd/Crocker Brewster. 2nd. 401p. emb Victorian cloth. G1. $200.00

GAUGUIN, Paul. *Noa Noa*. 1924. Paris. ils. VG/wrp. O7. $95.00

GAULT, W.P. *Ohio at Vicksburg*. 1906. Columbus. 1st ed. ils/map. 374p. VG. B18. $75.00

GAULT, William Campbell. *Cat & Mouse*. 1988. St Martin. 1st ed. NF/NF. P3. $15.00

GAULT, William Campbell. *Come Die With Me*. 1959. Random. 1st ed. VG. P3. $20.00

GAULT, William Campbell. *Death in Donegal Bay*. 1984. Walker. 1st ed. NF/NF. P3. $15.00

GAULT, William Campbell. *Ring Around Rosa*. 1955. Dutton. 1st ed. VG/VG. P3. $30.00

GAUNT. *Pre-Raphaelite Tragedy*. 1942. Harcourt. G. D2. $20.00

GAUSSEN, L. *World's Birthday*. 1865. London. Nelson. 270p. gilt cloth. K5. $26.00

GAVIT, Bernard C. *Intro to the Study of Law*. 1951. Brooklyn. Foundation. M11. $35.00

GAWRON, Jean Mark. *Apology for Rain*. 1974. Doubleday. 1st ed. F/F. P3. $15.00

GAY, Romney. *Romney Gay's Big Picture Book*. 1947. Grosset Dunlap. 4to. ils. F/VG+. M5. $65.00

GAY, Romney. *Romney Gay's Box of Books*. 1941. Grosset Dunlap. 8vo. G+/box. M5. $30.00

GAY, Romney. *Tommy Grows Wise*. 1939. Grosset Dunlap. 1st ed. 12mo. unp. pict brd. VG. T5. $30.00

GEDGE, Pauline. *Stargate*. 1982. Macmillan. 1st ed. NF/NF. P3. $20.00

GEIGER, Maynard J. *Palou's Life of Fray Junipero Serra*. 1955. WA. Am Franciscan Hist. 1st ed. sgn. 547p. map ep. gilt bl cloth. NF. T10. $150.00

GEIKIE, A. *Landscape in History*. 1905. Macmillan. 352p. cloth. G. D8. $12.00

GEIS, Darlene. *Colorslide Tour of Mexico*. 1961. Colombia Record. photo. unp. laminated brd. F3. $15.00

GEISEL, Theodor. *And to Think That I Saw It on Mulberry Street*. 1937. NY. 9th. pict brd. VG. M5. $45.00

GEISEL, Theodor. *Cat & the Hat Song Book*. 1967. Random. 1st ed. ils. VG. P2. $200.00

GEISEL, Theodor. *Happy Birthday to You!* 1959. Random. 1st ed. ils. VG/dj. D1. $385.00

GEISEL, Theodor. *If I Ran the Zoo*. 1950. Random. early ed. ils. VG/$2.50 price. D1. $225.00

GEISEL, Theodor. *McElligot's Pool*. 1947. Random. later prt. ils. VG+/torn. M5. $30.00

GEISEL, Theodor. *Seven Lady Godivas*. 1939. Random. 1st ed. 4to. ils. F/dj. B24. $475.00

GEISEL, Theodor. *Yertle the Turtle & Other Stories*. 1958. Random. 1st ed. 8vo. NF/dj. B24. $395.00

GEISEL, Theodor. *You're Only Old Once! A Book for Obsolete Children*. 1986. Random. 1st ed. F/clip. B17. $15.00

GEISEL, Theodor. *500 Hats of Bartholomew Cubbins*. 1938. Vanguard. early ed. ils. NF/clip. D1. $250.00

GELATT, R. *Fabulous Phonograph*. 1955. Lippincott. 1st ed. 320p. VG/VG. B5. $50.00

GEMELLI, Agostino. *La Lotta Contro Lourdes*. 1911. Firenze. Libreria Editirice Fiorentina. 352p. prt wrp. G1. $45.00

GEMMELL, David. *Last Guardian*. 1989. Legend. 1st. F/dj. P3. $25.00

GENESTOUX, Magdeleine. *Les Adventures de Passepartout*. 1925. Librairie Hachette. ils Cecil Aldin. VG. P2. $95.00

GENET & HAYES. *Robotic Observatories*. 1989. Mesa, AZ. 8vo. 292p. laminated brd. AN. K5. $15.00

GENTILCORE, R. Louis. *Animals & Maps*. 1969. Berkeley. ils. F/rpr. O7. $65.00

GENTLE, Mary. *Architecture of Desire*. 1993. Roc. 1st ed. F/F. P3. $20.00

GEORGE, David Lloyd. *War Memoirs of..., 1914-17*. 1933. Boston. 1st ed. 4 vol. F/dj. A17. $50.00

GEORGE, Elizabeth. *For the Sake of Elena*. 1992. Bantam. 1st ed. F/F. H11. $25.00

GEORGE, Elizabeth. *Great Deliverance*. 1988. Bantam. 1st ed. author's 1st novel. sgn. F/F. T2. $60.00

GEORGE, Elizabeth. *Payment in Blood*. nd. BOMC. VG/VG. P3. $10.00

GEORGE, Leopold. *Lehrbuch der Psychologie*. 1854. Berlin. Druck/Georg Reimer. 588p. VG. G1. $125.00

GEORGE, Peter. *Commander-1*. 1965. Delacorte. 1st ed. VG/VG. P3. $20.00

GERARD, Francis. *Secret Sceptre*. 1971. Tom Stacey. VG/VG. P3. $15.00

GERARD, John. *Herbal; or, General History of Plants*. 1975. NY. Dover. rpt of 1633 ed. 1677p. AN/dj. A10. $130.00

GERARD, Max. *Dali*. 1968. NY. Abrams. 1st ed. VG/VG. B5. $75.00

GERARD, Philip. *Hatteras Light*. 1986. Scribner. 1st ed. author's 1st novel. F/F. M23. $35.00

GERASIMOV, I. *Short History of Geographical Science in the Soviet Union*. 1976. Moscow. VG. O7. $20.00

GERBI, Antonello. *Dispute of the New World*. 1973. Pittsburgh. VG. O7. $35.00

GERBI, Antonello. *Nature in the New World*. 1986. Pittsburgh. VG. O7. $25.00

GERDTS, William H. *American Impressionism*. 1984. Abbeville. 1st ed. ils/pl. cloth. dj. D2. $85.00

GERHARD, Frederick. *Illinois as It Is*. 1857. Chicago/Phil. 1st ed. 3 fld maps. 451p. gilt blk cloth. VG. H3. $100.00

GERHARD, Peter. *Guide to the Historical Geography of New Spain*. 1972. Cambridge. VG. O7. $65.00

GERHHARD & GULICK. *Lower California Guidebook*. 1964. Arthur H Clark. 3rd ed/2nd prt. 8vo. 243p. F/dj. T10. $30.00

GERLACH, Arch C. *National Atlas of the United States of America*. 1990. US Geol Survey. lg folio. 417p. F. O7. $795.00

GERLACH, Larry. *Men in Blue*. 1980. Viking. 1st ed. F/VG. P8. $45.00

GERNSHEIM, Helmut. *History of Photography From the Earliest Use of the Camera*. 1955. Oxford. 359 photos mtd on coated stock. 395p. xl. VG. A4. $195.00

GERNSHEIM, Helmut. *Incunabula of British Photographic Literature...* 1984. np. 4to. ils. 159p. F/F. A4. $95.00

GERNSHEIM, Helmut. *Origins of Photography*. 1982. np. sq 4to. 191 photos. 280p. F/F/VG case. A4. $250.00

GERRITSEN, Tess. *Harvest.* 1996. Pocket. 1st ed. author's 1st novel. NF/NF. R16. $30.00

GERROLD, David. *Chess With a Dragon.* 1987. Walker. 1st ed. RS. F/F. P3. $20.00

GERROLD, David. *Day for Damnation.* 1984. Timescape. 1st ed. F/F. P3. $17.00

GERSHAM, Douglas H. *Lenton Lands.* 1988. Macmillan. 1st ed. F/F. M23. $25.00

GERT ZUR HEIDE, Karl. *Deep South Piano: Story of Little Brother Montgomery.* 1970. London. Studio Vista. 1st ed. F/wrp. B2. $25.00

GESELL, Arnold. *First Five Years of Life.* 1940. NY. 393p. VG/VG. A17. $7.50

GESELL & THOMPSON. *Infant Behavior: Its Genesis & Growth.* 1934. McGraw Hill. ils. panelled prt red cloth. VG. G1. $50.00

GESS, Denise. *Red Whiskey Blues.* 1987. Crown. 1st ed. author's 1st novel. F/F. B35. $20.00

GESSLER, Clifford. *Pattern of Mexico.* 1941. Appleton. 1st ed. 442p. dj. F3. $20.00

GESTON, Mark S. *Mirror to the Sky.* 1992. Morrow. UP of 1st ed. F/wrp. G10. $25.00

GEVITZ, Norman. *DO's: Osteopathic Medicine in America.* 1982. Baltimore. 1st ed. 183p. VG. A13. $30.00

GHEERBRANT, Alain. *Journey to the Far Amazon.* 1954. Simon Schuster. 2nd. 353p. dj. F3. $15.00

GIBB, G. *Saco Lowell Shops.* 1950. Cambridge, MA. 1st ed. sgn. ils/index. 835p. VG/VG. B5. $40.00

GIBBON, Edward. *Decline & Fall of the Roman Empire.* nd. AL Burt. 5 vol. VG. P12. $40.00

GIBBON & HERNDON. *Exploration of the Valley of the Amazon.* 1853. WA. 2 vol. pl. 3-quarter leather. VG. B5. $300.00

GIBBONS, Euell. *Stalking the Blue-Eyed Scallop.* 1965. David McKay. sgn. 8vo. 332p. G/fair. B11. $15.00

GIBBONS, Kaye. *Cure for Dreams.* 1991. Algonquin. 1st ed. sgn. F/F. B35. $50.00

GIBBONS, Kaye. *Ellen Foster.* 1987. Algonquin. 1st ed. F/F. M23. $175.00

GIBBONS, Kaye. *Family Life.* 1990. NC Wesleyan College. 1/500. sgn. F/wrp. C6. $55.00

GIBBONS, Kaye. *Frost & Flower: My Life With Manic Depression So Far.* 1995. Atlantic. 1st ed. 1/250. sgn. F. C2. $100.00

GIBBONS, Kaye. *Sights Unseen.* ARC. sgn. VG+/wrp. B30. $30.00

GIBBONS, Kaye. *Virtuous Woman.* 1989. Algonquin. 1st ed. F/F. M23. $40.00

GIBBS, James W. *Buckeye Horology.* 1971. Columbia, PA. ils. 128p. xl. G. B18. $25.00

GIBBS, Jim. *Disaster Log of Ships.* 1971. Bonanza. VG/VG. A16. $25.00

GIBSON, Edmund. *Codex Juris Ecclesiastic Anglicani...* 1713. London. 2nd vol only. contemporary calf. M11. $75.00

GIBSON, Edward. *Reach.* 1989. Doubleday. 1st ed. F/NF. G10. $10.00

GIBSON, Eva Katherine. *Zauberlinda the Wise Witch.* 1901. Robert Smith. 1st ed. 8vo. ils. VG. M5. $60.00

GIBSON, Hugh. *Rio.* 1938. Doubleday. sgn. 263p. VG/dj. F3. $15.00

GIBSON, James. *Dr Bodo Otto & Medical Background of American Revolution.* 1937. Springfield. 1st ed. 345p. NF. A13. $100.00

GIBSON, Walter. *Crime Over Casco & Mother Goose Murder.* 1979. Crime Club. 1st ed. F/F. P3. $50.00

GIBSON, Walter. *Norgil: More Tales of Prestidigitatio.* 1979. Mysterious. 1/250. sgn/#d. sgn also as Maxwell Grant. F/NF/box. P3. $125.00

GIBSON, William. *Count Zero.* 1986. Arbor. 1st ed. F/F. P3. $35.00

GIBSON, William. *Mona Lisa Overdrive.* 1988. London. Gollancz. 1st ed. sgn. F/F. T2. $65.00

GIBSON, William. *Neuromancer.* 1984. London. 1st Eng/1st hc ed. author's 1st book. sgn. F/F. A11. $275.00

GIBSON, William. *Virtual Light.* 1993. Bantam. 1st ed. F/F. M23. $30.00

GIBSON & STERLING. *Difference Engine.* 1991. Bantam. 1st ed. hc. F/F. P3. $20.00

GIDE, Andre. *Madeleine.* 1952. NY. 1st Am ed. F/F. A11. $55.00

GIDE, Andre. *Secret Drama of My Life.* 1951. Paris. 1st Eng-language ed. NF/wrp/glassine dj. A11. $85.00

GIDWANI. *Comparative Librarianship, Essays in Honour of DN Marshall.* 1973. Delhi. ils. 245p. F/VG. A4. $95.00

GIELGUD, Val. *Goggle-Box.* 1963. Collins Crime Club. 1st ed. VG. P3. $22.00

GIESY, J.U. *Jason, Son of Jason.* 1966. Avalon. NF/NF. P3. $20.00

GIESY, J.U. *Mystery Woman.* 1929. Whitman. hc. VG/VG. P3. $60.00

GIFFEN, J. Kelly. *Egyptian Sudan.* 1905. Chicago. Revell. 10 pl/1 map. 252p. xl. VG. W1. $25.00

GIFFORD, Barry. *Neighborhood of Baseball.* 1981. NY. 1st ed. sgn. F/NF. A11. $60.00

GIFFORD, Barry. *Quinzaine in Return for a Portrait of Mary Sun.* 1977. Berkeley. 1st ed. sgn. F/wht wrp. A11. $50.00

GIFFORD, Barry. *Wild at Heart.* 1990. Grove Weidenfeld. 1st ed. AN/dj. M22. $30.00

GIFFORD, Thomas. *Man From Lisbon.* 1977. McGraw Hill. 1st ed. VG/VG. P3. $25.00

GILB, Dagoberto. *Last Known Residence of Mickey Acuna.* 1994. Grove. 1st ed. F/F. A20. $30.00

GILBERT, A.W. *Potato.* 1917. NY. Macmillan. Rural Science series. 12mo. 16 pl. cloth. B1. $45.00

GILBERT, Anthony. *And Death Came Too.* 1977. Hamish Hamilton. VG/VG. P3. $15.00

GILBERT, Anthony. *Murder Anonymous.* 1968. Random. 1st ed. VG/VG. P3. $20.00

GILBERT, B. *Westering Man: The Life of Joseph Walker.* 1983. Atheneum. 1st ed. 8vo. 339p. F/dj. T10. $35.00

GILBERT, Bentley. *British Social Policy, 1914-1939.* 1970. Ithaca. 343p. dj. A13. $35.00

GILBERT, Henry. *King Arthur.* nd. Saalfield. hc. G. P3. $12.00

GILBERT, Michael. *Body of a Girl.* 1972. Harper Row. 1st ed. VG/VG. P3. $13.00

GILBERT, Michael. *Flash Point.* 1974. Harper Row. 1st ed. VG/VG. P3. $18.00

GILBERT, Michael. *Petrella at Q.* 1977. Harper Row. 1st ed. VG/tape rpr. P3. $13.00

GILBERT, Michael. *Queen Against Karl Mullen.* 1991. Carroll & Graf. 1st ed. F/F. P3. $19.00

GILBERT, Nan. *Sir Gruss, the Wooly Dog.* 1947. Whitman. 4to. VG+/G. M5. $25.00

GILBERT, Sarah. *Dixie Riggs.* 1991. Warner. 1st ed. rem mk. F/F. B35. $20.00

GILBERT, Sarah. *Hairdo.* 1989. Warner. UP. sgn. F. B35. $55.00

GILBERT, W.S. *Fifty Bab Ballads, Much Sound & Little Sense.* 1887. London. 317p. VG. A4. $20.00

GILBERT, Walter. *George Morland.* 1907. London. Blk. 1st ed. 50 pl. G+. B5. $55.00

GILBERT & GREGG. *Love, a Diptych.* 1994. Captain's Bookshelf. 1/30 hors commerce. sgns. F/wrp. C2. $150.00

GILBERT & JEFFERYS. *Crossties Through Carolina: Story of North Carolina...* 1969. Raleigh. 1st ed. 88p. VG/dj. A17. $30.00

GILBEY, Walter. *Harness Horse.* 1898. London. Vinton. G+. O3. $45.00

GILBOY, Bernard. *Voyage of Pleasure.* 1956. Cambridge. VG. O7. $25.00

GILCHRIST, Ellen. *Land Surveyor's Daughter.* 1979. Fayetteville. Lost Roads. 1st ed. sgn. author's 1st book. F/wrp. B4. $600.00

GILCHRIST, Ellen. *Light Can Be Both Wave & Particle.* 1989. Little Brn. 1st ed. 8vo. F/dj. w/pub letter. S9. $60.00

GILCHRIST, Ellen. *Net of Jewels.* 1992. Little Brn. 1st ed. F/VG+. A20. $20.00

GILCHRIST, Marie E. *Story of the Great Lakes.* 1942. Harper. G. A16. $50.00

GILDEN, Mel. *Harry Newberry & the Raiders...* 1989. Holt. 1st ed. F/F. P3. $15.00

GILES, Kenneth. *Death Among the Stars.* 1969. Walker. 1st ed. F/F. P3. $10.00

GILES, Nicki. *Fifth Rapunzel.* 1991. Hodder Stoughton. 1st ed. VG/VG. P3. $20.00

GILES, Nicki. *Marilyn Album.* 1991. Bison Group. hc. F/F. P3. $20.00

GILES, Valarius Cincinnatus. *Rags & Hope: the Recollections of Val C Giles...* 1961. Coward McCann. 1st ed. 280p. F/NF. M8. $45.00

GILES, W.E. *Cruise in a Queensland Labour Vessel to the South Seas.* 1968. Canberra/Honolulu. VG. O7. $20.00

GILES & PALMER. *Horseshoe Bend.* 1962. NY. 1st ed. VG/VG. B5. $35.00

GILES & YIESLA. *Shade Trees for Central & Northern United States...* 1992. Champaign. 296p. sc. M. B26. $30.00

GILKES, Lillian. *Cora Crane: Biography of Mrs Stephen Crane.* 1960. IN U. 1st ed. 416p. VG+/dj. M20. $25.00

GILL, Bartholomew. *McGarr & the Method of Descartes.* 1984. Viking. 1st ed. F/F. P3. $15.00

GILL, Bartholomew. *McGarr at the Dublin Horse Show.* 1979. Scribner. 1st ed. VG/VG. P3. $15.00

GILL, Elizabeth. *Crime Coast.* 1931. Crime Club. 1st ed. hc. VG. P3. $20.00

GILL, Eric. *Art & Love.* 1927. Bristol. Cleverdon. 1/35 (of 260). 8vo. sgn. F. w/extra suite of 6 pl. B24. $2,000.00

GILL, Eric. *Canticum Canticorum Salomonis Quod Hebraice Dicitur...* 1931. Weimar. Cranach. 1/268. tall 8vo. 31p. teg. fore-edge painting. dj. case. B24 $2,850.00

GILL, Eric. *Passion of Our Lord Jesus Christ...* 1934. London. Faber. 1/300. 5 engravings. 59p. bl cloth. NF/dj. B24. $350.00

GILL, Eric. *Procreant Hymn, by E Powys Mathers.* 1926. Golden Cockerel. 1/175. 8vo. 20p. wht buckram. F/dj. B24. $1,000.00

GILL, Eric. *Wood Engravings.* 1924. Ditchling. St Dominic. 1/150. 1 woodcut/34 engravings. linen brd. F. B24. $2,750.00

GILL, Graeme. *Rules of the Communist Party of the Soviet Union.* 1988. Armonk. ME Sharpe. M11. $35.00

GILL, Patrick; see Creasey, John.

GILL, Richard. *White Water & Black Magic.* 1940. Holt. 1st ed. 369p. cloth. F3. $25.00

GILLEN, Mollie. *Assasination of the Prime Minister.* 1972. NY. St Martin. M11. $45.00

GILLES, Helen Trybulowski. *Nigeria: From the Bight to Benin to Africa's Desert Sands.* 1944. NGS. photos. F/stiff wrp. P4. $8.50

GILLESPIE, John W. *New Plants from Fiji.* 1930-32. Honolulu. 3 parts. total 140 pl/2 photos. wrp. B26. $45.00

GILLESPIE, Robert B. *Hell's Kitchen.* 1987. Detective BC. VG. P3. $8.00

GILLESPIE, W.M. *Treatise on Land-Surveying.* 1855. Appleton. 6th. 84p tables. 424p. G. A17. $45.00

GILLETT, John M. *Gentians of Canada & Greenland.* 1963. Ottawa. 38 pl. 99p. F. B26. $26.00

GILLETT, Mary. *Army Medical Dept: 1775-1818.* 1981. WA. 299p. VG. A13. $40.00

GILLHAM, Skip. *Seaway Era Shipwrecks.* 1994. Ontario. Riverbank Traders. M. A16. $17.00

GILLIGAN, Edmund. *Gaunt Woman.* 1943. Scribner. 1st ed. VG/G. P3. $20.00

GILLMOR, Donald M. *Free Press & Fair Trial.* 1966. WA. Public Affairs. M11. $45.00

GILLMORE, Rufus. *Ebony Bed Murder.* 1932. Mystery League. 1st ed. xl. VG. P3. $12.00

GILMAN, Caroline. *Oracles From the Poets.* 1845. London/NY. 2nd. gilt bl cloth. NF. C6. $75.00

GILMAN, Charlotte Perkins. *Herland.* 1979. Pantheon. 1st ed. xl. dj. P3. $7.00

GILMAN, Dorothy. *Mrs Polifax & the Golden Triangle.* 1988. Doubleday. 1st ed. VG/VG. P3. $16.00

GILMAN, Robert Cham. *Starkahn of Rhada.* 1970. HBW. 1st ed. VG/VG. P3. $25.00

GILMOR, Frances. *Windsinger.* 1930. Milton Balch. 1st ed. inscr. 218p. G. B11. $30.00

GILMOR, Harry. *Four Years in the Saddle.* 1866. London. Longman Gr. 1st Eng ed. 310p. cloth/rebacked. M8. $150.00

GILMORE, R. *Ebony Bed Murder.* 1932. NY. 1st ed. VG/VG. B5. $20.00

GILMOUR, John. *British Botanists.* 1946 (1944). London. ils. 48p. VG/dj. B26. $15.00

GILMOUR, Margaret. *Ameliaranne at the Circus.* 1931. McKay. 1st ed. ils SB Pearse. unp. VG/dj. D1. $80.00

GILMOUR & WALTERS. *Wild Flowers: Botanising in Britain.* 1954. London. ils. 242p. dj. B26. $15.00

GILPATRICK, Guy. *Flying Stories.* 1946. Dutton. 1st ed. 8vo. 287p. gray cloth. NF. T10. $35.00

GILPATRICK, Guy. *Half Seas Over.* 1932. NY. 1st ed. VG/VG. B5. $42.50

GILPATRICK, Guy. *Last Glencannon Omnibus.* 1953. NY. 1st ed. VG/VG. B5. $40.00

GILPATRICK, Noreen. *Piano Man.* 1991. St Martin. 1st ed. 8vo. F/F. T10. $100.00

GILSON, Charles. *Robin of Sherwood.* nd. Children's Pr. hc. VG. P3. $10.00

GILSTRAP, John. *Nathan's Run.* 1996. Harper Collins. 1st ed. sgn. F/F. M23. $35.00

GIMBEL, Richard. *Thomas Paine: A Bibliographical Check List of Common Sense.* 1956. Yale. 124p. F. A4. $125.00

GINGRICH, Arnold. *Joys of Trout.* 1973. NY. 1st ed. sgn. VG/VG. w/2 letters & ephemera. B5. $40.00

GINGRICH, Arnold. *Well-Tempered Angler.* 1965. NY. 1st ed. VG/VG. B5. $30.00

GINSBERG, Allen. *Collected Poems, 1947-1980.* 1984. Harper. 1st ed. F/NF. B2. $40.00

GINSBERG, Allen. *Howl. Original Draft Facsimile, Transcript & Variant...* 1986. Harper. edit Barry Miles. F/NF. B2. $25.00

GINSBERG, Allen. *Kaddish..* 1962. Wiesbaden. 1st German ed. inscr Anselm Hollo. NF/wrp/dj. A11. $65.00

GINSBURG, Mirra. *Last Door to Aiya.* 1968. SG Phillips. 1st ed. F/F. P3. $23.00

GINSBURG, Mirra. *Ultimate Threshold.* 1979. HRW. 1st ed. VG/VG. P3. $20.00

GINSBURG, Ralph. *Unhurried View of Erotica.* 1958. np. 4to. 128p. VG. A4. $35.00

GINTHER, Pemberton. *Thirteenth Spoon.* 1932. Cupples Leon. VG. P3. $20.00

GIOVANNI, Nikki. *Gemini.* 1971. Bobbs Merrill. 1st ed. VG/VG. B4. $35.00

GIOVANNI, Nikki. *My House.* 1972. Morrow. 1st ed. F/NF. B4. $45.00

GIOVANNI, Nikki. *Racism 101.* 1994. Morrow. 1st ed. F/F. M23. $35.00

GIOVANNI, Nikki. *Women & the Men: Poems.* 1975. Morrow. 1st ed. 8vo. F/dj. S9. $35.00

GIOVINAZZO, Buddy. *Life Is Hot in Cracktown.* 1993. NY. Thunder. 1st ed. author's 1st book. F/F. H11. $30.00

GIRAUD, S. Louis. *Bookano Stories No 6.* ca 1936. London. Strand. 5 double-p popups. VG. D1. $340.00

GIRAUD, S. Louis. *Daily Express Children's Annual, No 2.* 1930s. London. Lane Pub. 5 popups. pict brd. NF. T10. $200.00

GISSING, George. *Books & the Quiet Life.* 1922. Portland. 2nd. VG. O7. $20.00

GITTINGS, Robert. *Peach Blossom Forest & Other Chinese...* 1951. Oxford. 1st ed. hc. VG/VG. P3. $20.00

GIVENS, Charles G. *Jig-Time Murders.* 1936. Bobbs Merrill. 1st ed. VG. P3. $25.00

GLADWIN, Harold Sterling. *History of the Ancient Southwest.* 1957. Portland, ME. Bond Wheelwright. 1st ed. sgn. ils. 383p. cloth. F/NF. B24. $125.00

GLAESSNER, Verina. *Kung Fu Cinema of Vengeance.* nd. Bounty. hc. VG. P3. $10.00

GLAISTER, Lesley. *Honour Thy Father.* 1991. Atheneum. 1st ed. F/F. M23. $20.00

GLANZ. *German Jew in America, an Annotated Bibliography.* 1969. np. 4to. 2527 entries. 208p. VG. A4. $35.00

GLASCOW, Ellen. *Deliverance.* 1904. Doubleday Page. 1st ed. VG. B10. $45.00

GLASCOW, Ellen. *Old Dominion Edition.* 1929. Doubleday Doran. VG. B10. $12.00

GLASCOW, Ellen. *Phases of an Inferior Planet.* 1898. NY. Harper. 1st ed. author's 2nd book. F. B4. $85.00

GLASGOW, Joseph A. *Some Memories: Christmas Stories of Virginia Circuit Judge.* 1935. McClure. ils. 90p. VG. B10. $35.00

GLASPELL, Susan. *Norma Ashe.* 1942. Lippincott. 1st ed. F/NF. B4. $50.00

GLASS, Francis. *Life of George Washington in Latin Prose.* 1835. Harper. 233p. full leather. xl. B10. $175.00

GLASSCHEIB, H.S. *March of Medicine: Aberrations & Triumphs of Healing Art.* 1963. London. 1st Eng trans. 360p. VG. A13. $25.00

GLASSCOCK, C.B. *Big Bonanza: Story of the Comstock Lode.* 1931. Portland. Binfords Mort. 8vo. 7 pl. 368p. map ep. F/NF. T10. $35.00

GLAUBKE, Robert. *Lost Treasure Trails.* 1954. Grosset Dunlap. 4to. VG/G. B17. $10.00

GLAZE, A.T. *Business History of Fond DuLac, Wisconsin.* 1905. Fond DuLac. 1st ed. ils/photos/index. 368p. G+. B5. $55.00

GLAZIER, Willard. *Down the Great River.* 1889. Phil. 12mo. 443p. G. T3. $40.00

GLAZIER, Willard. *Headwaters of the Mississippi.* 1894. np. 12mo. ils. 537p. gilt dk gr pict cloth. xl. G. T3. $30.00

GLAZIER, Willard. *Ocean to Ocean on Horseback.* 1903. Phil. 12mo. 544p. G. T3. $25.00

GLAZUNOV, Ilya. *Ilya Glazunov.* 1978. Moscow. ils. 267p. brd. D2. $80.00

GLEASON, O. *Gleason's Horse Book.* (1892). Hubbard. VG. O3. $68.00

GLEASON, O. *Gleason's Veterinary Hand-Book & System of Horse Taming.* 1890. Phil. 2 parts. 8vo. ils. 520p. F. B14. $75.00

GLEASON, Robert. *Wrath of God.* 1994. Harper Prism. UP. NF/wrp. M22. $15.00

GLENN, Lois. *Charles WS Williams: A Checklist.* 1975. Kent State. 128p. VG. A17. $12.50

GLENN, Rewa. *Botanical Explorers of New Zealand.* 1950. Wellington. 1st ed. ils. dj. B26. $48.00

GLENNAN, T. Keith. *Birth of NASA.* 1993. WA, DC. 1st ed. inscr. 389p. VG/dj. B18. $22.50

GLOBE, Alexander. *Peter Stent, London Printseller, Circa 1642-1665.* 1985. Vancouver. British Columbia U. 4to. 64p. F/dj. T10. $80.00

GLOERSEN, P. *Arctic & Antarctic Sea Ice, 1978-1987...* 1992. WA. NASA. F. O7. $45.00

GLOVER, John H. *Voyage of the Dayspring.* 1926. London. VG. O7. $40.00

GLUBB, John Bagot. *Soldier With the Arabs.* 1957. Hodder Stoughton. 1st ed. 8vo. ils/maps. 460p. F/dj. T10. $75.00

GLUCK, Louise. *Proofs & Theories: Essays on Poetry.* 1994. Ecco. 1st ed. F/F. M23. $35.00

GLUECK, Nelson. *Rivers in the Desert.* 1959. FSG. 1st ed. ils. 302p. VG/dj. W1. $22.00

GLUSKER & MORRIS. *Southern Album.* 1975. Oxmoor. ltd ed. sgns. 4to. VG/G. B11. $30.00

GLUT, Donald F. *Empire Strikes Back.* nd. BC. MTI. VG/VG. P3. $10.00

GLUT, Donald F. *Vampires of History.* 1972. Mirage. 1st ed. VG/VG. P3. $45.00

GOBLE, Paul. *Star Boy.* 1983. NY. 1st ed. ils. VG+. M5. $12.00

GOBOLD, E. Stanley. *Ellen Glasgow & the Woman Within.* 1972. LSU. photos. 322p. VG/VG. B10. $15.00

GOCHER, W.H. *Fasig's Tales of the Turf & Memoir/Tales of the Turf.* 1903. Hartford. 2 vol. VG. O3. $85.00

GODDARD, Anthea. *Vienna Pursuit.* 1976. Walker. NF/NF. P3. $8.00

GODDARD, Kenneth. *Balefire.* 1983. Bantam. 1st ed. author's 1st book. F/dj. N4/T2. $20.00

GODDEN, Rummer. *Impunity Jane.* 1954. Viking. 1st ed. ils Adrienne Adams. 48p. VG/VG. P2. $50.00

GODDEN, Rummer. *In Noah's Ark.* 1949. Viking. 1st ed. ils. 62p. NF/G+. P2. $30.00

GODDEN, Rummer. *Story of Holly & Ivy.* 1958. Viking. 1st ed. ils Adrienne Adams. 64p. VG/VG. P2. $45.00

GODEY, John. *Fatal Beauty.* 1984. Irwin. 1st ed. G/G. P3. $15.00

GODEY, John. *Nella.* 1981. Delacorte. 1st ed. G+/dj. N4. $17.50

GODEY, John. *Never Put Off 'Til Tomorrow What You Can Kill Today.* 1970. Random. 1st ed. VG/VG. P3. $25.00

GODEY, John. *Talisman.* 1976. Putnam. 1st ed. VG/VG. P3. $20.00

GODEY & HALE. *Lady's Book.* 1869. Phil. Godey. 3 fld pl. 522p. blk leather spine raised band. G. D1. $150.00

GODWIN, Frank. *King Arthur & His Nights...* 1927. Winston. 8vo. VG. B17. $5.00

GODWIN, Gail. *Dream Children.* 1976. Knopf. 1st ed. F/F. M19. $15.00

GODWIN, Gail. *Finishing School.* 1982. Viking. 1st ed. F/F. B4. $35.00

GODWIN, Parke. *Sherwood.* 1991. Morrow. 1st ed. NF/F. M23. $20.00

GODWIN, Parke. *Truce With Time.* 1988. Bantam. 1st ed. NF/NF. M23. $15.00

GODWIN, Parke. *Waiting for the Galactic Bus.* 1988. Doubleday. 1st ed. F/F. P3. $20.00

GODWIN, Tom. *Survivors.* 1958. Gnome. 1st ed. xl. dj. P3. $10.00

GODWIN & KAYE. *Masters of Solitude.* nd. BC. VG/VG. P3. $8.00

GOEBBELS, Joseph. *Vom Kaiserhof Zur Reich Kanzler.* 1934. Berlin. 1st German ed. 308p. VG/VG. B5. $85.00

GOELET, Frances. *Extracts From the Journal of...* 1870. Boston. xl. VG. O7. $20.00

GOELET, Frances. *Voyages & Travels of...* 1970. NY. VG. O7. $55.00

GOERKE, Heinz. *Linnaeus.* 1973 (1966). NY. ils. VG+/dj. B26. $30.00

GOETHE, Ann. *Midnight Lemonade.* 1993. Delacorte. 1st ed. author's 1st book. F/F. H11/M23. $25.00

GOETHE. *Renard the Fox.* nd. np. no pub. obl 32mo. 12 chromolitho pl. F/wrp. H3. $450.00

GOETZMANN, William H. *New Lands, New Man. America & the Second Great Age...* 1986. Viking. 1st ed. 8vo. 528p. half cloth. AN/dj. P4. $25.00

GOETZMANN & GOETZMANN. *West of the Imagination.* 1986. NY. VG. O7. $35.00

GOETZMANN & WILLIAMS. *Atlas of North American Exploration From Norse Voyages...* 1992. np. 4to. 100 maps/90 portraits. 224p. F/F. A4. $35.00

GOFF, Frederick R. *Early Printed Book of Low Countries.* 1958. WA. VG. O7. $15.00

GOFFIN, Robert. *Jazz From the Congo to the Metropolitan.* 1944. Doubleday. 1st ed. NF/NF. B2. $60.00

GOGOL, Nikolai. *Chickikov's Journeys; or, Home Life in Old Russia.* 1994. NY. 2 vol. 1/1200. ils/sgn Lucille Corcos. F/case. T10. $90.00

GOHM, Douglas. *Antique Maps of Europe, the Americas, West Indies...* 1972. London. Octopus. 167 maps. F/dj. O7. $45.00

GOINES, Donald. *Dopefiend. Story of a Black Junkie.* 1971. Los Angeles. true 1st prt (no banner blurb). NF/wrp. A11. $115.00

GOLD, Don. *Intermediate Two-Bids in Bridge: A Modern Alternative...* 1982. NY. 1st ed. 128p. VG/VG. S1. $8.00

GOLD, Eddie. *Golden Era Cubs.* 1985. Bonus Books. 1st ed. F/VG. P8. $20.00

GOLD, H. *Birth of a Hero.* 1951. NY. 1st ed. author's 1st book. F/F. A15. $50.00

GOLD, H.L. *Bodyguard.* nd. BC. VG/VG. P3. $8.00

GOLD, H.L. *Fifth Galaxy Reader.* 1961. BC. VG/VG. P3. $30.00

GOLD, H.L. *Galaxy Reader of SF.* 1952. Crown. 1st ed. hc. VG. P3. $35.00

GOLD, H.L. *Weird Ones.* 1965. Dobson. 1st ed. F/F. P3. $30.00

GOLD, Herbert. *Great American Jackport.* 1969. Random. 1st ed. F/NF. M19. $15.00

GOLD, Michael. *120 Million.* 1929. Internat. 1st ed. inscr. NF. B2. $150.00

GOLDBERG, Marshall. *Anatomy Lesson.* 1974. Putnam. 1st ed. NF/NF. H11. $30.00

GOLDBERG, Marshall. *Karamanov Equations.* 1972. Cleveland. World. 1st ed. author's 1st book. NF/NF clip. H11. $40.00

GOLDBERG, Martha. *Twirly Skirt.* 1954. Holiday. 1st ed. ils Helen Stone. 47p. VG/G. P2. $30.00

GOLDEN, Richard M. *Godly Rebellion: Parisian Cures & the Religious Fronde...* 1981. Chapel Hill. 8vo. 221p. red cloth/wht spine. M. P4. $20.00

GOLDENBERG, J. *Shipbuilding in Colonial America.* 1976. Charlottesville. VG. O7. $35.00

GOLDENWEISER, Alexander. *History, Psychology & Culture.* 1933. Knopf. 476p. maroon cloth. xl. VG. G1. $35.00

GOLDIN, Stephen. *Assault on the Gods.* 1977. Doubleday. F/F. P3. $15.00

GOLDIN, Stephen. *World Called Solitude.* 1981. Doubleday. 1st ed. F/F. P3. $15.00

GOLDING, William. *Close Quarters.* 1987. FSG. 1st ed. F/NF. M23. $15.00

GOLDING, William. *Darkness Visible.* 1979. FSG. 1st ed. F/F. B35. $18.00

GOLDING, William. *Paper Men.* 1984. FSG. 1st ed. F/F. P3. $15.00

GOLDING, William. *Rites of Passage.* 1980. FSG. 1st ed. F/NF. M23. $20.00

GOLDING, William. *Spire.* 1964. London. 1st ed. F/F. C6. $75.00

GOLDMAN, Francisco. *Long Night of White Chickens.* 1992. Atlantic. 1st ed. F/F. M23. $35.00

GOLDMAN, James. *Man From Greek & Roman...* 1974. Random. 1st ed. NF/NF. P3. $20.00

GOLDMAN, Judith. *James Rosenquist.* 1985. Viking. ils. cloth. dj. D2. $100.00

GOLDMAN, Laurel. *Sounding the Territory.* 1982. Knopf. 1st ed. author's 1st book. F/F. B4. $45.00

GOLDMAN, Lawrence Louis. *Tiger by the Tail.* 1946. David McKay. hc. VG/G. P3. $15.00

GOLDMAN, William. *Brothers.* 1987. Warner. 1st ed. F/F. H11. $25.00

GOLDMAN, William. *Color of Light.* 1984. Granada. 1st ed. VG/VG. P3. $23.00

GOLDMAN, William. *Edged Weapons.* 1985. Granada. F/F. P3. $20.00

GOLDMAN, William. *Father's Day.* 1971. HBJ. 2nd. VG/VG. P3. $13.00

GOLDMAN, William. *Hype & Glory.* 1990. Villard. 1st ed. VG. P3. $20.00

GOLDMAN, William. *Tinsel.* 1979. Delacorte. 1st ed. VG/VG. P3. $25.00

GOLDSBOROUGH, Robert. *Death on Deadline.* 1987. Bantam. 1st ed. F/F. H11. $40.00

GOLDSBOROUGH, Robert. *Last Coincidence.* 1989. Bantam. 1st ed. F/F. H11. $35.00

GOLDSBOROUGH, Robert. *Murder in E Minor.* 1986. Bantam. 1st ed. F/F. P3. $15.00

GOLDSCHEIDER, Ludwig. *Leonardo: Paintings & Drawings.* 1975. London. Phaidon. 8th. ils. cloth. dj. D2. $65.00

GOLDSCHMIDT, E. *Gothic & Renaissance Bookbindings.* 1928. London. Benn. 2 vol. 1st ed. 110 pl. taupe buckram. NF. C6. $500.00

GOLDSCHMIDT, Walter. *Sebei Law.* 1967. Berkeley. CA U. M11. $35.00

GOLDSMITH, Oliver. *Deserted Village.* 1865. Boston. JE Tilton. Keepsake ed. ils. 12mo. cloth. AN. B36. $35.00

GOLDSMITH, Oliver. *She Stoops to Conquer.* 1912. Hodder Stoughton. 1st Am ed. ils Hugh Thomson. F. T10. $150.00

GOLDSMITH, Oliver. *Vicar of Wakefield.* nd. Phil. McKay. 1st Am ed. ils Rackham. NF. A15. $75.00

GOLDSMITH, V.F. *Short Title Catalogue of Spanish & Portuguese Books...* 1974. 4to. 256p. F/NF. A4. $45.00

GOLDSTEIN, Lisa. *Dream Years.* 1985. Bantam. 1st ed. F/F. G10/P3. $15.00

GOLDSTEIN, Lisa. *Red Magician.* 1993. Tor. 1st hc ed. F/F. G10. $15.00

GOLDSTEIN, Lisa. *Strange Devices of Sun & Moon.* 1993. NY. Tor. 1st ed. F/dj. M23/P3. $20.00

GOLDSTEIN, Lisa. *Summer King, Winter Fool.* 1994. Tor. 1st ed. F/F. G10. $15.00

GOLDSTEIN, Richard. *Superstars & Screwballs.* 1991. Dutton. 1st ed. F/F. P8. $15.00

GOLDSTONE & PAYNE. *John Steinbeck: A Bibliographical Catalogue...* 1974. Austin, TX. 1/1200. 240p. VG. A4. $350.00

GOLDTHORPE. *From Queen to Empress: Victorian Dress 1837-1877.* Dec 1988-April 1989. Costume Inst. ils. cloth. F/F. D2. $25.00

GOLDWAITHE, Eaton K. *Once You Stop, You're Dead.* 1968. Morrow. 1st ed. VG/VG. P3. $18.00

GOLDWAITHE, Eaton K. *Scarecrow.* 1946. Books Inc. VG/G. P3. $10.00

GOLDWATER, Barry. *Conscience of a Conservative.* 1960. Shepardsville. 1st ed. inscr. F. N3. $45.00

GOLDWATER & RATHER. *According to Hoyle, 1742-1850.* 1983. 26p. VG/wrp. A4. $35.00

GOLDWATER. *Radical Periodicals in America 1890-1950...* 1964. Yale. 4to. 321 annotated entries. F. A4. $85.00

GOLENDOCK, P. *NY Yankees 1949-1964.* 1975. Englewood Cliffs. 1st ed. VG/VG. B5. $25.00

GOLLANCZ, Victor. *My Dear Timothy: An Autobiographical Letter...* 1953. NY. 1st ed. F/dj. A17. $15.00

GOLLER, Nicholas. *Tomorrow's Silence.* 1979. Macmillan. 1st ed. VG/VG. P3. $15.00

GONCHAROV, Ivan. *Voyage of the Frigate Pallada.* 1965. London. VG. O7. $55.00

GONDOR, Emery J. *You Are...A Puzzle Book for Children.* 1937. Modern Age. 1st ed. ils. VG/VG. D1. $135.00

GONNE, C.M. *Hints on Horses: How to Judge Them...* 1905. Dutton. 1st Am ed. O3. $35.00

GONZALEZ, Julio. *Catalogo de Mapas y Planos de Venezuela.* 1968. Madrid. 273 entries+8 indices. M/wrp. O7. $65.00

GOOCH, Brad. *City Poet: Life & Times of Frank O'Hara.* 1993. Knopf. 1st ed. rem mk. F/NF. B2. $25.00

GOOD, Howard E. *Black Swamp Farm.* 1967. OH State. 1st ed. ils BO Sutherland. 304p. VG/dj. B18. $15.00

GOOD, Kenneth. *Into the Heart.* 1991. Simon Schuster. 1st ed. 349p. F3. $20.00

GOOD, Ronald. *Geography of the Flowering Plants.* 1964 (1947). London. 3rd. ils/9 maps. torn dj. B26. $45.00

GOOD & PRATT. *World Geography of Petroleum.* 1950. Am Geographic Soc. fld map/photos. 464p. VG/torn. D8. $30.00

GOODALL, John S. *Paddy's Evening Out.* 1973. Atheneum. 1st ed. unp. NF/NF. M20. $25.00

GOODE, James. *Story of the Misfits.* 1963. Indianapolis. 1st ed. VG/VG. B5. $35.00

GOODE, Paul. *United States Soldiers' Home.* 1957. private prt. 1st ed. sgn. 8vo. 289p. VG. B11. $75.00

GOODING, E.G.B. *Flora of the Barbados.* 1965. London. ils. VG/dj. B26. $55.00

GOODING, John D. *Durango South Project.* 1980. Tucson, AZ. 4to. 200p. F/wrp. T10. $25.00

GOODIS, David. *Le Casse.* 1954. Paris. Gallimard. 1st French ed. blk/yel brd. VG. A11. $60.00

GOODKIND, Terry. *Wizard's First Rule.* 1994. NY. Tor. 1st ed. F/F. H11. $30.00

GOODMAN, Allegra. *Total Immersion.* 1989. Harper Row. 1st ed. F/F. M23. $20.00

GOODMAN, David Michael. *Western Panorama 1849-1875.* 1966. Glendale. Arthur Clark. 8vo. ils. 328p. gilt red cloth. F. T10. $100.00

GOODMAN, John Bartlett III. *Key to the Goodman Encyclopedia of the CA Gold Rush Fleet.* 1992. Los Angeles. Zamorano Club. only ed. 8vo. 31 fld charts. F/case. T10. $100.00

GOODNOW, Minnie. *Nursing History in Brief.* 1941. Phil. 325p. VG. A13. $20.00

GOODRICH, Charles. *Universal Traveler.* 1836. Hartford. fair. V4. $55.00

GOODRICH, L. *Graphic Art of Winslow Homer.* 1968. Smithsonian. 132 full-p ils. 136p. xl. VG/dj. T3. $20.00

GOODRUM, Charles A. *Best Cellar.* 1987. St Martin. 1st ed. VG/VG. P3. $15.00

GOODWIN, K.L. *Influence of Ezra Pound.* 1966. Oxford. 1st ed. assn copy. F/NF. V1. $35.00

GOODWIN, Maud Wilder. *White Aprons: Romance of Bacon's Rebellion.* 1901. Little Brn. 338p. G. B10. $12.00

GOOLD-ADAMS, Deenagh. *Cook Greenhouse Today.* 1969. London. ils/photos. VG. B26. $15.00

GORDAN. *Fifteenth-Century Books in Library of Howard L Goodhart...* 1955. Overbrook. 1/250. 4to. 160p. F. A4. $175.00

GORDIMER, Nadine. *Sport of Nature.* 1987. Knopf. ARC/1st Am ed. sgn. RS. F/dj. C2. $75.00

GORDON. *Gordon's Print Price Annual 1994.* 1994. 4to. NF. A4. $225.00

GORDON, Albert I. *Intermarriage Interfaith Interracial Interethnic.* 1964. Boston. Beacon. 1st ed. inscr/dtd. 420p. F/dj. B14. $60.00

GORDON, Armistead C. *Gay Gordons: Ballads of Ancient Scottish Clan.* 1902. Staunton. Shultx. 1/250. unp. VG. B10. $15.00

GORDON, Armistead C. *Memories & Memorials of William Gordon McCabe.* 1925. Richmond, VA. Old Dominion. 2 vol. 1st ed. cloth. VG. M8. $250.00

GORDON, Bernard L. *Man & the Sea.* 1970. Garden City. VG. O7. $20.00

GORDON, Caroline. *Aleck Maury Sportsman.* 1934. NY. 1st ed. VG/VG. B5. $145.00

GORDON, Caroline. *Glory of Hera.* 1972. Doubleday. 1st ed. F/NF. B4. $85.00

GORDON, Caroline. *Malefactors.* 1956. Harcourt Brace. 1st ed. 312p. G/G. B10. $25.00

GORDON, Caroline. *None Shall Look Back.* 1937. Scribner. 1st ed. 378p. VG. B10. $15.00

GORDON, Caroline. *Old Red & Other Stories.* 1963. NY. 1st ed. NF/NF. B4. $100.00

GORDON, Cyrus H. *Before the Bible: The Common Background of Greek & Hebrew...* 1962. NY. 1st ed. 4-line inscr. 319p. F/dj. B14. $55.00

GORDON, Donald. *Star-Raker.* 1962. Hodder Stoughton. 1st ed. VG/VG. P3. $20.00

GORDON, Elizabeth. *Bird Children.* 1912. Volland. 2nd. ils MT Ross. F. M5. $150.00

GORDON, Elizabeth. *Four-Footed Folk; or, The Children of the Farm & Forest.* 1914. Whitman. 8vo. ils. VG. M5. $55.00

GORDON, Elizabeth. *Happy Home Children.* 1924. Volland. ils Marion Foster. unp. VG. T5. $45.00

GORDON, Elizabeth. *I Wonder Why?* 1937 (1916). Rand McNally. 12mo. ils. VG. M5. $15.00

GORDON, Elizabeth. *Loraine & the Little People of Spring.* 1918. Rand McNally. 1st ed. ils Ella Lee. 64p. VG. P2. $40.00

GORDON, Elizabeth. *Really-So Stories.* 1924. Volland. 15th. 8vo. 96p. VG. T5. $40.00

GORDON, Elizabeth. *Taming of Giants.* 1950. Viking. 1st ed. ils Garry MacKensie. 57p. VG/G. P2. $20.00

GORDON, Elizabeth. *Witch of Scapefaggot Green.* 1948. Viking. 1st ed. ils William Pene DuBois. 76p. VG+/VG. P2. $75.00

GORDON, Harold J. Jr. *Hitler & the Beer Hall Putsch.* 1972. Princeton. 1st ed. 666p. VG/dj. A17. $20.00

GORDON, Lesley. *Pageant of Dolls* nd. ca 1950? Ward. 16 pl. NF/G. M5. $30.00

GORDON, Max. *Live at the Village Vanguard.* 1980. St Martin. 1st ed. F/F. B2. $25.00

GORDON, Richard. *Captain's Table.* 1954. Michael Joseph. 1st ed. VG/VG. P3. $30.00

GORDON, Richard. *Doctor & Son.* 1959. Michael Joseph. 1st ed. VG/VG. P3. $30.00

GORDON, Richard. *Doctor at Sea.* 1954. Michael Joseph. 13th. VG/VG. P3. $15.00

GORDON, Richard. *Doctor in Swim.* 1962. Michael Joseph. 1st ed. VG/VG. P3. $20.00

GORDON, Ruth. *My Side: The Autobiography of...* 1976. NY. 1st ed. 502p. F/dj. A17. $10.00

GORDON, Stuart. *Two-Eyes.* 1975. Sidgwick Jackson. 1st ed. VG/VG. P3. $20.00

GORDON & GORDON. *Informant.* 1973. Doubleday. 1st ed. hc. VG/G. P3. $15.00

GORDON & GORDON. *Operation Terror.* 1961. Crime Club. VG/VG. P3. $20.00

GOREN, Charles. *Charles Goren's Shortcut to Expert Bridge.* nd. NY. VG. S1. $3.00

GOREN, Charles. *Goren Point Count Bidding Wheel.* 1957. np. VG. S1. $3.00

GORES, Joe. *Come Morning.* 1986. Mysterious. 1st ed. RS. F/F. P3. $20.00

GORES, Joe. *Dead Man.* 1993. Mysterious. 1st ed. F/F. N4. $30.00

GORES, Joe. *Mostly Murder.* 1992. Mystery Scene. deluxe ed. 1/50. sgn/#d. leather. F/sans. P3. $50.00

GORES, Joe. *Wolf Time.* 1989. Putnam. 1st ed. sgn. F/F. T2. $35.00

GOREY, Edward. *Amphigorey.* 1972. Putnam. 1st ed. VG/VG. P3. $30.00

GOREY, Edward. *Broken Spoke.* 1979 (1976). London. Benn. 1st ed. ils. VG/VG. P2. $50.00

GOREY, Edward. *Case-Record From a Sonnetorium, by Merrill Moore.* 1951. Twayne. 1st ed. 8vo. F/dj. B24. $350.00

GOREY, Edward. *Curious Sofa, a Pornographic Work by Ogdred Weary.* 1961. NY. Obolensky. 1st ed. 12mo. unp. VG/wrp. T10. $115.00

GOREY, Edward. *Doubtful Guest.* 1957. Doubleday. 1st ed. sgn. prt brd. F/NF. B24. $350.00

GOREY, Edward. *Dwindling Party.* 1982. Random. 1st ed. unp. VG+. M20. $105.00

GOREY, Edward. *Eclectic Abecedarium.* 1983. Boston. Bromer. 1st ed. 1/300. sgn. author's 1st miniature book. F. B24. $175.00

GOREY, Edward. *Epiplectic Bicycle.* 1969. Dodd Mead. 1st ed. sgn. F/NF. B24. $95.00

GOREY, Edward. *Fatal Lozenge: An Alphabet.* 1960. NY. 1st ed. inscr. F/wrp. C2. $100.00

GOREY, Edward. *Figbash Acrobate.* 1994. Fantod. 1/500. sgn. F/pict wrp. B24. $45.00

GOREY, Edward. *Hapless Child.* 1961. NY. 1st ed. inscr. NF/wrp. C2. $125.00

GOREY, Edward. *Haunted Looking Glass.* 1959. Looking Glass Lib. VG/VG. P3. $45.00

GOREY, Edward. *Improvable Landscape: A Piermont Book.* 1986. Albondocani. 1/326. sgn. F/gr pict wrp. B24. $150.00

GOREY, Edward. *Insect God.* 1986. Beaufort. 1st ed thus. 16mo. F/VG. B17. $10.00

GOREY, Edward. *Light Metres, by Felicia Lamports. Drawings by Edward Gorey.* 1982. Everest House. 1/376. sgn. AN/case. B24. $185.00

GOREY, Edward. *Utter Zoo. An Alphabet.* 1967. Meredith. 1st ed. sgn. F/NF. B24. $110.00

GOREY, Edward. *Water Flowers.* 1982. NY. Cogdon Weed. stated 1st ed. F/VG+. H4. $25.00

GOREY, Edward. *Wuggly Ump.* 1963. Lippincott. 8vo. AN/dj. B24. $110.00

GORGAS, Josiah. *Civil War Diary of General Josiah Gorgas...* 1947. AL U. 1st ed. 208p. cloth. NF/VG. M8. $250.00

GORHAM, Bob. *Churchill Downs 100th Kentucky Derby.* 1973. Churchhill Downs. 4to. 247p. VG. O3. $45.00

GORKY, Maxim. *Foma Gordyeeff.* 1901. NY. 1st ed. VG. B5. $30.00

GORMAN, Ed. *Modern Treasury of Great Detective...* 1984. Carroll Graf. 1st ed. sgn. F/F. P3. $27.00

GORMAN, Ed. *Murder Straight Up.* 1986. NY. 1st ed. F/F. H11. $30.00

GORMAN, Ed. *New, Improved Murder.* nd. St Martin. 2nd ed. VG/VG. P3. $13.00

GORMAN, Ed. *Reason Why.* 1992. Mystery Scene. 1st ed. 1/100. sgn/#d. F/sans. P3. $20.00

GORMAN & GREENBERG. *Stalkers.* 1991. Severn. 1st Eng/1st hc ed. F/F. G10. $20.00

GORMAN & HORNER. *Digging Dinosaurs: Search That Unraveled the Mystery...* 1988. Workman. 210p. NF/wrp. D8. $12.00

GOSLING, Paula. *Hoodwink.* 1988. Macmillan. 1st ed. F/F. P3. $25.00

GOSLING, Paula. *Loser's Blues.* 1980. Macmillan. 1st ed. VG/VG. P3. $20.00

GOSNELL & SNOW. *On the Decks of Old Ironsides.* 1932. Macmillan. ils. 304p. VG. T7. $55.00

GOSS, Alice Dillon. *New Mother Goose.* 1912. Dodge. ils. VG. M5. $35.00

GOSS, Warren. *Lee Jed, a Boy's Adventures in the Army of '61-'65...* 1889. NY. Crowell. 1st ed. 404p. gr cloth. F. B14. $75.00

GOSSE, P.H. *Wonders of the Great Deep.* 1874. Quaker City Pub. ils. 385p. G+. P12. $15.00

GOSSEN, Gary. *Symbol & Meaning Beyond the Closed Community.* 1986. Inst Mesoamerican Studies. 1st ed. 267p. wrp. F3. $20.00

GOTLIEB, Phyllis. *Heart of Red Iron.* 1989. St Martin. 1st ed. VG/VG. P3. $16.00

GOTLIEB, Phyllis. *O Master Caliban!* 1976. Harper Row. 1st ed. F/F. P3. $20.00

GOTLIEB, Phyllis. *Why Should I Have All the Grief?* 1969. Macmillan. 1st ed. VG/VG. P3. $30.00

GOTTLIEB, Samuel Hirsch. *Overbooked in Arizona.* 1994. Scottsdale. Camelback Gallery. 1st hc ed. 1/501. sgn. F/F/case. T2. $50.00

GOUDY, Alice. *Jupiter & the Cats.* 1953. Scribner. 1st ed. ils Paul Brown. 90p. VG/G+. P2. $40.00

GOUGH, Laurence. *Accidental Deaths.* 1991. Viking. 1st ed. F/F. P3. $25.00

GOUGH, Laurence. *Death on a No 8 Hook.* 1988. Gollancz. 1st ed. NF/NF. P3. $22.00

GOUGH, Laurence. *Hot Shots.* 1989. Viking. 1st ed. rem mk. F/F. N4. $15.00

GOUGH, Laurence. *Serious Crimes.* 1990. Viking. 1st ed. F/F. P3. $25.00

GOULART, Ron. *Broken Down Engine.* 1971. Macmillan. 1st ed. VG/VG. P3. $30.00

GOULART, Ron. *Death in Silver.* 1975. Golden. F. P3. $8.00

GOULART, Ron. *Even the Butler Was Poor.* 1990. Walker. 1st ed. F/F. H11. $20.00

GOULART, Ron. *Odd Job #101.* 1975. Scribner. 1st ed. F/F. P3. $20.00

GOULD, Chester. *Dick Tracy, Ace Detective.* 1943. Whitman. hc. VG. P3. $20.00

GOULD, Frank W. *Grasses of SW United States.* 1981 (1951). Tucson. 4th. 343p. F/wrp. B26. $15.00

GOULD, Heywood. *Glitterburn.* 1981. St Martin. 1st ed. xl. dj. P3. $6.00

GOULD, Lois. *Medusa's Gift.* 1991. Knopf. 1st ed. rem mk. F/F. B35. $20.00

GOULD, S.J. *Bully for Brontasaurus: Reflections in Natural History.* 1991. Norton. 1st ed. 540p. F/dj. D8. $22.00

GOULD, S.J. *Ever Since Darwin: Reflections in Natural History.* 1977. NY. 1st ed. 285p. dj. A13. $30.00

GOULD, S.J. *Mismeasure of Man.* 1981. NY. 1st ed. 352p. VG/dj. A13. $30.00

GOULD, S.J. *Wonderful Life: The Burgess Shale & Nature of History.* 1989. Norton. 1st ed. F/dj. D8. $25.00

GOULDER, G. *John D Rockefeller: The Cleveland Years.* 1972. Cleveland. 1st ed. sgn. ils. 271p. VG/VG. B5. $25.00

GOULDING, M. *Fishes & the Forest.* 1980. Berkeley. 8vo. 279p. cloth. dj. B11. $20.00

GOULDSBOROUGH, John. *Reports...in All the Courts of Westminster...* 1653. London. Adams. 1st ed. contemporary sheep. M11. $250.00

GOURKE, John G. *MacKenzie's Last Fight With the Cheyennes.* 1966. NY. Argonaut. 8vo. ils. 56p. NF. T10. $45.00

GOVER, Paula K. *White Boys & River Girls.* 1995. Algonquin. 1st ed. rem mk. F/F. H11. $20.00

GOVERNMENT PRINTING OFFICE. *Album of American Battle Art 1755-1918.* 1947. Washington. 1st ed. 150 pl. 319p. VG. A17. $50.00

GOVERNMENT PRINTING OFFICE. *Navigation Laws of the United States.* 1927. 536p. VG. P12. $8.00

GOVERNMENT PRINTING OFFICE. *Poisonous Snakes of the World.* 1965. Washington, DC. lg 8vo. 212p. hc. G. B1. $25.00

GOW, Gordon. *Suspense in the Cinema.* 1968. NY. Castle. F/F. D2. $20.00

GOYTISOLO, Juan. *Party's Over.* 1966. Grove. 1st ed. F/F. M19. $20.00

GRABAR, Oleg. *Formation of Islamic Art.* 1973. Yale. 1st ed. ils. 233p. NF/dj. W1. $55.00

GRABAU, A.W. *Textbook of Geology, Part I, General Geology.* 1921. NY. DC Heath. 1st ed. VG. D8. $20.00

GRACE, Peter. *Polo.* 1991. NY. Howell. 1st ed. F/F. O3. $45.00

GRACY, Leonard R. *Duplicate Contract Bridge in the Home & Simple Tournament...* 1933. Phil. 68p. VG. S1. $8.00

GRADY, James. *Hard Bargains.* 1985. Macmillan. 1st ed. NF/NF. P3. $20.00

GRADY, James. *Six Days of the Condor.* 1974. Norton. 1st ed. VG/NF. M22. $40.00

GRADY, James. *Steeltown.* 1989. Bantam. 1st ed. F/F. P3. $19.00

GRAEME, David. *Monsieur Blackshirt.* 1935. Harrap. VG. P3. $25.00

GRAEME, David. *Sword of Monsieur Blackshirt.* 1936. Lippincott. 1st ed. 314p. VG+/dj. M20. $25.00

GRAF, Albert B. *Exotica 3.* 1963. Rutherford. 1828p. VG. B26. $145.00

GRAFTON, C.W. *Rope Began to Hang the Butcher.* 1944. Farrar Rinehart. 1st ed. VG. P3. $30.00

GRAFTON, Sue. *A Is for Alibi.* 1982. HRW. 1st ed. F/3 sm closed tears. P3. $700.00

GRAFTON, Sue. *B Is for Burglar.* 1985. HRW. 1st ed. F/F. P3. $475.00

GRAFTON, Sue. *C Is for Corpse.* 1986. Holt. ARC. inscr twice/sgn/dtd. VG/wrp. M22. $225.00

GRAFTON, Sue. *D Is for Deadbeat.* 1987. Holt. 1st ed. inscr/dtd 1987. F/dj. S9. $175.00

GRAFTON, Sue. *F Is for Fugitive.* 1989. Holt. 1st ed. F/F. A9/P3. $35.00

GRAFTON, Sue. *G Is for Gumshoe.* 1990. Holt. 1st ed. F/F. B2. $35.00

GRAFTON, Sue. *H Is for Homicide.* 1991. NY. Holt. 1st ed. F/F. H11. $35.00

GRAFTON, Sue. *I Is for Innocent.* 1992. Holt. 1st ed. F/F. H11. $30.00

GRAFTON, Sue. *J Is for Judgement.* 1993. NY. Holt. 1st ed. sgn. F/F. B11. $55.00

GRAFTON, Sue. *K Is for Killer.* 1994. Holt. 1st ed. F/F. N4/P3. $22.50

GRAFTON, Sue. *Keziah Dane.* 1968. Peter Owen. 1st ed. author's 1st book. F/VG. M19. $450.00

GRAHAM, Don. *No Name on the Bullet.* 1989. NY. 1st ed. VG/VG. B5. $25.00

GRAHAM, Frank. *Casey Stengel.* 1958. John Day. later prt. G+/G+. P8. $15.00

GRAHAM, Frank. *Great Hitters of Major Leagues.* 1969. Random. VG. P3. $10.00

GRAHAM, Frank. *Lou Gehrig, a Quiet Hero.* nd. Putnam. 26th. xl. P3. $8.00

GRAHAM, Henry H. *Quarterback.* ca 1920. Book Concern. 12mo. 63p. VG. A17. $7.00

GRAHAM, James; see Patterson, Harry.

GRAHAM, John Alexander. *Aldeburg.* nd. BC. F/F. P3. $8.00

GRAHAM, John D. *System & Dialectics of Art.* 1937. Delphic Studios. orig ed. 155p. xl. D2. $175.00

GRAHAM, Joseph A. *Sporting Dog.* 1924 (1904). Macmillan. 327p. gr cloth. VG. M20. $17.00

GRAHAM, Margaret. *Swing Shift.* 1951. Citadel. 1st ed. F/VG. B4. $50.00

GRAHAM, Mark Miller. *Reinterpreting Prehistory of Central America.* 1993. Niwot, CO. 1st ed. 336p. dj. F3. $40.00

GRAHAM, Sheilah. *Garden of Allah.* 1970. NY. Crown. 1st ed. F/NF. H11. $40.00

GRAHAM, T. *Elements of Chemistry.* 1843. Phil. royal 8vo. 749p. full leather. xl. T3. $28.00

GRAHAM, W.A. *Story of the Little Big Horn, Custer's Battle.* nd. Bonanza. rpt. F/laminated. E1. $35.00

GRAHAM, Whidden. *Crimson Hairs: An Erotic Mystery.* 1970. Grove. 1st ed. F/F. P3. $20.00

GRAHAM, Winston. *After the Act.* 1966. Doubleday. 1st ed. VG/VG. P3. $15.00

GRAHAM, Winston. *Angel, Pearl & Little God.* 1970. Literary Guild. VG/fair. $10.00

GRAHAM, Winston. *Merciless Ladies.* 1979. Bodley Head. 1st ed. VG/VG. P3. $20.00

GRAHAM, Winston. *Miller's Dance.* 1983. Doubleday. 1st ed. VG/VG. P3. $18.00

GRAHAM, Winston. *Spanish Armadas.* 1972. Collins. VG/VG. P3. $20.00

GRAHAM, Winston. *Woman in the Mirror.* 1975. Bodley Head. 1st ed. VG/VG. P3. $18.00

GRAHAM & TELEK. *Leaf Protein Concentrates.* 1983. Westport. AVI Pub. 8vo. ils. 844p. cloth. F. B1. $125.00

GRAHAME, Kenneth. *Dream Days.* 1899. NY/London. Lane. 1st ed. VG. C6. $75.00

GRAHAME, Kenneth. *Fun O' the Fair.* 1929. London. Dent. 30p. VG. M20. $52.00

GRAHAME, Kenneth. *Golden Age.* 1895. London. Lane. 1st ed. author's 2nd book. VG. C6. $120.00

GRAHAME, Kenneth. *Pagan Papers.* 1894. London. Mathews/Lane. 1/450. VG. C6. $150.00

GRAHAME, Kenneth. *Wind in the Willows.* 1933. Scribner. ils EH Shepard. VG/VG. B17. $10.00

GRAHAME, Kenneth. *Wind in the Willows.* 1940. Heritage. 1st prt thus. ils Rackham. 190p. VG+. C14. $20.00

GRAHAME, Robert; see Haldeman, Joe.

GRAMATKY, Hardie. *Little Toot.* 1939. NY. Putnam. 1st ed. 12mo. unp. G+. C14. $25.00

GRANFIELD, Robert. *Making Elite Lawyers, Visions of Law at Harvard & Beyond.* 1992. NY. UP. M11. $20.00

GRANGER, Bill. *British Cross.* 1983. Crown. 1st ed. F/F. H11. $35.00

GRANGER, Bill. *Burning the Apostle.* 1993. Warner. 1st ed. sgn. AN/dj. N4. $35.00

GRANGER, Bill. *El Murders.* 1987. Holt. 1st ed. F/F. P3. $17.00

GRANGER, Bill. *Hemingway's Notebook.* 1986. NY. Crown. 1st ed. F/F. H11. $25.00

GRANGER, Bill. *Last Good German.* 1991. Warner. 1st ed. VG/VG. P3. $19.00

GRANGER, Bill. *Schism.* 1981. Crown. 1st ed. F/F. A20. $25.00

GRANGER, Bill. *Shattered Eye.* 1982. Crown. 1st ed. F/dj. A20/H11. $25.00

GRANGER, Bill. *There Are No Spies.* 1986. Warner. 1st ed. VG/VG. P3. $17.00

GRANLUND, Nils T. *Blondes, Brunettes & Bullets.* 1957. McKay. 1st ed. NF/NF. H11. $40.00

GRANOVETTER, Matthew. *Murder at the Bridge Table.* 1988. NY. 310p. VG/wrp. S1. $8.00

GRANOVETTER & GRANOVETTER. *Tops & Bottoms.* 1982. NY. 182p. F/wrp. S1. $8.00

GRANT, Adele L. *Monograph of Genus Mimulus.* 1924. St Louis. rpt from Annuals of MO Botanical Garden 11. wrp. B26. $35.00

GRANT, Ambrose. *More Deadly Than the Male.* 1946. Eyre Spottiswoode. hc. VG. P3. $30.00

GRANT, Anne. *Memoirs of an American Lady.* 1901. NY. 2 vol. 1/350. 8vo. teg. half vellum. VG. T10. $250.00

GRANT, Audrey. *ACBL Introduction to Bridge Bidding, Club Series.* 1990. Memphis, TN. revised. pb. VG. S1. $8.00

GRANT, Bruce. *Concise Encyclopedia of the American Indian.* 1989. NY. Wings Books. 8vo. ils Bjorklund. 352p. F/dj. T10. $25.00

GRANT, Charles L. *Dark Cry of the Moon.* 1985. Donald Grant. 1st ed. sgn. F/F. T2. $35.00

GRANT, Charles L. *Final Shadows.* 1991. Doubleday. 1st ed. hc. F/F. P3. $20.00

GRANT, Charles L. *For Fear of the Night.* 1988. Tor. 1st ed. F/F. P3. $18.00

GRANT, Charles L. *Last Call of Mourning.* 1979. Doubleday. 1st ed. NF/NF. P3. $80.00

GRANT, Charles L. *Long Night of the Grave.* 1986. Donald Grant. 1st ed. sgn. F/F. T2. $35.00

GRANT, Charles L. *Night Visions 2: All Original Stories.* 1985. Dark Harvest. 1st ed. F/F. G10. $75.00

GRANT, Charles L. *Nightmare Seasons.* 1982. Doubleday. 1st ed. F/F. P3. $50.00

GRANT, Charles L. *Pet.* 1986. NY. Tor. 1st ed. sgn. F/F. T2. $32.00

GRANT, Charles L. *Ravens of the Moon.* 1978. Doubleday. 1st ed. VG/VG. P3. $20.00

GRANT, Charles L. *Shadows 3.* 1980. Doubleday. 1st ed. F/F. P3. $30.00

GRANT, Charles L. *Soft Whisper of the Dead.* 1982. Donald Grant. 1st ed. sgn. F/F. T2. $30.00

GRANT, Charles L. *Something Stirs.* 1991. Tor. 1st ed. F/F. P3. $19.00

GRANT, Charles L. *Tales From the Nightside.* 1981. Arkham. 1st ed. 1/4121. sgn. F/F. T2. $45.00

GRANT, Cyril Fletcher. *Studies in North Africa.* 1923. Dutton. 1st Am ed. ils. 304p. VG. W1. $16.00

GRANT, Edward. *Planets, Stars & Orbs...* 1994. Cambridge. 1st ed. 8vo. 816p. F/F. K5. $40.00

GRANT, James. *Mace's Luck.* 1985. Piatkus. hc. NF/NF. P3. $20.00

GRANT, Joan. *Lord of the Horizon.* 1944. Methuen. 3rd ed. VG. P3. $12.00

GRANT, Landon. *Marshal of Mustang.* nd. MacDonald. hc. VG/VG. P3. $15.00

GRANT, Linda. *Blind Trust.* 1990. Scribner. 1st ed. F/F. H11. $30.00

GRANT, Linda. *Love Nor Money.* nd. BC. F/F. P3. $8.00

GRANT, Madison. *Knife in Homespun America.* 1984. York, PA. 1st ed. pres. VG/VG. B5. $50.00

GRANT, Maxwell (house name); see Dent, Lester; Gibson, Walter; Lynds, Dennis.

GRANT, Michael. *Classical Greeks.* 1989. Scribner. F/F. P3. $27.00

GRANT, Michael. *Founders of the Western World.* 1991. Scribner. 1st ed. F/F. P3. $28.00

GRANT, Michael. *Line of Duty.* 1991. Doubleday. 1st ed. F/F. H11. $30.00

GRANT, Michael. *Rise of the Greeks.* 1988. Scribner. 1st ed. VG. P3. $28.00

GRANT, Robert. *Fourscore, an Autobiography.* 1934. Houghton Mifflin. G/worn. M11. $65.00

GRANT, Ulysses S. *Personal Memoirs.* 1885. NY. 2 vol. 1st ed. ils/maps. marbled edges. full calf. VG. H3. $125.00

GRANT, Verne. *Organismic Evolution.* 1977. San Francisco. ils/tables. 418p. F. B26. $28.00

GRANT, Verne. *Plant Speciation.* 1981 (1971). NY. 2nd. ils. sc. VG. B26. $40.00

GRANT, Vernon. *Tinker Tim the Toy Maker.* 1934. Whitman. ils. rebacked spine o/w VG. M5. $55.00

GRANTLAND, Keith; see Beaumont, Charles.

GRASS, Gunther. *Dog Years.* 1963. HBW. 1st ed. NF/NF. B35. $25.00

GRASS, Gunther. *Flounder.* 1977. HBJ. 1st ed. NF/NF. B35. $20.00

GRASS, Gunther. *Local Anaesthetic.* 1970. HBW. 1st ed. F/F. B35. $32.00

GRASS, Gunther. *Rat.* 1986. HBJ. 1st ed. F/F. B35. $18.00

GRASS, Gunther. *Tin Drum.* 1962. Pantheon. 1st ed. F/NF. B2. $45.00

GRASSET, Joseph. *Semi-Insane & the Semi-Responsible.* 1907. NY. Funk Wagnall. gilt gr cloth. G. M11. $125.00

GRATTAN, C. Hartley. *Southeast Pacific Since 1900.* 1963. Ann Arbor. xl. VG. O7. $10.00

GRATTON, L. *Non-Solar X- & Gamma-Ray Astronomy.* 1970. Dordrecht, Holland. Reidel. ils. 425p. dj. K5. $28.00

GRAU, Shirley Ann. *Black Prince AOS.* 1955. NY. 1st ed/1st issue. sgn. NF/NF. A11. $85.00

GRAVER, Elizabeth. *Have You Seen Me?* 1991. Pittsburgh U. 1st ed. author's 1st book. F/F. B4. $50.00

GRAVES, Anna Melissa. *Far East Is Not Very Far.* 1942. private prt. 1st ed. sgn. 8vo. 317p. VG. B11. $40.00

GRAVES, John. *Goodbye to a River.* 1960. NY. 1st ed. VG/VG. B5. $45.00

GRAVES, Robert. *But It Still Goes On.* 1930. London. Cape. 1st ed/2nd state. 8vo. gilt gr cloth. F/NF. T10. $200.00

GRAVES, Robert. *Claudius the God.* 1935. Smith Haas. 1st ed. G. P3. $25.00

GRAVES, Robert. *Collected Poems.* 1961. Doubleday. 1st ed. F/F. B35. $32.00

GRAVES, Robert. *Greek Myths.* 1988. Moyer Bell. hc. F/F. P3. $25.00

GRAVES, Robert. *Hercules My Shipmate.* 1945. Creative Age. 1st ed. 464p. VG/dj. M20. $47.00

GRAVES, Robert. *Isles of Unwisdom.* 1950. Cassell. 1st ed. VG/VG. P3. $20.00

GRAVES, Robert. *Lars Porsena.* 1927. Dutton. 1st Am ed. red cloth. F. B2. $40.00

GRAVES, Robert. *Love Respelt Again.* 1969. NY. 1st Am ed. 1/1000. sgn. NF/VG. C6. $80.00

GRAVES, Robert. *More Deserving Cases.* 1962. Marlborough College. 1/750. sgn. orig full morocco. F. C6. $125.00

GRAVES, Robert. *Original Rubaiyat of Omar Khayamm.* 1968. Garden City. 1st ed. 1/500. F/case. C2. $125.00

GRAVES, Robert. *Penny Fiddle.* 1960. Doubleday. 1st ed. ils Ardizzone. 63p. VG/dj. M20. $22.00

GRAVES, Robert. *Poems 1926-1930.* 1931. London. 1st ed. 1/1000. VG/VG. C6. $100.00

GRAVES, Robert. *Poems 1970-1972.* 1973. Doubleday. 1st Am ed. F/F. B4. $45.00

GRAVES, Robert. *Shout.* 1929. London. Mathews Marrot. 1/530. sgn. NF/VG. C6. $175.00

GRAVES, Valerie; see Bradley, Marion Zimmer.

GRAVES & PINCHOT. *White Pine: A Study.* 1896. NY. 1st ed. ils. 102p. VG. B5. $32.50

GRAY, A.W. *Bino's Blues.* 1995. Simon Schuster. 1st ed. author's 2nd book. rem mk. F/F. H11. $20.00

GRAY, A.W. *Man Offside.* 1991. Dutton. 1st ed. VG/VG. P3. $20.00

GRAY, Alasdair. *Poor Things.* 1992. HBJ. 1st Am ed. F/F. G10. $25.00

GRAY, Alasdair. *Ten Tales Tall & True.* 1993. Harcourt Brace. 1st Am ed. ils. F/F. G10. $20.00

GRAY, Carole. *Christmas Diorama.* 1992. np. 4 popups w/ties. F. A4. $25.00

GRAY, Charles. *Off at Sunrise: Overland Journal of Charles Glass Gray.* 1976. Huntington Lib. 1st ed. 8vo. ils. bl cloth. F/dj. T10. $45.00

GRAY, Colin S. *Leverage of Sea Power.* 1992. Macmillan. VG/VG. A16. $15.00

GRAY, David. *Gallops & Gallops 2.* 1898 & 1903. Century. 12mo. G. O3. $45.00

GRAY, Edward F. *Leif Eriksson: Discoverer of America.* 1930. NY. sgn. VG. O7. $75.00

GRAY, F. Griswold. *Horse & Buggy Days.* 1936. private prt. pres. O3. $85.00

GRAY, Harold. *Little Orphan Annie & the Gila Monster Gang.* nd. Whitman. hc. VG. P3. $10.00

GRAY, Harold. *Little Orphan Annie Bucking the World.* 1929. Cupples Leon. 8vo. VG. B17. $30.00

GRAY, Harold. *Little Orphan Annie in the Circus.* 1927. Cupples Leon. 8vo. F/VG. B17. $55.00

GRAY, Harold. *Pop-Up Little Orphan Annie & Jumbo the Circus Elephant.* 1935. Bl Ribbon. Pleasure Books. unp. VG. M20. $225.00

GRAY, Harold. *Pop-Up Little Orphan Annie.* 1935. Chicago. Bl Ribbon. 3 popups. VG. B5. $125.00

GRAY, J.A.C. *Amerika Samoa.* 1960. Annapolis. VG. O7. $20.00

GRAY, James Kendricks; see Fox, Gardner F.

GRAY, John Chipman. *Nature & Sources of the Law. Second Edition.* 1985. Birmingham. Legal Classics Lib. facsimile of 1927 ed. M11. $65.00

GRAY, John. *Near Eastern Mythology.* 1969. Hamlyn. 1st ed. ils. 141p. NF/dj. W1. $24.00

GRAY, Lewis H. *Ill Wind: Naval Airship Shenandoah in Novel County, OH.* 1989. Baltimore, MD. 1st ed. sgn. 154p. VG/wrp. B18. $15.00

GRAY, Martin. *For Those I Loved.* 1972. Boston. photos. 351p. VG. A17. $9.50

GRAY, Richard. *System of English Ecclesiastical Law.* 1743. London. J Stagg. last ed. contemporary mottled calf. worn. M11. $150.00

GRAY, Roland Palmer. *Songs & Ballads of the Maine Lumberjacks...* 1924. Cambridge. Harvard. 1st ed. sgn. 8vo. 181p. VG. B11. $50.00

GRAY, Thomas. *Elegy Written in a Country Church Yard.* 1938. London. LEC. 1st ed thus. intro H Walpole. ils AM Parker. F/case. C2. $200.00

GRAY, Westmoreland. *Hell's Stomping Grounds.* 1935. Lippincott. 1st ed. F/NF double djs. B4. $85.00

GRAY, Wood. *Hidden Civil War, Story of the Copperheads.* 1942. Viking. 8vo. 314p. T10. $35.00

GRAYDON, William. *Justices & Constables Assistant. Being General Collection...* 1805. Harrisburgh. John Wyeth. working copy. M11. $150.00

GRAYSMITH, Robert. *Sleeping Lady.* 1990. Dutton. 1st ed. VG/VG. P3. $20.00

GRAYSON, C.J. *Decisions Under Uncertainty: Drilling Decisions...* 1960. Harbard. 402p. cloth. F/chip. D8. $10.00

GRAYSON, Richard. *Death En Voyage.* 1986. Gollancz. 1st ed. NF/NF. P3. $20.00

GREAVES, Margaret. *Lucky Coin.* 1989. Steward Tabori Chang. ils Liz Underhill. ils. VG. B17. $9.00

GREELEY, Andrew M. *Cardinal Sins.* 1981. Warner. xl. dj. P3. $5.00

GREELEY, Andrew M. *Final Planet.* 1987. Warner. F/F. P3. $17.00

GREELEY, Andrew M. *God Game.* 1986. Warner. 1st ed. F/F. P3. $17.00

GREELEY, Horace. *Hints Toward Reforms.* 1850. NY. 1st ed. 400p. cloth. G. A17. $25.00

GREELY, Adolpus W. *Three Years of Arctic Service.* 1886. London. 2 vol. ils/fld map. G. M17. $110.00

GREEN, B.A. *Bibliography of the Tennessee Walking Horse.* 1960. Nashville. 1st ed. pres. VG. O3. $125.00

GREEN, Ben K. *More Horse Tradin'.* 1972. NY. 1st ed. VG/VG. B5. $30.00

GREEN, Ben K. *Village Horse Doctor.* 1971. NY. 1st ed. VG/G. B5. $30.00

GREEN, Donald E. *Panhandle Pioneer: Henry C Hitch, His Ranch & His Family.* 1980. Norman. 1st ed/2nd prt. 294p. AN/dj. P4. $25.00

GREEN, Edith Pinero. *Rotten Apples.* 1977. Dutton. 1st ed. VG/VG. P3. $15.00

GREEN, George Dawes. *Caveman's Valentine.* 1994. Warner. 1st ed. F/F. H11/M23. $50.00

GREEN, George Dawes. *Juror.* 1995. Warner. 1st ed. NF/F. H11. $25.00

GREEN, Gerald. *Last Angry Man.* 1956. Scribner. 1st ed. NF/NF. H11. $45.00

GREEN, Henry. *Doting.* 1952. London. 1st ed. VG+/VG. A11. $55.00

GREEN, Henry. *Nothing.* 1950. London. 1st ed. NF/NF. A11. $95.00

GREEN, J.R. *Short History of the English Peoples.* 1894. NY. 4 vol. xl. G. O7. $50.00

GREEN, Joseph. *Conscience Interplanetary.* 1972. Doubleday. 1st ed. F/F. P3. $15.00

GREEN, Kate. *Shooting Star.* 1992. Harper Collins. 1st ed. AN/dj. M22. $7.00

GREEN, Mason A. *Springfield Memories.* 1876. Springfield, MA. Whitney Adams. 8vo. 110p. gilt gr cloth. F. K1. $30.00

GREEN, N.W. *Mormonism Rise & Progress.* 1874. Hartford. 1st ed. 3-quarter leather. VG. B5. $50.00

GREEN, Paul. *Common Glory...* 1948. UNC. inscr. ils. VG/G. B10. $35.00

GREEN, Paul. *Lonesome Road: Six Plays for the Negro Theatre.* 1926. NY. McBride. 1st ed. 217p. VG. M8. $150.00

GREEN, Roger Lancelyn. *Ten Tales of Detection.* 1968. Dent Dutton. 2nd. VG/VG. P3. $20.00

GREEN, Terence M. *Barking Dogs.* 1988. St Martin. 1st ed. author's 1st novel. F/NF. G10. $12.00

GREEN, Tim. *Outlaws.* 1995. Turner. ARC. F/pict wrp. G10. $20.00

GREEN, William M. *Salisbury Manuscript.* 1973. Bobbs Merrill. 1st ed. F/F. p3. $15.00

GREENAWAY, Kate. *Almanack for 1884.* 1883. London. Routledge. 16mo. NF. B24. $140.00

GREENAWAY, Kate. *Almanack for 1885.* 1884. London. Routledge. 16mo. aeg. wht imitation morocco. F. B24. $175.00

GREENAWAY, Kate. *Almanack for 1888.* 1987. London. Routledge. 16mo. 12 half-p ils. aeg. gitl brn cloth. F. B24. $200.00

GREENAWAY, Kate. *Almanack for 1890.* 1889. London. Routledge. 16mo. 12 half-p ils. bl ep. aeg. gilt gr cloth. F. B24. $200.00

GREENAWAY, Kate. *Day in a Child's Life.* nd. Routledge. 1st ed. 4to. VG. M5. $150.00

GREENAWAY, Kate. *Greenaway's Babies.* 1907. Saalfield Muslin Book. G+. M5. $40.00

GREENAWAY, Kate. *Kate Greenaway's Alphabet.* ca 1885. London. Routledge. pict brd. B24. $140.00

GREENAWAY, Kate. *Language of Flowers.* nd. Routledge. 1st ed/1st state. cloth spine/pict brd. VG. M5. $100.00

GREENAWAY, Kate. *Marigold Garden.* nd. Warne. early prt. VG+. S13. $45.00

GREENAWAY, Kate. *Pied Piper of Hamelin.* 1993. Derrydale. 8vo. rem mk. F. B17. $7.50

GREENBAUM, Florence. *Jewish Cook Book. 1,600 Recipes According to Jewish Dietary.* 1925. NY. 5th. 8vo. 438p. gray cloth. NF. B14. $55.00

GREENBERG, Martin. *Coming Attractions.* 1957. Gnome. 1st ed. VG/VG. P3. $25.00

GREENBERG, Martin. *Five SF Novels.* 1952. Gnome. 1st ed. VG/VG. P3. $45.00

GREENBERG, Martin. *International Relations Through SF.* 1978. Franklin Watts. 1st ed. VG/VG. P3. $15.00

GREENBERG, Martin. *Journey to Infinity.* 1951. Gnome. 1st ed. NF/NF. P3. $45.00

GREENBERG, Martin. *New Adventures in Sherlock Holmes.* 1987. Carroll Graf. 1st ed. F/F. P3. $25.00

GREENBERG, Martin. *Robot & the Man.* 1953. Gnome. 1st ed. VG. P3. $25.00

GREENBERG, Martin. *Tony Hillerman Companion: A Comprehensive Guide...* 1994. Harper Collins. AP/1st ed. sgn. F/wrp. T2. $35.00

GREENBERG & GORMAN. *Cat Crimes II.* nd. Quality BC. VG/VG. P3. $10.00

GREENBERG & GREENBERG. *Guide to Corals & Fishes of Florida, Bahamas & Carribean.* 1986. Miami. Seahawk. ils. G. D8. $5.00

GREENBERG & NOLAN. *Bradbury Chronicles.* 1991. Roc. 1st ed. F/F. P3. $20.00

GREENBERG & PRONZINI. *Arbor House Treasury of Mystery...* 1981. BOMC. VG. P3. $18.00

GREENBERG & PRONZINI. *Cloak & Dagger.* 1988. Avenel. 2nd. F/F. P3. $15.00

GREENE, A.C. *Christmas Tree.* 1978. Nonesuch. 1/300. prt/sgn Ferguson. gilt orange cloth. miniature. B24. $100.00

GREENE, A.C. *900 Miles on the Butterfield Trail.* 1994. Denton. 1st ed. 293p. map ep. F/F. T10. $35.00

GREENE, Graham. *Bear Fell Free.* 1935. London. Grayson. 1/250. sgn. NF/NF. C2. $1,000.00

GREENE, Graham. *Brighton Rock & End of the Affair.* 1987. Peerage. F/F. P3. $15.00

GREENE, Graham. *Burnt-Out Case.* 1961. NY. 1st Am ed. F/NF. A11. $25.00

GREENE, Graham. *Comedians.* 1966. London. 1st ed. NF/NF. C6. $50.00

GREENE, Graham. *Doctor Fischer of Geneva.* 1980. Simon Schuster. 1st ed. NF/NF. M22/P3. $15.00

GREENE, Graham. *End of the Affair.* 1951. London. 1st ed. NF/VG+. C6. $95.00

GREENE, Graham. *Getting to Know the General.* 1984. NY. 1st ed. 4to. 249p. dj. F3. $15.00

GREENE, Graham. *Heart of the Matter.* 1948. Canada. Viking. 1st ed. VG. P3. $50.00

GREENE, Graham. *Heart of the Matter.* 1948. London. 1st ed. NF/VG. C6. $85.00

GREENE, Graham. *Honorary Consul.* 1973. Simon Schuster. 1st ed. F/NF. M22. $40.00

GREENE, Graham. *Human Factor.* 1978. Bodley Head/Clarke Irwin. 1st ed. VG/VG. P3. $25.00

GREENE, Graham. *Human Factor.* 1978. Simon Schuster. 1st ed. F/NF. M19. $17.50

GREENE, Graham. *In Search of a Character.* 1961. Bodley Head. 1st ed. VG. P3. $25.00

GREENE, Graham. *Monsignor Quixote.* 1982. Lester & Orpen Denys. 1st ed. G/G. P3. $15.00

GREENE, Graham. *Our Man in Havana.* 1958. Viking. 1st Am ed. F/VG. M22. $75.00

GREENE, Graham. *Reflections.* 1990. London. 1st ed. VG/VG. C4. $35.00

GREENE, Graham. *Shades of Greene.* 1975. Bodley Head/Heinemann. 1st ed. NF. P3. $20.00

GREENE, Graham. *Shipwrecked.* 1953. Viking. 1st ed. NF/VG. M22. $35.00

GREENE, Graham. *Tenth Man.* 1985. Simon Schuster. 1st ed. F/F. P3. $20.00

GREENE, Graham. *This Gun for Hire.* 1982. Viking. F/F. P3. $18.00

GREENE, Graham. *19 Stories.* 1947. London. 1st ed. sgn. VG/VG. C2. $300.00

GREENE, Jerome. *Battles & Skirmishes of the Great Sioux War 1876-1877.* 1993. Norman, OK. 1st ed. 8vo. 228p. T10. $25.00

GREENE, Jerome. *Lakota & Cheyenne: Indian Views of Great Sioux War...* 1994. Norman, OK. 1st ed. 8vo. 164p. M/M. T10. $30.00

GREENE, Julia. *Flash Back.* 1983. Severn House. VG/VG. P3. $20.00

GREENE, Merle. *Ancient Maya Relief Sculpture.* 1967. Mus Primitive Art. 1st ed. 1/4000. 60p. VG. F3. $30.00

GREENE, William B. *Mutual Banking: A Simple Plan to Abolish Interest of Money.* 1895? Columbus Junction, IA. Fulton. VG+/wrp. B2. $85.00

GREENER, Leslie. *Discovery of Egypt.* 1989. Dorset. 32 pl. 216p. NF/dj. W1. $16.00

GREENEWALT, Crawford H. *Hummingbirds.* 1960. Doubleday. 4to. portfolio. NF. T10. $100.00

GREENFIELD, Eloise. *Daydreamers.* 1981. Dial. 1st prt. ils Tom Feelings. AN/dj. C8. $75.00

GREENFIELD, Eloise. *Grandmamma's Joy.* 1980. NY. Collins. 1st ed. ils. AN/dj. C8. $55.00

GREENFIELD, Eloise. *Rosa Parks.* 1973. Crowell. 1st ed. ils Eric Marlow. VG/VG. B4. $35.00

GREENFIELD, Eloise. *Sister.* 1974. Crowell. 1st ed. inscr. ils Moneta Barnett. F/NF. B4. $85.00

GREENFIELD, Howard. *Marc Chagall.* 1967. 1st ed. VG/VG. S13. $18.00

GREENHAW, Wayne. *Elephants in the Corn Field: Ronald Reagan...* 1982. Macmillan. 1st ed. 288p. VG. B10. $10.00

GREENLEAF, Simon. *Treatise on the Law of Evidence. Vol III.* 1853. Little Brn. 1st ed. contemporary sheep. M11. $150.00

GREENLEAF, Stephen. *Beyond Blame.* 1986. Villard. 1st ed. VG/VG. P3. $25.00

GREENLEAF, Stephen. *Blood Type.* 1992. Morrow. 1st ed. F/F. H11. $20.00

GREENLEAF, Stephen. *Fatal Obsession.* 1983. Dial. 1st ed. NF/VG. N4. $30.00

GREENLEAF, Stephen. *Grave Error.* 1979. Dial. 1st ed. VG/VG. P3. $18.00

GREENLEAF, Stephen. *Toll Call.* 1987. Villard. 1st ed. VG/VG. P3. $20.00

GREENLEAVES, Winifred. *Trout Inn Mystery.* 1929. Lincoln MacVeagh. 1st ed. NF. P3. $35.00

GREENSMITH, J.T. *Petrology of the Sedimentary Rocks.* 1978. Allen Unwin. 6th. 241p. VG/wrp. D8. $8.00

GREENWELL, Rose Agnes. *Flora of Nelson County, KY.* 1935. WA, DC. 204p. wrp. B26. $20.00

GREENWOOD, Frederick. *Imagination in Dreams & Their Study.* 1894. London. John Lane. 198p. w/16p catalog. gr cloth. G1. $75.00

GREENWOOD, Grace. *New Life in New Lands: Notes of Travel.* 1873. NY. JB Ford. 1st ed. 8vo. F. T10. $100.00

GREENWOOD, John. *Fleet Histories Series Vol II.* 1992. Freshwater. M. A16. $25.00

GREENWOOD, John. *Missing Mr Mosley.* 1985. Walker. F/F. P3. $15.00

GREENWOOD, John. *Namesakes II.* 1973. Cleveland. Freshwater. VG/dj. A16. $70.00

GREENWOOD, John. *Namesakes of the '80s, Vol I.* 1980. Cleveland. Freshwater. VG/dj. A16. $60.00

GREENWOOD, L.B. *Sherlock Holmes & the Case of Sabina Hall.* 1988. Simon Schuster. 1st ed. VG/VG. P3. $20.00

GREENWOOD, Major. *Authority of Medicine: Old & New.* 1943. Cambridge. 1st ed. 32p. stiff wrp. A13. $20.00

GREENWOOD. *Researchers's Guide to American Genealogy, 2nd Edition.* 1990. np. 52 charts/reproductions. 623p. F/F. A4. $25.00

GREER, Carl Richard. *What a Buckeye Cover Man Saw in Europe.* 1923. Hamilton, OH. Becket Paper Co. sgn. 8vo. 190p. VG. B11. $25.00

GREER. *Kissing the Rod. 17th-Century Women's Verse.* 1989. NY. 477p. F/wrp. A17. $10.00

GREGG, Alexander. *History of the Old Cheraws.* 1925. SC. gr cloth. VG. B30. $125.00

GREGG, Cecil Freeman. *Inspector Higgins Goes Fishing.* 1951. Methuen. 1st ed. VG. P3. $20.00

GREGG, Josiah. *Commerce of the Prairies.* 1958. OK U. ils/fld map. 469p. VG. A4. $45.00

GREGG, Linda. *Chosen by the Lion.* 1994. Graywolf. 1st ed. sgn. F/F. C2. $25.00

GREGG, Linda. *Sacraments of Desire, Poems.* 1991. Graywolf. 1st ed. sgn. F/F. C2. $30.00

GREGORY, Dick. *Dick Gregory's Bible Tales.* 1974. Stein Day. 1st ed. 187p. dj. R11. $30.00

GREGORY, Dick. *Shadow That Scares Me.* 1968. Doubleday. 1st ed. VG. R11. $10.00

GREGORY, Franklin L. *Valley of Adventure.* 1940. Triangle. ffe removed. VG. P3. $10.00

GREGORY, J.C. *Nature of Laughter.* 1924. Harcourt Brace. 241p. gr cloth. G1. $45.00

GREGORY, Jackson. *Case for Mr Paul Savoy.* 1933. Scribner. 1st ed. VG. P3. $20.00

GREGORY, Robert. *Diz.* 1992. Viking. 1st ed. F/F. P8. $17.50

GREGORY, W. *American Newspapers 1821-1936.* 1967. Kraus Rpt Corp. brn cloth. T3. $140.00

GREGORY. *Gregory's Dictionary: New & Complete Dictionary...* 1822. NY. 3 vol. 140 pl. brn full leather. VG. B30. $350.00

GREIG, Francis. *Heads You Lose.* 1982. Crown. RS. F/F. P3. $15.00

GREIG, J.Y.T. *Psychology of Laughter & Comedy.* 1923. Dodd Mead. 1st Am ed. 304p. panelled maroon cloth. VG. G1. $35.00

GRENDON, Stephen; see Derleth, August.

GRENFELL, Wilfred. *Romance of Labrador.* 1934. NY. 1st ed. ils/pl. pict bl cloth. VG. H3. $40.00

GRENSER, Wodeman Ludwig. *Ueber Aether-Einathmungen Wahrend der Geburt.* 1847. Leipzig. 68p. prt yel wrp. B14. $1,000.00

GRESHAM, Elizabeth. *Puzzle in Porcelain.* 1945. Curtis. VG/wrp. B10. $7.00

GRESHAM, Grits. *Complete Book of Bass Fishing.* 1971. Outdoor Life/Harper Row. photos. G. P12. $7.50

GRESHAM, William Lindsay. *Houdini.* nd. HRW. 11th. VG/VG. P3. $15.00

GRESSITT, J. Linsley. *California Academy-Lingman Dawn-Redwood Expedition.* 1953. San Francisco. ils. 34p. F/wrp. B26. $27.50

GRETT, Willis Ray. *Aeronautical Meteorology.* 1925. NY. Ronald. ils/figures. 144p. G. K5. $14.00

GREW, Joseph C. *Report From Tokyo.* 1942. NY. 88p. dj. A17. $8.50

GREY, Daria. *God Loves a Dumbbell.* ca 1930s. NY. Pegasus. 1st ed. ils. F/VG. B4. $100.00

GREY, Richard. *Memoria Technica; or, New Method of Artificial Memory...* 1796. Dublin. Graisberry Campbell. 12mo. contemporary calf. G1. $75.00

GREY, Zane. *Border Legion.* nd. Black. VG. P3. $8.00

GREY, Zane. *Call of the Canyon.* 1924. Musson. 1st Canadian ed. F/G. A18. $30.00

GREY, Zane. *Captives of the Desert.* 1953. London. Hodder Stoughton. 1st Eng ed. VG/chip. A18. $20.00

GREY, Zane. *Desert Gold.* nd. Grosset Dunlap. VG/VG. P3. $20.00

GREY, Zane. *Hash Knife Outfit.* 1933. Harper. 1st ed. inscr. F/F case. M19. $1,500.00

GREY, Zane. *Ken Ward in the Jungle.* nd. Grosset Dunlap. VG. P3. $8.00

GREY, Zane. *Last of the Plainsmen.* nd. Grosset Dunlap. VG/G. P3. $15.00

GREY, Zane. *Last Trail.* nd. Triangle. hc. NF/NF. P3. $13.00

GREY, Zane. *Light of Western Stars.* nd. Grosset Dunlap. VG/VG. P3. $20.00

GREY, Zane. *Majesty's Rancho.* 1944. Musson. 1st ed. VG. P3. $20.00

GREY, Zane. *Nevada.* 1928. Harper. 1st ed. VG. P3. $40.00

GREY, Zane. *Rainbow Trail.* 1981. Ian Henry. F/F. P3. $10.00

GREY, Zane. *Reef Girl.* 1977. Harper Row. 1st ed. NF/NF. A18. $30.00

GREY, Zane. *Riders of the Purple Sage.* nd. Black. VG. P3. $8.00

GREY, Zane. *Shepherd of Guadaloupe.* nd. Grosset Dunlap. VG/VG. P3. $13.00

GREY, Zane. *Spirit of the Border.* 1943. Triangle. 18th. VG/VG. P3. $13.00

GREY, Zane. *Stairs of Sand.* 1945. Musson. VG. P3. $12.00

GREY, Zane. *Thunder Mountain.* 1936. NY. 1st ed. pres. NF/G+. C6. $110.00

GREY, Zane. *Vanishing American.* 1925. Musson. 1st ed. VG/G. P3. $35.00

GREY, Zane. *Wild Horse Mesa.* 1928. Musson. hc. G. P3. $7.00

GREY, Zane. *Young Lion Hunter.* nd. Grosset Dunlap. VG/VG. P3. $20.00

GREY, Zane. *Young Pitcher.* 1911. Harper. 248p. VG+. M20. $92.00

GRIBBIN & ORGILL. *Sixth Winter.* 1979. Simon Schuster. 1st ed. VG/VG. P3. $15.00

GRIBBLE, Leonard. *Case of the Marsden Rubies.* 1932. Harrap. 2nd. VG/VG. P3. $25.00

GRIDLEY, Marion. *Indians of Yesterday.* 1940. Donohue. folio. ils Lone Wolf. VG/VG. B17. $15.00

GRIERSON, Francis D. *Lady of Despair.* 1933. Collins Crime Club. 6th. G. P3. $10.00

GRIERSON, Francis D. *Murder in the Garden.* nd. Grosset Dunlap. decor brd. VG. P3. $15.00

GRIFFIN, Appleton P.C. *Discovery of the Mississippi: Bibliographical Account...* 1883. NY. Barnes rpt. 20p. xl. partially unopened. O7. $65.00

GRIFFIN, Charles. *Skull-Collectors of Formosa.* 1931. Ottawa. Canadian Geog Soc. removed. F. P4. $22.50

GRIFFIN, Gwyn. *Operational Necessity.* nd. BOMC. VG/VG. P3. $10.00

GRIFFIN, John Howard. *John Howard Griffin Reader.* 1968. Houghton Mifflin. 488p. VG+/VG. R11. $15.00

GRIFFIN, Martin. *Frank R Stockton: A Critical Biography.* 1965. Kennikat. rpt of 1939 ed. 178p. A17. $15.00

GRIFFIS, William E. *Sir William Johnson & the Six Nations.* 1891. NY. 1st ed. 12mo. 227p. gilt bl cloth. VG. H3. $125.00

GRIFFIS, William Elliot. *Mikado's Empire...* 1976. NY. 1st ed. 645p. gr cloth. VG. B14. $85.00

GRIFFITH, Fuller. *Lithographs of Childe Hassam: A Catalog.* 1962. Smithsonian. photos/pl. 66p. D2. $60.00

GRIFFITH, Linda. *Thumbelina.* 1977. CA. Inter-visual Communications. probable 1st ed. 16mo. NF. T5. $45.00

GRIFFITH, NORTON & SCHAUB. *Flight of Vengeance.* 1992. Tor. 1st ed. F/F. P3. $22.00

GRIFFITHS, Ella. *Murder on Page Three.* 1984. Quartet Crime. NF/NF. P3. $18.00

GRIFFITHS, J.N.R. *Golden Years of Bridge: Classic Hands From the Past.* 1981. London. 127p. M. S1. $12.00

GRIFFITHS, John. *Loyal & Dedicated Servant.* 1981. Playboy. 1st ed. VG/VG. P3. $18.00

GRIFFON, T. Wynne. *History of the Occult.* 1991. Mallard. hc. VG. P3. $15.00

GRIFFTH, David Wark. *Rise & Fall of Free Speech in America.* 1916. Los Angeles. unp. G/wrp. B18. $15.00

GRIGSON, Geoffrey. *Englishman's Flora.* 1955. London. Phoenix House. 1st ed. 1/50. sgn. 478p. F/case. C2. $750.00

GRIMBLE, Arthur. *Return to the Islands.* 1957. London. Murray. 1st ed. 8vo. ils/map. F/NF. T10. $50.00

GRIMES, Martha. *Deer Leap.* 1985. Little Brn. 1st ed. F/F. P3. $16.00

GRIMES, Martha. *Five Bells & Bladebone.* 1987. Little Brn. 1st ed. VG/VG. P3. $16.00

GRIMES, Martha. *I Am the Only Running Footman.* 1986. Boston. Little Brn. 1st ed. F/NF. B4. $45.00

GRIMES, Martha. *Old Contemptibles.* 1991. Little Brn. 1st ed. VG/VG. P3. $20.00

GRIMES, Martha. *Old Silent.* 1989. Little Brn. 1st ed. F/F. P3. $19.00

GRIMES, Martha. *Send Bygraves.* 1989. Putnam. 1st ed. decor brd. VG. P3. $15.00

GRIMM & GRIMM. *Dornroschen.* 1948. Zurich. Schiele Globi. ils Herbert Leupin. VG. D1. $85.00

GRIMM & GRIMM. *Fairy Tales by the Brothers Grimm.* 1931. LEC. 1/1500. ils/sgn Kredel. designed/sgn Koch. F/case. B24. $250.00

GRIMM & GRIMM. *Grimm Fairy Tales.* 1962. NY. LEC. 4 vol. 8vo. ils/sgn Lucille Corcos. F/case. T10. $250.00

GRIMM & GRIMM. *Grimm's Fairy Tales.* 1920. Ward Lock. decor brd. VG. P3. $10.00

GRIMM & GRIMM. *Hansel & Gretel.* 1946. Grosset Dunlap. ils Julian Wehr. sbdg. VG. D1. $150.00

GRIMM & GRIMM. *Little Brother & Little Sister.* 1917. Dodd Mead. 1st ed. ils Rackham. 251p. VG. D1. $275.00

GRIMM & GRIMM. *One Hundred Fairy Tales.* 1980. Franklin Lib. aeg. leather spine. NF. P3. $20.00

GRIMM & GRIMM. *Snow White & the Seven Dwarfs.* 1972. FSG. 1st ed. ils NE Burkert. F/VG+. B4. $100.00

GRIMM & GRIMM. *Tales From Grim.* 1936. Coward McCann. 4th. ils Wanda Gag. VG/VG. D1. $60.00

GRIMM & GRIMM. *Tischlein Deck Dich.* 1948. Zurich. Schiele Globi. ils Herbert Leupin. unp. pict brd. VG. D1. $85.00

GRIMM & ROY. *Human Interest Stories of...Gettysburg.* 1927. Times & News Pub. photos. 60p. G+. B10. $65.00

GRIMSHAW, James A. *Robert Penn Warren: A Descriptive Bibliography 1922-1979.* 1981. VA U. 1st ed. F/F. B10. $35.00

GRIMSLEY, Jim. *Winter Birds.* 1994. Algonquin. 1st ed. F/F. M23. $30.00

GRIMWOOD, Ken. *Into the Deep.* 1995. Morrow. 1st ed. F/F. H11. $25.00

GRIMWOOD, Ken. *Replay.* 1986. Arbor. 1st ed. F/NF. G10. $30.00

GRIMWOOD, Ken. *Replay.* 1986. Arbor. 1st ed. VG/VG. P3. $20.00

GRINNELL, Charles E. *Law of Deceit & Incidents in Its Practice...* 1886. Boston. Little Brn. gr cloth. G. M11. $125.00

GRINNELL, David; see Wollheim, Donald.

GRIS, Henry. *New Soviet Psychic Discoveries.* 1979. Souvenir. 1st ed. VG. P3. $20.00

GRISANTI, Mary Lee. *Art of the Vatican.* 1983. NY. Excalibur. 1st Am ed. 143p. F/F. T10. $20.00

GRISCOM, George L. *Fighting With Ross' Texas Cavalry Brigade...* 1976. Hill Jr College. 1st ed. 255p. cloth. NF/NF. M8. $95.00

GRISEWOOD, R. Norman. *Zarlah the Martian.* 1909. Fenno. hc. copyright p removed. G. P3. $50.00

GRISHAM, John. *Chamber.* 1994. Doubleday. 1st ed. inscr. F/F. B30. $35.00

GRISHAM, John. *Firm.* 1991. Doubleday. ARC. inscr. NF/wrp. B30. $400.00

GRISHAM, John. *Firm.* 1991. Doubleday. 1st ed. F/F. M19. $175.00

GRISHAM, John. *Pelican Brief.* 1992. Doubleday. 1st ed. F/F. N4. $65.00

GRISHAM, John. *Pelican Brief.* 1992. Doubleday. 1st ed. F/NF. H11. $50.00

GRISMER, Karl H. *Story of Sarasota.* 1946. Tampa. FL Grower. sgn. lg 8vo. VG. B11. $100.00

GRIST, Brooks D. *Echoes of Yesterday.* 1979. Tulare. 1st ed. 8vo. ils. 138p. F/dj. T10. $25.00

GRIST, Brooks D. *Tales by the Campfire.* 1974. Tulare, CA. 8vo. 175p. bl cloth. F/dj. T10. $25.00

GRISTEIN. *Women in Chemistry & Physics...* 1993. 721p. F. A4. $95.00

GROB, Gerald. *Inner World of American Psychiatry, 1890-1940.* 1985. New Brunswick. 1st ed. 310p. dj. A13. $35.00

GROBANI. *Guide to Football Literature.* 1975. np. 334p. F. A4. $55.00

GROOM, Arthur. *Boy's Book of Heroes.* ca 1950. London. Birn Bros. ils F Stocks May. 124p. G. A17. $10.00

GROOM, Winston. *Forrest Gump.* 1985. Garden City. 1st ed. author's 5th book. sgn. F/F. A11. $375.00

GROOM, Winston. *Gone the Sun.* 1988. Doubleday. 1st ed. F/F. H11. $30.00

GROOM, Winston. *Gump & Co.* 1995. NY. Pocket. 1st ed. sgn. 2nd Gump book. F/dj. S9. $35.00

GROOMS, Red. *Red Grooms' Ruckus Rodeo.* 1987. Abrams. probable 1st ed. 4to. F. B17. $10.00

GROOS, Karl. *Die Spiele der Menschen.* 1899. Jena. Gustav Fischer. 538p. later brn buckram. G1. $75.00

GROPIUS, Walter. *Town Plan for the Development of Selb.* 1969. np. 1st am ed. ils/charts/plans. VG. M17. $80.00

GROSE, Francis. *Military Antiquities Respecting a History of English Army...* 1812. London. 2 vol. 3rd. folio. pl. full diced calf. VG. C6. $750.00

GROSS, Al. *Progress Report of Wisconsin Prairie Chicken Investigations.* 1930. Madison, WI. Conservation Dept. 112p. VG/wrp. A10. $30.00

GROSS, Anthony. *Etching, Engraving & Intaglio Printing.* 1970. Oxford. ils. 184p. F/NF. A4. $45.00

GROSS, Louis S. *Redefining the American Gothic.* 1989. Umi Research. 1st ed. hc. F/F. P3. $35.00

GROSS, Milt. *Nize Baby.* 1926. Doran. 1st ed. VG. P3. $30.00

GROSSINGER, Jennie. *Art of Jewish Cooking.* 1958. NY. 1st ed. F/dj. B14. $75.00

GROSSMAN & HAMLET. *Birds of Prey of the World.* 1964. NY. 1st ed. ils. VG/VG. B5. $55.00

GROSZ, George. *Little Yes & a Big No.* 1946. Dial. 1st ed. NF/NF. B2. $85.00

GROTH, John. *Studio: Asia.* 1952. Cleveland. ARC/1st ed. ils. 208p. VG/dj. B18. $25.00

GROTH, John. *Studio: Europe.* 1945. NY. 283p. cloth. VG. A17. $12.50

GROTIUS, Hugo. *Law of War & Peace...* 1925. Bobbs Merrill. gr cloth. M11. $125.00

GROTIUS, Hugo. *Rights of War & Peace...* 1738. London. Innys Manby. contemporary calf. worn. M11. $1,500.00

GROTTA-KURSKA, Daniel. *Biography of JRR Tolkien: Architect of Middle Earth.* 1978. Running Pr. expanded 1st ed. F/NF. G10. $15.00

GROUT, Donald J. *Short History of Opera.* 1947. NY. 2 vol. 1st ed. ils/musical scores. gilt blk cloth. F/G case. H3. $85.00

GROVE. *Of Brooks & Books.* 1945. np. 1/1500. 94p. NF/NF. A4. $55.00

GROVER, Eulalie Osgood. *Overall Boys: First Reader.* 1905. Chicago. 1st ed. ils Bertha Corbett. 120p. G. A17. $20.00

GROVER, Paula K. *White Boys & River Girls.* 1995. Chapel Hill. Algonquin. AP. author's 1st book. NF/wrp. S9. $30.00

GROVER, Robert. *Here Goes Kitten.* 1964. Grove. 1st ed. sgn. F/F. B11. $65.00

GROVER, Robert. *Maniac Responsible.* 1963. Grove. 1st ed. 222p. VG/dj. M20. $20.00

GRUBB, Davis. *Fools' Parade.* 1969. NAL/World. 1st ed. sgn. VG/VG. P3. $40.00

GRUBB, Davis. *Night of the Hunter.* 1953. NY. 1st ed. VG/G. B5. $45.00

GRUBB, Davis. *Shadow of My Brother.* 1966. Hutchinson. 1st ed. NF/NF. P3. $25.00

GRUBB, Davis. *Watchman.* 1961. NY. 1st ed. VG/VG. B5. $30.00

GRUBER, Frank. *Bridge of Sand.* 1963. Dutton. 1st ed. VG/VG. P3. $25.00

GRUBER, Frank. *Laughing Fox.* 1943. Tower. VG/VG. P3. $20.00

GRUBER, Frank. *Run, Fool, Run.* 1966. Dutton. 1st ed. VG/VG. P3. $30.00

GRUDGE, Elizabeth. *Dean's Watch.* 1964. Hodder Stoughton. 3rd ed. VG/VG. P3. $10.00

GRUDGE, Elizabeth. *Pilgrim's Inn.* nd. BC. VG/VG. P3. $8.00

GRUDGE, Elizabeth. *White Witch.* 1958. Coward McCann. 1st ed. NF/NF. P3. $25.00

GRUELLE, Johnny. *Johnny Gruelle's Golden Book.* 1925. Donohue. 4to. ils. 95p. VG. D1. $75.00

GRUELLE, Johnny. *Man in the Moon Stories.* 1922. Cupples Leon. ils/8 pl. VG. M5. $195.00

GRUELLE, Johnny. *Marcella.* 1929. Volland. 1st ed. 94p. VG. M20. $45.00

GRUELLE, Johnny. *Original Raggedy Ann Stories.* 1930s. Donohue. rpt. 95p. VG+/dj. M20. $50.00

GRUELLE, Johnny. *Raggedy Ann in Cookie Land.* 1931. Volland. 1st ed. ils Gruelle. 95p. VG. M20. $105.00

GRUELLE, Johnny. *Raggedy Ann's Alphabet Book.* 1925. Chicago. Donohue. 12mo. ils. VG. C8. $75.00

GRUELLE, Johnny. *Raggedy Ann's Magical Wishes.* 1930s. Donahue. 94p. VG+/dj. M20. $65.00

GRUELLE, Johnny. *Raggedy Ann's Picture Book.* 1940. McLoughlin. 16p. NF. M5. $95.00

GRUELLE, Johnny. *Wooden Willie.* 1927. Donohue. 95p. VG. D1. $125.00

GRUENBERG, Sidonie M. *Wonderful Story of How You Were Born.* nd. Doubleday. revised ed. 8vo. ils. 39p. F/VG. C14. $10.00

GRUENFELD, Lee. *All Fall Down.* 1994. NY. Warner. 1st ed. F/NF. H11. $20.00

GRUENFELD, Lee. *Irreparable Harm.* 1993. Warner. 1st ed. author's 1st book. F/F. H11. $25.00

GRUENTHER, Alfred M. *Duplicate Contract Complete: A Guide to Playing...* 1933. NY. 1st prt. 328p. VG. S1. $20.00

GRUMBACH, Doris. *Chamber Music.* 1979. London. 1st ed. inscr. F/F. A11. $40.00

GRUMBACH, Doris. *Company She Kept: A Revealing Portrait of Mary McCarthy.* 1967. Coward McCann. 1st ed. author's 3rd book. VG/VG. S13. $20.00

GRUMBACH, Doris. *Company She Kept: A Revealing Portrait of Mary McCarthy.* 1967. Coward McCann. 1st ed. F/VG. B4. $45.00

GRUMBACH, Doris. *Ladies.* 1984. Dutton. 1st ed. rem mk. F/dj. S9. $25.00

GRUNFELD, Frederic V. *Hitler File: Social History of Germany...1918-45.* 1974. NY. 1st Am ed. 374p. VG/dj. A17. $27.50

GRZIMEK, H.C.B. *Grimek's Animal Life Encyclopedia, Vol 3.* 1972. Van Nostrand. 8vo. ils. 541p. F/F. B1. $60.00

GUENTHER, Konrad. *Naturalist in Brazil.* 1931. Houghton Mifflin. 400p. VG. A10. $37.50

GUERBER, H.A. *Norsemen.* 1986. Avenel. 2nd ed. VG/VG. P3. $10.00

GUERIN, Daniel. *Negroes on the March.* 1956. NY. Weissman. 1st ed. 190p. wrp. R11. $20.00

GUERIN, Marcel. *L'Oeuvre Grave de Manet.* 1969 (1944). Da Capo. ils. cloth. dj. D2. $175.00

GUEST, C.Z. *First Garden.* 1976. Putnam. 1st ed. sgn. ils Cecil Beaton. F/NF. B4. $85.00

GUEST, Edgar A. *Path to Home When Day Is Done.* 1919. Reilly Lee. hc. VG. P3. $20.00

GUEST, Judith. *Ordinary People.* 1976. Viking. 1st ed. author's 1st book. F/F. H11. $40.00

GUILD, Nicholas. *Chain Reaction.* 1983. St Martin. 1st ed. VG/VG. P3. $15.00

GUILES, Fred Lawrence. *Norman Jean: The Life of Marilyn Monroe.* 1969. McGraw Hill. VG. P3. $20.00

GUILEY, Rosemary Ellen. *Moonscapes.* 1991. Prentic Hall. 192p. VG/VG. K5. $13.00

GUILLEN, Michael. *Five Equations That Changed the World.* 1995. Hyperion. 1st ed. F/F. M23. $30.00

GUINNESS & SADLER. *Mr Jefferson, Architect.* 1973. NY. 1st ed. 177p. F. B14. $55.00

GUINTHER & TAYLOR. *Positive Flying.* 1978. NY. 1st ed. 229p. G/dj. B18. $12.50

GULICK, Paul. *Strings of Steel.* nd. Grosset Dunlap. MTI. VG. P3. $20.00

GULLETT, D.W. *History of Dentistry in Canada.* 1971. Toronto. 308p. dj. A13. $35.00

GUMUCHIAN. *Les Livres de l'EnFrance.* 1985. 2 vol. 4to. ils. F/F. A4. $325.00

GUNN, James E. *Alternate Worlds.* 1975. Prentice Hall. VG/VG. P3. $35.00

GUNN, James E. *Dreamers.* 1980. Simon Schuster. 1st ed. VG/VG. N4. $17.50

GUNN, James E. *End of the Dreams.* 1975. Scribner. 1st ed. F/F. P3. $15.00

GUNN, James E. *Joy Makers.* 1984. Crown. F/F. P3. $13.00

GUNN, James E. *Some Dreams Are Nightmares.* 1974. Scribner. 1st ed. F/F. P3. $15.00

GUNN, Victor. *Death's Doorway.* 1973. Collins. VG/VG. P3. $15.00

GUNTHER, Max. *Doom Wind.* 1986. Contemporary. 1st ed. VG/VG. P3. $18.00

GUNZ, D. *Maryland Germans: A History.* 1948. Princeton. 1st ed. ils. 476p. VG/VG. B5. $45.00

GUPTA, Yogi. *Yoga & Long Life.* 1969. NY. Yogi Gupta NY Center. sgn. 8vo. VG/G. B11. $15.00

GUPTILL, Arthur L. *Norman Rockwell: Illustrator.* 1975. NY. 4to. 208p. F/dj. T3. $25.00

GUPTILL, Arthur L. *Oil Painting Step-by-Step.* 1953. Watson Guptill. 1st ed. sgn. VG. D2. $40.00

GURGANUS, Allan. *Oldest Living Confederate Widow Tells All.* 1989. Knopf. 1st ed. author's 1st book. F/NF. H11. $40.00

GURGANUS, Allan. *White People.* 1991. Knopf. 1st ed. sgn. F/NF. B2. $50.00

GURNEY, A.R. *Gospel According to Joe.* 1974. Harper Row. 1st ed. NF/VG. M23. $15.00

GURNEY, David. *F Certificate.* 1968. Bernard Beis. 1st ed. hc. F. P3. $10.00

GUTHRIE, A.B. *The Way West.* 1949. NY. Sloane. author's 2nd book. G/G R16. $40.00

GUTHRIE, A.B. Jr. *Arfive.* 1971. Houghton Mifflin. 1st ed. F/F. A18. $30.00

GUTHRIE, A.B. Jr. *Big It.* 1960. Boston. 1st ed. VG/VG. B5. $40.00

GUTHRIE, A.B. Jr. *Blue Hen's Chick.* 1965. NY. 1st ed. VG/VG. B5. $30.00

GUTHRIE, A.B. Jr. *Fair Land, Fair Land.* 1982. Houghton Mifflin. 1st ed. sgn. F/F. A18. $100.00

GUTHRIE, A.B. Jr. *Genuine Article.* 1977. Houghton Mifflin. 1st ed. F/F. A18. $40.00

GUTHRIE, A.B. Jr. *Last Valley.* 1975. Houghton Mifflin. 1st ed. F/F. A18. $40.00

GUTHRIE, A.B. Jr. *Playing Catch-Up.* 1985. Houghton Mifflin. 1st ed. sgn. F/F. A18. $100.00

GUTHRIE, A.B. Jr. *These Thousand Hills.* 1956. Boston. 1st ed. VG/VG. B5. $20.00

GUTHRIE, Woody. *Bound for Glory.* 1943. NY. 1st ed. G/dj. B5. $65.00

GUTMANN, Joseph. *Hebrew Manuscript Painting.* 1978. Braziller. 1st ed. ils. 119p. F/dj. W1. $30.00

GUTTERSON, David. *Snow Falling on Cedars.* 1994. Harcourt. 1st ed. sgn. F/F. C2. $100.00

Book-collecting ought not to be a mere trade, or a mere fad; its object is to secure the comforts of home for examples really rare or beautiful, or interesting as relics.

Andrew Lang
1844 – 1912

HAASE, John. *Seasons & Moments*. 1971. S&S. 1st. inscr. F/F. B11. $30.00

HABENSTEIN & LAMERS. *Funeral Customs in World Over*. 1960. Bulfin. ils. 973p. VG/dj. B29. $25.00

HABER, Joyce. *Users*. 1976. Delacorte. 1st. NF/dj. M25. $25.00

HABERLY, L. *Farewells*. 1927. Long Crendon. Seven Acres. 1/300 hand-prt. VG. T9. $145.00

HABERLY, L. *Pursuit of the Horizon*. 1948. Macmillan. 1st. 8vo. 239p. gilt brn cloth. F. K7. $48.00

HABERSTEIN & LERNESS. *History of American Funeral Directing*. 1963. Bulfin. F/dj. M2. $15.00

HACKETT, John. *Third World War*. 1978. Sidgwick Jackson. 1st. VG/dj. P3. $20.00

HADDAM, Jane; see Papazoglou, Orania.

HADDOX, John. *Antonio Caso: Philosopher of Mexico*. 1971. Austin, TX. 1st. 128p. dj. F3. $20.00

HADEN & KAISER. *Pat Haden*. 1977. Morrow. 1st. inscr. photos. F/VG. P8. $25.00

HADER & HADER. *Cat & the Kitten*. 1940. Macmillan. 1st/2nd prt. 8vo. 98p. gr cloth. VG/dj. D1. $85.00

HADER & HADER. *Mighty Hunter*. 1947 (1943). London. Hale. 1st. ils. NF/VG. C8. $35.00

HADER & HADER. *Quack Quack*. 1961. Macmillan. 1st. 4to. 47p. NF/VG+. P2. $40.00

HADER & HADER. *Rainbow's End*. 1945. Macmillan. VG. B15. $50.00

HADFIELD, R.L. *Phantom Ship*. 1973. Geoffrey Bles. 1st. G+. P3. $18.00

HADLEY, Arthur. *Joy Wagon*. 1958. Viking. 1st. F/dj. M2. $25.00

HADVIELD, Robert A. *Work & Position of the Metallurgical Chemist*. 1921. Sheffield. 8vo. 97p. VG. K3. $35.00

HAECKEL, Ernst. *Evolution of Man: Popular Exposition of Principle Points...* 1896 & 1897. Appleton. 2 vol. leather/marbled brd. G. H1. $110.00

HAEUSSLER, Armin. *Story of Our Hymns*. 1952. Eden. 1099p. G. B29. $7.00

HAFEZ, E.S.E. *Reproduction in Farm Animals*. 1987. Lea Febiger. 5th. 649p. B1. $22.50

HAGANS & SEIBEL. *Complicated Watches*. 1945. Denver. Roberts. 136p. decor cloth. VG. K3. $25.00

HAGBERG, David. *Crossfire*. 1991. Tor. 1st. NF/dj. P3. $22.00

HAGEDORN, Hermann. *Leonard Wood, a Biography*. 1931. NY. 2 vol. 1st. ils/photos/appendix/index. B5. $60.00

HAGEDORN, Hermann. *Roosevelt in the Badlands*. 1921. Houghton Mifflin. dj. A19. $65.00

HAGER, Jean. *Grandfather Medicine*. 1989. St Martin. 1st. author's 1st mystery. F/F. L3. $200.00

HAGER, Jean. *Night Walker*. 1990. St Martin. 1st. sgn. F/NF. A24. $60.00

HAGER, Jean. *Redbird's Cry*. 1994. Mysterious. 1st. F/F. L3. $45.00

HAGERMANN, E.R. *Fighting Rebels & Redskins...Col Geo B Sanford 1861-62*. 1969. OK U. 1st. maps. 355p. F/dj. M4. $25.00

HAGGARD, H. Rider. *Allan & the Ice Gods*. 1927. Doubleday. 1st AM. VG. M2. $75.00

HAGGARD, H. Rider. *Ayesha: The Return of She*. 1905. Doubleday Page. 1st. G+. P3. $40.00

HAGGARD, H. Rider. *Classic Adventures*. 1986. New Orchard. 1st. F/dj. P3. $20.00

HAGGARD, H. Rider. *Cleopatra*. 1889. London. VG. M2. $95.00

HAGGARD, H. Rider. *Finished*. 1917. Longman Gr. 1st. VG. M19. $35.00

HAGGARD, H. Rider. *Heart of the World*. 1896. London. 1st. F. M2. $150.00

HAGGARD, H. Rider. *Jess*. 1896. Smith Elder. G+. P3. $60.00

HAGGARD, H. Rider. *Joan Haste*. 1895. Longmans. 1st Am. VG-. M2. $60.00

HAGGARD, H. Rider. *Montezuma's Daughter*. 1894. Longmans. 1st Am. VG. M2. $100.00

HAGGARD, H. Rider. *Nada the Lily*. 1892. London. 1st. VG. M2. $200.00

HAGGARD, H. Rider. *Wanderer's Necklace*. 1914. Longmans. 1st. VG/dj. M2. $90.00

HAGGARD, H. Rider. *Yellow God*. 1908. Cupples Leon. 1st. VG. M2. $125.00

HAGGARD, William. *Arena*. 1961. Washburn. 1st. VG/dj. P3. $15.00

HAGGARD, William. *Hard Sell*. 1965. Cassell. 1st. NF/dj. P3. $25.00

HAGGARD, William. *Median Line*. 1979. Cassell. NF/dj. P3. $20.00

HAGUE, Michael. *Cinderella & Other Tales From Perrault*. 1989. 4to. 23 full-p pl. 88p. F/F. A4. $25.00

HAGUE, Michael. *Magic Moments*. 1990. Little Brn. 1st. sgn. as new/sans. A20. $40.00

HAHN, Emily. *Eve & the Apes*. 1988. NY. 1st. 180p. F/NF. S15. $10.00

HAHNEMANN, Samuel. *Organon of Homoeopathic Medicine*. 1843. NY. 2nd Am. 8vo. 212p. cloth. VG. M1. $250.00

HAIG-BROWN, Roderick L. *Return to the River*. 1946. Toronto. McClelland Stuart. 1st. F/VG+. A18. $80.00

HAIG-BROWN, Roderick L. *Silver: Life Story of an Atlantic Salmon*. 1931. London. Black. ils JP Moreton. 96p. cloth. VG. M12. $45.00

HAIG-BROWN, Roderick L. *Western Angler*. 1939. Derrydale. 2 vol. 1/950. gilt red cloth. VG+. M20. $500.00

HAIGH & NEWTON. *Wools of Britain*. 1950. London. Pitman. 78p. cloth. VG. A10. $22.00

HAILEY, Arthur. *Airport*. 1968. Doubleday. 1st. NF/VG. N4. $27.50

HAILEY, Arthur. *Strong Medicine*. 1984. Doubleday. 1st. NF/NF. N4. $17.50

HAINES, John. *Stone Harp*. 1971. Wesleyan U. 1st. assn copy. F/NF. V1. $45.00

HAINING, Peter. *Lucifer Society*. 1972. Taplinger. 1st. F/dj. M2. $35.00

HAINING, Peter. *Mystery!* 1977. Stein Day. 1st. F/dj. M2. $20.00

HAINING, Peter. *Nightmare Reader*. 1973. Doubleday. 1st. F/dj. M2. $15.00

HAINING, Peter. *Werewolf! Horror Stories of the Man-Beast*. 1987. London. Severn. 1st. F/F. M21. $20.00

HAIRE, Frances. *Folk Costume Book*. 1937. 1st. ils Gertrude Moser. VG+. S13. $20.00

HAITES, Erik F. *Western River Transportation*. 1975. Johns Hopkins. 209p. T7. $45.00

HAITT, Ben. *Fish Poems*. 1968. Sacramento. Runcible Spoon. 1/200. 12mo. F/wrp. A17. $15.00

HAKLUYT, Richard. *Hakluyt's Voyages: Principal Navigations, Voyages...* 1965. Viking. 8vo. 522p. brn cloth. P4. $45.00

HALACY, D.S. *Colonization of the Moon.* 1969. Van Nostrand Reinhold. xl. K5. $10.00

HALBERSTAM, David. *Breaks of the Game.* 1981. Knopf. 1st. VG+/VG+. P8. $20.00

HALBERSTAM, David. *Noblest Roman.* 1961. Houghton Mifflin. 1st. F/F. B4. $250.00

HALBERSTAM, David. *Summer of '49.* 1989. NY. Morrow. 1st. NF/NF. R16. $25.00

HALBERT, Sherrill. *In Re, Dr Morse's History.* 1965. Sacramento Book Collectors Club. 1/300. as new. K7. $15.00

HALCOMB & SARIS. *Headgear of Hitler's Germany Vol 1: Heer-Kriegsmarine...* 1989. San Jose. 1st. ils. 348p. VG. S16. $40.00

HALDANE, Charlotte. *Last Great Empress of China.* 1963. Bobbs Merrill. 1st. 304p. F. W3. $38.00

HALDANE, J.B.S. *Last Judgment.* 1927. Harper. 1st. VG/dj. M2. $17.00

HALDEMAN, Joe. *Buying Time.* 1989. Morrow. 1st. F/F. H11. $25.00

HALDEMAN, Joe. *Mindbridge.* 1976. St Martin. 1st. sgn. F/F. B11. $45.00

HALE, Christopher. *Murder in Tow.* 1943. Doubleday Crime Club. 1st. F/NF. M15. $45.00

HALE, Edward Everett. *Brick Moon.* 1971. Barre, MA. Imp Soc. ils/sgn Michael McCurdy. 2-tone gilt cloth. F/case. T10. $60.00

HALE, James. *After Midnight Ghost Book.* 1981. Watts. 1st Am. VG/dj. M2. $22.00

HALE, Janet Campbell. *Jailing of Cecelia Capture.* 1985. Random. 1st. author's 2nd novel. F/F. L3. $45.00

HALE, Kathleen. *Puss in Boots.* nd. Fld Books Ltd. Peepshow Book. fld 3-D panorama. VG+. M20. $150.00

HALE, Louise Closser. *American's London.* 1920. Harper. 1st. ils. 349p. VG/dj. A25. $18.00

HALE, Mason E. Jr. *Monograph of the Lichen Relicina.* 1975. WA, DC. ils/figures. wrp. B26. $12.50

HALE, Sarah Jospheha. *Ladies' New Book of Cookery: A Practical System...* 1852. NY. Long. 3rd. 474p. lib buckram. B10. $100.00

HALE, Sarah Jospheha. *Mrs Hale's New Cookbook.* 1857. 1st. VG. E6. $125.00

HALE, William Harlan. *Horizon Cookbook & Ils History of Eating & Drinking...* 1968. Am Heritage. 768p. VG/G. B10. $35.00

HALEY, Alex & Malcolm X. *Autobiography of Malcolm X.* 1965. NY. Grove. 1st. VG/clip. B4. $850.00

HALEY, Alex. *Queen: Story of an American Family.* 1992. NY. Morrow. 1st. F/F. T12. $50.00

HALEY, Alex. *Roots.* 1976. Doubleday. 1st. F/NF. D10. $100.00

HALEY, Alex. *Roots.* 1976. Doubleday. 1st. VG/VG. R14. $25.00

HALEY, Gail. *Wonderful, Magical World of Marguerite.* 1964. Sayre Ross. 1st. ils. w/uncut paper doll. NF/VG/box. P2. $175.00

HALEY, Nelson Cole. *Whale Hunt.* 1948. NY. 1st. 304p. map ep. A17. $12.50

HALIFAX, Lord. *Lord Halifax's Ghost Book.* 1944. Didier. 1st. VG. P3. $20.00

HALKER, Clark D. *For Democracy, Workers & God: Labor-Song Poems...* 1991. IL U. 1st. F/F. V4. $25.00

HALL, A. Daniel. *Genus Tulipa.* 1940. London. 1st. 171p. A10. $125.00

HALL, Baynard R. *Frank Freeman's Barber Shop: A Tale.* 1853. Auburn. Alden Beardsley. ils Rush B Hall. 8vo. 343p. G. K7. $60.00

HALL, C. *Introduction to Electron Microscopy.* 1983. Malabar. 2nd. 397p. F. B1. $35.00

HALL, C.A. *Evolution of the Echinoid Genus Astrodapsis.* 1962. Berkeley. CA. ils/5 pocket maps & charts. F/wrp. M12. $25.00

HALL, Charles A.M. *Common Quest.* 1965. Westminster. 332p. VG/dj. B29. $6.50

HALL, Donald. *Principal Products of Portugal.* 1995. Beacon. 1st. sgn. F/dj. V1. $30.00

HALL, Donald. *Their Ancient, Glittering Eyes.* 1992. Ticknor Fields. F/F. A20. $25.00

HALL, Edward T. *Dance of Life: Other Dimension of Time.* 1983. Anchor. 232p. VG/dj. B29. $13.00

HALL, Eliza Calvert. *Aunt Jane of Kentucky.* 1907. Little Brn. 1st. 12mo. VG+. C8. $75.00

HALL, Eliza Calvert. *Land of Long Ago.* 1909. Little Brn. 1st. 295p. VG+. H1. $15.00

HALL, Hal. *Cinematographic Annual 1930. Vol 1.* 1930. Am Soc Cinematographers. photos. 600+. NF/sans. C9. $175.00

HALL, James Norman. *Doctor Dogbody's Leg.* 1940. Boston. 1st. G/dj. B5. $35.00

HALL, James W. *Bones of Coral.* 1991. Knopf. 1st. sgn. F/F. T2. $30.00

HALL, James W. *Tropical Freeze.* 1989. Norton. 1st. sgn. F/F. M15/T2. $45.00

HALL, James W. *Under Cover of Daylight.* 1987. Norton. 1st. F/F. M15. $75.00

HALL, James. *Racers to the Sun.* 1960. Obolensky. 1st. F/dj. M2. $15.00

HALL, Manly D. *Shadow Forms.* 1925. Hall. 1st. VG. M2. $30.00

HALL, Marshall. *Lectures on the Nervous System & Its Diseases.* 1836. Phil. Carey Hart. 1st Am. 240p. contemporary calf. VG. G1. $325.00

HALL, Melvin. *Journey to the End of an Era: An Autobiography.* 1947. Scribner. 1st. 438p. cloth. W1. $24.00

HALL, Parnell. *Detective.* 1987. DIF. 1st. sgn. author's 1st book. F/F. A24. $65.00

HALL, Parnell. *Strangler.* 1989. 1st. F/F. N4. $25.00

HALL, Radclyffe. *Well of Loneliness.* 1928. Paris. Pegassus. 1st French (in Eng). gilt cloth. M24. $85.00

HALL, Ruth. *Passionate Crusader: Life of Marie Stopes.* 1977. HBJ. 1st Am. photos. 351p. VG+/dj. A25. $20.00

HALL, S.C. *Book of Hand-Woven Coverlets.* 1931. Boston. ils. 278p. VG. M4. $25.00

HALL, Trowbridge. *Egypt in Silhouette.* 1928. McMillan. 1st. 8vo. 378p. VG. W1. $18.00

HALL, William. *Christmas Pony.* 1948. Knopf. 1st. ils Roger Duvoisin. 4to. VG/G. P2. $35.00

HALL & NORDHOFF. *Bounty Trilogy.* (1962). Boston. Wyeth Ed/later prt. 633p. P4. $40.00

HALL & SHARP. *Wolf & Man: Evolution in Parallel.* 1978. Academic. ils/photo/map/drawings. 210p. F/VG+. M12. $37.50

HALL-DUNCAN, Nancy. *History of Fashion Photography.* 1979. NY. Alpine Book Co. 240p. cloth. dj. D11. $100.00

HALLAHAN, William H. *Keeper of the Children.* 1978. Morrow. 1st. F/F. M21. $55.00

HALLAHAN, William H. *Ross Forgery.* 1973. Bibliomystery. 1st. xl. VG/dj. K3. $10.00

HALLAHAN, William H. *Search for Joseph Tully.* 1974. Bobbs Merrill. 1st. F/F. M21. $65.00

HALLECK, Fitz-Greene. *Fanny.* 1819. NY. 1st. 8vo. 49p. prt wrp. G. M1. $525.00

HALLECK, R.P. *History of American Literature.* 1911. Am Book Co. 1st/later issue. VG gilt bl cloth. M24. $25.00

HALLENBECK, Cleve. *Alvar Nunez Cabeza de Vaca: Journey & Route...1534-1536.* 1940. Glendale. AH Clark. 9 maps/charts/14p index. teg. NF. O7. $275.00

HALLET, Jean-Pierre. *Congo Kitabu.* 1966. Random. 5th. sgn pres. 16 pl/map ep. 436p. VG/dj. W1. $25.00

HALLIBURTON, Richard. *New Worlds to Conquer.* 1929. Bobbs Merrill. ils. 368p. F3. $15.00

HALLIBURTON, Richard. *Royal Road to Romance.* 1930. NY. sgn. VG. B14. $30.00

HALLIDAY, F.E. *Cult of Shakespeare.* 1960. Yoseloff. 1st Am. 218p. VG/dj. M20. $22.00

HALLIDAY, Samuel B. *Lost & Found; or, Life Among the Poor.* 1860. Phinney Blakeman Mason. 8vo. 356p. cloth. M1. $85.00

HALLIGAN, James. *Fundamentals of Agriculture.* 1911. Boston. Heath. 492p. cloth. VG. A10. $6.00

HALLOWELL, Priscilla. *Dinah & Virginia.* 1956. Viking. 1st. 8vo. NF/dj. M5. $35.00

HALPER, Albert. *Only an Inch From Glory.* 1943. Harper. 1st. F/NF. B2. $50.00

HALPERIN, Irving. *Here I Am: A Jew in Today's Germany.* 1971. Westminster. 140p. VG/dj. S3. $22.00

HALPERN, Jay. *Jade Unicorn.* 1979. Macmillan. 1st. F/dj. M2. $20.00

HALSEY, Francis W. *Authors of Our Day in Their Homes.* 1902. NY. James Pott. 1st/1st state. teg. F. M24. $75.00

HALSEY, Francis W. *Forgotten Books of the American Nursery.* 1911. Boston. Goodspeed. 1/700. ils. xl. VG. A4. $75.00

HALSEY, Mina Deane. *Tenderfoot in Southern California.* 1914. NY. Little Ives. 1st. ils. 162p. VG. A25. $32.00

HALSMAN, Philippe. *Photographs.* 1979. Internat Center Photography. ils. NF/lg wrp. C9. $75.00

HALSTEAD, Bruce W. *Poisonous & Venomous Marine Animals of the World.* 1965. WA. 3 vol. VG+. S15. $295.00

HALSTED, William. *Results of Operations for Cure of Cancer to Breast...* 1894. Baltimore. 1st. ils. 54p. A13. $150.00

HALTER, Jon C. *Bill Bradley: One to Remember.* 1975. Putnam. 1st. F/VG+. P8. $30.00

HAMADA, Shoji. *Catalogue of 77 Tea Bowls by Hamada Shoji.* 1972. Japan Folk Arts Mus. 1st. Japanese text. 77 full-p mc pl. 177p. F/F case. W3. $245.00

HAMBIDGE, G. *Hunger Signs in Crops.* 1941. WA. 1st. tall 8vo. 327p. cloth. NF. A22. $30.00

HAMBURGER, Michael. *Variations: Travelling in Suffolk.* 1981. Blk Swan. 1st. F/F. B4. $65.00

HAMBY, W.B. *Case Reports & Autopsy Records of Ambroise Pare.* 1960. Springfield. 1st Eng trans. 214p. A13. $150.00

HAMILL, Katherine. *Swamp Shadow.* 1936. Knopf. 1st. F/NF. B4. $85.00

HAMILL, Pete. *Gift.* 1973. Random. 1st. author's 2nd novel. F/F. D10. $35.00

HAMILTON, Alexander. *Works of..., Comprising His Most Important Offical Reports.* 1810. NY. Williams Whiting. 1st. 3 vol in 1. thick 8vo. new half calf. F. M1. $950.00

HAMILTON, Allan McLane. *Nervous Diseases: Their Description & Treatment.* 1878. Phil. Henry Lea. heavy 8vo. 512p+catalog. panelled brn cloth. xl. G1. $175.00

HAMILTON, Angus. *Korea.* 1904. Scribner. 1st. ils. 313p. xl. G+. W3. $42.00

HAMILTON, Charles. *Bench & the Ballot.* 1973. Oxford. 1st. 258p. F/VG+. B4. $60.00

HAMILTON, Charles. *Braddock's Defeat: Journal of Capt Robert Cholmey...* 1959. Norman, OK. 1st. 134p. as new/clip. H1. $65.00

HAMILTON, Charles. *Collecting Autographs & Manuscripts.* 1970. OK U. 2nd. F/VG. M24. $50.00

HAMILTON, Clarence. *Outlines of Music History.* 1913. Oliver Ditson. 308p. VG. B29. $6.50

HAMILTON, Edith. *Mythology.* 1942. Little Brn. 38th prt. 497p. F/NF. W2. $30.00

HAMILTON, Frank. *Treatise on Military Surgery & Hygiene.* 1865. NY. 648p. A13. $750.00

HAMILTON, Franklin; see Silverberg, Robert.

HAMILTON, Henry W. *Sioux of the Rosebud.* 1971. Norman, OK. photos John Anderson. F. A19. $35.00

HAMILTON, Henry. *History of the Homeland: Story of British Background.* 1947. London. Allen Unwin. 1st. maps. gr buckram. VG. B22. $15.00

HAMILTON, Jane. *Book of Ruth.* 1988. Ticknor Fields. 1st. author's 1st book. F/F. T11. $175.00

HAMILTON, Joyce. *White Water: Colorado Jet Boat Expedition 1960.* 1963. Caxton. 2nd. 8vo. VG/dj. F7. $80.00

HAMILTON, K.G.A. *Leafhoppers of Ornamental & Fruit Trees in Canada.* 1985. Ottawa. Agriculture Canada. 193 mc photos. 71p. VG/wrp. B1. $18.50

HAMILTON, Luther. *Reasons for the Unitarian Belief.* 1830. Boston. Bowles. 1st. 12mo. 137p. cloth. M1. $100.00

HAMILTON, Mary E. *Policewoman: Her Service & Ideals.* 1924. Stokes. 1st. sgn pres. 200p. VG/fair. A25. $22.00

HAMILTON, Robert. *WH Hudson: The Vision of Earth.* 1946. London. Dent. 1st. F/dj. Q1. $40.00

HAMILTON, Roberts. *Mayflower.* 1846. Saxton Kelt. 1st. aeg. gilt emb blk morocco. F. M24. $275.00

HAMILTON, Virginia. *All Jahdu Storybook.* 1991. HBJ. 1st. sgn. F/F. B3. $35.00

HAMILTON, Virginia. *In the Beginning: Creation Stories From Around the World.* 1988. HBJ. 1st. sm 4to. 161p. F/F clip. C14. $30.00

HAMILTON, Virginia. *MC Higgins, the Great.* 1974. Macmillan. 1st. F/F. B4. $150.00

HAMILTON, Virginia. *Paul Robeson: Life & Times of a Free Black Man.* 1974. Harper Row. 1st prt. NF/dj. M25. $25.00

HAMILTON, Virginia. *WEB DuBois: A Biography.* 1972. NY. Crowell. 4th. 8vo. F/F. C8. $25.00

HAMILTON, W.C. *Statistics in Physical Science.* 1964. Ronald. 1st. 230p. F. D8. $20.00

HAMILTON, William Rowan. *Mathematical Papers. Vol III. Algebra.* 1967. Cambridge. 1st. sgn RE Ingram. 672p. VG. K3. $90.00

HAMILTON-PATERSON, James. *That Time in Malomba.* 1990. Soho. 1st Am. F/F. M25. $25.00

HAMLIN, Augustus Choate. *Battle of Chancellorsville.* 1896. Bangor, ME. 9 mc maps. rebound. G. B18. $125.00

HAMLIN, Talbot. *Greek Revival Architecture in America.* 1947 (1944). London/NY. Oxford. 2nd. ils/pl/figures. cloth. D2. $65.00

HAMMEL, Eric. *Guadalcanal: Decision at Sea, Naval Battle of Guadalcanal...* 1988. NY. 1st. maps. 480p. VG/VG. S16. $25.00

HAMMETT, Dashiell. *Adventures of Sam Spade.* 1945. World. 1st. VG/VG. M22. $45.00

HAMMETT, Dashiell. *Battle of Aleutians.* 1944. Adak. Intelligence Section, US Infantry. 1st. F/stapled wrp. M15. $300.00

HAMMETT, Dashiell. *Big Knockover.* 1966. Random. 1st. F/dj. M15. $100.00

HAMMETT, Dashiell. *Maltese Falcon.* 1934. Modern Lib. 1st thus. NF. M22. $30.00

HAMMETT, Dashiell. *Novels of...* 1965. NY. Knopf. Omnibus ed. F/dj. M15. $100.00

HAMMETT, Dashiell. *Woman in the Dark.* 1988. Knopf. 1st thus. F/F. T11. $55.00

HAMMILL, Joel. *Trident.* 1981. Arbor. 1st. F/dj. M2. $12.00

HAMMITZSCH, Horst. *Zen in the Art of the Tea Ceremony.* 1981. St Martin. 104p. F/dj. W3. $28.00

HAMMOND, G.P. *Adventures of Alexander Barclay, Mountain Man...1845-1850.* 1976. Denver. Rosenstock. ils/photos/3 fld pocket maps. 246p. F. M4. $50.00

HAMMOND, Gerald. *Stray Shot.* 1989. St Martin. 1st Am. F/F. N4. $15.00

HAMMOND, L.H. *In the Vanguard of a Race.* 1922. NY. Council of Women for Home Missions. xl. clip ep. G+. B2. $25.00

HAMMOND, William A. *Sleep & Its Derangements.* 1873. Lippincott. 318p. bevelled ruled gr cloth. G. G1. $135.00

HAMMOND, William A. *Spinal Irritation.* 1870. Appleton. 1st separate. 42p. VG/prt olive wrp. G1. $100.00

HAMNER, Earl Jr. *Fifty Roads to Town.* 1953. Random. 1st. F/VG. B4. $200.00

HAMPE, Theodor. *Crime & Punishment in Germany...* 1929. London. Routledge. trans Malcolm Letts. ils. gr cloth. M11. $50.00

HAMPSON, John. *Man About the House.* 1935. London. 1/285. sgn. F/F. T9. $45.00

HANAUER, J. *Folk-Lore of the Holy Land: Moslem, Christian & Jewish.* 1910. London. Duckworth. 326p. teg. NF/NF. W3. $135.00

HANAWALT, Barbara A. *Crime & Conflict in English Communities 1300-1348.* 1979. Cambridge. VG/dj. M11. $45.00

HANBURY, Harold Greville. *Vinerian Chair & Legal Education.* 1958. Oxford. Basil Blackwell. M11. $85.00

HANCHETT, William. *Lincoln Murder Conspiracies.* 1983. 303p. dj. O8. $9.50

HANCOCK, H. Irving. *Making the Last Stand for Old Glory.* 1916. Altemus. 1st. VG/dj. M2. $100.00

HANCOCK, Thomas. *Principles of Peace Exemplified...* 1830. Providence. HH Brn. 315p. worn. V3. $25.00

HAND, G.J. *English Law in Ireland 1290-1324.* 1967. Cambridge. M11. $85.00

HAND, Sherman. *Collector's Encyclopedia of Carnival Glass.* 1978. Collector Books. 256p. mc pl. w/price guide. F/F. H1. $65.00

HANDLER, David. *Boy Who Never Grew Up.* 1992. Doubleday. 1st. sgn. F/dj. M15. $40.00

HANDLIN & LAYTON. *Let Me Hear Your Voice: Portraits of Aging Immigrant Jews.* 1983. WA U. photos Rochelle Casserd. 110p. VG/dj. S3. $25.00

HANEY, Lynn. *Naked at the Feast.* 1981. Dodd. 1st. F/F. B2. $25.00

HANFF, Helene. *84 Charling Cross Road.* 1975 (1970). NY. Deluxe ed. F/F. C8. $30.00

HANKE, Lewis. *Spanish Struggle for Justice in the Conquest of America.* 1959. PA U. 2nd. 217p. dj. F3. $25.00

HANKE, W. *Biology & Physiology of Amphibians.* 1990. Stuttgart. 413p. F. S15. $40.00

HANKINS, Maude McGehee. *Daddy Gander.* 1928. Volland. 1st. ils VE Cadie. 8vo. ils brd. pict box. R5. $200.00

HANNA, A.J. *Prince in Their Midst.* 1947. Norman. 2nd. sgn. 276p. VG. B11. $25.00

HANNA, Phil Townsend. *California Through Four Centuries: Handbook of...Dates.* 1935. Farrar Rinehart. 1st. sgn. ils/index. 212p. VG. B19. $40.00

HANNA, Phil Townsend. *Libros Californianos; or, Five Feet of California Books.* 1932. Jake Zeitlin/Primavera. 1st. 74p. VG. B19. $70.00

HANNA, Warren L. *Lost Harbor: Controversy Over Drake's California Anchorage.* 1979. Berkeley. 1st. inscr. 8vo. map ep. bl cloth. F/dj. P4. $45.00

HANNAH, Barry. *Airships.* 1978. Knopf. 1st. author's 3rd book. F/F. D10. $85.00

HANNAH, Barry. *Airships.* 1978. Knopf. 1st. inscr. NF/NF. R14. $90.00

HANNAH, Barry. *Boomerang.* 1989. Houghton Mifflin. 1st. as new. A20. $25.00

HANNAH, Barry. *Captain Maximus.* 1985. Knopf. 1st. F/F. H11. $30.00

HANNAH, Barry. *Geronimo Rex.* 1972. Viking. 1st. inscr. author's 1st book. NF/dj. L3. $175.00

HANNAH, Barry. *Hey Jack!* 1987. Dutton. 1st. F/F. H11. $35.00

HANNAH, Barry. *Nightwatchmen.* 1973. Viking. 1st. F/NF. B2. $85.00

HANNAH, Barry. *Ray.* 1980. Knopf. 1st. sgn. author's 3rd novel. F/F. D10. $55.00

HANNAH, Barry. *Tennis Handsome.* 1983. Knopf. 1st. sgn. author's 5th novel. F/F. D10. $45.00

HANNAM, Alberta. *Paint the Wind.* 1959. London. Michael Joseph. 1st Eng. 192p. F/NF. K7. $45.00

HANNEMAN, Audre. *Ernest Hemingway.* 1967. Princeton. 1st. F/dj. Q1. $100.00

HANNOCK, Ralph. *Rainbow Republics: Central America.* 1947. Coward McCann. 1st. 305p. dj. F3. $25.00

HANNON, Ezra; see Hunter, Evan.

HANS, Fred. *Great Sioux Nation, a Complete History of Indian Life...* 1907. Donohue. 1st. ils. 575p. VG. J2. $475.00

HANSBERRY, Lorraine. *Movement: Documentary of a Struggle for Equality.* 1964. S&S. later prt. photos. F/dj. M25. $75.00

HANSBERRY, Lorraine. *Sign in Sidney Brustein's Window.* 1965. Random. 1st. NF/dj. M25. $60.00

HANSEN, Chuck. *US Nuclear Weapons.* 1988. NY. Orion. 1st. ils. 232p. NF/dj. K3. $25.00

HANSEN, James R. *Engineer in Charge.* 1987. Washington, DC. 4to. 620p. VG. K5. $50.00

HANSEN, Joseph. *Obedience.* 1988. Mysterious. 1st Am. NF/VG. M22. $10.00

HANSEN, Joseph. *Strange Marriage.* 1965. Los Angeles. Argyle Books. ne. 8vo. 176p. F/VG. H1. $45.00

HANSEN, Ron. *Assassination of Jesse James.* 1983. Knopf. 1st. F/F. T11. $85.00

HANSEN, Ron. *Desperadoes.* 1979. Knopf. 1st. author's 1st book. F/F. T11. $110.00

HANSEN & MILLER. *Wild Oats in Eden.* 1962. Santa Rosa. self pub. photos Ansel Adams/John Lebaron/Beth Winter. 147p. NF. K7. $50.00

HANSFORD, S.H. *Chinese Jade Carving.* nd. London. Humphries. 1st/2nd imp. photos. 145p. F/F. W3. $86.00

HANSON, Earl Parker. *South From the Spanish Main.* 1967. NY. Delacorte. 1st. maps. VG/dj. K3. $20.00

HANSON, Margaret Brock. *Powder River Country.* 1981. Frontier Prt. sgn. dj. A19. $65.00

HANSON, Maurice F. *College Reunion.* 1955. Coward McCann. 1st. VG. O3. $25.00

HARANG, L. *Aurorae.* 1951. John Wiley. sm 4to. 166p. VG. K5. $30.00

HARCOURT, Helen. *Florida Fruits & How to Raise Them.* 1886. Louisville. revised/enlarged. 347p. gilt cloth. VG. B26. $65.00

HARCOURT, L.W. Vernon. *His Grace the Steward & Trial of Peers, a Novel Inquiry...* 1907. London. Longman Gr. gilt bl cloth. VG. M11. $175.00

HARDENOFF, Jeanne. *Sing Song Scuppernong.* 1974. HRW. 1st. 59p. F/F. D4. $25.00

HARDIN, John Wesley. *Life of John Wesley Hardin From Original Manuscript...* 1896. Smith Moore. 1st. 144p. G/dj. J2. $195.00

HARDING, A.R. *Deadfalls & Snares: A Book of Instruction for Trappers...* (1907). Columbus, OH. Harding. 218p. H7. $15.00

HARDING, A.R. *Fur Farming: Book of Information...* (1909). Columbus, OH. Harding. revised. 278p. G. H7. $15.00

HARDING, A.R. *Mink Trapping: Book of Instruction...* (1906). Columbus, OH. Harding. 171p+15p appendix. G. H7. $15.00

HARDING, Alan. *Law-Making & Law-Makers in British History...* 1980. London. Royal Historical Soc. M11. $45.00

HARDING, Anthony. *Racer's & Driver's Reader.* 1972. Arco. photos. F/F. P8. $35.00

HARDING, Bertia. *Phantom Crown.* 1934. Bobbs Merrill. 1st. sgn. 381p. VG. B11. $25.00

HARDING, G. Lankester. *Antiquities of Jordan.* 1967. NY. Praeger. revised. 8vo. ils/pl/maps. 215p. VG/dj. W1. $24.00

HARDING, George L. *Brief History of the California Spanish Press.* nd. Grabhorn. 1/100. lg folio fld once. ils. NF/self wrp. R3. $150.00

HARDWICH, T. Fredrick. *Manual of Photographic Chemistry...* 1858. NY. 4th. G. M17. $50.00

HARDY, Alice Dale. *Riddle Club at Home (#1).* 1924. Grosset Dunlap. 246p. cloth. VG/dj. M20. $25.00

HARDY, Alister. *Great Waters: Voyage of Natural History to Study Whales...* 1967. NY. Harper Row. 1st Am. VG/dj. P4. $65.00

HARDY, Forsyth. *Scandinavian Film.* 1952. London. Falcon. 62p+32p photos. A17. $15.00

HARDY, Helen Henriques. *Louisiana's Fabulous Foods & How to Cook Them.* nd. LA. Hope Pub. G/wrp. A16. $17.50

HARDY, James. *Surgery of the Aorta & Its Branches.* 1960. Phil. 1st. 386p. A13. $50.00

HARDY, Thomas. *Changed Man.* 1913. London. Macmillan. 1st. map/etching. gr cloth. VG. S13. $75.00

HARDY, Thomas. *Famous Tragedy of the Queen of Cornwall.* 1923. London. Macmillan. 1st. NF/G. M23. $50.00

HARDY, Thomas. *Far From Madding Crowd.* 1937. 1st thus. VG+. S13. $15.00

HARDY, Thomas. *Human Shows Far Phantasies.* 1925. London. Macmillan. 1st. 8vo. gr brd. VG/NF. M23. $75.00

HARDY, Thomas. *Jude the Obscure.* 1896. London. Osgood McIlvaine. 1st/mixed states. 517p. gilt gr cloth. B24. $150.00

HARDY, Thomas. *Late Lyrics & Earlier.* 1922. London. 1st. VG. S13. $50.00

HARDY, Thomas. *Life's Little Ironies.* 1894. Harper. 1st. gilt gr cloth. VG. M24. $100.00

HARDY, Thomas. *Poems of the Past & Present.* 1902. Harper 1st Am. gilt gr cloth. M24. $165.00

HARDY, Thomas. *Tess of the D'Urbervilles.* 1892. NY. Harper. 1st Am. gilt tan cloth. M24. $450.00

HARDY, Thomas. *Woodlanders.* 1887. NY. 1st Am hc. 12mo. bl half cloth/marbled brd. VG. A11. $185.00

HARDY & PINNEY. *Vineyards & Wine Cellars of California: Essay...* 1994. BC of CA. 1/450. 4to. ils. purple brd. F/box. R3. $200.00

HARE, Cyril. *English Murder.* 1951. Little Brn. 1st Am. F/dj. M15. $70.00

HARGRAVE, Lydon Lane. *Report on Archaeological Reconnaissance...* 1935. Berkeley. 8vo. 56p. stiff wrp. F7. $75.00

HARGREAVES, Bruce J. *Succulent Spurges of Malawi.* 1987. np. ils/maps/drawings. cbdg. F. B26. $20.00

HARING, C.H. *Spanish Empire in America.* 1947. NY. Oxford. map ep. F. O7. $75.00

HARING, C.H. *Trade & Navigation Between Spain & Indies...* 1964 (1918). Gloucester. Peter Smith. double-p map. F. O7. $55.00

HARIOT, Thomas. *Brief & True Report of the New Found Land of Virginia.* 1951. Ann Arbor. Clements Lib. facsimile 1588 ed. 1/500. 8vo. unp. M/case. H13. $65.00

HARJO, Joy. *In Mad Love & War.* 1990. Middletown. Wesleyan U. 1st author's 2nd book. F/F clip. L3. $75.00

HARJO, Joy. *She Had Some Horses.* 1983. NY/Chicago. Thunder's Mouth. 1st hc issue. F/F. L3. $250.00

HARJO, Joy. *Woman Who Fell From the Sky.* 1994. Norton. 1st. inscr/dtd. F/clip. L3. $75.00

HARKER, A. *Metamorphism: A Study of Transformations of Rock-Masses.* 1939. Dutton. 2nd. 185 diagrams. 362p. F. D8. $20.00

HARLAND, Marion. *Complete Cookbook.* 1906 (1903). ils. 709p. VG. E6. $65.00

HARLAND, Marion. *House & Home: A Complete Housewife's Guide.* ca 1889. Clawson Bros. 532p. fair. B10. $65.00

HARLOW, A. *Road of the Century.* 1947. NY. 1st. VG/G. B5. $50.00

HARMAN, F. Ward. *Ship Models Illustrated, With Working Guide to Modeling.* 1943. NY. Marine Model Co. 1st. 128p. VG/dj. P4. $45.00

HARMAN, H.H. *Modern Factor Analysis.* 1967. Chicago. 474p. NF/dj. D8. $30.00

HARMER, Jenny. *North Australian Plants. Part 1: Wildflowers...* 1970s. np. photos. 132p. glossy photo brd. as new. B26. $21.00

HARMETZ, Aljean. *Making of the Wizard of Oz.* 1977. Knopf. photos. NF/dj. C9. $40.00

HARNSBERGER, Caroline. *Mark Twain's Clara.* 1982. Evanston, IL. Ward Schori. 1st. gr cloth. F/dj. M24. $20.00

HAROLD, Childe. *Childe's Book of Abridged Wisdom.* 1905. Paul Elder. 1st. French fld p/cords. VG. P2. $100.00

HARPENDING, Asbury. *Great Diamond Hoax.* 1958. Norman, OK. 1st thus. Western Frontier Lib series. VG/dj. M24. $15.00

HARPER, Michael. *Photographs, Negatives: History as Apple Tree.* 1972. SF. Scarab. 1st. assn copy. F/dj. V1. $25.00

HARPER, Wilhellmina. *Gunniwolf & Other Merry Tales.* 1936. McKay/Jr Literary Guild. 1st thus. 104p. G+/G. P2. $65.00

HARPER, Wilhelmina. *Gunniwolf & Other Merry Tales.* 1937. London. Harrap. 1st. lg 8vo. G+. C8. $20.00

HARPER, Wilhelmina. *Little Book of Necessary Ballads.* 1930. Harper. 1st. 86p. NF. D4. $35.00

HARPER, Wilhelmina. *Selfish Giant & Other Stories.* 1935. McKay. probable 1st. ils Kate Seredy. 86p. VG/G+. P2. $80.00

HARPER, Wilhelmina. *Uncle Sam's Story Book.* 1944. McKay/Jr Literary Guild. 1st thus. 144p. NF/VG-. P2. $20.00

HARRE, T. Everett. *Behold the Woman.* 1916. Lippincott. NF. M2. $15.00

HARRIGAN, Edward. *Ten Little Mulligan Guards.* 1874. McLoughlin. 10 mc pl. pict wrp. M1. $225.00

HARRING, Harro. *Dolores: Novel of South America.* 1846. NY/Montevideo. 4 parts as issued. inscr. 4to. R12. $675.00

HARRINGTON, Alan. *Paradise 1.* 1978. Little Brn. 1st. F/dj. M2. $15.00

HARRINGTON, H.D. *Manual of Plants in Colorado.* 1964 (1954). Chicago. 2nd. map. 666p. gilt emb tan cloth. F. B26. $63.00

HARRINGTON, James. *Aphorismes Politiques.* 1795. Paris. Didot Jeune. 8vo. ftspc. brd. R12. $475.00

HARRINGTON, Ollie. *Bootsie & Others.* 1958. Dodd Mead. 1st. NF. M25. $75.00

HARRINGTON, William. *Cromwell File.* 1986. St Martin. 1st. NF/VG. N4. $17.50

HARRIS, Albert W. *Blood of the Arab.* 1941. Chicago. private prt. 1st. VG. O#. $125.00

HARRIS, Beth Coombe. *In the Grip of the Druids.* 1930s. London. VG. M2. $50.00

HARRIS, Burton. *John Colter, His Years in the Rockies.* 1952. Scribner. 1st. 180p. VG/dj. J2. $225.00

HARRIS, Clare. *Away From Here & Now.* 1947. Dorrance. 1st. F/dj. M2. $35.00

HARRIS, Credo. *Motor Rambles in Italy.* 1912. Moffat Yard. 1st. photos. VG. K3. $20.00

HARRIS, Dorothy Joan. *House Mouse.* 1974. London. Warne. 1st Eng. 8vo. ils Barbara Cooney. 46p. VG/dj. T5. $30.00

HARRIS, Frank. *Contemporary Portraits.* 1915. NY. Mitchell Kennerley. 1st Am. inscr Joseph Conrad. teg. gilt gr cloth. F. M24. $1,350.00

HARRIS, Frank. *Oscar Wilde, His Life & Confessions.* 1918. NY. 1st trade. 2 vol. gilt gr cloth. VG. K7. $65.00

HARRIS, Helena J. *Southern Sketches. Cecil Gray; or, The Soldier's Revenge.* 1866. New Orleans. 1st. 12mo. 20p. emb lib stp on title. prt wrp. M1. $300.00

HARRIS, Henry. *California's Medical Story.* 1932. SF. JW Stacey. inscr pres. ils. NF. R3. $100.00

HARRIS, Jessie W. *Everyday Foods.* 1939. Houghton Mifflin. G. A16. $10.00

HARRIS, Joel Chandler. *Chronicles of Aunt Minervy Ann.* 1899. Toronto. Wm Briggs. 1st Canadian. ils AB Frost. VG+/wrp. C8. $150.00

HARRIS, Joel Chandler. *Daddy Jake, the Runn-away & Other Stories.* 1889. NY. Century. 1st. 4to. 145p. glazed brd. G. D1. $200.00

HARRIS, Joel Chandler. *Stories From Uncle Remus.* 1934. Saalfield. sm 4to. F/VG. M5. $125.00

HARRIS, Joel Chandler. *Tales From Uncle Remus.* 1935. Houghton Mifflin. sgn by daughter-in-law/dtd 1948. red brd. VG. B11. $100.00

HARRIS, Joel Chandler. *Uncle Remus & Brer Rabbit.* 1907. Stokes. 1st thus. obl 4to. gr cloth/label. R5. $375.00

HARRIS, Joel Chandler. *Uncle Remus: His Songs & Sayings.* 1957. NY. LEC. 1/1500. ils/sgn Seong Moy. F/case. T10. $90.00

HARRIS, Joel Chandler. *Uncle Remus: New Stories of the Old Plantation.* 1905. NY. McClure Phillips. 1st. ils Frost/Conde/Verbeck. teg. red textured cloth. R5. $275.00

HARRIS, John W. *Africa: Slave or Free?* 1969 (1919). NY. Negro U. rpt. 8vo. 244p. VG. W1. $25.00

HARRIS, John. *Chapter of Kings by Mr Collins Illustrated by 38 Engravings.* 1818. London. J Harris. 1st. 16mo. gilt red leather. R5. $485.00

HARRIS, John. *Scenes in America for the Amusement & Instruction...* 1822. London. J Harris. 2nd. 85 #d engravings/fld map. leather-backed pict brd. R5. $225.00

HARRIS, Joseph. *Gardening for Young & Old.* 1905 (1882). Orange Judd. 191p. gilt bdg. A10. $50.00

HARRIS, MacDonald. *Hemingway's Suitcase.* 1990. S&S. 1st. NF/F. A20. $20.00

HARRIS, R.J. *Primer of Multivariate Statistics.* 1975. NY. Academic. 1st. 332p. NF. D8. $30.00

HARRIS, Robert. *Selling Hitler.* 1986. Pantheon. 1st Am. ils. 8vo. 402p. F/dj. K3. $20.00

HARRIS, Rosemary. *Child in the Bamboo Grove.* 1971. Faber. 1st. sm 4to. F/dj. M5. $65.00

HARRIS, Rosemary. *Tower of the Stars.* 1980. London. 1st. F/jd. M2. $12.00

HARRIS, Seale. *Woman's Surgeon, J Marion Sims.* 1950. NY. 1st. VG/VG. B5. $35.00

HARRIS, Thomas A. *I'm OK — You're OK.* 1969. Harper Row. author's 1st book. 278p. NF/NF. W2. $30.00

HARRIS, Thomas L. *Conversation in Heaven. A Wisdom Song.* 1984. Fountaingrove, CA. private prt. 1st. 8vo. cloth. M1. $125.00

HARRIS, Thomas L. *Star-Flowers, a Poem of the Woman's Mystery.* 1986. Fountaingrove, CA. private prt. 1st. 8vo. 121p. cloth. M1. $85.00

HARRIS, Thomas. *Black Sunday.* 1975. Putnam. 1st. author's 1st book. F/NF. H11. $165.00

HARRIS, Thomas. *Red Dragon.* 1981. Putnam. 1st. F/dj. B3. $60.00

HARRIS, Thomas. *Red Dragon.* 1981. Putnam. 1st. NF/NF. D10/T11. $50.00

HARRIS, Thomas. *Silence of the Lambs.* 1988. St Martin. 1st. F/F. B3. $60.00

HARRIS, W.S. *Life in a Thousand Worlds.* nd (1905). Beaver Springs, PA. Am Pub. 8vo. 344p. H1. $30.00

HARRIS, Wilfred. *Neuritis & Neuralgia.* 1926. London. Milford/Oxford. 418p. pebbled bl cloth. VG. G1. $50.00

HARRIS & HARRIS. *Blackfellow Bundi: A Native Australian Boy.* 1939. Whitman. 1st. ils Kurt Wiese. 63p. F/VG. P2. $65.00

HARRIS & HARRIS. *Complete Etchings of Rembrandt.* 1970. Bounty Books. VG/VG. M17. $20.00

HARRIS & HARRIS. *Eldon House: 5 Women's Views of the 19th Century.* 1994. Toronto. Champlain Soc. 1st. 8vo. 517p. red cloth. F. P4. $125.00

HARRIS & WEEKS. *X-Raying the Pharoahs: Most Important Breakthrough...* 1973. NY. 1st. ils. 195p. dj. A13. $100.00

HARRISON, Chip; see Block, Lawrence.

HARRISON, Colin. *Bodies Electric.* 1993. NY. Crown. 1st. F/F. B3. $30.00

HARRISON, Edith Ogden. *Princess of Sayrane.* 1910. McClurg. 1st. VG. M2. $45.00

HARRISON, Edith. *Below the Equator.* 1918. McClurg. 1st. photos. 288p. red cloth. F3. $20.00

HARRISON, Everett F. *Introduction to the New Testament.* 1982. Eerdmans. 507p. VG/dj. B29. $8.50

HARRISON, Fairfax. *Belair Stud 1747-1761.* 1929. Richmond. 1st. w/card. O3. $175.00

HARRISON, Gordon. *Mosquitoes, Malaria & Man: A History...* 1978. NY. 314p. F/NF. S15. $15.00

HARRISON, Harry. *Spaceship Medic.* 1970. London. Faber. 1st. sgn. F/F. T2. $125.00

HARRISON, Harry. *Stainless Steel Rat's Revenge.* 1970. Walker. 1st. NF/dj. M2. $40.00

HARRISON, Harry. *Two Tales & 8 Tomorrows: Science Fiction Stories.* 1965. London. Gollancz. 1st. sgn. F/NF. T2. $95.00

HARRISON, Harry. *West of Eden.* 1984. Bantam. 1st. F/dj. M2. $22.00

HARRISON, Harry. *Year 2000.* 1970. Doubleday. 1st. F/dj. M2. $20.00

HARRISON, Jamie. *Edge of Crazies.* 1995. Hyperion. 1st. sgn. author's 1st book. F/A. A23. $45.00

HARRISON, Jim. *Dalva.* 1988. Dutton/Lawrence. 1st. author's 7th novel. F/F. D10. $45.00

HARRISON, Jim. *Farmer.* 1976. Viking. 1st. inscr. author's 3rd novel. F/F. D10. $150.00

HARRISON, Jim. *Good Day to Die.* 1973. S&S. 1st. F/F. D10. $250.00

HARRISON, Jim. *Julip.* 1994. Boston. 1st. sgn. F/F. A11. $75.00

HARRISON, Jim. *Legends of the Fall.* 1979. Delacorte. 1st. VG/dj. Q1. $75.00

HARRISON, Jim. *Letters to Yesenin & Returning to Earth.* 1979. Los Angeles. Sumac Poetry series. NF/sans/wrp. T11. $75.00

HARRISON, Jim. *Locations.* 1968. NY. 1st. sgn. F/wrp. A11. $135.00

HARRISON, Jim. *Selected & New Poems: 1961-1981.* 1982. Delacorte. 1st. ils Russell Chatham. F/dj. V1. $110.00

HARRISON, Jim. *Sundog.* 1984. Dutton. 1st. sgn. F/F. H11. $80.00

HARRISON, Jim. *Warlock.* 1981. Delacorte. 1st. F/F. T11. $75.00

HARRISON, Jim. *Wolf.* 1971. S&S. 1st. sgn. author's 1st novel. F/NF. L3. $275.00

HARRISON, Kathryn. *Thicker Than Water.* 1991. Random. 1st. author's 1st book. F/F. R13. $35.00

HARRISON, Orlando. *How to Grow & Market Fruit.* 1911. Berlin, MD. 142p. VG. A10. $28.00

HARRISON, Paul Carter. *Drama of Mommo.* 1972. NY. Grove. 1st. 245p. F/F. B4. $50.00

HARRISON, Peter. *Brick Pavement: The Architects' & Builders' Companion.* 1994. Raleigh. self pub. 167p. M. A10. $30.00

HARRISON, Peter. *Seabirds: An Identification Guide.* 1893. Boston. 1st. 88 mc pl. 448p. F/F. S15. $38.00

HARRISON, R.K. *Archaeology of the New Testament.* 1964. Assn. 138p. VG/dj. B29. $8.00

HARRISON, Richard E. *Know Your Garden Series: Climbers & Trailers.* 1973. Cape Town. photos. 115p. VG/dj. B26. $37.50

HARRISON, Robert. *Dublin Dissector; or, Manual of Anatomy.* 1835. Phil. 1st Am. 314p. wrp. A13. $45.00

HARRISON, Whit; see Whittington, Harry.

HARRISON, William. *Roller Ball Murder.* 1974. Morrow. 1st. NF/dj. P3. $20.00

HARRISON & HARRISON. *Trees & Shrubs.* 1965. Rutland/Tokyo. Tuttle. 4to. 582 mc pl. F/VG. A22. $20.00

HARRISON & LOBBAN. *Seaweed Edology & Physiology.* 1994. Cambridge. 8vo. 366p. NF. B1. $45.00

HARRON, Robert. *Rockne: Idol of American Football.* 1931. Burt. 1st. photos/scores/rosters. G. P8. $20.00

HARRY, Eric. *Arc Light.* 1994. S&S. 1st. sgn. F/F. A23. $36.00

HARSHBERGER, John W. *Botanists of Philadelphia & Their Work.* 1899. Phil. 457p. gilt bl cloth. VG. B26. $295.00

HART, Carolyn. *Scandal in Fair Haven.* 1994. Bantam. 1st. sgn. VG/VG. A23. $35.00

HART, Carolyn. *Southern Ghost.* 1992. Bantam. 1st. sgn. F/F. A23. $35.00

HART, Cyril. *Verderers & Forest Laws of Dean.* 1971. Newton Abbot. David & Charles. M11. $45.00

HART, Francis Russell. *Admirals of the Caribbean.* 1922. Houghton Mifflin. inscr. 203p. map ep. P4. $60.00

HART, Henry H. *Venetian Adventurer...Life & Times of Marco Polo.* 1942. Stanford. ils/maps/index/bibliography. 284p. bl/rust cloth. P4. $65.00

HART, James. *Man Who Invented Hollywood...DW Griffith.* 1972. Louisville. 1st. 170p. VG. A17. $18.50

HART, Jerome. *In Our Second Century.* 1931. Pioneer. 1st ed. 454p. G. A17. $20.00

HART, Josephine. *Damage.* 1991. Knopf. 1st. sgn. F/F. R14. $50.00

HART, Liddell. *Colonel Lawrence: Man Behind the Legend.* 1937. Dodd Mead. 6th. 406p. VG. W1. $32.00

HART, R. *Leavening Agents: Yeast, Leaven, Salt-Rising...* 1912. VG. E6. $20.00

HART, Robert W. *Philippines Today.* 1928. Dodd Mead. photos. 191p. VG. P1. $25.00

HART, William. *Told Under a White Oak Tree by Bill Hart's Pinto Pony.* 1922. Houghton Mifflin. 1st. ils J Montgomery Flagg. 51p. VG/dj. J2. $65.00

HARTE, Bret. *Echoes of the Foothills.* 1875. 1st Am. VG. S13. $45.00

HARTE, Bret. *Jack Hamilton's Meditation.* 1899. 1st Am. VG. S13. $45.00

HARTE, Bret. *Lectures of Bret Harte.* 1909. NY. Chas Kozlay. 1st/trade issue. gilt brn cloth. M24. $75.00

HARTE, Bret. *Luck of Roaring Camp & Other Sketches.* 1899. Grosset Dunlap. ne. 256p. xl. G. W2. $95.00

HARTE, Bret. *Sally Dows & Other Stories.* 1893. 1st Am. VG. S13. $45.00

HARTE, Bret. *Trent's Trust.* 1903. 1st Am. VG. S13. $45.00

HARTE, Bret. *Under the Redwoods.* 1901. 1st Am. VG. S13. $45.00

HARTER & THOMPSON. *John Irving.* 1986. Twayne. 1st. F/F. T11. $30.00

HARTFORD, John. *Steamboat in a Cornfield.* 1986. NY. Crown. 1st. photos. F/F. D4. $25.00

HARTHAN, John P. *Bookbindings.* 1961. London. 2nd. VG. T9. $20.00

HARTLEY, Cecil B. *Heroes & Patriots of the South.* 1860. Phil. Evans. 320p. dk gr cloth. VG. K7. $50.00

HARTLEY, L.P. *Arm of Mrs Egan.* 1951. London. 1st. VG. M2. $20.00

HARTLEY, L.P. *Hireling.* 1957. London. 1st. VG/dj. T9. $35.00

HARTLEY, Margaret L. *Southwest Review Reader.* 1974. SMU. 242p. VG/VG. B19. $25.00

HARTLEY & INGILBY. *Vanishing Folkways.* 1971. S Brunswick. 1st Am. ils. 128p. VG/dj. B18. $15.00

HARTMAN, David. *Maimonides: Torah & Philosophic Quest.* 1977. JPS. 2nd imp. 296p. VG+/G+. S3. $25.00

HARTMAN, Joan. *Chinese Jade of Five Centuries.* 1969. 1st. photos. NF/clip. S13. $35.00

HARTMANN, Ernest L. *Biology of Dreaming.* 1967. Springfield, IL. C Thomas. 206p. VG/dj. G1. $50.00

HARTMANN, William. *Desert Heart: Chronicles of the Sonoran Desert.* 1989. Fisher Books. 1st. ils/index/notes. 216p. F/F. B19. $50.00

HARTMANN, William. *In the Stream of Stars: Soviet/American Space Art Book.* 1990. Workman. 1st. F/dj. M2. $30.00

HARTMANN & KESTER. *Plant Propagation Principles & Practices.* 1968. Prentice Hall. 2nd. 702p. dj. A10. $28.00

HARTNEY, Harold E. *Up & at 'Em.* 1940. Harrisburg. 2nd. inscr. 333p. G+. B18. $65.00

HARTNOLL, Phyllis. *Oxford Companion to the Theatre.* 1951. London. 1st. VG/dj. T9. $25.00

HARTUNG, Marion T. *First Book of Carnival Glass...Tenth Book of Carnival Glass.* 1962-1973. Emporia, KS. self pub. 10 vol. 8vo. 100 patterns per book. VG or better. H1. $175.00

HARUF, Kent. *Tie That Binds.* 1984. HRW. 1st. inscr/dtd 1984. F/F. B3. $50.00

HARVESTER, Simon. *Nameless Road.* 1969. Walker. 1st. 199p. VG/dj. M20. $15.00

HARVEY, Henry. *History of the Shawnee Indians From Year 1681 to 1854.* 1855. Cincinnati. Ephraim Morgan. 1st/2nd issue. 316p. D11. $250.00

HARVEY, Peggy. *Great Recipes From the World's Great Cooks.* 1964. Gramercy. VG/dj. A16. $10.00

HARVEY, Peggy. *Horn of Plenty.* 1964. Boston. Little Brn. 1st. ils. VG/dj. A16. $10.00

HARVEY, Samuel. *History of Hemostasis.* 1929. NY. 1st. 128p. A13. $50.00

HARVEY, W.F. *Debatable Tumours in Human & Animal Pathology.* 1940. Edinburgh. 1st. 124p. dj. A13. $25.00

HARVEY-GIBSON, R.J. *Outlines of the History of Botany.* 1919. London. 274p. xl. B26. $49.00

HARWELL, Richard. *Margaret Mitchell's Gone With the Wind Letters 1936-1949.* 1976. Macmillan. dj. A19. $20.00

HASAN, Sana. *Enemy in the Promised Land.* 1986. Pantheon. 1st. tall 8vo. 335p. cloth. VG/dj. W1. $20.00

HASELTON, Scott E. *Cacti for the Amateur.* 1958 (1938). Pasadena. ils. 132p. brn cloth. B26. $17.50

HASKELL, W.E. *News Print: Origina of Papermaking & Manufacturing...* 1921. Int'l Paper Co. 72p. G. A17. $30.00

HASLUCK, Paul. *Greenhouse & Conservatory Construction & Heating.* 1907. London. Cassell. 160p. VG. A10. $40.00

HASSALL, John. *Our Diary or Teddy & Me.* ca 1905. London. Thomas Nelson. 4to. pict brd. R5. $335.00

HASSE, Carl. *Hand-Atlas der Sensiblen und Motorischen Gebiete...* 1895. Wiesbaden. Bergmann. 36 mc lithos. xl. VG. G1. $150.00

HASSELL, M.P. *Dynamics of Arthropod Predator-Prey Stystems.* 1978. Princeton. 237p. F/wrp. B1. $20.00

HASSIN, George B. *Histopathology of the Peripheral & Central Nervous System.* 1933. Baltimore. Wm Wood. heavy 8vo. 491p. panelled pebbled bl cloth. VG. G1. $50.00

HASSLER, Jon. *Love Hunter.* 1988. Morrow. 1st. NF/dj. M25. $50.00

HASSLER, Jon. *Simon's Night.* 1979. Atheneum. 1st. NF/dj. M25. $75.00

HASSRICK, P.H. *Frederic Remington: Paintings, Drawings & Sculpture...* 1973. Abrams. ils. 218p. F/dj. M4. $45.00

HASTINGS, George T. *Trees of Santa Monica.* 1956. Santa Monica. self pub. 1st. VG/sans. O4. $25.00

HASTINGS, Howard L. *Top Horse of Crecent Ranch.* 1942. Cupples Leon. 1st. VG. O3. $18.00

HASTINGS, Margaret. *Court of Common Pleas in 15th-Century England...* 1971 (1947). Hamden. Archon. facsimile. M11. $45.00

HASTINGS, Max. *Das Reich: March of the 2nd Panzer Division Through France.* 1981. NY. 1st. photos/notes/index. 264p. VG/VG. S16. $30.00

HASTINGS, Max. *Overlord: D-Day, June 6, 1944.* 1984. S&S. 1st Am. 368p. VG/dj. M20. $15.00

HASTINGS, Milo. *City of Endless Night.* 1974 (1920). Hyperion. rpt. F. M2. $35.00

HATA & IZAWA. *Japanese Naval Aces & Fighter Units in World War II.* 1989. Annapolis. photos/index. 442p. VG/VG. S16. $25.00

HATCH, Eric. *Year of the Horse.* 1960. Crown. 1st. VG/VG. O3. $22.00

HATCH, Gardner. *American Ex-Prisoners of War.* 1988. Paducah. 184p. VG. S16. $50.00

HATCHER, Harlan. *Western Reserve: Story of New Connnecticut in Ohio.* 1949. Bobbs Merrill. 1st. 365p. VG+/dj. M20. $25.00

HATFIELD, Bud. *Wealth Within Reach.* 1992. Dallas. World. 1st. inscr. F/F. A23. $36.00

HATFIELD, Mrs. Mark O. *More Remarkable Recipes.* 1970. Beaverton. Criterion. 1st. sgn. F/F. A23. $36.00

HATHAWAY, B.A. *1001 Questions & Answers on Arithmetic.* 1887. Lebanon, OH. 161p. G+. B18. $25.00

HATHAWAY, N. *Unicorn.* 1980. Viking. ils/photos. 191p. F/VG+. M12. $45.00

HATT, D.E. *Sitka Spruce: Songs of Queen Charlotte Islands.* 1919. Vancouver. RP Latta. 51p. VG/prt wrp. P4. $25.00

HATZAN, A. Leon. *True Story of Hiawatha & History of the Six Nation Indians.* 1925. Toronto. 1st. 8vo. ils. 298p. gilt red cloth. F/VG. H3. $85.00

HAUSER, Hillary. *Women in Sports: Scuba Diving.* 1976. NY. Harvey House. 1st. photos. 80p. VG+. A25. $8.00

HAUSTEIN, Erik. *Cactus Handbook.* 1988. Seacaucus, NJ. 320p. F/dj. B26. $22.50

HAVIARAS, Stratis. *Crossing the River.* 1976. Cleveland. 1st. sgn. NF/decor gray wrp. A11. $55.00

HAVIGHURST, Walter. *Voices on the River.* 1964. Macmillan. 1st. ils. 310p. T7. $28.00

HAVILAND, Virginia. *Favorite Fairy Tales Told in Denmark.* 1971. Little Brn. 1st. 90p. F/G. P2. $25.00

HAVILAND, Virginia. *Favorite Fairy Tales Told in France.* 1959. Little Brn. 1st. ils Roger Duvoisin. 92p. NF/VG-. P2. $30.00

HAVILAND. *Samuel Langhorne Clemens: A Centennial for Tom Sawyer.* 1976. ils. 95p. F. A4. $45.00

HAVLICEK & RYAN. *Hondo: Celtic Man in Motion.* 1977. Prentice Hall. 1st. VG/dj. P8. $35.00

HAWES, Charles Boardman. *Dark Frigate.* 1923. Atlantic Monthly. 1st. 8vo. VG+. M5. $75.00

HAWGOOD, J.A. *America's Western Frontiers. Exploration & Settlement...* 1967. NY. 1st. ils. 440p. F/dj. M4. $20.00

HAWKER, C.E. *Chats About Wine.* 1907. London. Daly. 154p. fair. B10. $25.00

HAWKES, Jacquetta. *Province Island.* 1959. RAndom. 1st. NF/dj. M2. $20.00

HAWKES, John. *Adventures in the Alaskan Skin Trade.* 1985. NY. S&S. 1st prt. rem mk. VG/dj. P4. $25.00

HAWKES, John. *Death, Sleep & the Traveler.* 1974. New Directions. 1st. F/dj. D10. $50.00

HAWKES, John. *Passion Artist.* 1979. Harper Row. 1st. F/F. B35. $30.00

HAWKESWORTH, Ed. *Adventurer.* 1788. Dublin. Moore. 4 vol. new/corrected. tall 12mo. tree calf. H13. $325.00

HAWKEY, Raymond. *Evolution.* 1987. Putnam. 1st Am. popup/ils Christos Kondeatis. 4to. F. P2. $35.00

HAWKING, Stephen W. *Brief History of Time: From Big Bang to Black Holes.* 1988. Bantam. 1st. intro Carl Sagan. F/F. B4. $250.00

HAWKINS, Daisy Waterhouse. *Old Point Lace & How to Copy It.* 1878. London. Chatto Windus. 12mo. 17 fld charts. gilt cloth. VG. T10. $175.00

HAWKINS, John. *General History of the Science & Practice of Music.* 1853. London. Novello. New Ed. 3 vol. cloth. VG. T10. $150.00

HAWKINS & WHITE. *Stonehenge Decoded.* 1966 (1965). Doubleday. revised. G/dj. K5. $20.00

HAWLEY, R. *Practice of Silvaculture.* 1946 (1921). VG/torn. E6. $15.00

HAWLEY, Walter A. *Oriental Rugs.* 1913. John Lane. 1st. 11 full-p pl/80 pl/4 maps. 4to. 320p. teg. buckram. T10. $200.00

HAWORTH, P.L. *Trailmakers of the Northwest.* 1921. Harcourt. ils. 277p. cloth. VG. M12. $30.00

HAWTHORNE, Hildegarde. *Life of Thomas Paine.* 1949. Longmans. 1st. VG/dj. W2. $15.00

HAWTHORNE, Julian. *Nathaniel Hawthorne & His Wife.* 1884. Cambridge. Riverside. 1st. 2 vol. 1/350 on lg paper. uncut. M24. $300.00

HAWTHORNE, Nathaniel. *Marble Faun; or, The Romance of Monte Beni.* 1931. LEC. 2 vol. 1/1500. ils/sgn Straus. NF. M19. $50.00

HAWTHORNE, Nathaniel. *Our Old Home: A Series of English Sketches.* 1863. Ticknor Fields. 1st/1st state. gilt brn cloth. NF. M24. $150.00

HAWTHORNE, Nathaniel. *Snow Image: A Childish Miracle.* 1854. NY. James Gregory. thin 12mo. 31p. gilt bl cloth. VG. T10. $300.00

HAWTHORNE, Nathaniel. *Tales of the White Hills.* 1877. Boston. Osgood. 1st thus. gilt gr cloth. M24. $100.00

HAWTHORNE, Nathaniel. *Tanglewood Tales.* 1853. Ticknor Reed Fields. 1st/1st prt. gilt brn cloth (1st bdg). G. M24. $300.00

HAWTHORNE, Nathaniel. *Tanglewood Tales.* 1921. Phil. Penn. 1st thus. ils Sterrett/10 mc pl. 261p. VG. D1. $285.00

HAWTHORNE, Nathaniel. *Twice-Told Tales.* 1842. Boston. James Munroe. 1st thus/1st issue. pub pres. 2 vol. blk cloth. M24. $3,500.00

HAWTHORNE, Nathaniel. *Wonder-Book for Girls & Boys.* 1852. Ticknor Reed Fields. 1st/2nd prt. gilt bl cloth. VG. M24. $500.00

HAWTHORNE, Nathaniel. *Wonder-Book for Girls & Boys.* 1893. Riverside. 1/250. ils Walter Crane. 210p. teg. VG/dj. D1. $700.00

HAXARD, F. *Profitable Pigeon Breeding.* 1922. 1st. ils. VG. E6. $25.00

HAY. *Sambo Sahib: Story of Little Black Sambo & Helen Bannerman.* 1981. 1st. 205p. F/F. A4/D1. $75.00

HAY, Henry. *Cyclopedia of Magic.* 1949. Phil. 498p. VG/dj. S1. $10.00

HAY, Thomas Robson. *Hood's Tennessee Campaign.* 1929. NY. Neale. 1st. 272p. cl. cloth. NF. M8. $125.00

HAYAT, M.A. *Principles & Techniques of Electron Microscopy.* 1978. Van Nostrand. 318p. F/F. B1. $40.00

HAYCRAFT, Howard. *Murder for Pleasure: Life & Times of Detective Story.* 1941. Appleton Century. 1st. NF/G+. N4. $40.00

HAYDEN, Robert. *Kaleidoscope: Poems by American Negro Poets.* 1967. HBW. 1st. VG/dj. M25. $50.00

HAYDEN, Robert. *Night-Blooming Cereus.* 1972. London. 1st. 1/150. sgn Hayden/Paul Breman. F/wrp. w/prospectus. A11. $185.00

HAYDEN & WAKE. *Bonnie & Clyde Book.* 1972. S&S. 69 photos. cloth. F/dj. C9. $45.00

HAYES, Helen. *Gathering of Hope.* 1983. Phil. Fortress. sgn. VG/VG. B11. $18.00

HAYES & YOUNG. *Norman & the Nursery School.* nd (1949). Platt Munk. sm 4to. unp. NF/VG. C14. $18.00

HAYLEY & SMITH. *Life on the Texas Range.* 1952. TX Pr. 1st. 112p. VG/VG case. J2. $235.00

HAYMAKER, Webb. *Bing's Local Diagnosis in Neurological Diseases.* 1956. St Louis. Mosby. 2nd Eng-language. 478p. xl. G1. $65.00

HAYMAKER & WOODHALL. *Peripheral Nerve Injuries: Principles of Diagnosis.* 1945. Phil. Saunders. 1st. 227p. prt gray cloth. G1. $100.00

HAYS, H.R. *Dangerous Sex: Myth of Feminine Evil.* 1964. Putnam. 1st. 316p. VG. A25. $10.00

HAYTHORNTHWAITE, Philip F. *British Infantry of the Napoleonic Wars.* 1987. ils. VG/VG. M17. $25.00

HAYWOOD, Carolyn. *Eddie Makes Music.* 1957. Morrow. 1st. 191p. VG/G+. P2. $30.00

HAYWOOD, Carolyn. *Taffy & Melissa Molasses.* 1969. Morrow. 1st. sgn. F/VG+. P2. $35.00

HAYWOOD, Gar Anthony. *Fear of the Dark.* 1988. St Martin. 1st. author's 1st book. F/NF. A24. $75.00

HAYWOOD, Gar Anthony. *Fear of the Dark.* 1988. St Martin. 1st. sgn. F/NF. M15. $100.00

HAYWOOD, Gar Anthony. *Not Long for This World.* 1990. St Martin. 1st. F/NF. A24/M23. $50.00

HAYWOOD & OSTLER. *Spencer Haywood: Rise, Fall & Recovery.* 1992. Amistad. ARC. F/F. w/promo material. B4. $35.00

HAZARD. *Frontier in American Literature.* 1941 (1927). rpt. 328p. F/VG. A4. $45.00

HAZARD, Caroline. *Brief Pilgrimage in the Holy Land...* 1909. Houghton Mifflin. 1st. 138p. VG. V3. $17.50

HAZARD, Caroline. *Scallop Shell of Quiet.* 1908. Houghton Mifflin. 1st. VG. V3. $14.00

HAZARD, Paul. *Books, Children & Men.* 1972. Boston. Horn Book. 1/3000. 202p. VG/VG. A4. $45.00

HAZELTINE, H.D. *Maitland, Selected Essays.* 1936. Cambridge. gilt bl cloth. VG. M11. $85.00

HAZELTON, Harry. *Ocean Spectres; or, Brides of the Bahamas.* 1863. Boston. Elliott Thomes Talbot. 8vo. bl prt wrp. R12. $75.00

HAZO, Samuel. *Past Won't Stay Behind You. Poems.* 1993. Fayetteville, AR. 1st. F/F. R13. $15.00

HAZZARD, Shirley. *Bay of Noon.* 1970. Little Brn. 1st. F/F. B35. $16.00

HAZZARD, Shirley. *Transit of Venus.* 1980. Viking. 1st. sgn. F/dj. Q1. $50.00

HEACOX, K. *Alaska's National Parks.* 1990. Portland. Graphic Arts. ils Hirschmann. 160p. NF. M12. $30.00

HEAD, Francis. *Life in Germany; or, Visit to Springs of Germany...* 1848. NY. Leavitt Trow. 228p. lacks rear ep. A17. $25.00

HEAD, Henry. *Aphasia & Kindred Disorders of Speech.* 1963 (1926). NY/London. Hafner. rpt. 2 vol. tan cloth. VG/dj. G1. $200.00

HEADLEY & JOHNSON. *HM Stanley's Wonderful Adventures in Africa.* nd (1890). ils. VG. M17. $35.00

HEAL, Edith. *Robin Hood.* 1928. Rand McNally. Windemere series. 1st thus. gilt bl cloth/mc pl. VG. M5. $75.00

HEALD, C.B. *Injuries & Sport.* 1931. London. 1st. 543p. A13. $200.00

HEALY, Jeremiah. *Right to Die.* 1991. Pocket. 1st. F/F. P3. $20.00

HEALY, Jeremiah. *Right to Die.* 1991. Pocket. 1st. sgn. NF/dj. A24. $30.00

HEALY, Jeremiah. *So Like Sleep.* 1987. Harper Row. 1st. sgn. author's 3rd book. F/dj. A24. $40.00

HEALY, Jeremiah. *Staked Goat.* 1986. Harper Row. 1st. F/F. A20. $25.00

HEALY, Jeremiah. *Staked Goat.* 1986. Harper Row. 1st. sgn. author's 2nd book. F/dj. A24. $45.00

HEALY, Raymond. *New Tales of Time & Space.* 1951. Holt. 1st. VG/dj. M2. $12.00

HEANEY, Howell J. *Thirty Years of Bird & Bull: A Bibliography 1958-1988.* 1988. Newtown. Bird & Bull. 1/300. 4to. 106p. w/portfolio. case/box. B24. $400.00

HEANEY, Seamus. *Haw Lantern.* 1987. FSG. 1st. F/F. A24. $30.00

HEANEY, Seamus. *Haw Lantern.* 1987. London. Faber. 1st. inscr/dtd 1988. F/F. w/ephemera. R14. $190.00

HEANEY, Seamus. *Sweeney Ashtray.* 1983. Derry. Field Day Pub. 1st. F/dj. Q1. $200.00

HEARD, H.F. *Lost Cavern.* 1948. Vanguard. 1st. F/dj. M2. $40.00

HEARN, Lafcadio. *Chin Chin Kobakama.* (1905). Tokyo. Hasegawa. 1st. trans Kate James. crepe paper/silk tie/glassine wrp. D1. $300.00

HEARN, Lafcadio. *Exotics & Retrospectives.* 1898. Boston. Little Brn. 1st. teg. olive pict cloth. F. M24. $250.00

HEARN, Lafcadio. *Gleanings in Buddha Fields, Studies of Hand & Soul...* 1897. Houghton Mifflin. 1st. teg. gilt bl cloth. M24. $225.00

HEARN, Lafcadio. *Historical Sketchbook & Guide to New Orleans...* 1885. NY. WH Coleman. 1st/1st prt. map A. bdg A. F/brick-red prt cb wrp. M24. $1,250.00

HEARN, Lafcadio. *In Ghostly Japan.* 1899. Boston. Little Brn. 1st. photos/ils. 241p. VG. W3. $155.00

HEARN, Lafcadio. *Japan's Religions: Shinto & Buddhism.* 1966. New Hyde Park. 1st. 356p. NF/VG. W3. $65.00

HEARN, Lafcadio. *Japan: An Interpretation.* 1904. Macmillan. 1st. ils/notes/index. 541p. VG. W3. $125.00

HEARN, Lafcadio. *Japanese Miscellany.* 1901. Little Brn. 1st. teg. gilt gr cloth. F. M24. $250.00

HEARN, Lafcadio. *Letters From the Raven.* 1970. Brentano. 1st. teg. gilt quarter blk cloth. F. M24. $75.00

HEARN, Lafcadio. *Out of the East, Reveries & Studies in New Japan.* 1895. Houghton Mifflin. 1st/1st prt. silver stp yel cloth. F. M24. $150.00

HEARN, Lafcadio. *Romance of the Milky Way.* 1905. Houghton Mifflin. 1st. gray decor cloth. NF. M24. $125.00

HEARN, Michael. *Wizard of Oz, the Critical Heritage Series.* 1983. 320p. F/wrp. A4. $45.00

HEARTMAN, C. *Cuisinne d'Amour: A Cookbook for Lovers.* 1952 (1942). VG/G. E6. $20.00

HEARTMAN, Charles F. *Census of First Editions & Source Materials by Edgar A Poe.* 1932. Metuchen, NJ. private prt. 1st. 2 vol. gr brd/label. VG. M24. $300.00

HEAT-MOON, William Least. *Blue Highways.* 1982. Atlantic/Little Brn. 1st. NF/VG. H11. $55.00

HEATH, Dunbar Isidore. *Phoenician Inscriptions. Part I.* 1873. London. Quaritich. 1st. 8vo. 103p. VG. W1. $65.00

HEATH, Francis. *Fern Paradise: Plea for Culture of Ferns.* 1880. London. Low Searle. 474p. VG. A10. $50.00

HEATH, Robert Galbraith. *Studies in Schizophrenia: Multidisciplinary Approach...* 1954. Harvard. thick 8vo. 620p. gr cloth. G1. $50.00

HEATH-STUBBS & WRIGHT. *Faber Book of Twentieth Century Verse.* 1953. London. 1st. VG/dj. T9. $20.00

HEATTER, Maida. *Maida Heatter's Book of Desserts.* 1973. 1st. F/G+. E6. $12.00

HEBDEN, Mark. *Killer for the Chairman.* 1972. HBJ. 1st. F/NF. H11. $20.00

HEBDEN, Mark. *Pel Under Pressure.* 1983. NY. Walker. 1st. F/F. H11. $25.00

HECHT, Ben. *Cat That Jumped Out of the Story.* 1947. Winston. 1st. VG-. P2. $50.00

HECHT, Ben. *Kingdom of Evil.* 1924. Covici Friede. 1st. 1/2000. #d. ils Angarola/12 full-p ils. VG. M19. $100.00

HECKSCHER, Morrison. *American Rococo, 1750-1775: Elegance in Ornament.* 1991. NY. Abrams. 4to. 288p. F/wrp. T10. $25.00

HEDIN, Sven. *Riddles of the Gobi Desert.* 1933. nY. ils. 382p. VG+. W3. $96.00

HEDREN, Paul. *With Crook in the Black Hills, Stanley J Morrow's 1876...* 1985. Pruett. 1st. photos/maps. 90p. VG/dj. J2. $225.00

HEDRICK, U.P. *Grapes & Wines From Home Vineyards.* 1946. NY. OUP. 2nd. 326p. VG+/dj. A10. $30.00

HEDRICK, U.P. *History of Agriculture in State of New York.* 1933. Geneva, NY. 1st. ils. 462p. gilt gr cloth. xl. B26. $65.00

HEDRICK, U.P. *Pears of New York.* 1921. JB Lyon/Dept Agric. 29th Annual Report. 80 mc pl. 636p. gilt gr cloth. A10. $185.00

HEGARTY, Reginald B. *Birth of a Whaleship.* 1964. Free Public Lib. sgn. photos/plans/drawings. 159p. T7. $60.00

HEGEMANN, Elizabeth Compton. *Navaho Trading Days.* 1966. NM U. ils/bibliography. 288p. VG. B19. $20.00

HEGGEN, Thomas. *Mister Roberts.* 1946. Houghton Mifflin. 1st. NF/dj. B4. $275.00

HEGI, Ursula. *Floating in My Mother's Palm.* 1990. Poseidon. 1st. NF/F. H11. $50.00

HEGLAR, Mary Schnall. *Grand Prix Champions.* 1973. Bond/Parkhurst. photos. VG. P8. $35.00

HEIDE, Florence Parry. *Treehorn's Treasure.* 1981. Holiday House. 1st. ils Edward Gorey. unp. VG/clip. M20. $60.00

HEIGHWAY, O. *Leila Ada, the Jewish Convert.* 1853. Phil. VG. E6. $60.00

HEILBRUN, Carolyn G. *No Word From Winifred.* 1986. Dutton. 1st. NF/NF. P3. $20.00

HEILBRUN, Carolyn G. *Question of Max.* 1976. Knopf. 1st. NF/dj. M25. $25.00

HEILBRUN, Carolyn G. *Sweet Death, Kind Death.* 1984. Dutton. 1st. F/dj. M25. $15.00

HEILBRUN, Carolyn G. *Writing a Woman's Life.* 1988. Norton. 1st. F/NF. R13. $20.00

HEIM, Katherine. *True Story of Mary, Wife of Lincoln.* 1928. London/NY. A19. $30.00

HEIMER, Mel. *Long Count.* 1969. Atheneum. 1st. photos. VG+/dj. P8. $25.00

HEIN, Wolfgang-Hagen. *Alexander Von Humboldt: Life & Work.* 1987. Ingelheim Rhein. ils. 334p. F/dj. B26. $45.00

HEINDEL, Max. *Rosicrucian Mysteries: The Rosicrucian Fellowship.* 1916. London. 12mo. 228p+14p catalog. gilt/blk pict gr cloth. VG. H3. $45.00

HEINE, Heinrich. *Poems of...* 1957. LEC. 1st thus. 1/1500. intro Louis Untermeyer. ils Fretz Kredel. F/case. Q1. $150.00

HEINE, Heinrich. *Poetry & Prose of Heinrich Heine.* 1948. Citadel. 1st thus. 8vo. 874p. F/dj. H1. $22.50

HEINE, Susanne. *Women & Early Christianity.* 1988. Augsburg. 182p. VG. B29. $8.00

HEINEMANN, Larry. *Close Quarters.* 1977. FSG. 1st. author's 1st book. F/NF. A24. $100.00

HEINEMANN, Larry. *Paco's Story.* 1986. FSG. 1st. F/F. A20. $35.00

HEINIGER, Ernst A. *Grand Canyon.* 1975. WA/NY. Luce. 1st. folio. wht brd. dj+3-D glasses. F7. $60.00

HEINLEIN, Robert A. *Assignment in Eternity.* 1955. London. SF Club. 1st Eng. author's 2nd book. VG/dj. Q1. $200.00

HEINLEIN, Robert A. *Cat Who Walks Through Walls.* 1985. Putnam. 1st. NF/NF. N4. $25.00

HEINLEIN, Robert A. *Door Into Summer.* 1957. Doubleday. 1st. VG/dj. M2. $325.00

HEINLEIN, Robert A. *Farmer in the Sky.* 1962. London. Gollancz. 1st Eng. VG/dj. Q1. $125.00

HEINLEIN, Robert A. *I Will Fear No Evil.* 1970. Putnam. 1st. VG/dj. M2. $95.00

HEINLEIN, Robert A. *Job: A Comedy of Justice.* 1984. Ballantine. 1st. NF/F. A20. $15.00

HEINLEIN, Robert A. *Space Cadet.* 1954 (1948). Scribner. 8vo. ils Clifford N Geary. 252p. VG/G+. T5. $24.00

HEINLEIN, Robert A. *Starship Troopers.* 1959. Putnam. 1st. VG/dj. M2. $500.00

HEINLEIN, Robert A. *Stranger in a Strange Land.* 1961. Putnam. 1st. F/VG. Q1. $750.00

HEINLEIN, Robert A. *Time for the Stars.* 1956. Scribner. 1st. VG/dj. M2. $75.00

HEINRICH, B. *Bumble-Bee Economics.* 1979. Harvard. sgn pres. ils/tables. 245p. pict cloth. F/NF. M12. $30.00

HEINRICH, Willi. *Cross of Iron.* 1956. Bobbs Merrill. 1st. VG+/dj. A20. $35.00

HEINS, Henry H. *Golden Anniversary Bibliography.* 1964. Donald Grant. revised. 8vo. 418p. F/dj. B24. $200.00

HEINSOHN & LEWIN. *Heinsohn Don't You Ever Smile?* 1976. Doubleday. 1st. VG/G+. P8. $15.00

HEINTZ, Wulff D. *Double Stars.* 1978. Dordrecht, Holland. Reidel. revised. 174p. K5. $20.00

HEISENBERG, Werner. *Cosmic Radiation.* 1946. NY. Dover. 192p. NF. K3. $50.00

HEISENBERG, Werner. *Nuclear Physics.* 1953. NY. Philosophical Lib. 1st Eng language. 8vo. 225p. VG/dj. K3. $25.00

HEISENFELT, Kathryn. *Shirley Temple & the Spirit of Dragonwood.* 1945. Whitman. 248p. cloth. VG/dj. M20. $25.00

HEITLER, W. *Quantum Theory of Radiation.* 1966. Oxford/Clarendon. 3rd. 8vo. 430p. K3. $20.00

HEIZER, Robert. *Sources of Stones Used in Prehistoric Mesoamerican Sites.* 1976. Ramona. Bellena. rpt. maps/photos. F3. $20.00

HEKKING, Johanna M. *Pigtails.* 1937. Stokes. 1st. ils Molly Castle. VG/VG. D1. $60.00

HELD, Peter; see Vance, Jack.

HELL, Richard. *Across the Years.* 1991. Amsterdam. Soyo. 1/500. sgn. 12mo. w/CD. M/wooden box. B4. $150.00

HELL, Richard. *Go Now.* 1996. NY. Scribner. 1st. sgn. author's 1st novel. F/NF. R16. $40.00

HELL, Richard. *Go Now.* 1996. Scribner. 1st. sgn. F/F. B4. $100.00

HELLER, Joseph. *God Knows.* 1984. Franklin Lib. 1st/ltd. sgn. full leather. F. Q1. $75.00

HELLER, Joseph. *God Knows.* 1984. Knopf. 1st. F/VG+. A20. $25.00

HELLER, Joseph. *Picture This.* 1988. Putnam. 1st. F/F. T12. $25.00

HELLER, Joseph. *Something Happened.* 1974. Knopf. ARC. author's 2nd novel. RS. F/F. w/promo material. B4. $125.00

HELLER, Joseph. *Something Happened.* 1974. Knopf. 1st. F/F. N4. $40.00

HELLMAN, Lillian. *Maybe.* 1980. Little Brn. 1st. VG+/dj. A20. $20.00

HELLMAN, Lillian. *Scoundrel Time.* 1976. Little Brn. 1st. F/F. B35. $30.00

HELLMAYR, Charles E. *Birds of the James Simpson-Roosevelts Asiatic Expedition.* 1929. Chicago. Field Mus Natural Hist Pub 263. 144p. VG. S15. $15.00

HELLSTROM & RYWELL. *Smith & Wesson: Story of the Revolver.* (1953). Harriman, TN. Pioneer. stated 1st. 136p. VG. H7. $12.50

HELM, MacKinlay. *Angel Mo' & Her Son, Roland Hayes.* 1942. Little Brn. 1st. VG. M25. $35.00

HELME & PAUL. *Jerry: Story of an Exmoor Pony.* 1930. Scribner. 1st Am. VG. O3. $48.00

HELMS, Mary. *Middle America.* 1975. NY. Prentice Hall. 1st. 367p. dj. F3. $30.00

HELPER, Hinton Rowan. *Impending Crises of the South.* (1860). NY. AB Burdick. 50th thousand. 418p. cloth. VG. M20. $75.00

HELPER, Hinton Rowan. *Three Americas Railway.* 1881. St Louis. WS Bryan. 1st. 8vo. 473p. cloth. xl. M1. $125.00

HELPRIN, Mark. *Dove of the East.* 1975. Knopf. 1st. author's 1st book. NF/dj. D10/Q1. $75.00

HELPRIN, Mark. *Soldier of the Great War.* 1991. HBJ. 1st. F/F. A24. $35.00

HELPRIN, Mark. *Swan Lake.* 1989. Houghton Mifflin/Ariel. 1st. sm 4to. 81p. F/F. A24. $35.00

HELPRIN, Mark. *Winter's Tale.* 1983. HBJ. 1st. author's 4th book/2nd novel. F/NF. D10. $35.00

HELWEG-LARSEN, Kjeld. *Columbus Never Came.* 1964. London. Jarrolds. 2nd. inscr. 240p. map ep. dj. F3. $20.00

HEMINGWAY, Ernest. *By-Line: Ernest Hemingway: Selected Articles...* 1967. NY. 1st. edit Wm White. F/F. A11. $55.00

HEMINGWAY, Ernest. *Dangerous Summer.* 1985. London. Hamish Hamilton. 1st. F/dj. Q1. $50.00

HEMINGWAY, Ernest. *Dangerous Summer.* 1985. Scribner. 1st. F/clip. A24. $35.00

HEMINGWAY, Ernest. *Dateline: Toronto.* 1985. NY. 1st. edit Wm White. F/F. A11. $45.00

HEMINGWAY, Ernest. *Death in the Afternoon.* 1932. Scribner. 1932A/1st. G+/G-. B5. $250.00

HEMINGWAY, Ernest. *Farewell to Arms.* 1947. Paris. Albatross. 1st. VG-/dj. A11. $55.00

HEMINGWAY, Ernest. *Fifth Column.* 1969. Scribner. 1st thus. F/dj. Q1. $125.00

HEMINGWAY, Ernest. *For Whom the Bell Tolls.* 1940. 1st/1st state. VG/G. M19. $100.00

HEMINGWAY, Ernest. *For Whom the Bell Tolls.* 1940. Scribner. 1st/1st prt. beige cloth. F/2nd state dj. M24. $275.00

HEMINGWAY, Ernest. *For Whom the Bell Tolls.* 1942. LEC. 1/1500. ils/sgn Lynd Ward. NF/damaged box. B2. $125.00

HEMINGWAY, Ernest. *Islands in the Stream.* 1970. Scribner. 1st. F/F clip. D10. $60.00

HEMINGWAY, Ernest. *Islands in the Stream.* 1970. Scribner. 1st. VG/NF. A24. $35.00

HEMINGWAY, Ernest. *Moveable Feast.* 1964. NY. Scribner. 1st. photos. NF/dj. Q1. $75.00

HEMINGWAY, Ernest. *Moveable Feast.* 1964. Scribner. 1st. F/dj. D10. $175.00

HEMINGWAY, Ernest. *Moveable Feast.* 1964. Scribner. 1st. VG/VG. B5. $50.00

HEMINGWAY, Ernest. *Sun Also Rises.* 1926. Scribner. 1st/1st prt/1st issue. blk cloth/gold labels. F. M24. $850.00

HEMMING, John. *Red Gold: Conquest of the Brazilian Indians, 1500-1760.* 1978. Harvard. 1st. tall 8vo. 677p. as new/dj. H1. $25.00

HEMMING, John. *Search for El Dorado.* (1978). London. Micheal Joseph. 1st. 4to. 223p. dj. F3. $25.00

HEMPEL, Amy. *At the Gates of the Animal Kingdom.* 1990. Knopf. 1st. F/NF. R13. $20.00

HEMPEL, Amy. *Reasons to Live.* 1985. Knopf. 1st. author's 1st book. F/F. M25. $35.00

HEMSLEY, H. *Rock & Alpine Gardens.* 1910. London. Simpkin. 2nd. 92p. brd. A10. $32.00

HENDERSON, Alice Corbin. *Turquoise Trail.* 1928. Houghton Mifflin. 1st. VG/G. L3. $100.00

HENDERSON, Andrew. *Field Guide to the Palms of the Americas.* 1995. Princeton. ils/photos/maps. M. B26. $75.00

HENDERSON, Frank D. *Official Roster of Soldiers of American Revolution...* 1929. Columbus. 447p. buckram. VG. B18. $35.00

HENDERSON, Mariana. *DG Rossetti.* 1973. London/NY. Academy/St Martin. 104p. brd. dj. D2. $35.00

HENDERSON, Mrs. L.R. *Magic Aeroplane.* (1911). Reilly Britton. ils Emile a Nelson. 96p. G/torn. D1. $185.00

HENDERSON, Peter. *Garden & Farm Topics.* 1884. Henderson. 1st. 244p. A10. $28.00

HENDERSON, Peter. *Gardening for Profit.* 1893. Orange Judd. revised. 376p. VG. A10. $28.00

HENDERSON, Peter. *Gardening for Profit.* 1991. Chillicothe, IL. Am Botanist. rpt. 496p. M. A10. $26.00

HENDERSON, Peter. *Practical Floriculture, Cultivating Plants...* 1869. NY. inscr. 249p. VG. B14. $55.00

HENDERSON, Peter. *Practical Floriculture, Cultivating Plants...* 1869. NY. 1st. VG. E6. $25.00

HENDERSON, Randall. *Sun, Sand & Solitude.* 1968. Los Angeles. 1st. tan cloth. VG+. F7. $40.00

HENDERSON, W. *Modern Domestic Receipt Book.* 1857. ils. G+. E6. $135.00

HENDERSON, Zenna. *Pilgrimage: Book of the People.* 1978. Gregg. 1st thus. F. M2. $35.00

HENNESSEY, William J. *Russel Wright, American Designer.* 1983. MIT Pr. 2nd. 1985. 96p. F. H1. $35.00

HENRI, Florette. *Black Migration: Movement North 1900-1920.* 1975. Anchor/Doubleday. 1st. 419p. F/NF. B4. $65.00

HENRI, Raymond. *Iwo Jima: Springboard to Final Victory.* 1945. NY. 96p. VG/VG. S16. $75.00

HENRIQUES, H.S.Q. *Jews & the English Law.* 1974 (1908). Clifton. Augustus M Kelley. facsimile. M11. $75.00

HENRY, B.C. *Cross & the Dragon.* 1885. NY. Randolph. 2nd. ils/map. 482p. VG. W3. $110.00

HENRY, Charles. *Hostage.* 1959. Random. 1st. 237p. VG/dj. M20. $12.00

HENRY, Clark W. *Cross & the Eternal Order: A Study of Atonement...* 1944. Macmillan. 1st. fwd CH Dodd. 319p. xl. VG. B29. $14.00

HENRY, Gordon Jr. *Light People.* 1994. Norman. 1st. Am Indian Literature Critical Studies series. F/F. L3. $35.00

HENRY, H.M. *Police Control of the Slave in South Carolina.* 1914. Emory, VA. 1st. 216p. VG. B4. $50.00

HENRY, Marguerite. *Birds at Home.* 1942. Donohue. 12 full-p pl. NF. A17. $20.00

HENRY, Marguerite. *Born to Trot.* 1950. Rand McNally. 1st. sgn. F/VG. C8. $65.00

HENRY, Marguerite. *Dear Readers & Riders.* 1969. Rand McNally. 1st. VG. O3. $35.00

HENRY, Marguerite. *Justin Morgan Had a Horse.* 1945. Chicago. Wilcox Follett. 1st. folio. F/NF. B4. $175.00

HENRY, Marguerite. *Justin Morgan Had a Horse.* 1945. Wilcox Follett. 1st. ils Wesley Dennis. 4to. VG/dj. from $50 to $65.00

HENRY, Marguerite. *Misty of Chincoteague.* 1947. Rand McNally. 1st. ils Wesley Dennis. NF/G+. C8. $65.00

HENRY, Marguerite. *Stormy, Misty's Foal.* 1963. Rand McNally. 1st. ils Wesley Dennis. NF/VG. M19. $35.00

HENRY, Marguerite. *Stormy, Misty's Foal.* 1963. Rand McNally. 1st. lg 8vo. F/NF. C8. $50.00

HENRY, R.S. *Story of the Confederacy.* 1931. 1st. ils/index/map ep. 514p. O8. $18.50

HENRY, Samuel. *Foxhunting Is Different.* 1938. Derrydale. 1/950. ils Paul Brown. VG. T10. $100.00

HENRY, Will. *San Juan Hill.* 1962. Random. 1st. F/VG. B4. $100.00

HENRY, Will. *Sons of the Western Frontier.* 1967. Chilton. 2nd. F/VG+. T11. $20.00

HENRY VII (King of England). *Assertio Septem Sacramentorum Adversus Mart.* 1562. Paris. Desboys. 16mo. early calf. R12. $875.00

HENSEL, W.U. *Christina Riots & the Treason Trials of 1851...* 1911. Lancaster, PA. New Era. 2nd/revised. 4to. 158p. VG+. B4. $500.00

HENSHALL, J.A. *Bass, Pike, Perch & Other Game Fishes of America.* 1923. Stewart Kidd. 1st/3rd prt. 410p. VG. W2. $120.00

HENSHALL, J.A. *Camping & Cruising in Florida.* 1884. Cincinnati. R Clarke. 8vo. ils. 248p. pict cloth. G. M12. $95.00

HENSHAW, Henry W. *Book of Birds.* 1921. NGS. ils LA Fuertes. 195p. VG. S15. $20.00

HENSLEY, Joe L. *Fort's Law.* 1987. Doubleday. 1st. NF/NF. M22. $10.00

HENSLOW, T. Geoffrey. *Garden Instruction.* 1940. London. Quality. 1st. 324p. VG. A10. $25.00

HENSLOW, T. Geoffrey. *Gardens of Fragrance.* 1928. London. Warne. 224p. dj. A10. $28.00

HENSON, Matthew A. *Negro Explorer at the North Pole.* 1912. NY. Stokes. 8vo. 200p. bl cloth. P4. $750.00

HENTHOFF, Nat. *Boston Boy.* 1986. KNopf. 1st. F/F. A20. $20.00

HENTY, G.A. *In the Heart of the Rockies.* nd. London. Foulsham Henty Lib. 12mo. 223p. bl cloth. NF/torn. F7. $20.00

HENTZ, Caroline Lee. *Planter's Northern Bride.* 1854. Phil. TB Peterson. 8vo. 579p. cloth. VG. K7. $45.00

HEPBURN, Andrew. *Great Houses of American History.* 1974. Bramhall. 1st. 244p. VG. A8. $20.00

HEPBURN, Katherine. *Making of African Queen.* 1987. Knopf. 1st. F/F. A20. $25.00

HEPPER, F. Nigel. *Royal Botanic Gardens, Kew.* 1982. Owings Mills, MD. ils. 195p. F/dj. B26. $24.00

HERBERT, A.G. *Throne of David: Study of Fulfillment of Old Testament...* 1956. Faber. 275p. G/torn. B29. $9.50

HERBERT, Frank. *Heretics of Dune.* 1984. Putnam. ltd ed. 480p. VG. W2. $40.00

HERBERT, Frank. *Nebula Winners Fifteen.* 1981. Harper. 1st. F/dj. M2. $25.00

HERBERT, Frank. *White Plague.* 1982. Putnam. 1st. F/dj. M2. $15.00

HERBERT, H.W. *Captains of the Old World.* 1852. Scribner. 8vo. 364p. bl brd. G. K7. $40.00

HERBERT, H.W. *Frank Forester's Fish & Fishing of the United States...* 1850. NY. Stringer Townsend. 1st Am. 43 pl. 359+16p. gilt red cloth. NF. H7. $125.00

HERBERT, James. *Sepulchre.* 1988. Putnam. 1st Am. NF/dj. M2. $15.00

HERBERT & RANSOM. *Jesus Incident.* 1979. Putnam. ne. 405p. VG/VG. W2. $30.00

HERFORD, Oliver. *Child's Primer of Natural History.* 1899. Scribner. 1st. all edges tinted. pict brd. R5. $150.00

HERFORD, Oliver. *Most Timid in the Land.* 1992. SF. Chronicle. 2nd. thin obl 4to. ils/sgn Sylvia Long. F/dj. T10. $50.00

HERGE. *Adventures of Tintin, Flight 714.* 1968. Methuen. 1st ed. hc glazed pict brd. VG. M5. $40.00

HERGESHIMER, Joseph. *Balisand.* 1924. Knopf. 1st. F/VG+. B4. $150.00

HERGESHIMER, Joseph. *Cytherea.* 1922. London. Heinemann. 1st Eng. F/F. B4. $135.00

HERLIHY, James Leo. *Midnight Cowboy.* 1965. S&S. 1st. F/F. B4. $150.00

HERM, Gerhard. *Celts: People Who Came Out of the Darkness.* 1976. St Martin. 1st Am. ils/maps. 312p. as new/F. H1. $15.00

HERMANN, Paul. *Conquest by Man.* 1954. Harper. 1st. 455p. dj. F3. $15.00

HERR, Charlotte B. *Wise Mamma Goose.* 1913. Volland. early. ils Frances Beem. 12mo. NF. M5. $55.00

HERR, Michael. *Dispatches.* 1977. Knopf. 1st. author's 1st book. NF/clip. D10. $90.00

HERR, Michael. *Winchell.* 1990. Knopf. 1st. F/F. A20. $25.00

HERRESHOFF, L. Francis. *Sensible Cruising Designs.* 1973. diagrams/notes. VG/VG. M17. $45.00

HERRIES, J.W. *Storm Island & Other Stories.* 1947. London. 1st. inscr. F/NF. M2. $35.00

HERRIMAN, G. *Krazy Kat.* 1946. NY. Holt. 1st. ils. VG/worn. B5. $85.00

HERRING, D.W. *Lure of the Clock.* 1963. NY. Crown. ils. 121p. K3. $25.00

HERRIOT, James. *James Herriot's Cat Stories.* 1994. St Martin. 1st. 161p. F/F. W2. $15.00

HERRON, Carolivia. *Thereafter Johnnie.* 1991. Random. 1st. author's 1st novel. NF/NF. R13. $25.00

HERSCHEL, John F.W. *Outlines of Astronomy.* 1881 (1849). London. Longman Gr. new ed. xl. rebound. K5. $100.00

HERSEY, John. *Call.* 1985. Knopf. 1st. F/F. B4. $45.00

HERSEY, John. *Fling.* 1990. Knopf. 1st. F/F. B4. $45.00

HERSEY, John. *Hiroshima.* 1946. Knopf. VG/worn. K3. $20.00

HERSEY, John. *Hiroshima.* 1946. Knopf. 1st. NF/VG. M19. $35.00

HERSEY, John. *Hiroshima: Story of Six Human Beings Who Survived...* 1946. NY. 118p. VG/G. S16. $17.50

HERSEY, John. *Wall.* 1957. LEC. 1st thus. 1/1500. ils/sgn Raymond Holden. wht buckram. F/case. Q1. $75.00

HERSEY, John. *War Lover.* 1959. Knopf. 1st. G/VG. B35. $18.00

HERSHEY, Scott F. *Science of National Life...Wealth of Nations.* 1885. Chicago. 547p. full calf. A17. $20.00

HERT, C. *Tracking the Big Cats.* 1955. Caxton. ils/photos/map ep. cloth. VG. M12. $45.00

HERTER, Christian A. *Diagnosis of Organic Nervous Diseases.* 1892. Putnam. 12mo. 628p. gr cloth. xl. VG. G1. $50.00

HERTER & HERTER. *Bull Cook & Authentic Historical Recipes & Practices.* 1963 (1960). VG. E6. $20.00

HERTRICH, William. *Palms & Cycads: Their Culture in Southern California...* 1960 (1951). San Marino, CA. 2nd. ils. VG/dj. B26. $59.00

HERTZLER, Arthur. *Surgical Operations With Local Anesthesia.* 1912. NY. 1st. 209p. A13. $100.00

HERTZLER, Arthur. *Surgical Pathology of the Diseases of the Neck.* 1937. Phil. 1st. 237p. A13. $40.00

HERTZLER, Arthur. *Ventures in Science of a Country Surgeon.* 1944. private prt. 1st. 304p. A13. $35.00

HERVEY, John. *American Harness Racing. Book I.* 1948. NY. Hartenstein. 206p. VG. O3. $58.00

HERZOG, Arthur. *IQ 83.* 1978. S&S. 1st. NF/F. H11. $20.00

HERZOG, Arthur. *Make Us Happy.* 1978. Crowell. 1st. F/rpr. B35. $25.00

HERZOG, Yaacov. *People That Dwells Alone.* 1975. Sanhedrin. 283p. VG/G. S3. $23.00

HESS, H.H. *Stillwater Igneous Complex, Montana.* 1960. GSA Memoir 80. 6 pocket maps. 230p. NF. D8. $22.00

HESS, Joan. *Much Ado in Maggody.* 1989. St Martin. 1st. F/F. M22. $30.00

HESS, Joan. *O Little Town of Maggody.* 1993. Dutton. 1st. sgn. F/F. A23. $38.00

HESSLER & PISCO. *Lehrbuch der Technischen Physik.* 1866. Wein. Wilhelm Braumiller. ils. half leather/marbled brd. K3. $75.00

HESTON, Charlton. *Actor's Journals 1956-1976.* 1978. Dutton. 1st. sgn. G/G clip. A23. $25.00

HESTON, Charlton. *Beijing Diary.* 1990. S&S. 1st. sgn. A23. $36.00

HETH, Edward Harris. *Wonderful World of Cooking.* 1956. S&S. VG/dj. A16. $16.00

HETRICH, William. *Camellias in the Huntington Gardens.* 1954-59. San Marino. Huntington Botanical Gardens. 1st. 3 vol. ils. F/djs. T10. $150.00

HETRICH, William. *Camellias in the Huntington Gardens.* 1954-59. San Marino. Huntington Lib. 3 vol. VG/djs. A22. $95.00

HEUMAN, William. *Girl From Frisco.* 1955. Morrow. 1st. F/NF. B4. $65.00

HEUVELMANS, B. *In the Wake of Sea Serpents.* 1968. NY. ils/map. 645p. F/VG. M12. $37.50

HEWARD, Constance. *Ameliaranne Goes Touring.* 1941. London. Harrap. 1st. ils Pearse. 8vo. cloth. dj. R5. $125.00

HEWETT, Edgar L. *Ancient Life in the American Southwest.* 1930. Bobbs Merrill. 1st. 392p. map ep. bl cloth. VG/G+. F7. $45.00

HEWETT, Edgar L. *Chaco Canyon & Its Monuments.* 1936. Albuquerque. 1st. VG/G. B5. $55.00

HEWETT & MAUZY. *Landmarks of New Mexico.* 1940. Albuquerque. 1st. VG/G. B5. $55.00

HEWETT-BATES, J.S. *Bookbinding for Schools.* 1935. Peoria. Manual Arts. 2nd revised. VG/dj. K3. $20.00

HEWINS, Jack. *Borleske: Never Far From Hope.* 1966. Superior. 1st. photos. VG+/VG. P8. $20.00

HEWITT, Foster. *Hello Canada! And Hockey Fans in the United States.* 1950. Thomas Allen. 1st. VG. P8. $25.00

HEWLETT, Maurice. *Earthwork Out of Tuscany.* 1911. Portland. 1st. 1/700. VG/dj. T9. $15.00

HEY, William. *Practical Observations in Surgery, Illustrated...* 1805. Phil. 1st Am. 332p. A13. $300.00

HEYDT, Henry J. *Studies in Jewish Evangelism.* 1951. Am Brd Missions to Jews. 237p. VG/G. S3. $25.00

HEYER, Georgette. *April Lady.* 1957. Putnam. 1st Am. 254p. VG/dj. M20. $45.00

HEYER, Georgette. *Bath Tangle.* 1955. Putnam. 1st. 312p. VG/dj. M20. $45.00

HEYER, Georgette. *Death in the Stocks.* 1970. Dutton. 1st Am. 263p. cloth. VG/dj. M20. $25.00

HEYER, Georgette. *My Lord John.* 1975. Dutton. 1st. VG/VG. P3. $20.00

HEYER, Georgette. *Simon & the Coldheart.* 1979. Dutton. VG/VG. P3. $20.00

HEYER, Georgette. *Sylvester.* 1957. Putnam. 1st. 309p. VG/dj. M20. $45.00

HEYERDAHL, Thor. *American Indians in the Pacific: Theory Behind Kon-Tiki...* 1953. Rand McNally. 4to. 820p. brn cloth. VG. K7. $150.00

HEYLINGER, William. *Don Strong: Patrol Leader.* 1918. Grosset Dunlap. 287p. VG/dj. M20. $22.50

HEYMANS, Margriet. *Cats & Dolls.* 1976. Addison-Wesley. 1st. unp. VG/dj. M20. $25.00

HEYWARD, DuBose. *Porgy.* 1925. 1st. gilt blk cloth. VG. S13. $50.00

HIAASEN, Carl. *Double Whammy.* 1987. NY. Putnam. 1st. VG+/VG. R16. $45.00

HIAASEN, Carl. *Double Whammy.* 1987. Putnam. 1st. F/F. M22. $70.00

HIAASEN, Carl. *Native Tongue.* 1991. Knopf. 1st. NF/NF. A20. $35.00

HIAASEN, Carl. *Stormy Weather.* 1995. Knopf. 1st. sgn. F/F. A23. $40.00

HIAASEN, Carl. *Strip Tease.* 1993. Knopf. 1st. F/F. from $25 to $30.00

HIAASEN, Carl. *Tourist Season.* 1986. Putnam. 1st. inscr. F/dj. M15. $175.00

HIBBARD & HULME. *Familiar Garden Flowers.* 1900. London. Cassell. 5 vol. A10. $125.00

HICHENS, Robert. *Barbary Sheep. A Novel.* 1907. Harper. 1st. ils. 253p. VG. W1. $18.00

HICHENS, Robert. *Black Spaniel.* 1905. Stokes. 1st. VG. M2. $25.00

HICKERSON, Thomas F. *Highway Curves & Earthwork.* 1926. McGraw Hill. aeg. 12mo. 382p. limp bdg. A8. $12.00

HICKES, John Edwards. *Adventures of a Tramp Printer.* 1950. KS City. 1st. 285p. VG/G. B5. $40.00

HICKEY, D.R. *War of 1812: Forgotten Conflict.* 1989. IL U. 1st. ils/maps. F/dj. M4. $30.00

HICKEY & SMITH. *Operation Avalanche: Salerno Landings.* 1983. NY. ils/maps. 379p. VG/VG. S16. $25.00

HICKS, Elias. *Journal of the Life & Religious Labours.* 1832. NY. Isaac T Hopper. 1st. 451p. worn leather. V3. $55.00

HICKS, Granville. *Only One Storm.* 1942. Macmillan. 1st. author's 1st novel. F/F. B4. $125.00

HICKS, Granville. *Small Town.* 1946. Macmillan. 1st. F/NF. B4. $85.00

HICKS, Jimmie. *WW Robinson: Biography & Bibliography.* 1970. Zamarano Club. 1st. ils/bibliography. 83p. F. B19. $75.00

HICKS, Sam. *Desert Plants & People.* 1966. San Antonio. Naylor. 1st. 8vo. cloth. G+/dj. A22. $30.00

HIEB, David. *Fort Laramie, National Monument, Wyoming.* 1954. GPO. 1st. photos/maps. VG. J2. $25.00

HIELSCHER, Kurt. *Italia Natura ed Arte.* 1925. Milan. 304 full-p sephia photos. gilt cloth. VG. A17. $25.00

HIEMEYER, Fritz. *Flora Von Augsburg.* 1978. Augsburg. Naturwissenschaftlicher. 8vo. cloth. VG. A22. $15.00

HIGGERS, Jim. *Adventures of Theodore...* 1901. Chicago. 1st. 210p. pict cloth. G+. B18. $95.00

HIGGINS, D.S. *Rider Haggard: A Biography.* 1983. Stein Day. 1st Am. NF/dj. M2. $35.00

HIGGINS, Ethel Bailey. *Our Native Cacti.* 1931. NY. ils. 170p. pict cloth. B26. $20.00

HIGGINS, George V. *Cogan's Trade.* 1974. Knopf. 1st. F/F. N4. $25.00

HIGGINS, George V. *Defending Billy Ryan.* 1992. Holt. 1st. F/F. B4. $45.00

HIGGINS, George V. *Friends of Eddie Coyle.* 1972. Knopf. 1st. bl cloth (assumed 2nd issue). F/dj. Q1. $40.00

HIGGINS, George V. *Friends of Richard Nixon.* 1975. Atlantic/Little Brn. 1st. NF/NF. M22. $15.00

HIGGINS, George V. *On Writing.* 1990. Holt. 1st. F/F. M22. $15.00

HIGGINS, George V. *Patriot Game.* 1982. Knopf. 1st. sgn. NF/VG. R14. $35.00

HIGGINS, George V. *Trust.* 1989. Holt. 1st. NF/VG+. A20. $20.00

HIGGINS, George V. *Wonderful Years, Wonderful Years.* 1988. Holt. 1st. F/NF. M22. $10.00

HIGGINS, J.W. *Guide to Geology & Oil Fields of Los Angeles...* 1958. Los Angeles. 2 pocket maps. 204p. NF. D8. $40.00

HIGGINS, Jack; see Patterson, Harry.

HIGGINSON, A.H. *Foxhunting: Theory & Practice.* 1948. photos. VG/VG. M17. $25.00

HIGGINSON, John. *Working Class in the Making: Belgian Colonial Labor Policy.* 1989. WI U. 1st. as new. V4. $12.50

HIGGINSON, T.W. *Army Life in a Black Regiment.* 1935. MI U. 235p. F/G. M4. $35.00

HIGHAM, Charles. *Adventures of Conan Doyle.* 1976. NY. Norton. 1st. F/NF. M23. $25.00

HIGHAM, Charles. *Adventures of Conan Doyle: Life of Creator Sherlock Holmes.* 1976. Norton. 1st?/3rd prt. VG/NF. R10. $10.00

HIGHAM, Charles. *Elizabeth & Phillip.* 1991. Doubleday. ne. F/NF. W2. $25.00

HIGHSMITH, Patricia. *Found in the Street.* 1986. London. Heinemann. 1st. F/dj. Q1. $60.00

HIGHSMITH, Patricia. *Ripley Under Ground.* 1970. Doubleday. 1st. NF/VG. M22. $20.00

HIGHTOWER, Florence. *Ghost of Follonsbee's Folly.* (1958). Houghton Mifflin. 7th. 8vo. 218p. G+. T5. $12.00

HIGHWATER, Jamake. *Anpao: An American Indian Odyssey.* 1977. Lippincott. 1st. author's 4th book using Indian name. F/NF. L3. $100.00

HIGHWATER, Jamake. *Fodor's Indian America.* 1975. NY. McKay. 1st/only. NF/NF. L3. $100.00

HIGHWATER, Jamake. *I Wear the Morning Star.* 1986. Harper Row. 1st. F/F clip. L3. $65.00

HIJIKATA, Hisakatsu. *Society & Life in Palau.* 1993. Tokyo. Sasakawa Peace Found. 1st. ils. 273p. F. W3. $38.00

HIJORTSBERG, William. *Falling Angel.* 1978. Harper. 1st. VG/dj. M2. $50.00

HIJUELOS, Oscar. *Mambo Kings Play Songs of Love.* 1989. FSG. 1st. inscr. F/dj. B3. $80.00

HIJUELOS, Oscar. *Mr Ives' Christmas.* 1995. Harper Collins. 1st. sgn. F/F. A23. $40.00

HIJUELOS, Oscar. *Our House in the Last World.* 1983. NY. Persea. 1st. author's 1st book. F/F. D10. $185.00

HIJUELOS, Oscar. *Our House in the Last World.* 1983. Persea. 1st. sgn. F/F. B4. $250.00

HILBERG, Raul. *Destruction of the European Jews.* 1961. London. WH Allen. 788p. VG/G+. S3. $35.00

HILEGAS, Mark. *Future as Nightmare: HG Wells & the Anti-Utopians.* 1967. Oxford. 1st. NF/dj. M2. $35.00

HILL, Geoffrey. *Tenebrae.* 1978. London. 1st. sgn. F/NF. A11. $125.00

HILL, George. *Yearbook of the Dept of Agriculture 1899.* 1900. GPO. 880p. cloth. A10. $30.00

HILL, Grace Brooks. *Corner House Girls' Odd Find (#5).* 1916. Barse Hopkins. lists 8 titles. 252p. VG+/dj. M20. $30.00

HILL, Herbert. *Anger & Beyond: Negro Writer in the United States.* 1966. Harper Row. 1st. F/F. M25. $45.00

HILL, Ingrid. *Dixie Church Interstate Blues.* 1989. Viking. ARC. author's 1st book. RS. F/F. w/promo material. R13. $25.00

HILL, John; see Koontz, Dean R.

HILL, Joseph. *Bookmakers of Old Birmingham.* 1971. Burt Franklin. rpt. ils. VG. K3. $15.00

HILL, Ray. *OJ Simpson.* 1975. Random. revised/1st prt. phtos. F/VG+. P8. $30.00

HILL, Reginald. *No Man's Land.* 1985. London. 1st. VG/VG. T9. $45.00

HILL, Sallie F. *Progressive Farmer's Southern Cookbook.* 1961. Progressive Farmer. 470p. G. B10. $12.00

HILL, W.E. *Among Us Cats.* 1926. Harper Row. 1st. mtd mc frontis/full-p ils. VG/poor. P2. $125.00

HILL & WHEELER. *Grassland Seeds.* 1957. Van Nostrand. 734p. VG/dj. A10. $30.00

HILLARY, Louise. *Yak for Christmas.* 1968. Hodder Stoughton. 1st. sgn pres. ils/map ep. 208p. VG/dj. W3. $54.00

HILLER, Brett. *Voyages of Torres: Discovery of Southern Coastline..* 1980. St Lucia. U Queensland. 194p. VG/dj. P4. $50.00

HILLER, L. *Surgery Through the Ages: Pictorial Chronicle.* 1944. NY. 1st. 177p. A13. $75.00

HILLER, Mary. *Automata & Mechanical Toys.* 1988. London. Bloomsbury. 200p. NF/dj. K3. $25.00

HILLERMAN, Tony. *Best of the West.* 1991. Harper Collins. 1st. sgn. F/F. A23/B3. $60.00

HILLERMAN, Tony. *Blessingway.* 1990. Armchair Detective. 1st. sgn. F/F. A23. $50.00

HILLERMAN, Tony. *Blessingway.* 1970. Harper Row. 1st. F/NF. M15. $1,250.00

HILLERMAN, Tony. *Coyote Waits.* 1990. Harper Row. 1st. sgn. F/F/case. B3. $350.00

HILLERMAN, Tony. *Dance Hall of the Dead.* 1991. Armchair Detective. 1st trade. M/dj. A18. $25.00

HILLERMAN, Tony. *Fly on the Wall.* 1971. Harper Row. 1st. F/dj. M15. $800.00

HILLERMAN, Tony. *Great Taos Bank Robbery.* 1973. Albuquerque. NM U. 1st/1 of 2 states. gray bdg. F/dj. M15. $500.00

HILLERMAN, Tony. *Joe Leaphorn Mysteries.* 1989. Harper Row. Omnibus ed. F/dj. M15. $35.00

HILLERMAN, Tony. *New Mexico, Rio Grande & Other Essays.* 1992. Graphic Arts Center. 1st. M/dj. A18. $35.00

HILLERMAN, Tony. *Skinwalkers.* 1986. Harper Row. 1st. F/F. M15. $75.00

HILLERMAN, Tony. *Talking God.* 1989. Harper Row. 1st. F/dj. M15. $45.00

HILLERMAN, Tony. *Talking God.* 1989. Harper Row. 1st. sgn. F/F. M25. $60.00

HILLERMAN, Tony. *Thief of Time.* 1988. Harper Row. 1st. NF/F. A20. $30.00

HILLERMAN, Tony. *Words, Weather & Wolfmen.* 1989. Gallup. Southwesterner Books. 1st. 1/350. sgns. F/dj. M15. $150.00

HILLES, M.W. *Pocket Anatomist: Being Complete Description of Anatomy...* 1860. Phil. 1st Am. 12mo. 263p. A13. $50.00

HILLIER & SHINE. *Walt Disney's Mickey Mouse Memorabilia.* 1986. NY. Abrams. 4to. 235 mc ils. 180p. F/F. A4. $75.00

HILLIS, Newell Dwight. *Quest of John Chapman. Story of a Forgotten Hero.* 1904. NY. 349p. G. B18. $32.50

HILLS, Marjorie. *Live Alone & Like It: A Guide for the Extra Woman.* 1936. Bobbs Merrill. 1st/later prt. ils Cipe Pineless. 149p. VG/dj. A25. $18.00

HILLS, Rick. *Limbo River.* 1990. Pittsburgh. 1st. author's 1st story collection. F/F. R13. $20.00

HILTON, James. *Lost Horizon.* 1936. Grosset Dunlap. MTI. VG/VG. B5. $35.00

HILTON, James. *Nothing So Strange.* 1947. Atlantic/Little Brn. 1st. NF/torn. M25. $25.00

HIMES, Chester. *Case of Rape.* 1980. Targ. 1/350. sgn. F/glassine dj. A24. $100.00

HIMES, Chester. *Cast the First Stone.* 1952. Coward McCann. 1st. VG. M25. $100.00

HIMES, Chester. *Cotton Comes to Harlem.* 1965. Putnam. 1st. NF/dj. M25. $100.00

HIMES, Chester. *Pinktoes.* 1965. Putnam/Stein Day. 1st. NF/VG. M19. $65.00

HIMES, Chester. *Quality of Hurt.* 1972. NY. ARC. sgn assoc copy w/TLS. RS. F/F. A11. $675.00

HIMES, Chester. *Real Cool Killers.* 1985. London. Allison Busby. 1st hc ed. F/dj. M15. $45.00

HIMES, Joshua V. *Views of the Prophecies & Prophetic Chronology...* 1841. Boston. Moses Dow. 1st. 16mo. 252p. cloth. M1. $125.00

HINCKLEY, F. Lewis. *Directory of Antique Furniture.* 1963. photo. VG/VG. S13. $25.00

HIND, Robert. *Ruby Pendant: Story of Texas Life.* ca 1880. London. James B Knapp. 1st. mc stp bl pict cloth. M24. $125.00

HINDE, Thomas. *Lewis Carrol: Looking-Glass Letters.* 1991. NY. Rizzoli. 1st Am. sm 8vo. 160p. F/F. T5. $35.00

HINDS, N.E.A. *Geomorphology: The Evolution of Landscape.* 1943. Prentice Hall. 1st. ils. 894p. VG. D8. $20.00

HINDUS, Milton. *Worlds of Maurice Samuel: Selected Writings.* 1977. JPS. 444p. VG/dj. S3. $25.00

HINE, L. *Baptists in Southern California.* 1966. Judson. 1st. VG/sans. O4. $15.00

HINE, Robert F. *William Andrew Spalding.* 1961. San Marino, CA. Huntington Lib. 1st. F/F. O4. $15.00

HINE, Robert V. *Bartlett's West, Drawing the Mexican Boundary.* 1968. New Haven/London. Yale. ils. 155p. F/VG. K7. $30.00

HINE, Robert V. *California's Utopian Colonies.* 1966. New Haven/London. Yale. 8vo. 209p. VG. K7. $8.00

HINES, Alan. *Square Dance.* 1984. Harper. 1st. sgn. author's 1st book. NF/dj. R13. $30.00

HINKE. *Oz in Canada, a Bibliography.* 1982. 1/1000. intro Peter E Hanff. F. A4. $135.00

HINTON, Alan. *Shells of New Guinea & Central Indo-Pacific.* 1975. Hong Kong. rpt 1972 Australian. 44 full-p pl. 94p. VG/VG. S15. $24.00

HINTON, Richard J. *John Brown & His Men.* 1894. index/ils. 752p. O8. $12.50

HINTZ, Howard W. *Quaker Influence in American Literature.* 1940. Revell. 90p. G. V3. $12.00

HIROKAWA, Taishi. *Sonomama Sonomama: High Fashion in Japanese Countryside.* 1987. SF. Chronicle. wrp. D11. $60.00

HIRSCH, Edwin W. *Power to Love: A Psychic & Physiologic Study...* 1935. Knopf. 3rd. ils. 363p. VG/dj. A25. $20.00

HIRSCH, Joe. *Kentucky Derby: Chance of a Lifetime.* 1988. NY. McGraw Hill. 1st. 4to. 221p. VG/VG. O3. $45.00

HIRSCH, Susan E. *Roots of the American Working Class.* 1978. Pittsburgh. 1st. VG/worn. V4. $15.00

HIRSCHFELD, Al. *Show Business Is No Business.* 1951. S&S. 1st. 8vo. 141p. F/NF. T10. $50.00

HIRSCHFELD, Burt. *Masters Affair.* 1971. Arbor. 1st. author's 2nd book. F/F. H11. $20.00

HIRST, Stephen. *Life in a Narrow Place.* 1976. NY. McKay. 1st/2nd prt. 8vo. photos. yel cloth. dj. F7. $35.00

HISSEY, James John. *Through Ten English Countries.* 1894. London. Bentley. 1st. VG. O3. $95.00

HISSEY, Jane. *Little Bear Lost.* nd (1989). Hutchinson. 1st. sm 4to. unp. VG. C14. $12.00

HITCHCOCK, Alfred. *My Favorites in Suspense.* 1959. Random. 1st. blk cloth. NF/VG. A24. $30.00

HITCHCOCK, Alfred. *Stories My Mother Never Told Me.* 1963. Random. 1st. NF/VG. A24. $25.00

HITCHCOCK, E.C. *Saddle Up.* 1937. Scribner. 304p. gilt cloth. VG. M20. $25.00

HITCHCOCK & STANDLEY. *Flora of the District of Columbia & Vicinty.* 1919. GPO. 327p. VG. A10. $45.00

HITLER, Adolf. *Mein Kampf.* 1939. Stackpole. 1st unexpurgated in Eng language. VG. M19. $85.00

HITLER, Adolf. *Mein Kampf.* 1939. Munich. pres Mayor of Heidelberg in 1940. teg. leather. case. B18. $95.00

HITTELL, John S. *History of City of San Francisco & Incidentally of...CA.* 1878. SF. Bancroft. 1st. pres to JW Dwinelle. 8vo. gilt brn cloth. F. R3. $900.00

HITTI, Philip K. *Near East in History, a 5000 Year Story.* 1961. Princeton. Van Nostrand. 1st rpt. 8vo. 574p. VG/dj. W1. $35.00

HJORTSBERG, William. *Alp.* 1969. S&S. 1st. author's 1st book. NF/NF. L3. $85.00

HJORTSBERG, William. *Falling Angel.* 1978. HBJ. 1st. F/dj. M21. $60.00

HJORTSBERG, William. *Gray Matters.* 1971. S&S. 1st. author's 3rd novel. NF/NF. M22. $40.00

HO & TSOU. *China in Crisis.* 1968. Chicago. 3 vol in 2. F. W3. $48.00

HOAGLAND, Edward. *Heart's Desire.* 1988. Summit. 1st. F/NF clip. T11. $60.00

HOBAN, Lillian. *Arthur's Honey Bear.* 1974. Harper Row. 1st. 64p. F/VG. P2. $25.00

HOBAN, Russell. *Bread & Jam for Frances.* 1964. Harper Row. probable 1st. 31p. VG/VG. P2. $65.00

HOBAN, Russell. *Egg Thoughts & Other Frances Songs.* 1972. Harper Row. 1st. 32p. F/F. D4. $35.00

HOBAN, Russell. *Medusa Frequency.* 1987. Atlantic Monthly. 1st Am. F/dj. Q1. $30.00

HOBAN, Russell. *Ridley Walker.* 1980. SUmmit. 1st Am. F/dj. M2. $50.00

HOBAN, Tana. *A, B, See.* (1982). NY. Greenwillow. stated 1st. unp. VG+/VG. C14. $10.00

HOBAN, Tana. *Look! Look! Look!* 1988. Greenwillow. 1st. F/F. C8. $35.00

HOBART, Lois. *Mexican Mural: Story of Mexico, Past & Present.* 1963. NY. Harcourt Brace. 1st. 224p. dj. F3. $10.00

HOBBIE & HOBBIE. *Art of Holly Hobbie, Drawing on Affection.* 1986. 1st collected. 100 mc pl. 127p. F/F. A4. $35.00

HOBBS, Lois Zortmann. *Corny Cornpicker Finds a Home.* 1959. John Deere. 1st. Golden format. sq 8vo. M8. $75.00

HOBBS, MEANS & WILLIAMS. *Outline of Structural Geology.* 1976. John Wiley. 1st. 571p. VG/dj. D8. $15.00

HOBBS, Robert. *Robert Smithson: Sculpture.* 1981. Cornell. ils/photos/bibliography/index. cloth. dj. D2. $125.00

HOBBS, William Herbert. *Peary.* 1936. NY. Macmillan. 1st. 27 maps/13 halftones/10 records. bl cloth. P4. $95.00

HOBBS & PASCHALL. *Teacher's Bible Commentary.* 1972. Broadman. 817p. VG/dj. B29. $16.00

HOBBS & WHALLEY. *Beatrix Potter: V&A Collection, the Leslie Linder Bequest.* nd. London. 4to. ils. 240p. F/F. A4. $145.00

HOCHWALT, A.F. *Farmer's Dog: For Work, for Profit & for Sport.* 1922. Cincinnati. Sportsmen's Digest. 1st. 12mo. VG. H7. $15.00

HOCHWALT, A.F. *Working Dog & His Education: A Treatise...* 1921. Cincinnati. Sportsmen's Review. 1st. 116p. VG. H7. $15.00

HODGE, Frederick Webb. *Handbook of American Indians, North of Mexico.* 1907. Smithsonian. 1st. 2 vol. ils. VG/VG. J2. $475.00

HODGE, Frederick Webb. *History of Hawikuh.* 1937. Ward Ritchie. A19. $55.00

HODGE & UMARU. *Hausa. Basic Course.* 1963. WA. Foreign Service Inst. 399p. xl. VG. W1. $12.00

HODGES, George W. *Swamp Angel.* 1958. New Voice. 1st. inscr. F/F. B4. $150.00

HODGES, Henry. *Technology in the Ancient World.* 1974. London. BC Assoc. 4to. ils. 260p. NF/VG. K3. $65.00

HODGES, Margaret. *Little Humpbacked Horse.* 1980. FSG. 1st. 8vo. unp. F/NF clip. C14. $14.00

HODGKISS & TATHAM. *Keyguide to Information Sources in Cartography.* 1986. 253p. NF. A4. $195.00

HODGSON, Fred T. *Estimating Frame & Brick Houses, Barns, Stables...* 1910. NY. David Williams. 12mo. VG. O3. $40.00

HODGSON, Fred T. *Up-to-Date Hardwood Finisher, in Two Parts.* 1904. Chicago. Drake. 1st. ils. 209p. B18. $22.50

HODGSON, Moira. *Cooking With Fruits & Nuts.* 1973. NY. Crowell. 1st. VG/dj. A16. $17.50

HODGSON, William Hope. *Ghost Pirates.* 1976 (1909). Hyperion. rpt. F. M2. $45.00

HODGSON & WILLIAMS. *Growing Bromeliads.* 1990. Portland. ils/photos. F/dj. B26. $25.00

HODSON, Geoffrey. *Kingdom of the Gods.* 1952. Madras. Theosophical Pub. 1st. 8vo. 247p. F. T10. $50.00

HODSON, J.L. *Annual Report of Adjutant General of State of Maine...1866.* 1867. Augusta. 588p. leather spine/marbled brd. M4. $55.00

HOEHLING, A.A. *Jeannette Expedition: Ill-Fated Journey to the Arctic.* 1969. London. Abelard Schuman. 8vo. 224p. VG/dj. P4. $45.00

HOEHLING, A.A. *They Sailed Into Oblivion.* 1962. NY. VG/VG. B5. $15.00

HOEHN, Reinhardt. *Curiousities of the Plant Kingdom.* 1980. Universe. 4to. 212p. NF/dj. A22. $30.00

HOEKEMA, Anthony A. *Created in God's Image.* 1988. Eerdmans. 264p. VG/dj. B29. $17.00

HOEXTER, Corrine K. *From Canton to California: Epic of Chinese Immigration.* 1976. Four Winds. 1st. 8vo. ils. gilt red cloth. F. R3. $40.00

HOFFMAN, Alice Spencer. *Children's Shakespeare.* 1911. London. 1st thus. ils Chas Folkard. VG. M5. $145.00

HOFFMAN, Alice. *Drowning Season.* 1979. Dutton. 1st. author's 2nd book. VG/dj. A24. $75.00

HOFFMAN, Alice. *Fortune's Daughter.* 1985. Putnam. 1st. sgn. F/F. D10. $50.00

HOFFMAN, Alice. *Illumination Night.* 1987. Putnam. 1st. F/dj. B4. $45.00

HOFFMAN, Alice. *Property of...* 1977. FSG. 1st. sgn. author's 1st book. F/NF. D10. $110.00

HOFFMAN, Alice. *Property of...* 1977. FSG. 1st. VG/NF. M25. $35.00

HOFFMAN, Alice. *Turtle Moon.* 1992. Putnam. 1st. inscr. F/F. R13. $35.00

HOFFMAN, Alice. *White Horses.* 1982. Putnam. 1st. sgn. F/F. D10. $50.00

HOFFMAN, Andrew Jay. *Twain's Heroes, Twain's Worlds.* 1988. Phil. PA U. 1st. bl cloth. F/dj. M24. $20.00

HOFFMAN, B.R. *Luther & the Mystics.* 1976. Augsburg. 285p. VG/dj. B29. $8.50

HOFFMAN, Bob. *High Protein Road to Better Nutrition.* 1961 (1940). York. Strength & Health Magazine. 7th. photos. 255p. VG/dj. A25. $8.00

HOFFMAN, Carl. *Saipan: Beginning of the End.* 1950. WA. fld mc maps/charts/photos. 286p. VG. S16. $85.00

HOFFMAN, Carl. *Seizure of Tinian.* 1951. WA. fld mc maps/photos/index. VG. S16. $85.00

HOFFMAN, E.T.A. *Selected Writings of ETA Hoffman.* 1969. Chicago. 2 vol. ils. xl. VG/VG case. A4. $45.00

HOFFMAN, G.W. *Geography of Europe Including Asiatic USSR.* 1969. Ronald. ils. cloth. 669p. VG. D8. $10.00

HOFFMAN, Heinrich. *Adolf Hitler. Bilder Aus dem Leben des Fuhrers.* 1936. Hamburg. photos. 132p. VG-/tattered. B18. $125.00

HOFFMAN, Heinrich. *Der Struwwelpeter.* ca 1960s. London. Blackie. 8vo. 24p. pict brd. VG/VG. D1. $40.00

HOFFMAN, Heinrich. *Slovenly Peter.* nd. Winston. ils. gilt wine cloth. VG. M5. $75.00

HOFFMAN, Malvina. *Heads & Tales.* 1936. Scribner. 1st. inscr pres. photos. VG/dj. w/TLS+ephemera. A25. $175.00

HOFFMAN, Malvina. *Heads & Tales.* 1936. Scribner. 1st. photos. 416p. teg. VG+/VG. A25. $80.00

HOFFMAN, W.S. *Paul Mellon, Portrait of an Oil Baron.* 1974. Chicago. 1st. 204p. NF/dj. D8. $18.50

HOFFMAN, Walter James. *Graphic Art of the Eskimos.* 1897. GPO. 8vo. ils/figures/82 pl. professionally rebound. P4. $225.00

HOFFMAN & HOFFMAN. *We Married an Englishman.* 1938. NY. Carrick Evans. 1st. sgns. 8vo. 314p. cloth. VG. W1. $35.00

HOFFMAN & JOHNSON. *Reports of Land Cases Determined...1853...* 1975. SF. Yosemite Collections. rpt. 1/50. sgn/edit Johnson. 8vo. cloth. F. R3. $100.00

HOFFMANN, E.T. *Nutcracker.* 1984. Crown. ltd. 1/250. 4to. ils/sgn/#d Sendak. 102p. w/orig litho. M/case. D1. $1,200.00

HOFFMANN, E.T. *Tales of Hoffmann.* 1943. Heritage. ils Hugo Steiner-Prag. 344p. F/VG case. H1. $20.00

HOFFMANN, Professor. *Modern Magic: A Practical Treatise on Art of Conjuring.* nd. Phil. ils. 563p. decor cloth. dj. B18. $37.50

HOFFMEISTER, Donald F. *Mammals of the Grand Canyon.* 1971. Chicago. 8vo. 183p. stiff wrp. VG. F7. $12.00

HOFMANN, Charles. *American Indians Sing.* 1967. John Day. ils. 96p. xl. VG. K7. $25.00

HOGAN, Desmond. *Link With the River.* 1989. FSG. 1st. F/NF. R13. $15.00

HOGAN, Inez. *Monkey Twins, They Saw It All!* 1944 (1943). Dutton. 2nd. sm 8vo. NF. C8. $30.00

HOGAN, Inez. *Mule Twins.* 1939. Dutton. probable 1st. 8vo. 49p. VG/VG. D1. $60.00

HOGAN, Inez. *Nicodemus Runs Away.* 1946. Shakespeare Head Pr. 1st thus. 12mo. VG+. C8. $125.00

HOGAN, Inez. *Twin Deer.* 1943 (1941). Dutton. 2nd. 12mo. G+. C8. $27.50

HOGAN, James. *Code to the Lifemaker.* 1983. Del Rey. 1st. sgn. F/dj. M2. $35.00

HOGAN, Linda. *Mean Spirit.* 1990. Atheneum. 1st. F/dj. A24. $30.00

HOGAN, Linda. *Seeing Through the Sun.* 1985. Amherst. MA U. 1st. NF/wrp. L3. $45.00

HOGBIN, H. Ian. *Experiments in Civilization: Effects of European Culture...* 1970. NY. Schocken. ils/2 maps. 268p. VG/worn. P4. $35.00

HOGES, Margaret. *Saint George & the Dragon.* 1984. Little Brn. stated 1st. ils Hyman. F/dj. M5. $52.00

HOGG, Ian. *Fighting Tanks.* 1977. NY. ils. 160p. VG/VG. S16. $25.00

HOGG, James. *Jabobite Relics of Scotland.* 1819. Edinburgh. Blackwood Cadell Davies. 1st. tall 8vo. 424p. H13. $295.00

HOGNER, Dorothy Childs. *Summer Roads to Gaspe.* 1939. Dutton. 1st. ils Nils Hogner. 288p. VG. A25. $15.00

HOGUE, Arthur R. *Origins of the Common Law.* 1966. Bloomington. IU. 1st. M11. $45.00

HOHLER, Robert T. *I Touch the Future.* 1986. Random. 1st. 8vo. 262p. VG/dj. K5. $17.00

HOHMAN, Elmo Paul. *American Whaleman: Study of Life & Labor in Whaling...* 1928. Longmans. photos. 355p. VG. S15. $70.00

HOIG, Stan. *Western Odyssey of John Simpson Smith, Frontiersman...* 1974. Clark. 1st. 254p. VG/VG. J2. $155.00

HOKE, Helen. *Doctor the Puppy Who Learned.* 1944. Messner. 1st. NF/VG-. P2. $45.00

HOLBEIN, Hans. *Celebrated Hans Holbein's Alphabet of Death.* 1856. Paris. Prt for Edwin Tross. gilt gr cloth. Q1. $250.00

HOLBEIN. *Selected Drawings From Collection of Her Majesty...* 1954. ils. stp for USAF/For Salvage Only. VG/G. M17. $15.00

HOLBERG, Ruth. *Hester & Timothy Pioneers.* 1937. Doubleday Doran. 1st. 128p. VG/VG. P2. $30.00

HOLBROOK, James G. *Survey of Metropolitan Trial Courts.* 1956. LA. 434p. gilt fabricoid. D11. $30.00

HOLBROOK, M.L. *Parturition Without Pain: Code of Directions...* 1871. NY. 1st. 159p. A13. $125.00

HOLBROOK, Stewart H. *Old Post Road.* 1962. McGraw Hill. 1st. American Trails series. 8vo. 273p. VG. T10. $25.00

HOLBROOK, Stewart H. *Wild Bill Hickok Tames the West.* 1952. Random. dj. A19. $20.00

HOLCOMB, William Hartley. *Old Mission Rhymes.* 1900. San Diego. Frye Garrett Smith. A19. $40.00

HOLDEN, George Parker. *Idyl of the Split-Bamboo.* 1920. Cincinnati. Stewart Kidd. 1st. ils. 278p. VG. B18. $150.00

HOLDEN, Reuben. *Yale in China.* 1964. New Haven. 1st. photos/addenda/9 appendix. 327p. NF. W3. $68.00

HOLDEN, William Curry. *Spur Ranch, a Study...* 1934. Christopher Pub. 1st. 229p. VG. J2. $275.00

HOLDER, C.F. *Life in the Open: Sport With Rod, Gun, Horse & Hound...* 1906. Putnam. 8vo. photos. 401p. gilt pict cloth. NF. M12. $60.00

HOLDSTOCK, Robert. *Eye Among the Blind.* 1977. Doubleday. 1st Am. F/dj. M2. $22.00

HOLDSWORTH, W.S. *Charles Dickens as a Legal Historian.* 1929. Yale. 2nd. maroon cloth/morocco label. M11. $85.00

HOLDSWORTH, W.S. *Historians of Anglo-American Law.* 1966 (1928). Hamden. Archon. facsimile. M11. $75.00

HOLL, Adelaide. *Sylvester, the Mouse With the Musical Ear.* 1973 (1961). Golden/Western. 1st thus. lg 4to. VG+/VG. C8. $45.00

HOLLAND, Isabelle. *God, Mrs Muskrat & Aunt Dot.* 1983. Phil. Westminster. 1st. 8vo. 77p. VG. T5. $25.00

HOLLAND, Ray P. *Now Listen, Warden.* 1946. NY. Barnes. A19. $15.00

HOLLAND, Ray P. *Shotgunning in the Lowlands.* 1945. NY. as Barnes. stated 1st. 1/3500. 4to. 213p. F/VG box. H7. $60.00

HOLLAND, Rupert Sargent. *Historic Railroads.* (1927). Macrae Smith. 1st probable. lg 8vo. NF. C8. $60.00

HOLLEY, Marietta. *Samatha Among the Colored Folks.* 1894. NY. ils. G+. M17. $45.00

HOLLEY, O.L. *Life of Benjamin Franklin.* 1848. Boston. 468p. O8. $12.50

HOLLICK, Frederick. *Outlines of Anatomy & Physiology...* ca 1846. Phil. TB Peterson. 4to. orig leather/pict brd. M1. $150.00

HOLLIDAY, J.S. *World Rushed In.* 1981. S&S. 1st. 8vo. 559p. brn leatherette. VG. K7. $25.00

HOLLIDAY, J.S. *World Rushed In: California Gold Rush Experience.* 1981. S&S. 2nd. F/NF clip. O4. $25.00

HOLLIDAY, Laurel. *Heart Songs: Intimate Diaries of Young Girls.* 1978. Guerneville. Bluestocking Books. 1st. 191p. sc. VG+. A25. $20.00

HOLLIDAY, Michael; see Creasey, John.

HOLLIDAY, Robert Cortes. *Literary Lanes & Other Byways.* 1925. Doran. 1st. 219p. gr cloth. NF/dj. B22. $18.00

HOLLING, Holling C. *Book of Cowboys.* 1936. Platt Munk. 1st. F/dj. C8/M19. $65.00

HOLLING, Holling C. *Book of Indians.* 1935. Platt Munk. 1st. VG/G. O3. $45.00

HOLLING, Holling C. *Minn of the Mississippi.* 1951. Houghton Mifflin. 1st. ils. 87p. VG/VG. J2. $185.00

HOLLING, Holling C. *Paddle to the Sea.* 1945 (1941). London. Collins. 1st. VG/VG. C8. $75.00

HOLLINGSWORTH, Adelaide. *Home Cook Book.* 1895. ils. G+. M17. $25.00

HOLLO, Anselm. *Heavy Jars.* 1977. W Branch. Toothpaste. 1/100. sgn. F. B2. $35.00

HOLLON, W.E. *Beyond the Cross Timbers. Travels of Randolph B Marcy.* 1955. OK U. 1st. ils. F/dj. M4. $40.00

HOLLON, W.E. *Great American Desert.* 1966. Oxford. 1st. ils/notes/index. 284p. NF/VG. w/2 TLS. B19. $35.00

HOLLOWAY, David. *Stalin & the Bomb.* 1994. New Haven. Yale. ils. M/dj. K3. $30.00

HOLLOWAY, Laura C. *Mothers.* 1891. Baltimore. RH Woodward Co. A19. $35.00

HOLMAN, Felice. *I Hear You Smiling & Other Poems.* 1973. Scribner. 1st. 62p. F/F. D4. $30.00

HOLMAN, Russell. *Freshman.* 1925. Grosset Dunlap. 1st/photoplay. F/VG. B4. $185.00

HOLMAN, William. *Library Publications.* 1965. SF. Roger Beacham. 1st. 1/350. folio. M24. $350.00

HOLMAN & MARKS. *Pioneering in Northwest. Niobrara-Virginia City Wagon Road.* 1924. Sioux City. Deitch Lamar. 150p. prt cloth. D11. $40.00

HOLME. *Kate Greenaway Book, a Collection of Illustrations, Verse...* 1976. 144p. F/VG. A4. $45.00

HOLME, Bryan. *Enchanted Garden.* 1982. NY. Oxford. 8vo. ils. F/clip. A22. $20.00

HOLME, Bryan. *Horses.* 1951. Studio. 1st. photos. VG. O3. $35.00

HOLMER, W.J. *Undersea Victory: Influence of Submarine Operations...* 1966. Garden City. 1st. ils/maps. 595p. VG/dj. B5. $35.00

HOLMES, Bruce T. *Anvil of the Heart.* 1983. Haven. 1st. F/dj. M2. $20.00

HOLMES, Charles M. *Principles & Practice of Horse-Shoeing.* 1949. Leeds, England. Farriers Journal. 1st. VG. O3. $38.00

HOLMES, James William. *Voyaging: 50 Years on the Seven Seas in Sail.* 1972. Dodd Mead. 8vo. 207p. silvered gr cloth. NF/VG. P4. $25.00

HOLMES, John Clellon. *Go.* 1952. Scribner. 1st. inscr. VG/VG+. B4. $1,350.00

HOLMES, John Clellon. *Horn.* 1958. Random. 1st. F/NF. B2. $100.00

HOLMES, John Clellon. *Nothing More to Declare.* 1967. NY. 1st. Holme's copy. F/NF. A11. $65.00

HOLMES, Kenneth. *Covered Wagon Women, Diaries & Letters...1840-1890.* 1983-93. Arthur H Clarke. 11 vol. 1st. fld maps. F. w/prospectus. A4. $595.00

HOLMES, L.P. *Black Sage.* 1950. Doubleday. 1st. F/NF. B4. $100.00

HOLMES, L.P. *Hill Smoke.* 1959. Dodd Mead. 1st. F/VG. B4. $65.00

HOLMES, Maurice. *Captain James Cook, RN, FRS: A Bibliographical Excursion.* 1952. London. Francis Edwards. 1/500. 11 full-p photos. 103p. cloth. D11. $100.00

HOLMES, Oliver Wendell. *Astraea: Balance of Illusions.* 1850. Ticknor Reed Fields. 1st/2nd prt/state A (B?). gilt brn wavy-grain cloth. F. M24. $125.00

HOLMES, Oliver Wendell. *Common Law. Edited by Mark DeWolfe Howe.* 1968. Macmillan. VG/dj. M11. $75.00

HOLMES, Oliver Wendell. *Dedication of New Building & Hall of Boston Medical Lib...* 1881. Boston. Riverside. bl cloth/bl-gray wrp bdg in. NF. M24. $200.00

HOLMES, Oliver Wendell. *One Hoss Shay.* 1905. Houghton Mifflin. 1st thus. ils Howard Pyle. VG/G-. P2. $100.00

HOLMES, Samuel Jackson. *Negro's Struggle for Survival: A Study in Human Ecology.* 1937. Berkeley, CA. 1st. 296p. cloth. cl. VG. M8. $85.00

HOLMES, W.J. *Undersea Victory.* 1966. Garden City. 1st. VG/VG. B5. $40.00

HOLMES, William. *National Gallery of Art in Washington: Catalogue of...* 1922. GPO. 25 full-p pl w/tissue guards. bl cloth. VG/VG+. B22. $12.00

HOLST, Adolf. *Die Glucklichen Mausleut.* (1929). Oldenburg. Cerhard Stalling. orange cloth. G. D1. $150.00

HOLST, Adolf. *Die Wunderwiese.* ca 1920s. Koln. Hermann Schaffstein. ils Ritter. VG. D1. $350.00

HOLT, Samuel; see Westlake, Donald E.

HOLTE, Clarence L. *Nubian Baby Book.* 1971. Nubian. 1st. ils Robert Pious. wht cloth. F/wrp band. B4. $100.00

HOLTON, Isaac. *New Granada.* (1967). Carbondale, IL. 1st this. 223p. dj. M20. $15.00

HOLTON, Leonard. *Flowers by Request.* 1964. Dodd Mead. 1st. xl. NF/dj. M25. $45.00

HOLWAY, John. *Voices From the Great Black Baseball Leagues.* 1975. Dodd Mead. 1st. photos. F/dj. B4. $100.00

HOLWAY, John. *Voices From the Great Black Baseball Leagues.* 1975. Dodd Mead. 1st. 363p. cloth. NF/dj. M20. $85.00

HOLWAY, Mary Gordon. *Art of the Old World in New Spain & Mission Days of Alta...* 1922. SF. AM Robertson. 1/1000. 8vo. ils/photos. tan cloth. VG. K7. $25.00

HOLYBAND, Claudius. *French Litteton (A Most Easie, Perfect & Absolute Way...* 1953. Cambridge. only modern ed. M11. $65.00

HOLZMAN & LEONARD. *View From the Bench.* 1980. Norton. 1st. photos. VG/dj. P8. $25.00

HOME, H.H. *Citrus Fruits & Their Culture.* 1904. Jacksonville. 1st. ils. 597p. VG. B5. $60.00

HOME, Henry (of Kames). *Elements of Criticism.* 1883. NY. revised. 486p. NF. A17. $10.00

HOMER. *Iliad.* 1962. Chicago. 1st thus. ils Baskin. 526p. F/VG. H1. $30.00

HOMER. *Illustrated Odyssey.* 1980. London. 1st. VG/VG. T9. $20.00

HOMEWOOD, Harry. *O God of Battles.* 1983. Morrow. 1st. F/F. H11. $25.00

HOMSHER, Lola A. *History of Albany County, Wyoming to 1880.* 1965. The Lusk Herald. 1st. 110p. VG/pict wrp. J2. $95.00

HONCE. *Vincent Starrett Library: Astonishing Result...* 1941. Golden Eagle. 1/100. ils. 85p. VG. A4. $350.00

HONEY, W.B. *Dresden China.* 1946. Troy, NY. Rosenfeld. 1st. 61 pl. 223p. F. T10. $100.00

HONNYWILL, Eleanor. *Challenge of Antarctica.* 1969. London. Methuen. 1st. 160p. VG/dj. P4. $30.00

HONNYWILL, Eleanor. to *Stand at the Pole: Dr Cook-Admiral Peary North Pole...* 1981. NY. Stein Day. 8vo. 288p. half cloth. P4. $20.00

HONOUR, Hugh. *New Golden Land: European Images of America...* 1975. Pantheon. ils/12 3-column p of notes. as new/dj. O7. $50.00

HOOD, Hugh. *Strength Down Centre.* 1970. Prentice Hall. 1st. photos. VG/G+. P8. $27.50

HOOD, Thomas. *New Comic Annual, for 1831.* (1831). London. Hurst Chance. 1st. 16mo. 192p. full contemporary calf. M1. $200.00

HOOD, Thomas. *Poems by...* 1871. London. Moxon. lg paper ed. ils Birket Foster. 109p. half gr morocco. B24. $300.00

HOOKER, J.D. *Life & Letters of Sir Joseph Hooker.* 1918. London. 2nd. 2 vol. ils/map/4 portraits. gilt navy cloth. VG. B26. $200.00

HOOPES, Chad L. *What Makes a Man: Annie E Kennedy & John Bidwell Letters...* 1973. Fresno, CA. Valley Pub. 1st. F/NF. O4. $25.00

HOOPES, Donelson. *Winslow Homer Watercolors.* 1969. 4to. ils. VG/VG. S13. $25.00

HOOPES, Roy. *Cain: The Biography of James M Cain.* 1982. NY. 1st. 684p. F/dj. A17. $30.00

HOOTON, Earnest H. *Apes, Men & Morons.* 1937. Putnam. 1st. sgn. F. B14. $45.00

HOOVER, H.M. *Rains of Zenda.* 1977. Viking. 1st. F/dj. M2. $20.00

HOOVER, Herbert Clark. *Remedy for Disappearing Game Fishes.* 1930. NY. Huntington. 1st. 1/990. ils Harry Cimino. 42p. NF. H7. $65.00

HOOVER, Herbert T. *South Dakota Leaders.* 1989. Vermillion, SD. SD U. A19. $22.00

HOOVER, J. Edgar. *Study of Communism.* 1962. HRW. 1st. F/VG+. A20. $25.00

HOPE, Bob. *Confessions of a Hooker. My Lifelong Love Affair With Golf.* 1985. Doubleday. 1st. Gerald Ford sgn/dtd 1997. VG/VG. A23. $80.00

HOPE, Bob. *Don't Shoot, It's Only Me.* 1990. Putnam. 1st. sgn. F/F. A23. $45.00

HOPE, Bob. *Five Women I Love.* 1966. Doubleday. 1st. 255p. F. W2. $15.00

HOPE, Brian; see Creasey, John.

HOPE, Christopher. *White Boy Running.* 1988. FSG. 1st. F/F. B3. $30.00

HOPE, Laura Lee. *Bobbsey Twins at the Seashore (#3).* nd. Chicago. Goldsmith. 1st. F/poor. T12. $19.00

HOPE, Laura Lee. *Bobbsey Twins in Echo Valley (#36).* (1943). Grosset Dunlap. early ed. 12mo. VG+/VG. C8. $22.50

HOPE, Laura Lee. *Bobbsey Twins on a Ranch.* 1935. Grosset Dunlap. 1st. inscr. VG/poor. T12. $10.00

HOPE, Laura Lee. *Bobbsey Twins on an Airplane Trip (#26).* (1933). Grosset Dunlap. pre-1943 prt. 12mo. VG/VG. C8. $35.00

HOPE, Laura Lee. *Outdoor Girls Around the Campfire.* 1923. Grosset Dunlap. 1st. 214p. pict bdg. VG/VG. H1. $20.00

HOPE, Laura Lee. *Outdoor Girls in a Winter Camp.* 1913. Grosset Dunlap. 8vo. 208p. pict cloth. lists to Outdoor Girls in FL. VG. T10. $25.00

HOPKINS, Charles H. *Rise of the Social Gospel in American Protestantism.* 1950. Yale. 352p. VG. B29. $12.00

HOPKINS, Edward J. *Organ: Its History & Construction.* 1855. London. Robert Cocks. 1st. thick 4to. 600p. cloth/rebacked orig spine. T10. $150.00

HOPKINS, Lee Bennett. *Hey-How for Halloween!* 1974. HBJ. 7th. sgn. 8vo. 31p. VG/G. T5. $24.00

HOPKINS, Lee Bennett. *Me! A Book of Poems.* 1970. NY. Seabury. 1st. 32p. F/NF. D4. $30.00

HOPKINS, Lee Bennett. *Side by Side.* 1988. S&S. 1st. sgn. F/F. D4. $45.00

HOPKINS, Lee Bennett. *This Street's for Me!* 1970. NY. Crown. 1st. ils Ann Grifalconi. F/F. D4. $30.00

HOPKINS, Robert. *Darwin's South America.* 1969. John Day. 1st. 224p. dj. F3. $20.00

HOPMAN, Harry. *Lobbing Into the Sun.* 1975. Bobbs Merrill. 1st. ils. F/VG. P8. $15.00

HOPWOOD, John A. *Pussy Cat Dirty Nose.* 1928. McLoughlin. 4to. pict brd. R5. $85.00

HORAN, James D. *Across the Cimarron.* 1956. Crown. 1st. 301p. cloth. VG/dj. M20. $30.00

HORAN, James D. *Confederate Agent.* 1960. 326p. O8. $18.50

HORAN, James D. *Pinkertons: Detective Dynasty That Made History.* 1967. NY. ARC/1st. photos. 564p. F/dj. M4. $40.00

HORDER, Thomas. *Clinical Pathology in Practice With Short Account Vaccine...* 1910. London. 1st. 216p. A13. $75.00

HORDER, W. Garrett. *Quaker Worthies.* 1896. London. Headley Bros. 224p. V3. $15.00

HORGAN, J.J. *City of Flight: History of Aviation in St Louis.* 1984. Gerald. 1/175. sgn/#d. photos/ils. leather. F. M4. $90.00

HORGAN, Paul. *Centuries of Santa Fe.* 1956. Dutton. 1st. VG+/VG+ clip. T11. $30.00

HORGAN, Paul. *Devil in the Desert.* 1952. Longman Gr. 1st. F/VG. A18. $30.00

HORGAN, Paul. *Everything to Live For.* 1968. FSG. 1st. F/NF. T11. $25.00

HORGAN, Paul. *Josiah Gregg & His Vision of the Early West.* 1979. FSG. 1st. 116p. VG+/dj. M20. $20.00

HORGAN, Paul. *Lamy of Santa Fe.* 1975. FSG. 1st. F/F. T11. $60.00

HORGAN, Paul. *Lamy of Santa Fe: His Life & Times.* 1975. NY. FSG. 1st. sgn. 523p. VG/VG. B14. $55.00

HORGAN, Paul. *Memories of the Future.* 1966. FSG. 1st. F/dj. Q1/T11. $45.00

HORGAN, Paul. *Mexico Bay.* 1982. FSG. 1st ed. inscr. NF/NF. T11. $65.00

HORGAN, Paul. *One Red Rose for Christmas.* 1952. Longman Gr. 1st. VG+/VG. A18. $30.00

HORGAN, Paul. *Thin Air Mountain.* 1977. FSG. 1st. F/VG+. T11. $35.00

HORLER, Sidney. *Peril.* 1930. Mystery League. 1st. VG. M2. $20.00

HORN. *World Encyclopedia of Cartoons.* 1980. 4to. ils. 676p. F/F. A4. $50.00

HORN, Huston. *Pioneers.* 1975. Time-Life. leather. A19. $20.00

HORN, M.A. *Digest of Hygiene for Mother & Daughter...* 1947. Wilmington. Hygienic Prod. 39th prt. ils. 93p+ads. VG+. A25. $20.00

HORN, Stanley Fitzgerald. *Decisive Battle of Nashville.* 1956. LSU. 1st. inscr. 181p. cloth. NF. M8. $35.00

HORNER, Harlan Hoyt. *Lincoln & Greeley.* 1953. 1st. 432p. O8. $18.50

HORNUNG, Clarence P. *Treasury of American Design.* (1976). Abrams. 2 vol. 4to. F/dj (Mylar w/end sleeves). H1. $50.00

HORNUNG, E.W. *Mr Justice Raffles.* 1909. NY. 1st Am. gilt cloth. G. A17. $20.00

HORNUNG, E.W. *Raffles.* 1901. Scribner. 1st Am. NF. M22. $35.00

HORNUNG, E.W. *Thief in the Night.* 1905. Raffles. 1st. VG. M22. $20.00

HOROWITZ, David. *First Frontier.* 1978. S&S. hc. dj. A19. $25.00

HORRISON, Samuel Elliot. *John Paul Jones: A Sailor's Biography.* 1959. Little Brn. 1st. 453p. F/dj. H1. $16.00

HORSCHI, Josef. *Steinzeug.* 1978. German text. photos. VG/VG. M17. $25.00

HORSLEY, Terrence. *Sporting Pageant: A Gun, a Rifle & an Aeroplane.* (1947). London. Witherby Ltd. 1st. photos. 205p. VG. H7. $15.00

HORT, Alfred. *Via Nicaragua: Sketch of Travel.* 1987. Conway, NH. facsimile. 267p. F3. $25.00

HORTENSE, Queen. *Memoirs...* 1927. 2 vol. stp Sample Copy. G+. M17. $30.00

HORTON, John J. *Jonathan Hale Farm, a Chronicle...* 1961. Cleveland. Western Reserve Hist Soc. 1st. photos/map. 160p. VG. B18. $12.50

HORTON, Richard. *Complete Measurer.* 1862. London. Weale. 319p. cloth. A10. $25.00

HORTON & JACKSON. *Ohio Valley Flood of March-April 1913.* 1913. WA. ils/fld map/charts/fld panorama. 96p. wrp. B18. $22.50

HOSILLOS, Lucilla. *Philippine-American Literary Relations, 1898-1941.* 1969. Quezon City. U Philippines. 4to. VG+. P1. $15.00

HOSMER, George L. *Practical Astronomy.* 1948 (1910). John Wiley. 4th. 355p. K5. $20.00

HOTMAN, Francois. *Franco-Gallia; or, Account of Ancient Free State of France.* 1711. London. Goodwin. 8vo. calf. R12. $475.00

HOUEL, J. *Elements de la Theorie des Quaternions.* 1874. Paris. Gauthier. half leather. xl. K3. $35.00

HOUGEN, John. *Story of the Famous 34th Infantry Division.* 1949. San Angelo. 1st. maps/photos. 981p. VG. S16. $125.00

HOUGH, Emerson. *Covered Wagon.* nd. Grosset Dunlap. 1st thus/photoplay. NF/dj. M2. $30.00

HOUGH, Emerson. *Maw's Vacation.* 1921. St Paul. 1st. ils. 62p. G+. B5. $35.00

HOUGH, Frank O. *If Not Victory.* 1939. NY. Carrick Evans. 1st. F/NF. B4. $85.00

HOUGH, Franklin. *Elements of Forestry.* 1882. Cincinnati. Clarke. 381p. cloth. VG. A10. $35.00

HOUGH, George A. *Disaster on Devil's Bridge.* 1963. Marine Hist Assn. 146p. VG/prt wrp. P4. $30.00

HOUGH, J.L. *Geology of the Great Lakes.* 1958. Urbana. 313p. cloth. VG. D8. $25.00

HOUGH, Richard. *Buller's Victory.* 1984. Morrow. 1st Am. F. T11. $25.00

HOUGH, Stella V. *Woman's Exchange Recipes.* 1946. Detroit. Arnold Powers. G. A16. $17.50

HOUGH, Walter. *Antiquities of the Upper Gila & Salt River Valleys in AZ...* 1907. GPO. 8vo. ils. 96p. VG. K7. $50.00

HOUGHTON, George. *Golf Addict Among the Scots.* 1967. Country Life. 1st. ils Houghton. F/VG+. P8. $35.00

HOUGHTON, Norris. *Moscow Rehearsals.* 1936. Harcourt Brace. 1st. sgn. 291p. G. H1. $25.00

HOUK, R. *Eastern Wildflowers.* 1989. SF. Chronicle. 108p. F/F. B1. $27.50

HOUNIHAN. *Hounihan's Baker's & Confectioner's Guide & Treasure...* ca 1877. Staunton, VA. self pub. ils. G+. E6. $100.00

HOURANI, Albert. *History of the Arab Peoples.* 1991. Cambridge. Belknap Pr of Harvard. 39 ils/12 maps. as new/dj. O7. $35.00

HOUSE, E.M. *Philip Dru: Administrator.* 1912. Huebsch. 1st. VG. M2. $100.00

HOUSE, Edward J. *Hunter's Camp-Fires.* 1909. Harper. 1st. 402p. F. H7. $250.00

HOUSEHOLD, Geoffrey. *Salvation of Pablo Gabar & Other Stories.* 1940. Little Brn. 1st Am. F/dj. B4. $175.00

HOUSEHOLD, Geoffrey. *Sending.* 1980. Little Brn. 1st. F/F. M21. $40.00

HOUSEHOLD, Geoffrey. *Third Hour.* 1938. Little Brn. 1st Am. F/VG. B4. $200.00

HOUSEMAN, A.E. *More Poems.* 1936. London. Cape. 1st. NF/NF. B2. $45.00

HOUSEMAN, Laurence. *Echo de Paris, a Study From Life.* 1923. London. Cape. sm 8vo. 60p. VG. K7. $195.00

HOUSEMAN, Laurence. *Princess Badoura.* nd (1913). London. Hodder Stoughton. ils Dulac/10 tipped-in pl. 4to. whit pict cloth. VG. T10. $400.00

HOUSHOLDER, B. *Grand Slam of North American Wild Sheep.* 1974. Phoenix. N Am Sheep Hunt Assn. sgn pres. 220p. F. M12. $95.00

HOUSTON, Edwin J. *Elements of Physical Geography.* 1884 (1875). Phil. Eldredge. 4to. woodcuts/maps. 160p. quarter leather. G. K5. $30.00

HOUSTON, James. *Gig.* 1969. Dial. 1st. author's 2nd novel. F/NF. B4. $100.00

HOUSTON, James. *Men in My Life.* 1987. Creative Arts. F/dj. M2. $15.00

HOUSTON, James. *Songs of the Dream People.* 1972. Atheneum. 1st. 83p. F/F. D4. $35.00

HOUSTON, S.D. *Maya Glyps.* 1990. Berkeley. 2nd. 4to. wrp. F3. $15.00

HOVELL, Mark. *Rats & How to Destroy Them.* 1924. London. John Bale. 466p. VG. H7. $35.00

HOW, R.W. *Adventures at Friendly Farm.* 1952. Coward McCann. VG/G. O3. $18.00

HOWARD, Albert. *Farming & Gardening for Health & Disease.* 1945. London. Faber. 2nd. 282p. VG. A10. $25.00

HOWARD, Cecil. *Pizarro & the Conquest of Peru.* 1968. Am Heritage. 2nd. 153p. F3. $15.00

HOWARD, Clark. *Arm.* 1967. LA. Sherbourne. 1st. F/F. H11. $40.00

HOWARD, Elizabeth. *North Winds Blow Free.* 1949. Morrow. 1st. 8vo. 192p. G+. T5. $20.00

HOWARD, George E. *On Development of King's Peace & English Local Peace...* early 1890s. 65p. prt/sewn wrp. M11. $65.00

HOWARD, Hamilton G. *Civil War Echoes.* 1907. 1st. 298p. O8. $35.00

HOWARD, J.H. *Childhood Delight.* ca 1880s. McLoughlin. 4to. sc. VG. M5. $150.00

HOWARD, Joseph Kinsey. *Strange Empire.* 1952. Morrow. 1st. 601p. cloth. VG/dj. M20. $40.00

HOWARD, Robert E. *Red Nails.* 1979. Berkley Putnam. 1st. NF/dj. M2. $20.00

HOWARD, Robert West. *Waggonmen.* 1964. Putnam. 1st. VG/G. O3. $48.00

HOWARTH, David. *D-Day: The Sixth of June, 1944.* 1959. McGraw Hill. 1st. 251p. VG/dj. M20. $15.00

HOWE, Henry. *Historical Collections of Ohio...* 1848 (1847). Cincinnati. 599p+ads. w/fld map. VG. M20. $150.00

HOWE, Henry. *History of Wayne County, Ohio.* 1977. Knightstown, IN. The Bookmark. A19. $15.00

HOWE, Irving. *UAW & Walter Reuther.* 1949. Random. 1st. F/F. V4. $35.00

HOWE, Mark DeWolfe. *Holmes-Pollock Letters, Correspondence of Mr Justice Holmes.* 1941. Cambridge. 1st. 2 vol. crimson cloth. box. M11. $100.00

HOWE, Walter. *Mining Guild of New Spain & Its Tribunal General.* 1968 (1949). Greenwood. rpt. 534p. F3. $30.00

HOWE & MARKHAM. *Paul Outerbridge Jr: Photographs.* 1980. NY. Rizzoli. ils. 160p. cloth. dj. D11. $175.00

HOWELL, A.B. *Aquatic Mammals: Their Adaptations to Life in the Water.* 1930. Springfield. Thomas. ils/figures. 338p. gilt pict cloth. F/VG. M12. $60.00

HOWELL, Arthur H. *Birds of Arkansas.* 1911. WA. USDA. 4 pl. 100p. VG. S15. $15.00

HOWELL, John Thomas. *Marin Flora: Manual of Flowering Plants & Ferns...* 1949. Berkeley, CA. 1st. inscr. VG/G+. O4. $20.00

HOWELL, William. *William E Howell's Real Estate Tract Directory...* 1888. LA. Times-Mirror Prt House. 279p. orange brd. D11. $1,000.00

HOWELLS, John Mead. *Architectural Heritage of the Piscataqua.* 1937. NY. 240p. bl cloth. VG. B14. $125.00

HOWELLS, John Mead. *Architectural Heritage of the Piscataqua.* 1965. Architectural Pub. VG/VG. B5. $37.50

HOWELLS, Victor. *Naturalist in Palestine.* 1956. London. 180p. VG/dj. S15. $18.50

HOWELLS, W.D. *Certain Delightful English Towns...* 1906. NY. 1st trade. ils. 290p. teg. VG. B18. $35.00

HOWELLS, W.D. *Questionable Shapes.* 1903. Harper. 1st. VG. M2. $30.00

HOWES, Edith. *Cradle Ship.* 1916. London. Cassell. 1st. ils FM Anderson. 8vo. bl cloth. dj. R5. $175.00

HOWES, Paul Griswold. *Giant Cactus Forest & Its World.* 1954. NY. DSP. ils/drawings. VG/dj. from $25 to $30.00

HOWITT, S. *Orme's Collection of British Field Sports...* 1955. Guildford. Chas Traylen. facsimile 1807 London. obl folio. half leather. B24. $850.00

HOWLAND, Mrs. E. *American Economical Housekeeper & Family Receipt Book.* 1850 (1845). self pub. rebacked. E6. $150.00

HOWSE, Derek. *Francis Place & the Early History of Greenwich Observatory.* 1975. NY. Science Hist Pub. 1st. pl. VG/dj. K3. $30.00

HOWSE & THROWER. *Buccaneer's Atlas: Basil Ringrose's South Sea Waggoner.* 1992. Berkeley. 1st. 107 charts. 314p. as new/dj. P4. $95.00

HOYLE, Trevor. *Last Gasp.* 1983. Crown. 1st. F/dj. M2. $15.00

HOYNE, Thomas Temple. *Intrigue on the Upper Level.* 1934. Reilly Lee. 1st. VG/mc Canon dj. M2. $50.00

HOYT, A.M. *Toto & I: Gorilla in the Family.* 1941. Lippincott. ils/photos. 238p. cloth. F/NF. M12. $27.50

HOYT, E.P. *Battle of Leyte Gulf: Death Knell of Japanese Fleet.* 1972. NY. ils. 314p. VG. S16. $25.00

HOYT, E.P. *Japan's War: Great Pacific Conflict.* 1986. NY. 514p. VG/VG. S16. $25.00

HOYT, E.P. *Peabody Influence: How a Great Family Helped to Build Am.* 1968. photos. VG/VG. M17. $25.00

HOYT, Edwin J. *Buckskin Joe.* 1966. NE U. 1st. edit Glenn Shirley. cloth. VG+/dj. M20. $45.00

HOYT, Edwin. *Guadalcanal.* 1982. NY. maps/photos/index. VG/VG. S16. $25.00

HOYT, Henry. *Frontier Doctor.* 1929. Houghton Mifflin. 1st. 260p. VG. J2. $185.00

HOYT, Richard. *Manna Enzyme.* 1982. Morrow. 1st. NF/VG+. N4. $20.00

HUARD, Frances Wilson. *My Home in the Field of Mercy.* 1917. NY. Doran. 1st. ils Chas Huard. 269p. VG+. A25. $20.00

HUBBARD, B. *Mush You Malemutes.* 1938 (1932). lg 8vo. photos. VG. E6. $20.00

HUBBARD, Elbert. *Ali Baba.* 1926 (1913). East Aurora, NY. ltd. ils/pl. 114p. teg. 3-quarter leather. F/fair. H3. $125.00

HUBBARD, Elbert. *Little Journeys to the Homes of Eminent Painters.* 1902 (1899). Putnam. 16mo. 497p. gilt full suede. VG. H1. $35.00

HUBBARD, Elbert. *Little Journeys to the Homes of Famous Women.* 1928. Roycrofters. A19. $20.00

HUBBARD, Elbert. *Little Journeys to the Homes of the Great.* 1928. Roycrofters. A19. $20.00

HUBBARD, Elbert. *Selected Writings of...* 1928. NY. Wm H Wish Co. Memorial ed. VG/dj. A19. $350.00

HUBBARD, Eleanore Mineah. *Peter Piper's Playmates.* 1930. Chicago. Whitman. 8vo. 62p. F. B24. $150.00

HUBBARD, Harlan. *Shantyboat.* 1954. NY. VG/VG. B5. $37.50

HUBBARD, Jim. *American Refuges.* 1991. MN U. 1st. as new/dj. V4. $25.00

HUBBARD, L. Ron. *Dianetics.* 1950. NY. 1st. VG. B5. $60.00

HUBBARD, L. Ron. *Mission Earth Vol 1, Invaders Plan.* 1985. Bridge. 1st. F/NF. W2. $30.00

HUBBARD, L. Ron. *Mission Earth Vol 6, Death Quest.* 1986. Bridge. 1st. F/F. W2. $30.00

HUBBARD, L. Ron. *Science of Survival: Simplified, Faster Dianetic Techniques.* 1951. Wichita, KS. Hubbard Dianetic Found. 4th. inscr. VG/shabby. B4. $2,500.00

HUBBARD, L. Ron. *Scientology Handbook Based on Works of...* 1994. Bridge. 871p. as new. B29. $35.00

HUBBARD, William. *Narrative of Indian Wars in New England.* 1801. Worcester. leather. A15. $40.00

HUBBARD & KIMBALL. *Introduction to Study of Landscape Design.* nd. np. ils HG Ripley. 36 pl. 406p. decor cloth. xl. G. B18. $37.50

HUCK. *Children's Literature in the Elementary School.* 1979. 3rd. 4to. 813p. VG. A4. $45.00

HUCKER, Charles. *China's Imperial Past.* 1975. Stanford. 1st. 474p. F/F. W3. $46.00

HUDSON, Christopher. *Playing in the Sand.* 1989. London. 1st. VG/VG. T9. $10.00

HUDSON, Derek. *Arthur Rackham: His Life & Work.* 1916. Scribner. 4to. 181p. F/dj. B24. $65.00

HUDSON, Derek. *Lewis Carroll.* 1977. Clarkson Potter. 1st. ils/photos. 271p. A4/D1. $65.00

HUDSON, Harry K. *Bibliography of Hard-Cover Boys' Books.* 1977. self pub. revised/enlarged. 280p. G+/wrp. H1. $85.00

HUDSON, Norman. *American Antiques.* 1972. 1st. ils. NF/VG. S13. $25.00

HUDSON, Travis. *Breath of the Sun.* 1980. Banning, CA. Malki Mus Pr. 1st. F/F. O4. $20.00

HUDSON, W.H. *Green Mansions.* 1976. Heritage. 1st. F/case. M2. $20.00

HUDSON, W.H. *Purple Land: Being Narrative...Richard Lamb's Adventures...* (1911). London. Duckworth. 8vo. 355p. decor cloth. NF. M12. $20.00

HUESTON, Ethel. *Coasting Down East.* 1924. Dodd Mead. 26 pl/text drawings. 304p. T7. $48.00

HUFFAKER, Clair. *Flaming Lance.* 1958. S&S. 1st. VG/clip. B4. $125.00

HUFFMAN, Eugene Henry. *Now I Am Civilized.* 1930. Los Angeles. Wetzel. 1st. sgn. ils Herbert Rasche. F/VG. B4. $850.00

HUGEL, Avon Chew. *Chew Bunch in Browns Park.* 1970. Scrimshaw. 1st. 1/1000. 103p. VG. J2. $185.00

HUGGINS, Nathan Irvin. *Harlem Renaissance.* 1971. Oxford. 1st. NF/dj. M25. $35.00

HUGGLER, Tom. *Grouse of North America.* 1990. Minocqua. 1/4000. sgn. M/dj. A17. $45.00

HUGHES, Colin; see Creasey, John.

HUGHES, Graham. *Modern Silver Throughout the World 1880-1967.* 1967. World. 480 ils. 256p. cloth. dj. D2. $115.00

HUGHES, J.P. *How You Got Your Name: Origin & Meaning of Surnames.* 1959. London. VG/VG. M17. $15.00

HUGHES, Langston. *Ask Your Mama: 12 Moods for Jazz.* 1961. Knopf. 1st. NF/dj. M8. $200.00

HUGHES, Langston. *Big Sea.* 1940. Knopf. 1st. gr brd. VG. M25. $50.00

HUGHES, Langston. *Black Misery.* 1969. Eriksson. 1st. NF/dj. M25. $75.00

HUGHES, Langston. *Black Misery.* 1969. Paul Eriksson. 1st. 57p. VG/dj. D4. $65.00

HUGHES, Langston. *Laughing to Keep From Crying.* 1952. Holt. later prt. NF/dj. M25. $60.00

HUGHES, Langston. *Montage of a Dream Deferred.* 1951. Holt. 1st. blk brd. G. M25. $45.00

HUGHES, Langston. *One Way Ticket.* 1949. NY. 1st. VG/VG. B5. $100.00

HUGHES, Langston. *Simple Speaks His Mind.* 1950. S&S. 1st. VG/VG. M19. $175.00

HUGHES, Langston. *Simple Takes a Wife.* 1953. S&S. 1st. decor brd. sans. A24/M25. $200.00

HUGHES, Langston. *Simple Takes a Wife.* 1954. London. Gollancz. 1st. NF/dj. Q1. $150.00

HUGHES, Langston. *Tambourines to Glory.* 1958. John Day. 1st. inscr/dtd 1963. F/NF. B4. $650.00

HUGHES, Langston. *Ways of White Folks.* 1934. Knopf. 1st. sgn/dtd 1934. orange/blk brd. VG. M25. $250.00

HUGHES, Monica. *Isis Pedlar.* 1983. Atheneum. 1st Am. F/dj. M2. $17.00

HUGHES, Robert R. *Introduction to Clinical Electro-Encephalography.* 1961. Bristol. John Wright. 4to. ils. 118p. panelled red cloth. VG. G1. $30.00

HUGHES, Suckey. *Washi: World of Japanese Paper.* 1978. Tokyo. 1st. 227 pl/maps/glossary. 360p. F/VG. W3. $185.00

HUGHES, Ted. *Cave Birds, an Alchemical Cave Drama.* 1978. Viking. 1st. 62p. coth. NF/NF. D4. $35.00

HUGHES, Ted. *Earth-Owl & Other Moon-People.* 1963. London. Faber. 1st. sgn. 46p. F/F. D4. $100.00

HUGHES, Ted. *Five Autumn Songs for Children's Voices.* 1968. Devonshire. Gilbertston. 1st. 1/150 (of 500 total). sgn. 10p. F/wrp. D4. $165.00

HUGHES, Ted. *Moon-Whales & Other Moon Poems.* 1976. Viking. 1st. 80p. NF/NF. D4. $40.00

HUGHES, Ted. *Rain-Charm for the Duchy.* 1992. London. Faber. 1st. FNF. A24. $25.00

HUGHES, Ted. *Season Songs.* 1975. Viking. 1st. ils Leonard Baskin. 77p. F/F. D4. $65.00

HUGHES, Ted. *Season Songs.* 1976. London. Faber. 1st. 75p. NF/dj. D4. $45.00

HUGHES & ROWE. *Colouring, Bronzing & Patination of Metal.* 1991. Watson Guptill. 372p. cloth. dj. D2. $75.00

HUGO, Victor. *Hunchback of Notre Dame.* nd. AL Burt. 416p. VG/tattered. M20. $40.00

HUGO, Victor. *Les Miserables.* nd. Donohue. ne. 1000p. VG. W2. $350.00

HUGO, Victor. *Notre-Dame de Paris.* 1955. LEC. 1st thus. 1/1500. ils/sgn Bernard Lamotte. F/glassine/case. Q1. $100.00

HUGO, Victor. *Toilers of the Sea.* 1960. LEC. 1st thus. 1/1500. ils/sgn Tranquillo Marangoni. F/dj/case. Q1. $125.00

HUIE, William Bradford. *He Slew the Dreamer.* 1970. Delacorte. 1st. sgn. F/F. B35. $45.00

HUIE, William Bradford. *Hiroshima Pilot.* 1964. xl. G/dj. K3. $10.00

HULBACH, Vladimir. *Sinbad the Sailor, Retold From the Classic...* 1975. London. Hamlyn. ils Vladimir Jachaj. 56p. cloth. VG. W1. $15.00

HULFISH, David S. *Cyclopedia of Motion Picture Work.* 1911. Chicago. 1st hc. 600+p. VG+. A11. $165.00

HULL, Burling. *Thirty-Three Rope Ties & Chain Releases.* ca 1930s. NY. Magno Novelty. 8vo. 46p. F/ils wrp. B24. $75.00

HULL, E. Mayne. *Planets for Sale.* 1954. Fell. 1st. VG/dj. M2. $25.00

HULL, F.M. *Bee Flies of the World.* 1973. Smithsonian. 687p. clip dj. B1. $50.00

HULL, Robert Charlton. *Search for Adele Parker.* 1974. Libra. 1st. 188p. VG/VG. J2. $95.00

HULTGREN, Arland J. *Christ & His Beliefs: Christology & Redemption in New Test.* 1987. Fortress. 285p. VG. B29. $12.00

HULTON & QUINN. *American Drawings of John White, 1577-1590.* 1964. Chapel Hill. NC U. 2 vol. 1st. 1/600. 160 pl. gilt red cloth. F/cloth case. C6. $850.00

HUME, H. Harold. *Camellias in America.* 1955. Harrisburg. McFarland. revised. 422p. A10. $75.00

HUME, H. Harold. *Camellias.* 1951. Macmillan. 1st. 8vo. ils/pl. 271p. VG/torn. A22. $20.00

HUMMEL, Arthur. *Eminent Chinese of the Ch'ing Period 1644-1912.* 1970. Taipei. 1103p. F. W3. $68.00

HUMPHREY, George. *Human Foot & Human Hand.* 1861. London. 1st. 216p. A13. $250.00

HUMPHREY, Zephine. *'Allo Good-By.* 1940. Dutton. 1st. 284p. VG/dj. A25. $10.00

HUMPHREYS, A.A. *Virginia Campaign of 1864 & 1865.* 1883. 1st. 9 lg fld maps. 451p. O8. $21.50

HUMPHREYS, Henry Noel. *Origin & Progress of Art of Writing.* 1855. London. Day. 4to. 28 pl. mid-Victorian papier-mache bdg. R12. $475.00

HUMPHREYS, W.J. *Ways of the Weather.* 1942. Lancaster, PA. Cattell. 4to. 400p. G/dj. K5. $18.00

HUMPHRIES, Jefferson. *Conversations With Reynolds Price.* 1991. Jackson, MS. 1st. sgn Reynolds Price. F/F. R13. $35.00

HUMPHRIES, Sydney. *Oriental Carpets, Runners & Rugs & Some Jacquard Repros.* 1910. London. Adam/Chas Blk. 1st. thick 4to. 427p. polished wht linen. VG. T10. $200.00

HUNG, William. *Tu Fu: China's Greatest Poet.* 1952. Harvard. 1st. 300p. F/VG. W3. $65.00

HUNGERFORD, Edward. *Wells Fargo Advancing the American Frontier.* 1949. Random. 1st. 274p. pict cloth. VG. B14. $45.00

HUNGERFORD, Edwin. *Men of Eire: Story of Human Effort.* 1946. NY. 2nd. 346p. map ep. VG/dj. B18. $20.00

HUNGERFORD, James. *Falcon Rover.* 1866. NY. Beadle. Beadle Dime Novel #112. 8vo. orange wrp. R12. $60.00

HUNNICUTT, Ellen. *In the Music Library.* 1987. Pittsburgh. 1st. NF/NF. R13. $20.00

HUNNICUTT, R.P. *Firepower: History of the American Heavy Tank.* 1988. Novato. 224p. VG/VG. S16. $45.00

HUNNISETT & POST. *Medieval Coroner.* 1961. Cambridge. M11. $85.00

HUNNISETT & POST. *Medieval Legal Records, Edit in Memory of CAF Meekings.* 1978. London. Her Majesty's Stationary Office. M11. $75.00

HUNT, Barbara. *Little Night Music.* 1947. Rinehart. 1st. F/VG. B4. $75.00

HUNT, Edward Eyre. *Greathouse.* 1937. Harcourt. 1st. NF/dj. M2. $20.00

HUNT, Frazier. *Untold Story of Douglas MacArthur.* 1954. Devin Adair. 1st. sgn. VG/G. A23. $40.00

HUNT, Irene. *Trail of Apple Blossoms.* 1968. Chicago. Follett. 1st. 8vo. 64p. VG/VG. T5. $24.00

HUNT, John M. *Creating an Australian Garden.* 1986. Kenhurst, NSW. ils/photos. 168p. F/dj. B26. $24.00

HUNT, John. *Ascent of Everest.* 1953. London. 1st. 300p. F/G. A17. $20.00

HUNT, Kyle; see Creasey, John.

HUNT, Mabel Leigh. *Benjie's Hat.* 1938. Stokes. 1st. ils Grace Paull. 119p. VG/dj. P2. $35.00

HUNT, Mabel Leigh. *Johnny-Up & Johnny-Down.* 1962. Lippincott. Weekly Reader BC. 1st. 94p. VG. V3. $8.50

HUNT, Mabel Leigh. *Michael's Island.* 1940. Stokes. 1st. ils Kate Seredy. 266p. VG/dj. P2. $50.00

HUNT, Mabel Leigh. *Young Man of the House.* 1944. Lippincott. 1st. 171p. VG/dj. V3. $22.00

HUNT, Rockwell D. *Fifteen Decisive Events of California History.* 1959. Los Angeles. 1st. F. O4. $25.00

HUNT, Thomas. *Ghost Trails of California.* 1974. Palo Alto, CA. 1st. Images of Am series. 4to. ils. F/VG. O4. $25.00

HUNT, W.R. *Alaska: A Bicentennial History.* 1976. NY. 1st. photos/maps. 200p. F/dj. M4. $20.00

HUNT, W.R. *Arctic Passage: Turbulent History of the Land & People...* (1975). NY. 1st. ils/map. gr cloth. VG/clip. H3. $40.00

HUNT & MOORE. *Atlas of Neptune.* 1994. Cambridge. F/F. K5. $20.00

HUNT & SANCHEZ. *Short History of California.* 1929. NY. Crowell. 8vo. 671p. gilt red cloth. xl. VG. K7. $50.00

HUNT & THOMPSON. *North to the Horizon: Arctic Doctor & Hunter 1913-1917.* 1980. Camden. 117p. F/dj. A17. $20.00

HUNTER, Ben. *Baja Feeling.* nd. Ontario, CA. Brasch. 1st. F/F. O4. $20.00

HUNTER, Evan. *Another Part of the City.* 1986. Mysterious. 1st. NF/NF. M22. $15.00

HUNTER, Evan. *Beauty & the Beast.* 1983. Holt. 1st. F/F. N4. $35.00

HUNTER, Evan. *Cinderella.* 1986. Holt. 1st. F/F. B4. $50.00

HUNTER, Evan. *Cut Me In.* 1954. Abelard Schuman. 1st. VG. M25. $25.00

HUNTER, Evan. *Downtown.* 1991. Morrow. 1st Am. F/F. N4. $25.00

HUNTER, Evan. *Easter Man.* 1972. Doubleday. 1st. VG/VG. M22. $15.00

HUNTER, Evan. *Every Little Crook & Nanny.* 1972. Doubleday. 1st. inscr. VG/VG. M22. $35.00

HUNTER, Evan. *Ice.* 1983. Arbor. 1st. sgn. F/NF. B3. $50.00

HUNTER, Evan. *Jigsaw.* 1970. Doubleday. 1st. VG/dj. M25. $25.00

HUNTER, Evan. *Let's Hear It for the Deaf Man.* 1973. Doubleday. 1st. F/F. M25. $17.50

HUNTER, Evan. *Mischief: A Novel of the 87th Precinct.* 1993. Morrow. 1st. sgn. VG/VG. A23. $40.00

HUNTER, Evan. *Pusher.* 1991. Armchair Detective. 1st in hc. as new/dj. N4. $30.00

HUNTER, Evan. *Puss in Boots.* 1987. Holt. 1st. F/dj. M15. $35.00

HUNTER, Evan. *Rumplestiltskin.* 1981. Viking. 1st. F/F. N4. $45.00

HUNTER, Evan. *Snow White & Rose Red.* 1985. HRW. 1st. F/dj. M15. $30.00

HUNTER, Evan. *Strangers When We Meet.* 1958. S&S. 1st. F/NF. B4. $100.00

HUNTER, Evan. *Streets of Gold.* 1974. Harper Row. 1st. VG+/F. A20. $30.00

HUNTER, Evan. *Tricks.* 1987. Arbor. 1st. F/F. A20. $25.00

HUNTER, J.A. *Hunter's Tracks.* 1947. Appleton Century Croft. 1st. 8vo. photos. 240p. F/VG. H1. $55.00

HUNTER, J.A. *Hunter.* 1952. Harper. A19. $25.00

HUNTER, J.M. *Trail Drivers of Texas.* 1925. 2nd/revised. 1044p. VG. A15. $175.00

HUNTER, Jim Catfish. *Catfish: My Life in Baseball.* 1988. McGraw Hill. 1st. F/F. T12. $70.00

HUNTER, John. *Treatise on Blood, Inflammation & Gun-Shot Wounds.* 1840. Phil. 611p. half leather. A13. $200.00

HUNTER, Kristin. *Landlord.* 1966. Scribner. 1st. NF/NF. M25. $60.00

HUNTER, Louis. *Steamboats on the Western Rivers.* 1949. Cambridge. ils/pl/tables. 684p. dj. T7. $85.00

HUNTER, Robert. *Violence & the Labor Movement.* 1914. Macmillan. 1st. F. V4. $25.00

HUNTER, Stephen. *Black Light.* 1996. Doubleday. 1st. sgn. F/F. A23. $40.00

HUNTER, Stephen. *Day Before Midnight.* 1989. Bantam. 1st. F/F. H11. $60.00

HUNTER, Stephen. *Spanish Gambit.* 1985. Crown. 1st. 389p. F/F. W2. $35.00

HUNTER, W.S. *Hunter's Eastern Townships Scenery, Canada East.* 1860. Montreal. John Lovell. 1st. lg 4to. cloth. VG. M1. $1,750.00

HUNTER & FERGUSON. *Ancient America & the Book of Mormon.* 1950. Oakland, CA. Kolob Book. 1st. 8vo. 448p. VG/dj. K7. $45.00

HUNTER & ROSE. *Album of Gun-Fighters.* 1951. Hunter Rose. 1st. 236p. ES. VG/dj. J2. $475.00

HUNTFORD, Roland. *Amundsen Photographs.* 1987. NY. 199p. F/dj. A17. $30.00

HUNTINGTON, Dwight W. *Our Wild Fowl & Waders.* (1910). NY. Amateur Sportsman. 1st. sgn pres. 207p. red cloth. VG. H7. $60.00

HUNTINGTON, James. *On the Edge of Nowhere: A Thrilling True Story...Alaska.* 1966. NY. Crown. 8vo. 183p. VG/worn. P4. $25.00

HUNTINGTON, Nathaniel G. *System of Modern Geography...* 1835. Hartford. 306p. prt brd/leather spine. G. B14. $55.00

HURD, Clement. *Race Between the Monkey & the Duck.* 1946 (1940). Wonder. lg 8vo. NF. C8. $35.00

HURD, Edith Thacher. *Dinosaur My Darling.* 1978. Harper Row. 1st. ils Don Freeman. 32p. NF/VG+. P2. $35.00

HURD, Edith Thacher. *Faraway Christmas.* 1958. lee Shepard. 1st. ils Clement Hurd. NF/VG. P2. $40.00

HURLEY & LEGG. *Once More on My Adventure: Life of Frank Hurley.* 1966. Sydney/London. Ure Smith Pty Ltd. 8vo. 227p. VG/dj. P4. $85.00

HURLEY & PONTING. *Antarctic Photographs.* 1979. Macmillan. photos. 129p. dj. P4. $85.00

HURLIMANN, Bettina. *Picture-Book World.* 1968. London. Oxford. 1st Eng. 4to. red/wht pict brd. dj. R5. $100.00

HURLIMANN, Bettina. *Seven Houses: My Life With Books.* 1976. London. Bodley Head. photos. 216p. F/NF. A4. $65.00

HURLIMANN, Bettina. *Three Centuries of Children's Books in Europe.* 1967. London. Oxford. ils. 297p. F/F. A4. $60.00

HURLIMANN, Martin. *Frankreich Landschaft und Baukunst.* 1931. Berlin-Zurich. 1st. 304 full-p photos. lg 4to. A17. $35.00

HURNARD, Noami D. *King's Pardon for Homicide Before AD 1307.* 1969. Clarendon. VG/dj. M11. $65.00

HURRELL, George. *Portfolios of George Hurrell.* 1991. Graystone. photos. wht cloth. dj. O3. $85.00

HURST, Earl Oliver. *Big Book of Space.* 1959 (1953). Grosset Dunlap. 4to. 26p. VG. K5. $12.00

HURST, Fannie. *Every Soul Hath Its Song.* 1916. NY. Harper. 1st. F/F. B4. $400.00

HURST, Fannie. *Star-Dust: Story of an American Girl.* 1921. Harper. 1st. F/NF. B4. $400.00

HURST, S.B.H. *Commera Ali.* 1922. Harper. 1st. VG. M2. $25.00

HURSTON, Zora Neale. *Complete Stories.* 1995. Harper. 1st. F/F. R13. $25.00

HURSTON, Zora Neale. *Gilded Six-Bits.* 1986. Redpath. 1st thus. Perfect Present series. F/wrp/envelope. Q1. $40.00

HURSTON, Zora Neale. *Moses, Man of the Mountain.* 1939. Lippincott. 1st. NF/VG. B4. $750.00

HURSTON, Zora Neale. *Tell My Horse.* 1938. Phil. 2nd. VG/dj. B5. $165.00

HUSMANN, George. *American Grape Growing & Wine Making.* 1907. Orange Judd. 4th. 269p. A10. $55.00

HUSSEY, A. *Voyage of the Racoon: A Secret Journal of Visit to Oregon...* 1958. SF. BC of CA. 1/400. ils H Gusk. marbled brd/morocco spine. F. w/prospectus. R3. $135.00

HUSSEY, Christopher. *Eton College.* 1923. London. 2nd. lg 4to. ES. half leather. VG. T10. $100.00

HUSTE, Annemarie. *Annemarie's Cooking School Cookbook.* 1974. Houghton Mifflin. 1st. sgn. VG/dj. A16. $12.00

HUSTON, James. *Out of the Blue: US Army Airborne Operations in WWII.* 1982. TN. ils/maps. 327p. VG/VG. S16. $21.50

HUTCHENS, Alma R. *Indian Herbology of North America.* 1983 (1969). Windsor, Ontario. 9th. ils/glossary/index. 382p. B26. $47.50

HUTCHENSON, Horace G. *Life of Sir John Lubbock.* 1914. London. Lord Avebury. 2 vol. ils/2 pl/fld pedigree. bl cloth. VG. B26. $69.00

HUTCHEON, Wallace S. *Robert Fulton: Pioneer of Undersea Warfare.* 1981. Annapolis. Naval Inst. ils. 191p. dj. T7. $25.00

HUTCHINS, Pat. *Wind Blew.* 1974. Macmillan. 1st. 32p. NF/dj. D4. $40.00

HUTCHINSON, I.W. *Calling of Bride.* nd. Stirling. Eneas Mackay. inscr. 32p. VG. P4. $75.00

HUTCHINSON, Jonathan. *Extracts From the Letters of Jonathan Hutchinson...* 1844. London. Harvey Darton. 2nd. 376p. V3. $15.00

HUTCHINSON, Veronica S. *Chimney Corner Poems.* 1929. Minton Balch. 1st. ils Lois Lenski. 4to. G. P2. $30.00

HUTCHINSON, Veronica S. *Henny Penny.* 1976. Little Brn. 1st thus. ils Leonard B Lubin. unp. F/F. T5. $45.00

HUTCHINSON, W.H. *California: Two Centures of Man, Land & Growth Golden State.* 1969. Palo Alto. Am W Pub. ils/collated John Barr Tompkins. 352p. F/NF. K7. $25.00

HUTCHINSON, William T. *Cyrus Hall McCormick, Harvest, 1856-1884.* 1935. Appleton. 1st. photos/charts/maps. 793p. VG. K3. $20.00

HUTTON, Harold. *Vigilante Days.* 1978. Chicago. Swallow. dj. A19. $45.00

HUTTON, Laurence. *From the Books of Laurence Hutton.* 1892. NY. Harper. 1st. teg. dk gr cloth. M24. $35.00

HUXLEY, Aldous. *After Many a Summer Dies the Swan.* 1939. Chatto Windus. 1st. VG. M25. $45.00

HUXLEY, Aldous. *After Many a Summer Dies the Swan.* 1939. Harper. 1st Am. VG/G torn. M25. $60.00

HUXLEY, Aldous. *Ape & Essence.* 1948. Harper. 1st. F/NF. M25. $45.00

HUXLEY, Aldous. *Art of Seeing.* 1942. Harper. 1st. F/VG. M19. $35.00

HUXLEY, Aldous. *Brave New World.* 1932. Doubleday. 1st Am. VG/dj. B4. $350.00

HUXLEY, Aldous. *Devils of Loudon.* 1952. Harper. 1st. F/VG. T12. $75.00

HUXLEY, Aldous. *Ends & Means.* 1937. NY. Harper. 1st Am. NF. B24. $50.00

HUXLEY, Aldous. *Gioconda Smile. A Play.* 1948. Chatto Windus. AP. gray-gr plain wrp. B24. $65.00

HUXLEY, Aldous. *Leda.* (1920). NY. Doran. 1st Am. 1/500. sgn. linen-backed lavender brd. M24. $225.00

HUXLEY, Aldous. *Music at Night & Other Essays.* 1931. NY. Fountain. 1st. 1/842. sgn. quarter blk cloth/marbled brd. F. M24. $150.00

HUXLEY, Aldous. *On the Margin.* 1923. Chatto Windus. 1st. gray-gr cloth. F/NF. M24. $125.00

HUXLEY, Anthony. *Plant & Planet.* 1974. Readers Union. 428p. F/VG. S15. $10.00

HUXLEY, E. *Whipsnade: Captive Breeding for Survival.* 1981. London. Collins. ils/photos. 159p. F/F. M12. $17.50

HUXLEY, Elspeth. *Out in the Midday Sun: My Kenya.* 1987. Viking. 1st Am. 8vo. 262p. NF/dj. W1. $25.00

HUXLEY, Francis. *Raven & the Writing Desk.* 1976. ils. 191p. F/F. A4. $85.00

HUXLEY, Francis. *Way of the Sacred.* 1989. London. 1st. VG/VG. T9. $15.00

HUXLEY, Julian. *From an Antique Land. Ancient & Modern in the Middle East.* 1955. London. Parrish. 3rd. 8vo. 66 pl/maps. 310p. VG. W1. $14.00

HUXLEY, Thomas H. *American Address With a Lecture on Study of Biology.* 1877. Appleton. 1st. ils. 164p. G. K3. $35.00

HUXLEY & LEARY. *Visionary Experience & How to Change Behavior.* 1962. Copenhagen. Munksgaard. 2nd separate prt. 8vo. 39p. wht self-wrp. M1. $750.00

HUYGHE, Rene. *Watteau's Universe.* 1968. Paris/Woodbury. Screpel/Barron. ils. 118p. clear plastic dj. D2. $40.00

HYAMS, Edward. *Astrologer.* 1950. London. Lognman. 1st. F/VG+. B4. $100.00

HYAMS, Joe. *Flight of the Avenger.* 1993. Harcourt Brace. 1st. inscr George Bush. F/F. A23. $125.00

HYAMS, Paul R. *King, Lords & Peasants in Medieval England...* 1980. Clarendon. M11. $65.00

HYDE, George. *Sioux Chronicle.* 1956. Norman, OK. 1st. 334p. VG/dj. J2. $80.00

HYDE, George. *Spotted Tail's Folk, a History of the Brule Sioux.* 1961. Norman, OK. 1st. 329p. VG/VG. J2. $95.00

HYDE, J.A. Lloyd. *Oriental Lowestoft Chinese Export Porcelains...* 1954. Newport, Eng. Ceramic Book Co. 2nd. 1/1500. ils. 166p. VG. W3. $150.00

HYDE, Joe. *Love, Time & Butter.* 1971. NY. Richard Baron. VG/dj. A16. $12.00

HYDE, Robert. *McTodd.* 1903. Macmillan. 1st. VG. M2. $22.00

HYDE, Robert. *Winds of Gobi.* 1930. Brewer Warren. 1st. VG. M2. $25.00

HYDE & JETT. *Navajo Wildlands.* 1969. Sierra Club. 8vo. 158p. VG. F7. $20.00

HYDEN, Dorothea Hoaglin. *These Pioneers.* 1938. Los Angeles. 1st. inscr. VG. O4. $20.00

HYGINUS, Gaius Julius. *Poeticon Astronomicon.* 1985. Greenbrae, CA. Allen. 1/140. trans Livingston/Smith. F/case. w/prospectus. B24. $350.00

HYLAND & LOCKWOOD. *Estates of Beverly Hills, Holmby Hills, Bel-Air...* 1984. Beverly Hills. Margrant Pub. 1st. ils. 161p. dj. D11. $125.00

HYLANDER, C.J. *Cruisers of the Air.* 1931. NY. 1st. photos/drawings. 308p. B18. $95.00

HYLL, Thomas. *First Garden Book.* 1946. Herrin, IL. 3rd. 98p. cloth. A10. $40.00

HYMAN, Marc. *No Time for Sergeants.* 1954. 1st. author's 1st book. NF/VG. S13. $50.00

There is a superstition in the book trade that all books about Lincoln sell, that all books about dogs sell, and that all books by and about doctors sell. Ergo, say the publishers and booksellers, the crafty inkster who can combine these favorite subjects, and produce a book about Lincoln's doctor's dog, is going to clean up.

Vincent Starrett
1886 – 1974

ICARDI, Aldo. *American Master Spy.* 1954. Stalwart Ent. 1st. VG/G. E6. $25.00

IDEL, Albert E. *Great Blizzard.* 1948. Holt. BC. VG/G. P8. $30.00

IGLAUER, Edith. *Strangers Next Door.* 1991. Harbour. 1st. VG/dj. N2. $10.00

IGNATIUS, David. *Siro.* 1991. NY. FSG. 1st. F/F. H11. $35.00

ILES, Greg. *Black Cross.* 1995. Dutton. 1st. F/NF. N4. $35.00

ILLINGWORTH, Frank. *Highway to the North.* 1955. NY. Philosophical Lib. 8vo. ils/fld map. 293p. VG/dj. P4. $20.00

ILLINGWORTH, Frank. *North of the Circle.* 1951. Philsophical Lib. 8vo. 253p. VG. P4. $25.00

ILLSON, Willard Rouse. *Harrod's Old Fort, 1791.* 1929. KY Hist Soc. 1st. 12p. B10. $25.00

IMBER, Jonathan. *Abortion & the Private Practice of Medicine.* 1986. New Haven. 1st. 164p. A13. $30.00

IMHOLTE, John Quinn. *First Volunteers: History of 1st MN Volunteer Regiment...* 1963. Minneapolis. Ross & Haines. 1st. NF/clip. A14. $28.00

IMPEY, Rose. *Letter to Santa Claus.* Nov 1989. Delacorte. 1st. ils Sue Porter. VG+. B36. $9.00

INAYAT KHAN, Hazrat. *Sufi Message of Hazrat Inayat Khan. Vol XI: Philosophy...* 1964. London. Barrie Rockliff. 8vo. 259p. VG/tattered. W1. $18.00

INGALLS, Fay. *Valley Road: Story of Virginia Hot Springs.* 1949. Cleveland. World. 2nd. F/NF. B20. $12.50

INGE, William. *Come Back, Little Sheba.* 1950. NY. Random. 1st. author's 1st book. F/clip. Q1. $200.00

INGERSOLL, Ernest. *Country Cousins: Short Studies in Natural History of US.* 1884. NY. Harper. 1st. 252p. gilt bl cloth. VG+. B20. $45.00

INGERSOLL, Ernest. *Dragons & Dragon Lore.* 1928. Payson Clarke. 1st. ils. paper brd/blk cloth spine. VG+. B20. $75.00

INGERSOLL, Ernest. *Silver Caves.* 1900. Dodd Mead. 1st. 8vo. 216p. NF/dj. J3. $75.00

INGERSOLL, Robert Green. *Complete Lectures of...* nd. Chicago. J Regan. 411p. reading copy. H1. $12.00

INGLIS, Andrew F. *Behind the Tube.* 1990. Boston. Focal. 527p. VG. C5. $20.00

INGLIS, Brian. *History of Medicine.* 1965. Cleveland. 1st. 196p. dj. A13. $50.00

INGLIS & WEST. *Alternative Health Guide.* 1983. Knopf. 1st Am. 352p. VG/dj. P12. $12.00

INGOLD, Ernest. *House in Mallorca.* 1950. SF. Paul Elder. 48p. patterned cloth. D11. $50.00

INGOLDSBY, Thomas. *Jackdaw of Rheims.* 1913. London. ils Chas Folkard. G. M17. $20.00

INGRAM, Rex Llopis. *Mars in the House of Death.* 1939. Knopf. 1st. VG/dj. C9. $78.00

INGRAMS, Richard. *Dr Johnson by Mrs Thrale: Anecdotes in Their Orig Form.* 1984. Chatto Windus/Hogarth. 1st. F/dj. H13. $55.00

INGSTAD, Helge. *Nunamiut: Among Alaska's Inland Eskimos.* 1954. Norton. 1st. photos. 303p. VG. S14. $17.50

INMAN, Arthur Crew. *Inman Diary.* 1985. Cambridge. Harvard. 2 vol. 1st. gilt bl cloth. F/case/pub wrp band. F1. $35.00

INMAN, Henry. *Stories of the Old Santa Fe Trail.* 1881. Kansas City, MO. Ramsey Millett Hudson. 1st. 8vo. ils. 287p. cloth. O1. $150.00

INNES, Hammond. *Conquistadors.* 1970 (1969). NY. Knopf. rpt. 8vo. 336p. red cloth. dj. F7. $25.00

INNES, Hammond. *Wreck of the Mary Deare.* 1956. Knopf. 1st Am. VG/G. L4. $22.00

INNES, Lowell. *Pittsburgh Glass 1797-1891.* 1976. Houghton Mifflin. 1st. 4to. 522p. blk cloth. VG/dj. H1. $175.00

INNES, Michael. *Hare Sitting Up.* 1959. London. Gollancz. 1st. F/VG. M15. $40.00

INNES, Michael. *Honeybath's Heaven.* 1977. London. Gollancz. 1st. F/dj. C15. $25.00

INNIS & INNIS. *Gold in the Blue Ridge: Story of the Beale Treasure.* 1973. WA. ils/maps. F/dj. M4. $28.00

INTERNATIONAL BRIDGE ASSOC. *Bridge Writer's Choice 1964: Their Favorite Hands.* VG. S1. $10.00

IOESCO, Eugene. *Story Number 1.* 1968. Harlan Quist. 1st. ils Etienne Delessert. NF/dj. D4. $55.00

IOONS, Walter. *Diamond Dreams.* 1995. Little Brn. 1st. F/dj. P8. $40.00

IPCAR, Dahlov. *Brown Cow Farm.* (1959). Doubleday. early ed. 42p. brd. F/dj. D4. $30.00

IRBY, Kenneth. *Relation.* 1970. Blk Sparrow. 1st. 1/26 (201 total). sgn/lettered. F/dj. w/ils. L3. $125.00

IREDALE, Tom. *Birds of New Guinea.* 1956. Melbourne. Georgian House. 2 vol. 1st. 35 mc pl/fld map. teg. NF. B20. $375.00

IRELAND, Alexander Jr. *Book-Lover's Enchiridion.* 1884. London. Simpkin Marshall. 4th. 8vo. 492p. gilt bl cloth. VG. H4. $30.00

IRIS, Scharmel. *Spanish Earth.* (1964). Chicago. Ralph Fletcher Seymour. inscr/sgn. gilt bl linen. F/NF. H4. $75.00

IRONS, W.V. *Water Resources of the Upper Colorado River Basin.* 1964. GPO. 1036p. A10. $25.00

IRVING, Blanche M. *Five Deer on Loco Mountain Road: People & Places...* 1982. Sunstone. 1st. sgn. ils. 64p. F/sans. B19. $20.00

IRVING, Clifford. *Final Argument.* 1993. S&S. 1st. F/NF. T12. $20.00

IRVING, Frederick. *Safe Deliverance.* 1942. Boston. 1st. 308p. A13. $25.00

IRVING, John. *Cider House Rules.* 1985. Morrow. 1st. F/F. H11. $35.00

IRVING, John. *Cider House Rules.* 1985. Morrow. 1st. NF/dj. S18. $25.00

IRVING, John. *Hotel New Hampshire.* 1981. Dutton. 1st. F/dj. B30. $30.00

IRVING, John. *Prayer for Owen Meany.* 1989. Morrow. 1st/ltd. 543p. F/dj. W2. $35.00

IRVING, John. *Prayer for Owen Meany.* 1989. Toronto. Dennys. 1st Canadian. NF/F. H11. $35.00

IRVING, John. *Widow for One Year.* 1998. Unicycle. 1/1200. sgn/#d. special leather. AN. B30. $160.00

IRVING, John. *World According to Garp.* 1978. Dutton. 1st. author's 4th novel. gilt quarter cloth. F/dj. M24. $125.00

IRVING, Pierre. *Life & Letters of Washington Irving.* 1883. Putnam. 3 vol. Memorial ed. 1/300. ils/tissue guards. VG. H4. $60.00

IRVING, Washington. *Astoria; or, Anecdotes of an Enterprise Beyond Rocky Mtns.* 1964. U OK. 556p. VG/dj. J2. $95.00

IRVING, Washington. *Chronicle of Conquest of Granada.* 1829. Phil. Lea Carey. 2 vol. sm format prt. 8vo. full calf. H4. $125.00

IRVING, Washington. *History of New York From the Beginning of the World...* 1820. London. John Murray. 1st Eng. 8vo. 520p. maroon morocco. O1. $225.00

IRVING, Washington. *Oliver Goldsmith, a Biography.* 1872. Phil. Lippincott. 8vo. 427p. teg. cloth. w/facs letter. VG. H13. $175.00

IRVING, Washington. *Rip Van Winkle & Legend of Sleepy Hollow.* 1974. ils Felix OC Darley. VG/dj. M17. $20.00

IRVING, Washington. *Rip Van Winkle.* 1993. Creative Eds. probable 1st. folio. VG/dj. B17. $15.00

IRVING, Washington. *Rip Van Winkle: Legend of the Kaatskill Mountains.* 1923. Lippincott. 7th. ils Edna Cook. VG. T12. $30.00

IRVING, Washington. *Tales of Alhambra.* nd. Granada, Spain. red leather. M17. $15.00

IRVING, Washington. *Wolfert's Roost & Other Papers, Now First Collected.* 1855. Putnam. 12mo. 384p+12p ads. pict olive cloth. VG. K1. $50.00

IRVING, Washington. *Wolfert's Roost & Other Papers.* 1855. NY. Putnam. 1st/1st prt/1st bdg. gilt gr cloth. NF. M24. $100.00

IRWIN, Constance. *Fair Gods & Stone Faces.* 1963. St Martin. 1st. 346p. dj. F3. $25.00

IRWIN, David. *Alone Across the Top of the World.* 1935. Winston. 1st. 8vo. 254p. G. S14. $20.00

IRWIN, Frank. *Herbal Woodcuts & Legends.* 1971. Tilton, NH. Hillside. mini. 1/250. sgn/#d. 56p. pink pict cloth. B24. $95.00

IRWIN, Inez Haynes. *Maida's Little Island.* 1939. Grosset Dunlap. VG/dj. M20. $20.00

IRWIN, Jim. to *Rule the Night: Discovery Voyage of Astronaut...* (1973). Phil/NY. inscr pres. F/VG. H4. $200.00

IRWIN, Wallace. *Letters of a Japanese Schoolboy.* 1909. Doubleday Page. 1st. cream cloth. F. M24. $50.00

ISAACS, Susan. *Magic Hour.* 1991. Harper Collins. 1st. F/dj. T12. $15.00

ISAACS, Susan. *Shining Through.* 1988. Harper Row. 1st. sgn. NF/dj. B30. $25.00

ISCHLONDSKY, Naum Efimovich. *Neuropsyche und Himrind.* 1930. Berlin. Urban & Schwarzenberg. 2 vol. buckram. G1. $75.00

ISEMAN, John W. *Aviation Manual: A Practical Handbook.* 1930. NY. Popular Science. 1st. 698p. G+. B18. $47.50

ISHERWOOD, Christopher. *Diaries 1939-60.* 1996. London. 1st. edit K Bucknell. dj. T9. $35.00

ISHERWOOD, Christopher. *Down There on a Visit.* 1962. S&S. 1st. VG/G. B30. $25.00

ISHERWOOD, Christopher. *Memorial: Portrait of a Family.* 1946. Norfolk. 1st. dj. T9. $65.00

ISHERWOOD, Christopher. *People One Ought to Know.* 1982. London. Macmillan. 1st. unp. brd. F/dj. D4. $35.00

ISHERWOOD, Christopher. *Prater Violet.* 1946. London. Methuen. 1st. NF/dj. A24/T9. $50.00

ISHIGURO, Kazuo. *Remains of the Day.* 1986. NY. Knopf. 1st Am. F/dj. C9. $90.00

ISLAS, Arturo. *Migrant Souls.* 1990. NY. Morrow. 1st. F/F. H11. $20.00

ISRAEL, Lee. *Estee Lauder: Beyond the Magic.* 1985. Macmillan. 1st. NF/dj. W2. $30.00

ISSLER, Anne Roller. *Stevenson at Silverado.* 1974. Valley Pub. revised/3rd prt. F/wrp. W2. $15.00

ISTVAN, Kafer. *Az Egyetemi Nyomda Negyszza Eve.* (1977). Magyar. Helikon. 4to. Hungarian text. ils. 247p+index. F/dj. H4. $75.00

ITIX, Charles. *Looking Good: A Guide for Men.* 1977. Hawthorn. later prt. photos Bruce Weber. VG/dj. C9. $60.00

IVANOFF, Pierre. *Monuments of Civilization: Maya.* 1973. Grosset Dunlap. 2nd. 191p. dj. F3. $40.00

IVERSON, Peter. *When Indians Became Cowboys: Native Peoples & Cattle...* 1994. U OK. photos. 266p. AN. J2. $45.00

IVES, A.G.L. *British Hospitals.* 1948. London. 1st. 50p. A13. $20.00

IVES, George. *Bibliography of Oliver Wendell Holmes.* 1907. Houghton Mifflin. 1/530. 337p. F1. $65.00

IVES, J. Moss. *Ark & the Dove: Beginning of Civil & Religious Liberties...* 1936. London. ils. VG/G. M17. $20.00

IVES, Morgan; see Bradley, Marion Zimmer.

IVINS, William M. *Prints & Books: Informal Papers.* 1926. Cambridge. 8vo. 'Withdrawn' on ffe. 375p. H4. $20.00

IVY, A.C. *Observations on Krebiozen in the Treatment of Cancer.* 1956. Chicago. Regnery. 1st. 88p. F/worn. N2. $12.50

IWASAKI, Chihiro. *Momoko & the Pretty Bird.* 1973. Follett. 1st. ils. F/NF. M5. $15.00

IZANT, Grace Goulder. *This Is Ohio.* (1953). Cleveland/NY. World. 1st. inscr/dtd pres. 264p. w/business card. H4. $20.00

IZZARD, Bob. *Adobe Walls Wars: Fascinating Yet True Story...* 1993. TX. 1st. maps. 116p. stiff wrp. E1. $30.00

IZZEDDIN, Nejla. *Arab World: Past, Present & Future.* 1953. Chicago. Regnery. 1st. 8vo. ils. 412p. cloth. VG. W1. $25.00

IZZI, Eugene. *Booster.* 1989. St Martin. 1st. F/dj. A23. $30.00

IZZI, Eugene. *Invasions.* 1990. NY. Bantam. 1st. F/dj. B2/H11. $30.00

IZZI, Eugene. *Prowlers.* 1991. Bantam. 1st. F/F. H11. $30.00

– J –

JABLOKOV, Alexander. *Deeper Sea*. 1992. Morrow. 1st ed. F/F. G10/P3. $22.00

JACCACI, A.F. *Saharan Caravan*. 1893. Scribner. ils. VG. P4. $15.00

JACKH, Ernest. *Rising Crescent: Turkey, Yesterday, Today & Tomorrow*. 1944. Farrar Rhinehart. 1st ed. ils. 278p. xl. VG. W1. $24.00

JACKMAN, Stuart. *Davidson Affair*. 1966. Eerdmans. VG/VG. P3. $13.00

JACKOBS, Harvey. *Egg of the Glak & Other Stories*. 1969. NY. 1st ed. F/F. A17. $10.00

JACKSON, Basil. *Epicenter*. 1971. Norton. 2nd. NF/NF. P3. $10.00

JACKSON, Bruce. *Thief's Primer*. 1969. Macmillan. 1st ed. F/F. H11. $45.00

JACKSON, C.S. *Picturemaker of the Old West: William H Jackson*. 1947. Scribner. NF/G. D2. $60.00

JACKSON, Charles. *Outer Edges*. 1948. NY. 1st ed. 240p. F/dj. A17. $15.00

JACKSON, Donald Dale. *Gold Dust*. 1980. NY. 1st ed. 361p. F/F. E1. $40.00

JACKSON, Donald. *Voyages of the Steamboat Yellow Stone*. 1985. Ticknor Fields. dj. A16. $15.00

JACKSON, G. *Peggy Stewart at School*. 1918. Goldsmith. ils Norman Rockwell. VG/VG. B17. $10.00

JACKSON, G. Gibbard. *World's Aeroplanes & Airships*. 1929. London. Sampson Low. probable 1st ed. 244p. fair. B18. $65.00

JACKSON, Gordon. *History & Archaeology of Ports*. 1983. London. Windmill. 25 ils. VG/dj. T7. $35.00

JACKSON, Helen Hunt. *Ramona*. 1884. Roberts. 1st ed. F. A18. $500.00

JACKSON, Holbrook. *Anatomy of Bibliomania*. 1930-1931. London. Soncino. 2 vol. 1/1000. VG. A4. $200.00

JACKSON, J. Hughlings. *Selected Writings of JH Jackson*. 1958. NY. Basic. 2 vol. 1st Am ed. gr cloth. VG/dj. G1. $275.00

JACKSON, John W. *Pennsylvania Navy, 1775-1781*. 1974. Rutgers. 1st ed. 514p. VG/dj. B18. $22.50

JACKSON, John. *Hit on the House*. 1994. Atlantic Monthly. 1st ed. F/F. M22. $10.00

JACKSON, Jon A. *Blind Pig*. 1978. Random. 1st ed. rem mk. F/F. B4. $100.00

JACKSON, Jon. *Ridin' With Ray*. 1995. Santa Barbara. 1st ed. 1/300. sgn. AN. C2. $60.00

JACKSON, Joseph Henry. *Bad Company*. 1939. NY. 1st ed. ils/photos. 346p. F/VG. E1. $40.00

JACKSON, Joseph Henry. *Tintypes in Gold, Four Studies...* 1939. NY. 1st ed. 191p. F/G. E1. $45.00

JACKSON, K.C. *Textbook of Lithology*. 1970. McGraw Hill. 522p. cloth. VG. D8. $20.00

JACKSON, Leroy. *Peter Patter Book*. 1918. Rand McNally. 1st ed. ils Blanche Fisher Wright. VG. P2. $85.00

JACKSON, Mae. *Can I Poet With You*. 1969. NY. Blk Dialogue Pub. 1st ed. tall 8vo. NF/stapled wrp. B4. $75.00

JACKSON, Richard. *Black Literature & Humanism in Latin America*. 1988. Athens, GA. 1st ed. 166p. dj. F3. $15.00

JACKSON, Shirley. *Hangsaman*. 1951. Farrar Strauss. 1st ed. F/VG. B4. $125.00

JACKSON, Shirley. *We Have Always Lived in the Castle*. 1962. Viking. 1st ed. F/NF clip. B4. $150.00

JACKSON, W.T. *Wagon Roads West*. 1952. Berkeley. 1st ed. 422p. VG/fair. B5. $25.00

JACKSON. *Norman Rockwell Identification & Value Guide*. 1980. np. 12mo. 16p. G/wrp. T3. $5.00

JACOB, Edmond. *Ras Shamra et l'Ancien Testament*. 1960. Neuchatel, Switzerland. Delachaux Niestle. 1st ed. ils. 132p. VG/wrp. W1. $18.00

JACOB, Francois. *Logic of Life, a History of Heredity*. 1973. NY. 1st Eng trans. 348p. dj. A13. $40.00

JACOB, OBST & RICHTER. *Completely Ils Atlas of Reptiles & Amphibians...* 1988. Neptune City. TFH Pub. 4to. pict brd. NF. B1. $125.00

JACOBI, Carl. *Disclosures in Scarlet*. 1972. Arkham. 1st ed. 1/3127. F/F. T2. $30.00

JACOBI, Carl. *Revelations in Black*. 1974. Neville Spearman. F/F. P3. $25.00

JACOBS, Flora Gill. *Dollhouse Mystery*. (1958). Coward McCann. 11th. inscr. ils. 96p. NF/NF. C14. $15.00

JACOBS, James Ripley. *Beginning of the US Army 1783-1812*. 1947. Princeton, NJ. 1st ed. 419p. NF. E1. $35.00

JACOBS, Joseph. *Buried Moon*. nd. Bradbury. stated 1st prt. 4to. 13 double-p ils. NF. C14. $14.00

JACOBS, Joseph. *Indian Fairy Tales*. 1892. London. David Nutt. 1st ed. 8vo.VG. M5. $110.00

JACOBS, Joseph. *Master of All Masters*. 1972. Thistle Book. ils Anne Rockwell. unp. VG. T5. $15.00

JACOBS, T.C.H. *Appointment With the Hangman*. 1936. MacAulay. 1st ed. VG. P3. $30.00

JACOBS, T.C.H. *Documents of Murder*. 1933. MacAulay. hc. VG. P3. $25.00

JACOBS, T.C.H. *Red Eyes of Kali*. nd. Stanley paul. hc. xl. dj. P3. $12.00

JACOBS, W.W. *Night Watches*. 1914. Scribner. 1st ed. decor brd. VG. P3. $45.00

JACOBSEN, Jerome V. *Educational Foundations of the Jesuits in 16th-C New Spain*. 1938. Berkeley. 1st ed. 8vo. 292p. gilt maroon cloth. F. T10. $50.00

JACOBSEN, Johan A. *Alaskan Voyage 1881-1883*. 1977. Chicago. VG. O7. $65.00

JACOBSON, Mark. *Gojiro*. 1991. Atlantic. 1st ed. F/F. H11. $30.00

JACOBSON, Timothy. *Making Medical Doctors: Science & Medicine...* 1987. Tuscaloosa, AL. 1st ed. 349p. dj. A13. $30.00

JACOBY, Arnold. *Senor Kon-Tiki: Life & Adventure of Thor Heyerdahl*. 1967. NY. 1st ed. F/F. B4. $50.00

JACOBY, Arnold. *Senor Kon-Tiki: Life & Adventure of Thor Heyerdahl*. 1967. NY. 1st prt. 424p. VG/dj. E1. $30.00

JACOBY & JACOBY. *Jacoby on Card Games*. 1986. NY. 239p. F/dj. S1. $6.00

JACQUEMARD, Simonne. *Night Watchman*. 1964. HRW. 1st ed. hc. VG. P3. $13.00

JACQUES, Brian. *Bellmaker*. 1994. NY. Philomel. 1st ed. sgn. ils Allan Curless. F/dj. T10. $50.00

JACQUES, Florence. *Francis Lee Jaques: Artist of the Wilderness World*. 1973. NY. 1st ed. F/F. B5. $125.00

JACQUIER, Henry. *Piracy in the Pacific*. 1976. NY. VG. O7. $20.00

JAEGER, Gustav. *Entdeckund der Seele*. 1884. Leipzig. Ernst Gunthers. 410p. xl. VG. G1. $50.00

JAENSCH, E.R. *Uber die Wahrnehmung des Raumes...* 1911. Leipzig. Johann Ambrosius Barth. 488p. prt brn wrp. VG. G1. $85.00

JAFEK, Bev. *Man Who Took a Bite Out of His Wife*. 1993. Overlook/Penguin. UP. F. B35. $30.00

JAFFE, Rona. *After the Reunion.* nd. BC. hc. VG/VG. P3. $5.00

JAFFE, Rona. *Best of Everything.* 1958. Simon Schuster. 2nd. NF/NF. B35. $30.00

JAFFE, Rona. *Mazes & Monsters.* 1981. Delacorte. 1st ed. VG/VG. P3. $20.00

JAFFE, Susanne. *Other Anne Fletcher.* 1980. NAL. hc. VG/VG. P3. $15.00

JAGO, William. *Science & Art of Bread-Making.* 1895. London. fair. V4. $80.00

JAGO, Willie. *Team Tactics at Bridge.* 1996. Australia. pb. 190p. M. S1. $12.00

JAGODA, Robert. *Friend in Deed.* 1977. Norton. 1st ed. sgn. F/F. B35. $30.00

JAHN, Michael. *Murder at the Museum of Natural History.* 1994. St Martin. 1st ed. F/NF. N4. $20.00

JAKES, John. *Furies.* nd. BC. hc. VG/VG. P3. $8.00

JAKUBOWSKI, Maxim. *New Crimes 3.* 1991. Carrol Graf. F/F. P3. $19.00

JAKUBOWSKI, Maxim. *100 Great Detectives.* 1991. Carroll Graf. 1st Am ed. F/F clip. M22. $25.00

JAMES, Alice. *Catering for Two: Comfort & Economy for Small Households.* 1906. Putnam. VG. H7. $20.00

JAMES, Arthur W. *Commonwealth Vs the Buck Boys.* 1930. Garrett Massie. G. B10. $35.00

JAMES, Bill C. *Jim Miller, the Untold Story of a Texas Badman.* 1989. Wolfe City, TX. 1/300. sgn. F. E1. $40.00

JAMES, Bill C. *Mysterious Killer, James Brown Miller 1861-1909.* 1976. Carrollton, TX. 1/250. sgn/#d. F/stiff wrp. E1. $40.00

JAMES, Bill. *Great American Baseball Stat Book.* 1987. Ballantine. 1st ed. VG+. P8. $15.00

JAMES, Cary. *King & Raven.* 1995. Tor. 1st ed. F/F. P3. $24.00

JAMES, Edward T. *American Plutarch.* 1964. NY. 1st ed. 408p. VG. E1. $20.00

JAMES, George Wharton. *California Romantic & Beautiful.* 1914. Page. 2nd. ils/map. VG. P12. $50.00

JAMES, George Wharton. *In & Around the Grand Canyon.* 1901. Boston. photos. VG. M17. $50.00

JAMES, George Wharton. *Indians of the Painted Desert Region.* 1907. Little Brn. later ed. inscr. 8vo. photos. NF. T10. $225.00

JAMES, George Wharton. *Our American Wonderlands.* 1915. Chicago. 1st ed. inscr. 8vo. 297p. bl cloth. F. T10. $150.00

JAMES, Grace. *Green Willow & Other Japanese Fairy Tales.* 1910. Macmillan. 1st ed. ils Warwick Goble. 281p. VG. D1. $450.00

JAMES, Grace. *Green Willow.* 1923. London. Macmillan. 3rd ils ed/1st medium 8vo ed. 16 mc pl. NF. A20. $85.00

JAMES, Henry. *English Hours.* nd. Houghton Mifflin. 1st ed. ils Pennell. teg. leather/marbled brd. VG. A20. $75.00

JAMES, Henry. *In the Cage.* 1898. Chicago. Herbert Stone. 1st Am ed. 229p. F. A4. $235.00

JAMES, Henry. *Outcry.* 1911. NY. Scribner. 1st Am ed. NF. A4. $115.00

JAMES, Henry. *Tragic Muse.* 1890. London. Macmillan. 1st Eng ed. 3 vol. 1/500. pub cloth. NF. B24. $2,500.00

JAMES, Henry. *Travelling Companions.* 1919. Boni Liveright. 1st ed. 309p. VG. M20. $32.00

JAMES, Jamie. *Music of the Spheres.* 1993. Grove. 1st ed. rem mk. F/F. B35. $18.00

JAMES, Jesse Jr. *Jesse James, My Father...* 1906 (1899). Cleveland. rpt. F/wrp. E1. $95.00

JAMES, M.R. *Best Ghost Stories of MR James.* 1946. Tower. 5th. hc. F/F. P3. $20.00

JAMES, M.R. *Wailing Well.* 1928. Mill House. 1/157. VG. C6. $300.00

JAMES, Mrs. T.D. *Matsuyama Mirror (Kagami) #10.* nd. London. Griffith Farran. ils. 22p. crepe paper. VG. D1. $110.00

JAMES, P.D. *Children of Men.* 1993. Knopf. 1st ed. F/F. H11. $30.00

JAMES, P.D. *Devices & Desires.* 1990. Knopf. 1st Am trade ed. VG/VG. M22. $10.00

JAMES, P.D. *Innocent Blood.* nd. BOMC. hc. VG/VG. P3. $10.00

JAMES, P.D. *Innocent Blood.* 1980. Scribner. 1st ed. VG/VG. M22. $15.00

JAMES, P.D. *Maul & the Pear Tree.* 1986. Mysterious. 1st ed. hc. VG. P3. $18.00

JAMES, P.D. *Skull Beneath the Skin.* 1982. Lester Orpen Denys. 1st ed. VG/VG. P3. $17.00

JAMES, P.D. *Skull Beneath the Skin.* 1982. Scribner. 1st ed. F/F clip. H11. $30.00

JAMES, P.D. *Unsuitable Job for a Woman.* nd. BC. VG/VG. P3. $8.00

JAMES, Peggy Seitz. *Stow, Ohio: Shadows of Its Past.* 1972. Ann Arbor. ils/notes/index. 307p. VG. B18. $22.50

JAMES, Peter. *Possession.* 1988. Doubleday. 1st ed. NF/NF. P3. $18.00

JAMES, Peter. *Prophecy.* 1994. St Martin. 1st Am ed. F/F. G10. $10.00

JAMES, Philip. *Children's Books of Yesterday.* 1933. London. The Studio. ils. 128p. gr cloth. VG. D1. $75.00

JAMES, Will. *Big Enough.* 1931. NY. 1st ed. G+. B5. $65.00

JAMES, Will. *Cowboy in the Making.* 1937. NY. 1st ed. VG. B5. $45.00

JAMES, Will. *Lone Cowboy: My Life Story.* 1937. Scribner. ils Will James. 431p. VG+. M20. $67.00

JAMES, Will. *Smoky.* 1929. Scribner. 1st ed thus. ils Will James. 263p. VG+. M20. $87.00

JAMES, Will. *Three Mustangers.* 1933. NY. 1st/A ed. ils. 338p. pict gr cloth. VG. H3. $100.00

JAMES, Will. *Young Cowboy.* 1935. Scribner. later prt. xl. VG/G. M5. $16.00

JAMES, William. *Psychology.* 1892. Holt. 1st ed/3rd prt. 12mo. gr cloth. VG. G1. $85.00

JAMES & SHANNON. *Sheriff AJ Royal, Fort Stockton, Texas.* 1984. np. 1/300. 1st ed. sgn/#d. photos. F. E1. $50.00

JAMES. *Dictionary of American Bibliography, Supplement 3, 1941-45.* 1973. np. 879p. xl. VG. A4. $75.00

JAMES. *Notable American Women 1607-1950.* 1974. Harvard. 3 vol. 2125p. VG/case. A4. $85.00

JANCE, J.A. *Desert Heat.* 1993. Avon. 1st ed. pb. sgn. F/wrp. T2. $10.00

JANCE, J.A. *Failure to Appear.* 1993. Morrow. 1st ed. sgn. F/F. T2. $30.00

JANCE, J.A. *Hour of the Hunter.* 1991. Morrow. 1st ed. sgn. F/F. T2. $40.00

JANCE, J.A. *Tombstone Courage.* 1994. Morrow. 1st ed. RS. F/F. P3. $20.00

JANCE, J.A. *Without Due Process.* 1992. Morrow. 1st ed. F/F. P3. $20.00

JANE, Fred T. *Jane's Fighting Ships 1906-1907.* 1970. NY. rpt. 300p. F/F. E1. $50.00

JANE, Mary C. *Mystery in Old Quebec.* nd. Weekly Reader. VG/VG. P3. $8.00

JANES, E.C. *Story of Knives.* 1968. NY. 1st ed. 127p. NF/NF. E1. $30.00

JANICK, J. *Horticultural Science.* 1963. San Francisco. WH Freeman. 8vo. 472p. cloth. dj. B1. $35.00

JANIFER, Laurence. *Reel.* 1983. Doubleday. 1st ed. RS. F/F. P3. $20.00

JANKOVICH, Miklos. *They Rode Into Europe.* 1971. London. Harrap. 1st ed. VG/VG. O3. $48.00

JANNERSTEN, Eric. *Card Reading: The Art of Guesssing Right at Bridge Table.* 1972. NY. 207p. VG/wrp. S1. $5.00

JANNERSTEN, Eric. *Find the Mistakes: A Bridge Quiz.* 1982. London. 160p. F/dj. S1. $15.00

JANNERSTEN & KELSEY. *Only Chance.* 1980. London. 171p. VG. S1. $10.00

JANNEY, Russell. *Miracle of the Bells.* 1946. McLeod. G/G. P3. $8.00

JANOVY, John Jr. *Vermilion Sea: Naturalist's Journey in Baja, CA.* 1992. Houghton Mifflin. 1st ed. 8vo. 226p. F/dj. B24. $20.00

JANOWITZ, Tama. *American Dad.* 1981. Putnam. 1st ed. F/F. H11. $65.00

JANOWITZ, Tama. *Cannibal in Manhattan.* 1987. Crown. 1st ed. F/F. B35/H11. $20.00

JANOWITZ, Tama. *Slaves of New York.* 1986. Crown. 1st ed. F/F. M19. $25.00

JANSON, H.W. *History of Art, 4th Ed.* 1991. Abrams. F/F. P3. $50.00

JAQUES, Florence Page. *Canoe Country.* 1958. MN U. 5th. VG. B17. $5.00

JARDIN, Rex. *Devil's Mansion.* 1931. Fiction League. G. P3. $10.00

JARES, Joe. *Whatever Happened to Gorgeous George.* 1974. Englewood Cliffs. 1st ed. VG/VG. B5. $20.00

JARRELL, Randall. *Animal Family.* 1965. Pantheon. 12mo. VG/G. B17. $7.50

JARRELL, Randall. *Pictures From an Institution.* 1974 (1954). Faber. 290p. F/F. B10. $12.00

JARRELL, Randall. *Seven-League Crutches.* 1951. Harcourt Brace. ARC/1st ed. RS. F/NF. B4. $250.00

JARVIS, George O. *Surgical Adjuster, for Reducing Dislocations...* 1846. Derby, CT. 80p. VG/prt wrp (lacks back). B14. $175.00

JASIENICA, P. *Commonwealth of Both Nations: The Silver Age.* 1987. NY/Miami. Am Inst Polish Culture/Hippocrene. 1st ed. 338p. AN/dj. P4. $20.00

JASON, Leon. *Heckle & Jeckle.* 1957. Wonder. TVTI. VG. P3. $8.00

JASPERS, Karl. *Psychologie der Weltanschauungen.* 1925. Berlin. Julius Springer. 3rd. 486p. buff wrp. G1. $50.00

JASSAU, J.J. *Textbook of Practical Astronomy.* 1932 (1932). McGraw Hill. 3rd. 8vo. 226p. cloth. G. K5. $18.00

JASTROW, Morris. *War & the Bagdad Railway.* 1917. Phil. VG. O7. $45.00

JAY, Charlotte. *Arms for Adonis.* 1960. Collins Crime Club. 1st ed. VG/VG. P3. $25.00

JAY, Charlotte. *Man Who Walked Away.* 1958. Collins Crime Club. hc. VG/torn. P3. $20.00

JAYNE, Walter. *Healing Gods of Ancient Civilizations.* 1925. New Haven. 1st ed. 569p. VG. A13. $150.00

JAYNE, William. *Abraham Lincoln.* 1908. Chicago. 16mo. 58p. quarter leather/blk brd. xl. G. T3. $20.00

JEANS, James. *Astronomy & Cosmogony.* 1961 (1928). Philosophical Lib. rpt of 1929 2nd ed. 428p. G. K5. $10.00

JEFFARES, Norman. *Man & Poet (WB Yeats).* 1949. London. 1st ed. assn copy. VG. V1. $20.00

JEFFERIES, Roderic. *Deadly Petard.* 1983. St Martin. 1st ed. VG/VG. P3. $15.00

JEFFERIES, Roderic. *Two-Faced Death.* 1976. Collins Crime Club. 1st ed. F/F. P3. $35.00

JEFFERS, Alex. *Safe as Houses.* 1995. Boston. Faber. AP. sgn. author's 1st novel. F/wrp. S9. $30.00

JEFFERS, Robinson. *Californians.* 1916. Macmillan. 1st ed. author's 1st commercial book. 217p. NF. T10. $350.00

JEFFERS, Robinson. *Cawdor.* 1983. Yolla Bolly. 1/240. sgns. F/case. S9. $275.00

JEFFERS, Robinson. *Dear Judas & Other Poems.* 1929. NY. 1st ed. F/NF. C6. $120.00

JEFFERS, Robinson. *Medea.* 1946. Random. 1st ed. F/F. B35. $60.00

JEFFERS, Robinson. *Solstice.* 1935. NY. 1st ed. 1/320. sgn. F/NF. C2. $300.00

JEFFERS, Robinson. *Themes in My Poems.* 1956. San Francisco. 1st ed. 1/350. 6 woodcuts. w/prospectus. F. B24. $275.00

JEFFEYS, J.G. *Wilful Lady.* 1975. Walker. 1st ed. hc. F/F. P3. $15.00

JEFFRIES, Ewel. *Short Biography of John Leeth.* 1904. Cleveland. 1/267. #d. 70p. F. E1. $165.00

JEKEL, Pamela. *Columbia.* 1986. St Martin. 1st ed. 8vo. 428p. map ep. F/F. T10. $30.00

JEKYLL, Gertrude. *Some English Gardens.* 1905. London. 3rd. 50 full-p pl. teg. gilt stp cloth. B26. $210.00

JEKYLL, Gertrude. *Wall & Water Gardens.* 1901. Scribner. 1st Am ed. 8vo. contemporary half leather. T10. $100.00

JELLICOE, G.A. *Motopia: Study in Evolution of Urban Landscape.* 1961. VG/VG. M17. $45.00

JEN, Gish. *Typical American.* 1991. Houghton Mifflin. 1st ed. author's 1st book. F/F. B35. $35.00

JENKINS, Cecil. *Message From Sirius.* 1961. Collins Crime Club. 1st ed. F/F. P3. $35.00

JENKINS, Dan. *Saturday America.* 1970. Boston. 1st ed. VG/VG. B5. $20.00

JENKINS, Dorothy H. *Children Make a Garden.* 1936. Doubleday. 1st ed. 8vo. VG. M5. $28.00

JENKINS, Elizabeth. *Mystery of King Arthur.* 1975. CMG. 1st ed. VG/VG. P3. $20.00

JENKINS, Geoffrey. *Grue of Ice.* 1962. Collins. 1st ed. F/F. P3. $30.00

JENKINS, Geoffrey. *Southtrap.* 1979. Collins. 1st ed. NF/NF. P3. $25.00

JENKINS, Geoffrey. *Twist of Sand.* 1959. Collins. 1st ed. hc. VG/G. P3. $20.00

JENKINS, Herbert. *Malcolm Sage Detective.* nd. Roy. hc. G/G. P3. $15.00

JENKINS, John H. *Basic Texas Books.* 1983. Austin. 1st ed. 648p. F/F. E1. $95.00

JENKINS, John H. *I'm Frank Hamer.* 1968. Austin, TX. 1st ed. sgn. 305p. F/F. E1. $110.00

JENKINS, Peter. *Walk Across America.* 1979. NY. 1st ed. photos. F/F. A17. $10.00

JENKINS, Rolland. *Mediterranean Cruise.* 1924. Knickerbocker. 2nd. 8vo. 40 pl. 279p. cloth. VG. W1. $18.00

JENKINS, Will F. *Forgotten Planet.* 1984. Crown. 1st ed. F/F. P3. $13.00

JENKINS, Will F. *Four From Planet 5.* 1974. Wht Lion. 1st ed. VG/VG. P3. $25.00

JENKINS, Will F. *Murder of the USA.* 1946. Crown. 1st ed. hc. VG/G. P3. $45.00

JENKINS, Will F. *Space Platform.* 1953. Shasta. 1st ed. sgn. NF/NF. B35. $125.00

JENKINS & REES. *Bibliography of History of Wales.* 1931. Cardiff. 218p. VG. A4. $145.00

JENKINSON, Michael. *Ghost Towns of New Mexico, Playthings of the Wind.* 1967. Albuquerque. 1st ed. 156p. F. E1. $35.00

JENKS, Almet. *Huntsman at the Gate.* 1952. Lippincott. 1st ed. VG/G. O3. $45.00

JENKS, George F. *Studies in Cartography: A Festschrift in Honor of GF Jenks.* 1987. Monograph 37. edit PP Gilmartin. brn cloth. M. O7. $35.00

JENNEY & SHELLEY. *Fortunes of Heaven by Percy Bysshe Shelley.* nd. London. Arthur Stockwell. sgn pres. 98p. silver/gray cloth. VG/G. B11. $45.00

JENNINGS, Gary. *Killer Storms.* 1970. Lippincott. 8vo. 207p. xl. dj. K5. $11.00

JENNINGS, Herbert Spencer. *Suggestions of Modern Science Concerning Education.* 1918. Macmillan. 12mo. bl buckram. G1. $37.00

JENNINGS, James R. *Freight Rolled.* 1969. San Antonio. 1st ed. photos. 99p. F/F. E1. $15.00

JENNINGS, John J. *Theatrical & Circus Life; or, Secrets of the Stage...* 1882. St Louis. 1st ed. 608p. fair. B18. $75.00

JENNINGS, John. *Banners Against the Wind.* 1954. Little Brn. 1st ed. VG/VG. P3. $15.00

JENNINGS, John. *Chronicle of the Calypso, Clipper.* 1955. Little Brn. 1st ed. VG/VG. P3. $15.00

JENNINGS, John. *Pepper Tree.* 1950. Little Brn. 1st ed. VG/VG. P3. $15.00

JENNINGS, N.A. *Texas Ranger.* 1972. Dallas. revised. fwd J Frank Dobie. hc. F. E1. $35.00

JENNINGS & NORBECK. *Prehistoric Man in the New World.* 1964. Chicago. 1st ed. 633p. dj. F3. $30.00

JENNISON, Christopher. *Wait 'Til Next Year.* 1974. Norton. 1st ed. F/VG+. P8. $35.00

JENSEN, Amy. *Guatemala.* 1955. Exposition. 1st ed. 263p. dj. F3. $15.00

JENSEN, Jen. *Life & Works of...* 1964. Chicago. 1st ed. VG/VG. B5. $145.00

JENSEN, Paul M. *Boris Karloff & His Films.* 1974. as Barnes. 1st ed. VG/VG. P3. $25.00

JENSEN. *America's Yesterdays: Images in Photographic Archives...* 1978. cloth. F/VG. D2. $65.00

JEPSON, Selwyn. *Keep Murder Quiet.* 1940. Michael Joseph. 1st ed. xl. VG. P3. $12.00

JEPSON, Selwyn. *Man Dead.* 1951. Doubleday. VG. P3. $18.00

JEPSON, Selwyn. *Rogues & Diamonds.* 1925. Lincoln McVeagh/Dial. 1st ed. VG. P3. $35.00

JERKINS, Karen A. *Tender Moments.* 1988. Vantage. 1st ed. F/VG. B4. $45.00

JERNIGAN, Muriel Molland. *Forbidden City.* nd. BC. VG/VG. P3. $8.00

JEROME, V.J.A. *Lantern for Jeremy.* 1952. Masses Mainstream. 1st ed. NF/NF. B2. $30.00

JESSETT, Thomas E. *Reports & Letters of Herbert Beaver 1836-1838.* 1959. Portland. 1/750. F. E1. $60.00

JESSUP, M.K. *Case for the UFO.* 1955. NY. 1st ed. NF/G. N3. $20.00

JESSUP, Richard. *Cincinnati Kid.* 1963. Boston. 1st ed. author's 1st novel. NF/NF. C2. $30.00

JESSUP, Richard. *Foxway.* 1971. Little Brn. 1st ed. VG/VG. P3. $15.00

JETER, K.W. *Death Arms.* 1987. Morrigan. 1st ed. F/F. P3/T2. $30.00

JETER, K.W. *Farewell Horizontal.* 1989. St Martin. 1st ed. F/F. P3. $17.00

JETER, K.W. *In the Land of the Dead.* 1989. Morrigan. 1st ed. F/F. P3/T2. $30.00

JETER, K.W. *Infernal Devices.* 1987. St Martin. 1st ed. F/F. P3. $25.00

JETER, K.W. *Madlands.* 1991. St Martin. 1st ed. F/F. P3. $19.00

JETER, K.W. *Wolf Flow.* 1992. St Martin. 1st ed. F/F. P3. $19.00

JEVONS, Marshall. *Murder at the Margin.* 1978. Horton. 1st ed. 168p. VG/VG. B10. $15.00

JEWERY, Mary. *Warne's Model Cookery & Housekeeping Book.* 1868. London. Warne. People's ed. 12mo. sgn Mrs Geo Westinghouse. VG. T10. $100.00

JOBE, Joseph. *Extended Travels in Romantic America...* 1966. Lausanne. 223p. F/case. A17. $45.00

JOBE, Joseph. *Guns: An Illustrated History of Artillery.* 1971. Greenwich. 1st ed. ils/photos. 217p. VG. E1. $45.00

JOBSON, Hamilton. *Shadow That Caught Fire.* 1972. Scribner. 1st ed. F/F. P3. $15.00

JOBSON, Hamilton. *Waiting for Thursday.* 1977. Collins Crime Club. 1st ed. VG/VG. P3. $20.00

JOE, Yolanda. *He Say She Say.* 1996. Doubleday. ARC. F/wrp. B4. $35.00

JOGUES, Isaac. *Narrative of the Captivity.* 1857. Appleton. 8vo. 358p. VG. T10. $150.00

JOHN, Augustus. *Chiaroscuro: Fragments of Autobiography.* 1952. NY. 1st ed. 285p. F/dj. A17. $17.50

JOHN, Laurie. *Cosmology Now.* 1976. NY. Taplinger. 8vo. VG/dj. K5. $17.00

JOHNS, A. Wesley. *Man Who Shot McKinley.* 1970. S Brunswick/NY. 1st ed. 293p. VG/dj. B18. $22.50

JOHNS, Anne page. *Fur Tree & Other Poems.* 1943. Dietz. VG/VG. B10. $12.00

JOHNS, E.B. *Camp Travis & Its Part in the World War.* 1919. NY. 1st ed. photos. 337p. G. E1. $110.00

JOHNS, Foster. *Victory Murders.* nd. Economy Book League. VG. P3. $13.00

JOHNS, Francis A. *Bibliography of Arthur Waley.* 1968. Rutgers. 1st ed. photo portfolio. 187p. VG. A17. $15.00

JOHNS, John Edwin. *Florida During the Civil War.* 1963. Gainesville. 1st ed. 265p. NF/NF. M8. $85.00

JOHNS, Masterton. *Beyond Time.* 1966. Arcadia. hc. VG/VG. P3. $15.00

JOHNS, W.E. *Biggles, Pioneer Air Fighter.* nd. Dean. hc. VG/VG. P3. $15.00

JOHNS, W.E. *Biggles Flies North.* 1947. Oxford. 3rd. G. P3. $10.00

JOHNS, W.E. *Biggles in the Blue.* 1953. Brock. 1st ed. VG/G. P3. $15.00

JOHNS, W.E. to *Outer Space.* 1957. Hodder Stoughton. 1st ed. VG/G. P3. $20.00

JOHNS, William Allen. *Willie Tolbert: A Memoir.* 1971. Dietz. photos. 61p. VG/G. B10. $15.00

JOHNSON, Alvin. *Touch of Color & Other Tales.* 1963. NY. 1st ed. F/F. A17. $9.50

JOHNSON, Brita Elizabeth. *Maher-Shalal-hash-Baz; or, Rural Life in Old Virginia.* 1923. Claremont, VA. Sigfried Olson. 328p. VG/G. B10. $20.00

JOHNSON, Clifton. *Highways & Byways of the Great Lakes.* 1911. NY. 12mo. 382p. gilt stp gr cloth. VG. T3. $30.00

JOHNSON, Clifton. *Highways & Byways of the Mississipi Valley.* 1906. Macmillan. 1st ed. photos. VG. P12. $50.00

JOHNSON, Crockett. *Barnaby.* 1943. Holt. 1st ed. 361p. VG/G. P2. $45.00

JOHNSON, Curt. *Artillery: The Big Guns Go to War.* 1975. London. 1st ed. 144p. F/F. E1. $35.00

JOHNSON, Curt. *Best Little Magazine Fiction, 1970.* 1970. NYU. 1st ed. hc. F/F. B35. $85.00

JOHNSON, Denis. *Angels.* 1983. Knopf. 1st ed. author's 1st novel. F/F. M19. $45.00

JOHNSON, Denis. *Resucitation of a Hanged Man.* 1991. Faber. 1st ed. F/VG+. A20. $15.00

JOHNSON, Diane. *Loving Hands at Home.* 1968. HBW. 1st ed. NF/VG. B4. $50.00

JOHNSON, Diane. *Lying Low.* 1978. Knopf. 1st ed. F/F. M19. $17.50

JOHNSON, Dorothea. *Dorothea Johnson's Entertaining & Etiquette.* 1979. Washington, DC. Acropolis. 2nd. sgn. 8vo. VG/VG. B11. $10.00

JOHNSON, Dorothy M. *All the Buffalo Returning.* 1979. Dodd Mead. 1st ed. F/F. A18. $35.00

JOHNSON, E. Richard. *Case Load — Maximum.* 1971. Harper Row. 1st ed. VG/VG. P3. $20.00

JOHNSON, Gerald W. *Incredible Tale.* 1950. NY. BC. F/worn. E1. $5.00

JOHNSON, Grace. *Roman Collar Detective.* 1956. Bruce. 2nd. hc. VG/VG. P3. $13.00

JOHNSON, Hildegard Binder. *Carta Marina: World Geography in Strassburg, 1525.* 1963. Minneapolis. 1st ed. map. 159p. F. O7. $55.00

JOHNSON, J. *Typography; or, Printers Instructor.* 1824. London. 2 vol. rebound. VG. B5. $195.00

JOHNSON, Jack. *Jack Johnson: In the Ring & Out.* 1927. Chicago. 1st ed. VG+. A15. $65.00

JOHNSON, Lady Bird. *White House Diary.* 1970. NY. 1st ed. sgn. F. E1. $95.00

JOHNSON, Lee. *Heads for Death.* 1966. John Gifford. 1st ed. VG/G. P3. $15.00

JOHNSON, Lyndon Baines. *Vantage Point.* 1971. HRW. 1st ed. 8vo. ils. 636p. F/dj. T10. $30.00

JOHNSON, M.L.; see Malzberg, Barry.

JOHNSON, Margaret S. *Red Joker.* 1950. Morrow. 1st ed. 8vo. 95p. G. C14. $6.00

JOHNSON, Martin. *Congorilla.* 1932. Brewer Warren Putnam. 3rd. sgn Osa/Martin Johnson. 41 pl. 318p. G. B11. $50.00

JOHNSON, Mel; see Malzberg, Barry.

JOHNSON, Milton. *Price of Discontent.* 1929. Gordonsville. Johnson Pub. 319p. VG/G. B10. $10.00

JOHNSON, Owen. *Stover at Yale.* 1940. Grosset Dunlap. VG/G. P12. $8.00

JOHNSON, Peter H. *Parker: America's Finest Shotgun.* 1985. Harrisburg. Hardcover Classic. 3rd. 260p. F/F. E1. $45.00

JOHNSON, Robert Lee. *Contract Bridge Bidding: The Latest Point Count Bidding...* 1952. Hollywood, CA. 36p. VG. S1. $3.00

JOHNSON, Ronald. *American Table.* 1984. Morrow. 1st ed. F/NF. C2. $35.00

JOHNSON, Rossiter. *Campfires & Battlefields: A Pictorial Narrative...* 1967. NY. Civil War Pr. 6th. VG/dj. T10. $40.00

JOHNSON, Samuel. *Letters of Samuel Johnson 1731-1784.* 1992-1994. Princeton. 5 vol. ils. F/F. A4. $125.00

JOHNSON, SCOTT & SICKELS. *Anthology of Children's Literature.* 1948. Houghton Mifflin. ils NC Wyeth. VG/torn. B17. $45.00

JOHNSON, Stanley. *Doomsday Deposit.* 1980. Dutton. hc. F/F. P3. $13.00

JOHNSON, Stephen. *History of Cardiac Surgery 1896-1955.* 1970. Baltimore. 1st ed. 201p. dj. A13. $100.00

JOHNSON, Thomas M. *Wearing the Edged Weapons of the 3rd Reich.* 1977. Columbia. 1st ed. 63p. F/pict wrp. E1. $40.00

JOHNSON, V.W. *Catskill Fairies.* 1876 (1875). Harper. ils Alfred Fredricks. 163p. aeg. pict bdg. G+. P2. $60.00

JOHNSON, Warren. *Muddling Toward Frugality.* 1978. Sierra Club. 1st ed. 252p. F/dj. A17. $14.50

JOHNSON, William. *Focus on the SF Film.* 1972. Prentice Hall. 1st ed. F/F. P3. $25.00

JOHNSON & LEONARD. *Railroad to the Sea.* 1939. Iowa City. 1st ed. ils. 277p. VG/VG. B5. $45.00

JOHNSON & MALONE. *Dictionary of American Biography.* 1929-1944.. 21 (of 22) vol. 1st prt. 4to. xl. VG. A4. $795.00

JOHNSON & MASTERS. *Human Sexual Response.* 1966. Little Brn. 1st ed. F/NF. B35. $40.00

JOHNSON & WHITE. *Confederate Military History: Maryland & West Virginia.* 1976. Bl & Gray. rpt of 1899 ed. cloth. F/dj. M8. $20.00

JOHNSON. *Civil War Battles.* 1981. NY. 4to. 160p. VG/dj. T3. $20.00

JOHNSON. *Thoreau's Complex Weave...* 1986. VA U. F/F. A4. $45.00

JOHNSTON, Annie Fellows. *Little Colonel Doll Book.* 1910. Boston. Page. 1st ed. ils MG Johnston. worn. D1. $375.00

JOHNSTON, Annie Fellows. *Little Colonel's Christmas Vacation.* 1931 (1905). Page. 8vo. tan pict cloth. VG. M5. $20.00

JOHNSTON, Annie Fellows. *Little Colonel's House Party.* 1930 (1900). Page. 8vo. tan pict cloth. VG. M5. $20.00

JOHNSTON, Annie Fellows. *Little Colonel Stories.* 1930 (1902). Page. 8vo. ils. tan pict cloth. VG. M5. $20.00

JOHNSTON, Annie Fellows. *Little Colonel.* 1908 (1904). Page. 5th/Ils Holiday Ed. 8vo. gilt cloth. VG. M5. $40.00

JOHNSTON, Charles. *Brink of Jordan.* 1972. Hamilton. 1st ed. 8vo. map. 179p. VG/dj. W1. $16.00

JOHNSTON, Hank. *Death Valley Scotty, Fastest Con in the West.* 1974. Corona del Mar, CA. 1st ed. photos. 160p. F/F. E1. $40.00

JOHNSTON, J.F. *Hillforts of the Iron Age in England & Wales.* 1976. Liverpool. 1st ed. VG/VG. B5. $40.00

JOHNSTON, Joe. *Adventures of Teebo: A Tale of Magic & Suspense.* 1984. Random. 1st ed. 8vo. unp. C14/P3. $10.00

JOHNSTON, Joseph Eggleston. *Narrative of Military Operations, Directed During War...* 1874. Appleton. 1st ed. 602p. full sheep. VG. M8. $250.00

JOHNSTON, Leah C. *San Antonio: St Anthony's Town.* 1947. San Antonio. 1st ed. photos. F/chip. E1. $30.00

JOHNSTON, Mary. *Aubrey.* 1902. Boston. 1st ed. ils Yohn. gilt cloth. NF. A17. $12.50

JOHNSTON, Mary. *Exile.* 1927. Little Brn. 1st ed. VG/VG. B4. $75.00

JOHNSTON, Mary. *Fortunes of Garin.* 1915. Houghton Mifflin. 1st ed. 375p. G+. B10. $12.00

JOHNSTON, Mary. *Lewis Rand.* 1908. Houghton Mifflin. 1st ed. 8vo. ils FC Yohn. T10. $50.00

JOHNSTON, Mary. *to Have & to Hold.* 1900. Houghton Mifflin. 1st ed. VG. H4. $40.00

JOHNSTON, S. Paul. *Horizons Unlimited.* 1941. NY. 1st ed. 354p. G. B18. $15.00

JOHNSTON, Swift P. *Notes on Astronomy: A Complete Elementary Handbook...* 1892. London. Heywood. 2nd. 86p. G. K5. $28.00

JOHNSTON, Terry C. *Borderlords.* 1985. Jameson. 1st ed. F/F. A18. $35.00

JOHNSTON, Velda. *Etruscan Smile.* nc. BC. VG/VG. $8.00

JOHNSTON, Velda. *Flight to Yesterday.* nd. Quality BC. F/F. P3. $10.00

JOHNSTON, Velda. *I Came to a Castle.* 1969. Dodd Mead. 1st ed. VG/VG. P3. $20.00

JOHNSTON, Velda. *Late Mrs. Fonsell.* nd. BC. hc. VG/VG. P3. $8.00

JOHNSTON, Velda. *Man at Windemere.* nd. BC. hc. VG/VG. P3. $8.00

JOHNSTON, Velda. *People on the Hill.* 1971. Dodd Mead. 2nd. VG/torn. P3. $8.00

JOHNSTON, Velda. *Room With Dark Mirrors.* 1975. Dodd Mead. 1st ed. VG/VG. P3. $15.00

JOHNSTON, Velda. *Shadow Behind the Curtain.* nd. BC. VG/VG. P3. $8.00

JOHNSTON, Velda. *Stone Maiden.* nd. BC. VG/VG. P3. $8.00

JOHNSTON, William. *Barney.* 1970. Random. 1st ed. VG/VG. P3. $13.00

JOHNSTON, William. *Dr. Kildare: The Magic Key.* 1964. Whitman. TVTI. VG. P3. $8.00

JOHNSTON, William. *Great Indian Uprising.* 1967. Whitman. TVTI. VG. P3. $10.00

JOHNSTON, William. *Who's Got the Button?* 1968. Whitman. TVTI. VG. P3. $13.00

JOHNSTONE, William. *Creative Art in Britain.* 1950. London. Macmillan. 1st revised ed. 291p. tan cloth. NF/dj. B22. $10.00

JOLIVET, P. *Insects & Plants.* 1986. Brill/Flora & Fauna Pub. 8vo. ils. VG/wrp. B1. $22.50

JOLLY, David C. *Antique Maps, Sea Charts, City Views...* 1984. Boorkline. O7. $45.00

JOLY, Henri. *L'Homme et l'Animal.* 1886. Paris. Hachette. 2nd. inscr. 12mo. 312p. G1. $40.00

JONES, Bill. *Wallace Story.* (1966). AM S Pub. probable 1st ed. 471p. gilt bl cloth. F/NF. B22. $15.00

JONES, Billy M. *Health-Seekers in the Southwest, 1817-1900.* 1967. Norman. 1st ed. ils/photos. 254p. F/VG. E1. $30.00

JONES, Bobby. *Bobby Jones on Golf.* 1966. Garden City. 1st ed. VG/VG. B5. $50.00

JONES, Bobby. *Golf Is My Game.* 1960. Garden City. 1st ed. VG/VG. B5. $50.00

JONES, Courtway. *Witch of the North.* 1992. Pocket. 1st ed. 8vo. F/dj. T10. $35.00

JONES, D.F. *Fall of Colossus.* nd. BC. VG/VG. P3. $8.00

JONES, D.F. *Fall of Colossus.* 1974. Putnam. 1st ed. NF/VG. M22. $12.00

JONES, D.F. *Xeno.* 1979. British SF BC. VG/VG. P3. $10.00

JONES, D.J. *Introduction to Microfossils.* 1956. Harper. ils. 406p. cloth. F. D8. $25.00

JONES, Dave. *Making & Repairing Western Saddles.* 1982. NY. Aero. 4to. VG/VG. O3. $25.00

JONES, Diana Wynne. *Eight Days of Luke.* 1988. Greenwillow. 1st Am ed. F/F. G10. $15.00

JONES, Diana Wynne. *Everad's Ride.* 1995. Framingham. NESFA. 1st ed. 1/175. sgns. F/F/case. T2. $30.00

JONES, Diana Wynne. *Magicians of Caprona.* 1982. Macmillan. 2nd. NF/NF. P3. $15.00

JJONES, Douglas C. *Come Winter.* 1989. Holt. 1st ed. 8vo. F/dj. T10. $25.00

JONES, Douglas C. *Courtmartial of George Armstrong Custer.* 1976. NY. 1st ed. 291p. F/VG. E1. $80.00

JONES, Douglas C. *Creek Called Wounded Knee: A Novel.* 1978. NY. 1st ed. 236p. VG/VG. E1. $60.00

JONES, Douglas C. *Elkhorn Tavern.* 1980. HRW. 1st ed. F/NF. M23. $25.00

JONES, Douglas C. *Hickory Cured.* 1987. Holt. 1st ed. F/F. M23. $12.00

JONES, Douglas C. *Winding Stair.* 1979. HRW. 1st ed. F/NF. M23. $15.00

JONES, E. Morse. *Roll of the British Settlers in South Africa.* 1971. Cape Town. Balkema. 2nd. 4to. 174p. VG/dj. W1. $18.00

JONES, Elwyn. *Barlow Comes to Judgement.* nd. BC. hc. VG/VG. P3. $5.00

JONES, Fred. *Farm Gas Engines & Tractors.* 1963. McGraw Hill. 4th. 518p. VG+. A10. $35.00

JONES, Gayl. *Eva's Man.* 1976. Random. 1st ed. author's 2nd book. NF/NF. B4. $85.00

JONES, Gayl. *White Rat.* 1977. Random. 1st ed. F/F. B4. $75.00

JONES, Guy. *There Was a Little Man.* 1948. Random. 1st ed. VG/VG. P3. $30.00

JONES, H. Spencer. *Life on Other Worlds.* 1940. Macmillan. 299p. cloth. G. K5. $12.00

JONES, Harold. *100th Anniversary of the Army Medical Library, WA.* 1936. WA. 1st ed. VG. A13. $40.00

JONES, Harry E. *Luger Variations.* 1967. Los Angeles. sgn. 307p. VG/VG. B11. $35.00

JONES, Helen L. *Robert Lawson, Illustrator.* 1972. Boston. Little Brn. 1st ed. ils Robert Lawson. 121p. VG/G+. T5. $55.00

JONES, Howard M. *Major American Writers.* 1948. Harcourt. 1828p. cream cloth. VG. B22. $7.00

JONES, James. *From Here to Eternity.* 1951. Scribner. 1st ed. 1/1500. sgn pres. F/F. B24. $500.00

JONES, James. *Go to the Widowmaker.* 1967. Delacorte. 1st ed. F/NF. H11. $50.00

JONES, James. *Viet Journal.* 1974. Delacorte. 1st ed. F/F. M19. $20.00

JONES, Jessie Orton. *Secrets.* 1956 (1945). Viking. 4th. ils EO Jones. unp. VG. T5. $25.00

JONES, John William. *Personal Reminiscences, Anecdotes & Letters of RE Lee.* 1876. Appleton. 2nd. 509p. VG. M8. $85.00

JONES, Kenneth Glyn. *Search for the Nebulae.* 1975. Chalfont St Giles, UK. Alpha Academic. 84p. cloth. VG. K5. $26.00

JONES, LeRoi. *Home.* 1968. MacGibbon Kee. 1st ed. NF/NF. M19. $50.00

JONES, LeRoi. *System of Dante's Hell.* 1965. Grove. 1st ed. author's 1st novel. F/NF. M19. $65.00

JONES, Louis Thomas. *Highlights of Pueblo Land.* 1968. San Antonio. 1st ed. photos. 106p. F/F. E1. $20.00

JONES, Louis Thomas. *Indians at Work & Play.* 1971. San Antonio. 1st ed. biblio/index/notes. 156p. F/F. E1. $20.00

JONES, N.E. *Squirrel Hunters of Ohio.* 1898 (1897). Robert Clarke. 363p. gilt gr cloth. VG+. M10. $185.00

JONES, Nettie. *Fish Tales.* 1983. Random. 1st ed. F/NF. B4. $45.00

JONES, Nettie. *Mischief Makers.* 1989. Weidenfeld Nicholson. 1st ed. F/F. B4. $35.00

JONES, O.S. *Disposition of Oil Field Brines.* 1945. Lawrence, KS. 192p. F. D8. $8.00

JONES, O.S. *Fresh-Water Protection From Polution Arising in Oil Fields.* 1950. Lawrence, KS. 132p. F. D8. $10.00

JONES, P. Mansell. *French Introspectives From Montaigne to Andre Gide.* 1970. Kennikat. 115p. A17. $8.50

JONES, R.W. *Cop Out.* 1987. St Martin. 1st ed. VG/VG. P3. $17.00

JONES, Raymond F. *Cybernetic Brains.* 1962. Avalon. 1st ed. F/VG. M19. $45.00

JONES, Raymond F. *Cybernetic Brains.* 1962. Avalon. 1st ed. xl. dj. P3. $7.00

JONES, Raymond F. *Renaissance.* 1951. Gnome. 1st ed. VG/VG. P3. $60.00

JONES, Raymond F. *Secret People.* 1956. Avalon. 1st ed. F/F. P3. $40.00

JONES, Raymond F. *Son of the Stars.* 1952. Avalon. 1st ed. VG/fair. P3. $20.00

JONES, Raymond F. *Stories of Great Physicians.* 1963. Whitman. hc. VG. P3. $8.00

JONES, Raymond F. *Voyage to the Bottom of the Sea.* 1965. Whitman. TVTI. VG. P3. $10.00

JONES, Raymond F. *World of Weather.* 1961. Whitman Badger. hc. NF. P3. $12.00

JONES, Richard Glyn. *Solved!* 1987. BOMC. VG/VG. P3. $10.00

JONES, Richard Glyn. *Unsolved!* nd. BOMC. VG/VG. P3. $10.00

JONES, Robert Kenneth. *Shudder Pulps.* 1975. Fax. 1st ed. hc. NF/NF. P3. $35.00

JONES, Shirley. *Impressions.* 1984. S Croyden. Red Hen. 1/40. sm volio. sgns. 8 aquatints on handmade. F/box. B24. $2,000.00

JONES, Stephen. *Best Horror From Fantasy Tales.* 1990. Carroll Graf. 1st ed. F/F. P3. $18.00

JONES, Thomas Goode. *Last Days of the Army of Northern Virginia.* 1893. np. 1st ed. 46p. VG/wrp. M8. $350.00

JONES, Thomas. *Hoyle's Games Improved.* 1779. London. 216p. VG. S1. $250.00

JONES, Thomas. *Pugilist at Rest.* 1993. Little Brn. 1st ed. sgn. F/F. B35. $75.00

JONES, Tristan. *Heart of Oak.* 1984. St Martin. 282p. VG/dj. T7. $18.00

JONES, Tristan. *Steady Trade: A Boyhood at Sea.* 1982. St Martin. 1st ed. F/F. M23. $20.00

JONES, V.S. Vernon. *Aesop's Fables.* 1926. Doubleday. early rpt. 12mo. pict label. VG. B17. $65.00

JONES, Virgil Carrington. *Roosevelt's Rough Riders.* 1971. NY. 1st ed. ils. 354p. VG/G. E1. $35.00

JONES, Wilfred. *Epic of Kings: Hero Tales of Ancient Persia.* 1926. Macmillan. 1st ed. 9 pl. 333p. NF. A17. $20.00

JONES & JONES. *Ithaca Sojourners.* 1980. Old Mariner's Pr. sgn. 8vo. 70p. VG. B11. $15.00

JONES & JONES. *Small Rain: Verses From the Bible.* 1953. Viking. 9th. obl 8vo. unp. VG+. C14. $10.00

JONG, Erica. *Fanny.* 1980. NAL. 1st ed. NF/NF. B35. $30.00

JONG, Erica. *Fruits & Vegetables.* 1971. HRW. ARC/1st ed. inscr. author's 1st book. RS. F/dj. w/promo material. B4. $300.00

JONG, Erica. *Witches.* nd. BC. hc. VG/VG. P3. $10.00

JONSON, Ben. *Works of...* 1756. London. Prt for Midwinter. 7 vol. orig calf. G. A17. $100.00

JORDAN, Anne Devereaux. *Fires of the Past.* 1991. St Martin. 1st ed. F/NF. G10. $10.00

JORDAN, Bill. *No Second Place Winner.* 1977. Shreveport, LA. sgn. 8vo. 114p. F/F. B11. $45.00

JORDAN, Cathleen. *Tales From Alfred Hitchcock...* 1988. Morrow. 1st ed. hc. NF/NF. P3. $15.00

JORDAN, David. *Food & Game Fishers.* 1902. 1st ed. teg. VG+. S13. $55.00

JORDAN, David. *Nile Green.* 1973. John Day. 1st ed. VG/VG. P3. $13.00

JORDAN, George. *From Major Jordan's Diaries.* 1961. NY. rpt of 1952 ed. 284p. stiff wrp. A17. $8.50

JORDAN, Gilbert J. *Yesterday in the Texas Hill Country.* 1979. College Station. 1st ed. 171p. leather. F. E1. $40.00

JORDAN, Joe. *Bluegrass Horse Country.* 1940. Lexington. 1st trade ed. sgn. VG. O3. $65.00

JORDAN, June. *Civil Wars.* 1981. Boston. Beacon. 1st ed. NF/VG. R11. $13.00

JORDAN, June. *Passion: New Poems 1977-1980.* 1980. Boston. Beacon. 1st ed. F/NF clip. B4. $50.00

JORDAN, June. *Some Changes.* 1971. Dutton. ARC. inscr. author's 2nd book. RS. F/VG+. B4. $250.00

JORDAN, Nina. *Puzzle & Riddle Book.* 1935. Racine. ils. 86p. VG. A17. $7.50

JORDAN, Pat. *Black Coach.* 1971. Dodd Mead. 248p. VG+/VG+. R11. $15.00

JORDAN, Robert. *Dragon Reborn.* 1991. Tor. 1st ed. F/F. P3. $23.00

JORDAN, Robert. *Shadow Rising.* 1992. NY. Tor. 1st ed. F/F. H11. $50.00

JORDAN, W.K. *Philanthrophy in England, 1480-1660: A Study...* 1959. London. 1st ed. 410p. VG. A13. $25.00

JORDAN & PRICE. *Animal Structures.* 1903. Appleton. 1st ed. 99p. gr cloth. F. B14. $45.00

JORDANOFF, A. *Illustrated Aviation Dictionary.* 1942. NY. 1st ed. ils. 415p. bl cloth. VG/dj. B14. $95.00

JORGENSEN, H.R. *Red Laquer Case.* 1933. World Syndicate. hc. VG. P3. $20.00

JOSCELYN, Archie. *Golden Bowl.* 1931. Internat Fiction Lib. hc. VG/fair. P3. $25.00

JOSCELYN, Archie. *Golden Bowl.* 1931. Internat Fiction Lib. 246p. VG/VG. M20. $32.00

JOSEFOVICI, U. *Die Psychische Vererbung.* 1912. Leipzig. Englemann. 156p. red cloth. VG. G1. $40.00

JOSEPH, Franz. *Star Fleet Technical Manual.* 1975. Ballantine. 1st ed. TVTI. F. P3. $40.00

JOSEPH, Meryl. *Who Won Second Place at Omaha.* 1975. Random. 1st ed. photos. NF/dj. S9. $125.00

JOSEPH & LIPPINCOTT. *Point to the Stars.* 1972 (1963). McGraw Hill. 2nd ed. xl. K5. $7.00

JOSHI, G.N. *Constitution of India.* 1952. Macmillan. 2nd. G/worn. M11. $45.00

JOSHI, S.T. *HP Lovecraft Annotated Bibliography.* 1981. Kent State. hc. VG. P3. $30.00

JOSLIN, Sesyle. *Baby Elephant's Baby Book.* 1964. HBW. 1st ed. 12mo. unp. NF/VG. C14. $15.00

JOURDAN, Catherine R. *ABC of Duplicate Bridge Direction.* 1967. Waltham, MA. 96p. sbdg. VG. S1. $5.00

JOYCE, James. *Dubliners.* 1969. Modern Lib. VG/VG. P3. $13.00

JOYCE, James. *Exiles: A Play in Three Acts.* 1921. London. Egoist. 2nd. 8vo. gilt blk cloth. VG. T10. $50.00

JOYCE, James. *Haveth Childers Everywhere.* 1930. Paris. 1/500 on Vidalon paper. F/F/VG case. C6. $700.00

JOYCE, James. *James Joyce Miscellany. Second Series.* 1959. Carbondale. 1st ed. 8vo. NF/prt wrp. S9. $25.00

JOYCE, James. *Shorter Finnegan's Wake.* 1967. Viking. ARC/1st Am ed. RS. VG/VG. B4. $85.00

JOYCE, John A. *Jewels of Memory.* 1896. WA, DC. 2nd. ffe missing. VG. B18. $35.00

JOYCE, William. *Day With Wilbur Robinson.* 1990. Harper Row. 1st ed. rem mk. VG/dj. M20. $20.00

JOYCE, William. *Mother Goose.* 1984. Random. 1st ed. 4to. ils. NF. C14. $12.00

JUDA, L. *Wise Old Man: Turkish Tales of Nasreddin Hodja.* (1963). Edinburgh. Thomas Nelson. probable 1st ed. 112p. NF/VG. C14. $12.00

JUDD, B.I. *Handbook of Tropical Forage Grasses.* 1979. Garland. 12mo. photos/drawings. 116p. F. B1. $20.00

JUDD, Frances K. *In the Sunken Garden.* nd. Books Inc. decor brd. VG. P3. $10.00

JUDD, Frances K. *Message in the Sand Dunes.* 1938. Cupples Leon. VG. P3. $15.00

JUDD, Frances K. *Strange Echo.* nd. Grosset Dunlap. decor brd. VG. $5.00

JUDD, Frances K. *When the Key Turned.* nd. Books Inc. hc. VG/VG. P3. $12.00

JUDD, Naomi. *Love Can Build a Bridge.* 1993. NY. 1st ed. sgn. F. B5. $25.00

JUDSON, Clara Ingram. *George Washington.* 1952. Follett. 2nd. ils Frankberg. VG/VG. B17. $4.50

JUDSON, Clara Ingram. *Mighty Soo.* 1955. Follett. ils Robert Frankenberg. VG/VG. A16. $16.00

JUNDD, Henry P. *Intro to the Hawaiian Language.* 1962. Honolulu. VG. O7. $10.00

JUPP, Ursula. *Home Port Victoria.* 1967. Victoria, Canada. private prt. sgn. 8vo. 168p. gr cloth. F/F. B11. $40.00

JUPTNER, Joseph P. *US Civil Aircraft.* 1962. Los Angeles. Aero Pub. 2 vol. ils. VG/dj. B18. $125.00

JUST, Ward. *In the City of Fear.* 1982. Viking. 1st ed. F/VG+. A20. $17.00

JUSTER, Norton. *Dot & the Line.* 1963. Random. 1st ed. ils. NF/VG. P2. $25.00

JUSTUS, May. *Gabby Gaffer.* 1975. Minneapolis. Dillon. rpt. 8vo. 106p. VG+/VG. T5. $25.00

JUSTUS, May. *Jumping Johnny & Skedaddle.* 1958. Row Peterson. ils Henneberger. 96p. VG. T5. $20.00

KABOTIE, Fred. *Hopi Indian Artist.* 1977. Flagstaff. Mus of AZ. 1st ed. 149p. gilt cloth. F/dj. T10. $75.00

KAESE & LYNCH. *Milwaukee Braves.* 1954. Putnam. 1st ed. VG/G+. P8. $225.00

KAFALLO, Ivan Demitrius. *Profane Chronicles.* 1994. Wexford Barrow. UP. F/pict wrp. B35. $25.00

KAFKA, Franz. *Castle.* 1969. Modern Lib. VG/VG. P3. $15.00

KAFKA, Franz. *Dearest Father.* 1954. Schocken. 1st ed. F/NF. B2. $50.00

KAFKA, Paul. *Love Enter.* 1993. Houghton Mifflin. 1st ed. sgn. AN/dj. B4. $50.00

KAGAN, Solomon. *Contributions of Early Jews to American Medicine.* 1934. Boston. 1st ed. 63p. VG. A13. $65.00

KAHL, Virginia. *Maxie.* 1956. Scribner. 1st ed. ils. cloth. VG/worn. M5. $30.00

KAHN, David. *Codebreakers.* 1967. NY. 1st ed. VG/VG. B5. $50.00

KAHN, David. *Codebreakers.* 1968. Macmillan. later prt. NF/dj. N4. $30.00

KAHN, E.J. *Big Drink.* 1960. NY. 1st ed. VG/VG. B5. $25.00

KAHN, Fritz. *Design of the Universe.* 1954. NY. Crown. ils/diagrams. 373p. cloth. VG. K5. $8.00

KAHN, James. *Timefall.* 1987. St Martin. 1st ed. RS. F/F. P3. $20.00

KAHN, Joan. *Chilling & Killing.* 1978. Houghton Mifflin. 1st ed. VG/VG. P3. $18.00

KAHN, Joan. *Edge of the Chair.* nd. BOMC. VG/VG. P3. $10.00

KAHN, Joan. *Hanging by a Thread.* 1969. Houghton Mifflin. 1st ed. VG/VG. P3. $15.00

KAHN, Joan. *Some Things Strange & Sinister.* nd. Ellery Queen Mystery Club. hc. VG. P3. $5.00

KAHN, Joan. *Some Things Weird & Wicked.* 1976. Pantheon. 1st ed. F/F. G10. $15.00

KAHN, Joan. *Trial & Terror.* nd. BOMC. VG/VG. P3. $15.00

KAHN, Peggy. *Christmastime at Santa's Workshop.* 1990s. Random. 8vo. F. B17. $7.00

KAHN, Roger. *Boys of Summer.* 1972. NY. Harper Row. 1st ed. VG/VG. R16. $40.00

KAHN, Roger. *But Not to Keep.* 1979. Harper Row. 1st ed. VG/VG. A20. $12.00

KAHN, Roger. *Seventh Game.* 1982. NAL. 1st ed. VG+/VG+. A20. $10.00

KAHRL, William J. *California Water Atlas.* 1979. Sacramento. State of CA. folio. 118p. ES. M. O7. $575.00

KAI-SHEK, Chiang. *Soviet Russia in China.* 1957. FSC. 1st ed. F/NF. B35. $22.00

KAIL, Aubrey. *Medicial Mind of Shakespeare.* 1986. Balgowlah, NSW. 1st ed. 320p. dj. A13. $50.00

KAINS, Josephine; see Goulart, Ron.

KAKONIS, Tom. *Criss Cross.* 1990. NY. 1st ed. F/NF. H11. $30.00

KAKONIS, Tom. *Criss Cross.* 1990. St Martin. 1st ed. VG/VG. P3. $20.00

KAKONIS, Tom. *Double Down.* 1991. Dutton. 1st ed. F/dj. N4. $27.50

KAKONIS, Tom. *Michigan Roll.* 1988. NY. 1st ed. author' 1st book. NF/F. H11. $40.00

KAKONIS, Tom. *Shadow Counter.* 1993. Dutton. 1st ed. AN/F. N4. $17.50

KALLEN, Lucille. *No Lady in the House.* nd. BC. VG/VG. P3. $8.00

KALLEN, Lucille. *Piano Bird.* nd. BC. VG/VG. P3. $8.00

KALLEN, Lucille. *Tanglewood Murder.* 1980. Wyndham. 1st ed. F/F. P3. $15.00

KALOGRIDIS, Jeanne. *Covenant With the Vampire.* 1994. Delacorte. 1st ed. F/F. P3. $20.00

KALPAKIAN, Laura. *Graceland.* 1992. Grove Weidenfeld. ARC. 8vo. F/pict wrp. S9. $25.00

KALS, W.S. *How to Read the Night Sky.* (1974). Doubleday. 4th. 155p. VG/VG. K5. $12.00

KALTENBORN, H.V. *Kaltenborn Edits the News.* 1937. Modern Age. 1st ed. NF/stiff pict wrp. B4. $150.00

KAMEN, Gloria. *Ringdoves — From the Fables of Bidpai.* 1988. Atheneum. 1st ed. 8vo. 32p. F/NF. C14. $25.00

KAMES, Henry Home. *Elements of Criticism...With Analyses...* 1851. NY. Huntington Mason. contemporary sheep. M11. $125.00

KAMINSKY, Stuart M. *Bullet for a Star.* nd. BC. VG/VG. P3. $8.00

KAMINSKY, Stuart M. *Buried Caesars.* 1989. Mysterious. 1st ed. F/F. A20/P3. $18.00

KAMINSKY, Stuart M. *Catch a Falling Clown.* 1981. St Martin. 1st ed. F/F. P3. $40.00

KAMINSKY, Stuart M. *Down for the Count.* 1985. St Martin. 1st ed. F/F. P3. $25.00

KAMINSKY, Stuart M. *Fala Factor.* 1984. St Martin. 1st ed. F/F. P3. $30.00

KAMINSKY, Stuart M. *He Done Her Wrong.* 1983. St Martin. 1st ed. F/F. B2/P3. $35.00

KAMINSKY, Stuart M. *High Midnight.* 1981. St Martin. 1st ed. F/F. P3. $40.00

KAMINSKY, Stuart M. *Howard Hughes.* nd. BC. VG/VG. P3. $8.00

KAMINSKY, Stuart M. *Man Who Walked Like a Bear.* 1990. Scribner. 1st ed. F/F. A20/T2. $20.00

KAMINSKY, Stuart M. *Never Cross a Vampire.* 1980. St Martin. 1st ed. F/NF. T2. $50.00

KAMINSKY, Stuart M. *Opening Shots.* 1991. Mystery Scene. ltd deluxe 1st ed. 1/50. sgn/#d. leather. sans. F. P3. $50.00

KAMINSKY, Stuart M. *Rostrikov's Vacation.* 1991. Scribner. 1st ed. F/F. T2. $25.00

KAMINSKY, Stuart M. *When the Dark Man Calls.* 1983. St Martin. 1st ed. F/F. P3/T2. $30.00

KAMPEN, M.E. *Religion of the Maya.* 1981. Netherlands. EJ Brill. 1st ed. 36p. wrp. F3. $35.00

KANDEL, Aben. *Black Sun.* 1929. Harper. 1st ed. NF/NF. B35. $150.00

KANDEL, Lenore. *Love Book.* 1966. San Francisco. Stolen Paper. NF/wrp. B2. $35.00

KANE, Frank. *Bullet Proof.* 1951. Washburn. 1st ed. VG/VG. M22. $55.00

KANE, Frank. *Grave Danger.* 1954. Washburn. VG/torn. P3. $13.00

KANE, Frank. *Red Hot Ice.* 1955. Ives Washburn. hc. VG. P3. $25.00

KANE, Harnett T. *Amazing Mrs Bonaparte.* 1963. Doubleday. 1st ed. sgn. 310p. VG/dj. M20. $27.00

KANE, Harnett T. *Gentlemen, Swords & Pistols.* 1951. Morrow. 1st ed. VG/VG. P3. $20.00

KANE, Harnett T. *Louisiana Hayride.* 1941. Morrow. 4th. 471p. cloth. VG/ragged. M20. $30.00

KANE, Harnett T. *Natchez on the Mississippi.* 1947. Morrow. photos. 373p. G/poor. B10. $15.00

KANE, Harnett T. *New Orleans Woman.* 1946. Doubleday. sgn. 8vo. 344p. VG/G. B11. $20.00

KANE, Harnett T. *Plantation Parade.* 1946. Morrow. 3rd. sgn. G/G. P3. $25.00

KANE, Harnett T. *Romantic South.* 1961. Coward McCann. America Vista series. photos. 385p. B10. $15.00

KANE, Harnett T. *Scandalous Mrs Blackford.* 1951. Messner. 1st ed. VG/VG. P3. $15.00

KANE, Henry. *Conceal & Disguise.* 1966. Macmillan. 1st ed. NF/NF. P3. $20.00

KANE, Henry. *Hang by Your Neck.* 1949. Simon Schuster. 1st ed. VG/VG. P3. $20.00

KANE, Henry. *Little Red Phone.* 1982. Arbor House. 1st ed. VG/VG. P3. $18.00

KANE, Henry. *Operation Delta.* 1967. Michael Joseph. 1st ed. VG/VG. P3. $25.00

KANE, Henry. *Report for a Corpse.* 1948. Simon Schuster. 1st ed. VG/torn. P3. $15.00

KANE, Henry. *Virility Factor.* 1971. McKay. 1st ed. VG/VG. P3. $20.00

KANER, H. *Sun Queen.* 1946. Kaner. VG/VG. P3. $30.00

KANFER, Stefan. *International Garage Sale.* 1985. Norton. 1st ed. NF/NF. H11. $20.00

KANIN, Garson. *Do Re Me.* 1955. Little Brn. 1st ed. F/NF. B4. $100.00

KANIN, Garson. *One Hell of an Actor.* 1977. Doubleday. 1st ed. VG+/VG+. A20. $15.00

KANT, Immanuel. *Philosophy of Law, an Exposition of Fundamental Principles.* 1974. Clifton. Kelley. facsimile of 1887 Eng ed. M11. $65.00

KANTAR, Edwin B. *Defensive Bridge Play Complete.* 1974. N Hollywood. lg format. 528p. VG/wrp. S1. $15.00

KANTOR, Alfred J. *Book of Alfred J Kantor.* 1971. McGraw Hill. 1st ed. F/F. B35. $49.00

KANTOR, MacKinlay. *Andersonville.* 1955. 1st/special Cival War BC ed. sgn. VG/rubbed. S13. $65.00

KANTOR, MacKinlay. *Gettysburg.* 1952. Random. 189p. VG/G. B10. $25.00

KANTOR, MacKinlay. *Lee & Grant at Appomattox.* 1950. Random. 9th. 175p. VG. B10. $12.00

KANTOR, MacKinlay. *Signal 32.* 1950. Random. 1st ed. NF/VG. M22. $20.00

KANTOR, MacKinlay. *Story Teller.* 1967. Doubleday. 1st ed. sgn. F/F. B11. $20.00

KANUSS, William H. *Story of Camp Chase: A History of the Prison...* 1906. Nashville. ME Church. 1st ed. 407p. cloth. NF. M8. $250.00

KAPLAN, E.H. *Field Guide to Coral Reefs of the Caribbean & Florida.* 1982. Houghton Mifflin. 289p. cloth. VG. D8. $18.00

KAPLAN, Fred. *Dickens: A Biography.* nd. Morrow. 4th. hc. F/F. P3. $25.00

KAPP, Kit S. *Central America Early Maps Up to 1860.* 1974. Kapp. 1st ed. 23 maps. 106p. wrp. F3. $30.00

KARAKE, Dosabhai Framji. *History of the Parsis...* 1977. NY. AMS. 2 vol. rpt of 1884 ed. VG. W1. $65.00

KARDINER, Abram. *Individual & His Society.* 1939. Columbia. 503p. panelled ochre cloth. VG. G1. $50.00

KARIG, Walter. *Zotz!* 1947. Rinehart. VG/torn. P3. $10.00

KARL, Frederick R. *William Faulkner: American Writer.* 1989. NY. 1st ed. 1131p. F/dj. A17. $17.50

KARPIN, Fred L. *Contract Bridge: The Play of the Cards.* 1958. MA. 506p. VG. S1. $10.00

KARPINSKI. *Italian Chiaroscuro Woodcuts...Volume XII.* 1971. Penn State. 4to. ils. 209p. VG. A4. $95.00

KARROW, P.F. *Pleistocene Geology of the Scarborough Area.* 1967. Ontario Dept Mines. 108p. prt brd. VG. D8. $12.00

KARSH, Yousuf. *Karsh.* 1983. NYGS. 1st ed. sgn. F/dj. S9. $175.00

KARSH, Yousuf. *Yousuf Karsh & John Fisher See Canada.* 1960. Rand McNally. 1st ed. ils. NF/dj. S9. $30.00

KARSTEN, Rafae. *Toba Indians of the Bolivian Grand Chaco.* 1970. Netherlands. Anthropological Pub. 126p. wrp. F3. $25.00

KASER, David. *Book for a Sixpence: Circulating Lib of America.* 1980. Beta Phi Mu. 194p. quarter cloth. A17. $17.50

KASPAROV, Garry. *Unlimited Challenge: The Autobiography of Garry Kasparov.* 1990. np. ils. F/F. A4. $20.00

KASTENBAUM, Robert. *Is There Life After Death?* 1984. Methuen. VG. P3. $18.00

KASTLE, Herbert. *Cross-Country.* 1975. WH Allen. 1st ed. VG/VG. P3. $20.00

KASTLE, Herbert. *Millionaires.* 1972. WH Allen. 1st ed. VG/VG. P3. $15.00

KATO, Ken. *Yamato: Rage in Heaven.* 1990. Warner. 1st ed. rem mk. NF/NF. G10. $5.00

KATZ, Bobbi. *Upside Down & Inside Out: Poems From Your Pockets.* 1973. Franklin Watts. 1st ed. 12mo. ils cloth. F/VG. C14. $15.00

KATZ, David. *Der Vibrationsinn.* 1923. Hierosolymis. German/Hebrew text. prt buff wrp. G1. $50.00

KATZ, Michael J. *Big Freeze.* 1991. Putnam. 1st ed. F/F. P3. $22.00

KATZ, Richard. *Von Hund Zu Hund.* 1956. Zurich. Albert Muller. 1st ed. German text. gilt cloth. F/worn. A17. $12.50

KATZ, Robert. *Ziggurat.* 1977. Houghton Mifflin. 1st ed. VG/VG. P3. $15.00

KATZ, Sali Barnett. *Hispanic Furniture: An American Collection From the SW.* 1986. Architectural Book Pub. ils. 224p. AN/dj. T10. $35.00

KATZ, William. *Facemaker.* 1988. McGraw Hill. 1st ed. NF/NF. P3. $17.00

KATZ, William. *Open House.* nd. BC. VG/VG. P3. $8.00

KATZEFF, Paul. *Full Moons: Fact & Fantasy...* 1981. Citadel. 1st ed. xl. dj. K5. $20.00

KATZENBACH, John. *In the Heat of the Summer.* 1982. NY. 1st ed. author's 1st book. NF/NF. H11. $20.00

KAUFMAN, Frederick. *Forty-Two Days & Nights on the Iberian Peninsula.* 1987. HBJ. 1st ed. F/F. H11. $40.00

KAUFMAN, Sue. *Diary of a Mad Housewife.* 1967. NY. Random. 1st ed. red H stp on front fly. NF/VG+. B4. $85.00

KAVAN, Anna; see Ferguson, Helen.

KAVANAGH, Dan. *Flaubert's Parrot.* 1985. Knopf. 1st ed. F/F. H11. $65.00

KAVANAGH, Dan. *History of the World in 10½ Chapters.* 1989. Knopf. 1st ed. clip. F/F. H11. $35.00

KAVANAGH, Dan. *Talking It Over.* 1991. Knopf. 1st ed. F/F. H11. $30.00

KAVENEY, Roz. *Tales From the Forbidden Planet.* 1987. Titan. 1st ed. F/F. P3. $25.00

KAY, Gertrude Alice. *Us Kids & the Circus.* 1928. Saalfield. unp. VG. M20. $72.00

KAY, Gertrude Alice. *When the Sandman Comes.* nd. Chicago. Stanton VanVliet. 8vo. 183p. G+. T5. $30.00

KAY, Guy Gavriel. *Song for Arbonne.* 1992. Canada. Viking. 1st ed. F/F. P3. $25.00

KAY, Guy Gavriel. *Summer Tree.* 1984. McClelland Stewart. 1st ed. VG/VG. P3. $25.00

KAY, Guy Gavriel. *Tigana.* 1990. Roc. 1st ed. F/F. P3. $20.00

KAY, Guy Gavriel. *Wandering Fire.* nd. BC. VG/VG. P3. $8.00

KAY, Ross. *Go Ahead Boys & the Mysterious Old House (#3).* 1916. Barse Hopkins. 232p. VG+/dj. M20. $40.00

KAY, Terry. *Year the Lights Came On.* 1976. Houghton Mifflin. 1st ed. VG. M23. $20.00

KAYE, M.M. *Death in Cyprus.* 1984. Allen Lane. VG/VG. P3. $20.00

KAYE, M.M. *Death in Kenya.* 1983. Allen Lane. VG/VG. P3. $17.00

KAYE, M.M. *Death in Zanzibar.* 1983. St Martin. 1st ed. hc. VG/VG. P3. $15.00

KAYE, M.M. *Fair Pavilions.* 1978. Allen Lane. 1st ed. VG/VG. P3. $25.00

KAYE, M.M. *Fair Pavilions.* 1978. St Martin. 1st Am ed. F/F. B4. $85.00

KAYE, M.M. *Shadow of the Moon.* 1957. Longman. 1st ed. VG/VG. P3. $30.00

KAYE, Marvin. *Devils & Demons.* nd. BC. VG/VG. P3. $10.00

KAYE, Marvin. *Ghosts.* 1981. Doubleday. 1st ed. VG/VG. P3. $25.00

KAYE, Marvin. *Laurel & Hardy Murders.* 1977. Dutton. 1st ed. VG/VG. P3. $20.00

KAYE, Marvin. *Lively Game of Death.* 1974. Arthur Barker. VG/VG. P3. $20.00

KAYE, Marvin. *Masterpieces of Terror & Supernatural.* 1985. Doubleday. 2nd. VG/VG. P3. $16.00

KAYE, Marvin. *Possession of Immanuel Wolf.* 1981. Doubleday. 1st ed. VG/G. P3. $13.00

KAYE, Marvin. *Stein & Day Handbook of Magic.* nd. BOMC. VG/VG. P3. $10.00

KAYE, Marvin. *Wintermind.* 1982. Doubleday. 1st ed. F/F. P3. $15.00

KAYE, Marvin. *Witches & Warlocks.* nd. BC. VG/VG. P3. $10.00

KAYE, Mollie. *Black Bramble Wood.* 1938. Collins. 1st ed. ils Margaret Tempest. VG. M5. $45.00

KAYTOR, Marilyn. *21: Life & Times of New York's Favorite Club.* 1975. Viking. 1st ed. 191p. blk cloth. B22. $5.00

KAZANTZAKIS, Nikos. *Report to Greco.* 1965. Simon Schuster. 1st ed. F/F. M19. $20.00

KAZANTZAKIS, Nikos. *Symposium.* 1974. Crowell. 1st ed. F/F. B35. $25.00

KEANE, John B. *Bodhran Makers.* 1992. NY. 4 Walls 8 Windows. 1st ed. F/F. M23. $20.00

KEARNEY, Patrick. *History of Erotic Literature.* 1982. np. 4to. 192p. F/F. A4. $45.00

KEARNEY & KUTLER. *Super Soaps.* 1977. Grosset Dunlap. 1st ed. F/F. P3. $20.00

KEARY, C.F. *Dawn of History: An Introduction to Pre-Historic Study.* 1904. Scribner. new ed. 367p. VG. W1. $12.00

KEATES, J.S. *Cartographic Design & Production.* 1973. London. Longman. 1st ed. ils. F/dj. O7. $30.00

KEATING, Bern. *Alaska.* 1969. WA. NGS. 1st ed. 208p. bl cloth. NF/dj. P4. $10.00

KEATING, H.R.E. *Bedside Companion to Crime.* 1989. Mysterious. 1st ed. F/F. P3. $20.00

KEATING, H.R.E. *Body in the Billiard Room.* 1987. Hutchinson. 1st ed. F/F. P3. $20.00

KEATING, H.R.E. *Death & the Visiting Firemen.* 1973. Crime Club. 1st ed. VG/VG. P3. $20.00

KEATING, H.R.E. *Inspector Ghote Hunts the Peacock.* 1968. Dutton. 1st ed. F/F. P3. $20.00

KEATING, H.R.E. *Under a Monsoon Cloud.* 1986. Viking. 1st ed. NF/NF. P3. $16.00

KEATING, H.R.E. *Whodunit?* 1982. Van Nostrand Reinhold. 1st ed. VG/VG. P3. $25.00

KEATS, Ezra Jack. *Peter's Chair.* 1967. Harper Row. 8vo. pict brd. VG. B17. $6.50

KEATS, Ezra Jack. *Snowy Day.* 1962. NY. Viking. 1st ed. 8vo. VG+/VG. C8. $100.00

KEDDIE, Niccki R. *Roots of Revolution: An Interpretive History of Modern Iran.* 1981. Yale. 1st ed. ils. 321p. VG. W1. $12.00

KEDOURIE, Elie. *Islam in the Modern World & Other Stories.* 1981. HRW. 1st Am ed. 332p. NF/dj. W1. $22.00

KEEBLE, John. *Broken Ground.* 1987. Harper Row. 1st ed. VG/VG. P3. $18.00

KEEBLE, John. *Yellowfish.* 1980. Harper Row. 1st ed. VG/VG. A20. $16.00

KEEGAN, John. *Churchill's Generals.* 1991. NY. 1st Am ed. 368p. M/dj. A17. $12.50

KEEGAN, John. *Six Armies in Normandy: From D-Day to Liberation...* 1982. NY. 3rd. 365p. dj. A17. $10.00

KEEL, John A. *Jadoo.* 1957. Messner. 1st ed. VG. P3. $20.00

KEELE & POYNTER. *Short History of Medicine.* 1961. London. 1st ed. 160p. dj. A13. $40.00

KEENAN, Brian. *Evil Cradling: The Five-Year Ordeal of a Hostage.* 1992. Viking. 1st Am ed. 297p. VG/dj. W1. $18.00

KEENANA, Henry F. *Iron Gate.* 1891. Appleton. 1st ed. VG. B10. $45.00

KEENE, Carolyn. *Dana Girls: By the Light of the Study Lamp.* nd. Grosset Dunlap. VG. P3. $8.00

KEENE, Carolyn. *Dana Girls: Circle of Footprints.* nd. Grosset Dunlap. VG. P3. $8.00

KEENE, Carolyn. *Dana Girls: Curious Coronation.* nd. Grosset Dunlap. VG. P3. $8.00

KEENE, Carolyn. *Dana Girls: Haunted Lagoon (#21).* 1959. Grosset Dunlap. lists to #22. 182p. VG+/dj. M20. $25.00

KEENE, Carolyn. *Dana Girls: Mystery at the Crossroads.* 1954. Grosset Dunlap. gr bdg. VG. P3. $8.00

KEENE, Carolyn. *Dana Girls: Mystery of the Bamboo Bird.* nd. Grosset Dunlap. VG. P3. $8.00

KEENE, Carolyn. *Dana Girls: Portrait in the Sand (#12).* 1943. Grosset Dunlap. 1st ed. 216p. VG/dj. M20. $40.00

KEENE, Carolyn. *Dana Girls: Winking Ruby Mystery.* 1957. Grosset Dunlap. VG. P3. $8.00

KEENE, Carolyn. *Nancy Drew Cookbook.* 1975 (1973). Grosset Dunlap. inscr. 159p. VG. M20. $100.00

KEENE, Carolyn. *Nancy Drew: Broken Anchor.* 1983. Wanderer Books. blk stp orange cloth. VG/G+. P12. $5.00

KEENE, Carolyn. *Nancy Drew: Bungalow Mystery.* nd. Grosset Dunlap. VG. P3. $4.00

KEENE, Carolyn. *Nancy Drew: Clúe in the Crossword Cipher.* nd. Grosset Dunlap. VG. P3. $4.00

KEENE, Carolyn. *Nancy Drew: Clue in the Diary.* 1932. Grosset Dunlap. VG. P3. $15.00

KEENE, Carolyn. *Nancy Drew: Clue in the Jewel Box.* nd. Grosset Dunlap. VG. P3. $4.00

KEENE, Carolyn. *Nancy Drew: Clue of the Black Keys (#28).* 1960 (1951). Grosset Dunlap. Cameo ed. 181p. VG+/dj. M20. $45.00

KEENE, Carolyn. *Nancy Drew: Hidden Staircase.* 1980. Grosset Dunlap. G+. P12. $4.00

KEENE, Carolyn. *Nancy Drew: Mystery of the Glowing Eye.* 1974. Grosset Dunlap. NF. P12. $4.00

KEENE, Carolyn. *Nancy Drew: Mystery of the Ivory Charm (#13).* 1937A (1936). Grosset Dunlap. 3rd. 216p. VG+/dj. M20. $250.00

KEENE, Carolyn. *Nancy Drew: Mystery of the Lost Dogs.* 1977. Grosset Dunlap. VG. B17. $15.00

KEENE, Carolyn. *Nancy Drew: Password to Larkspur Lane (#10).* 1934B. Grosset Dunlap. 5th. 220p. VG+/dj. M20. $225.00

KEENE, Carolyn. *Nancy Drew: Secret of the Twin Puppets.* 1977. Grosset Dunlap. VG. B17. $15.00

KEEP, Josiah. *West Coast Shells.* 1891. San Francisco. Carson. 12mo. gilt brn cloth. G. T10. $25.00

KEEPING, Charles. *Tinker Tailor Folk Song Tales.* 1969. World. 1st Am ed. ils. F/dj. P2. $30.00

KEEPING, Charles. *Tinker Tailor Folk Song Tales.* 1969. World. 1st Am ed. 4to. unp. F/clip. C14. $25.00

KEES, Hermann. *Ancient Egypt.* 1977. Chicago. 25 pl/11 maps. 392p. VG. W1. $12.00

KEES, Weldon. *State of the Nation: 11 Interpretations by Saroyan...* 1940. Cincinnati. 1st ed. 1/99. sgn all 7 contributors. F/wrp. C2. $200.00

KEESHAN, Robert. *She Loves Me, She Loves Me Not.* 1963. Harper. probable 1st ed. ils Sendak. NF/VG+. C8. $65.00

KEIL, Charles. *Urban Blues.* 1966. Chicago. 1st ed. F/NF. B2. $35.00

KEILLOR, Garrison. *Lake Wobegon Days.* 1985. Viking. 1st ed. F/F. M23. $20.00

KEILLOR, Garrison. *WLT: A Radio Romance.* 1991. Viking. 1st ed. F/VG+. A20. $10.00

KEIM, Randolph. *Sherman.* 1904. WA. 1/12000. VG. V4. $75.00

KEITH, Agnes Newton. *Children of Allah Between the Sea & Sahara.* 1966. Little Brn. 1st Am ed. 467p. VG/dj. W1. $12.00

KEITH, Arthur Berriedale. *Sovereignty of the British Dominions.* 1929. London. Macmillan. G/worn. M11. $85.00

KEITH, Arthur. *Darwinism & What It Implys.* 1928. London. 1st ed. 56p. VG. A13. $45.00

KEITH, Brandon. *Affair of the Gentle Saboteur.* 1966. Whitman. TVTI. VG. P3. $13.00

KEITH, Brandon. *Affair of the Gunrunner's Gold.* 1967. Whitman. TVTI. G. P3. $7.00

KEITH, Brandon. *Message From Moscow.* 1966. Whitman. TVTI. VG. P3. $10.00

KEITH, David. *Matter of Accent.* 1943. Dodd Mead. VG. P3. $25.00

KEITH, Thomas. *New Treatise on the Use of the Globes...* 1826. NY. Wood. 4th Am from last London ed. scuffed leather. K5. $120.00

KELEMEN, Pal. *Medieval American Art.* 1956. Macmillan. 2 vol. 1st ed. 306 pl. gilt red cloth. NF. T10. $150.00

KELEMEN, Pal. *Medieval American Art.* 1956. NY. Macmillan. 1st 1-vol ed. 308p. map ep. NF/NF. T10. $65.00

KELL, John McIntosh. *Recollections of a Naval Life...* 1900. Neale. 1st ed. 307p. cloth. VG. M8. $350.00

KELLAND, Clarence Budington. *Mark Tidd, Editor.* 1917. Harper. ils. F. M5. $15.00

KELLAND, Clarence Budington. *Mark Tidd's Citadel (#6).* 1916. Grosset Dunlap. 279p. VG+/dj. M20. $20.00

KELLEAM, Joseph E. *Hunters of Space.* 1960. Avalon. 1st ed. hc. F/F. P3. $20.00

KELLEAM, Joseph E. *Little Men.* 1960. Avalon. 1st ed. F/F. P3. $20.00

KELLEAM, Joseph E. *When the Red King Woke.* 1966. Avalon. 1st ed. F/F. P3. $20.00

KELLER, Frances Ruth. *Contented Little Pussy Cat.* 1949. Platt Munk. ils Adele Werber/Doris Laslo. VG. B17. $12.50

KELLER, Harry. *Official Detective Omnibus.* 1948. DSP. 1st ed. hc. VG. P3. $20.00

KELLER, Helen. *Song of the Stone Wall.* 1910. NY. 1st ed. VG. B5. $55.00

KELLER, Helen. *World I Live In.* 1908. Century. 12mo. 4 pl. 196p. prt gr cloth. G1. $50.00

KELLER, John. *Game of Draw Poker.* 1887. NY. 84p. VG. S1. $25.00

KELLER & SCHOENFELD. *Principles of Psychology: A Systematic Text...* 1950. Appleton Century. 431p. olive cloth/painted labels. G1. $35.00

KELLERMAN, Jonathan. *Butcher's Theater.* 1986. Bantam. 1st ed. F/NF. N4. $35.00

KELLERMAN, Jonathan. *Devil's Waltz.* 1993. Bantam. 1st ed. sgn. NF/NF. M22. $35.00

KELLERMAN, Jonathan. *Private Eyes.* 1992. Bantam. 1st ed. NF/NF. P3. $22.00

KELLERMAN, Jonathan. *Time Bomb.* 1990. Bantam. 1st ed. F/F. A20. $20.00

KELLEY, David. *Astronomical Identities of Mesoamerican Gods.* 1980. Miami. 1st ed. 54p. F3. $20.00

KELLEY, Donald R. *Historians & the Law in Postrevolutionary France.* 1984. Princeton. M11. $27.50

KELLEY, F.C. *Life & Times of Kin Hubbard.* 1952. NY. 1st ed. dj. A17. $10.00

KELLEY, Leo P. *Luke Sutton: Outrider.* 1984. Doubleday. 1st ed. F/F. P3. $13.00

KELLEY, Leo P. *Time 110100.* 1972. Walker. 1st ed. F/F. P3. $15.00

KELLEY, Robert. *Racing in America 1937-1959.* 1960. NY. Jockey Club. 1/1000. VG. O3. $150.00

KELLEY, Susan. *Summertime Soldiers.* 1986. Walker. 1st ed. author's 2nd book. F/F. H11. $40.00

KELLEY, William Melvin. *Dancers on the Shore.* 1964. Doubleday. 1st ed. F/F. B2. $50.00

KELLNER, Bruce. *Bibliography of the Work of Carl Van Vechten.* 1980. Westport. 258p. VG. A17. $15.00

KELLOGG, M. Bradley. *Wave & the Flame.* 1987. Gollancz. 1st ed. VG/VG. P3. $20.00

KELLOGG, Marjorie. *Tell Me That You Love Me, Junie Moon.* 1968. FSG. 1st ed. F/F clip. B4. $100.00

KELLOGG, Robert H. *Life & Death in Rebel Prisons: Andersonville, Florence...* 1868. Hartford. ils. 424p. gilt cloth. VG. B14. $75.00

KELLOGG, W.K. *Kellogg's Funny Jungleland.* 1909. Kellogg. moveables. cereal giveaway. VG. D1. $40.00

KELLY, J. Frederick. *Early Domestic Architecture of Connecticut.* 1924. New Haven. Yale. 4to. 48 pl/242 text ils. tan buckram. VG. T10. $175.00

KELLY, J.B. *Arabia, the Gulf & the West.* 1980. NY. Basic. 1st Am ed. 8vo. 5 maps. F/dj. W1. $35.00

KELLY, Mary Ann. *My Old Kentucky Home, Good Night.* 1978. Exposition. 1st ed. sgn. 8vo. 32 pl. VG/G. B11. $25.00

KELLY, Mary. *Dead Man's Riddle.* 1967. Walker. VG/VG. P3. $18.00

KELLY, Mary. *Girl in the Alley.* 1974. Walker. 1st ed. VG/VG. P3. $15.00

KELLY, Pat. *River of Lost Dreams: Navigation on the Rio Grande.* 1986. Lincoln, NE. 8vo. ils/index. 149p. F/dj. T10. $25.00

KELLY, S.J. *History of St Paul's Protestant Episcopal Church...* 1945. E Cleveland. 160p. VG. B18. $9.50

KELLY, Susan. *Hope Against Hope.* 1991. Scribner. 1st Am ed. author's 1st novel. AN/dj. M22. $15.00

KELLY, Susan. *Summertime Soldiers.* 1986. Walker. 1st ed. author's 2nd novel. F/F. T2. $20.00

KELLY, Susan. *Trail of the Dragon.* 1988. Walker. 1st ed. F/F. T2. $15.00

KELLY, Vince. *Achieving a Vision: Life Story of PW Tewksbury.* (1941). Australia. George M Dash. sgn pres ed. 8vo. 220p. VG/worn. B11. $50.00

KELLY, W.K. *Decameron of Boccaccio.* 1869. London. marbled brd/brn half leather. VG. B30. $68.00

KELLY, Walt. *At the Mercy of the Elephants.* 1990. Eclipse. 1st ed. F. P3. $20.00

KELLY, Walt. *Diggin' Fo' Square Roots.* 1990. Eclipse. 1st ed. F. P3. $20.00

KELLY, Walt. *Pogo & Albert.* 1989. Eclipse. 1st ed. F. P3. $20.00

KELLY & KELLY. *Dancing Diplomats.* 1950. NM U. 1st ed. ils Gustave Baumann. 254p. dj. F3. $25.00

KELSEY, H.W. (Hugh). *Bridge: The Mind of the Expert.* 1981. London. NF/NF. S1. $12.00

KELSEY, H.W. (Hugh). *Countdown to Better Bridge.* 1986. Louisville. 184p. VG/wrp. S1. $7.00

KELSEY, H.W. (Hugh). *Instant Bridge.* 1975. Toronto. 70p. VG/wrp. S1. $5.00

KELSEY, H.W. (Hugh). *Simple Squeezes.* 1985. England. 120p. F/dj. S1. $15.00

KELSEY, H.W. (Hugh). *Simple Squeezes.* 1985. London. 120p. VG/wrp. S1. $8.00

KELSEY, H.W. (Hugh). *Test Your Pairs Play.* 1985. London. 80p. F/wrp. S1. $4.00

KELSEY, Vera. *Satan Has Six Fingers.* 1943. Crime Club. VG. P3. $15.00

KELSEY, Vera. *Whisper Murder!* nd. Collier. hc. VG. P3. $15.00

KELTON, Elmer. *Good Old Boys.* 1985. TX Christian U. 1st ed thus. M/M. A18. $10.00

KEMELMAN, Harry. *Day the Rabbi Resigned.* 1992. Fawcett Columbine. 1st ed. F/F. P3. $20.00

KEMELMAN, Harry. *Thursday the Rabbi Walked Out.* 1978. Morrow. 1st ed. NF/NF. P3. $25.00

KEMELMAN, Harry. *Wednesday the Rabbi Got Wet.* 1976. Morrow. 3rd ed. VG/VG. P3. $12.00

KEMELMAN, Harry. *Weekend With the Rabbi.* nd. BC. VG/VG. P3. $10.00

KEMP, Harry. *Chanteys & Ballads.* 1920. Brentano. 1st ed. sgn. 12mo. 173p. bl cloth. VG. B11. $50.00

KEMP, Oliver. *Wilderness Homes.* 1908. NY. Outing. 1st ed. 163p. VG. B5. $60.00

KEMP, Sarah. *Over the Edge.* 1979. Crime Club. 1st ed. VG/VG. P3. $18.00

KEMPSON, Ewart. *Contract Bridge: How to Play It.* ca 1952. London. 160p. VG. S1. $8.00

KEMPSON, Ewart. *First Pocket Book of Bridge Problems.* 1961. NY. 79p. VG. S1. $6.00

KEMPSON, Ewart. *Quintessence of CAB: CAB System of Bidding.* 1959. London. 160p. VG/dj. S1. $12.00

KEMPSON, Ewart. *Second Book of Bridge Problems.* 1962. NY. 80p. VG/dj. S1. $7.00

KEMPTON, Murray. *Part of Our Time.* 1955. NY. 1st ed. dj. A17. $10.00

KENDALL, Aubyn. *Art & Archaeology of Pre-Columbian Middle America.* 1977. Boston. Hall. 1st ed. 324p. F3. $60.00

KENDEIGH, S. Charles. *Parental Car & Its Evolution in Birds.* 1952. IL Biological Monographs. 356p. prt bl wrp. G1. $40.00

KENDRAKE, Carleton; see Gardner, Erle Stanley.

KENDREW, James. *Cries of York, for Amusement of Young Children.* ca 1811-20. York. 32mo. 28 woodcuts. 32p. F/tan self wrp/paper fld. B24. $225.00

KENDRICK, Baynard. *Flames of Time.* 1948. Scribner. 1st ed. VG/G. P3. $35.00

KENDRICK, Tony. *Neon Tough.* 1988. Putnam. 1st ed. NF/NF. P3. $20.00

KENDRICK, Tony. *81st Site.* 1980. NAL. 1st ed. VG/VG. P3. $18.00

KENDRICK. *Early Reading of Thomas Wentworth Higginson.* 1939. np. 4to. 218p. cloth. A4. $195.00

KENEALLY, Thomas. *Confederates.* 1980. Harper Row. 1st ed. F/F clip. M23. $30.00

KENEALLY, Thomas. *Place at Whitton.* 1965. Walker. 1st ed. VG/VG. P3. $18.00

KENEALLY, Thomas. *Playmaker.* 1987. Simon Schuster. 1st ed. VG/VG. P3. $20.00

KENEALLY, Thomas. *Schindler's List.* 1982. 1st ed. sgn. F/VG. M19. $250.00

KENNEDY, Adam. *Just Like Humphrey Bogart.* 1978. Viking. 1st ed. VG/VG. P3. $15.00

KENNEDY, John Fitzgerald. *Profiles in Courage.* 1956. NY. 1st ed. ils. F/NF. B14. $150.00

KENNEDY, Joseph. *Preliminary Report: Eighth Census 1860.* 1862. WA. 8vo. 294p. gr cloth. xl. VG. T3. $35.00

KENNEDY, Leigh. *Journal of Nicholas the American.* 1987. London. Cape. 1st ed. xl. VG/VG. M21. $65.00

KENNEDY, Margaret. *Constant Nymph.* 1925. Doubleday Page. G. P3. $7.00

KENNEDY, Margaret. *Fool of the Family.* 1930. Doubleday Doran. 1st ed. NF/VG. B4. $65.00

KENNEDY, Robert F. to *Seek a Newer World.* 1967. Doubleday. 1st ed. F/NF. M23. $30.00

KENNEDY, Roger G. *Mission: History & Architecture of Missions of North Am.* 1993. Houghton Mifflin. 1st ed. photos. 240p. F/dj. A17. $30.00

KENNEDY, William. *Billy Phelan's Greatest Game.* 1978. NY. 1st ed. F/NF. C6. $60.00

KENNEDY, William. *Hurrah for the Life of a Sailor!* 1900. Edinburgh. Blackwood. 47 pl/maps. 356p. VG. T7. $75.00

KENNEDY, William. *Legs.* 1974. Coward McCann. 1st ed. author's 2nd novel. VG/G. M22. $50.00

KENNEDY, William. *Quinn's Book.* 1988. Viking. 1st ed. F/F. H11. $30.00

KENNEDY, William. *Riding the Yellow Trolley Car.* 1993. Viking. 1st trade ed. F/F. B35. $22.00

KENNEDY & ROSS. *Bibliography of Negro Migration.* 1934. Columbia. 1st ed. 251p. cloth. VG+. M8. $75.00

KENNEY, Charles. *Hammurabi's Code.* 1995. Simon Schuster. 1st ed. F/F. M23. $25.00

KENNEY. *Catalogue of Rare Astronomical Books in San Diego State...* 1988. 1/1000. ils. 336p. F/F cloth case. A4. $125.00

KENT, Charles W. *Revival of Interest in Southern Letters.* 1900. BF Johnson. 27p. wrp. B10. $25.00

KENT, James. *Lectures on Homoepathic Philosophy.* 1900. Lancaster. 1st ed. 290p. VG. A13. $100.00

KENT, Louise Andre. *He Went With Magellan.* 1943. Houghton Mifflin. 1st ed. inscr. 200p. cloth. VG+/dj. B22. $5.00

KENT, Rockwell. *Beowulf.* 1932. Random. 1/950. sgn w/thumbprint. VG. T10. $425.00

KENT, Rockwell. *Birthday Book.* 1931. 1/1850. sgn. silk brd. VG+. S13. $250.00

KENT, Rockwell. *Canterbury Tales.* 1934. NY. 1st ed. VG/G. B5. $40.00

KENT, Rockwell. *It's Me Oh Lord.* 1955. NY. 1st ed. VG. B5. $70.00

KENT, Rockwell. *N by E.* 1930. Random. 1/900. sgn. 8 full-p pl. 245p. silver bl cloth. F/case. B24. $375.00

KENT, Rockwell. *Northern Christmas.* 1941. NY. 1st ed. VG/VG. B5. $37.50

KENT, Rockwell. *Rockwell Kent's Greenland Journal.* 1962. NY. 1/1000. NF/case. w/suite of 6 orig lithos (1 sgn). C6. $225.00

KENT, Rockwell. *Salamina.* nd. Harcourt Brace. 8vo. 336p. xl. dj. B11. $30.00

KENT, Rockwell. *Voyaging Southward From the Strait of Magellan.* 1924. Putnam. 1st trade ed. ils. teg. F/bl dj. B24. $475.00

KENT, Rockwell. *1938 International Exhibition of Paintings.* nd. Carnegie Inst. 12mo. ils. VG/wrp. T10. $25.00

KENYON, Michael. *May You Die in Ireland.* 1965. Morrow. 2nd ed. hc. F/F. P3. $12.00

KENYON, Michael. *Whole Hog.* 1967. Collins Crime Club. 1st ed. VG/G. P3. $15.00

KER, N.R. *Medieval Manuscripts in British Libraries.* 1969. London. Clarendon. 10 pl. 437p. xl. A17. $20.00

KERENYI, C. *Greece in Colour.* 1957. McGraw Hill. 1st ed. atlas folio. 32 tipped-in pl. VG. W1. $45.00

KERN. *Tale of a Cat as Told by Himself.* 1902. np. ils. 92p. VG. A4. $85.00

KEROUAC, Jack. *Scripture of the Golden Eternity.* 1960. Totem. 1st ed/3rd state. VG/wrp. M19. $45.00

KEROUAC, Jan. *Baby Driver.* 1981. NY. 1st ed. VG/VG. B5. $20.00

KERR, Archibald William. *Shadow of Drumcarnett.* 1929. Alexander-Ouseley. VG. P3. $30.00

KERR, Ben; see Block, Lawrence.

KERR, E. *Yoknapatawph: Faulkner's Little Postage Stamp of Native...* 1969. NY. 1st ed. VG/VG. B5. $42.50

KERR, James. *Clinic.* nd. BC. VG/VG. P3. $8.00

KERR, P.F. *Optical Mineralogy.* 1959. McGraw Hill. 3rd. 442p. VG. D8. $20.00

KERR, Philip. *March Violets.* 1989. Viking. 1st ed. NF/NF. P3. $18.00

KERR, Robert Nolan. *Tunes for Little Players: A Piano Book.* 1947. Phil. ils. 35p. G/wrp. A17. $6.50

KERR & RIVKIN. *Hello, Hollywood.* 1962. Doubleday. 1st ed. sgns. VG+. D2. $25.00

KERSH, Gerald. *Fowlers End.* 1957. Simon Schuster. 1st ed. NF/NF. P3. $50.00

KERSH, Gerald. *Night & the City.* 1948. World Forum. 2nd. VG. P3. $10.00

KERSH, Gerald. *Prelude to a Certain Midnight.* 1947. Heinemann. 1st ed. VG. P3. $30.00

KERSH, Gerald. *Sergeant Nelson of the Guards.* 1945. Winston. VG. P3. $20.00

KERSH, Gerald. *Weak & the Strong.* 1946. Simon Schuster. 1st ed. F/NF. B35. $25.00

KESEY, Ken. *Further Inquiry.* 1990. Viking. 1st ed. F/F. B35. $25.00

KESEY, Ken. *Sailor Song.* 1992. Viking. 1st ed. sgn. F/F. A18. $50.00

KESSEL, John. *Meeting in Infinity: Allegories & Extrapolations.* 1992. Arkham. 1st ed. F/F. T2. $22.00

KESSLER, Ronald. *Richest Man in the World: Study of Adnan Khashoggi.* 1986. Warner. 1st ed. xl. dj. W1. $20.00

KESTERTON, David. *Darkling.* 1982. Arkham. 1st ed. 1/3126. author's 1st novel. F/F. P3/T2. $13.00

KETCHAM, Hank. *I Wanna Go Home!* 1965. 1st ed. NF/VG. S13. $20.00

KETCHUM, Philip. *Death in the Night.* 1939. Phoenix. ffe removed. G. P3. $10.00

KETCHUM, Philip. *Wyatt Earp.* 1956. Whitman. VG. P3. $15.00

KETCHUM, Richard. *Winter Soldiers.* 1973. London. MacDonald. 1st ed. F/clip. M23. $20.00

KETTELL, T.P. *Southern Wealth & Northern Profits.* 1860. NY. royal 8vo. 173p. brn cloth. G. T3. $55.00

KETTERER, Bernadine. *Manderley Mystery.* 1937. Eldon. 1st ed. VG. P3. $20.00

KEUNING, J. *Willem Jansz Blaeu: A Biography & History of His Work.* 1973. Amsterdam. Theatrvm Orbis Terrarvm. 8vo. 23 maps. AN/dj. O7. $45.00

KEVERNE, Richard. *More Crook Stuff.* 1938. Constable. 1st ed. VG. P3. $60.00

KEVORKIAN, Jack. *Story of Dissection.* 1959. NY. 1st ed. 80p. dj. A13. $50.00

KEYES, Daniel. *Minds of Billy Milligan.* 1981. Random. 2nd. VG/VG. P3. $15.00

KEYES, Frances Parkinson. *All This Is Louisiana.* 1950. Harper. inscr to Taylor Caldwell. 317p. VG/dj. M20. $75.00

KEYES, Francis Parkinson. *Once on Esplanade.* 1947. Dodd Mead. 1st ed. sgn. ils Addison Burbank. VG/dj. M20. $125.00

KEYES, T. *Battle of Disneyland.* 1974. WH Allen. 1st ed. VG/VG. P3. $20.00

KEYHOE, Donald. *Aliens From Space.* nd. BC. VG. P3. $8.00

KEYHOE, Donald. *Flying Saucers From Outer Space.* 1953. Holt. 1st ed. VG/G. P3. $18.00

KEYNES, Geoffrey. *Letters of Sir Thomas Browne.* 1946. London. 440p. dj. A13. $50.00

KEYSTONE, Oliver. *Arsenic for the Teacher.* 1950. Phoenix. VG. P3. $10.00

KHAN, K.S. Khaja. *Studies in Tasawwuf.* 1977. Lahore. rpt of 2nd revised ed. 8vo. 260p. VG/dj. W1. $14.00

KHAYYAM, Omar. *Rubaiyat.* nd. Crowell. ils Willy Pogany. teg. full leather. VG. T10. $125.00

KHAYYAM, Omar. *Rubaiyat.* nd. NY. Crowell. ils Willy Pogany. teg. F/dj/box. T10. $150.00

KHAYYAM, Omar. *Rubaiyat.* 1909. Hodder Stoughton. ils Edmund Dulac. gilt cloth. VG. T10. $350.00

KHAYYAM, Omar. *Rubaiyat.* 1940. NY. ils Szyk. padded leather. G. V4. $45.00

KHEIRALLAH, George. *Arabia Reborn.* 1952. Albuquerque. 1st ed. ils. 307p. VG/dj. W1. $45.00

KHORANA. *Africa in Literature for Children & Young Adults.* 1994. 363p. F. A4. $65.00

KIBLER, James E. *Poetry of William Gilmore Simms.* 1979. Rpt Co. ARC. 478p. VG. B10. $35.00

KIBLER, James E. *Pseudonymous Publications of William Gillmore Simms.* 1976. GA U. ARC. 102p. VG. B10. $25.00

KIDD, John. *On the Adaptation of External Nature to Physical Condition.* 1833. London. Pickering. 375p. contemporary bl cloth. G1. $135.00

KIDDER, D.P. *Ancient Egypt: Its Monuments & History.* 1854. NY. Carlton Phillips. 12mo. map ftspc. 214p. VG. T10. $50.00

KIDDER, T. *Road to Yuba City.* 1974. NY. ARC/1st ed. RS. F/NF. A15. $75.00

KIDDER, Tracy. *Among Schoolchildren.* 1989. Houghton Mifflin. 1st ed. F/F. A20. $18.00

KIDWELL, Claudia B. *Cutting a Fashionable Fit.* 1979. Smithsonian. sgn. F. D2. $35.00

KIENZLE, William X. *Assault With Intent.* nd. BC. VG/VG. P3. $8.00

KIENZLE, William X. *Rosary Murders.* 1979. Hodder Stoughton. 1st ed. VG/VG. P3. $22.00

KIENZLE, William X. *Shadow of Death.* 1983. Andrews McMeel. 1st ed. VG/VG. P3. $15.00

KIEREIN, John. *Kamikaze No Trump.* 1977. Boulder. 45p. VG/wrp. S1. $8.00

KIERNAN, Thomas. *Miracle at Coogans Bluff.* 1975. Crowell. 1st ed. VG+/VG+. P8. $35.00

KIES. *Occult in the Western World, an Annotated Bibliography.* 1986. np. 244p. F. A4. $45.00

KIG, Charles. *Campaigning With Crook.* 1967. Norman. 2nd. 12mo. 166p. F/dj. T10. $25.00

KIJEWSKI, Karen. *Copy Kat.* 1992. Doubleday. 1st ed. F/F. H11. $35.00

KIJEWSKI, Karen. *Kat's Cradle.* 1992. Doubleday. 1st ed. AN/dj. N4. $40.00

KIJEWSKI, Karen. *Wild Kat.* 1994. Doubleday. 1st ed. F/F. A20. $12.00

KILBOURN, William. *Pipeline.* 1970. Clarke Irwin. VG/VG. P3. $15.00

KILEY. *Hemingway: Old Friend Remembers.* 1965. np. 19 photos. 198p. F/VG. A4. $75.00

KILIAN, Crawford. *Icequake.* 1979. Douglas McIntyre. 1st ed. NF/NF. P3. $30.00

KILIAN, Crawford. *Tsunami.* 1983. Douglas McIntyre. 1st ed. F/F. P3. $20.00

KILLION, C.E. *Honey in the Comb.* 1951. Killion. 8vo. photos. 114p. cloth. NF. B1. $25.00

KILMER, Joyce. *Trees & Other Poems.* 1917. 1st ed. VG+. S13. $25.00

KILPATRICK, Franklin P. *Human Behavior From the Transactional Point of View.* 1952. Hanover, NH. 4to. 259p. prt gray cloth. G1. $35.00

KILPATRICK, James Jackson. *Southern Case for School Segregation.* 1962. Crowell Collier. 1st ed. 220p. VG/VG. B10. $15.00

KILUPAILA. *Bibliography of Hydrometry.* 1961. Notre Dame. 998p. xl. VG. A4. $185.00

KILWORTH, Gary. *Angel.* 1993. Gollancz. 1st ed. F/F. G10. $25.00

KILWORTH, Gary. *Downers.* 1991. Methuen. 1st ed. F/F. P3. $20.00

KILWORTH, Gary. *Hunter's Moon.* 1989. Unwin Hyman. 1st ed. F/F. P3. $22.00

KILWORTH, Gary. *In Solitary.* 1977. Faber. 1st ed. F/F. P3. $20.00

KIMBLE, George H.T. *Our American Weather.* (1955). McGraw Hill. 3rd. 322p. G/dj. K5. $12.00

KIMBROUGH, Emily. *Floating Island.* 1968. Harper Row. 1st ed. sgn. ils Vasiliu. F/dj. B14. $45.00

KIMMEL, S. *Mad Booths of Maryland.* 1940. Indianapolis. 1st ed. VG/VG. B5. $40.00

KINCAID, Jamaica. *Lucy.* 1990. FSC. ARC. sgn. F/wrp. B4. $50.00

KINCAID, Jamaica. *Lucy.* 1990. FSC. 1st ed. sgn. F/F. B4. $85.00

KINCAID, Nanci. *Crossing Blood.* 1992. Putnam. 1st ed. author's 1st novel. F/F. M23. $25.00

KINDER, Gary. *Light Years.* 1987. Atlantic Monthly. 1st ed. VG. P3. $19.00

KINER, Ralph W. *Kiner's Korner.* 1987. Arbor. 1st ed. F/VG+. P8. $25.00

KINERT, Reed. *Little Helicopter.* 1947. Macmillan. possible 1st ed. 8vo. unp. VG/VG clip. C14. $15.00

KING, Alfred Castner. *Mountain Idylls & Other Poems.* 1901. NY. 120p. G. A17. $25.00

KING, Ben. *Southland Melodies.* 1911. Forbes. 128p. VG. B10. $125.00

KING, Charles. *Campaigning With Crook.* 1967. Norman. 2nd. 12mo. 166p. F/dj. T10. $25.00

KING, Charles. *Mama's Boy.* 1992. NY. Pocket. 1st ed. author's 1st book. F/F. H11. $25.00

KING, Dick. *Ghost Towns of Texas.* 1953. Naylor. 1st ed. cloth. VG/dj. M20. $25.00

KING, Evan. *Children of the Black-Haired People.* 1955. NY. 1st ed. dj. A17. $15.00

KING, Florence. *Southern Ladies & Gentlemen.* 1975. Stein Day. 1st ed. 216p. reading copy. B10. $12.00

KING, Florence. *When Sisterhood Was in Flower.* 1982. Viking. 1st ed. 190p. VG/VG. B10. $25.00

KING, Francis. *Voices in an Empty Room.* 1984. Hutchinson. 1st ed. VG/VG. P3. $19.00

KING, Frank. *Case of the Painted Girl.* 1949. Nimmo. VG. P3. $20.00

KING, Grace. *Memories of a Southern Woman of Letters.* 1932. NY. 1st ed. 398p. VG-/torn. B18. $22.50

KING, Henry C. *Background of Astronomy.* 1957. London. Watts. 1st ed. G/dj. K5. $12.00

KING, Henry C. *Pictorial Guide to the Stars.* 1967. Crowell. 1st ed. 4to. 167p. cloth. G. K5. $15.00

KING, J.C.H. *Artifical Curiosities From the Northwest Coast of America.* 1981. London. 1st ed. 87 pl. 119p. NF/dj. T10. $100.00

KING, Jaime. *Ancient Mexico.* 1987. Albquerque. 2nd. 134p. wrp. F3. $10.00

KING, Joe. *San Francisco Giants.* 1958. Prentice Hall. 1st ed. VG. P8. $12.50

KING, Larry L. *Of Outlaws, Con Men, Whores, Politicians & Other Artists.* 1980. NY. Viking. 1st ed. 8vo. 274p. F/dj. T10. $25.00

KING, Laurie. *Monstrous Regiment of Women.* 1995. Scribner. 1st ed. sgn. F/F. T2. $35.00

KING, Laurie. *to Play the Fool.* 1995. St Martin. 1st ed. sgn. F/F. T2. $35.00

KING, Laurie. *With Child.* 1996. St Martin. 1st ed. sgn. F/F. T2. $25.00

KING, Lester. *Medical World of the 18th Century.* 1958. Chicago. 1st ed. 346p. VG. A13. $65.00

KING, Martha Bennett. *Bean Blossom Hill.* 1957. Container Corp of Am. 1st ed. 36p. VG/G. T5. $40.00

KING, Martin Luther. *Strength to Love.* 1963. NY. 1st ed. VG/VG. B5. $35.00

KING, Martin Luther. *Why We Can't Wait.* 1964. Harper Row. 1st ed. photos. NF/NF. R11. $60.00

KING, P.B. *Evolution of North America.* 1977. Princeton. fld map. NF/dj. D8. $30.00

KING, Rufus. *Lethal Lady.* 1948. Detective BC. VG. P3. $20.00

KING, Rufus. *Murder in the Wilett Family.* 1931. Crime Club. VG. P3. $20.00

KING, Rufus. *Valcour Meets Murder.* 1932. Crime Club. 1st ed. VG. P3. $30.00

KING, Stephen. *Bare Bones: Conversations on Terror With Stephen King.* 1988. McGraw Hill. 1st ed. F/F. T2. $20.00

KING, Stephen. *Carrie.* 1974. Doubleday. 1st ed. xl. poor. P3. $75.00

KING, Stephen. *Christine.* 1983. Viking. 1st ed. VG/VG. P3. $60.00

KING, Stephen. *Cujo.* 1981. Viking. 1st ed. F/F. B4. $125.00

KING, Stephen. *Cujo.* 1981. Viking. 1st ed. 319p. VG. B18. $45.00

KING, Stephen. *Cycle of the Werewolf.* 1983. Land of Enchantment. hc. NF/NF. P3. $125.00

KING, Stephen. *Danse Macabre.* 1981. Everest. 1st ed. F/F. P3. $100.00

KING, Stephen. *Danse Macabre.* 1981. Everest. 1st ed. VG/G. P3. $60.00

KING, Stephen. *Dark Half.* 1989. Viking. 1st ed. F/F. P3. $30.00

KING, Stephen. *Dark Tower II: The Drawing of the Three.* 1987. Donald Grant. ltd ed. 1/800. sgn. ils/sgn Phil Hale. AN/AN. B24. $475.00

KING, Stephen. *Dark Tower II: The Drawing of the Three.* 1987. Donald Grant. 1st ed. F/F. P3. $100.00

KING, Stephen. *Dark Tower III: Waste Lands.* 1991. Donald Grant. ltd ed. 1/1250. sgn. ils/sgn Ned Dameron. AN/dj/case. B24. $350.00

KING, Stephen. *Dark Tower III: Waste Lands.* 1991. Donald Grant. 1st ed. F/F. P3. $45.00

KING, Stephen. *Dark Tower: Gunslinger.* 1982. Donald Grant. ltd ed. F/NF. B4. $575.00

KING, Stephen. *Dark Tower: Gunslinger.* 1982. Donald Grant. ltd ed. VG/VG. P3. $450.00

KING, Stephen. *Dead Zone.* 1979. Viking. 1st ed. F/F. B4. $150.00

KING, Stephen. *Different Seasons.* 1982. Viking. 1st ed. VG/VG. P3. $75.00

KING, Stephen. *Dolan's Cadillac.* 1989. Lord John. 1st ed. 1/1000. sgn. F. B24. $275.00

KING, Stephen. *Dolores Claiborne.* 1993. Viking. 1st ed. F/F. N4/P3. $25.00

KING, Stephen. *Eyes of the Dragon.* 1987. Viking. 1st ed. F/NF. H11. $40.00

KING, Stephen. *Firestarter.* 1980. Phantasia. 1st ed. 1/725. sgn/dtd. cover ils/sgn Michael Whelan. F/dj/case. B24. $550.00

KING, Stephen. *Four Past Midnight*. 1990. Viking. 1st ed. F/F. P3. $23.00

KING, Stephen. *Gerald's Game*. 1992. Viking. 1st ed. F/F. P3. $23.00

KING, Stephen. *It*. 1986. Viking. 1st ed. NF/NF. P3. $45.00

KING, Stephen. *Misery*. 1987. London. Hodder Stoughton. 1st ed. F/NF. T2. $25.00

KING, Stephen. *Misery*. 1987. NY. Viking. 1st ed. F/F. H11. $50.00

KING, Stephen. *My Pretty Pony*. 1989. Vernona, Italy. Stamperia Valonega. 1st trade ed. AN/case. M21. $65.00

KING, Stephen. *Needful Things*. 1991. Viking. 1st ed. F/F. P3. $25.00

KING, Stephen. *Night Shift*. 1978. Doubleday BC. NF/VG. M21. $15.00

KING, Stephen. *Pet Sematary*. 1983. Doubleday. 1st ed. F/F. P3. $50.00

KING, Stephen. *Pet Sematary*. 1983. Doubleday. 1st ed. NF/VG. N4. $35.00

KING, Stephen. *Pet Sematary*. 1983. Hodder Stoughton. 1st ed. VG/VG. P3. $75.00

KING, Stephen. *Shining*. 1977. Doubleday. 1st ed. author's 3rd book. F/F. A4. $250.00

KING, Stephen. *Skeleton Crew*. 1985. Putnam. 1st ed. F/F. P3. $60.00

KING, Stephen. *Skeleton Crew*. 1985. Scream. 1/1000. sgn. ils/sgn JK Potter. F/F. B4. $400.00

KING, Stephen. *Stand*. 1978. Doubleday. 1st ed. NF/NF. M19/P3. $175.00

KING, Stephen. *Stand*. 1990. Doubleday. 8th. F/F. P3. $23.00

KING, Stephen. *Thinner*. 1984. NAL. 1st ed. F/F. T2. $70.00

KING, Stephen. *Tommyknockers*. 1987. Putnam. 1st ed. F/NF. N4. $35.00

KING, Stephen. *Tommyknockers*. 1987. Putnam. 1st ed. VG/VG. P3. $25.00

KING, Tabitha. *Caretakers*. 1984. Methuen. 1st ed. F/F. P3. $50.00

KING, Thomas Butler. *War Steamers. Report No 681*. 29th Congresss, 1st session. disbound. VG. A16. $250.00

KING, W.J. Harding. *Mysteries of the Libyan Desert*. 1925. London. Seeley. 8vo. ils/map. xl. VG. W1. $65.00

KING & POLIKARPUS. *Down Town*. 1985. Arbor. 1st ed. F/F. P3. $20.00

KING & SHERATON. *Is Salami Better Than Sex?* sgn. VG/VG. K2. $30.00

KING & STRAUB. *Talisman*. 1984. Viking. 1st ed. NF/NF. H11/P3. $40.00

KINGSBURY, Donald. *Moon Goddess & the Son*. 1986. Baen. 1st ed. hc. F/F. P3. $20.00

KINGSBURY. *Records of the Virginia Company of London, Court Book...* 1906. GPO. 635p. VG. A4. $245.00

KINGSLEY, Charles. *Heroes or Greek Fairy Tales*. nd. SB Gundy. decor brd. VG. P3. $45.00

KINGSLEY, Charles. *Saint's Tragedy; or, True Story of Elizabeth of Hungary*. 1848. London. JW Parker. 1st ed. author's 1st book. 271p. Victorian cloth. VG. T10. $200.00

KINGSMILL, Hugh. *Return of William Shakespeare*. 1929. Indianapolis. VG/G. B5. $20.00

KINGSOLVER, Barbara. *Animal Dreams*. 1990. Harper Collins. 1st ed. F/F. H11. $55.00

KINGSOLVER, Barbara. *Pigs in Heaven*. 1993. Harper Collins. 1st ed. F/F. M23. $25.00

KINGSTON, William H.G. *Mark Seaworth: Tale of the Indian Ocean...* 1855. NY. Francis. 3 steel engravings. 401p. VG. T7. $40.00

KINNAIRD, Clark. *This Must Not Happen Again!* 1945. Pilot. VG/VG. P3. $20.00

KINNELL, Galway. *Three Poems*. 1976. NY. 1st ed. 1/100. sgn. wrp. C2. $75.00

KINNEY, Charles; see Gardner, Erle Stanley.

KINNEY, Richard. *Harp of Silence*. 1962. Pantheon. sgn. 8vo. 64p. gilt bl brd. VG. B11. $8.00

KINNEY, Thomas. *Devil Take the Foremost*. 1947. Crime Club. 1st ed. VG. P3. $10.00

KINSCELLA, Hazel G. *Music on the Air*. 1934. Viking. possible 1st ed. 438p. bl cloth. F. B22. $6.00

KINSELLA, W.P. *Iowa Baseball Confederacy*. 1986. Boston. 1st ed. VG/VG. B5. $20.00

KINSLEY, Peter. *Three Cheers for Nothing*. 1964. Dutton. 1st ed. author's 1st novel. NF/VG. M22. $10.00

KINTNER, Elvan. *Letters of Robert Browning & Elizabeth Barrett Browning...* 1969. Cambridge. 2 vol. VG/G. V4. $45.00

KIPLING, Rudyard. *Animal Stories*. 1953. Macmillan. VG. P3. $20.00

KIPLING, Rudyard. *Captain's Courageous*. 1897. NY. 1st Am ed. VG. C6. $95.00

KIPLING, Rudyard. *Choice of Kipling's Verse Made by TS Eliot...* 1943. Scribner. 1st Am ed. F/VG. B4. $65.00

KIPLING, Rudyard. *Debits & Credits*. 1926. Macmillan. 1st ed. 8vo. gilt red cloth. NF/dj. T10. $100.00

KIPLING, Rudyard. *Diversity of Creatures*. 1917. London. Macmillan. 1st ed. teg. F/VG. T10. $150.00

KIPLING, Rudyard. *Five Nations*. 1903. London. 1st ed. VG. M19. $50.00

KIPLING, Rudyard. *Independence*. 1923. London. Macmillan. 1st ed. 8vo. 32p. F/stiff gray prt wrp. T10. $100.00

KIPLING, Rudyard. *Jungle Book*. 1894. Century. 1st Am ed. 303p. VG+. P2. $100.00

KIPLING, Rudyard. *Jungle Book*. 1928. Doubleday Doran. hc. decor brd. G. P3. $20.00

KIPLING, Rudyard. *Jungle Books, Vol I & II*. 1948. Doubleday. 2 vol. ils Aldren Watson. VG/G. M21. $30.00

KIPLING, Rudyard. *Kipling's Fantasy Stories*. 1992. Tor. 1st ed. F/F. P3. $18.00

KIPLING, Rudyard. *Kipling's SF*. 1992. Tor. 1st ed. hc. F/F. P3. $18.00

KIPLING, Rudyard. *Light That Failed*. 1891. London. 1st ed. VG. C6. $95.00

KIPLING, Rudyard. *Light That Failed*. 1924. Doubleday Page. G. P3. $15.00

KIPLING, Rudyard. *Puck of Pook's Hill*. 1906. Doubleday. 1st ed. ils Rackham. VG+. M5. $28.00

KIPLING, Rudyard. *Second Jungle Book*. 1906. Macmillan. 9th. VG. P3. $25.00

KIPLING, Rudyard. *Selected Prose & Poetry of...* 1937. NY. 1030p. gilt cloth. NF. A17. $15.00

KIPLING, Rudyard. *Tour of Inspection*. 1928. Anthoensen. 1st book ed. 1/93. sm 8vo. 51p. NF. B24. $185.00

KIRCK. *Neale Books: An Annotated Bibliography*. 1977. np. ils. 254p. F. A4. $85.00

KIRK, George E. *Short History of the Middle East...* 1955. London. Methuen/Praeger. 3rd. 8vo. 14 maps. 292p. G. W1. $12.00

KIRK, Michael. *Cut in Diamonds*. 1986. Doubleday Crime Club. 1st ed. NF/NF. P3. $13.00

KIRK, Michael. *Mayday From Jalaga*. 1983. Crime Club. 1st ed. VG/VG. P3. $15.00

KIRK, Russell. *Creature of the Twilight*. 1966. Fleet. 1st ed. VG/VG. P3. $35.00

KIRK, Russell. *Lord of the Hollow Dark.* 1979. St Martin. 1st ed. NF/NF. P3. $25.00

KIRK, Russell. *Princess of All Lands.* 1979. Arkham. 1st ed. 1/4220. F/F. T2. $45.00

KIRK, Russell. *Watchers at the Strait Gate: Mystical Tales.* 1984. Arkham. 1st ed. 1/3459. F/F. T2. $15.00

KIRKBRIDE, Thomas S. *On the Construction, Organization & General Arrangements...* 1880. Phil. 2nd. 320p. red cloth. VG. B14. $100.00

KIRKBRIDGE, Ronald. *Winds, Blow Gently.* 1945. Frederick Fell. 1st ed. VG/VG. P3. $20.00

KIRKLAND, Charles P. *Liability of Government of Great Britain...* 1863. NY. Randolph. 1st ed thus. VG. M8. $45.00

KIRN, Walter. *My Hard Bargain.* 1990. Knopf. 1st ed. F/F. B35. $30.00

KIRSCHNER, Edwin J. *Zeppelin in the Atomic Age.* 1957. Urbana. 1st ed. ils. 80p. VG/dj. B18. $47.50

KIRST, Hans Hellmut. *Heroes for Sale.* 1982. Collins. 1st ed. F/F. P3. $20.00

KIRST, Hans Hellmut. *Night of the Generals.* 1963. Collins. 1st ed. VG/VG. P3. $20.00

KIRST, Hans Hellmut. *Time for Truth.* 1974. Coward McCann. 1st ed. F/NF. H11. $25.00

KIRST, Hans Hellmut. *Wolves.* 1968. Coward McCann. 1st ed. VG/VG. P3. $25.00

KIRSTEIN, Lincoln. *Portrait of Mr B: Photographs of George Balanchine.* 1984. Ballet Soc. 1st ed. 154p. cloth. dj. M20. $32.00

KISER, Ellis. *Atlas of the City of Yonkers, Westchester County, New York.* 1907. Phil. Mueller. lg folio. 25 double-p maps. O7. $165.00

KISHON, Ephraim. *Look Back, Mrs Lot!* 1961. Atheneum. 1st Am ed. F/clip. B4. $50.00

KISTER. *Best Encyclopedias: A Guide to General & Specialized...* 1986. np. 356p. xl. VG. A4. $25.00

KITTO, John. *Palestine From the Patriarchal Age to the Present Time.* 1900. NY. Collier. 8vo. ils. 426p. teg. VG. W1. $12.00

KITTREDGE, Mary. *Cadaver.* 1992. St Martin. 1st ed. 3rd in Edwina Crusoe series. F/NF. M22. $15.00

KITZINGER, Ernest. *Portraits of Christ.* 1940. King Penguin. hc. VG. P3. $25.00

KIVELSON, Margaret. *Solar System.* 1986. Englewood Cliffs. 1st prt. 4to. 436p. K5. $20.00

KJELGAARD, Jim. *Coming of the Mormons.* 1963. NY. Random. Landmark ed. 8vo. 183p. NF/dj. T10. $25.00

KLAVAN, Andrew. *Darling Clementine.* 1988. Permanent Pr. ltd prt. 1/2000. author's 2nd novel. AN/dj. M22. $50.00

KLAVAN, Andrew. *Don't Say a Word.* 1991. Pocket. 1st ed. F/F. H11. $25.00

KLAVAN, Andrew. *Don't Say a Word.* 1991. Pocket. 1st ed. VG/VG. P3. $20.00

KLAVAN, Andrew. *Face of the Earth.* 1980. Viking. 1st ed. F/F. H11. $40.00

KLAVAN, Andrew. *Face of the Earth.* 1980. Viking. 1st ed. VG/VG. P3. $20.00

KLAVAN, Andrew. *Scarred Man.* 1990. Doubleday. 1st ed. F/F. M22. $30.00

KLEBER, L.O. *Suffrage Cookbook.* 1915. Pittsburgh. 1st ed. 243p. G. B5. $55.00

KLEIN, Dave. *Great Infielders of the Major League.* 1972. Random. VG. P3. $8.00

KLEIN, Emil. *Enjoy Your Bridge.* 1947. London. 191p. VG. S1. $5.00

KLEIN, Gerard. *Overlords of War.* nd. BC. NF/NF. P3. $5.00

KLEIN, Herman. *Herman Klein & the Gramophone.* 1990. Amadeus. photos/notes/index. 618p. F/dj. A17. $25.00

KLEIN, Joe. *Payback.* 1984. Knopf. 1st ed. inscr. F/F. B4. $350.00

KLEIN, T.E.D. *Ceremonies.* 1984. Viking. 1st ed. VG+/dj. M21. $25.00

KLEIN, T.E.D. *Dark Gods.* 1985. Viking. 1st ed. VG+/dj. M21. $30.00

KLEIN, Zachary. *Still Among the Living.* 1990. Harper Row. 1st ed. F/F. P3. $19.00

KLEIN & PELLET. *That Pellet Woman.* 1965. NY. Stein Day. 1st ed. 8vo. 379p. VG/dj. T10. $45.00

KLEINFIELD, S. *Biggest Company on Earth (AT&T).* 1981. NY. 1st ed. VG/VG. B5. $20.00

KLEINPELL, R.M. *Miocene Stratigraphy of California.* 1938. Am Assn Petroleum Geol. 1st ed. 450p. VG. D8. $25.00

KLETT & MUYBRIDGE. *One City: Two Visions, San Francsico Panoramas 1878-1990.* 1990. np. 11p text. 2 10-ft accordian-fld photos. VG. A4. $125.00

KLINCK, Carl. *Robert Service: A Biography.* 1976. NY. 1st ed. VG/VG. B5. $22.50

KLINE, Fred. *I, Dodo.* 1968. San Francisco. 1st ed. 16mo. 1/200. wrp. A17. $7.50

KLINE, Otis Adelbert. *Maza of the Moon.* 1930. McClurg. 1st ed. VG/dj. M21. $60.00

KLINE, Otis Adelbert. *Outlaws of Mars.* 1961. Avalon. 1st ed. VG/VG. P3. $30.00

KLINE, Otis Adelbert. *Planet of Peril.* nd. Grosset Dunlap. VG. P3. $30.00

KLINE, Otis Adelbert. *Port of Peril.* 1949. Grandon. VG/VG. P3. $35.00

KLINE, Otis Adelbert. *Swordsman of Mars.* 1960. Avalon. 1st ed. VG/VG. P3. $30.00

KLINEFELTER, Walter. *Third Display of Old Maps & Plans...* 1973. LaCrosse. Sumac. 1/300. ils. F/dj. O7. $55.00

KLINGER, Ron. *Improve Your Bridge Memory.* 1964. London. 93p. VG/wrp. S1. $5.00

KLINGER, Ron. *Playing to Win at Bridge: Practical Problems...* 1976. London. 125p. VG/wrp. S1. $6.00

KLINGER, Ron. *World Championship Pairs Play.* 1983. London. 167p. F/dj. S1. $12.00

KLINGER, Ron. *100 Winning Bridge Tips.* 1987. London. 128p. VG/wrp. S1. $6.00

KLOMAN & TULLY. *It's a Great Relief.* 1934. Vanguard. ARC/1st ed. rebound half leather. w/promo material. B4. $85.00

KLUCKHOHN, Clyde. *to the Foot of the Rainbow.* 1927. Century. 1st ed. 8vo. ils. 276p. stp gr cloth. F/dj. T10. $85.00

KLUDAS, Arnold. *Great Passenger Ships of the World Vol 3, 1924-1935.* 1986. Wellingborough. Patrick Stephens. VG/dj. A16. $25.00

KLUDAS, Arnold. *Great Passenger Ships of the World.* 1986. Wellingborough. Patrick Stephens. 6 vol. VG/VG. A16. $240.00

KLUGE, Alexander. *Battle.* 1967. NY. 1st ed. trans from German. F/dj. A17. $8.50

KLUGE, P.F. *Eddie & the Cruisers.* 1980. Viking. 1st ed. author's 2nd book. rem mk. NF/F. H11. $25.00

KLUGER, Richard. *Sheriff of Nottingham.* 1992. Viking. 1st ed. VG/VG. P3. $23.00

KNAPP, Arthur Jr. *Race Your Boat Right.* 1952. Van Nostrand. 1st ed. sgn. 8vo. 296p. B11. $35.00

KNEALE, Nigel. *Year of the Sex Olympics.* 1976. Ferret Fantasy. 1st ed. F/F. P3. $20.00

KNEBEL, Fletcher. *Bottom Line.* 1974. Doubleday. 1st ed. G/dj. N4. $17.50

KNEBEL, Fletcher. *Night of Camp David.* 1965. Harper Row. 1st ed. F/NF. H11. $35.00

KNEBEL, Fletcher. *Trespass.* 1969. Doubleday. 1st ed. VG/VG. P3. $20.00

KNEBEL, Fletcher. *Vanished.* 1968. Doubleday. 1st ed. F/NF. H11. $40.00

KNEEBONE, John T. *Southern Liberal Journalists & Issue of Race 1920-1944.* 1985. UNC. pub pres. 312p. F/F. B10. $25.00

KNEIPP, Marianne. *Reflections & Observations, Essays of Denton A Cooley, MD.* 1984. Austin, TX. 1st ed. 240p. dj. A13. $25.00

KNERR, M.E.; see Smith, George O.

KNIGHT, Austin M. *Modern Seamanship.* 1917. NY. 8vo. ils. 712p. cloth. G-. T3. $14.00

KNIGHT, Austin M. *Modern Seamanship.* 1943. Van Nostrand. 10th. 847p. VG. P12. $10.00

KNIGHT, C. Morley. *Hints on Driving.* 1895. London. Bell. 2nd. 212p. cloth. VG. A10. $20.00

KNIGHT, Charles. *William Caxton, the First English Printer.* 1844. London. Knight. 1st ed. 12mo. 240p. contemporary half leather. T10. $150.00

KNIGHT, Clayton. *Lifeline in the Sky.* 1957. NY. 1st ed. inscr. 268p. cloth. VG/dj. B18. $125.00

KNIGHT, Clifford. *Affair of the Corpse Escort.* 1946. David McKay. 1st ed. VG/fair. P3. $20.00

KNIGHT, Clifford. *Affair of the Scarlet Crab.* 1937. Dodd Mead. 1st ed. VG. P3. $20.00

KNIGHT, Clifford. *Affair of the Sixth Button.* 1947. McKay. 1st ed. VG/G. P3. $18.00

KNIGHT, Clifford. *Death & Little Brother.* 1952. Dutton. 1st ed. VG. P3. $15.00

KNIGHT, Damon. *Best From Orbit.* 1975. Berkley Putnam. 1st ed. VG/VG. P3. $18.00

KNIGHT, Damon. *Best of Damon Knight.* 1978. Taplinger. VG/VG. P3. $20.00

KNIGHT, Damon. *Beyond Tomorrow.* 1965. Harper Row. 1st ed. VG/VG. P3. $20.00

KNIGHT, Damon. *Dark Side.* nd. BC. VG/VG. P3. $8.00

KNIGHT, Damon. *Dimension X.* 1970. Simon Schuster. 1st ed. VG/G. P3. $20.00

KNIGHT, Damon. *Nebula Award Stories.* nd. BC. VG/VG. P3. $8.00

KNIGHT, Damon. *One Side Laughing.* 1991. St Martin. 1st ed. F/F. P3. $17.00

KNIGHT, Damon. *Orbit 7.* 1970. Putnam. 1st ed. xl. dj. P3. $8.00

KNIGHT, Damon. *SF Argosy.* 1972. Simon Schuster. 1st ed. VG/VG. P3. $25.00

KNIGHT, Damon. *Tomorrow & Tomorrow.* nd. Simon Schuster. 2nd ed. VG. P3. $10.00

KNIGHT, Damon. *Tomorrow & Tomorrow.* 1974. Gollancz. 1st ed. F/F. M19. $17.50

KNIGHT, Damon. *World & Thorinn.* 1980. Berkley Putnam. 1st ed. xl. dj. P3. $5.00

KNIGHT, David; see Prather, Richard S.

KNIGHT, Edgar W. *Henry Harrisse on Collegiate Education.* 1947. Chapel Hill. VG/wrp. O7. $45.00

KNIGHT, Eric. *Flying Yorkshireman.* 1938. Harper. 1st ed. VG/dj. M21/P3. $15.00

KNIGHT, Eric. *Sam Small Flies Again.* 1942. Harper. 1st ed. VG. P3. $15.00

KNIGHT, Kathleen Moore. *Death Blew Out the Match.* 1935. Crime Club. 1st ed. G. P3. $20.00

KNIGHT, Kathleen Moore. *High Rendezvous.* 1954. Crime Club. 1st ed. ffe removed. VG/VG. P3. $18.00

KNIGHT, Kathleen Moore. *Intrigue for Empire.* 1944. Crime Club. 1st ed. VG. P3. $15.00

KNIGHT, Kathleen Moore. *Port of Seven Strangers.* 1945. Detective BC. VG. P3. $10.00

KNIGHT, Kathleen Moore. *Stream Sinister.* 1945. Detective BC. VG. P3. $10.00

KNIGHT, Kathryn Lasky. *Dark Swan.* 1994. NY. 1st ed. F/F. H11. $20.00

KNIGHT, Kathryn Lasky. *Mumbo Jumbo.* 1991. Summit. 1st ed. F/F. H11. $25.00

KNIGHT, Marjorie. *Alexander's Birthday.* 1940. Dutton. 1st ed. ils Howard Simon. 120p. VG/G. T5. $30.00

KNIPPEL, Dolores. *Poems for the Very Young Child.* 1932. Racine. ils Ellsworth. 125p. VG. A17. $7.50

KNOBLOCH, Irving W. *Preliminary Verified List of Plant Collectors in Mexico.* 1983. Plainfield, NJ. 179p. VG/orange wrp. w/sgn letter. B26. $30.00

KNOCK, Florence. *Passiflorals for Your Garden.* 1965. Kansas City. photos/line drawings. 100p. xl. B26. $20.00

KNOTTS, Raymond. *And the Deep Blue Sea.* 1944. Farrar Rinehart. 1st ed. VG/VG. P3. $30.00

KNOWLAND, Helen. *Madame Baltimore.* 1949. Dodd Mead. 1st ed. VG. P3. $10.00

KNOWLES, John. *Doing Better & Feeling Worse: Health in the United States.* 1977. NY. 1st ed. 287p. VG. A13. $30.00

KNOX, Bill. *Draw Batons!* 1973. Doubleday Crime Club. 1st ed. NF/NF. P3. $15.00

KNOX, Calvin; see Silverberg, Robert.

KNOX, George William. *Development of Religion in Japan.* 1907. NY. 204p. red cloth. NF. B14. $75.00

KNOX & SWEET. *On a Mexican Mustang, Through TX, From Gulf to Rio Grande.* 1883. Hartford, CT. ils. 672p. professional rpr. E1. $200.00

KNUDSON, Albert C. *Doctrine of God.* 1930. NY. Abingdon Cokesbury. 1st ed. sgn. 8vo. 434p. VG/G. B11. $40.00

KNYSTAUTAS, A. *Natural History of the USSR.* 1987. McGraw Hill. 4to. 224p. F/F. B1. $38.50

KOBOTIE, Fred. *Hopi Indian Artist.* 1977. Flagstaff. Mus of N AZ. 1st ed. ils. 2-tone cloth. F/dj. T10. $75.00

KOCH, H.W. *Hitler Youth: Origins & Development 1922-1945.* 1975. NY. 348p. VG/dj. A17. $20.00

KOCH, Rudolf. *Die Bergpredigt Jesu Christi in der Lutherschen Übersetzung.* ca 1915. Leipzig. Xenien. 4to. mottled vellum. F. B24. $285.00

KOCH, Vivienne. *William Carlos Williams.* 1950. New Directions. 1st ed. assn copy. NF/VG. V1. $35.00

KOCHER, Theodore. *Text-Book of Operative Surgery.* 1895. London. Blk. VG. H7. $125.00

KOEBEL, W.H. *In the Maoriland Bush.* ca 1911. London. 8vo. 316p. VG. N3. $25.00

KOEMAN, C. *Handleiding Voor die Studie van de Topografische Kaarten...* 1963. Groningen. Wolters. Dutch/Eng text. 34 maps/fld index. F. O7. $75.00

KOEMAN, I.C. *Joan Blaeu & His Grand Atlas.* 1970. Amsterdam. 28 maps. M/stiff wrp. O7. $30.00

KOERS, Albert W. *International Regulation of Marine Fisheries...* 1973. West Byfleet. Fishing News Ltd. M11. $50.00

KOFFKA, Kurt. *Die Grundlagen der Psychischen Entwicklung...* 1921. Osterwieck am Harz. AW Zickfeldt. 278p. cloth. G1. $100.00

KOFFKA, Kurt. *Principles of Gestalt Psychology.* 1935. Harcourt Brace. 720p. bl-gr cloth. ES. G1. $50.00

KOFOED, Jack. *Moon Over Miami.* 1955. Random. 1st ed. sgn pres. 8vo. 272p. VG/VG. B11. $65.00

KOGAN & WENDT. *Bet a Million.* 1948. Indianapolis. 1st ed. VG/VG. B5. $22.50

KOGER, Lisa. *Farlanburg Stories.* 1990. Norton. 1st ed. F/F. M23. $20.00

KOGOS, Fred. *Dictionary of Yiddish Slang & Idioms.* 1967. NY. Citadel. 1st ed. F/F. H11. $25.00

KOHLER, Wolfgang. *Dynamics in Psychology.* 1940. Liveright. sm 8vo. 158p. panelled bl cloth. G. G1. $35.00

KOHLER, Wolfgang. *Gestalt Psychology: Intro to New Concepts...* 1929. Liveright. 404p. bl cloth. VG. G1. $50.00

KOIE & RECHINGER. *Symbolae Afganicae V.* 1963. Copenhagen. ils. 267p. wrp. B26. $30.00

KOJA, Kathe. *Skin.* 1993. Delacorte. 1st ed. F/F. G10. $20.00

KOLAGA, Walter A. *All About Rock Gardens & Plants.* 1966. NY. ils. 385p. VG/dj. B26. $15.00

KOLB, E.L. *Through the Grand Canyon From WY to Mexico.* 1958. Macmillan. new ed. sgn. 8vo. 344p. VG. B11. $45.00

KOLLER, Larry. *Salt-Water Fishing.* 1954. Bobbs Merrill. photos. VG/G. P12. $12.00

KOLUPAEV, Victor. *Hermit's Swing.* 1980. Macmillan. 1st ed. VG/VG. P3. $15.00

KOMIE, Lowell B. *Judge's Chambers & Other Stories.* 1987. Chicago. Academy Chicago Pub. M11. $45.00

KONEFSKY, Samuel J. *Constitutional World of Mr Justice Frankfurter.* 1949. Macmillan. M11. $45.00

KOOCK, Mary Faulk. *Cuisine of the Americas.* 1967. Austin. sgn. 8vo. VG/VG. B11. $10.00

KOONTZ, Dean R. *Bad Place.* 1990. Putnam. 1st ed. NF/NF. N4. $22.50

KOONTZ, Dean R. *Blood Risk.* 1973. Bobbs Merrill. 1st ed. F/G+. M19. $175.00

KOONTZ, Dean R. *Blood Risk.* 1973. Bobbs Merrill. 1st ed. rem mk. NF/NF. B4. $200.00

KOONTZ, Dean R. *Chase.* 1972. Random. 1st ed. as by KR Dwyer. F/F. H11. $240.00

KOONTZ, Dean R. *Cold Fire.* 1991. Putnam. 1st ed. F/F. P3. $23.00

KOONTZ, Dean R. *Dark Rivers of the Heart.* 1994. Knopf. ARC of 1st trade ed. F/pict wrp. G10. $60.00

KOONTZ, Dean R. *Door to December.* 1988. London. 1st hc ed. F/F. T2. $50.00

KOONTZ, Dean R. *Dragon Tears.* 1993. London. Headline. 1st ed. F/F. T2. $50.00

KOONTZ, Dean R. *Dragon Tears.* 1993. Putnam. 1st ed. VG/VG. P3. $23.00

KOONTZ, Dean R. *Dragonfly.* 1975. Random. 1st ed. as by KR Dwyer. F/NF. H11. $165.00

KOONTZ, Dean R. *Dragonfly.* 1975. Random. 1st ed. NF/NF. H11. $135.00

KOONTZ, Dean R. *Eyes of Darkness.* 1989. Dark Harvest. 1st hc ed. F/F. T2. $35.00

KOONTZ, Dean R. *Face of Fear.* 1977. Bobbs Merrill. 2nd. xl. dj. P3. $30.00

KOONTZ, Dean R. *Face of Fear.* 1989. London. Headline. 1st hc ed. F/F. T2. $45.00

KOONTZ, Dean R. *Funhouse.* nd. Doubleday. BC. VG/dj. M21. $15.00

KOONTZ, Dean R. *House of Thunder.* 1988. Dark Harvest. 1st ed. F/NF. M19. $75.00

KOONTZ, Dean R. *How to Write Best-Selling Fiction.* 1981. 1st ed. NF/NF. S13. $50.00

KOONTZ, Dean R. *Key to Midnight.* 1989. Dark Harvest. 1st ed. F/F. T2. $35.00

KOONTZ, Dean R. *Mask.* 1989. London. Headline. 1st hc ed. F/F. T2. $65.00

KOONTZ, Dean R. *Midnight.* 1989. London. Headline. 1st ed. F/F. T2. $45.00

KOONTZ, Dean R. *Midnight.* 1989. Putnam. 1st ed. F/F. H11. $40.00

KOONTZ, Dean R. *Midnight.* 1989. Putnam. 1st ed. VG/VG. P3. $25.00

KOONTZ, Dean R. *Mr Murder.* 1993. London. Headline. 1st ed (precedes Am). F/F. T2. $70.00

KOONTZ, Dean R. *Mr Murder.* 1993. Putnam. 1st ed. VG/VG. P3. $24.00

KOONTZ, Dean R. *Night Chills.* 1976. Atheneum. 1st ed. F/F. P3. $300.00

KOONTZ, Dean R. *Oddkins.* 1988. Warner. 1st ed. F/F. P3. $50.00

KOONTZ, Dean R. *Oddkins: A Fable for All Ages.* 1988. London. Headline. 1st ed. F/pict wrp. T2. $20.00

KOONTZ, Dean R. *Servants of Twilight.* nd. Quality BC. VG/VG. P3. $15.00

KOONTZ, Dean R. *Shadowfires.* nd. BC. F/F. P3. $10.00

KOONTZ, Dean R. *Shadowfires.* 1990. Dark Harvest. F/F. P3. $45.00

KOONTZ, Dean R. *Shattered.* 1973. Random. 1st ed. xl. dj. VG. P3. $30.00

KOONTZ, Dean R. *Strange Highways.* 1995. Warner. ARC of 1st Am trade ed. F/pict wrp. G10. $60.00

KOONTZ, Dean R. *Surrounded.* 1974. Bobbs Merrill. 1st ed. G/G. P3. $200.00

KOONTZ, Dean R. *Trapped.* 1993. Eclipse. 1st ed. ils Anthony Bilau. F/NF. G10. $10.00

KOONTZ, Dean R. *Voice of the Night.* 1980. Doubleday. 1st ed. xl. dj. P3. $35.00

KOONTZ, Dean R. *Wall of Masks.* 1975. Bobbs Merrill. 1st ed. as by Brian Coffey. F/NF. H11. $240.00

KOONTZ, Dean R. *Watchers.* 1987. Putnam. 1st ed. F/F. T2. $50.00

KOONTZ, Dean R. *Winter Moon.* 1994. Headline. 1st ed. F/F. P3. $40.00

KOOP & ROSA. *Rowdy Joe Lowe: Gambler With a Gun.* 1989. Norman, OK. 1st ed. 188p. F/F. E1. $30.00

KOPAL, Zdenek. *Astronomical Centers of the World.* 1988. Cambridge. 1st prt. VG/VG. K5. $30.00

KOPAL, Zdenek. *Man & His Universe.* 1972. NY. Morrow. 31 pl. 313p. VG/VG. K5. $17.00

KORMAN, Justine. *Who Framed Roger Rabbit Storybook.* 1988. Golden. 2nd. MTI. VG. P3. $8.00

KORN, Bertram. *Early Jews of New Orleans.* 1969. 1st ed. ltd. sgn. VG/VG. S13. $45.00

KORNBLUTH, C.M. *Best of...* 1977. Taplinger. 1st ed. hc. F/F. P3. $15.00

KORNBLUTH, C.M. *Mile Beyond the Moon.* nd. BC. VG/VG. P3. $10.00

KORNBLUTH, C.M. *Mindworm.* 1955. Michael Joseph. 1st ed. VG/VG. P3. $75.00

KORNBLUTH, C.M. *Not This August.* nd. BC. VG/VG. P3. $10.00

KORNBLUTH, C.M. *Syndic.* 1953. BC. VG/VG. P3. $10.00

KORNBLUTH, C.M. *Syndic.* 1953. Doubleday. 1st ed. NF/NF. P3. $75.00

KORNBLUTH, C.M. *Takeoff.* 1952. Doubleday. 1st ed. VG/G. P3. $60.00

KORNBLUTH & POHL. *Space Merchants.* 1953. Ballantine. 1st ed. NF/VG+. G10. $150.00

KOROWICZ, Marek Stanislaw. *Some Present Aspects of Sovereigny in International Law.* 1961. Leyden. AW Sythoff. 120p. wrp. M11. $25.00

KORSTEN, Frans. *Catalogue of the Library of Thomas Baker.* 1990. Cambridge. M11. $85.00

KOSINSKI, Jerzy. *Being There.* 1970. HBJ. 1st ed. F/F. H11. $60.00

KOSINSKI, Jerzy. *Passion Play.* 1979. St Martin. VG/VG. P3. $30.00

KOSINSKI, Jerzy. *Passion Play.* 1979. St Martin. 1st ed. inscr. NF/NF. M19. $100.00

KOSINSKI, Jerzy. *Steps.* 1968. Random. 1st ed. F/F. M19. $85.00

KOSTER, Henry. *Travels in Brazil.* 1968. Carbondale. rpt of 1816 ed. 182p. dj. F3. $15.00

KOSTER, R.M. *Mandragon.* 1979. Morrow. 1st ed. VG/VG. P3. $18.00

KOTKER, Norman. *Earthly Jerusalem.* 1969. Scribner. 1st ed. 8vo. 307p. map ep. VG/dj. W1. $12.00

KOTZWINKLE, William. *Christmas at Fontaine's.* 1982. Putnam. 1st ed. ils Joe Servello. F/F. T2. $15.00

KOTZWINKLE, William. *Fata Morgana.* nd. BOMC. hc. VG/VG. P3. $10.00

KOTZWINKLE, William. *Game of Thirty.* 1994. Houghton Mifflin/Seymour Lawrence. 1st ed. F/NF. G10. $12.00

KOTZWINKLE, William. *Hot Jazz Trio.* 1989. Houghton Mifflin/Seymour Lawrence. 1st ed. F/F. T2. $25.00

KOTZWINKLE, William. *Jack in the Box.* 1980. Putnam. 1st ed. VG/VG. P3. $18.00

KOTZWINKLE, William. *Midnight Examiner.* 1989. Houghton Mifflin. 1st ed. F/F. P3. $18.00

KOVAR, Edith. *Fairy Gold & Other Stories.* 1931. Whitman. lg 4to. ils. VG. M5. $60.00

KOZAKIEWICZOWIE, Helena. *Renaissance in Poland.* 1976. Warsaw. Arkady. ils/pl/map. 330p. cloth. dj. D2. $80.00

KRABBE, Tim. *Vanishing.* 1993. Random. 1st Am ed. AN/dj. M22. $25.00

KRAFT, James L. *Like Unto: A Philosophical Review of Vacation Journey...* 1939. private prt. 12mo. 56p. VG. P4. $15.00

KRAMER, Jane. *Off Washington Square: Reporter Looks at Greenwich Village.* 1963. DSP. ARC. author's 1st book. F/NF. B4. $85.00

KRAMISH, Arnold. *Griffin: Greatest Untold Espinage Story of WWII.* 1986. Boston. 1st ed. 294p. F/dj. A17. $9.50

KRANTZ, John. *Portrait of Medical History & Current Medical Problems.* 1962. Baltimore. 1st ed. 156p. VG. A13. $20.00

KRANTZ, Judith. *Scruples.* 1978. Crown. 1st ed. F/NF. B4. $85.00

KRANZ, Jacqueline. *American Nautical Art & Antiques.* 1975. Crown. rem mk. G. A16. $40.00

KRASILOVSKY, Phyllis. *Cow Who Fell in the Canal.* 1957. Doubleday. 1st ed. ils Peter Spier. pict brd. G+. T5. $30.00

KRASNER, William. *Stag Party.* 1957. Harper. 1st ed. VG/VG. P3. $20.00

KRAUS, Rene. *Europe in Revolt.* 1942. NY. 1st prt. 563p. dj. A17. $10.00

KRAUS & KRAUS. *Gothic Choirstalls of Spain.* 1986. London. Kegan Paul. 1st ed. photos. 218p. F/F. T10. $35.00

KRAUS. *History of Way & Williams...1895-1898.* 1984. KNA Pr. 1/500. F. A4. $125.00

KRAUSE, Herbert. *Oxcart Trail.* 1954. Bobbs Merrill. 1st ltd Minnesota ed. inscr/sgn twice. F/F. A18. $35.00

KRAUSE, Herbert. *Wind Without Rain.* 1939. Bobbs Merrill. 1st ed. inscr. NF/NF. A18. $35.00

KRAUSE & LEMKE. *United States Paper Money.* 1981. Iola, WI. 4to. 204p. VG. T3. $8.00

KRAUSKOPF, K.B. *Introduction to Geochemistry.* 1967. McGraw Hill. 721p. cloth. VG. D8. $30.00

KRAUSS, Bob. *Exceptional View of Life: Easter Seal Story.* 1977. Honolulu. 1st ed. ils. 64p. dj. A17. $10.00

KRAUSS, Ruth. *Bundle Book.* 1951. Harper. early ed. ils Helen Stone. unp. G+. T5. $30.00

KRAUSS, Ruth. *Bundle Book.* 1951. NY. Harper. 1st ed. ils Helen Stone. unp. VG/torn. D1. $60.00

KRAUSS, Ruth. *Hole Is to Dig.* 1952. Harper. 1st ed. ils Maurice Sendak. 48p. VG/worn. D1. $200.00

KRAUSS, Ruth. *How to Make an Earthquake.* nd. NY. Harper. 8vo. 28p. G+. C14. $5.00

KRAUSS, Ruth. *Open House for Butterflies.* 1960. Harper. 1st ed. ils Maurice Sendak. unp. VG/torn. D1. $200.00

KREIDOLF, Ernst. *Lenzgekind.* 1926. Zurich. ils Ernst Kriedolf. unp. VG. D1. $120.00

KREISLER, Fritz. *Four Weeks in the Trenches: War Story of a Violinist.* 1915. Boston. Houghton Mifflin. 1st ed. inscr/dtd July 1915. silvered cloth. F. B14. $250.00

KREITH, Frank. *Radiation Heat Transfer.* 1962. Scranton. Internat TB Co. 236p. VG+. P4. $25.00

KREMENTZ, Jill. *Very Young Gardener.* 1991. Dial. 1st ed. sm 4to. F/F. C8. $35.00

KRENKEL, Roy G. *Cities & Scenes From the Ancient World.* 1974. Owlswick. 1st ed. F/F. T2. $35.00

KRENSKY, Stephen. *Witching Hour.* 1981. Atheneum. 1st ed. 8vo. 155p. F/NF. C14. $15.00

KRESS, Nancy. *Beggars and Choosers.* 1994. Tor. 1st ed. F/F. P3. $23.00

KRESS, Nancy. *Beggars in Spain.* 1993. Easton. 1st ed. sgn. leather. F. M23. $100.00

KRESS, Nancy. *Beggars in Spain.* 1993. Morrow. 1st trade ed. F/NF. G10. $15.00

KRESS, Nancy. *Brain Rose.* nd. Quality BC. hc. VG/VG. P3. $10.00

KRESS, Nancy. *Golden Grove.* 1984. Bluejay. 1st ed. hc. NF/NF. P3. $20.00

KRESS, Nancy. *White Pipes.* 1985. Bluejay. 1st ed. F/F. T2. $25.00

KRETSCHMER, Konrad. *Die Italienis Chen Portolane des Mittelalters...* 1962 (1909). Hildescheim. G Olms. ils. F. O7. $75.00

KREUTZER, W. *Notes & Observations Made During 4 Years' Service...* 1872. Phil. 1st ed. ils/map. 368p. G+. B5. $135.00

KREYMBORG, Al. *Plays for Merry Andrews.* 1920. NY. 1st ed. 1/50. VG. A15. $40.00

KRIEGER, L.C.C. *Mushroom Handbook.* 1967. Dover. 12mo. 32 mc pl/126 ils. 560p. VG/wrp. B1. $20.00

KROCH, Adolph. *Great Bookstore in Action.* 1940. Chicago. inscr. cloth. VG. A4. $35.00

KROEBER, Theodora. *Inland Whale.* 1959. Bloomington. IU. 1st ed. 8vo. ils. 205p. F/VG clip. T10. $45.00

KROEBER, Theodora. *Ishi in Two Worlds: Biography of the Last Wild Indian...* 1969. Berkeley. 9th. 8vo. 258p. F/NF. T10. $25.00

KROLL, Harry Harrison. *Darker Grows the Valley.* 1947. Bobbs Merrill. 1st ed. VG/G. P3. $10.00

KROLL, Harry Harrison. *Their Ancient Grudge.* 1946. Bobbs Merrill. 1st ed. 8vo. gilt bl cloth. VG/VG. T10. $25.00

KROLL, Steven. *Hand-Me-Down Doll.* 1983. Holiday House. possible 1st ed. 8vo. unp. VG+. T5. $20.00

KROMBEIN, K.V. *Catalog of the Hymenoptera in America North of Mexico.* 1979. Smithsonian. 3 vol. 4to. VG. B1. $200.00

KRONHAUSEN. *Erotic Book of Plates.* 1970. 185 pl. 213p. F/NF. A4. $125.00

KRONHEIM. *Aunt Friendly's Nursery Book.* nd. Warne. 12mo. gilt brn cloth. VG. M5. $125.00

KRONKE, Horst. *Die Welt der Schiffahrt en Miniature.* 1992. Herford. Koehlers Verlagsgesellschaft. AN. A16. $34.00

KRUCKEBERG, Arthur R. *Gardening With Native Plants of the Pacific Northwest.* 1982. Seattle. ils. VG/dj. B26. $50.00

KRUGER, Mary. *Death on the Cliff Walk.* 1994. Kensington. 1st ed. author's 1st book. F/F. H11. $30.00

KRUGER, Paul. *Finish Line.* 1968. Simon Schuster. 1st ed. VG/VG. P3. $20.00

KRUGER, Paul. *If the Shroud Fits.* 1969. Simon Schuster. 1st ed. VG/VG. P3. $20.00

KRUM, Charlotte. *Jingling ABC's.* 1929. Row Peterson. 1st ed. 8vo. ils. rpr p. VG. M5. $60.00

KRUMBEIN & SLOSS. *Stratigraphy & Sedimentation.* 1951. San Francisco. WH Freeman. 1st ed. 497p. G. D8. $14.00

KRUMGOLD, Joseph. *...And Now Miguel.* (1953). TY Crowell. 2nd. 245p. NF. C14. $12.00

KRUMMEL & SADIE. *Music Printing & Publishing.* 1990. np. ils. 629p. F/F. A4. $35.00

KRYNINE, D.P. *Soil Mechanics.* 1941. McGraw Hill. 1st ed/4th imp. 451p. G. D8. $15.00

KRYZHANOVSHII, O.L. *Lepidopterous Fauna of the USSR & Adjacent Countries.* 1988. Smithsonian. 8vo. trans from Russian. 405p. F/dj. B1. $48.00

KUBASTA. *Circus Life.* 1960. London. Bancroft. 1st ed. folio. popup. NF. T10. $250.00

KUBASTA. *Der Fliegende Koffer.* 1962. Prague. Artia. obl 4to. 8 double-p popups. cloth spine. VG. T10. $175.00

KUBASTA. *Sleeping Beauty.* 1961. London. Bancroft. moveables. G+. P2. $110.00

KUBASTA. *Tip+Top on the Farm.* 1961. London. Bancroft. 6 double-p popups. NF. T10. $200.00

KUBE-MCDOWELL, Michael P. *Alternities.* nd. BC. hc. VG. P3. $8.00

KUBE-MCDOWELL, Michael P. *Quiet Pools.* 1990. Ace. hc. F/F. P3. $18.00

KUCHLER, A.W. *Portenial Natural Vegetation of the Conterminous US.* 1964. NY. 117 photos. VG/case. B26. $58.00

KUHLKEN, Ken. *Loud Adios.* 1991. NY. 1st ed. F/F. H11. $40.00

KUHLMAN, Charles. *Legend Into History: The Custer Mystery.* 1977. Ft Collins. new ed. 249p. NF. E1. $55.00

KUHN, Alfred. *Das Alte Spanien: Landscaft, Geschichte, Kunst.* 1925. Berlin. Neufeld Henius. 267 ils. 336p. VG. W1. $45.00

KUHN, Herbert. *On the Track of Prehistoric Man.* 1955. Random. 1st ed. 211p. dj. F3. $15.00

KUHN, Thomas. *Sources for History of Quantum Physics: An Inventory...* 1967. Phil. 1st ed. 176p. VG. A13. $25.00

KUHNS, William T. *Memories of Old Canton.* 1937. np. 1st ed. 64p. xl. G. B18. $27.50

KUIPER, Gerald P. *Earth as a Planet.* 1964 (1954). Chicago. 4th. 4to. 751p. VG/dj. K5. $40.00

KUKLICK, Bruce. to *Everything a Season.* 1991. Princeton. later prt. F/F. P8. $20.00

KULPE, Oswald. *Introduction to Philosophy: Handbook for Students...* 1897. London. Sonnenschein. 1st Eng-language ed. 12mo. brn cloth. VG. G1. $50.00

KUMMEL & TEICHERT. *Stratigraphic Boundary Problems: Permian & Traissic...* 1970. Lawrence, KS. 474p. cloth. AN/dj. D8. $30.00

KUMMER, Frederic Arnold. *Courage Over the Andes.* (1940). Winston/Jr Literary Guild. 8vo. 251p. NF. C14. $6.00

KUMMER, Frederic Arnold. *First Days of Knowledge.* 1923. Doran. 1st ed. VG. P3. $20.00

KUMMER, Frederic Arnold. *Song of Sixpence.* 1913. Watt. 1st ed. VG. P3. $15.00

KUNDERA, Milan. *Immortality.* 1991. Grove Weidenfeld. 1st ed. F/F. A20. $10.00

KUNDERA, Milan. *Joke.* 1969. NY. 1st Am ed. author's 1st book. F/NF. C2. $100.00

KUNETKA & STRIEBER. *War Day.* 1984. HRW. 1st ed. NF/NF. N4. $30.00

KUNG, Dinah. *Left in the Care of.* 1997. NY. Carroll & Graf. ARC. author's 1st novel. NF. R16. $35.00

KUNHARDT, C.P. *Steam Yachts & Launches: Their Machinery & Management.* 1887. Forest & Stream. 1st ed. 97 ils. 239p. G. A17. $45.00

KUNHARDT, Dorothy. *Brave Mr Buckingham.* 1935. Harcourt Brace. 1st ed. ils. unp. beige cloth. VG/dj. D1. $120.00

KUNHARDT, Philip. *Life in Camelot: The Kennedy Years.* nd. Little Brn. BC. 319p. blk brd/spine. NF/VG. B22. $7.50

KUNICZAK, W.S. *Sempinski Affair.* 1969. Doubleday. 1st ed. RS. VG/VG. P3. $20.00

KUNKEL & GARDNER. *What Do You Advise? Guide to the Art of Counseling.* 1946. Ives Washburn. 314p. prt gr cloth. VG/dj. G1. $35.00

KUNTSLER, James Howard. *Embarrassment of Riches.* 1985. NY. Dial. 1st ed. rem mk. F/NF. B4. $50.00

KUNZ, George Frederick. *Gems & Precious Stones of North America.* 1892. NY. Scientific Pub Co. 2nd. ils Louis Prang. gilt cloth. F. B14. $350.00

KUNZ, George Frederick. *Rings for the Finger.* 1917. Lippincott. 1st ed. ils/pl. 381p. F. B14. $400.00

KUNZOG, John C. *One-Horse Show. Chronicle of Early Circus Days.* 1942. Jamestown, NY. self pub. 1st ed. sgn. gilt gr cloth. F/VG. H3. $125.00

KURAN, Aptullah. *Sinan: Grand Old Master of Ottoman Architecture.* 1987. Int Turkist Study/Ada. 1st ed. pres. photos. 319p. NF/dj. W1. $70.00

KURATA, Shigeo. *Nepenthes of Mount Kinabulu.* 1976. Sabah, Malaysia. ils/photos. 80p. sc. VG/dj. B26. $20.00

KUREISHI, Hanif. *Buddha of Suburbia.* 1990. Viking. 1st ed. author's 1st novel. F/F. M23. $30.00

KURELEK, William. *Prairie Boy's Summer.* 1975. Montreal. Tundra. 1st ed. sm 4to. F/F. C8. $35.00

KURTEN, Bjorn. *How to Deep-Freeze a Mammoth.* nd. Columbia. 2nd. VG/VG. P3. $17.00

KURTZ, Katherine. *Bastard Prince.* 1994. Ballantine. 1st ed. F/F. G10. $10.00

KURTZ, Katherine. *Bishop's Heir.* nc. BC. VG/VG. P3. $8.00

KURTZ, Katherine. *Harrowing of Gwynedd.* 1989. Del Rey. 1st ed. hc. F/F. P3. $18.00

KURTZ, Katherine. *Quest for Saint Camber.* nd. Del Rey. 6th. VG/VG. P3. $15.00

KURYLO, Friedrich. *Ferdinand Braun: A Life of the Nobel Prizewinner...* 1981. Cambridge. 289p. dj. A13. $25.00

KURZWEIL, Allen. *Case of Curiosities.* 1992. HBJ. 1st ed. rem mk. F/F. H11. $30.00

KUSCHE, Lawrence David. *Bermuda Triangle Mystery — Solved.* 1975. Harper Row. 1st ed. VG/VG. P3. $18.00

KUSHNER, Ellen. *Thomas, the Rhymer.* 1990. Morrow. 1st ed. F/F. G10. $45.00

KUSKIN, Karla. *Philharmonic Gets Dressed.* nd. Harper Row. 8vo. unp. F/VG clip. C14. $6.00

KUTTNER, Henry. *Best of...* nd. BC. VG/VG. P3. $10.00

KUTTNER, Henry. *Fury.* 1950. Grosset Dunlap. VG/VG. P3. $45.00

KUTTRUFF, Karl. *Ships of the Great Lakes, a Pictorial History.* 1976. Detroit. Wayne State. VG. A16. $40.00

KVAMME, Torstein O. *Christmas Caroler's Book in Song & Story.* 1935. Chicago. ils. 80p. G/wrp. A17. $5.00

KWITNY, Jonathan. *Shakedown.* 1977. Putnam. 1st ed. VG/VG. P3. $15.00

KYLE, David A. *Book of SF Ideas & Dreams.* 1977. Hamlyn. VG/VG. P3. $20.00

KYLE, David A. *Pictorial History of SF.* 1977. Hamlyn. 2nd. hc. VG/VG. P3. $20.00

KYLE, Duncan. *Black Camelot.* 1978. Collins. 1st ed. F/F. P3. $15.00

KYLE, Duncan. *Dancing Men.* 1986. Holt. 1st ed. F/F. P3. $20.00

KYLE, Duncan. *Stalking Point.* 1981. St Martin. 1st ed. F/F. P3. $16.00

KYLE, Elisabeth. *On Lennox Moor.* 1954. Jr Literary Guild. BC. 8vo. 188p. VG/G. T5. $15.00

KYLE & SHAMPO. *Medicine & Stamps.* 1970. Chicago. 1st ed. 216p. VG. A13. $40.00

KYNE, Peter B. *Enchanted Hill.* 1924. Cosmopolitan. 1st ed. ils Dean Cornwell. F/VG. A18. $40.00

KYNE, Peter B. *Kindred of the Dust.* 1922. Copp Clark. hc. VG. P3. $20.00

KYNE, Peter B. *Never the Twain Shall Meet.* 1923. Cosmopolitan. 1st ed. ils Dean Cornwell. F/F. A18. $35.00

KYNE, Peter B. *Pride of Palomar.* 1921. Cosmopolitan. 1st ed. sgn. ils Ballinger/Cornwell. VG/VG. A18. $50.00

KYNE, Peter B. *They Also Serve.* 1927. Cosmopolitan. 1st ed. ils Baldridge/Brown. F/F. A18. $25.00

KYNE, Peter B. *Tide of Empire.* 1928. Cosmopolitan. 1st ed. ils WS Broadhead. F/VG. A18. $40.00

KYSOR, Harley D. *Aircraft in Distress.* 1956. Phil. 1st ed. sgn. 432p. G. B18. $22.50

– L –

L'AMOUR, Louis. *Education of a Wandering Man.* 1989. Bantam. 1st. F/F. A20. $15.00

L'AMOUR, Louis. *Guns of the Timberlands.* 1955. Jason. 1st. F/NF. B4. $2,250.00

L'AMOUR, Louis. *Jubal Sackett.* 1985. Bantam. 1st. 375p. VG+/clip. M20. $30.00

L'AMOUR, Louis. *Sitka.* 1957. Appleton-Century-Crofts. 1st. F/NF. B4. $1,500.00

L'ENGLE, Madeleine. *Acceptable Time.* 1989. FSG. 1st. F/F. B3. $20.00

L'ENGLE, Madeleine. *House Like a Lotus.* 1984. FSG. 1st. NF/NF clip. B3. $25.00

L'ENGLE, Madeleine. *Other Side of the Sun.* 1971. FSG. 1st. NF/NF. B3. $60.00

L'ENGLE, Madeleine. *Ring of Endless Light.* 1980. FSG. 1st. 324p. F/VG+. P2. $50.00

L'ENGLE, Madeleine. *Young Unicorns.* 1968. FSG. 1st. NF/VG. B3. $75.00

L'HEUREUX, John. *No Place for Hiding.* 1971. Doubleday. 1st. sgn. NF/VG. R14. $35.00

L'HEUREUX, John. *Woman Run Mad.* 1988. Viking. 1st. sgn. rem mk. NF/F. R14. $30.00

L'HOTE, Henri. *Search for the Tassili Frescoes...* 1959. NY. 1st Am. ils/maps. 236p. decor cloth. VG/dj. B18. $25.00

LA CHAPELLE, Mary. *House of Heros & Other Stories.* 1988. Crown. 1st. inscr. author's 1st book. F/NF. R13. $35.00

LA CLAIR, Earl E. *Wood & the Wool.* 1966. Francestown, NH. Golden Quill. inscr/orig poem. F/F. B11. $18.00

LA FLESCHE, Francis. *Middle Five.* 1900. Boston. Sm Maynard. 1st. author's 1st book. NF. L3. $250.00

LA FONTAINE. *Fables of La Fontaine.* (1940). NY. Harper. 1st. ils Andre Helle. 39p. VG. D1. $100.00

LA FONTAINE. *Fables.* 1893. Paris. ils. VG. M17. $30.00

LA GARGE, Oliver. *Enemy Gods.* 1937. Boston. 1st ed. F/taped. A17. $20.00

LA LANNE, Jack. *Abundant Health & Vitality After 40.* 1962. Prentice Hall. 1st. sgn. 224p. VG/VG. B11. $35.00

LA MOTTA, Jake. *Raging Bull: My Story.* 1970. Prentice Hall. 1st. F/F. B4. $200.00

LA POINT, James. *Legends of the Lakota.* 1976. SF. Indian Historian Pr. 1st. F. L3. $100.00

LA RAME, Louis. *Bimbi.* 1910. Lippincott. 1st thus. ils Maria Kirk. gilt red cloth. F. M5. $35.00

LABADIE, Emile L. *Native Plants for Use in California Landscape.* 1978. Sierra City, CA. 2nd. ils. 244p. as new. B26. $16.00

LABAT, Gaston. *Regional Anesthesia.* 1928. Phil. 2nd. 567p. A13. $100.00

LABOCETTA, Mario. *Tales of Hoffmann.* nd. NY. Dodd Mead/H Piazza. 10 full-p ils. G+. C14. $20.00

LACH, Alma. *Campbell Kids at Home.* 1954. Rand McNally. 1st Elf (#493). VG. P2. $20.00

LACHAMBRE & MACHURON. *Andree's Balloon Expedition in Search of North Pole.* 1898. NY. Stokes. 1st Am. 306p. P4. $145.00

LACHOUQUE, Henry. *Waterloo.* 1972. ils. VG/VG. M17. $27.50

LACK, D. *Population Studies of Birds.* 1966. Clarendon. ils/figures/photos. 341p. cloth. VG. M12. $45.00

LACKINGTON, J. *Confessions of J Lackington, Late Bookseller...* 1808. NY. Wilson Hitt. 16mo. 189p. F. T10. $250.00

LACOUTURE, Jean. *Ho Chi Min: A Political Biography.* 1968. Random. 1st Am. VG/VG. V4. $25.00

LACY, Ed. *Hotel Dwellers.* 1966. Harper Row. 1st. F/dj. M15. $45.00

LADA-MOCARSKI, Valerian. *Bibliography of Books on Alaska Published Before 1868.* 1969. Yale. ils. 567p. cloth. dj. D11. $250.00

LADD, George Eldon. *Theology of the New Testament.* 1975. Eerdmans. 661p. G. B29. $9.00

LAFEVER, Minard. *Modern Builder's Guide: Ils by 87 Copperplate Engravings.* 1833. Sleight/Collins Hannaay. 1st. lg 4to. 146p. full contemporary calf. M1. $1,000.00

LAFFERTY, R.A. *Does Anyone Else Have Anything Further to Add?* 1974. Scribner. 1st. F/dj. M2. $25.00

LAFFERTY, R.A. *Not to Mention Camels.* 1976. Bobbs Merrill. 1st. F/dj. M2. $25.00

LAGARDE, Andre. *Latin Church in the Middle Ages.* 1915. Scribner. 600p. VG. B29. $8.50

LAGERBERG, Torsten. *Vare Ville Planter.* 1950-1958. Oslo. revised/enlarged. 8 vol in 9. ils. xl. half morocco. B26. $185.00

LAGUARDIA, Robert. *Red Tempestuous Life of Susan Hayward.* 1985. Macmillan. 1st. VG/VG. W2. $25.00

LAHR, Bert. *Notes on a Cowardly Lion: Biography of Bert Lahr.* 1969. 408p. F/NF. A4. $35.00

LAI, LIM & YUNG. *Island: Poetry & History of Chinese Immigrants...1910-40.* 1980. SF. Hoc Doi. sgns. 8vo. F/paper wrp. R3. $20.00

LAJITHA, E. *March of Japan.* ca 1938. ils. xl. G+. E6. $15.00

LAKE, Nancy. *Daily Dinners.* 1892. London. Warne. G. A16. $35.00

LAMB, Brian M. *Guide to Cacti of the World.* 1991. NY. ils/photos/map. M/dj. B26. $40.00

LAMB, Bruce. *Wild Bunch.* 1993. Worland, WY. High Plains. A19. $30.00

LAMB, Charles. *Essays of Elia.* 1899. E Aurora. Roycroft. 1/100 (of 970). 14 hand-colord initials. full suede. B24. $200.00

LAMB, E. *Flowering of Your Cacti.* 1955. London. ils/photos. 12mo. glossy pict brd. B26. $17.50

LAMB, Frank W. *Indian Baskets of North America.* 1972. Riverside. 1st. ils/maps/photos. 155p. NF/dj. K7. $50.00

LAMB, Harold. *Curved Saber.* 1964. Doubleday. 1st. NF/dj. M2. $75.00

LAMB, Harold. *Durandal.* 1931. Doubleday. 1st. F/dj. M2. $50.00

LAMB, Harold. *Nur Mahal.* 1935. Doubleday Doran. 325p. VG/dj. W1. $18.00

LAMB, Hugh. *Terror by Gaslight: More Victorian Tales.* 1976. Taplinger. 1st Am. F/dj. M2. $22.00

LAMB, S.H. *Native Trees & Shrubs of the Hawaiian Islands.* 1987. Sunstone. 2nd. 159p. NF. B1. $26.50

LAMB, Ursula. *Martin Fernandez dei Navarrette Clears the Deck...* 1980. Coimbra. 17p. as new/wrp. O7. $15.00

LAMB, Wally. *She's Come Undone.* 1992. Pocket. 1st. F/F. H11. $40.00

LAMB, Wally. *She's Come Undone.* 1992. Pocket. 1st. NF/clip. A24. $35.00

LAMB & LAMB. *Ils Reference on Cacti & Other Succulents.* 1974-79. London. Blanford. 5 vol. 8vo. cloth. F/djs. A22. $150.00

LAMB & LAMB. *Pocket Encyclopedia of Cacti in Colour.* 1969. Poole. ARC. sgns. 326 mc photos. 217p. F/dj. B26. $15.00

LAMB & LARRICK. to *Ride a Butterfly: Original Pictures, Stories...* 1991. NY. Doubleday/Dell Pub Group. 1st. 96p. F/NF. C14. $16.00

LAMBERT, Gerard B. *Yankee in England.* 1957. ils. xl. VG. M17. $25.00

LAMBERT, Janet. *Candy Kane.* (1943). Grosset Dunlap. rpt. 8vo. 185p. G. T5. $14.00

LAMBERT, Janet. *Parri MacDonald: That's My Girl.* 1964. Dutton. 1st. 190p. VG+/dj. M20. $30.00

LAMBERT, Janet. *Penny Parish: Up Goes the Curtain.* 1946. Dutton. 2nd. 189p. VG/dj. M20. $20.00

LAMBERT, Janet. *Practically Perfect.* (1947). Grosset Dunlap. 8vo. 192p. gray tweed brd. VG/VG. T5. $15.00

LAMBERT, Janet. *Star Dream.* (1951). Grosset Dunlap. 8vo. 190p. VG. C8/T5. $12.50

LAMBERT, Oscar D. *Pioneer Leaders of Western Virginia.* 1935. Parkersburg, WV. 10 biographies. 226p. gilt cloth. G+. B18. $22.50

LAMBERT, Reita. *Right to the Heart.* 1939. Caxton. 1st. F/F clip. B4. $175.00

LAMMERS & VERHEY. *On Moral Medicine: Theological Perspectives...* 1987. Eerdmans. 657p. VG. B29. $18.50

LAMON, H. *Turkey Raising.* 1924 (1922). photos. VG. E6. $25.00

LAMONT, Helen Otis. *Story of Shelter Island in the Revolution.* 1975. Shelter Island. Hist Soc. sgn. 64p. VG/wrp. B11. $18.00

LAMOTT, Anne. *Hard Laughter.* 1980. NY. Viking. 1st author's 1st book. VG+/clip. B4. $100.00

LAMOTT, Anne. *Joe Jones.* 1985. SF. Northpoint. 1st. F/NF. M23. $30.00

LAMPELL, Millard. *The Wall.* 1961. Knopf. 1st. F/NF. B2. $35.00

LAMPORT, Felicia. *Light Metres.* 1982. Everest House. ils Gorey. 122p. VG/dj. M20. $50.00

LAMPORT, Felicia. *Scrap Irony.* 1961. Houghton Mifflin. 1st. 128p. F/NF. D4. $45.00

LAMSON, Peggy. *Roger Baldwin, Founder of Am Civil Liberties Union.* 1976. Houghton Mifflin. 1st. F/NF. B2. $30.00

LAMSON & VANDERZWAAG. *Challenge of Arctic Shipping...* 1990. Montreal/Kingston. McGill-Queen's U. 282p. bl cloth. P4. $35.00

LANCASTER, Roy. *Travels in China: A Plantsman's Paradise.* 1993 (1989). Woodbridge, Suffolk. ils. 520p. as new/dj. B26. $80.00

LANCASTER-BROWN, Peter. *Halley & His Comet.* 1985. Poole. Blanford. 1st. ils. NF/dj. K3. $20.00

LANCIANI, Rodolfo. *Ancient Rome in Light of Recent Discoveries.* 1889. Boston. 3rd. 329p. gilt cloth. A17. $25.00

LANCMAN, E. *Chinese Portraiture.* 1966. Tokyo. Tuttle. 1st. 188p. F/dj. W3. $65.00

LANCOUR, Gene. *Globes of Llarun.* 1980. Doubleday. 1st. inscr. F/F. T12. $15.00

LANCOUR, Gene. *War Machines of Kalinth.* 1977. Doubleday. 1st. F/dj. M2. $10.00

LANDA, M.J. *Jew in Drama.* 1927. Morrow. 1st. 340p. VG+. S3. $24.00

LANDE, Carl H. *Rebuilding a Nation.* 1987. WA Inst Pr. 592p. M/VG. P1. $15.00

LANDELS, J.G. *Engineering in the Ancient World.* 1978. Berkeley. 1st. 8vo. 224p. F/dj. K3. $20.00

LANDESBERGER, Franz. *Rembrandt, the Jews & the Bible.* 1961. JPS. 2nd. ils/biblio/index. 190p. VG. S3. $33.00

LANDIS, C.S. *Woodchucks & Woodchuck Rifles.* 1951. NY. 1st. VG/G. B5. $45.00

LANDOR, A. Henry Savage. *Across Widest Africa.* 1907. NY. Scribner. 1st. 2 vol. 150+ pl/missing fld map. teg. VG. W1. $95.00

LANDOR, A. Henry Savage. *Explorer's Adventures in Tibet.* 1910. Harper. 1st. ils. pict cloth. VG. W3. $120.00

LANDOR, A. Henry Savage. *In the Forbidden Land: Account of Journey Into Tibet.* 1899. NY/London. Harper. 1st. 2 vol. photos/pl/lg fld map. VG. W3. $245.00

LANDOR, Walter Savage. *Imaginary Conversations.* 1936. Verona. Officina Bodoni. 1/1500. sgn Hans Mardersteig. VG. T10. $60.00

LANDSMAN, Anne Cheek. *Needlework Designs From American Indians.* 1977. Barnes/Yoseloff. 4to. 122 full-p designs+36p text. as new/dj. K7. $35.00

LANDSTROM, Bjorn. *Bold Voyages & Great Explorers.* 1964. Doubleday. 1st. F/rpr. O7. $30.00

LANE, Edward William. *Thousand & One Nights, Commonly Called, in England...* 1865. Warne Routledge. new ed. 3 vol. 8vo. ils. cloth. VG. W1. $175.00

LANE, Ronald. *Rudder's Rangers: The Second US Ranger Battalion.* 1979. Manassas. Ranger Assoc. 1st. sgn Margaret Rudder. F/F. A23. $40.00

LANE, Rose Wilder. *Discovery of Freedom.* 1943. NY. 1st. VG/dj. B5. $45.00

LANE, Walter Paye. *Adventures & Recollections of Gen Walter P Lane...* 1970 (1887). Austin, TX. Pemberton. rpt. 180p. cloth. F/NF. M8. $45.00

LANE-POOLE, Stanley. *Speeches & Table-Talk of the Prophet Mohammad.* 1882. Macmillan. 16mo. 196p. cloth. VG. W1. $45.00

LANES, Selma G. *Art of Maurice Sendak.* 1980. Abrams. 1st. obl 4to. ils. 278p. F/prt plastic. from $150.00 to $165.00

LANG, Andrew. *Arabian Nights Entertainment.* 1898. Longman Gr. 1st. ils HJ Ford. aeg. 424p. gilt bl cloth. F. D1. $850.00

LANG, Andrew. *Arabian Nights.* 1968. Santa Rose, CA. Classic. 1st. ils Wm Dempster. 218p. VG. W1. $15.00

LANG, Andrew. *Ballads & Lyrics of Old France.* 1898. Postland, ME. Mosher. 1/925. 12mo. teg. full blk leather/raised bands. NF. H3. $125.00

LANG, Andrew. *Blue Fairy Book.* 1889. London. Longman Gr. 1st. ils HJ Ford/GP Jacomb Hood. aeg. gilt bl cloth. R5. $220.00

LANG, Andrew. *Books & Bookmen.* 1892. Longman Gr. new ed. ils. 177p. G. K3. $20.00

LANG, Andrew. *Library.* 1881. London. Macmillan. 1st. mc pl/woodcuts. 184p. VG. K3. $30.00

LANG, Andrew. *Price Prigio & Prince Ricardo.* 1961. 1st thus. ils Watkins-Pitchford. VG/VG. S13. $16.00

LANG, Andrew. *Princess Nobody: A Tale of Fairyland.* 1884. London. Longman Gr. 1st thus. 4to. ils Richard Doyle. 56p text. cloth. R5. $475.00

LANG, Andrew. *True Story Book.* (1893). Longman Gr. 2nd. ils Bogle/Davis/etc. 337p. VG. D1. $85.00

LANG, Daniel. *From Hiroshima to the Moon.* 1959. S&S. ils. 496p. VG. K3. $20.00

LANG, Mrs. Andrew. *Book of Saints & Heroes.* 1912. Longman Gr. 1st. edit Andrew Lang. VG. M19. $45.00

LANG, Rev. Dr. *On the Origin & Migrations of the Polynesian Nation...* nd. np. 8vo. VG. P4. $55.00

LANGBEIN, John H. *Torture & the Law of Proof, Europe & England...* 1977. Chicago. M11. $65.00

LANGDON, Stephen. *Sumerian Grammatical Texts.* 1917. Phil. U Mus. 1st. 44p. VG/wrp. W1. $45.00

LANGDON-DAVIES, John. *Behind the Spanish Barricades.* 1936. Secker Warburg. 1st. G. V4. $30.00

LANGE, John; see Crichton, Michael.

LANGE & TAYLOR. *American Exodus.* 1939. NY. Reynal Hitchcock. ils. 158p. cloth. D11. $250.00

LANGER, Susanne. *Cruise of the Little Dipper.* 1923. Norcross. ils Helen Sewell. 176p. G. P2. $25.00

LANGERLOF, Selma. *Story of Gosta Berling.* 1928. Doubleday Doran. Marbacka ed. 473p. VG. A25. $10.00

LANGFORD, N.P. *Discovery of Yellowstone Park, 1879, Diary...* 1905. Langford. 1st. sgn. 122p. VG. J2. $375.00

LANGLEY, Noel. *Tale of the Land of Green Ginger.* 1937. Morrow. 1st. 4to. 143p. VG/VG. D1. $135.00

LANGLOIS, Dora. *In the Shadow of Pa-Menkh.* 1908. London. VG. M2. $50.00

LANGMAN, Ida K. *Selected Guide to Literature on Flowering Plants of Mexico.* 1964. Phil. 1015p. as new/dj. B26. $62.50

LANGMORE, Diane. *Missionary Lives: Papua, 1874-1914.* 1989. Honolulu. 8vo. 408p. map ep. as new/sans. P4. $35.00

LANGSTAFF, J. Brett. *Oxford 1914.* 1965. NY. 1st. inscr. 317p. VG+/dj. B18. $25.00

LANGSTAFF, John. *Over in the Meadow.* 1957. Harcourt Brace. 1st. VG/G. C8. $25.00

LANGSTAFF & LANGSTAFF. *Jim Along, Josie.* 1970. HBJ. 1st. 127p. cloth. F/F. D4. $50.00

LANGTON, Jane. *Dark Nantucket Noon.* 1975. Harper Row. 1st. F/dj. M15. $100.00

LANGTON, Jane. *Memorial Hall Murder.* 1978. Harper Row. 1st. F/F. M15. $50.00

LANGTON, Jane. *Transcendental Murder.* 1964. Harper Row. 1st. author's 1st novel. VG/dj. M15. $175.00

LANIER, Sidney. *Boy's King Arthur.* 1968 (1924). ils NC Wyeth. VG/dj. S13. $30.00

LANKS, Herbert. *By Pan American Highway Through S Am.* 1942. Appleton. 1st. xl. F3. $10.00

LANNER & LANNER. *Pinon Pine: A Natural & Cultural History...* 1981. Reno, NV. ils/map/photo. F/NF. M12. $22.50

LANNING, George. *Pedestal.* 1967. London. Michael Joseph. 1st. VG/NF. Q1. $40.00

LANNING, John. *Pedro de la Torre.* 1974. LSU. 1st. 145p. dj. F3. $25.00

LANNING, John. *18th-Century Enlightenment in University of San Carlos...* 1956. Cornell. 1st. 372p. F3. $20.00

LANSDALE, Joe R. *Magic Wagon.* 1986. Doubleday. 1st. xl. G+/VG+. M21. $40.00

LANSDALE, Joe R. *Savage Season.* 1990. Ziesing. 1st hc. F/F. M22. $50.00

LANTZ, Sherlee. *Pageant of Pattern for Needlepoint Canvas.* 1973. Atheneum. 1st. 4to. 509p. 16 mc pl/150 photos/351 diagrams. F/dj. T10. $125.00

LANVAL, Marc. *Inquiry Into Intimate Lives of Women.* 1950 (1937). NY. Cadillac. 1st Am. chart. 243p. VG. A25. $12.00

LANZMAN, Claude. *Shoah: Oral History of the Holocaust, Complete Text of Film.* 1985. Pantheon. ils. 200p. VG/dj. S3. $24.00

LAO TZU. *Way of Life.* 1944. John Day. 1st. VG/dj. M25. $45.00

LAPIDE, Phinn E. *Prophet of San Nicandro.* 1953. Beechhurst. ils. 240p. VG/VG. S3. $25.00

LAQUEUR, W. *Struggle for the Middle East.* 1969. Macmillan. 1st Am. 360p. VG/dj. W1. $22.00

LAQUIAN, Aprodicio A. *Slums Are for People.* 1971. Honolulu. 245p. cloth. M/VG. P1. $15.00

LARDNER, Dionysius. *Popular Astronomy.* 1856. London. Walton Maberly. ils. 369p. gilt cloth. K5. $60.00

LARDNER, Dionysius. *Treatise on Hydrostatics & Pneumatics.* 1832. Phil. Carey Lea. 1st Am from 1st London. lg 12mo. 273p. rebound. K3. $40.00

LARDNER, Ring. *Bib Ballads.* 1915. Volland. 1st. presumed 1/500. teg. ils tan cloth. VG. M24. $100.00

LARDNER, Ring. *Ecstasy of Owen Muir.* 1954. Cameron Kahn. 1st. F/NF. B2. $35.00

LARDNER, Ring. *Say It With Oil.* 1923. Doran. 1st. NF/F. B4. $300.00

LARDNER, Ring. *Some Champions: Sketches & Fiction.* 1976. NY. 1st. F/F. A11. $85.00

LARGE, E.C. *Asleep in the Afternoon.* 1939. Holt. 1st. F/dj. M2. $90.00

LARKIN, David. *Fantastic Creatures of Edward Julius Detmold.* intro Keith Nicholson. 4to. 40 full-p pl. M/dj. B24. $75.00

LARKIN, Margaret. *Seven Shapes in a Gold Mine.* 1960. London. Readers Union. 213p. F3. $15.00

LARKIN, Philip. *All What Jazz.* 1985. Farrar Straus. reissue w/new intro. F/dj. Q1. $40.00

LARKINS, William. *US Navy Aircraft 1921-1941 & US Marine Corps Aircraft...* 1988. NY. 2 vol in 1. ils/index. VG/VG. S16. $35.00

LARMOTH, Jeanine. *Murder on the Menu.* 1972. Scribner. VG/dj. A16. $35.00

LAROUSSE. *Larousse Encyclopedia of Mythology.* 1959. photos. VG/VG. M17. $30.00

LAROUSSE. *Larousse Encyclopedia of Renaissance & Baroque Art.* 1967. ils. VG/VG. M17. $22.50

LAROUSSE. *Wines & Vineyards of France.* 1991. NY. 1st. VG/VG. T9. $26.00

LARSEN, Jeanne. *Silk Road.* 1989. Holt. 1st. F/dj. M2. $20.00

LARSEN, Lucinda Christenson. *Lucinda's Party Foods.* 1960. Caxton. VG. A16. $12.00

LARSON, Arthur. *Eisenhower: The President Nobody Knew.* 1968. Scribner. 1st. NF/clip. A20. $20.00

LARSON, Dewey B. *Quasars & Pulsars.* 1971 (1959). Portland, OR. 180p. Vg/dj. K5. $25.00

LARSON, Jennifer. *Leaf From Francisco Palou's Noticias de la Nueva California.* 1990. Orinda. Golden Key. 1/150. pict wrp. D11. $50.00

LARSON, T.A. *History of Wyoming.* 1965. NE U. 1st. 619p. VG/VG. J2. $135.00

LARTEGUY, Jean. *Centurions.* 1962. Dutton. 2nd. NF/VG+. A20. $20.00

LASANSKY, Mauricio. *Nazi Drawings.* 1976. IA. revised. 16p+30 full-p pl. cloth. A17. $27.50

LASCELLES, G. *Falconry With Coursing by Harding Cox.* (1901). London. Longman. new imp. 2 vol in 1. ils GE Lodge. gilt polished calf. M12. $125.00

LASH, Joseph P. *Eleanor & Franklin.* 1971. Norton. 1st. tall 8vo. 32 pl. 765p. F/dj. H1. $22.50

LASH, Joseph P. *World of Love.* 1984. Franklin Lib. 1st. sgn. full leather. F. Q1. $35.00

LASKER, David. *Boy Who Loved Music.* 1979. Viking. 1st. ils Joe Lasker. VG/dj. T5. $35.00

LASKI, Marghanita. *Little Boy Lost.* 1949. London. 1st. VG/dj. w/sgn Christmas card. T9. $35.00

LASSWELL, Mary. *Mrs Rassmusson's One-Arm Cookery.* 1946. Boston. VG/VG. B5. $30.00

LASSWELL, Mary. *One on the House.* 1949. Houghton Mifflin. 1st. ils George Price. 263p. VG. A25. $8.00

LATH, J.A. *Adventure & Mystery: Cortez Emerald Mystery.* 1935. Cupples Leon. 189p. VG/dj. M20. $20.00

LATH, J.A. *Lost City of the Aztecs.* 1934. Cupples Leon. 1st. NF. M2. $35.00

LATHAM, Aaron. *Crazy Sundays: F Scott Fitzgerald in Hollywood.* 1971. Viking. 1st. NF/dj. M25. $35.00

LATHAM, Hiram. *Trans-Missouri Stock Raising.* 1962. Old West Pub. rpt. A19. $30.00

LATHEM, E.C. *Robert Frost 100.* 1974. Boston. Godine. 1st. pict wrp. M24. $25.00

LATHEN, Emma. *Longer the Thread.* 1971. S&S. 1st. F/NF. B2. $35.00

LATHEN, Emma. *Pick Up Sticks.* 1970. Inner Sanctum. 1st. NF/dj. M25. $22.50

LATHROP, Dorothy. *Animals of the Bible.* 1937. Stokes. 1st. 4to. gr cloth. G+. D1. $150.00

LATHROP, Dorothy. *Hide & Go Seek.* 1938. Macmillan. 1st. pres/sgn. teal-gr cloth. dj. R5. $200.00

LATHROP, Dorothy. *Puffy & the Seven Leaf Clover.* 1954. Macmillan. 1st. 34p. VG/VG. P2. $75.00

LATHROP, Dorothy. *Skittle-Skattle Monkey.* 1945. Macmillan. 12mo. ils. VG/dj. D1. $150.00

LATHROP, Dorothy. *Sung Under the Silver Umbrella.* 1935. NY. 1st. VG/fair. B5. $30.00

LATHROP, Elise. *Early American Inns & Taverns.* 1935 (1926). Tudor. 365p. VG/ragged. M20. $20.00

LATHROP, Elise. *Historic Houses of Early America.* 1933. NY. 110 photos. 464p. VG. M4. $30.00

LATHROP, Elise. *Historic Houses of Early America.* 1935 (1927). Tudor. 464p. NF/dj/box. M20. $45.00

LATHROP, Leonard. *Farmer's Library; or, Essays...* 1826. Windsor. Spooner. 2nd. 300p. leather brd. VG. A10. $200.00

LATOURETTE, Kenneth. *Christianity in Revolutionary Age...* 1976. Zondervan. 2 vol. VG. B29. $40.00

LATOURETTE, Kenneth. *History of Christian Missions in China.* 1929. Macmillan. 1st. bibliography/fld map. 930p. F/VG. W3. $145.00

LATROB, C.J. *Rambler in Oklahoma: Latrobe's Tour With Washington Irving.* 1955. OK City. ils/maps. 92p. VG. M4. $20.00

LATTA, Estelle. *Controversial Mark Hopkins.* 1963. Duke. Cothran Hist Research Found. 2nd revised. NF/G+. O4. $15.00

LATTA, F.F. *Black Gold in the Joaquin.* 1949. Caldwell. 1st. VG. O4. $15.00

LATTAUER, V.S. *Commonsense Horsemanship.* 1974. NY. Arco. rpt. VG/G. O3. $25.00

LATTAUER, V.S. *More About the Forward Seat.* 1939. London. Hurst Blackett. 1st. VG. O3. $45.00

LATTAUER & KOURNAKOFF. *Defense of the Forward Seat.* 1934. Boots & Saddles Riding School. ltd. sgns. half leather. O3. $150.00

LATTIMORE, Eleanor Frances. *More About Little Pear.* 1971. Morrow. 1st. lg 12mo. VG/VG+. C8. $22.50

LATTIMORE, Eleanor Frances. *Two Helens.* 1967. Morrow. 1st. 8vo. 128p. VG/G. T5. $25.00

LATTIMORE & LATTIMORE. *Silks, Spices & Empire.* 1968. Delacorte. 1st. maps. VG/dj. K3. $20.00

LATYMER, Hugo. *Mediterranean Gardener.* 1990. Barron's. tall 8vo. F/dj. A22. $30.00

LAUBER, Lynn. *White Girls.* 1990. Norton. 1st. author's 1st book. F/F. R13. $25.00

LAUBER, Lynn. *21 Sugar Street.* 1993. Norton. 1st. inscr. F/F. R13. $35.00

LAUBER, Patricia. *Runaway Flea Circus.* 1958. Random. 1st. 72p. VG/dj. M20. $30.00

LAUBIN & LAUBIN. *American Indian Archery.* 1990. OK U. ils/photos. 179p. F/dj. M4. $12.00

LAUFE, Leonard. *Obstetric Forceps.* 1968. NY. 1st. ils. 141p. A13. $75.00

LAUFER, Berthold. *Chinese Pottery of the Han Dynasty.* 1970. Rutland/Tokyo. 2nd (rpt 1909). 339p. F/dj. W3. $86.00

LAUGHLIN, Clara E. *So You're Going to France!* 1927. Houghton Mifflin. 1st. ils. 611p. VG. A25. $10.00

LAUGHLIN, Clarence John. *Ghosts Along the Mississippi.* 1961. NY. Bonanza. sgn. 220p. cloth. dj. D11. $150.00

LAUGHLIN, Robert. *Of Wonders Wild & New.* 1976. Smithsonian. 4to. xl. wrp. F3. $15.00

LAUMER, Keith. *Nine by Laumer.* 1967. Doubleday. 1st. F/NF. M2. $50.00

LAURENCE, Dan H. *Shaw, Books & Libraries.* 1976. Austin. HRC. 1st. 1/500. red cloth/label. F. M24. $30.00

LAURENTS, Arthur. *Way We Were.* 1972. Harper Row. 1st. sgn. F/VG. M19. $25.00

LAURITZEN, Jonreed. *Ordeal of the Young Hunter.* 1954. Little Brn. 1st. 246p. cloth. VG+/dj. M20. $25.00

LAUSANNE, Edita. *Great Book of Wine.* 1974. Galahad. revised. F/F. W2. $95.00

LAUT, Agnes C. *Through Our Unknown Southwest.* 1925. McBride. 5th. 271p. blk cloth. G+. F7. $22.50

LAVELL, Edith. *Linda Carlton's Ocean Flight (#2).* 1931. AL Burt. 283p. cloth. VG/dj (lists 3 titles). M20. $85.00

LAVENDER, David. *River Runners of the Grand Canyon.* 1986. Tucson. 2nd. sm 4to. bl cloth. F. F7. $35.00

LAVENDER, David. *Rockies.* 1968. Harper Row. 1st. 404p. VG/dj. M20. $25.00

LAVER, James. *Adventures in Monochrome: Anthology of Graphic Art.* ca 1950. London. Studio. 128p. G. A17. $15.00

LAVIN, Mary. *House in Clewe Street.* 1945. Little Brn. 21st. sgn. author's 2nd book. F/VG. L3. $200.00

LAVIN, Mary. *Shrine & Other Stories.* 1977. London. 1st. VG/VG. T9. $25.00

LAWES & MILTON. *Mask of Comus.* 1937. Nonesuch. 1/950. ils MRH Farrar. VG/worn box. B5. $95.00

LAWLISS, Chuck. *Civil War Sourcebook: A Traveler's Guide.* 1991. NY. Harmony. 1st. 308p. stiff prt wrp. M8. $20.00

LAWRENCE, A.B. *History of Texas; or, Emigrant's Guide...* 1844. NY. Nafis Cornish. 12mo. 275p. old calf. M1. $500.00

LAWRENCE, D.H. *Collected Letters of...* 1962. NY. Viking. 1st. 2 vol. edit HT Moore. F/djs. Q1. $100.00

LAWRENCE, D.H. *Lady Chatterly's Lover.* 1959. Grove. 1st Am Complete/Authorized from 3rd Manuscript Version. W2. $1,500.00

LAWRENCE, D.H. *Man Who Died.* 1931. London. 1/2000. VG/partial laid in. T9. $85.00

LAWRENCE, D.H. *My Skirmish With Jolly Roger.* 1929. Random. 1st. 1/600. F/F glassine dj as issued. D10. $300.00

LAWRENCE, D.H. *Reflections on the Death of Porcupine & Other Essays.* 1925. Phil. Centaur. 1st. 1/925. VG. Q1. $150.00

LAWRENCE, G.H.M. *B-P-H: Botanico-Periodicum-Huntianum.* 1968. Pittsburgh. Hunt Botanical Lib. 1063p. NF. B1. $35.00

LAWRENCE, George. *Adanson: Bicentennial Michel Adanson's Familles des Plantes.* 1963 & 1965. Pittsburgh. Hunt. 2 vol. F. A10. $55.00

LAWRENCE, Louise. *Star Lord.* 1978. Harper. 1st. F/dj. M2. $15.00

LAWRENCE, Mildred. *Crissy at the Wheel.* 1966 (1952). HBW. ils Marvin Bileck. 200p. VG/dj. T5. $22.00

LAWRENCE, T.E. *Letters of...* 1939. Doubleday Doran. 1st. edit David Garnett. VG. W1. $30.00

LAWRENCE, T.E. *Minorities.* 1971. London. 1st. edit JM Wilson/pref C Day Lewis. VG/VG. T9. $35.00

LAWRENCE, T.E. *Mint: A Day-Book of the RAF Depot...* 1955. London. Jonathan Cape. 1st/1st under his own name. F/dj. Q1. $100.00

LAWRENCE, W.G. *Ceramic Science for the Potter.* 1972. Chilton. 1st. 239p. F. D8. $30.00

LAWRENCE, W.J.C. *Practical Plant Breeding.* 1937. London. ils. 155p. cloth. B26. $10.00

LAWRENCE, W.J.C. *Practical Plant Breeding.* 1951. Allen Unwin. 3rd/6th imp. 12mo. 161p. B1. $19.00

LAWRENCE, William. *Treatise on Ruptures, Containing Anatomical Description...* 1811. Phil. 1st Am. 412p. full leather. A13. $350.00

LAWSON, A.C. *Atlas of Maps & Seismograms Accompanying Report...1906.* 1970. WA. Carnegie. rpt 1908 ed. sbdg. NF. B1. $45.00

LAWSON, John Howard. *Processional! A Jazz Symphony of American Life.* 1925. NY. Seltzer. 1st. NF. B2. $40.00

LAWSON, Marie A. *Sea Is Blue.* 1946. Viking. 1st. ils. cloth. VG/dj. M20. $25.00

LAWSON, Robert. *Fabulous Flight.* 1949. Little Brn. 1st. 8vo. 152p. bl cloth. VG. T5. $35.00

LAWSON, Robert. *I Hear America Singing.* 1937. Winston. 1st. VG. M5. $30.00

LAWSON, Robert. *Rabbit Hill.* 1944. Viking. 1st. 128p. VG/G. P2. $95.00

LAWSON, Robert. *Rabbit Hill.* 1944. Viking. 1st. 8vo. VG+. M5. $50.00

LAWSON, Robert. *Smeller Martin.* 1950. Viking. 1st. 157p. VG/G. P2. $65.00

LAWSON, Robert. *Tough Winter.* 1954. Viking. 1st. ils. 8vo. 128p. VG/torn. D1. $60.00

LAWTON, Manny. *Some Survived: Epic Account of Japanese Captivity WWII.* 1984. Algonquin. 3rd. 295p. as new/dj. P1. $14.00

LAWTON, Thomas. *Chinese Figure Painting.* 1973. Freer Gallery. 1st. ils. 236p. F. W3. $125.00

LAYCOCK, Thomas. *Essay on Hysteria: Being Analysis of Irregular & Aggravated.* 1840. Phil/New Orleans. Haswell. 2 vol in 1. 1st Am. 8vo. 192p. G1. $300.00

LAYDEN & SNYDER. *It Was a Different Game.* 1969. Prentice Hall. 1st. photos. P8. $15.00

LAYMAN, Richard. *Dashiell Hammett: A Descriptive Bibliography.* 1979. Pittsburgh. 1st. 185p. cloth. F. A17. $30.00

LAYNE, J. Gregg. *Western Wayfaring: Routes of Exploration & Trade...* 1954. Automobile Club S CA. 1st. 1/100. ils/index. 63p. NF/sans. B19. $100.00

LAZZARO, G. Di San. *Klee.* 1957. Praeger. 1st Am. 12mo. 304p. F/dj. H1. $25.00

LE BLANC, Maurice. *Arsene Lupin: Super-Sleuth.* 1927. NY. Macaulay. 1st Am. NF/VG. B4. $100.00

LE BLANC, Maurice. *Crystal Stopper.* 1913. Doubleday. 1st. VG. M2. $25.00

LE CARRE, John. *Call for the Dead.* 1962. Walker. 1st. F/F. B35. $250.00

LE CARRE, John. *Clandestine Muse.* 1986. Newark, VT. Janus. 1st. 1/250. sgn. F/handmade wrp. Q1. $275.00

LE CARRE, John. *Honorable Schoolboy.* 1977. Hodder Stoughton. 1st. VG/VG clip. M22. $45.00

LE CARRE, John. *Little Drummer Girl.* 1983. Knopf. 1st. F/F. from $40 to $50.00

LE CARRE, John. *Little Drummer Girl.* 1983. Knopf. 1st. NF/dj. P3. $25.00

LE CARRE, John. *Looking-Glass War.* 1965. Heinemann. 1st. VG/dj. A24. $80.00

LE CARRE, John. *Naive & Sentimental Lover.* 1971. Hodder Stoughton. 1st. F/clip. M15. $100.00

LE CARRE, John. *Night Manager.* 1993. Knopf. 1st. F/NF. A20. $20.00

LE CARRE, John. *Perfect Spy.* 1986. Knopf. 1st Am. sgn. F/F. M15. $150.00

LE CARRE, John. *Russia House.* 1989. Knopf. 1st. F/F. B35. $30.00

LE CARRE, John. *Secret Pilgrim.* 1991. Knopf. 1st. F/F. B35. $22.00

LE CARRE, John. *Small Town in Germany.* 1968. Coward McCann. 1st Am. F/dj. M15. $50.00

LE CARRE, John. *Small Town in Germany.* 1968. Coward McCann. 1st Am. VG/VG. M22. $25.00

LE CARRE, John. *Spy Who Came in From the Cold.* 1964. Coward McCann. 1st Am. sgn. 256p. F/F. W2. $450.00

LE CARRE, John. *Tinker, Tailor, Soldier, Spy.* 1974. Knopf. 1st Am. NF/NF. N4. $30.00

LE CONTE, J. *Journal of Ramblings Through High Sierra of California...* 1930 (1875). SF. Sierra Club. rpt. 1/1500. ils. 152p. cloth/brd. F/VG. M12. $125.00

LE FANU, J. Sheridan. *Uncle Silas.* 1947. London. F/dj. M2. $35.00

LE GALLIENE, Richard. *Quest of the Golden Girl.* 1896. London/NY. John Lane/Bodley Head. 1st Am. gilt dk gr cloth. NF. M24. $150.00

LE GALLIENNE, Eva. *At 33.* 1940 (1934). Longman Gr. sgn ep. 262p. gilt bl cloth. G. H1. $18.00

LE GALLIENNE, Richard. *Old Country House.* 1902. Harper. 144p. leather. A10. $25.00

LE GEAR. *List of Geographical Atlases in Library of Congress...* nd. 9 vol. rpt of 1958-92 eds. 1/150. F. A4. $325.00

LE GRAND. *Augustus Rides the Border.* 1947. Bobbs Merrill. 1st. 134p. VG/dj. M20. $30.00

LE GUIN, Ursula K. *Buffalo Gals, Won't You Come Out Tonight.* 1994. Pomegranate. 1st. sgn. ils/sgn SS Boulet. F/dj. A24. $45.00

LE GUIN, Ursula K. *City of Illusions.* 1971. London. Gollancz. 1st. NF/dj. Q1. $100.00

LE GUIN, Ursula K. *Compass Rose.* 1982. Harper. 1st. F/dj. M2. $25.00

LE GUIN, Ursula K. *Dispossessed.* 1986. Easton. 1st thus. F/sans. M21. $40.00

LE GUIN, Ursula K. *Eye of the Heron.* 1983. Harper Row. 1st. F/VG. B3. $20.00

LE GUIN, Ursula K. *Gwilan's Harp.* 1981. Lord John. 1/300. sgn/#d. VG. M2. $50.00

LE GUIN, Ursula K. *Malafrena.* 1979. Putnam. 1st. sgn. F/F. R14. $45.00

LE GUIN, Ursula K. *Rocannon's World.* 1975. Garland. 1st hc. F/sans. M2. $50.00

LE GUIN, Ursula K. *Rocannon's World.* 1979. Gollancz. 1st. author's 1st book. F/dj. Q1. $75.00

LE GUIN, Ursula K. *Tehanu, the Last Book of Earthsea.* 1990. Atheneum. 1st. F/F. B3. $25.00

LE HURAY, Peter. *Treasury of English Church Music Vol 2 1545-1650.* 1965. Blandford. 282p. VG/dj. B29. $10.50

LE LIONNAIS, Francois. *Encyclopedie Essentielle.* 1959. Paris. Robert Delpire. 112p. NF. K3. $15.00

LE MAIR, Willebeek. *Old Dutch Nursery Rhymes.* 1917. London. Augener. obl 4to. 42p. gilt bl cloth/pict label. VG. D1. $200.00

LE MASTER, Richard. *Wildlife in Wood.* 1978. 1st. photos. VG/VG. M2. $35.00

LE MAY, Alan. *Unforgiven.* 1957. 1st. VG/VG. S13. $50.00

LE NEVE FOSTER, C. *Text-Book of Ore & Stone Mining.* 1901. Chas Griffin. 4th/revised. 700+ ils. 765p. cloth. D8. $60.00

LE NOBLE, Pierre. *La Cassette Ouverte de L'Illustre Criole...* 1691. Villefranche. Du Four. 12mo. brd. R12. $225.00

LE QUEUX, William. *Closed Box.* 1908. Dodge. G+. M2. $17.00

LE QUEUX, William. *Golden Tree.* 1931. Fiction League. 1st Am. F/NF. M15. $50.00

LE QUEUX, William. *Great White Queen.* nd. Shaw. VG. M2. $95.00

LE ROUX, Hugues. *Acrobats & Mountebanks.* 1890. London. trans AP Morton. ils Jules Garnier. gilt gr silk. VG. A11. $175.00

LE VAYER DE BOUTIGNY, R.-R. *Dissertations sur l'Autorite des Rois...* 1682. Cologne. Marteau. 12mo. brd. R12. $300.00

LEA, Henry Charles. *Ordeal, With Additional Original Documents in Translation...* 1973. Phil. 199p. sewn wrp. M11. $20.00

LEA, Tom. *Hands of Cantu.* 1964. Little Brn. 1st. F/VG+ clip. T11. $45.00

LEA, Tom. *Selection of Paintings & Drawings From the Nineteen-Sixties.* 1969. Encino. 1st ltd Rio Bravo of 200. sgns. F/case. A18. $175.00

LEA, Tom. *Wonderful Country.* 1952. Little Brn. 1st. NF/VG+. T11. $75.00

LEA & MASTERS. *Sex Crimes in History: Evolving Concepts...* 1966. NY. Matrix House. 1st thus. 323p. VG/dj. A25. $20.00

LEACH, Brownie. *Kentucky Derby Diamond Jubilee.* 1949. NY. 1st. 192p. lg 4to. F. A17. $25.00

LEACH, C. *Aids to Goatkeeping.* 1946 (1926). G+. E6. $12.00

LEACH, David G. *Rhododendrons of the World.* 1962. Allen Unwin. 4to. 544p. VG/torn. A22. $65.00

LEACH, Julian G. *Insect Transmission of Plant Diseases.* 1940. McGraw Hill. ils. 615p. F/dj. B26. $37.50

LEACH, Maria. *God Had a Dog.* 1961. Rutgers. 1st. VG/G. B5. $45.00

LEACH, Sally. *Scholar at Work, an Exhibit.* 1970. Austin. 1st. bl cloth. F. M24. $65.00

LEAF, Munro. *Arithmetic Can Be Fun.* 1949. Lippincott. stated 1st. 4to. VG. M5. $20.00

LEAF, Munro. *Manners Can Be Fun.* 1936. Lippincott. 31st imp. 45p. cloth. VG/dj. M20. $22.00

LEAF, Munro. *Story of Ferdinand.* 1936. Viking. 3rd. VG+/VG. M5. $42.00

LEAKEY, John. *West That Was.* 1967. Lincoln, NE. A19. $10.00

LEAR, Edward. *Book of Nonsense.* 1980. Viking/Met Mus Art. sm 4to. unp. F/G+ clip. C14. $20.00

LEAR, Edward. *Jumblies.* 1968. NY. Young Scott Books. 1st. ils/sgn Edward Gorey. tan pict cloth. dj. as new. R5. $45.00

LEAR, Edward. *Jumblies.* 1972. 2nd. ils Gorey. VG/VG. M17. $40.00

LEAR, Edward. *Le Hibou et la Poussiquette.* 1961. Little Brn. 1st. 31p. NF/VG clip. C14. $20.00

LEAR, Edward. *New Vestments.* 1970. NJ. Bradbury. 1st. ils Arnold Lobel. 32p. F/NF. D4. $35.00

LEAR, Edward. *Nonsense Songs.* nd. London/NY. Warne. ne. ils LL Brooke. unp. cloth. F/F. D4. $50.00

LEAR, Edward. *Owl & the Pussycat.* 1983. Macmillan. 1st. unp. NF/dj. M20. $25.00

LEAR, Edward. *Quangle Wangle's Hat.* 1969. Heinemann. 1st. ils Helen Oxenbury. 32p. VG+/VG+. D4. $65.00

LEAR, Edward. *Teapots & Quails.* 1953. MA. Harvard. 1st. ils. intro/edit Angus Davidson/Philip Hofer. VG+/dj. D4. $35.00

LEAR, Floyd Seyward. *Treason in Roman & Germanic Law, Collected Papers.* 1965. Austin. VG/dj. M11. $65.00

LEARNARD, Rachel. *Mrs Roo & the Bunnies.* 1953. Houghton Mifflin. ARC/1st. ils Tom Funk. 31p. F/NF. D4. $35.00

LEARY, Timothy. *Jail Notes.* 1970. NY. 1st. intro Allen Ginsberg. VG/VG. B5. $45.00

LEARY. *Book-Peddling Parson: Account of Life & Works of Mason Lock.* 1984. 158p. F/F. A4. $35.00

LEASON & SUTTON. *Big Book of Dogs.* nd (1952). Grosset Dunlap. 4to. unp. NF. C14. $12.00

LEAVITT, David. *Equal Affections.* 1989. Weidenfeld Nicholson. 1st. sgn. F/F. R14. $40.00

LEAVITT, David. *Family Dancing.* 1984. Knopf. 1st. sgn. F/F. L3. $125.00

LEAVITT, Gertrude Stevens. *Story of Frances E Willard.* 1905. Portland. HL Nelson. 1st. photos. 32p. VG+. A25. $22.00

LEAVITT, Robert Greenleaf. *Forest Trees of New England.* 1932. Jamaica Plain. Arnold Arboretum. 8vo. G+. A22. $15.00

LEBARON, Anthony; see Laumer, Keith.

LEBAS, F. *Rabbit: Husbandry, Health & Production.* 1986. Rome. ils. 235p. NF. S15. $13.50

LECKY, W.E.H. *History of Ireland in the 18th Century.* 1972. Chicago. 8vo. 494p. gilt bl/red cloth. F/dj. H13. $85.00

LEDERER, William J. *Mirages of Marriages.* 1968. Norton. 1st. 473p. NF/NF. W2. $55.00

LEDOUX, Louis. *Art of Japan.* 1927. NY. Japan Soc. 85p. VG. W3. $42.00

LEDYARD, Gleason H. *And to the Eskimos.* 1962. Chicago. 4th. 254p. F/dj. A17. $15.00

LEE, Anna. *Natural Foods Cookbook.* 1972. London. Hamlyn. VG/dj. A16. $7.00

LEE, Charles E. *Blue Riband.* ca 1935. London. Sampson Low. 67 halftones. VG. T7. $50.00

LEE, Fred J. *Casey Jones: True Story of John Luther Casey Jones.* 1939. Southern Pub. 1st. 298p. pict cloth. VG/dj. M20. $50.00

LEE, Frederic P. *Azalea Book.* 1958. Van Nostrand. 8vo. 324p. VG/torn. A22. $35.00

LEE, Frederic P. *Azalea Handbook.* 1953. Am Horticultural Soc. tall 8vo. cloth. VG/tattered. A22. $20.00

LEE, Gus. *China Boy.* 1991. Dutton. 1st. sgn. F/F. R14. $60.00

LEE, Hanna. *Memoir of Pierre Toussaint, Born a Slave in St Domingo.* 1854. Boston. Crosby Nichols. 2nd. 124p. NF. B4. $375.00

LEE, Harper. to *Kill a Mockingbird.* 1960. London. Heinemann. 1st Eng. NF/dj. B4. $500.00

LEE, Harper. to *Kill a Mockingbird.* 1993. Harper Collins. 35th Anniversary/later prt. inscr. F/F. A23. $250.00

LEE, Mary Catherine. *Lois Mallet's Dangerous Gift.* 1902. Houghton Mifflin. 1st. 116p. V3. $15.00

LEE, Mrs. N.K.M. *Cook's Own Book, Being Complete Culinary Encyclopedia.* 1972. NY. Arno. G/dj. A16. $10.00

LEE, Nathaniel. *Lee's Plays.* 1726-1734. London. 3 vol. leather. VG. A15. $50.00

LEE, Norman E. *Harvests & Harvesting Through the Ages.* 1960. London. ils. 208p. F/dj. B26. $20.00

LEE, Rebecca Lawrence. *Concha: My Dancing Saint.* 1966. Riverside, CA. 1st. 1/300. inscr/sgn/#d. xl. VG. O4. $25.00

LEE, Robert E. *Recollections & Letters of General Robert E Lee.* 1926. 471p. O8. $14.50

LEE, Robert. *Victory at Guadalcanal.* 1981. Novato. photos/map/index. 260p. VG/VG. S16. $17.50

LEE, Ruth Webb. *Antique Fakes & Reproductions.* 1966. Lee Publications. enlarged/revised 8th. 317p. gilt bl cloth. F/clip. H1. $45.00

LEE, Stan. *Bring on the Bad Guys.* 1976. 253p. F. M13. $16.00

LEE, Stan. *Marvel Masterworks, X-Men 1-10.* 1987. Marvel Comics. 1st. F/dj. M2. $35.00

LEE, Tanith. *Dreams of Dark & Light.* 1986. Arkham. 1st. collects 23 stories. F/F. T2. $45.00

LEE, Vincent. *Building of Sacsayhuaman & Other Papers.* 1987-89. Wilson, WY. 1st. sgn. 4to. 108p. wrp. F3. $25.00

LEE, Vincent. *Investigations in Bolivia.* 1992. Wilson, WY. 1st. sgn. 105p. wrp. F3. $25.00

LEE, Vincent. *Vira Vira: A New Chachapoyas Site.* 1993. Wilson, WY. sgn. 40p text+maps/photos. F3. $20.00

LEE, W. Storrs. *Great California Deserts.* 1963. Putnam. 1st. NF/VG clip. O4. $15.00

LEE, William F. *Stan Kenton, Artist in Rhythm.* 1980. Los Angeles. Creative Pr. 1st. 727p. VG/dj. M20. $35.00

LEECH, M. *Reveille in Washington.* 1941. 1st. 483p. O8. $9.50

LEECH, Samuel. *Thirty Years From Home; or, Voice From the Main Deck...* 1844. Boston. Tappan Dennet. 12mo. 305p. brn cloth. P4. $150.00

LEEDALE, G.F. *Euglenoid Flagellates.* 1967. Prentice Hall. 242p. dj. B1. $32.00

LEESE & LEESE. *Desert Plants: Cacti & Succulents in the Wild...* 1959. London. photos/drawings. 220p. VG. B26. $20.00

LEFANU, W.R. *Bio-Bibliography of Edward Jenner 1749-1823.* 1951. London. Harvey Blythe. 1st. 1/1000. 29 pl. 176p. NF. K3. $95.00

LEFCOURT, Peter. *Deal.* 1991. Random. 1st. F/F. M22. $20.00

LEFFINGWELL, William Bruce. *Shooting on Upland, Marsh & Stream.* 1890. Rand McNally. 1st. 473p. gilt bdg. VG. H7. $150.00

LEGGE, James. *Record of Buddhist Kingdoms: Being Account by Chinese Monk.* 1975 (1886). SF. rpt. notes/index. 123p. F/NF. W3. $48.00

LEGMAN, G. *Love & Death: Study in Censorship.* 1949. Breaking Point. 1st? 95p. G/wrp. A17. $15.00

LEGRAND, Edy. *Petite Histoire de Lafayette.* ca 1935. Paris. Tolmer. obl 4to. pict brd. VG. D1. $165.00

LEGSTRAND & ROLEN. *Long Pony Race.* 1966. Knopf. 1st Am. VG/G. O3. $10.00

LEHANE, Dennis. *Drink Before the War.* 1994. Harcourt Brace. 1st. sgn. F/F. D10. $60.00

LEHMANN, John. *Edward Lear & His World.* 1977. Scribner. 1st. sm 4to. bl brd. NF/dj. T5. $45.00

LEHY, Frank. *Notre Dame Football: The T Formation.* 1949. Prentice Hall. 1st. photos/diagrams. VG. P8. $25.00

LEIBER, Fritz. *Knight & Knave of Swords.* 1988. Morrow. 1st. F/dj. M2. $20.00

LEIBERT, Herman W. *Dr Johnson's First Book.* 1950. New Haven. Yale. 1/150. 8vo. F/heavy paper wrp. H13. $85.00

LEICHHARDT, F.W. Ludwig. *Letters of...* 1968. Cambridge. Hakluyt Soc. 8vo. 1175p. bl cloth. VG. P4. $70.00

LEICHMAN, Seymour. *Boy Who Could Sing Pictures.* 1968. Doubleday. 1st. sm 4to. VG/NF. C8. $35.00

LEIGH, Randolph. *Forgotten Waters: Adventures in Gulf of California.* 1941. Lippincott. 1st. VG. O4. $25.00

LEIGHTEN, Peter. *Moon Travelers.* nd. London. Oldbourne. 8vo. 240p. NF/dj. K3. $20.00

LEINSTER, Murray; see Jenkins, Will F.

LEIPOLD, L. Edmond. *Famous Scientists & Astronauts.* 1968 (1967). Minneapolis. TS Denison. 4th. 8vo. 80p. xl. K5. $14.00

LEIRIS, Galerie Louise. *Picasso.* 1960. France. self pub. French text. A19. $10.00

LEITER, S. *Art of Kabuki: Famous Plays in Performance.* 1979. CA U. photos/trans/bibliography/index. F/VG. W3. $38.00

LEITHAUSER, Brad. *Hence.* 1989. Knopf. 1st. NF/dj. M21. $20.00

LEITHAUSER, Joachim. *World Beyond the Horizon.* 1955. Knopf. 1st. 412p. dj. F3. $20.00

LEITNER, Irving. *Baseball Diamond in the Rough.* 1972. NY. 1st. VG/dj. B5. $30.00

LEJARD, Andre. *Art of the French Book, From Early Manuscripts to Present.* 1947. Paris. ils. 166p. G+. B18. $37.50

LEJEUNE, Anthony. *Gentlemen's Clubs of London.* 1979. photos. VG. M17. $25.00

LEM, Stanislaw. *Chain of Chance.* 1978. Harcourt. 1st. F/dj. M2. $15.00

LEMAITRE, Canon Georges. *Primeval Atom.* 1950. Van Nostrand. 186p. cloth. K5. $25.00

LEMAITRE, Georges. *Four French Novelists.* 1969. Kennikat. 419p. F. A17. $7.50

LEMAN, A.E. *Diseases of Swine.* 1986. IA State. 6th. 930p. cloth. F. B1. $60.00

LEMAN, Rhoda. *Book of the Night.* 1984. HRW. 1st. F/NF. M21. $25.00

LEMMON, Ken. *Cool Greenhouse Plants.* 1967. London. Garden BC. 192p. VG/dj. A10. $22.00

LEMOINE, Ann. *Wild Girl of the Wood.* nd (ca 1812). London. Roe Lemoine. Chapbook. 28p. Sawyer bdg. H13. $95.00

LEMPRIERE, J. *Universal Biography.* 1810. NY. Sargeant. 2 vol. 1st Am. thick tall 8vo. contemporary full calf. H13. $250.00

LENARD, Philipp. *Great Men of Science.* 1933. Macmillan. trans from 2nd German. 8vo. 389p. G. K5. $30.00

LENIN, N. *Imperialism: The State & Revolution.* 1926. Vanguard. VG/dj. V4. $30.00

LENIN, V.I. *Toward the Seizure of Power.* 1932. NY. Intern'l. 1st. 2 vol. F/dj. B2. $60.00

LENK, Torsten. *Flintlock: Its Origin & Development.* 1965. Bramhall. photos. VG/VG. M17. $40.00

LENNON, Florence Becker. *Victoria Through the Looking Glass: Life of Lewis Carroll.* 1945. S&S. 1st. 387p. F/G. H1. $18.00

LENNOX, Charlotte Ramsey. *Female Quixote; or, Adventures of Arabella.* 1810. London. 2 vol. new ed. 12mo. full tan calf/rebacked. H13. $395.00

LENOTRE, G. *Paris Revolutionnaire.* 1908. Paris. 4 vol. Premiere Serie. 12mo. ils. teg. 3-quarter red leather. H3. $150.00

LENSKI, Lois. *Cotton in My Sack.* 1949. Lippincott. 1st 191p. VG/G+. P2. $120.00

LENSKI, Lois. *I Like Winter.* (1950). NY. Walck. 24mo. unp. bl cloth. G+. T5. $35.00

LENSKI, Lois. *Journey Into Childhood: Autobiography of Lois Lenski.* 1972. Lippincott. 1st. 208p. VG/clip. M20. $25.00

LENSKI, Lois. *Little Airplane.* (1938). London. Oxford. 1st. 8vo. beige cloth. VG. D1. $60.00

LENSKI, Lois. *Surprise for Davy.* 1947. Oxford. 1st. 12mo. VG. M5. $55.00

LENSKI, Lois. *Susie Mariar.* (1939). Oxford. obl 8vo. unp. G. T5. $20.00

LENSKI, Louis. *Songs of Mr Small.* 1954. 1st. VG. M17. $25.00

LENSKI, R.C.H. *Interpretation of St John's Gospel.* 1956. Warburg. 1444p. G. B29. $9.50

LENT, Henry B. *Full Steam Ahead!* 1933. Macmillan. 1st. ils Earle Winslow. pict cloth. VG. C8. $40.00

LENTRICCHIA, Melissa. *No Guarantees.* 1990. Morrow. 1st. inscr. F/NF. R13. $40.00

LENTZ, Harold B. *Sleeping Beauty.* 1933. Bl Ribbon. 1 double-p popup at center. 8vo. mc pict brd. R5. $250.00

LENZ, Ellis Christian. *Rifleman's Progress.* 1946. Huntington, WV. Standard pub. 1st. 4to. 162p. F/VG. H7. $50.00

LENZ, Sidney. *Lenz on Bridge: Volume Two.* 1927. NY. 2nd. 456p. VG. S1. $15.00

LENZNER, R. *Great Getty: Life & Loves of J Paul Getty...* 1985. Crown. 283p. NF/G. D8. $22.00

LEONARD, Charles. *Stolen Squadron.* 1942. Doubleday Crime Club. 1st. F/dj. M15. $45.00

LEONARD, Elmore. *Bandits.* 1987. Arbor. 1st. sgn. F/NF. B2. $35.00

LEONARD, Elmore. *City Primeval. High Noon in Detroit.* 1980. Arbor. 1st. F/NF. Q1. $60.00

LEONARD, Elmore. *Double Dutch Treat.* 1986. Arbor. 1st. F/F. A20. $25.00

LEONARD, Elmore. *Dutch Treat.* 1977. Arbor. 1st. VG/VG. A20. $25.00

LEONARD, Elmore. *Fifty-Two Pickup.* 1974. Delacorte. 1st. VG/dj. M15. $150.00

LEONARD, Elmore. *Get Shorty.* 1990. Delacorte. 1st. F/F. from $25 to $30.00

LEONARD, Elmore. *Glitz.* 1985. Arbor. 1st. NF/NF. M22. $15.00

LEONARD, Elmore. *Glitz.* 1985. Mysterious. 1st. 1/500 special bdg. sgn. F/sans/case. M15. $60.00

LEONARD, Elmore. *Hombre.* 1989. Armchair Detective. 1st thus. M/dj. A18. $20.00

LEONARD, Elmore. *Killshot.* 1989. Arbor. 1st. VG+/NF. N4. $22.50

LEONARD, Elmore. *LaBrava.* 1983. Arbor. 1st. F/F. B35. $40.00

LEONARD, Elmore. *Maximum Bob.* 1991. Delacorte. 1st. F/F. B35. $25.00

LEONARD, Elmore. *Split Images.* 1981. NY. Arbor. 1st. F/F. M15. $65.00

LEONARD, Elmore. *Swag.* 1976. Delacorte. 1st. NF/dj. M25. $75.00

LEONARD, Elmore. *Touch.* 1987. Arbor. 1st. F/F. M22/P3. $20.00

LEONARD, Elmore. *Unknown Man No 89.* 1977. London. Secker Warburg. 1st Eng. F/dj. M15. $150.00

LEONARD, Elmore. *Unknown Man No 89.* 1993. Armchair Detective. 1/100. sgn/#d. F/case. M19. $50.00

LEONARD, George. *Ultimate Athlete.* 1975. Viking. 1st. ils. F/VG. P8. $17.50

LEONARD, Jonathan. *Ancient America.* 1967. Time. 1st. 4to. 192p. F3. $15.00

LEONARD, L.L. *International Regulation of Fisheries.* 1944. WA. Carnegie. ils/maps/figures. 201p. VG. M12. $22.50

LEONARDO, Richard. *History of Surgery.* 1943. NY. 1st. 100 pl. 504p. A13. $350.00

LEONIS, Shelia. *Thread in the Maze.* ca 1965. London. Rider. 1st. 12mo. 96p. NF/dj. W1. $12.00

LEOPOLD, Aldo. *Aldo Leopold's Wilderness: Selected Early Writings.* 1990. Harrisburg. 1st. ils. F/dj. M4. $18.00

LEOPOLD, Aldo. *Sand County Almanac, Etc.* 1949. Oxford. ils CW Schwartz. 226p. pict cloth. NF. M12. $125.00

LEOPOLD, Aldo. *Wildlife of Mexico.* 1959. Berkeley. ils CW Schwartz. 568p. cloth. xl. VG. M12. $60.00

LERICHE, Rene. *Surgery of Pain.* 1939. London. 1st. 512p. A13. $300.00

LERNER, J. *Review of Amino Acid Transport Processes in Animal Cells...* 1978. Orono. 234p. B1. $35.00

LEROY, L.W. *Biostratigraphy of the Majfi Section, Egypt.* 1953. GSA Memoir 54. 73p. cloth. F. D8. $16.00

LESBERG, Sandy. *Great Classic Recipes of Europe.* 1972. NJ. Prentice Hall. G/dj. A16. $20.00

LESBERG, Sandy. *Specialty of the House.* 1970. Prentice Hall. G/fair. A16. $15.00

LESCOVET. *Remonstrances Prononcees avx Ovvertvres Pvbliqves...* 1619. Paris. Cramoisy. 8vo. quarter vellum. R12. $350.00

LESIEUTRE, Alain. *Spirit & Splendour of Art Deco.* 1974. NY. Paddington. 1st. ils. 304p. VG/VG. B5. $37.50

LESLEY, Craig. *River Song.* 1989. Houghton Mifflin. 1st. sgn. M/dj. A18. $50.00

LESLEY, Craig. *Sky Fisherman.* 1995. Houghton Mifflin. 1st. sgn. M/dj. A18. $35.00

LESLIE, Eliza. *Directions for Cookery in Its Various Branches.* 1839. Phil. Carey Hart. 8th. 468p. modern lib buckram. B10. $250.00

LESLIE, Eliza. *Maid of Canal Street & the Bloxhams. By Miss Leslie.* 1851. Phil. Hart. 1st. 8vo. 115p. later calf-backed cloth. M1. $125.00

LESLIE, Eliza. *75 Receipts for Pastry, Cake, Sweetmeats.* 1835 (1827). G. E6. $150.00

LESLIE, Frank. *Report on the Fine Arts.* 1868. GPO. pres. folio. purple prt wrp. R12. $225.00

LESLIE, John. *Narrative of Discovery & Adventure in Polar Seas & Regions.* 1833. NY. Harper. ils/fld chart. 373p. full calf. T7. $115.00

LESLIE, R.F. *Miracle at Square Top Mountain.* 1979. Dutton. ils/maps. 243p. cloth/brd. F/VG. M12. $15.00

LESSA, William A. *Drake's Island of Thieves, Ethnological Sleuthing.* 1975. Honolulu. 1st. ils/maps/tables. 289p. NF/dj. P4. $30.00

LESSING, Doris. *Briefing for a Descent Into Hell.* 1971. London. Cape. 1st. sgn. F/clip. D10. $125.00

LESSING, Doris. *Fifth Child.* 1988. Knopf. 1st. NF/VG+. M21. $10.00

LESSING, Doris. *In Pursuit of the English.* 1961. S&S. 1st. sgn. author's 4th book pub in US. NF/VG. D10. $75.00

LESSING, Doris. *Memoirs of a Survivor.* 1975. Knopf. 1st Am. 8vo. F/dj. T10. $100.00

LESTER, Julius. *Falling Pieces of the Broken Sky.* 1990. NY. Arcade. 1st. rem mk. F/F. B4. $35.00

LESTER, Julius. *Long Journey Home: Stories From Black History.* 1972. 156p. VG/VG. A4. $75.00

LESTER, Pauline. *Marjorie Dean: College Freshman.* 1922. NY. AL Burt. 1st. ils. 278p. VG+. A25. $16.00

LESTER, Pauline. *Marjorie Dean: High School Senior.* 1917. AL Burt. 1st. ils. 302p. VG. A25. $15.00

LESTER, Pauline. *Marjorie Dean: High School Sophomore.* 1917. NY. AL Burt. 1st. 256p. VG/dj. A25. $20.00

LESY, Michael. *Wisconsin Death Trip.* 1973. NY. 1st. VG/VG. B5. $50.00

LETCHER, Owen. *Big Game Hunting in North-Eastern Rhodesia.* 1987. NY. rpt. F/F. S15. $12.00

LEUPOLD, H.C. *Exposition of Genesis. Vol 1: Chapters 1-19.* 1950. Baker. 578p. G. B29. $9.50

LEVANDER, F.W. *Total Solar Eclipse 1905.* 1906. London. Eyre Spottiswoode. 8vo. 64p. K5. $60.00

LEVEL, Maurice. *Tales of Mystery & Horror.* 1920. McBride. VG. M2. $32.00

LEVENSON, Sam. *Sex & the Single Child.* 1969. S&S. 1st. lg 8vo. VG+/VG. C8. $15.00

LEVERTOV, Denise. *Pig Dreams.* 1981. Countryman Pr. 1st. 47p. F/F. D4. $30.00

LEVI, Carlo. *Words Are Stones.* 1958. Farrar Straus. 1st. F/VG. M19. $25.00

LEVI & REGGE. *Dialoggo.* 1989. Princeton. 1st. F/clip. B35. $20.00

LEVIATAN. *Collection of References Pertaining to Miniature Books.* 1985. 1/500. 459 entries. 76p. F. A4. $85.00

LEVICK, James J. *Early Friends & Their Services in America.* 1883. Phil. WH Pile. 36p. V3. $20.00

LEVIEN, Michael. *Naval Surgeon: Voyages of Dr Edward H Cree, Royal Navy...* 1982. NY. 1st Am. 276p. A13. $45.00

LEVIN, Ira. *Boys From Brazil.* 1976. Random. 1st. NF/NF. M22. $50.00

LEVIN, Ira. *Rosemary's Baby.* 1967. Random. 1st. author's 2nd novel. F/dj. D10/H11. $100.00

LEVIN, Ira. *This Perfect Day.* 1970. Random. 1st. F/dj. M2. $25.00

LEVIN, Meyer. *Beginnings of Jewish Philosophy.* 1971. Behrman. ils. 192p. VG. S3. $25.00

LEVIN, Meyer. *Citizens.* 1940. Viking. 1st. NF/NF. B4. $200.00

LEVINE, Daniel. *Bird: Making of an American Sports Legend.* 1988. McGraw Hill. 1st. photos. F/F. P8. $25.00

LEVINE, Israel. *Francis Bacon (1561-1626).* 1925. London. Parsons. 1st. sm 8vo. 181p. VG/dj. K3. $12.00

LEVINE, Philip. *5 Detroits.* 1970. Unicorn. 1st. 1/500. F/sans. R14. $125.00

LEVINGER, Lee J. *Jewish Chaplain in France.* 1921. Macmillan. 220p. VG. S3. $25.00

LEVINSOHN, John L. *Frank Morrison Pixley of the Argonaut.* 1989. SF. BC of CA. 1/450. 8vo. gray linen. R3. $90.00

LEVINSON, Edward. *I Break Strikes! Technique of Pearl L Bergoff.* 1936. Robert McBride. 2nd. VG/VG. V4. $30.00

LEVISON, Eric. *Eye Witness.* 1921. Bobbs Merrill. 1st. F/VG. M15. $65.00

LEVITAN, Tina. *Laureates: Jewish Winners of the Nobel Prize.* 1960. Twayne. ils/biblio/index. 236p. VG/G. S3. $22.00

LEVORSEN, A. *Geology of Petroleum.* 1967. Freeman. 2nd. F/dj. D8. $20.00

LEVY, Barry. *Quakers & the American Family.* 1988. NY. Oxford. 1st. 340p. VG/dj. V3. $15.50

LEVY, Deborah. *Ophelia & the Great Idea.* 1989. NY. Viking. ARC. author's 1st story collection. F/F. w/promo material. R13. $25.00

LEVY, Ferdinand. *Flashes From the Dark.* 1941. Dublin. Sgn of 3 Candles. 1st. F/NF. B4. $225.00

LEVY, Newman. *Sandy MacPherson: Book Collector.* 1940. 1/750. sgn. wrp. K3. $15.00

LEWANDOWSKY, Max Heinrich. *Untersuchungen Uber die Leitungsbahnen...* 1904. Jena. Gustav Fischer. folio. assn copy. 13 photo pl. G/cloth case. G1. $250.00

LEWIN, Michael Z. *Hard Line.* 1982. Morrow. 1st. F/F. B2. $35.00

LEWIN, R.S. *Elements of Mining.* 1941. John Wiley. 2nd/2nd prt. 579p. G. D8. $18.00

LEWIN, Ralph A. *Genetics of Algae.* 1976. Berkeley. ils. 360p. F/dj. B26. $37.50

LEWIN, Ronald. *Rommel as Military Commander.* 1968. Batsford/Van Nostrand. 1st. 262p. VG/dj. M20. $15.00

LEWINSOHN, Richard. *Science, Prophecy & Prediction.* 1961. NY. Bell. 318p. xl. dj. K3. $15.00

LEWIS, Alfred Henry. *Confessions of a Detective.* 1906. NY. as Barnes. 1st. F/case. M15. $75.00

LEWIS, Arthur H. *It Was Fun While It Lasted.* 1973. Trident. 1st. F/F. B4. $85.00

LEWIS, Bernard. *Islam & the Arab World.* 1976. Knopf/Am Heritage. 1st Am. 360p. VG/torn. W1. $65.00

LEWIS, C.S. *All My Road Before Me: The Diary, 1922-27.* edit W Hooper. VG/VG. M17. $25.00

LEWIS, C.S. *Case for Christianity.* 1974. Macmillan. 56p. VG. B29. $7.50

LEWIS, C.S. *Christian Behaviour: Further Series of Broadcast Talks.* 1943. Geoffrey Bles. 1st. F/VG. A18. $50.00

LEWIS, C.S. *English Literature in the 16th Century Excluding Drama.* 1954. Oxford. 1st. F/VG. A18. $75.00

LEWIS, C.S. *Horse & His Boy.* 1956 (1954). London. Bles. 2nd. sm 8vo. VG. C8. $35.00

LEWIS, C.S. *Last Battle.* 1962. Macmillan. F/dj. M2. $17.00

LEWIS, C.S. *Letters to an American Lady.* 1967. Eerdmans. 1st Am. F/clip. A18. $35.00

LEWIS, C.S. *Letters to Malcolm: Chiefly on Prayer.* 1964. Geoffrey Bles. 1st. F/clip. A18. $35.00

LEWIS, C.S. *Magician's Nephew.* 1960 (1955). London. Bodley Head. 3rd. sm 8vo. NF/G+. C8. $35.00

LEWIS, C.S. *Prince Caspian: Return to Narnia.* 1951. Geoffrey Bles. 1st. ils Pauline Baynes. VG. A18. $150.00

LEWIS, C.S. *Reflections on the Psalms.* 1958. Geoffrey Bles. 1st. F/F. A18. $60.00

LEWIS, C.S. *Screwtape Letters & Screwtape Proposes a Toast.* 1961 (1942). 1st thus. lg 12mo. VG/dj. C8. $45.00

LEWIS, C.S. *Silver Chair.* 1961 (1953). Macmillan. 3rd. 8vo. 208p. VG/VG. T5. $45.00

LEWIS, C.S. *Surprised by Joy: The Shape of My Early Life.* 1955. Geoffrey Bles. 1st. F/clip. A18. $125.00

LEWIS, C.S. *Voyage of the Dawn Trader.* 1960 (1952). Macmillan. 2nd. 210p. bl cloth. VG/G. T5. $65.00

LEWIS, C.S. *Voyage of the Dawn Trader.* 1970 (1952). Macmillan. 9th. NF/VG+. C8. $35.00

LEWIS, Cecil Day. *Otterbury Incident.* 1948. Putnam. 1st. ils Ardizzone. 148p. VG/VG. P2. $70.00

LEWIS, Charles Lee. *Famous Old-World Sea Fighters.* 1929. Boston/London. ils. 362p. T7. $35.00

LEWIS, D.B. Wyndham. *Francois Villon.* 1928. Coward McCann. 1st Am. gilt bdg. NF/dj. Q1. $40.00

LEWIS, David. *We, the Navigators.* 1972. Honolulu. 345p. bl cloth. VG. P4. $45.00

LEWIS, Deborah; see Grant, Charles L.

LEWIS, Edward R. Jr. *Reflections of Canton in Pharmacist's Show Globe.* 1967. Canton. self pub. sgn. 256p. F/VG. B11. $65.00

LEWIS, G.R. *Stannaries: A Study of Medieval Tin Miners of Cornwall...* 1965 (1908). Truro. Bradford Barton Ltd. facsimile. M11. $75.00

LEWIS, George Andrew. *Origin & Treatment of Stammering.* 1910. Akron. 8th. 199p. G. A17. $15.00

LEWIS, H. Spencer. *Thousand Years of Yesterday.* 1935. Amorc. VG. M2. $22.00

LEWIS, Henry. *Valley of the Mississippi Illustrated.* 1967. Minneapolis. 1/2000. ils/pl. 423p. F/dj. M4/O7. $60.00

LEWIS, Isabel Martin. *Handbook of Solar Eclipses.* 1925. NY. Duffield. 1st. ils. VG/torn. K3. $25.00

LEWIS, Jerry D. *Tales of Our People: Great Stories of the Jew in America.* 1969. Bernard Geis. 332p. VG/dj. S3. $23.00

LEWIS, John N.C. *Small Boat Conversions.* 1951. London. Hart Davis. ils/plans/photos. 207p. T7. $25.00

LEWIS, Lange. *Juliet Dies Twice.* 1943. Bobbs Merrill. 1st. NF. M25. $35.00

LEWIS, Lange. *Passionate Victims.* 1952. Bobbs Merrill. 1st. VG/rpr. M25. $45.00

LEWIS, Lloyd. *Sherman: Fighting Prophet.* 1932. Harcourt Brace. 1st. 690p. VG/dj. M20. $40.00

LEWIS, Oscar. *Death in the Sanchez Family.* 1969. Random. 1st. 8vo. F/NF. T10. $35.00

LEWIS, Oscar. *Life in a Mexican Village: Tepoztlan Restudied.* 1951. Urbana. 2nd. 512p. F3. $15.00

LEWIS, Oscar. *Sacramento River.* nd. HRW. 1st. ils Michael Hampshire. NF/VG clip. O4. $15.00

LEWIS, Preston. *Lady & Doc Holliday.* 1989. Diamonds. 197p. as new/dj. J2. $95.00

LEWIS, Ralph. *Inductive Preaching: Helping People Listen.* 1983. Crossway. 223p. G/dj. B29. $7.50

LEWIS, Richard. *In a Spring Garden.* 1965. Dial. 1st. ils Ezra Jack Keats. 32p. cloth. NF/dj. D4. $35.00

LEWIS, Richard. *Still Waters of the Air: Poems by 3 Modern Spanish Poets.* 1970. NY. Dial. 1st. ils/sgn bookplate Ed Young. F/F. D4. $25.00

LEWIS, Richard. *There Are Two Lives: Poems by Children of Japan.* 1970. S&S. 1st. trans Kimura. F/F. W3. $36.00

LEWIS, Shari. *One-Minute Greek Myths.* 1987. Doubleday. 1st. 48p. F. C14. $10.00

LEWIS, Sinclair. *Ann Vickers.* 1933. Doubleday Doran. 1st. 1/2350 on rag paper. 562p. cloth. VG+/dj. M20. $185.00

LEWIS, Sinclair. *Bethel Merraday.* 1940. NY. 1st. VG/VG. B5. $40.00

LEWIS, Sinclair. *Cass Timberlane.* 1945. Random. 1st. F/VG. M19. $35.00

LEWIS, Sinclair. *Dodsworth.* 1929. Harcourt Brace. 1st. F/G. M23. $200.00

LEWIS, Sinclair. *Elmer Gantry.* 1927. NY. Harcourt. 1st. 8vo. cloth/bl brd. G. M23. $50.00

LEWIS, Sinclair. *God-Seeker.* 1949. Random. 1st. F/VG. M19. $45.00

LEWIS, Sinclair. *It Can't Happen Here.* 1935. Doubleday Doran. 1st. 458p. VG+/dj. M20. $30.00

LEWIS, Sinclair. *Keep Out of the Kitchen.* 1929. ARC (of article for *Cosmopolitan*). 34p. bl brd. VG. M20. $425.00

LEWIS, Sinclair. *Man From Main Street.* 1953. Random. 1st. 317p. VG/dj. M20. $35.00

LEWIS, Sinclair. *Man Who Knew Coolidge.* 1928. Harcourt Brace. 1st. NF/VG. M23. $100.00

LEWIS, Sinclair. *Prodical Parents.* 1938. Doubleday Doran. 1st. VG/VG. M19. $45.00

LEWIS, Sinclair. *World So Wide.* 1951. Random. 1st. NF/NF. B35. $30.00

LEWIS, Thomas. *Pain.* 1942. Macmillan. 1st Am. 192p. panelled pebbled red buckram. G1. $75.00

LEWIS, Thomas. *Vascular Disorders of the Limbs.* 1936. London. 1st. 111p. A13. $75.00

LEWIS, Wilmarth Sheldon. *Three Tours Through London...1748-1776.* 1941. Yale. sgn. ils. VG. M17. $20.00

LEWIS, Wilmarth. *Collector's Progress.* 1951. Knopf. 1st. ils. VG/dj. K3. $25.00

LEWIS & LEWIS. *Jayhawker: A Play.* 1935. Doubleday. 1st. 163p. VG/dj. M20. $125.00

LEWIS & LITAI. *China Builds the Bomb.* 1991. Stanford. rpt. M/wrp. K3. $20.00

LEWIS & MURAKAMI. *R MacDonald: Narrative of His Early Life on the Columbia...* 1923. Spokane. 1st. 1/1000. 8vo. 333p. red cloth. NF. P4. $250.00

LEWIS & PACELLA. *Modern Trends in Child Psychiatry.* 1945. NY. Internat U. 1st. ils. 341p. VG+. A25. $20.00

LEWIS & SCHARY. *Storm in the West.* 1963. Stein Day. 1st. 192p. VG/dj. M20. $45.00

LEWISOHN, Ludwig. *Last Days of Shylock.* 1931. Harper. 1st. 221p. VG. S3. $30.00

LEY, Willy. *Conquest of Space.* 1950. Viking. VG. M2. $20.00

LEY, Willy. *Events in Space.* 1969. McKay. 8vo. 180p. dj. K5. $13.00

LEY, Willy. *Harnessing Space.* 1963. Macmillan. 8vo. 314p. VG/dj. K5. $15.00

LEY, Willy. *Rockets, Missiles & Men in Space.* 1968. Viking. sm 4to. 557p. xl. dj. K5. $20.00

LEYARD, John. *Journal of Capt Cook's Last Voyage...* 1963. Chicago. Quadrangle. facsimile. F. O7. $55.00

LEYDET, Francois. *Coyote: Defiant Sondog of the West.* 1977. OK U. 224p. F/F. S15. $25.00

LEYDET, Francois. *Time & the River Flowing.* 1968. Ballantine/Sierra Club. 8vo. 160p. VG/wrp. F7. $12.00

LEYMARIE, Jean. *Fauvism.* 1959. d'Art Albert Skira. 71 tipped-in mc pl. F/F. H1. $47.50

LI, H.L. *Trees of Pennsylvania, the Atlantic States & Lake States.* 1972. Phil. 8vo. 276p. F/wrp. B1. $20.00

LI CHIIAO-P'ING. *Chemical Arts of Old China.* 1948. Easton, PA. Journal Chemical Ed. 1st. tall 8vo. 215p. xl. VG. H1. $35.00

LIANG, Yen. *Tommy & Dee-Dee.* 1953. Oxford. 1st. sq 8vo. F/VG. M5. $35.00

LIBBY, Bill. *Great American Race Drivers.* 1970. Cowles. photos/records/stats. VG/G+. P8. $45.00

LIBBY, Bill. *We Love You Lakers.* 1972. Sports Magazine Pr. 1st. photos. VG+. P8. $15.00

LIBBY & WEST. *Basketball My Way.* 1973. Prentice Hall. 1st. photos. VG/G+. P8. $30.00

LICHAUCO, Alejandro. *Lichauco Paper: Imperialism in the Philippines.* 1973. Monthly Review. 1st. 111p. cloth. M/VG. P1. $8.00

LICHINE, Alex. *Wines of France.* 1951. Knopf. 1st. 316p. VG/G+. B10. $45.00

LICHT, Hans. *Sexual Life in Ancient Greece.* 1956. London. Routledge Kegan. 8th. photos. 557p. VG. A25. $20.00

LICHTENBERG, G.G. *Lichtenberg Reader.* 1959. trans Mautner/Hatfield. VG/VG. M17. $17.50

LICHTENBERG, Jacqueline. *Unto Zeor, Forever.* 1978. Doubleday. 1st. NF/dj. M2. $20.00

LIDA. *Bourru, L'Ours Brun.* 1936. Flammarion. Albums du Pere Castor. ils Rojankovsky. VG. M5. $55.00

LIDA. *Martin Pecheur.* 1938. Flammarion. ils Rojankovsky. obl 8vo. VG. M5. $42.00

LIDA. *Spiky the Hedgehog.* 1938. Harper. 1st. sq 4to. VG+/dj. P2. $75.00

LIDDEL-HART, B.H. *Rommel Papers.* 1953. NY. fld maps/index. 454p. VG/torn. S16. $35.00

LIDDELL & LIDDELL. *Greek-English Lexicon: A Supplement.* 1968. Oxford. edit EA Barber. 153p. VG. B29. $30.00

LIDDIC & HARBAUGH. *Camp on Custer, Transcribing the Custer Myth.* 1995. Clark. 1/500. sgn Liddic. 189p. as new. J2. $325.00

LIDE & JOHANSES. *Thord Firetooth.* 1937. Lee Shepard. 1st. 236p. VG/G. P2. $20.00

LIDELL, John A. *Treatise on Apoplexy, Cerebral Hemorrhage, Cerebral...* 1990. NY. Classics Neurology/Neurosurgery Lib. facsimile. G1. $65.00

LIDTKE, Vernon L. *Alternative Culture: Socialist Labor in Imperial Germany.* 1985. Oxford. 1st. VG/VG. V4. $25.00

LIE, F. *Military History of Modern China 1924-49.* 1965. Princeton. 1st. F/F. E6. $18.00

LIEBERMAN, William S. *Nelson A Rockefeller Collection: Masterpieces of Modern Art.* 1981. NY. Hudson Hills. photos Lee Boltin. 255p. cloth. dj. D2. $65.00

LIEBHERR, James K. *Zoogeography of Caribbean Insects.* 1988. Cornell. 285p. F. S15. $20.00

LIEBIG, Justus. *Address to Agriculturists of Great Britain.* 1845. Liverpool. Baines. 32p. wrp. A10. $25.00

LIEBKNECHT, Karl. *Briefe aus Dem Felde, aus der Untersuchungshaft...* 1919. Berlin. Wochenschrift Die Aktion. 1st. VG. B2. $125.00

LIEBLING, A.J. *Normandy Revisited.* 1958. S&S. 1st. 243p. VG/dj. M20. $8.00

LIFF, Flora Gregg. *Peoples of the Blue Water.* 1954. Harper. 1st. 271p. VG/G+. F7. $27.50

LIFTON, B.J. *Place Called Hiroshima.* 1985. Tokyo. 1st. ils E Hosoe. F/dj. K3. $20.00

LIGHTMAN, Alan. *Einstein's Dreams.* 1993. Pantheon. 1st. inscr. F/F. B2. $75.00

LIGHTNER, Otto. *History of Business Depressions.* 1932. NY. 1st. VG. B5. $25.00

LIGHTNER, Theodore A. *Highlights of the Culbertson System.* 1931. NY. 1st. 238p. VG. S1. $15.00

LIGOTTI, Thomas. *Nocturary.* 1994. Carroll Graf. 1st Am. F/NF. R10. $10.00

LIKINS, Mrs. J.W. *Six Years' Experience as a Book Agent in California.* 1992. SF. BC of CA. tall 8vo. ils. terra-cotta cloth. R12. $50.00

LIKINS, William M. *Trail of the Serpent.* 1928. Uniontown, PA. Watchman. 1st. 123p. stiff prt wrp. M8. $250.00

LILIENTHAL, Alfred H. *There Goes the Middle East.* 1957. NY. Devin Adair. 1st. 8vo. 12 pl. 300p. VG. W1. $12.00

LILIENTHAL, Howard. *Thoracic Surgery: Surgical Treatment of Thoracic Disease.* 1925. Phil. 1st. 2 vol. A13. $250.00

LILLIGRIDGE, Will. *Ben Blair.* 1907. NY. AL Burt. A19. $25.00

LILLYS, William. *Persian Miniatures: Story of Rustam.* 1958. Rutland/Tokyo. Art Treasures of Asia series. VG. W3. $28.00

LIMNELIUS, George. *Medbury Fort Murder.* 1929. Doubleday Crime Club. 1st Am. F/dj. M15. $90.00

LIMOJON DE SAINT-DIDIER. *La Ville et la Republique de Vnise.* 1680. Lyne. 12mo. vellum. R12. $450.00

LINCOLN, Abraham. *Addresses of Abraham Lincoln.* 1929. Kingsport, TN. 22x16mm. 139p. aeg. gilt red leather. B24. $150.00

LINCOLN, Abraham. *Discoveries & Inventions: A Lecture...1860.* 1915. SF. John Howell. 1/1000. 24p. gilt brd. D11. $30.00

LINCOLN, Abraham. *His Talk With Lincoln.* 1922. Riverside. 1/530. 33p. F. O8. $27.50

LINCOLN, Abraham. *President's Words*. 1865. Boston. Walker Fuller. 186p. F. O8. $21.50

LINCOLN, Almira H. *Familiar Lectures on Botany...* 1829. Hartford. Huntington. 1st. 338p. tree calf. A10. $95.00

LINCOLN, Joseph. *Back Numbers*. 1932. NY. 1st. VG/VG. B5. $45.00

LINCOLN, Joseph. *Old Home House*. 1907. NY. 1st. VG. B5. $55.00

LINCOLN, Joseph. *Storm Girl*. 1937. NY. 1st. sgn pres. VG/VG. B5. $35.00

LINDBERG. *Annotated McGuffey, Selections From...Readers 1836-1920*. 1976. 4to. ils. 380p. xl. VG/VG. A4. $50.00

LINDBERGH, Anne Morrow. *Flower & the Nettle: Diaries & Letters 1936-39*. 1976. Harcourt. 1st. 605p. white cloth/bl spine. as new/dj. B22. $12.00

LINDBERGH, Anne Morrow. *Gifts From the Sea*. 1955. Pantheon. 1st. F/F case. B35. $55.00

LINDBERGH, Anne. *Three Lives to Live*. 1992. Little Brn. 1st. sm 8vo. NF/NF. C8. $30.00

LINDBERGH, Charles A. *Of Flight & Life*. 1948. Scribner. 1st. VG/dj. B4. $85.00

LINDBERGH, Charles A. *We*. 1927. Putnam. 1st trade. VG/VG. B4. $150.00

LINDBERGH, Charles. *We*. 1927. Scribner. 1st. VG/dj/box. B5. $50.00

LINDBURG, D.C. *Macaques*. 1980. Van Nostrand. 8vo. 384p. F/F. B1. $25.00

LINDEMAN, E.B. *Space: A New Direction for Mankind*. 1969. Harper. sgn. F/dj. M2. $15.00

LINDER. *History of the Writings of Beatrix Potter*. 1979. ils. 472p. F/F. A4. $165.00

LINDER, Kurt. *Hunting Book of Wolfgang Birkner*. 1969. Winchester. 1/250. facsimile. plates loose as issued. box w/20p booklet. B24. $200.00

LINDGREN, Astrid. *Springtime in Noisy Village*. 1966. Viking. 1st Am. sm 4to. VG+/G+. C8. $35.00

LINDGREN & WILDES. *Century of Electrical Engineering & Computer Science at MIT*. 1985. Cambridge, MA. 1st. ils. 4to. 423p. VG/dj. K3. $25.00

LINDLEY, Harlow. *History of the Ordinance of 1787 & Old Northwest Territory*. 1937. Marietta. 95p. VG/wrp. B18. $15.00

LINDMAN, M. *Snipp, Snapp, Snurr & the Magic Horse*. 1933. Whitman. 1st. 4to. cloth. VG. M5. $60.00

LINDOP, Audrey. *Sight Unseen*. 1969. Doubleday. 1st. F/dj. M2. $13.00

LINDSAY, Alexander J. *Survey & Excavations North & East of Navajo Mountain...* 1968. Flagstaff. ils/79 tables. 399p. F/orange wrp. F7. $45.00

LINDSAY, Cynthia. *Dear Boris: Life of William Henry Pratt, aka Boris Karloff*. 1975. Knopf. photos. NF/dj. C9. $50.00

LINDSAY, Vachel. *General William Booth Enters Heaven & Other Poems*. 1916 (1913). Macmillan. rpt. sgn/dtd 1916. VG+. B4. $85.00

LINDSAY, Vachel. *Springfield Town Is Butterfly Town...* 1969. Kent State. 1st. ils. pref Louis Untermeyer. unp. F/F. D4. $125.00

LINDSAY & MAMET. *Owl: Story for Children*. 1987. NY. Kipling. 1st. ils Stephen Alcorn. F/NF. R13. $25.00

LINDSELL, Harold. *Battle for the Bible*. 1976. Zondervan. 218p. VG/dj. B29. $8.00

LINDSEY, A.A. *Natural Areas in Indiana & Their Preservation*. 1969. Purdue. 594p. xl. NF. S15. $17.00

LINDSEY, David. *Cold Mind*. 1983. Harper Row. 1st. NF/F. A20. $35.00

LINDSEY, David. *Heat From Another Sun*. 1984. Harper Row. 1st. F/F. N4. $30.00

LINDSEY, David. *Heat From Another Sun*. 1984. Harper Row. 1st. sgn. VG/VG. A23. $42.00

LINDSEY, David. *Spinal*. 1986. Atheneum. 1st. NF/F. A20. $30.00

LINDSEY, Robert. *Gathering of Saints*. 1988. S&S. 1st. 397p. VG/VG. J2. $85.00

LINEBARGER, Paul. *Instrumentality of Mankind*. 1989. Gollancz. F/dj. P3. $30.00

LINEBARGER, Paul. *Quest of the Three Worlds*. 1989. Gollancz. 1st. F/dj. P3. $25.00

LINEBARGER, Paul. *Rediscovery of Man*. 1988. Gollancz. 1st. F/dj. P3. $30.00

LINFORTH, James. *Route From Liverpool to Great Salt Lake Valley*. (1855). Los Angeles. Westernlore. facsimile. 1/350. fld map. 120p. VG/dj. K7. $145.00

LING, Max Freedom. *Growing Into the Light*. 1955. DeVorss. 1st. 177p. F. H1. $20.00

LINGENFELTER, Richard E. *Presses of the Pacific Islands 1817-1867: A History...* 1967. LA. Plantin. 1/500. photos/woodcuts/fld map. 131p. D11. $75.00

LINGO, Ada E. *Murder in Texas*. 1935. Houghton Mifflin. 1st. inscr. F/clip. M15. $125.00

LININGTON, Elizabeth. *Greenmask!* 1964. Harper. 1st. author's 1st book. F/NF. M19. $45.00

LININGTON, Elizabeth. *Something Wrong*. 1967. Harper Row. 1st. NF/NF. M19. $25.00

LINK, P.S. *Basic Petroleum Geology*. 1987. OGCI Pub. 493 figures. 425p. F/dj. D8. $30.00

LINKE, Lilo. *Peoples of the Amazon*. 1965. London. Adventurers Club. 189p. dj. F3. $20.00

LINKLATER, Eric. *Voyage of the Challenger*. 1972. Doubleday. ils/photos. 288p. VG/dj. P4/S15. $30.00

LINSDALE, Jean. *Natural History of Magpies*. 1937. Cooper Ornithological Club. ils. 234p. F. S15. $40.00

LINTON, Calvin D. *Bicentennial Almanac*. 1975. Thomas Nelson. dj. A19. $35.00

LIONNI, Leo. *Alphabet Tree*. 1968. Pantheon. 1st. 4to. unp. VG/G+. T5. $32.00

LIONNI, Leo. *Fish Is Fish*. 1970. Pantheon. 1st. ils. VG/G+. P2. $30.00

LIPMAN, Jean. *American Folk Painters of Three Centuries*. 1980. 1st. ils. F/F. S13. $55.00

LIPMAN, Jean. *Rufus Porter: Rediscovered Artist, Inventor, Journalist*. 1980. NY. Potter/Crown. photos/ils/genealogy/checklist. 212p. cloth. dj. D2. $65.00

LIPMAN & WINCHESTER. *Flowering of American Folk Art 1776-1876*. 1974. ils. VG/VG. M17. $45.00

LIPOWSKI, Z.J. *Delirium: Acute Brain Failure in Man*. 1980. Springfield, IL. Chas Thomas. thick 8vo. 568p. VG/worn. G1. $50.00

LIPP & VON REIS. *New Plant Sources of Drugs & Foods From NY Botanical...* 1982. Cambridge. Harvard. 1st. 8vo. 363p. F/dj. A22. $25.00

LIPPINCOTT, David. *Salt Mine*. 1979. Viking. 1st. NF/F. H11. $15.00

LIPPINCOTT, Mary S. *Life & Letters of Mary S Lippincott*. 1893. Phil. WH Pile. 294p. V3. $12.00

LIPSCHITZ, Max A. *Faith of a Hassid*. 1967. NY. Jonathan David. ils Steinsnyder/Yanich. 346p. VG/G+. S3. $30.00

LIPSCOMB, Ken. *Duke Casanova*. 1958. NY. Exposition. 1st. F/NF. B4. $125.00

LIPSON. *NY Times, Parent's Guide to Best Books for Children*. 1988. 4to. ils. 421p. F/F. A4. $45.00

LIPTON, Morris A. *Psychopharmacology: Generation of Progress*. 1978. NY. Raven. 1732p. bl-gr cloth. G1. $50.00

LIPTZIN, S. *Germany's Stepchildren*. 1944. 1st. VG/VG. E6. $15.00

LISH, Gordon. *Dear Mr Capote*. 1983. HRW. 1st. F/F. B35. $35.00

LISH, Gordon. *Dear Mr Capote*. 1983. HRW. 1st. sgn. author's 1st book. F/F. L3. $125.00

LISH, Gordon. *Mourner at the Door.* 1988. Viking. 1st. F/F. B35. $25.00

LISH, Gordon. *What I Know So Far.* 1984. HRW. 1st. F/F. R14. $25.00

LISS, Howard. *Strange But True Hockey Stories.* 1972. Random. Pro Hockey Lib series. photos. VG. P8. $10.00

LISTER, Raymond. *Craftsman in Metal.* 1968. as Barnes. 1st Am. 208p. VG+/dj. M20. $15.00

LISTER & LISTER. *Those Who Came Before: SW Archeology in National Park...* 1983. AZ U. 1st. ils/bibliography/index. 184p. B19. $45.00

LISTON, Robert. *Elements of Surgery.* 1837. Phil. 1st Am. 540p. full leather. A13. $200.00

LITTAUER, Vladimir S. *Development of Modern Riding.* 1991. Howell. 1st. VG/VG. O3. $25.00

LITTLE, George. *American Cruisers Own Book.* 1859. Phil. JB Smith. 384p. emb cloth. P4. $75.00

LITTLE, Jean. *When the Pie Was Opened.* 1968. Little Brn. 1st. 83p. cloth. NF/dj. D4. $25.00

LITTLE, W.J. *On the Nature & Treatment of Deformities of Human Frame...* 1993. NY. Classics Neurology/Neurosurgery Lib. facsimile. G1. $75.00

LITTLE & WADSWORTH. *Common Trees of Puerto Rico & the Virgin Islands.* 1964. USDA. 548p. VG. B1. $68.00

LITTLEJOHN, D. *Hitler Youth.* 1987. SC. ils. 377p. VG/VG. S16. $22.50

LITTLER, Gene. *Real Score.* 1976. Waco. Word. 1st. inscr. VG/VG. A23. $50.00

LITTLETON, Thomas. *Littleton's Tenures, in French & English.* 1671. London. John Streater/James Flesher. contemporary calf. M11. $850.00

LITVAG, Irving. *Master of Sunnybank: Biography of Albert Payson Terhune.* 1977. Harper Row. 1st. VG/dj. M20. $40.00

LIVEING, Edward. *On Megrim, Sick-Headache & Some Allied Disorders...* 1986. Birmingham. Classics Neurology/Neurosurgery Lib. facsimile. G1. $85.00

LIVELY, Penelope. *Moon Tiger.* 1988. Grove. 1st Am. F/F. R13/R14. $25.00

LIVELY, Penelope. *Next to Nature, Art.* 1982. Heinemann. 1st. F/F. A24. $45.00

LIVELY, Penelope. *Pack of Cards.* 1989. NY. Grove. 1st Am. F/F. R14. $20.00

LIVELY, Penelope. *Passing On.* 1990. NY. 1st Am. F/dj. R13. $15.00

LIVELY, Penelope. *Revenge of Samuel Stokes.* 1981. London. Heinemann. 1st. F/NF. R13. $25.00

LIVERMOORE, Mary. *My Story of the War.* nd. np. 1st ed. mc pl of Civil War battle flags. F. O8. $22.50

LIVERSIDGE, Douglas. *Prince Charles: Monarch in the Making.* 1975. London. Barker. 1st. F/F. T12. $35.00

LIVERSIDGE, Douglas. *Whale Killers.* 1963. London. Jarrolds. ils. 191p. dj. T7. $24.00

LIVINGSTON, Armstrong. *Monster in the Pool.* 1929. AL Burt. F/NF. M2. $25.00

LIVINGSTON, F.V. *Bibliography of the Works of Rudyard Kipling.* 1927. NY. Edgar Wells. 1st. teg. gilt brn cloth. F. M24. $75.00

LIVINGSTON, Myra. *Child as Poet: Myth or Reality?* 1984. Boston. Horn Book. 1st. inscr. 354p. F/F. D4. $30.00

LIVINGSTON, Myra. *Higgledy-Piggledy.* 1986. NY. McElderry. 1st. inscr. ils Peter Sis. 32p. F/F. D4. $35.00

LIVINGSTON, Myra. *Learical Lexicon.* 1985. Atheneum. 1st. sgn. 64p. F/F. D4. $30.00

LIVINGSTON, Myra. *Listen, Children, Listen.* 1972. HBJ. 1st. 96p. F/F. D4. $35.00

LIVINGSTON, Myra. *Way Things Are & Other Poems.* 1974. Atheneum. 1st. 40p. NF/NF. D4. $30.00

LIVINGSTON, Myra. *4-Way Stop & Other Poems.* 1976. Atheneum. 1st. 40p. F/F. D4. $30.00

LIVINGSTON & WEST. *Hybrids & Hybridizers.* 1978. Newton Square, PA. ils/photos. 256p. F/dj. B26. $29.00

LIVINGSTONE, David. *Livingstone's Travel & Researches in South Africa...* 1859. Phil. Bradley. 8vo. 440p. cloth. G. W1. $28.00

LLOYD, B.E. *Lights & Shades in San Francisco.* 1876. SF. AL Bancroft. 1st. thick 4to. ils. aeg. gilt blk calf. F. R3. $600.00

LLOYD, Hugh. *Hal Keen: Copperhead Trail Mystery (#3).* 1930s. Grosset Dunlap. 218p. orange cloth. VG/dj (lists 6 titles). M20. $60.00

LLOYD, J. Ivester. *Beagling.* 1954. London. Herbert Jenkins. 1st. VG/G. O3. $45.00

LLOYD, J.W. *Muskmelon Production.* 1928. Orange Judd. 12mo. 10 pl. 126p. B1. $14.00

LLOYD & LLOYD. *Lloyd on Lloyd.* 1985. Beaufort. 1st. sgn. A23. $48.00

LOBECK, A.K. *Geomorphology: An Introduction...* 1939. NY. McGraw Hill. 1st/7th imp. 731p. VG. D8. $35.00

LOBEL, Arnold. *Comic Adventures of Mother Hubbard & Her Dog.* 1968. Bradbury. 1st. 32p. F/F. D4. $35.00

LOBEL, Arnold. *Days With Frog & Toad.* 1979. Harper. 1st. 8vo. NF/VG. C8. $50.00

LOBEL, Arnold. *Gregory Griggs & Other Nursery Rhyme People.* 1978. Greenwillow. 1st. sgn pres+sgn drawing on title p. cloth. dj. R5. $175.00

LOBEL, Arnold. *Gregory Griggs & Other Nursery Rhyme People.* 1978. Greenwillow. 1st. 48p. F/F. D4. $45.00

LOBEL, Arnold. *Mouse Soup.* 1977. Harper Row. 1st. 64p. F/NF. P2. $45.00

LOBEL, Arnold. *Rose in My Garden.* 1984. Greenwillow. 1st. 39p. F/F. D4. $50.00

LOBLEY, Douglas. *Ships Through the Ages.* 1972. London. Octopus. ils. 144p. dj. T7. $20.00

LOCK, M. *East Asian Medicine in Urban Japan.* 1980. CA U. 1st. ils/figures/tables. F/F. W3. $58.00

LOCK & SCHALLY. *Hypothalamus & Pituitary in Health & Disease.* 1972. Springfield, IL. Chas Thomas. lg 8vo. red cloth. VG/dj. G1. $75.00

LOCKE, A. *Tigers of Trengganu.* (1954). Scribner. 1st. 181p. F/clip. H7. $35.00

LOCKE, E.W. *Three Years in Camp & Hospital.* 1870. Boston. 408p. O8. $18.50

LOCKE, Edwin A. *Food Values: Practical Tables for Use in Private Practice.* 1928. NY. Appleton. 2nd. 110p. VG/dj. A25. $25.00

LOCKE, George. *Worlds Apart.* 1972. London. 1st. F. M2. $15.00

LOCKE, John. *Some Thoughts Concerning Education.* 1809. London. Sherwood Neely. lg 12mo. 255p. G. H13. $195.00

LOCKE, William J. *Golden Journey of Mr Paradyne.* 1924. Dodd Mead. 1st. VG. M2. $27.00

LOCKE & STERN. *When Peoples Meet: Race & Culture Contacts.* 1949. Hinds Hayden Eldredge. rpt. 825p. NF/VG clip. B4. $150.00

LOCKHART, James L. *Porkey, an Arkansas Razorback.* 1939. Whitman. ils. NF/VG. M5. $40.00

LOCKHART, Robert Bruce. *Scotch: The Whiskey of Scotland in Fact & Story.* 1951. Putnam. 1st. 184p. VG. B10. $35.00

LOCKHART, Theodore. *In Search of Roots.* 1970. Dorrance. 1st. F/VG clip. B4. $100.00

LOCKRIDGE, Richard. *Death on the Hour.* 1974. Lippincott. 1st. inscr. NF/dj. Q1. $75.00

LOCKRIDGE, Richard. *Inspector's Holiday.* 1971. Lippincott. 1st. inscr. VG/dj. Q1. $50.00

LOCKRIDGE, Richard. *Murder in False-Face.* 1968. Phil/NY. Lippincott. 1st. F/NF. Q1. $60.00

LOCKRIDGE, Richard. *Preach No More.* 1971. Lippincott. 1st. inscr. NF/dj. Q1. $50.00

LOCKRIDGE, Richard. *Something Up a Sleeve.* 1972. Lippincott. 1st. inscr. VG/dj. Q1. $50.00

LOCKRIDGE, Richard. *Twice Retired.* 1970. Lippincott. 1st. inscr. NF/dj. Q1. $50.00

LOCKRIDGE & LOCKRIDGE. *Cats & People.* 1950. Phil. inscr. 286p. gr cloth. VG. B14. $35.00

LOCKRIDGE & LOCKRIDGE. *Voyage Into Violence.* 1956. Lippincott. 1st. 191p. VG/dj. M20. $12.00

LOCKWOOD, Charles. *Hell at 50 Fathoms.* 1962. NY. 1st. VG/VG. B5. $40.00

LOCKWOOD, Douglas. *Front Door: Darwin 1869-1969.* 1969. London/Adelaide. Angus Robertson/Rigby. 1st. 8vo. 288p. map ep. VG. P4. $25.00

LOCKWOOD, Frank C. *Pioneer Portraits: Selected Vignettes.* 1968. AZ U. 1st. ils/index. 240p. F/F. B19. $25.00

LOCKYER, Herbert. *All the Apostles of the Bible.* 1972. Zondervan. 278p. VG/dj. B29. $9.00

LOCKYER, Herbert. *All the Miracles of the Bible.* 1961. Zondervan. 316p. F. B29. $9.50

LOCKYER, J. Norman. *Dawn of Astronomy.* 1973. Cambridge. MIT. facsimile 1894 London. VG/dj. K5. $75.00

LOCKYER & LOCKYER. *Life & Work of Sir Norman Lockyer.* 1928. London. Macmillan. 17 pl. 474p. G. K5. $125.00

LOCSIN & LOCSIN. *Oriental Ceramics Discovered in the Philippines.* 1967. Rutland/Tokyo. 1st. ils/pl. gray line. NF/VG. W3. $585.00

LODEWIJK, Tom. *Book of Tulips.* 1979. Vendome. 4to. ils. 128p. F/NF. A22. $30.00

LODEWIJKS, J.M. *Tropical Fish in the Aquarium.* 1974. London. Blandford. revised. ils/drawings. 127p. pict brd. NF. M12. $15.00

LODGE, O.R. *Recapture of Guam.* 1954. WA. ils/fld maps. 214p. VG. S16. $85.00

LODGE, Oliver. *Past Years: An Autobiograpy.* 1931. London. Hodder Stoughton. 1st. ils. 364p. VG. K3. $35.00

LODGE & SPENS. *Terms & Vacations.* 1938. London. Oxford. 1st. 250p. VG/dj. A25. $40.00

LOEB, Charles. *Future Is Yours.* 1947. Cleveland. Future Outlook League. 1st. F/VG. B2. $45.00

LOEHR, Max. *Chinese Painting After Sung.* 1967. Yale U Art Gallery. ils. 38p. silk bdg. F. W3. $42.00

LOEHR, Max. *Ritual Vessels of Bronze Age China.* 1968. NYGS. ils. 183p. gilt gray cloth. NF/VG. W3. $52.00

LOFTING, Hugh. *Doctor Dolittle & the Green Canary.* (1950). Lippincott. 1st thus. 276p. VG/VG. D1. $85.00

LOFTING, Hugh. *Doctor Dolittle's Circus.* (1924). Stokes. 1st. 8vo. 379p. VG. from $80 to $125.00

LOFTING, Hugh. *Story of Mrs Tubbs.* 1923. Stokes. 1st. 92p. VG. P2. $150.00

LOFTUS, Agustus. *Diplomatic Reminiscences of Lord Augustus Loftus PC, GCB.* 1892. London. Cassell. 1st. 2 vol. half morocco. xl. VG. W1. $95.00

LOGAN, John. *Great Conspiracy.* 1886. 1st. inscr. 806p. O8. $87.50

LOGAN, Rayford W. *Negro in American Life & Thought: Nadir 1877-1901.* 1954. Dial. 1st. 380p. F/F. B4. $125.00

LOGAN, S.A. *Old Saint Jo: Gateway to the West 1799-1932.* 1979. St Joseph. ils/photos. 464p. NF. M4. $20.00

LOGSDON, Gene. *Gardener's Guide to Better Soil.* 1975. Emmaus. Rodale. 1st. 246p. dj. A10. $16.00

LOGUE, Christopher. *Children's Book of Comic Verse.* 1979. London. Batsford. 1st. 162p. NF/F. D4. $25.00

LOHMAN, Fred. *Mother Goose.* 1938. Saalfield. 116p. VG+/dj. D4. $85.00

LOKEN, Marty. *Davis Boats.* 1981. Seattle, WA. Center for Wooden Boats. photos/plans/drawings. wrp. T7. $10.00

LOMASK, Milton. *Aaron Burr.* 1979-1982. NY. 1st. 2 vol. ils. VG+/djs. B18. $37.50

LOMAX, Louis E. *Negro Revolt.* 1962. Harper. 1st. NF/dj. M25. $25.00

LOMBARDI, Felipe Rojas. *A-to-Z No-Cookbook.* 1972-. RL Creations. ils Dorothy Ivens. VG/VG. B10. $15.00

LONDON, A. *Complete American-Jewish Cookbook.* 1971 (1952). 3,500 recipes. F/VG. E6. $15.00

LONDON, Charmian. *Book of Jack London.* 2 vol. 1st. inscr. NF. M19. $850.00

LONDON, Jack. *Adventure.* 1911. Macmillan. 1st. inscr/dtd 1913. VG/lacks dj/custom case. B4. $2,500.00

LONDON, Jack. *Before Adam.* 1907. Macmillan. 1st. VG. M19. $125.00

LONDON, Jack. *Burning Daylight.* 1910. Macmillan. 1st. G. M19. $75.00

LONDON, Jack. *Call of the Wild.* 1903. London. Heinemann. 1st Eng. VG. B2. $75.00

LONDON, Jack. *Call of the Wild.* 1903. Macmillan. 1st/1st prt/Eng issue. teg. gilt bl cloth. M24. $225.00

LONDON, Jack. *Chinago.* 1911. Leslie Judge. 1st. VG. M19. $125.00

LONDON, Jack. *Dream of Debs.* nd. Chicago. Kerr. 1st. VG/wrp. B2. $150.00

LONDON, Jack. *Essays of Revolt.* 1926. Vanguard. 1st. NF. M19. $75.00

LONDON, Jack. *Game.* 1905. Macmillan. 1st. Metro stp. VG. M19. $100.00

LONDON, Jack. *John Barleycorn.* 1913. NY. Century. 1/5342. G+. B2. $150.00

LONDON, Jack. *Mutiny of the Elsinore.* 1914. Macmillan. 1st. VG. M19. $150.00

LONDON, Jack. *Red One.* 1918. Macmillan. 1/5342. G+. B2. $300.00

LONDON, Jack. *Sea-Wolf.* 1904. Macmillan. 1st. VG. B2. $60.00

LONDON, Jack. *Smoke & Shorty.* 1920. 1st Eng (no Am issued). VG. M19. $175.00

LONDON, Jack. *South Sea Tales.* 1911. Macmillan. 1st. G. M19. $100.00

LONDON, Jack. *Star Rover.* 1915. Macmillan. 1st. F/NF. B4. $750.00

LONDON, Jack. *Tales of the Fish Patrol.* 1906. 1st Eng. NF. M19. $250.00

LONDON, Jack. *When God Laughs.* nd. Internat Fiction Lib. F/dj. M2. $27.00

LONDON, Rose. *Cinema of Mystery.* 1975. Bounty. F/NF. M2. $12.00

LONG, Esmond. *History of American Pathology.* 1962. Springfield. 1st. 460p. A13. $75.00

LONG, Frank Belknap. *In Mayan Splendor.* 1977. Arkham. 1st. 1/3000. ils Stephen Fabian. NF/F. M19. $25.00

LONG, Frank Belknap. *Rim of the Unknown.* 1972. Arkham. 1st. NF/dj. Q1. $75.00

LONG, Huey. *My First Days in the White House.* 1935. Harrisburg. 1st. VG/VG. B5. $95.00

LONG, John Luther. *Madame Butterfly.* 1898. NY. Century. 1st. quarter gr cloth/pict label. uncut. M24. $250.00

LONG, Joseph W. *American Wild-Fowl Shooting.* 1879. Orange Judd. 330p. G. H7. $50.00

LONG, Lydia Belknap; see Long, Frank Belknap.

LONG LANCE, Chief Buffalo Child. *Long Lance.* 1928. NY. Cosmopolitan. 1st. NF. L3. $85.00

LONG LANCE, Chief Buffalo Child. *Long Lance: Autobiography of a Blackfoot Indian Chief.* 1956. London. Faber. 1st. 241p. VG/dj. M20. $25.00

LONGFELLOW, Henry Wadsworth. *Courtship of Miles Standish & Other Poems.* 1858. Boston. Ticknor Fields. 1st/1st prt. 12mo. gilt cloth. M24/T10. $450.00

LONGFELLOW, Henry Wadsworth. *Hanging of the Crane.* 1907. Houghton Mifflin. Centennial/1st thus. 1/1000. unp. F/VG. D4. $45.00

LONGFELLOW, Henry Wadsworth. *Hiawatha's Childhood.* 1984. FSG. 1st Am. ils Errol LeCain. F/F. D4. $30.00

LONGFELLOW, Henry Wadsworth. *Nuremberg.* 1888. Phil. Gebbie. 1st Am. pub sgn/#d. full vegetable vellum. M24. $125.00

LONGFELLOW, Henry Wadsworth. *Song of Hiawatha.* nd. Merson. ne. 262p. NF/VG. W2. $75.00

LONGFELLOW, Henry Wadsworth. *Song of Hiawatha.* 1911. Chicago. Rand McNally. lg 8vo. 242p. M/glassine wrp/box. B24. $325.00

LONGFELLOW, Henry Wadsworth. *Tales of a Wayside Inn.* 1863. Boston. Ticknor Fields. 1st/1st prt/1st state ads. teg. gr cloth. M24. $225.00

LONGFELLOW, Samuel. *Few Verses of Many Years.* 1887. Cambridge. private prt. 1st. 16mo. 104p. prt wrp. M1. $150.00

LONGFORD, Elizabeth. *Elizabeth.* 1983. Toronto. Musson. 1st. NF. T12. $35.00

LONGFORD, Elizabeth. *Royal House of Windsor.* 1974. London. Weidenfeld Nicolson. 1st. F/F. T12. $50.00

LONGGOOD, William. *Poisons in Your Food.* 1960. S&S. 1st. 277p. VG+/dj. H1. $12.50

LONGRIGG, Roger. *History of Horse Racing.* 1972n. Stein Day. 1st. photos. G+. P8. $50.00

LONGSTREET, Stephen. *War Cries on Horseback.* 1970. Doubleday. 1st. 8vo. 335p. xl. VG/dj. K7. $18.00

LONGSTRETH, T.M. *Missouri Clipper.* 1941. Appleton. 1st. 282p. cloth. VG/dj. M20. $40.00

LONGSTRETH, T.M. *Reading the Weather.* 1941 (1915). Macmillan. 8vo. 195p. G. K5. $12.00

LONGUS. *Daphnis & Chloe.* 1931. 1st. ils John Austen. VG. M19. $25.00

LONGYEAR, Barry B. *City of Baraboo.* 1980. Berkley Putnam. 1st. F/dj. M2. $15.00

LONSDALE, G. *20 Years in Soviet Secret Service.* 1965. 1st Am. VG/VG. E6. $13.00

LONTZ, Vernon E. *Arctic Interlude: True Stories of Alaska.* 1900. NY. Vantage. photos. VG/dj. P4. $25.00

LOOFBOUROW, Leon L. *In Search of God's Gold.* 1950. Stockton, CA. 1st. G/fair. O4. $15.00

LOOK, A. *U-Boom: Uranium on the Colorado Plateau.* 1956. Bell pr. 224p. G/dj. D8. $20.00

LOOMIS, Elias. *Treatise on Meteorology.* 1868. Harper. 8vo. 305p. contemporary leather. K5. $75.00

LOOMIS & PARMALEE. *Decoys & Decoy Carvers of Illinois.* 1969. N IL U. 1st. 426 photos. 506p. F/F case. M4. $175.00

LOOSE, G. *Guide to American Bird Names, Origins, Meanings...* 1989. Virginia Beach. 146p. F/wrp. B1. $14.00

LOPEZ, Barry. *Crossing Open Ground.* 1988. Scribner. 1st. sgn. M/dj. A18. $40.00

LOPEZ, Barry. *Crow & Weasel.* 1990. Northpoint. 1st state w/gold stp bdg. sgn. ils Pohrt. M/dj. A18. $100.00

LOPEZ, Barry. *Desert Notes: Reflections in the Eye of a Raven.* 1976. Sheed Andrews & McMeel. 1st. F/NF. B4. $350.00

LOPEZ, Barry. *Field Notes: Grace Note of the Canyon Wren.* 1994. Knopf. 1st. sgn. M/dj. A18. $35.00

LOPEZ, Barry. *Of Wolves & Men.* 1978. Scribner. 1st. F/NF. B2. $100.00

LOPEZ, Barry. *River Notes: Dance of Herons.* 1979. Andrews McMeel. 1st. sgn. F/dj. A18. $100.00

LOPEZ, Barry. *Winter Count.* 1981. Scribner. 1st. F/NF. T11. $65.00

LOPEZ, Salvador P. *Literature & Society: Essays on Life & Letters.* 1940. Manila. Philippine Book Guild. 224p. cloth. VG/G. P1. $10.00

LOPEZ ENGUIDANOS, Jose. *Coleccion de Vaciados de Estatuas Antiguas Que Posee...* 1794. Madrid. 1st/only. folio. 84 engravings. contemporary bdg. R15. $4,500.00

LORAND, Rhoda L. *Love, Sex & the Teenager.* 1968. Macmillan. 5th. 243p. VG. A25. $8.00

LORANT, Stefan. *New World: First Pictures of America...* 1946. Duell Sloan. 1st. 4to. 292p. F3. $50.00

LORD, Bette Bao. *Legacies.* 1990. Knopf. 1st. F/F. A20. $15.00

LORD, Ernest E. *Shrubs & Trees for Australian Gardens.* 1978 (1948). Melbourne. 4th. photos. VG+/dj. B26. $54.00

LORD, Isabel Ely. *Everybody's Cookbook.* 1924. Holt. 1925 prt. 916p. recent red cloth. T10. $35.00

LORD, John. *Beacon Lights of History. First Series: Jewish Heroes...* 188. NY. Fords Howard Hulbert. 524p. fair. B29. $10.00

LORD, Sheldon; see Block, Lawrence.

LORD, W. *Miracle of Dunkirk.* 1962. NY. 1st Am. 323p. VG/VG. S16. $20.00

LORD & LORD. *Forever the Land.* 1950. Harper. 1st. 394p. dj. A10. $25.00

LORENTZ, H.A. *Einstein Theory of Relativity.* 1920. NY. Brentano. 8vo. 64p. VG. K3. $22.00

LORIMER, Norma. *By the Waters of Egypt.* ca 1910. Stokes. 1st. ils/maps. 314p. G. W1. $10.00

LORIMER, Norma. *There Was a King in Egypt.* 1918. Brentanos. 1st. NF/dj. M2. $35.00

LORING, Brent; see Worts, George F.

LOSE, Phyllis. *No Job for a Lady.* 1979. NY. Macmillan. 1st. sgn. VG/VG. O3. $35.00

LOSKE, Lothar M. *Die Sonnenuhren.* 1959. Berlin. Springer. ils. 12mo. 88p. VG+. K3. $22.00

LOSSING, Benson J. *Our Great Continent.* 1889. NY. Gay Bros. A19. $50.00

LOSSING, Benson J. *Pictorial Field-Book of Revolution; or, History...* 1969 (1860). rpt. 2 vol. 1100 ils. F. M4. $55.00

LOTI, Pierre. *Iceland Fisherman.* 1931. Stockholm. LEC. 1/1500. ils/sgn Yngve Berg. NF. M19. $35.00

LOTT, Bret. *Man Who Owned Vermont.* 1987. Viking. 1st. sgn. NF/NF. R14. $45.00

LOTTMAN, Herbert R. *Left Bank.* 1982. London. 1st. VG/VG. T9. $25.00

LOUGHBOROUGH, Mary Ann. *My Life in Vicksburg With Letters of Trial & Travel.* 1864. NY. Appleton. 1st. 196p. cloth. NF. M8. $250.00

LOUGHRAN, Peter. *Dearest.* 1983. Stein Day. 1st. F/dj. M2. $20.00

LOUIRIE, Dick. *Stumbling.* 1973. Crossing. sgn pres. 8vo. 111p. VG/glossy wrp. H1. $35.00

LOUIS, Joe. *How to Box.* 1948. McKay. 1st. ils/photos. VG. P8. $75.00

LOUSLEY, J.E. *Flora of the Isles of Scilly.* 1971. Newton Abbott. 8vo. 336p. F/F. A22. $25.00

LOVE, Jeannette F. *Fall & Rise of Cushan & Other Poems.* 1911. Stoneman. 1st. NF. B4. $650.00

LOVECRAFT, H.P. *Dunwich Horror.* 1963. Salk City. 1st. VG/VG. B5. $35.00

LOVECRAFT, H.P. *Something About Cats & Other Pieces.* 1949. Arkham. 1st. F/dj. w/sgn postcard. B24. $225.00

LOVELACE, Maud Hart. *Betsy-Tacy.* 1940. Crowell. ils Lenski. VG+/G+. M5. $75.00

LOVELACE, Maud Hart. *Early Candelight.* 1929 (1929). John Day. 3rd. 322p. VG. T5. $45.00

LOVELACE & RICE. *Music & Worship in the Church.* 1960. Abingdon. 220p. G/dj. B29. $6.50

LOVELL, J. *Flower & the Bee, Plant Life & Pollination.* 1918. 1st. photos. VG. E6. $25.00

LOVELL, Mary S. *Sound of Wings: Life of Amelia Earhart.* 1989. St Martin. 1st. photos. 420p. VG/VG. A25. $18.00

LOVESEY, Peter. *Last Detective.* 1991. Doubleday. 1st. F/F. M23. $30.00

LOVETT, C. *Lewis Carroll's Alice: Annotated Checklist...* 1990. ils. 556p. F. A4. $225.00

LOVETT, C. *Robinson Crusoe: Bibliographical Checklist...* 1991. 1198 entries. 322p. F. A4. $125.00

LOVETT, Sarah. *Dangerous Attachments.* 1995. Villard. 1st. sgn. author's 1st book. F/F. A23. $50.00

LOW, Frances H. *Queen Victoria's Dolls.* 1894. London. sm 4to. ils Alan Wright. VG. C8. $125.00

LOW, Joseph. *Mother Goose Riddle Rhymes.* 1953. Harcourt Brace. 1st. 48p. VG+/dj. D4. $45.00

LOWE, Samuel. *New Story of Peter Rabbit.* 1926. Whitman. legal pirated ed. ils Wright/Vetsch. VG. D1. $75.00

LOWE & STEENBERGH. *Ecology of the Saguaro: II.* 1977. Tucson. 8vo. 243p. G. A22. $30.00

LOWELL, James Russell. *Branded Hand.* 1845. Salem, OH. Anti-Slavery Bugle. 1st/variant issue. F. M24. $165.00

LOWELL, James Russell. *Conversations on Some of the Old Poets.* 1845. Cambridge. John Owen. 1st. 16mo. contemporary calf. M1. $475.00

LOWELL, James Russell. *Impressions of Spain.* 1899. Houghton Mifflin. 1st/2nd prt. teg. quarter vellum (2nd state). M24. $225.00

LOWELL, James Russell. *Liberty Bell.* 1844. Boston. Anti-Slavery Fair. 1st. yel glazed prt brd/rebacked. M24. $125.00

LOWELL, Percival. *Occult Japan; or, The Way of the Gods.* ca 1894. Houghton Mifflin. 4th. 379p. VG. W3. $125.00

LOWELL, Robert. *History.* 1973. FSG. 1st. F/dj. M25. $45.00

LOWELL, Robert. *Old Glory.* 1965. NY. 1st. F/VG+. A11. $35.00

LOWERY, George H. *Louisana Birds.* 1955. LSU. 3rd. sgn. VG/VG. B11. $40.00

LOWRY, Robert. *Find Me in Fire.* 1948. Garden City. 1st. sgn. NF/VG+. A11. $250.00

LOWRY, Shannon. *Northern Lights: Tales of Alaska's Lighthouses...* 1992. Harrisburg. Stackpole. 1st. 118p. M/dj. P4. $30.00

LOWRY & WHITE. *Century of Speed the Red Mile 1875-1975.* 1975. Lexington Trots Breeders. 1st. sgn pres from White. VG. O3. $65.00

LOZOWICK, Louis. *William Gropper.* 1983. Phil. Art Alliance. 1st. F/NF. B2. $75.00

LUARD, Nicholas. *Gondar.* 1988. Gondor. 1st. VG/VG. T9. $10.00

LUBBOCK, Basil. *Blackwall Frigates.* 1924. ils. VG. M17. $15.00

LUBBOCK, Basil. *Log of the Cutty Sark.* 1974. Glasgow. Brn, Son & Ferguson. later ed. 332p. bl cloth. VG. P4. $65.00

LUBBOCK, John. *Pre-Historic Times, as Illustrated by Ancient Remains...* 1872. Appleton. New Ed. 8vo. 649p. emb cloth. T10. $150.00

LUCAS, A. *Ancient Egyptian Materials & Industries.* 1934. London. Arnold. 8vo. 447p. VG. W1. $65.00

LUCAS, Annabelle. *Wild Flowers of the Witwatersrand.* 1987. Cape Town. ils Barbara Pike. 113p. F. B26. $22.50

LUCAS, Dione. *Cordon Bleu Cook Book.* 1951 (1947). Little Brn. sgn. 322p. VG/worn. M20. $30.00

LUCAS, E.V. *Another Book of Verses for Children.* 1925. Macmillan. 1st reissue. 8vo. 431p. gray cloth. NF. M5. $35.00

LUCAS, E.V. *Four & Twenty Toilers.* 1900. NY. McDevitt-Wilson. 1st. obl 4to. pict cloth. R5. $285.00

LUCAS, E.V. *If Dogs Could Write: Second Canine Miscellany.* 1930. Lippincott. ne. 16mo. 95p. G/dj. H7. $20.00

LUCAS, E.V. *Lucas' Annual.* 1914. Macmillan. 1st. VG. M2. $15.00

LUCAS, E.V. *Verena in the Midst.* 1920. Doran. 1st Am. F/pict dj. B4. $125.00

LUCAS, George; see Foster, Alan Dean.

LUCAS, Jim G. *Dateline: Viet Nam.* 1966. NY. Award. 1st. F/F. H11. $45.00

LUCAS, Robert Irwin. *Tarentum Pattern Glass.* 1981. self pub. 1st. 422p. ES. as new/dj. H1. $35.00

LUCAS, Walter A. *Popular Picture & Plan Book of Railroad Cars & Locomotives.* 1951. Simmons-Boardman. 1st. 4to. 288p. H1. $45.00

LUCE, Edward. *Keogh, Comanche & Custer.* 1939. np. ltd. sgn. facsimiles/photos. 127p. G. J2. $785.00

LUCIE-SMITH, Edward. *Art Deco Painting.* 1990. ils. VG/VG. M17. $35.00

LUCIW & LUCIW. *Ahapius Honcharenko & the Alaska Herald.* 1963. Toronto. Slavia Lib. 120p. VG/prt wrp. P4. $32.50

LUCKINGHAM, Bradford. *Phoenix: History of Southwestern Metropolis.* 1989. AZ U. 1st. ils/index/notes. 316p. F/F. B19. $20.00

LUCRETIUS, Carus Titius. *Titi Lucretii Cari de Rerum Natura.* 1773. Birminghamiae. Johannis Baskerville. 12mo. 214p. new bdg. K3. $90.00

LUDECKE, Heinz. *Albrech Durer.* 1970. ils. VG/G. M17. $20.00

LUDLOW, Fitz Hugh. *Hasheesh Eater.* 1857. NY. Harper. 1st. author's 1st book. gilt purple-brn cloth. F. M24. $400.00

LUDLUM, Robert. *Bourne Supremacy.* 1986. Random. 1st. 597p. NF/NF. W2. $20.00

LUDLUM, Robert. *Bourne Ultimatum.* 1990. Random. 1st. 611p. F/F. W2. $30.00

LUDLUM, Robert. *Chancellor Manuscript.* 1977. Dial. 1st. VG/NF. T11. $55.00

LUDLUM, Robert. *Cry of the Halidon.* 1974. Delacorte. 1st. F/VG+. T11. $65.00

LUDLUM, Robert. *Gemini Contenders.* 1976. NY. Dial. 1st. F/NF. T11. $40.00

LUDLUM, Robert. *Holcroft Covenant.* 1978. NY. Richard Marek. 1st. F/dj. Q1. $75.00

LUDLUM, Robert. *Icarus Agenda.* 1988. Random. 1st. NF/NF. B35. $18.00

LUDLUM, Robert. *Matarese Circle.* 1979. Richard Marek. 1st. F/dj. Q1. $40.00

LUDLUM, Robert. *Matlock Paper.* 1973. NY. Dial. 1st. F/dj. M15. $100.00

LUDLUM, Robert. *Road to Gandolfo.* 1975. Dial. 1st. F/all 3 djs present. from $125 to $150.00

LUDLUM, Robert. *Road to Omaha.* 1992. Random. 1st. F/dj. Q1. $25.00

LUDLUM, Robert. *Scarlatti Inheritance.* 1971. World. 1st. author's 1st book. VG+/fair. N4. $75.00

LUDLUM, Robert. *Scorpio Illusion.* 1993. Bantam. 1st. NF/dj. Q1. $25.00

LUDWIG, Emil. *Cleopatra: Story of a Queen.* 1937. Viking. 1st. 8vo. 342p. VG. W1. $18.00

LUDWIG, Emil. *Goethe: History of a Man 1749-1832.* 1928. NY. 1st. 8vo. ils. teg. 3-quarter leather. F. H3. $50.00

LUEDERS, Edward. *Clam Lake Papers.* 1977. NY. 1st. VG/dj. B5. $25.00

LUGARD, Lord. *Dual Mandate in British Tropical Africa.* 1965. London. Cassell. 5th. 8vo. cloth. NF/dj. W1. $35.00

LUGER, Richard. *Letters to the Next President.* 1988. S&S. 1st. F/F. B35. $16.00

LUI, Garding. *Inside Los Angeles Chinatown.* 1948. np. 8vo. ils. blk stp red cloth. F. R3. $85.00

LUKEMAN, Tim. *Koren.* 1981. Doubleday. 1st. F/dj. M2. $17.00

LUKENBILL & STEWART. *Youth Literature, Interdisciplinary, Annotated Guide...* 1988. 481p. VG. A4. $125.00

LUMAN, Duncan. *New Worlds for Old.* 1979. Morrow. 1st. F/dj. M2. $15.00

LUMLEY, Brian. *Blood Brothers.* 1992. Tor. 1st. F/dj. M2. $30.00

LUMMIS, Charles F. *Bullying the Moque.* 1968. Flagstaff, AZ. 1st. NF/VG. O4. $20.00

LUMMIS, Charles F. *Flowers of Our Lost Romance.* 1929. Houghton Mifflin. 1st. VG. O4. $60.00

LUMMIS, Charles F. *Land of Poco Tiempo.* 1893. Scribner. 1st. 310p. decor cloth. D11. $100.00

LUMMIS, Charles F. *Man Who Married the Moon & Other Pueblo Indian Folk-Stories.* 1894. Century. 1st. ils. VG+. A18. $125.00

LUMMIS, Charles F. *Mesa, Canon & Pueblo.* 1925. Century. 1st. G. O4. $25.00

LUNA, Kris. *Steller Radium Discharge.* 1952. London. 1st. F/dj. M2. $10.00

LUNDAHL, Gene. *Jargon's Journey.* 1966. Denver. 1st. 1/300. sgn. F/dj. A17. $15.00

LUNDQUIST, Carl. *United We Stood.* 1985. Todd Honeywell. 1st. F/VG+. P8. $20.00

LUNGWITZ, A. *Text-Book of Horseshoeing for Horseshoers & Veterinarians.* 1902. Phil. ils. 168p. G-. B18. $25.00

LUPOFF, Richard. *Forever City.* 1987. Walker. 1st. F/dj. M2. $20.00

LUPOFF & THOMAS. *All in Color All for a Dime.* 1970. New Rochelle. 1st. VG/VG. A4. $25.00

LURIA, A.R. *Higher Cortical Functions in Man.* 1977. NY. Basic. 1st Eng-language/5th prt. blk cloth. VG/dj. G1. $50.00

LURIA, A.R. *Nature of Human Conflicts or Emotion, Conflict & Will...* 1932. NY. Liveright. 321p. bl cloth. VG/dj. G1. $65.00

LURIE, Alison. *Don't Tell the Grown-Ups.* 1990. Little Brn. 1st. F/dj. A24. $25.00

LURIE, Alison. *Foreign Affairs.* 1984. Franklin Lib. ltd. sgn. leather. F. from $40 to $50.00

LURIE, Alison. *Real People.* 1969. Random. 1st. F/NF. M19. $35.00

LURIE, Alison. *Truth About Lorin Jones.* 1988. Little Brn. 1st trade. F/F. T12. $35.00

LURIE, Alison. *Women & Ghosts.* 1994. Doubleday. 1st. sgn. F/F. A23. $40.00

LUSK, Clayton R. *Revolutionary Radicalism: Its History, Purpose & Tactics.* 1920. Albany. JB Lyon. 4 vol. B2. $150.00

LUSTBADER, Eric V. *French Kiss.* 1989. Fawcett. 1st. F/dj. M2. $20.00

LUTHER, Martin. *Acta...Agust(ana).* 1518. Leipzig. Lotter. 4to. woodcut. vellum/manuscript brd. R12. $875.00

LUTHER, Martin. *An die Pfarrherrn Wider den Wucher zu Predigen.* 1540. Wittenberg. Klug. 4to. woodcut title border. brd. R12. $1,675.00

LUTHER, Martin. *Luther's Works, Vol 26: Lectures on Galatians Chapters 1-4.* nd. np. Am ed. as new/dj. B29. $15.00

LUTHER, Seth. *Address on Origin & Progress of Avarice...* 1834. Boston. self pub. 1st. 8vo. 43p. modern cloth. M1. $1,000.00

LUTHER, Tal. *High Spots of Custer & Battle of the Little Big Horn.* 1967. KS City Posse Westerners. 1st. 1/250. sgn. VG. J2. $145.00

LUTRELL, Estelle. *Mission of San Xavier Del Bac: An Historical Guide.* 1922. Kimball. 1st? LC Powell bookplate. F/wrp. B19. $25.00

LUTZ, W.J. *William D Wittliff: Bibliography.* 1975. Dallas. sgn. 49p. F. M4. $35.00

LUTZE, Eberhard. *Veit Stoss.* 1940. Berlin. Keutscher Kunstverlag. 2nd. ils. D2. $35.00

LUXFORD, Nola. *Kerry Kangaroo.* 1957. Whittlesey. 1st. sm 4to. cloth. dj. M5. $22.00

LUYS, Jules Bernard. *Brain & Its Functions. International Scientific Series 39.* 1882. NY. Appleton. 1st Eng-language/1st prt/Am issue. 327p. xl. VG. G1. $85.00

LUYTEN, Willem J. *Search for Faint Blue Stars, I-XXX.* 1956-1962. Minneapolis. The Observatory. 161p. cloth. K5. $30.00

LYBACK, Johanna R.M. *Indian Legends.* 1925. Lyons Carnahan. ils Alexander Key. M5. $45.00

LYDON, Sandy. *Chinese Gold: Chinese in Monterey Bay Region.* 1985. Capitola book Co. lg obl 8vo. ils. gilt bl cloth. F/dj. R3. $40.00

LYLE, R.C. *Royal Newmarket.* 1945. London. Putnam. 1st. ils Lionel Edwards/10 mc pl. VG/fair. O3. $145.00

LYNCH, Kenneth. *Benches.* 1971. Canterbury, CT. Arch Handbook. 80p. VG. A10. $30.00

LYNCH, Kenneth. *Garden Ornaments.* 1974. Canterbury, CT. Arch Handbook. 768p. VG. A10. $35.00

LYNCH, Patricia. *Brogeen & the Bronze Lizard.* 1970. Macmillan. 1st Am. 8vo. ils HB Vestal. F/dj. T10. $25.00

LYND & LYND. *Middletown: A Study in American Culture.* 1929. Harcourt Brace. 1st. gilt cloth. dj. M24. $75.00

LYNDE, Francis. *Flight of the Gray Goose.* 1927. Scribner. 1st. 216p. VG/dj. M20. $45.00

LYNDE, Francis. *Scientific Sprague.* nd. AL Burt. VG. M2. $17.00

LYNDS, Dennis. *Deadly Innocents.* 1986. Walker. 1st. F/F. P3. $15.00

LYNN, Elizabeth. *Dancers of Arun.* 1979. Berkley. 1st. F/dj. M2. $25.00

LYNN, Elizabeth. *Sardonyx Net.* 1981. Putnam. 1st. F/dj. M2. $25.00

LYNN, F.J. *Ecology & Economic Impact of Poisonous Plants...* 1988. Westview. 428p. B1. $26.50

LYNN. *Fantasy Literature for Children & Young Adults...* 1989. 3rd. 818p. NF. A4. $145.00

LYON, G.F. *Brief Narrative of Unsuccessful Attempt to Reach Repulse...* 1825. London. John Murray. 1st. 198p. rebound. P4. $395.00

LYON, W.E. *Youth in the Saddle.* nd (1955). Barnes. VG/VG. O3. $10.00

LYONS, A.B. *Plant Names Scientific & Popular...* 1900. Detroit. Nelson Baker. 469p. A10. $45.00

LYONS, James R. *Intellectual Legacy of Paul Tillich.* 1969. Wayne State. 4 essays. 115p. VG/G+. S3. $22.00

LYONS, Mary E. *Sorrow's Kitchen. Life & Folklore of Zora Neale Hurston.* 1990. Scribner. 1st. F/NF. R13. $15.00

LYONS & NOGUCHI. *Physical Evidence.* 1990. Putnam. 1st. F/F. N4. $22.50

LYONS & WOODHALL. *Atlas of Peripheral Nerve Injuries.* 1949. Phil. 1st. 4to. 339p. A13. $200.00

LYSAGHT, A.M. *Joseph Banks in Newfoundland & Labrador, 1766.* 1971. LA. CA U. 1st. ils/pl/maps. VG. K3. $65.00

LYTLE, Andrew. *Novel, Novella & Four Stories.* 1958. NY. 1st. sgn pres. VG/dj. B5. $125.00

– M –

MAAS, Peter. *Manhunt.* 1986. Random. 1st. F/F. M22. $10.00

MAASS, Walter. *Country Without a Name: Austria Under Nazi Rule 1938-45.* 1979. NY. maps/biblio/index. 178p. VG/VG. S16. $17.50

MABEY, Richard. *Oxford Book of Nature Writing.* 1995. Oxford. 260p. as new/dj. S15. $15.00

MABIE, Hamilton W. *Fairy Tales Every Child Should Know.* 1926. Doubleday. ils MH Frye. VG. M5. $55.00

MABIE, Hamilton W. *Myths Every Child Should Know.* 1914. Doubleday Page. ils Mary Hamilton Frye. F. M19. $35.00

MABIE, Peter. *A to Z Book.* (1929). Whitman. 4to. NF/pict wrp. D1. $60.00

MABIE, Peter. *Parade of the Toy Soldiers.* 1931. Whitman. 8vo. cb stock. VG. D1. $95.00

MACAPAGAL, Diosdado. *Democracy in the Philippines.* 1976. Manila. photos/index. 216p. F. P1. $20.00

MACARTHUR, Arthur. *After the Afternoon.* 1941. Appleton. NF. M2. $25.00

MACARTHUR, D. Wilson. *They Sailed for Senegal.* 1938. Stokes. 1st. F/VG. B4. $100.00

MACARTHUR, David. *Thunderbolt Man.* 1947. London. 1st. F. M2. $22.00

MACARTHUR, John. *Our Sufficiency in Christ: Three Deadly Influences...* 1991. Word. 282p. VG/dj. B29. $9.00

MACARTNEY, Carol. *Easy Stages Cook Book.* 1972. London. Octopus. G/dj. A16. $15.00

MACASKILL, Wallace R. *Out of Halifax.* 1937. NY. Derrydale. 1st. sgn/#d. 98 pl. F. B11. $185.00

MACAULAY, David. *Underground.* 1976. Houghton Mifflin. 1st. sgn. 112p. VG+/VG. P2. $40.00

MACAULEY, Robie. *Secret History of Time to Come.* 1979. Knopf. 1st. F/dj. M2. $15.00

MACBRIDE, Roger Lee. *West From Home.* 1974. Harper. dj. A19. $35.00

MACCOBY, Eleanor E. *Development of Sex Differences.* 1966. Stanford. 1st. 351p. VG+. A25. $15.00

MACDONALD, Aeneas. *Whiskey.* 1934. Duffield Gr. 1st Am. 135p. VG. B10. $35.00

MACDONALD, Betty. *Nancy & Plum.* 1952. Lippincott. 1st. sm 8vo. VG+/dj. C8. $75.00

MACDONALD, G.A. *Volcanoes.* 1972. Prentice Hall. 510p. F. D8. $18.00

MACDONALD, George. *At the Back of the North Wind.* 1871. NY. Routledge. 1st Am/later prt. gilt pict red cloth. VG. M24. $350.00

MACDONALD, George. *At the Back of the North Wind.* 1909. ils Maria Kirk. NF. M19. $35.00

MACDONALD, George. *At the Back of the North Wind.* 1924. Macmillan. 1st thus. ils Francis Bedford. VG. M5. $30.00

MACDONALD, George. *Golden Key.* 1976. FSG. 1st. ils Sendak. 86p. bl brd. F/F. D1. $75.00

MACDONALD, George. *Princess & Curdie.* nd (1883). Lippincott. 1st Am. 8vo. VG. M5. $75.00

MACDONALD, George. *Princess & the Goblin.* 1920. McKay. early ed. ils JW Smith. 4to. top edge orange. gr cloth. R5. $250.00

MACDONALD, Golden; See Brown, Margaret Wise.

MACDONALD, Gordon. *Restoring Your Spiritual Passion.* 1986. Nelson. 223p. VG/dj. B29. $6.00

MACDONALD, John D. *Barrier Island.* 1986. Knopf. 1st. F/F. N4. $27.50

MACDONALD, John D. *Barrier Island.* 1986. Knopf. 1st. VG. P3. $18.00

MACDONALD, John D. *Blue City.* 1st. VG/NF. M22. $200.00

MACDONALD, John D. *Cinnamon Skin.* 1982. Harper. 1st. F/NF. N4. $27.50

MACDONALD, John D. *Condominium.* 1977. Lippincott. 1st. F/NF. N4. $35.00

MACDONALD, John D. *Free Fall in Crimson.* 1981. Harper. 1st. VG. P3. $30.00

MACDONALD, John D. *Ivory Grin.* 1952. Knopf. 1st. VG. M25. $50.00

MACDONALD, John D. *Lonely Silver Rain.* 1985. Knopf. 1st. F/F. from $20 to $30.00

MACDONALD, John D. *One More Sunday.* 1984. Knopf. 1st. 311p. NF/VG. W2. $20.00

MACDONALD, John D. *Scarlet Ruse.* 1980. Lippincott Crowell. 1st Am hc. F/dj. M15. $100.00

MACDONALD, John D. *Three for McGee.* 1967. Doubleday. 1st. VG/VG+ clip. B4. $250.00

MACDONALD, John D. *Wine of the Dreamers.* 1951. NY. Greenberg. 1st. author's 1st hc book. F/dj. B4/L3. $250.00

MACDONALD, John Ross; see Millar, Kenneth.

MACDONALD, Ross; see Millar, Kenneth.

MACDONALD, Wilson. *Miracle Songs of Jesus.* 1921. Toronto. Ryerson. 2nd. VG. T12. $100.00

MACDONELL, Anne. *Italian Fairy Book.* 1911. London. Fisher Unwin. 1st. ils Morris Williams. 8vo. gr cloth. R5. $375.00

MACDOUGAL, A. *Secret of Successful Restaurants.* 1929. 1st. VG. E6. $25.00

MACDOUGAL, Bonnie. *Breach of Trust.* 1996. Pocket. 1st. author's 1st. novel. NF/NF. R16. $30.00

MACEWEN, William. *Pyogenic Infective Diseases of the Brain & Spinal Cord.* 1893. Glasgow. Maclehouse. heavy 8vo. 354p. pebbled gr cloth. G1. $500.00

MACEY, Peter. *Alien Culture.* 1977. London. 1st. F/dj. M2. $12.00

MACFALL, Haldane. *Beautiful Children.* ca 1910. TC Jack. 33 mc pl. VG. M19. $45.00

MACFARLAN, Allan. *American Indian Legends.* 1968. LEC/Ward Ritchie. 1/1500. ils/sgn Everett jackson. w/prospectus. M/box. K7. $140.00

MACGRATH, Harold. *Cellini Plaque.* 1925. Grosset Dunlap. 252p. VG/dj. M20. $15.00

MACGREAGOR-MORRIS, Pamela. *World's Show Jumpers.* 1967. Barnes. 1st Am. VG/G. O3. $25.00

MACGREGOR, Alexander. *Highland Superstitions.* 1922. Enease MacKay. VG. B2. $30.00

MACGREGOR, Geddes. *Bible in the Making.* 1959. Lippincott. 447p. VG/dj. B29. $12.00

MACGREGOR, James. *Father Lacombe.* 1975. Hurtig. 1st. F/F. T12. $20.00

MACH, Ernest. *Space & Geometry in Light of Physiological...Inquiry.* 1943. Lasalle. Open Court. 8vo. 148p. K3. $18.00

MACHADO DE CASTRO, Joaquim. *Ao Rey Fidelissimo Dom Jose I Nosso Senhor, Collocando...* 1775. Lisbon. Regia Off Typografica. 1st/only. unbound. R15. $650.00

MACHEN, Arthur. *Chronicle of Clemedy.* 1923. Soc Pantagruelists. 1/1050. sgn/#d. 331p. VG. B11. $85.00

MACHEN, Arthur. *Hill of Dreams.* 1907. Estes. 1st Am. VG. M2. $75.00

MACHEN, Arthur. *100 Merrie Tales.* 1924. Carbonnell. 2 vol. 1/1250. sgn. ils/sgn Clara Tice. VG/dj. B5. $150.00

MACHEN, J. Gresham. *Christianity & Liberalism.* 1974. Eerdmans. 189p. VG. B29. $7.00

MACHIAVELLI. *Tvtte le Opere.* 1650 (1550). np. 5 works in 1. 4to. double-p woodcut. calf. R12. $650.00

MACHIAVELLI, Niccolo. *Prince.* 1954. NY. LEC. 1st thus. 1/1500. full leather. NF/case. Q1. $200.00

MACINNES, Helen. *Above Suspicion.* 1941. Little Brn. 1st. VG. N4. $20.00

MACINNES, Helen. *Hidden Target.* 1980. HBJ. 1st. F/G. T12. $10.00

MACINNES, Helen. *I & My True Love.* 1953. Harcourt Brace. 1st. F/NF. B4. $85.00

MACINTYRE, Donald. *Narvik.* 1959. London. 1st. ils/maps. 224p. VG/VG. S16. $25.00

MACINTYRE, Donald. *Wings of Neptune, Story of Naval Aviation.* 1964. NY. 1st Am. 268p. VG/dj. B18. $22.50

MACK, Burton L. *Lost Gospel: Book of Q & Christian Origins.* 1993. Harper Collins. 275p. F/wrp. B29. $9.00

MACK, Burton L. *Mack & Christian Origins: Myth of Innocence.* 1988. Fortress. 432p. VG. B29. $13.50

MACK, Connie. *Connie Mack's Baseball Book.* 1950. NY. 1st. sgn. VG/VG. B5. $40.00

MACK, R.E. *From Lace to Leaf, a Volume of Poems With Illustrations.* ca late 1800s. NY. ils. VG. M17. $20.00

MACKAY, Douglas. *Honourable Company: History of Hudson's Bay Company.* 1936. Bobbs Merrill. 8vo. blk cloth. VG/worn. P4. $75.00

MACKELLAR, Thomas. *American Printer: A Manual of Typography.* 1870. Phil. Mackellar Smith. 5th. ils. VG. K3. $60.00

MACKENZIE, D.R. *Movement & Dispersal of Agriculturally Important Biotic...* 1985. Baton Rouge. Claitor's Pub. 611p. F. B1. $45.00

MACKENZIE, Norman. *Secret Societies.* 1967. NY. 1st Am. ils. 350p. F/F. W3. $135.00

MACKENZIE, Robert. *19th Century: A History.* 1880. London. Nelson. 1st. 8vo. 463p. brn cloth. VG. T10. $50.00

MACKENZIE. *Mackenzie's Five Thousand Receipts in All Useful...Arts.* 1853. Phil. Troutman Hayes. rebound. A16. $70.00

MACKEY, Sandra. *Saudis: Inside the Desert Kingdom.* 1987. Houghton Mifflin. 1st. 433p. VG. W1. $22.00

MACKEY & SOOY. *Early California Costumes 1769-1850.* 1949. Stanford. 2nd. 8vo. xl. VG. O4. $15.00

MACKINSTRY, Elizabeth. *Aladdin & the Wonderful Lamp.* 1935. Macmillan. 1st. 4to. unp. NF/G+ clip. C14. $38.00

MACLACHLAN, Colin. *Criminal Justice in 18th-Century Mexico.* 1974. Berkeley. 1st. 141p. dj. F3. $30.00

MACLAREN, Malcom. *Rise of the Electrical Industry in the 19th Century.* 1943. Princeton. 1st. 225p. VG/dj. B5. $45.00

MACLAREN, Sherrill. *Braehead.* 1986. Toronto. McClelland Stewart. dj. A19. $40.00

MACLAURIN, C. *Mere Mortals.* 1925. Doran. 8vo. 291p. VG/dj. K3. $15.00

MACLAURIN, C. *Post Mortem.* nd. Doran. 8vo. 260p. K3. $15.00

MACLAURIN, Colin. *Account of Sir Isaac Newton's Philosophical Discoveries.* 1750 (1748). London. Millar. 2nd. 8vo. 412p. rebound modern leather. K5. $450.00

MACLAY, Edgar Stanton. *History of the United States Navy.* 1894. NY. Appleton. 2 vol. ils. rebacked. T7. $125.00

MACLEAN, A.D. *Winter's Tales 24.* 1974. St Martin. 1st Am. F/dj. M2. $15.00

MACLEAN, Alistair. *Athabasca.* 1980. Doubleday. 1st Am. F/F. N4. $25.00

MACLEAN, Alistair. *Bear Island.* 1971. Collins. 1st. F/F. N4. $30.00

MACLEAN, Alistair. *Bear Island.* 1971. London. Collins. 1st. VG/dj. P3. $25.00

MACLEAN, Alistair. *Captain Cook.* 1972. Doubleday. 1st. F/dj. B26/M19. $25.00

MACLEAN, Alistair. *Carvan to Vaccares.* 1970. London. Collins. 1st Am. F/dj. Q1. $35.00

MACLEAN, Alistair. *Force 10 From Navarone.* 1968. Doubleday. 1st Am. VG+/VG. N4. $25.00

MACLEAN, Alistair. *Guns for Navarone.* 1957. Doubleday. 1st. VG/VG. R14. $35.00

MACLEAN, Alistair. *HMS Ulysses.* 1955. London. Collins. 1st Eng (true 1st). gilt red cloth. F/VG+. T11. $95.00

MACLEAN, Alistair. *Last Frontier.* 1959. London. Collins. 1st. F/VG+. T11. $50.00

MACLEAN, Alistair. *Puppet on a Chain.* 1969. Doubleday. 1st Am. NF/VG. N4. $25.00

MACLEAN, Alistair. *Seawitch.* 1977. Doubleday. 1st Am. F/NF. N4. $25.00

MACLEISH, Archibald. *Collected Poems, 1971-1952.* 1952. Houghton Mifflin. rpt. sgn. F/dj. M24. $65.00

MACLEISH, Archibald. *Fall of the City: A Verse Play for Radio.* 1937. Farrar Rinehart. 8vo. 33p. orange brd. NF/torn glassine dj. T10. $45.00

MACLEISH, Archibald. *Songs for Eve.* 1954. Houghton Mifflin. 1st. sgn. gilt red cloth. F/dj. M24. $75.00

MACLEISH, Roderick. *Prince Ombra.* (1982). Congdon Weed. 3rd. F/NF. M21. $7.50

MACLEISH & VAN DOREN. *Dialogues.* 1964. Dutton. 1st. edit Warren Bush. F/F. B35. $35.00

MACLEOD, Barbara. *Children's Twilight Tales.* 1942. NY. Henry Harrison. 1st. inscr/dtd 1942. NF. C14. $25.00

MACLEOD, Charlotte. *An Owl Too Many.* 1991. Mysterious. 1st. F/F. N4. $20.00

MACLEOD, Charlotte. *Recycled Citizen.* 1988. Mysterious. 1st. F/F. N4. $20.00

MACLEOD, Charlotte. *Silver Ghost.* 1988. Mysterious. 1st. F/F. N4. $20.00

MACLEOD, Charlotte. *Something the Cat Dragged in.* 1983. Doubleday. 1st. F/NF. Q1. $30.00

MACLEOD, Fiona. *Dominion of Dreams.* 1900. Stokes. 1st Am. VG. M2. $50.00

MACLEOD. *Moral Tale: Children's Fiction & American Culture 1820-60.* 1975. 196p. F. A4. $30.00

MACMANUS, Seamus. *Ballads of a Country Boy.* 1905. MH Gill. 1st. inscr/dtd 1909. 100p. gilt gr cloth. H1. $75.00

MACMANUS, Seamus. *Top O' the Mornin'.* 1920. Stokes. 1st. VG. M2. $20.00

MACMICHAEL, William. *Gold Headed Cane.* 1953. Springfield, IL. 7th. 186p. uncut. VG/worn. K3. $25.00

MACMINN, George R. *Theater of the Golden Era in California.* 1941. Caxton. ils. 529p. yel stp blk cloth. D11. $60.00

MACNEICE, Louis. *One for the Grave.* 1968. Oxford. ARC. RS. dj. V1. $25.00

MACOBOY, S. *Ultimate Rose Book.* 1993. Abrams. folio. ils. 472p. F/F. E6. $25.00

MACPHERSON, James. *Fingal, an Ancient Epic Poem in Six Books...* 1762. London. Beckett DeHondt. 2nd. tall 4to. 270p. full polished calf/rebacked. H13. $375.00

MACPHERSON, Margaret L. *Australia Calling.* 1946. Dodd Mead. 1st. sgn. 197p. VG/VG. M20. $20.00

MACPHERSON & STUART-WORTLEY. *Partridge: Natural History, Shooting, Cookery.* 1894. Longman Gr. 2nd. 276p. pict bdg. xl. VG. H7. $20.00

MACQUITTY, William. *Tutankhamun: The Last Journey.* 1978. NY. Quartet Books. BC. 5th. ils. 50p. NF/dj. W1. $18.00

MACRAE, Stuart. *Winston Churchill's Toyshop: Invention & Making...* 1971. NY. photos/index. 228p. VG/VG. S16. $24.00

MACSHERIDAN, C. *Stag Cook Book: Man's Cook Book for Men.* 1922. Doran. 197p. B10. $25.00

MACSWIGGAN, A.E. *Fairy Lamps.* 1962. Fountainhead. 1st. sgn. 170p. VG/dj. M20. $45.00

MACVEY, John. *Colonizing Other Worlds.* 1984. Stein Day. 1st. F/dj. M2. $15.00

MADAULE, Jacques. *Albigensian Crusade.* 1967. NY. Fordham. 8vo. 177p. VG/dj. W1. $22.00

MADDAMS, W.F. *Interesting Newer Mammillarias.* nd. np. Mammillarian Soc. photos. brn cloth. F. B26. $17.50

MADDEN, Betty I. *Art, Crafts & Architecture in Early Illinois.* 1974. Urbana. 1st. ils. 297p. VG/dj. B18. $22.50

MADDEN, John. *First Book of Football.* 1988. Crown. 1st. sgn. F/F. A23. $40.00

MADDEN, John. *One Size Doesn't Fit All.* 1988. Villard. 1st. sgn. F. A23. $40.00

MADDISON, Francis. *Sir William Dugdale 1605-1686.* 1953. Warick. Warwickshire County Council. 92p. prt sewn wrp. M11. $45.00

MADISON, Charles A. *Yiddish Literature: Its Scope & Major Writers.* 1968. NY. Ungar. 540p. VG/G+. S3. $28.00

MADISON, Lucy Foster. *Washington.* 1925. Phil. Penn Pub. 1st. 8vo. 399p. G+. C14. $17.00

MADS, George. *Winchester Book.* 1985. Brownesboro, TX. sgn. 655p. M. A17. $50.00

MAE, Verta. *Vibration Cooking; or, Travel Notes of a Geechee Girl.* 1970. Doubleday. 1st. 190p. F/F. B4. $85.00

MAETERLINCK, Maurice. *Hours of Gladness.* 1912. London. Allen. 1st. ils Detmold. lg 4to. gilt wht cloth. R5. $400.00

MAETERLINCK, Maurice. *Inner Beauty.* 1910. London. 1st. half leather. VG+. S13. $50.00

MAETERLINCK, Maurice. *Life of the Bee.* nd. Bl Ribbon. rpt. VG. E6. $12.00

MAGEE, David. *Infinite Riches: Adventures of a Rare Book Dealer.* 1973. NY. Eriksson. 1st. ils. 274p. VG+/dj. K3. $25.00

MAGEE, David. *Jam Tomorrow.* 1941. Houghton Mifflin. 1st. author's 1st book. F/dj. Q1. $75.00

MAGNAN, Valentin. *Recherches sur les Centres Nerveux...* 1893. Paris. Masson. 8vo. 572p. xl. VG. G1. $175.00

MAGNER, D. *Magner's Standard Horse & Stock Book.* 1900. Akron. Saalfield. 1st. 1181p. rebacked. VG. O3. $95.00

MAGNI, Laura. *Goodnight Stories From the Big Tree.* 1990. Derrydale. 1st Am. 192p. NF. C14. $20.00

MAGNIAUX, Phillippe. *Adventures of Charlie Chaplin, the Gold Rush.* 1975. Drake. ils. lg laminated brd. NF/sans. C9. $75.00

MAGOUN, F. Alexander. *Frigate Constitution & Other Historic Ships.* 1928. Marine Research Soc. 154p. cloth. VG. M20. $200.00

MAGRIEL, P. *Backgammon.* 1976. NY. 1st. VG/VG. B5. $60.00

MAGRIEL, P. *Pavlova: Illustrated Monograph.* 1948. photos. VG/G+. M17. $25.00

MAHAN, A.T. *Gulf & Inland Waters.* 1883. Scribner. 1st. 12mo. 267p. VG. M1. $125.00

MAHAN, A.T. *Types of Naval Officers.* 1902. London. Sampson Low. 7 pl. 500p. T7. $80.00

MAHAN, D.H. *Summary of the Course of Permanent Fornication...* 1850. West Point, NY. Lith at US Mill Academy. 1st. 372p. M1. $550.00

MAHFOUZ, Naguib. *Atlas of Mahfouz's Obstetric & Gynaecological Museum.* 1949. Altricham, Eng. 1st. 3 vol. 1276p. A13. $200.00

MAHLER, Raphael. *History of Modern Jewry 1780-1815.* 1971. Schocken. 742p. VG/dj. S3. $40.00

MAHONEY, Latimer. *Illustrators of Children's Books 1744-1945.* 1947. ltd. 4to. ils. 544p. VG. A4. $145.00

MAHONEY, Latimer. *Illustrators of Children's Books 1744-1945.* 1947. Horn Book. 1st. 4to. VG/home-made case. D1. $175.00

MAHONEY & WHITNEY. *Realms of Gold.* 1929. Doubleday Doran. various ils. 796p. VG. P2. $50.00

MAILER, Norman. *Advertisements for Myself.* 1959. Putnam. 1st. VG/VG. R14. $40.00

MAILER, Norman. *American Dream.* 1965. Dial. 1st. NF/dj. Q1. $60.00

MAILER, Norman. *Ancient Evenings.* 1983. Little Brn. 1st. F/F. B35. $35.00

MAILER, Norman. *Barbary Shore.* 1951. NY. Rinehart. 1st. NF/dj. from $110 to $150.00

MAILER, Norman. *Cannibals & Christians.* 1966. Dial. 1st. VG/VG. R14. $35.00

MAILER, Norman. *Deer Park.* 1967. NY. Dial. 1st. F/clip. Q1. $100.00

MAILER, Norman. *Executioner's Song.* 1979. Little Brn. 1st. F/F. H11. $60.00

MAILER, Norman. *Genius & Lust.* 1976. Grove. 1st. F/dj. Q1. $40.00

MAILER, Norman. *Harlot's Ghost.* 1991. Random. 1st. sgn. F/F. R14. $60.00

MAILER, Norman. *Naked & the Dead.* 1948. 1st. author's 1st book. rem mk. VG/torn. A15. $75.00

MAILER, Norman. *Of a Fire on the Moon.* 1970. Little Brn. 1st. NF/clip. Q1. $40.00

MAILER, Norman. *Oswald's Tale: An American Mystery.* 1995. Random. 1st. sgn. VG/VG. A23. $50.00

MAILER, Norman. *Pieces & Pontifications.* 1983. NEL. 1st. sgn. F/dj. A24. $45.00

MAILER, Norman. *Prisoner of Sex.* 1971. Boston. 1st. VG/VG. T9. $20.00

MAILER, Norman. *St George & the Godfather.* 1983. Arbor. 1st. F/F. A24. $35.00

MAILER, Norman. *Tough Guys Don't Dance.* 1984. Random. 1st. F/F. A20. $25.00

MAILLET. *Telliamed; or, World Explain'd.* 1797. Baltimore. Pechin for Porter. 8vo. calf. R12. $250.00

MAILS, Thomas E. *Fools Crow.* 1979. Doubleday. 1st. F/dj. A19. $50.00

MAINE, Charles Eric. *Crisis 2000.* 1956. London. 1st. F/dj. M2. $25.00

MAINE, Henry Sumner. *Ancient Law, Its Connection With Early History of Society...* 1908. London. gilt gr cloth. G. M11. $50.00

MAIR, John. *Fourth Forger.* 1938. London. Cobden Sanderson. 1st. ils. VG. K3. $45.00

MAITLAND, F.W. *Bracton's Note Book: A Collection of Cases...* 1983 (1887). Littleton. facsimile. M11. $350.00

MAITLAND, F.W. *Constitutional History of England.* 1908. Cambridge. 1st. cloth. M11. $125.00

MAITLAND, F.W. *Domesday Book & Beyond, Three Essays in Early History...* 1921. Cambridge. bl cloth. M11. $85.00

MAITLAND, F.W. *English Law & the Renaissance.* 1901. London. Cambridge. gilt crimson cloth. M11. $100.00

MAITLAND, F.W. *Equity, a Course of Lectures...* 1969. Cambridge. VG/dj. M11. $85.00

MAITLAND, F.W. *Roman Canon Law in the Church of England, Six Essays.* 1968 (1898). Burt Franklin. facsimile. M11. $75.00

MAITLAND, F.W. *Why the History of English Law Is Not Written.* 1888. London. 20p. sewn wrp. M11. $125.00

MAJDALANY, Fred. *Cassino: Portrait of a Battle.* 1957. London. ils/biblio/index. 270p. VG/VG. S16. $24.00

MAJNO, Guido. *Healing Hand: Man & Wound in the Ancient World.* 1975. Cambridge. 1st. 571p. A13. $50.00

MAJOR, Clarence. *All-Night Visitors.* 1969. Olympia. 1st. f/VG clip. B4. $100.00

MAJOR, Clarence. *Painted Turtle: Woman With Guitar.* 1988. Sun Moon. 1st. sgn. F/F. R14. $40.00

MAJOR, John. *Oppenheimer Hearing.* 1971. Stein Day. ils. 8vo. 336p. VG/ils wrp. K3. $15.00

MAJOR, Ralph H. *Classic Descriptions of Disease.* 1932. Thomas. 630p. dj. A17. $30.00

MAKEMSON, Maud. *Book of the Jaguar Priest.* 1951. NY. Schuman. 1st. 238p. dj. F3. $45.00

MAKSHEV, O.A. *Patriotic War of 1812 in Paintings.* 1912. Paris. Lapina. folio. crimson cloth portfolio. F. B24. $250.00

MAKUCK, Peter. *Where We Live.* 1982. BOA Ed. 1/10 (of 1200). sgns. w/holograph poem. F. V1. $100.00

MALAMUD, Bernard. *Dubin's Lives.* 1979. Franklin Lib. 1st. decor gr leather. F/sans. T11. $40.00

MALAMUD, Bernard. *Natural.* 1963. Eyre Spottiswoode. 1st Eng. author's 1st book. F/dj. Q1. $450.00

MALAMUD, Bernard. *Pictures of Fidelman.* 1969. Farrar. 1st. NF/clip. M25. $25.00

MALAMUD, Bernard. *Tenants.* 1971. FSG. 1st. NF/NF. R14. $35.00

MALAMUD, Bernard. *Two Fables.* 1978. Pawlet, VT. 1/320. sgn/#d. F. B2. $100.00

MALAURIE, Jean. *Last Kings of Thule: Year Among the Eskimos of Greenland.* 1956. ils/photos. VG/VG. M17. $30.00

MALCOLM, Fiona. *Child's Own Visions.* 1916. London. Harrap. 1st. ils Anderson/4 mtd pl. cloth. R5. $175.00

MALET, Andre. *Thought of Rudolf Bultmann.* 1969. Doubleday. 440p. VG/torn. B29. $8.50

MALET, Lucas. *Tall Villa.* 1919. Doran. 1st. VG. M2. $25.00

MALING, Arthur. *Taste of Treason.* 1983. Harper Row. 1st. F/F. H11. $20.00

MALL, Thomas. *History of the Martyrs Epitomised...* 1747. Boston. Rogers Fowle. 1st Am. 2 vol. later bdg. M1. $225.00

MALLAN, Lloyd. *Men, Rockets & Space Rats.* 1956 (1955). NY. Messner. 2nd. 8vo. 335p. G/dj. K5. $30.00

MALLARD, Robert Q. *Plantation Life Before Emancipation.* 1892. Richmond, VA. Whittet Shepperson. 1st. 237p. cloth. NF. M8. $250.00

MALLARME, Stephane. *Selected Letters.* 1988. Chicago. 1st. trans R Lloyd. VG/dj. T9. $15.00

MALLET, Thierry. *Glimpses of the Barren Lands.* 1930. NY. Fevillon Freres. 1st. 142p. VG. H7. $15.00

MALLONEE, R.C. *Naked Flagpole.* 1980. CA. 1st. ils/maps. 204p. VG/VG. S16. $25.00

MALLORY, William Wyman. *Geologic Atlas of the Rocky Mountain Region, US of Am.* 1972. Rocky Mtn Assn Geolog. full-p maps. 331p. gilt cloth. D11. $40.00

MALM, William. *Japanese Music & Musical Instruments.* 1974. Rutland/Tokyo. ils/pl/figures/4 append/glossary. 299p. F/F. W3. $56.00

MALONE, Michael. *Painting the Roses Red.* 1974. Random. ARC. author's 1st novel. RS. F/F. B4. $250.00

MALONE, Michael. *Psychetypes: A New Way of Exploring Personality.* 1977. Dutton. 1st. F/F. B4. $250.00

MALONE, Michael. *Uncivil Seasons.* 1983. Delacorte. 1st. F/F. M22. $65.00

MALONEY, Richard C. *Fifty Notable Ship Portraits at Mystic Seaport.* 1963. Marine Hist Assn. ils. 63p. P4. $25.00

MALORY, Thomas. *Le Morte d'Arthur.* 1955. NY. Heritage. 4to. 757p. patterned brd/blk linen spine. F/G case. H13. $65.00

MALOUF, David. *Johnno.* 1975. Queensland. correct 1st. author's 1st novel. NF/NF. L3. $150.00

MALTBY, Lucy Mary. *It's Fun to Cook.* (1938). Phil. Winston. 8vo. 399p. VG/G+. T5. $25.00

MALZBERG, Barry. *Herovit's World.* 1973. Random. 1st. F/dj. M2. $25.00

MAMET, David. *Some Freaks.* 1989. NY. Viking. 1st. F/F. R14. $35.00

MAMET, David. *Village.* 1994. Little Brn. 1st. F/F. R13. $20.00

MAMET, David. *Writing in Resturants.* 1986. Viking. 1st. sgn. F/F. D10. $60.00

MAMMANA, Dennis. *Star Hunters.* 1990. Phil. Running Pr. 160p. F/F. K5. $20.00

MANCHESTER, William. *Death of a President November 20-November 25, 1963.* 1967. Harper Row. 1st. F/F. H11. $25.00

MANDERS, Olga Sarah. *Mrs Manders' Cook Book.* 1968. NY. Viking. G/dj. A16. $15.00

MANFRED, Frederick. *Man Who Looked Like the Prince of Wales.* 1965. Trident. 1st. NF/dj. M25. $45.00

MANFRED, Frederick. *Riders of Judgment.* 1957. Random. 1st. VG/dj. w/author's photo. M25. $35.00

MANFRED, Frederick. *This Is the Year.* 1947. Doubleday. 1st. VG/dj. M25. $45.00

MANFRED, Frederick. *Wanderlust: A Trilogy.* 1962. Swallow. 1st thus. NF/dj. A18. $50.00

MANGAN, F. *Pipeliners: Story of El Paso Natural Gas.* 1977. El Paso. Guynes. ils/photos. 354p. cloth. NF/dj. D8. $35.00

MANGAN, Terry William. *Colorado on Glass...As Seen by the Camera.* 1975. Denver. Sundance Ltd. 1st. 1/250. sgn. 406p. brd. cloth case. w/contact prt. D11. $500.00

MANGELSDORF, Paul. *Corn: Its Origin, Evolution & Improvement.* 1974. Cambridge. Harvard. 262p. VG/dj. A10. $20.00

MANGLAPUS, Raul S. *Philippines: Silenced Democracy.* 1976. Maryknoll, NY. Orbis Books. 203p. cloth. M/VG. P1. $10.00

MANGUEL, Alberto. *Seasons.* 1987. Doubleday. ils Warabe Aska. 48p. F/F. D4. $30.00

MANKOWITZ, Wolf. *Wedgwood.* 1966 (1953). Spring Books. 284p. gilt bl cloth. NF/plastic dj. H1. $65.00

MANLEY, William Lewis. *Death Valley in '49.* 1894. San Jose, CA. Pacific Tree & Vine. 1st. 498p. VG. K7. $250.00

MANLOVE. *Impulse of Fantasy Literature.* 1983. 188p. F/F. A4. $45.00

MANN, Arthur. *Baseball Confidential.* 1951. NY. 1st. VG/VG. B5. $25.00

MANN, Edward Andrew. *Portals.* 1974. S&S. 1st. F/dj. M2. $10.00

MANN, Felix. *Acupuncture: Ancient Chinese Art of Healing.* 1963. Random. fwd Aldous Huxley. 174p. F/VG. W3. $42.00

MANN, Heinrich. *Henry, King of France.* 1939. Knopf. 1st Am. F/VG+. B4. $125.00

MANN, Heinrich. *Small Town Tyrant.* 1944. Creative Age. 1st Am. VG/VG. B4. $250.00

MANN, M.T. *Rev JT Mann of Fitzgerald, Georgia...* ca 1907. np. 1st. NF/prt wrp. M8. $1,250.00

MANN, Thomas. *Doctor Faustus.* 1948. Knopf. 1st. NF/VG. M19. $25.00

MANN, Thomas. *Holy Sinner.* 1951. Knopf. 1st. 336p. blk cloth. F/VG. B22. $12.00

MANN, Thomas. *Sketch of My Life.* 1960. Knopf. 1st. F/VG. M19. $25.00

MANN, Thomas. *Transposed Heads: A Legend of India.* 1977. Kentfield, CA. Allen. 1/140. 4to. 108p. Indian cloth. F. B24. $475.00

MANNIN, Ethel. *Lovely Land: Hashemite Kingdom of Jordan.* 1965. London. Hutchinson. 1st. 17 pl. VG/dj. W1. $24.00

MANNING, Elise W. *Farm Journal's Friendly Food Gifts From Your Kitchen.* 1978. Doubleday. G/dj. A16. $7.50

MANNING, J. Russell. *Illustrated Stock Doctor.* 1882. Phil. Hibbard. leather. G. O3. $48.00

MANNING, R. *What Kinda Cactus Izzat?* 1957 (1941). Phoenix. 7th or later. 108p. VG. B26. $6.00

MANNING-SANDERS, Ruth. *Book of Sorcerers & Spells.* 1975 (1973). London. Methuen. rpt. sm 4to. 125p. VG. T5. $25.00

MANO, D. Keith. *Horn.* 1969. Houghton Mifflin. 1st. sgn. NF/NF. R14. $45.00

MANSFIELD, Katherine. *Dove's Nest.* 1923. London. Constable. 1st/2nd issue. gr cloth. F. M24. $85.00

MANSFIELD, Katherine. *In a German Pension.* 1926. Knopf. 1st Am. gr cloth/label. F. M24. $75.00

MANSFIELD, Katherine. *Poems.* 1924. Knopf. 1st Am. gr linen/orange decor brd/label. F/dj. M24. $200.00

MANSO, Peter. *Mailer: His Life & Times.* 1985. S&S. 1st. F/F. T12. $20.00

MANTEGAZZA, Paolo. *Sexual Relations of Mankind.* 1932. Anthropological Pr. 1st. 1/1500. sm 4to. handmade/untrimmed paper. F. H1. $35.00

MANTEL, Hilary. *Fludd.* 1989. London. Viking. 1st. F/NF. B3. $15.00

MANTHEY, Gerda. *Fuchsias.* 1991. Portland. ils. 204p. as new/dj. B26. $39.00

MANTLE, Mickey. *All My Octobers.* 1994. NY. Harper Collins. 1st. NF/VG. R16. $25.00

MANTZ & MURRY. *Life of Katherine Mansfield.* 1933. London. Constable. 1st. 349p. VG. A25. $15.00

MANWOOD, John. *Treatise of the Laws of the Forest, Wherein Is Declared...* 1665. London. Prt for Co of Stationers. 3-quarter sheep. M11. $650.00

MANZONI, Alessandro. *I Promessi Sposi (The Betrothed).* 1951. Verona. Officina Bodoni. LEC. 1/1500. sgn Hans Mardersteig/Bramanti. F/VG case. T10. $150.00

MARA, Bernard; see Moore, Brian.

MARACOTTA, Lindsay. *Everything We Wanted.* 1984. Crown. 1st. 356p. NF/NF. W2. $20.00

MARAMOROSCH, K. *Invertebrate Tissue Culture.* 1976. Academic. 393p. cloth. VG. B1. $65.00

MARASCO, Robert. *Burnt Offerings.* 1973. Delacorte. 1st. author's 1st book. 260p. F/F. W2. $30.00

MARAT, Jean-Paul. *Discours...Sur la Defense of Louis XVI.* 1792. Paris. Impirmerie de Marat. 8vo. brd. R13. $550.00

MARBURY, Mary Orvis. *Favorite Flies & Their Histories.* 1988. Secaucus. facsimile 1892 ed. F/F. A17. $25.00

MARCEL, Pierre. *Biblical Doctrine of Infant Baptism.* 1959. James Clarke. 256p. VG/torn. B29. $7.50

MARCET, Jane Haldimand. *Conversations on Vegetable Physiology...* 1829. London. Longman Rees. 2 vol. A10. $95.00

MARCH, Daniel. *Home Life in the Bible.* 1873. ils. VG. M17. $25.00

MARCH & TAMBIMUTTU. *TS Eliot: A Symposium.* 1949. Chicago. 1st. 259p. F/dj. A17. $35.00

MARCOS, Ferdinand E. *Today's Revolution: Democracy.* 1971. Manila. sm 8vo. 152p. M/VG. P1. $15.00

MARCOSSON, I.F. *Anaconda.* 1957. Dodd Mead. 370p. cloth. VG. D8. $18.00

MARCUS, G.J. *Naval History of England.* 1961. Little Brn. 18 maps. 494p. T7. $35.00

MARCUS, J.S. *Art of Cartography.* 1991. Knopf. 1st. author's 1st book. F/F. A24. $35.00

MARCUS, Joyce. *Inscriptions of Calakmul.* 1987. Ann Arbor. 1st. 4to. 205p. wrp. F3. $25.00

MARECHAUX, Pascal. *Arabia Felix: Images of Yemen & Its People.* 1980. NY. Barron. 1st Am. NF/dj. W1. $45.00

MAREK, George. *Opera as Theater.* 1962. NY. 1st. inscr. VG/VG. T9. $50.00

MAREY, E.J. *Animal Mechanism: Treatise Terrestrial & Aerial Locomotion.* 1874. London. King. 1st Eng-language ed. 12mo. 283p+32p catalog. red cloth. G1. $125.00

MARGOLIN & WYLIE. *Ring of Dancers: Images of Faroese Culture.* 1981. Phil. 1st. 182p. rust cloth. P4. $25.00

MARGOLIS & SENDAK. *Some Swell Pup.* 1976. FSG. 1st. unp. VG/VG. D1. $55.00

MARGULIES, Leo. *Flying Wildcats.* 1943. Hampton. 1st. VG. M2. $35.00

MARIA, Father Vincent. *San Francisco Bay 1775.* 1971. SF. John Howell. A19. $45.00

MARIANO & MOZINO. *Noticias de Nutka.* 1913. Mexico City. Imprenta Y Fototipia Secretaria Fomento. 117p. wrp. P4. $500.00

MARIO, Queena. *Murder in the Opera House.* 1934. NY. 1st. VG/VG. B5. $50.00

MARIO, Thomas. *Playboy's Host & Bar Book.* 1971. Chicago. Playboy. VG. A16. $15.00

MARION, Frances. *Powder Keg.* 1953. Little Brn. 1st. inscr. F/VG+. B4. $275.00

MARIS, Jesse. *Remembering.* 1951. np. 1st. sgn pres. ils/photos. 84p. VG. B5. $50.00

MARITAIN, Jacques. *France My Country, Through the Disaster.* 1941. Longman Gr. 1st trans ed. 8vo. 117p. VG/dj. T10. $50.00

MARK, Stuart A. *Southern Hunting in Black & White: Nature, History...* 1991. Princeton. 1st. 327p. M/dj. A17. $15.00

MARK, Yudel. *Grammar of Standard Yiddish.* 1978. Congress Jewish Culture. Yiddish text. 394p. VG+. S3. $27.00

MARKBREIT & STEINBERG. *Born to Referee.* 1988. Morrow. 1st. photos. F/VG. P8. $12.50

MARKENS, Isaac. *Hebrew in America, a Series of Historical...Sketches.* 1888. self pub. VG. E6. $100.00

MARKHAM, Clements R. *Narrative of Proceedings of Pedrarias Davila...* 1865. London. Hakluyt Soc. 8vo. fld map. 88p. gilt bl cloth. P4. $395.00

MARKHAM, Edwin. *Man With the Hoe & Other Poems.* 1899. Doubleday McClure. 1st collected/2nd issue. 8vo. 134p. cloth. case. M1. $200.00

MARKHAM, Edwin. *Man With the Hoe & Other Poems.* 1900. Doubleday. inscr to RJ Hinton/dtd 1900. NF. Q1. $125.00

MARKHAM, Edwin. *Shoes of Happiness & Other Poems.* 1913. Doubleday Page. sgn. VG. M20. $25.00

MARKHAM, Ernest. *Raspberries & Kindred Fruits.* 1936. London. Macmillan. 68p. VG/dj. A10. $28.00

MARKMAN & MARKMAN. *Flayed Gods.* 1992. Harper. 1st. 456p. xl. dj. F3. $15.00

MARKMANN & SHERWIN. *Book of Sports Cars.* 1959. Putnam. 1st. 323p. cloth. VG/clip. M20. $30.00

MARKOFF, Alexander. *Russians on the Pacific Ocean.* 1955. LA. Glen Dawson. 1/300. decor cloth. D11. $75.00

MARKS, David. *Treatise on Faith of Freewill Baptists...* 1834. Dover. 1st. 18mo. 156p. F. M1. $200.00

MARKS, J.; see Highwater, Jamake.

MARKS, Lis. *Ghostly Towers.* 1986. Dial. 1st. ils Angela Barrett. F. T10. $50.00

MARKS, Paul Mitchell. *And Die in the West.* 1989. Morrow. 1st. 480p. VG/VG. J2. $225.00

MARKS, Richard Lee. *Three Men of the Beagle.* 1991. Knopf. 1st. 8vo. index/bibliography/map ep. NF/dj. P4. $35.00

MARKS-HIGHWATER, J.; see Highwater, Jamake.

MARKSON, David. *Ballad of Dingus Magee.* 1965. Bobbs Merrill. 1st. sgn. F/dj. Q1. $60.00

MARKSON, David. *Going Down.* 1970. HRW. 1st. sgn. F/dj. Q1. $50.00

MARKSON, David. *Malcolm Lowry's Volcano.* 1978. Times Books. 1st. sgn. F/F. Q1. $60.00

MARKSON, David. *Springer's Progress.* 1977. HRW. 1st. sgn. F/dj. Q1. $50.00

MARKSON, David. *Wittgenstein's Mistress.* 1988. Elmwood Park, IL. Dalkey Archive. 1st. sgn. F/dj. Q1. $50.00

MARKUS, Kurt. *Buckaroon.* 1987. Little Brn. 1st. 127p. VG/VG. J2. $195.00

MARKUS, Rixi. *Common-Sense Bridge.* 1972. NY. 1st Am. 171p. VG/dj. S1. $6.00

MARLIN, J. *Appeal to the Heart.* 1985. Putnam. 1st. 138p. F/F. W2. $15.00

MARLOWE, Dan J. *Operation Flashpoint.* 1972. London. Wht Lion. 1st hc. F/dj. M15. $45.00

MARLOWE, Derek. *Dandy in Aspic.* 1966. Putnam. 1st. author's 1st book. F/NF. H11. $25.00

MARLOWE, Hugh; see Patterson, Harry.

MAROGER, Jacques. *Secret Formulas & Techniques of the Masters.* 1948. Studio. trans from French. 200p. gray cloth. B14. $45.00

MAROIS, Blanche. *Le Premier Livre.* 1928. Neuvieme Ed/Pour Les Petis Enfants. ils. VG. M17. $30.00

MARON, Margaret. *Bootlegger's Daughter.* 1992. Mysterious. 1st. F/F. D10. $55.00

MARON, Margaret. *Bootlegger's Daughter.* 1992. Mysterious. 1st. NF/dj. Q1. $50.00

MARON, Margaret. *Corpus Christmas.* 1989. Doubleday. 1st. F/F. D10. $45.00

MARON, Margaret. *Death of a Butterfly.* 1984. Doubleday Crime Club. 1st. VG+/VG+. N4. $50.00

MARON, Margaret. *Past Imperfect.* 1991. Doubleday. 1st. F/F. D10. $35.00

MARON, Margaret. *Shooting at Loons.* 1994. Mysterious. 1st. sgn. F/F. R13. $35.00

MARON, Margaret. *Southern Discomfort.* 1993. Mysterious. 1st. sgn. F/F. A23. $40.00

MARQUEZ, Gabriel Garcia. *Autumn of the Patriarch.* 1976. Harper Row. 1st Am. F/NF. D10. $75.00

MARQUEZ, Gabriel Garcia. *Collected Stories.* 1984. Harper Row. 1st. F/F. B3/D10. $45.00

MARQUEZ, Gabriel Garcia. *El Amor en los Tiempos de Colera.* 1985. Mexico. 1st/Editorial Diana issue. F/F. A11. $65.00

MARQUEZ, Gabriel Garcia. *El Otono del Patriarca.* 1975. Buenos Aires. Editorial Sudamericana. 1st Latin Am. F/NF wrp. B4. $450.00

MARQUEZ, Gabriel Garcia. *General in His Labyrinth.* 1990. NY. 1st. VG/VG. T9. $15.00

MARQUEZ, Gabriel Garcia. *Innocent Erendira & Other Stories.* 1978. Harper Row. 1st author's 5th book. F/F clip. H11. $65.00

MARQUEZ, Gabriel Garcia. *La Hojarasca.* 1955. Bogota. Ediciones SLB. 1st. author's 1st book. VG/self wrp. L3. $25.00

MARQUEZ, Gabriel Garcia. *Love in the Time of Cholera.* 1988. London. Cape. 1st. F/F. D10. $50.00

MARQUEZ, Gabriel Garcia. *Of Love & Other Demons.* 1995. Knopf. 1st Am. trans Edith Grossman. F/dj. Q1. $25.00

MARQUIS, Thomas B. *Keep the Last Bullet for Yourself.* 1976. Two Continents. 1st. 203p. cloth. VG/dj. M20. $28.00

MARQUIS, Thomas B. *Rain-in-the-Face, Curley, the Crow.* 1934. Cactus Pony Pub. VG/wrp. J2. $28.00

MARR-JOHNSON, Diana. *Rainbow's Pop-Up Book.* 1960. London. Dean. ils Janet/Anne Grahame-Johnstone. pict brd. unused. R5. $75.00

MARRIC, J.J.; see Creasey, John.

MARRINER, John. *Black Sea & Blue River.* 1968. Hart Davis. 16 pl/28 maps. 240p. VG. W1. $20.00

MARSDEN, Brian G. *Catalog of Cometary Orbits.* 1983. Hillside, NJ. Enslow. 1st trade. VG/glossy wrp. K5. $15.00

MARSDEN, C. *Grow Cacti: A Practical Handbook.* 1958 (1955). London. enlarged 2nd. 4 mc pl. 178p. VG/dj. B26. $24.00

MARSDEN, John. *Fury of the Northmen: Saints & Shrines & Sea-Raiders...* 1995. NY. St Martin. 1st Am. M/dj. P4. $25.00

MARSH, Andrew. *Marsh's Manual of Reformed Phonetic Short-Hand.* 1868. SF. Bancroft. 1st. gilt blk cloth. NF. M24. $850.00

MARSH, Dave. *Glory Days.* 1986. Pantheon. 1st. F/F. A20. $10.00

MARSH, George P. *Lectures on the English Language.* 1860. NY. Scribner. 1st. 8vo. 697p. cloth. M1. $225.00

MARSH, George. *Toilers of the Trails.* 1921. Penn Pub. 1st. 245p. VG. J2. $65.00

MARSH, J.B.L. *Story of the Jubilee Singers.* 1877. 7th. VG. M17. $35.00

MARSH, Ngaio. *Colour Scheme.* 1943. London. Collins. 1st. NF/worn. B2. $80.00

MARSH, Ngaio. *Death at the Bar.* 1940. Little Brn. 1st Am. F/VG. M15. $125.00

MARSH, Ngaio. *Death of a Peer.* 1940. Little Brn. 1st. NF/VG. M22. $75.00

MARSH, Ngaio. *When in Rome.* 1970. Little Brn. 1st. F/NF. M19. $25.00

MARSH, O.C. *Dinocerata: Monograph of Extinct Order of Gigantic Mammals.* 1886. USGS. ils/55 pl/fld pl/200 figures. 243p. xl. VG. M12. $95.00

MARSHALIS & STEWART. *Sweet Swing Blues on the Road.* 1994. Norton. 1st. inscr. 190p. F/F. B4. $85.00

MARSHALL. *America's Great Comic Strip Artists.* nd. mc ils. 295p. F. M13. $85.00

MARSHALL, A.J. *Biology & Comparative Physiology of Birds.* 1960-61. NY/London. 2 vol. VG. S15. $65.00

MARSHALL, Alan; see Westlake, Donald E.

MARSHALL, Catherine. *Friends With God: Stories & Prayers of the Marshall Family.* 1956. Whittlesey. 1st. 48p. NF/VG clip. C14. $18.00

MARSHALL, Don B. *California Shipwrecks.* 1978. Seattle. Superior Pub. 1st. inscr. ils. 175p. dj. T7. $35.00

MARSHALL, Edison. *Love Stories of India.* 1950. Farrar. 1st. VG/dj. M2. $20.00

MARSHALL, John A. *American Bastille: Hist of Illegal Arrests & Imprisonment...* 1870. Phil. Evans Stoddart. 4th. 728p. cloth. NF. M8. $85.00

MARSHALL, Marguerite Mooers. *Arms & the Girl.* 1942. Triangle/Blakiston. 1st thus/4th prt. 285p. VG/VG. A25. $20.00

MARSHALL, Mel. *Delectable Egg & How to Cook It.* 1968. NY. Trident. 1st. G/dj. A16. $15.00

MARSHALL, Paule. *Daughters.* 1991. Atheneum. 1st. sgn. author's 6th book. F/F. D10. $45.00

MARSHALL, Paule. *Soul Clap Hands & Sing.* 1961. NY. Atheneum. 1st. sgn. author's 2nd book. F/NF. D10. $165.00

MARSHALL, R. *Arctic Wilderness.* 1956. Berkeley. ils/photos/fld map. 171p. decor cloth. VG/VG. M12. $30.00

MARSHALL, Roger. *Race to Win.* 1980. NY. Norton. 1st. 8vo. 370p. F/VG. P4. $15.00

MARSHALL, S.L. *Pork Chop Hill.* nd. Nashville. BC. 22 maps/index. 315p. F/NF. W3. $28.00

MARSHALL, S.L.A. *Crimsoned Prairie: Indian Wars on the Great Plains.* 1972. Scribner. 1st. 256p. VG/worn. M20. $20.00

MARSHALL, W. Taylor. *Cataceae With Ils Keys of All Tribes...* 1941. Pasadena. 1st. ils. 227p. VG+. B26. $95.00

MARSHALL & WOODS. *Glossary of Succulent Plant Terms.* 1945 (1938). Pasadena. 2nd. ils/photos. 112p. maroon cloth. B26. $35.00

MARSTEN, Richard; see Hunter, Evan.

MARTENS & SISSON. *Jack London, First Editions, Illustrated...* 1979. 1/1000. ils. 167p. NF. A4. $625.00

MARTIN, A.E. *Bridal Bed Murders.* 1953. S&S. 1st. NF/VG. H11. $15.00

MARTIN, Albro. *James J Hill & the Opening of the Northwest.* 1992. MN Hist Soc. 676p. M/wrp. A17. $22.50

MARTIN, Alfred. *First Corinthians.* 1989. Loizeaux. 152p. F/dj. B29. $90.00

MARTIN, C.L. *Sketch of Sam Bass, the Bandit...* 1956 (1880). OK U. new ed/1st prt. ils. 166p. F/dj. M4. $35.00

MARTIN, Christopher. *Amistad Affair.* 1970. London. Abelard Schuman. 240p. dj. T7. $20.00

MARTIN, David. *Crying Heart Tattoo.* 1982. HRW. 1st. F/F. T12. $20.00

MARTIN, Douglas D. *Yuma Crossing.* 1954. Albuquerque. 1st. 8vo. VG+/dj. F7. $30.00

MARTIN, Douglas. *Telling Line: Essays on 15 Contemporary Book Illustrators.* 1989. London. Julia MacRae. 1st. 4to. 320p. F/dj. T10. $75.00

MARTIN, Edward W. *Secrets of the Great City.* 1868. Phil. 522p+2p ads. G. A17. $35.00

MARTIN, Edward. *Always Be on Time.* 1959. Harrisburg. 1st. inscr. 183p. VG/torn. B18. $27.50

MARTIN, Franklin. *South America From a Surgeon's Point of View.* 1922. NY. 1st. 325p. A13. $50.00

MARTIN, Fred. *Travel Book.* 1976. SF. Arion. 1/200. sgn. prt/sgn Andrew Hoyem. F/Lucite case. B24. $400.00

MARTIN, George. *Fevre Dream.* 1950. Farrar. 1st. VG/dj. M2. $45.00

MARTIN, George. *Verdi: His Music, Life & Times.* 1963. Dodd Mead. tall 8vo. 633p. as new/dj. H1. $20.00

MARTIN, Henry Byam. *Polynesian Journal.* 1981. Salem. ils. VG/VG. M17. $20.00

MARTIN, Jack; see Etchison, Dennis.

MARTIN, James E. *95 File.* 1973. S&S. 1st. sgn. 247p. VG+/dj. M20. $20.00

MARTIN, John. *Heirs of Hippocrates.* 1980. IA City. Friends of U IA Lib. 4to. 474p. F. K3. $65.00

MARTIN, L.C. *Theory of the Microscope.* 1967 (1966). London. Blackie. lg 8vo. 488p. VG/dj. K5. $55.00

MARTIN, Linda. *Way We Wore: Fashion Ils of Children's Ware...1870-1970.* 1978. ils. VG/VG. M17. $30.00

MARTIN, Percy. *Mexico's Treasure House (Guanajuato).* 1906. NY. Cheltenham. 1st. 256p. silvered/gilt red cloth. F3. $55.00

MARTIN, Pete. *Hollywood Without Make-Up.* 1948. Lippincott. 1st. VG. M25. $25.00

MARTIN, Robert Bernard. *Accents of Persuasion: Charlotte Bronte's Novels.* 1966. Faber. 2nd. cloth. VG+/dj. M20. $25.00

MARTIN, Robert. *Judas Journey.* 1956. Dodd Mead. 1st. 212p. cloth. VG/dj. M20. $25.00

MARTIN, Steve. *Cruel Shoes.* 1979. Putnam. 1st. F/F. H11. $35.00

MARTIN, Thomas Commerford. *Inventions, Researches & Writings of Nikola Tesla.* 1952. Milwaukee. rpt 1894 ed. 496p. A17. $20.00

MARTIN, Valerie. *Set in Motion.* 1978. FSG. 1st. author's 2nd book. NF/dj. L3. $75.00

MARTIN, William W. *Manual Ecclesiastical Architecture.* 1897. Jennings Graham. ils. 429p. fair. B29. $8.00

MARTIN, William. *Nerve Endings.* 1984. Crown. 1st. sgn. F/G. B11. $25.00

MARTIN, William. *These Were God's People: Bible History.* 1966. Southwest Co. 506p. G. B29. $7.00

MARTIN & MARTIN. *Black Extended Family.* 1978. Chicago. 1st. 129p. F/VG clip. B4. $45.00

MARTIN & MARTIN. *Lightning, a Cowboy's Colt.* 1948. Kansas City, MO. 4to. VG+. C8. $17.50

MARTIN & SACHS. *Electric Boats & Navigation.* 1894. NY. Shelley. ils. 224p. VG. T7. $145.00

MARTINEAU, Alice. *Herbaceous Garden.* 1913. Williams Norgate. 2nd imp. 8vo. 298p. A22. $60.00

MARTINEAU, Mrs. Philip. *Reminiscences of Hunting & Horses.* 1930. London. Benn. 1st. VG. O3. $58.00

MARTINEZ, Buck. *From Worst to First: Toronto Blue Jays in 1980.* 1985. Toronto. 1st. F. T12. $25.00

MARTINEZ, Oscar J. *Border People: Life & Society in the US-Mexican Borderlands.* nd. AZ U. 1st. as new/dj. V4. $20.00

MARTINEZ, Raymond J. *Mysterious Marie Laveau Voodoo Queen & Folk Tales...* ca 1980s. Jefferson, LA. Hope Pub. rpt. ils. 96p. VG+. A25. $10.00

MARTINS DE SIQUEIRA, Luis. *Informacao em Direito com Que se Satisfas per Parte...* 1630. Lisbon. Rodriguez. 1st/only. sm folio. 18th-C mottled calf. R15. $650.00

MARTONE, Michael. *Alive & Dead in Indiana.* 1984. Knopf. 1st. author's 1st book. F/F. H11. $35.00

MARTY, Martin E. *Health & Medicine in the Lutheran Tradition.* 1986. Crossroad. 178p. G/dj. B29. $7.00

MARUKI, Toshi. *Hiroshima No Pika.* nd. np. 1st Am. ils. F/dj. K3. $25.00

MARUKI & MARUKI. *Art of Ira Maruki & Toshiko Maruki.* 1985. 1st. photos. 128p. M/dj. K3. $50.00

MARUKI & MARUKI. *Atomic Bomb.* 1959. Niji Shobo. Eng/Japanese text. 18 repro paintings. 22p. K3. $75.00

MARX, Groucho. *Beds.* 1930. NY. 1st. VG. B5. $75.00

MARX, Harpo. *Harpo Speaks.* 1961. NY. 1st. VG/VG. B5. $40.00

MARX, Joseph Laurence. *Nagasaki, the Necessary Bomb.* 1971. 1st. VG/dj. K3. $20.00

MARX, Karl. *Poverty of Philosophy.* 1920. Charles Kerr. 1st. VG. V4. $22.50

MARX, Karl. *Salaires Prix, Profits.* 1899. Paris. Girard Briere. 8vo. orig prt wrp. R12. $60.00

MARX, Karl. *World Without Jews.* 1959. Philosophical Lib. VG/VG. V4. $17.50

MARX, Robert F. *Shipwrecks of the Western Hemisphere.* 1970s. NY. World. ils. 482p. dj. T7. $35.00

MARYANSKI, Richard A. *Antique Picture Frame Guide.* 1973. Cedar Forest. 80p. cloth. VG/dj. M20. $25.00

MARYE, George Thomas. *From '49 to '83 in California & Nevada.* 1923. SF. Robertson. pre-pub copy (pastebrd cover/cloth tape spine). K7. $50.00

MARZALEK, J.J. *Sherman: Soldier's Passion for Order.* 1993. NY. 1st. 635p. F/dj. M4. $20.00

MARZIO, Peter C. *Democratic Art.* 1979. Boston. Godine. 4to. 357p. M/dj. B24. $50.00

MASEFIELD, John. *South & East.* 1929. 1st. ils J Parsons. NF/G. M19. $35.00

MASELLA, Jack. *Racing Cancer.* 1963. Exposition. 1st. inscr. VG+. P8. $35.00

MASO, Carole. *Ghost Dance.* 1986. Northpoint. 1st. sgn. author's 1st book. F/F. L3. $75.00

MASON, Arthur. *Wee Men of Ballwooden.* 1930. Doubleday. stated 1st. ils Lawson. VG. M5. $38.00

MASON, Bobbie Ann. *Girl Sleuth.* 1975. Old Westbury. Feminist. 1st. inscr. prt wrp. R14. $175.00

MASON, Bobbie Ann. *In Country.* 1985. Harper Row. 1st. author's 1st novel. NF/NF. T11. $40.00

MASON, Bobbie Ann. *Spence & Lila.* 1988. Harper Row. 1st. F/NF. T11. $25.00

MASON, Charles. *Report of the Commissioner of Patents for Year 1855.* 1856. Nicholson. 488p. cloth. A10. $30.00

MASON, F. Van Wyck. *Harpoon in Eden.* 1969. Doubleday. 1st. 430p. bl cloth. H1. $20.00

MASON, F. Van Wyck. *Spider House.* 1932. Mystery League. 1st. NF/VG. M22. $75.00

MASON, Grace Sartwell. *His Wife's Job.* 1919. Appleton. 1st. F/F. B4. $125.00

MASON, J. Monck. *Comments on Plays of Beumont & Fletcher.* 1798. London. Harding. 1st. half leather/brd. VG. K3. $90.00

MASON, Mike. *Mystery of Marriage: as Iron Sharpens Iron.* 1985. Multnomah. 185p. F/dj. B29. $6.00

MASON, R.H. *Photography Yearbook.* 1979. Argus. 1st. 276p. F/NF. W2. $60.00

MASON, Susanna. *Selections From Letters & Manuscripts...* 1836. Phil. Rackliff Jones. 1st. 312p. V3. $30.00

MASON, Theodore C. *Battleship Sailor.* 1982. ils. VG. M17. $15.00

MASON, William M.A. *Poems.* 1771. York. new ed. VG. A15. $50.00

MASON & PACKER. *Illustrated Dictionary of Jewelery.* 1974. ils. VG/VG. M17. $30.00

MASPERO, Gaston. *Art in Egypt.* 1912. London. Heinemann. 12mo. 4 mc pl/photos. 314p. gilt gr cloth. VG. T10. $25.00

MASPERO, Gaston. *Popular Stories of Ancient Egypt.* 1967. New Hyde Park, NY. U Books. 316p. VG. W1. $30.00

MASQUERIER, Lewis. *Sociology; or, Reconstruction of Society...* 1877. NY. self pub. 1st. 12mo. cloth. M1. $325.00

MASSEY, A.B. *Orchids in Virginia.* 1953. Blacksburg, VA. 8vo. wrp. A22. $10.00

MASSMAN. *Bibliomidgets of Achille J St Onge: Memorial & Bibliography.* 1979. 1/1000. sgn. 100p. F/case. A4. $225.00

MASSON, Madeleine. *Birds of Passage.* 1950. Cape Town. HB Timmins. 1st. ils. 190p. VG. A25. $12.00

MASTERS, Anthony. *Literary Agents, the Novelist as Spy.* 1987. Oxford. 1st. VG/VG. T9. $20.00

MASTERS, Edgar Lee. *Fate of the Jury.* 1929. Appleton. 1st. F/VG. M23. $50.00

MASTERS, Edgar Lee. *Lee: A Dramatic Poem.* 1926. Macmillan. 1st. VG. M23. $50.00

MASTERS, Edgar Lee. *Maximilian: A Play in Five Acts.* 1902. Boston. Badger/Gorham. 1st. 12mo. 154p. xl. M1. $125.00

MASTERS, Edgar Lee. *Skeeters Kirby.* 1923. Macmillan. 1st. NF/VG+. M23. $75.00

MASTERS, John. *Deceivers.* 1952. Viking. 1st Am. F/dj. Q1. $60.00

MASTERS, John. *High Command.* 1983. Morrow. 1st Am. 404p. F/F. W2. $30.00

MASTERSON, Elsie. *Blueberry Hill Cookbook.* 1959. Crowell. 1st. sgn. VG/clip. M20. $75.00

MASTERSON, V.V. *Katy Railroad & the Last Frontier.* 1952. Norman, OK. dj. A19. $50.00

MASTERSON, William H. *William Blount.* 1954. Baton Rouge. LSU. 1st. 378p. cloth. NF/dj. M8. $65.00

MATEER, Mrs. A.H. *Handbook of New Terms & Newspaper Chinese.* 1917. Shanghai. 309p. VG. W3. $58.00

MATERA, Lia. *Prior Convictions.* 1991. S&S. 1st. as new/dj. N4. $25.00

MATHER, Berkely. *Spy for a Spy.* 1968. Scribner. 1st. F/F. H11. $35.00

MATHER, Cotton. *Essays to Do Good.* 1822. Lexington, KY. Skillman. 1st thus. 12mo. w/subscriber list. full calf. case. T10. $400.00

MATHER, Fred. *Men I Have Fished With: Sketches of Character...* 1897. NY. Forest/Stream. 1st. 371p. gilt gr cloth. G. H7. $65.00

MATHER, Helen. *Light Horsekeeping: How to Get a Horse & How to Keep It.* 1970. Dutton. 1st. G/G. O3. $15.00

MATHES, W. Michael. *Mexico on Stone: Lithography in Mexico, 1826-1900.* 1984. SF. BC of CA. 1/550. ils. pict brd/cloth spine. D11. $75.00

MATHESON, Donald H. *Something New in Model Boat Building.* 1950s. London. Hutchinson. ils. 80p. T7. $38.00

MATHESON, Richard. *Earthbound.* 1989. NY. Tom Doherty. 1st. inscr. F/F. A23. $50.00

MATHESON, Richard. *Earthbound.* 1994. Tor. 1st. as new/F. N4. $20.00

MATHESON, Richard. *What Dreams May Come.* 1978. Putnam. 1st. F/dj. M2. $65.00

MATHESON, Richard. *7 Steps to Midnight.* 1993. NY. Forge. 1st. sgn. F/F. A23. $50.00

MATHEWS, Jack. *Memoirs of a Bookman.* 1990. Athens, OH. 1st. NF/dj. K3. $15.00

MATHEWS, John Joseph. *Sundown.* 1934. Longman Gr. 1st. inscr. author's 2nd book. NF. L3. $750.00

MATHEWS, John Joseph. *Talking to the Moon.* 1945. Chicago. 1st. author's 3rd book. NF/G. L3. $175.00

MATHEWS, John Joseph. *Wah'Kon-Tah.* 1932. OK U. 1st. 539p. VG/dj. M20. $35.00

MATHIAS & MATHIAS. *Revision of the Andean Genus Niphogrton.* 1951. Berkeley. ils. 22p. VG/wrp. B26. $9.00

MATOS MOCTEZUMA, Eduardo. *Great Temple of the Aztecs.* 1988. Thames Hudson. 1st. 4to. 192p. dj. F3. $35.00

MATSCHAT, Cecile. *Seven Grass Huts: An Enginner's Wife in Central...America.* 1939. NY. ils. 218p. F3. $10.00

MATTES, Merrill J. *Platte River Narratives: A Descriptive Bibliography...* 1988. IL U. 1st. lg format. 632p. M/sans. A18. $95.00

MATTHES, F.E. *Incomparable Valley...Yosemite.* 1950. Berkeley. 1st paper-bound ed. photos Ansel Adams. 160p. VG. D8. $22.00

MATTHEWS, Basil. *Clash of Color: A Study in Problem of Race.* 1924. Missionary Ed Movement of US/Canada. G/G. V4. $15.00

MATTHEWS, Brander. *Americanisms & Criticisms.* 1892. NY. Harper. 1st. gilt dk gr cloth. F. M24. $35.00

MATTHEWS, Brander. *Intro to the Study of American Literature.* 1896. NY. Am Book Co. 1st/later issue. gilt sage gr cloth. VG. M24. $15.00

MATTHEWS, David. *Feel of Feeling.* 1976. Vantage. 1st. inscr dedication to Nikki Giovanni. F/NF. B4. $150.00

MATTHEWS, Greg. *Further Adventures of Huckleberry Finn.* 1983. NY. Crown. 1st. author's 1st book. F/F. T11. $45.00

MATTHEWS, Janet Snyder. *Edge of the Wilderness.* 1983. Tulsa, OK. Caprine. inscr. 464p. F/F. B11. $40.00

MATTHEWS, John. *Grail: Quest for the Eternal.* 1981. ils. VG/VG. M17. $30.00

MATTHEWS, L. Harrison. *Life of Mammals.* 1969. Universe. 2 vol. VG. S15. $40.00

MATTHEWS, Mrs. M.M. *10 Years in Nevada.* 1880. Buffalo. 1st. ils. 343p. G+. B5. $175.00

MATTHEWS, William. *Sleek for the Long Flight.* 1972. 1st. F/NF. V1. $35.00

MATTHIESSEN, Peter. *African Silences.* 1991. Random. 1st. F/F. M23. $25.00

MATTHIESSEN, Peter. *African Silences.* 1991. Random. 1st. sgn. F/F. D10. $50.00

MATTHIESSEN, Peter. *At Play in the Fields of the Lord.* 1965. Random. 1st. F/dj. Q1. $125.00

MATTHIESSEN, Peter. *Baikal.* 1992. London. Thames Hudson. 1st Eng. F/F. T11. $50.00

MATTHIESSEN, Peter. *Far Tortuga.* 1975. Random. 1st. sgn. author's 5th fiction book. F/F. D10. $75.00

MATTHIESSEN, Peter. *In the Spirit of Crazy Horse.* 1983. Viking. 1st. NF/NF. M19. $125.00

MATTHIESSEN, Peter. *Killing Mr Watson.* 1990. Random. 1st. sgn. F/F. D10. $60.00

MATTHIESSEN, Peter. *Men's Lives: The Surfmen & Baymen of the South Fork.* 1986. Random. 1st. sgn. F/F. D10. $110.00

MATTHIESSEN, Peter. *Nine-Headed Dragon River.* 1986. Boston. Shambala. 1st. NF/NF. D10. $40.00

MATTHIESSEN, Peter. *On the River Styx & Other Stories.* 1989. Collins Harvill. 1st. F/F. B3. $35.00

MATTHIESSEN, Peter. *Oomingmak: Expedition to Musk Ox Island in Bering Sea.* 1967. Hastings. 1st. F/F. C6. $60.00

MATTHIESSEN, Peter. *Race Rock.* 1954. London. 1st. author's 1st novel. F/NF clip. L3. $300.00

MATTHIESSEN, Peter. *Sand Rivers.* 1981. Viking. 1st. photos. F/dj. Q1. $75.00

MATTHIESSEN, Peter. *Shorebirds of North America.* 1967. NY. 1st. NF/VG clip. B4. $250.00

MATTHIESSEN, Peter. *Snow Leopard.* 1978. Franklin Lib. 1st (preceeds trade). sgn. F/sans. R14. $150.00

MATTHIESSEN, Peter. *Snow Leopard.* 1978. Viking. 1st. sgn. F/F. D10. $95.00

MATTHIESSEN & PORTER. *Tree Where Man Was Born/The African Experience.* 1972. Viking. true 1st. sgn. F/F. D10. $100.00

MATTISON, Alice. *Great Wits.* 1988. Morrow. 1st. sgn. F/F. R14. $45.00

MATTISON, Ray H. *Army Post of the Northern Plains 1865-1885.* 1965. OR Trail Mus Assn. 27p. as new. J2. $25.00

MAUCHLINE, John. *Introductory Hebrew Grammar.* 1967. Clark. 192p. VG. B29. $10.00

MAUDSLAY & MAUDSLAY. *Glimpse at Guatemala & Some Notes on Ancient Monuments...* 1992. Flo Silver. rpt of 1899 ed. ils/pl/fld map. F3. $40.00

MAUGHAM, W. Somerset. *Ashenden; or, The British Agent.* 1928. Doubleday Doran. 1st Am. orange stp bl cloth. VG. M24. $100.00

MAUGHAM, W. Somerset. *Cakes & Ale & 12 Short Stories.* 1967. Doubleday. 1st Am. F/F. B4. $125.00

MAUGHAM, W. Somerset. *Christmas Holiday.* 1939. Doubleday. 1st Am. F/NF clip. B4. $150.00

MAUGHAM, W. Somerset. *Ex Libris.* 1936. NY Times 1st Nat Book Fair. 1st. VG. K3. $15.00

MAUGHAM, W. Somerset. *France at War.* 1940. London. Heinemann. 1st. xl. K3. $10.00

MAUGHAM, W. Somerset. *Magician.* 1909. Duffield. 1st Am. NF. B4. $300.00

MAUGHAM, W. Somerset. *Mr Maugham Himself.* 1954. Doubleday. ne. 688p. NF. W2. $60.00

MAUGHAM, W. Somerset. *Princess September & the Nightingale.* 1939. London. Oxford. 1st thus. 8vo. F/VG. C8. $50.00

MAUGHAM, W. Somerset. *Razor's Edge.* 1944. Doubleday Doran. ne. 343p. NF. W2. $200.00

MAUGHAM, W. Somerset. *Razor's Edge.* 1944. Doubleday Doran. 1st. 1/750. sgn. gilt maroon cloth. F. M24. $250.00

MAUGHAM, W. Somerset. *Summing Up.* 1938. Doubleday. 1st Am. F/NF. B4. $150.00

MAUGHAM, W. Somerset. *Theatre.* 1937. NY. Doubleday. 1st. F/NF clip. B4. $150.00

MAUGHAM, W. Somerset. *Then & Now.* 1946. Doubleday. 1st. F/VG. M35. $35.00

MAUGHAM, W. Somerset. *Unconquered.* 1944. NY. House of Books. only ed. 1/300. sgn. NF/NF. B4. $275.00

MAULDIN, Henry K. *Your Lakes, Valleys & Mountains: History of Lake Co.* 1960. SF. East Wind Prt. ils/map. 64p. NF/wrp. K7. $20.00

MAUNDY, Talbot. *Cock O' the North.* 1929. Bobbs Merrill. 1st. VG. M2. $35.00

MAUNDY, Talbot. *Winds of the World.* 1932. London. VG. M2. $10.00

MAUPIN, Armstead. *Sure of You.* 1989. Harper Row. 1st. F/F. R14. $25.00

MAURER, M. *World War II Combat Squadrons of the USAF: Official...* 1992. NY. rpt. 841p. VG/VG. S16. $35.00

MAURICEAU, A.M. *Married Woman's Private Medical Companion.* 1855. NY. 16mo. cloth. F. M1. $200.00

MAURO, Frederic. *Portugal et l'Atlantique au XVIIme Siecle 1570-1670...* 1960. Paris. SEVPEN. 22 maps. 550p. F/wrp. O7. $55.00

MAUROIS, Andre. *Country of 36 Thousand Wishes.* 1930. Appleton. 1st Am. ils Adrienne Segur. 66p. VG. D1. $75.00

MAUROIS, Andre. *Fatapoufs & Thinifers.* 1940. Holt. 1st. ils Jean Bruller. 92p. G. P2. $30.00

MAUROIS, Andre. *My Latin American Diary.* 1953. London. Falcon. 1st. 89p. dj. F3. $15.00

MAUROIS, Andre. *Private Universe.* 1932. London. 1st. inscr by trans. VG. T9. $30.00

MAUS, Cynthia P. *Old Testament & the Fine Arts.* 1954. Harper. 826p. VG/dj. B29. $7.00

MAVOR, James W. *Voyage to Atlantis.* 1969. Putnam. 8vo. 320p. bl cloth. VG/dj. P4. $30.00

MAWSON, T. *Art & Craft of Garden Making.* 1901. London. 2nd enlarged. ils/pl. VG. E6. $100.00

MAXIMOV, N.A. *Plant in Relation to Water.* 1929. Allen Unwin. 1st. 8vo. VG. A22. $40.00

MAXON, William R. *Studies of Tropical American Ferns Nos 1 to 7.* 1908-22. WA, DC. 7 parts. 298p. B26. $68.00

MAXWELL, A.E. *Frog & the Scorpion.* 1986. Doubleday. 1st. F/dj. M15. $100.00

MAXWELL, Alice. *Recipes of Guam.* 1954. Agana. self pub. ils. VG. E6. $30.00

MAXWELL, Arthur. *Uncle Arthur's Bedtime Stories.* 1950. 5 vol. orange bdg. VG+. S13. $75.00

MAXWELL, Gavin. *Ring of Bright Water.* 1960. London. 1st. VG/VG. T9. $30.00

MAXWELL, Margaret F. *Passion for Freedom: Life of Sharlot Hall.* 1982. Tucson. 8vo. 234p. F/VG. F7. $35.00

MAXWELL, William. *Old Man at the Railroad Crossing & Other Tales.* 1966. Knopf. 1st. NF/dj. D10. $65.00

MAXWELL, William. *Outermost Dream.* 1989. Knopf. 1st. F/F. D10. $35.00

MAXWELL, William. *Over by the River & Other Stories.* 1977. Knopf. 1st. sgn. F/F. R14. $90.00

MAXWELL, William. *So Long, See You Tomorrow.* 1980. Knopf. 1st. F/F. D10. $50.00

MAXWELL & MAXWELL. *Legal Bibliography of British Commonwealth of Nations...* 1955. London. Sweet & Maxwell. 2nd. M11. $150.00

MAXXE, Robert; see Rosenblum, Robert.

MAY, Robert L. *Rudolph, the Red-Nosed Reindeer.* 1939. Montgomery Ward. 1st. 1/200. ils Denver Gillen. 8vo. 32p. pres bdg. R5. $485.00

MAY, Robert L. *Rudolph, the Red-Nosed Reindeer.* 1939. NY. Maxton Pub. 1st commercial (after MW). inscr. 8vo. red pict brd. dj. R5. $975.00

MAY, Robin. *Gold Rushes: From California to the Klondike.* 1977. London. Wm Luscombe. 1st Eng. F/F. O4. $20.00

MAY, Walter. *Die Geschichte vom Rotkappchen (Little Red Riding Hood).* 1940. Zurich. Albert Miller. sm 4to. pict brd. F/dj. B24. $350.00

MAYARD, L. *Tropical Cooking (Cuisine des Pays Clauds).* nd. ca 1962. Haiti. VG/G+. E6. $25.00

MAYBEE, Betty Lou. *Barbie's Fashion Success (#3).* 1962. Random. 188p. glossy brd. VG/ragged. M20. $12.50

MAYBEE, Betty Lou. *Barbie's Hawaiian Holiday (#6).* 1963. Random. 172p. pict brd (lists 6 titles). VG. M20. $18.00

MAYER, Marianna. *Iduna & the Magic Apples.* 1988. Macmillan. 1st. obl 8vo. unp. burgundy brd. VG. T5. $20.00

MAYER, Marianna. *Unicorn & the Lake.* 1982. Dial. 1st. ils Michael Hague. unop. VG+. T5. $35.00

MAYER, MAYER & MAYER. *Clockwork Universe.* 1980. NY. Neale Watson. ils. 321p. VG/dj. K3. $40.00

MAYER, Mercer. *Ah-Choo.* 1976. Dial. 1st. obl 12mo. VG/VG. P2. $30.00

MAYER, Mercer. *Boy, a Dog & a Frog.* 1967. Dial. 1st. 24mo. unp. whit brd. VG+. T5. $35.00

MAYHAR, Ardath. *Lords of the Triple Moons.* 1983. Atheneum. 1st. F/dj. M2. $20.00

MAYHAR, Ardath. *World Ends in Hickory Hollow.* 1985. Doubleday. 1st. F/dj. M2. $27.00

MAYHEW & MAYHEW. *Greatest Plague of Life.* 1847. London. David Bogue. 12mo. ils Cruikshank. contemporary half leather. T10. $350.00

MAYLE, Peter. *Dog's Life.* 1995. Knopf. 1st. sgn. F/F. A23. $35.00

MAYLE, Peter. *Hotel Pastis.* 1993. Knopf. 1st. sgn. VG/VG. A23. $40.00

MAYNARD, Kenneth. *Lamb's Mixed Fortunes.* 1987. Weidenfeld Nicolson. 1st. F/NF. Q1. $50.00

MAYNARD, Olga. *Bird of Fire.* 1962. Dodd Mead. 2nd prt. sgn. F/NF. L3. $45.00

MAYNE, Peter. *Alleys of Marrakesh.* 1954. London. Travel Book. 8vo. 172p. VG. W1. $12.00

MAYNE, William. *Swarm in May.* 1955. London. Oxford. 1st 199p. VG/G. P2. $35.00

MAYO, Eleanor. *Forever Strangers.* 1958. Norton. 1st. F/dj. B4. $45.00

MAYO, Herbert. *Nervous System & Its Functions.* 1992. NY. Classics Neurology/Neurosurgery. facsimile. F. G1. $65.00

MAYO, Herbert. *Observations on Injuries & Diseases of the Rectum.* 1833. London. 1st. 220p. quarter leather. VG. A13. $150.00

MAYO, Jim; see L'Amour, Louis.

MAYONE DIAS, Eduardo. *Cantares de Alem-Mar.* 1982. Coimbre. Ordem DeUniversidade. 1/1000. 223p. wrp. F3. $10.00

MAYOR, Joseph B. *Epistle of St James.* 1978. Baker. 2nd (rpt 1897). Greek text. 256p. G. B29. $11.00

MAYR, Ernst. *Growth of Biological Thought.* 1982. Harvard. 8vo. 974p. F/wrp. K3. $15.00

MAYS, Benjamin E. *Negro's God, as Reflected in His Literature.* 1938. Boston. Chapman Grimes. 269p. G. B18. $35.00

MAYS & SIMMONS. *People of the Sun.* 1979. Albuquerque. 1st. 4to. F/NF. L3. $35.00

MAZZUCHELLI. *La Vita di Pietro Aretino.* 1741. Padua. Comino. 8vo. quarter calf. R12. $350.00

MCALPINE, J.F. *Manual of Nearctic Diptera, Vol 2.* 1987. Canadian Gove Pub Center. 287 pl. B1. $68.50

MCANDREW, H.J. *History of Critical Conservation North American Waterfowl.* 1950. Berkeley. private prt. 2 vol. 160 tipped-in mc photos/drawings. 429p. VG. M12. $125.00

MCBAIN, Ed; see Hunter, Evan.

MCBANE, Susan. *Know Your Pony.* 1992. Ward Lock Riding School. 1st. VG. O3. $15.00

MCBETH, George. *Poems From Oby.* 1983. Atheneum. 1st. 1/750. F/F. B35. $60.00

MCBRIDE, Barrie St. Clair. *Farouk of Egypt: A Biography.* 1968. Barnes. 1st Am. 8vo. 238p. NF/dj. W1. $22.00

MCBRIDE, Mary Margaret. *Encyclopedia of Cooking. 12 Volumes.* 1960. Evanston. Homeakers Inst. G. A16. $30.00

MCCABE, James Dabney. *Life & Campaigns of General Robert E Lee.* (1866). Atlanta, National Pub. 1st. 717p. later cloth. VG. M8. $125.00

MCCABE, Neal and Constance. *Baseball's Golden Age.* 1993. NY. Harry Abrams Pub. 1st. sm 4to. pict. 198p. NF/NF. R16. $45.00

MCCABE, Olivia. *Rose Fairies.* 1911. Rand McNally. 1st. ils Hope Dunlap. 4to. gilt gr cloth/label. R5. $200.00

MCCAFFREY, Anne. *Coelura.* 1983. CA. Underwood Miller. 1st. F/F. A24. $35.00

MCCAFFREY, Anne. *White Dragon.* 1978. Del Rey. 1st. VG/dj. M2. $45.00

MCCAGUE, J. *Cumberland.* 1973. NY. 1st. Rivers of Am series. VG/VG. B5. $32.50

MCCALL, Anthony; see Kane, Henry.

MCCALLEY & MILLER. *From Here to Obscurity.* 1975. np. ils. ils ep. VG+/torn. B18. $25.00

MCCALLUM & MCCALLUM. *Wire That Fenced the West.* 1979. Norman, OK. A19. $15.00

MCCAMMON, Robert R. *Mine.* 1990. Pocket Books. 1st. NF/NF. N4. $30.00

MCCAMMON, Robert R. *Usher's Passing.* 1984. HRW. 1st. NF/dj. N4. $35.00

MCCANDLESS & SENZAKI. *Buddhism & Zen.* 1953. NY. Philos Lib. 90p. VG/dj. W3. $30.00

MCCANN, Edson. *Preferred Risk.* 1955. S&S. 1st. F/dj. M2. $35.00

MCCANN, Lee. *Nostradamus.* 1941. Creative Age. 1st. VG/dj. M2. $15.00

MCCARRY, Charles. *Last Supper.* 1983. Dutton. 1st. 389p. F/F. W2. $30.00

MCCARRY, Charles. *Miernik Dossier.* 1973. Saturday Review. 1st. NF/dj. M25. $45.00

MCCARTHY, Cormac. *Child of God.* 1973. Random. 1st. author's 3rd book. F/dj. Q1. $850.00

MCCARTHY, Cormac. *Crossing.* 1994. Knopf. 1st. 1/1000. sgn. F/dj. Q1. $350.00

MCCARTHY, Cormac. *Outer Dark.* 1968. Random. 1st. author's 2nd novel. F/NF. D10. $850.00

MCCARTHY, Cormac. *Stonemason.* 1994. Hopewell. Ecco. 1/350. sgn. F/case. B3. $325.00

MCCARTHY, Cormac. *Suttree.* 1979. Random. 1st. author's 4th novel. NF/dj. Q1. $850.00

MCCARTHY, Mary. *Group.* 1963. HBW. 1st. F/NF. H11. $60.00

MCCARTHY, Mary. *Ideas & the Novel.* 1980. HBJ. 1st. F/F. B35. $28.00

MCCARTHY, Mary. *Memories of a Catholic Girlhood.* 1957. Harcourt Brace. 1st. 245p. blk cloth. F/VG. H1. $20.00

MCCARTHY James Remington. *Matter of Time.* 1947. NY. Harper. ils. 8vo. 230p. K3. $35.00

MCCAUSLAND, Elizabeth. *AH Mauerer: Biography of America's First Modern Painter.* 1951. Wyn. 1st. 289p. VG/ragged. M20. $35.00

MCCAUSLAND, Hugh. *Old Sporting Characters & Occasions From Sporting & Road...* 1948. Batchworth. 1st. 172p. cloth. VG/dj. M20. $30.00

MCCLANE, A.J. *McLane's New Standard Fishing Encyclopedia.* 1974. NY. 1156p. dj. A17. $27.50

MCCLANE, A.J. *Practical Fly Fisherman.* 1953. NY. 1st. 257p. NF/taped. A17. $85.00

MCCLELLAN, Edwin. *Woman in the Crested Kimono: Life of Shibue Io...* 1985. New Haven. Yale. 1st. 192p. VG/dj. A25. $15.00

MCCLELLAN, George B. *McClellan's Own Story.* 1887. NY. 1st. 678p. O8. $65.00

MCCLELLAND, Lucille Hudin. *Textbook for Psychiatric Technicians.* 1967. St Louis. Mosby. 1st. ils. VG+. A25. $15.00

MCCLINTON, K.M. *Chromolithographs of Louis Prang.* 1973. NY. 1st. ils. 246p. F/dj. M4. $30.00

MCCLINTON, K.M. *Lalique for Collectors.* 1975. Scribner. 1st. 152p. as new/dj. H1. $48.00

MCCLOSKEY, Robert. *Blueberries for Sal.* 1949. Viking. 3rd. sgn pres. obl 4to. pict brd. dj. R5. $225.00

MCCLOSKEY, Robert. *Lentil.* 1946. Viking. 2nd. sgn pres. lg 4to. gray cloth. dj. R5. $150.00

MCCLOSKEY, Robert. *Make Way for Ducklings.* 1941. Viking. 2nd. 4to. VG/G. P2. $100.00

MCCLOSKEY, Robert. *Make Way for Ducklings.* 1950. NY. Viking. 10th. sgn pres. brn cloth. dj. R5. $250.00

MCCLOSKEY, Robert. *One Morning in Maine.* Jan 1953. Viking. 2nd. 1953 Caldecott Honor. lg 4to. gray cloth. dj. R5. $75.00

MCCLURE, Alfred J.P. *Steamin' to Bells Around the Middle Sea.* 1900. self pub. 1/350. sgn. VG. B11. $150.00

MCCLURE, James. *Artful Egg.* 1984. Pantheon. 1st. F/F. H11. $25.00

MCCLURE, James. *Four & Twenty Virgins.* 1973. London. Gollancz. 1st. F/dj. M15. $85.00

MCCLURE, James. *Song Dog.* 1991. Mysterious. 1st Am. F/F. A24. $15.00

MCCLURE, James. *Steam Pig.* 1971. Harper Row. 1st. author's 1st book. F/F. H11. $35.00

MCCLURE, Michael. *Gargoyle Cartoons.* 1971. Delacorte. 1st. inscr. NF/VG. R14. $40.00

MCCLURE, Michael. *Jaguar Skies.* 1975. New Directions. 1st. inscr. F/NF. R14. $45.00

MCCLURE, Robert. *Diseases of the American Horse, Cattle & Sheep.* 1890. Phil. Keystone. G. O3. $38.00

MCCLURE, Roy. *Burns, Shock, Wound Healing & Vascular Injuries.* 1943. Phil. 1st. 272p. A13. $75.00

MCCLURE. *With Stanley in Africa.* 1891. ils. VG. M17. $40.00

MCCLURKEN, James M. *Gah-Baeh-Jhagwah-Buk: The Way It Happened.* 1992. Lansing. 1st. photos/maps. 130p. M/dj. A17. $25.00

MCCOMAS & TUOHY. *Collector's Guide & History to Lionel Trains.* TM Prod/Chilton. 6 vol (complete). VG to F. H1. $145.00

MCCONNELL, Duncan. *Granpappy's Pistol; or, to Hell With Gun Collecting.* 1956. Coward McCann. 1st. sgn. 152p. VG/dj. M20. $50.00

MCCONNELL, James V. *Worm Returns.* 1965. Prentice Hall. ils. VG/worn. K3. $20.00

MCCORKLE, Jill. *Cheerleader.* 1984. Algonquin. 1st. sgn. VG/VG. L1. $200.00

MCCORKLE, Jill. *Ferris Beach.* 1990. Algonquin. 1st. sgn. VG/VG. L1. $75.00

MCCORKLE, Jill. *July 7.* 1984. Algonquin. 1st. author's 1st book. F/dj. from $150 to $175.00

MCCORKLE, Jill. *Tending to Virginia.* 1987. Algonquin/Taylor Pub. 1st. sgn. VG/VG. L1. $85.00

MCCORMICK, Charles H. *Nest of Vipers: McCarthyism & Higher Education...* 1989. IL U. 1st. M/dj. V4. $20.00

MCCORMICK, Donald. *Blood on the Sea.* 1962. London. Muller. ils. 158p. dj. T7. $22.00

MCCORMICK, Harriet Hammond. *Landscape Art Past & Present.* 1923. Scribner. 1/1200. A10. $200.00

MCCORMICK, Richard C. *Arizona: Its Resources & Prospects.* 1865. NY. Van Nostrand. fld map. 22p. prt wrp. D11. $150.00

MCCORMICK, Wilfred. *Rocky McCune: Phantom Shortstop.* 1963. McKay. 1st. cloth. 178p. Vg/dj. M20. $45.00

MCCOWEN, Alec. *Young Gemini.* 1979. London. Elm Tree. 1st. F/F. T12. $20.00

MCCOY, Horace. *Scalpel.* 1952. Appleton Century. 1st. F/dj. from $50 to $85.00

MCCOY, Horace. *They Shoot Horses, Don't They?* 1935. S&S. 1st. inscr/dtd 1935. author's 1st book. NF/VG. L3. $2,000.00

MCCOY, J.J. *Hunt for the Whooping Cranes.* 1966. NY. photos/maps/drawings. 223p. VG/VG. S15. $20.00

MCCOY, John T. *Airplanes.* 1936. Rand McNally. ils/drawings. VG/stiff wrp. B18. $45.00

MCCRACKEN, Harold. *Frederic Remington: Artist of the Old West...* (1947). 4to. full-p pl. 205p. xl. VG/VG. A4. $65.00 M4.

MCCRACKEN, Harold. *God's Frozen Children: Animals, Men & Mummies...* 1930. NY. 1st ed. inscr. 291p. dj. B5. $45.00 M4.

MCCRACKEN, Harold. *Portrait of the Old West With Bibliographical Checklist...* 1952. NY. 1st. ils. 232p. F/dj. T10. $125.00

MCCRUMB, Sharyn. *Hangman's Beautiful Daughter.* 1992. Scribner. 1st. F/F. D10. $40.00

MCCRUMB, Sharyn. *If Ever I Return, Pretty Peggy-O.* 1990. Scribner. 1st. F/F. D10. $50.00

MCCRUMB, Sharyn. *Missing Susan.* 1991. Ballantine. 1st. F/F. D10. $50.00

MCCRUMB, Sharyn. *She Walks These Hills.* 1994. Scribner. 1st. sgn. F/F. A23. $42.00

MCCRUMB, Sharyn. *Windsor Knot.* 1990. Ballantine. 1st. F/F. B3/Q1. $50.00

MCCRUMB, Sharyn. *Zombies of the Gene Pool.* 1992. S&S. 1st. F/F. A23. $42.00

MCCULLERS, Carson. *Mortgaged Heart.* 1971. Houghton Mifflin. 1st. F/NF. D10. $50.00

MCCULLOCH, Hugh. *Men & Measures of Half a Century.* 1889. np. 1st. 542p. O8. $21.50

MCCULLOUGH, Colleen. *Creed for the Third Millenium.* 1985. NY. Harper Row. 1st. F/F. T12. $12.50

MCCULLOUGH, Colleen. *First Man in Rome.* 1990. Morrow. 1st. F/F. T12. $20.00

MCCULLY, Emily Arnold. *Mirette on the High Wire.* 1992. Putnam. 1st. 1993 Caldecott Award. pict brd. dj. R5. $65.00

MCCUNE, Shannon. *Korea: Land of Broken Calm.* 1966. Princeton. ils/maps. 221p. VG/dj. W3. $38.00

MCCURRACH, James C. *Palms of the World.* 1970. Stuart. Horticultural Books. rpt. 4to. cloth. G. A22. $55.00

MCCUTCHEON, George B. *Prince of Graustark.* 1914. 1st. ils Keller. NF. M19. $35.00

MCDANIEL, Bruce W. *Dune & Desert Folk.* nd. Los Angeles. ils. unp. cloth/vignette. B26. $24.00

MCDERMOTT, Alice. *Bigamist's Daughter.* 1982. Random. 1st. F/F. B4. $125.00

MCDERMOTT, Alice. *That Night.* 1987. FSG. 1st. F/NF. R14. $30.00

MCDERMOTT, Gerald. *Anansi the Spider, a Tale from the Ashanti.* 1973 (1972). Holt Rinehart. 2nd. obl 8vo. F/NF. C8. $22.50

MCDERMOTT, Gerald. *Stone-Cutter, a Japanese Folk Tale.* 1975. Viking. 1st. 4to. unp. red cloth. NF/VG. T5. $30.00

MCDEVITT, Jack. *Talent for War.* 1989. London. 1st hc. F/dj. M2. $25.00

MCDONALD, Edward D. *Bibliography of Writings of Norman Douglas.* 1927. Phil. Centaur Book Shop. 1/300. VG. K3. $25.00

MCDONALD, Gregory. *Fletch Too.* 1986. Warner. 1st. F/F. N4. $25.00

MCDONALD, Gregory. *Flynn's In.* 1984. Mysterious. 1st. F/F. A20. $25.00

MCDONALD, Gregory. *Running Scared.* Obolensky. 1964 1st. VG/VG. A20. $45.00

MCDONALD, Lucile. *Search for the Northwest Passage.* 1958. Portland. Binford Mort. 8vo. 137p. VG. P4. $45.00

MCDONELL, Katherine. *Journals of William Lindsay: An Ordinary 19th-C Physician...* 1989. Indianapolis. 216p. A13. $30.00

MCDOUGALL, Bonnie. *Popular Chinese Literature & Performing Arts...1949-1979.* 1984. CA U. 450p. F/F. W3. $48.00

MCDOUGALL, W.B. *Grand Canyon Wild Flowers.* 1964. Flagstaff. 8vo. cloth. NF. A22. $20.00

MCDOUGALL & MOIR. *Selected Correspondence of Glasgow Colonial Society...1840.* 1994. Toronto. Champlain Soc. 8vo. 1272p. red cloth. F. P4. $85.00

MCDOWELL, Roddy. *Double Exposure.* 1966. NY. 1st. VG/VG. B5. $30.00

MCELRATH, Jean. *Aged in Sage.* 1964. NV U. A19. $25.00

MCELROY, John. *Struggle for Missouri.* 1913. WA, DC. National Tribune. A19. $45.00

MCELROY, Joseph. *Ancient History: A Paraphase.* 1971. Knopf. 1st. NF/dj. M25. $35.00

MCELWEE, William. *Murder of Sir Thomas Overbury.* 1952. Faber. 1st. 280p. VG/dj. M20. $35.00

MCEWAN, Ian. *Child in Time.* 1987. Houghton Mifflin. 1st. F/F. B35. $18.00

MCEWAN, Ian. *Comfort of Strangers.* 1981. S&S. ARC/1st. author's 4th book. F/F. w/pub promo material. D10. $50.00

MCEWAN, Ian. *First Love, Last Rites.* 1975. Random. 1st Am. author's 1st book. F/F. L3. $85.00

MCEWAN, Ian. *In Between the Sheets.* 1979. S&S. 1st Am. NF/NF. R14. $30.00

MCEWAN, Ian. *Innocent.* 1990. Doubleday. 1st. F/F. H11. $30.00

MCEWEN, J.D. *Brazil: Description of People, Country & Happenings...* 1915. np. Witness Pr. 1st. ils. 259p. F3. $30.00

MCFARLAND, Dennis. *Music Room.* 1990. Houghton Mifflin. 1st. author's 1st novel. F/dj. A24. $40.00

MCFARLAND, J. Horace. *How to Grow Roses.* 1946. Harrisburg. Horace McFarland. 21st. 192p. VG. H1. $15.00

MCFARLANE, Brian. *Stanley Cup.* 1971. Scribner. 1st Am. photos. VG/VG. P8. $30.00

MCFEE, William. *Law of the Sea.* 1950. Lippincott. VG. M11. $50.00

MCFIE, H. *Wasa-Wasa: Tale of Trails & Treasure in Far North.* 1951. NY. 288p. F/dj. M4. $20.00

MCGARGAR & COLBY. *Lost Victory: A Firsthand Account...Vietnam.* 1989. Chicago. 438p. map ep. VG+/dj. B18. $17.50

MCGARRITY, Mark. *Death on a Cold, Wild River.* 1993. Morrow. 1st. F/dj. Q1. $40.00

MCGARRITY, Mark. *Lucky Shuffles.* 1973. Grossman. 1st. F/F. M25. $25.00

MCGAUGH, James L. *Psychobiology: Behavior From Biological Perspective.* 1971. Academic. 366p. gray cloth. G1. $50.00

MCGIFFERT, Arthur C. *Protestant Thought Before Kant.* 1911. Scribner. 261p. VG. B29. $7.50

MCGINLEY, Phyllis. *Love Letters of Phyllis McGinley.* 1954. Viking. sgn. VG/VG. B11. $8.50

MCGINNIS, R.A. *Beet-Sugar Technology.* 1971 (1951). Ft Collins. 2nd. ils. 835p. VG+. B26. $14.00

MCGINNIS, Vera. *Rodeo Road: My Life as a Pioneer Cowgirl.* 1974. Hastings. 1st. 225p. VG+/dj. M20. $35.00

MCGINNISS, Joe. *Dreaming Team.* 1972. Random. 1st. F/F. A20. $20.00

MCGLASHAN, C.F. *History of the Donner Party: A Tragedy of the Sierra.* 1881. Bancroft. 4th. ils. 261p. D11. $250.00

MCGLASHAN, C.F. *History of the Donner Party: A Tragedy of the Sierra.* 1973 (1880). Fresno, CA. rpt. F/F. O4. $15.00

MCGOVERN, William Montgomery. *Jungle Paths & Inca Ruins.* 1927. NY. Century. 1st. 8vo. 526p. F. T10. $75.00

MCGOWAN, Edward. *Narrative of..., Including Full Account Author's Adventures.* 1857. SF. self pub. 1st. 7 full-p woodcuts. rebound brd/prt wrp. R3. $900.00

MCGRATH, Patrick. *Blood & Water & Other Tales.* 1988. Poseidon. 1st. inscr. F/F. R14. $60.00

MCGRATH, Patrick. *Grotesque.* 1989. Poseidon. 1st. F/F. M22. $45.00

MCGRATH, Patrick. *Spider.* 1990. Poseidon/S&S. 1st. sgn. F/dj. A24. $35.00

MCGROATRY, John S. *California of the South.* 1933. Los Angeles. 1st. 5 vol. NF. O4. $150.00

MCGROATRY, John S. *California Plutarch Vol 1.* 1935. Los Angeles. 1st. 4to. half leather. U xl. G+. O4. $60.00

MCGROATRY, John S. *California: Its History & Romance.* 1911. Los Angeles. 8th. inscr. VG. O4. $20.00

MCGROATRY, John S. *Wander Songs.* 1908. Los Angeles. Grafton. VG. O4. $20.00

MCGUANE, Thomas. *Bushwhacked Piano.* 1971. S&S. 1st. author's 2nd book. NF/NF clip. T11. $120.00

MCGUANE, Thomas. *Keep the Change.* 1989. Houghton Mifflin. 1st. F/NF. R13. $20.00

MCGUANE, Thomas. *Ninety-Two in the Shade.* 1973. FSG. 1st. author's 3rd book. F/F. Q1. $75.00

MCGUANE, Thomas. *Nobody's Angel.* 1982. Random. 1st. author's 5th novel. F/dj. D10. $60.00

MCGUANE, Thomas. *Nothing But Blue Skies.* 1992. Houghton Mifflin. 1st. 1/300. sgn/#d. F/case. Q1. $125.00

MCGUANE, Thomas. *Outside Chance.* 1990. Houghton Mifflin. 1st. F/NF. A20. $20.00

MCGUANE, Thomas. *Panama.* 1978. FSG. 1st. F/NF. B3. $40.00

MCGUANE, Thomas. *Something to Be Desired.* 1984. Random. 1st. author's 6th novel. F/F. from $30 to $40.00

MCGUANE, Thomas. *Sporting Club.* 1968. S&S. 1st. sgn. author's 1st book. NF/dj. R13. $250.00

MCGUANE, Thomas. *Sporting Club.* 1969. S&S. 1st. author's 1st book. F/dj. Q1. $75.00

MCGUANE, Thomas. to *Skin a Cat.* 1986. Dutton/Lawrence. 1st. F/F. R13. $25.00

MCGUANE, Thomas. to *Skin a Cat.* 1987. Secker Warburg. 1st Eng. F/F. T11. $30.00

MCGUCKIN, Jack. *Split Second From Hell.* 1979. Perkasie. 1st. photos. 197p. VG/VG. S16. $30.00

MCGUFFEY READER. *McGuffey's New Fifth Eclectic Reader.* 1866. leather. torn ep o/w VG. A4. $35.00

MCGUFFEY READER. *McGuffey's Readers.* facsimile. 7 vol. F/VG case. A4. $75.00

MCGUFFEY READER. *McGuffey's Smaller Eclectic Primer.* 1867 (1849). VanAntwerp. 34p. sc. M5. $110.00

MCGUGAN, B.M. *Forest Lepidoptera of Canada.* 1958-1965. Dept Forestry of Canada. 4 vol in 1 (orig covers bdg in). 840p. F. S15. $35.00

MCHENRY, George. *Cotton Trade: Negro Slavery in the Confederate States.* 1863. London. Saunders Otley. inscr. 292p. xl. B11. $200.00

MCHENRY & ROPER. *Smith & Wesson Hand Guns.* 1958. Stackpole. 1st. 233p. VG/torn. J2. $195.00

MCHUGH, Tom. *Time of the Buffalo.* 1972. NY. 339p. VG/VG. S15. $30.00

MCHUGH, Vernon. *From Hell to Heaven: Memoirs From Patton's 3rd Army.* 1980. Ardmore. 35p. VG/VG. S16. $15.00

MCILVANNEY, William. *Big Man.* 1985. Morrow. 1st Am. F/F. M25. $25.00

MCILVANNEY, William. *Papers of Tony Veitch.* 1983. Pantheon. 1st Am. F/dj. M25. $35.00

MCILVANNEY, William. *Strange Loyalties.* 1991. Morrow. 1st Am. F/dj. M25. $25.00

MCILVOY, Kevin. *Fifth Station.* 1988. Algonquin. 1st. F/F. B35. $12.00

MCINERNEY, Jay. *Bright Lights, Big City.* 1984. Vintage Contemporaries. 1st. F/wrp. B2. $50.00

MCINERNEY, Jay. *Story of My Life.* 1988. Atlantic Monthly. 1st. F/F. B35/P3. $20.00

MCINERNY, Ralph. *Seventh Station.* 1977. Vanguard. 1st. VG/VG. M22. $30.00

MCINTOSH, J.T. *One in Three Hundred.* 1954. Doubleday. 1st. VG/dj. M2. $25.00

MCINTYRE, John T. *Ashton-Kirk, Special Detective.* 1914. Phil. 1st. VG+. B2. $50.00

MCINTYRE, Nancy Fair. *It's a Picnic!* 1969. Viking. G/dj. A16. $15.00

MCINTYRE, Vonda N. *Search for Spock.* 1984. Boston. Gregg. 1st. sgn. F/F. B11. $40.00

MCISSAC, F.J. *Tony Sarg Marionette Book.* 1921. NY. Huebsch. 1st. 12mo. 58p. NF. D1. $85.00

MCKAY, Claude. *Harlem Shadows.* 1922. Harcourt Brace. 1st. VG+. B4. $300.00

MCKAY, Martha Nicholson. *When the Tide Turned in the Civil War.* 1929. Indianapolis. Hollenbeck. 1st. 66p. F/F. B4. $100.00

MCKAY, Paul. *Pilgrim & the Cowboy.* 1989. NY. 1st. 214p. F/dj. S15. $25.00

MCKEARIN & MCKEARIN. *American Glass.* 1941. Crown. 1st. 622p. G/dj. H1. $65.00

MCKEARIN & WILSON. *American Bottles & Flasks & Their Ancestry.* 1978. Crown. 1st/1st prt. 779p. gilt bl cloth. F/dj. H1. $150.00

MCKECHNIE, Hector. *Judicial Process Upon Brieves, 1219-1532.* 1956. Glasgow. Jackson. 31p. prt stapled wrp. M11. $35.00

MCKEE, Alexander. *King Henry VIII's Mary Rose.* 1974. Stein Day. 346p. VG/clip. P4. $25.00

MCKEE, Mrs. *Royal Cookery Book.* 1983. Arlington. 1st. 239p. photos. clip dj. B10. $15.00

MCKEE, Ruth Eleanor. *Lord's Anointed: A Novel of Hawaii.* 1935. Doubleday Doran. 1st. VG/VG. A25. $20.00

MCKEE. *McKee's Price Guide to Children's Literature.* 1970. 82p. VG. A4. $55.00

MCKELVEY, Blake. *Urbanization of America.* 1963. Rutgers. 2nd. 8vo. 370p. red cloth. T10. $25.00

MCKELVEY, Susan Delano. *Botanical Exploration of Trans-Mississippi West 1790-1850.* 1955. Jamaica Plain. Arnold Arboretum of Harvard. 10 fld maps. 1144p. D11. $200.00

MCKENDRY, Maxine. *Seven Centuries Cookbook.* 1973. McGraw Hill. G/dj. A16. $25.00

MCKENNA, Dolores. *Tom Mitten's Cousins.* 1923. NY. Samuel Gabriel. 8vo. pict brd. box. R5. $200.00

MCKENNA, Richard. *Left-Handed Monkey Wrench.* 1984. Annapolis. Naval Inst. 1st. F/dj. Q1. $50.00

MCKENNA, Richard. *Sand Pebbles.* 1962. Harper Row. 1st. F/NF. T11. $85.00

MCKENNA, Rollie. *Portrait of Dylan.* 1982. Owings Mills. Stemmer. inscr/dtd. photos. 112p. cloth. dj. D11. $60.00

MCKENNON, Joe. *Horse Dung Trail: Sage of American Circus.* 1975. Carnival Pub. sgn. 528p. VG/dj. M20. $50.00

MCKEOWN, Martha Ferguson. *Alaska Silver.* 1951. NY. Macmillan. 2nd. 274p. map ep. dj. P4. $23.00

MCKILLUP, Patricia. *Stepping From the Shadows.* 1982. Atheneum. 1st. F/dj. M2. $30.00

MCKINLEY, Clare. *Misty the Wonder Pony.* nd (1956). Rand McNally. lg 4to. unp. VG+. C14. $17.00

MCKINLEY, Robin. *Door in the Hedge.* 1981. Greenwillow. 1st. 8vo. 216p. NF/NF. T5. $30.00

MCKNIGHT, Reginald. *I Get on the Bus.* 1990. Little Brn. 1st. sgn/dtd 1993. F/F. R13. $40.00

MCKOWN, Robin. *Congo: River of Mystery.* 1968. NY. McGraw Hill. 1st. lg 8vo. ils. 144p. VG/dj. W1. $18.00

MCKUEN, Rod. *Lonesome Cities.* 1967. NY. special deluxe sgn ed. VG/box. B5. $45.00

MCLAGLEN, Victor. *Express to Hollywood.* 1934. London. Jerrold. 1st. inscr. G+. B4. $250.00

MCLANATHAN, Richard. *Brandywine Heritage.* 1971. Brandywine River Mus. 1st. 121p+18 mc pl. sq 4to. dj. A17. $25.00

MCLAREN, Moray. *Bonnie Prince Charlie.* 1972. Saturday Review. 1st. 224p. VG/dj. M20. $18.00

MCLAREN, Samuel Bruce. *Scientific Papers.* 1925. Cambridge. 1st. xl. K3. $30.00

MCLAURIN, Tim. *Keeper of the Moon.* 1991. Norton. 1st. sgn. F/F. R13. $35.00

MCLAURIN, TIm. *Woodrow's Trumpet.* 1989. Norton. 1st. sgn. NF/NF. R13. $40.00

MCLEAN, Joseph E. *William Rufus Day, Supreme Court Justice From Ohio.* 1946. John Hopkins. 172p. G/wrp. B18. $12.50

MCLEAN, Rauri. *Joseph Cundall, a Victorian Publisher, Notes on His Life...* 1976. 4to. ils. 104p. F/NF. A4. $65.00

MCLEAN, Rauri. *Victorian Publishers' Bookbindings in Paper.* 1983. 4to. ils. 112p. F/F. A4. $135.00

MCLEAN, Ruari. *Modern Book Design From William Morris to Present Day.* 1959. Essential Books. 116p+16 pl. xl. F/dj. A17. $15.00

MCLENNAN, William E. *Settlement Men's Clubs.* 1917. np. 20p. VG. A25. $15.00

MCLEOD, Alexander. *Pigtails & Gold Dust: Panorama of Chinese Life...* 1947. Caxton. 1st. VG. O4. $35.00

MCLEOD, Alexander. *Pigtails & Gold Dust: Panorama of Chinese Life...* 1948. Caxton. 2nd. 8vo. gilt bl cloth. F/dj. R3. $50.00

MCLEOD, George. *Notes on Surgery of the War in the Crimea...* 1858. London. 1st. 439p. xl. A13. $450.00

MCLEOD, Robert R. *In the Acadian Land: Nature Studies.* 1899. Boston. Bralee Whidden. 1st. ils. 166p. cloth. K3. $30.00

MCLEOD & REHBOCK. *Darwin's Laboratory: Evolutionary Theory & Natural History.* 1994. Honolulu. 1st. 540p. bl cloth. P4. $45.00

MCLINTOCK, Barbara. *Heartaches of a French Cat.* 1989. Boston. Godine. 1st. thin 4to. F/clip. T10. $50.00

MCLINTOCK, Elizabeth. *Japanese Tea Garden, Golden Gate Park, San Francisco, CA.* 1977. SF. John McLaren Soc. 8vo. ils. F/wrp. R3. $10.00

MCLOUGHLIN BROTHERS. *All About Santa.* 1896. NY. narrow 4to. stiff die-cut covers. R5. $275.00

MCLOUGHLIN BROTHERS. *Doings of Kriss Kringle.* 1897. NY. 8vo. 10p. mc paper wrp. R5. $150.00

MCLOUGHLIN BROTHERS. *Little Pigs.* ca 1890s. ils anonymously. heavy cb stock. G. D1. $75.00

MCLOUGHLIN BROTHERS. *Old Woman & Her Pig.* (1890). NY. Little Pig series. unp. G/wrp. D1. $40.00

MCLOUGHLIN BROTHERS. *Rip Van Winkle.* ca 1880. NY. ils Thomas Nast. VG/pict wrp. D1. $285.00

MCLOUGHLIN BROTHERS. *Snapshots at Santa Claus.* 1906. NY. Mistletoe series. 4to. mc pict paper cover. R5. $150.00

MCLOUGHLIN BROTHERS. *Ten Little Mulligan Guards.* ca 1870. obl 4to. pict wrp. R5. $285.00

MCLOUGHLIN BROTHERS. *Three Blind Mice.* ca 1860. NY. Aunt Jenny series. 8vo. pict wrp. R5. $150.00

MCLOUGHLIN BROTHERS. *Visit From Santa Claus.* ca 1899. McLoughlin. 4to. pict wrp. R5. $300.00

MCLUHAN, Marshall. *War & Peace in the Global Village.* 1966. 1st. F/NF. M19. $50.00

MCLUHAN, T.C. *Dream Tracks, the Railroad & the American Indian 1890-1930.* 1985. Harry Adams. 1st. 208p. VG/dj. J2. $75.00

MCLUHAN, T.C. *Touch the Earth.* 1971. Toronto. New Pr. 1st. inscr/dtd 1971. F/VG clip. L3. $275.00

MCMANUS, Edgar J. *Black Bondage in the North.* 1973. Syracuse. 1st. 236p. F/F. B4. $50.00

MCMATH, Robert C. *Populist Vanguard: A History of Southern Farmer's Alliance.* 1975. Norton. trade pb. VG/dj. V4. $12.50

MCMILLAN, Carol. *Our Own Mother Goose.* 1934. Reid/Koehne Studios. 36p. lg sc. VG. M5. $42.00

MCMILLAN, George. *Old Breed: History of First Marine Division in WWII.* 1949. WA, DC. 1st. ils/maps. 483p. VG. S16. $150.00

MCMILLAN, George. *Uncommon Valor: Marine Divisions in Action.* 1986. Nashville. photos/maps. 256p. VG/VG. S16. $27.50

MCMILLAN, Priscilla Johnson. *Marina & Lee.* 1977. Harper. 1st. inscr. NF/F. B4. $125.00

MCMILLAN, Terry. *Disappearing Acts.* 1989. Viking. 1st. F/F. B2. $175.00

MCMILLAN, Terry. *Mama.* 1987. Houghton Mifflin. 1st. inscr/dtd 1987. author's 1st book. F/dj. Q1. $350.00

MCMURRICH, J. Playfair. *Leonardo Da Vinci: Anatomist (1452-1519).* 1930. Baltimore. 1st. 265p. A13. $125.00

MCMURTRY, Larry. *All My Friends Are Going to Be Strangers.* 1972. S&S. 1st. NF/NF. T11. $135.00

MCMURTRY, Larry. *Anything for Billy.* 1988. S&S. 1st. F/F. A23. $42.00

MCMURTRY, Larry. *Anything for Billy.* 1989. London. Collins. 1st. sgn. F/F. from $50 to $60.00

MCMURTRY, Larry. *Buffalo Girls.* 1990. S&S. 1st. sgn. F/F. A23/D10/R14. $60.00

MCMURTRY, Larry. *Cadillac Jack.* 1982. S&S. 1st. F/F. M19. $45.00

MCMURTRY, Larry. *Cadillac Jack.* 1992. S&S. 1st. sgn. F/F. A23. $75.00

MCMURTRY, Larry. *Daughter of the Tejas.* 1965. Greenwich. NYGS. 1st/2nd state. NF/NF clip 2nd state. T11. $125.00

MCMURTRY, Larry. *Desert Rose.* 1983. S&S. 1st. sgn. F/F. A23. $75.00

MCMURTRY, Larry. *Evening Star.* 1992. S&S. 1st. sgn. F/F. A23. $40.00

MCMURTRY, Larry. *Flim Flam.* 1987. S&S. 1st. F/F. D10. $45.00

MCMURTRY, Larry. *Horseman, Pass By.* 1961. Harper. 1st. inscr. author's 1st book. NF/NF. L3. $1,750.00

MCMURTRY, Larry. *Late Child.* 1995. S&S. ARC. sgn. F/F. D10. $50.00

MCMURTRY, Larry. *Lonesome Dove.* 1985. S&S. 1st. F/F. T11. $200.00

MCMURTRY, Larry. *Moving On.* 1970. S&S. 1st. NF/dj. M25/T11. $75.00

MCMURTRY, Larry. *Pretty Boy Floyd.* 1994. S&S. 1st. sgn. F/F. A23. $42.00

MCMURTRY, Larry. *Some Can Whistle.* 1989. S&S. 1st. F/F. T11/T12. $20.00

MCMURTRY, Larry. *Somebody's Darling.* 1978. S&S. 1st. rem mk. NF/F. D10. $40.00

MCMURTRY, Larry. *Somebody's Darling.* 1978. S&S. 1st. sgn. F/F. A23. $90.00

MCMURTRY, Larry. *Streets of Laredo.* 1993. NY. S&S. 1st. F/F. T12. $25.00

MCMURTRY, Larry. *Streets of Laredo.* 1993. S&S. 1st. sgn. F/F. A23. $45.00

MCMURTRY, Larry. *Terms of Endearment.* 1975. S&S. 1st. F/dj. B24. $400.00

MCMURTRY, Larry. *Texasville.* 1987. S&S. 1st. inscr. NF/NF. R14. $50.00

MCMURTRY, Larry. *Texasville.* 1987. S&S. 1st. sgn. F/F. A23. $40.00

MCNAIRN, Jack. *San Francisco's Celestial Sons.* 1980. Boonville, CA. self pub. ils/map Chinatown. F/stapled wrp. R3. $15.00

MCNALLY, Dennis. *Desolate Angel: A Biography of Jack Kerouac...* 1979. Random. 1st. F/clip. Q1. $40.00

MCNALLY, Raymond. *Clutch of Vampires.* 1974. NYGS. 1st. 8vo. F/dj. T10. $50.00

MCNALLY, Raymond. *Dracula Was a Woman.* 1983. McGraw Hill. 1st. F/dj. M2. $30.00

MCNALLY & MCNALLY. *This Is Mexico.* 1947. Dodd Mead. 1st. 4to. dj. F3. $15.00

MCNARRY, Donald. *Ship Models in Miniature.* 1975. Praeger. ils. 176p. dj. T7. $25.00

MCNEER, May. *Story of the Southern Highlands.* nd (1945). Harper. 4to. unp. VG+. C14. $18.00

MCNEIL, Marion. *Round the Mulberry Bush.* 1933. Saalfield. ils Fern Bisel Peat. VG. from $55 to $75.00

MCNEILL, Elizabeth. *Nine & a Half Weeks: A Memoir of a Love Affair.* 1978. Dutton. 1st. F/F. B4. $150.00

MCNICKLE, D'Arcy. *Surrounded.* 1936. Dodd Mead. 1st. author's 1st book. NF. L3. $750.00

MCNICKLE & FEY. *Indians & Other Americans.* 1959. Harper. 1st. G/G. L3. $75.00

MCNULTY, John. *Third Avenue, New York.* 1946. Little Brn. 1st. F/VG+ clip. B4. $125.00

MCPEEK & MCPEEK. *Verlys of America Decorative Glass 1935-1951.* 1972. self pub. 1st. 66p. VG. H1. $45.00

MCPHAIL, David. *Oh, No, Go.* 1973. Atlantic/Little Brn. 1st. 4to. NF/G+. P2. $35.00

MCPHEE, John. *Alaska: Images of the Country.* 1981. Sierra Club. 1st. folio. F/F. B4. $100.00

MCPHEE, John. *Basin & Range.* 1981. FSG. 1st. F/F. T11. $45.00

MCPHEE, John. *Coming Into the Country.* 1977. Farrar Straus. 1st. F/clip. Q1. $60.00

MCPHEE, John. *Crofter & Laird.* 1970. FSG. 1st. NF/NF clip. T11. $100.00

MCPHEE, John. *Deltoid Pumpkin Seed.* 1973. Farrar Straus. 1st. F/F. H11. $45.00

MCPHEE, John. *Giving Good Weight.* 1979. FSG. 1st. F/F. D10. $40.00

MCPHEE, John. *Headmaster.* 1966. FSG. 1st. author's 2nd book. F/NF. B3. $300.00

MCPHEE, John. *Headmaster.* 1966. NY. 1st. VG/dj. B5. $95.00

MCPHEE, John. *La Place de la Concorde Suisse.* 1984. FSG. 1st. F/F. D10. $45.00

MCPHEE, John. *Levels of the Game.* 1969. FSG. 1st. VG+/dj. P8. $35.00

MCPHEE, John. *Levels of the Game.* 1970. London. Macdonald. 1st Eng. F/dj. Q1. $75.00

MCPHEE, John. *Pieces of the Frame.* 1975. FSG. 1st. F/F. B4. $200.00

MCPHEE, John. *Roomful of Hovings & Other Profiles.* 1968. FSG. 1st. NF/NF. B3. $125.00

MCPHEE, John. *Sense of Where You Are.* 1965. FSG. 1st. photos. VG. P8. $45.00

MCPHEE, John. *Wimbledon, a Celebration.* 1972. Viking. 1st. photos Alfred Eisenstaedt. VG/VG. R14. $60.00

MCPHERSON, James Alan. *Atlas of the Civil War.* 1994. 223p. O8. $18.50

MCPHERSON, James Alan. *Hue & Cry.* 1969. Atlantic/Little Brn. 1st. F/NF. B4. $150.00

MCQUADE, James. *Misty.* 1972. Sherbourne. 1st. sgn. VG/dj. M2. $25.00

MCQUAID, Clement. *Gamblers Digest.* 1971. Northfield, IL. 320p. VG/dj. S1. $8.00

MCQUARRIE, Ralph. *Star Wars, Return of the Jedi Portfolio.* 1983. Ballantine. ils. oversize portfolio. NF. C9. $100.00

MCQUINN, Donald E. *Targets.* 1980. Macmillan. 1st. F/F. H11. $35.00

MCQUOWN, F.R. *Fine-Flowered Cacti.* 1965. London. 1st. 30 photos/8 drawings. VG/dj. B26. $25.00

MCRAVEN, Charles. *Building With Stone.* 1990. Alpine. 2nd. 192p. VG. A8. $10.00

MCTAGGART, M.F. *Mount & Man: A Key to Better Horsemanship.* 1925. Country Life. 1st. ils Lionel Edwards. VG. O3. $20.00

MCTEER, May. *Story of the Great Plains.* 1943. 1st. lithos CH DeWitt. VG+/worn. S13. $20.00

MCTIGUE. *Child's Garden of Delights: Pictures, Poems & Stories...* 1987. ils. 271p. F/F. A4. $35.00

MCVAUGH, Rogers. *Edward Palmer: Plant Explorer of American West.* 1956. Norman. photos/lists/2 maps. 430p. VG+/dj. B26. $29.00

MCWHINEY, Grady. *Braxton Bragg & Confederate Defeat. Vol 1.* 1969. NY. 1st. ils/map. 421p. VG/dj. B18. $20.00

MCWHORTER, L.V. *Hear Me, My Chiefs, Nez Perce Legend & History.* 1952. Caxton. 1st. photos. 640p. VG/dj. J2. $295.00

MCWHORTER, L.V. *Yellow Wolf: His Own Story.* 1940. Caxton. 1st. sgn. NF. L3. $450.00

MCWHORTER, L.V. *Yellow Wolf: His Own Story.* 1940. Caxton. 1st. 324p. VG. J2. $95.00

MEACHUM, Walter E. *Old Oregon Trail, the Road That Won an Empire.* 1924. Ryder Bros. 1st. 33p. VG. J2. $55.00

MEACHUM, Walter E. *Old Oregon Trail, the Road That Won an Empire.* 1948. Am Pioneer Trails Assn. G. A19. $35.00

MEAD. *Thomas Pynchon: Biography of Primary & Secondary Materials.* 1989. 1/957. ils. 184p. F/F. A4. $125.00

MEAD, J.R. *Hunting & Trading on the Great Plains 1859-1875.* 1986. OK U. 1st. photos/maps. F/dj. M4. $30.00

MEAD, Margaret. *Continuities in Cultural Evolution.* 1964. New Haven. Yale. 1st. 8vo. VG/dj. w/card: Compliments of Author. T10. $50.00

MEAD, Margaret. *Growing Up in New Guinea: Comparative Study...* 1930. Morrow. 1st. F/NF. B4. $275.00

MEAD, Richard. *Medical Precepts & Cautions.* 1755. London. Brindley. 2nd. 8vo. 311p. F. T10. $200.00

MEAD, Sheperd. *Big Ball of Wax.* 1954. S&S. 1st. F/dj. M2. $20.00

MEADE, L.T. *Bad Little Hannah, a Story of Girls.* ca 1908. NY. AL Burt. 373p. VG. A25. $15.00

MEADE, L.T. *Bunch of Cousins & the Barn Boys.* nd (1923). London. Chambers. 12mo. VG+. C8. $25.00

MEADE, L.T. *Girl of the People.* ca 1915. NY. Hurst. 1st thus? 271p. VG. A25. $10.00

MEADE, L.T. *World of Girls.* (1886). London. Cassell. 39 Thousand prt. 12mo. VG. C8. $45.00

MEADE, Martha L. *Recipes From the Old South.* 1961. Bramhall. G/dj. A16. $12.00

MEADE, Mary. *Mary Meade's Cooking Fun.* 1965. Chicago. Tribune. ils Becky Krehbiel. 4to. 32p. VG+. M5. $20.00

MEADOWCRAFT, Enid La Monte. *By Wagon & Flatboat.* 1938. Crowell. 1st. 170p. VG/G+. P2. $35.00

MEADOWS & MILLS. *Antarctic.* 1994. Oxford/Santa Barbara. Clio. 8vo. 383p. M/sans. P4. $87.50

MEAGHER, Maude. *Green Scamander.* 1933. Houghton Mifflin. 1st. VG/dj. M2. $35.00

MEANS, Philip Ainsworth. *Ancient Civilizations of the Andes.* 1931. Scribner. 1st. 586p. G. F3. $45.00

MEANS, Philip Ainsworth. *Spanish Main.* 1935. Scribner. ils. 278p. T7. $45.00

MEANY, Tom. *Incredible Giants.* 1955. Barnes. sgn. VG/VG. B11. $65.00

MEAR & SWAN. *In the Footsteps of Scott.* 1987. London. Cape. 1st Eng. 306p. map ep. gilt bl. P4. $35.00

MEARS, Eliot Grinnell. *Resident Orientals on the American Pacific Coast...* 1928. Chicago U. 8vo. gilt red cloth. F. R3. $90.00

MEASE, James. *Memoirs of Philadelphia Society for Promoting Agriculture.* 1816. Phil. Warner. 543p. leather spine missing pieces. scarce. A10. $75.00

MEBANE, John. *Collecting Brides' Baskets & Other Glass Fancies.* 1976. Wallace-Homestead. ne. 174p. VG/glossy wrp. H1. $45.00

MECHI, John J. *Series of Letters on Agricultural Improvements.* 1845. London. Longman. 122p. cloth. A10. $45.00

MEDINA, J.T. *Discovery of the Amazon According to Account Friar Gaspar...* 1934. Am Geog Soc. trans from 1894 ed. 467p. M4. $35.00

MEDUNA, Ladislas. *Die Entwicklung der Zirbeldruse im Sauglingsalter...* 1925. Munchen/Berlin. Bergmann/Springer. 1st separate. inscr. 547p. G1. $85.00

MEDWAY, Lord. *Wild Mammals of Malaya & Offshore Islands...* 1969. London. Oxford. ils. 127p. cloth. VG. M12. $60.00

MEE, John L. *Three Little Frogs.* 1924. Chicago. Volland. 1st. ils John Rae. sq 12mo. mc brd. R5. $75.00

MEEKINGS, C.A.F. *1235 Surrey Eyre, Vol I, Introduction.* 1979. Guildford. Surrey Record Soc. M11. $65.00

MEERPOL & MEERPOL. *We Are Your Sons: Legacy of Ethel & Julius Rosenberg...* 1975. Houghton Mifflin. 419p. VG/dj. S3. $24.00

MEEUSE, A.D.J. *All About Angiosperms.* 1987. Eburon. 8vo. 212p. F/wrp. B1. $25.00

MEGAW & MEGAW. *Celtic Art: From Its Beginnings to the Book of Kells.* 1989. photos. VG/VG. M17. $27.50

MEIGHN, Moira. *Little Book of Conceited Secrets & Delights...* 1928. London. Medici Soc. 1st. ils. 79p. VG+. A25. $20.00

MEIGNAN, Victor. *From Paris to Pekin Over Siberian Snows...* 1889. London. Swann. 2nd. ils/notes. 428p. gilt pict cloth. VG. W3. $265.00

MEIGS, Charles. *Obstetrics: Science & the Art.* 1849. Phil. 1st. 685p. recent leatherette/orig label. A13. $250.00

MEIGS, Cornelia. *Trade Wind.* 1955 (1927). Little Brn. 8vo. 309p. xl. VG. T5. $12.00

MEIGS. *Critical History of Children's Literature, a Survey...* 1953. ils. 648p. VG/VG. A4. $95.00

MEIJER, W. *Spinoza een Levensbeeld.* nd. Amsterdam. sm 4to. Dutch text. 34p. wrp in brd. S3. $19.00

MEIR, Golda. *My Life.* 1975. Putnam. 1st. F/F. B35. $15.00

MEIROWSKY, Arnold M. *Neurological Surgery of Trauma.* 1965. WA, DC. Office Surgeon General. 4to. gray cloth. G1. $50.00

MELKONIAN, Michael. *Algal Cell Mobility.* 1992. NY. ils. 236p. as new. B26. $29.00

MELLIN, Jeanne. *Horseback Riding.* 1970. Grosset Dunlap. rpt. VG. O3. $25.00

MELLIN, Jeanne. *Morgan Horse Handbook.* 1973. Brattleboro. Stephen Green. ARC/1st. F/F. O3. $45.00

MELLING, Elizabeth. *Crime & Punishment, a Collection of Examples...* 1969. Maidstone. Kent County Council. M11. $50.00

MELLOW, James R. *Charmed Circle: Gertrude Stein & Company.* 1974. Praeger. 1st. 528p. red brd/gray cloth. B22. $10.00

MELVILLE, George W. *In the Lena Delta: A Narrative...* 1884. Boston. Houghton Mifflin. 8vo. 497p. brn cloth. P4. $225.00

MELVILLE, Herman. *Billy Budd & Other Prose Pieces.* 1924. London. Constable. 1st. F/torn. B4. $400.00

MELVILLE, Herman. *Redburn: His First Voyage.* 1849. NY. Harper. 1st/2nd state (18p ads dated Oct 1849). glt brn cloth. M24. $750.00

MELVIN, Jean Sutherland. *American Glass Paperweights & Their Makers.* 1967. Thomas Nelson. 192p. as new/dj/Fcase. H1. $80.00

MENCKEN, H.L. *Book of Prefaces.* 1917. Knopf. 1st. VG. A20. $50.00

MENCKEN, H.L. *Christmas Story.* 1946. Knopf. 1st. F/dj. Q1. $75.00

MENCKEN, H.L. *Prejudices.* 1926. Knopf. 1st. VG/fair. M23. $50.00

MENDEL, Gregor. *Experiments in Plant-Hybridisation.* 1925. Cambridge. rpt. 41p. VG/wrp. B26. $9.00

MENDELL, Ronald. *Who's Who in Basketball.* 1973. Arlington. 1st. VG+/dj. P8. $25.00

MENDELL & PHARES. *Who's Who in Football.* 1974. Arlington. 1st. biographical sketches. VG+. P8. $20.00

MENDELSSOHN, Kurt. *Riddle of the Pyramids.* 1975. London. BC Assoc. ils. 224p. NF/dj. W1. $12.00

MENDELSSOHN, Moses. *Phedon, ou Entretiens sur la Spiritualite...* 1772. Paris/Bayeux. Saillant Lepelley. tall 8vo. gilt calf. R12. $375.00

MENDOZA, George. *Inspector.* 1970. Doubleday. 1st. ils Peter Parnall. obl 4to. VG+/dj. P2. $35.00

MENDOZA & ROCKWELL. *Norman Rockwell's Americana ABC.* nd (1975). Dell/Abrams. unp. NF. C14. $8.00

MENGE, J.J. *Erstes Lese-, Lehr- und Vebungsbuch fur Deutsche...* 1874. NY/Cincinnati. 1st. 8vo. 64p. G. T10. $75.00

MENGEL, Willi. *Ottmar Mergenthaler & the Printing Revolution.* 1954. 1st. ils. decor bdg. VG. K3. $18.00

MENKE, Frank G. *All-Sports Record Book.* 1950. Barnes. 1st. G+/G. P8. $6.00

MENKE, Frank G. *Down the Stretch.* 1945. Smith Durell. 1st. 209p. VG/dj. M20. $30.00

MENKEN, Alice Davis. *On the Side of Mercy: Problems in Social Readjustment.* 1933. Convici Friede. 1st. ils. 224p. VG/dj. A25. $15.00

MENNINGER, Edwin A. *Flowering Trees of the World...* 1962. Hearthside. 1st. 8vo. F/VG. A22. $75.00

MENPES, Mortimer. *Japan: Record in Color.* 1904. London. 200 full-p engravings. 207p. teg. gold-tooled cloth. NF. W3. $75.00

MERCER, Alexander Gardiner. *Bible Characters.* 1885. Putnams. 335p. VG. B29. $8.00

MERCER, F.A. *Gardens & Gardening.* 1937. London. Studio. 134p. VG. A10. $22.00

MERCER, Samuel A.B. *Sumero-Babylonian Year-Formulae.* 1946. London. Luzac. 1st. 4to. 2 fld charts. 121p. VG. W1. $35.00

MERCHANT, Paul; see Ellison, Harlan.

MEREDITH, D. *Grasses & Pastures of South Africa.* 1955. np. ils/figures/maps. 771p. VG/dj. B26. $122.50

MEREDITH, D. *Search at Lock Ness: Expedition of the NY Times...* (1977). NY. ils/map/drawings. 183p. cloth/brd. NF/F. M12. $25.00

MEREDITH, De Witt. *Voyages of the Velero III. Pictorial Version...* 1939. Los Angeles. private prt. 1st. inscr. 286p. P4. $165.00

MEREDITH, George. *Last Poems.* Oct 1909. Scribner. 1st Am. 64p. teg. gilt bdg. G. H1. $16.00

MEREDITH, George. *Shaving of Shagpat.* 1955. NY. LEC. 1st thus. 1/1500. ils/sgn Honore Guilbeau. F/glassine/case. Q1. $125.00

MEREDITH, Isabel. *Girl Among the Anarchists.* 1903. London. Duckworth. 1st. B2. $85.00

MEREDITH, Owen. *Lucile.* 1868. Ticknor Fields. ils George DuMaurier. aeg. gilt brn cloth. G. H1. $28.00

MEREDITH, Scott. *Bar 1 Roundup of Best Western Stories.* 1952. Dutton. 1st. VG/dj. M2. $12.00

MEREDITH, William. *Earth Walk.* 1970. Knopf. 1st. F/dj. V1. $45.00

MERILLAT, Herb. *Guadalcanal Remembered.* 1982. NY. maps/photos/notes/biblio/index. 298p. VG/VG. S16. $15.00

MERINO, Jose Maria. *Beyond the Ancient Cities.* 1987. FSG. 1st Am. F/F. B4. $45.00

MERRELL, David J. *Ecological Genetics.* 1981. NM U. 1st. as new/dj. V4. $12.50

MERRIAM, D.F. *Computer Applications in the Earth Sciences.* 1981. NY. Plenum. 385p. F/G. D8. $25.00

MERRIAM, D.F. *Geostatistics, a Colloquium.* 1970. NY. Plenum. 177p. F/G. D8. $25.00

MERRIAM, Eve. *Emma Lazarus: Woman With a Torch.* 1956. Citadel. 160p. G+/fair. S3. $20.00

MERRIAM, Harold. *Montana Adventure, the Recollections of Frank B Linderman.* 1968. NE U. 1st. 224p. VG/VG. J2. $125.00

MERRIEN, Jean. *Lonely Voyages.* 1954. London. 1st. 8vo. 280p. map ep. VG/dj. P4. $35.00

MERRILL, Anthony F. *Rammed-Earth House.* 1947. Harper. 1st. 230p. dj. A10. $40.00

MERRILL, Dean. *Clergy Couples in Crisis: Impact of Stress...* 1985. Word. 216p. VG/dj. B29. $7.50

MERRILL, Judith. *Path Into the Unknown.* 1968. Delacorte. 1st Am. VG/dj. M2. $10.00

MERRILL, Judith. *9th Annual Year's Best Science Fiction.* 1964. S&S. 1st. F/dj. M2. $25.00

MERRIMAN, Charles E. *Who's It in America.* 1906. NY. Dodge. 1st. cream pict cloth. NF/VG. M24. $65.00

MERRIMAN, Henry Seton. *Vultures.* 1902. Harper. 1st Am. F/NF. B4. $125.00

MERRYMAN, Mildred Plew. *Bonbon & Bonbonette.* 1924. Rand McNally. 1st. 96p. VG+. P2. $95.00

MERSAND, Joseph. *Traditions in American Literature: A Study of Jewish...* 1939. Modern Chapbooks. biblio/index. 247p. VG. S3. $25.00

MERSERVE & SANDBURG. *Photographs of Abraham Lincoln.* 1944. Harcourt Brace. 1st. photos. 126p. F/dj. H1. $60.00

MERTENS, J.M. *Living Snakes of the World.* 1987. Sterling. 480p. dj. B1. $50.00

MERTON, Robert K. *On the Shoulders of Giants.* 1985. HBJ. 8vo. 300p. F/dj. K3. $15.00

MERTON, Robert K. *Sociology of Science.* 1974. Chicago. 2nd. VG/dj. K3. $40.00

MERTON, Thomas. *Alaskan Journal of Thomas Merton.* 1988. Isla Vista, CA. Turkey Pr. 1st. 1/140 deluxe. Japanese linen. F/case. Q1. $250.00

MERTON, Thomas. *Disputed Questions.* 1960. NY. 1st. 297p. F/VG. W3. $45.00

MERTON, Thomas. *Seasons of Celebration.* 1965. Farrar. 1st. F/NF. B2. $35.00

MERTON, Thomas. *Seeds of Contemplation.* 1949. New Directions. 1st. F/dj. Q1. $250.00

MERTON, Thomas. *Silent Life.* 1957. FSC. 1st. F/NF. B3. $60.00

MERTON, Thomas. *Thomas Merton on Peace.* 1971. NY. 1st. VG/VG. B5. $40.00

MERTZ, Barbara Gross. *Into the Darkness.* 1990. S&S. 1st. 298p. F/NF. W2. $20.00

MERTZ, Barbara Gross. *Jackal's Head.* 1968. Meredith. 1st. VG/VG. P3. $40.00

MERTZ, Barbara Gross. *Lion in the Valley.* 1986. Warner. 1st. sgn. VG/VG. A23. $42.00

MERTZ, Barbara Gross. *Naked Once More.* 1989. Warner. 1st. F/F. H11. $25.00

MERTZ, Barbara Gross. *Night Train to Memphis.* 1994. Warner. 1st. sgn. VG/VG. A23. $40.00

MERTZ, Barbara Gross. *Sea King's Daughter.* 1975. Dodd Mead. VG/VG. P3. $25.00

MERTZ, Barbara Gross. *Search the Shadows.* 1987. Atheneum. ARC. NF/wrp. B3. $30.00

MERYMAN, Richard. *Andrew Wyeth.* 1968. 1st. folio. NF/VG. S13. $150.00

MESERVE & SANDBURG. *Photographs of Abraham Lincoln.* 1944. NY. Harcourt Brace. photos. 30p. cloth. dj. D11. $75.00

MESSICK, Dale. *Brenda Starr, Girl Reporter.* 1943. Racine. Whitman. authorized ed. ils. 248p. VG. A25. $8.00

MESSNER, Reinhold. *Antarctica: Both Heaven & Hell.* 1991. Seattle. Mountaineers. 1st Am. 8vo. 381p. M/dj. P4. $35.00

METALIOUS, Grace. *Peyton Place.* 1956. S&S. 1st. 378p. VG. W2. $140.00

METCALF, Arthur. *Arm's Length.* 1930. Scribner. 1st. VG. M2. $22.00

METCALF, Arthur. *Green Devil.* 1912. Pilgrim. 1st. sgn. VG. M2. $35.00

METCALF & FLINT. *Destructive & Useful Insects.* 1951. McGraw Hill. 3rd. 1071p. A10. $22.00

METCALFE, C.R. *Anatomy of the Monocotyledons.* 1960. Oxford. Clarendon. 731p. VG/dj. A10. $65.00

METCHNIKOFF, Elie. *Prolongation of Life: Optimistic Studies.* 1908. NY. 1st Am. 343p. A13. $75.00

METHVEN, Barbara. *Microwaving for One & Two.* 1981. Cy DeCosse. VG. B10. $10.00

METRAUX, Alfred. *History of the Incas.* 1969. Pantheon. 1st Am. 205p. dj. F3. $20.00

METTLER, Frederick Albert. *Neuroanatomy.* 1948. St Louis. Mosby. 2nd revised/enlarged. tall 8vo. ils. 536p. VG. G1. $65.00

METZ, Alice Hulett. *Early American Pattern Glass.* 1961 (1958). self pub. 3rd. sgn. 243p. sbdg. G. H1. $25.00

METZ, Alice Hulett. *Much More Early American Pattern Glass.* 1965. self pub. 1st. sgn. 232p. sbdg. G. H1. $48.00

METZGER & RUBIN. *Shaker Industries.* 1977. Butternut. 1/225. 68x60mm. M/prt wrp. B24. $100.00

MEW, Egan. *Chelsea & Chelsea-Derby China.* nd. Jack/Dodd Mead. 92p. cloth/pict label. VG. M20. $22.00

MEWSHAW, Michael. *Blackballed.* 1986. Atheneum. 1st. F/F. A20. $10.00

MEYER, Elise. *You Can Be a Better Cook Than Mama Ever Was.* 1968. Doubleday. A16. $10.00

MEYER, F.B. *Our Daily Homily.* 1966. Revell. 469p. fair. B29. $8.00

MEYER, J.B. *William Carey: Shoemaker Who Became Father & Founder...* nd. Partridge. 160p. xl G. B29. $9.50

MEYER, Milton W. *Diplomatic History of the Philippine Republic.* 1965. Honolulu. 321p. M/VG. P1. $35.00

MEYER, Nicholas. *Seven-Per-Cent Solution.* 1974. Dutton. 1st. VG/VG. P3. $25.00

MEYER, Nicholas. *West End Horror.* 1976. Dutton. 1st. VG/dj. M2. $15.00

MEYER, Roy W. *History of the Santee Sioux.* 1967. Lincoln, NE. 8vo. 434p. bl cloth. NF. K7. $48.00

MEYER. *Treasury of Great Children's Book Illustrators.* 1987. 4to. ils/93 mc pl. 272p. F/VG. A4. $85.00

MEZZROW & WOLFE. *Really the Blues.* 1946. Random. 1st. sgn Mezzrow. VG/NF. B2. $350.00

MIAN, Mary. *Take Three Witches.* 1971. Houghton Mifflin. 1st. sgn. F/F. B11. $40.00

MICHAEL. *Musical Instruments in the Dayton C Miller Flute Collection.* 1982. Lib of Congress. 349p. 4to. F. A17. $22.50

MICHAEL, Barbara; see Mertz, Barbara Gross.

MICHAEL, Bryan; see Moore, Brian.

MICHAEL, Paul. *American Movies Reference Book, the Sound Era.* 1969. Prentice Hall. 600+p. NF/dj. C9. $50.00

MICHAEL, W.H.C. *Mississippi Flotilla: What the Gunboats Accomplished...* 1886. Omaha, NE. 1st. 19p. VG/prt wrp. M8. $250.00

MICHAELS, Leonard. *Going Places.* 1969. FSG. 1st. inscr. author's 1st book. F/F. L3. $125.00

MICHAELS, Leonard. *I Would Have Saved Them if I Could.* 1975. FSG. 1st. author's 2nd book. F/F. B4. $75.00

MICHAELS, Leonard. *Shuffle.* 1990. FSG. 1st. F/F. B35. $12.00

MICHAUX, F.A. *Travels to the West of Alleghany Mountains...* 1805. London. Shury. 294p. VG. A10. $350.00

MICHEAUX, Oscar. *Story of Dorothy Stanfield.* 1946. Book Supply. 1st. F/F. B4. $200.00

MICHEL, Henri. *Second World War.* 1975. NY. 947p. VG/VG. S16. $45.00

MICHELET, Jules. *Bird.* 1879. London. revised. ils Giacomelli. 350p. VG. S15. $80.00

MICHELET, M. *Life of Martin Luther.* 1856. NY. Kelley. 314p. gr cloth. VG. M20. $40.00

MICHELMORE, Peter. *Swift Years: The Robert Oppenheimer Story.* 1969. Dodd Mead. ils. 8vo. 273p. VG/dj. K3. $15.00

MICHENER, E.A. *How to Grow Food for Your Family.* 1942. NY. Barnes. 139p. xl. A10. $13.00

MICHENER, James A. *About Centennial: Some Notes on the Novel.* 1974. Random. 1st. NF/NF. T11. $75.00

MICHENER, James A. *Alaska.* 1988. Random. ltd. 868p. NF/NF. W2. $50.00

MICHENER, James A. *Bridge at Andau.* 1957. Random. 1st. NF/G+. M19. $50.00

MICHENER, James A. *Caravans.* 1963. Random. 1st. sgn/dtd 1995. NF/NF. R14. $175.00

MICHENER, James A. *Caribbean.* 1989. Random. 1st. F/F. A20. $20.00

MICHENER, James A. *Centennial.* 1974. Random. 1st. F/NF. B2. $65.00

MICHENER, James A. *Chesapeake.* 1978. Random. 1st. sgn on tipped-in leaf. F/F. B2. $125.00

MICHENER, James A. *Covenant.* 1980. Random. 1st. F/dj. Q1. $60.00

MICHENER, James A. *Drifters.* 1971. Random. 1st. NF/dj. A24. $60.00

MICHENER, James A. *Eagle & the Raven.* 1990. Austin. State House. sgn. F/F. B3. $45.00

MICHENER, James A. *Fires of Spring.* 1949. Random. 1st. NF/VG. B4. $600.00

MICHENER, James A. *Firstfruits: Harvest of 25 Years of Israeli Writing.* 1973. JPS. F/NF. H11. $55.00

MICHENER, James A. *Floating World.* 1954. Random. 1st/4th prt. ils. 403p. F/clear plastic dj. W3. $75.00

MICHENER, James A. *Fodor's Modern Guides/Hawaii 1961.* 1961. McKay. intro Michener. F/NF pink dj. A24. $50.00

MICHENER, James A. *Iberia.* 1968. Random. 1st. F/dj. Q1. $75.00

MICHENER, James A. *Japanese Prints: From the Early Masters to the Modern.* 1959. Rutland/Tokyo. Tuttle. 1st. VG/VG. B5. $110.00

MICHENER, James A. *Legacy.* 1987. Random. 1st. F/F. N4. $25.00

MICHENER, James A. *Michener Miscellany.* 1973. Random. 1st. F/NF. T11. $75.00

MICHENER, James A. *Miracle in Seville.* 1995. Random. 1/500. sgn. ils John Fulton. F/sans/F case. R14. $175.00

MICHENER, James A. *Modern Japanese Print.* 1968. Tuttle. 1st trade. ils. 57p. F. W3. $110.00

MICHENER, James A. *My Lost Mexico.* 1992. Austin. State House. 1/350. sgn. F/case. B3. $150.00

MICHENER, James A. *Novel.* 1991. Random. 1st. F/dj. Q1. $30.00

MICHENER, James A. *Presidential Lottery.* 1969. NY. Random. 1st. blk cloth. F/NF. T11. $75.00

MICHENER, James A. *Rascals in Paradise.* 1957. NY. Random. 1st. NF/VG+. T11. $95.00

MICHENER, James A. *Recessional.* 1994. Random. 1st trade. 484p. F/F. W2. $45.00

MICHENER, James A. *Sayonara.* 1954. Random. 1st. NF/NF. M19. $50.00

MICHENER, James A. *Sayonara.* 1954. Random. 1st. VG/VG. B3/P3. $45.00

MICHENER, James A. *Sayonara.* 1954. VT/Japan. Tuttle. 1st thus. prt for Am occupation forces. NF/dj. D10. $90.00

MICHENER, James A. *Space.* 1982. Random. ltd 1st. 622p. F/NF. W2. $120.00

MICHENER, James A. *Tales of the South Pacific.* 1951. London. Collins. 1st Eng. F/VG+. B4. $450.00

MICHENER, James A. *Voice of Asia.* 1951. Random. 1st/1st state. NF/NF. T11. $165.00

MICHENER, James A. *Watermen.* 1979. Random. 1st. ils John Moll. NF/NF. A24. $50.00

MICKLETHWAIT & PEPPIN. *Dictionary of British Book Illustrations, the 20th Century.* 1983. London. 1st. VG/VG. T9. $50.00

MIDDENDORF, John William. *Henley Royal Regatta.* 1964. Baltimore. Barton Cotton. 1/1000. ils. unp. T7. $35.00

MIDDLEKAUFF, R. *Glorious Cause: American Revolution 1763-1789.* 1982. Oxford. 1st prt. ils/map. 696p. F/dj. M4. $30.00

MIDDLETON, Christopher. *Vindication of Conduct of Capt Christopher Middleton...* 1967. Wakefield. rpt (London 1742). 206p. 48p. xl. P4. $25.00

MIDDLETON, Christopher. *Voyages in Search of a Northwest Passage 1741-1747...* 1994. London. Hakluyt Soc. 2nd Series #177. 8vo. 333p. bl cloth. P4. $50.00

MIDDLETON, Don. *Roy Rogers & the Gopher Creek Gunman.* 1945. Racine. Whitman. Ils Erwin Hess. sm 8vo. VG+/dj. C8. $22.50

MIDDLETON, W.E. Knowles. *History of the Barometer.* 1964. Johns Hopkins. sm 4to. 489p. dj. K5. $125.00

MIDGLEY, John. *Goodness of Beans, Peas & Lentils.* 1992. Random. 1st Am. VG/VG. B10. $9.00

MIDGLEY, John. *Goodness of Olive Oil.* 1992. Random. 65p. VG/VG. B10. $10.00

MIERS, Earl Schenck. *Career Coach.* 1941. Westminster. 1st. ils. VG/G+. P8. $25.00

MIERS, Earl Schenck. *Composing Sticks & Mortar Boards.* 1941. Rutgers. 1st trade. 97p. A17. $12.50

MIERS, Earl Schenck. *General Who Marched to Hell.* 1990. Dorset. A19. $20.00

MIGHELS, Ella Sterling. *Fairy Tale of the White Man, Told From Gates of Sunset by...* 1915. SF. Pacific Pub. 8vo. 72p. VG/wrp. K7. $45.00

MIHALAS, D. *Galactic Astronomy.* 1968. SF. Freeman. 1st. 257p. VG. D8. $10.00

MIKI, Fumio. *Haniwa: Clay Sculpture of Protohistoric Japan.* 1960. Tuttle. 1st. 12 full-p mc pl/80 full-p gravure. 161p. F/NF. W3. $135.00

MILAN, Galleria del Levante. *Il Contributo Russo Alle Avanguardie Plastiche.* 1964. Curato. Carlo Belloi. Italian text. 117p. xl. D2. $45.00

MILES, Babe. *Bluebells & Bittersweet Gardening...* 1969. Van Nostrand. 168p. cloth. VG. A10. $20.00

MILES, Barry. *Ginsberg: A Biography.* 1989. NY. 1st. 588p+photos. F/dj. A17. $15.00

MILES, Miska. *Annie & the Old One.* (1971). Little Brn. 3rd. NF/NF. C8. $22.50

MILES, Miska. *Apricot ABC.* 1969. Atlantic/Little Brn. 1st. ils Peter Parnall. VG+/VG+. P2. $35.00

MILES, Miska. *Pony in the Schoolhouse.* 1964. Little Brn. 1st. F/VG. C8. $22.50

MILES, Nelson. *Personal Recollections & Observations of General...Miles...* 1896. Werner Co. 1st. ils Fredrick Remington. 590p. VG. J2. $475.00

MILES, William. *Horse's Foot & How to Keep It Sound.* 1856. NY. Saxton. G. O3. $45.00

MILHAM, Willis I. *Meteorology: A Text-Book on the Weather...* 1925 (1912). NY. Macmillan. 8vo. 549p. cloth. G. K5. $15.00

MILHAM, Willis I. *Time & Timekeepers.* 1941. Macmillan. Imperial ed. 339 figures. 616p. VG. K3. $40.00

MILL, James. *Analysis of the Phenomena of the Human Mind.* 1869. London. new ed. 2 vol. red cloth. B14. $125.00

MILL, John Stuart. *Dissertations & Discussions Political, Philosophical...* 1859. London. John Parker. 1st. 8vo. cloth. M1. $175.00

MILLAIS, J.G. *Far Away Up the Nile.* 1924. London. Longman. ils/drawings. 254p. cloth. VG. M12. $150.00

MILLAR, C.E. *Soil Fertility.* 1955. NY. Wiley. 436p. dj. A10. $20.00

MILLAR, David P. *From Snowdrift to Shellfire.* 1984. Sydney. David Ell. 1st. 4to. 160p. VG/dj. P4. $110.00

MILLAR, Kenneth. *Barbarous Coast.* 1956. Knopf. 1st. VG+/VG+. B2. $200.00

MILLAR, Kenneth. *Chill.* 1964. Knopf. 1st. F/NF. M15. $125.00

MILLAR, Kenneth. *Goodbye Look.* 1969. Knopf. 1st. F/dj. M25. $60.00

MILLAR, Kenneth. *Lew Archer.* 1977. Mysterious. 1st hc. 1/250. sgn. F/dj/case. Q1. $250.00

MILLAR, Kenneth. *On Crime Writing.* 1973. Santa Barbara. Capra. 1st. 1/250. sgn. F. Q1. $250.00

MILLAR, Kenneth. *Self-Portrait.* 1981. Santa Barbara. Capra. 1st. 1/250. sgn. fwd/sgn Eudora Welty. F. Q1. $200.00

MILLAR, Margaret. *Banshee.* 1983. Morrow. 1st. F/F. M22. $20.00

MILLAR, Margaret. *Iron Gates.* 1945. Random. 1st. VG. M22. $12.00

MILLARD, S.T. *Goblets & Goblets II.* c 1938. Topeka, KS. Central Pr. 1st. sgn/dtd 1940. 8vo. 177 pl. unp. ES. G+. H1. $90.00

MILLAY, Edna St Vincent. *Collected Sonnets.* 1941. Harper. 1st. 8vo. 161p. VG+. H1. $15.00

MILLAY, Edna St. Vincent. *Buck in the Snow.* 1928. Harper. 1st. F/NF. M23. $40.00

MILLAY, Edna St. Vincent. *Conversations at Midnight.* 1937. Harper. 1st. NF/dj. B35. $28.00

MILLAY, Edna St. Vincent. *Fatal Interview.* 1931. Harper. 1st. F/F. Q1. $75.00

MILLER, A.K. *Ordovician Cephalopod Fauna of Baffin Island.* 1954. Geological Soc of Am. 8vo. 234p. gilt cloth. P4. $65.00

MILLER, Albert G. *Fury & the Mustangs.* nd. Grosset Dunlap. pict brd. VG. O3. $10.00

MILLER, Anne Archbold. *Little Old Outlaws.* 1910. McClurg. 1st. ils HG Reed/WN Peoples. VG. M5. $85.00

MILLER, Arthur. *Enemy of the People.* 1951. Viking. 1st. sgn. VG/VG. R14. $90.00

MILLER, Arthur. *Situation Normal.* 1944. Reynal Hitchcock. 1st. sgn. NF/VG. R14. $225.00

MILLER, Arthur. *Timebends.* 1987. Grove. 1st. sgn. NF/NF. R14. $75.00

MILLER, Basil. *Ten Slaves Who Became Famous.* 1951. Zondervan. 1st. 71p. F/NF. B4. $85.00

MILLER, Charlotte. *50 Drawings of Canaletto From the Royal Lib Windsor Castle.* 1983. Johnson Rpt Co. 1/520. atlas folio. 44p+50 facsimile pl. A17. $350.00

MILLER, Daniel. *Early History of the Reformed Church in Pennsylvania.* 1906. self pub. 12mo. 280p. gilt cloth. G. H1. $30.00

MILLER, Debbie S. *Midnight Wilderness: Journeys in Alaska's Arctic...* 1990. SF. Sierra Club. 8vo. 238p. half cloth. P4. $20.00

MILLER, E.D. *Modern Polo.* 1902. London/NY. Hurst Blackett/Scribner. 2nd. G. O3. $25.00

MILLER, Edgar G. *American Antique Furniture.* 1966. Dover. 2 vol. rpt. VG. M17. $45.00

MILLER, F.T. *Photographic History of the Civil War.* 1910. 10 vol. 4to. orig cloth. VG. A4. $650.00

MILLER, Gloria Bley. *Thousand Recipe Chinese Cookbook.* 1988. NY. Weathervane. M/dj. A16. $18.00

MILLER, H. *Old Red Sandstone; or, New Walks in Old Field...* (1878). NY. Carter. new enlarged. ils. 403p. VG. M12. $30.00

MILLER, Henry. *Crazy Cock.* 1991. Grove Weidenfeld. 1st. F/F. B35. $16.00

MILLER, Henry. *Dear, Dear Brenda.* 1986. Morrow. 1st. F/F. T11. $20.00

MILLER, Henry. *Moloch; or, This Gentile World.* 1992. Grove. 1st. F/F. B35. $16.00

MILLER, Henry. *Opus Pistorum.* 1983. Grove. 1st. F/F. D10. $45.00

MILLER, Henry. *Remember to Remember.* 1947. New Directions. 1st. F/F. D10. $250.00

MILLER, Henry. *Remember to Remember.* 1952. London. Grey Walls. 2nd Eng. yel brd. VG/dj. Q1. $50.00

MILLER, Henry. *Tropic of Cancer.* 1961. Grove. 1st thus. intro Karl Shapiro. VG/VG. R14. $40.00

MILLER, Henry. *Tropic of Capricorn.* 1964. Calder. 1st Eng. NF/VG. M19. $25.00

MILLER, Henry. *13 California Towns From the Original Drawings.* 1947. SF. BC of CA. 1/300. obl 4to. marbled brd/gray cloth. NF. R3. $150.00

MILLER, Janet. *Jungles Preferred.* 1931. Houghton Mifflin. 1st. 8vo. 321p. cloth. VG. W1. $9.00

MILLER, Joaquin. *True Bear Stories.* 1990. Rand McNally. ils. NF. M19. $65.00

MILLER, Judith. *Antiques Directory.* 1985. 4to. ils. NF/NF. S13. $25.00

MILLER, Lynn R. *Work Horse Handbook.* 1981. np. Mill Pr. 224p. VG. O3. $25.00

MILLER, Max. *Harbor of the Sun.* 1940. Doubleday Doran. 1st. VG. O4. $15.00

MILLER, Maxine Adams. *Bright Blue Beads. An American Family in Persia.* 1965. Caldwell. Caxton. 4th. 8vo. 11 pl. VG. W1. $12.00

MILLER, Merle. *On Being Different: What It Means to Be Homosexual.* 1971. Random. 1st. F/VG+. B4. $50.00

MILLER, Nolan. *Why I Am So Beat.* 1954. Putnam. 1st. F/NF. B4. $125.00

MILLER, Olive Beaupre. *Engines & Brass Bands.* 1933. Doubleday Doran. 1st. 376p. VG/dj. M20. $30.00

MILLER, Olive Thorne. *Bird-Lover in the West.* 1894. Boston/NY. 1st. 277p. gr cloth. VG. S15. $30.00

MILLER, Ray. *Real Corvette, an Illustrated History...* 1975. Oceanside, CA. 1st. ils. 320p. VG/dj. B18. $35.00

MILLER, Ray. *V-8 Affair.* 1972. Avalon. Evergreen. ils. 303p. VG/dj. B18. $35.00

MILLER, Raymond C. *Kilowatts at Work: History of Detroit Edison Company.* 1957. Wayne. 467p. F/dj. A17. $20.00

MILLER, Richard Gordon. *History & Atlas of Fishes of the Antarctic Ocean.* 1993. Carson City. Foresta Inst Ocean/Mtn Studies. 792p. M/dj. P4. $95.00

MILLER, Richard L. *Truth About Big-Time Football.* 1953. Sloane. 1st. G+. P8. $17.50

MILLER, Robert Ryal. *For Science & National Glory.* 1968. Norman, OK. 1st. ils. VG/dj. K3. $35.00

MILLER, Samuel. *Dilemma of Modern Belief.* 1963. Harper. 1st. sgn. F/VG. B11. $18.00

MILLER, Samuel. *Notes on Hospital Practice: Phil & NY Hospitals.* 1881. Phil. 1st. 3 vol in 1. A13. $75.00

MILLER, Sue. *Family Pictures.* 1990. Harper Row. 1st. F/F. R14. $25.00

MILLER, Sue. *Family Pictures.* 1990. Harper Row. 1st. F/NF. B3. $20.00

MILLER, Sue. *Good Mother.* 1986. Harper Row. 1st. sgn. NF/NF. M22. $40.00

MILLER, Sue. *Inventing the Abbotts.* 1981. Harper Row. 1st. F/F. R14. $40.00

MILLER, T. *Castles & the Crown.* 1963. NY. 1st. VG/VG. B5. $25.00

MILLER, Thomas W. *Chronic Man.* 1990. Madison, CT. International U. 2 vol. 8vo. blk cloth. VG/dj. G1. $65.00

MILLER, Walter M. *Canticle for Leibowitz.* 1960. Lippincott. VG/dj. M2. $50.00

MILLER, Warren H. *Camping Out.* (1918). NY. Doran. 1st. 322p. VG. H7. $15.00

MILLER & SNELL. *Why the West Was Wild, a Contemporary Look.* 1963. KS State Hist Soc. 1st. ils/pl/map. 685p. VG/dj. J2. $495.00

MILLET, Allan. *Semper Fidelis: History of the US Marine Corps.* 1982. NY. 782p. VG/VG. S16. $35.00

MILLETT, Kate. *Basement: Meditations on Human Sacrifice.* 1979. S&S. 1st. ils. VG/G. A25. $20.00

MILLETT, Kate. *Going to Iran.* 1982. GMG. 1st. ils. rem mk. VG/G. A25. $8.00

MILLHAUSER, Steven. *Barnum Museum.* 1990. Poseidon. 1st. F/F. R14. $35.00

MILLHAUSER, Steven. *Edwin Mullhouse.* 1972. Knopf. 1st. author's 1st book. F/NF. B2. $175.00

MILLHAUSER, Steven. *From the Realm of Morpheus.* 1986. Morrow. 1st. F/F. R14. $35.00

MILLHAUSER, Steven. *In the Penny Arcade.* 1986. Knopf. 1st. author's 3rd book. F/F. D10. $50.00

MILLIGAN, David. *Color Book of Wine.* 1974. Octopus. 1st. F/F. W2. $20.00

MILLIKAN, Robert A. *Autobiography of Robert A Millikan.* 1950 (1950). Prentice Hall. 2nd. 8vo. 311p. G. K5. $40.00

MILLIKEN, R. *No Conceivable Injury.* 1986. Australia. Penguin. 1st. VG/wrp. K3. $20.00

MILLIN, Sarah Gertrude. *God's Stepchildren.* 1927. Grosset Dunlap. 1st thus/10th prt. 319p. VG. A25. $15.00

MILLIS, Walter. *Martial Spirit.* 1931. Cambridge. Literary Guild of Am. 8vo. 427p. gilt maroon cloth. T10. $25.00

MILLS, C. Wright. *Sociological Imagination.* 1959. Oxford. 1st. 234p. F/dj. H1. $22.50

MILLS, E.A. *Watched by Wild Animals.* 1922. Doubleday. ils W James. 243p. cloth. VG+. M12. $30.00

MILLS, J.V.G. *Ying-Yai Sheng-Lan: Overall Surveys of Ocean Shores.* 1970. Cambridge. ils/maps. 393p. F/dj. M4. $25.00

MILLS, William Stowell. *Story of the Western Reserve of Connecticut.* 1900. NY. 1st. 134p. VG. B18. $37.50

MILNE, A.A. *Chloe-Mar.* 1946. 1st. VG/VG. S13. $40.00

MILNE, A.A. *Christopher Robin Verses.* 1932. Dutton. stated 1st. ils Ernest Shepard. gilt bl cloth. G. M5. $65.00

MILNE, A.A. *Enchanted Places.* 1975. Dutton. 1st Am. 169p. F/G. M5. $75.00

MILNE, A.A. *House at Pooh Corner.* 1928. London. Methuen. 1st. F/VG+. B4. $500.00

MILNE, A.A. *House at Pooh Corner.* 1928. Methuen. 1/350. sgn Milne/Shepard. 4to. bl cloth/wht brd/label. dj. F5. $3,000.00

MILNE, A.A. *Now We Are Six.* 1927. London. Methuen. 1st Eng. ils Ernest Shepard. teg. maroon cloth. dj. D1. $350.00

MILNE, A.A. *Winnie the Pooh/House at Pooh Corner (titled in Russian).* 1965. Moscow. 1st thus. ils Diodorov/Kalinovskiy. 8vo. gilt wheat cloth. dj. R5. $125.00

MILNE, Caleb. *I Dream of the Day...: Letters From Caleb Milne...* 1945. Longman. 1st. intro Marjorie Kinnan Rawlings. F/clip. B4. $100.00

MILORADOVICH, Milo. *Art of Fish Cookery.* 1949. Doubleday. 1st. 457p. G-. B10. $10.00

MILSOM, S.F.C. *Historical Foundations of the Common Law.* 1969. London. Butterworths. 1st. M11. $125.00

MILSOM, S.F.C. *Legal Framework of English Feudalism.* 1976. Cambridge. M11. $125.00

MILSOM, S.F.C. *Studies in History of Common Law.* 1985. London. Hambledon. M11. $45.00

MILTON, John. *Complete Poetical Works...* 1899. Boston. 8vo. 417p. teg. 3-quarter leather. VG. H3. $45.00

MILTON, John. *Comus.* 1921. London. Heinemann. 1st. 1/550. ils/sgn Rackham. teg. VG. B24. $950.00

MILTON, John. *Histoire Entiere & Veritable Dv Procez de Charles Stuart...* 1650. London. JG. 4to. full calf. gilt bdg. R12. $750.00

MILTON, John. *L'Allegro & Il Penseroso.* 1954. NY. LEC. 1st thus. 1/1780. ils Wm Blake. F/glassine/case. Q1. $150.00

MILTON, John. *Masque of Comus.* 1954. Cambridge. LEC. 1st thus. 1/1500. ils Edmund Dulac. F/case. Q1. $175.00

MILTON, John. *Paradise Lost.* 1905. London/NY. Routledge. ils Wm Strang. VG. B5. $60.00

MILTON, Nancy. *Giraffe That Walked to Paris.* 1992. Crown. 1st. obl 4to. unp. NF/F. T5. $24.00

MINAMIKI, George. *Chinese Rites Controversy: From Beginnings to Modern Times.* 1985. Loyola. 1st. 353p. F/F. W3. $40.00

MINAMOTO, Toyomune. *Daitokuji.* 1958. Tokyo. 1st. Japanese text. ils Sakamoto. 205p. F/NF. W3. $125.00

MINER, Earl. *Intro to Japanese Court Poetry.* 1968. Stanford. notes/glossary. 173p. F/F. W3. $58.00

MINER, Ellis D. *Uranus: The Planet, Rings & Satellites.* 1990. NY. Ellis Horwood. 334p. VG. K5. $25.00

MINER, V. Alchech. *From My Grandmother's Kitchen, a Sephardic Cookbook.* 1984. photos. sc. VG. E6. $18.00

MINGUS, Charles. *Beneath the Underdog.* 1971. Knopf. 1st. F/NF. B2. $50.00

MINGUS, Charles. *Beneath the Underdog.* 1971. Knopf. 1st. NF/dj. M25. $45.00

MINKOFF, George. *Bibliography of the Black Sun Press.* 1970. Great Neck. self pub. 1st. F/sans. B2. $75.00

MINNEY, R. *Next Stop-Peking: Record of a 16,000-Mile Journey...* 1957. London. 1st. ils/photos. 192p. VG/VG. W3. $36.00

MINNICH, J.W. *Inside Rock Island Prison From December 1863 to June 1865.* 1908. Nashville. ME Church. 1st. 59p. NF/prt wrp. M8. $350.00

MINNICK, Sylvia Sun. *Samfow: San Goaquin Chinese Legacy.* 1988. Fresno. panorama W Pub. 4to. sgn. gilt red cloth. F/dj. R3. $30.00

MINNIGH, L.W. *Gettysburg, What They Did Here.* 1924. Gettysburg. NA Meligakes. w/map. A19. $50.00

MINOT, Susan. *Lust & Other Stories.* 1989. Houghton Mifflin. 1st. NF/F. A20. $25.00

MINOT, Susan. *Lust & Other Stories.* 1989. Houghton Mifflin. 1st. sgn. F/F. R14. $40.00

MINTON & MINTON. *Venomous Reptiles.* 1969. Scribner. 275p. NF/VG. S15. $30.00

MINTZ, M. *Martial Arts Films.* 1978. NY. ils/index/notes. 243p. F/VG. W3. $36.00

MIRABEAU. *Considerations sur l'Ordre de Cincinnatus/Memoire.* 1784. London/np. 2 works in 1. tall 8vo. calf. R12. $750.00

MIRABEAU. *Plan de Division du Royaume.* 1798. Paris. Baudouin. 8vo. wrp. R12. $225.00

MIRABEAU. *Sur La Liberte de La Presse, Imite De L'Anglois, De Milton.* 1789. London. unrecorded 2nd. 8vo. stitched. R12. $650.00

MIRALLIE, Charles. *De l'Aphasie Sensorielle.* 1896. Paris. Steinheil. 220p. ils/woodcuts. contemporary brd. xl. VG. G1. $125.00

MIRICK, B.L. *History of Haverhill, Massachusetts.* 1832. Haverhill. AW Thayer. 1st. quarter purple muslin/tan brd. M24. $450.00

MIRSKY, Jeannette. *Elisha Kent Kane & the Seafaring Frontier.* 1954. Little Brn. 1st. 201p. dj. T7. $18.00

MIRSKY, Jeannette. *Western Crossings.* 1946. Balboa Mackenzie. 1st. ils. 365p+13p index. VG+/dj. B18. $22.50

MIRSKY & NIVENS. *World of Eli Whitney.* 1952. Macmillan. 1st. 346p. F/dj. H1. $17.50

MISHIMA, Sumie Seo. *Broader Way: A Woman's Life in New Japan.* 1953. John Day. 1st. 247p. VG/dj. A25. $22.00

MISHIMA, Yukio. *Confessions of a Mask.* 1958. NY. New Directions. 1st. NF/VG. A24. $85.00

MISHIMA, Yukio. *Five Moderns No Plays.* 1957. NY. Knopf. 1st Am. trans from Japanese. F/clip. Q1. $75.00

MISHIMA, Yukio. *Runaway Horses.* 1973. Knopf. 1st Am. trans from Japanese. F/dj. Q1. $50.00

MISHIMA, Yukio. *Temple of the Golden Pavilion.* 1959. Knopf. 1st. ils Fumi Komatsu. F/dj. Q1. $75.00

MISKELLA, William. *Practical Japanning & Enameling.* 1928. Chicago. 256p. A17. $30.00

MISS READ; see Stuart, Dora Jessie.

MISTH, Mary Stuart. *Virginia Cookery-Book.* 1885 (1884). Harper. 352p. orig cloth over modern buckram/new ep. B10. $150.00

MISTRY, Rohanton. *Swimming Lessons.* 1987. Houghton Mifflin. 1st. NF/NF. A20. $30.00

MITCHEL, John. *Jail Journal.* 1913. Dublin. MH Hill. VG+. B2. $150.00

MITCHELL, C. Bradford. *Touching the Adventures & Perils...* 1970. NY. Am Hull Insurance. ils. 234p. dj. T7. $25.00

MITCHELL, David. *Pirates.* 1976. NY. Dial. 1st. ils/index/bibliography. 208p. VG/dj. P4. $25.00

MITCHELL, Don. *Thumb Tripping.* 1970. Little Brn. 1st. F/VG. B4. $85.00

MITCHELL, Ehrman B. *Ponies for Young People.* 1960. Van Nostrand. 1st. VG/VG. O3. $15.00

MITCHELL, Ethelyn. *Nip & Tuck at Play.* 1938. Lyons & Carnaha. 46p. VG/wrp. M20. $12.00

MITCHELL, George. *Little Babs.* 1919. Volland. 1st. ils Arthur Henderson. 12mo. pict brd. pub box. R5. $200.00

MITCHELL, J. Leslie. *Cairo Dawns.* 1931. Bobbs Merrill. 1st Am. VG. M2. $30.00

MITCHELL, Jan. *Cooking a la Longchamps.* 1964. Doubleday. 1st. G/dj. A16. $20.00

MITCHELL, Joseph. *Old Mr Flood.* 1948. DSP. 1st. inscr/dtd 1948. F/VG. B4. $650.00

MITCHELL, Joseph. *Up in the Old Hotel & Other Stories.* 1992. Pantheon. 1st. F/F clip. B4. $55.00

MITCHELL, Juliet. *Psychoanalysis & Feminism.* 1974. NY. Pantheon. 1st. F/VG. B2. $30.00

MITCHELL, Lebbeus. *Bobby in Search of a Birthday.* 1916. Volland. 1st. ils Joseph Pierre Nuyttens. VG. T5. $45.00

MITCHELL, Mairin. *Elcano: First Circumnavigator.* 1958. London. Herder. as new. O7. $35.00

MITCHELL, Margaret. *Gone With the Wind.* 1936. Macmillan. VG. W2. $1,250.00

MITCHELL, Richard. *Thought Control in Pre-War Japan.* 1976. Cornell. 226p. F/dj. W3. $36.00

MITCHELL, S.A. *Eclipses of the Sun.* 1932 (1923). NY. Columbia. 3rd. G/dj. K5. $80.00

MITCHELL, Silas Weir. *Fat & Blood: How to Make Them.* 1879. Lippincott. 2nd revised. 12mo. flexible panelled mauve cloth. G. G1. $185.00

MITCHELL, Silas Weir. *Injuries of Nerves & Their Consequences.* 1872. Phil. 1st. 377p. A13. $600.00

MITCHELL, Silas Weir. *Injuries of Nerves & Their Consequences.* 1983 (1872). Birmingham. Classics Neurology/Neurosurgery. facsimile. G1. $75.00

MITCHELL-HODGES, F.A. *Danger My Ally.* 1954. London. Elek Books. 1st. 255p. dj. F3. $35.00

MITCHENER, C.H. *Ohio Annals.* 1876. Dayton. 358p. G-. B18. $95.00

MITCHUM, S.W. Jr. *Romme's Last Battle.* 1983. NY. 1st. ils. 212p. VG/VG. S16. $22.50

MITFORD, Jessica. *American Way of Death.* 1963. NY. S&S. 1st. F/NF. M24. $65.00

MITSCHERLICH. *Doctors of Infamy: Story of Nazi Medical Crimes.* 1949. Schuman. 172p+16p photos. G. A17. $20.00

MITTEN, Homer H. *Enchanted Canyon Fairy Story.* 1932. LA. Suttonhouse. ltd. 1/400. sgn pres. ils/sgn Eulalie. gilt gr cloth. R5. $350.00

MIX, Tom. *West of Yesterday.* 1923. Times-Mirror Pr. 1st. 162p. VG. J2. $185.00

MIYOSHI, Masao. as *We Saw Them: First Japanese Embassy to the United States.* 1979. Berkeley. 1st. ils. wht cloth brd/bl cloth spine. F. R3. $25.00

MIZWA, Stephen P. *Nicholas Copernicus, 1543-1943.* 1969. Port WA. Kennikat. reissue. ils. VG. K3. $20.00

MO, Timothy. *Monkey King.* 1986. Morrow. 1st Am. NF/NF. M23. $35.00

MO, Timothy. *Redundancy of Courage.* 1991. Chatto Windus. 1st. F/dj. A24. $35.00

MOCHI, Ugo. *Hoofed Mammals of the World.* 1953. Scribner. folio. 40 pl. cloth brd. F. B24. $375.00

MOERMAN, Daniel E. *American Medical Ethnobotany.* 1977. NY. Garland. 527p. xl. A10. $45.00

MOFFAT, James. *Theology of the Gospels.* 1913. Scribner. 220p. VG. B29. $7.50

MOFFAT, Robert U. *John Smitt Moffat CMG Missionary: A Memoir.* 1969 (1921). Negro U. rpt. 8vo. 8 pl/1 map. 388p. VG. W1. $25.00

MOFFETT, Cleveland. *Possessed.* 1920. McCann. 1st. G+. M2. $27.00

MOHAMMAD REZA PAHLAVI, Shah. *Answer to History: Shah of Iran.* 1980. Stein Day. 1st. 8vo. 204p. NF/dj. W1. $16.00

MOHLENBROCK & VOIGT. *Flora of Southern Illinois.* 1959. Carbondale. 390p. dj. A10. $24.00

MOHR, John H. *Medical Guide in Treating All Internal & External Diseases.* 1868. Reading, PA. Owens Steam Pr. 16mo. 262p. G. O3. $125.00

MOHR & ROTH. *Timber Pines of the Southern United States.* 1897 (1896). WA, DC. revised. 176p. new buckram. B26. $75.00

MOJTABAI, A.G. *Stopping Place.* 1979. S&S. 1st. 349p. F/F. W2. $30.00

MOKLER, Alfred James. *Ft Casper, Comprising a Description of Killing Lt Collins...* 1939. Prairie. 1st. 74p. VG/pict wrp. J2. $115.00

MOKLER, Alfred James. *Transition of the West: Portrayal of Indian Problem...* 1927. Lakeside. is. 228p. cloth. D11. $125.00

MOLESWORTH & MOSELEY. *Wing to Wing, Air Combat in China 1943-45.* 1990. NY. 1st. 207p. VG/dj. B18. $32.50

MOLEY, Raymond. *American Century of John C Lincoln.* 1962. Duell Sloan. 1st. sgn. 209p. VG/VG. B11. $25.00

MOLFINO, Francesco. *Fisiopatologia Della Ghiandola Pineale.* 1935. Roma. Luigi Pozzi. 132p. VG/stiff tan wrp. G1. $50.00

MOLLEMA, J.C. *De Nederlandsche Vlag op de Wereldzeen...* 1930s. Amsterdam. Scheltens Giltay. ils/maps. NF. O7. $125.00

MOLLISON, P.L. *Blood Transfusion in Clinical Medicine.* 1851. Oxford. 1st. 456p. A13. $35.00

MOLLO, Andrew. *Armed Forces of World War II: Uniforms, Insignia...* 1981. NY. photos/pl/table of ranks/index. 312p. VG/VG. S16. $40.00

MOLLO, Victor. *Bridge in the Menagerie.* 1967. NY. 1st Am. 152p. VG/dj. S1. $8.00

MOLLOY, Hercules. *Oedipus in Disneyland.* 1972. 1st. ils. VG. S13. $18.00

MOLLOY, Robert. *Medical Electrical Equipment: Principles, Installation...* 1958. NY. 1st. 312p. A13. $75.00

MOLONEY, Alfred. *CMG: Sketch of the Forestry of West Africa.* 1887. Sampson Low Marston. 527p. gr cloth. VG. M20. $25.00

MOLONY, E. *Portrait of Rivers: Itchen, Trent, Crouch, Wye, Ouse, Avon.* nd. London. Dobson. ils/photos. 139p. NF/F. M12. $15.00

MOLTMANN, Jurgen. *Gospel of Liberation.* 1974. Word. 136p. VG/dj. B29. $9.50

MOMADAY, Natachee Scott. *Ancient Child.* 1989. Doubleday. ARC. sgn. author's 2nd novel. F/F. D10. $55.00

MOMADAY, Natachee Scott. *Colorado.* 1973. Chicago. Rand McNally. 1st. folio. photos David Muench. F/VG. L3. $100.00

MOMADAY, Natachee Scott. *Gourd Dancer.* 1976. Harper Row. 1st. F/NF. L3. $100.00

MOMADAY, Natachee Scott. *House Made of Dawn.* 1968. Harper Row. 1st. F/NF. L3. $350.00

MOMADAY, Natachee Scott. *Owl in the Cedar Tree.* 1965. np. Ginn. 1st. F. L3. $125.00

MOMADAY, Natachee Scott. *Way to Rainy Mountain.* 1969. Albuquerque. NM U. 1st. F/F. L3. $200.00

MONACHAN, John; see Burnett, W.R.

MONAGHAN, Frank. *French Travellers in the United States 1765-1932.* 1961. NY. Antiquarian. 1/750. ils. F. O7. $55.00

MONAGHAN, Jay. *Book of the American West.* 1969. S&S. new prt. 608p+reading list. F/VG dj. A17. $27.50

MONAGHAN. *Common Heritage, Noah Webster's Blue-Black Speller.* 1983. 304p. F. A4. $35.00

MONDEY, David. *Rockets & Missiles.* 1971. Grosset Dunlap. 1st Am. 4to. 75p. VG. K5. $12.00

MONES & MULL. *Independent Oilman: From Spivey-Grabs to Cheyenne Wells...* 1982. Wichita, KS. 291p. cloth. as new/dj. D8. $25.00

MONETTE, Paul. *Borrowed Time: An Aids Memoir.* 1988. HBJ. 1st. rem mk. NF/F. R14. $25.00

MONRO, Edward. *Sacred Allegories.* 1888. London. Mastes. thick 8vo. full calf. F. T10. $75.00

MONROE, Harriet. *Valeria & Other Poems.* 1892. Chicago. McClurg. trade ed. author's 1st book. VG+. B2. $125.00

MONSARRAT, Nicholas. *East Coast Corvette.* 1943. Lippincott. 1st. 153p. dj. T7. $15.00

MONSON, William. *Sir William Monson's Naval Tracts: In Six Books...* 1703. London. Churchill. folio. modern cloth. P4. $600.00

MONTAGNE, Prosper. *New Larousse Gastronomique.* 1983. London. Hamlyn. VG/dj. A16. $35.00

MONTAGU. *Essay on Writings & Genius of Shakespeare.* 1770. London. Hughs. 8vo. 3-quarter calf. R12. $125.00

MONTAGUE, Richard. *Oceans, Poles & Airman.* 1971. Random. 1st. 307p. G+/dj. B18. $15.00

MONTANA, Joe. *Audibles.* 1986. Morrow. 1st. F/F. P8. $15.00

MONTECINO, Marcel. *Big Time.* 1990. Morrow. 1st. F/F. H11. $30.00

MONTECINO, Marcel. *Crosskiller.* 1988. Arbor. 1st. author's 1st novel. F/F. D10. $65.00

MONTECINO, Marcel. *Crosskiller.* 1988. Arbor. 1st. sgn. author's 1st book. F/F. H11. $140.00

MONTEITH, James. *Manual of Geography.* 1868. BArnes. sm 4to. ils/maps. 124p. G+. H1. $20.00

MONTESQUIEU, C. *Considerations Sur les Causes de la Grandeur Romains.* 1755. Paris. A15. $30.00

MONTESQUIEU. *Reflections on Causes of Grandeur & Declension of Romans.* 1734. London. Innys Manby. 8vo. calf. R12. $750.00

MONTGOMERY, Bernard L. *Eighth Army: El Alamein to River Sangro.* 1946. Berlin. 1/100 pres to US Army. fld maps. 158p. VG/VG. S16. $125.00

MONTGOMERY, Elizabeth Rider. *Three Miles an Hour.* 1952. Dodd Mead. 2nd. 245p. VG/dj. A25. $15.00

MONTGOMERY, Elizabeth. *Land Divided.* 1938. London. Hutchinson. 1st. 2 full-p maps. 288p. VG. W1. $12.00

MONTGOMERY, Field Marshal V. *Normandy to the Baltic List Army Group.* 1948. Boston. 1st. maps. 351p. VG/G. B5. $45.00

MONTGOMERY, Frances Trego. *Billy Whiskers in the South.* 1917. Saalfield. ils Will Fitzgerald. 4to. gr cloth. R5. $135.00

MONTGOMERY, Frances Trego. *On a Lark to the Planets.* 1922. Akron. 186p. pict yel bdg. VG. B14. $45.00

MONTGOMERY, L.M. *Anne of Avonlea.* 1909. Page. 3rd imp (same month as 1st). gilt cloth/mc pl. VG. M5. $65.00

MONTGOMERY, L.M. *Anne of Green Gables.* 1935 (1908). Grosset Dunlap. pre-1963 prt. lg 12mo. VG/dj. C8. $25.00

MONTGOMERY, L.M. *Anne's House of Dreams.* 1917. 1st. VG. M17. $50.00

MONTGOMERY, L.M. *Chronicles of Avonlea.* 1912. Page. 2nd imp. gilt cloth/mc pl. VG. M5. $60.00

MONTGOMERY, L.M. *Emily of New Moon.* 1934. Toronto. 1st. xl. NF/G. T12. $40.00

MONTGOMERY, L.M. *Tangled Web.* 1931. McClelland Stewart. 324p. VG+/dj. M20. $15.00

MONTGOMERY, Rutherford. *Capture of the Golden Stallion.* nd. Grosset Dunlap. Famous Horse Stories series. VG. O3. $12.00

MONTGOMERY, Rutherford. *Golden Stallion & the Wolf Dog.* nd. Grosset Dunlap. Famous Horse Stories series. VG. O3. $15.00

MONTGOMERY, Rutherford. *High Country.* (1938). Derrydale. rpt/ltd. photos. leather. VG. M17. $25.00

MONTGOMERY, Rutherford. *Tom Pittman USAF.* 1957. DSP. 1st. 152p. VG/dj. M20. $20.00

MONTHAN & MONTHAN. *Art & Indian Individualists: Art of 17 Contemporary...* 1975. Northland. 1st. ils. 198p. cloth. dj. D11. $100.00

MONZERT, L. *Independent Liquorist or Art of Preparing Cordials...* 1866. VG. E6. $75.00

MOODEY, Marion McCook. *Here Comes the Peddler.* nd (1947). Holiday. sm 4to. unp. F/VG+. C14. $14.00

MOODIE, Susanna. *Roughing It in the Bush.* Oct 1938. London. Thomas Nelson. A19. $45.00

MOODIE, William. *Old English, Scotch & Irish Songs, With Music.* ca 1900. Glasgow. Bryce. Mite series. 31x22mm. 127p. aeg. Zaehnsdorf bdg. B24. $350.00

MOODY, Ralph. *Stagecoach West.* 1967. Crowell. 1st. VG. O3. $35.00

MOON, Marjorie. *Children's Books of Mary (Belson) Elliott, a Biography.* 1987. 30 pl. 172p. F/F. A4. $95.00

MOON & MOON. *One Little Indian.* 1950. Whitman. 1st. sm 4to. VG/dj. M5. $60.00

MOONEY, James. *Ghost-Dance Religion & the Sioux Outbreak of 1890.* 1973. Rio Grande Classic. rpt. ils/maps/figures. VG. M4. $45.00

MOONEY, James. *Historical Sketch of the Cherokee.* 1975. Chicago. Adeline. ils. 265p. cloth. D11. $35.00

MOONEY & OLBRECHTS. *Swimmer Manuscript: Cherokee Sacred Formulas...* 1932. WA. BAE. ils. 319p. prt wrp. D11. $30.00

MOONEY & SHIPTON. *National Index of American Imprints Through 1800.* 1969. Am Antiquarian Soc. 2 vol. 1028p. F. A4. $200.00

MOORCOCK, Michael. *Cure for Cancer.* 1971. Holt. 1st. F/dj. M2. $30.00

MOORCOCK, Michael. *Land Leviathan.* 1974. Doubleday. 1st Am. F/dj. M2. $30.00

MOORE, Alexander. *Life Cycles in Atchalan.* 1973. NY. Teachers College. 1st. 220p. wrp. F3. $15.00

MOORE, Anne Carroll. *Art of Beatrix Potter.* (1955). London. Warne. ils. F/dj. B15. $75.00

MOORE, Anne Carroll. *Century of Kate Greenaway.* 1946. NY/London. ils Kate Greenaway. VG/glassine dj/wrp. D1. $85.00

MOORE, Anne Carroll. *My Roads to Childhood, Views & Reviews...* 1939. 399p. VG/VG. A4. $55.00

MOORE, Anne Carroll. *Roads to Childhood.* 1920. Doran. probable 1st. narrow 8vo. brn brd. VG. T5. $55.00

MOORE, Bernard. *Wines of North America.* 1983. Chartwell. 1st Am. 192p. VG/VG. B10. $35.00

MOORE, Brian. *Answer From Limbo.* 1962. Little Brn. 1st. sgn. NF/clip. Q1. $150.00

MOORE, Brian. *Black Robe.* 1985. Dutton. 1st. F/F. H11. $45.00

MOORE, Brian. *Catholics.* 1972. McClelland Stewart. UP/1st Canadian. NF/wrp. D10. $75.00

MOORE, Brian. *Emperor of Ice-Cream.* 1965. McClelland Stewart. 1st. NF/NF. P3. $25.00

MOORE, Brian. *Emperor of Ice-Cream.* 1965. Viking. 1st. VG/dj. M25. $35.00

MOORE, Brian. *Feast of Lupercal.* 1957. Little Brn. 1st. NF/NF. B35. $65.00

MOORE, Brian. *I Am Mary Dunne.* 1968. Toronto. McClelland Stuart. 1st Canadian. sgn. F/clip. Q1. $150.00

MOORE, Brian. *Lies of Silence.* 1990. London. 1st. sgn. VG/VG. T9. $45.00

MOORE, Brian. *Lies of Silence.* 1990. London. Bloomsbury. 1st. sgn. F/F. D10. $50.00

MOORE, Brian. *Lies of Silence.* 1990. London. Bloomsbury. 1st. 1/150. sgn/#d. marbled brd/gilt spine. F/glassine. Q1. $125.00

MOORE, Brian. *Lonely Passion of Judith Hearne.* 1956. Atlantic/Little Brn. ARC/1st Am. RS. F/dj. D10. $225.00

MOORE, Brian. *Luck of Ginger Coffey.* 1960. Atlantic/Little Brn. 1st. NF/dj. M25. $45.00

MOORE, Brian. *Revolution Script.* 1970. HRW. 1st. NF/dj. M25. $50.00

MOORE, Brian. *Revolution Script.* 1971. HRW. 1st. inscr. F/dj. Q1. $100.00

MOORE, Brian. *Temptation of Eileen Hughes.* 1981. Toronto. McClelland Stewart. 1st Canadian. sgn. F/dj. Q1. $75.00

MOORE, Christopher. *Practical Demon-Keeping.* 1992. St Martin. 1st. sgn. author's 1st book. F/dj. A24. $40.00

MOORE, Clement C. *Night Before Christmas.* 1935. Platt Munk. 28 full-p ils. gr cloth. G. B14. $25.00

MOORE, Clement C. *Night Before Christmas.* 1942. Phil. Winston. 1st thus. 4to. dj. R5. $85.00

MOORE, Clement C. *Night Before Christmas.* 1954. Garden City. 1st. ils Roger Duvoisin, pict brd. dj. R5. $100.00

MOORE, Clement C. *Night Before Christmas, or A Visit of St. Nicholas.* 1899 (1896). McLoughlin. prt on linen. VG. M5. $145.00

MOORE, Donald J. *Martin Buber: Prophet of Religious Secularism.* 1974. JPS. biblio. 264p. VG/dj. S3. $24.00

MOORE, Edward C. *Outline of th History of Christian Thought Since Kant.* 1912. Scribner. 249p. VG. B29. $10.00

MOORE, Edward. *Fables for the Female Sex.* 1771. London. Davies Dodsley. 4th. tall 8vo. 173p. contemporary tree calf. H13. $295.00

MOORE, Elaine T. *Winning Your Spurs.* 1954. Little Brn. 1st. VG/fair. O3. $25.00

MOORE, Evelyn. *Sancocho.* 1947. Panama. Star & Herald. 2nd. 214p. pict cloth. F3. $25.00

MOORE, Frank. *Women of the War: Their Heroism & Self-Sacrifice.* 1866. Hartford. Scranton. 1st. 596p. cloth. M8. $85.00

MOORE, George. *Brook Kerith. A Syrian Story.* 1929. Macmillan. 1st thus. 1/500. sgn. ils/sgn Stephen Gooden. F/case. B24. $200.00

MOORE, George. *Sister Teresa.* 1901. London. Fisher Unwin. 1st. teg. gr cloth. untrimmed. F. M24. $35.00

MOORE, Harry T. *Intelligent Heart.* 1954. NY. 1st. VG/VG. T9. $40.00

MOORE, Isabel. *Talks in a Library With Laurence Hutton.* 1909. NY. 458p. VG. A17. $12.50

MOORE, John Hamilton. *New Practical Navigator...* 1800. Newburyport. Edmund M Blunt. 2nd. 8vo. 570p. VG. M1. $550.00

MOORE, John W. *Roster of North Carolina Troops in Civil War.* 1882. Raleigh. 4 vol. 1st. Vol 1-3 in modern buckram. C6. $200.00

MOORE, John William. *Notes on Raiatean Flowering Plants.* 1963. Honolulu. tall 8vo. VG/wrp. A22. $20.00

MOORE, John. *Incian Paul.* 1945. Harcourt Brace. 1st. F/NF. B4. $100.00

MOORE, Lorrie. *Anagrams.* 1986. Knopf. 1st. author's 1st novel. NF/dj. A24. $50.00

MOORE, Lorrie. *Self-Help.* 1985. Knopf. 1st. author's 1st book. F/F. D10. $160.00

MOORE, Margaret. *Dangerous Conceits.* 1989. Walker. 1st Am. as new/dj. N4. $20.00

MOORE, Marianne. *Like a Bulwark.* 1957. London. Faber. 1st. F/dj. Q1. $75.00

MOORE, Marianne. *Marianne Moore Reader.* 1961. Viking. 1st. F/NF. A24. $30.00

MOORE, Marianne. *Nevertheless.* 1944. NY. 1st. VG/G. B5. $100.00

MOORE, Marianne. *Occasionem Cognosce.* 1963. Lunenburg. Stinehour. 1/175. stn/#d. F/sewn wrp. B2. $250.00

MOORE, N. Hudson. *Collector's Manual.* 1935 (1905). Tudor. 329p. VG+/dj/case. M20. $60.00

MOORE, N. Hudson. *Old China Book.* 1935 (1903). Tudor. 300p. cloth. VG/ragged. M20. $20.00

MOORE, N. Hudson. *Old Glass: European & American.* 1935 (1924). Tudor. 394p. cloth. VG+/torn dj/case. M20. $40.00

MOORE, N. Hudson. *Old Pewter, Brass, Copper & Sheffield Plate.* 1905. Stokes. 1st. 229p. cloth/pict label. VG+. M20. $35.00

MOORE, Nancy. *Unhappy Hippotamus.* 1957. Vanguard. 1st. ils Edward Leight. 4to. VG/G+. P2. $30.00

MOORE, Patrick. *Return of Halley's Comet.* 1984. Norton. 1st. F. T12. $15.00

MOORE, Robin. *Country Team.* 1967. NY. Crown. 1st. inscr/dtd 1967. F/VG. B4. $200.00

MOORE, Robin. *French Connection.* 1969. Little Brn. 1st. F/VG. M19. $25.00

MOORE, Robin. *Green Berets.* 1965. NY. Crown. 1st. inscr/dtd 1978. NF/VG+ clip. B4. $275.00

MOORE, Ruth. *Earth We Live On, Story of Geological Discovery.* 1956. Knopf. 416p. D8. $14.50

MOORE, Ruth. *Niels Bohr, the Man, His Science & the World They Changed.* 1966. NY. Knopf. 1st. VG/dj. K3. $20.00

MOORE, Susanna. *My Old Sweetheart.* 1982. Houghton Mifflin. 1st. author's 1st book. F/F. D10. $75.00

MOORE, Susanna. *Sleeping Beauties.* 1993. Knopf. 1st. F/dj. Q1. $25.00

MOORE, Susanna. *Sleeping Beauties.* 1993. Knopf. 1st. sgn. author's 3rd novel. F/F. D10. $35.00

MOORE, Susanna. *Whiteness of Bones.* 1989. NY. Doubleday. 1st. F/NF. B4. $50.00

MOORE, Thomas Jr. *Sky Is My Witness.* 1943. NY. 135p. VG. S16. $60.00

MOORE, Ward. *Bring the Jubilee.* 1955. Heinemann. 1st. VG/dj. M2. $30.00

MOORE. *Checklist of Writings of Daniel DeFoe.* 1971. revised. 299p. F. A4. $65.00

MOOREHEAD, A. *Darwin & the Beagle.* 1969. Harper Row. 1st/5th imp. ils. F/NF. D8. $25.00

MOOREHEAD, Alan. *Fatal Impact.* 1966. Harper Row. 1st. 230p. VG+/dj. M20. $18.00

MOOREHEAD, Alan. *Traitors.* 1952. Hamish Hamilton. 1st. ils. VG/dj. K3. $30.00

MOORHOUSE, Geoffrey. *Fearful Void.* 1974. Lippincott. 1st. 8vo. 20 pl/2 full-p maps. 288p. NF/dj. W1. $18.00

MORAN, Jim. *US Marine Corps Uniforms & Equipment in WWII.* 1992. London. ils. 138p. VG/VG. S16. $40.00

MORAN DE BUTRON, Jacinto. *La Azucena de Quito.* 1732. Mexico. Imprenta Real Superior Govierno. woodcut. limp vellum. D11. $200.00

MORAND, Paul. *Champions du Monde.* 1930. Abbeville. Grasset. 1/56 on Rives. 4to. F/wrp/cloth case. T10. $90.00

MORAVIA, Alberto. *Five Novels.* 1955. FSG. 1st. F/VG. A20. $15.00

MORAVIA, Alberto. *Times of Desecration.* 1985. FSG. 1st. F/F. A20. $25.00

MORE, Cresacre. *Life of Sir Thomas More, ...By His Great Grandson.* 1726. London. Woodman Lyon. 8vo. engraved ftspc. calf/rebacked. R12. $375.00

MORE, Edward. *Utopia; or, A Philosphical Romance, in Two Books...* 1743. Glasgow. Robert Foulis. sm 4to. 139p. mottled calf/leather label. H13. $285.00

MOREAU, Georges. *Theorie des Moteurs a Gaz.* 1902. Paris. Beranger. 8vo. 224p. orig cloth. VG. K3. $90.00

MOREAU, Jeanne. *Jeanne Moreau.* 1989. Haga. Japanese text. photos. NF/dj. C9. $75.00

MORELOCK, J.D. *Army Times Book of Great Land Battles, From Civil War...* 1994. Berkley Books. 1st. 8vo. 311p. F/dj. T10. $25.00

MORENO, H.J. *Moreno's Cictionary of Spanish-Names California Cities...* 1916. San Luis Obispo. 1st. VG. O4. $25.00

MORETON, C. Oscar. *Old Carnations & Pinks.* 1955. London. Rainbird. 51p. dj. A10. $55.00

MOREY, Sheena. *Pat 'n' Penny.* 1946. Chicago. obl 4to. VG. M5. $30.00

MOREY, Walt. *Scrub Dog of Alaska.* 1971. NY. Dutton. 1st Am. inscr. 8vo. 212p. bl cloth. VG/dj. P4. $30.00

MORFIT, Campbell. *Chemical & Pharmaceutical Manipulations...* 1849. Phil. 482p. blk cloth. VG. B14. $200.00

MORGA, A.D. *Sucesos de las Filipinas.* 1971. Cambridge. edit/trans JS Cummins. ils. 347p. F/dj. M4. $20.00

MORGAN, A.T. *Yazoo; or, On the Picket Line of Freedom in the South.* 1884. WA, DC. self pub. 1st. 512p. ES. later cloth. VG. M8. $350.00

MORGAN, Al. *Cast of Characters.* 1957. Dutton. 1st. F/VG. M25. $25.00

MORGAN, Charles S. *Master in Sail & Steam.* 1981. Concord, MA. self pub. ils. 89p. wrp. T7. $12.00

MORGAN, Dale. *Great Salt Lake.* 1947. Indianapolis. 1st. sgn. VG/G+. B5. $65.00

MORGAN, Dale. *Jedediah Smith & the Opening of the West.* 1953. Bobbs Merrill. 1st. 458p. VG/torn. J2. $285.00

MORGAN, David P. *Canadian Steam!* 1961. Kalmbach. 1st. unp. cloth. VG/dj. M20. $28.00

MORGAN, Elizabeth. *Making of a Woman Surgeon.* 1980. Putnam. 1st. photos. 368p. VG/dj. A25. $18.00

MORGAN, F.R. *Teddy Bear's House Underground.* 1908. Donohue. 12mo. mc pict brd. R5. $150.00

MORGAN, F.R. *Teddy Bears on Rollers & What Happened.* 1908. Donohue. 12mo. 16p. mc pict brd. R5. $150.00

MORGAN, G. Campbell. *Acts of the Apostles.* 1924. REvell. 547p. G. B29. $11.00

MORGAN, G. Campbell. *Analyzed Bible.* 1909. Revell. 477p. VG. B29. $9.50

MORGAN, G. Campbell. *Peter & the Church.* 1938. Revell. 96p. VG. B29. $7.50

MORGAN, George Hallenbrooke. *Annals, Comprising Memoirs, Incidents & Statistics...* 1858. Harrisburg. 1st/1st prt. 400p. EX. rebound. H1. $95.00

MORGAN, Janet. *Agatha Christie.* 1985. Knopf. 1st Am. NF. W2. $20.00

MORGAN, L.H. *American Beaver & His Works.* 1868. Lippincott. 1st. 24 pl/fld map. 330p. B1. $235.00

MORGAN, Lael. *Woman's Guide to Boating & Cooking.* 1968. Freeport, ME. Bond Wheelwright. 1st. ils. 246p. VG/dj. A25. $12.00

MORGAN, Murry. *One Man's Gold Rush: A Klondike Album.* 1967. Seattle/London. 2nd. map 213p. VG/dj. P4. $35.00

MORGAN, Ruth. *Cooking for Compliments.* 1968. London. Hamlyn. VG/dj. A16. $10.00

MORGAN, Speer. *Whipping Boy.* 1994. Houghton Mifflin. 1st. sgn. F/F. A23. $40.00

MORGAN & STRICKLAND. *Arizona Memories.* 1984. Tucson. sgn pres. 354p. VG/VG. B11. $35.00

MORGAN. *Oxford Illustrated History of Britain.* 1987. ils. VG/VG. M17. $25.00

MORGENSTERN, Christian. *Three Sparrows & Other Nursery Poems.* 1968. Scribner. 1st. ils/sgn Nonny Hogrogian. trans Max Knight. F/NF. D4. $45.00

MORGENSTERN, Soma. *In My Father's Pastures.* 1947. JPS. 369p. G/G. S3. $22.00

MORIN, Edgar. *Rumor in Orleans.* 1971. Pantheon. 1st Am. 276p. VG/G. S3. $26.00

MORISON, Samuel Eliot. *Conservative American Revolution.* 1976. VG. M17. $40.00

MORISON, Samuel Eliot. *European Discovery of America, Vol I & Vol II.* 1971 & 1974. Oxford. 2 vol. F/dj. O7. $35.00

MORISON, Samuel Eliot. *Maritime History of Massachusetts, 1783-1860.* 1941. Houghton Mifflin. 1st thus. 420p. VG/ragged. M20. $20.00

MORISON, Samuel Eliot. *Portuguese Voyages to American in 15th Century.* 1965. NY. Octagon. rpt. 6 maps. as new. O7. $55.00

MORISON, Samuel Eliot. *Spring Tides.* 1965. Houghton Mifflin. 1st. VG/VG. M17. $20.00

MORISON, Samuel Eliot. *Victory in the Pacific 1945.* 1975. Boston. photos/map/index. 407p. VG/VG. S16. $30.00

MORLEY, Christopher. *Haunted Bookshop.* 1955. Lippincott. 253p. F. W2. $55.00

MORLEY, Griswold S. *Covered Bridges of California.* 1938. Berkeley. ils/photos. 92p. silvered gray cloth. F. K7. $85.00

MORLEY, Henry. *Ideal Commonwealths.* 1885. Routledge. 1st. VG. M2. $100.00

MORLEY, John. *Edmund Burke: A Historical Study.* 1867. Macmillan. 312p. VG. H1. $65.00

MORLEY, John. *Rousseau.* 1873. London. Chapman Hall. 1st. 2 vol. 8vo. brick cloth. VG. T10. $100.00

MORLEY, Margaret W. *Carolina Mountains.* 1913. Boston. 1st. ils/map ep. pict cloth. VG. B18. $35.00

MORLEY, Sylvanus G. *Excavation of the Cannonball Ruins in Southwestern Colorado.* 1908. np. Archaeological Inst of Am. fld map. prt wrp. D11. $15.00

MORPURGO, J.E. *Barnes Wallis.* 1972. London. 1st. 400p. VG/dj. B18. $47.50

MORRELL, David. *Covenant of the Flame.* 1991. 1st. sgn/dtd. F/F. A15. $30.00

MORRELL, David. *First Blood.* 1972. Evans. 1st. F/F. C2. $100.00

MORRELL, David. *First Blood.* 1972. Evans. 1st. F/NF. M25. $75.00

MORRELL, David. *League of Night & Fog.* 1987. Dutton. 1st. F/dj. M2/N4. $30.00

MORRELL, David. *Testament.* 1975. NY. Evans. 1st. author's 2nd novel. G+/dj. M21. $15.00

MORRELL, David. *Testament.* 1975. NY. Evans. 1st. F/NF. M15. $45.00

MORRELL, Gipson. *Mr Bear Squash You All Flat.* 1950. Wonder. ils Angela. unp. glossy brd. VG+. M20. $150.00

MORRIS, Alan. *Bloody April.* 1967. London. 1st. ils. map ep. 208p. VG-/dj. B18. $22.50

MORRIS, Charles. *San Francisco Calamity by Earthquake & Fire.* 1906. Phil/Chicago/Toronto. John Winston. salesman sample book. 104p+ad. bl cloth. K7. $75.00

MORRIS, Eugene. *Against the Grain.* 1988. McGraw Hill. 1st. photos. F/VG+. P8. $20.00

MORRIS, Henry. *Human Anatomy: Complete Systematic Treatise...* 1893. Phil. 1st Am. 1286p. full leather. A13. $40.00

MORRIS, Henry. *Omnibus.* 1967. North Hills. Bird & Bull. 1/500. 8vo. Sangorski Sutcliffe bdg. w/prospectus. B24. $400.00

MORRIS, Ivan. *World of the Shining Prince: Court Life in Ancient Japan.* 1964. Knopf. 1st Am. 336p. F/VG. W3. $68.00

MORRIS, J.E. *North Wales.* 1911. London. Blk. Beautiful Britain series. ils. VG. M17. $20.00

MORRIS, James. *Conundrum.* 1974. London. 1st. VG/VG. T9. $25.00

MORRIS, James. *Islam Inflamed: A Middle East Picture.* 1969. NY. Panthon. 1st. 8vo. 7 maps. 326p. VG/torn. W1. $18.00

MORRIS, Jan; see Morris, James.

MORRIS, Jim. *Sheriff of Purgatory.* 1979. Doubleday. 1st. F/dj. M2. $15.00

MORRIS, Josephine. *Household Science & Arts.* 1913. Am Book Co. 256p. VG. B10. $25.00

MORRIS, Mary McGarry. *Dangerous Woman.* 1991. Franklin Lib. 1st/ltd issue. sgn. full leather. F. Q1. $40.00

MORRIS, Phillip Quinn. *Mussels.* 1989. Random. 1st. author's 1st novel. F/F. M23. $25.00

MORRIS, Phillip Quinn. *Thirsty City.* 1990. Random House. 1st. F/F. B4. $45.00

MORRIS, Ronald L. *Wait Until Dark. Jazz & the Underworld, 1880-1940.* 1980. Bowling Gr. Popular. 1st. F/NF. B2. $35.00

MORRIS, Stephen. *King of Vermont.* 1989. Morrow. 1st. F/F. R14. $30.00

MORRIS, W.F. *GB: Story of the Great War.* 1929. Dodd Mead. 1st Am. NF/VG. B4. $100.00

MORRIS, William Alfred. *Medieval English Sheriff to 1300.* 1968 (1927). Manchester. facsimile. M11. $65.00

MORRIS, William. *Doom of King Acrisius.* 1902. NY. RH Russell. 1st. ils Edward Burne-Jones. VG. B2. $75.00

MORRIS, William. *Early Poems of Wm Morris.* 1913. London. Blackie. 4to. 194p. F/glassine/pub cb box. C6. $325.00

MORRIS, William. *News From Nowhere; or, Epoch of Rest...* nd. Humboldt Lib. G. V4. $30.00

MORRIS, Willie. *James Jones: A Friendship.* 1978. Doubleday. 1st. NF/NF. A20. $30.00

MORRIS, Willie. *My Dog Skip.* 1995. Random. 1st. sgn. F/F. A23. $40.00

MORRIS, Willie. *Prayer for the Opening of the Little League Season.* 1995. Harcourt Brace. 1st. sgn. F/F. A23. $40.00

MORRIS, WOOD & WRIGHT. *Persia.* 1969. London. Thames Hudson. 1st. folio. 216p. VG/torn. W1. $45.00

MORRIS, Wright. *About Fiction.* 1975. Harper Row. 1st. inscr. F/F. R14. $45.00

MORRIS, Wright. *Deep Sleep.* 1953. Scribner. 1st. F/NF. B4. $300.00

MORRIS, Wright. *Love Among the Ruins.* 1957. Harcourt Brace. 1st. F/F. B4. $150.00

MORRIS, Wright. *Love Among the Ruins.* 1957. Harcourt Brace. 1st. F/NF. B24. $100.00

MORRIS, Wright. *Will's Boy.* 1981. Harper. 1st. F/F. B4. $50.00

MORRIS & MORRIS. *Men & Pandas.* 1967. NY. ils. 223p. VG. S15. $16.00

MORRISON, Arthur. *Red Triangle.* 1903. LC Page. 1st. VG+. N4. $65.00

MORRISON, Gertrude W. *Girls of Central High on Lake Luna (#2).* 1914. Grosset Dunlap. VG/dj (lists 7 titles). M20. $20.00

MORRISON, Toni. *Beloved.* 1987. Knopf. 1st. F/F. B4/C2. $75.00

MORRISON, Toni. *Bluest Eye.* 1979. Chatto Windus. 1st Eng. sgn. author's 1st book. F/dj. Q1. $350.00

MORRISON, Toni. *Jazz.* Chatto Windus. sgn. F/F. Q1. $150.00

MORRISON, Toni. *Song of Solomon.* 1977. Knopf. 1st. NF/dj. B4. $100.00

MORRISON, Toni. *Song of Solomon.* 1978. Chatto Windus. 1st Eng. F/F. Q1. $100.00

MORRISON, Toni. *Tar Baby.* 1981. Knopf. ARC. inscr. NF/dj. D10. $160.00

MORRISON, Toni. *Tar Baby.* 1981. Knopf. 1st. F/VG. M19. $35.00

MORRISON, Tony. *Pathways to the Gods.* 1978. Harper. 1st. 208p. dj. F3. $20.00

MORROW, Bradford. *Almanac Branch.* 1991. Linden. 1st. author's 2nd novel. F/F. B3. $40.00

MORROW, Bradford. *Come Sunday.* 1988. Weidenfeld Nicolson. 1st. sgn. F/F. D10. $65.00

MORROW, Bradford. *Posthumes.* 1982. Santa Barbara. Cadmus. 1st. sgn Morrow/Ginzel. 1/150. F/F. D10. $145.00

MORROW, E. Frederic. *Way Down South Up North.* 1973. Pilgrim. 1st. 128p. F/F. B4. $65.00

MORSE, Arthur D. *While Six Million Died: Chronicle of American Apathy.* 1968. Random. BC. 420p. VG/G+. S3. $24.00

MORSE, Benjamin, M.D.; see Block, Lawrence.

MORSE, Howard H. *Historic Old Rhinebeck.* 1908. NY. self pub. 1st. sgn. 448p. G. B11. $18.00

MORSE, Melvin. *Closer to the Light: Learning From Near-Death Experiences...* 1990. Villard. 206p. VG/dj. B29. $9.50

MORSE, Sidney. *Household Discoveries: An Encyclopedia...* 1909. NY. Success Co. G. A16. $50.00

MORSE, Sidney. *New Household Discoveries.* 1917. NY. Success Co. G. A16. $47.50

MORSE, Theresa A. *Best I Ever Tasted.* 1969. Doubleday. VG/dj. A16. $10.00

MORSE. *Beatrix Potter's Americans, Selected Letters.* 1982. 216p. F/VG. A4. $60.00

MORTIMER, John. *Summer's Lease.* 1988. Franklin Lib. 1st. sgn. full leather. F. Q1. $60.00

MORTOFT, Francis. *Francis Mortoft: His Book. Being His Travels...* 1925. London. Hakluyt Soc. 8vo. 216p. bl cloth. P4. $95.00

MORTON, H.V. *Through Lands of the Bible.* 1938. Dodd Mead. 1st. 8vo. 452p. VG. W1. $10.00

MORTON, Harry. *Whale's Wake.* 1982. Honolulu. 8vo. 396p. gilt bdg. M/dj. P4. $32.50

MORTON, Julia F. *Plants Poisonous to People in Florida & Other Warm Areas.* 1977 (1971). Miami. Fairchild Tropical Garden. 8vo. VG/dj. A22. $25.00

MORTON, Leah. *I Am a Woman — And a Jew.* 1926. NY. JH Sears. 362p. VG. S3. $35.00

MORTON, Rosalie Slaughter. *Doctor's Holiday in Iran.* 1940. Funk Wagnall. 8vo. 355p. xl. W1. $10.00

MOSCOW, Alvin. *Collision Course: Andrea Doria & the Stockholm.* 1959. NY. 1st. inscr. 316p. F/dj. B18. $22.50

MOSELEY, Walter. *Red Death.* 1991. Norton. 1st. F/F. T11. $45.00

MOSER, Barry. *Ghost Horse of the Mounties.* 1991. Godine. 1st. VG/NF. B3. $20.00

MOSES, Robert. *Public Works: A Dangerous Trade.* 1970. McGraw Hill. sgn. 952p. full leather. w/ephemera. B11. $150.00

MOSHER, Howard Frank. *Disappearances.* 1977. Viking. 1st. author's 1st novel. F/NF. T11. $75.00

MOSHKIN, V.A. *Castor.* 1986. New Delhi. ils/figures/tables. 315p. F/dj. B26. $22.50

MOSKOWITZ, Sam. *Charles Fort: A Radical Corpuscle.* 1976. Moskwitz. 1/300. NF/stapled wrp. R10. $25.00

MOSKOWITZ, Sam. *Modern Masterpieces of Science Fiction.* 1974 (1966). Hyperion. rpt. F. M2. $25.00

MOSKOWITZ, Sam. *Strange Horizons.* 1976. Scribner. 1st. F/dj. M2. $25.00

MOSLEY, Diana. *Loved Ones, Pen Portraits.* 1985. London. 1st. VG/VG. T9. $25.00

MOSLEY, Walter. *Black Betty.* 1994. Norton. ARC. sgn. F/F. D10. $40.00

MOSLEY, Walter. *Devil in a Blue Dress.* 1990. Norton. 1st. sgn. author's 1st book. F/dj. from $75 to $100.00

MOSLEY, Walter. *Red Death.* 1991. Norton. 1st. author's 2nd book. F/dj. A24. $50.00

MOSLEY, Walter. *White Butterfly.* 1992. Norton. 1st. F/dj. B2. $75.00

MOSLEY, Walter. *White Butterfly.* 1992. Norton. 1st. sgn. author's 3rd book. F/dj. A24. $100.00

MOSS, C. *Portraits in Wild: Behavior Studies East African Mammals.* 1975. Houghton Mifflin. ils/pl. 363p. cloth. F/NF. M12. $22.50

MOSS, Howard. *Instant Lives.* 1974. Saturday Review/Dutton. 1st. ils Gorey. 84p. VG/clip. M20. $35.00

MOSS, James A. *Field Service.* Aug 1917. Menasha, WI. George Banta. 186p+ads. tan cloth. F. H1. $20.00

MOSSMAN, Isaac Van Dorsey. *Pony Expressman's Recollections.* 1955. np. Champoeg. 1/500. 55p+fld pocket map. D11. $50.00

MOSZKOWSKI, Alexander. *Einstein: Einblicke in Seine Gedankenwelt.* 1922. Berlin. Fontane. 1st. 240p. K3. $30.00

MOTLEY, John Lothrop. *Life & Death of John of Barneveld...* 1879. NY. 2 vol. VG. A17. $18.50

MOTLEY, Willard. *Let No Man Write My Epitaph.* 1958. Random. 1st. NF/NF. B4. $65.00

MOTT, Valentine. *Ligature of the Arteria Ilica Communis, at Its Origin.* 1827. Phil. 422p. half leather. A13. $150.00

MOTTRAM, R.H. *Castle Island.* 1931. Chatto Windus. 1st. 415p. cloth. VG/dj. M20. $35.00

MOTZ & NATHANSON. *Constellations: An Enthusiast's Guide to the Night Sky.* 1988. Doubleday. 411p. VG/dj. K5. $30.00

MOUNTEVANS, Admiral Lord. *Man Against the Desolate Antarctic.* 1951. NY. Funk. ils. 172p. dj. T7. $22.00

MOUNTFIELD, D. *History of Polar Exploration.* 1974. NY. ils/maps. 208p. VG/dj. M4. $20.00

MOURELLE, Don Francisco A. *Voyage of the Sonora From the 1775 Journal of...* 1987. Fairfield. Ye Galleon. 1/301. facsimile 1920 SF ed. w/fld pocket map. M/sans. P4. $40.00

MOURSE, Hosea Ballou. *Gilds of China.* 1909. London. 1st. 2 photos/notes/bibliography. 92p. VG. W3. $110.00

MOURSE, Hosea Ballou. *Trade & Administration of the Chinese Empire.* 1908. NY/Bombay. Longman Gr. 1st. 451p. xl Cornell Club. VG. W3. $135.00

MOUSSY & TRUFFAUNT. *400 Blows.* 1969. Grove. 100+ photos. VG+. C9. $30.00

MOWAT, Farley. *Black Joke.* 1963. Little Brn. 1st Am. 8vo. 218p. VG. T5. $20.00

MOWAT, Farley. *Grey Seas Under.* 1958. Little Brn. 1st Am. NF/NF. T11. $50.00

MOWAT, Farley. *Polar Passion.* 1967. Toronto. McClelland Stewart. 4to. 302p. gray cloth. VG/dj. P4. $55.00

MOWAT, Farley. *Snow Walker.* 1975. Toronto. McClelland Stewart. 1st. NF/VG. B3. $30.00

MOWBRAY, Jay Henry. *Illustrious Career & Heroic Deeds of Colonel Roosevelt.* 1910. Berton. 1st. 363p. VG. J2. $65.00

MOYER, John W. *Famous Frontiersmen.* nd (1972). Hubbard. probable 1st. 116p. F. C14. $20.00

MOYES, Patricia. *Angel Death.* 1981. HRW. 1st Am. F/dj. N4. $30.00

MOYLE, J.B. *Institutes of Justinian. Fifth Edition.* 1955. Clarendon. 2 vol. VG/dj. M11. $175.00

MOYLE & MOYLE. *Northland Wild Flowers.* 1993. MN U. 6th. ils. 236p. F. S15. $14.00

MOYZISCH, L.C. *Operation Cicero.* 1950. London. Wingate. 1st. NF/VG. B4. $200.00

MOZART. *Grundliche Violinschule.* 1770. Augsburg. Lotter. 4to. 3 full-p pl/fld table prt music. modern calf. R12. $2,750.00

MRAZKOVA, Daniela. *Another Russia: Through the Eyes of New Soviet Photographer.* 1986. Facts on File. 1st. VG/VG. V4. $30.00

MUCHA, Jiri. *Alphonse Maria Mucha.* 1989. ils/fld ils. VG/VG. M17. $40.00

MUCK. *Einhundert Jahre, Berliner Philharmonisches Orchester...* 1982. 3 vol. lg 4to. ils. F. A4. $150.00

MUCKENSTURM, L. *Louis' Salads & Chafing Dishes.* 1906. 1st. tall narrow 4to. VG. E6. $55.00

MUDIMBE, V.Y. *Between Tides.* 1973. S&S. 1st. F/F. A20. $15.00

MUEGGLER, Walter F. *Aspen Community Types of Intermountain Region.* 1988. Ogden. 32 mc photos/map. 135p. VG/wrp. B26. $14.00

MUELLER, Ralph. *Report After Action: Story of 103rd Infantry Division.* 1945. Innsbruck. 1st. ils/maps. VG/torn. S16. $75.00

MUENCH, J. *Along Yosemite Trails.* 1948. Hastings. ils/photos/map ep. 101p. cloth. VG/G. M12. $17.50

MUENCH, Paul. *Hindenburg's March to London.* 1916. Winston. 1st Am. VG/wrp. M2. $75.00

MUHAMMAD, Elijah. *Message to the Blackman.* 1965. 1st. author's 1st book. F/G. M19. $100.00

MUIR, John. *Our National Parks.* 1909. Boston. 1st. ils/2p map. 382p. G+. B5. $95.00

MUIR, John. *Rambles of a Botanist Among Plants & Climates of CA.* 1974. Mariposa, CA. Rocking K. 1/50. prt/sgn Wm Kimes. gr cloth. F. K7. $85.00

MUIR, John. *South of Yosemite. Selected Writings.* 1968. Garden City, NY. Am Mus Natural Hist. bl cloth brd/blk spine. NF/dj. K7. $45.00

MUIR, John. *Travels in Alaska.* 1915. Boston. 1st. VG/VG. B5. $80.00

MUIR, John. *Travels in Alaska.* 1971. NY. ils/photos. 327p. cloth. F. M12. $20.00

MUIR, Marcie. *Bibliography of Australian Children's Books.* 1970. 1st. ils. 1038p. F/NF. A4. $155.00

MUIR, Percy. *Victorian Illustrated Books.* 1989. London. rpt. F/F. A4. $85.00

MUIRDEN, James. *Sky Watcher's Handbook.* 1993. NY. Freeman. 8vo. ils. 408p. VG/dj. K5. $30.00

MUKERJEE, Radhakamal. *Culture & Art of India.* 1969. NY. Praeger. 1st. photos/bibliography/maps/index. F/NF. W3. $75.00

MUKHERJEE, Bharati. *Holder of the World.* 1993. Knopf. 1st. sgn. F/F. R14. $35.00

MUKHERJEE, Bharati. *Jasmine.* 1989. Grove Weidenfeld. 1st. F/F/wrp band. R14. $30.00

MULDOON, Paul. *Faber Book of Contemporary Irish Poetry.* 1986. London. 1st. VG/VG. T9. $20.00

MULLAHY & THOMPSON. *Psychoanalysis: Evolution & Development.* 1950. Hermitage. 1st. 250p. VG/dj. A25. $15.00

MULLER, Dan. *My Life With Buffalo Bill.* 1948. Reilly Lee. 1st. 303p. VG/dj. J2. $95.00

MULLER, Katherine K. *Wild Flowers of Santa Barbara.* 1958. Santa Barbara. unp. sbdg. F. B26. $9.00

MULLER, Marcia. *Cavalier in White.* 1986. St Martin. 1st. F/F. M15. $50.00

MULLER, Marcia. *Eye of the Storm.* 1988. Mysterious. UP. NF/beige wrp. Q1. $60.00

MULLER, Marcia. *There Hangs the Knife.* 1988. St Martin. 1st. rem mk. F/VG+. N4. $15.00

MULLER, Marcia. *Trophies & Dead Things.* 1990. Mysterious. 1st. F/F. P3. $18.00

MULLER, Marcia. *Trophies & Dead Things.* 1990. Mysterious. 1st. sgn. F/F. T2. $35.00

MULLER, Orrie. *Orientalisches Tagebuch. Impressionen Rande Dreier Welten.* 1932. Bremen. Leumer. 1st. 8vo. G/torn dj/stiff wrp. W1. $12.00

MULLER, Richard. *American Greenhouse Construction.* 1927. NY. DeLaMare. 143p. VG. A10. $32.00

MULLER, W. Max. *Egyptian Mythology.* 1923. Boston. ils. VG. M17. $20.00

MULLER & PRONZINI. *Chapters & Hearse: Suspense Stories About World of Books.* 1985. Morrow. 1st. sgn. F/dj. M15. $45.00

MULLER & PRONZINI. *Kill or Cure.* 1985. Macmillan. 1st. F/dj. Q1. $30.00

MULLER-BROCKMAN, J. *Grid Systems in Graphic Design.* 1981. Eng/German text. ils. VG/VG. M17. $20.00

MULLETT, J.C. *Five Years' Whaling Voyage 1848-1853.* 1977. Ye Galleon. rpt. ils. 48p. T7. $45.00

MULLIGAN, B.O. *Maples Cultivated in the United States & Canada.* 1958. Am Assn Botanical Gardens & Aboretums. 56p. wrp. $23.00

MULLIKEN, Robert S. *Selected Papers of Robert S Mulliken.* 1975. Chicago/London. 4to. 1127p. VG. K3. $35.00

MULLINS, P. *Rocking Horse: History of Moving Toy Horses.* 1992. Great Britain. 1st. sq 4to. ils. 376p+48p servey. F/case. M4. $90.00

MULLINS & REED. *Union Bookshelf: A Selected Civil War Bibliography.* 1982. Broadfoot. 81p. F. A17. $25.00

MUMFORD, John Kimberly. *Oriental Rugs.* 1900. Scribner. 1st. 24 tissue-guarded pl/2 maps/table. maroon buckram. T10. $250.00

MUNARI, Bruno. *ABC.* 1960. World. 1st. ils. VG. P2. $35.00

MUNARI, Bruno. *Circus in the Mist.* 1969 (1968). World. 1st Am. NF/NF. C8. $125.00

MUNBY, A.N.L. *Portrait of an Obsession: Life of Sir Thomas Phillips.* 1967. Putnam. 1st. NF/dj. K3. $25.00

MUNDY, Talbot. *C-I-D.* 1932. Century. 1st. NF. M19. $25.00

MUNDY, Talbot. *Winds of the World.* 1917. Bobbs Merrill. 1st. VG. M19. $25.00

MUNK, J.A. *Activities of a Lifetime.* 1924. Times-Mirror. 1st. ils. 221p. NF. B19. $75.00

MUNK, J.A. *Southwest Sketches.* 1920. Putnam/Knickerbocker. 8vo. 311p. VG. F7. $50.00

MUNK, J.A. *Story of the Munk Library...* 1927. LA. Times-Mirror. 1st. 8vo. 78p. brn Victorian cloth. xl. T10. $45.00

MUNN, Henry Toke. *Tales of the Eskimo.* nd. London. 196p+19 photos. dj. A17. $40.00

MUNNINGS, A.J. *Pictures of Horses & English Life.* 1927. London/NY. Eyre Spottiswoode/Scribner. 1st. VG. O3. $750.00

MUNRO, Alice. *Friend of My Youth.* 1990. Knopf. ARC. sgn. F/wrp/box. R13. $45.00

MUNRO, Hugh. *Compendious System of Theory & Practice of Modern Surgery.* 1792. London. 1st. lg fld table. recent quarter leather/new ep. A13. $300.00

MUNROE, David Hoadley. *Grand National, 1839-1930.* 1931. Huntington. 1st regular. 147p. cloth. VG. M20. $50.00

MUNSEY. *Disneyana: Walt Disney Collectibles.* 1974. 4to. ils. 385p. NF/VG. A4. $150.00

MUNTANER, Ramon. *Chronicle of Muntaner.* 1920-21. Hakluyt Soc. 1st Eng. 2 vol. 8vo. gilt bdg. P4. $125.00

MUNTEAN, Michaela. *Runaway Soup & Other Stories.* 1987. Golden. 1st. sm 4to. unp. F. C14. $12.00

MUNTHE, Axel. *Story of San Michele.* 1930. Lodnon. rpt. inscr. VG/VG. T9. $65.00

MUNZ, Philip A. *California Spring Wildflowers.* 1974 (1961). Berkeley. ils/photos. 122p. sc. VG. B26. $7.50

MURAKAMI, Haruki. *Wild Sheep Chase.* 1989. Kodansha. 1st Am ed. trans Alfred Birnbaum. NF/dj. A24. $30.00

MURBARGER, Nell. *Ghosts of the Glory Trail.* June 1965. LA. Westernlore. dj. A19. $50.00

MURCOCK, Harold. *Earl Percy Dines Abroad: A Boswellian Episode.* 1924. Boston. 1/550. VG/G case. M17. $45.00

MURCOCK, John R. *Arizona Characters in Silhouette.* 1939. Fray Marcos DeNiza. inscr. 8vo. 151p. F7. $55.00

MURDOCH, Iris. *Good Apprentice.* 1985. London. 1st. VG/VG. T9. $25.00

MURIE, O.J. *Elk of North America.* (1957). Stackpole. 2nd. ils. 376p. gilt pict cloth. F. M12. $37.50

MURIE, O.J. *Jackson Hole With a Naturalist.* 1963. Frontier. 1st. 55p. VG/wrp. J2. $40.00

MURIE & MURIE. *Wapiti Wilderness.* 1966. Knopf. dj. A19. $40.00

MURKY, Norman. *Scottish Hand-Loom Weavers 1790-1850: A Social History.* nd. John Donald Pub. 1st. VG/VG. V4. $15.00

MURPHEY, Robert Cushman. *Bird Islands of Peru.* 1925. Putnam. 1st. 362p. xl. F3. $20.00

MURPHY, Arthur. *Works of Cornelius Tacitus.* 1805. London. Stockdale. 8 vol. tall 8vo. fld maps. H13. $495.00

MURPHY, Dallas. *Apparent Wind.* 1991. Pocket. 1st. as new/dj. N4. $22.50

MURPHY, Dallas. *Lover Man.* 1987. Scribner. 1st. sgn. F/F. M22. $20.00

MURPHY, Edward. *Lectures on Principles & Practice of Midwifery.* 1852. London. 1st. 616p. A13. $500.00

MURPHY, George. *Soviet Mongolia.* 1966. CA U. 1st. 224p. F/dj. W3. $48.00

MURPHY, John. *Roentgen Ray as Therapeutic Force...* 1903. Louisville. 1st. xl. A13. $50.00

MURPHY, Pat. *Falling Woman.* 1986. NY. Tor. 1st. sgn. F/F. T2. $100.00

MURPHY, Robert Cushman. *Fish-Shape Paumanok: Nature & Man on Long Island.* 1964. Am Philosophical Soc. 1st. sgn. ils/pict ep. 67p. VG/dj. B18. $15.00

MURRAY, J.W. *Distribution & Ecology of Living Benthic Foraminiferids.* 1973. Heinemann. 274p. VG/dj. D8. $35.00

MURRAY, Janet. *Traditional Scots Recipes: With a Fine Feeling for Food.* 1972. NY. Bramhall. G/dj. A16. $10.00

MURRAY, Jim. *Jim Murray Collection.* 1988. Taylor. 1st. intro Vin Scully. F/F. P8. $20.00

MURRAY, Lindley. *Power of Religion on the Mind...* 1838. NY. Trustees of Residuary Estate of Lindley Murray. 376p. V3. $16.50

MURRAY, Robert. *Ft Laramie: Visions of a Grand Old Post.* 1974. Ft Collins, CO. Old Army. dj. A19. $50.00

MURRAY, Robert. *Military Posts of Wyoming.* 1974. Old Army. 1st. sgn. ils/photos/map. 82p. VG/VG. J2. $195.00

MURRAY, Spencer. *Cruising the Sea of Cortez.* 1963. Desert Southwest Inc. 1st. photos Ralph Poole. VG. O4. $25.00

MURRAY, Thomas Boyles. *Pitcairn: The Island, the People & the Pastor...* ca 1858. London. Soc for Promoting Christian Knowledge. 11th. full calf. P4. $175.00

MURRAY, Thomas Boyles. *Pitcairn: The Island, the People & the Pastor...* 1860. London. The Soc. 12th. ils. 414p. T7. $120.00

MURRAY, V.T. *Fifty Masterpieces of Mystery.* nd. London. 1st. VG. M2. $35.00

MURRAY, William. *Treatise on Emotional Disorders of Sympathetic System...* 1867. NY. Simpson. 1st Am. 95p. prt pebbled ochre cloth. xl. G1. $225.00

MURRAY, William. *When the Fat Man Sings.* 1987. Bantam. 1st. F/clip. M22. $15.00

MURREY, T. *Valuable Cooking Receipts.* 1880. 1st. VG. E6. $45.00

MUSE, Maude B. *Materia Medica Pharmacology & Therapeutics.* 1941. Phil. Saunders. 3rd. 12mo. VG/dj. A22. $25.00

MUSGRAVE, Thomas. *Castaway on the Auckland Isles.* 1866. London. Hutchinson. ils. 251p. dj. T7. $18.00

MUSIAL, Stan. *Stan Musial: The Man's Own Story.* 1964. Doubleday. 1st. 328p. VG/dj. M20. $45.00

MUSTON, Michael. *Manhattan on the Rocks.* 1989. Holt. 1st. F/F. B35. $12.00

MUZIK, T.J. *Weed Biology & Control.* 1970. McGraw Hill. 273p. cloth. B1. $18.50

MYER, Albert J. *Manual of Signals.* 1868. NY. mc pls of signal flags. 417p. O8. $55.00

MYER, F.S. *Handbook of Ornament.* 3rd Am. ils. VG. M17. $20.00

MYERS, Edward H. *Disruption of the Methodist Episcopal Church 1844-46.* 1875. Nashville/Macon. 12mo. 216p. xl. VG. B14. $35.00

MYERS, Gustavus. *History of the Supreme Court.* 1925. Kerr. VG/dj. V4. $25.00

MYERS, Joan. *Santiago: Saint of Two Worlds.* 1991. Albuquerque. 1st. 4to. 73p. 83 photo pl/map. F/dj. T10. $50.00

MYERS, John Myers. *Dead Warrior.* 1956. Little Brn. 1st. VG/dj. M2. $50.00

MYERS, John Myers. *Deaths of the Bravos.* 1962. Little Brn. 1st. 467p. VG/dj. M20. $18.00

MYERS, John Myers. *Doc Holliday, Life...of America's Legendary Desparadoes...* 1955. Little Brn. 1st. 287p. VG/VG. J2. $125.00

MYERS, John Myers. *Print in Wild Land.* 1967. Doubleday. sm 8vo. 274p. as new/dj. K7. $25.00

MYERS, R.D. *Handbook of Drug & Chemical Stimulation of Brain.* 1974. Van Nostrand Reinhold. 8vo. red cloth. VG/dj. G1. $50.00

MYERS, R.M. *Children of Pride.* 1972. New Haven. 1st. VG/G. B5. $50.00

MYERS, William. *Journal of a Cruise to California & Sandwich Islands...* 1955. BC of CA. 1/400. lg 4to. gilt beige cloth. F. R3. $275.00

MYERS, William. *Sketches of California & Hawaii by...* 1970. BC of CA. 1/450. lg 4to. 2-tone beige cloth. F. R3. $200.00

MYLAR, Isaac L. *Early Days at the Mission San Juan Bautista.* 1929. Watsonville, CA. Evening Pajaronian. 1/300. sgn. gilt maroon cloth. VG. K7. $50.00

MYRER, Anton. *Big War.* 1957. NY. 463p. VG. S16. $28.50

MYRER, Anton. *Once an Eagle.* 1968. HRW. 1st. 817p. VG. W2. $35.00

MYRICK, David F. *San Francisco's Telegraph Hill.* 1972. Howell North. 1st. 4to. ils. NF/VG. O4. $20.00

MYRICK, Herbert. *Sugar: A New & Profitable Industry in the US.* 1897. NY. Orange Judd. 160p. VG. A10. $35.00

A book collector has friends everywhere. The bookseller from who you buy books is, more frequently than not, your friend. There is a bond between you that transcends the commercial transaction. For you've established something (call it rapport) between you that is personal, almost spiritual if you will. He understands your interests and your needs and the compulsion which brings you to him. (And let it be freely admitted, his magnet is as compelling to the bibliophile as the bar is to the boozer.) The bookseller becomes inextricably identified with you, your library, your intellectual life.

William Targ

NABOKOV, Vladimir. *Laughter in the Dark.* 1960. New Directions. 1st. VG/dj. B30. $25.00

NABOKOV, Vladimir. *Transparent Things.* 1972. McGraw Hill. 1st. NF/VG. B30. $25.00

NABUCO, Carolina. *Life of Joaquinn Nabuco.* 1950. Stanford. 8vo. 373p. map ep. bl cloth. VG/dj. P4. $35.00

NADOLNY, Sten. *Discovery of Slowness.* 1987. NY. Viking. 1st Am. F/dj. T11. $20.00

NAETHER, Carl A. *Book of the Pigeon.* 1939. Phil. McKay. 1st. 8vo. VG/fair. A2. $25.00

NAIPAUL, V.S. *Among the Believers: An Islamic Journey.* 1981. NY. Knopf. 1st trade. 430p. VG. W1. $18.00

NAIPAUL, V.S. *Bend in the River.* 1979. Knopf. 1st Am. F/dj. A24. $55.00

NAIPAUL, V.S. *Guerrillas.* 1975. Knopf. 1st Am/2nd prt. G/dj. P12. $8.00

NAIPAUL, V.S. *Way in the World.* 1984. Knopf. 1st. VG/dj. M17. $17.50

NAIR, P. Thankappan. *Peacock: National Bird of India.* 1977. Calcutta. Firma KLM Private Ltd. 1st. 304p. VG/dj. N2. $25.00

NAISBITT, John. *Global Paradox.* 1994. Morrow. 1st sm 4to. 394p. F/dj. W2. $35.00

NAITUM, Duane. *Songs From the Storyteller's Stone.* 1994. Seattle. Duane Niatum. sgn. F/bl ils wrp. O11. $35.00

NAKAYAMA, Shigeru. *History of Japanese Astronomy: Chinese Background...* 1969. Cambridge. 8vo. 329p. VG/dj. K5. $45.00

NALBANDOV, A.V. *Reproductive Physiology.* 1964. Freeman. 2nd. 316p. xl. G. S5. $12.00

NANCE, C. Roger. *Archaeology of La Calsada.* 1992. Austin. U TX. 8vo. 234p. F/dj. P4. $45.00

NANCY, Ted L. *Letters From a Nut.* 1997. Avon. 1st. unp. NF/dj. W2. $35.00

NANSEN, Fridtjof. *In Northern Mists. Vol 1.* 1911. NY. Stokes. 1st. 384p. VG. B5. $95.00

NAPIER, Robina. *Johnsoniana: Anecdotes of Late Samuel Johnson, LLD...* 1884. London. Geo Bell. 1st. tan linen. H13. $145.00

NAPIER, Simon. *Back Woods Blues.* 1968. Blues Unlimited. 1st. NF/wrp. B2. $50.00

NARANJO & ORSTEIN. *On the Psychology of Meditation.* 1971. NY. VG/VG. M17. $40.00

NASH, D.W. *Pharoah of the Exodus.* 1863. London. JR Smith. 1st. 8vo. ftspc. 319p. gilt dk gr cloth. NF. H5. $200.00

NASH, F.O.H. *Kattie of the Balkans.* 1931. London/NY. 1st. F/dj. B20. $35.00

NASH, Gerald D. *American West Transformed: Impact of Second World War.* 1985. IN U. 1st. 8vo. 304p. F/dj. B20. $15.00

NASH, Jay Robert. *Look for the Woman.* 1981. Evans. 1st. photos. VG/dj. C9. $30.00

NASH, Joseph. *Mansions of England in the Olden Time.* 1912. London. Heinemann. New ed. 104 full-p pl. gilt red cloth. B20. $85.00

NASH, N. Richard. *Cry Macho.* 1975. Delacorte. 1st. NF/F. T12. $15.00

NASH, Ogden. *Good Intentions.* 1942. Little Brn. 1st. 8vo. 180p. F/NF. B20. $50.00

NASH, Paul W. *Gilded Fly: Short Stories.* 1993. Typographeum. 1/100. ils EL James. dj. T9. $35.00

NASH, PUGACH & TOMASSON. *Social Security: First Half Century.* 1988. Albuquerque. 1st. F/NF. N2. $15.00

NASH & OFFEN. *Dillinger, Dead or Alive.* 1970. Chicago. Regnery. 1st. ils. 204p. VG/dj. B5. $30.00

NASHIF, Huda. *Pre-School Education in the Arab World.* 1985. London/Sydney/Dover. Croom Helm. 1st. 8vo. 204p. NF/dj. W1. $18.00

NASMITH, George G. *Timothy Eaton.* 1923. McClelland Stewart. 1st. VG. P3. $35.00

NASMYTH, Spike. *2355 Days: A POW's Story.* 1991. NY. Orion. 1st. photos. 264p. F/dj. R11. $15.00

NATHAN, Robert. *Enchanted Voyage.* 1936. Knopf. 1st. 8vo. 187p. NF/dj. B20. $75.00

NATHAN, Robert. *Selected Poems.* 1935. Knopf. 1st. 38p. gilt bl cloth/paper label. F/dj. F1. $40.00

NATHAN, Robert. *Winter Tide: Sonnets & Poems.* 1940. Knopf. 1st. 1/2500. 54p. F/dj. B20. $50.00

NATIONAL GEOGRAPHIC SOCIETY. *Mountain Worlds.* 1988. WA. 1st. sq 4to. 320p. F/dj. M4. $30.00

NATIONAL GEOGRAPHIC SOCIETY. *Song and Garden Birds of North America.* 1966. NGS. Wash., DC. Color ils. NF/VG. R16. $25.00

NAUEN, Elinor. *Diamonds Are a Girl's Best Friend.* 1994. Faber. 1st. AN/dj. P8. $25.00

NAUGLE & SHERRY. *Concordance to the Poems of Samuel Johnson.* 1973. Ithaca. Cornell. 1st. Eng/Latin text. F. H13. $45.00

NAUMANN, Rudolf. *Architectur Kleinasiens.* 1971. Tubingen. Wasmuth. ils/maps/2 pocket maps. 508p. cloth. VG/case. Q2. $75.00

NAUMOFF, Lawrence. *Night of the Weeping Women.* 1988. Atlantic Monthly. 1st. author's 1st book. rem mk. NF/F. B3. $35.00

NAUMOFF, Lawrence. *Silk Hope.* 1994. Harcourt. 1st. F/F. H11. $20.00

NAUMOV, N.P. *Ecology of Animals.* 1972. U IL. 650p. xl. VG. S5. $75.00

NAUS, Burt. *Visionary Leadership.* 1992. Josse Bass. 1st. sm 4to. 237p. F/dj. W2. $20.00

NAVA, Michael. *How Town.* 1990. Harper Row. 1st. NF/dj. G8. $12.50

NAVE, Orville. *Nave's Topical Bible.* 1970. Moody. 1464p. VG. B29. $13.00

NAVRATILOVA & VECSEY. *Martina.* 1985. Knopf. 4th. photos. 287p. VG/dj. P12. $8.00

NAYLOR, Gloria. *Bailey's Cafe.* 1992. HBJ. 1st. sgn. F/dj. M25. $50.00

NAYLOR, Gloria. *Linden Hills.* 1985. Ticknor Fields. 1st. F/dj. A24/H11. $45.00

NAYLOR, Gloria. *Women of Brewster Place.* 1982. Viking. 1st. author's 1st book. NF/NF. B3. $300.00

NAYLOR, James Ball. *In the Days of St Clair.* 1908. Saalfield. ils. 420p. decor cloth. VG. B18. $19.50

NAYLOR, James Ball. *Ralph Marlowe.* 1901. Akron. 4th. 412p. G. B18. $15.00

NAYLOR, Maria. *Authentic Indian Designs.* 1975. Dover. ils. G. A19. $25.00

NEAL, Larry. *Hoodoo Hollerin' Bebop Ghosts.* 1974. WA, DC. Howard U. 1st. inscr/dtd 1975. F/NF. L3. $40.00

NEARING, Scott. *Twilight of Empire.* 1930. Vanguard. 1st. VG. B2. $25.00

NEBENZAHL, Kenneth. *Bibliography of Printed Battle Plans...1775-1795.* 1975. Chicago. NF/dj. M10. $22.50

NEBLETTE, C.B. *Photography: Its Principles & Practice.* 1943. London. Chapman Hall. 4th/rpt. 8vo. ils. 865p. G. K5. $50.00

NECKER, C. *Natural History of Cats.* 1970. Barnes. 8vo. ils. 326p. NF/G. M12. $22.50

NEE, Watchman. *Spiritual Man.* 1969. Christian Fellowship. 3 vol. VG/wrp. B29. $12.50

NEEDHAM, Joseph. *Science, Religion & Reality.* 1955. NY. 355p. A13. $40.00

NEEDHAM, Richard. *Wit & Wisdom of Richard Needham.* 1977. Edmonton. Hurtig. 1st. sgn. NF/wrp. A26. $10.00

NEELY, Barbara. *Blanche Among the Talented Tenth.* 1994. St Martin. 1st. F/dj. C9. $30.00

NEELY, Richard. *Madness of the Heart.* 1976. NY. Crowell. 1st. NF/F. H11. $25.00

NEELY, Robert D. *Laws of Dickens & Their Clerks.* 1938. Boston. Christopher Pub. red cloth. M11. $65.00

NEERGAARD, Ebbe. *Story of Danish Film.* 1963. Denmark. Danish Inst. photos. VG/wrp. C9. $48.00

NEF, Karl. *Outline of History of Music.* 1964 (1935). NY. Columbia. 2nd. 400p. VG/glassine. C5. $12.50

NEFF, Terry A. *Proud Heritage: 2 Centuries of American Art...* 1987. Chicago. ils. VG/dj. M17. $40.00

NEHRBASS, Richard. *Perfect Death for Hollywood.* 1991. Harper Collins. 1st. F/F. H11. $25.00

NEIDELMAN, Edna H. *American's Lincoln: From the Hearts of Many Poets.* (1966). Pageant. 135p. VG/dj. B10. $15.00

NEIDER, Charles. *Great West.* Bonanza. rpt. ils. 457p. VG/dj. B19. $20.00

NEIHARDT, John G. *Black Elk Speaks.* 1932. NY. Morrow. 1st. 280p. G+. B5. $75.00

NEIHARDT, John G. *Poetic Values: Their Reality & Our Need of Them.* 1925. Macmillan. 1st. F. A18. $40.00

NEIHARDT, John G. *Sixth Grandfather: Black Elk's Teachings.* 1984. Lincoln, NE. VG/dj. A19. $25.00

NEIHARDT, John G. *Song of Hugh Glass.* 1915. Macmillan. 1st. F. A18. $50.00

NEIHARDT, John G. *Splendid Wayfaring: Story of Exploits...Jedediah Smith...* 1924. NY. later prt. 290p. B18. $37.50

NEILL, John. *Outlines of the Arteries With Short Description.* 1945. Phil. Barrington. pres. 6 hand-colored pl. 30p. VG. G7. $95.00

NEILL, John. *Outlines of the Veins & Lymphatics With Short Descriptions.* 1847. 1st. ils. VG. E6. $125.00

NEIMAN, LeRoy. *Horses.* 1979. Abrams. sgn pres/dtd. ils. 350p. D2. $395.00

NELSON, Albert F.J.H. *There Is Life on Mars.* 1956. NY. Citadel. 8vo. 152p. VG/dj. K5. $30.00

NELSON, Arty. *Technicolor Pulp.* 1995. NY. Warner. 1st. author's 1st book. F/F. H11. $30.00

NELSON, Arty. *Technicolor Pulp.* 1995. NY. Warner. 1st. author's 1st book. F/NF. R16. $35.00

NELSON, B. *Galapagos: Islands of Birds.* 1968. NY. 338p. cloth. F/dj. C12. $35.00

NELSON, Donald A. *Television Antennas: Design, Construction, Installation...* 1951. Indianapolis. Howard Sams. 8vo. VG/wrp. A2. $14.00

NELSON, Gil. *Trees of Florida.* 1994. Sarasota. ils. 352p. sc. AN. B26. $20.00

NELSON, Robert L. *Partners With Power, Social Transformation of Lg Law Firm.* 1988. Berkeley. M11. $35.00

NELSON, Thomas Jr. *Letters of..., Governor of Virginia.* 1874. Richmond. 1st. 1/500. later cloth. VG. M8. $250.00

NELSON, William E. *Americanization of the Common Law...1760-1830.* 1975. Cambridge. Harvard. M11. $35.00

NELSON, Willie. *Autobiography: Willie.* 1988. S&S. 334p. G/dj. C5. $12.50

NEMEC, David. *Beer & Whisky League.* 1994. NY. Lyons Burford. 1st. F/dj. G10. $18.00

NEMEC, David, et. al. *20th Century Baseball Chronicle.* 1993. Chicago. PUblications International. 4to. gte. 608p. color pict. NF/deluxe cover art. R16. $95.00

NEPOS, Cornelius. *Quae Extant.* 1684. Leyden. Jacobi Hackii. 16mo. 306p. contemporary vellum. K1. $100.00

NERUDA, Pablo. *Extravagaria.* 1974. NY. Farrar. 1st Am. F/dj. B2. $35.00

NESBIT, E. *Daphne in Fitzroy Street.* 1909. Doubleday Page. 1st. red cloth/label. VG/dj. B27. $150.00

NESBIT, William. *How to Hunt With the Camera.* 1926. NY. 337p. VG. A17. $30.00

NESBITT, Alexander. *Lettering: History & Technique of Lettering as Design.* 1950. Prentice Hall. 1st. 4to. 300p. F/dj. O10. $30.00

NESMITH, J.H. *Soldiers Manual.* 1963. Washington. 73p. VG. S16. $25.00

NESMITH, Robert I. *Dig for Pirate Treasure.* 1958. Bonanza. 8vo. 302p. VG/dj. B11. $18.00

NESSELL, C.W. *Restless Spirit.* 1963. Minneapolis, MN. 112p. wht cloth. H6. $24.00

NESTLE, Joan. *Restricted Country.* 1987. Ithaca. Firebrand. 1st. sgn. 189p. VG+. A25. $20.00

NETHERTON & NETHERTON. *Fairfax County in Virginia: Pictorial History.* (1986). Donning. photos. 216p. VG/VG. B10. $35.00

NEUBERGER, Max. *Essays in the History of Medicine.* 1930. NY. 1/300. 210p. A13. $50.00

NEUBERGER, Max. *History of Medicine. Vol 1.* 1910. London. Frowde. 1st. 4to. G7. $150.00

NEUGEBOREN, Jay. *Stolen Jew.* 1981. HRW. 1st. F/dj. T12. $45.00

NEUMANN, Robert. *Passion: Six Literary Marriages.* 1932. Harcourt Brace. 1st Am. 8vo. 213p. F/dj. B20. $25.00

NEUNZIG, H.H. *Moths of America North of Mexico...* 1990. lg 8vo. ils/pl. 165p. NF. B1. $40.00

NEUSTADT, Egon. *Lamps of Tiffany.* (1970). Fairfield. folio. 224p. F/clip. H1. $200.00

NEVE, J.L. *Churches & Sects of Christendom.* 1944. Lutheran. 509p. G. B29. $13.50

NEVEROV, Howard. *Federigo; or, The Power of Love.* 1954. Atlantic/Little Brn. 1st. NF/VG. L3. $55.00

NEVILLE, Dorothy. *Carr P Collins, Man on the Move.* 1963. Dallas, TX. Park Pr. inscr/sgn Collins. 185p. F. W2. $20.00

NEVILLE, Emily Cheney. *Fogerty.* 1969. Harper Row. early ed. 182p. cloth. F/dj. D4. $30.00

NEVIN, David. *Mexican War.* 1979. Time-Life Old West. 1st. maps. 240p. F. M4. $20.00

NEVIN, David. *1812.* 1996. NY. Tom Doherty. 1st. bl cloth. F/dj. T11. $25.00

NEVINS, A. *Polk: Diary of a President 1845-1849...* 1952. NY. 512p. NF/poor. M4. $30.00

NEVINS, Francis M. Jr. *120-Hour Clock.* 1986. NY. Walker. 1st. F/NF. A23. $25.00

NEVINSON, Henry W. *More Changes, More Chances.* ca 1925. NY. Harcourt Brace. 1st. ils. 427p. VG. W1. $45.00

NEVIUS, Laird. *Discovery of Modern Anaesthesia.* 1894. NY. 1st. 112p. A13. $250.00

NEWBERRY, Clare Turlay. *Barkis.* 1938. Harper. 1st. 12mo. 30p. VG/dj. D1. $150.00

NEWBERRY, Clare Turlay. *Marshmallow.* 1942. Harper. 1st. lg 4to. pict dj. R5. $150.00

NEWBOLT, Frank. *Etchings of Van Dyck.* 1906. London. Newnes/Scribner. ils/pl. cloth spine/brd. D2. $45.00

NEWCOMB, Harvey. *Negro Pew: Being an Inquiry Concerning Propriety...* 1837. Boston. Knapp. 1st. 8vo. 108p. O1. $200.00

NEWCOMB, Rexford. *Old Mission Churches & Historic Houses of California.* 1925. Phil. Lippincott. 1st. ils. 363p. cloth. D11. $100.00

NEWELL, R.C. *Biology of Intertidal Animals.* 1970. Am Elsevier. 555p. xl. G. S5. $50.00

NEWELL, William Wells. *Games & Songs of American Children.* 1883. Harper. 1st. 242p. beige cloth. VG. B20. $150.00

NEWELL & SMITH. *Mighty MO: The USS Missouri.* 1969. NY. Bonanza. 3rd. sm 4to. bl cloth. NF/dj. M7. $20.00

NEWHAFER, Richard. *No More Bugles in the Sky.* 1966. NAL. stated 1st. VG/dj. R11. $60.00

NEWHALL, Nancy. *Elequent Light.* 1963. SF. Sierra Club. 1st. photos. F/dj. T10. $150.00

NEWHALL & NEWHALL. *Master of Photography.* 1958. Braziller. VG/dj. S5. $25.00

NEWHAN, Ross. *California Angels.* 1982. S&S. 1st. sgn Gene Autry. F/dj. P8. $100.00

NEWMAN, Christopher. *Dead End Game.* 1994. Putnam. 1st. F/dj. P8. $15.00

NEWMAN, Daisy. *I Take Thee, Serenity.* 1982. Houghton Mifflin. BC. 314p. VG/dj. V3. $9.50

NEWMAN, Daisy. *Procession of Friends: Quakers in America.* 1972. Doubleday. 1st. 460p. xl. dj. V3. $18.00

NEWMAN, G.F. *Sir, You Bastard.* 1970. S&S. 1st. F/F. H11. $30.00

NEWMAN, John Henry. *Apologia pro Vita Sua...* 1931. Macmillan. Modern Readers series. 1st. 380p. G/dj. H10. $17.50

NEWMAN, Katherine S. *Declining Fortunes.* 1993. Harper Collins. 1st. sm 4to. 257p. F/dj. W2. $35.00

NEWMAN, Kim. *Anno Dracula.* 1992. London. S&S. 1st. sgn label on title p. F/dj. M15. $150.00

NEWMAN, Kim. *Anno Dracula.* 1993. Carroll Graff. 1st Am. F/dj. S18. $40.00

NEWMAN, Ralph. *Man & Nature, Selected Essays of Giorgio Del Vecchio.* 1969. Notre Dame. cloth. M11. $45.00

NEWMAN, Ralph. *Selective Checklist of Carl Sandburg's Writings.* 1952. Chicago. 1st thus/offprt. 1/500. NF. M8. $28.00

NEWQUIST, Roy. *Conversations With Joan Crawford.* 1980. Citadel. 1st. NF/dj. T12. $15.00

NEWSOM, Samuel. *Dwarfed Tree Manual for Westerners.* 1964 (1960). Tokyo. 5th. ils. 133p. VG/dj. B26. $20.00

NEWTON, A. Edward. *Bibliography & Pseudo-Bibliography.* 1936. Phil. U PA. 2nd. VG/G. B5. $27.50

NEWTON, A. Edward. *Dr Johnson, a Play.* 1923. Boston. Atlantic Monthly. 1st. ils. H13. $45.00

NEWTON, A. Edward. *Rare Books, Original Drawings, Autograph Letters of...* 1941. Parke-Bernet Galleries. 4 vol. sm 4to. F/dj as issued. O10. $135.00

NEYHART, Louise A. *Henry's Lincoln.* 1958 (1945). Holiday House. 1st thus. ils Chas Banks Wilson. F/fair. M5. $10.00

NGUYEN, Thai. *Is South Vietnam Viable?* 1962. Manila. Carmelo & Bauermann. 314p. VG. R11. $75.00

NIATUM, Duane. *Ascending Red Cedar Moon.* 1973. NY. Harper Row. ARC/1st. inscr. F/dj. L3. $125.00

NIBLACK, Albert P. *Coast Indians of Southern Alaska & N British Columbia...* 1887. GPO. 100+ pl/fld charts. 161p. brn cloth. VG. O1. $75.00

NICHOL, B.P. *Once: A Lullaby.* 1986. Greenwillow. 1st. obl 8vo. unp. F/dj. T5. $30.00

NICHOLS, Anne. *Abie's Irish Rose.* 1929. Grosset Dunlap. MTI. F/NF. B4. $100.00

NICHOLS, John. *American Blood.* 1987. NY. Holt. 1st. inscr. F/dj. B2. $45.00

NICHOLS, John. *Fragile Beauty: John Nichols' Milagro Country...* 1987. Gibbs Smith. 1st. ils. 146p. NF/dj/swrp. B19. $30.00

NICHOLS, John. *Ghost in the Music.* 1979. Holt. 1st. inscr/dtd 1987. F/dj. M25. $35.00

NICHOLS, John. *Ghost in the Music.* 1979. NY. Holt. 1st. NF/F. H11. $30.00

NICHOLS, John. *Minor Lives: A Collection of Biographies...* 1971. Harvard. 1st. portrait ftspc. 367p. gilt bl cloth. F/dj. H13. $95.00

NICHOLS, John. *Nirvana Blues.* 1981. HRW. 1st. F/dj. T12. $85.00

NICHOLS, Leigh; see Koontz, Dean R.

NICHOLS, P. *Cancer: Its Proper Treatment: Value of Escharotics...* 1941. VG. E6. $18.00

NICHOLS, R.F. *Franklin Pierce: Young Hickory of the Granite Hills.* 1958. Penn State. ils. 625p. NF. M4. $40.00

NICHOLS & O'NEAL. *Architecture in Virginia, 1776-1959: Old Dominion's...* (1958). VA Mus Fine Arts. unp. sbdg. VG. B10. $25.00

NICHOLSON, William S. *Historic Homes & Churches of Virginia's Eastern Shore.* (1984). Atlantic. ils/photos. 176p. VG/VG. B10. $45.00

NICKERSON, Jane. *Florida Cookbook.* 1973. Gainsville, FL. 1st. VG/dj. A16. $12.00

NICKLAUS, Jack. *My 55 Ways to Lower Your Golf Score.* 1964. S&S. 1st. ils. NF/dj. P12. $12.00

NICOLSON, Harold. *Paul Verlaine.* 1921. Boston. 1st Am. author's 1st book. G/dj. Q1. $175.00

NICOLSON, Nigel. *Flight of the Mind/Question of Things Happening...* 1975 & 1976. London. Hogarth. 2 vol. 1st. VG/dj. M10. $50.00

NIEBUHR, Rheinhold. *Nature & Destiny of Man: A Christian Interpretation...* 1941-43. Scribner. 2 vol. 1st Am. G. H10. $35.00

NIEKRO & NIEKRO. *Knuckleballs.* 1986. Freundlich. 1st. F/dj. P8. $25.00

NIELSEN, Helen. *After Midnight.* 1966. Gollancz. 1st Eng. VG/G. G8. $17.50

NIELSEN, Helen. *Fifth Caller.* 1959. Morrow. 1st. VG/dj. G8. $15.00

NIELSEN, Kay. *In Powder & Crinoline Fairy Tales.* 1913. Hodder Stoughton. 1st. lg 4to. teg. glassine dj/pub box. R5. $2,000.00

NIETHAMMER, Carolyn. *Daughters of the Earth.* 1977. Macmillan. F/dj. A19. $25.00

NIGHBERT, David. *Strikezone.* 1989. St Martin. 1st. F/dj. P8. $25.00

NIGHTINGALE, Gay. *Growing Cyclamen.* 1982. Portland. ils/photos. F/dj. B26. $20.00

NIJINSKA & RAWLINSON. *Bronislava Nijinska: Early Memoirs.* 1981. HRW. 1st. F/dj. T12. $60.00

NIKOLSKII, George V. *Theory of Fish Populatin Dynamics.* 1969. Oliver Boyd. 323p. xl. VG. S5. $25.00

NILES, Blair. *Colombia: Land of Miracles.* 1924. NY. Century. 1st. 389p. cloth. dj. F3. $15.00

NIMS, John Frederick. *Iron Pastoral.* 1947. NY. Wm Sloane. 1st. inscr. author's 1st book. F/dj. B2. $35.00

NIMS-SMITH, Dwight L. *Photographer & the River, 1889-90.* 1967. Santa Fe. 1st. 1/600. 12mo. VG/dj. F7. $100.00

NIN, Anais. *Henry & June.* 1986. HBJ. 1st. F/NF. B3. $20.00

NIRVANA. *Chocolate Making: Comprehensive Treatise.* ca 1920s?. London. 16mo. photos/ads. 167p. VG. E6. $35.00

NISBET, H.B. *Herder & the Philosophy & History of Science.* 1970. Cambridge. 1st. 358p. A13. $25.00

NISSEN, Claus. *Die Botanische Buchillustration, Ihre Geschichte...* nd. 2 vol in 1. 1/225. 4to. 2387 entries. F. A4. $250.00

NISWANDER, Adam. *Charm.* 1993. Phoenix. Integra. 1st. sgn. author's 1st novel. F/dj. T2. $25.00

NIVEN, J. *Martin Van Buren: Romantic Age of American Politics.* 1983. OUP. 1st. ils. F/dj. M4. $35.00

NIVEN & POURNELLE. *Football.* 1985. Ballantine. 1st. F/dj. S13. $15.00

NIXON, Alan. *Attack on Vienna.* 1972. St Martin. 1st. F/dj. P3. $13.00

NIXON, Alan. *Item 7.* 1970. S&S. 1st. F/dj. P3. $13.00

NIXON, Cornelia. *Now You See It.* 1991. Boston. Little Brn. 1st. author's 1st book. F/dj. H11. $20.00

NIXON, John Lowery. *Dark & Deadly Pool.* 1987. Delacorte. 2nd. G+/dj. B36. $8.00

NIXON, N.F. *Subliminal Perception: Nature of a Controversy.* 1917. London. McGraw Hill. 362p. NF/dj. G1. $88.00

NIXON, Pat. *Century of Medicine in San Antonio.* 1936. San Antonio. 1st. 405p. A13. $65.00

NIXON, Paul. *Warath.* 1987. Kenthurst, NSW. photos. 80p. F. B26. $27.50

NIXON, Richard M. *Inaugural Address of..., President of the United States.* (1969). Worcester. St Onge. 1/1500. photo ftspc. 44p. aeg. gilt bl leather. B24. $30.00

NIXON, Richard M. *Real War.* 1980. NY. Warner. 341p. map ep. F/NF. R11. $17.00

NIXON, Richard M. *Six Crises.* 1962. Doubleday. 1st. inscr. 8vo. 460p. VG+/dj. B20. $250.00

NOAKES, Aubry. *Sportsmen in a Landscape.* 1994. Lippincott. 1st Am. VG/dj. O3. $45.00

NOAKES, Vivien. *Edward Lear, a Biography.* 1986. 4to. ils/60 mc pl. 216p. F/F. A4. $95.00

NOAKES, Vivien. *Painter Edward Lear.* 1991. Newton Abbot. 1st. dj. T9. $20.00

NOBLE, Daniel. *Brain & Its Physiology...* 1995. NY. Classics of Neurology/ Neurosurgery Lib. sm 8vo. G1. $65.00

NOBLE, Lorraine. *Four-Star Scripts: Actual Shooting Scripts...* 1936. Doubleday Doran. 1st. VG+. C9. $60.00

NOBLE, Peter. *Fabulous Orson Welles.* 1956. Hutchinson. 1st. photos. VG/clip. C9. $180.00

NOBLE-IVES, Sarah. *Story of Teddy the Bear.* ca 1923. Springfield, MA. lg 4to. 6 full-p mc pl. pict brd. R5. $225.00

NOCK, O. *World Atlas of Railways.* 1983. NY. Bonanza. rpt. VG/dj. B9. $20.00

NOEL, Lucie. *James Joyce & Paul L Leon.* 1950. Gotham Book Mart. 1st. F/bl prt wrp. M24. $125.00

NOEL-BAKER, F. *Spy Web.* 1955. 1st. intro Philbrick. F/G+. E6. $15.00

NOFI, Albert A. *Opening Guns: Ft Sumter to Bull Run...Vol I.* 1988. Gallery/WH Smith. 1st. NF/dj. A14. $14.00

NOGUCHI, Yone. *Selected Poems of...* 1921. Four Seas/Elkin Mathews. 1st Am. teg. NF/case. Q1. $250.00

NOHL, J. *Black Death: A Chronicle of the Plague.* 1924. NY. ils/index. 284p. VG. B5. $35.00

NOLAN, Keith William. *Battle for Hue: Tet, 1968.* 1983. Novato. Presidio Pr. 201p. NF/VG. R11. $15.00

NOLAN, Liam. *Small Man of Nanataki.* 1966. Dutton. 1st. sm 8vo. 162p. NF/VG. W2. $10.00

NOLAN, William A. *Surgeon's World.* 1972. Random. 1st. 8vo. 366p. NF/VG. C14. $15.00

NOLAN, William F. *Hammett: A Life at the Edge.* 1983. Congdon Weed. 1st. VG/dj. P3. $17.00

NOLAN, William F. *McQueen.* 1984. Congdon Weed. 1st. NF/dj. T11. $10.00

NOLL, Mark A. *Scandal of the Evangelical Mind.* 1994. IVP. 274p. VG/dj. B29. $12.50

NOON, Jeff. *Pollen.* 1996. NY. Crown. 1st. F/F. H11. $30.00

NOON, Jeff. *Vurt.* 1995. NY. Crown. 1st Am. author's 1st book. F/dj. A24/H11. $30.00

NORDANG, Bruno. *Patagonia Year.* 1938. Knopf. 1st Am. 253p. dj. F3. $20.00

NORDHOFF, Charles. *California: For Health, Pleasure & Residence.* 1873. Harper. 255p. pict cloth. B18. $65.00

NORDHOFF, Charles. *Communistic Societies of the United States.* 1875. Harper. 1st. B2. $150.00

NORDHOFF, Charles. *Communistic Societies of the United States.* 1962 (1875). rpt. ils/map. 439p. F/dj. M4. $50.00

NORDHOFF, Charles. *History of Playing Cards.* 1977. Buffalo. Hillside. 1/250. hand-colored ils. 48p. orange pict cloth. B24. $95.00

NORDHOFF, Charles. *Peninsular California: Some Account of the Climate...* 1888. NY. Harper. 1st. ils/maps. 130p. D11. $100.00

NORDYKE, Lewis. *John Wesley Hardin: Texas Gunman.* 1957. Morrow. 1st. 278p. VG/dj. B5. $25.00

NORFLEET, Frank J. *Norfleet: Actual Experiences of a Texas Rancher's...Chase...* 1924. Sugar Land, TX. 8vo. ils. cloth. VG. O1. $65.00

NORGAARD, Erik. *With Love to You: History of the Erotic Postcard.* 1969. Clarkson Potter. 1st Am. ils. 120p. pict brd. B18. $20.00

NORMAN, Charles. *Hornbeam Tree & Other Poems.* 1988. Holt. 1st. ils Ted Rand. F/dj. D4. $25.00

NORMAN, Howard. *Bird Artist.* 1994. FSG. 1st. F/dj. R14. $45.00

NORMAN, Howard. *Bird Artist.* 1994. London. Faber. true 1st. 8vo. F/dj. S9. $85.00

NORMAN, Howard. *How Glooskap Outwits the Ice Giants.* 1989. Little Brn. 1st. ils Michael McCurdy. VG/NF. A24. $45.00

NORMAN, Howard. *Kiss in the Hotel Joseph Conrad & Other Stories.* 1989. NY. Summit. 1st. author's 1st collection short fiction. F/dj. O11. $50.00

NORMAN, Howard. *Northern Lights.* 1987. Summit. 1st. author's 1st book. NF/NF. B3. $175.00

NORMAN, Howard. *Who-Paddled-Backward-With Trout.* 1987. Little Brn. 1st. F/dj. O11. $100.00

NORMAN, John. *Medicine in the Ghetto.* 1969. NY. 1st. 333p. A13. $50.00

NORMAN, Rick. *Fielder's Choice.* 1991. August. 1st. sgn. F/dj. P8. $45.00

NORRIE, Ian. *Traveller's Guide to Celebration of London.* 1984. NY. Historical Times. 1st Am. 8vo. 217p. F. B11. $15.00

NORRIS, Charles. *Bread.* 1923. Dutton. 1st. inscr. G. M19. $25.00

NORRIS, Frank. *McTeague: A Story of San Francisco.* 1899. Doubleday McClure. 1st/2nd issue. wht stp red cloth. F. M24. $300.00

NORRIS, Joel. *Serial Killers.* 1988. NY. Dolphin. 1st. F/dj. A23. $30.00

NORRIS, Kathleen. *Belle-Mere.* 1931. Doubleday. 1st. F/NF. B2. $50.00

NORRIS, Kathleen. *Certain People of Importance.* 1922. Doubleday. 1st. F/dj. B2. $75.00

NORRIS, Kathleen. *Little Ships.* 1925. Doubleday. 1st. F/dj. B2. $40.00

NORRIS, Kathleen. *Red Silence.* 1929. Doubleday. 1st. F/dj. B2. $60.00

NORRIS, Kenneth S. *Hawaiian Spinner Dolphin.* 1994. CA U. 408p. F/dj. S15. $30.00

NORRIS & WASHINGTON. *Last of the Scottsboro Boys.* 1979. NY. 1st. 281p. VG/dj. B5. $20.00

NORTH, Andrew; see Norton, Andre.

NORTH, Anthony; see Koontz, Dean R.

NORTH, Arthur Walbridge. *Camp & Camino in Lower California: A Record...* 1910. Baker Taylor. 1st. ils/index. 346p. VG+. B19. $45.00

NORTH, Darian. *Criminal Seduction.* 1993. Dutton. 1st. author's 1st book. NF/F. H11. $25.00

NORTH, Dick. *Lost Patrol.* 1978. Alaska Northwest. 1st. ils. 138p. VG. S14. $10.00

NORTH, Mary Remsen. *Down the Colorado River, by a Lone Girl Scout.* 1930. Putnam. 1st. 8vo. orange cloth. VG/dj. F7. $75.00

NORTH, Sterling. *Abe Lincoln: Log Cabin to White House.* 1956. Random. 5th. Landmark Book #61. VG/dj. P12. $15.00

NORTHEND, Mary Harrod. *Historic Doorways of Old Salem.* 1926. Houghton Mifflin. 1st. photos. 96p. gilt cloth. B18. $22.50

NORTHROP, N.B. *Pioneer History of Medina County.* 1972. Portland, IN. rpt of 1861. 224p. VG. B18. $55.00

NORTHUMBERLAND, Eighth Duke. *Shadow of the Moor.* 1990. Stocksfield. Spredden. 12mo. 69p. VG/dj. O3. $25.00

NORTON, Alice; see Norton, Andre.

NORTON, Andre. *Brother to Shadows.* 1993. Morrow. 1st. 1F/dj. T10. $30.00

NORTON, Andre. *Dread Companion.* 1970. HBJ. 1st. F/dj. T10. $75.00

NORTON, Andre. *Gate of the Cat.* 1987. Ace. 1st. F/dj. T10. $45.00

NORTON, Andre. *Imperial Lady.* 1989. NY. Tor. 1st. F/dj. A24. $20.00

NORTON, Andre. *Jargoon Pard.* 1974. NY. Atheneum. 1st. NF/dj. M21. $30.00

NORTON, Andre. *Plague Ship.* 1956. Gnome. 1st. blk-lettered gray cloth. F/dj. T10. $250.00

NORTON, Bettina A. *Edwin Whitefield, 19th-Century North American Scenery.* 1977. Barre Pub. 1st. ils. 158p. G+. B18. $17.50

NORTON, Charles Eliot. *Historical Studies of Church Buildings in Middle Ages.* 1880. NY. Harper. 1st. 331p. G. H10. $45.00

NORTON, Charles. *Handbook of Florida.* 1892. NY. Longmans. 49 maps/plans/fld map. 392p. VG. B14. $55.00

NORTON, J.E. *Bibliography of Works of Edward Gibbon.* 1970. 272p. F. A4. $45.00

NORTON, Mary. *Borrowers.* 1991. HBJ. 1st. ils Michael Hague. F/dj. B17. $20.00

NORWICH, John Julius. *Sahara.* 1968. Weybright Talley. ils/pl. 240p. NF/dj. W1. $30.00

NOSSITER, Bernard D. *Fat Years & Lean: American Economy Since Roosevelt.* 1990. Harper Row. 1st. 271p. VG. S5. $12.00

NOTESTEIN, Lucy Lilian. *Wooster of the Miffle West.* 1937. London. Yale. 1st. ils. 333p. VG/dj. B18. $22.50

NOTESTEIN, Wallace. *English People on Eve of Colonization 1603-1630.* 1954. Harper. 1st. ils. 302p. VG/dj. S17. $10.00

NOTT, C. *Sketches of the War: Series of Letters...* 1865 (1863). G+. E6. $65.00

NOTTINGHAM, Stratton. *Wills & Administrations of Accomack County, VA 1663-1800.* 1973. Polyanthos. 494p. VG. B10. $50.00

NOURSE, Alan. *Fourth Horseman.* 1983. Harper Row. 1st. F/dj. T12. $25.00

NOURSE, J.E. *Narrative of the Second Arctic Expedition...* 1879. WA. 12 text maps/lg fld map mtd on cloth. 644p. new cloth. M4. $165.00

NOVA, Craig. *Incandescence.* 1979. Harper. 1st. F/dj. M25. $25.00

NOVAK, Joseph; see Kosinski, Jerzy.

NOVLE, Joan Russell. *Recollection of Virginia Woolf.* 1972. London. Peter Owen. 1st. 207p. VG/dj. M10. $12.50

NOVOMEYSKY, M.A. *Given to Salt: Struggle for the Dead Sea Concession.* 1958. London. Parrish. ils. 286p. cloth. VG/dj. Q2. $26.50

NOWLIN, William. *Bark Covered House; or, Back in the Woods Again...* 1876. Detroit. Prt for Author. 12mo. 250p. dk brn cloth. K1. $1,250.00

NOWOSIELSKI, Sophie. *Memoirs of a Woman Solider: In the Hurricane of War.* 1929. photos. VG. E6. $25.00

NOYCE, Wilfrid. *South Col: A Personal Story of Ascent of Everest.* 1955. Wm Sloane. 1st. F/VG. M19. $17.50

NOYES, Alfred. *Pageant of Letters.* 1940. NY. Sheed Ward. 1st. 8vo. 356p. cloth. F/dj. O10. $25.00

NOYES, Stanley. *Shadowbox.* 1970. Macmillan. 1st. F/NF. H11. $15.00

NOYES, William. *Wood & Forest.* 1912. Peoria. 2nd. 294p. B26. $35.00

NUGENT, Beth. *Live Girls.* 1996. Knopf. 1st. rem mk. F/sans. R14. $25.00

NULAND, Sherwin. *Doctors: Biography of Medicine.* 1988. NY. 1st. 519p. A13. $30.00

NUNN, Kem. *Pomona Queen.* 1992. NY. Pocket. 1st. F/NF. B3. $20.00

NURSE, H.A. *Poultry Houses, Coops & Equipment.* 1914. St Paul. Webb. 96p. VG/wrp. A10. $20.00

NUSBAUM, Deric. *Deric With the Indians.* 1927. Putnam. 1st. sm 8vo. G. C14. $10.00

NUSEIBEH, Hazem Zaki. *Palestine & the United Nations.* 1981. NY/London/Melbourne. 1st. 8vo. 200p. cloth. NF/dj. W1. $18.00

NUSSER, Richard. *Walking After Midnight.* 1989. NY. Villard. 1st. F/F. H11. $20.00

NUTT, Katherine F. *Gold, Guns & Grass: South Park & Fairplay, Colorado...* 1983. Flagstaff. 1st. ils/map/biblio. F/wrp. B19. $12.50

NUTTALL, T. *Popular Handbook of the Birds of the United States & Canada.* 1903 (1891). Boston. revised/annotated. 2 vol in 1. xl. VG. C12. $42.00

NUTTING, Anthony. *Arabs: Narrative History From Mohammed to Present.* 1964. NY. Potter. 1st Am. tall 8vo. 13 maps/charts. 424p. VG/dj. W1. $28.00

NUTTING, Anthony. *Gordon, Martyr & Misfit.* 1967. London. Rpt Soc. 2nd. gilt simulated leather. VG. M7. $25.00

NUTTING, Wallace. *Clock Book.* 1934 (1924). Garden City. 8vo. 312p. gilt tan cloth. F. B20. $60.00

NUTTING, Wallace. *Virginia Beautiful.* (1935). Garden City. later ed. 300+ photos. 262p. VG+/dj. H7. $30.00

NUTTING, Wallace. *Virginia Beautiful.* 1930. Framingham, MA. sgn. photos. 306p. VG. B18. $25.00

NYE, Bud. *Stay Loose.* 1959. Doubleday. 1st. VG/G. P8. $30.00

NYE, Nelson. *Champions of the Quarter Tracks.* 1959. Coward McCann. 1st. VG/fair. O3. $85.00

NYE, Nelson. *Horse Thieves.* 1987. Evans. 1st. 179p. F/F. B19. $15.00

NYE, Nelson. *Your Western Horse.* 1968. AS Barnes. 3rd. VG/dj. A21. $35.00

NYE, Robert. *Merlin.* 1979. Putnam. 1st Am. 215p. gilt blk cloth. F/dj. F1. $25.00

O'BRIAN, Patrick. *Wine-Dark Sea.* 1993. Norton. 1st Am ed. sgn. F/F. w/author's bookmark. B4. $250.00

O'BRIEN, C. *From Three Yachts.* 1950. Rupert Hart Davis. 239p. dj. T7. $24.00

O'BRIEN, Flann. *Third Policeman.* 1967. Walker. 1st Am ed. F/NF. B2. $45.00

O'BRIEN, Frederick. *White Shadows in the South Seas.* 1924. NY. Century. 8vo. 7 pl. cloth. VG. W1. $10.00

O'BRIEN, N. *Revolution From the Heart.* 1987. Oxford. 1st ed. sgn. 310p. VG/dj. W1. $18.00

O'BRIEN, Tim. *In the Lake of the Woods.* 1994. Houghton Mifflin. 1st ed. F/F. T2. $25.00

O'BRIEN, Tim. *Nuclear Age.* 1985. Knopf. 1st ed. F/F. M19. $25.00

O'BRIEN, Tim. *Things They Carried.* 1990. Houghton Mifflin. 1st ed. F/F. M19. $35.00

O'BRIEN. *Herbert Hoover: A Bibliography.* 1993. np. 2643 annotated entries. 401p. F. A4. $75.00

O'CALLAGHAN, E.B. *Lists of Inhabitants of Colonial New York.* 1979. Baltimore. G. V4. $25.00

O'CONNELL, Carol. *Mallory's Oracle.* 1994. Putnam. AP/1st Am ed. author's 1st book. F/wrp. T2. $40.00

O'CONNELL, Carol. *Mallory's Oracle.* 1994. Putnam. UP. RS. F/wrp. M23. $40.00

O'CONNELL, Jack. *Box Nine.* 1992. Mysterious. 1st ed. author's 1st novel. AN/dj. M22. $40.00

O'CONNELL, Jack. *Wireless.* 1993. Mysterious. 1st ed. F/F. P3. $20.00

O'CONNOR, Betty. *Better Homes & Gardens Story Book.* 1950. Meredeth. 4to. VG. B17. $20.00

O'CONNOR, Flannery. *Complete Stories.* 1971. FSG. 1st ed. VG/NF clip. B4. $45.00

O'CONNOR, Flannery. *Habit of Being: Letters of Flannery O'Connor.* 1979. FSG. UP. intro Sally Fitzgerald. F/wrp. B4. $200.00

O'CONNOR, Flannery. *Memoir of Mary Ann.* 1961. FSG. 1st ed. VG/VG. S13. $85.00

O'CONNOR, Flannery. *Running in the Family.* 1982. FSG. 1st ed. NF/VG+. S13. $30.00

O'CONNOR, Jack. *Arms & Ammunition Annual 1952.* 1952. Outdoor Life. sc. G+. P12. $10.00

O'CONNOR, Jack. *Art of Hunting Big Game in North America.* 1967. Outdoor Life. ils. VG. P12. $15.00

O'CONNOR, Jack. *Hunting Rifle.* 1970. Winchester. 1st ed. 314p. cloth. VG+/dj. M20. $25.00

O'CONNOR, John. *Adobe Book.* 1973. Santa Fe. 1st ed. 130p. VG/VG. B5. $45.00

O'CONNOR, R. *Hell's Kitchen.* 1958. NY. 1st ed. VG/VG. B5. $20.00

O'CONNOR, Robert. *Buffalo Soldiers.* 1993. Knopf. 1st ed. author's 1st novel. F/F. B4/H11. $50.00

O'CROULEY. *Description of the Kingdom of New Spain.* 1972. John Howell Books. F/F. D2. $85.00

O'DELL, Scott. *Hawk That Dare Not Hunt.* 1975. Houghton Mifflin. 1st ed. F/F. B17. $20.00

O'DELL, Scott. *Island of the Blue Dolphins.* 1960. Houghton Mifflin. 23rd. VG/VG. B17. $6.50

O'DELL, Scott. *Treasure of Topo-El-Bampo.* 1972. Houghton Mifflin. 8vo. 48p. VG. C14. $6.00

O'DONNELL, Barrett; see Malzberg, Barry.

O'DONNELL, E.P. *Great Big Doorstop.* 1941. Houghton Mifflin. 1st ed. F/NF. B4. $250.00

O'DONNELL, Elliott. *Casebook of Ghosts.* 1969. Taplinger. 1st ed. NF/NF. P3. $20.00

O'DONNELL, K.M.; see Malzberg, Barry.

O'DONNELL, Lillian. *Aftershock.* 1977. Detective BC. VG. P3. $8.00

O'DONNELL, Lillian. *Casual Affairs.* 1985. Putnam. 1st ed. F/F. P3. $17.00

O'DONNELL, Lillian. *Falling Star.* 1979. Putnam. 1st ed. F/F. P3. $20.00

O'DONNELL, Lillian. *Good Night to Kill.* 1989. Putnam. 1st ed. F/F. P3. $18.00

O'DONNELL, Lillian. *Ladykiller.* 1984. Putnam. 1st ed. VG/VG. P3. $18.00

O'DONNELL, Lillian. *Wicked Designs.* 1980. Putnam. 1st ed. VG/VG. P3. $13.00

O'DONNELL, Peter. *Dead Man's Handle.* 1985. London. Souvenir. 1st ed. sgn. F/F. T2. $55.00

O'DONNELL, Peter. *Death of a Jester.* 1987. London. Titan. 1st ed. F/wrp. T2. $15.00

O'DONNELL, Peter. *Dragon's Claw.* 1985. Mysterious. 1st Am ed. 1/250. sgn. F/sans/case. T2. $65.00

O'DONNELL, Peter. *I, Lucifer.* 1975. Pan. 3rd. VG. P3. $5.00

O'DONNELL, Peter. *Iron God.* 1989. London. Titan. 1st ed. F/wrp. T2. $15.00

O'DONNELL, Peter. *Last Day in Limbo.* 1984. Mysterious. 1st Am ed. 1/250. sgn. F/F/case. T2. $35.00

O'DONNELL, Peter. *Modesty Blaise.* 1965. Souvenir. 1st ed. NF/NF. P3. $30.00

O'DONNELL, Peter. *Night of Morningstar.* 1987. Mysterious. 1st Am ed. 1/250. sgn. F/sans/case. T2. $35.00

O'DONNELL, Peter. *Puppet Master.* 1987. London. Titan. 1st ed. ils Romero. F/pict wrp. T2. $15.00

O'DONNELL, Peter. *Silver Mistress.* 1981. Cambridge. Archival. 1st Am ed. F/F. T2. $20.00

O'DONNELL, Peter. *Silver Mistress.* 1984. Mysterious. ltd ed. 1/250. sgn. F/sans/case. T2. $35.00

O'DONNELL, Peter. *Warlords of Phoenix.* 1987. London. Titan. 1st ed. F/pict wrp. T2. $15.00

O'DONNELL, Peter. *Xanadu Talisman.* 1984. Mysterious. 1st Am ed. 1/250. sgn/#d. F/sans/case. T2. $35.00

O'DONOGHUE & SPRINGER. *Adventures of Phoebe Zeit-Geist.* 1968. Grove. 1st ed. 150p. bl cloth. AN/dj. B22. $12.00

O'DONOVAN, Edmond. *Mern Oasis: Travels & Adventures East of Caspian...* 1883. NY. 2 vol. maps. VG. B5. $250.00

O'FAOLAIN, Sean. *Talking Trees & Other Stories.* 1970. Boston. 1st ed. F/F. A17. $20.00

O'FARRELL, William. *Repeat Performance.* 1947. Triangle. VG/VG. P3. $15.00

O'FLAHERTY, Liam. *Fairy Goose & Two Other Stories.* 1927. Crosby Gaige. 1/1190. sgn. F/VG. C6. $75.00

O'GORMAN, Ned. *Harvesters Vase.* 1968. Harcourt Brace. 1st ed. assn copy. F/NF. V1. $20.00

O'GRADY, Timothy. *Motherland.* 1989. Holt. 1st Am ed. F/F. A20. $18.00

O'GRADY, Tom. *In the Room of the Just Born.* 1989. Dolphin Moon. sgn. 72p. VG. B10. $10.00

O'HANLON, Redmond. *Into the Heart of Borneo: Account of a Journey...* 1984. Salamander. 1st ed. F/F. C2. $150.00

O'HARA, Frank. *Homage to Frank O'Hara.* 1980. Creative Age. revised ed. photos. V1. $15.00

O'HARA, John. *Farmers Hotel.* 1951. Random. 1st ed. VG/VG. P3. $60.00

O'HARA, John. *Lockwood Concern.* 1965. NY. 1st ed. 1/300. sgn. F/case. C2. $150.00

O'HARA, John. *North Frederick.* 1955. Random. 1st ed. VG/VG. P3. $50.00

O'HARA, John. *Pipe Night.* 1946. Faber. 1st ed. F/F. M19. $85.00

O'HARA, John. *Sermons & Soda Water.* 1960. Random. 1st ed. 3 vol. F/NF case. B35. $25.00

O'HARA, Kenneth. *View to a Death.* 1958. Cassell. 1st ed. VG/VG. P3. $25.00

O'HARA, Kevin. *Exit & Curtain.* 1952. Hurst Blackett. 1st ed. xl. VG. P3. $10.00

O'HARA, Mary. *Flica's Friend: Autobiography of...* 1982. NY. ils. 284p. F/dj. A17. $10.00

O'HARA. *Making Watercolor Behave.* 1932. VG. D2. $15.00

O HENRY. *Four Million.* 1907. McClure. 3rd ed. VG. P3. $20.00

O'KANE, John. *Ship of Sulaiman.* 1972. Columbian. 1st Am ed. 250p. NF/dj. W1. $22.00

O'KEEFE, John A. *Tektites & Their Origin.* 1976. Amsterdam. Elsevier. ils/pl. 254p. VG/dj. K5. $75.00

O'LEARY, Patrick. *Door Number Three.* 1995. Tor. 2nd. F/F. P3. $24.00

O'MALLEY, Austin. *Ethics of Medical Homide & Mutilation.* 1922. NY. 285p. VG. A13. $75.00

O'MALLEY & SAUNDERS. *Leonardo da Vinci on the Human Body.* 1982. Greenwich/Crown. rpt of 1952 ed. 506p. cloth. dj. D2. $60.00

O'MARIE, Carol Anne. *Missing Madonna.* nd. BC. VG/VG. P3. $8.00

O'NAIR, Mairi. *Girl With the X-Ray Eyes.* 1935. Mills Boon. 1st ed. xl. VG. P3. $15.00

O'NAN, Stewart. *Snow Angels.* 1994. Doubleday. 1st ed. sgn. F/F. B4. $125.00

O'NEAL, Bill. *American Assn.* 1991. Eakin. 1spb. VG+. P8. $15.00

O'NEIL, Daniel J. *Contract Bridge Made Simple.* 1961. NY. revised. lg format. 187p. VG/wrp. S1. $5.00

O'NEIL, Dennis. *Private Files of the Shadow.* 1989. DC Comics. hc. VG/VG. P3. $25.00

O'NEIL, Dennis. *Shadow 1941: Hitler's Astrologer.* 1988. Marvel Graphic Novel. 1st ed. VG/VG. P3. $25.00

O'NEIL, Dennis. *Stacked Deck, the Greatest Joker Story.* 1990. Longmeadow. 1st ed. rpt of comics. aeg. leahter. F. P3. $60.00

O'NEIL, George. *That Bright Heat.* 1928. Boni Liveright. 1st ed. sgn. 12mo. G. B11. $8.00

O'NEILL, Brian. *Easter Week.* 1939. NY. Internat. 1st ed. NF/wrp. B2. $45.00

O'NEILL, Dennis J. *Whale of a Territory.* 1966. NY. 1st ed. 249p. VG/torn. B18. $15.00

O'NEILL, Eugene. *All God's Chillun Got Wings & Welded.* 1924. NY. 1st ed. NF. B4. $75.00

O'NEILL, Eugene. *Emperor Jones.* 1928. NY. 1/750. sgn. VG/worn box. B5. $200.00

O'NEILL, Eugene. *Gold: A Play in Four Acts.* 1920. Boni Liveright. 1st ed. inscr/dtd 1938. NF. B24. $750.00

O'NEILL, Eugene. *Hughie.* 1959. New Haven. Yale. 1st ed. F/F. B4. $200.00

O'NEILL, Eugene. *Iceman Cometh.* 1946. Random. 2nd. VG+/VG+. P10. $20.00

O'NEILL, Eugene. *Lazarus Laughed.* 1927. NY. VG/VG. C6. $60.00

O'NEILL, Eugene. *Marco Millions.* 1927. Boni Liveright. 1st ed. F/F. B4. $275.00

O'NEILL, Eugene. *Nine Plays.* ca 1931. NY. Nobel Prize ed. 867p. cloth. dj. A17. $15.00

O'NEILL, Eugene. *Strange Interlude.* 1928. Boni Liveright. 1st ed. NF/dj. B24. $150.00

O'NEILL, John. *Prodigal Genius.* 1944. NY. sgn. VG/VG. B5. $45.00

O'NEILL, William L. *Everyone Was Brave: Rise & Fall of Feminism in America.* 1969. Quadrangle. 1st ed. F/F. B35. $35.00

O'REILLY, Victor. *Games of the Hangman.* 1991. Grove Weidenfeld. 1st ed. F/F. H11. $35.00

O'REILLY, Victor. *Rules of the Hunt.* 1995. Putnam. 1st ed. F/F. H11. $25.00

O'SHAUGHNESSY, Edith. *Diplomat's Wife in Mexico.* 1917. NY. Harper. 8vo. 356p. VG. P4. $25.00

O'SHAUGHNESSY, Michael. *Monster Book of Monsters.* 1988. Bonanza. 1st ed. F/F. P3. $15.00

O'SHAUGHNESSY, Perri. *Motion to Suppress.* 1995. Delacorte. 1st ed. F/F. H11. $25.00

OAKLEY, Graham. *Church Mice at Bay.* 1979 (1978). Atheneum. 1st Am ed. ils. unp. tan cloth. NF/NF. T5. $45.00

OAKLEY, Imogen Brashear. *Awake, America! & Other Verse.* 1934. Macrea Smith. sgn. ils/sgn Thornton Oakley. 8vo. 74p. VG. B11. $40.00

OATES, Joyce Carol. *Angel of Light.* 1981. Dutton. 1st ed. F/F. P3. $25.00

OATES, Joyce Carol. *Anonymous Sins & Other Poems.* 1969. LSU. 1st ed. F/NF. A15. $40.00

OATES, Joyce Carol. *Assassins.* 1975. Vanguard. 1st ed. F/F. H11. $35.00

OATES, Joyce Carol. *Assignation.* 1988. Ecco. 1st ed. F/F. B4. $45.00

OATES, Joyce Carol. *Childworld.* 1976. Vanguard. 1st ed. inscr. F/F. B4. $125.00

OATES, Joyce Carol. *Edge of Impossibility.* 1972. Vanguard. 1st ed. sgn. F/VG clip. B4. $100.00

OATES, Joyce Carol. *Fabulous Beasts.* 1975. LSU. 1st ed. ils AG Smith. F/F. B4. $125.00

OATES, Joyce Carol. *Foxfire: Confessions of a Girl Gang.* 1993. NY. 2nd. 328p. F/F. A17. $9.50

OATES, Joyce Carol. *Garden of Earthly Delights.* 1967. Vanguard. 1st ed. sgn. NF/NF. B4. $150.00

OATES, Joyce Carol. *Goddess & Other Women.* 1974. Vanguard. 1st ed. VG/VG. P3. $30.00

OATES, Joyce Carol. *Hungry Ghosts.* 1974. Blk Sparrow. 1/350. sgn/#d. F/acetate dj. S9. $60.00

OATES, Joyce Carol. *I Lock My Door Upon Myself.* 1990. Ecco. 1st ed. sgn. F/F. B4. $85.00

OATES, Joyce Carol. *Martya: A Life.* 1986. Dutton. 1st ed. F/F. H11. $25.00

OATES, Joyce Carol. *On Boxing.* 1987. Dolphin/Doubleday. 1st trade ed. sgn. F/F. B4. $85.00

OATES, Joyce Carol. *Poisoned Kiss & Other Stories.* 1976. Gollancz. 1st ed. F/F. P3. $20.00

OATES, Joyce Carol. *Raven's Wing.* 1986. 1st ed. VG/VG. K2. $14.00

OATES, Joyce Carol. *Solstice.* 1985. Dutton. 1st ed. F/F. H11. $25.00

OATES, Joyce Carol. *Son of the Morning.* 1978. Vanguard. 1st ed. VG/VG. P3. $30.00

OATES, Joyce Carol. *Them.* 1969. Vanguard. 1st ed. NF/VG. M19. $35.00

OATES, Joyce Carol. *Wheel of Love.* 1967. Vanguard. ARC. sgn. F. w/photo & promo material. B4. $200.00

OATES, Joyce Carol. *Women Whose Lives Are Food.* 1978. VG/dj. K2. $35.00

OATES, Joyce Carol. *Wonderland.* 1971. Vanguard. ARC. inscr. RS. F/F. B4. $200.00

OATES, Joyce Carol. *Wonderland.* 1971. Vanguard. 1st ed. F/F. H11. $45.00

OATES, Stephen B. *Confederate Cavalry West of the River.* 1961. Austin, TX. 1st ed. 234p. cloth. NF/VG. M8. $165.00

OATES, William Calvin. *War Between the Union & the Confederacy...* 1974. Dayton, OH. Morningside Bookshop. rpt. 808p. NF. M8. $45.00

OBERG, Arthur. *Anna's Song.* 1980. WA U. 1st ed. F/F. V1. $10.00

ODELL & ROSING. *Future of Oil.* 1980. London/NY. Kogan Page/Nichols. 1st ed. ils. 265p. xl. VG/dj. W1. $30.00

ODETS, Clifford. *Clash by Night.* 1942. Random. 1st ed. inscr. NF. B4. $250.00

OEMLER, A. *Truck-Farming at the South.* 1883. NY. Orange Judd. 270p. VG. A10. $50.00

OFFUTT, Chris. *Same River Twice.* 1993. Simon Schuster. 1st ed. F/F. A20. $22.00

OGBURN, Charlton Jr. *Marauders.* 1959. NY. 1st ed. 307p. dj. A17. $10.00

OGDEN, Robert Morris. *Hearing. Illustrated With Diagrams.* 1924. London. Cape. 1st ed. russet buckram. G1. $35.00

OGILVIE, J.S. *Album Writer's Friend.* 1881. NY. 64p. decor cloth. G. B18. $15.00

OGRIZEK, Dore. *United States.* 1950. NY. ils. 518p. G. A17. $10.00

OJIKE, Mbonu. *My Africa.* 1946. John Day. 8vo. 350p. red cloth. VG/worn. P4. $20.00

OKRENT, Daniel and Lewine, Harris. *The Ultimate Baseball Book.* 1991. NY. Houghton Mifflin. 4to. 394 p. ils. NF/sc. R16. $28.00

OKSENBERG, Michel. *China's Developmental Experience.* 1973. Columbia. 1st ed. 8vo. 219p. VG/dj. W1. $20.00

OKUDA, Seiiti. *Japanese Industrial Arts.* 1941. Tokyo. Brd Tourist Industry. 12mo. 106p. VG/wrp. W1. $12.00

OLAFSON, Frederick A. *Society, Law & Morality.* 1961. Englewood Cliffs. M11. $25.00

OLCOTT, Anthony. *Murder at the Red October.* 1981. Chicago. 1st ed. NF/NF. H11. $20.00

OLCOTT, Frances Jenkins. *Adventures of Haroun er Raschid & Other Tales...* 1923. Henry Holt. 1st ed. 363p. red cloth. VG. M20. $75.00

OLDENBURG, Chloe Warner. *Leaps of Faith.* 1985. Pepper Pike, OH. 183p. G+/dj. B18. $15.00

OLDERMAN, Murray. *Nelson's 20th-Century Encyclopedia of Baseball.* 1963. Nelson. 1st ed. VG. P8. $15.00

OLDRIN, John. *Chipmunk Terrace.* 1958. Viking. sgn. 79p. VG+/dj. M20. $20.00

OLDRIN, John. *Eight Rings on His Tail.* 1956. Viking. 1st ed. sgn. 79p. VG+/dj. M20. $25.00

OLDRIN, John. *Round Meadow.* 1951. Viking. 1st ed. sgn. 80p. VG+/dj. M20. $25.00

OLDS, C. Burnell. *Trees & Shrubs of Claremont.* 1955. Claremont. VG. B26. $17.50

OLDS, Sharon. *Father.* 1992. Knopf. UP. sgn. F. V1. $35.00

OLEKSAK & OLEKSAK. *Beisbol.* 1991. Masters. 1st ed. F/VG+. P8. $65.00

OLIVER, Chad. *Shadows in the Sun.* 1985. Crown. 1st ed. F/F. P3. $13.00

OLIVER, Chad. *Shores of Another Sea.* 1984. Crown. F/F. P3. $15.00

OLIVER, Katherine Elspeth. *Claw.* 1914. Los Angeles. Out West Magazine. 1st ed. 384p. gilt red cloth. VG. T10. $45.00

OLIVER, Nola Nance. *This Too Is Natchez.* 1953. Hastings. photos. 72p. VG/fair. B10. $12.00

OLIVER, Paul. *Blues Fell This Morning: Meaning of the Blues.* 1960. Horizon. 1st ed. intro Richard Wright. F/VG+ clip. B4. $85.00

OLIVER, Paul. *Shelter in Africa.* 1971. Praeger. F/VG. D2. $65.00

OLIVIER, Charles P. *Comets.* 1930. Baltimore. Williams Wilkins. 1st ed. 8vo. 246p. G/dj. K5. $100.00

OLMSTEAD, A.T. *History of Palestine & Syria to the Macedonian Conquest.* 1931. Scribner. 1st ed. 664p. VG. W1. $85.00

OLMSTED, Lorena Ann. *Setup for Murder.* 1962. Avalon. 1st ed. xl. dj. P3. $5.00

OLNEY, Ross R. *Tales of Time & Space.* 1969. Whitman. VG. P3. $5.00

OLSEN, Elder. *Olson's Penny Arcade.* 1975. Chicago. 1st ed. assn copy. F/NF. V1. $10.00

OLSEN, Elder. *Plays & Poems 1948-1958.* 1958. Chicago. 1st ed. assn copy. F/NF. V1. $15.00

OLSEN. *Painting the Marine Scene in Watercolor.* 1967. VG/VG. D2. $10.00

OLSHAKER, Mark. *Einstein's Brain.* 1981. Evans. 1st ed. F/F. P3. $15.00

OLSON, Kenneth E. *Music & Musket: Bands & Bandsmen of the American Civil War.* 1981. Greenwood. 1st ed. 299p. VG/VG. B10. $25.00

OLSON, Lyla M. *Improvised Equipment in Home Care of the Sick.* Jan 1944. Phil. Saunders. 419 ils. 264p. VG. B14. $45.00

OLSON, Sigurd. *Lonely Land.* 1961. NY. 1st ed. VG/VG. B5. $25.00

OLSON, Toby. *Changing Appearance: Poems 1965-1970.* 1975. Membrane. NF/wrp. V1. $20.00

OLSON, Toby. *Dorit in Lesbos.* 1990. Simon Schuster. 1st ed. F/F. A20. $18.00

OLSON, Toby. *Vectors.* 1972. Ziggurat-Membrane/Albatross. F/wrp. V1. $15.00

OMAN, C. *History of Art of War in Middle Ages.* 1924. London. 2 vol. 2nd. VG+. A15. $125.00

OMMANNEY, F.D. *Isle of Cloves: A View of Zanzibar.* 1956. Phil/NY. Lippincott. 230p. VG/dj. P4. $25.00

OMURA, Bunji. *Last Genro: Prince Saionji, Man Who Westernized Japan.* 1938. Lippincott. 1st ed. VG. W1. $25.00

OMWAKE, John. *Conestoga Six-Horse Bell Teams of Eastern Pennsylvania.* 1930. Cincinnati. 4to. VG. O3. $195.00

ONDAATJE, Michael. *Cinnamon Peeler.* 1991. Knopf. 1st ed. F/F. M23. $20.00

ONDAATJE, Michael. *English Patent.* 1992. Knopf. 1st ed. rem mk. NF/F. M23. $25.00

ONDAATJE, Michael. *In the Skin of the Lion.* 1987. NY. 1st ed. sgn. F/F. C2. $50.00

OPIE & OPIE. *Tail Feathers From Mother Goose, Opie Rhyme Book.* 1988. Little Brn. 1st ed. ils. 125p. AN/VG. T5. $40.00

OPPENHEIM, E. Phillips. *Battle of Basinghall Street.* 1935. McClelland Stewart. 1st Canadian ed. VG/dj. P3. $30.00

OPPENHEIM, E. Phillips. *Berenice.* 1911. Little Brn. NF. P3. $25.00

OPPENHEIM, E. Phillips. *Curious Happenings to the Rookie Legatees.* 1940. Triangle. 2nd. VG/VG. P3. $20.00

OPPENHEIM, E. Phillips. *Devil's Paw.* 1936. Hodder Stoughton. 12th. VG/VG. P3. $20.00

OPPENHEIM, E. Phillips. *Dumb Gods Speak.* 1937. McClelland Stewart. 1st ed. VG/VG. P3. $30.00

OPPENHEIM, E. Phillips. *Envoy Extraordinary.* 1937. Little Brn. 1st ed. VG. P3. $20.00

OPPENHEIM, E. Phillips. *Evil Shepherd.* nd. Review of Reviews. VG. P3. $10.00

OPPENHEIM, E. Phillips. *Gabriel Samara, Peacemaker.* 1925. McClelland Stewart. 1st ed. VG. P3. $25.00

OPPENHEIM, E. Phillips. *General Besserley's Second Puzzle Box.* 1940. Little Brn. 1st ed. VG. P3. $30.00

OPPENHEIM, E. Phillips. *Golden Beast.* 1926. Little Brn. 1st ed. VG. P3. $20.00

OPPENHEIM, E. Phillips. *Great Impersonation.* 1938. Triangle. 2nd. VG/VG. P3. $15.00

OPPENHEIM, E. Phillips. *Man From Sing Sing.* 1944. Tower. 2nd. VG/VG. P3. $15.00

OPPENHEIM, E. Phillips. *Matorni's Vineyard.* 1928. Little Brn. G. P3. $12.00

OPPENHEIM, E. Phillips. *Ostrekoff Jewels.* 1932. McClelland Stewart. 1st ed. VG/VG. P3. $30.00

OPPENHEIM, E. Phillips. *Passionate Quest.* 1924. Little Brn. 1st ed. VG. P3. $18.00

OPPENHEIM, E. Phillips. *Pawns Count.* 1918. McClelland Goodchild. G. P3. $20.00

OPPENHEIM, E. Phillips. *Pulpit in the Grill Room.* 1939. Little Brn. 1st ed. VG. P3. $20.00

OPPENHEIM, E. Phillips. *Shy Plutocrat.* 1941. Little Brn. 1st ed. VG. P3. $25.00

OPPENHEIM, E. Phillips. *Spymaster.* 1938. Little Brn. 1st ed. VG. P3. $20.00

OPPENHEIM, E. Phillips. *Tempting of Tavernake.* 1912. Little Brn. 1st ed. VG. P3. $20.00

OPPENHEIM, E. Phillips. *Wrath to Come.* 1924. Little Brn. 2nd. 355p. G. B10. $12.00

OPPENHEIM, E. Phillips. *Wrath to Come.* 1924. McClelland Stewart. 1st ed. VG. P3. $25.00

OPPENHEIM, E. Phillips. *Zeppelin's Passenger.* 1918. McClelland Goodchild Stewart. 1st ed. G. P3. $20.00

OPPENHEIM, Janet. *Other World: Spiritism & Psychical Research in England...* 1985. Cambridge. 1st ed. 503p. VG/dj. A13. $45.00

OPPENHEIMER, Joel. *Names & Local Habitations.* 1988. Jargon Soc. 1st ed. F/F. V1. $20.00

OPPENHEIMER, Joel. *Poems 1962-68.* 1969. IN. 1st ed. VG/dj. A17. $9.50

OPPENHEIMER, Joel. *Wrong Season.* 1973. Bobbs Merrill. 1st ed. F/VG. P8. $40.00

ORCHARD, Vincent. *Derby Stakes: A Complete History 1900 to 1953.* (1954). London. 1st ed. ils. 325p. gilt bl cloth. F/G. H3. $80.00

ORCUTT, William Dana. *Book in Italy.* 1928. Harper. 1/750. 128p. T10. $100.00

ORCUTT, William Dana. *In Quest of the Perfect Book.* 1926. Little Brn. 1st ed. 1/365p. sgn. 316p. half vellum. F/split case. T10. $250.00

ORCUTT, William Dana. *Kingdom of Books.* 1927. Little Brn. 1st trade ed. 8vo. ils. gilt brn cloth. NF. T10. $45.00

ORCZY, Baroness. *Beau Brocade.* 1953. Hodder Stoughton. 36th. xl. dj. P3. $5.00

ORCZY, Baroness. *Bronze Eagle.* 1915. Doran. 1st ed. NF. P3. $30.00

ORCZY, Baroness. *Scarlet Pimpernel: Four Complete Novels.* 1950. Hodder Stoughton. 7th. G. P3. $20.00

ORDE, A.J. *Little Neighborhood Murder.* 1989. Doubleday. 1st ed. author's 1st book. F/F. H11. $25.00

ORGA & ORGA. *Ataturk.* 1962. London. Joseph. 1st ed. 304p. VG. W1. $28.00

ORGILL, Douglas. *Man in the Dark.* 1980. Ian Henry. hc. VG/VG. P3. $20.00

ORIOL, Laurence. *Murder to Make You Grow Up.* 1968. MacDonald. 1st ed. VG/VG. P3. $22.00

ORIOL, Laurence. *Short Circuit.* 1967. MacDonald. 1st ed. VG/VG. P3. $15.00

ORR, A. *In the Ice King's Palace.* 1986. Tor. hc. F/F. P3. $16.00

ORR, A. *World in Amber.* 1985. Bluejay. 1st ed. VG/VG. P3. $20.00

ORR, Bobby. *Bobby Orr: My Game.* 1974. Little Brn. 1st ed. VG/VG. P3. $20.00

ORR, Gregory. *We Must Make a Kingdom of It.* 1986. Wesleyan. 1st ed. F/VG+. V1. $10.00

ORR, H. Winnett. *On the Contributions of Hugh Owen Thomas, Sir Robert Jones.* 1949. Springfield. 1st ed. 253p. VG. A13. $60.00

ORR, James L. *Smithville Days.* 1922. Smithville, OH. 1st ed. 128p. G. B18. $45.00

ORSINI, Abe. *Life of the Blessed Virgin Mary...* 1861. NY. Virtue. 24 pl. 764p. aeg. emb gilt morocco. VG. W1. $65.00

ORTELIUS, Abraham. *Thesaurus Geographicus.* 1596. Antwerp. Ex Officina Plantiniana. folio. unp. K1. $1,000.00

ORTLOFF, Henry Stuart. *Garden Bluebook of Annuals & Biennials.* 1931. Doubleday. hc. VG. P3. $8.00

ORUI & TOBA. *Castles in Japan.* 1935. Tokyo. 12mo. 106p. xl. VG. W1. $12.00

ORVIS, Kenneth. *Night Without Darkness.* 1965. McClelland Stewart. VG. P3. $8.00

ORWELL, George. *Dickens, Dali & Others.* 1946. 1st ed. VG/G+. S13. $18.00

ORWELL, George. *Keep the Aspidistra Flying.* 1936. London. Gollancz. 1st ed. bl cloth. F/yel dj. B24. $1,850.00

ORWELL, George. *Shooting an Elephant.* 1950. Harcourt Brace. 1st Am ed. F/VG+. H4. $100.00

ORWELL, George. *Such, Such Were the Joys.* 1953. NY. Harcourt Brace. ARC/1st Am ed. RS. F/NF. H4. $75.00

ORWELL, George. *1984.* 1949. Harcourt. 1st Am ed. VG/VG. M22. $85.00

ORWELL, George. *1984.* 1949. Saunders. 1st Canadian ed. VG/VG. M19. $100.00

OSBORN. *Questioned Documents, Second Edition.* 1929. np. 1052p. NF. A4. $125.00

OSBORN, David. *Love & Treason.* 1982. NAL. 1st ed. VG/VG. P3. $15.00

OSBORNE, Denise. *Murder Offscreen.* 1994. Holt. 1st ed. F/F. M23. $25.00

OSBORNE, John. *Patriot for Me.* 1966. London. Faber. 1st ed. F/F. B4. $125.00

OSBORNE, John. *Time Present & the Hotel in Amsterdam.* 1968. London. Faber. 1st ed. F/F. B4. $125.00

OSBORNE, Lilly de Jongh. *Four Keys to El Salvador.* 1956. Funk Wagnall. 1st ed. 221p. dj. F3. $25.00

OSKISON, John. *Tecumseh & His Times.* 1938. NY. 1st ed. ils. 244p. VG/G. B5. $45.00

OSLER, Mirabel. *Gentle Plea for Chaos.* 1989. NY. 1st Am ed. ils. 176p. F/dj. B26. $20.00

OSLER, William. *Aphorisms.* 1950. Schuman. 1st ed. edit WB Bean. F/dj. A15. $30.00

OSLER, William. *Diagnosis of Abdominal Tumors.* 1900. London. 1st ed. NF. A9. $95.00

OSLER, William. *Principles & Practice of Medicine.* 1899. NY. 3rd. gr cloth. F. B14. $125.00

OSLER, William. *Principles & Practice of Medicine.* 1912. NY. 8th. 1225p. cracked inner hinge. A13. $75.00

OSLER, William. *Science & Immortality.* 1905. Boston. 1st ed. 12mo. 54p. VG. A13. $125.00

OSMOND, Andrew. *Saladin!* 1976. Doubleday. hc. VG/VG. P3. $10.00

OSSENDOWSKI, Ferdinand. *Beasts, Men & Gods.* 1923. Dutton. 2nd. 8vo. 325p. cloth. VG. W1. $16.00

OSSENDOWSKI, Ferdinand. *Slaves of the Sun.* 1928. Dutton. 1st ed. 5 maps. 489p. xl. VG. W1. $28.00

OSSWALD & REED. *Hundreds of Turkeys.* 1941. Heath. TB. NF. M5. $12.00

OSSWALD & REED. *Little Crow.* 1950. Heath. 8vo. ils. NF/wrp. M5. $12.00

OSTER, Jerry. *Club Dead.* 1988. Harper Row. 1st ed. F/F. P3. $16.00

OSTER, Jerry. *Internal Affairs.* 1990. Bantam. 1st ed. sgn. F/F. P3. $25.00

OSTER, Jerry. *Municipal Bonds.* 1981. Houghton Mifflin. 1st ed. VG/VG. P3. $20.00

OSTER, Jerry. *Nowhere Man.* 1987. Harper Row. 1st ed. F/F. P3. $18.00

OSTER, Jerry. *Rancho Maria.* 1986. Harper Row. 1st ed. F/F. P3. $15.00

OSTER, Jerry. *Saint Mike.* 1987. Harper Row. 1st ed. NF/NF. P3. $16.00

OSTER, Jerry. *Sweet Justice.* 1985. Harper Row. 1st ed. F/F. P3. $18.00

OSTER, Jerry. *Violet Love.* 1991. Bantam. 1st ed. NF/NF. P3. $20.00

OSTRANDER, Isabel. *Twenty-Six Clues.* 1919. WJ Watt. 277p. VG/dj. M20. $45.00

OSTRANDER, Shelia. *Psychic Discoveries Behind the Iron Curtain.* nd. Laffont. VG. P3. $15.00

OSTRIKER, Alicia. *Woman Under the Surface.* 1982. Princeton. 1st ed. sgn/Dtd. F/dj. V1. $35.00

OSTROW, Albert A. *Complete Card Player.* 1945. NY. 2nd. 771p. VG. S1. $5.00

OTIS, James. *Captain Tom the Privateersman.* 1899. Dana Estes. 1st ed. 163p. VG. M20. $17.50

OTIS, James. *Toby Tyler; or, Ten Weeks With the Circus.* 1923. Harper. hc. VG/VG. P3. $15.00

OTT, Gil. *Children.* 1981. Tamarisk. ltd ed. 1/250. VG+/wrp. V1. $10.00

OTTIN, Merry. *Land of Emperors & Sultans.* ca 1964. Crown. 1st ed. folio. ils. 300p. VG/torn. W1. $85.00

OTTO, Whitney. *How to Make an American Quilt.* 1991. Villard. 1st ed. author's 1st book. F/F. C2/M19. $50.00

OTTO, Whitney. *Now You See Her.* 1994. Villard. 1st ed. 8vo. F/dj. w/photo & promo material. S9. $40.00

OTTOS, Svend. *Giant Fish & Other Stories.* 1982. Larousse. trans Joan Tate. VG. B17. $6.50

OTTUM, Bob. *See the Kid Run.* 1978. Simon Schuster. 1st ed. F/F. P3. $15.00

OTWAY, Howard. *Evangelist.* 1954. Harper. 1st ed. F/VG. H11. $40.00

OUELLETTE, Pierre. *Deus Machine.* 1993. Villard. 1st ed. F/NF. G10. $10.00

OUIDA. *Nurnberg Stove.* 1916. Lippincott. 12mo. ils Maria L Kirk. VG. B17. $4.00

OURSLER, William. *Marijuana: The Facts — The Truth.* 1968. NY. Eriksson. 240p. F/dj. B14. $55.00

OURSLER, William. *Narcotics: America's Peril.* 1952. Doubleday. 1st ed. VG. P3. $25.00

OUTCAULT, R.F. *My Resolutions: Buster Brown.* 1906. NY. 1st ed. VG. A15. $50.00

OUTHWAITE. *Outrolling the Map: Story of Exploration.* 1935. np. ils Gordon Grant/56 maps. 351p. VG. A4. $25.00

OVENDEN. *Pre-Raphaelite Photography.* 1972. F/F. D2. $45.00

OVERHOLSER, Stephen. *Track of a Killer.* 1982. Walker. 1st ed. F/F. A18. $10.00

OVERHOLSER, Wayne D. *Best Western Stories of...* 1984. S IL U. 1st ed. edit Pronzini/Greenberg. M/M. A18. $20.00

OVERHOLSER, Wayne D. *Gun for Johnny Deere.* 1963. Macmillan. 1st ed. F/F. A18. $12.50

OVERHOLSER, Wayne D. *Trial of Billy Peale.* 1962. Macmillan. 1st ed. F/F. A18. $12.50

OVERTON, Grant. *American Nights Entertainment.* 1923. Appleton Doran. 1st ed. VG. P3. $35.00

OWEN, Iris M. *Conjuring Up Philip.* 1976. Harper Row. 1st ed. VG. P3. $15.00

OWEN, Mrs. Octavius Freire. *Heroines of History.* 1854. NY. Carlton. ils. 386p. VG. B14. $45.00

OWEN & RAMSAY. *Nuts & Their Uses/Story of Citrus Fruits.* 1928. Dansville, NY. ils. 128p. decor cloth. VG. B26. $20.00

OWEN & SRB. *General Genetics.* 1955. San Francisco. ils. 50p. B26. $17.50

OWENS, Bill. *Working (I Do It for the Money).* 1977. Simon Schuster. 1st ed. VG/wrp. S9. $50.00

OWENS, George. *Judas Pool.* 1994. Putnam. 1st ed. F/F. H11. $20.00

OXENHAM, John. *Carette of Sark.* nd. Hodder Stoughton. VG/G+. P3. $8.00

OZ, Amos. *In the Land of Israel.* 1983. HBJ. 1st ed. F/F. B35. $20.00

OZ, Amos. *Touch the Water, Touch the Wind.* 1973. HBJ. 1st ed. F/F. B35. $20.00

OZICK, Cynthia. *Shawl.* 1989. Knopf. 1st ed. F/NF. B4. $35.00

To attract a collector, a book must appeal to his eye, his mind, or his imagination.

Graham Pollard
1903 – 1976

– P –

PACE, A. *Luigi Castiglioni's Viaggio.* 1983. Syracuse. trans A Pace/edit Joseph Ewan. F/dj. B26. $38.00

PACE, Mildred Mastin. *Old Bones the Wonder Horse.* 1955. Whittlesey. 3rd. 8vo. F/VG. M5. $12.00

PACK, Graham. *Two Kinds of Time.* 1950. Houghton Mifflin. 8vo. ils. 725p. VG/dj. W1. $18.00

PACK, Robert. *Clayfield Rejoyces, Clayfield Laments.* 1987. Godine. 1st ed. F/NF. V1. $10.00

PACK, Robert. *Nothing But Light.* 1972. Rutgers. 1st ed. sgn. F/VG+. V1. $20.00

PACKARD, Frank L. *Broken Waters.* 1925. Copp Clarke. VG. P3. $20.00

PACKARD, Frank L. *Doors of Night.* 1922. Copp Clarke. VG. P3. $25.00

PACKARD, Frank L. *Jimmie Dale & the Blue Envelope.* 1930. Copp Clarke. VG. P3. $20.00

PACKARD, Frank L. *Pawned.* 1921. Copp Clark. 1st Canadian ed. VG. P3. $20.00

PACKARD, Frank L. *Tiger Claws.* 1928. Copp Clarke. 1st ed. VG. P3. $25.00

PADDOCK, Paul. *China Diary: Crisis Diplomacy in Dairen.* 1977. IA State. 8vo. 274p. VG. W1. $18.00

PADEN, Irene. *Wake of the Prairie Schooner.* 1943. Macmillan. 1st ed. 8vo. red cloth. F/NF. T10. $65.00

PADEN, Irene. *Wake of the Prairie Schooner.* 1943. NY. Macmillan. sgn. 8vo. 514p. VG. B11. $40.00

PADEV, Micheal. *Escape From the Balkins.* 1943. NY. Bobs & Merill. 1st. G+/G. R16. $25.00

PADFIELD, P. *Titanic & the Californian.* 1966. NY. 1st ed. VG/VG. B5. $35.00

PADGETT, Abigail. *Child of Silence.* 1993. Mysterious. 1st ed. author's 1st novel. F/F. T2. $75.00

PADGETT, Abigail. *Strawgirl.* 1994. Mysterious. 1st ed. author's 2nd novel. sgn. F/F. T2. $40.00

PADGETT, Lewis. *Mutant.* 1953. Gnome. 1st ed. VG/VG. P3. $100.00

PADGETT, Lewis. *Tomorrow & Tomorrow/Fairy Chessmen.* 1951. Gnome. 1st ed. VG/VG. P3. $85.00

PADGETT, Ron. *Great Balls of Fire.* nd. HRW. 1st ed. F/VG+. V1. $20.00

PADOVER, Saul. *Letters of Karl Marx.* 1979. Englewood Cliffs. 1st ed. 576p. F/F. A17. $15.00

PAGE, Charles N. *Feathered Pets: A Treatise on Food, Breeding & Care...* 1898. Des Moines. self pub. 142p. A17. $25.00

PAGE, Charlotte A. *Under Sail & in Port.* 1950. Peabody Mus. 8 pl. 88p. VG. T7. $70.00

PAGE, Elizabeth. *Tree of Liberty.* 1939. Farrar Rinehart. 1st ed. 985p. G+. B10. $50.00

PAGE, Gertrude Cook. *Illusion & Other Poems.* 1940. Dietz. inscr. 83p. VG. B10. $7.50

PAGE, Irvine. *Speaking to Doctor: His Responsibilities & Opportunities.* 1972. Minneapolis. 1st ed. 320p. VG. A13. $20.00

PAGE, Jesse. *Land of the Peaks & the Pampas.* 1913. London. 1st ed. ils/pl. 368p. VG. H3. $50.00

PAGE, Russell. *Education of a Gardner.* 1983 (1962). London. ils. 381p. VG/dj. B26. $25.00

PAGE, Thomas Nelson. *In Ole Virginia; or, Marse Chan & Other Stories.* 1888 (1887). Scribner. inscr. 230p. VG/case. B10. $200.00

PAGE, Thomas Nelson. *John Marvel Assistant.* 1909. Scribner. 1st ed. 573p. VG. B10. $25.00

PAGE, Thomas Nelson. *Old Gentleman of the Black Stock.* 1901. Scribner. ils HC Christy. teg. G+. B10. $25.00

PAGE, Thomas Nelson. *Red Rock: Chronicle of Reconstruction.* 1898. NY. 1st ed. 584p. gilt cloth. VG-. A17. $17.50

PAGE, Thomas Nelson. *Robert E Lee the Southerner.* 1908. Scribner. 1st ed. sgn. 12mo. 312p. xl. VG. B11. $100.00

PAGE, Thomas Nelson. *Two Little Confederates.* 1932. Scribner. 1st ed. ils JW Thomason. 189p. NF. D1. $85.00

PAGE, Thomas Nelson. *Washington & Its Romance.* 1923. NY gr cloth. xl. VG. B30. $15.00

PAGE, Thomas. *Hephaestus Plague.* 1973. Putnam. 1st ed. xl. dj. P3. $5.00

PAGE, Thomas. *Spirit.* 1977. Rawson. 1st ed. NF/NF. P3. $20.00

PAHIR, C. *Atlantic Salmon Fishing.* 1937. NY. Derrydale. 1/950. fair. B5. $200.00

PAIGE, Richard; see Koontz, Dean R.

PAIN, Barry. *Stories & Interludes.* 1892. Harper. G. P3. $100.00

PAINE, Albert Bigelow. *Hollow Tree Snowed-In Book.* 1924 (1910). ils Conde. VG. S13. $15.00

PAINE, Albert Bigelow. *Tent Dwellers.* 1921. Harper. B-V ed. 279p. VG/dj. M20. $32.00

PAINE, Swift. *Eilly Orrum, Queen of the Comstock.* 1929. Bobbs Merrill. 8vo. photos. 309p. G. T10. $45.00

PAINE, Swift. *Eilly Orrum, Queen of the Comstock.* 1949. Palo Alto. Pacific Books. later ed. 8vo. 309p. red cloth. VG. T10. $35.00

PAINE, Thomas. *Common Sense.* 1928. NY. Rimington Hooper. 1/376. 130p. gilt blk cloth. case. K1. $45.00

PAINE, Thomas. *Complete Writings of...* 1945. NY. 2 vol. 1st ed. 8vo. gilt blk cloth. VG/rpr case. H3. $50.00

PAINTER, A. *Coyote in the Garden.* 1988. Confluence. 1st ed. F/NF. V1. $10.00

PAINTER, F.V.N. *Poets of the South: A Series of Biographical...* 1903. Am Book Co. 237p. G. B10. $25.00

PAINTER, F.V.N. *Poets of Virginia.* 1907. BF Johnson. 336p. NF. B10. $35.00

PALAZZO, Tony. *Bianco & the New World.* 1957. Viking. 1st ed. 64p. VG+/VG+. P2. $30.00

PALAZZO, Tony. *Mister Whistler's Secret.* 1953. Viking. 1st ed. 8vo. 52p. G+. C14. $7.00

PALEY, Grace. *Enormous Changes at the Last Minute.* 1974. FSG. 1st ed. F/F. B4. $85.00

PALEY, Grace. *Little Disturbances of Man.* 1959. Doubleday. 1st ed. sgn. F/NF. B4. $350.00

PALLEN, R. *Birds of Caribbean.* 1961. NY. 1st ed. 98 pl. VG/VG. B5. $45.00

PALLEY, Reese. *Porcelain Art of Edward Marshall Boehm.* 1976. Abrams. sgn. obl 4to. 89 mc pl. 312p. F/VG. B11. $55.00

PALLIS, Marco. *Peaks & Lamas.* 1949. Knopf. revised. 64 pl/4 maps. VG. W1. $45.00

PALLISTER, Charles. *Sensationalist.* 1991. Ballantine. 1st ed. author's 1st book. F/F. H11. $30.00

PALLOTTINO, Massimo. *Etruscan Painting.* 1952. Geneva. Skira. 1st ed. 64 tipped-in pl. 139p. VG/torn. W1. $45.00

PALMER, Albert W. *Orientals in American Life.* 1934. NY. Friendship. 12mo. 212p. VG. W1. $10.00

PALMER, Beverly W. *Selected Letters of Charles Sumner.* 1990. Boston. 2 vol. F/dj. A17. $45.00

PALMER, Edwin Henry. *Song of the Reed & Other Pieces.* 1877. London. Truebner. 1st ed. 8vo. 200p. teg. morocco. F. W1. $85.00

PALMER, Eve. *Field Guide to Trees of Southern Africa.* 1983 (1977). London. 2nd. 32 pl/700 drawings, 383p. VG. B26. $30.00

PALMER, Frederick. *Bliss, Peacemaker: Life & Letters of General Tasker H Bliss.* 1934. NY. 1st ed. ils. 476p. xl. G. B18. $25.00

PALMER, Frederick. *So a Leader Came.* 1932. Long Smith. 1st ed. VG. P3. $40.00

PALMER, Joe. *This Was Racing.* 1953. NY. 1st ed. ils. 270p. brn/orange cloth. F/VG. H3. $30.00

PALMER, Joel. *Journal of Travels Over the Rocky Mountains.* 1983. Ye Galleon. 1st ed thus. M/sans. A18. $17.50

PALMER, Robin. *Mickey Never Fails.* (1939). Boston. DC Heath. 1st ed. 8vo. ils Walt Disney Studios. 102p. G+. C14. $20.00

PALMER, Robin. *Wings of the Morning: Verses From the Bible.* 1968. NY. Walck. 1st ed. 8vo. unp. VG+/dj. C14. $7.00

PALMER, Thomas. *Dream Science.* 1990. Ticknor. 1st ed. author's 2nd book. F/F. H11. $25.00

PALMER, William J. *Detective & Mr Dickens.* nd. Quality BC. F/F. P3. $10.00

PALMER, William J. *Highwayman & Mr Dickens.* 1992. St Martin. 1st ed. NF/NF. P3. $19.00

PALMER & PIERCE. *Cambios: Spirit of Transformation in Spanish Colonial Art.* 1992. NM U. 1st ed. 4to. 148p. AN/dj. T10. $50.00

PALMER & WILLIAMS. *Dictionary of National Biography 1951-1960.* 1971. 1176p. xl. VG. A4. $85.00

PALMQUIST, Peter E. *With Nature's Children: Emma B Freemen.* 1976. Interface CA Corp. 8vo. unp. F/wrp. T10. $40.00

PANATI, Charles. *Links.* 1978. Houghton Mifflin. 1st ed. VG/G. P3. $10.00

PANCAKE, John S. *Destructive War: British Campaign in the Carolinas 1780-82.* 1985. AL U. 1st ed. ils/map ep. 293p. VG/dj. B18. $17.50

PANERO, Jose L. *Systematics of Pappobolus.* 1992. Ann Arbor. ils. 195p. VG/wrp. B26. $25.00

PANG, Eul-Soo. *In Pursuit of Honor & Power.* 1988. Tuscaloosa. 1st ed. 341p. dj. F3. $20.00

PANGBORN, Edgar. *Davy.* 1964. St Martin. 1st ed. VG/VG. P3. $60.00

PANGBORN, Edgar. *Good Neighbors & Other Strangers.* 1972. Macmillan. 1st ed. NF/NF. P3. $25.00

PANGBORN, Edgar. *Trial of Callista Blake.* 1961. St Martin. 1st ed. VG/G+. P3. $40.00

PANGBORN, Edgar. *West of the Sun.* 1953. Doubleday. 1st ed. VG/VG. P3. $35.00

PANOFSKY, Erwin. *Life & Art of Albrecht Durer.* 1955. ils. VG/VG. S13. $18.00

PANSHIN, Alexei. *Farewell to Yesterday's Tomorrow.* 1975. Berkeley Putnam. 1st ed. VG/VG. P3. $18.00

PANSHIN, Alexei. *World Beyond the Hill.* 1989. Tarcher. F/F. P3. $60.00

PANTZER, Eugene E. *Antun Gustav Matos.* 1981. Twayne. 1st ed. 144p. xl. VG. A17. $7.50

PANUM, Peter. *Observations Made During the Epidemic on Measles...1846.* 1940. NY. 1st Eng trans. 111p. VG. A13. $60.00

PAPAIOANNOU, Kostas. *Byzantine & Russian Painting.* 1973. Funk Wagnall. 8vo. 207p. F/dj. T10. $45.00

PAPAZOGLOU, Orania. *Sanctity.* 1986. Crown. 1st ed. F/dj. N4. $30.00

PAPE, Max. *Art of Driving.* 1982. London. Allen. 1st ed. VG/VG. O3. $45.00

PAPER, Gordon. *Chain Reaction.* 1978. Viking. 1st ed. hc. F/F. P3. $15.00

PARACELSUS. *Selected Writings, Editied With Intro by Jolande Jacobi.* 1951. NY. 1st Eng trans. 347p. VG. A13. $100.00

PARDEY & PARDEY. *Seraffyn's Mediterranean Adventure.* 1981. NY. Norton. ils/maps. 256p. dj. T7. $22.00

PARDIES, Ignace Gaston. *Dell'anima Delle Bestie, e sue Funzioni.* 1694. Venezia. Per Andrea Poletti. sm 8vo. 187p. G1. $185.00

PARDOE, Julia. *Romance of the Harem.* 1839. Phil. 2 vol. 1st Am ed. VG. C6. $120.00

PARDON & WILKS. *How to Play Solo Whist: Its Methods & Principles...* 1893. London. New ed. VG. S1. $20.00

PARETSKY, Sara. *Bitter Medicine.* 1987. NY. 1st ed. F/F. C2. $40.00

PARETSKY, Sara. *Blood Shot.* 1988. Delacorte. 1st ed. NF/NF. M22. $25.00

PARETSKY, Sara. *Blood Shot.* 1988. Delacorte. 1st ed. sgn. F/F. T2. $45.00

PARETSKY, Sara. *Burn Marks.* 1990. Delacorte. 1st ed. F/F. H11/N4. $30.00

PARETSKY, Sara. *Deadlock.* 1984. Dial. 1st ed. NF/NF. P3. $250.00

PARETSKY, Sara. *Guardian Angel.* nd. Delacorte. 5th. VG/VG. P3. $15.00

PARETSKY, Sara. *Killing Orders.* 1985. Morrow. 1st ed. sgn. F/F. C2. $175.00

PARETSKY, Sara. *Tunnel Vision.* 1994. Delacorte. 1st ed. sgn. F/F. T2. $35.00

PARGETER, Edith Mary. *Confession of Brother Haluin.* 1988. Stoddart. 1st ed. VG/VG. P3. $35.00

PARGETER, Edith Mary. *Dead Man's Ransom.* 1984. Morrow. 1st ed. NF/NF. H11. $30.00

PARGETER, Edith Mary. *Devil's Novice.* 1984. Morrow. 1st Am ed. F/F. B4. $100.00

PARGETER, Edith Mary. *Fallen Into the Pit.* 1990. MacDonald. VG/VG. P3. $30.00

PARGETER, Edith Mary. *Heretic's Apprentice.* 1989. Stoddart. 1st ed. VG/VG. P3. $30.00

PARGETER, Edith Mary. *Hermit of Eyton Forest.* 1987. Stoddart. 1st ed. hc. F/F. P3. $35.00

PARGETER, Edith Mary. *Holy Thief.* nd. Mysterious. 3rd. sgn. VG/VG. P3. $25.00

PARGETER, Edith Mary. *Leper of St Giles.* 1982. Morrow. 1st Am ed. F/F. B4. $100.00

PARGETER, Edith Mary. *Monk's Hood.* 1981. Morrow. 1st Am ed. F/F. B4. $125.00

PARGETER, Edith Mary. *Potter's Field.* 1989. Stoddart. 1st ed. VG/VG. P3. $30.00

PARGETER, Edith Mary. *Sanctuary Sparrow.* 1983. Morrow. 1st ed. VG/VG. P3. $30.00

PARIS, John. *Kimono.* 1921. London. Collins. 1st ed. 12mo. 345p. G. W1. $10.00

PARIS, W. Francklyn. *Napoleon's Legion.* 1928. Funk Wagnall. popular ed. sgn. 8vo. 240p. gr cloth. VG. B11. $75.00

PARISH, Edmund. *Hallucinations & Illusions: Study of Fallacies...* 1897. London. Walter Scott. 12mo. 390p. VG. G1. $75.00

PARISH, Elijah. *Sacred Geography; or, Gazetteer of the Bible...* 1813. Boston. Armstrong. 1st ed. 8vo. unp. contemporary calf. VG. W1. $125.00

PARISH, H.J. *Victory With Vaccines: Story of Immunization.* 1968. Edinburgh. 1st ed. 245p. dj. A13. $50.00

PARISH, James Robert. *Hollywood Character Actors.* 1978. Arlington. 1st ed. VG/VG. P3. $35.00

PARISH, James Robert. *Jeanette MacDonald Story.* 1976. NY. 1st ed. VG/VG. B5. $40.00

PARISH, James Robert. *Leading Ladies.* 1977. Arlington. 1st ed. VG/VG. P3. $35.00

PARK, Jordan; see Kornbluth, C.M.

PARK, No-Yong. *Oriental View of American Civilization.* 1945. Hale Cushman Flint. 12mo. inscr in Eng/Chinese. 128p. red cloth. T10. $50.00

PARK, Paul. *Coelestis.* 1993. Harper Collins. 1st ed. hc. F/F. P3. $30.00

PARK, Paul. *Sugar Rain.* 1989. Morrow. 1st ed. F/F. G10. $15.00

PARK, Ruth. *Witch's Thorn.* 1952. Houghton Mifflin. 1st ed. VG/VG. P3. $35.00

PARKER, Charles. *Paris Furniture Master Ebenistes.* 1956. Eng. Newport. 1st ed. 1/1000. ils. 104p. VG. B5. $75.00

PARKER, Constance-Anne. *Mr Stubbs, the Horse Painter.* 1971. London. JA Allen. 1st ed. ils. 203p. NF/dj. B14. $55.00

PARKER, Dorothy. *Enough Rope.* 1926. Boni Liveright. 1st ed. F/F. B4. $850.00

PARKER, Dorothy. *Viking Portable Library of Dorothy Parker.* 1944. Viking. 1st ed. intro WS Maugham. F/NF. B4. $55.00

PARKER, Helen F. *Arthur's Aquarium.* 1873. Boston. 152p. red cloth. gilt spine. G. B14. $35.00

PARKER, Herbert. *Courts & Lawyers of New England.* 1931. NY. Am Hist Soc. 4 vol. ils/photos. buckram. worn. M11. $250.00

PARKER, John. *Tidings Out of Brazil.* 1957. NM U. 1st ed. 1/1000. 48p. F3. $35.00

PARKER, Louis N. *Disraeli: A Play.* nd. Copp Clarke. VG. P3. $10.00

PARKER, Pat. *Movement in Black: Collected Poetry of Pat Parker 1961-1978.* 1978. Oakland. Diana. 1st ed. fwd Audre Lord. intro Judy Grahn. F/NF. B4. $85.00

PARKER, Robert B. *All Our Yesterdays.* 1994. Delacorte. ARC/1st ed. sgn. F/pict wrp. T2. $20.00

PARKER, Robert B. *All Our Yesterdays.* 1994. Delacorte. 1st ed. F/F. N4. $25.00

PARKER, Robert B. *Catskill Eagle.* 1985. Delacorte. 1st ed. sgn. rem mk. F/F. T2. $25.00

PARKER, Robert B. *Catskill Eagle.* 1985. Delacorte. 1st ed. VG/VG. P3. $18.00

PARKER, Robert B. *Crimson Joy.* 1988. Delacorte. 1st ed. VG/VG. P3. $20.00

PARKER, Robert B. *Double Deuce.* 1992. Putnam. 1st ed. NF/NF. N4. $25.00

PARKER, Robert B. *Early Autumn.* 1981. Delacorte. 1st ed. NF/dj. P3. $45.00

PARKER, Robert B. *Headquarters Budapest.* 1944. NY. index. 345p. VG/tape rpr. A17. $10.00

PARKER, Robert B. *Judas Goat.* 1978. Houghton Mifflin. 1st ed. F/F. T2. $75.00

PARKER, Robert B. *Judas Goat.* 1978. Houghton Mifflin. 1st ed. VG/VG. P3. $40.00

PARKER, Robert B. *Looking for Rachel Wallace.* 1980. Delacorte. 3rd. NF/NF. P3. $20.00

PARKER, Robert B. *Pale Kings & Princes.* 1987. Delacorte. 1st ed. F/F. P3. $16.00

PARKER, Robert B. *Pastime.* 1991. NY. Putnam. 1st ed. sgn. F/F. B11. $35.00

PARKER, Robert B. *Pastime.* 1991. Putnam. 1st ed. VG/VG. P3. $20.00

PARKER, Robert B. *Perchance to Dream.* 1991. Putnam. F/F. P3. $20.00

PARKER, Robert B. *Playmates.* 1989. Putnam. 1st ed. F/dj. M22. $20.00

PARKER, Robert B. *Playmates.* 1989. Putnam. 1st ed. sgn. VG/VG. B11. $35.00

PARKER, Robert B. *Playmates.* 1989. Putnam. 1st ed. VG/VG. P3. $18.00

PARKER, Robert B. *Poodle Springs.* 1989. Putnam. 1st ed. sgn. F/F. T2. $25.00

PARKER, Robert B. *Promised Land.* 1976. Houghton Mifflin. 1st ed. inscr. F/F. T2. $150.00

PARKER, Robert B. *Stardust.* 1990. Putnam. 1st ed. sgn. AN/dj. N4. $30.00

PARKER, Robert B. *Taming a Sea-Horse.* 1986. Dealcorte. 1st ed. NF/NF. P3. $16.00

PARKER, Robert B. *Valediction.* 1984. Delacorte/Lawrence. 1st ed. sgn. F/F. T2. $35.00

PARKER, Robert B. *Walking Shadow.* 1994. Putnam. 1st ed. RS. F/F. P3. $20.00

PARKER, Robert B. *Widening Gyre.* 1983. Delacorte. 1st ed. F/F. H11. $35.00

PARKER, Robert B. *Widening Gyre.* 1983. Delacorte/Lawrence. 1st ed. sgn. F/F. T2. $45.00

PARKER, Robert B. *Wilderness.* 1979. Delacorte/Lawrence. AP/1st ed. sgn. F/prt wrp. T2. $125.00

PARKER, Samuel. *Parker's Exploring Tour Beyond the Rocky Mountains.* 1967. Minneapolis. Ross Haines. facsimile. 1/2000. 380p. fld map. AN/dj. P4. $15.00

PARKER, T.J. *Laguna Heat.* 1985. NY. 1st ed. F/NF. H11. $35.00

PARKER, T.J. *Little Saigon.* 1988. St Martin. 1st ed. F/F. P3. $19.00

PARKER, T.J. *Little Saigon.* 1988. St Martin. 1st ed. VG+/VG+. A20. $15.00

PARKER, T.J. *Pacific Beat.* 1991. St Martin. 1st ed. F/F. A20. $12.00

PARKER, Watson. *Gold in the Black Hill.* 1966. Norman. 1st ed. sgn. 259p. VG/VG. B5. $35.00

PARKER & PARKER. *Year at the Races.* 1990. Viking. 1st ed. sgns. F/F. T2. $125.00

PARKER & SMITH. *Modern Turkey.* 1940. London. Routledge. 8vo. 18 pl/maps. 259p. cloth. VG. W1. $22.00

PARKES, Oscar. *British Battleships 1860-1950.* 1970-1973. London. Seeley. revised. 450 plans/photos. 701p. AN. T7. $120.00

PARKHURST. *Painter in Oil: A Complete Treatise...* 1898. VG. D2. $40.00

PARKINSON, C. Northcote. *Law & the Profits.* 1960. Houghton Mifflin. M11. $12.50

PARKINSON, Virginia. *Pointers for Little Persons Book Two: Safety...* 1943. NY. Schilling. ils. 28p. F/NF. A17. $17.50

PARKMAN, Francis. *Journals of Francis Parkman.* 1947. NY. 2 vol. 1st ed. edit M Wade. F/NF. A15. $60.00

PARKS, Gordon. *Gordon Parks: Whispers of Intimate Things.* 1971. Viking. 1st ed. photos. unp. VG+/VG. R11. $18.00

PARKS, Joseph Howard. *John Bell of Tennessee.* 1950. LSU. F/VG. B30. $20.00

PARKS. *Elizabethan Club of Yale University & Its Library.* 1986. Yale. 4to. 280p. F. A4. $85.00

PARLETT, David. *Solitaire: Aces Up & 399 Other Card Games.* 1979. NY. 367p. VG. S1. $5.00

PARNALL, Peter. *Dog's Book of Birds.* 1977. Scribner. 1st ed. 16mo. unp. F/G. C14. $8.00

PARNELL, Frank H. *Monthly Terrors: An Index to Weird Fantasy Magazines.* 1985. Greenwood. VG. P3. $100.00

PARR, Charles McKew. *So Noble a Captain: Life & Times of Ferdinand Magellan.* 1953. Crowell. 1st ed. inscr. 8vo. 15 pl/map ep. 423p. VG/G. B11. $65.00

PARRISH, Frank. *Bird in the Net.* 1988. Harper Row. 1st ed. VG/VG. P3. $16.00

PARRISH, Frank. *Death in the Rain.* 1984. Dodd Mead. 1st ed. lacks ffe. xl. VG/VG. N4. $10.00

PARRISH, Frank. *Fly in the Cobweb.* 1986. Harper Row. F/F. P3. $15.00

PARRISH, Maxfield. *Palgrenes Golden Treasury.* 1941. Garden City. VG/G. B5. $65.00

PARRISH, Randall. *Case & the Girl.* nd. AL Burt. hc. VG/VG. P3. $25.00

PARRISH, Randall. *Devil's Own.* nd. Donohue. VG/VG. P3. $18.00

PARRY, Judge. *Don Quixote.* 1924. NY. ils Walter Crane. VG. M17. $40.00

PARRY, Michel. *Savage Heroes.* 1980. Taplinger. 1st ed. F/F. P3. $22.00

PARSONS, Allen P. *Complete Book of Fresh-Water Fishing.* 1969. Outdoor Life/Harper Row. photos. VG/G+. P12. $20.00

PARSONS, Elsie Clew. *Isleta Paintings.* 1962. Smithsonian. 1st ed. 4to. 299p. VG/dj. T10. $250.00

PARSONS, Herbert Collins. *Puritan Outpost: History of Town & People of Northfield, MA.* 1937. NY. 1st ed. ils. 546p. VG. B18. $22.50

PARSONS, J. *Smith & Wesson Revolvers.* 1957. NY. 1st ed. VG/G. B5. $60.00

PARSONS, John Herbert. *Introduction to Study of Colour Vision.* 1924. Cambridge. 2nd. tall 8vo. 324p. VG/dj. G1. $60.00

PARTEE, Charles. *Adventure in Africa. Story of Don McClure.* 1990. Ministry. sgn. 8vo. F/F. B11. $12.00

PARTINGTON, J.R. *History of Greek Fire & Gunpowder.* (1960). Cambridge, Eng. ils. 381p. gilt red cloth. VG. H3. $150.00

PARTON, Dolly. *Coat of Many Colors.* 1994. Harper. 1st ed. AN/dj. H4. $15.00

PARTON, James. *Life & Times of Aaron Burr.* 1858. np. VG. M17. $50.00

PARTON, James. *Life of Horace Greeley.* 1869. Boston. 8vo. 598p. gr cloth. xl. T3. $15.00

PARTRIDGE, Norman. *Slippin' Into Darkness.* 1994. Baltimore. CD Pub. 1st ed. 1/500. sgn. ils/sgn AM Clark. F/F. T2. $65.00

PASCALIS, Felix. *Annual Oration, Delivered Before the Chemical Society...* 1802. Phil. 48p. modern wrp. B14. $175.00

PASTERNAK, Boris. *Safe Conduct.* 1959. Elek. 1st ed. VG/VG. M19. $35.00

PATCHEN, Kenneth. *Journal of Albion Moonlight.* 1944. United Book Guild. hc. NF. V1. $25.00

PATCHEN, Kenneth. *Journal of Albion Moonlight.* 1946. NY. sgn twice w/orig poem. VG/VG. B5. $100.00

PATCHEN, Kenneth. *Poemscapes.* 1958. Highlands, NC. Jonathan Williams. 1st ed. 1/42. sgn. F/wrp. B4. $850.00

PATCHEN, Kenneth. *Red Wine & Yellow Hair.* 1949. New Directions. 1st ed. assn copy. RS. F/VG. V1. $55.00

PATCHEN, Kenneth. *Selected Poems.* 1946. New Directions. 1st ed. RS. VG+/VG. V1. $100.00

PATCHETT, M.E. *Adam Troy, Astoman.* 1954. Lutterworth. G+/dj. P3. $15.00

PATCHETT, M.E. *Kidnappers of Space.* 1953. Lutterworth. 1st ed. G+/dj. P3. $15.00

PATCHIN, Frank Gee. *Pony Rider Boys With the Texas Rangers.* nd. Saalfield. VG/VG. P3. $15.00

PATER, Walter. *Greek Studies: A Series of Essays.* 1911. London. Macmillan. Lib ed. crown 8vo. gilt bl cloth. NF. T10. $25.00

PATER, Walter. *Marius the Epicurean.* 1898. NY. G. A17. $15.00

PATERSON, Antionette Mann. *Infinite Worlds of Giordano Bruno.* 1970. Springfield, IL. Charles Thomas. 1st ed. inscr. 8vo. VG/VG. B11. $25.00

PATON, Alan. *Case History of a Pinky.* (1965). Johannesburg. SA Inst Race Relations. NF/stapled wrp. B4. $125.00

PATRICK, Keats. *Death Is a Tory.* 1935. Bobbs Merrill. 1st ed. VG/VG. P3. $45.00

PATRICK, Richard North. *Degree of Guilt.* 1993. Knopf. 1st ed. F/F. H11. $30.00

PATRICK, Richard North. *Escape the Night.* 1983. Random. 1st ed. F/F. H11. $35.00

PATRICK, Vincent. *Family Business.* 1985. Poseidon. 1st ed. F/F. H11. $35.00

PATRICK, Vincent. *Pope of Greenwich Village.* 1979. Seaview. 1st ed. author's 1st book. NF/F. H11. $30.00

PATRICK, William. *Spirals.* 1983. Houghton Mifflin. 1st ed. RS. F/F. P3. $15.00

PATRICK & RANSOME. *Red Dancing Shoes.* 1993. Tambourine. 1st ed. sgn. AN/dj. B4. $45.00

PATROUCH, Joseph F. *SF of Isaac Asimov.* 1974. Doubleday. 1st ed. hc. VG/VG. P3. $22.00

PATTEN, Brian. *Sly Cormorant & the Fishes.* 1977. Middlesex, Eng. Cormorant. 1st ed. NF/VG. C8. $50.00

PATTEN, John. *Pre-Industrial England: Geographical Essays.* 1979. Folkstone. Kent Dawson. 1st ed. 8vo. 245p. F/F. T10. $35.00

PATTEN, Lewis B. *Gene Autry & the Ghost Riders.* 1955. Whitman. G. P3. $12.00

PATTEN, William. *Book of Sport.* 1901. NY. Taylor. ltd ed. 1/1500. folio. binding copy. O3. $185.00

PATTEN. *George Cruikshank: A Revaluation.* 1974. Princeton. ils. 302p. NF. A4. $85.00

PATTERSON, Harry. *Dillinger.* 1983. Hutchinson. 1st ed. F/F. P3. $20.00

PATTERSON, Innis. *Eppworth Case.* 1930. Farrar Rinehart. 1st ed. VG/VG. P3. $30.00

PATTERSON, James. *Along Came a Spider.* 1993. Little Brn. ARC. VG/prt wrp. M22. $25.00

PATTERSON, James. *Along Came a Spider.* 1993. Little Brn. 1st ed. NF/NF. P3. $22.00

PATTERSON, James. *Black Market.* 1986. Simon Schuster. 1st ed. NF/NF. P3. $20.00

PATTERSON, James. *Jericho Commandment.* 1979. Crown. 1st ed. author's 2nd novel. F/F. T2. $40.00

PATTERSON, James. *Midnight Club.* 1989. Little Brn. 1st ed. F/F. T2. $15.00

PATTERSON, Leonardo. *Magic of Middle American Culture Before 1492.* 1992. Austria. Bavariadruck. 1st ed. pl. wrp. F3. $65.00

PATTERSON, Richard North. *Degree of Guilt.* 1993. Knopf. 1st ed. sgn. F/F. T2. $35.00

PATTERSON, Richard North. *Escape the Night.* 1983. Random. 1st ed. VG/VG. P3. $25.00

PATTERSON, Richard North. *Eyes of a Child.* 1995. Knopf. 1st ed. NF/NF. P3. $24.00

PATTERSON, Richard North. *Outside Man.* 1981. Atlantic/Little Brn. 1st ed. NF/NF. H11. $45.00

PATTERSON, Richard North. *Private Screening.* 1985. Villard. 1st ed. F/F. H11. $45.00

PATTISON, Barrie. *Seal of Dracula.* nd. Bounty. F/F. P3. $15.00

PATTON, Frances Gray. *Good Morning, Miss Dove.* 1954. Dodd Mead. 1st ed. F/NF. B4. $175.00

PATTOU, Edith. *Hero's Song.* 1991. HBJ. 1st ed. F/F. P3. $17.00

PAUL, Aileen. *Kid's Gardening: A First Indoor Gardening Book for Children.* 1972. Doubleday. 1st ed. 8vo. ils. F/VG. M5. $12.00

PAUL, Barbara. *But He Was Already Dead When I Got There.* 1986. Scribner. 1st ed. F/F. P3. $14.00

PAUL, Barbara. *Cadenza for Caruso.* 1984. St Martin. 1st ed. VG/VG. P3. $20.00

PAUL, Barbara. *Chorus of Detectives.* 1987. St Martin. 1st ed. VG/VG. P3. $18.00

PAUL, Barbara. *Fare Play.* 1995. Scribner. 1st ed. F/F. P3. $20.00

PAUL, Elliot. *Black & the Red.* 1956. Random. 1st ed. 277p. VG/dj. M20. $27.00

PAUL, Elliot. *Desperate Scenery.* 1954. Random. 1st ed. F/clip VG. A18. $25.00

PAUL, Henry E. *Outer Space Photography for the Amateur.* 1976. NY. Amphoto. 4th. 152 photos. 155p. VG/dj. K5. $18.00

PAUL, Jim. *What's Called Love.* 1993. Villard. ARC. w/promo material. F/F. B35. $18.00

PAUL, Raymond. *Who Murdered Mary Rogers?* 1971. Prentice Hall. hc. VG. P3. $20.00

PAULEY, Bruce F. *Hitler & the Forgotten Nazis: A History...* 1981. NC U. biblio/index. 292p. VG/dj. A17. $20.00

PAULHAN, Frederic. *L'Activite Mentale et les Elements de l'Esprit.* 1889. Paris. Germer Bailliere. 8vo. 588p. later blk cloth. VG. G1. $75.00

PAULL, Mrs. George A. *Marjorie's Doings.* 1900. Jacobs. 12mo. gr cloth. VG. M5. $22.00

PAULSEN, Martha. *Toyland.* 1944. Saalfield. ils Julian Wehr. spbg. F/chip. T10. $175.00

PAVLOV, Ivan Petrovich. *Lectures on Conditioned Reflexes.* (1928). NY. Internat Pub. 1st Eng-language ed. 414p. blk cloth. VG. G1. $85.00

PAWIAK, Janina. *Historical Atlas of Poland.* 1981. Warsaw. Dept State Cartographical Pub. 54p of maps. F/dj. O7. $35.00

PAXSON, Diana L. *White Raven.* 1988. Morrow. 1st ed. VG/VG. P3. $10.00

PAXSON, Diana L. *Wolf & the Raven.* 1993. Morrow. 1st ed. NF/dj. M21. $15.00

PAXTON, Harry. *Whiz Kids.* 1950. McKay. 1st ed. F/VG+. P8. $250.00

PAYES, Rachel Cosgrove. *Forsythia Finds Murder.* 1960. Avalon. 1st ed. xl. dj. P3. $8.00

PAYNE, David. *Early From the Dance.* 1989. Doubleday. VG+/F. A20. $13.00

PAYNE, Laurence. *Malice in Camera.* 1983. Crime Club. 1st ed. F/F. P3. $15.00

PAYNE, Robert. *Forever China.* 1945. Dodd Mead. 2nd. 8vo. 573p. VG. W1. $18.00

PAYNE, Robert. *Holy Sword: Story of Islam From Muhammad to Present.* 1959. Harper. 1st ed. 16 pl/2 maps. 335p. VG/dj. W1. $20.00

PAYNE, Robert. *Mao Tse-Tung: Ruler of Red China.* 1950. NY. Schuman. 8vo. 4 pl. 303p. VG. W1. $18.00

PAYNE, Robert. *Portrait of a Revolutionary: Mao Tse-Tung.* 1961. Abelard-Schuman. 8vo. 311p. VG/dj. W1. $18.00

PAZ, Ireneo. *Life & Adventures of Celebrated Bandit Joaquin Murieta...* 1925. Chicago. Regan. 1st ed. 1/975. 174p. red ribbed cloth. NF. T10. $85.00

PEABODY, H.G. *Glimpse of the Grand Canyon.* 1900. KS City. worn. V4. $35.00

PEAGRAM, William Mead. *Past-Times.* 1909. Baltimore. Saumenig. 141p. G. B10. $12.00

PEAKE, Mervyn. *Gormenghast.* 1967. Weybright Talley. hc. VG. P3. $20.00

PEAKE, Mervyn. *Ride a Cock-Horse & Other Nursery Rhymes.* 1940. Chatto Windus. 1st ed. 4to. pict brd. NF/NF. D1. $650.00

PEAKE, Mervyn. *Titus Groan.* 1946. Reynal Hitchcock. 1st ed. NF/NF. P3. $250.00

PEARCE, Hamilton. *Story of the Kidnaping of Billy Whitla.* 1909. Cleveland. 204p. fair. B18. $32.50

PEARCE, Michael. *Manmur Zapt & the Camil of Destruction.* 1993. Collins Crime Club. 1st ed. NF/NF. P3. $25.00

PEARING, Blanche. *In the City by the Lake.* 1892. Chicago. 1st ed. 192p. G. A17. $15.00

PEARIS, Leonard M. *Insect Pests of Farm, Garden & Orchard.* 1941. NY. 4th. ils. 549p. VG. B26. $27.50

PEARL, Jack. *Dam of Death.* 1967. Whitman. TVTI. VG. P3. $8.00

PEARL, Jack. *Fear Formula.* 1968. Whitman. TVTI. F. P3. $13.00

PEARL, Jack. *Space Eagle: Operation Star Voyage.* 1970. Whitman. VG. P3. $10.00

PEARMAN, G.I. *Greenhouse.* 1988. Melbourne. 8vo. 752p. pict brd. F. B1. $35.00

PEARS, Tim. *In the Place of the Fallen Leaves.* 1995. Donald Fine. 1st ed. F/F. M23. $35.00

PEARSON, C. *Indomitable Goose.* 1960. Minneapolis. G/G. B5. $40.00

PEARSON, E. *Studies in Murder.* 1924. NY. 1st ed. VG/VG. B5. $37.50

PEARSON, E. *Trial of Lizzie Borden.* 1937. NY. 1st ed. VG/G. B5. $70.00

PEARSON, John. *Kindness of Dr Avicenna.* 1982. HRW. 1st ed. F/F. P3. $15.00

PEARSON, John. *Life of Ian Fleming.* 1966. McGraw Hill. 1st ed. VG/VG. P3. $30.00

PEARSON, Karl. *Grammar of Science.* 1900. London. 2nd. 548p. VG. A13. $50.00

PEARSON, Ridley. *Angel Maker.* 1993. Delacorte. 1st ed. F/F. M22. $15.00

PEARSON, Ridley. *Probable Cause.* 1990. St Martin. 1st ed. F/F. P3. $20.00

PEARSON, Ridley. *Probable Cause.* 1990. St Martin. 1st ed. sgn. NF/NF. B2. $35.00

PEARSON, Ridley. *Seizing of Yankee Green Mall.* 1987. NY. 1st ed. NF/F. H11. $35.00

PEARSON, Ridley. *Undercurrents.* 1988. St Martin. 1st ed. VG/VG. P3. $18.00

PEARSON, T.R. *Call & Response.* 1989. NY. Linden. 1st ed. sgn. F/F. B4. $45.00

PEARSON, Virginia. *Play a Tune With Betty & Billy.* nd. Boston Music Co. 21p. NF. C14. $20.00

PEARSON, William. *Chessplayer.* 1984. Viking. 1st ed. F/F. H11. $25.00

PEARSON, William. *Chessplayer.* 1984. Viking. 1st ed. hc. VG/VG. P3. $15.00

PEARSON, William. *Hunt the Man Down.* nd. BC. VG/VG. P3. $8.00

PEARSON, William. *Trial of Honor.* 1967. NAL. 1st ed. xl. dj. P3. $5.00

PEARTH, Dorothy L. *Ferns & Flowering Plants of Westmoreland Co, PA.* 1975. Pittsburgh. ils. 115p. sc. B26. $17.50

PEARY, Danny. *We Played the Game.* 1994. Hyperion. 1st ed. F/F. P8. $25.00

PEASE, Arthur S. *Flora of Northern NH.* 1964. Cambridge. New Eng Botanical Club. 2 maps. 278p. wrp. B26. $35.00

PEASE, Howard. *Tod Moran: Fog Horns.* 1937. Doubleday. later ed. 295p. VG/dj. M20. $12.50

PEASE, Josephine Van Dolzen. *This Is the World.* 1956. Chicago. rpt. ils. 72p. F/F. A17. $7.50

PEAT, Fern Bisel. *Mother Goose, Her Best-Known Rhymes.* 1933. Saalfield. 4to. VG+. C8. $75.00

PEAT, Fern Bisel. *Three Little Kittens.* 1937. Saalfield. 12 pl. VG/stiff wrp. M5. $40.00

PEAT, H.R. *Inexcusable Lie.* 1923. Donnelley. 1st ed? inscr. VG. A15. $15.00

PEATTIE, Donald C. *Audubon's America.* 1940. Boston. 1st ltd ed. sgn. 329p. teg. gilt cloth. VG/case. H3. $75.00

PEATTIE, Roderick. *Look to the Frontier: A Geography for Peace Table.* 1970. Kennikat. 246p. F. A17. $7.50

PECK, George. *Peck's Bad Boy & His Pa.* 1900. WB Conkey. 1st/only complete ed. ils Williams. G+. P12. $15.00

PECK, George. *Peck's Irish Friend.* 1900. WB Conkey. ils Williams. G+. P12. $15.00

PECK, Richard E. *Final Solution.* 1973. Doubleday. 1st ed. VG/VG. P3. $15.00

PEDERSEN & PIHL. *Early Physics & Astronomy.* 1974. NY. Am Elsevier. 1st ed. 8vo. 413p. VG/VG. K5. $40.00

PEDLER, Kit. *Brainrack.* 1974. Souvenir. 1st ed. F/F. P3. $25.00

PEDRAZAS, Allan. *Harry Chronicles.* 1995. St Martin. 1st ed. F/F. M23. $50.00

PEDRETTI, Carlo. *Codex Huygens & Leonardo da Vinci's Art Theory.* 1968. Kraus Rpt. ils. linen. D2. $65.00

PEDRETTI, Carlo. *Leonardo da Vinci Inedito. Tre Saggi.* 1968. Florence. Barbera. ils/pl. 97p dj. D2. $70.00

PEDRETTI, Carlo. *Leonardo: A Study in Chronology & Style.* 1973. Berkeley. sgn. 199 pl. 192p. dj. D2. $55.00

PEEL, Lynnette J. *Rural Industry in the Port Phillip Region 1835-1880.* 1974. Carlton. VG. O7. $20.00

PEET. *Who's the Author? A Guide to Authorship of Novels...* 1901. np. 321p. VG. A4. $35.00

PEET, Bill. *Bill Peet: An Autobiography.* nd. Houghton Mifflin. 2nd. 4to. 190p. xl. VG. C14. $12.00

PEFFER, Nathaniel. *Far East: A Modern History.* 1958. Ann Arbor. 8vo. 489p. VG. W1. $15.00

PEI, Meg. *Salaryman.* 1992. Viking. 1st ed. author's 1st book. F/F. H11. $30.00

PEISSEL, Michel. *Lost World of Quintana Roo.* 1963. Dutton. 1st ed. 306p. dj. F3. $20.00

PELHAM, D. *Human Body.* 1983. Viking. 1st ed. moveables. VG. P2. $40.00

PELL, Franklyn. *Hangman's Hill.* 1946. Dodd Mead. 1st ed. VG/VG. P3. $23.00

PELLAPRAT, Henri-Paul. *Modern French Culinary Art.* 1966. np. VG/VG. B30. $60.00

PELLEGRINO, Charles. *Her Name Titanic.* 1988. McGraw Hill. VG/VG. A16. $15.00

PELLEGRINO, Charles. *Unearthing Atlantis.* 1991. Random. 1st ed. VG. P3. $23.00

PELLER, Hugo. *Stork Shee Rose on Christmas Eve.* 1977. Attic Pr. 1/150. miniature. teg. sgn Peller bdg. F/double-clamshell box. B24. $950.00

PELLETIER, C. *Bubble Reputation.* 1993. NY. Crown. 1st ed. F/F clip. B4. $45.00

PELLETIER, C. *Marriage Made at Woodstock.* 1994. Crown. 1st ed. F/F. A20. $10.00

PELLICO, Silvio. *Le Mie Prigioni.* 1869. Milan. Edoardo Sonzogno Editore. ils Tony Johannot. VG. T10. $100.00

PELLOW, Thomas. *Adventures of Thomas Fellow...* 1890. Fisher Unwin/Macmillan. 1st ed. 10 pl. xl. VG. W1. $45.00

PENA, Amado. *Pena on Pena.* 1995. Waco, TX. WRS Pub. 1st ed. ils. AN/dj. T10. $30.00

PENDEXTER, Hugh. *Red Belts.* 1920. Doubleday Page. 1st ed thus. 246p. VG/fair. B10. $15.00

PENDLETON, Louis. *Corona of the Nantahalas: A Romance.* 1895. Merriam. 1st ed. 99p. G. B10. $35.00

PENDRAY, G. Edward. *Men, Mirrors & Stars.* 1935. Funk Wagnalls. 1st ed. 8vo. 339p. G/dj. K5. $28.00

PENFIELD, F.C. *East of Suez.* 1907. NY. Century. 8vo. ils/map. xl. VG. W1. $12.00

PENFIELD & ROBERTS. *Speech & Brain Mechanisms.* 1959. Princeton. ils. maroon cloth. VG/worn. G1. $65.00

PENFOLD. *Africa: Maps & Plans in the Public Record Office.* 1982. London. HMSO. 440p. F/NF. A4. $135.00

PENICK, I. *Empire Strikes Back: A Pop-Up Book.* 1980. Random. VG. P3. $15.00

PENLEY, Norman. *Miss Melbourn's Milton.* nd. Modern Pub. VG. P3. $25.00

PENN, John. *Deadly Sickness.* 1985. Scribner. 1st ed. F/F. P3. $15.00

PENN, John. *Outrageous Exposures.* 1988. Collins. 1st ed. VG/VG. P3. $20.00

PENNAK, R.W. *Fresh-Water Invertebrates of the United States.* 1953. Ronald Pr. 8vo. ils. 769p. cloth. xl. B1. $20.00

PENNELL, Francis W. *Scrophulariaceae of Eastern North America.* 1935. Phil. 155 distributional maps/ils. 650p. wrp. B26. $45.00

PENNELL, Joseph Stanley. *History of Rome Hanks & Kindred Matters.* 1944. Scribner. 1st ed. 363p. VG/G. B10. $10.00

PENNELL, Joseph. *Adventures of an Illustrator.* 1925. Little Brn. 1st trade ed. 4to. beige cloth. xl. VG. T10. $75.00

PENNELL, Joseph. *Quaint Corners in Philadelphia.* 1922. Wanamaker. VG. P12. $18.00

PENNEY, Clara Louisa. *List of Books Printed Before 1601 in Lib Hispanic Soc of Am.* 1929. np. 290p. VG. A4. $65.00

PENNY, Marie. *Children's Corner.* 1933. Greenberg. 1st ed. sm 8vo. F/G. M5. $35.00

PENROSE, Margaret. *Campfire Girls on the Program.* nd. NY. 202p. F. A17. $10.00

PENROSE, Margaret. *Dorothy Dale, Girl of Today.* 1908. Cupples Leon. G+. P12. $5.00

PENROSE, Margaret. *Dorothy Dale & Her Chums.* 1909. Cupples Leon. G+. P12. $5.00

PENTECOST, Hugh; see Phillips, Judson.

PENZER. *Annotated Bibliography of Sir Richard Francis Burton.* nd. rpt. 1/225. ils. 367p. F. A4. $85.00

PENZLER, Otto. *Detectionary.* nd. BC. VG/VG. P3. $10.00

PEPER & RIKOFF. *Hunting Moments of Truth.* 1973. Winchester. 1st ed. ils Milton C Weiler. VG/VG. P12. $15.00

PEPPER, Charles. *Life-Work of Louis Klopsch.* nd. Christian Herald. probable 1st ed. 395p. VG. B22. $12.00

PEPPIN, Brigid. *Golden Age of Fantastic Illustration.* 1975. Watson Guptill. 1st Am ed. ils. 192p. VG+/VG+. P2. $100.00

PEPPIN & MICKLETHWAIT. *Dictionary of British Book Illustrator, the 20th Century.* 1983. London. ils. 336p. VG/VG. A4. $95.00

PERCY, Walker. *Lancelot.* 1977. FSG. 1st ed. NF/F. B35. $29.00

PERCY, Walker. *Lost in the Cosmos.* 1983. FSG. 1st ed. NF/NF. A20/B35. $18.00

PERCY, Walker. *Love in the Ruins.* 1971. FSG. 1st ed. F/NF. B35. $60.00

PERCY, Walker. *Second Coming.* 1980. FSG. 1st ed. VG/VG. P3. $18.00

PERCY, Walker. *Thanatos Syndrome.* 1987. FSG. VG/VG-. P3. $15.00

PERELMAN, S.J. *Dream Department.* 1943. Random. 1st ed. F/NF. B2. $125.00

PERELMAN, S.J. *Rising Gorge.* 1961. Simon Schuster. 1st ed. VG/G. P12. $12.00

PPEREZ, Bernard. *First Three Years of Childhood.* 1888 (1878). NY. Kellogg. 2nd Eng-language ed. 12mo. 292p. G1. $40.00

PEREZ DE RIBAS, Andres. *My Life Among the Savage Nation of New Spain.* 1968. Ward Ritchie. 8vo. 256p. gilt red cloth. F. T10. $75.00

PERINN. *Ayn Rand: First Descriptive Bibliography.* 1990. ils. 100p. F/VG. A4. $65.00

PERKINS, Al. *Ian Fleming's Chitty-Chitty Bang-Bang.* nd. Beginner Books BC. VG. P3. $4.00

PERKINS, Charles Elliott. *Pinto Horse.* 1937. Fisher Skofield. ils Edward Borein. F. T10. $150.00

PERKINS, Jack. *Pied Piper of Hamlin.* 1931. McLoughlin. Jr Color Classics. ils. F. M5. $20.00

PERKINS, Lucy Fitch. *Colonial Twins of Virginia.* 1924. Houghton Mifflin. 1st ed. ils. pict cloth. VG+/fair. M5. $40.00

PERKINS, Lucy Fitch. *Filipino Twins.* 1923. Houghton Mifflin. 1st ed. ils. VG+/G. M5. $40.00

PERKINS, Marlin. *Zoo Parade.* 1954. Rand McNally. 1st ed. ils Bransom/Fleishman. 95p. VG. C14. $18.00

PERKINS & TANIS. *Native Americas of North America.* 1975. Scarecrow. 558p. F3. $35.00

PERLES, Alfred. *Great True Spy Adventures.* 1960. Arco. 2nd. VG. P3. $15.00

PERLMAN. *Immortal Eight: American Painting From Eakins...* 1979. F/F. D2. $25.00

PERNA, Albert F. *Glider Gladiators of WWII.* 1970. Freeman, SD. 1st ed. ils. 383p. F/dj. B18. $20.00

PERNICK, Martin. *Calculus of Suffering: Pain, Professionalism & Anesthesia...* 1985. NY. 1st ed. 421p. VG. A13. $35.00

PERON, Eva. *My Mission in Life.* 1953. Vantage. 1st Am ed. trans Ethel Cherry. VG+/VG. B4. $125.00

PEROWNE, Barry. *Raffles in Pursuit.* 1934. Cassell. 1st ed. xl. VG. P3. $15.00

PEROWNE, Barry. *Raffles of the MCC.* 1979. St Martin. 1st ed. VG/VG. P3. $15.00

PEROWNE, Stewart. *Jerusalem & Bethlehem.* 1965. London. Phoenix. Cities of the World series. 1st ed. 8vo. VG. W1. $12.00

PERRAULT, Charles. *Beauty & the Beast.* 1980. Gr Tiger. ils Michael Hague. 74p. VG. D1. $85.00

PERRAULT, Charles. *Histoire De Peau D'Ane.* 1902. Hammersmith. 1st ed thus. 1/230. VG. C6. $400.00

PERRAULT, Charles. *Perrault's Classic French Fairy Tales.* 1967. Meridith. 1st ed. 8vo. 224p. NF. C14. $10.00

PERRAULT, Charles. *Sleeping Beauty.* 1919. London. Heinemann. 1st ed. ils/sgn Rackham. VG/case. D1. $1,500.00

PERRETT, Bryan. *Knights of the Black Cross: Hitler's Panzerwaffe...* 1986. NY. 1st Am ed. 266p. brd. VG/dj. B18. $15.00

PERRY, Anne. *Hyde Park Headsman.* 1994. Fawcett. 1st Am ed. F/F. B4. $35.00

PERRY, Gaylord. *Me & the Spitter.* 1974. Saturday Review. later prt. VG+/VG+. P8. $50.00

PERRY, George Sessions. *Hackberry Cavalier.* 1945. Viking. 1st ed. VG/VG. A18. $20.00

PERRY, George Sessions. *Texas: A World in Itself.* 1942. Whittlesey. 8th. sgn. 293p. NF/dj. T10. $45.00

PERRY, John. *American Ferryboats.* 1957. NY. Wilfred Funk. VG/VG. A16. $35.00

PERRY, Ritchie. *Fall Guy.* 1972. Houghton Mifflin. 1st ed. VG/VG. P3. $18.00

PERRY, Ritchie. *One Good Death Deserves Another.* 1976. Collins Crime Club. 1st ed. VG/VG. P3. $15.00

PERRY, Ronald. *Denizens.* 1980. Random. 1st ed. Nat Poetry Series. F/F. V1. $10.00

PERRY, Thomas. *Island.* 1987. Putnam. 1st ed. VG+/F. A20. $22.00

PERRY, Thomas. *Vanishing Act.* 1995. Random. 1st ed. F/F. P3. $23.00

PERSICO, Joseph E. *Piercing of the Reich.* 1979. Viking. 1st ed. hc. VG/VG. P3. $18.00

PERSICO, Joseph E. *Spiderweb.* 1979. Crown. 1st ed. VG/VG. P3. $15.00

PERTWEE, Roland. *Hell's Loose.* 1929. Houghton Mifflin. VG. P3. $8.00

PERVIVAL, Olive. *Our Old-Fashioned Flowers.* 1947. Pasadena. ils. 245p. VG+. B26. $35.00

PESCE, Angelo. *Colours of the Arab Fatherland.* 1975. Falcon. 1st ed. ils. 143p. VG/dj. W1. $30.00

PESETSKY, Bette. *Author From a Savage People.* 1983. Knopf. 1st ed. author's 2nd book. F/F. B4. $35.00

PESETSKY, Bette. *Stories Up to a Point.* 1981. Knopf. 1st ed. rem mk. F/F. B4. $50.00

PESHA. *Great Lakes Ships Book 2.* Great Lakes Maritime Inst. G/wrp. A16. $20.00

PESOTTA, Rose. *Bread Upon the Waters.* 1944. NY. 1st ed. 435p. VG/torn. B18. $35.00

PETAJA, Emil. *Stardrift.* 1971. Fpci. 1st ed. sgn. F/F. P3. $30.00

PETER, Lily. *Great Riding.* 1966. Robert Moore Allen. sgn. 8vo. 269p. F/G. B11. $20.00

PETER & SOUTHWICK. *Cleveland Park: Early Residential Neighborhood...* 1958. Community Lib Comm. ils/map. 60p. VG/wrp. B10. $12.00

PETERKIN, Julia. *Plantation Christmas.* 1934. Houghton Mifflin. 12mo. VG/VG. B17. $30.00

PETERKIN & ULMANN. *Roll, Jordan, Roll.* 1933. NY. Ballou. 1st trade ed/1st issue. NF/NF. B4. $850.00

PETERS, Elizabeth; see Mertz, Barbara Gross.

PETERS, Ellis; see Pargeter, Edith Mary.

PETERS, Harry. *Currier & Ives, Printmakers to the American People...* 1976. 4 vol. rpt. 4to. ils. cream buckram. box. A4. $400.00

PETERS, Ludovic. *Tarakian.* 1963. Abelard Schuman. 1st ed. VG/G+. P3. $20.00

PETERS, Ludovic. *Two After Malic.* 1966. Walker. 1st ed. VG/VG. P3. $13.00

PETERS, Robert. *Poet as Ice-Skater.* 1975. San Francisco. 1/1000. 52p. wrp. A17. $9.50

PETERSE, Richard G. *Lost Cities of Cibola.* 1980. Chicago. Franciscan Herald. 8vo. ils. 292p. gilt cloth. NF/dj. T10. $50.00

PETERSEN, Eugene T. *Mackinac Island: Its History in Pictures...* 1973. Mackinac Island, MI. State Park Comm. ils. dj. T7. $35.00

PETERSEN, Herman. *Covered Bridge.* 1950. Crowell. 1st ed. VG/VG. P3. $20.00

PETERSEN, Marjorie. *Stornaway East & West.* 1966. Van Nostrand. VG/VG. A16. $10.00

PETERSEN, William. *Hippocratic Wisdom: Modern Appreciation of Ancient Medical.* 1946. Springfield. 1st ed. 263p. VG. A13. $50.00

PETERSHAM & PETERSHAM. *Miki & Mary: Their Search for Treasures.* 1934. Viking. 1st ed. ils. G+. P2. $80.00

PETERSHAM & PETERSHAM. *Off to Bed (7 Stories for Wide-Awakes).* (1954). WI. EM Hale/Cadmus. rpt. unp. VG. T5. $15.00

PETERSHAM & PETERSHAM. *Stories From the Old Testament.* 1938. Winston. 1st ed. ujnp. cloth. VG/dj. M20. $42.00

PETERSHAM & PETERSHAM. *Story Book of Foods From the Field.* 1936. 1st ed. NF/VG+. S13. $20.00

PETERSHAM & PETERSHAM. *Story of the Presidents of the United States of America.* 1953. NY. Macmillan. 1st ed. 4to. 80p. NF. C14. $10.00

PETERSON, Audrey. *Nocturne Murder.* 1987. Arbor. 1st ed. VG/VG. P3. $18.00

PETERSON, Frederick. *Ancient Mexico.* 1961. Putnam. 2nd. 313p. dj. F3. $20.00

PETERSON, Hans. *Liselott & the Quiffin.* 1964. London. Methuen. 1st ed. 12mo. 156p. G+/G+. T5. $20.00

PETERSON, Hans. *Magnus in Danger.* nd. Pantheon. stated 1st Am ed. 8vo. 135p. VG+. C14. $8.00

PETERSON, Harold L. *Pageant of the Gun.* 1967. Doubleday. ils/photos. gitl bdg. VG/VG. P12. $10.00

PETERSON, Keith; see Klavan, Andrew.

PETERSON, Robert. *Leaving Taos.* 1980. Harper Row. 1st ed. Nat Poetry series. F/F. V1. $20.00

PETERSON, Susan. *Living Tradition of Maria Martinez.* 1978. NY. Kodansha. 2nd. VG/VG. B5. $45.00

PETERSON, William J. *Steamboating on the Upper Mississippi.* 1968. Iowa City. State Hist Soc. sgn. 8vo. 64 pl. 575p. map ep. A4/B11. $85.00

PETIEVICH, Gerald. *Earth Angels.* 1989. NAL. 1st ed. NF/NF. P3. $18.00

PETIEVICH, Gerald. *Paramour.* 1991. Dutton. 1st ed. xl. dj. P3. $5.00

PETIEVICH, Gerald. *Quality of the Informant.* 1985. Arbor. 1st ed. F/F. H11. $30.00

PETIEVICH, Gerald. *Shakedown.* 1988. Simon Schuster. 1st ed. F/F. P3. $17.00

PETIEVICH, Gerald. *To Live & Die in LA.* 1984. Arbor. 1st ed. F/F. H11. $55.00

PETIT, Christopher. *Robinson.* 1994. Viking. 1st ed. F/F. P3. $21.00

PETRARCH. *Le Rime del Petrarca.* 1822. Pickering. teg. full brn morocco. miniature. T10. $150.00

PETRY, Ann. *Street.* 1946. Houghton Mifflin. 1st ed. author's 1st book. F/NF. B4. $450.00

PETSOPOULOS, Yanni. *Tulips, Arabesques & Turbans: Decorative Arts...* 1982. Abbeville. 1st ed. 224p. VG/dj. W1. $65.00

PETTEE, F.M. *Palgrave Mummy.* 1929. Payson Clarke. 1st ed. hc. VG. P3. $30.00

PETTEE, F.M. *Who Bird & Other Whimsies.* 1920. Chicago. Whitman. possible 1st ed. unp. F/box lacks end pieces. T5. $35.00

PETTES, G.W. *American or Standard Whist.* 1881. Boston. 2nd. 268p. VG. S1. $10.00

PETTES, G.W. *American Whist Illustrated Containing Laws & Principles...* 1890. Boston. 2nd 367p. VG. S1. $12.00

PETTES, Helen. *Mouse's Tail.* 1917. Cupples Leon. ils Julia Greene. NF. M5. $42.00

PETTIJOHN, F.J. *Sedimentary Rocks.* 1957. Harper. 2nd. 40 pl. 718p. VG. D8. $30.00

PETTIJOHN & POTTER. *Paleocurrent & Basin Analysis.* 1963. Academic Pr. 1st ed. 30 pl/130 figures. 296p. VG/dj. D8. $35.00

PETZAL, David. *Experts' Book of the Shooting Sports.* 1972. Simon Schuster. 1st ed. photos. NF/VG. P12. $12.50

PETZINGER, T. *Oil & Honor: The Texaco-Pennzoil Wars.* 1887. Putnam. 1st ed. 495p. VG/dj. D8. $15.00

PEYTON, John Lewis. *Rambling Reminiscences of a Residence Abroad...* 1888. Staunton. SM Yost. 298p. VG. B10. $25.00

PEYTON, Richard. *At the Track.* 1987. Bonanza. hc. F/F. P3. $13.00

PFLUGER, Edward. *Die Sensorischen Functionen des Ruckenmarks...* 1853. Berlin. Hirschwald. 146p. modern brd. VG. G1. $575.00

PHEAR, J.B. *Treatise on Rights of Water, Including Public & Private...* 1859. London. Norton. emb cloth. M11. $250.00

PHELAN, Nancy. *Welcome the Wayfarer: Traveller in Modern Turkey.* 1965. Macmillan. 1st ed. 8vo. 16 pl. NF/dj. W1. $12.00

PHELPS, Earle Bernard. *Disinfection of Sewage & Dewage Filter Effluents.* 1909. GPO. 8vo. fld plan/index. 91p. F/new wrp. T10. $25.00

PHELPS, Earle Bernard. *Pollution of Atreams by Sulphite Pulp Waste.* 1909. GPO. 8vo. 37p. F/new wrp. T10. $25.00

PHELPS, Elizabeth Stuart. *Trixy.* 1904. Houghton Mifflin. 1st ed. inscr. F/NF. B4. $125.00

PHELPS, Richard H. *Newgate of Connecticut, Its Origin & Early History...* 1901. Hartford. Am Pub. gilt maroon cloth. M11. $125.00

PHILBRICK, W.R. *Slow Dancer.* 1984. St Martin. 1st ed. VG/VG. P3. $18.00

PHILIP & UPGREN. *Star Catalogues: Centennial Tribute to AN Vyssotsky.* 1989. NY. Davis. ils. 100p. VG. K5. $25.00

PHILIPS, Shine. *Big Spring: Causual Biography of a Prairie Town.* 1942. Prentice Hall. 1st ed. 8vo. 231p. tan cloth. NF. T10. $35.00

PHILIPSON, John. *Harness: As It Has Been, As It Is...* 1882. Newcastle. 1st ed. O3. $85.00

PHILLIPS, Alexander M. *Mislaid Charm.* 1947. Prime. 1st ed. VG/chip 1st state (yellow dj). P3. $25.00

PHILLIPS, Caryl. *Cambridge.* 1992. Knopf. 1st ed. F/F. M23. $20.00

PHILLIPS, Conrad. *Empty Cot.* 1958. Arthur Barker. 1st ed. VG/VG. P3. $25.00

PHILLIPS, Conrad. *Unrepentant.* 1958. Arthur Barker. 1st ed. VG/VG. P3. $25.00

PHILLIPS, Hubert. *Bridge Is Only a Game.* 1959. London. 96p. VG. S1. $10.00

PHILLIPS, Hubert. *Brush Up Your Bridge.* 1939. London. 119p. VG. S1. $8.00

PHILLIPS, Jayne Anne. *Counting.* 1978. NY. Vehicle Eds. 1st ed. 1/526. author's 2nd book. VG/wrp. B4. $150.00

PHILLIPS, Jayne Anne. *Fast Lanes.* 1984. NY. Vehicle Eds. 1/200. sgn. F/wrp. B4. $85.00

PHILLIPS, Jayne Anne. *Fast Lanes.* 1987. Dutton. 1st ed. F/F. H11. $35.00

PHILLIPS, Jayne Anne. *How Mickey Made It.* 1981. St Paul. Bookslinger. 1/150. sgn/#d. special bdg. F. B2. $150.00

PHILLIPS, Jayne Anne. *Machine Dreams.* 1984. Dutton. ARC. F/F. w/photo. B4. $50.00

PHILLIPS, Jayne Anne. *Machine Dreams.* 1984. Dutton. 1st ed. author's 1st novel. F/F. H11. $40.00

PHILLIPS, Jayne Anne. *Machine Dreams.* 1984. Dutton. 1st ed. F/F. B35. $42.00

PHILLIPS, Jayne Anne. *Shelter.* 1994. Houghton Mifflin. ARC. F/F. B4. $45.00

PHILLIPS, Jayne Anne. *Shelter.* 1994. Houghton Mifflin. 1st ed. F/F. H11. $30.00

PHILLIPS, Judson. *Backlash.* 1976. Dodd Mead. 1st ed. VG/VG. P3. $20.00

PHILLIPS, Judson. *Cannibal Who Overate.* 1962. Red Badge Detective. VG+/VG+. P10. $10.00

PHILLIPS, Judson. *Champagne Killer.* 1972. Dodd Mead. 1st ed. VG/VG. P3. $20.00

PHILLIPS, Judson. *Deadly Joke.* 1971. Dodd Mead. 1st ed. VG/VG. P3. $20.00

PHILLIPS, Judson. *Deadly Trap.* 1978. Dodd Mead. 1st ed. NF/NF. P3. $15.00

PHILLIPS, Judson. *Death by Fire.* 1986. Dodd Mead. 1st ed. F/F. P3. $16.00

PHILLIPS, Judson. *Death Syndicate.* 1941. Triangle. VG. P3. $15.00

PHILLIPS, Judson. *Escape a Killer.* 1971. Dodd Mead. 1st ed. VG/VG. P3. $20.00

PHILLIPS, Judson. *Honeymoon With Death.* 1975. Dodd Mead. 1st ed. VG/VG. P3. $15.00

PHILLIPS, Judson. *Judas Freak.* 1974. Dodd Mead. G+/dj. P3. $15.00

PHILLIPS, Judson. *Murder Arranged.* 1978. Dodd Mead. 1st ed. VG/VG. P3. $18.00

PHILLIPS, Judson. *Murder in High Places.* 1983. Dodd Mead. 1st ed. VG/VG. P3. $15.00

PHILLIPS, Judson. *Murder in Luxury.* 1981. Dodd Mead. 1st ed. VG/VG. P3. $18.00

PHILLIPS, Judson. *Murder Round the Clock.* 1985. Dodd Mead. 1st ed. F/NF. H11. $25.00

PHILLIPS, Judson. *Past, Present & Murder.* 1982. Dodd Mead. VG/VG. P3. $15.00

PHILLIPS, Judson. *Plague of Violence.* 1970. Dodd Mead. 1st ed. VG/VG. P3. $18.00

PHILLIPS, Judson. *Power Killers.* 1974. Dodd Mead. 1st ed. VG/G+. P3. $13.00

PHILLIPS, Judson. *Remember to Kill Me.* 1984. Dodd Mead. 1st ed. VG/VG. P3. $15.00

PHILLIPS, Judson. *Sniper.* nd. Detective BC. VG. P3. $8.00

PHILLIPS, Judson. *Vanishing Senator.* 1972. Dodd Mead. 1st ed. xl. dj. P3. $8.00

PHILLIPS, Lance. *Saddle Horse.* 1970. Barnes. later prt. VG/VG. O3. $45.00

PHILLIPS, P. Lee. *List of Works on Cartography.* 1901. WA. GPO. 90p. F. O7. $95.00

PHILLIPS, Paul C. *Medicine in the Making of Montana.* 1962 Missoul. a. 1st ed. 564p. NF. N3. $15.00

PHILLIPS, Stanley S. *Excavated Artifacts From Battlefields & Campsites...* 1986. np. 4to. 199p. VG. T3. $20.00

PHILLIPS, W. Glasgow. *Tuscaloosa.* 1994. Morrow. 1st ed. sgn. F/F. M23. $40.00

PHILLIPS, Wendell. *Oman: A History.* 1967. Reynal/Morrow. 1st ed. ils/2 full-p maps. VG/torn. W1. $45.00

PHILLIPS, Wendell. *Qataban & Sheba: Exploring Ancient Kingdoms...* 1955. Harcourt. 1st ed. sgn. 362p. VG/dj. W1. $22.00

PHILLIPS, Wendell. *Qataban & Sheba: Exploring Ancient Kingdoms...* 1955. Harcourt. 1st ed. 362p. cloth. VG+. B22. $7.00

PHILLIPS, Wendell. *Unknown Oman.* 1966. McKay. 1st Am ed. pres. 8vo. ils. 319p. VG. W1. $30.00

PHILLIPS & STEAVENSON. *Splendour of the Heavens.* 1931. NY. McBride. 4to. 976p. G/tattered. K5. $250.00

PHILLIPS-BIRT, Douglas. *When Luxury Went to Sea.* 1971. St Martin. 1st Am ed. VG/VG. A16. $40.00

PIAGET, Jean. *Child's Conception of Physical Causality.* 1930. London. Kegan Paul. 1st English-language ed/later issue. bl-gr cloth. G1. $100.00

PIAGET, Jean. *La Formation du Symbole Chez l'Enfant...* (1945). Paris. Delachaux Niestle. 312p. prt yel wrp. G1. $75.00

PIAGET, Jean. *Moral Judgment of the Child.* 1932. Harcourt Brace/Kegan Paul. 1st Eng-language ed. 418p. G1. $50.00

PICANO, Felice. *Mesmerist.* 1977. Delacorte. 1st ed. F/F. H11. $40.00

PICANO, Felice. *Mesmerist.* 1977. Delacorte. 1st ed. VG/VG. P3. $25.00

PICARD, Barbara. *French Legends, Tales & Fairy Stories.* 1955. Walck. 1st ed. 8vo. VG/VG. B17. $5.00

PICARD, Jean. *De Prisca Celtopaedia, Libri Doctrina, Quam Vel in Graecia.* 1556. Paris. Matthew David. only ed. 4to. suede. VG. B14. $880.00

PICASSO, Pablo. *Hunk of Skin.* 1968. City Lights. 1st Am ed. VG+. V1. $40.00

PICK, Bernhard. *Talmud: What It Is & What It Knows About Jesus...* 1877. NY. John B Alden. 147p. decor tan cloth. VG. B14. $55.00

PICKARD, Nancy. *Afraid of the Time.* 1992. Mystery Scene Short Story. 1st ed. 1/100. sgn. F/sans. P3. $20.00

PICKARD, Nancy. *But I Wouldn't Want to Die There.* 1993. Pocket. 1st ed. F/F. P3. $20.00

PICKARD, Nancy. *27-Ingredient Chile Con Carne Murders.* 1993. Delacorte. 1st ed. F/F. P3. $18.00

PICKERING, James S. *Asterisks, a Book of Astronomical Footnotes.* 1964. Dodd Mead. 8vo. 214p. VG/dj. K5. $25.00

PICKNEY, Darryl. *High Cotton.* 1992. Farrar. 1st ed. F/F. B2. $50.00

PIDDINGTON, R.A. *Limits of Mankind: Philosophy of Population.* 1956. Bristol, Eng. 153p. F/dj. B14. $75.00

PIDGIN, C.F. *Blennerhassett.* 1901. Boston. 1st ed. ils. F. A17. $10.00

PIENKOWSKI, Jan. *Robot.* 1981. Dell. 1st Am ed. 4to. F. B17. $22.00

PIERCE, David M. *Angels in Heaven.* 1992. Mysterious. 1st ed. VG/VG. P3. $18.00

PIERCE, John J. *Old Genre.* 1994. Greenwood. F. P3. $55.00

PIERCE, Josephine H. *Fire on the Hearth.* 1951. Springfield, MA. 254p. VG/dj. B18. $22.50

PIERCE, Ovid Williams. *Devil's Half.* 1968. Doubleday. 1st ed. inscr/dtd 1973. F/NF. M23. $20.00

PIERCE, R.V. *People's Common Sense Medical Advisor.* 1895. Buffalo. 12mo. ils. 1008p. blk cloth. VG. T3. $30.00

PIERCY, Marge. *Available Light.* 1988. Knopf. 1st ed. sgn. F/NF. V1. $25.00

PIERCY, Marge. *Braided Lives.* 1982. Summit. 2nd. VG/VG. P3. $13.00

PIERCY, Marge. *Dance the Eagle to Sleep.* 1970. Doubleday. 1st ed. author's 2nd novel. F/NF. H11. $45.00

PIERCY, Marge. *He, She & It.* 1991. Knopf. 1st ed. F/F. H11. $25.00

PIERCY, Marge. *High Cost of Living.* 1978. Harper Row. 1st ed. F/F. H11. $40.00

PIERCY, Marge. *Mars & Her Children.* 1992. Knopf. 1st ed. sgn. F/F. V1. $25.00

PIERCY, Marge. *Moon Is Always Female.* 1989. Knopf sgn. F/wrp. V1. $15.00

PIERCY, Marge. *Summer People.* 1989. Summit. 1st ed. F/F. H11. $30.00

PIERCY, Marge. *Woman on the Edge of Time.* 1976. Knopf. 1st ed. inscr. F/F. B4. $85.00

PIERSOL, George. *Gateway of Honor: American College of Physicians 1915-59.* 1962. Phil. 1st ed. 646p. VG. A13. $35.00

PIERSON, Willard J. *Practical Methods for Observing & Forecasting Ocean Waves.* 1955. Hydrographic Office. 284p. VG. P12. $20.00

PIGGOTT, Stuart. *Earliest Wheeled Transport...* 1983. Cornell. 1st Am ed. 4to. 272p. VG/dj. W1. $18.00

PIKE, Christopher. *Season of Passage.* 1992. Tor. 1st ed. NF/NF. P3. $20.00

PIKE, James A. *Other Side.* nd. Laffont. hc. VG. P3. $15.00

PIKE, James. *Prostrate State: South Carolina Under Negro Government.* 1935. NY. VG. B30. $35.00

PILEGGI, Nicholas. *Wiseguy.* 1985. Simon Schuster. 1st ed. F/F. H11. $25.00

PILGRIM, Mariette S. *Oogaruk the Aleut.* 1949. Caxton. sgn. ils HH Wilson. 8vo. 223p. F/G. B11. $35.00

PILKINGTON, James. *Artist's Guide & Mechanics Own Book...* 1841. Boston. 490p. VG. B14. $100.00

PILLSBURY, W.B. *Attention. Library of Philosophy Series.* 1908. Macmillan. 1st Eng-language ed. 346p. panelled crimson cloth. G1. $75.00

PINCHER, Chapman. *Not With a Bang.* 1965. Weidenfeld Nicolson. hc. G/torn. P3. $10.00

PINCHON, Edgcumb. *Viva Villa!* (1933). Grosset Dunlap. 383p. G. F3. $15.00

PINCHOT, Giffort. *To the South Seas: Cruise of the Schooner Mary Pinchot...* 1930. Winston. 1st ed. sgn. ils/map ep. 500p. gilt bl brd. VG. B11. $85.00

PINI & PINI. *Elfquest Book 1.* 1981. Donning. 1st/ltd ed. sgn. hc. F/box. P3. $225.00

PINI & PINI. *Elfquest Book 2.* 1982. Donning. 1st/ltd ed. sgn. F/box. P3. $150.00

PINI & PINI. *Elfquest Book 3.* 1983. Donning. 1st/ltd ed. sgn. F/box. P3. $100.00

PINI & PINI. *Elfquest Book 4.* 1984. Donning. 1st/ltd ed. sgn. F/box. P3. $75.00

PINKERTON, Allan. *Detective & the Somnambulist.* 1877. Belford. 1st Canadian ed. fair. P3. $40.00

PINKERTON, Allan. *Spy of the Rebellion.* 1883. NY. ils. VG. B30. $42.50

PINKERTON, Allan. *Spy of the Rebellion.* 1911. Dillingham. hc. VG. P3. $20.00

PINKWATER, Daniel. *Fish Whistle.* 1939. Addison Wesley. 1st ed. sgn/sketch. F/F. B11. $25.00

PINNER, David. *Ritual.* 1967. New Authors Ltd. 1st ed. F/F. P3. $13.00

PINTER, Harold. *Poems & Prose 1949-1977.* 1978. Grove. 1st ed. F/F. V1. $20.00

PIOZZI, Hester Lynch. *Anecdotes of the Late Samuel Johnson, LLD...* 1786. London. T Cadell. 1st ed. 8vo. modern calf. F. T10. $450.00

PIPER. *English Face.* 1975. VG/G. D2. $25.00

PIPER, Evelyn. *Nanny.* nd. BC. VG/VG. P3. $8.00

PIPER, Evelyn. *Stand-In.* 1970. McKay Washburn. 1st ed. VG/VG. P3. $15.00

PIPER, H. Beam. *Murder in the Gun Room.* 1953. Knopf. 1st ed. NF/VG. B2. $150.00

PIPER, John F. *Marine Electrical Installation.* 1943. Cornell. 3rd. ils. gilt red bdg. G+. P12. $10.00

PIPER, Watty. *Brimful Book: A Collection of Mother Goose Rhymes...* 1939. Platt Munk. folio. ils. VG. B17. $17.50

PIPER, Watty. *Children's Hour on the Farm.* 1929. Platt Munk. 16mo. VG. M5. $15.00

PIPER, Watty. *Children's Hour With the Birds.* 1929. Platt Munk. 16mo. VG. M5. $15.00

PIPER, Watty. *Nursery Tales Children Love.* 1933. Platt Munk. lg 4to. VG+. M5. $55.00

PIPER, Watty. *Stories That Never Grow Old.* 1952 (1938). Platt Munk. ils Hauman. unp. VG/torn. T5. $45.00

PIRIE, David. *Vampire Cinema.* 1977. Crescent. VG/VG. P3. $20.00

PIRSIG, Robert M. *Lila.* 1991. Bantam. 1st ed. F/F. M23. $25.00

PISERCHIA, Doris. *Spaceling.* nd. BC. F/F. P3. $8.00

PITCHFORD, Kenneth. *Color Photos of the Atrocities.* 1973. Atlantic. 1st ed. assn copy. VG. V1. $15.00

PITTENGER, Peggy Jett. *Back Yard Foal.* 1967. Barnes. sm 4to. VG. O3. $25.00

PITTER, Ruth. *Spirit Watches.* 1940. Macmillan. 1st ed. F/NF. V1. $35.00

PITTS, Lilla Belle. *Singing & Rhyming.* 1950. Ginn. 8vo. ils Eloise Wilkin. VG. B17. $7.50

PITZ, Henry. *Brandywine Tradition.* 1968. Weathervane. 1st ed thus. ils. 252p. G+. T5. $32.00

PITZ, Henry. *Drawing Trees.* 1956. 1st ed. VG/VG. S13. $45.00

PITZ, Henry. *King Arthur & His Noble Knights.* 1949. Lippincott. 1st imp. 8vo. F/VG. B17. $7.50

PIZER. *Theodore Dreiser: A Primary & Secondary Bibliography.* 1975. np. 525p. F. A4. $65.00

PLAIDY, Jean. *Prince of Darkness.* 1978. Hale. 1st ed. VG/VG. P3. $12.00

PLATH, Sylvia. *Bed Book.* 1976. Harper. 1st Am ed. NF/VG. C8. $40.00

PLATH, Sylvia. *Bell Jar.* 1971. Harper Row. 1st Am ed. author's only novel. VG+/NF. B4. $85.00

PLATH, Sylvia. *Colossus & Other Poems.* 1967. Knopf. 2nd. F/NF. V1. $20.00

PLATH, Sylvia. *Crossing the Water.* 1971. Harper Row. 2nd. F/NF. V1. $10.00

PLATH, Sylvia. *Letters Home.* 1975. Harper Row. 1st ed. photos. 402p. NF/clip. S9. $30.00

PLATO. *Collected Dialogues of...* 1987. Princeton. 13th. hc. F/F. P3. $33.00

PLATT, Kin. *Body Beautiful Murder.* 1976. Random. 1st ed. VG/G+. P3. $18.00

PLATT, Kin. *Terrible Love Life of Dudley Cornflow.* 1976. Bradbury. 1st ed. VG/VG. P3. $15.00

PLATT, Ruthorford. *Walt Disney Secrets of Life.* 1957. NY. ils. 124p. VG/wrp. A17. $5.00

PLAYLE, Margaret. *Second Rucksack Book.* 1954. London. ils. 192p. VG/dj. A17. $8.50

PLEASANTS, W. Shepard. *Stingaree Murders.* 1932. Mystery League. 1st ed. VG. P3. $15.00

PLEDGE, H.T. *Science Since 1500: A Short History of Mathematics...* 1940. London. 1st ed. 357p. VG. A13. $20.00

PLIMPTON, George. *Paper Lion.* 1966. Harper Row. 1st ed. F/F. B35. $25.00

PLIMPTON, George. *Rabbit's Umbrella.* 1955. Viking. 1st ed. ils Wm Pene DuBois. F/VG+. B4. $250.00

PLOMER, Henry R. *Short History of English Printing 1476-1898.* 1900. London. Kegan Paul. 1/50. 8vo. 330p. full vellum. NF. T10. $250.00

PLOMER, Henry R. *Wynkyn de Worde & His Contemporaries From Death of Caxton...* 1925. London. Grafton. 1st ed. 8vo. ils. 264p. F. T10. $250.00

PLOWDEN, David. *End of an Era.* 1992. Norton. AN. A16. $50.00

PLOWRIGHT, Teresa. *Dreams of an Unseen Planet.* 1986. Arbor. 1st ed. author's 1st novel. F/F. G10/P3. $20.00

PLUMLY, Stanley. *Boy on the Step.* 1989. Ecco. 1st ed. AN/dj. V1. $20.00

PLUNKET, Robert. *My Search for Warren Harding.* 1983. 1st ed. author's 1st book. VG+/VG+. S13. $18.00

PODHAJSKY, Alois. *Die Spanische Hofreitschule.* 1959. Wien. Holzhausens. VG/G. O3. $45.00

PODHAJSKY, Alois. *Lipizzaners.* 1970. Doubleday. 2nd Am. VG/VG. O3. $48.00

PODHAJSKY, Alois. *My Dancing White Horses.* 1966. NY. HRW. 3rd. VG/VG. O3. $35.00

PODHAJSKY, Alois. *Spanish Riding School of Vienna.* 1956. Vienna. Eng text. VG/wrp. O3. $25.00

PODMORE, Frank. *Apparitions & Thought-Transference...* 1894. London. Walter Scott. 12mo. 401p. prt mauve cloth. VG. G1. $65.00

PODRUG, Junius. *Frost of Heaven.* 1992. Arlington Hts. Dark Harvest. 1st ed. inscr. F/F. H11. $45.00

POE, Edgar Allan. *Chapter on Autography.* 1926. NY. 1/750. F/NF. C6. $60.00

POE, Edgar Allan. *Fall of the House of Usher.* 1986. Marshall Cavendish. hc. decor brd. F. P3. $25.00

POE, Edgar Allan. *Masque of the Red Death & Other Tales.* 1932. Halcyon. 1st ed thus. 1/175. ils JB Wright. NF. C6. $300.00

POE, Edgar Allan. *Murders in the Rue Morgue.* nd. JH Sears. VG. P3. $20.00

POE, Edgar Allan. *Seventy-Seven Tales/One Complete Novel/Thirty One Poems.* 1985. Amaranth. aeg. leather. F/sans. G10. $15.00

POE, Edgar Allan. *Tales of Edgar Allan Poe.* 1979. Franklin Lib. gilt bdg/leather spine. NF. P3. $20.00

POE, Edgar Allan. *Tales.* 1928. NY. 1st ed. ils 520p. F/dj. A17. $9.50

POE, Edgar Allan. *Works...* 1864. NY. 4 vol. G+. M17. $120.00

POESCH. *Art of the Old South: Painting, Sculpture, Architecture.* 1983. F/F. D2. $35.00

POGANY, Willy. *Golden Cockerel.* 1938. NY. 1st ed. ils. VG. B5. $45.00

POGANY, Willy. *Gulliver's Travels.* 1917. Macmillan. 1st ed. 8vo. VG. M5. $75.00

POGANY, Willy. *My Poetry Book, an Anthology of Modern Verse...* 1957. Winston. 2nd ed thus. 8vo. VG. M5. $12.00

POGANY, Willy. *Wimp & the Woodle & Other Stories.* 1935. Sutton House. 1st ed. ils. VG. B5. $45.00

POGANY & POGANY. *Peterkin.* 1940. McKay. 1st ed. ils Willy Pogany. VG+/ragged dj. M20. $110.00

POHL, Frederik. *Best of Frederik Pohl.* nd. BC. VG/VG. P3. $8.00

POHL, Frederik. *Beyond the Blue Event Horizon.* 1980. Del Rey. VG/VG. P3. $18.00

POHL, Frederik. *Black Star Rising.* nd. BC. VG/VG. P3. $8.00

POHL, Frederik. *Chernobyl.* 1987. Bantam. 1st ed. VG/G. P3. $15.00

POHL, Frederik. *Coming of the Quantum Cats.* nd. BC. VG/VG. P3. $8.00

POHL, Frederik. *Cool War.* 1981. Del Rey. 1st ed. VG/VG. P3. $15.00

POHL, Frederik. *Day the Martians Came.* 1989. Easton. 1st ed. sgn. full leather. F/swrp. P3. $60.00

POHL, Frederik. *Heechee Rendezvous.* 1984. Del Rey. 1st ed. F/F. P3. $20.00

POHL, Frederik. *Homegoing.* 1989. Easton. 1st ed. sgn. leather. F/wrp. P3. $60.00

POHL, Frederik. *Jem.* 1979. St Martin. 1st ed. VG/VG. P3. $15.00

POHL, Frederik. *Merchants' War.* 1985. Gollancz. 1st ed. F/F. P3. $20.00

POHL, Frederik. *Midas World.* 1983. St Martin. 1st ed. F/F. P3. $20.00

POHL, Frederik. *Narabedla Ltd.* 1988. Ballantine. 1st ed. F/F. H11. $25.00

POHL, Frederik. *Nebula Winners 14.* 1980. Harper. 1st ed. NF/NF. P3. $30.00

POHL, Frederik. *Outnumbering the Dead.* 1990. Legend. 1st ed. hc. F/F. P3. $25.00

POHL, Frederik. *Second If Reader of SF.* 1968. Doubleday. 1st ed. VG/VG. P3. $25.00

POHL, Frederik. *SF Roll of Honor.* 1975. Random. 1st ed. F/F. P3. $15.00

POHL, Frederik. *Starburst.* 1982. Del Rey. 1st ed. VG/VG. P3. $15.00

POHL, Frederik. *Stopping at Slowyear.* 1991. Axolotl. 1st ed. sgn. F/F. P3. $45.00

POHL, Frederik. *Way the Future Was.* 1978. Del Rey. VG/VG. P3. $15.00

POHL, Frederik. *World at the End of Time.* 1990. Del Rey. 1st ed. F/F. P3. $18.00

POHL & KORNBLUTH. *Presidential Year.* 1956. Ballantine. 1st ed. F/F. P3. $400.00

POHL & KORNBLUTH. *Town Is Drowning.* 1955. Ballantine. 1st ed. VG. P3. $375.00

POHL & WILLIAMSON. *Land's End.* nd. BC. VG/VG. P3. $8.00

POHL & WILLIAMSON. *Singers of Time.* 1991. Doubleday. 1st ed. VG/VG. P3. $22.00

POHL & WILLIAMSON. *Starbild Trilogy.* nd. BC. VG/VG. P3. $10.00

POINDEXTER, Miles. *Ayer Incas.* 1930. NY. 2 vol. 1st ed. ils. VG/G+. B5. $65.00

POLASEK, Emily. *Bohemian Girl in America.* 1982. Rollins. inscr. 8vo. 120p. VG/VG repro. B11. $25.00

POLE, William. *Philosophy of Whist.* 1884. London. 2nd. 218p. VG. S1. $8.00

POLE, William. *Pole on Whist. Theory of Modern Scientific Game of Whist.* 1889. NY. Authorized Am ed. 5th. 128p. VG. S1. $6.00

POLIDORI, John William. *Vampyre.* 1973. Hertfordshire. Gubblecote. 1/1000. 8vo. 42p. F. T10. $100.00

POLITE, Carlene. *Les Flagellants.* 1966. Paris. Christian Bourgois. 1/15. author's 1st novel. F/dj. B4. $450.00

POLITE, Carlene. *Sister X & the Victims of Foul Play.* 1975. FSG. 1st ed. F/NF. B4. $45.00

POLITI, Leo. *Bunker Hill.* 1964. Palm Desert. Desert Southwest Inc. 1st ed. ils. gilt gray cloth. dj. T10. $250.00

POLITI, Leo. *Mission Bell.* (1953). Scribner. later prt. 32p. F/dj. T10. $45.00

POLITI, Leo. *Mission Bell.* 1953. Scribner. ils. pict lib bdg. NF/clip. T10. $135.00

POLITI, Leo. *Pedro the Angel of Olivera St.* 1946. Scribner. 1st ed. 12mo. VG/VG. D1. $125.00

POLITZ, Edward A. *Forty-First Thief.* 1975. Delacorte. 1st ed. VG/VG. P3. $15.00

POLK. *Island of California: A History of the Myth.* 1991. np. 57 pl. 398p. F/F. A4. $125.00

POLLACK, Rachel. *Temporary Agency.* 1994. St Martin. 1st ed. F/F. M23. $35.00

POLLARD, A.O. *Unofficial Spy.* 1936. Hutchinson. xl. dj. P3. $13.00

POLLARD, Alfred W. *Romance of King Arthur.* 1917. Macmillan. VG. P3. $40.00

POLLARD, Edward A. *First Year of the War: Southern History of the War.* 1863 (1862). Charles Richardson. 368p. gilt gr cloth. VG. M20. $77.00

POLLARD, Edward A. *Second Year of the War.* 1864 (1863). Charles Richardson. 386p. gilt cloth. VG. M20. $87.00

POLLARD, Edward A. *War in America.* 1864. London. 12mo. 354p. gr cloth. G. T3. $70.00

POLLOCK, Channing. *Fool.* nd. Grosset Dunlap. MTI. VG. P3. $10.00

POLLOCK, Dale. *Skywalking.* nd. Harmony. VG/VG. P3. $15.00

POLLOCK, J.C. *Mission MIA.* 1982. Crown. 1st ed. F/F. P3. $16.00

POLLOCK, John Hackett. *Athens Aflame.* ca 1920. Dublin. Martin Lester. 1/500. 8vo. 49p. NF. T10. $65.00

POLLOCK, John Hackett. *Smoking Flax.* ca 1920. Dublin. Martin Lester. 1/500. 8vo. 59p. NF. T10. $50.00

POLLOCK, John Hackett. *Tale of Thule: Together With Some Poems.* ca 1920. Dublin. Talbot. 1/500. 8vo. 56p. VG. T10. $50.00

POLNER, Murray. *Branch Rickey.* 1982. Atheneum. 1st ed. F/F. P8. $50.00

POLWHELE, Richard. *History of Devonshire.* 1793, 1797 & 1806. London. Caddell Johnson Dilly. 3 vol in 1. 1st ed. C6. $500.00

POLZER, Charles. *Kino Guide.* 1968. Tucson. SW Mission Research Center. 1/200. cloth. F3. $30.00

POMERANCE. *Ludwig Bemelmans, a Bibliography.* 1993. NY. Heinemann. 4to. ils. 413p. F/F. A4. $75.00

POMERANZ, Herman. *Medicine in the Shakespearean Plays & Dicken's Doctors.* 1936. NY. 1st ed. 416p. VG. A13. $100.00

POMEROY, Earl. *Pacific Slope.* 1966. Knopf. 2nd. 8vo. ils/fld map/index. xl. VG. T10. $15.00

PONDER, Zita Inez. *Bandaged Face.* 1929. MacAulay. 1st ed. G. P3. $30.00

PONICSAN, Darryl. *Cinderella.* 1973. Liberty. 1st ed. MTI. VG/VG. S13. $30.00

PONICSAN, Darryl. *Goldengrove.* 1971. Dial. 1st ed. NF/VG. B4. $45.00

PONSOT, Marie. *Fables of La Fontaine.* (1957). Grosset Dunlap. ils. pict ep. VG. T5. $25.00

POOL & POOL. *Who Financed Hitler?* 1978. NY. 1st prt. 535p. dj. A17. $12.50

POOLE, Stafford. *In Defense of the Indians.* 1974. DeKalb, IL. 1st ed. 385p. dj. F3. $45.00

POOR, Charles Lane. *Men Against the Rule.* 1937. Derrydale. 1/950. ils. 157p. VG/dj. B5. $70.00

POORTVLIET, Rien. *Dutch Treat, the Artist's Life...* 1981. Abrams. folio. xl. VG/VG. B17. $7.50

POP, Alexander. *Poetical Works of...* nd. Ward Lock. marbled brd. 3-quarter leather. VG. S13. $50.00

POPE, Alexander. *Works of...* 1871. London. Murray. 10 vol. ils/index. gilt cloth. NF. A17. $95.00

POPE, Dudley. *Buccaneer.* 1981. Musson. 1st ed. F/F. P3. $22.00

POPE, Dudley. *England Expects.* 1959. Weidenfeld Nicolson. 1st ed. VG/VG. P3. $30.00

POPE, Dudley. *Ramage.* 1965. Weidenfeld Nicolson. 3rd. xl. dj. P3. $8.00

POPE, Dudley. *Ramage's Devil.* 1982. Secker Warburg. 1st ed. VG/VG. P3. $20.00

POPE, Edwin. *Ted Williams: The Golden Year 1957.* 1970. Prentice Hall. later prt. sgn. VG+/VG+. P8. $275.00

POPE, Saxton. *Adventurous Bowmen: Field Notes on African Archery.* 1926. NY. ils. 233p. VG. B14. $100.00

POPE, Saxton. *Study of Bows & Arrows.* 1914. Berkeley. 20 pl. 64p. G/G. B5. $145.00

POPE & WNELEY. *China.* 1944. Smithsonian. 85p. VG. P4. $22.50

POPHAM, A.E. *Correggio's Drawings.* 1957. London. Oxford. ils/pl. 218p. cloth. D2. $275.00

POPKIN, Zelda. *Journey Home.* nd. BC. VG/VG. P3. $8.00

PORGES. *Edgar Rice Burroughs.* 2 vol. photos/art/covers/ads. 1309p. F. M13. $40.00

PORTER, Anna. *Mortal Sins.* 1988. NAL. 1st ed. rem mk. NF/dj. N4. $15.00

PORTER, Burton P. *Old Canal Days.* 1942. Columbus, OH. 1st/Premiere ed. sgn. ils. 469p. ES. G+. B18. $65.00

PORTER, Connie. *All-Bright Court.* 1991. Houghton Mifflin. 1st ed. author's 1st novel. F/F. M23. $20.00

PORTER, Eliot. *Galapagos the Flow of Wildness.* 1968. Sierra Club. 2 vol. 1st ed. VG/G box. B5. $125.00

PORTER, Gene Stratton. *Birds of the Bible.* 1909. Cincinnati. Jennings Graham. ils. 467p. VG. A4. $400.00

PORTER, Gene Stratton. *Daughter of the Land.* 1918. Garden City. 1st ed. ils. pict cloth. G. A17. $30.00

PORTER, Gene Stratton. *Freckles.* nd. Grosset Dunlap. VG. P3. $15.00

PORTER, Gene Stratton. *Laddie.* (1913). Tor/Country Life. 1st Canadian ed. 4 pl. VG-. A17. $50.00

PORTER, Gene Stratton. *Magic Garden.* nd. Grosset Dunlap. VG. P3. $20.00

PORTER, Gene Stratton. *Magic Garden.* 1927. Garden City. 1st ed. VG/VG. B5. $80.00

PORTER, Gene Stratton. *Music of the Wild.* 1910. Doubleday Page. 426p. VG. M20. $77.00

PORTER, Gene Stratton. *Song of the Cardinal.* May 1903. Indianapolis. 1st ed. lg 8vo. photos. gilt cloth. NF. A17. $175.00

PORTER, Gene Stratton. *Song of the Cardinal.* 1915. NY. sgn. ils. teg. gilt full red leather. VG. H3. $225.00

PORTER, Gene Stratton. *Tales You Won't Believe.* 1925. NY. G. V4. $125.00

PORTER, Gene Stratton. *White Flag.* 1923. Doubleday Page. 1st ed. F/NF. B4. $350.00

PORTER, Joyce. *Dead Easy for Dover.* 1979. St Martin. VG/VG. P3. $22.00

PORTER, Joyce. *Dover & the Unkindest Cut of All.* 1967. Scribner. 1st ed. VG/VG. P3. $25.00

PORTER, Joyce. *Dover Goes to Pott.* 1968. Jonathan Cape. 1st ed. VG. P3. $13.00

PORTER, Joyce. *Dover One.* 1964. Scribner. 1st ed. VG/VG. P3. $40.00

PORTER, Joyce. *Dover Three.* 1965. Scribner. 1st ed. VG/VG. P3. $25.00

PORTER, Joyce. *Neither a Candle Nor a Pitchfork.* 1970. McCall. VG/VG. P3. $25.00

PORTER, Katherine Anne. *Christmas Story.* 1967. Delacorte. ARC. inscr. gilt brd. F/dj. w/letter. B24. $275.00

PORTER, Katherine Anne. *Collected Stories of...* 1965. HBW. 2nd. inscr to nephew/dtd 1971. VG/VG. B4. $250.00

PORTER, Katherine Anne. *Days Before.* 1952. Harcourt Brace. 1st ed. NF/F. B4. $85.00

PORTER, Katherine Anne. *Flowering Judas & Other Stories.* 1935. Harcourt Brace. 1st trade ed. F/dj. B24. $450.00

PORTER, Katherine Anne. *French Song Book.* 1933. Harrison of Paris. 1st ed. 1/595. inscr/sgn to LD Wolfe. NF. B4. $400.00

PORTER, Katherine Anne. *Leaning Tower & Other Stories.* 1944. Harcourt Brace. 1st ed. F/NF. B4. $100.00

PORTER, Katherine Anne. *Leaning Tower & Other Stories.* 1944. Harcourt Brace. 1st ed. 242p. VG/VG. B10. $85.00

PORTER, Katherine Anne. *Pale Horse, Pale Rider.* 1939. Harcourt Brace. 1st ed. F/NF. B24. $235.00

PORTER, Katherine Anne. *Ship of Fools.* 1962. Atlantic/Little Brn. 1st ed. F/NF. H11. $55.00

PORTER, Miriane. *Sally Gabble & the Fairies.* 1929. Macmillan. 1st ed. ils Helen Sewell. VG/VG. P2. $110.00

PORTER & PORTER. *All Under Heaven: The Chinese World.* 1983. Pantheon. 1st ed. 192p. decor cloth. VG+/dj. B18. $25.00

PORTER & PORTER. *In Sickness & Health: The British Experience 1650-1850.* 1988. NY. 1st ed. 324p. dj. A13. $40.00

PORTER & WIGGINS. *Flora of the Galapagos Islands.* 1971. Stanford. ils. 998p. VG+/dj. B26. $110.00

PORTIS, Charles. *Gringos.* 1991. Simon Schuster. 1st ed. F/F. A18. $20.00

PORTIS, Charles. *True Grit.* 1968. NY. 1st ed. F/F. B5. $25.00

POSNER, David. *Sandpipers, Selected Poems 1965-1975.* nd. FL U. 1st ed. F/VG+. V1. $20.00

POST, Emily. *Children Are People.* 1940. NY. 1st ed. 383p. F/dj. A17. $10.00

POST, Emily. *How to Behave Though a Debutant.* 1928. Doubleday Doran. 1st ed. cloth. F/F. B4. $175.00

POST, George E. *Flora of Syria, Palestine & Sinai...* 1932-33. Beirut. 2nd ed. 2 vol. ils/5 maps. B26. $110.00

POST, Kenneth. *Florist Crop Production & Marketing.* 1950 (1949). NY. 427 photos/diagrams. VG. B26. $45.00

POSTON, Charles D. *Building a State in Apache Land.* 1963. Tempe. 1st ed. 8vo. 174p. red cloth. NF. T10. $35.00

POSY, Arnold. *Israeli Tales & Legends.* 1948. Block. 8vo. VG/G. B17. $4.00

POTOK, Chaim. *Chosen.* 1992. Knopf. 1st ed. sgn. rem mk. F/F case. B35. $40.00

POTOK, Chaim. *Promise.* 1969. Knopf. 1st ed. author's 2nd book. F/NF. H11. $30.00

POTTER, Beatrix. *Fairy Caravan.* 1929. Phil. McKay. 1st Am ed. ils Potter. 225p. VG. D1. $450.00

POTTER, Beatrix. *Pie & the Patty-Pan.* 1905. London. 1st ed. VG. M17. $325.00

POTTER, Beatrix. *Roly-Poly Pudding.* 1908. Warne. 1st Am ed. 8vo. 70p. red cloth cloth. VG. D1. $400.00

POTTER, Beatrix. *Tale of Little Pig Robinson.* 1930. McKay. 1st Am ed. 8vo. gr cloth. VG. D1. $350.00

POTTER, Beatrix. *Tale of Peter Rabbit.* 1916. Saalfield. ils Virginia Albert. unp. VG. M20. $10.00

POTTER, Dennis. *Ticket to Ride.* 1985. Faber. 1st Am ed. author's 2nd novel. NF/VG. M22. $30.00

POTTER, Jonathan. *Collecting Antique Maps: An Introduction to History...* 1992. London. Studio/4to. ils. 192p. F/dj. O7. $35.00

POTTER & ROLAND. *Annotated Bibliography of Canadian Medical Periodicals...* 1979. Toronto. 1st ed. 77p. dj. A13. $45.00

POTTERTON, David. *Culpepper's Color Herbal.* 1983. NY. sc. M. B26. $15.00

POTTINGER, Stanley. *The Fourth Procedure.* 1995. NY. Ballantine. 1st. author's 1st novel. NF/NF. $35.00

POTTLE, Frederick A. *Boswell in Holland 1763-1764.* 1952. Heinemann. lg 8vo. 14 pl. 428p. vellum/gilt bl cloth. K1. $75.00

POTTLE, Frederick A. *Boswell in Holland 1763-1764.* 1952. NY. 1st ed. ils. F/dj. A17. $15.00

POTTLE, Frederick A. *Boswell on the Grand Tour: Germany & Switzerland, 1764.* 1953. London. Heinemann. lg 8vo. 1/1000. 354p. gilt bl cloth. K1. $75.00

POULIN, A. *Nameless Garden.* 1978. Croissant. 1st ed. 1/50. sgn/#d. F/wrp. V1. $45.00

POULLE, Emmanuel. *Bibliotheque Scientifique d'un Imprimeur Humaniste...* 1963. Geneva. Librairie Droz SA. 4to. 104p. cream cloth. K1. $35.00

POULSEN, Svend. *Poulsen on the Rose.* 1955 (1941). London. 1st Eng ed. 7 pl. VG/dj. B26. $15.00

POUND, Ezra. *ABC of Reading.* 1934. Yale. 1st Am ed. NF. B4. $85.00

POUND, Ezra. *Cavalcanti Poems.* 1966. London. Faber. 1st ed. sgn. 105p. teg. F/case. B24. $2,250.00

POUND, Ezra. *Ezra Pound & James Laughlin: Selected Letters...* 1994. np. 335p. F/F. A4. $30.00

POUND, Ezra. *Imaginary Letters.* 1930. Blk Sun. 1/50 on Japan vellum. sgn. pub's copy. 56p. F/F/case. C6. $3,000.00

POUND, Ezra. *Lustra.* 1916. London. 2nd. rem bdg. F. C2. $100.00

POUND, Ezra. *Lustra.* 1916. London. Elkin Mathews. 1st ed/1st imp. 1/200. tan cloth. F/case/chemise. B24. $2,500.00

POUND, Ezra. *Personae.* 1909. London. Elkin Mathews. 1st ed. F. B24. $750.00

POUND, Ezra. *Redondillas; or, Something of That Sort.* 1967. New Directions. 1st ed. 1/110. sgn. F/orig plain dj. B24. $1,850.00

POUND, Reginald. *Harley Street.* 1967. London. 1st ed. 198p. dj. A13. $25.00

POURNELLE, Jerry. *Nebula Winners 16.* 1982. HRW. 1st ed. VG/VG. P3. $20.00

POURNELLE, Jerry. *Step Farther Out.* 1980. WH Allen. 1st ed. VG. P3. $20.00

POURNELLE, Jerry. *Storms of Victory.* 1987. Ace. 1st ed. VG/VG. P3. $17.00

POWELL, Anthony. *Kindly Ones.* 1962. Little Brn. 1st ed. F/F. B35. $35.00

POWELL, Anthony. *Soldier's Art.* 1966. London. Heinemann. 1st ed. F/F. C2. $75.00

POWELL, Danny. *Parting the Curtains: Interviews With Southern Writers.* 1994. John K Blair. 1st ed. photos Jill Krementz. F/F. A20. $28.00

POWELL, Dawn. *Golden Spur.* 1962. Viking. 1st ed. F/NF. B4. $400.00

POWELL, Donald M. *Peralta Grant.* 1960. Norman, OK. 1st ed. sgn. ils. 186p. F/NF. T10. $65.00

POWELL, E. Alexander. *Yonder Lies Adventure!* 1932. Macmillan. 1st ed. 452p. VG. W1. $18.00

POWELL, Fay Ellen. *Kitty Colette.* 1988. Saltbush. 1/200. F/sans. B19. $20.00

POWELL, G. Harold. *Letters From the Orange Empire.* 1990. Hist Soc of CA. 1st trade ed. 1/350. 142p. VG. B19. $30.00

POWELL, Gertrude Eliza Clark. *Looking Back & Remembering.* 1987. private prt. 1st ed. ils. 85p. NF. B19. $45.00

POWELL, J.W. *Report of the US Geological Survey...1882-1883.* 1884. WA. folio. 473p. G. T3. $62.00

POWELL, J.W. *Seventh Annual Report of the Bureau of Ethnology...* 1891. GPO. xl. 409p. gr cloth. T10. $50.00

POWELL, J.W. *Sixth Annual Report of the Bureau of Ethnology 1884...* 1888. WA. 669p. gilt olive gr cloth. G+. M20. $95.00

POWELL, J.W. *Thirteenth Annual Report of the US Geological Survey...* 1893. GPO. 4to. 2 fld pocket maps. T10. $150.00

POWELL, Lawrence Clark. *Act of Enchantment.* nd (1961). Stagecoach. 1/300. hc. NF/VG. B19. $32.50

POWELL, Lawrence Clark. *Arizona: A Bicentennial History.* 1976. Norton. 1st ed. ils. 154p. NF/NF. B19. $25.00

POWELL, Lawrence Clark. *Blue Train.* 1977. Capra. 1st ed. author's 1st novel. 128p. VG+/dj. B19. $45.00

POWELL, Lawrence Clark. *Bookman's Progress: Selected Writings of...* 1968. Ward Richie. 255p. F/NF. A4. $45.00

POWELL, Lawrence Clark. *Books in My Baggage.* 1960. World. 1st ed. inscr. 257p. NF. B19. $35.00

POWELL, Lawrence Clark. *Books West Southwest.* 1957. Ward Ritchie. 1st ed/1st state (blk cloth backstrip). 157p. NF. B19. $50.00

POWELL, Lawrence Clark. *California Classics: Creative Literature...* 1971. Ward Ritchie. 1st ed. inscr. 393p. NF. B19. $65.00

POWELL, Lawrence Clark. *El Morro.* 1984. Capra. 1st ed. 129p. VG+. B19. $30.00

POWELL, Lawrence Clark. *Eucalyptus Fair.* 1992. Books West Southwest. 1st ed. 1/50. sgn/#d. 277p. M/case. B19. $100.00

POWELL, Lawrence Clark. *Evening Redness.* 1991. Capra. 1/100. sgn/#d. 436p. leather spine. NF/case. B19. $75.00

POWELL, Lawrence Clark. *Ex Libris: Notes on My Family's Bookplates.* 1984. Bajada. 1st ed. 38p. F/sans. B19. $50.00

POWELL, Lawrence Clark. *Fortune & Friendship.* 1968. RR Bowker. 1st ed. inscr. 227p. NF. B19. $40.00

POWELL, Lawrence Clark. *From the Heartland.* 1976. Northland. ils. 167p. NF. B19. $40.00

POWELL, Lawrence Clark. *Holly & the Fleece.* 1995. Capra. 1st ed. 125p. M. B19. $20.00

POWELL, Lawrence Clark. *Land of Fact.* 1992. Hist Soc S CA. 1st ed. 1/150. sgn LCP/Ward Ritchie. M/sans. B19. $100.00

POWELL, Lawrence Clark. *Landscape & Literature.* 1990. DeGolyer Lib. 1st ed. 1/750. sgn. NF/sans. B19. $40.00

POWELL, Lawrence Clark. *Le Monde Passe, la Figure de ce Monde Passe.* 1983. private prt. 1st ed. 81p. F/sans. B19. $25.00

POWELL, Lawrence Clark. *Life Goes On: Twenty More Years of Fortune...* 1986. Scarecrow. ils. 186p. NF/NF. B19. $45.00

POWELL, Lawrence Clark. *Little Package.* 1964. World. 1st ed. 319p. NF. B19. $55.00

POWELL, Lawrence Clark. *My Haydn Commonplace Book.* 1983. private prt. 1st ed. 1/200 (not intended for sale). 50 p. NF. B19. $50.00

POWELL, Lawrence Clark. *My Mozart Commonplace Book.* 1980. private prt. 1/300. 73p. w/pres card. VG+. B19. $35.00

POWELL, Lawrence Clark. *My New Mexico Literary Friends.* 1986. Pr of Palace of Governors. 1st ed. 27p. bl cloth. NF. B19. $95.00

POWELL, Lawrence Clark. *Orange Grove Boyhood.* 1988. Capra. 1st ed. ils. 80p. NF. B19. $25.00

POWELL, Lawrence Clark. *Passion for Books.* 1958. World. ltd ed. 154p. F/NF case. B19. $110.00

POWELL, Lawrence Clark. *Philosopher Pickett.* 1942. CA U. 1st ed. inscr. 178p. NF/clip. B19. $95.00

POWELL, Lawrence Clark. *Portrait of My Father.* 1986. Capra. 1st ed. 111p. NF. B19. $35.00

POWELL, Lawrence Clark. *River Between.* 1979. Capra. 1st ed. sgn. VG/tattered. B19. $20.00

POWELL, Lawrence Clark. *Vein of Silk, Vein of Steel.* 1975. private prt. 1st ed. F/sans. B19. $65.00

POWELL, Lawrence Clark. *Where Water Flows.* 1980. Northland. 1st ed. 64p. NF. B19. $20.00

POWELL, Mary Lucas. *Status & Health in Prehistory: A Case Study...* 1988. Smithsonian. 8vo. ils/tables/pl. F/F. T10. $25.00

POWELL, P.H. *Murder Premeditated.* 1951. Herbert Jenkins. hc. xl. dj. P3. $10.00

POWELL, Padgett. *Edisto.* 1983. FSG. 1st ed. author's 1st novel. F/F. B4. $75.00

POWELL, Padgett. *Edisto.* 1984. FSG. 1st ed. sgn. F/F. B35. $100.00

POWELL, Padgett. *Typical.* 1991. FSG. 1st ed. sgn. F/F. B35. $50.00

POWELL, Padgett. *Woman Named Drown.* 1987. FSG. 1st ed. sgn. F/F. B35. $55.00

POWELL, Philip. *Soldiers, Indians & Silver.* 1952. CA U. 1st ed. 317p. xl. F3. $25.00

POWELL, Richard R. *Compromises of Conflicting Claims, a Century of CA Law...* 1977. Dobbs Ferry. Oceana. M11. $45.00

POWELL, Talmage. *Mission Impossible: Money Explosion.* 1970. Whitman. TVTI. VG. P3. $10.00

POWELL, Talmage. *Mission Impossible: Priceless Particle.* 1969. Whitman. TVTI. w/sgn label. VG. P3. $20.00

POWELL, Thomas Reed. *Constitution in Transition.* 1941. IL U. 15p. stapled self wrp. M11. $25.00

POWELL, Thomas Reed. *Our Academic Heritage.* 1942. np. Vermont Alumnus. rpt. 4p. M11. $5.00

POWER, Susan. *Grass Dancer.* 1994. Putnam. ARC. F/wrp. B4. $50.00

POWER, Susan. *Grass Dancer.* 1994. Putnam. 1st ed. F/F. M23. $40.00

POWERS, J.F. *Prince of Darkness & Other Stories.* 1947. Doubleday. 1st ed. author's 1st book. F/NF. C2. $100.00

POWERS, J.L. *Black Abyss.* 1966. Arcadia. VG/VG. P3. $13.00

POWERS, John R. *Do Black Patent Leather Shoes Really Reflect Up?* 1975. Chicago. Regnery. 1st ed. author's 2nd book. F/F. H11. $50.00

POWERS, John R. *Junk-Drawer Corner-Store Front-Porch Blues.* 1992. Dutton. 1st ed. F/F. H11. $20.00

POWERS, Richard. *Prisoner's Dilemma.* 1988. NY. Beech Tree/Morrow. 1st ed. F/NF. B2. $100.00

POWERS, Stephen. *A Foot & Alone: A Walk From Sea to Sea by Southern Route.* 1872. Hartford. Columbian Book Co. 1st ed. 12 pl. 327p. cloth. VG+. T10. $275.00

POWERS, Tim. *Anubis Gates.* 1989. Shingletown. Mark Ziesing. 1st Am hc ed. inscr. F/F. T2. $35.00

POWERS, Tim. *Dinner at Deviant's Palace.* nd. BC. VG/VG. P3. $10.00

POWERS, Tim. *Dinner at Deviant's Palace.* 1985. Ace. 1st hc ed. F/F. T2. $12.00

POWERS, Tim. *Drawing of the Dark.* 1991. Eugene. Hypatia. 1st hc ed. 1/275. sgn. intro/sgn KW Jeter. F/sans. T2. $70.00

POWERS, Tim. *On Stranger Tides.* 1987. Ace. 1st ed. sgn. F/F. T2. $45.00

POWERS, Tim. *Skies Discrowned.* 1993. Huntington Beach. James Cahill. 1st hc ed. 1/300. sgns. F/F. T2. $75.00

POWERS, Tim. *Stress of Her Regard.* 1989. Ace. 1st ed. inscr. F/F. T2. $45.00

POWYS, John. *Cowper & Llewellyn: Confessions of Two Brothers.* 1916. Rochester. 1st ed. F/F. C2. $75.00

POYER, David C. *Stepfather Bank.* 1987. St Martin. 1st ed. F/F. P3. $17.00

POYER, Joe. *North Cape.* 1969. Doubleday. 1st ed. xl. dj. P3. $5.00

POYNTER, Noel. *Medicine & Man.* 1971. London. 1st ed. 195p. VG. A13. $25.00

PRAGER, Arthur. *Rascals at Large.* 1971. Doubleday. 1st ed. VG/VG. P3. $25.00

PRASHER. *Indian Library Literature, an Annoted Bibliography.* 1971. New Delhi. 3550 engries. 504p. VG/dj. A4. $65.00

PRATCHETT, Terry. *Strata.* 1994. Doubleday. 1/500. sgn/#d. F/F. P3. $45.00

PRATHER, Richard S. *Amber Effect.* 1986. Tor. 1st ed. F/F. P3. $13.00

PRATHER, Richard S. *Kubla Khan Caper.* 1966. Trident. 1st ed. VG/VG. P3. $25.00

PRATT, Ambrose. *Lore of the Lyrebird.* 1937. Melbourne. 8vo. fwd Colin Mackenzie. 71p. cloth. VG. B14. $30.00

PRATT, Caroll C. *Logic of Modern Psychology.* 1939. Macmillan. inscr. 185p. bl cloth. G1. $35.00

PRATT, Charles Stuart. *Bye-O-Baby Ballads.* nd. Lathrop. later rpt. 8vo. ils Childe Hassam. G+. M5. $90.00

PRATT, Fletcher. *All About Famous Inventors...* 1955. Random. hc. VG. P3. $20.00

PRATT, Fletcher. *Civil War in Pictures.* nd. BC. VG. P3. $10.00

PRATT, Fletcher. *Double in Space.* 1951. Doubleday. 1st ed. NF/NF. P3. $40.00

PRATT, Fletcher. *Fighting Ships of the US Navy.* 1941. Garden City. G/dj. A16. $30.00

PRATT, Fletcher. *Night Work.* 1946. Holt. 1st ed. VG. P3. $30.00

PRATT, Fletcher. *Rockets, Jets, Guided Missiles...* 1951. Random. G. P3. $20.00

PRATT, Fletcher. *Undying Fire.* 1953. Ballantine. 1st ed. F/F. P3. $45.00

PRATT, Fletcher. *Witches Three.* 1952. Twayne. 1st ed. VG/VG. P3. $45.00

PRATT, Theodore. *Murder Goes to the World's Fair.* nd. Eldon. hc. VG. P3. $25.00

PRAWY, Marcel. *Vienna Opera.* 1969. Praeger. 4to. 224p. wht cloth. dj. K1. $45.00

PREISS, Byron. *Microverse.* 1989. Bantam. 1st ed. F/F. G10. $30.00

PREISS, Byron. *Planets.* 1985. Bantam. hc. F/F. P3. $25.00

PREISS, Byron. *Raymond Chandler's Philip Marlowe.* 1988. Knopf. 1st ed. F/F. P3. $19.00

PREISS, Byron. *Universe.* 1987. Bantam. 4to. 335p. VG/VG. K5. $15.00

PRENTIS, Joseph. *Monthly Kalander.* 1992. Chillicothe, IL. Am Botanist. 65p. stiff wrp. A10. $18.00

PRESCOTT, Philander. *Recollections of Philander Prescott, Frontiersman...* 1966. Lincoln, NE. 8vo. 272p. NF/NF. T10. $35.00

PRESCOTT, William Hickling. *History of the Conquest of Mexico.* 1957. Heritage. 8vo. ils Miguel Ovarrubias. prt brd/cloth spine. F. T10. $35.00

PRESCOTT, William Hinkling. *History of the Conquest of Peru.* 1874. Lippincott. 2 vol. 12mo. teg. later quarter red leather. T10. $75.00

PRESS & SIEVER. *Earth.* 1978. WH Freeman. 2nd. 649p. F. D8. $20.00

PRESTON, Howard Willis. *Rhode Island & the Sea.* 1932. Providence. State Bureau of Information. T7. $35.00

PRESTON, Thomas W. *Historical Sketches of the Holston Valleys.* 1926. Kingsport. 186p. VG/VG. B10. $50.00

PREUSS, Paul. *Human Error.* 1985. Tor. 1st ed. hc. F/F. P3. $15.00

PREUSS, Paul. *Starfire.* 1988. Tor. 1st ed. F/F. P3. $18.00

PREUSSLER, Otfried. *Satanic Mill.* nd. Macmillan. 3rd. VG/VG. P3. $14.00

PREYER, Wilhelm. *Ein Merkwurdiger Fall von Fascination.* 1895. Stuttgart. Ferdinand Enke. VG/prt yel wrp. G1. $75.00

PRICE, Alfred. *World War II Fighter Conflict.* 1975. London. MacDonald. 160p. VG+/dj. B18. $32.50

PRICE, Anthony. *Colonel Butler's Wolf.* 1973. Crime Club. 1st ed. xl. dj. P3. $6.00

PRICE, Anthony. *For the Good of the State.* 1987. Mysterious. 1st ed. F/F. P3. $17.00

PRICE, Anthony. *Gunner Kelly.* 1984. Doubleday Crime Club. 1st ed. VG/torn. P3. $12.00

PRICE, Derek J. de Solla. *Science Since Babylon.* 1961. New Haven. 1st ed. 149p. VG. A13. $20.00

PRICE, E. Hoffman. *Strange Gateways.* 1967. Arkham. 1st ed. 1/2007. F/F. T2. $125.00

PRICE, Emerson. *Inn of That Country.* 1939. Caldwell. 1st ed. author's 1st book. F/F. A17. $20.00

PRICE, Eugenia. *New Moon Rising.* 1969. Lippincott. 1st ed. sgn. F/NF. B4. $45.00

PRICE, Eva Jane. *China Journal 1889-1900.* 1989. Scribner. 1st ed. 8vo. 289p. AN/dj. P4. $22.50

PRICE, Fred W. *Moon Observer's Handbook.* 1988. Cambridge. photos. 309p. F/F. K5. $35.00

PRICE, Margaret Evans. *Legends of the Seven Seas.* 1929. Harper. 1st ed. 168p. bl cloth. fairl. T5. $15.00

PRICE, Margaret Evans. *Little Red Riding Hood & Other Old-Time Fairy Tales.* 1926 (1921). Rand McNally. lg 4to. VG. M5. $35.00

PRICE, Margaret Evans. *Sleeping Beauty & Other Old-Time Fairy Tales.* 1926 (1921). Rand McNally. lg 4to. ils. VG. M5. $35.00

PRICE, Molly. *Iris Book.* 1966. Princeton. ils/photos. VG/dj. B26. $22.00

PRICE, Nancy. *Sleeping With the Enemy.* 1987. Simon Schuster. 1st ed. F/F. H11. $40.00

PRICE, Reynolds. *Back Before Day.* 1989. 1/400. sgn. VG/VG. C4. $50.00

PRICE, Reynolds. *Blue Calhoun.* 1st ed. NF/NF. B30. $23.00

PRICE, Reynolds. *Clear Pictures.* 1989. np. ils. 304p. F/F. A4. $25.00

PRICE, Reynolds. *Collected Stories.* 1993. Atheneum. 1st ed. sgn. F/F. C2. $75.00

PRICE, Reynolds. *Kate Vaiden.* 1987. London. 1st ed. VG/VG. C4. $45.00

PRICE, Reynolds. *Love & Work.* 1968. Atheneum. 1st ed. F/F. B2. $40.00

PRICE, Reynolds. *Mustian.* 1983. Atheneum. 1st ed. F/NF. B4. $65.00

PRICE, Reynolds. *Use of Fire.* 1990. Atheneum. 1st ed. F/F. M23. $20.00

PRICE, Richard. *Breaks.* 1983. Simon Schuster. 1st ed. xl. dj. P3. $10.00

PRICE, Richard. *Clockers.* 1992. Houghton Mifflin. 1st ed. F/F. H11. $45.00

PRICE, Richard. *Wanderers.* 1974. Houghton Mifflin. 1st ed. author's 1st novel. F/F clip. B35. $60.00

PRICE, Richard. *Wanderers.* 1974. Houghton Mifflin. 1st ed. author's 1st novel. F/F. H11. $90.00

PRICE. *Civl War Handbook.* 1961. Fairfax, VA. 8vo. 72p. G. T3. $9.00

PRICHARD, James B. *Archaeology & the Old Testament.* 1959. Princeton. 2nd. 8vo. ils/map. VG/dj. W1. $22.00

PRICHARD, James Cowles. *Researches Into the Physical History of Mankind.* 1836-1847. Sherwood Gilbert Piper. 5 vol. 3rd. ils/1 fld map. G. W1. $95.00

PRIDDELL, Guy. *We Began at Jamestown.* 1968. Richmond. Dietz. 1st ed. inscr. 8vo. 198p. orange cloth. F/VG. B11. $40.00

PRIDEAUX. *Bibliography of the Works of Robert Louis Stevenson.* 1917. np. 411p. VG. A4. $125.00

PRIDGEN, Tim. *Courage: Story of Modern Cockfighting.* 1938. ils. VG. M17. $40.00

PRIEST, Christopher. *Glamour.* 1984. Jonathan Cape. 1st ed. sgn. F/F. P3. $30.00

PRIESTLY, J.B. *Black-Out in Gretley.* 1943. Clipper Books. F/F. P3. $30.00

PRIESTLY, J.B. *Bright Day.* 1946. Heinemann. 2nd. VG. P3. $15.00

PRIESTLY, J.B. *Carfitt Crisis.* 1976. Stein Day. 1st ed. VG/VG. P3. $15.00

PRIESTLY, J.B. *Doomsday Men.* 1938. London. Heinemann. 1st ed. VG. M22. $20.00

PRIESTLY, J.B. *Faraway.* 1932. Macmillan. 1st ed. hc. VG. P3. $25.00

PRIESTLY, J.B. *Festival at Farbridge.* 1951. Heinemann. 1st ed. VG. P3. $30.00

PRIESTLY, J.B. *Good Companions.* 1929. Harper. 1st ed. VG. P3. $35.00

PRIESTLY, J.B. *It's an Old Country.* nd. BC. VG/VG. P3. $10.00

PRIESTLY, J.B. *Lost Empires.* 1965. Atlantic/Little Brn. 1st Am ed. VG/VG. M22. $15.00

PRIESTLY, J.B. *Magicians.* 1954. Harper. 1st ed. VG/VG. P3. $40.00

PRIESTLY, J.B. *Salt Is Leaving.* 1975. Harper Row. VG/VG. P3. $15.00

PRIESTLY, J.B. *Shapes of Sleep.* 1962. Heinemann. 1st ed. NF/NF. P3. $25.00

PRILL, David. *Unnatural.* 1995. St Martin. 1st ed. author's 1st book. F/M. M23. $40.00

PRINCE, Leslie. *Ferrier & His Craft.* 1980. London. Allen. 1st prt. VG. O3. $35.00

PRINCE, Morton. *Clinical & Experimental Studies in Personality.* 1929. Cambridge. Sci-Art Pub. 8vo. 559p. dj. G1. $125.00

PRINCE, Pamela. *Once Upon a Time.* 1988. Harmony. 1st ed. ils JW Smith. 47p. NF/NF. T5. $30.00

PRINCE, Pamela. *Sweet Dreams, the Art of Bessie Pease Gutmann.* 1985. Harmony. 11th. rem mk. F/VG. B17. $9.00

PRINGLE, Elizabeth W.A. *Chronicles of Chicora Wood.* 1940. Boston. purple cloth. VG. B30. $25.00

PRINGLE, Terry. *Preacher's Boy.* 1988. Algonquin. 1st ed. rem mk. F/F. H11. $35.00

PRINGLE, Terry. *Tycoon.* 1990. Algonquin. 1st ed. F/F. H11. $20.00

PRIOR, M. *Poems on Several Occasions.* 1709. London. Tomson. 1st authorized ed. 8vo. 328p. F. T10. $250.00

PROCTER, Maurice. *Body to Spare.* nd. BC. VG/VG. P3. $8.00

PROCTER, Maurice. *His Weight in Gold.* 1966. Harper Row. 1st ed. F/F. P3. $18.00

PROCTER, Maurice. *Rogue Running.* 1966. Harper Row. 1st ed. F/F. P3. $18.00

PROCTOR, M. *Natural History of Pollination.* 1996. Portland. 39 tables. 487p. sc. M. B26. $25.00

PROCTOR, Mary. *Everyman's Astronomy.* 1939. Scientific BC. 23 pl. 246p. G/dj. K5. $13.00

PROCTOR, Richard A. *Mysteries of Time & Space.* 1883. NY. Worthington. 1st Am ed. 8vo. 418p. G. K5. $45.00

PRODDOW, Penelope. *Hermes, Lord of Robbers.* 1971. Doubleday. 1st ed. ils Barbara Cooney. NF/VG+. P2. $55.00

PROFATT, John. *Curiosities & Law of Wills.* 1884. San Francisco. Whitney. gilt gr cloth. M11. $75.00

PRONZINI, Bill. *Blowback.* 1977. Random. 1st ed. NF/NF. M22. $65.00

PRONZINI, Bill. *Breakdown.* 1991. Delacorte. 1st ed. F/F. P3. $20.00

PRONZINI, Bill. *Cat's Paw.* 1991. Mystery Scene Short Story. 1st ed. 1/100. sgn. F/sans. P3. $20.00

PRONZINI, Bill. *Crime & Crime Again.* 1990. Bonanza. NF/NF. P3. $12.00

PRONZINI, Bill. *Demons.* 1993. Delacorte. 1st ed. F/F. P3. $20.00

PRONZINI, Bill. *Gallows Land.* 1983. Walker. 1st ed. sgn. F/F. A18. $15.00

PRONZINI, Bill. *Hard-Boiled.* 1995. Oxford. 1st ed. F/F. P3. $25.00

PRONZINI, Bill. *Masques.* 1981. Arbor. 1st ed. VG/VG. N4. $30.00

PRONZINI, Bill. *Nightshades.* 1984. St Martin. 1st ed. F/F. P3. $25.00

PRONZINI, Bill. *Panic!* 1972. Random. 1st ed. VG/VG. P3. $40.00

PRONZINI, Bill. *Quicksilver.* 1984. St Martin. 1st ed. F/F. P3. $25.00

PRONZINI, Bill. *Shackles.* 1988. St Martin. 1st ed. VG/VG. P3. $25.00

PRONZINI, Bill. *Shattershot.* 1982. St Martin. 1st ed. F/F. P3. $30.00

PRONZINI, Bill. *Small Felonies.* 1988. St Martin. 1st ed. F/F. P3. $20.00

PRONZINI, Bill. *Snowbound.* 1974. Putnam. 1st ed. VG/VG. P3. $30.00

PRONZINI, Bill. *Stacked Deck.* 1991. Mystery Scene. 1st ed. 1/50. leather. F/sans. P3. $50.00

PRONZINI, Bill. *Stalker.* 1971. Random. 1st ed. author's 1st book. NF/NF. H11. $55.00

PRONZINI, Bill. *Tales of the Dead.* nd. Bonanza. 3rd. F/F. P3. $12.00

PROPPER, Milton. *Divorce Court Murder.* 1934. Harper. 1st ed. NF/NF double djs. B4. $125.00

PROPPER, Milton. *Handwriting on the Wall.* 1941. Harper. 1st ed. F/NF double djs. B4. $75.00

PROSE, Francine. *Glorious Ones.* 1974. Atheneum. ARC. inscr. RS. F/F. B4. $150.00

PROUDLEY & PROUDLEY. *Heathers in Colour.* 1978 (1974). Poole, Dorset. ils/photos. 192p. F/dj. B26. $16.00

PROULX, E. Annie. *Fences & Gates, Walkways, Walls & Drives.* 1983. 1st ed. author's 2nd book. NF. S13. $75.00

PROULX, E. Annie. *Gardener's Journal & Record Book.* 1983. Rodale. simultaneous wrp ed. F. B4. $185.00

PROULX, E. Annie. *Gourmet Gardner: Growing Choice Fruits & Vegetables...* 1987. Fawcett Columbine. 1st ed. F/wrp. B4. $150.00

PROULX, E. Annie. *Heart Songs & Other Stories.* 1988. Scribner. ARC/1st ed. author's 1st book. RS. F/NF. S9. $750.00

PROULX, E. Annie. *Postcards.* 1992. Scribner. ARC. author's 1st novel. RS. F/F. B4. $500.00

PROULX, E. Annie. *Shipping News.* 1993. Scribner. UP. sgn. F/wrp. B4. $350.00

PROUST, Marcel. *Remembrance of Things Past.* 1934. Random. 2 vol. VG/tattered box. P3. $40.00

PROUST, Marcel. *Swann's Way.* 1954. LEC. 1st ed. ils/sgn Bernard Lamotte. 441p. NF/case. C2. $75.00

PROVENSEN & PROVENSEN. *Animal Fair.* 1952. Simon Schuster. 1st ed. ils. VG. P2. $40.00

PROVENSEN & PROVENSEN. *Golden Bible for Children, the New Testament.* 1953. Golden. folio. G. B17. $4.00

PROVENSEN & PROVENSEN. *Karen's Curiosity.* (1963). Golden. ils. 24mo. unp. G+/torn. T5. $25.00

PROVENSEN & PROVENSEN. *Peaceable Kingdom: The Shaker Abecedarius.* 1978. NY. Viking. 1st ed. F/VG+. C8. $40.00

PROWELL, Sandra West. *By Evil Means.* 1993. Walker. 2nd. F/F. P3. $35.00

PROWELL, Sandra West. *Killing of Monday Brown.* 1994. NY. Walker. AP. 8vo. F/red wrp. S9. $30.00

PROWELL, Sandra West. *Killing of Monday Brown.* 1994. Walker. 1st ed. sgn. F/F. T2. $30.00

PRYOR, William Clayton. *Steamship Book.* 1934. Harcourt Brace. G. A16. $17.50

PTOLEMAEUS, Claudius. *Cosmographia.* 1966. Amsterdam. facsimile. folio. M/dj. O7. $225.00

PTOLEMAEUS, Claudius. *Geographica.* 1966. Amsterdam. facsimile of 1540 ed. 48 double-p maps. M/dj. O7. $295.00

PUBLIUS. *Works...* 1822. Pickering. contemporary calf. miniature. T10. $100.00

PUCKETT, Andrew. *Bloodstains.* 1989. Crime Club. 1st ed. NF/NF. P3. $15.00

PUCKETT, Andrew. *Terminius.* 1990. Collins Crime Club. 1st ed. F/F. P3. $18.00

PUCKETT, David H. *Memories.* 1987. Vantage. 1st ed. F/F. B4. $100.00

PUDNEY, John. *Suez: De Lesseps' Canal.* 1969. London. Dent. 242p. xl. VG/dj. W1. $16.00

PUFFER, Ethel D. *Psychology of Beauty.* 1905. Houghton Mifflin. 286p. prt pebbled crimson cloth. G1. $35.00

PUHARICH, Andrija. *Sacred Mushroom: Key to the Door of Eternity.* 1959. Doubleday. 1st ed. F/NF. B2. $45.00

PUISEUX, P. *La Terre et la Lune.* 1980. Paris. Gauthier-Villars. sm 4to. 176p. xl. K5. $60.00

PUNCH, Walter. *Keeping Eden.* 1992. Boston. Little Brn/MA Horticulture Soc. 277p. AN/dj. A10. $50.00

PUNER, Helen Walker. *Daddies: What They Do All Day.* 1957. Lee Shepard. 7th. 4to. 95p. VG+/G. C14. $10.00

PUNER, Helen Walker. *Sitter Who Didn't Sit.* 1949. Lee Shepard. 1st ed. ils Duvoisin. unp. VG/torn. T5. $35.00

PUNSHON, E.R. *It Might Lead Anywhere.* 1949. Gollancz. 2nd. VG/VG. P3. $20.00

PURCELL, Richard J. *Connecticut in Transition 1775-1818.* 1963. Middletown, CT. Wesleyan U. 8vo. 305p. F/NF. H4. $40.00

PURDY, Carl. *My Life & Times.* 1976. np. ils/photos. 228p. sc. VG. B26. $25.00

PURDY, James. *Eustace Chisholm & the Works.* 1967. NY. 1st ed. F/F. A17. $15.00

PURDY, James. *Mourners Below.* 1981. Viking. 1st ed. F/F. A20. $8.00

PURSER, Philip. *Four Days to the Fireworks.* 1965. Walker. 1st ed. VG/VG. P3. $13.00

PURVES, David Laing. *English Circumnavigators: Most Remarkable Voyages...* 1874. London. Nimmo. ils/4 fld maps. 831p. VG. T7. $60.00

PURVEY, Margery. *Royal Society: Concept & Creation.* 1967. London. 1st ed. 246p. dj. A13. $30.00

PUSHKAREV & TUNNARD. *Man-Made America: Chaos or Control?* 1967.. Yale. 5th. ils. VG/VG. M17. $25.00

PUSHKIN, Alexander. *Golden Cockerel.* 1950. LEC. 1/1500. ils/sgn Edmund Dulac. 42p. F/chemise/case. B24. $350.00

PUTNAM, George Haven. *Books & Their Makers During the Middle Ages.* 1962. rpt of 1896-97 ed. 2 vol. VG/box. B30. $100.00

PUTNAM, H. Phelps. *Collected Poems.* 1970. FSG. 1st ed. F/NF. V1. $20.00

PUTNAM, Mary Traill Spence. *Record of an Obscure Man.* 1861. Ticknor Fields. 1st ed. 8vo. 216p. gilt brn cloth. K1. $35.00

PUTNAM & UHLE. *Pre-Inca Pottery of Nazca, Peru.* 1994. Falcon Hill. rpt. ils. sbdg. F3. $20.00

PUZO, Mario. *Fools Die.* 1978. Putnam. 1st ed. F/NF. H11. $40.00

PUZO, Mario. *Godfather.* 1969. Putnam. 1st ed. NF/VG. H11. $120.00

PUZO, Mario. *Sicilian.* 1984. Linden. 1st ed. NF/dj. H11/N4. $20.00

PYE, Henry James. *Summary of the Duties of a Justice of the Peace...* 1810. London. contemporary speckled calf. M11. $350.00

PYE, Peter. *Sail in a Forest.* 1961. London. Hart Davies. ils/map. 174p. dj. T7. $24.00

PYLE, Ernie. *Last Chapter.* 1946. 1st ed. VG+/chip. S13. $15.00

PYLE, Howard. *Book of King Arthur.* 1970. Classic. hc. VG. P3. $10.00

PYLE, Howard. *Merry Adventures of Robin Hood.* 1920. Scribner. ils. VG. M19. $45.00

PYLE, Howard. *Merry Adventures of Robin Hood.* 1966. Golden. 2nd. 4to. 284p. VG+. C14. $10.00

PYLE, Howard. *Pepper & Salt; or, Seasoning for Young Folks.* 1886. NY. Harper. 1st ed. 4to. 121p. tan cloth. NF. B24. $600.00

PYLE, Howard. *Wonder Clock.* (1915). Harper. ils Howard Pyle. 8vo. 318p. VG. T5. $45.00

PYLE, Katharine. *Tales of Folk & Fairies.* 1919. Little Brn. 1st ed. VG. N4. $35.00

PYM, Roland. *Sleeping Beauty.* 1951. Houghton Mifflin. Peepshow fld book. VG. P2. $65.00

PYNCHON, Thomas. *Crying of Lot 49.* 1966. Lippincott. 1st ed. F/NF. B2. $125.00

PYNCHON, Thomas. *Gravity's Rainbow.* 1973. Viking. 1st ed. author's 3rd book. NF/clip. C2. $375.00

PYTHON, Monty. *Brand New Monty Python Book.* nd. Eyre Methuen. VG/G. P3. $20.00

The instinct to collect, like the process of fermentation, cannot be put out of existence by legislation nor can it be deprived of its vitality by the frowns of those who are insensitive to its urge. As long as people collect and as long as there are books there will be book collectors.

Lawrence C. Wroth
1884 – 1970

– Q –

QUACKENBUSH, Robert. *Sherlock Chick's First Case.* 1986. Parents Magazine. 1st. 8vo. ils. F. M5. $10.00

QUAIFE, Milo. *Absolom Grimes: Confederate Mail Runner.* 1926. Yale. 1st. xl. VG. E6. $30.00

QUAIFE, Milo. *Chicago's Highways Old & New.* 1923. Chicago. DF Keller. 1st. ils/fld map. 278p. G. B18. $25.00

QUAIFE, Milo. *Development of Chicago, 1674-1914.* 1916. Caxton Club. 1/175. ils. 290p. NF. A4. $450.00

QUAIFE, Milo. *Far Hunters in the Far West.* 1924. Lakeside Classic. VG. J2. $165.00

QUAIFE, Milo M. *John Askin Papers.* 1928 & 1931. Detroit Lib Comm. 2 vol. 1/1000. thick 8vo. ils. 3-quarter leather. F. O7. $250.00

QUAIFE, Milo. *Pictures of Gold Rush California.* 1949. Lakeside Classic. 1st thus. teg. dk red cloth. VG/sans. T11. $35.00

QUAIFE, Milo. *Wau-Bun, the Early Days in the North West.* 1932. Lakeside Classic. 609p. VG. J2. $65.00

QUAIN, Richard. *Diseases of the Rectum.* 1854. London. 1st. 4 hand-colored pl. 285p. A13. $200.00

QUALE. *Collector's Book of Children's Books.* 1971. lg 4to. 144p. NF/NF. A4. $155.00

QUAMMEN, David. *Song of the Dodo: Island Biography in Age Extinctions.* 1996. Scribner. 702p. xl. VG. S5. $20.00

QUAMMEN, David. *Soul of Victor Tronko.* 1987. NY. Doubleday. 1st. sgn. F/NF. B3. $40.00

QUAMMEN, David. *Natural Acts.* 1985. NY. Lyons. 1st. F/NF. B3. $50.00

QUAMMEN, David. *To Walk the Line.* 1970. Knopf. 1st. sgn/#d bookplate. author's 1st book. F/NF. B3. $100.00

QUANDT, William B. *Saudi Arabia in the 1980s. Foreign Policy, Security & Oil.* 1981. WA, DC. Brookings Inst. 1st. dbl-p map. 190p. VG/wrp. W1. $6.00

QUANTIC, Diane Dufva. *Nature of the Place: A Study of Great Plains Fiction.* 1995. NE U. 1st. M/dj. A18. $25.00

QUARLES, Benjamin. *Frederick Douglass.* 1948. WA, DC. Assoc Pub. 1st. F/NF clip. B4. $185.00

QUARLES, E.A. *American Pheasant Breeding & Shooting.* 1916. Willmington, DE. Hercules Powder. 1st. ils. 132+8P. G/wrp. H7. $17.50

QUARLES, Garland R. *Some Worthy Lives: Mini-Biographies...* 1988. Winchester-Frederick Co Hist Soc. 280p. AN. B10. $25.00

QUARRINGTON, Paul. *Home Game.* 1983. Canada. Doubleday. 1st. VG/dj. P8. $30.00

QUASHA, George. *Somapoetics.* 1973. Fremont. Sumac. 1st. 1/1000. inscr. NF. L3. $35.00

QUAYLE, Dan. *Standing Firm.* 1994. Harper Collins. 8vo. 402p. F. W2. $40.00

QUAYLE, Eric. *Collector's Book of Books.* 1971. NY. Clarkson Potter. 1st Am. 144p. cloth. F/dj. O10. $40.00

QUAYLE, Eric. *Early Children's Books: A Collector's Guide.* 1983. Totowa, NJ. Barnes Noble. 8vo. gr cloth/label. as new/dj. R5. $85.00

QUAYLE, Eric. *Little People's Pageant of Cornish Legends.* 1986. S&S. 1st Am. ils Michael Foreman. 108p. F/dj. D4. $35.00

QUAYLE, Eric. *Magic Ointment & Other Cornish Legends.* 1986. London. Andersen. 1st. 108p. F/sans. D4. $30.00

QUAYLE, Eric. *Shining Princess.* 1989. Arcade. 1st. 8vo. ils Michael Forman. VG/dj. B17. $15.00

QUEEN, Ellery. *Double, Double.* 1950. Little Brn. 1st. F/NF. M15. $100.00

QUEEN, Ellery. *Ellery Queen's Aces of Mystery.* 1975. NY. Dial. 1st. 8vo. cloth. F/dj. O10. $17.50

QUEEN, Ellery. *Ellery Queen's Champions of Mystery.* 1977. Dial. 1st. F/dj. N4. $25.00

QUEEN, Ellery. *French Powder Mystery.* 1941. Triangle. rpt. VG. N4. $15.00

QUEEN, Ellery. *Murderer Is a Fox.* 1948. London. Gollancz. 1st/2nd imp. VG. T12. $30.00

QUEEN, Ellery. *Origin of Evil.* 1951. Lodnon. 1st. NF/dj. M2. $30.00

QUEEN, Ellery. *Queen's Awards, Sixth Series.* 1951. Little Brn. 1st. VG. M22. $10.00

QUEEN, Ellery. *Queen's Bureau of Investigation.* 1954. Little Brn. 1st. VG/dj. M20. $65.00

QUEEN, Ellery. *Siamese Twin Mystery.* 1933. NY. Stokes. 1st. VG/professionally restored. Q1. $1,000.00

QUEENY, E.M. *Cheechako: Story of an Alaskan Bear Hunt.* 1941. NY. 1/1250. intro Nash Buckingham. F. M4. $135.00

QUEENY, E.M. *Prairie Wings: Pen & Camera Flight Studies...* 1946. NY. Ducks Unlimited. 1st. 4to. 256p. G. H10. $125.00

QUEKETT, John. *Lectures on Histology.* 1852. London. 1st. 215p. A13. $75.00

QUENNELL, Peter. *Mayhew's Characters.* nd. London. Spring Books. M20. $17.00

QUENNELL, Peter. *Prodical Rake: Memoirs of William Hickey.* 1962. Dutton. 1st/3rd prt. 8vo. 452p. VG. W2. $12.00

QUENNELL, Peter. *Samuel Johnson: His Friends & Enemies.* 1973. McGraw Hill. 1st Am. 8vo. 272p. gilt brn cloth. F/dj. H13. $45.00

QUENTIN, Patrick. *Man in the Net.* 1956. S&S. 1st. F/clip. M15. $45.00

QUENTIN, Patrick. *Puzzle for Fiends.* 1946. NY. S&S. 1st. F/NF. M15. $45.00

QUENTIN, Patrick. *Puzzle for Players.* 1938. S&S. 1st. F/VG clip. M15. $135.00

QUERLE, Anthony James. *Allah il Allah!* ca 1930s. Sampson Low. 1st? 255p. Vg/wrp. M7. $25.00

QUERRY, Ronald B. *Growing Old at Willie Nelson's Picnic.* 1983. TX A&M. 1st. sgn. F/F. B3. $75.00

QUICK, Dorothy. *Fifth Dagger.* 1947. Scribner. 1st. VG/G. G8. $40.00

QUICK, Herbert. *Brown Mouse.* 1915. Bobbs Merrill. 1st. ils JA Coughlin. 310p. G. G11. $12.00

QUICK, Herbert. *Invisible Woman.* 1924. Bobbs Merrill. 1st. F/VG. A18. $30.00

QUICK, Herbert. *Virginia of the Air Lanes.* 1909. Bobbs Merrill. 1st. ils Wm R Leigh. 424p. G. G11. $10.00

QUICK, Jim. *Fishing the Nymph.* 1960. Ronald. G. A19. $25.00

QUIGG, Jane. *Miss Brimble's Happy Birthday.* 1955. Oxford. 1st. 95p. VG/G. C14. $10.00

QUIGLEY, Martin. *Magic Shadows: Story of the Origin of Motion Pictures.* 1948. WA, DC. Georgetown U. 1st. ils. VG/dj. C9. $90.00

QUIGLEY, Martin. *Original Colored House of David.* 1981. Houghton Mifflin. 1st. F/VG. P8. $30.00

QUIGLEY, Martin. *Today's Game.* 1956. Viking. 1st. F/VG. P8. $27.50

QUILLER-COUCH, Arthur. *New Oxford Book of English Verse.* 1961. OUP. new ed. sm 8vo. 1166p. F/VG. W2. $360.00

QUILLER-COUCH, Arthur. *Sleeping Beauty & Other Fairy Tales.* 1910. Hodder Stoughton. 1st. ils Edmund Dulac. aeg. 129p. rb morocco/raised bands. F. D1. $750.00

QUIN-HARKIN, Janet. *Peter Penny's Dance.* 1976. Dial. 1st. lg 8vo. VG/VG. C8. $12.50

QUINBY. *Richard Harding Davis: A Bibliography.* 1924. np. 1/1000. 31 pl. 315p. VG. A4. $135.00

QUINBY & STEVENSON. *Catalogue of Botanical Books in Collection RMM Hunt.* nd. 3 vol in 2. 1/400. ils. F. A4. $150.00

QUINCY, John. *Lexicon Physico-Medicum; or, New Medicinal Dictionary.* 1767. London. 482p. VG. B14. $150.00

QUINCY, Josiah. *Essays on the Soiling of Cattle.* 1866. Boston. Williams. 121p. cloth. A10. $35.00

QUINCY, Josiah. *Speeches Delivered in Congress of the United States...* 1874. Little Brn. 8vo. pres from edit. 412p. gilt gr cloth. VG. O1. $75.00

QUINCY, William S. *Three-Masted Schooner James Miller.* 1986. Mystic Seaport Mus. ils/3 fld plans. 48p. wrp. T7. $17.00

QUINE, C.R. *Old Portage & the Portage Path.* 1953. np. 35p. VG/wrp. B18. $25.00

QUINE, Judith Balaban. *Bridesmaids: Grace Kelly, Princess of Monaco...* 1989. NY. Weidenfeld Nicholson. 1st. F/dj. T12. $25.00

QUINN, Dan; see Lewis, Alfred Henry.

QUINN, David. *North America From Earliest Discovery to First Settlements.* 1977. Harper Row. New Am Nation series. 1st. 81 ils/maps. F/dj. O7. $45.00

QUINN, David. *Roanoke Voyuges 1584-1590.* 1955. London. Hakluyt Soc. 1st. 2 vol. 8vo. gilt bl cloth. NF. P4. $165.00

QUINN, P.T. *Money in a Garden, a Vegetable Manual.* 1871. 1st. woodcuts. xl. VG. E6. $30.00

QUINN, P.T. *Pear Culture for Profit.* 1869. NY. Tribune. 136p. A10. $38.00

QUINN, Vernon. *Leaves: Their Place in Life & Legend.* 1937. NY. Stokes. 211p. VG. A10. $32.00

QUINN, Vernon. *Seeds: Their Place in Life & Legend.* 1936. NY. Stokes. 188p. cloth. VG. A10. $28.00

QUINTANILLA, Luis. *Franco's Black Spain.* 1946. Reynal Hitchcock. 1st. 4to. VG/VG. B2. $85.00

QUIRING, Daniel. *Collateral Circulation (Anatomical Aspects).* 1949. Phil. 1st. 142p. xl. A13. $15.00

QUIRK, John. *Hard Winners.* 1965. Random. 1st. VG/VG. P3. $22.00

QUIRK, Lawrence J. *Claudette Colbert, an Illustrated Biography.* 1985. Crown. 1st. 212p. VG+/dj. M20. $15.00

QUISUMBING, E.A. *Complete Writings of... on Philippine Orchids.* 1981. Manila. 2 vol. ils/pl. edit HI Valmayor. as new. B26. $45.00

It is because the passion for books is a sentimental passion that people who have not felt it always fail to understand it.

Andrew Lang
1844 – 1912

– R –

RAAB, Lawrence. *Mysteries of the Horizon.* 1972. Doubleday. 1st ed. F/VG+. V1. $15.00

RAABE, Tom. *Biblioholism: The Literary Addiction.* 1991. Golden. Fulcrum. 1st ed. pb. F/pict wrp. T2. $15.00

RABAN, Jonathan. *Arabia: Journey Through the Labyrinth.* 1979. Simon Schuster. 1st ed. 344p. VG/dj. W1. $20.00

RABAN, Jonathan. *Old Glory: An American Voyage.* 1981. Simon Schuster. 409p. dj. T7. $22.00

RABE, David. *Crossing Guard.* 1995. Hyperion. UP. NF. B35. $30.00

RABELAIS, Francois. *Gargantua & Pantagruel.* 1990. Norton. 2nd. F/F. P3. $30.00

RABKIN, Eric S. *Fantastic Worlds.* 1979. Oxford. 1st ed. VG/VG. P3. $20.00

RABOFF, Ernest. *Paul Klee, Art for Children.* 1969. Doubleday. VG/VG. B17. $5.00

RACE, Elizabeth. *Little Gumdrop.* nd. McNight. 8vo. ils. unp. VG. C14. $10.00

RACINA, Thom. *Great Los Angeles Blizzard.* 1977. Putnam. 1st ed. VG/VG. P3. $15.00

RACKHAM, Arthur. *Arthur Rackham Fairy Book.* 1987. Weathervane. VG/VG. P3. $15.00

RACKHAM, Arthur. *Midsummer-Night's Dream.* 1912. Doubleday Page. 3rd imp. 4to. G. B17. $80.00

RACKHAM, Arthur. *Peter Pan in Kensington Gardens, Retold for Little People.* 1958. Scribner. 12mo. ils. xl. G. B17. $7.50

RACKHAM, Arthur. *Rhinegold & the Valkyrie.* 1939. Garden City. 8vo. bl cloth. VG/G. B17. $45.00

RACKHAM, Arthur. *Some British Ballads.* (1920). Dodd Mead. 1st Am ed. ils Rackham. 170p. gilt bl cloth. F. T10. $250.00

RACKHAM, B. *Book of Porcelain.* 1910. London. Blk. 1st ed. 28 tipped-in pl. VG. B5. $90.00

RACZ, Attila. *Courts & Tribunals, a Comparative Study.* 1980. Budapest. Akademiai Kiado. M11. $45.00

RADCLIFFE, Charles Bland. *Vital Motion as Mode of Physical Motion.* 1876. Macmillan. sm 8vo. 252p. prt cloth. G1. $75.00

RADCLIFFE, J.N. *Friends, Ghosts & Sprites.* 1854. London. early 3-quarter leather. VG. A9. $125.00

RADEKA, Lynn. *Legendary Towns of the Old West.* 1990. NY. 1st ed. photos. 176p. F/F. E1. $30.00

RADER. *South of Forty, From Mississippi to Rio Grande...* 1947. OK U. 4to. describes 3793 titles. 336p. VG/dj. A4. $225.00

RADFORD, P.J. *Antique Maps.* 1965. Denmead. Radford. 33 maps. NF/rpr. O7. $35.00

RADIGUET, Raymond. *Devil in the Flesh.* 1948. Blk Sun. 1st ed. trans Kay Boyle. VG/VG. M22. $35.00

RADIN, Edward D. *Lizzie Borden: The Untold Story.* 1961. Simon Schuster. cloth. worn. M11. $35.00

RADIN, Paul. *Indians of South America.* 1942. Doubleday Doran. 1st ed. 324p. F. E1. $45.00

RADIN & WEI. *Precision's One Club Complete.* 1981. 169p. VG/wrp. S1. $5.00

RADLEY, Shelia. *Quiet Road to Death.* nd. BC. VG/VG. P3. $10.00

RADLEY, Shelia. *Who Saw Him Die?* 1987. Scribner. 1st ed. VG/VG. P3. $15.00

RADOK, Rainier. *Australia's Coast: Environmental Atlas Guide...* 1976. Adelaide. Rigby. 33 pl. NF. O7. $50.00

RAE, Hugh C. *Harkfast.* 1976. St Martin. 1st ed. hc. F/F. P3. $20.00

RAE, Hugh C. *Sullivan.* 1978. Constable. 1st ed. VG/VG. P3. $18.00

RAE, John. *Statues of Henry VII.* 1869. London. John Camden Hotten, contemporary morocco. M11. $225.00

RAEMAEKERS, Louis. *Kultur in Cartoons.* 1917. NY. dk gr cloth. xl. VG. B30. $20.00

RAFERT, Stewart. *Miami Indians of Indiana.* 1996. IN Hist Soc. 352p. M. M20. $30.00

RAFFERTY, Milton D. *Historical Atlas of Missouri.* 1982. Norman, OK. 1st ed. maps/references. 113p. F/stiff wrp. E1. $25.00

RAGO, Henry. *Sky of Late Summer.* 1963. Macmillan. 1st ed. F/NF. V1. $20.00

RAGSDALE, Kenneth Baxter. *Quicksilver, Terlingua & the Chisos Mining Company.* 1976. College Sta, TX. 1st ed. photos. 327p. F/F. E1. $30.00

RAHEB, Barbara J. *Diary of a Victorian Cat.* 1993. Pennywright. 1/300. ils. gilt morocco. miniature. B24. $55.00

RAHEB, Barbara J. *Haunted House.* 1992. Agoura Hills. Pennyweight. gilt leatherette. miniature. F. B24. $250.00

RAHMAN, Fazlur. *Islam.* 1979. Chicago. 2nd. 8vo. 285p. VG. W1. $22.00

RAHT, Carlysle Graham. *Romance of Davis Mountains & Big Bend Country.* 1919. El Paso. Rathbooks. ils/26 pl. 382p. gilt bl cloth. K1. $100.00

RAINE, Richard. *Night of the Hawk.* 1968. Heinemann. 1st ed. VG/VG. P3. $22.00

RAINE, William MacLeod. *Broad Arrow.* 1945. Triangle. VG. P3. $12.00

RAINE, William MacLeod. *For Honor & Life.* 1933. Houghton Mifflin. 1st ed. F/F. A18. $25.00

RAINE, William MacLeod. *Guns of the Frontier: Story of How the Law Came to the West.* (1946). Cleveland, OH. Forum. 1st ed. 282p. F. E1. $35.00

RAINE, William MacLeod. *Gunsight Pass.* 1946. Triangle. VG. P3. $8.00

RAINE, William MacLeod. *Hell & High Water.* 1973. Tom Stacey. hc. VG/VG. P3. $15.00

RAINE, William MacLeod. *Outlaw Trail.* 1947. London. Hodder Stoughton. 1st ed. VG/clip. A18. $20.00

RAINE, William MacLeod. *Plantation Guns.* 1945. Hodder Stoughton. 1st ed. F/VG. A18. $20.00

RAINE, William MacLeod. *This Nettle Danger.* 1947. Houghton Mifflin. 1st ed. F/VG+. A18. $30.00

RAINE, William MacLeod. *Trail's End.* 1947. World. VG/VG. P3. $15.00

RAINE, William MacLeod. *45-Caliber Law: Way of Life of the Frontier Officer.* nd. np. pict bdg. F. E1. $35.00

RAJAB, Jehan. *Palestinian Costume.* 1989. Kegan Paul. 1st ed. 160p. NF/dj. W1. $45.00

RAK, Mary Kidder. *Cowman's Wife.* 1934. Boston. 1st ed. ils/map ep. 269p. NF/worn. E1. $45.00

RAKOCY, Bill. *Images Paso Del Norte, 400 Years of Pictorial Borderland...* 1980. El Paso. 1st ed. sgn/dtd. 301p. F. E1. $100.00

RAKOSI, Carl. *Ere-Voice.* 1971. New Directions. 1st ed. sgn. NF. V1. $35.00

RALEIGH, Walter. *Cabinet-Council.* 1658. Johnson. 12mo. 200p. rebound calf. K1. $300.00

RALLING, C. *Voyage of Charles Darwin: His Autobiographical Writings...* 1979. Mayflower Books. 1st Am ed. 183p. F/dj. D8. $12.00

RALPHSON, George H. *With the Canadians at Vimy Ridge.* 1919. Donohue. Over There series. G+. P12. $6.00

RAMAGE, Edwin S. *Atlantis: Fact or Fiction?* 1978. IN U. 1st ed. NF/NF. M23. $20.00

RAMANUJAN, A.K. *Striders.* 1966. London. 1st ed. assn copy. F/NF. V1. $20.00

RAMBO, Ralph. *Trailing the California Bandit, Tiburcio Vasquez 1835-75.* 1968. San Jose, CA. 1st ed. sgn. ils/maps. 40p. F/stiff wrp. E1. $45.00

RAME, David. *Road to Tunis.* 1944. Macmillan. 1st ed. 296p. VG. W1. $18.00

RAME, David. *Road to Tunis.* 1944. NY. 1st ed. 296p. VG/VG. B5. $25.00

RAMPLING, Anne; see Rice, Anne.

RAMSAY, Diana. *Deadly Discretion.* 1973. Collins. 1st ed. F/F. P3. $25.00

RAMSAY, Jay; see Campbell, Ramsey.

RAMSBOTTOM, J. *Book of Roses.* 1941. Middlesex, Eng. ils. 30p. brd. B26. $15.00

RAMSEY, Dan. *How to Forecast the Weather.* 1983. Tab pb. 213p. K5. $10.00

RAMSEY, Guy. *Aces All.* 1955. London. 205p. VG. S1. $15.00

RAMSLAND, Katherine. *Prism of the Night: A Biography of Anne Rice.* 1991. NY. 1st ed. 85p. F/F. A17. $20.00

RAMSLAND, Katherine. *Vampire Companion.* 1993. Ballantine. 1st ed. F/F. P3. $30.00

RAND, Ayn. *Atlas Shrugged.* 1957. NY. 1st ed. VG/torn. A15. $150.00

RAND, Ayn. *For the New Intellectual.* 1961. NY. 1st ed. VG/VG. B5. $45.00

RAND, Ayn. *Fountainhead.* nd. Bobbs Merrill. VG. P3. $15.00

RAND, Ayn. *Goal of My Writing.* 1963. Nathaniel Branden Inst. 10p. VG/wrp. B4. $100.00

RAND, Clayton. *Sons of the South.* 1961. HRW. 1st ed. inscr. 212p. NF. T10. $35.00

RAND, Edward. *Popular Flowers & How to Cultivate Them.* 1874 (1870). Boston. Shepard. 208p. VG. A10. $40.00

RAND, George Hart. *Sherman Hale, the Harvard Half-Back.* 1910. Fenno. 326p. VG+/dj. M20. $40.00

RAND MCNALLY. *Commercial Atlas & Marketing Guide. 81st Edition.* 1950. Chicago. xl. G. O7. $45.00

RANDALL, Bob. *Fan.* 1977. Random. 1st ed. VG/VG. P3. $18.00

RANDALL, Homer. *Army Boys in the French Trenches.* 1919. World. VG/G+. P12. $6.00

RANDALL, Homer. *Army Boys on the Firing Line.* 1919. Saalfield. G+/G+. P12. $8.00

RANDALL, J.G. *Lincoln & the South.* 1946. Baton Rouge. 1st ed. 161p. VG/dj. B18. $15.00

RANDALL, Marta. *Sword of Winter.* 1983. Timescape. 1st ed. VG/VG. P3. $20.00

RANDALL, Robert. *Dawning Light.* 1959. Gnome. 1st ed. xl. dj. P3. $15.00

RANDAU, Carl. *Visitor.* 1945. Tower. 1st ed. hc. NF/NF. P3. $20.00

RANDIER, Jean. *Nautical Antiques for the Collector.* 1976. London. Barrie Jenkins. VG/VG. A16. $65.00

RANDISI, Robert J. *Alone With the Dead.* 1995. St Martin. 1st ed. F/F. P3. $22.00

RANDISI, Robert J. *Dead of Brooklyn.* 1991. St Martin. 1st ed. NF/NF. P3. $19.00

RANDISI, Robert J. *Eyes Have It.* 1984. Mysterious. 1st ed. F/F. P3. $25.00

RANDISI, Robert J. *No Exit From Brooklyn.* 1987. St Martin. 1st ed. F/NF. T2. $20.00

RANDISI, Robert J. *Separate Cases.* 1990. Walker. 1st ed. NF/F. N4. $20.00

RANDISI & WALLACE. *Deadly Allies.* 1992. Doubleday Perfect Crime. 1st ed. F/F. P3. $20.00

RANDOLPH, Buckner Magill. *Ten Years Old & Under...1873-1880.* 1935. Ruth Hill. 127p. VG. B10. $45.00

RANDOLPH, J. Ralph. *British Travelers Among the Southern Indians 1660-1763.* 1973. np. 1st ed. 183p. F/dj. E1. $35.00

RANDOLPH, Marion. *Breathe No More.* 1944. Tower. VG/G+. P3. $13.00

RANDOLPH, Mary. *Virginia Housewife; or, Methodical Cook.* 1984. Birmingham. facsimile of 1828 ed. silk moire ep. aeg. A17. $20.00

RANDOLPH, Vance. *Down in the Holler.* 1953. Norman. 1st ed. VG/worn. B5. $32.50

RANKE, Herman. *Art of Ancient Egypt.* 1936. Allen Unwin. 1st ed. tall 8vo. 232 pl. VG/dj. W1. $22.00

RANKIN, E.B. *Modern Base Ball Science.* 1915. Nat Base Ball Reg Bureau. G+. P8. $350.00

RANKIN & SCHEER. *Rebels & Redcoats: Living Story of the American Revolution.* 1957. World. 1st ed. inscr Rankin. 8vo. 572p. F/F. B11. $50.00

RANKINE, John. *Fingalnam Conspiracy.* 1973. Sidgwick Jackson. 1st ed. hc. F/F. P3. $35.00

RANKINE, John. *Never the Same Door.* 1967. Dobson. 1st ed. F/F. P3. $20.00

RANNEY, Edward. *Stonework of the Maya.* 1974. Albuquerque. 1st ed. 119p. wrp. F3. $20.00

RANSOM, Bill. *Burn.* 1995. Ace. 1st ed. AN/dj. M22. $20.00

RANSOM, Bill. *Last Call.* 1983. Bl Begonia. 1/300. sgn. F/wrp. V1. $15.00

RANSOM, Bill. *Virvax.* 1993. Ace. 1st ed. NF/VG+. G10. $5.00

RANSOM, J.E. *Fossils in America.* 1964. Harper Row. 1st ed. 402p. F/dj. D8. $18.00

RANSOM, John Crowe. *Armageddon.* 1923. Charleston. Poetry Soc of SC. 1st ed. VG/stapled wrp. C2. $450.00

RANSOM, John Crowe. *Grace After Mead.* 1924. Hogarth. 1st ed. 1/400. F. B24. $650.00

RANSOM, John Crowe. *Poems About God.* 1919. Holt. 1st ed. poet's 1st book. assn copy. F/glassine. V1. $550.00

RANSOM, John Crowe. *Poems About God.* 1919. NY. 1st ed. author's 1st book. VG+. C2. $175.00

RANSOM, M.A. *Sea of the Bear: Journal of a Voyage to Alaska & the Arctic.* 1921. US Naval Inst. 1st ed. 119p. bl cloth. NF/dj. B22. $8.50

RANSOME, Stephen. *Alias His Wife.* 1965. Dodd Mead. 1st ed. VG/G+. P3. $15.00

RANSOME, Stephen. *False Bounty.* 1948. Crime Club. 1st ed. G. P3. $15.00

RANSOME, Stephen. *Frazer Aquittal.* 1955. Crime Club. 1st ed. VG/VG. P3. $20.00

RANSOME, Stephen. *Lilies in Her Garden Grew.* 1973. Lythway. hc. F/F. P3. $15.00

RANSOME, Stephen. *Shroud Off Her Back.* 1953. Doubleday. 1st ed. lacks ffe. VG. P3. $10.00

RANSOME, Stephen. *Warning Bell.* 1960. Crime Club. 1st ed. VG/G+. P3. $20.00

RANSTEAD, Herbert E. *True Story & History of 53rd Regiment...* 1910. np. 1st ed. 104p. VG/wrp. M8. $650.00

RAO, N.S.S. *Biological Nitrogen Fixation.* 1988. Montreaux. Gordon Breach. 337p. brd. F/F. B1. $50.00

RAPER, J.R. *Without Shelter: Early Career of Ellen Glasgow.* 1971. LSU. 273p. VG/VG. B10. $15.00

RAPHAEL, Morris. *Battle in the Bayou Country.* 1976. Detroit. 2nd. sgn. 199p. VG/dj. B18. $15.00

RAPHAEL, Rick. *Thirst Quenchers.* 1966. British SF BC. hc. xl. dj. P3. $5.00

RAPP, George. *Thoughts on the Destiny of Man...* 1824. New Harmony, IN. sm 8vo. 96p. plain bl wrp. C6. $2,000.00

RAPPORT, Leonard. *Fakes & Facsimiles: Problems of Identification.* Jan 1979. Am Archivist. ils. 58p. G/wrp. T3. $20.00

RAPPORT, S. *History of Egypt.* 1904. London. Grollier. 1st ed. 1/200. 1200 ils/pl. 3-quarter morocco. VG. W1. $350.00

RASCOE, Burton. *Belle Starr, the Bandit Queen.* 1941. NY. 1st ed. ils/photos/index. 340p. F. E1. $60.00

RASCOE, Jesse. *Pegleg's Lost Gold.* 1973. Ft Davis, TX. 1st ed. 102p. F/wrp. E1. $25.00

RASHER, Mrs. *Mrs Rasher's Curtain Lectures.* 1884. JS Ogilvie. 1st ed. G+. P12. $18.00

RASMUSSEN, Halfdan. *Halfdan's ABC.* 1982 (1967). Copenhagen. Carlsen Litho. Danish text. unp. NF. C14. $20.00

RASOR, Dina. *Pentagon Underground.* 1985. NY. 1st ed. 310p. E1. $15.00

RASWAN, Carl. *Drinkers of the Wind.* 1961. NY. Ariel. 2nd. VG/G. O3. $35.00

RATCHFORD, Fannie E. *Story of Champ d'Asile, as Told by Two of the Colonists.* 1969. Austin, TX. facsimile. 180p. F/case. E1. $40.00

RATCLIFF, J. *Yellow Magic, the Story of Penicillin.* 1945. NY. 173p. VG. A13. $30.00

RATCLIFFE, J.A. *Physics of the Upper Atmosphere.* 1960. Academic. 8vo. photos/diagrams. 586p. VG/dj. K5. $45.00

RATH, Ida Ellen. *Rath Trail.* 1961. Wichita. 1st ed. 204p. E1. $30.00

RATHBONE, Julian. *Carnival!* 1976. Michael Joseph. 1st ed. VG/VG. P3. $20.00

RATHBONE, Julian. *Diamonds Bid.* 1967. Walker. 1st ed. F/F. P3. $15.00

RATHBONE, Julian. *Euro-Killers.* 1979. Pantheon. 1st ed. VG/VG. P3. $15.00

RATHBONE, Julian. *Ravishing Monarchist.* 1978. St Martin. 1st ed. NF/NF. P3. $20.00

RATHBONE, Julian. *Watching the Detectives.* 1983. Pantheon. 1st ed. VG/VG. P3. $14.00

RATHBONE, Julian. *With My Knives I Know I'm Good.* 1970. Putnam. 1st ed. VG/VG. P3. $25.00

RATHBONE, Julian. *Zdt.* 1986. Heinemann. 1st ed. NF/NF. P3. $22.00

RATHBONE, Perry T. *Mississippi Panorama...* 1950. City Art Mus of St Louis. new/revised. 228p. VG/G. B10. $15.00

RATHJEN, Carl Henry. *Flight of Fear.* 1969. Whitman. TVTI. VG. P3. $8.00

RATIGAN, William. *Great Lakes Shipwrecks & Survivals.* 1969. Grand Rapids. Eerdmans. new revised ed. VG/VG. A16. $20.00

RATIGAN, William. *Straits of Mackinac!* 1957. Grand Rapids. Eerdmans. G/G. A16. $15.00

RATTAN, Volney. *Popular California Flora...* 1988. San Francisco. 8th revised. ils. VG. B26. $18.00

RAUCHER, Herman. *Maynard's House.* 1980. Putnam. 2nd. F/F. P3. $15.00

RAUCHER, Herman. *Summer of '42.* 1971. Putnam. 1st ed. F/F. B4. $150.00

RAVEN, Neil. *Evidence.* 1987. Scribner. 1st ed. F/F. H11. $20.00

RAVEN, Simon. *Before the Cock Crow.* 1986. Muller Blond Wht. 1st ed. VG/VG. P3. $25.00

RAVEN, Simon. *Rich Pay.* 1965. Putnam. 1st ed. VG/VG. P3. $20.00

RAVEN & RAVEN. *Genus Epilobium (Onagraceae) in Australia...* 1976. Christchurch. sgns. ils/sgn Keith R West. photos/map. 322p. B26. $55.00

RAVEN. *British Fiction 1750-1770, a Chronological Check-List...* 1987. DE U. 1363 entries. 359p. F/VG. A4. $50.00

RAWLINGS, Charles. *In Our Neck O' the Woods.* 1972. Sheridan, WY. F/VG. N3. $20.00

RAWLINGS, Marjorie Kinnan. *Cross Creek.* 1942. Scribner. 1st ed. VG/VG. M19. $50.00

RAWLINGS, Marjorie Kinnan. *Cross Creek Cookery.* 1942. NY. 1st ed. VG/VG. P3. $50.00

RAWLINGS, Marjorie Kinnan. *Secret River.* 1956. Scribner. 2nd. 8vo. ils. NF. C14. $12.00

RAWLINGS, Marjorie Kinnan. *Sojourner.* 1953. Scribner. 1st ed. VG/VG. P3. $40.00

RAWLINGS, Marjorie Kinnan. *When the Whippoorwill.* 1940. Scribner. 1st ed. NF/VG. B4. $350.00

RAWLINGS, Rover. *Last Airmen.* 1989. NY. 1st ed. 241p. VG+/dj. B18. $15.00

RAWN, Melanie. *Golden Key.* 1966. DAW. 1st ed. F/F. P3. $25.00

RAWN, Melanie. *Stronghold.* 1990. DAW. 1st ed. F/F. P3. $22.00

RAWSON, Clayton. *Footprints on the Ceiling.* 1979. Gregg. VG/VG. P3. $25.00

RAWSON, Clayton. *Headless Lady.* 1940. Putnam. 1st ed. VG. P3. $45.00

RAWSON, Clayton. *No Coffin for the Corpse.* 1979. Gregg. 1st ed. VG/VG. P3. $25.00

RAY, Clarence E. *Rube Burrow, King of Outlaws & Train Robbers.* nd. Chicago. 181p. NF/wrp. E1. $45.00

RAY, David. *Kangaroo Paws.* 1995. Thomas Jefferson U. 1st ed. F/sans. V1. $20.00

RAY, Gordon N. *Buried Life: Study of Relation Between Thackeray...* 1962. Harvard. 148p. dj. A17. $7.50

RAY, Isaac. *Treatise on the Medical Jurisprudence of Insanity.* 1962. Cambridge. 376p. VG. A13. $50.00

RAY, Man. *Man Ray: Self Portrait.* 1963. Boston. 1st ed. ils/photos. 398p. F/dj. A17. $75.00

RAY, Robert. *Cage of Mirrors.* 1980. Lippincott Crowell. 1st ed. VG+/VG. A20. $18.00

RAY, Robert. *Hit Man.* 1988. St Martin. 1st ed. F/F. P3. $19.00

RAY, Robert. *Merry Christmas, Murdock.* 1989. Delacorte. 1st ed. F/VG+. A20. $8.00

RAY, Tom. *Yellowstone Red.* 1948. Dorrance. 1st ed. sgn. VG/VG. P3. $30.00

RAY, Worth S. *Down in the Cross Timbers.* 1947. Austin, TX. 1st ed. 1/500. inscr. ils. 160p. F. E1. $80.00

RAYER, F.G. *Tomorrow Sometimes Comes.* 1951. Home & Van Thal. 1st ed. VG. P3. $15.00

RAYMO, Chet. *In the Falcon's Claw.* 1990. Viking. 1st ed. rem mk. F/F. M23. $15.00

RAYMOND, Alex. *Flash Gordon & the Planet Mongo.* 1974. Nostalgia. 1st ed. VG/VG. P3. $35.00

RAYMOND, Jehan. *Le Cur, Compositions Decoratives.* ca 1900. Chicago. G Broes Van Dort. folio. 48 pl. VG. T10. $250.00

RAYMOND, M. *God Goes to Murderer's Row.* 1951. Bruce. 1st ed. VG/VG. P3. $10.00

RAYMOND, Nancy. *Smoky.* 1945. Fideler. 4to. VG/VG. B17. $22.50

RAYMONT, J.E.G. *Plankton & Productivity in the Oceans.* 1967. Pergamon. 2nd. 8vo. 2 fld ils/tables/graphs. dj. B1. $30.00

RAYTER, Joe. *Stab in the Dark.* 1955. Morrow. 1st ed. G+/dj. P3. $15.00

READ, Conyers. *Lord Burghley & Queen Elizabeth.* 1960. Knopf. 1st ed. 603p. VG/dj. M20. $20.00

READ, Herbert. *Herbert Read: An Intro to His Various Works...* nd. Faber. F/NF. V1. $20.00

READ, Opie. *Arkansas Planter.* 1896. Chicago. 1st ed. VG. B5. $75.00

READ, Piers Paul. *Season in the West.* 1988. Random. 1st ed. F/F. H11. $20.00

READE, Hamish. *Comeback for Stark.* 1968. Putnam. 1st ed. NF/NF. P3. $10.00

READING, Robert S. *Indian Civilizations.* 1961. San Antonio, TX. 2nd. 200p. F/F. E1. $20.00

REAGAN, Ronald. *Where's the Rest of Me.* 1965. NY. 1st ed. VG/VG. B5. $35.00

REAGAN, Thomas B. *Caper.* 1969. Putnam. 1st ed. VG/VG. P3. $20.00

REAVER, Chap. *Mote.* 1990. Delacorte. 1st ed. sgn. F/VG. B11. $20.00

REBELL, Fred. *Escape to the Sea.* 1939. London. Murray. ils. 254p. VG. T7. $30.00

REBEN, Martha. *Healing Woods.* 1952. NY. 1st ed. sgn. VG/VG. B5. $25.00

RECHY, John. *This Day's Death.* 1969. Grove. 1st ed. F/F. B2. $35.00

RECORD, S.J. *Ecomomic Woods of the United States.* 1912. Wiley. 8vo. ils. 117p. cloth. NF. B1. $25.00

RED FOX. *Memoirs of Chief Red Fox.* 1971. McGraw Hill. 2nd. 8vo. 209p. F/dj. T10. $25.00

REDFIELD, James. *Celestine Prophecy.* 1994. NY. Warner. 1st ed. F/F. I11. $30.00

REDMOND, Juanita. *I Served on Bataan.* 1943. Phil. 3rd imp. 167p. G. A17. $7.50

REDMOND, Paul J. *Flora of Worchester County, MD.* 1932. WA, DC. 104p. NF/wrp. B26. $20.00

REDONDI, Pietro. *Galileo: Heretic.* 1987. Princeton. trans Raymond Rosenthal. 356p. VG/dj. K5. $30.00

REED, David. *Anna.* nd. BC. VG. P3. $10.00

REED, Earl. *Dune Country.* 1916. John Lane. 1st ed. inscr. VG. A20. $95.00

REED, Earl. *Silver Arrow.* 1926. Reilly Lee. 1st ed. inscr. VG. A20. $75.00

REED, Ennis. *Poems.* 1964. CA U. 1st ed. assn copy. F/NF. V1. $20.00

REED, Ishmael. *Shrovetide in Old New Orleans.* 1978. Doubleday. 1st ed. sgn. F/F. B30. $45.00

REED, John F. *Campaign to Valley Forge: July 1, 1777-December 19, 1777.* 1965. Phil. inscr. 8vo. 11 maps. 448p. F/F. T10. $45.00

REED, John. *Ten Days That Shook the World.* 1919. Boni Liveright. G+. B5. $50.00

REED, Kit. *Catholic Girls.* 1987. Donald Fine. 1st ed. F/F. P3. $15.00

REED, Kit. *Fort Privilege.* 1985. Doubleday. 1st ed. NF/NF. P3. $18.00

REED, Kit. *Tiger Rag.* 1973. Dutton. 1st ed. VG/VG. P3. $20.00

REED, Robert. *Exaltation of Larks.* 1995. Tor. 1st ed. F/F. P3. $22.00

REED, Robert. *Hormone Jungle.* 1987. Donald Fine. 1st ed. F/F. P3. $20.00

REED, Robert. *Leeshore.* 1987. Donald Fine. 1st ed. NF/NF. P3. $17.00

REED, Sarah N. *Romance of Arlington House.* 1908. Chapple. 110p. VG-. B10. $12.00

REED, W. Maxwell. *Patterns in the Sky.* 1951. Morrow. 8vo. 125p. xl. dj. K5. $10.00

REED & SONDERGAARD. *Fun for Fidelia.* 1950. Heath. ils. VG. M5. $12.00

REES, John. *Shaping of Psychiatry by War.* 1945. NY. 1st ed. 158p. VG. A13. $40.00

REES-MOGG. *How to Buy Rare Books: A Practical Guide...* 1985. np. 4to. ils/pl. 160p. F/F. A4. $85.00

REESE, A.M. *Alligator & Its Allies.* 1915. NY. 1st ed. sgn. 358p. VG. B5. $130.00

REESE, John. *Singalee.* 1969. Doubleday. 1st ed. VG/VG. P3. $15.00

REESE, John. *Sunblind Range.* 1968. Doubleday. 1st ed. VG/VG. P3. $15.00

REESE, John. *Sure Shot Shapiro.* 1968. Doubleday. 1st ed. VG/VG. P3. $15.00

REESE, Kitty. *Mystery Trivia Quiz Book.* 1985. Bell. hc. VG. P3. $12.00

REESE, Terence. *Modern Bidding & the ACOL System.* 1960 (1956). London. rpt. 128p. VG. S1. $7.00

REESE, Terence. *Precision Bidding & Precision Play.* 1973. NY. 153p. VG. S1. $4.00

REEVE, Arthur B. *Craig Kennedy Listens in.* 1923. Harper. 1st ed. VG/fair. P3. $45.00

REEVE, J. Stanley. *Foxhunter's Journal.* 1952. Dorrance. 1/550. VG/case. O3. $125.00

REEVE, J. Stanley. *Foxhunting Recollections.* 1928. Lippincott. 1st trade ed. VG. O3. $45.00

REEVE & REEVE. *New Mexico: Land of Many Cultures.* 1969. Boulder, CO. 1st ed. photos/maps. 231p. F/NF. E1. $30.00

REEVES, Hubert. *Stellar Evolution & Nucleosynthesis.* 1968. NY. Gordon Breach. 8vo. 99p. VG. K5. $25.00

REEVES, James J. *History of the Twenty-Fourth Regiment of NJ Volunteers.* 1889. Camden, NJ. Chew. 1st ed. 45p. NF/wrp. M8. $150.00

REEVES, John. *Murder Before Matins.* 1984. Doubleday. 1st ed. F/F. P3. $13.00

REEVES, John. *Murder by Microphone.* 1978. Doubleday. 1st ed. VG/VG. P3. $15.00

REEVES, John. *Murder With Muskets.* 1985. Canada. Doubleday. 1st ed. VG/VG. P3. $18.00

REEVES, Robert. *Peeping Thomas.* 1990. Crown. 1st ed. sgn. F/F. B4. $35.00

REEVES & THORNTON. *Medical Book Illustration: A Short History.* 1983. NY. 1st ed. 142p. dj. A13. $75.00

REEVES-STEVENS, Garfield. *Nighteyes.* 1989. Doubleday. 1st ed. F/F. G10. $10.00

REGAN, David. *Mourning Glory.* 1981. Devin-Adair. 1st ed. F/F. B4. $100.00

REGAN, Tom. *All That Dwell Therein.* 1982. CA U. 1st ed. VG/VG. P3. $10.00

REGINALD, R. *Cumulative Paperback Index 1939-1959.* 1973. Gale Research. G. P3. $200.00

REICH, John. *Italy Before Rome: The Making of the Past.* 1979. Oxford. Elsevier/Phaidon. 4to. 151p. AN/dj. P4. $25.00

REICH, Oswald. *Dog, Goat & Horse Training.* 1963. NY. Exposition. 67p. VG/VG. O3. $45.00

REICHARD, Gladys. *Navajo Shepherd & Weaver.* 1936. NY. 1st ed. photos. VG. M17. $75.00

REICHLER, Joseph. *Baseball's Great Moments.* 1985. Bonanza. hc. VG/VG. P3. $10.00

REICHLER, Joseph. *Inside the Majors.* 1952. Hart. ils/photos. 192p. VG. A17. $20.00

REID, Alastair. *Ounce Dice Trice.* 1958. Little Brn. stated 1st ed. 4to. 57p. VG/fair. C14. $14.00

REID, Alastair. *Supposing.* 1960. Little Brn. 1st ed. 8vo. ils Birnbaum. 48p. VG+/G+. C14. $9.00

REID, J.H. Stewart. *Mountains, Men & Rivers.* 1954. Ryerson. 1st ed. VG/VG. P3. $25.00

REID, Jesse Walton. *History of the 4th Regiment of SC Volunteers...* 1892. Greenville, SC. Shannon. 1st ed. 143p. NF/prt wrp. M8. $1,750.00

REID, Mayne. *War-Trail.* 1857. Robert DeWitt. ils. G+. P12. $35.00

REILLY, Helen. *Compartment K.* 1955. Detective BC. hc. VG. P3. $8.00

REILLY, Helen. *Death Demands an Audience.* 1941. Dial. VG. P3. $20.00

REILLY, Helen. *Follow Me.* 1960. Random. 1st ed. NF/NF. P3. $25.00

REILLY, Helen. *Not Me, Inspector.* 1959. Random. 1st ed. VG/VG. P3. $30.00

REIMAN, Terry. *Vamp Till Ready.* 1954. Harper. 1st ed. NF/NF. P3. $15.00

REIMER, E.F. *Matching Mountains With the Boy Scout Uniform.* 1929. NY. 1st ed. ils. 197p. VG/worn. B5. $95.00

REINA, Ruben. *Gift of Birds.* 1991. Phil. 1st ed. photos. wrp. F3. $40.00

REINACH, Theodore. *Jewish Coins.* 1966. Chicago. Argonaut. 1st Am ed. 8vo. 11 pl. 77p. NF/dj. W1. $20.00

REINER, Carl. *Enter Laughing.* 1958. NY. 1st ed. author's 1st book. VG/G. B5. $30.00

REINHARDT, Richard. *Out West on the Overland Train.* 1967. Palo Alto. 209p. VG. B18. $17.50

REINHARDT, Richard. *Workin' on the Railroad.* 1970. Am W Pub. 1st ed. 318p. F/F. E1. $45.00

REISER, Stanley. *Medicine & the Reign of Technology.* 1978. Cambridge. 1st ed. 317p. dj. A13. $50.00

REITSCH, Hanna. *Flying Is My Life.* 1954. NY. 1st Am ed. 246p. VG/dj. B18. $150.00

REJAUNIER, Jeanna. *Motion & the Act.* 1972. Nash. 1st ed. F/F. B35. $20.00

RELLING, William. *Deadly Vintage.* 1995. Walker. 1st ed. F/F. M23. $40.00

REMARQUE, Erich Maria. *All Quiet on the Western Front.* 1969. LEC. 1st ed. 1/1500. ils/sgn John Groth. F/case. C2. $75.00

REMENHAM, John. *Going Wrong.* 1990. Mysterious. 1st ed. NF/NF. P3. $19.00

REMENHAM, John. *Peacemaker.* 1947. MacDonald. 1st ed. VG/tape rpr. P3. $23.00

RENAUL, Lynn. *Racing Around Kentucky.* 1995. Louisville. 214p. AN. O3. $15.00

RENAULT, Mary. *Kings Must Die.* 1958. Pantheon. 1st ed. F/NF. B2. $45.00

RENDA, Gunsel. *History of Turkish Painting.* 1988. Seattle/London. Palasar. 444p. NF/dj. W1. $145.00

RENDEL, Robert. *That Extra Trick.* 1932. Boston. 126p. VG. S1. $12.00

RENDELL, Ruth. *Asta's Book.* 1993. Bristol. Scorpion. 1/99 (119 total). sgn. quarter leather. F. B4. $150.00

RENDELL, Ruth. *Bridesmaid.* 1989. Doubleday. 1st ed. VG/VG. P3. $23.00

RENDELL, Ruth. *Crocodile Bird.* 1993. Crown. 1st Am ed. sgn. F/NF. N4. $40.00

RENDELL, Ruth. *Fever Tree & Other Stories of Suspense.* 1982. NY. 1st Am ed. VG/G. V4. $15.00

RENDELL, Ruth. *Going Wrong.* 1990. NY. 1st ed. inscr. F/F. V4. $50.00

RENDELL, Ruth. *New Girl Friend.* 1985. Hutchinson. F/F. P3. $20.00

RENDELL, Ruth. *Talking to Strange Men.* 1987. Pantheon. 1st ed. F/F. P3. $17.00

RENDELL, Ruth. *Unkindness of Ravens.* 1985. Pantheon. 1st Am ed. NF/VG clip. M22. $8.00

RENDELL, Ruth. *Veiled One.* 1988. Hutchinson. 1st ed. F/F. P3. $18.00

RENEHAN, E.J. *John Burroughs: American Naturalist.* 1992. Post Mills. Chelsea Gr. 1st ed. photos. 356p. half cloth. F/F. B1. $35.00

RENICK & RENICK. *Tommy Carries the Ball.* 1940. Scribner. later rpt. ils F Machetanz. VG/VG. B17. $4.00

RENNERT, Vincent Paul. *Western Outlaws. Vivid Accounts of the Deeds & Misdeeds...* 1968. np. 152p. F/dj. E1. $35.00

RENOIR, Jean. *Notebooks of Captain Georges.* 1966. Boston. 1st ed. VG/dj. A17. $9.50

RESHAW, Patrick. *Wobblies: Story of Syndicalism in the US.* 1967. NY. ils. 312p. G+/dj. B18. $17.50

RESNICK, Mike. *Dinosaur Fantastic.* nd. BC. F/F. P3. $8.00

RESNICK, Mike. *Shaggy BEM.* 1988. Nolacon. 1st ed. hc. F/F. P3. $20.00

RESNICK, Mike. *Will the Last Person to Leave...* 1992. Tor. 1st ed. F/F. P3. $20.00

RESNICOW, Herbert. *Gold Gamble.* 1988. St Martin. 1st ed. VG/VG. P3. $18.00

RESTON, James Jr. *Collision at Home Plate.* 1991. Burlingame. 1st ed. VG+/VG+. P8. $17.50

REVEILLE-PARISE, J.-H. *Hygiene de l'Esprit: Physiologie et Hygiene des Hommes.* (1880). Paris. J-B Bailliere. 12mo. 435p. early bl silk. G1. $50.00

REVERE, Lawrence. *Playing Blackjack as a Business.* 1971. Las Vegas. 171p. VG. S1. $5.00

REVESZ, Gesa. *Psychology of a Musical Prodigy.* 1925. London. Harcourt Brace/Kegan Paul. 180p. gr cloth. dj. G1. $65.00

REVI, Albert C. *American Art Nouveau Glass.* 1968. Nashville. Nelson. ils/drawings/pl. 476p. cloth. dj. D2. $60.00

REVKIN, Andrew. *Burning Season.* 1990. Houghton Mifflin. 1st ed. 317p. dj. F3. $15.00

REXROTH, Kenneth. *100 Poems From the Japanese.* 1955. New Directions. 1st ed. NF/VG. M19. $45.00

REY, H.A. *Stars: A New Way to See Them.* 1962. Houghton Mifflin. 4to. VG/G. B17. $8.50

REY, H.A. *Where's My Baby?* 1943. Houghton Mifflin. sm 4to. scarce. M5. $20.00

REYES, Carlos. *Prisoner.* 1973. Capra. 1st ed. Chapbook series. F/wrp. V1. $15.00

REYNOLDS, Chang. *Pioneer Circuses of the West.* 1966. Los Angeles. photos /biblio/index. 212p. F/F. E1. $30.00

REYNOLDS, Francis J. *Master Tales of Mystery Vol 1.* nd. Collier. hc. VG. P3. $15.00

REYNOLDS, Francis J. *New Encyclopedia Atlas & Gazetter of the World...* 1917. NY. Collier. folio. fld world map (poor). F. O7. $65.00

REYNOLDS, James. *Andrea Palladio.* 1948. NY. 1st ed. VG/VG. B5. $35.00

REYNOLDS, James. *Gallery of Ghosts.* 1965. Grosset Dunlap. VG/VG. P3. $15.00

REYNOLDS, Mack. *Compounded Interest.* 1983. NESFA. 1st ed. 1/1000. NF/NF. G10. $10.00

REYNOLDS, Mack. *Star Trek: Mission to Horatius.* 1968. Whitman. TVTI. G. P3. $15.00

REYNOLDS, Maxine; see Reynolds, Mack.

REYNOLDS, Quentin. *Dress Rehearsal: Story of Dieppe.* 1943. NY. 3rd. 278p. dj. A17. $9.50

REYNOLDS, Sheri. *Bitterroot Landing.* 1994. Putnam. 1st ed. author's 1st book. F/F. M23. $25.00

REYNOLDS, V. *Apes: Gorilla, Chimpanzee, Orangutan & Gibbon...* 1967. NY. Dutton. stated 1st ed. 8vo. ils. 296p. VG/VG. B1. $30.00

REYNOLDS, William J. *Naked Eye.* 1990. Putnam. 1st ed. sgn. F/F. P3. $28.00

RHEIMS, Bettina. *Modern Lovers.* 1990. Paris. Audiovisuel. 1st ed. French text. 57 full-p pl. F/dj. S9. $125.00

RHEIMS, Maurice. *Strange Life of Objects.* 1961. Atheneum. 1st Am ed. 274p. cloth. M20. $27.00

RHINE, J.B. *New Frontiers of the Mind.* 1937. Farrar Rinehart. pl. 275p. gray cloth. VG/dj. G1. $65.00

RHINEHART, Luke. *Book of Est.* 1976. NY. HRW. 1st ed. inscr. NF/NF. B4. $150.00

RHINEHART, Luke. *Dice Man.* 1971. Morrow. 1st ed. VG/VG. P3. $30.00

RHINEHART, Mary Roberts. *Nomad's Land.* 1926. Doran. 8vo. 27 pl. 287p. VG. W1. $18.00

RHODE, Deborah. *Justice & Gender, Sex Discrimination & the Law.* 1989. Harvard. M11. $25.00

RHODES, Daniel. *Adversary.* 1988. St Martin. 1st ed. author's 2nd novel. F/F. T2. $15.00

RHODES, Daniel. *Next, After Lucifer.* 1987. St Martin. 1st ed. author's 1st novel. F/F. T2. $15.00

RHODES, Eugene Manlove. *Bransford in Arcadia; or, The Little Eohippus.* 1914. Holt. 1st ed. VG. A18. $100.00

RHODES, Eugene Manlove. *Proud Sheriff.* 1968. OK U. 1st ed. pref WH Hutchinson. intro HH Knibbs. F/F. A18. $20.00

RHODES, Eugene Manlove. *Rhodes Reader: Stories of Virgins, Villains & Varmits.* 1957. OK U. 1st ed. intro WH Hutchinson. F/clip. A18. $40.00

RHODES, Eugene Manlove. *Stepsons of Light.* 1969. Norman, OK. rpt. 322p. F/F. E1. $30.00

RHODES, Eugene Manlove. *Stepsons of Light.* 1969. OK U. 1st ed. intro WH Hutchinson. rem mk. F/clip. A18. $10.00

RHODES, Eugene Manlove. *West Is West.* 1917. NY. 1st ed. ils Harvey Dunn. F/NF. C2. $175.00

RHODES, Henry T.F. *Alphonse Bertillon, Father of Scientific Detection.* 1956. London. Harrap. M11. $35.00

RHODES, Jack. *Inter-City Bus Lines of the Southwest.* 1988. TX A&M. 8vo. 158p. F/dj. T10. $35.00

RHODES, May D. *Hired Man on Horseback.* 1938. Houghton Mifflin. 1st ed. 263p. cloth. VG/dj. M20. $20.00

RHODES, Richard. *Making Love: An Erotic Odyssey.* 1992. Simon Schuster. 1st ed. F/F. A20. $15.00

RIBOT, Theodule Armand. *Diseases of Personality.* 1887. NY. Fitzgerald. 1st Eng-language ed. 8vo. 52p. bl wrp. G1. $50.00

RIBOT, Theodule Armand. *Evolution of General Ideas.* 1899. Chicago. Open Court. 1st Eng-language ed. 231p. prt gr cloth. G1. $65.00

RIBOT, Theodule Armand. *L'Evolution des Idees Generales.* 1897. Paris. Germer Bailliere/Felix Alcan. 260p. later gray cloth. G1. $75.00

RIBOT, Theodule Armand. *La Logique des Sentiments.* 1905. Paris. Felix Alcan. 200p. early marbled brd. G1. $75.00

RIBOUD, Barbara Chase. *Echo of Lions.* 1989. Morrow. 1st ed. F/F. B4. $35.00

RIBOUD, Barbara Chase. *From Memphis & Peking.* 1974. Random. 1st ed. author's 1st book. rem mk. NF/NF clip. B4. $65.00

RICE, Anne. *Beauty's Release.* 1985. Dutton. 1st ed. F/F. B4. $200.00

RICE, Anne. *Belinda.* 1986. Arbor. 1st ed. sgn. F/F. B4. $100.00

RICE, Anne. *Claiming of Sleeping Beauty.* 1987. London. Macdonald. 1st ed. sgn. F/F. B4. $125.00

RICE, Anne. *Cry to Heaven.* 1982. Knopf. 1st ed. VG/VG. P3. $45.00

RICE, Anne. *Exit to Eden.* 1985. Arbor. 1st ed. VG/VG. P3. $65.00

RICE, Anne. *Feast of All Saints.* 1979. NY. 1st ed. author's 2nd book. F/F. M19. $125.00

RICE, Anne. *Feast of All Saints.* 1979. NY. 1st ed. VG/VG. B5. $40.00

RICE, Anne. *Feast of All Saints.* 1979. Simon Schuster. 1st ed. author's 2nd book. rem mk. NF/NF. H11. $80.00

RICE, Anne. *Interview With the Vampire.* 1976. Knopf. 1st ed. author's 1st book. F/F. B4. $750.00

RICE, Anne. *Lasher.* 1993. Knopf. 1st ed. F/F. H11. $45.00

RICE, Anne. *Queen of the Damned.* 1988. Knopf. 1st ed. VG/VG. P3. $25.00

RICE, Anne. *Tale of the Body Thief.* 1992. Knopf. 1st ed. VG/VG. P3. $25.00

RICE, Anne. *Taltos.* 1994. Canada. Knopf. 1st ed. F/F. P3. $25.00

RICE, Anne. *Vampire Lestat.* 1985. NY. 1st ed. F/F. B5. $95.00

RICE, Anne. *Vampire Lestat.* 1985. NY. 1st ed. inscr. VG/VG. M19. $250.00

RICE, Anne. *Vampire Lestat.* 1985. NY. 1st ed. NF/NF. S13. $75.00

RICE, Anne. *Witching Hour.* 1990. Knopf. 1st ed. F/F. H11. $45.00

RICE, Craig. *Having Wonderful Crime.* 1943. Simon Schuster. 1st ed. VG. P3. $20.00

RICE, Craig. *Knocked for a Loop.* 1957. Simon Schuster. G. P3. $15.00

RICE, Craig. *Sunday Pigeon Murders.* 1945. Tower. 2nd. VG/G+. P3. $20.00

RICE, Craig. *Thursday Turkey Murders.* 1943. Simon Schuster. 1st ed. hc. VG. P3. $20.00

RICE, David Talbot. *Constantinople: From Byzantium to Istanbul.* 1965. Stein Day. 1st Am ed. 214p. xl. VG. W1. $25.00

RICE, David Talbot. *Icons.* 1990. Secaucus, NJ. 1st ed. 143p. VG/dj. W1. $65.00

RICE, Elmer. *Flight to the West.* 1941. Coward McCann. 1st ed. F/VG+. B4. $100.00

RICE, John. *Health for 7,500,000 People: Annual Report of the Dept...* 1938. NY. 1st ed. 390p. VG. A13. $45.00

RICE, Philip E. *America's Favorite Fishing.* 1971. Outdoor Life/Harper Row. ils. VG. P12. $9.00

RICE, Philip E. *Game Bird Hunting.* 1982. Outdoor Life. sc. ils/photos. G+. P12. $4.00

RICE, Philip E. *Outdoor Life Gun Data Book.* 1975. Outdoor Life/Harper Row. VG/G+. P12. $8.00

RICE, Prudence. *Macanche Island, El Peten, Guatemala.* 1987. Gainesville, FL. 1st ed. 267p. dj. F3. $40.00

RICE, Robert. *Business of Crime.* 1956. FSC. 1st ed. VG. P3. $15.00

RICH, Adrienne. *On Lies, Secrets & Silence: Selected Prose 1966-1978.* 1979. Norton. 1st ed. F/NF. V1. $15.00

RICH, Adrienne. *What Is Found There: Notebooks on Poetry & Politics.* 1993. Norton. 1st ed. F/F. V1. $20.00

RICH, Ben E. *Mr Durant of Salt Lake City, That Mormon.* 1893. Salt Lake City. George Cannon. 1st ed. 12mo. 320p. gilt bl cloth. VG. T10. $125.00

RICH, Edwin Gile. *Why-So Stories.* nd. Maynard Sm. 2nd. 207p. gilt red cloth. VG. B22. $4.00

RICH, Virginia. *Nantucket Diet Murders.* 1985. Delacorte. 1st ed. F/F. T2. $25.00

RICHARD, Adrienne. *Accomplice.* 1973. Little Brn. 1st ed. 8vo. 174p. F/VG. C14. $15.00

RICHARD, James. *Snow King.* 1957. Lee Shepard. VG/fair. O3. $25.00

RICHARD, John. *Where's Jack? A Christmas Pop-Up Book.* 1993. np. ils/tab-operated mechanicals/popups. F. A4. $30.00

RICHARD, Mark. *Fishboy.* 1993. Doubleday. 1st ed. sgn. F/F. M23. $45.00

RICHARDS, Allen. *To Market to Murder.* 1961. Macmillan. 1st ed. hc. VG/VG. P3. $15.00

RICHARDS, Dorothy. *Beversprite. My Years Building an Animal Sanctuary.* 1977. NY. Chronicle. 1st ed. sgn. 8vo. 191p. VG/VG. B11. $25.00

RICHARDS, Eva Alvey. *Arctic Mood: A Narrative of Arctic Adventures.* 1949. Caldwell, ID. Caxton. 1st ed. 8vo. 282p. map ep. NF. T10. $35.00

RICHARDS, Gregory B. *SF Movies.* 1984. Bison. 1st ed. VG/VG. P3. $15.00

RICHARDS, John R. *Inside Dope on Football Coaching.* 1917. Chicago. TE Wilson. ils. 114p. VG. B14. $45.00

RICHARDS, Laura E. *Daughter of Jehu.* 1918. Appleton. 1st ed. F/NF. B4. $100.00

RICHARDS, Laura E. *Digging Out.* 1966. McGraw Hill. 1st ed. F/VG+. B4. $85.00

RICHARDS, Laura E. *Isla Heron.* 1896. Boston. Estes Lauriat. 5th thousand. 109p. G. A17. $10.00

RICHARDS, Leverett G. *TAC: Story of Tactical Air Command.* 1961. NY. 1st ed. 254p. F/VG. B18. $22.50

RICHARDS, R.R. *Championship Bridge.* 1928. NY. 114p. VG. S1. $15.00

RICHARDS, Robert. *California Crusoe; or, Lost Treasure Found.* 1854. London/NY. 1st ed. 12mo. 162p. gilt cloth. lacks ffe. T10. $500.00

RICHARDSON, A.D. *Personal History of Ulysses S Grant.* 1868. Hartford. 8vo. ils. 560p. VG. T3. $50.00

RICHARDSON, Donald. *Greek Mythology for Everyone.* 1989. Avenel. F/F. P3. $10.00

RICHARDSON, Frederick. *Billy Bunny's Fortune.* 1936. Wise-Algonquin. later reissue. ils. F. M5. $40.00

RICHARDSON, Gladwell. *Two Guns, Arizona.* 1968. Santa Fe, NM. photos/sources. 28p. F/stiff wrp. E1. $30.00

RICHARDSON, Robert. *Bellringer Street.* 1988. St Martin. BC. F/F. N4. $7.50

RICHARDSON & WHITAKER. *Adventure South.* 1942. Detroit. 1st ed. sgns. 330p. VG/VG. B5. $35.00

RICHEAL, Kip. *Pittsburgh Pirates: Still Walking Tall.* 1993. Sagamore. 1st ed. AN/dj. P8. $12.50

RICHELSON, Geraldine. *Star Wars Storybook.* nd. Random. 14th. VG. P3. $10.00

RICHET, Charles. *Our Sixth Sense.* ca 1929. London. Rider. 1st ed. 227p. blk cloth. G1. $37.50

RICHTER, Conrad. *Early Americana & Other Stories.* 1936. Knopf. 1st ed. F/NF. A18/C2. $75.00

RICHTER, Conrad. *Early Americana & Other Stories.* 1978. Gregg. 1st ed thus. intro WA Bloodworth. F/F. A18. $25.00

RICHTER, Conrad. *Fields.* 1946. Knopf. 1st ed. F/NF. A18. $60.00

RICHTER, Conrad. *Free Man.* 1943. Knopf. 1st ed. inscr. NF/NF. A18. $60.00

RICHTER, Conrad. *Lady.* 1957. Knopf. 1st ed. F/clip. A18. $15.00

RICHTER, Conrad. *Rawhide Knot & Other Stories.* 1978. Knopf. 1st ed. fwd Harvina Richter. F/F. A18. $40.00

RICHTER, Conrad. *Town.* 1950. Knopf. 1st ed. F/F. A18. $75.00

RICHTER, Conrad. *Tracy Cromwell.* 1942. Knopf. 1st ed. F/VG. A18. $40.00

RICHTER, Conrad. *Trees.* 1940. Knopf. 1st ed. F/NF. A18. $75.00

RICHTER, Ed. *Making of a Big League Pitcher.* 1963. Chilton. 1st ed. VG+/VG. P8. $45.00

RICKARDS, Colin. *Bowler Hats & Stetsons.* nd. Bonanza. 1st ed thus. VG/dj. E1. $25.00

RICKARDS, Colin. *Buckskin Frank Leslie, Gunman of Tombstone.* 1964. El Paso, TX. 1st ed. 1/450. 45p. E1. $85.00

RICKARDS, Colin. *Mysterious Dave Mather.* 1968. Santa Fe. 1st ed. 1/1500. photos. 42p. F. E1. $65.00

RIDDICK. *Guide to Indian Manuscripts, Materials From Europe...* 1993. 286p. F. A4. $65.00

RIDDLE, Donald W. *Lincoln Runs for Congress.* 1948. Rutgers. 1st ed. 217p. VG/torn. B18. $15.00

RIDDLE, Kenyon. *Records & Maps of the Old Santa Fe Trail.* 1963. Stuart. Southeastern Prt. 8vo. 8 fld map. 147p. M. O7. $100.00

RIDEOUT, Walter. *Radical Novel in the United States, 1900-1954.* 1960. 1/250. sgn. F/VG. A4. $450.00

RIDER, Bevan. *More Expeditious Conveyance.* 1984. London. Allen. 1st ed. F/F. O3. $25.00

RIDER, J.W. *Hot Tickets.* 1987. Arbor. 1st ed. author's 2nd book. F/F. H11. $25.00

RIDER, Rowland W. *Roll Away Saloon, Cowboy Tales of the Arizona Strip.* 1985. Logan, UT. ils/photos. 114p. F/stiff pict wrp. E1. $10.00

RIDGE, John Rollin. *Life & Adventures of Joaquin Murieta, Celebrated CA Bandit.* 1955. Norman, OK. 1st WFL ed. 12mo. 159p. VG/dj. E1/T10. $25.00

RIDGE & RIDGE. *America's Frontier Story: A Documentary History...* 1969. NY. 1st ed. photos/notes. 655p. F/F. E1. $30.00

RIDGELY, Frances S. *Animalitos.* 1959. Pageant. 1st ed. sgn. ils Barry Martin. 63p. VG. B11. $45.00

RIDGELY, Frances S. *City Is Not Builded in a Day.* 1968. Springfield, IL. Vachel Lindsay Assoc. sgn. 8vo. 34p. VG/wrp. B11. $30.00

RIDLEY, Bromfield. *Battles & Sketches of the Army of Tennessee.* 1978. Dayton. F. V4. $35.00

RIDLEY, H. *LM Montgomery: A Biography.* 1956. Toronto. 1st ed. VG/VG. B5. $30.00

RIDLEY, John. *Stray Dogs.* 1997. NY. Ballantine. 1st. author's 1st book. F/NF. R16. $40.00

RIDLEY, Thomas. *View of the Civile & Ecclesiastical Law...* 1676. Oxford. Hall Davis. 396p. modern gilt calf/morocco spine label. K1. $200.00

RIDPATH, John Clark. *History of the World.* 1890. Jones Bros. 4 vol. ils. VG. P12. $50.00

RIDPATH, Michael. *Free to Trade.* 1994. Harper Collins. 1st ed. author's 1st novel. F/F. M22. $15.00

RIED, P.R. *Men of Colditz.* 1954. Phil. 1st ed. VG/VG. B5. $20.00

RIES, Karl. *Die Maulwurte (The Moles) 1919-1935.* 1970. Mainz. 1st ed. 151p. VG. B18. $22.50

RIESE, Randall. *Unabridged Marilyn.* 1990. Bonanza. 1st ed. F/F. P3. $15.00

RIESE, Walther. *Concept of Disease, Its History, Its Versions & Nature.* 1953. NY. 1st ed. 343p. dj. A13. $30.00

RIESEBERG, Harry E. *Adventures in Underwater Treasure Hunting.* 1965. NY. Frederick Fell. ils. 140p. dj. T7. $24.00

RIESENBERG, Felix. *Gold Road: California's Spanish Mission Trail.* 1962. NY. 1st ed. Am Trail series. 315p. F/dj. A17. $25.00

RIFKIN, Shepard. *Murder Vine.* 1970. Dodd Mead. 1st ed. VG/VG. P3. $15.00

RIGELSFORD, Adrian. *Dr Who: The Monsters.* 1992. Dr Who Books. F/F. P3. $25.00

RIGGS, Elias. *Outline of a Grammar of the Turkish Language.* 1856. Constantinople. AB Churchill. 1st/only ed. 12mo. 56p. brn cloth. VG. C6. $200.00

RIGGS, James. *Hello Doctor: Brief Biography of Charles Bernstein.* 1936. Roycroft. apparant 1st/only ed. 120p. bl bdg. B22. $6.50

RIGNANO, Eugenio. *Upon the Inheritance of Acquired Characters...* 1911. Chicago. 1st Eng trans. 413p. A13. $50.00

RIHANI, Ameen. *Chant of Mystics & Other Poems.* 1921. NY. White. 1st ed. narrow 12mo. lacks part of spine strip o/w VG. W1. $25.00

RIKER, Ben. *Pony Wagon Town Along US 1890.* 1948. Bobbs Merrill. 1st ed. sgn. 8vo. 312p. bl brd. VG. B11. $35.00

RILEY, Edward Miles. *Journal of John Harrower, an Indentured Servant...* 1963. Colonial Williamsburg. 1st ed. sgn. 8vo. 202p. bl cloth. G/G. B11. $45.00

RILEY, J. *Authentic Narrative of Loss of the American Brig Commerce.* 1833. Hartford. 8vo. ils. 271p. leather. G. T3. $42.00

RILEY, James Whitcomb. *Child-World.* 1897. Bowen Merrill. 1st ed/later prt. 209p. VG. M20. $62.00

RILEY, James Whitcomb. *Home Again With Me.* 1908. Bobbs Merrill. ils HC Christy. fair. P12. $75.00

RILEY, James Whitcomb. *Riley Songs of Home.* 1910. Grosset Dunlap. 8vo. ils Will Vawter. 190p. cloth. NF. B36. $35.00

RILEY, James Whitcomb. *Runaway Boy.* 1906. Bobbs Merrill. 8 pl. VG+. M5. $85.00

RILKE, Rainer Maria. *Thirty-One Poems.* 1946. NY. Beechhurst. 1st ed. VG/G. V1. $20.00

RINEHART, Mary Roberts. *Album.* 1933. Farrar Rinehart. 1st ed. G. P3. $30.00

RINEHART, Mary Roberts. *Doctor.* 1936. Farrar Rinehart. 1st ed. VG. P3. $20.00

RINEHART, Mary Roberts. *Door.* nd. Farrar Rinehart. VG. P3. $25.00

RINEHART, Mary Roberts. *Lost Ectasy.* nd. Grosset Dunlap. MTI. VG. P3. $20.00

RINEHART, Mary Roberts. *Man in Lower Ten.* 1940. Triangle. VG. P3. $10.00

RINEHART, Mary Roberts. *Red Lamp.* 1925. Doran. 1st ed. G. P3. $20.00

RINEHART, Mary Roberts. *Street of Seven Stars.* 1914. Houghton Mifflin. 1st ed. 377p. VG. M20. $27.00

RINEHART, Mary Roberts. *Swimming Pool.* 1952. Rinehart. 1st ed. VG/VG. P3. $25.00

RINEHART, Mary Roberts. *Temperamental People.* 1924. Doran. 1st ed. F/NF. B4. $85.00

RINEHART, Mary Roberts. *Yellow Room.* 1945. Farrar Rinehart. 1st ed. VG. P3. $15.00

RING, Douglas; see Prather, Richard.

RING, Ray. *Arizona Kiss.* 1991. Little Brn. 1st ed. F/F. P3. $18.00

RING, Ray. *Telluride Smile.* 1988. NY. Dodd Mead. 1st ed. author's 1st book. F/F. H11. $50.00

RINGELBLUM & SLOAN. *Notes From the Warsaw Ghetto.* 1958. NY. 1st ed. maps/index. VG/VG. B5. $35.00

RINGGOLD, Cadwalader. *Series of Charts With Sailing Directions.* 1852. WA. JT Towers. 4th ed. 6 lg fld maps+8 pl. VG+. O7. $2,000.00

RINGGOLD, Jennie Parks. *Frontier Days in Southwest, Pioneer Days in Old Arizona.* 1952. San Antonio. 1st ed. 197p. VG. E1. $40.00

RINGWALD, Donald C. *Hudson River Day Line.* 1965. Howell-North. G/dj. A16. $80.00

RINKER, H.L. *Warman's Americana & Collectibles.* 1984. 8vo. ils. 550p. G. T3. $7.00

RIOS, Eduardo Enrique. *Life of Fray Antonio Margil, OFM.* 1959. Academy Francisco Hist. 1st ed. 8vo. 159p. gilt bl cloth. F. T10. $50.00

RIPLEY, Alexandra. *Charleston.* 1981. Doubleday. 1st ed. NF/NF. B35. $75.00

RIPLEY, Alexandra. *Scarlett.* 1991. Warner. 1st ed. F/F. H11. $30.00

RIPLEY, Alexandra. *Scarlett.* 1991. Warner. 1st ed. VG/VG. P3. $25.00

RIPLEY, K.B. *Sand in My Shoes.* 1931. NY. 1st ed. VG. B5. $30.00

RIPLEY, Robert L. *Believe It or Not!* 1929. Simon Schuster. 1st ed. pres. ils. 172p. red stp gr cloth. K1. $125.00

RIPLEY, W.L. *Dreamsicle.* 1993. Little Brn. 1st ed. F/F. H11. $30.00

RIRINGO, Charles. *History of...Billy the Kid.* 1967. Austin. facsimile. 142p. NF. E1. $65.00

RIRINGO, Charles. *Riata & Spurs.* 1927. NY. 1st ed/1st issue. G. E1. $150.00

RIRINGO, Charles. *Two Evilsims: Pinkertonism & Anarchism.* 1967. Austin. facsimile. 109p. F/sans. E1. $60.00

RISCHBIETER. *Art & the Stage in the 20th Century.* 1968. NYGS. folio. F/VG. D2. $90.00

RISTER, Carl Coke. *Oil! Titan of the Southwest.* 1949. Norman, OK. 1st ed. photos/fld map. 467p. F. E1. $75.00

RISTER, Carl Coke. *South-Western Frontier 1865-1881.* 1928. Cleveland. 336p. F/case. E1. $300.00

RISTER, Carl Coke. *Southern Plainsmen.* 1938. Norman, OK. 1st ed. 298p. F/chip. E1. $100.00

RISTOW, Walter W. *Guide to the History of Cartography...* 1973. WA. Lib of Congress. 3rd. sgn. F/wrp. O7. $45.00

RISTOW & SKELTON. *Nautical Charts on Vellum in Library of Congress.* 1977. WA. Lib of Congress. 33 charts/12 ils. F. O7. $85.00

RITCHIE, Jack. *Adventures of Henry Turnbuckle.* 1987. Carbondale. SIU. 1st ed. F/F. H11. $30.00

RITTENHOUSE, Jack D. *Disturnell's Treaty Map: Map That Was Part of Guadelupe...* 1985. Santa Fe. Stagecoach. fld map. gilt bl cloth. F. O7. $125.00

RITTENHOUSE, Jack D. *Outlaw Days at Cabezon, New Mexico.* 1964. Santa Fe. ltd ed. sgn. 28p. F/stiff wrp. E1. $50.00

RITTER, Hans. *Die Letzien Karawanen in Der Sahara.* 1985. Atlantis. special ed. folio. ils. 211p. NF/dj. W1. $45.00

RITTER, Mary Bennett. *More Than Gold in California 1849-1933.* 1933. Berkeley. private prt. 1st ed. inscr/dtd. 451p. F. E1. $100.00

RITTER VON RITTERSHAIN, G. *Geistesleben. Betrachtungen Uber die Geistige Thatigkeit...* 1871. Wien. Wilhelm Braumuller. 116p. prt yel wrp. G1. $150.00

RITZ, David. *Blue Notes Under a Green Felt Hat.* 1989. NY. Donald Fine. 1st ed. rem mk. NF/F. H11. $15.00

RIVERA, Diego. *My Art, My Life.* 1960. 1st ed. photos. VG/VG. S13. $20.00

RIVERS, Thomas. *Miniature Fruit Garden; or, Culture of Pyramidian...* 1870. 15th. ils. VG. E6. $35.00

RIVERS-COFFEY, Rachel. *Horse Like Mr Ragman.* 1977. Scribner. 1st. VG/G. O3. $20.00

RIVES, Amelie. *Barbara Dering.* 1893. Lippincott. reading copy. B10. $8.00

RIVES, Amelie. *Trix & Over-The-Moon.* 1909. Harper. 1st ed. ils F Walter Taylor. 165p. VG. B10. $25.00

RIVES, Reginald. *Coaching Club.* 1935. Derrydale. 1/300. sgn. O3. $995.00

RIVKIN, S. *Mama Meichulim, Traditional Jewish Cooking Made Easy.* 1960. G+. E6. $20.00

RIZK, Salom. *Syrian Yankee.* 1952. Doubleday. sgn. 8vo. 317p. VG/torn. W1. $16.00

RIZZI, Timothy. *Night Stalker.* 1992. Donald Fine. 1st sign. author's 1st novel. NF/NF-. R16. $45.00

ROAD, Alan. *Doctor Who: Making of a TV Series.* 1982. Andre Deutsch. TVTI. NF. P3. $20.00

ROARK, R.J. *Formulas for Stress & Strain.* 1938. McGraw Hill. 1st. 326p. G. D8. $9.00

ROARK & YOUNG. *Formulas for Stress & Strain.* 1975. McGraw Hill. 5th. 624p. VG. D8. $20.00

ROBACK, A.A. *Popular Psychology With Chapters on Intelligence.* 1928. Cambridge. Sci-Art Pub. 267p. VG/dj. G1. $35.00

ROBACK, A.A. *Psychology of Character...* 1927. Harcourt Brace. 1st ed/Am issue. 596p. gr cloth. VG. G1. $75.00

ROBACKER, Earl F. *Old Stuff in Up-Country Pennsylvania.* 1973. Cranbury, NJ. 1st ed. 283p. F/F. E1. $30.00

ROBACKER, Earl F. *Pennsylvania Dutch Stuff.* 1960. NY. rpt. F/VG. E1. $30.00

ROBARTS, Edith. *Gulliver in Giantland.* nd. London. Sisley's Ltd. 16mo. ils. VG+. M5. $35.00

ROBB, Charles. *Red O'Leary Wins Out.* 1927. NY. 1st. ils. 287p. VG/dj. B5. $25.00

ROBBINS, A. *Journal...of the Brig Commerce...Upon the Western Coast...* 1818. Hartford. 16mo. fld map. 275p. full leather. G. T3. $40.00

ROBBINS, Archibold. *Journal Comprising Account of Loss of Brig Commerce...* 1825. Hartford. 18th. 275p. G. B5. $60.00

ROBBINS, Clifton. *Mystery of Mr Cross.* 1933. Appleton. VG. N4. $20.00

ROBBINS, Harold. *Memories of Another Day.* 1979. S&S. 1st trade. F/F. T12. $25.00

ROBBINS, Harold. *Pirate.* 1974. Simon Schuster. 1st ed. NF/NF. B35. $30.00

ROBBINS, Harold. *79 Park Avenue.* 1955. Knopf. 1st ed. author's 4th book. F/VG. H11. $40.00

ROBBINS, John. *Tooth Fairy Is Broke.* 1988. Darnstown, MD. Clark-Davis. 1st. ils/sgn Rae Owings. lg 8vo. F/F. C8. $45.00

ROBBINS, Leonard A. *Index to Adventure Magazine Volume 1 & Volume 2.* nd. Starmont. VG. P3. $150.00

ROBBINS, Leonard A. *Pulp Magazine Index First Series, Volume 1.* nd. Starmont. VG. P3. $100.00

ROBBINS, Leonard A. *Pulp Magazine Index Second Series.* nd. Starmont. VG. P3. $120.00

ROBBINS, Tom. *Another Roadside Attraction.* 1971. Doubleday. 1st. author's 1st book. F/NF. D10. $495.00

ROBBINS, Tom. *Jitterbug Perfume.* 1984. Bantam. 1st ed. VG/VG. P3. $16.00

ROBBINS, Tom. *Skinny Legs & All.* 1990. Bantam. 1st. F/F. R14. $25.00

ROBBINS. *Law: A Treasury of Art & Literature.* 1990. np. sm folio. 198 pl. F/NF clip. A4. $85.00

ROBERSON, Jennifer. *Lady of the Forest: Novel of Sherwood.* 1992. Zebra. 1st ed. sgn. F/F. T2. $22.00

ROBERT, Otto. *Outlaws of Cave-in-Rock.* 1924. Clark. 1st. ils/maps/facsimiles. 364p. VG. J2. $900.00

ROBERT & WARDE. *Code for Collector of Beautiful Books.* 1936. LEC. 1st. VG. K3. $20.00

ROBERTS, Brian B. *Chronological List of Antarctic Expeditions.* 1958. Cambridge. Scott Polar Research Inst. prt wrp. P4. $75.00

ROBERTS, Catherine. *Real Book About Making Dolls & Doll Clothes.* (1951). Garden City. 8vo. 191p. G+. T5. $15.00

ROBERTS, Charles G.D. *In the Morning of Time.* 1922. McClelland Stewart. 1st ed. G. P3. $35.00

ROBERTS, Dan W. *Rangers & Sovereignty.* 1914. San Antonio. 1st ed. photos. 190p. F/case. E1. $200.00

ROBERTS, Dorothy James. *Return of the Stranger.* 1958. Appleton Century Crofts. VG/VG. P3. $20.00

ROBERTS, E.H. *Viability of Seeds.* 1972. Syracuse. 12 separately authored chapters. 448p. F. S15. $12.00

ROBERTS, E.M. *Great Meadow.* 1930. Viking. 1/295. 338p. teg. VG/lacks glassine wrp/box. B10. $75.00

ROBERTS, E.M. *Kentucky Poetry Review.* Fall 1981. np. Special Roberts issue. NF/stiff wrp. V1. $10.00

ROBERTS, Edwards. *Shoshone & Other Western Wonders.* 1888. Harper. A19. $35.00

ROBERTS, Gail. *Atlas of Discovery.* 1973. London. Aldus. 1st ed. ils. 192p. M/dj. O7. $45.00

ROBERTS, Gillian. *Caught Dead in Phil.* 1987. Scribner. 1st ed. F/F. C2. $75.00

ROBERTS, Gillian. *I'd Rather Be in Philadelphia.* 1992. Ballantine. 1st ed. F/F. H11. $25.00

ROBERTS, Gillian. *With Friends Like These...* nd. BC. VG/VG. P3. $8.00

ROBERTS, Katharine. *Center of the Web.* nd. Collier. VG. P3. $15.00

ROBERTS, Keith. *Furies.* 1966. London. Hart Davis. 1st ed. author's 1st book. VG/VG. scarce. M21. $200.00

ROBERTS, Keith. *Kiteworld.* 1985. Gollancz. 1st ed. F/F. P3. $25.00

ROBERTS, Keith. *Lordly Ones.* 1986. Gollancz. 1st ed. VG/VG. P3. $30.00

ROBERTS, Keith. *Winterwood & Other Hauntings.* 1989. Morrigan. 1st ed. F/F. P3. $30.00

ROBERTS, Kenneth. *Battle of Cowpens.* 1958. Garden City. 1st ed. F/F. B5. $30.00

ROBERTS, Kenneth. *Boon Island.* 1956. Doubleday. 1st. F/NF. H11. $25.00

ROBERTS, Kenneth. *Don't Say That About Maine.* 1951. Waterville, ME. Colby College. F/stapled wrp in dj. B4. $150.00

ROBERTS, Kenneth. *Lydia Bailey.* 1947. Doubleday. 1st ed. 1/1050. sgn. F/glassine dj/case. B24. $250.00

ROBERTS, Kenneth. *Oliver Wiswell.* 1940. Doubleday Doran. 1st. NF/dj. Q1. $50.00

ROBERTS, Lee; see Martin, Robert.

ROBERTS, Les. *Infinite Number of Monkeys.* 1987. NY. 1st ed. F/F. H11. $30.00

ROBERTS, Les. *Pepper Pike.* 1988. St Martin. 1st ed. F/F. P3. $16.00

ROBERTS, Lionel. *In-World.* 1968. Arcadia. F/F. P3. $20.00

ROBERTS, Martha. *These Go in Flight.* 1970. Golden Quill. inscr. 56p. VG/VG. B10. $8.00

ROBERTS, Nancy. *Appalachian Ghosts.* 1978. Doubleday. 1st ed. VG/VG. P3. $12.00

ROBERTS, Ned H. *Muzzle-Loading Cap Lock Rifle.* 1952. Bonanza. rpt. 308p. F/NF. E1. $40.00

ROBERTS, Norman C. *Baja California Plant Field Guide.* 1989. La Jolla. ils/map/photos. as new/photo wrp. B26. $23.00

ROBERTS, O.W. *Narrative of Voyages & Excursions on East Coast...* 1965 (1827). Gainesville. rpt. ils/fld map. 302p+9p index. gilt cloth. NF. M12. $17.50

ROBERTS, Oral. *Exactly How You May Receive Your Healing Through Faith.* 1958. Oral Roberts Evang Assn. 1st. sgn. 12mo. VG/VG. B11. $15.00

ROBERTS, Paul William. *River in the Desert: Modern Travels in Ancient Egypt.* 1993. Random. 1st ed. 394p. NF/dj. W1. $20.00

ROBERTS, Ruby Altizer. *Forever Is Too Long.* 1946. Wings. inscr. 91p. VG/fair. B10. $10.00

ROBERTS, S.C. *Holmes & Watson: A Miscellany.* 1953. Oxford. 1st ed. VG/VG. P3. $75.00

ROBERTS, Susan. *Magician of the Golden Dawn.* 1978. Comtemporary Books. VG/VG. P3. $20.00

ROBERTS, Thomas. *Birds of Minnesota.* 1932. Minneapolis. 2 vol. 1st. 4to. ils. F. C6. $185.00

ROBERTS, W. Adolphe. *Haunting Hand.* 1926. Macaulay. 1st. VG/VG. B4. $1,000.00

ROBERTS, W. Adolphe. *Single Star.* 1949. Bobbs Merrill. 1st. F/VG+. B4. $175.00

ROBERTS & ROBERTS. *Moreau de St Merys American Journey 1793-1798.* 1947. Doubleday. 1st ed. VG/G+. P12. $20.00

ROBERTS & SEELY. *Tidewater Dynasty.* 1981. HBJ. BC. VG/VG. B10. $8.00

ROBERTS. *Jean Stafford: A Biography.* 1988. np. 28 photos. 294p. NF/NF. A4. $25.00

ROBERTSON, Dale. *Son of the Phantom.* 1946. Whitman. G. P3. $15.00

ROBERTSON, Don. *By Antietam Creek.* 1960. Prentice Hall. 1st ed. VG/VG. B11. $25.00

ROBERTSON, Don. *Ideal, Genuine Man.* 1987. Philtrum. 1st ed. F/NF clip. G10. $25.00

ROBERTSON, Don. *Rare Birds of the West Coast.* 1980. Pacific Grove. photos/maps/11 mc pl. 496p. NF/NF. S15. $25.00

ROBERTSON, E. Arnot. *Sign Post.* 1944. Canada. Macmillan. 1st ed. VG. P3. $13.00

ROBERTSON, Giles. *Giovanni Bellini.* 1968. Oxford. Clarendon. pl/biblio. 171p. cloth. D2. $125.00

ROBERTSON, James I. *Concise Illustrated History of the Civil War.* 1971. Nat Hist Soc. sm 4to. ils. 50p. G/wrp. T3. $6.00

ROBERTSON, Keith. *Henry Reed, Inc.* 1958. Viking. 1st. ils Robert McCloskey. VG/VG-. P2. $65.00

ROBERTSON, Keith. *Three Stuffed Owls.* 1957 (1954). Viking. 3rd. 8vo. 198p. VG. T5. $20.00

ROBERTSON, Mary Elsie. *Clearing.* 1982. Atheneum. 1st. F/F. B4. $45.00

ROBERTSON, Mary Elsie. *What I Have to Tell You.* 1989. Doubleday. 1st. 322p. F/F. W2. $25.00

ROBERTSON, Morgan. *Down to the Sea.* 1905. Harper. 1st. VG. M2. $40.00

ROBERTSON, Morgan. *Where Angels Fear to Tread.* 1889. Century. 1st. VG. M2. $65.00

ROBERTSON, Morgan. *Wreck of the Titan.* 1912. NY. VG. B5. $45.00

ROBERTSON, P. *Book of Firsts.* 1974. NY. 4to. ils. 256p. brn cloth. VG/dj. T3. $20.00

ROBERTSON, R.B. *Of Whales & Men.* 1954. Alfred Knopf. 300p. gilt bl bdg. VG. P12. $15.00

ROBERTSON, W. Graham. *Year of Songs for a Baby in a Garden.* 1906. London. John Lane. inscr/dtd 1905. 110p. olive-gr cloth. B24. $450.00

ROBERTSON & ROBERTSON. *Cowman's Country: Fifty Frontier Ranches in TX Panhandle...* 1981. Paramount. 1st ed. sgns. photos/biblio. 184p. F. E1. $75.00

ROBESON, Kenneth; see Goulart, Ron.

ROBESON, Paul. *Paul Robeson Speaks: Writings, Speeches, Interviews 1918-74.* 1978. Brunner/Mazel. 1st. edit PS Foner. F/F. M25. $75.00

ROBIE, Virginia. *Historic Styles of Furniture.* 1916. ils. VG. M17. $25.00

ROBIN, Robert. *Above the Law.* 1992. NY. Pocket. 1st ed. F/F. H11. $20.00

ROBINS, George. *Lays of the Hertfordshire Hunt.* 1916. London. Humphreys. 12mo. G. O3. $18.00

ROBINSON, Bob. *Show Your Horse.* 1978. St Louis. Saddle & Bridle. 1st ed. 200p. sc. VG. O3. $12.00

ROBINSON, Brooks. *Putting It All Together.* 1971. Hawthorn. 1st ed. F/VG+. P8. $30.00

ROBINSON, Douglas H. *Dangerous Sky: History of Aviation Medicine.* 1973. Seattle. ils. 292p. VG/dj. B18. $25.00

ROBINSON, E.A. *Amaranth.* 1934. Macmillan. 1st ed. 105p. VG+/dj. M20. $25.00

ROBINSON, E.A. *Critical Study.* 1952. Macmillan. 1st ed. F/NF. V1. $20.00

ROBINSON, E.A. *Man Who Died Twice.* 1924. Macmillan. 1st ed. ltd. sgn. tall 8vo. F. T10. $150.00

ROBINSON, E.A. *Sonnets 1889-1927.* 1928. Macmillan. 1st collected ed. 8vo. F/NF. T10. $50.00

ROBINSON, E.A. *Tristam.* 1927. Macmillan. 1st ed. red cloth. NF. V1. $25.00

ROBINSON, Francis. *Atlas of the Islamic World Since 1500.* 1982. Facts on File. 1st ed folio. 238p. VG/dj. W1. $65.00

ROBINSON, Frank M. *Power.* nd. BC. VG/VG. P3. $10.00

ROBINSON, Frank. *Extra Innings.* 1988. McGraw Hill. 1st ed. F/F. P8. $17.50

ROBINSON, Heath. *Heath Robinson at War.* 1942. London. Methuen. 1st. 48p. prt paper wrp. paper dj. R5. $275.00

ROBINSON, Heath. *Heath Robinson's Book of Goblins.* 1934. London. Hutchinson. 1st. 7 full-p pl. 4to. dk bl cloth. R5. $400.00

ROBINSON, Heath. *Inventions.* 1973. Duckworth. 1st. ils. 147p. VG/VG. D1. $30.00

ROBINSON, Henry Morton. *Cardinal.* 1950. Simon Schuster. 1st ed. inscr. F/F. B4. $200.00

ROBINSON, Jane. *Edward G Robinson's World of Art.* 1975. Harper Row. 1st ed. ils/phtos. 117p. cloth. dj. D2. $35.00

ROBINSON, John Louis. *David Lipscomb: Journalist in Texas.* 1872. Nortex. sgn. 60p. F/G. E1. $25.00

ROBINSON, Kim Stanley. *Blue Mars.* 1996. London. Harper Collins. 1st ed. sgn. F/F. M23. $100.00

ROBINSON, Kim Stanley. *Escape From Kathmandu.* 1989. Tor. 1st ed. F/F. P3. $18.00

ROBINSON, Kim Stanley. *Future Primitive: The New Ecotopias.* 1994. Tor. 1st ed. F/F. G10. $20.00

ROBINSON, Kim Stanley. *Gold Coast.* 1988. Tor. 1st ed. F/F. P3. $20.00

ROBINSON, Kim Stanley. *Planet on the Table.* 1986. Tor. 1st ed. F/F. P3. $20.00

ROBINSON, Kim Stanley. *Red Mars.* 1993. Bantam. UP. sgn. F/red wrp. M23. $500.00

ROBINSON, Kim Stanley. *Remaking History.* 1991. Tor. 1st ed. F/F. G10. $25.00

ROBINSON, Kim Stanley. *Short Sharp Shock.* 1990. Ziesing. 1st ed. F/F. P3. $20.00

ROBINSON, Lynda S. *Murder at the God's Gate.* 1995. Walker. 1st ed. F/F. M23. $35.00

ROBINSON, M.S. *MacPherson Collection: Pageant of Sea of Maritime Prints...* 1950. London. Halton. 4to. 16 mc pl/210 halftones. 264p. T7. $150.00

ROBINSON, Marilyn. *Housekeeping.* 1980. FSG. 1st ed. inscr. author's 1st novel. F/F. B4. $100.00

ROBINSON, Peter. *Dedicated Man.* 1991. Scribner. 1st Am ed. sgn. F/F. T2. $25.00

ROBINSON, Peter. *Gallows View.* 1987. Viking. 1st ed. VG/VG. P3. $18.00

ROBINSON, Peter. *Necessary End.* 1989. Canada. Viking. 1st ed. VG/VG. P3. $25.00

ROBINSON, Ruth E. *Buy Books Where, Sell Books Where.* 1981-1982. np. 4to. 226p. G. T3. $5.00

ROBINSON, Spider. *Time Pressure.* 1987. Ace. 1st ed. F/F. P3. $20.00

ROBINSON, Thomas. *Common Law of Kent; or, Customs of Gavelkind.* 1788. London. modern quarter calf. M11. $450.00

ROBINSON, Tom. *Buttons.* 1938. Viking. 1st trade ed. ils Peggy Bacon. VG/VG. P2. $60.00

ROBINSON, Tom. *Greylock & the Robins.* 1946. Viking/Jr Literary Guild. 1st ed thus. ils Lawson. VG. M5. $55.00

ROBINSON, Tom. *In & Out.* 1943. Viking. 1st. ils Marguerite deAngeli. 140p. G+. T5. $25.00

ROBINSON, Victor. *Encyclopedia of Sexualis: A Comprehensive Encyclopedia...* 1936. NY. 1st ed. 819p. VG. A13. $100.00

ROBINSON, Victor. *Pathfinders in Medicine.* 1929. NY. 2nd. 810p. A13. $125.00

ROBINSON, W.W. *Lawyers of Los Angeles.* 1959. Los Angeles. 1st. F/G. O4. $15.00

ROBINSON, Will G. *Gold Rush Centennial Ed.* 1961. Dakota Territory Centennial Commission. E1. $25.00

ROBINSON, Will H. *Story of Arizona.* 1919. Phoenix. Berryhill Co. 8vo. 458p. ribbed gr cloth. VG. T10. $50.00

ROBINSON, William Albert. *Voyage to Galapagos.* 1936. Harcourt Brace. photos/drawings. 279p. VG. T7. $28.00

ROBINSON, William Morrison. *Confederate Privateers.* 1928. New Haven. Yale. 372p. G. T10. $85.00

ROBISON, Mary. *Amateur's Guide to the Night.* 1983. Knopf. 1st ed. rem mk. F/F. B4. $35.00

ROBISON, Mary. *Subtraction.* 1991. Knopf. 1st. F/F. R13. $20.00

ROCHE, John P. *Quest for the Dream: Development of Civil Rights...* 1963. Macmillan. 1st ed. 308p. torn dj. R11. $12.00

ROCHE, Paul. *All Things Considered.* 1968. Weybright Talley. 1st ed. assn copy. F/NF. V1. $20.00

ROCHESTER, A. *Nursery Rhymes.* ca 1935. Raphael Tuck. obl 4to. stiff wrp w/diecuts of children. R5. $75.00

ROCHESTER, A. *Why Farmers Are Poor: Agricultural Crisis in the US.* 1940. Internat Pub. 1st. VG/VG. V4. $20.00

ROCK, J.F. *Sandalwoods of Hawaii.* 1916. Honolulu. ils. 43p. F/wrp. B26. $26.00

ROCKEFELLER, John D. Jr. *Last Rivet: Story of Rockefeller Center.* 1940. NY. 1st. ils. suede cloth. F. B5. $40.00

ROCKFELLOW, John A. *Log of an Arizona Trail Blazer.* 1933. Acme. 1st. ils. 201p. B19. $55.00

ROCKNE, Dick. *Bow Down to Washington.* 1975. Strode. 1st. VG/VG. P8. $30.00

ROCKWELL, Carey. *Danger in Deep Space.* nd. Grosset Dunlap. VG. P3. $15.00

ROCKWELL, Carey. *Sabotage in Space.* nd. Grosset Dunlap. VG. P3. $15.00

ROCKWELL, Carey. *Tom Corbett Space Cadet & Danger in Deep Space.* 1953. Grosset Dunlap. ils. VG/G. P12. $5.00

ROCKWELL, Carey. *Tom Corbett Space Cadet & Stand By for Mars!* 1952. Grosset Dunlap. ils. VG/poor. P12. $5.00

ROCKWELL, Carey. *Tom Corbett: Treachery in Outer Space (#6).* 1954. Grosset Dunlap. lists 8 titles. 210p. cloth. VG/dj. M20. $15.00

ROCKWELL, Norman. *Norman Rockwell: My Adventures as an Illustrator.* 1960. Doubleday. ils. NF/VG. A4. $40.00

ROCKWELL, Norman. *Norman Rockwell: My Adventures as an Illustrator.* 1960. Doubleday. 1st ed. sgn. 437p. xl. VG. B11. $50.00

ROCKWOOD, Roy. *Bomba & the Lost Explorers.* nd. Grosset Dunlap. VG/fair. P3. $12.00

ROCKWOOD, Roy. *Bomba at the Moving Mountain.* nd. Cupples Leon. VG/VG. P3. $18.00

ROCKWOOD, Roy. *Bomba on the Underground River.* nd. Cupples Leon. G. P3. $10.00

ROCKWOOD, Roy. *Bomba the Jungle Boy & the Cannibals.* nd. Cupples Leon. VG. P3. $15.00

ROCKWOOD, Roy. *Bomba the Jungle Boy Among the Slaves.* 1939. Clover Books. G+. P12. $8.00

ROCKWOOD, Roy. *Dave Dashaway, Air Champion.* 1915. Cupples Leon. G+. P12. $5.00

ROCKWOOD, Roy. *Dave Dashaway & His Hydroplane (#2).* 1913. Cupples Leon. lists 5 titles. 202p. VG/ragged. M20. $25.00

ROCKWOOD, Roy. *Great Marvel Series: By Air Express to Venus (#8).* 1929. Cupples Leon. lists 9 titles. 248p. VG/dj. M20. $95.00

ROCKWOOD, Roy. *Great Marvel Series: On a Torn-Away World (#6).* 1913. Cupples Leon. lists 7 titles. 246p. gr cloth. VG/2nd dj art. M20. $50.00

ROCKWOOD, Roy. *Great Marvel Series: Through Space to Mars (#4).* 1910. Cupples Leon. lists 6 titles. 248p. VG/dj. M20. $60.00

ROCKWOOD, Roy. *On a Torn-Away World.* nd. Whitman. VG. P3. $20.00

RODD, Ralph. *Midnight Murder.* 1931. Collins Crime Club. 1st ed. VG. P3. $20.00

RODDIS, Louis. *Short History of Nautical Medicine.* 1941. NY. 359p. VG. A13. $100.00

RODEN, H.W. *Too Busy to Die.* nd. Detective BC. VG. P3. $10.00

RODEN, H.W. *Wake for a Lady.* 1946. Morrow. 1st ed. VG/VG. P3. $30.00

RODENGEN, Jeffrey L. *Legends of Chris-Craft.* 1988. FL. Write Stuff Syndicate. 1st ed. AN/dj. A16. $100.00

RODENWALDT, Gerhart. *Acropolis.* 1957. Oxford. Blackwell. 2nd. 4to. 104 pl. VG/torn. W1. $35.00

RODINSON, M. *Israel & the Arabs.* 1968. Pantheon. 1st Am ed. sm 8vo. 239p. VG/torn. W1. $18.00

RODKINSON, Michael L. *New Edition of the Babylonian Talmud. Vol VII...* 1918. Boston. Talmud Soc. tall 8vo. xl. VG. W1. $12.00

RODMAN, Selden. *Mexican Traveler.* 1969. Meredith. 1st ed. 264p. dj. F3. $20.00

RODNEY, George B. *Coronado Trial.* nd. Grosset Dunlap. VG/G+. P3. $13.00

RODRIQUEZ, Manuel. *Rum & Roosters.* (1957). Crowell. 1st. 256p. dj. F3 $15.00

RODRIQUEZ, Mario. *Cadiz Experiment in Central America.* 1978. CA U. 1st ed. 316p. dj. F3. $20.00

ROE, A.S. *39th Massachusetts Volunteers 1862-1865.* 1914. Worcester. 1st ed. ils. 493p. VG. B5. $125.00

ROE, Frank Gilbert. *Indian & the Horse.* 1974. Norman, OK. 4th. 433p. E1. $30.00

ROE, Judy. *Same Old Grind.* 1975. Millbrae, CA. Les Femmes. simultaneous wrp ed. B4. $45.00

ROEDER, Ralph. *Juarez & His Mexico.* 1948. Viking. 2nd. 761p. F3. $15.00

ROEDIGER, Virginia More. *Ceremonial Costumes of the Pueblo Indians...* 1941. CA U. 1st. 4to. 40 full-p pl. 251p. buckrum. as new/dj. K7. $275.00

ROESLER, Hugo. *Atlas of Cardio-Roentgenology.* 1940. Springfield. 1st. 124p. A13. $100.00

ROESSNER, Michaela. *Vanishing Point.* 1993. Tor. 1st ed. F/F. G10. $15.00

ROETHKE, Theodore. *Garden Master.* 1975. Seattle, WA. F/VG. V1. $15.00

ROFF, Joe T. *Brief History of Early Days in North Texas...* 1930. Roff, OK. 40p. VG/stiff wrp. E1. $350.00

ROFFMAN, Jan. *Walk in the Dark.* 1970. Crime Club. 1st ed. VG/VG. P3. $15.00

ROGERS, Andrew D. *Bernhard Eduard Fernow: Story of North Am Forestry.* nd. Princeton. 623p. dj. A10. $35.00

ROGERS, David Banks. *Prehistoric Man of the Santa Barbara Coast.* 1929. Santa Barbara. Mus Nat Hist. ils/fld map. 452p. D11. $175.00

ROGERS, Ernest E. *Connecticut's Naval Office at New London.* 1933. New London, CT. New London Co Hist Soc. 1/750. ils. 357p. teg. T7. $55.00

ROGERS, Eugene. *Beyond the Barrier: Story of Byrd's Expedition...* 1990. Annapolis. Naval Inst. 1st/2nd prt. 8vo. M/dj. P4. $28.00

ROGERS, Francis M. *Europe Informed: An Exhibition of Early Books...* 1966. Harvard/Columbia. ils/index. F/wrp. O7. $45.00

ROGERS, Fred Blackburn. *Filings From an Old Saw: Reminiscences of San Francisco...* 1956. SF. John Howell. 1/750. 8vo. ftspc Stockton. gr cloth. F. R3. $45.00

ROGERS, J.E. *Shell Book.* 1951. Boston. Branford. revised. 8vo. ils. cloth. NF. B1. $35.00

ROGERS, J.M. *Topkapi Saray Museum: The Treasury.* 1987. Little Brn. 1st ed. folio. 124 pl. 215p. F/case. W1. $95.00

ROGERS, John William. *Finding Literature on the Texas Plains.* 1931. Dallas. 57p. F. E1. $125.00

ROGERS, John. *Red World: Memories of a Chippewa Boyhood.* 1974. Norman. 2nd ed/1st prt. 153p. F/VG. E1. $30.00

ROGERS, Pat. *Oxford Ils History of English Literature.* 1987. Oxford. readling list/index. F/dj. A17. $25.00

ROGERS, Robert William. *History of Babylonia & Assyria.* 1901. NY/Cincinnati. Eaton Mains/Jennings Pye. 2 vol. 2nd. VG. W1. $75.00

ROGERS, Walter Thomas. *Manual of Bibliography.* 1891. London. Grevel. new ed. 8vo. 213p. teg. VG. T10. $35.00

ROGERS, Will. *Autobiography of...* 1949. Houghton Mifflin. lacks ffe. G+/dj. P3. $18.00

ROGERS, Will. *Ether & Me or Just Relax.* 1929. NY. Putnam. 1st. NF/VG. L3. $125.00

ROGERS, Will. *Letters of a Self-Made Diplomat to His President. Vol I.* 19226. NY. Boni. ils. 263p. VG. A4. $35.00

ROGERS, Will. *Will Rogers Scrapbook.* 1976. Grosset Dunlap. ils. 191p. brn cloth. F/dj. T10. $45.00

ROGERS, William Ledyard. *Greek & Roman Naval Warfare...Strategy, Tactics...* 1964. Annapolis. 555p. F. A17. $25.00

ROGIN, Gilbert. *Fencing Master & Other Stories.* 1965. Random. 1st. rem mk. NF/F. B4. $50.00

ROGOW, Roberta. *Futurespeak: A Fan's Guide to Language of Science Fiction.* 1991. Paragon. 1st. 408p. NF/dj. M21. $15.00

ROHAN, Michael Scott. *Anvil of Ice.* 1986. Morrow. 1st Am. F/dj. M2. $25.00

ROHAN, Michael Scott. *Gates of Noon.* 1992. Gollancz. 1st ed. F/F. P3. $25.00

ROHEIM, Gaza. *Hungarian & Vogul Mythology.* 1954. NY. Augustin. 8vo. ils/map. VG. W1. $16.00

ROHMER, Sax. *Bat Wing.* nd. AL Burt. VG/VG. P3. $35.00

ROHMER, Sax. *Brood of the Witch Queen.* 1924. Doubleday Page. 1st ed. G. P3. $45.00

ROHMER, Sax. *Day the World Ended.* nd. AL Burt. NF/dj. M2. $60.00

ROHMER, Sax. *Dope.* 1919. AL Burt. 1st ed thus. VG. M21. $20.00

ROHMER, Sax. *Drums of Fu Manchu.* 1939. Crime Club. 1st ed. VG. P3. $75.00

ROHMER, Sax. *Fire Tongue.* 1931. Cassell. 2nd. VG. P3. $20.00

ROHMER, Sax. *Green Eyes of Bast.* 1920. McBride. 1st ed. G. P3. $45.00

ROHMER, Sax. *Insidious Dr Fu Manchu.* nd. AL Burt. 1st ed thus. VG. M21. $10.00

ROHMER, Sax. *Mask of Fu Manchu.* 1932. Crime Club. 1st ed. G. P3. $35.00

ROHMER, Sax. *Orchard of Tears.* 1969. Bookfinger. 1st Am. F/sans. M2. $25.00

ROHMER, Sax. *She Who Sleeps.* 1928. Doubleday Doran. 1st. VG. M19. $35.00

ROHMER, Sax. *Wrath of Fu Manchu.* 1973. Tom Stacey. 1st ed. NF/NF. P3. $30.00

ROHMER, Sax. *Yu'an Hee See Laughs.* nd. Collier. 1st ed thus. VG+. M21. $15.00

ROLFE, Edwin. *Collected Poems.* 1993. Urbana, IL. 1st ed. F/F. B2. $35.00

ROLFE, Frank. *Commercial Geography of Southern California.* 1915. Los Angeles. Rolfe. ils/fld maps. ES. NF. O7. $135.00

ROLFE, Fred. *Letter to Claud.* 1964. IA City. 1/150. F/wrp. A15. $50.00

ROLLAND, Sandy. *Raffles: His Sons & Daughters.* 1974. Burlington. 1st ed. 1/1000. sgn. VG. O3. $295.00

ROLLE, A. *John Charles Fremont.* 1991. OK U. 1st. ils. F/dj. M4. $30.00

ROLLE, Andrew F. *Road to Virginia City: Diary of James Knox Polk Miller.* 1960. OK U. 1st ed. ils Joe Beeler. 142p. F/F. E1. $40.00

ROLLER. *Exhibition of Works by Galileo Galilei...* 1980. Norman, OK. 4to. ils. NF/wrp. A4. $35.00

ROLLERSTON, Humphry. *Some Medical Aspects of Old Age.* 1922. London. 170p. xl. A13. $100.00

ROLLESTON, T.W. *Celtic Myths & Legends.* 1986. Bracken. 1st ed. VG. P3. $25.00

ROLLINS, Philip Ashton. *Cowboy: An Unconventional History of Civilization...* 1936. NY, NY. 3rd. ils/map/index. 402p. F. E1. $65.00

ROLLINS & SHAW. *Genus Lesquerella in North America.* 1973. Cambridge. ils/maps/tables. 288p. VG+. B26. $19.00

ROLLYSON, Carl. *Lillian Hellman: Her Legend & Her Legacy.* 1988. NY. 1st ed. 613p. F/F. A17. $15.00

ROLLYSON, Carl. *Nothing Ever Happens to the Brave: Story of Martha Gellhorn.* 1990. St Martin. 1st. F/F. R13. $15.00

ROLLYSON. *Lives of Norman Mailer.* 1991. np. photos. 425p. F/F. A4. $25.00

ROLT-WHEELER, Francis. *Book of Cowboys.* 1921. Lee Shepard. 1st ed. photos. F/chip. A18. $40.00

ROLVAAG, O.E. *When the Wind Is in the South & Other Stories.* 1984. Center for Western Studies. 1st ed. M/M. A18. $30.00

ROMAINE. *Guide to American Trade Catalogs 1744-1900.* 1960. np. 445p. VG. A4. $185.00

ROMANES, George J. *Animal Intelligence. Internat Scientific Series Vol 44.* 1883 (1882). NY. Appleton. 12mo. 520p. xl. VG. G1. $65.00

ROMANES, George J. *Examination of Weismannism.* 1899. Chicago. Open Court. 1st Am ed/2nd prt. 221p. VG. G1. $40.00

ROMANES, George J. *Mind & Motion & Monism.* 1895. Longman Gr. 1st Am ed. 12mo. 170p. panelled gr cloth. VG. G1. $50.00

ROMANO, Deane. *Flight From Time One.* 1972. Walker. 1st ed. VG/VG. P3. $15.00

ROMBAUER, Irma S. *Cookbook for Boys & Girls.* 1946. Bobbs Merrill. 1st. tall 8vo. VG. M5. $75.00

ROMBAUER, Irma S. *Joy of Cooking.* 1972. Bobbs Merrill. G. A16. $20.00

ROMBAUER, Marjorie Dick. *Legal Problem Solving: Analysis, Research & Writing.* 1973. St Paul. West Pub. M11. $35.00

ROMBERGER, J.A. *Meristems, Growth & Development in Woody Plants.* 1963. USDA. 214p. cloth. VG. B1. $27.00

ROME, Jesus. *Civilization of the Maya.* (1979-80). Crescent. 1st ed. 174p. dj. F3. $20.00

ROOME, Annette. *Bad Trip.* 1971. Dodd Mead. 1st ed. VG/VG. P3. $20.00

ROOME, Annette. *Real Shot in the Arm.* 1989. Crown. 1st ed. NF/NF. P3. $18.00

ROOME, Annette. *Triple Threat.* 1949. AA Wyn. 1st ed. VG/torn. P3. $20.00

ROONEY, Andy. *Word for Word.* 1986. Putnam. 1st ed. F/F. B35. $20.00

ROONEY, James. *Lame Horse: Causes, Symptoms & Treatment.* 1975. Barnes. VG/G. O3. $25.00

ROONEY, Mickey. *Life Is Too Short.* 1991. Villard. 1st. sgn. F/F. $50.00

ROONEY, Mickey. *Search for Sonny Skies.* 1994. Birch Lane. 1st. sgn. F/F. A23. $40.00

ROOS & ROOS. *Few Days in Madrid.* 1966. Deutsch. 1st ed. VG/VG. P3. $18.00

ROOSEVELT, Elliott. *Murder & the First Lady.* 1984. St Martin. 1st ed. F/F. B4. $45.00

ROOSEVELT, Elliott. *Murder at the Palace.* nd. BC. VG/VG. P3. $8.00

ROOSEVELT, Elliott. *Murder in the Blue Room.* 1990. St Martin. 1st ed. F/F. P3. $17.00

ROOSEVELT, Elliott. *Roosevelt Letters. Vol 1: Early Years 1887-1904.* 1949. 8vo. 470p. blk cloth. G. T3. $15.00

ROOSEVELT, Selwa 'Lucky.' *Keeper of the Gate.* 1990. Simon Schuster. 1st ed. sgn. VG/VG. B11. $12.00

ROOSEVELT, Robert Barnwell. *Game Birds of the North Carleton.* 1866. NY. A19. $75.00

ROOSEVELT, Robert Barnwell. *Superior Fishing; or, Striped Bass, Trout & Black Bass...* 1985. NM Hist Soc. facsimile 1865 ed. 310p. F/dj. A17. $22.50

ROOSEVELT, Theodore. *African Game Trails.* 1910. np. 1st ed. ils. 483p. half leather. VG. A4/S13. $45.00

ROOSEVELT, Theodore. *African Game Trails.* 1910. NY. 1st ed (p78 & p79 are blank). NF. A15. $125.00

ROOSEVELT, Theodore. *Book-Lover's Holidays in the Open.* 1925. Scribner. 8vo. 373p. VG. F7. $30.00

ROOSEVELT, Theodore. *Hunting Tales of a Ranchman.* 1908. Current Literay Pub. G+. P12. $10.00

ROOSEVELT, Theodore. *Letters to His Children.* 1919. NF. S13. $15.00

ROOSEVELT, Theodore. *Presidential Addresses & State Papers.* 1910. NY. 8 vol. index. 2359p. VG. A17. $50.00

ROOSEVELT, Theodore. *Ranch Life & the Hunting-Trail.* 1907. Century. sm 4to. ils Remington. teg. stp City of Boston. H7. $55.00

ROOSEVELT, Wyn. *Frontier Boys in the Grand Canyon.* 1908. NY. Platt Peck. ils Schneider. white cloth. VG. F7. $30.00

ROOT, Elihu. *Men & Policies, Addresses by Elihu Root.* 1925. Harvard. M11. $50.00

ROOT, Waverley. *Foods of France.* 1958. Knopf. 2nd. dj. B10. $50.00

ROOT, William Pitt. *Fireclock.* 1981. Four Zoas. ltd ed. 1/about 175. NF/wrp. V1. $15.00

ROOT, William Pitt. *Reasons for Going It on Foot.* 1981. Atheneum. 1st ed. F/F. V1. $15.00

ROOT, William Pitt. *Storm & Other Poems.* 1969. Atheneum. 1st. assn copy. poet's 1st book. F/dj. V1. $55.00

ROPER, Allen. *Ancient Eugenics.* 1975. Minneapolis. facsimile of 1913 ed. 76p. VG. A13. $30.00

ROPES, J.C. *Army Under Pope.* 1881. NY. 12mo. fld map. 229p. blk cloth. G. T3. $25.00

ROQUELAURE, A.N.; see Rice, Anne.

ROSA, Joseph G. *Gunfighter: Man or Myth?* 1969. Norman, OK. 229p. NF/dj. T10. $25.00

ROSA, Joseph G. *Guns of the American West.* 1985. NY. 1st Am ed. 192p. F/F. E1. $55.00

ROSA, Joseph G. *They Called Him Wild Bill Hickok.* 1964. Norman, OK. 1st ed. photos/index. 278p. F/VG. E1. $75.00

ROSA, Joseph G. *West of Wild Bill Hickok.* 1982. Norman. 1st ed. 23p. F/F. E1. $60.00

ROSA, Rodrigo Rey. *Pelcari Project.* 1991. London. Peter Owen. 1st. F/NF. A24. $30.00

ROSAND, David. *Titian: His World & His Legacy.* 1982. Columbian U. ils/pl. 349p. cloth. dj. D2. $75.00

ROSCOE, T. *US Destroyer Operations in WWII.* 1953. Annapolis. 1st ed. VG/VG. B5. $67.50

ROSCOE, Theodore. *I'll Grind Their Bones.* 1936. NY. Dodge. 1st ed. F/VG+. B4. $150.00

ROSCOE, Theodore. *To Live & Die in Dixie.* 1961. NY. 1st ed. VG/VG. B5. $25.00

ROSCOE, Theodore. *Web of Conspiracy.* 1960. Englewood Cliffs. 2nd. 562p. G+/torn. B18. $37.50

ROSCOE, Thomas. *Wanderings & Excursions in North Wales.* 1836. London. Tilt Simpkin. tall 8vo. 262p. aeg. full gr calf. K1. $250.00

ROSCOE, William. *Butterfly's Ball & the Grasshopper's Feast.* 1977. Boston. 1/150. sgn prt/ils Carah Chamberlain. F. B24. $250.00

ROSE, Billy. *Wine, Women & Works.* 1948. 1st ed. ils Salvador Dali. VG/VG. S13. $45.00

ROSE, J. Holland. *Development of European Nations 1870-1900.* 1905. Knickerbocker. 2 vol. 1st ed. maps/plans. teg. VG. W1. $75.00

ROSE, Mark. *Science Fiction.* 1976. Prentice Hall. 1st. NF/dj. M2. $22.00

ROSE, Turner. *Marked for Rest.* 1932. Samuel French. 25p. VG/stiff wrp. B10. $15.00

ROSE, Victor M. *Life & Services of General Ben McCulloch.* 1958. Phil. facsimile. photos. 260p. VG/case. E1. $65.00

ROSE, Victor M. *Texas Vendetta on the Sutton-Taylor Feud.* 1956. Houston, TX. rpt. 69p. F. E1. $75.00

ROSE, William K. *Astrophysics.* 1973. HRW. 3rd. 287p. VG. K5. $23.00

ROSEBAULT, Charles J. *Saladin, Prince of Chivalry.* 1930. Cassell. 1st ed. ils/pl/maps. 303p. VG. W1. $30.00

ROSEN, Charles. *Mile Above the Rim.* 1976. Arbor. 1st ed. F/F. B35. $20.00

ROSEN, George. *Reception of William Beumont's Discovery in Europe.* 1942. NY. 1st ed. 97p. VG. A13. $55.00

ROSEN, Gerald. *Dr Ebenezer's Book & Liquor Store.* 1980. NY. 1st ed. F/F. H11. $30.00

ROSEN, Marion. *Death by Education.* 1993. NY. 1st ed. F/F. H11. $25.00

ROSEN, Michael. *Down at the Doctor's.* 1987. NY. Simon Schuster. 1st ed. 8vo. unp. NF/NF. C14. $8.00

ROSEN, Richard. *Fadeaway.* 1986. Harper Row. 1st ed. F/F. P3. $16.00

ROSEN, Richard. *Saturday Night Dead.* 1988. Viking. 1st ed. F/F. H11. $30.00

ROSEN, Richard. *Saturday Night Dead.* 1988. Viking. 1st ed. VG/VG. P3. $17.00

ROSEN, Ruth Chier. *Wendy & Chip's Kitchen Debut.* 1956. ASF Ent. sbdg. VG. M5. $45.00

ROSENBACH, A.S.W. *Book Hunter's Holiday.* 1936. Houghton Mifflin. 1/760. sgn. F/glassine. T10. $200.00

ROSENBACH, A.S.W. *Collected Catalogues of Dr ASW Rosenbach 1904-1951.* 1967. 10 vol. NF. A4. $650.00

ROSENBACH, A.S.W. *Early American Children's Books...* nd. rpt of 1933 ed. 1/150. 104 ils/816 entries. 413p. F. A4. $85.00

ROSENBAUM, David. *Sasha's Trick.* 1995. Mysterious. 1st ed. F/F. H11. $25.00

ROSENBAUM, David. *Zaddick.* 1993. Mysterious. 1st ed. F/F. H11. $30.00

ROSENBERG, David A. *Marcos & Martial Law in the Philippines.* 1979. Ithaca. Cornell. 315p. F/VG. P1. $14.00

ROSENBERG, Joel. *Keepers of the Hidden Ways.* 1995. Morrow. 1st ed. F/F. w/pub material. G10. $10.00

ROSENBERG, Joel. *Not for Glory.* 1988. NAL. 1st ed. F/F. P3. $17.00

ROSENBERG, Nancy Taylor. *Interest of Justice.* 1993. Dutton. ARC. F/pict wrp. G10. $30.00

ROSENBERG, Nancy Taylor. *Interest of Justice.* 1993. Dutton. 1st ed. sgn. F/F. H11. $50.00

ROSENBLUM, Robert. *Good Thief.* 1975. Hart Davis MacGibbon. hc. VG/VG. P3. $20.00

ROSENBLUM, Robert. *Sweetheart Deal.* 1976. Putnam. 1st ed. F/F. P3. $15.00

ROSENBLUM. *World History of Photography.* 1984. 803 photos. 671p. F/F. A4. $165.00

ROSENDORFF, H.G. *Australian Contract Bridge Championships 1964 Perth.* nd. Sydney. VG/wrp. S1. $10.00

ROSENE, Walter. *Bobwhite Quail: Its Life & Management.* 1969. Rutgers. 418p+65 photos+5 mc pl+2 maps. F/dj. A17. $50.00

ROSENFELD, Alvin H. *Double Dying: Reflections on Holocaust Literature.* 1980. IU. 210p. VG+/dj. S3. $29.00

ROSENFELD, Lulla. *Death & the I Ching.* 1981. Potter. 1st ed. NF/NF. P3. $18.00

ROSENFELD, Morris. *Sail-Ho!* 1947. NY. Maloney. 1st ed. 4to. ils. 112p. VG. T7. $35.00

ROSENGARTEN, Frederick. *Book of Spices.* 1969. 1st ed. NF/NF. S13. $75.00

ROSENGARTEN, Joseph George. *German Soldier in the Wars of the United States.* 1886. Lippincott. 1st thus. 47p. half leather/marbled brd. M8. $85.00

ROSENKRANZ, George. *Everything You Always Wanted to Know About Trump Leads...* 1986. Louisville. 158p. F/wrp. S1. $7.00

ROSENQUIST, James. *James Rosenquist.* 1968. Nat Gallery Canada. ils. 92p. D2. $65.00

ROSENTHAL, Franz. *Aramaic Handbook.* 1967. Wiesbaden. Harrassowitz. 1st ed. 4 parts. 2 fld pl. VG/wrp. W1. $60.00

ROSENTHAL, Franz. *Grammar of Biblical Aramaic.* 1983. Wiesbaden. Harrassowitz. 5th. 100p. VG/wrp. W1. $16.00

ROSENTHAL, M.L. *She.* 1977. BOA Ed. 1/14 (pres). sgns. F. V1. $125.00

ROSENTHAL, Stuart. *Cinema of Federico Fellini.* 1976. AS Barnes/Tantivy. ils. NF. C9. $50.00

ROSETTI, Dante Gabriel. *Ballads & Sonnets.* 1881. London. 1st ed. NF. C6. $125.00

ROSKE, Ralph. *Everyman's Eden: History of California.* 1968. Macmillan. 1st ed. 8vo. ils/maps. VG/tattered. T10. $45.00

ROSKILL, S.W. *Navy at War, 1939-1945.* 1960. London. Collins. 43 photos/24 maps. 480p. T7. $40.00

ROSKILL, S.W. *Strategy of Sea Power.* 1962. London. Collins. VG/VG. A16. $37.50

ROSNER, Fred. *Studies in Torah Judaism: Modern Medicine & Jewish Law.* 1972. Yeshiva. 216p. VG. S3. $25.00

ROSNER, Paul. *Princess & the Goblin.* 1966. Sherbourne. 1st. VG/dj. M25. $35.00

ROSS, A.M. *Blindfold.* 1978. Little Brn. 1st ed. F/F. P3. $13.00

ROSS, Angus. *Bradford Business.* 1974. John Long. 1st ed. F/F. P3. $22.00

ROSS, Christian K. *Father's Story of Charley Ross, the Kidnapped Child.* 1876. Phil. 1st ed. 431p. decor cloth. G. B18. $35.00

ROSS, Clinton. *Zuleka: Being History of Adventure in Life of Am Gentleman.* 1897. Lamson Wolffe. 1st ed. 8vo. 222p. teg. VG. W1. $25.00

ROSS, D.A. *Introduction to Oceanography.* 1970. Appleton Century Crofts. 384p. VG. D8. $8.50

ROSS, Dudley T. *Devil on Horseback: Biography of the Notorious Jack Powers.* 1975. Valley Pub. 1st ed. 185p. F/F. E1. $30.00

ROSS, Frank A. *Bibliography of Negro Migration.* 1934. NY. 251p. VG+. M8. $75.00

ROSS, Frank. *Sleeping Dogs.* 1978. Atheneum. 1st ed. VG/VG. P3. $18.00

ROSS, Harry H. *Enchanting Isles of Erie.* 1949. np. 73p. VG. M20. $27.00

ROSS, Ivan T. *Requiem for a Schoolgirl.* 1961. Heinemann. 1st ed. VG/VG. P3. $28.00

ROSS, James R. *Jesse James.* 1988. Dragon. 1st ed. 280p. E1. $50.00

ROSS, Jonathan. *Burning of Billy Toober.* 1974. Walker. 1st ed. VG/VG. P3. $18.00

ROSS, Lillian. *Portrait of Hemingway.* 1961. S&S. 1st. G/G. B35. $16.00

ROSS, Lillian. *Takes.* 1983. NY. 1st ed. dj. A17. $7.50

ROSS, Martin. *Last Parallel: Marine's War Journal.* 1957. NY. 3rd. 333p. dj. A17. $8.50

ROSS, Marvin C. *West of Alfred Jacob Miller.* 1968. OK U. revised/enlarged ed. 208p. VG/worn. T10. $65.00

ROSS, Nancy Wilson. *Farthest Reach: Oregon & Washington.* 1949. Knopf. 5th. 8vo. fld map. VG/dj. T10. $25.00

ROSS, Nancy Wilson. *I, My Ancestor.* 1950. Random. 1st ed. VG/VG. P3. $15.00

ROSS, Patricia. *In Mexico They Say.* 1946. Knopf. 3rd. 211p. dj. F3. $15.00

ROSS, Sam. *He Ran All the Way.* 1947. NY. 1st. NF/VG clip. B4. $150.00

ROSS, W. Gillies. *Arctic Whalers Icy Seas.* 1985. Tor. 1st. 263p. F/dj. A17. $25.00

ROSS & KENNEDY. *Bibliography of Negro Migration.* 1934. NY. Columbia. 1st. 251p. cloth. VG+. M8. $75.00

ROSS & ROSS. *Imperial Glass.* 1971. Wallace-Homestead. 8vo. mc pl. sbdg. VG. H1. $26.00

ROSS & ROSS. *Long Road South.* 1968. Mitchell. 1st. 168p. F3. $15.00

ROSSELLINI, Roberto. *War Trilogy.* 1973. Grossman. 1st ed. F/dj. A17. $15.00

ROSSER, J. ALlyn. *Bright Moves.* 1990. Northeastern. 1st ed. sgn Charles Simic. F/wrp. V1. $15.00

ROSSETTI, Christina. *Goblin Market.* 1893. Macmillan. 1st. ils Laurence Housman. tall 12mo. aeg. gr cloth. R5. $550.00

ROSSETTI, Christina. *Goblin Market.* 1933. Lippincott. 1st. ils Rackham/4 full-p mc pl. red cloth/label. R5. $125.00

ROSSETTI, D.G. *Poems.* 1873. Leipzig. Tauchnitz. 1st Continental/1st state. full vellum. M24. $100.00

ROSSETTI, D.G. *Poems.* 1881. Ellis White. new ed. gilt bl cloth. M24. $100.00

ROSSETTI, W.M. *Life of John Keats.* 1887. London. Walter Scott. 1st. teg. gilt maroon cloth. F. M24. $75.00

ROSSHANDLER, Leo. *Man-Eaters & Pretty Ladies.* 1972. NY. 2nd. ils/photos/drawings. F3. $25.00

ROSSITER, Clinton. *Federalist Papers.* 1961. Penguin. 560p. prt wrp. M11. $75.00

ROSSITER, Oscar. *Tetrasomy Two.* 1974. Doubleday. 1st ed. F/F. P3. $13.00

ROSTAND, Robert. *D'Artagnan Signature.* 1976. Putnam. 1st ed. VG/torn. P3. $13.00

ROSTEN, Leo. *Silky!* 1979. Harper Row. 1st ed. VG/VG. P3. $20.00

ROSTLER, William. *Hidden Worlds of Zandra.* 1983. Doubleday. 1st ed. F/F. G10. $10.00

ROTERBERG, A. *New Era Card Tricks.* nd. NY. 284p. missing cover o/w contents VG. S1. $5.00

ROTH, Barry. *Annotated Bibliography of Jane Austen Studies.* 1985. VA U. 1st. as new. V4. $25.00

ROTH, Cecil. *Haggadah.* 1957. Jerusalem. Massadah Alumoth. 1st trade. 8vo. ils Szyk. box. B24. $250.00

ROTH, Gunther D. *Amateur Astronomer & His Telescope.* 1963. Van Nostrand. trans Alex Helm. xl. dj. K5. $14.00

ROTH, Henry. *Shifting Landscape: A Composite 1925-1987.* 1987. Jreidh Pub Soc. 2nd. VG/VG. V4. $22.50

ROTH, Holly. *Masks of Glass.* nd. BC. VG. P3. $4.00

ROTH, Holly. *Sleeper.* 1955. Simon Schuster. 1st ed. VG/torn. P3. $10.00

ROTH, Lillian. *I'll Cry Tomorrow.* 1954. Frederick Fell. 1st ed. NF/NF. B35. $40.00

ROTH, Philip. *Anatomy Lesson.* 1983. FSG. 1st ed. 1/300. sgn. F/case. C2. $125.00

ROTH, Philip. *Breast.* 1972. HRW. 1st ed. F/F. B35. $35.00

ROTH, Philip. *Counterlife.* 1986. Franklin Lib. 1st ed. sgn. leather. F. C2. $35.00

ROTH, Philip. *Deception.* 1990. S&S. 1st. F/F. T12. $15.00

ROTH, Philip. *Ghost Writer.* 1979. FSG. 1st ed. NF/NF. B35. $20.00

ROTH, Philip. *Goodbye, Columbus.* 1959. Houghton Mifflin. 1st ed. author's 1st book. F/clip. B24. $500.00

ROTH, Philip. *Great American Novel.* 1973. HRW. 1st ed. NF/NF. B35. $20.00

ROTH, Philip. *My Life as a Man.* 1974. HRW. 1st ed/3rd. F/F. B35. $20.00

ROTH, Philip. *Operation Shylock: A Confession.* 1993. Simon Schuster. 1st ed. F/F. H11. $25.00

ROTH, Philip. *Our Gang.* 1971. Random. 1st ed. F/F. B35. $35.00

ROTH, Philip. *Partrimony.* 1991. S&S. 1st. sgn. F/F. R14. $45.00

ROTH, Philip. *Portnoy's Complaint.* 1969. Random. 1st ed. F/NF. B35. $38.00

ROTH, Philip. *Professor of Desire.* 1977. NY. 1st ed. sgn. NF/NF. C6. $55.00

ROTH, Philip. *Reading Myself & Others.* 1975. FSG. 1st. F/F. B35. $18.00

ROTH, Philip. *Sabbath's Theater.* 1995. Houghton Mifflin. ARC. F/pict wrp. G10. $75.00

ROTH, Philip. *Zuckerman Unbound.* 1981. NY. 1st ed. 1/350. sgn. F/case. C2. $100.00

ROTH & ROTH. *James Dean.* 1983. Pomegranate Artbooks. 1st ed. inscr. photos by Sanford Roth. VG+/wrp. S9. $100.00

ROTHA, Paul. *Documentary Film.* 1968 (1952). NY. Communications Arts Books/Hastings. 3rd. F/VG. D2. $25.00

ROTHAUS, James. *Team History Series.* 1987. Creative Education. F. P8. $15.00

ROTHENBERG, Robert. *Group Medicine & Health Insurance in Action.* 1949. NY. 1st ed. 278p. VG. A13. $35.00

ROTHERHAM, E.R. *Flowers & Plants of New South Wales & Southern Queensland.* 1975. Sydney. 556 mc pl/map ep. 191p. F/dj. B26. $65.00

ROTHERY, Agnes. *Virginia: New Dominion.* 1940. Appleton Century. 1st ed. ils EH Suydam. 368p. VG/fair. B10. $20.00

ROTHMAN & SIMEONE. *Spine.* 1975. Phil. Saunders. 2 vol. 8vo. ils. bl cloth. VG. G1. $65.00

ROTHSCHILD, A. *Lincoln, Master of Men.* 1906. Riverside. 8vo. 531p. navy cloth. xl. VG. T3. $20.00

ROTHSTEIN, Andrew. *Munich Conspiracy (1938).* 1958. London. 1st ed. 320p. VG/dj. A17. $15.00

ROTHWELL, Richard P. *Mineral Industry in the US & Other Countries...* 1893. NY. inscr to Pres Cleveland. 628p. VG. B14. $125.00

ROUNTHWAITE & SEATON. *Pocket Book of Marine Engineering Rules & Tables.* 1899. London. Griffin. 5th. 128 tables. 471p. full leather. T7. $65.00

ROUNTREE, Harry. *Animal Fun ABC.* ca 1900. Graham. lg 4to. sc. M5. $55.00

ROUSANIERE, John. *America's Cup Book 1851-1983.* 1983. Norton. 1st ed. 4to. VG/dj. T7. $45.00

ROUSE, Blair. *Letters of Ellen Glasgow.* 1958. Harcourt Brace. 1st ed. 384p. VG/G. B10. $35.00

ROUSE, John E. *Criollo Spanish Cattle in the Americas.* 1977. Norman, OK. 1st ed. 301p. F/VG. E1. $40.00

ROUSE, Parke Jr. *Cows on Campus: Williamsburg in Bygone Days.* 1973. Richmond. Dietz. 1st ed. sgn. 8vo. 219p. VG/VG. B11. $40.00

ROUSSEL, Raymond. *How I Wrote Certain of My Books.* 1977. NY. Sun. VG/wrp. V1. $10.00

ROVIN, Jeff. *Adventure Heroes.* 1994. Facts on File. 1st. F/dj. M2. $35.00

ROVIN, Jeff. *Encyclopedia of Super Villains.* 1987. Facts on File. 1st. F/dj. M2. $35.00

ROVIN, Jeff. *Mars!* 1978. Corwin. 1st ed. F/NF. G10. $10.00

ROVIN, Jeff. *Mars!* 1978. LA. Corwin. 1st. 4to. 244p. VG. K5. $20.00

ROWAN, A.N. *Of Mice, Models & Men.* 1984. Albany. 8vo. 323p. VG. B1. $26.50

ROWBOTHAM, Sally Smith. *Virginia's Historic Trees...* 1931. np. phot. 22p. VG. B10. $45.00

ROWBOTTOM & SUSSKIND. *Electricity & Medicine: History of Their Interaction.* 1984. San Francisco. 1st ed. 303p. VG. A13. $60.00

ROWE, Anne E. *Enchanted Country: Northern Writers in the South 1865-1910.* 1978. LSU. 155p. VG/VG. B10. $15.00

ROWE, Anne. *Century of Change in Guatemalan Textiles.* 1981. NY. 1st ed. 151p. wrp. F3. $30.00

ROWE, John. *Hard Rock Men. Cornish & American Mining Frontier.* 1974. NY. 1st ed. ils/index. 322p. VG/VG. B5. $35.00

ROWLAND, Laura J. *Shinju.* 1994. Random. 1st ed. author's 1st book. F/F. H11. $30.00

ROWLEY, G. *Illustrated Encyclopedia of Succulents.* 1978. Crown. 4to. ils. hc. clip dj. B1. $40.00

ROWLINSON. *Tennyson's Fixations, Psychoanalysis & Topics...* 1994. VA U. 205p. F/F. A4. $35.00

ROWNTREE, Lester. *Flowering Shrubs of California.* 1948. Stanford. 2nd. 317p. VG/dj. A10. $25.00

ROWSE, A.L. *Shakespeare's Southampton.* 1965. Harper Row. 1st ed. 323p. VG/clip. M20. $25.00

ROWSWELL, A.K. *Diamond Laughs.* 1948. Ft Pitt Brewing. 1st ed. ils. G+. P8. $35.00

ROY, Claude. *Modigliani.* 1958. Cleveland. World. ils. 136p. cloth. dj. D2. $25.00

ROYSE, Isaac. *History of 115th Regiment of Illinois Volunteer Infantry...* 1900. Terre Haute. 1st ed. ils/maps. 405p. VG. B5. $175.00

ROYSTER, Vermont. *My Own, My Country's Time.* 1983. Algonquin. 8vo. 351p. brn cloth. VG/clip. P4. $22.50

RUARK, Robert. *Didn't Know It Was Loaded.* 1948. Garden City. 1st ed. VG/G. B5. $37.50

RUARK, Robert. *Honey Badger.* 1965. McGraw Hill. 1st ed. F/VG+. B4. $85.00

RUARK, Robert. *Old Man & Boy.* 1957. NY. 1st ed. VG/VG. B5. $40.00

RUARK, Robert. *Old Man's Boy Grows Older.* 1961. NY. 1st ed. VG/VG. B5. $40.00

RUARK, Robert. *Use Enough Gun.* 1966. NAL. 1st ed. F/NF. H11. $55.00

RUARK, Robert. *Use Enough Gun.* 1966. NAL. 1st ed. 333p. VG/dj. M20. $45.00

RUARK, Robert. *Women.* 1967. NY. 1st ed. VG/VG. B5. $50.00

RUBENS, Jeff. *Win at Poker.* 1968. NY. 218p. VG. S1. $10.00

RUBIN, Barry. *Revolution Until Victory?* 1994. Cambridge. Harvard. 1st ed. 271p. NF/dj. W1. $18.00

RUBIN, Louis. *No Place on Earth: Ellen Glasgow, James Branch Cabell...* 1959. TX U. sgn. 81p. VG. B10. $20.00

RUBINSTEIN, Gillian. *Galax-Arena.* 1995. Simon Schuster. 1st Am ed. F/F. G10. $10.00

RUBY & RUBY. *Chinook Indians...Civilization of the Am Indian Series.* 1976. Norman. 1st ed. photos/ils/index. 349p. F/F. E1. $50.00

RUBY & RUBY. *Indians of the Pacific Northwest.* 1981. Norman. 1st ed. biblio/maps. 294p. F/F. E1. $65.00

RUBY & RUBY. *Spokane Indians... Civilization of Am Indian Series.* 1970. Norman, OK. 1st ed. photos/map. 346p. F/F. E1. $50.00

RUDD, RUDD & WHITE. *And Three Small Fishes.* 1974. McClure. F/VG. B10. $8.00

RUDDER. *Literature in Spain in English Translation...* 1975. np. 637p. F/F. A4. $50.00

RUDINGER, N. *Rudinger Atlas of the Osseous Anatomy of the Human Ear.* 1874. Boston. 9 orig mtd photos. trans CJ Blake. red portfolio. B14. $325.00

RUDMAN, Mark. *Rider.* 1994. Wesleyan. 1st ed. F/wrp. V1. $10.00

RUDNIK, Raphael. *Lesson From the Cyclops.* 1967. Random. 1st ed. assn copy. F/NF. V1. $20.00

RUDOLPH, Marguerita. *Magic Sack.* (1967). McGraw Hill. ils Ralph Pinto. pict gr cloth. xl. G. T5. $12.00

RUDOLPH, Wolfgang. *Sailor Souvenirs.* 1985. Leipzig. ils. 151p. VG. T7. $22.00

RUE, Leonard Lee. *Game Birds of North America.* 1973. Outdoor Life/Harper Row. ils. VG/G+. P12. $14.00

RUEDEBUSCH, Emil F. *Old & New Ideal. Solution of Part of the Social Question...* 1897. Mayville, WI. 2nd. 347p. red cloth. VG. B14. $75.00

RUFF, Ann. *Unsung Heroes of Texas.* 1985. Lone Star. 126p. pb. F. E1. $15.00

RUGE, Friedrich. *Der Seekrieg 1939-45.* 1954. Stuttgart. Koehler. VG. A17. $15.00

RUGGERO, Ed. *28 North Yankee.* 1990. Pocket. 1st ed. F/F. H11. $25.00

RUGGLES, Eleanor. *Prince of Players: Edwin Booth.* 1953. Norton. 1st ed. cloth. VG. D2. $15.00

RUGOFF, Milton. *Beechers.* 1981. NY. 1st ed. 653p. dj. A17. $15.00

RUHEN, Olaf. *Tangaroa's Godchild.* 1962. Little Brn. 1st ed. 346p. VG/worn. P4. $25.00

RUKEYSER, Muriel. *Gates.* 1976. McGraw Hill. 1st ed. F/NF. V1. $20.00

RUKEYSER, Muriel. *Selected Poems.* 1951. New Directions. 1st ed. NF/NF. V1. $35.00

RULFO, Juan. *Burning Plain & Other Stories.* 1970. Austin, TX. 2nd. inscr. 175p. F3. $15.00

RUMBALL. *Rare Bibles: An Introduction for Collectors & a Checklist...* 1954. 2nd/final revised ed. 1/600. F. A4. $165.00

RUNDELL, Walter Jr. *Early Texas Oil.* 1977. TX A&M. 3rd. 4to. 260p. F/dj. T10. $35.00

RUNES, D. *Diary & Sundry Observations of Thomas Alva Edison.* 1948. NY. 247p. F/dj. A17. $20.00

RUNYON, Damon. *In Our Town. Twenty Seven Slices of Life.* 1946. NY. 1st ed. ils Garth Williams. 120p. silvered brn cloth. F. H3. $40.00

RUNYON, Damon. *Tents of Trouble.* 1911. NY. 1st ed. author's 1st book. G/sans. B5. $135.00

RUPORT, A. *Art of Cockfighting: A Handbook for the Beginner...* 1949. Devin-Adair. 1st ed. 211p. NF/dj. M20. $67.00

RUSCH, Kristine Katherine. *Best of Pulphouse: The Hardback Magazine.* 1991. St Martin. 1st ed. F/NF. G10. $10.00

RUSCH, Kristine Katherine. *Pulphouse: The Hardcover Magazine #4, SF.* 1989. Pulphouse. 1/1000. cloth. AN/sans. M21. $20.00

RUSH, James. *Philosophy of the Human Voice.* 1833. Phil. 2nd. ils. 432p. calf. VG. B14. $75.00

RUSH, James. *Philosophy of the Human Voice.* 1859. Lippincott. 5th. 677p. detached spine. G1. $50.00

RUSH, Norman. *Mating.* 1991. Knopf. 1st ed. inscr. F/F. B2. $65.00

RUSH, Oscar. *Open Range & Bunk House Philosophy.* 1930. Denver, CO. 2nd. 118p. professional rpr. w/sgn typewritten note. E1. $65.00

RUSHDIE, Salman. *Haroun & the Sea of Stories.* 1990. Viking. ARC. w/promo material. F/F. B35. $35.00

RUSHDIE, Salman. *Imaginary Homelands.* 1991. Viking/Granta. 1st ed. rem mk. F/F. B35. $35.00

RUSHDIE, Salman. *Jaguar Smile.* 1987. Viking. 1st ed. rem mk. F/F. B35. $25.00

RUSHDIE, Salman. *Moor's Last Sigh.* 1995. NY. ARC/1st Am ed. 1/1000. sgn. F/decor wrp/2-part case. C2. $75.00

RUSHDIE, Salman. *Satanic Verses.* 1988. Viking. 1st ed. F/F. B35. $55.00

RUSHFORTH, Peters. *Kindergarten.* 1979. Hamish Hamilton. 1st ed. author's 1st ed. AN/dj. C2. $75.00

RUSHKOFF, Douglas. *Ecstasy Club.* 1997. NY. Harper Collins. 1st. author's 1st novel. F/cover art. R16. $30.00

RUSK, Ralph Leslie. *Literature of the Middle Western Frontier.* 1962. Frederick Ungar. 1st ed thus. VG+. A18. $40.00

RUSKIN, John. *Unto This Last. Four Essays...* 1907. Hammersmith. 1st ed. 1/300. limp vellum. VG. C6. $225.00

RUSS, Joanna. *Zanzibar Cat.* 1983. Arkham. 1st ed. 1/3526. F/F. T2. $55.00

RUSSELL, Alan. *Hotel Detective.* 1994. Mysterious. 1st ed. F/F. H11/M23. $30.00

RUSSELL, Andy. *Grizzly Country.* 1967. Knopf. ils. VG/VG. P12. $7.00

RUSSELL, Andy. *Trails of a Wilderness Wanderer.* 1971. Knopf. 2nd. 8vo. 298p. F/dj. T10. $25.00

RUSSELL, B. *In Praise of Idleness.* 1935. NY. 1st ed. VG/G. B5. $25.00

RUSSELL, Bertrand. *Common Sense & Nuclear Warfare.* 1959. NY. 1st Am ed. NF/NF clip. N3. $15.00

RUSSELL, Bertrand. *Human Society in Ethics & Politics.* 1955. Simon Schuster. NF/VG. M19. $25.00

RUSSELL, Bertrand. *Wisdom of the West.* (1959). Doubleday. 320p. F/dj. B22. $9.00

RUSSELL, Charles Edward. *Greatest Trust in the World.* 1905. NY. 1st ed. 252p. G. E1. $40.00

RUSSELL, Charles Lord. *Diary of a Visit to the USA in the Year 1883.* 1910. NY. 8vo. ils. 220p. gr cloth. x. T3. $20.00

RUSSELL, Charles M. *Good Medicine, Memories of the Real West.* (1930). Garden City. ils. 162p. F/worn. E1. $55.00

RUSSELL, Charles M. *Trails Plowed Under.* (1936). NY. later ed. 211p. F/NF. E1. $45.00

RUSSELL, Don. *Lives & Legends of Buffalo Bill.* 1960. Norman, OK. 1st ed. biblio/index. 514p. VG/dj. E1. $65.00

RUSSELL, Edward C. *Bridge at a Glance: Auction-Contract.* 1930. np. sm format. 28p. VG/wrp. S1. $8.00

RUSSELL, Eric Frank. *Men, Martians & Machines.* 1984. Crown Classic of Modern SF Vol 1. F/F. G10. $10.00

RUSSELL, H. Diane. *Jacques Callot: Prints & Related Drawings.* 1975. np. ils. 351p. D2. $65.00

RUSSELL, Irwin. *Poems.* 1888. Century. 4th. 112p. VG. B10. $25.00

RUSSELL, Jacqueline. *If You Like Horses.* 1932. Houghton Mifflin. 12mo. G+. O3. $25.00

RUSSELL, James. *Evolution of Function of Public Health Administration...* 1895. Glasgow. 1st ed. 141p. xl. A13. $75.00

RUSSELL, Jeffrey Burton. *Devil: Perceptions of Evil From Antiquity...* 1977. Cornell. 1st ed. 8vo. 275p. F. T10. $35.00

RUSSELL, Mary La Fetra. *Mother Goose.* 1924. Gabriel. 4to. 12 linen p. VG. M5. $25.00

RUSSELL, Ray. *Haunted Castles: Complete Gothic Tales.* 1985. Maclay. 1st ed. F/F. R10. $10.00

RUSSELL, Ross. *Jazz Style in Kansas City & the Southwest.* 1971. Berkeley. 1st ed. NF/VG. B2. $30.00

RUSSELL, Thomas H. *Sinking of the Titanic.* 1912. LH Walter. ils. 320p. blk stp red bdg/pict label. fair. P12. $12.00

RUSSELL, Thomas H. *Sinking of the Titanic.* 1912. np. 8vo. ils. 320p. red cloth. VG. T3. $30.00

RUSSELL, W. Clark. *Frozen Pirate.* ca 1900. Lupton. gilt bl bdg. G+. P12. $4.00

RUSSELL, W.H. *Atlantic Telegraph.* 1972. David/Charles Rpts. VG/VG. A16. $47.50

RUSSELL, W.L. *Structural Geology for Petroleum Geologists.* 1955. McGraw Hill. 427p. F. D8. $25.00

RUSSELL, Walter. *Age of Innocence.* 1904. Dodd Mead. 1st ed. 8vo. VG. M5. $40.00

RUSSELL, Walter. *Book of Early Whispering.* 1949. Waynesboro, VA. U of Science & Philosophy. ltd ed. sgn. 103p. VG. B11. $15.00

RUSSELL-WOOD, A.J.R. *Fidalgos & Philanthropists: Santa Casa da Misericordia...* 1968. Berkley. 1st ed. 429p. dj. A13. $25.00

RUSSEN, David. *Iter Lunare.* 1976. Gregg. 1st separate Am ed. F/sans. G10. $15.00

RUSSO, Richard. *Nobody's Fool.* 1993. Random. 1st ed. F/F. M23. $25.00

RUST, Edwin Grey. *Those Dexters.* 1929. Michie. 1st ed. 82p. G. B10. $10.00

RUST, Fred Winslow. *Road Ahead & Bypaths.* 1944. Boston. Humphries. sgn. 12mo. VG. B11. $15.00

RUTH, Babe. *Babe Ruth's Baseball Book for 1932.* 1932. Syndicate. ils/photos. G+. P8. $150.00

RUTH, Babe. *Babe Ruth's Big Book of Baseball.* 1935. Reilly Lee. Quaker Oats premium. photos. VG. P8. $90.00

RUTHERFORD, Ward. *Hitler's Propaganda Machine.* 1978. Grosset Dunlap. 192p. split hinge. A17. $18.50

RUTLEDGE, Archibald. *Deep River: The Complete Poems.* 1960. Columbia, SC. 1st ed. 8vo. 635p. gilt gr buckram. F/VG. H3. $85.00

RUTLEDGE, Archibald. *From the Hills to the Sea.* 1958. Indianapolis. VG/VG. B5. $50.00

RUTLEDGE, Archibald. *Life's Extras.* 1946. Fleming. Revell. sgn. ils. VG. B10. $45.00

RUTLEDGE, Archibald. *Those Were the Days.* 1955. Richmond, VA. Dietz. 462p. VG. B18. $37.50

RUTT, Richard. *Korean Works & Days.* 1964. Tuttle. 1st ed. sgn. pl. 231p. F/F. B11. $30.00

RUTTER, Owen. *Triumphant Pilgrimage.* 1937. Lippincott. 1st ed. 8vo. pl/map. 296p. xl. VG. W1. $45.00

RUXTON, George F. *Life in the Far West.* 1983 (1849). Time Life. rpt. 312p. leather. E1. $20.00

RYAN, Abram J. *Poems: Patriotic, Religious, Miscellaneous.* 1880. John B Piet. A prt. ils. 347p. G. B10. $75.00

RYAN, David D. *Falls of the James.* 1975. Richmond, VA. 2nd. sgn. 8vo. G. B11. $10.00

RYAN, David D. *Four Days in 1865: Fall of Richmond.* 1993. Cadmus Comm. inscr. 161p. VG/VG. B10. $18.00

RYAN, J.C. *Revolt Along the Rio Grande.* 1964. San Antonio. 1st ed. map ep. 234p. F/NF. E1. $40.00

RYAN, Nolan. *King of the Hill.* 1992. Harper Collins. 1st ed. F/F. P8. $12.50

RYAN. *Civil War Literature of Ohio, a Bibliography...* 1994. rpt of 1991 ed. 1/300. 527p. F. A4. $60.00

RYDELL, Raymond A. *Cape Horn to the Pacific.* 1952. Berkeley. 213p. VG/dj. T7. $40.00

RYDER, Jonathan; see Ludlum, Robert.

RYDIORD, John. *Kansas Placenames.* 1972. OK U. 1st ed. 613p. pb. F. E1. $40.00

RYLANT, Cynthia. *Missing May.* 1992. Orchard Books. 2nd. 89p. F/F. T5. $25.00

RYMAN, Geoff. *Child Garden.* 1989. London. Unwin Hyman. 1st ed. sgn. F/dj. M21. $50.00

RYMAN, Rebecca. *Olivia & Jai.* 1990. NY. 1st ed. NF/F. H11. $20.00

RYNNING, Thomas H. *Gun Notches: Life Story of a Cowboy-Soldier.* 1931. NY. 332p. VG. E1. $45.00

In nature, the bird who gets up earliest catches the most worms; but in book-collecting, the prizes fall birds who know worms when they see them.

Michael Sadleir
1888 – 1987

– S –

SABATINI, Rafael. *Hounds of God.* 1928. McClelland Stuart. G. P3. $13.00

SABERHAGEN, Fred. *Fifth Book of Lost Swords.* 1989. Tor. 1st. F/F. P3. $17.00

SABERHAGEN, Fred. *Merlin's Bones.* 1995. Tor. 1st. F/dj. P3. $23.00

SABIN, Arthur J. *Red Scare in Court. New York Versus Intern'l Workers Order.* 1993. Phil. 1st. F/F. B2. $30.00

SABLJAK, Mark. *Bloody Legacy.* 1992. Granmercy. 1st. NF/dj. P3. $15.00

SACHAR, Howard M. *Egypt & Israel.* 1981. NY. Richard Marek. 384p. VG/G+. S3. $26.00

SACHAR, Howard M. *Emergence of the Middle East, 1914-1924.* 1969. Knopf. 1st. 518p. VG/dj. W1. $25.00

SACHAR, Howard M. *Israel: Establishment of a State.* 1952. British Book Centre. 332p. VG/fair. S3. $22.00

SACKS, B. *Be It Enacted: Creation of Territory of Arizona.* 1964. Phoenix. A19. $45.00

SACKS, Janet. *Best of Science Fiction Monthly.* 1975. London. 1st. F/dj. M2. $20.00

SACKS, Oliver. *Man Who Mistook His Wife for a Hat & Other Clinical Tales.* 1985. Summit. later prt. 233p. cloth. VG/dj. G1. $22.50

SACKTON, Alexander. *TS Eliot Collection of the University of Texas at Austin.* 1975. Austin. 1st. 1/1500. gilt brn cloth. glassine. M24. $50.00

SACKVILLE-WEST, V. *Saint Joan of Arc.* 1936. London. Cobden Sanderson. 1st. F/VG. B4. $150.00

SACRANIE, Raj. *Stories From Outer Space.* 1979. Chartwell. 1st. F/dj. P3. $10.00

SADAJI & SAITO. *Magic of Trees & Stones. Secrets of Japanese Gardening.* 1965. NY. Japan Pub. 2nd. 282p. dj. A10. $35.00

SADEN, Hans. *True History of His Captivity 1557.* 1929. NY. McBride. ils/3 maps. xl. F. O7. $45.00

SADLEIR, Michael. *Anthony Trollope, a Commentary.* 1927. Houghton Mifflin. 1st Am. lg 8vo. 432p. VG. H13. $85.00

SADLEIR, Michael. *XIX Century Fiction: A Bibliographical Record.* nd. 2 vol. rpt. 1/350. ils. F. A4. $185.00

SADLER, Mark; see Lynds, Dennis.

SADOWSKI, Yahya M. *Scuds or Butter? Political Economy of Arms Control...* 1993. WA, DC. Brookings Inst. 1st. 8vo. ils. VG/wrp. W1. $10.00

SAFIRE, William. *Freedom.* 1987. Doubleday. 1st. sgn. 1125p. NF. W2. $30.00

SAFIRE, William. *Full Disclosure.* 1977. Doubleday. 1st. VG/dj. P3. $15.00

SAFRAN, Alexandre. *Kabbalah: Law & Mysticism of Jewish Tradition.* 1975. Feldheim. 339p. VG. S3. $32.00

SAGAN, Carl. *Contact: A Novel.* 1985. S&S. 1st. VG/VG. K5. $20.00

SAGAN, Carl. *Dragons of Eden: Speculations on Evolution...* 1977. Random. 1st. 263p. NF/dj. D8. $10.00

SAGAN, Carl. *Pale Blue Dot.* 1994. Random. 8vo. 429p. G. K5. $15.00

SAGAN, Francoise. *Heart-Keeper.* 1968. Dutton. 1st. NF/dj. P3. $15.00

SAGAN, Francoise. *Painted Lady.* 1983. NY. Dutton. 1st. F/F. T12. $20.00

SAGE, Dana. *22 Brothers.* 1950. S&S. G/dj. P3. $20.00

SAGE, Leland L. *William Boyd Allison.* 1956. Iowa City. State Hist Soc IA. A19. $30.00

SAGE, Rufus B. *Rocky Mountain Life.* 1880. Boston. ils. VG. M17. $25.00

SAGGS, H.W.F. *Greatest That Was Babylon.* 1962. Hawthorn. 1st. tall 8vo. 64 b&w pl/line ils. 562p. F/G. H1. $45.00

SAGLE, Lawrence W. *Steam, Diesel & Electric Power of B&O RR, 1829-1964.* 1964. Standard Pr & Pub. 351p. VG/dj. M20. $45.00

SAINSBURY, Noel. *Billy Smith: Exploring Ace (#1).* 1928. Cupples Leon. 247p. VG+/dj (lists 3 titles). M20. $25.00

SAINSBURY, Noel. *Flying Ace Stories.* nd. Cupples Leon. VG. P3. $20.00

SAINSBURY, Noel. *Gridiron Grit.* 1934. NY. Cupples Leon. 1st. VG. T12. $15.00

SAINT, H.F. *Memoirs of an Invisible Man.* 1987. Atheneum. 1st. sgn. author's 1st novel. NF/NF. M22. $20.00

SAINT-DENIS, Ruth. *Lotus Light.* 1932. Boston. 1st. ils. VG. B5. $25.00

SAINT-GERMAIN, Christopher. *Doctor & Student 1531.* 1970. Menston. Scholar Pr. facsimile. M11. $75.00

SAINT-JOHN, Bayle. *Village Life in Egypt: With Sketches of the Said, Vol 1.* 1853. Boston. Ticknor Reed Fields. 1st. sm 8vo. W1. $145.00

SAINT-JOHN, H.C. *Notes & Sketches From the Wild Coasts of Nippon.* 1880. Edinburgh. Douglas. 50 engravings/1 fld map. 392p. cloth/leather label. T7. $175.00

SAINT-JOHN. *Osborne Collection of Early Children's Books 1566-1910.* 1958. Toronto Public Lib. 1/1500. 99 pl. 585p. VG. A4. $285.00

SAINTSBURY, George. *Notes on a Cellar-Book.* 1931. Macmillan. 3rd/5th prt. VG/VG. B10. $25.00

SAKI. *Short Stories of Saki.* 1958. Modern Lib. VG/dj. P3. $20.00

SALE, Roger. *Seattle, Past to Present.* 1976. Seattle. 2nd. 8vo. 273p. F/dj. T10. $25.00

SALES, Frances. *Ibrahim.* 1989. Lippincott. 1st Am. sm 4to. 31p. F/NF. C14. $17.00

SALINGER, J.D. *Raise High the Roof Beam, Carpenters.* 1963. Little Brn. 1st/3rd issue. VG/VG. R14. $40.00

SALISBURY, Albert. *Here Rolled the Covered Wagons.* 1948. Superior. dj. A19. $40.00

SALISBURY, Harrison E. *Long March.* 1985. Franklin Lib. 1st. sgn. full leather. F. Q1. $60.00

SALLIS, James. *Black Hornet.* 1994. NY. Carroll Graf. 1st. sgn. F/F. T2. $30.00

SALLIS, James. *Long-Legged Fly.* 1992. NY. Carroll Graf. 1st. sgn. author's 1st novel. F/NF. T2. $45.00

SALMON, Richard. *Trout Flies.* 1975. NY. 1/589. sgn twice. VG/dj/box. B5. $180.00

SALMOND, John A. *Miss Lucy of the CIO: Life & Time of Lucy Randolph Mason...* 1988. Athens, GA. 1st. F/F. B2. $25.00

SALOMONSKY, V.C. *Masterpieces of Furniture in Photographs...* 1953. Dover. rpt. VG. M17. $17.50

SALSBURY & WALSH. *Making of Buffalo Bill: Study in Heroics.* 1928. Bobbs Merrill. 1st. ils. 391p. stp cloth. dj. D11. $50.00

SALSLOW, James M. *Poetry of Michelangelo.* 1991. Yale. 1st. F/F. P3. $45.00

SALTEN, Felix. *Bambi.* July 1928. S&S. 1st Am. sm 8vo. gr pict cloth. VG. C8. $60.00

SALTEN, Felix. *Bambi.* 1942. Grosset Dunlap. 1st. ils Disney Studio. VG/dj. D1. $85.00

SALTER, James. *Arm of Flesh*. 1961. Harper. 1st. sgn. author's 2nd book. F/NF. D10. $365.00

SALTER, James. *Dusk & Other Stories*. 1988. Northpoint. 1st. F/F. from $35 to $45.00

SALTER, James. *Light Years*. 1975. Random. 1st. sgn. author's 4th novel. F/F. D10. $125.00

SALTER, James. *Solo Faces*. 1980. London. Collins. 1st. sgn. F/NF clip. R14. $100.00

SALWAY. *Peculiar Gift, Nineteenth Century Writings...* 1976. rpt 40 essays. ils. 573p. F/F. A4. $55.00

SALYER, Alfred Mark. *Salyer's Antics of the Ants Done in Verse & Prose*. 1924. NY. 121p. VG. S15. $25.00

SALZMAN, Mark. *Laughing Sutra*. 1991. Random. 1st. sgn. author's 2nd book. F/F. B3. $60.00

SAMBON, Arthur. *Catalogue des Fresques de Boscoreale*. 1903. Paris. Canessa. 4to. 26p. new cloth spine. xl. T10. $300.00

SAMPLE, Albert Race. *Race Hoss: Big Emma's Boy*. 1984. Austin, TX. Eakin. 2nd. 320p. F/NF clip. B4. $45.00

SAMPLE & SCHWARTZ. *Confessions of a Dirty Ballplayer*. 1970. Dial. 1st. photos. VG+/VG. P8. $20.00

SAMPSON, A. *Seven Sisters: Great Oil Companies & World They Shaped*. 1975. Viking. 334p. NF/G. D8. $25.00

SAMPSON, Emma Speed. *Billy & the Major*. 1918. Reilly Lee. 20th. 299p. VG+/dj. M20. $35.00

SAMPSON, Emma Speed. *Miss Minerva's Problem*. 1936. Reilly Lee. 311p. VG/dj. M20. $35.00

SAMPSON, G. *Historic Churches & Temples of Georgia*. 1987. Mercer U. ils from paintings/drawings. 111p. F/dj. M4. $20.00

SAMS, Ferrol. *Widow's Mite*. 1987. Peachtree. 1st. F/F. B35. $32.00

SAMUEL, Maurice. *Jews on Approval*. 1932. 1st. VG+. E6. $25.00

SAMUEL, Maurice. *Whatever Gods*. 1923. Duffield. sgn. 346p. VG. S3. $30.00

SAMUELSEN, Rube. *Rose Bowl Game*. 1951. Doubleday. 1st. inscr. VG. P8. $20.00

SANBORN, Ruth Burr. *Murder on the Aphrodite*. 1935. Macmillan. 1st. xl. VG. P3. $12.00

SANCHEZ, Thomas. *Mile Zero*. 1989. Knopf. ARC. sgn/dtd 1989. F/wrp/box. R14. $40.00

SANCHEZ, Thomas. *Mile Zero*. 1989. Knopf. 1st. inscr. F/F. A20. $30.00

SANCHEZ, Thomas. *Zoot-Suit Murders*. 1978. Dutton. 1st. F/NF. M19. $25.00

SANCHEZ, Thomas. *Zoot-Suit Murders*. 1978. Dutton. 1st. VG/dj. P3. $18.00

SAND, Algo. *Senor Bum in the Jungle*. 1932. NY. National Travel Club. 319p. F3. $15.00

SAND, George. *Tales of a Grandmother*. 1930. Lippincott. 1st thus. 12 mc pl. 384p. F/dj. H1. $45.00

SANDBORN, F.B. *Genius & Character of Emerson, Lectures at Concord...* 1885. Boston. Osgood. 1st. gilt brn cloth. M24. $125.00

SANDBURG, Carl. *Abraham Lincoln: The War Years*. 1939. Harcourt Brace. 4 vol. 14th prt. gilt bl cloth. F. H1. $50.00

SANDBURG, Carl. *Early Moon*. 1930. Harcourt Brace. 1st. ils James Daugherty. 137p. VG. D4. $50.00

SANDBURG, Carl. *Lincoln Preface*. 1953. NY. 16p. O8. $9.50

SANDBURG, Carl. *More Rootabagas*. 1993. Knopf. 1st. 94p. F/F. C14. $18.00

SANDBURG, Carl. *Poems of the Midwest*. 1946. Cleveland. World. 1st thus. 1/950. #d. VG. Q1. $50.00

SANDBURG, Carl. *Remembrance Rock*. 1948. Harcourt Brace. 1st regular after ltd sgn ed. NF/NF clip. D10. $50.00

SANDBURG, Carl. *Smoke & Steel*. 1920. NY. 1st. sgn. VG. B5. $40.00

SANDERS, Charles W. *Mournful Rides Again*. 1936. Wild West Club. xl. VG. P3. $10.00

SANDERS, Charles W. *Sanders' Pictorial Reader*. 1869. Ivison Phinney Blakeman. enlarged/revised. 12mo. 48p. gr paper brd. T10. $50.00

SANDERS, Dori. *Ideal Land for Farming*. 1990. Alonquin. 1st. sgn. F/wrp. R13. $35.00

SANDERS, Ed. *Tales of Beatnik Glory*. 1975. Stonehill. 1st. NF/VG+. B4. $45.00

SANDERS, George. *Stranger at Home*. 1946. S&S. 1st. VG/dj. P3. $45.00

SANDERS, Lawrence. *Capital Crimes*. 1989. Putnam. 1st. F/F. P3. $20.00

SANDERS, Lawrence. *Passion of Molly T.* 1984. Putnam. 1st. VG/dj. P3. $20.00

SANDERS, Lawrence. *Pleasures of Helen*. 1971. Putnam. 1st. F/F. H11. $30.00

SANDERS, Lawrence. *Seduction of Peter S.* 1983. Putnam. 1st. F/F. H11. $35.00

SANDERS, Lawrence. *Sullivan's Sting*. 1990. Putnam. 1st. F/F. T12. $20.00

SANDERS, Lawrence. *Third Deadly Sin*. 1981. Putnam. 1st. NF/dj. P3. $25.00

SANDERS, Lawrence. *Timothy Files*. 1987. Putnam. 1st. F/F. T12. $15.00

SANDERS, T.W. *Fruit & Its Cultivation in Garden & Orchard*. 1945. London. Collingridge. 5th. 288p. VG-. A10. $22.00

SANDERSON, Ivan. *Animal Treasure*. 1937. Viking. 1st. VG/VG. A20. $20.00

SANDERSON, Ivan. *How to Know the American Mammals*. 1951. Boston. ils LA Fuertes. 164p. VG/worn. S15. $20.00

SANDERSON, Ruth. *Story of the First Christmas*. 1994. Atlanta. Turner. 4 3-D mc scenes. ribbon ties. M. T10. $25.00

SANDES, R. *Downtown Jews, Portraits of Immigrant Generation*. 1969. NYC. 1st. photos. VG/VG. E6. $15.00

SANDFORD, John. *Eyes of Prey*. 1991. Putnam. 1st. F/F. H11. $40.00

SANDFORD, John. *Fool's Run*. 1989. Holt. 1st. sgn. F/F. A20. $60.00

SANDLIN, Tim. *Sex & Sunsets*. 1987. Holt. 1st. sgn. author's 1st book. F/dj. A24. $65.00

SANDLIN, Tim. *Skipped Parts*. 1991. Holt. 1st. sgn. F/F. B3. $40.00

SANDLIN, Tim. *Western Swing*. 1988. Holt. 1st. author's 2nd book. F/dj. A24. $30.00

SANDLIN, Tim. *Western Swing*. 19883. NY. Holt. 1st. sgn. F/F. R14. $45.00

SANDOZ, Mari. *Buffalo Hunter*. 1954. Hastings. 1st. NF/VG. T11. $45.00

SANDOZ, Mari. *Capital City*. 1939. Little Brn. 1st. NF/VG. T11. $65.00

SANDOZ, Mari. *Cheyenne Autumn*. 1953. McGraw Hill. 1st. F/NF clip. B4. $200.00

SANDOZ, Mari. *Crazy Horse: Strange Man of the Oglalas*. 1945. Lincoln. dj. A19. $30.00

SANDOZ, Mari. *Old Jules Country*. 1965. Hastings. 1st. VG/VG. P3. $15.00

SANDOZ, Mari. *Story Catcher*. 1968. Phil. Westminster. special ed. dj. A19. $150.00

SANDOZ, Mari. *Winter Thunder*. 1954. Phil. Westminster. A19. $25.00

SANDOZ, Maurice. *Maze*. 1945. Doubleday. ils Salvador Dali. dj. A19. $150.00

SANDOZ, Maurice. *On the Verge*. 1950. Doubleday. 1st. ils Salvador Dali. F/NF. B24. $150.00

SANDS, Oliver Jackson. *Story of Sport & Deep Run Hunt Club*. 1977. Richmond. 1/750. sgn/#d. VG. O3. $165.00

SANDSTROM, Eve. *Death Down River.* 1990. Scribner. 1st. sgn. F/F. A23. $38.00

SANDYS, Charles. *History of Gavelkind & Other Remarkable Customs...* 1851. London. John Russell Kent. fld tables. emb cloth. M11. $175.00

SANFORD, John. *View From the Wilderness: American Literature as History.* 1977. Capra. 1st. inscr. F/dj. T10. $35.00

SANGER, Majory Bartlett. *Checkerback's Journey: Migration of the Ruddy Turnstone.* 1969. Cleveland. 1st. 159p. F/VG. S15. $18.00

SANGER, Richard H. *Arabian Peninsula.* 1954. Cornell. 1st. sgn pres. ils/maps. 295p. VG/dj. W1. $45.00

SANSOM, William. *Last Hours of Sandra Lee.* 1961. Hogarth. 1st. F/clip. A24. $45.00

SANTEE, Ross. *Apache Land.* 1945. Scribner. 1st. inscr/2 mc sketches+hand-colored ils. 216p. VG/worn. B19. $950.00

SANTEE, Ross. *Apache Land.* 1957. Scribner. 1st. 216p. VG/dj. J2. $125.00

SANTEE, Ross. *Cowboy.* 1928. Grosset Dunlap. A19. $45.00

SANTEE, Ross. *Cowboy.* 1977. Lincoln/London. A19. $8.00

SANTESSON, Hans. *Fantastic Universe Omnibus.* 1960. Prentice Hall. 1st. VG/torn. M2. $15.00

SANZ, Carlos. *Australia: Su Decubrimiento y Determinacion.* 1973. Madrid. F/stiff wrp. O7. $35.00

SANZ, Carlos. *Bibliografia General de la Carta de Colon.* 1958. Madrid. Victoriano Suarez. 367p. F/wrp. O7. $125.00

SANZ, Charles. *Juan Sebastian Elcano: Autentico Protagonista Prima...* 1973. Madrid. Aguirre. ils/45 maps. NF/prt wrp. O7. $45.00

SAPIENZA, Marilyn. *Cosby Show Scrapbook.* 1986. Weekley Reader BC. TVTI. VG. P3. $4.00

SAPPER. *Island of Terror.* 1931. Musson. 1st. VG. P3. $25.00

SAPPER. *Tiny Carteret.* 1932. Musson/Hodder Stoughton. NF. P3. $15.00

SARAVIA, Antanasio. *Los Missioneros Muertos en el Norte de Nueva Espana.* 1943. Mexico. 2nd. 253p. wrp. F3. $15.00

SARAZEN, Gene. *Better Golf After Fifty.* 1967. NY. 1st. VG/VG. B6. $35.00

SARAZEN, Gene. *Golf Magazine's Your Long Game.* 1964. Harper Row. 1st. sgn. VG/VG. A23. $60.00

SARG, Tony. *Where Is Tommy?* 1932. Greenberg. 1st. obl 4to. VG. M5. $85.00

SARGENT, Charles Sprague. *Woods of the United States.* 1885. NY. 7 tables/28p index. 203p. gilt brn cloth. B26. $139.00

SARGENT, F.W. *On Bandaging & Other Operations of Minor Surgery...* 1867. Phil. 3rd. ils. 383p. A13. $350.00

SARGENT, Pamela. *Venus of Shadows.* 1988. Doubleday. 1st. F/F. P3. $20.00

SARGENT, Wyn. *People of the Valley. Life With Cannibal Tribe New Guinea.* 1974. NY. 1st/2nd prt. 302p. VG/dj. P4. $35.00

SARNER. *Checklist of Works of Herman Wouk.* 1995. 1/400. sgn. 18 pl. 156p. F/F. A4. $45.00

SAROYAN, William. *Hilltop Russians in San Francisco.* 1941. Stanford. JL Delkin. 1/500. 4to. ils. VG/dj. K7. $195.00

SAROYAN, William. *Human Comedy.* 1943. NY. Harcourt Brace. 1st. author's 1st novel. ils Don Freeman. F/VG. T12. $150.00

SAROYAN, William. *My Name Is Aram.* (1940). Harcourt Brace. later prt. sgn. VG/dj. Q1. $40.00

SAROYAN, William. *Sons Come & Go, Mothers Hang in Forever.* 1976. FRanklin Lib. true 1st/ltd. aeg. decor gilt leather. F/sans. T11. $45.00

SARRANTONIO, Al. *Campbell Wood.* 1986. Doubleday. 1st. F/F. P3. $18.00

SARTON, May. *After the Stroke.* 1988. Norton. 1st. F/F. B3. $30.00

SARTON, May. *Anger.* 1982. Norton. 1st. F/F. B3. $40.00

SARTON, May. *As We Are Now.* 1973. Norton. 1st. NF/NF. B3. $45.00

SARTON, May. *Faithful Are the Wounds.* 1955. Rinehart. 1st. NF/dj. A24. $55.00

SARTON, May. *Fur Person.* 1957. Rinehart. 3rd. ils Barbara Knox. 106p. VG/dj. A25. $15.00

SARTON, May. *Journal of a Solitude.* 1973. Norton. 1st. F/NF. B3. $75.00

SARTON, May. *Magnificent Spinster.* 1985. Norton. 1st. F/clip. A24. $25.00

SARTON, May. *Mrs Stevens Hears the Mermaids Singing.* 1965. Norton. 1st. NF/dj. A24. $45.00

SARTON, May. *Silence of Now.* 1988. Norton. 1st. F/F. B3. $20.00

SARTON, May. *World of Light: Portraits & Celebrations.* 1976. Norton. 1st. 254p. VG/clip. A25/M17. $18.00

SARTRE, Jean-Paul. *Age of Reason.* 1947. London. Hamish. 1st. NF. T12. $35.00

SARTRE, Jean-Paul. *Troubled Sleep.* 1951. NY. 1st. trans G Hopkins. VG/VG. T9. $15.00

SASEK, M. *This Is Australia.* 1970. Macmillan. 1st. 4to. VG. C8. $30.00

SASEK, M. *This Is Israel.* 1962. Macmillan. 1st. 4to. VG+/dj. C8. $25.00

SASEK, M. *This Is Munich.* 1963. Macmillan. 1st. VG/VG. C8. $30.00

SASEK, M. *This Is Washington DC.* 1969. London. Allen. 1st. 4to. NF/NF. C8. $60.00

SASSON, Jean P. *Princess: True Story of Life Behind Veil in Saudi Arabia.* 1992. Morrow. 1st. 8vo. ils. NF/dj. W1. $20.00

SASSOON, Siegfried. *Memoirs of a Fox-Hunting Man.* 1971. London. Folio Soc. 8vo. ils Lynton Lamb. olive cloth. F/case. T10. $50.00

SATCHELL, G.H. *Circulation in Fishes.* 1971. Cambridge. 131p. VG. S15. $15.00

SATO, Koji. *Zen Life.* 1972. photos. VG/VG. M17. $17.50

SATTERTHWAIT, Walter. *At Ease With the Dead.* 1991. Harper Collins. 1st. F/dj. Q1. $75.00

SATTERTHWAIT, Walter. *Wall of Glass.* 1987. St Martin. 1st. author's 1st book. F/VG clip. B3. $250.00

SATTLER, H.R. *Illustrated Dinosaur Dictionary.* 1983. Lee Shepard. 1st. 315p. VG/dj. D8. $21.00

SAUER, H.W. *Developmental Biology of Physarum.* 1982. London. 237p. dj. B1. $49.00

SAUL, John. *Creature.* 1989. Bantam. 1st. F/F. M21. $12.00

SAUNDERS, Charles Francis. *Finding the Worthwhile in the Southwest.* 1918. NY. McBride. 12mo. 231p. F7. $40.00

SAUNDERS, Charles Francis. *Little Book of California Missions.* 1935. McBride. 5th. VG. O4. $15.00

SAUNDERS, Charles Francis. *With the Flowers & Trees in California.* 1923. NY. ils EH Saunders. 286p. VG. S15. $12.00

SAUNDERS, George. *Civil Wars: Land in Bad Decline.* 1996. Random. 1st. sgn. F/F. A23. $42.00

SAUNDERS, George. *Your Horse: His Selection, Stabling & Care.* 1954. NY. Van Nostrand. 1st. VG/G. O3. $15.00

SAUNDERS, L.G. *Contract Bridge Primer: 55 Rules With Logical Reasons.* nd. Phil. 198p. VG. S1. $20.00

SAUNDERS, Marshall. *Beautiful Joe's Paradise, a Sequel to Beautiful Joe.* 1903 (1893). np. sm 12mo. ils Chas Livingston Bull. pict cloth. G. C8. $20.00

SAUNDERS, Roy. *Queen of the River.* (1961). London. Osbourne. ne. 160p. VG/dj. H7. $20.00

SAVAGE, Candace. *Aurora: The Mysterious Northern Lights.* 1995. Sierra Club. ils. 144p. VG/glossy wrp. K5. $20.00

SAVAGE, Ernest A. *Old English Libraries.* 1970. Barnes Noble. rpt. ils. 298p. VG. K3. $15.00

SAVAGE, Katharine. *People & Power: Story of Four Nations.* 1959. London. Oxford. 1st. F. T12. $20.00

SAVAGE, Les. *Doctor at Coffin Gap.* 1949. Doubleday. 1st. NF/NF. B4. $85.00

SAVAGE, Les. *Hide Hustlers.* 1950. Doubleday. 1st. F/F. B4. $100.00

SAVAGE, Richard. *Strangers' Meeting.* 1957. Mus Pr. 1st. VG/dj. P3. $20.00

SAVAGE, Thomas. *Some Put Their Trust in Chariots.* 1961. Random. 1st. NF/dj. M25. $25.00

SAVAGE, William W. *Cherokee Strip Livestock Association: Federal Regulation...* 1973. U MO Pr. 1st. 154p. cloth. NF/dj. M20. $32.00

SAVAGE, William W. *Comic Books & America 1945-1954.* 1990. Norman, OK. 1st. 8vo. buckram. F/F. C8. $20.00

SAVARIN, Julian J. *Waiters on the Dark.* 1972. St Martin. 1st Am. F/dj. M2. $15.00

SAVCHENKO, Vladimir. *Saucers Over the Moor.* nd. Children's BC. VG/dj. P3. $8.00

SAVELL, Isabelle Keating. *Daughter of Vermont: Biography of Emily Eaton Hepburn.* 1952. N River Pr. 1st. 184p. cloth. VG/dj. M20. $25.00

SAVELLE, Max. *Empires to Nations: Expansion in America 1713-1824...* 1974. MN U. 3 maps. as new/dj. O7. $35.00

SAVOURS, Ann. *Scott's Last Voyage Through the Antarctic Camera...* 1975. NY. Praeger. 160p. VG/dj. P4. $55.00

SAVOY, Gene. *On the Trail of the Feathered Serpent.* 1974. Bobbs Merrill. 1st. 217p. dj. F3. $20.00

SAWARD, Dudley. *Bernard Lovell: A Biography.* 1984. London. Hale. photos. VG/dj. K5. $26.00

SAWYER, Corinne Holt. *Murder by Owl Light.* 1992. DIF. 1st. F/dj. Q1. $35.00

SAWYER, Edith A. *Denise of the Three Pines.* 1922. Page. 1st. 315p. cloth. VG+/dj. M20. $32.00

SAWYER, Edmund Ogden Jr. *Our Sea Saga: Wood Wind Ships.* 1929. SF. self pub. inscr. 205p. VG/VG. B11. $75.00

SAWYER, George S. *Southern Institutes; or, Inquiry Into Origin...Slave Trade.* 1859. Lippincott. 8vo. 393p+6p ads. VG. K7. $125.00

SAWYER, Ruth. *Christmas Anna Angel.* 1944. Viking. 1st. ils Kate Seredy. G+/dj. P2. $50.00

SAWYER, Ruth. *Maggie Rose, Her Birthday Christmas.* 1952. Harper. 1st. 12mo. VG. C8. $135.00

SAWYER, Susan F. *Priestess of the Hills.* 1928. Meador. 1st. NF. M2. $25.00

SAWYER. *Story of Mary & Her Little Lamb as Told by Mary...* 1928. ils. 47p. NF. A4. $65.00

SAXON, Gladys Relyea. *California Camel Adventure.* 1955. Caxton. 1st. 183p. VG+/G+. P2. $15.00

SAXON, John A. *Liability Limited.* 1947. Mill. 1st. VG/dj. M25. $45.00

SAYERS, Dorothy L. *Busman's Honeymoon.* 1955. Gollancz. 16th. NF/dj. P3. $20.00

SAYERS, Dorothy L. *Gaudy Night.* 1935. London. Gollancz. 1st. G. M22. $15.00

SAYERS, Dorothy L. *Hangman's Holiday.* 1954. Gollancz. 18th. NF/dj. P3. $20.00

SAYERS, Dorothy L. *Mind of the Maker.* 1944. Methuen. 2nd. VG/dj. P3. $35.00

SAYERS, Dorothy L. *Nine Tailors.* 1934. Harcourt Brace. 1st Am. F/NF. M15. $450.00

SAYERS, Dorothy L. *Omnibus of Crime.* 1929. Payson Clarke. 1st. VG. M22/N4. $25.00

SAYERS, Dorothy L. *Three Great Lord Peter Novels.* 1978. Gollancz. TVTI. F/dj. P3. $25.00

SAYERS, Valerie. *Due East.* 1987. 1st. author's 1st book. F/F. M19. $35.00

SAYLES, John. *Anarchists' Convention.* 1979. Little Brn. 1st. F/dj. Q1. $75.00

SAYLOR, Steven. *Arms of Nemesis.* 1992. St Martin. 1st. sgn. F/dj. A24. $40.00

SCARLETT, Roger. *Murder Among the Angels.* 1932. Crime Club. VG. P3. $25.00

SCARRY, Richard. *Look & Learn Library.* 1978. Golden/Western. 1st probable. 4 vol. sm 4to. VG+/VG case. C8. $80.00

SCHAAP, Dick. *Massacre at Winged Foot.* 1974. Random. 1st. photos. VG/VG. P8. $20.00

SCHACHNER, Nathan. *Alexander Hamilton.* 1946. Appleton. VG. M2. $10.00

SCHACHNER, Nathan. *Sun Shines West.* 1943. Appleton Century. 1st. VG/dj. P3. $23.00

SCHACHNER, Nathan. *Thomas Jefferson: A Biography.* 1951. NY. 2 vol. ils. VG. M4. $35.00

SCHACHT, Al. *Clowning Through Baseball.* 1941. NY. inscr. ils Mullin. gray cloth. VG. B14. $47.50

SCHACHTER, Norm. *Close Calls.* 1981. Morrow. 1st. VG+/dj. P8. $20.00

SCHAEFER, Jack. *Great Endurance Horse Race: 600 Miles on a Single Mount...* 1963. Statecoach. 1st ltd of 750. F/F clip. A18. $150.00

SCHAFER, Joseph. *History of Agriculture in Wisconsin.* 1922. Madison. State Hist Soc. 1/1600. 212p. VG. A10. $35.00

SCHALDACH, William. *Fish.* 1937. Phil. 1st. 1/1500. VG. B5. $130.00

SCHARF, J. Thomas. *History of the Confederate States Navy.* 1886. Joseph McDonaough. 2nd. 824p. cloth. VG. M20. $135.00

SCHATZKI, Walter. *Children's Books, Old & Rare, Catalogue Number One.* 1974. rpt. 200+ entries. 46p. cloth. VG. A4. $95.00

SCHEIDL, Gerda Marie. *Crystal Ball.* 1993. North-South Books. 1st. 4to. 26p. F/VG+. C14. $14.00

SCHELL, Herbert. *History of South Dakota.* 1961. NE U. 1st. 424p. VG/dj. J2. $75.00

SCHEMBECHLER, Bo. *Bo.* 1989. Warner. 1st. inscr. F/F. A23. $40.00

SCHENCK, Hilbert. *Chronosequence.* 1988. Tor. 1st. F/F. P3. $18.00

SCHER, Paula. *Brownstone.* 1973. Pantheon. sm 4to. VG+/VG. C8. $17.50

SCHERER, James. *First Forty-Niner & Story of Golden Tea-Caddy.* 1925. NY. Minton Balch. ils. 127p. NF. K7. $45.00

SCHERF, Margaret. *Beautiful Birthday Cake.* 1971. Doubleday. 1st. VG/dj. M20/P3. $20.00

SCHERMELE, Willy. *Bunnikins.* ca 1952. London. Juvenile Prod. 4to. cloth. dj. R5. $125.00

SCHERMELE, Willy. *Fairyland Secrets.* ca 1950s. London. Juvenile Prod. ils. VG-. P2.

SCHERMELE, Willy. *Teddy Bears' Picnic.* ca 1961. London. Purnell. 4to. pict brd. dj. R5. $125.00

SCHERR, George H. *Journal of Irreproducible Results.* 1986. Dorset. 3rd. ils. VG. K3. $25.00

SCHERREN, H. *Ponds & Rock Pools With Hints on Collecting...* 1894. London. Rel Tract Soc. ils/figures. 208p. cloth. VG. M12. $37.50

SCHEVILL, Margaret Erwin. *Beautiful on the Earth.* 1947. Hazel Dreis. 1st. 1/500. sgn. ils. 155p. VG+. B19. $125.00

SCHEWEY, Don. *Caught in the Act: NY Actors Face to Face.* 1986. NY. 1st. 304p+54 full-p photos. xl. F/dj. A17. $17.50

SCHICKEL, Richard. *Harold Lloyd: Shape of Laughter.* 1974. NGS. 1st. 218p. dj. A17. $15.00

SCHIEL, Jacob H. *Journey Through the Rocky Mountains...* 1959. Norman, OK. dj. A19. $40.00

SCHIEPS, Paul. *Hold the Fort.* 1971. lg 8vo. 57p. ils bdg. O8. $9.50

SCHIFF, Stuart David. *Whispers II.* 1979. Doubleday. 1st. F/dj. P3. $25.00

SCHILKE, Fritz. *Trakehner Horses: Then & Now.* 1977. Norman. Am Trakenhner Assn. VG. O3. $65.00

SCHILLINGS, C.G. *With Flashlight & Rifle.* 1905. NY. 1st. 421p. VG. A17. $35.00

SCHILPP, Paul Arthur. *Albert Einstein: Autobiographical Notes.* 1979. Open Court. Centenial ed. 1st thus. F/dj. K3. $20.00

SCHILPP, Paul Arthur. *Albert Einstein: Philosopher-Scientist.* 1949. Evanston, IL. 1st. ils. VG. K3. $85.00

SCHINDLER, Harold. *Orrin Porter Rockwell.* 1993. Salt Lake City. A19. $16.00

SCHINE, Cathleen. *To the Birdhouse.* 1990. FSG. 1st. author's 2nd book. F/F. B3. $50.00

SCHISGALL, Oscar. *Devil's Daughter.* 1932. Fiction League. 1st. VG/dj. P3. $25.00

SCHIWETZ, E.M. *Buck Schiwetz' Memories: Paintings & Drawings...* 1978. TX A&M. ils/pl/drawings. 112p. F/dj. M4. $25.00

SCHLEE, Susan. *On Almost Any Wind.* 1978. Ithaca. 1st. 310p. VG/dj. P4. $25.00

SCHLERETH, Hewitt. *Common Sense Celestial Navigation.* 1975. Chicago. Regnery. 231p. dj. T7. $20.00

SCHLESINGER, Arthur. *Thousand Days.* 1965. Houghton Mifflin. 1st. inscr. F/price marked out. Q1. $100.00

SCHLESINGER, Max. *Historical Jesus of Nazareth.* 1876. NY. Somerby. 12mo. VG. B14. $55.00

SCHLICKE, C.P. *General George Wright, Guardian of the Pacific Coast.* 1988. OK U. 1st. photos/maps. F/dj. M4. $30.00

SCHMIDT, Nathaniel. *Prophet of Nazareth.* 1905. London/NY. Macmillan. 1st. 8vo. 422p. G. W1. $10.00

SCHMIDT, Stanley. *Alalog's Children of the Future.* 1982. Dial. 1st. NF/dj. M2. $15.00

SCHMIDT, Stanley. *Analog: Writers' Choice Vol 2.* 1984. Dial. 1st. VG/dj. P3. $15.00

SCHMIDT, Stanley. *From Mind to Mind.* 1984. Doubleday. 1st. F/dj. P3. $18.00

SCHMITT, Martin F. *Fighting Indians of the West.* 1948. Scribner. 270 photos. dj. A19. $50.00

SCHMITZ, James H. *Best of James H Schmitz.* 1991. NESFA. 1st. F/F. P3. $20.00

SCHMITZ, James H. *Tale of Two Clocks.* 1962. Torquil/Dodd Mead. 1st trade. VG/dj. M21. $75.00

SCHMUTZ, Ervin M. *Livestock-Poisoning Plants of Arizona.* 1968. Tucson. tall 8vo. 176p. F. A22. $20.00

SCHNACKENBERG, G. *Lamplit Answer.* 1985. FSG. 1st. F/dj. V1. $30.00

SCHNAPPER, M.B. *American Labor: Pictorial Social History.* nd. Public Affairs. 1st. VG/VG. V4. $45.00

SCHNELL, D.E. *Carnivorous Plants of the United States & Canada.* 1976. Winston-Salem. Blair. 125p. dj. B1. $27.50

SCHOENBERGER, Guido. *Drawings of Mathis Gothart Nithart.* 1948. NY. Bittner. 64p+44 pl. dj. A17. $35.00

SCHOENER, Allon. *Portal to America: The Lower East Side 1870-1925.* 1967. NY. 1st. photos. 256p. VG/dj. B18. $15.00

SCHOEPFLIN, Johann Daniel. *Vindiciae Typographicae.* 1760. Strasbourg. Bauer. lg 4to. 7 fld pl. gilt vellum. R12. $425.00

SCHOFIELD, Susan Clark. *Refugio, They Named You Wrong.* 1991. Algonquin. 1st. author's 1st book. F/F. B3. $30.00

SCHOLEFIELD, Alan. *Sea Cave.* 1983. Congdon Weed. 1st. VG/dj. P3. $20.00

SCHOLEM, Gershom. *Walter Benjamin: Story of a Friendship.* 1981. JPS. ils. 242p. VG+/VG. S3. $25.00

SCHOLES, Percy A. *Dr Burney's Musical Tours in Europe.* 1959. Oxford. 2 vol. 1st. gilt tan buckram. H13. $195.00

SCHOLES, Robert. *Structural Fabulation.* 1975. Notre Dame. 1st. F/dj. P3. $25.00

SCHONFELDER & SCHONFELDER. *Guide de la Flore Mediterraneene.* 1988. Fribourg, Switzerland. French text. 500 mc photos. 314p. F. B26. $39.00

SCHOOLCRAFT, Henry R. *Travels in Central Portions of the Mississippi Valley.* 1975. Millwood, KS. rpt. as new. O7. $55.00

SCHORR, Mark. *Ace of Diamonds.* 1984. NY. 1st. F/F. H11. $30.00

SCHORR, Mark. *Eye for an Eye.* 1989. St Martin. 1st. F/F. P3. $17.00

SCHOW, David J. *Kill Riff.* 1988. Tor. 1st. F/dj. M2/P3. $18.00

SCHRAER, H. *Biological Calcification.* 1970. NY. Appleton Century Crofts. 8vo. 462p. dj. B2. $45.00

SCHRAFT, Constance. *Instead of You.* 1990. Ticknor. ARC. F/NF. w/promo material. R13. $25.00

SCHRANTZ, W.L. *Jasper County, Missouri, in the Civil War.* 1923. Carthage. photos/map/new ep. G. M4. $95.00

SCHREIBER, Flora Rheta. *Sybil.* 1973. Regnery. 1st. 359p. NF. W2. $25.00

SCHREIBER, Martin. *Last of a Breed.* 1982. Cowboy Project. 1st. VG/case. J2. $175.00

SCHREIBER & SCHREIBER. *Vanished Cities.* 1957. Knopf. 1st. 8vo. 344p. VG. W1. $20.00

SCHREINER, Olive. *Trooper Peter Halket of Mashonaland.* 1897. Boston. Roberts Bros. 1st Am. gilt cream cloth. NF. M24. $45.00

SCHROEDER, Doris. *Annette & Mystery of Moonstone Bay.* 1962. Whitman. TVTI. VG. P3. $10.00

SCHROEDER, Doris. *Annie Oakley in the Ghost Town Secret.* 1957. Whitman. 1st. TVTI. VG. P3. $20.00

SCHROEDER, Doris. *Secret of Holiday Island.* 1960. Whitman. TVTI. G. P3. $10.00

SCHROEDER, Doris. *Spin & Marty Trouble at Triple-R.* 1958. Whitman. TVTI. VG. P3. $18.00

SCHROEDER, John Frederick. *Life & Times of Washington...* 1857. NY. Johnson Fry. 1st in 2 vol. 4to. full leather/raised bands. VG. H1. $250.00

SCHROEDINGER, Erwin. *Statistical Thermodynamics.* 1946. Cambridge. 12mo. 88p. VG/torn. K3. $25.00

SCHUBERT, Kurt. *Dead Sea Community: Its Origin & Teachings.* 1959. Harper. 178p. VG/G+. S3. $24.00

SCHUCK, H. *Novel, the Man & His Prizes.* 1950. Stockholm. Sohlmans Forlag. 8vo. 620p. rpr front hinge. K3. $25.00

SCHUELER, Donald. *Temple of the Jaguar.* 1993. Sierra Club Books. 1st. 253p. dj. F3. $25.00

SCHULBERG, Budd. *Disenchanted.* 1983. London. 2nd. sgn. F/F. A11. $60.00

SCHULBERG, Budd. *Waterfront.* 1955. Random. 1st. inscr/dtd 1993. NF/NF. R14. $70.00

SCHULER, Harold H. *South Dakota Capitol in Pierre.* 1985. Pierre, SC. A19. $20.00

SCHULER, Stanley. *American Barns: In a Class by Themselves.* 1984. photos. VG/VG. M17. $25.00

SCHULKIN, J. *Sodium Hunger: Search for a Salty Taste.* 1991. Cambridge. ils/figures/tables. 192p. F/F. M12. $27.50

SCHULLERY, Paul. *Bear Hunter's Century: Profiles From Golden Age...* 1988. Stackpole. 252p. F/dj. A17. $15.00

SCHULLERY, Paul. *Grand Canyon: Early Impressions.* 1981. Boulder. CO Assoc U Pr. 1st. 195p. orange cloth. F7. $25.00

SCHULLERY, Paul. *Old Yellowstone Days.* 1979. Boulder, CO. CO Assoc U Pr. A19. $15.00

SCHULMAN, J. Neil. *Alongside Night.* 1979. Crown. 1st. F/dj. M2. $15.00

SCHULMAN, Pauline. *Our Merciful Father: Life Story of a Jewish Woman...* 1959. Exposition. 159p. VG/G. S3. $22.00

SCHULTZ, LeRoy. *Barns, Stables & Outbuildings.* 1986. McFarland. 150p. cloth. F. A10. $40.00

SCHULTZ, Samuel J. *Old Testament Speaks: Complete Survey of Old Testament Hist.* 1980. Harper Collins. 3rd. 436p. as new/dj. B29. $10.00

SCHULZ, Charles M. *Charlie Brown Christmas.* 1965. World. F/dj. M13. $25.00

SCHULZ, Ellen D. *Texas Cacti.* 1930. San Antonio. TX Academy of Science. maroon cloth. VG. B26. $47.50

SCHULZ, Fritz. *Classical Roman Law.* 1961. Oxford. M11. $125.00

SCHURZ, Carl. *Abraham Lincoln: A Biographical Essay.* 1907. 1/1040. 134p. O8. $27.50

SCHUTT, Arthur. *Flying Business: A Life of Arthur Schutt.* 1976. Melbourne. Nelson. 1st. inscr. 12mo. 179p. F/F. T10. $35.00

SCHUTZ, Benjamin M. *All the Old Bargains.* 1985. Bluejay. 1st. sgn. F/dj. P3. $25.00

SCHUTZ, Benjamin M. *Embrace the Wolf.* 1985. Bluejay. 1st. F/dj. P3. $18.00

SCHUTZ, Benjamin M. *Fistful of Empty.* 1991. Viking. 1st. F/dj. P3. $18.00

SCHUYLER, George S. *Black No More: Being an Account of the Strange...* 1931. NY. Macaulay. 1st. F. B4. $400.00

SCHUYLER, Robert Livingston. *Frederic William Maitland, Historian...* 1960. Berkeley. 261p. prt sewn wrp. M11. $45.00

SCHWANTES, G. *Cultivation of the Mesembryanthemacae.* 1954. London. photos. VG/dj. B26. $35.00

SCHWARTZ, A. *Butterflies of Hispaniola.* 1989. Gainesville, FL. ils/distribution maps. 580p. pict cloth. F. M12. $27.50

SCHWARTZ, Delmore. *I Am Cherry Alive, the Little Girl Sang.* 1979. Harper Row. 1st. 32p. F/F. D4. $35.00

SCHWARTZ, Hans. *Evil: Historical & Theological Perspective.* 1995. Fortress. 226p. F/wrp. B29. $8.00

SCHWARTZ, John Burnham. *Bicycle Days.* 1989. Summit. 1st. F/F. H11. $25.00

SCHWARTZ, Stephen. *Perfect Peach.* 1977. Little Brn. 1st. 48p. gilt brd. F/G+. C14. $10.00

SCHWARTZ, Urs. *John F Kennedy 1917-1963.* 1964. London. Hamlyn. 1st Eng. ils. F/dj. Q1. $75.00

SCHWARTZ-NOBEL, Loretta. *Engaged to Murder.* 1987. Viking. 2nd. VG. P3. $15.00

SCHWARZ, Jeffrey. *Orang-Utan Biology.* 1988. Oxford. 383p. F. S15. $45.00

SCHWATKA, F. *Summer in Alaska in the 1880s...* 1988. Secaucus. Castle Books. 8vo. 418p. F/F. P4. $25.00

SCHWATKA, F. *Summer in Alaska: Popular Account of Travels in Alaska...* 1894 (1891). ils. VG. E6. $40.00

SCHWATKA, F. *Summer in Alaska: Popular Account of Travels of Alaska...* 1891. Phil. ils. 418p. rebound. F. M4. $80.00

SCHWEBELL, Gertrude C. *Where Magic Reigns.* 1957. Stephen Daye. 1st. 313p. VG/dj. M5. $20.00

SCHWEITZER, Albert. *Psychiatric Study of Jesus.* 1948. Beacon. 1st. VG. M19. $45.00

SCHWEITZER, Byrd Baylor. *Chinese Bug.* 1968. Houghton Mifflin. 1st. sm 4to. F/VG+. C14. $20.00

SCHWEITZER, Jerome M. *Restorative Dentistry: Clinical Photographic Presentation.* 1947. St Louis. 511p. 4to. A17. $27.50

SCHWIEBERT, E.G. *Luther & His Times.* 1950. Concordia. 892p. VG. B29. $15.00

SCITHERS, George. *Isaac Asimov's Marvels of Science Fiction.* 1979. Dial. 1st. VG/dj. P3. $15.00

SCOBEE, Barry. *Ft Davis, TX 1853-1960.* 1963. Hill Prt Co. 1st. sgn. 220p. VG. J2. $110.00

SCOGINS, C.E. *Red Gods Call.* 1926. Bobbs Merrill. ARC for Am Booksellers Convention. F/dj. M2. $50.00

SCOOT, Anna Miller. *Flower Babies Book.* 1914. Rand McNally. later prt. 8vo. VG. M5. $85.00

SCOPPETTONE, Sandra. *Everything You Have Is Mine.* 1991. Little Brn. 1st. author's 1st mystery. F/dj. A24. $35.00

SCOPPETTONE, Sandra. *Let's Face the Music & Die.* 1996. Little Brn. 1st. F/dj. P3. $22.00

SCOPPETTONE, Sandra. *Razzamatazz.* 1985. Franklin Watts. 1st. VG/VG. M22. $25.00

SCOPPETTONE, Sandra. *Suzuki Beane.* 1961. Garden City. 1st. VG. B5. $60.00

SCORTIA, Thomas N. *Artery of Fire.* 1972. Doubleday. 1st. F/dj. M2. $12.00

SCORTIA, Thomas N. *Best of Thomas N Scortia.* 1981. Doubleday. 1st. NF/dj. P3. $20.00

SCOTLAND, Jay; see Jakes, John.

SCOTT, Alastair. *Tracks Across Alaska: A Dogsled Journey.* 1990. NY. Atlantic Monthly. 1st Am. 8vo. 247p. M/dj. P4. $20.00

SCOTT, Alma. *Wanda Gag: Story of an Artist.* 1949. NM U. 1st. photos/ils. VG/VG. D1. $100.00

SCOTT, Anna M. *Year With the Fairies.* (1914). Volland. 1st. ils MT Ross. VG. D1. $275.00

SCOTT, C.A. Dawson. *Haunting.* 1985. Tabb House. NF/dj. P3. $20.00

SCOTT, Charles W. *Pieces of the Game: Human Drama of Americans Held Hostage...* 1984. Atlanta. Peachtree. 1st. F/G. T12. $6.00

SCOTT, Frank J. *Art of Beautifying Suburban Home Grounds of Small Extent.* 1881. NY. ils. 618p. pict cloth. VG. B18. $125.00

SCOTT, Fred. *Saipan Under Fire.* 1982. Foster. rpt. maps. sc. VG. S16. $15.00

SCOTT, Genio C. *Fishing in American Waters.* (1875). Orange Judd. 539p. VG. H7. $75.00

SCOTT, H.A. *Blue & White Devils: 3rd Infantry Division.* 1984. TN. 1st. ils/maps. 173p. VG/VG. S16. $30.00

SCOTT, Jack Denton. *Spargo.* 1971. Cleveland. World. 1st. F/F. H11. $20.00

SCOTT, Joanna. *Arrogance.* 1990. Linden. 1st. author's 3rd book. VG/VG. L1. $40.00

SCOTT, Joanna. *Fading, My Parmacheene Belle.* 1987. Ticknor Fields. 1st. author's 1st novel. VG/VG. L1. $85.00

SCOTT, Justin. *Treasure for Treasure.* 1975. Arthur Barker. 1st. VG/dj. P3. $35.00

SCOTT, Lynn H. *Covered Wagon & Other Adventures.* 1987. Omaha. 1st. F/F. B3. $20.00

SCOTT, Martha B. *Artist & the Sportsman.* 1968. Renaissance Eds. 1st. ils. F/VG+. P8. $25.00

SCOTT, Mary Hurlburt. *Oregon Trail Through Wyoming.* 1958. Powder River. inscr. map. A19. $100.00

SCOTT, Melissa. *Shadow Man.* 1995. Tor. 1st. F/dj. P3. $23.00

SCOTT, Morgan. *Rival Pitchers of Oakdale.* 1911. Hurst. 1st. VG. B2. $50.00

SCOTT, Natalie. *Gourmet's Guide to New Orleans.* 1939. New Orleans. Stafford. G/wrp. A16. $15.00

SCOTT, Paul. *Jewel in the Crown.* 1966. Morrow. 1st Am. NF/dj. M25. $25.00

SCOTT, Paul. *Male Child.* 1957. Dutton. 1st Am. VG/VG+. B4. $85.00

SCOTT, Peter. *Coloured Key to the Wildfowl of the World.* 1961. NY. ils. 91p. NF/dj. S15. $12.00

SCOTT, Renae. *Doing Community Outreach to Third World Women.* 1980. Casa Myrna Vazques. 1st. ils. VG+. A25. $15.00

SCOTT, Reva. *Samuel Brannan & the Golden Fleece.* 1944. Macmillan. 1st. inscr. G+. O4. $15.00

SCOTT, S. Gilbert. *Monograph on Adolescent Spondylitis...* 1942. London. 1st. 132p. A13. $65.00

SCOTT, Thomas. *Vindication of Divine Inspiration of Holy Scriptures...* 1797. NY. Forman for Davis. 8vo. contemporary calf. R12. $275.00

SCOTT, Walter. *Black Dwarf.* nd. Collins. VG. P3. $12.00

SCOTT, Walter. *Complete Poetical & Dramatic Works.* 1883. London. Rutlege. sm 8vo. intro Wm B Scott. ils. leather/marbled brd. G. H1. $35.00

SCOTT, Walter. *Ivanhoe.* 1933. Windermere. ils Milo WInter. F. M19. $35.00

SCOTT, Walter. *Ivanhoe.* 1950. Heritage. F/sans/case. P3. $45.00

SCOTT, Walter. *Lady of the Lake.* 1853. Little Brn. 8vo. 375p. bl cloth. F. B24. $150.00

SCOTT, Walter. *Poetical Works of Sir Walter Scott.* nd. Routledge. decor brd. G. P3. $20.00

SCOTT, Walter. *Talisman.* 1929. ils Rowland Wheelwright. VG/G. M19. $35.00

SCOTT-ELLIOTT, W. *History of Atlantis/Lost Lemuria.* 1925. London. Theosophical Pub. 6 fld pocket maps. F. O7. $75.00

SCRIBNER, Harvey. *My Mysterious Clients.* 1900. Cincinnati. Robert Clarke. 1st. inscr to brother. NF. M15. $125.00

SCRIPPS, John Locke. *Life of Abraham Lincoln.* 1961. 1st. 192p. O8. $9.50

SCRYMSOUR, Ella. *Perfect World.* 1922. Stokes. 1st. VG. M2. $32.00

SCUDDER. *Mr Bodley Abroad.* 1908 (1881). Rare Book Div of Lib of Congress. VG. A4. $45.00

SCULL, Penrose. *Great Ships Around the World.* 1960. NY. Ziff Davis. 4to. 400+ ils. 260p. T7. $35.00

SCULLY, Julia. *Disfarmer: Heber Springs Portraits, 1939-1946.* 1976. Danbury. Addison House. photos. 136p. cloth. dj. D11. $250.00

SCULLY & SCULLY. *Official Motorists' Guide to Mexico.* 1937. Dallas. Turner. 238p. dj. F3. $15.00

SEABORNE, E.A. *Detective in Fiction.* 1937. Clarke Irwin. 4th. VG. P3. $20.00

SEABROOK, W.P. *Modern Fruit Growing.* 1945. London. Benn. 7th. 307p. VG/dj. A10. $22.00

SEABROOK, William. *Dr Wood, Modern Wizard of the Laboratory.* 1941. Harcourt Brace. 1st. ils. 8vo. 335p. VG/dj. K3. $20.00

SEALE, Bobby. *Seize the Time: Story of Black Panther Party...* 1970. Random. 1st. sgn. 429p. F/F. B4. $300.00

SEALE, Patrick. *Abu Nidal, a Gun for Hire. Secret Life of...Terrorist.* 1992. Random. 1st. 339p. NF/dj. W1. $22.00

SEAMAN, Augusta Huiell. *Crimson Patch.* 1920. Century. 1st. 226p. cloth. VG. M20. $20.00

SEAMAN, Augusta Huiell. *Girl Next Door.* 1920 (1917). Century. 260p. cloth. VG/dj. M20. $35.00

SEAMAN, Louise. *Brave Bantam.* 1946. Macmillan. 1st. sgn. ils Helen Sewell. VG/dj. M20. $50.00

SEARGENT, David A. *Comets: Vagabonds of Space.* 1982. NY. Doubleday. 1st. F/F. T12. $25.00

SEARLES, Baird. *Films of Science Fiction & Fantasy.* 1988. Abrams. 1st. VG. P3. $75.00

SEARS, Edmund. *Zathu, a Tale of Ancient Galilee.* 1925. Cornhill. 1st. VG. M2. $17.00

SEARS, George W. *Woodcraft: Spirit of the Outdoors.* (1936). NY. Nessmuk Lib. 189p. VG. H7. $12.50

SEARS, Robert. *Wonders of the World, in Nature, Art & Mind.* 1853. NY. Edward Walker. New Ed. 8vo. ils. 528p. emb gilt cloth. T10. $125.00

SEARS, Victor H. *Principles & Technics for Complete Denture Construction.* 1949. St Louis. Mosby Co. 1st. 8vo. 416p. gilt bl cloth/red spine. F. H1. $22.50

SEATON, Albert. *Stalin as Military Commander.* 1975. NY. ils/notes/biblio/index. 312p. VG/VG. S16. $21.50

SEAVER, Jeannette. *Jeannette's Secrets of Everyday Good Cooking.* 1975. Knopf. 1st. ils. 8vo. 309p+index. dj. A16. $12.00

SEAWELL, Molly Elliot. *Twelve Naval Captains.* 1897. Scribner. 233p. gray cloth. F. K7. $35.00

SEBALD, William. *With MacArthur in Japan.* 1965. Toronto. George J McLeod Ltd. inscr. dj. A19. $30.00

SEBASTIAN, Tim. *Spy in Question.* 1988. Toronto. Doubleday. 1st Canadian. F/F. T12. $25.00

SECREST, William. *Lawmen & Desperadoes, a Compendium of Noted & Early...* 1994. Clark. 1st. photos/ils. 343p. as new. J2. $65.00

SEDGWICK, Mabel C. *Garden Month by Month.* 1907. Garden City. 1st. 516p. VG. A10. $30.00

SEEBER, Edward D. *Choix de Pieces Huguenotes (1685-1756).* 1930s. Bloomington, IN. IU. sgn. 80p. VG. B11. $150.00

SEELEY, Mabel. *Chuckling Fingers.* 1941. Crime Club. VG/fair. P3. $15.00

SEELEY, Mabel. *Eleven Came Back.* 1943. Crime Club. 1st. VG. P3. $20.00

SEELEY, Mabel. *Stranger Beside Me.* 1951. Doubleday. 1st. VG/VG. P3. $23.00

SEELEY, Mabel. *Woman of Property.* 1947. Doubleday. 1st. VG/dj. P3. $23.00

SEGAL, Erich. *Fairy Tale.* 1973. Harper Row. 1st. ils Dino Kotopoulis. VG/G+. T5. $20.00

SEGAL, Erich. *Love Story.* 1970. NY. special ltd sgn pres. VG/glassine dj. B5. $50.00

SEGAR, E.C. *Popeye With the Hag of the 7 Seas.* 1935. Chicago. Pleasure Books. 3 popups. pict brd. D1. $500.00

SEIBLE, C.W. *Helium, Child of the Sun.* 1968. Lawrence, KS. 138p. F/dj. D8. $15.00

SEIFERT, Howard. *Space Technology.* 1959. John Wiley. 8vo. 1250p. Vg/dj. K5. $100.00

SEISS, J.A. *Gospel in the Stars.* 1884 (1882). NY. Chas Cook. 4th. 8vo. 522p. cloth. K5. $100.00

SEKOROVA, Dagmar. *European Fairy Tales.* 1971. Lee Shepard. 1st. VG/dj. P3. $12.00

SELA, Owen. *Exchange of Eagles.* 1977. Pantheon. 1st. VG/dj. P3. $15.00

SELBY, Henry. *Zapolic Deviance.* 1974. Austin, TX. 1st. 166p. dj. F3. $10.00

SELBY, Hubert. *Demon.* 1976. Playboy. 1st. NF/VG. A20. $20.00

SELBY, Hubert. *Last Exit to Brooklyn Post-Trial Ed.* 1968. Calder Boyars. 2nd. VG/dj. P3. $25.00

SELBY, Hubert. *Room.* 1972. Calder Boyars. 1st. F/dj. P3. $45.00

SELBY, John. *Eagle & the Serpent.* 1977. Hippocrene Books. 1st. 163p. dj. F3. $15.00

SELDEN, G. *Garden Under the Sea.* 1957. Viking. 1st. VG/G. P2. $20.00

SELDEN, John. *Table-Talk...With a Biographical Preface & Notes...* 1860. London. John Russell Smith. 3rd (Singer) ed. emb gr cloth. M11. $125.00

SELDENI, Ioannis. *Ad Fletam Dissertatio, Reprinted From Edition of 1647...* 1925. Cambridge. cloth. M11. $125.00

SELDES, George. *You Can't Do That.* 1938. Modern Age Services. hc. VG. P3. $25.00

SELF, H. *Environment & Man in Kansas.* 1978. np. ils/maps. 288p. NF/dj. D8. $15.00

SELF, M.C. *American Quarter Horse in Pictures.* 1969. Phil. Smith. ils/photos/drawings. 157p. gilt cloth. F/G+. M12. $17.50

SELF, M.C. *Riding With Mariles.* 1960. McGraw Hill. 1st. VG/G. O3. $25.00

SELF, Will. *Cock & Bull.* 1992. London. Bloomsbury. 1st. F/dj. A24. $45.00

SELIGMAN, Kurt. *History of Magic.* 1948. Pantheon. VG/G. P3. $30.00

SELIGO, Hans. *Morocco.* 1966. Munich. Andermann. 1st. broad 8vo. 30 mc pl. 60p. NF. W1. $10.00

SELL & WEYBRIGHT. *Buffalo Bill & the Wild West.* 1955. Oxford. 1st. ils/photos. 278p. VG/dj. J2. $75.00

SELLINGS, Arthur. *Quy Effect.* 1966. Dobson. 1st. VG/dj. P3. $28.00

SELTZER, Charles Alden. *Land of the Free.* 1927. Gundy. 1st. VG. P3. $30.00

SELTZER, Charles Alden. *So Long, Sucker.* 1941. Doubleday Doran. 1st. G. P3. $20.00

SELVERSTON, Allen I. *Model Neural Networks & Behavior.* 1985. Plenum. tall 8vo. 458p. prt blk brd. G1. $50.00

SELVON, Samuel. *Lonely Londoner.* 1956. St Martin. 1st. NF/dj. M25. $35.00

SELWYN, E.W.H. *Photography in Astronomy.* 1950. Rochester, NY. Eastman Kodak. 1st. VG. K5. $15.00

SENAULT, Louis. *Hevres Nouvelles Dediees a Madame La Davphine.* 1680. Paris. Duval. 8vo. vignettes/borders. contemporary sharkskin/silver clasp. R12. $1,500.00

SENDAK, Maurice. *Caldecott & Co: Notes on Books & Pictures.* 1988. ils. 216p. F/F. A4. $65.00

SENDAK, Maurice. *Cunning Little Vixen.* 1985. Farrar. stated 1st. sm 4to. F/VG. M5. $75.00

SENDAK, Maurice. *Cunning Little Vixen.* 1985. NY. Farrar. 1/250. sgn. as new/box. R5. $200.00

SENDAK, Maurice. *Dear Mili.* 1988. FSG. 1st. unp. cloth. NF/dj. M20. $37.00

SENDAK, Maurice. *In the Night Kitchen.* nd (1970). Harper Row. 4to. unp. F. C14. $18.00

SENDAK, Maurice. *Ten Little Rabbits: A Counting Book.* (1970). Phil. Rosenbach Found. 1st. 32mo. NF. D1. $40.00

SENDAK, Maurice. *We Are All in the Dumps With Jack & Guy.* 1993. Harper Collins. 1st. unp. NF/dj. M20. $25.00

SENDAK & STOCKTON. *Bee-Man of Orn.* (1964). HRW. 1st stated. 8vo. 46p. NF/$3.50 dj. D1. $100.00

SENECA. *Hints & Points for Sportsmen.* 1895. Forest/Stream. 224+16p. VG. H7. $35.00

SENEFELDER, Alois. *Invention of Lithography.* 1911. NY. Fuchs Lang. 1st. 229p. NF. K3. $80.00

SENN, N. *In the Heart of the Arctics.* 1907. Chicago. inscr. ils. G. M4. $15.00

SENNETT, Mack. *King of Commedy.* 1954. Doubleday. 1st. photos. VG+/dj. C9. $75.00

SENOUR, Faunt le Roy. *Morgan & His Captors.* 1865. Cincinnati. CF Vent. 1st. 389p. cloth. VG. M8. $250.00

SEQUIN, E.C. *Medical Thermometry & Human Temperature.* 1876. NY. 1st. 446p. A13. $200.00

SERANNE, Ann. *Complete Book of Desserts.* 1963. Doubleday. G/dj. A16. $10.00

SEREDY, Kate. *Lazy Tinka.* 1962. Harrap. 1st. ils. VG/dj. M20. $30.00

SEREDY, Kate. *Lazy Tinka.* 1962. Viking. 1st. sq 8vo. 56p. VG+/VG. P2. $75.00

SEREDY, Kate. *Open Gate.* 1943. Viking. 1st. 280p. VG/G. P2. $50.00

SERFOZO, Mary. *Rain Talk.* 1990. NY. Margaret K McElderry Books. 1st. 8vo. F/F. C14. $16.00

SERGEANT, Philip. *Last Empress of the French. Life of Empress Eugenie.* nd. Phil. 8vo. ils. teg. 3-quarter dk red leather. F. H3. $75.00

SERLING, Rod. *Season to Be Wary.* 1967. Little Brn. 1st. xl. VG/dj. P3. $10.00

SERRA, Victoria. *Tia Victoria's Spanish Kitchen.* 1963. NY. Weathervane. VG/dj. A16. $15.00

SERVICE, Robert W. *Ballads of a Cheechako.* 1909. NY. Barse Hopkins. 1st. NF/VG. T11. $50.00

SERVICE, Robert W. *Rhymes of a Rebel.* 1952. NY. Dodd Mead. 1st. F/VG. T11. $60.00

SERVICE, Robert W. *Rhymes of a Red Cross Man.* 1916. Barse Hopkins. 192p. gilt gr cloth. P4. $30.00

SERVISS, Garrett P. *Columbus of Space.* 1974 (1911). Hyperion. rpt. F. M2. $30.00

SESSONS, Ruth Huntington. *Sixty-Odd: A Personal History.* 1936. Brattleboro. Stephen Daye. 1st. 429p. VG. A25. $12.00

SETH, Vikram. *Suitable Boy.* 1993. Harper Collins. 1st Am. F/F. B4. $45.00

SETLOWE, Richard. *Experiment.* 1980. Holt. 1st. F/dj. M2. $12.00

SETON, Anya. *Dragonwick.* 1944. Houghton Mifflin. 1st. inscr/dtd 1944. F/F clip. B4. $250.00

SETON, Ernest Thompson. *Trail of the Sandhill Stag.* 1920. Scribner. later prt. VG. A19. $25.00

SETON, Graham. *Eye for an Eye.* 1933. Farrar Rhinehart. 1st Am. F/NF. M15. $80.00

SETTLE, Mary Lee. *Charley Bland.* 1989. Franklin Lib. 1st. sgn. leather. F. B35. $45.00

SETTLE, Mary Lee. *Fight Night on a Sweet Saturday.* 1964. NY. Viking. 1st. F/NF. B4. $85.00

SETTLE, Raymond W. *March of the Mounted Riflemen, First United States...* 1940. Clark. 1st. ils/map. 380p. VG. J2. $325.00

SETTLE, Raymond W. *Saddles & Spurs.* 1972. Lincoln, NE. A19. $15.00

SETTLE & SETTLE. *Empire on Wheels.* 1949. Stanford. 1st. VG/VG. O3. $45.00

SETTLE & SETTLE. *War Drums & Wagon Wheels.* 1966. NE U. 1st. 268p. cloth. VG/dj. M20. $30.00

SEVERIN, Mark F. *Making a Bookplate.* 1949. The Studio. How to Do It series. ils. xl. G+. M17. $20.00

SEVERIN, Tim. *Brendan Voyage.* 1978. NY. McGraw Hill. 292p. cloth. VG/dj. P4. $30.00

SEVERIN, Tim. *Jason Voyage: Quest for the Golden Fleece.* 1985. NY. S&S. BC. 8vo. 263p. half cloth. VG/dj. P4. $25.00

SEVERN, Merlyn. *Ballet in Action.* 1938. Oxford. 1st. 4to. F/dj. w/sgn photo. T10. $50.00

SEWALL, Thomas. *Examination of Phrenology in Two Lectures...1837.* 1839. Boston. DS King. 2nd revised. 6 lithos (5 fld). 110p. brn cloth. G1. $185.00

SEWARD, John. *Spirit of Anecdote & Wit.* 1823. London. Walker/Bumpus. 4 vol. 1st. sm 8vo. early Regency-style bdg. H13. $245.00

SEWELL, Anna. *Black Beauty.* 1890. Boston. Geo Angell. 1st. stiff brd. M24. $350.00

SEWELL, Anna. *Black Beauty.* 1946. Garden City. Jr DeLuxe ed. VG. O3. $15.00

SEWELL, Anna. *Black Beauty: His Grooms & Companions.* 1890. Boston. Am Humane Edu Soc. 1st Am. prt brd. VG. B14. $250.00

SEXBY, Edward. *Killing No Murder.* 1749. London. 8vo. title in red/blk. quarter calf. R12. $150.00

SEXBY, Edward. *Killing No Murder.* 1792. London. Ridgway. tall 8vo. disbound. R12. $125.00

SEXBY, Edward. *Traicte Politique, ...Ou il est Prouve...* 1793 (1658). Paris. 16mo. gilt calf. R12. $150.00

SEXTON & SEXTON. *Samuel A Maverick.* 1964. San Antonio. 1st. sgn. VG/VG. B5. $15.00

SEYFFERT, O. *Spielzeug.* ca 1910. Berlin. Ernst Wasmuth. ils W Trier. pink silk ep. pict brd. VG. D1. $200.00

SEYMOUR, Alta Halverson. *Grandma for Christmas.* 1941. Westminster. ils Janet Smalley/Jeanne McLavy. VG. M5. $20.00

SEYMOUR, Charles. *Intimate Papers of Colonel House, Arranged as a Narrative.* 1926. Houghton Mifflin. 4 vol. 8vo. teg. gilt red buckram. VG. T10. $75.00

SEYMOUR, Frank C. *Flora of Vermont.* 1969. Burlington. 4th. 393p. VG. B26. $38.00

SEYMOUR, Gerald. *Glory Boys.* 1976. Random. 1st. VG/dj. P3. $25.00

SEYMOUR, Gerald. *Harry's Game.* 1975. Random. 1st. author's 1st book. F/F. H11. $35.00

SEYMOUR, Gerald. *Home Run.* 1989. Collins Harvill. 1st. NF/F. A20. $30.00

SEYMOUR, Gerald. *Song in the Morning.* 1987. Norton. 1st. VG/dj. P3. $18.00

SEYMOUR, Henry. *Intrigue in Tangier.* 1958. John Gifford. 1st. VG/dj. P3. $18.00

SEYMOUR, John. *Fat of the Land.* 1975. Shocken. 176p. dj. A10. $25.00

SEYMOUR, Peter. *Discovering Our Past.* 1986. Macmillan. popup John Strejan. ils Borje Svensson. NF. P2. $15.00

SEYMOUR, Ralph Fletcher. *Across the Gulf: Narration of Short Journey...* 1928. Chicago. Alderbrink. 1/425. sgn. fld map. 63p. G+. B11. $85.00

SEYNER, Antonio. *Historica del Levantamiento de Portugal.* 1644. Zaragoza. Pedro Lanaja. 1st. 276p. later speckled calf. R15. $2,000.00

SHAARA, Michael. *Broken Place.* 1968. NY. NAL. 1st. author's 1st book. F/NF. D10. $425.00

SHABAZZ, L. *Cooking for the Champ, Mohammed Ali's Favorite Recipes.* 1979. 1st. 4to. sc. VG. E6. $20.00

SHACOCHIS, Bob. *Next New World.* 1989. Crown. 1st. F/F. B2. $40.00

SHADOIAN, Jack. *Dreams & Dead Ends: American Gangster/Crime Film.* 1977. MIT. 366p. dj. A17. $12.50

SHAFAREVICH, Igor. *Socialist Phenomenon.* 1980. Harper. 1st. VG/dj. V4. $15.00

SHAFER, George D. *Ways of a Mud Daubner.* 1949. Stanford. 78p. NF/VG. S15. $12.00

SHAFFER, E.T.H. *Carolina Gardens.* 1939. Chapel Hill. 326p. cloth. A10. $40.00

SHAGAN, Steve. *Circle.* 1982. Morrow. 1st. VG/dj. P3. $18.00

SHAHN, Ben. *Sweet Was the Song.* 1965 (1956). NY. Odyssey. obl 24mo. NF/VG. C8. $25.00

SHAKESPEARE, William. *Complete Works of Shakespeare.* 1936. NY. Doubleday Doran. 2 vol. 1/750. sgn Kent. edit Wm Wright. B11. $550.00

SHAKESPEARE, William. *Complete Works...* nd (1952). Harcourt. sq tall 8vo. 1666p. bl cloth. B22. $12.00

SHAKESPEARE, William. *Flowers From Shakespeare's Garden.* 1906. London. Cassell. 1st. ils Walter Crane. 40p. VG. D1. $250.00

SHAKESPEARE, William. *Life of Henry VIII.* 1758. London. D Browne. 1st ils. 8vo. 116p. half calf. B24. $550.00

SHAKESPEARE, William. *Life of King Henry the Fifth.* 1909. Macmillan. rpt. 219p. G. W2. $1,100.00

SHAKESPEARE, William. *Starlight & Moonshine.* 1988. Orchard Books. 1st thus. glossy brd. F. T5. $20.00

SHALER, N.S. *First Book of Geology.* 1904 (1884). Boston. DC Heath. 8vo. 255p. xl. K5. $15.00

SHALLETT, S. *Old Nameless: Epic of a US Battlewagon.* 1943. NY. 177p. VG. S16. $21.50

SHALLIT, Joseph. *Lady, Don't Die on My Doorstep.* 1951. Lippincott. VG. P3. $15.00

SHAMBURGER, Page. *Tracks Across the Sky.* 1964. Phil. 1st. VG/VG. B5. $35.00

SHAMES, Laurence. *Florida Straits.* 1992. S&S. 1st. sgn. F/F. D10. $60.00

SHAMES, Laurence. *Hunger for More: Searching for Values in an Age of Greed.* 1989. Times Books. 1st. F/F. B4. $100.00

SHAND, P. Morton. *Book of French Wines.* 1928. London. Knopf. 247p. B10. $45.00

SHANGE, Ntozake. *Betsey Brown.* 1985. St Martin. 1st. 207p. NF/NF. W2. $20.00

SHANGE, Ntozake. *Ridn' the Moon in Texas.* 1987. St Martin. 1st. F/F. R14. $35.00

SHANKLAND, E.N. *Bird Book: Observations of Bird Life.* (1931). Saalfield. ils FB Peat. VG. B15. $100.00

SHANKS, Edward. *Dark Green Circle.* 1936. Bobbs Merrill. 1st. G+. M2. $10.00

SHANN, Renee. *Air Force Girl.* 1943. Triangel/Blakiston. 1st thus. 275p. VG/dj. A25. $35.00

SHANN, Renee. *Airman's Wife.* 1944. Phil. Triangle/Blakiston. 1st thus. 202p. VG/dj. A25. $22.00

SHANNON, Dell. *Blood Count.* 1986. Morrow. 1st. VG/dj. P3. $16.00

SHANNON, Dell. *Case Pending.* 1960. Harper. 1st. author's 1st book. VG/dj. M25. $35.00

SHANNON, Dell. *Extra Kill.* 1962. Morrow. VG/VG. M19. $25.00

SHANNON, Dell. *Felony at Random.* 1979. Morrow. 1st. VG/dj. P3. $20.00

SHANNON, Dell. *Knave of Hearts.* 1962. Morrow. 1st. NF/NF. M19. $25.00

SHANNON, Dell. *Murder by the Tale.* 1987. Morrow. 1st. VG/dj. P3. $20.00

SHANNON, Dell. *With Intent to Kill.* 1972. Morrow. 1st. VG/dj. P3. $20.00

SHANNON, Terry. *Little Wolf & the Rain Dancer.* 1954. Whitman. 1st. ils Charles Payzant. VG+. M5. $38.00

SHAPELEY, H. *Climactic Change, Evidence, Causes & Effects.* 1953. Harvard. 1st. 318p. VG. D8. $20.00

SHAPIRO, David. *Introduction to the Poetry (John Ashbery).* 1979. Columbia. 1st. assn copy. F/VG+. V1. $15.00

SHAPIRO, H.L. *Migration & Environment: Study of Physical Characteristics.* 1939. London. Oxford. 168 tables/77 graphs. 594p. cloth. VG/remnant. P4. $45.00

SHAPIRO, H.L. *Peking Man: The Discovery, Disappearance & Mystery...* 1974. S&S. 1st. 190p. VG/dj. D8. $22.00

SHAPIRO, Karl. *Poems 1940-1953* 1953. Random. rpt. sgn. VG/VG. B11. $45.00

SHAPIRO, Lionel. *6th of June.* 1955. Doubleday. 1st. NF. T12. $15.00

SHAPIRO. *Carson McCullers: Descriptive Listings...* 1980. Garland. ils. 324p. F. A4. $195.00

SHAPLEN, Robert. *Forest of Tigers.* 1956. Knopf. 1st. F/NF. H11. $40.00

SHAPLEY, Harlow. *Flights From Chaos.* 1930. Whittlesey. 1st. 8vo. 168p. K5. $25.00

SHARMA, P.V. *Geophysical Methods in Geology.* 1983 (1976). Elsevier, NY. 6th. 428p. VG. B1. $26.50

SHARP, Evelyn. *Other Side of the Sun (Fairy Stories).* 1900. Bodley Head. 1st. 8 full-p pl. 8vo. all edges gr. pict cloth. R5. $250.00

SHARP, Margery. *Britannia Mews.* 1946. Little Brn. 1st. VG/dj. P3. $30.00

SHARP, Margery. *Miss Bianca & the Bridesmaids.* 1972. Little Brn. 1st. 123p. VG/VG. P2. $40.00

SHARP, Margery. *Miss Bianca in the Antarctic.* 1971. Little Brn. 1st. ils Eric Blegvard. 134p. VG+/VG. P2. $40.00

SHARP, Margery. *Rescuers.* 1959. Little Brn. 1st. ils Garth Williams. 8vo. bl cloth. dj. R5. $100.00

SHARP, Marilyn. *Sunflower.* 1979. Marek. 1st. F/dj. P3. $15.00

SHARP, Samuel. *Critical Enquiry Into Present State of Surgery.* 1750. London. 2nd. 294p. full leather. A13. $600.00

SHARP, W. Watson. *Australia's Native Orchids.* 1970. Sydney. photos/line drawings. 144p. VG+/dj. B26. $26.00

SHARPE, Dinah. *My Horse; My Love.* 1892. Orange Judd. 1st. G. O3. $58.00

SHARPE, Tom. *Riotous Assembly.* 1971. Viking. 1st. author's 1st novel. F/NF. L3. $100.00

SHATRAW, Milton. *Thrashin' Time: Memories of a Montanan Boyhood.* 1970. Am West. 1st. 188p. VG/VG. J2. $55.00

SHAUB & SHAUB. *Treasures From the Earth: World of Rocks & Minerals.* 1975. Crown. 1st prt. 223p. VG. D8. $10.00

SHAW, Albert. *Abraham Lincoln: A Cartoon History.* 1929. 500+p. O8. $27.50

SHAW, Andrew; see Block, Lawrence.

SHAW, Bob. *Cosmic Kaleidoscope.* 1976. Gollancz. 1st. F/dj. P3. $35.00

SHAW, Bob. *Dark Night in Toyland.* 1989. Gollancz. 1st. F/dj. P3. $25.00

SHAW, Bob. *Killer Planet.* 1989. Gollancz. 1st. F/F. P3. $25.00

SHAW, Bob. *Medusa's Children.* 1979. Doubleday. 1st Am. F/dj. M2. $15.00

SHAW, Bob. *Obitsville Judgement.* 1990. Gollancz. 1st. F/F. P3. $25.00

SHAW, Bob. *Wreath of Stars.* 1977. Doubleday. 1st. NF/dj. P3. $20.00

SHAW, Ellen Eddy. *Gardening & Farming.* 1919. Toronto. Gundy. 376p. gilt cloth. VG. A10. $40.00

SHAW, Frank H. *Full Fathom Five: Book of Famous Shipwrecks.* 1930. Macmillan. 20 pl. 301p. T7. $35.00

SHAW, George Bernard. *Back to Methuselah, a Metabiological Pentateuch...* 1939. 4to. ils/sgn John Farleigh. 260p. VG. A4. $135.00

SHAW, George. *Roy Rogers Rodeo.* ca 1950s. London. Purnell. pub file copy. 5 double-p popups/ils. R5. $200.00

SHAW, Irwin. *Beggarman, Thief.* 1977. Delacorte. 1st. F/dj. Q1. $50.00

SHAW, Irwin. *Bread Upon the Waters.* 1981. Delacorte. 1st trade. 438p. NF/dj. W2. $10.00

SHAW, Irwin. *Bread Upon the Waters.* 1981. Delacorte. 1st. sgn. F/sans/F case. R14. $100.00

SHAW, Irwin. *Top of the Hill.* 1979. London. 1st. F/F. T12. $30.00

SHAW, Lloyd. *Cowboy Dances, a Collection of Western Square Dances.* 1940. Caldwell, ID. 2nd. sgn. 375p. VG/torn. B18. $17.50

SHAW, R.E. *Erie Water West: History of the Erie Canal 1792-1854.* 1966. KY U. 1st. ils. F/VG. M4. $25.00

SHAW, Richard J. *Trees & Flowering Shrubs of Yellowstone & Grand Teton...* 1964. Salt Lake City. 72 mc photos. cbdg. B26. $7.50

SHAW, Stanley. *Woman Tamer.* 1923. MacAulay. 1st. VG/dj. P3. $25.00

SHAW, T.E. *Odyssey of Homer.* 1935. London. Oxford. 1st Eng trade. gilt bl buckram. F/dj. Q1. $200.00

SHAW. *Childhood in Poetry: Forty-Year History of a Collection...* 1970. inscr. 28p. cloth. F. A4. $65.00

SHAW(N), Frank S.; see Goulart, Ron.

SHEA, Michael. *Tomorrow's Men.* 1982. Weidenfeld Nicolson. 1st. F/dj. P3. $20.00

SHEARING, Joseph. *Spectral Bride.* 1942. Smith Durrell. 1st. NF. M2. $25.00

SHECKLEY, Robert. *Dramocles.* 1983. HRW. 1st. F/dj. P3. $18.00

SHECKLEY, Robert. *Victim Prime.* 1987. Methuen. 1st. F/dj. P3. $20.00

SHEDLEY, Ethan. *Earth Ship & Star Song.* 1979. Viking. 1st. F/dj. M2. $15.00

SHEDLEY, Ethan. *Medusa Conspiracy.* 1980. Viking. 1st. VG+/dj. N4. $17.50

SHEED, Wilfrid. *Transatlantic Blues.* 1978. Dutton. 1st. 312p. NF/NF. W2. $20.00

SHEEHAN, J. Eastman. *General & Plastic Surgery With Emphasis on War Injuries.* 1945. NY. 1st. ils. 345p. A13. $150.00

SHEEHAN, Michael M. *Will in Medieval England, From Conversion of Anglo-Saxons...* 1963. Toronto. Pontifical Inst Mediaval Studies. 359p. prt wrp. M11. $50.00

SHEEHAN, Neil. *Bright & Shining Lie.* 1988. Random. 1st. NF/F. A20. $20.00

SHEEHAN, Perley Poore. *Abyss of Wonders.* 1953. Polaris. 1st. F/case. P3. $65.00

SHEEHAN, William. *Worlds in the Sky.* 1992. Tucson. 243p. VG. K5. $15.00

SHEERAN, James B. *Confederate Chaplain, a War Journal of James B Sheeran...* 1960. Milwaukee. 1st. 168p. VG. B18. $15.00

SHEETS, K.A. *American Fishing Books 1743-1993.* 1993. Ann Arbor. 1800+ titles. 111p. F/dj. M4. $35.00

SHEFFIELD, Charles. *Summertide.* 1990. Del Rey. F/dj. P3. $17.00

SHEFFIELD, J. *Works of..., Duke of Buckingham.* 1729. London. 2 vol. 2nd/corrected. A15. $45.00

SHEFNER, Vadim. *Unman/Kovrigin's Chronicles.* 1980. Macmillan. 1st. VG/dj. P3. $15.00

SHEHADEH, Raja. *Third Way. A Journal of Life in the West Bank...* 1982. London/Melbourne/NY. Quartet Books. 1st. 8vo. 143p. NF/dj. W1. $12.00

SHELBY, Philip. *Days of Drums.* 1996. NY. S7S. 1st. author's 1st novel. F/NF. R16. $30.00

SHELDON, Charles. *Wilderness of Denali: Explorations of a Hunter-Naturalist...* 1960. NY. new ed. 412p. F/dj. A17. $45.00

SHELDON, Charles. *Wilderness of North Pacific Coast Islands.* 1912. Scribner. 1st. 45 pl/5 maps. dk gr cloth. teg. F. B14. $250.00

SHELDON, Harold P. *Tranquility Revisited.* 1989. Derrydale. 1/2500. aeg. gilt leather. F. A17. $35.00

SHELDON, Roy. *House of Entropy.* 1953. Hamilton Panther. G/G. P3. $35.00

SHELDON, Sidney. *Doomsday Conspiracy.* 1991. Morrow. 1st. sgn. VG/VG. A23. $30.00

SHELDON, Sidney. *Doomsday Conspiracy.* 1991. Morrow. 1st. 412p. NF/NF. W2. $30.00

SHELDON, Sidney. *Other Side of Midnight.* 1974. Morrow. 1st. F/NF. H11. $35.00

SHELDON, Sidney. *Rage of Angels.* 1980. Morrow. 1st. VG/VG. P3. $20.00

SHELDON, Sidney. *Rage of Angels.* 1980. Morrow. 1st. 504p. NF/NF. W2. $30.00

SHELDON, Sidney. *Sands of Time.* 1988. Morrow. 1st. 412p. F/F. W2. $40.00

SHELL, Jacob. *Lumberman's Ready Calculator...* 1853 (1847). Harrisburg. Scheffer Beck. 41p. cloth. VG. A10. $35.00

SHELLEY, Bruce. *Call to Christian Character...* 1970. Zondervan. 186p. F/dj. B29. $6.00

SHELLEY, E.M. *Hunting Big Game With Dogs in Africa.* 1924. Columbus, MS. self pub. 1st. photos. 215p. F. H7. $100.00

SHELLEY, Mary. *Frankenstein.* 1983. Dodd Mead. 1st. ils Berni Wrightson. intro Stephen King. F/dj. P3. $30.00

SHELLEY, R.M. *Revision of the Milliped Family Eurymerodesmidae.* 1989. Phil. Am Entomological Soc. 112p. F/stiff wrp. B1. $22.00

SHELTON, Ferne. *Southern Appalachian Cookbook: Rare Time-Treated Recipes...* 1964. Hutcraft. 32p. VG. B10. $6.00

SHEN, W.H. *River Mechanics Vol II.* 1971. Ft Collins. VG. D8. $40.00

SHENK & SHENK. *Encyclopedia of Pennsylvania.* 1932. Harrisburg. 593p. gilt bdg. G. H1. $35.00

SHENSTONE, William. *Works of...* 1764. London. 2 vol. 1st collected. ils. A15. $75.00

SHEPARD, E.H. *Everybody's Pepys.* 1926. Harcourt Brace. VG. A20. $25.00

SHEPARD, J.W. *Christ of the Gospels.* 1954. Eerdmans. 650p. G. B29. $10.00

SHEPARD, Leslie. *Dracula Book of Great Vampire Stories.* 1977. Citadel. 1st. NF/dj. P3. $25.00

SHEPARD, Lucius. *Ancient Curse of the Baskervilles.* 1984. Bloomington, IN. Gaslight Pub. reissue/1st thus. F/sans. T2. $12.00

SHEPARD, Lucius. *Beyond the City: Idyll of a Suburb.* 1982. Bloomington, IN. Gaslight Pub. reissue/1st thus. F/sans. T2. $15.00

SHEPARD, Lucius. *Father of Stones.* 1989. Baltimore, MD. WA SF Assn. 1/500. sgn. ils/sgn JK Potter. F/F/case. T2 $65.00

SHEPARD, Lucius. *Jaguar Hunter.* 1988. Kerosina. 1st. F/F. P3. $30.00

SHEPARD, Lucius. *Kalimantan.* 1990. Legend. 1st. F/F. P3. $27.00

SHEPARD, Lucius. *Kalimantan.* 1990. London. Century. 1st. 1/300. sgn/#d. F/F/case. T2. $75.00

SHEPARD, Lucius. *Scalehunter's Beautiful Daughter.* 1988. Willimantic, CT. Ziesing. 1/300. sgn. F/F. T2. $75.00

SHEPARD, O. *Lore of the Unicorn.* 1967. London. Allen Unwin. ils/pl/figures. 312p. brd. F/VG. M12. $30.00

SHEPARD, Sam. *Five Plays.* 1967. Bobbs Merrill. 1st. NF/NF. D10. $235.00

SHEPARD. *Encyclopedia of Occultism & Parapsychology: A Compendium...* 1984. 3 vol. 1/1000. 2nd. F. A4. $250.00

SHEPHERD, John. *Simpson & Syme of Edinburgh.* 1969. Edinburgh. 1st. 288p. dj. A13. $40.00

SHEPHERD, John. *Spencer Wells: Life & Work of Victorian Surgeon.* 1965. Edinburgh. 1st. 132p. A13. $40.00

SHEPHERD, Michael; see Ludlum, Robert.

SHEPHERD & WREN. *Super Summer of Jamie McBride.* 1971. S&S. 1st. inscr Wren. NF/NF. M23. $35.00

SHEPLEY, J. *Hydrogen Bomb: The Men, the Menace, the Mechanism.* 1954. 1st. VG. E6. $20.00

SHERBURNE, Andrew. *Memoirs of Andrew Sherburne: A Pensioner of the Navy...* 1828. Utica. 1st. 12mo. 262p. calf/red label. F. B14. $150.00

SHERBURNE, James. *Hacey Miller.* 1971. Houghton Mifflin. 1st. sgn. VG/VG. B11. $30.00

SHERIDAN, Philip Henry. *Personal Memoirs..., General United States Army.* 1888. NY. Webster. 1st. 2 vol. cloth/shoulder strap insignia spine. M8. $250.00

SHERIDAN, Richard Brinsley. *Rivals.* 1953. London. LEC. 1st thus. 1/1500. ils/sgn RB Sussan. F/remnant glassine/F case. Q1. $100.00

SHERMAN, Dan. *Dynasty of Spies.* 1980. Arbor. 1st. VG/dj. P3. $20.00

SHERMAN, Dan. *Man Who Loved Mata Hari.* 1985. DIF. 1st. VG/dj. P3. $18.00

SHERMAN, Dan. *White Mandarin.* 1982. Arbor. 1st. VG/dj. P3. $20.00

SHERMAN, Eleazer. *Narrative of..., Giving an Account of His Life...* 1828. Providence, RI. Prt for Author. 1st. 16mo. old calf. M1. $200.00

SHERMAN, Fanny Jessop. *Admiral Wags.* 1944. Dodd Mead. sgn. ils Paul Brown. G. O3. $25.00

SHERMAN, Harold M. *Winning Point.* 1936. Saalfield. 1st. G+. P8. $12.50

SHERMAN, S.M. *History of the 133rd Regiment, OVI.* 1896. Columbus. 163p. G. B18. $135.00

SHERMAN, Steve. *Maple Sugar Murders.* 1987. Walker. 1st. VG/dj. P3. $12.00

SHERMAN, William C. *Air Warfare.* 1926. NY. 307p. VG. B18. $65.00

SHERMAN, William Tecumseh. *Memoirs of..., by Himself.* 1957. Bloomington, IN. IU. rpt. 2 vol in 1. NF/VG. M8. $65.00

SHERRINGTON, Charles. *Integrative Action of the Nervous System.* 1906. London. Constable. 1st/Eng issue. 411p. gilt ruled bl cloth. G1. $750.00

SHERROD, Robert. *History of Marine Corps Aviation in World War II.* 1952. WA, DC. 1st. maps/unit sketches/index. 496p. VG. S16. $40.00

SHERROD, Robert. *Tarawa: Story of a Battle.* 1944. NY. map/casualty list. 164p. VG. S16. $18.50

SHERWOOD, Martin. *Maxell's Demon.* 1976. NEL. 1st. F/dj. P3. $15.00

SHERWOOD, Martin. *Survival.* 1975. NEL. 1st. F/dj. P3. $15.00

SHERWOOD, Mrs. *Master Henry's Lesson.* nd (1850s). Troy, NY. Merriam & Moore. 12mo. 24p. 20 woodcuts. VG. T10. $50.00

SHERZER, Joel. *Kuna Way of Speaking.* 1990. Austin. 1st wrp ed. 260p. F3. $15.00

SHETTERLY, Will. *Elsewhere.* 1991. HBJ. 1st. F/dj. P3. $17.00

SHEW, Joel. *Children: Their Hydropathic Management in Health...* 1852. NY. Fowlers Wells. 1st. 8vo. 432p. cloth. F. M1. $200.00

SHEW, Spencer. *Second Companion to Murder.* 1961. Knopf. 1st. VG. P3. $25.00

SHEWAN, Andrew. *Great Days of Sail.* 1927. Boston/London. ils. 240p. T7. $50.00

SHEWEY, Don. *Caught in the Act: NY Actors Face to Face.* 1986. NY. 1st. 304p. xl. F/dj. A17. $17.50

SHIEL, M.P. *Purple Cloud.* 1946. World. NF/dj. P3. $30.00

SHIEL, M.P. *Xelucha.* 1975. Arkham. 1st. 1/4283. F/dj. P3. $25.00

SHIELD, G.O. *Cruisings in the Cascades.* 1889. Chicago. 1st. photos/ads. 339p. VG. B18. $275.00

SHIELDS, Carol. *Orange Fish.* 1990. Viking. 1st Am. F/F. R13. $35.00

SHIELDS, Carol. *Republic of Love.* 1992. Random. 1st Canadian/true 1st. sgn. author's 10th book. F/F. D10. $50.00

SHIELDS, Carol. *Stone Diaries.* 1994. Viking. 1st. F/F. B2. $85.00

SHIELDS, David. *Dead Languages.* 1989. Knopf. 1st. sgn. NF/dj. R13. $35.00

SHIELDS, G.O. *Battle of the Big Hole, a History of General Gibbon...* 1889. Rand McNally. 1st. photos. 120p. VG. J2. $425.00

SHIMA. *Japanese Children's Books at Library of Congress..1946-85.* 1987. 4to. 304 annotated entries. F/wrp. A4. $35.00

SHIMER, J.A. *This Changing Earth: An Intro to Geology.* 1968. Harper Row. 1st. 233p. F/dj. D8. $12.00

SHINER, Lewis. *Deserted Cities of the Heart.* 1988. Doubleday. 1st. F/dj. M2. $25.00

SHINER, Lewis. *Slam.* 1990. Doubleday. 1st. NF/NF. M22. $30.00

SHINN, Everett. *Christmas in Dickens.* 1941. NY. Garden City. 1st. 8vo. pict brd. dj. R5. $65.00

SHIPPEN, Katherine. *New Found World.* 1945. Viking/Jr Literary Guild. 1st thus. lg 8vo. 262p. VG/G. T5. $35.00

SHIPPEY, Lee. *Folks Ushud Know.* 1930. Sierra Madre, CA. 1st. sgn. ils AL Ewing. VG. O4. $20.00

SHIPPEY, Lee. *It's an Old California Custom.* 1948. Vanguard. 2nd. inscr. VG. O4. $15.00

SHIRAKAWA, Yoshikazu. *Himalayas. Photos & Text by Yoshikazu Shirakawa.* 1971. NY. Abrams. folio. pl/fld panoramas/fld map. dj/fld case. B24. $250.00

SHIRAS, George. *Hunting Wild Life With Camera & Flashlight.* 1936. NGS. 2nd. 950 photos. 450p. VG. S15. $30.00

SHIRCLIFE, Arnold. *Edgewater Beach Hotel Salad Book.* 1929 (1926). Hotel Monthly. 4th. 306p. B10. $20.00

SHIRLEY, Dame. *Shirley Letters From California Mines 1851-52.* 1922. SF. TC Russell. 1st thus. 8 hand-colored pl. 352p. F/dj. K7. $495.00

SHIRLEY, Orville. *Americans: Story of the 442nd Combat Team.* 1946. WA, DC. 1st. photos/map/roster. 151p. VG. S16. $95.00

SHIRLEY, Rodney W. *Early Printed Maps of the British Isles.* 1980. London. Holland. revised. ils. 188p. NF/dj. K3. $60.00

SHIVERS, Louise. *Here to Get My Baby Out of Jail.* 1983. Random. 1st. F/dj. R13. $50.00

SHOBIN, David. *Seeding.* 1982. Linden. 1st. F/dj. P3. $18.00

SHOCKLEY, Ann Allen. *Afro-American Women Writers 1746-1933: An Anthology...* 1988. Boston. Hall. 1st. pres sgn/dtd 1989. 465p. NF/dj. M8. $45.00

SHOEMAKER, Bill. *Shoemaker: America's Greatest Jockey.* 1988. Doubleday. 1st. photos. F/VG+. P8. $20.00

SHOHET, D. *Jewish Court in the Middle Ages, Studies...* 1931. 1st. G+. E6. $18.00

SHORT, Bobby. *Black & White Baby.* 1971. Dodd Mead. 1st. 304p. F/NF. B4. $45.00

SHORT, Christopher. *Blue-Eyed Boy.* 1966. Dodd Mead. 1st. VG/dj. P3. $20.00

SHORT, Luke. *Saddle by Starlight.* 1952. Houghton Mifflin. 1st. NF/dj. P3. $35.00

SHORT, Philip. *Dragon & the Bear.* 1982. Morrow. 1st. 519p. F/F. W2. $45.00

SHOUMATOFF, Alex. *Rivers Amazon.* 1978. Sierra Club. 1st. 258p. dj. F3. $20.00

SHOUP, D. *Marines in China 1927-28.* 1987. Archon. 1st. F/F. E6. $15.00

SHRIBER, Ione Sandberg. *Never Say Die.* 1950. Rhinehart. 1st. VG/dj. P3. $25.00

SHRINER, Charles. *Wit, Wisdom & Foibles of the Great.* 1918. Funk Wagnalls. 1st. sm 4to. 689p. VG. H1. $12.00

SHROCK, R.R. *Sequence in Layered Rocks: A Study of Features...* 1948. McGraw Hill. 1st. 507p. NF. D8. $30.00

SHROCK & TWENHOFEL. *Principles of Invertebrate Paleontology.* 1953. NY. McGraw Hill. 2nd. ils/figures. 816p. G. D8. $37.00

SHRROR, R. *History of Marine Corps Aviation in WWII.* 1952. WA. 1st. VG/G. B5. $25.00

SHUCK, Oscar T. *California Scrap-Book: A Repository of Useful Information...* 1869. SF. Bancroft. 1st. sheep/gilt blk label. M24. $350.00

SHUCK, Oscar T. *History of the Bench & Bar of California.* 1901. LA. Commercial Prt House. ils. 1152p. cloth. D11. $75.00

SHULEVITZ, Uri. *Oh What a Noise.* nd (1971). Macmillan. 1st. sm 4to. unp. G+. C14. $10.00

SHULEVITZ, Uri. *Toodlecreek Post Office.* 1990. FSG. 1st. 4to. unp. F/G+. C14. $14.00

SHULL, A.F. *Principles of Animal Biology.* 1946. McGraw Hill. 6th. 425p. B1. $35.00

SHULMAN, Albert M. *Gateway to Judaism: Encyclopedia Home Reference.* 1971. Yoseloff. 1056p. VG/G+. S3. $52.00

SHULMAN, Irving. *Velvet Knife.* 1959. Doubleday. 1st. VG/dj. M25. $25.00

SHULMAN, Max. *I Was a Teen-Age Dwarf.* 1959. Bernard Geis. 1st. VG/dj. M25. $75.00

SHUMATE, Albert. *San Francisco Scandal: California of George Gordon.* 1994. CA Hist Soc. 1st. photos/maps. as new. J2. $45.00

SHURA, Mary Francis. *In the Valley of the Frost Giants.* 1971. Lee Shepard. 1st. 48p. NF. C14. $17.00

SHURLY, E. *Cacti.* 1962 (1959). London. 2nd. 160p. F/dj. B26. $17.50

SHURTLEFF, Malcolm. *How to Control Plant Diseases in Home & Garden.* 1962. Ames, IA. 520p. dj. A10. $20.00

SHUSTER & SIEGEL. *Superman Archives Vol 1.* 1989. DC Archive Eds. 1st. F/dj. P3. $40.00

SHUTE, Henry A. *Brite & Fair.* 1968. Noone House. 1st thus. ils Tasha Tudor. 286p. VG/dj. M20. $75.00

SHUTE, Nevil. *Chequer Board.* 1947. McClelland Stewart. 1st. VG/G. P3. $25.00

SHUTE, Nevil. *In the Wet.* 1953. NY. 1st. VG/VG. B5. $40.00

SHUTE, Nevil. *Old Captivity.* 1940. Literary Guild. VG/dj. P3. $30.00

SHUTE, Nevil. *Ordeal.* 1939. Morrow. 1st. VG/dj. P3. $40.00

SHUTE, Nevil. *Pastoral.* 1944. Morrow. VG/dj. P3. $18.00

SHUTE, Nevil. *Rainbow & the Rose.* 1958. Morrow. VG/dj. P3. $35.00

SHUTTLESWORTH & WILLIAMS. *Moon: Steppingstone to Outer Space.* 1977. Doubleday. 8vo. 117p. xl. dj. K5. $15.00

SHWARTZ, Susan. *Grail of Hearts.* 1992. Tor. 1st. F/dj. P3. $22.00

SIA, Mary Li. *Chinese Chopsticks.* nd. Peking. Peking Internat Women's CLub. 2nd. G/dj. A16. $25.00

SIAS, Beverlee. *Skier's Cookbook.* 1971. NY. AS Barnes. G/dj. A16. $10.00

SIBLEY, Celestine. *Christmas in Georgia.* 1964. NY. Doubleday. 1st. sgn. F/VG. B11. $40.00

SIDDIQI, Mazheruddin. *Islamic State: Political Writings of Maulana Sayyid...* 1986. Karachi. Islamic Research Academy. 1st. 8vo. 82p. xl. VG. W1. $12.00

SIDDONS, Anne Rivers. *Fox's Earth.* 1981. S&S. 1st. VG/dj. P3. $20.00

SIDDONS, Anne Rivers. *Heartbreak Hotel.* 1976. S&S. 1st. author's 2nd book. F/F. H11. $85.00

SIDDONS, Anne Rivers. *King's Oak.* 1990. Harper Collins. 1st. F/F. H11. $20.00

SIDDONS, Henry. *Practical Ils of Rhetorical Gesture & Action.* 1968. Blom. facsimile 1822 London. 408p. 12mo. F. A17. $20.00

SIDEN, Harry. *Hockey Showdown.* 1972. Canada. Doubleday. 1st. F/VG. P8. $25.00

SIDGWICK, J.B. *Observational Astronomy for Amateurs.* 1982. Hillside, NJ. Enslow. 4th. 348p. VG/VG. K5. $20.00

SIDIS, Boris. *Psychopathological Researches: Studies...* 1802. NY. GE Stechert. tall 8vo. 10 fld pl. 330p. beveled ochre buckram. NF. G1. $175.00

SIDNEY, Margaret. *Five Little Peppers & How They Grew.* 1951. Whitman. ils Roberta Paflin. VG/dj. P3. $15.00

SIDNEY, Sage. *Stand-Ups: Adventures of Alice in Wonderland.* 1939. Saalfield. popups. unp. VG/pict wrp. M20. $60.00

SIEGBAHN, Manne. *Spectroscopy of X-Rays.* 1925. Oxford. 1st Eng text. 8vo. 287p. xl. K3. $30.00

SIEMENS, Georg. *History of the House of Siemens.* 1957. Freiburg. 1st. 2 vol. A13. $65.00

SIENKIEWICZ, Henryk. *Quo Vadis, a Narrative of the Time of Nero.* 1897. Boston. Little Brn. 2 vol. ils Howard Pyle. teg. djs. B24. $125.00

SIENKIEWICZ, Henryk. *Quo Vadis?* 1959. LEC. 1st thus. 1/1500. ils/sgn Salvatore Fiume. F/dj/case. Q1. $175.00

SIKORSKI, Helena. *Dark Side of the Moon.* 1946. London. Faber. 1st. gilt bl cloth. faded dj. M24. $35.00

SILK, J. Frederick. *Manual of Nitrous Oxide Anaesthesia.* 1888. London. 1st. 120p. A13. $150.00

SILK, Joseph. *Big Bang.* 1989. NY. Freeman. 1st thus. ils. 485p. VG/dj. K3. $20.00

SILKO, Leslie Marmon. *Almanac of the Dead.* 1991. S&S. 1st. F/dj. A24. $35.00

SILLER, Van. *Lonely Breeze.* 1965. Crime Club. 1st. VG/dj. P3. $20.00

SILLTOE, Alan. *Storyteller.* 1979. S&S. 1st. F/F. B3. $20.00

SILVA, Joseph; see Goulart, Ron.

SILVER, Eric. *Book of the Just: Unsung Heroes Who Rescued Jews...* 1992. Grove. biblio/index. 175p. VG+/VG+. S3. $28.00

SILVERBERG, Robert. *Book of the Skulls.* 1972. Scribner. 1st. F/F. M2. $25.00

SILVERBERG, Robert. *Calibrated Alligator.* 1969. HRW. 1st. NF/dj. P3. $25.00

SILVERBERG, Robert. *Conglomeroid Cocktail Party.* 1984. Arbor. 1st. F/dj. P3. $15.00

SILVERBERG, Robert. *Galactic Dreamers.* 1977. Random. 1st. NF/dj. P3. $15.00

SILVERBERG, Robert. *Gate of Worlds.* 1978. Gollancz. F/dj. P3. $20.00

SILVERBERG, Robert. *Infinite Jests.* 1974. Chilton. 1st. F/dj. P3. $18.00

SILVERBERG, Robert. *Lord Valentine's Castle.* 1979. Harper. 1st. sgn. F/dj. M2. $45.00

SILVERBERG, Robert. *Lost Race of Mars.* 1960. Winston. 1st. VG/dj. M2. $30.00

SILVERBERG, Robert. *New Dimensions 6.* 1976. Harper Row. 1st. F/dj. P3. $20.00

SILVERBERG, Robert. *Project Pendulum.* 1987. Walker. 1st. sgn. F/dj. P3. $25.00

SILVERBERG, Robert. *Recalled to Life.* 1977. Doubleday. 2nd? sgn. F/dj. P3. $35.00

SILVERBERG, Robert. *Robert Silverberg's Worlds of Wonder.* 1987. Warner. 1st. NF/dj. P3. $20.00

SILVERBERG, Robert. *Star of Gypsies.* 1986. DIF. 1st. F/dj. P3. $20.00

SILVERBERG, Robert. *Thebes of the Hundred Gates.* 1991. Axolotl. sgn. F/dj. P3. $40.00

SILVERBERG, Robert. *Thorns.* 1969. Rapp Whiting. 1st. VG/dj. P3. $20.00

SILVERBERG, Robert. *Time Hoppers.* 1967. Doubleday. 1st. NF/dj. P3. $50.00

SILVERBERG, Robert. *Tom O'Bedlam.* 1985. DIF. 1st. F/F. N4. $25.00

SILVERBERG, Robert. *Treasure Beneath the Sea.* 1960. Whitman. 1st. F. P3. $30.00

SILVERBERG, Robert. *World Inside.* 1971. Doubleday. 1st. NF/NF. M23. $30.00

SILVERBERG, Robert. *15 Battles That Changed the World.* 1963. Putnam. 1st. inscr. VG/dj. M2. $75.00

SILVERMAN, Kenneth. *Edgar A Poe: Mournful & Never-Ending Romance.* 1991. NY. 1st. 564p. dj. A17. $15.00

SIMAK, Clifford D. *City.* nd. SFBC. Nf/dj. M2. $20.00

SIMAK, Clifford D. *Cosmic Engineers.* 1950. Gnome. 1st. VG/dj. P3. $125.00

SIMAK, Clifford D. *Fellowship of the Talisman.* 1978. Del Rey. 1st. F/dj. P3. $20.00

SIMAK, Clifford D. *Mastodonia.* 1978. Del Rey. 1st. F/dj. P3. $20.00

SIMAK, Clifford D. *Project Pope.* 1981. Del Rey. 1st. F/dj. P3. $20.00

SIMAK, Clifford D. *Skirmish.* 1977. Berkley Putnam. 1st. F/dj. P3. $25.00

SIMAK, Clifford D. *Strangers in the Universe.* 1956. S&S. 1st. VG/dj. M2. $25.00

SIMAK, Clifford D. *Time & Again.* 1951. S&S. 1st. NF/dj. P3. $90.00

SIMAK, Clifford D. *Visitors.* 1980. Del Rey. 1st. F/NF. M23. $35.00

SIMAK, Clifford D. *Visitors.* 1980. Del Rey. 1st. VG/dj. P3. $20.00

SIMAK, Clifford D. *Where the Evil Dwells.* 1982. Del Rey. 1st. F/dj. P3. $20.00

SIMAK, Clifford D. *Wonder & Glory.* 1969. St Martin. VG/dj. P3. $35.00

SIMENON, Georges. *Blind Alley.* 1946. Reynal Hitchcock. 1st Am. VG/dj. Q1. $75.00

SIMENON, Georges. *Glass Cage.* 1973. Harcourt. 1st Am. F/F. M22. $15.00

SIMENON, Georges. *Grandmother.* 1964. HBJ. 1st. VG/dj. P3. $18.00

SIMENON, Georges. *In Case of Emergency.* 1959. Dell. MTI. 11 photos. VG. C9. $25.00

SIMENON, Georges. *Innocents.* 1973. HBJ. 1st. VG/dj. P3. $20.00

SIMENON, Georges. *Magician & the Widow: Two Novels.* 1955. Doubleday. 1st. VG/dj. P3. $30.00

SIMENON, Georges. *Maigret & the Black Sheep.* 1976. Hamish Hamilton. 1st. VG/dj. P3. $18.00

SIMENON, Georges. *Maigret & the Informer.* 1973. HBJ. 1st. VG/dj. P3. $20.00

SIMENON, Georges. *Maigret & the Nabour Case.* 1982. HBJ. 1st. VG/dj. P3. $15.00

SIMENON, Georges. *Maigret Abroad.* 1940. Routledge. 1st. VG. P3. $35.00

SIMENON, Georges. *Man Who Watched the Train Go By.* 1942. London. Routledge. 1st Eng. VG/dj. M15. $100.00

SIMENON, Georges. *Monsieur Monde Vanishes.* 1977. HBJ. 1st. VG/dj. P3. $20.00

SIMENON, Georges. *Move.* 1968. NY. HBW. 1st Am. F/F. T12. $100.00

SIMENON, Georges. *Rich Man.* 1971. HBJ. 1st. VG/VG. P3. $20.00

SIMENON, Georges. *Strangers in the House.* 1954. Doubleday. 1st. VG/dj. P3. $35.00

SIMENON, Georges. *When I Was Old.* 1971. HBJ. 1st. NF/dj. P3. $25.00

SIMMONDS, A. *Horticultural Who Was Who.* 1948. London. inscr. 80p. VG. A10. $40.00

SIMMONDS, N.W. *Evolution of Crop Plants.* 1976. London. ils/maps. VG+. B26. $32.50

SIMMONS, Andre. *Arab Foreign Aid.* 1981. E Brunswick, NY. Assoc U Pr. 1st. 8vo. 196p. G/dj. W1. $10.00

SIMMONS, Dan. *Carrion Comfort.* 1989. Dark Harvest. 1st. NF/NF. M19. $65.00

SIMMONS, Dan. *Hollow Man.* 1992. Bantam. 1st. F/dj. P3. $20.00

SIMMONS, Dan. *Summer of Night.* 1991. Putnam. 1st. F/F. M23. $40.00

SIMMONS, Diane. *Let the Bastards Freeze in the Dark.* 1980. Wyndham. 1st. VG/dj. P3. $15.00

SIMMONS, Geoffrey. *Adam Experiment.* 1978. Arbor. 1st. F/dj. P3. $15.00

SIMMONS, Matty. *Best of the Diners' Club Magazine.* 1962. Regents American. VG/dj. P3. $20.00

SIMO, Melanie L. *Loudon & the Landscape.* 1988. New Haven. 337p. dj. A10. $30.00

SIMON, Andre L. *Noble Grapes & the Great Wines of France.* 1957. McGraw Hill VG/dj. A16. $20.00

SIMON, Carly. *Fisherman's Song.* 1991. Doubleday. 1st. ils Margot Datz. F/F. B3. $30.00

SIMON, Leonard. *Irving Solution.* 1977. Arbor. 1st. F/dj. P3. $15.00

SIMON, Merrill. *God, Allah & the Great Land Grab: Middle East in Turmoil.* 1989. Jonathan David. biblio/index. 385p. VG. S3. $24.00

SIMON, Merrill. *Jerry Falwell & the Jews.* 1984. Jonathan David. 172p. VG/dj. S3. $22.00

SIMON, Paul. *At the Zoo.* 1991. NY. Doubleday. 1st. unp. NF/NF. C14. $17.00

SIMON, Philip J. *Log of the Mayflower.* 1957. Chicago. Priam. 208p. T7. $18.00

SIMON, Roger L. *California Roll.* 1985. Villard. 1st. F/dj. P3. $18.00

SIMON, Roger L. *Mama Tass Manifesto.* 1970. HRW. 1st. VG/dj. P3. $30.00

SIMON, Roger L. *Raising the Dead.* 1988. Villard. 1st. F/dj. p3. $16.00

SIMON, S.J. *Cut for Partners.* 1956. London. rpt. 128p. VG. S1. $20.00

SIMON & SIMON. *Tumblers With a Past.* 1967. np. self pub. 32 mc pl. sbdg. w/price guide. F. H1. $35.00

SIMONS, Arthur. *All About Greenhouses.* 1960. London. Garden BC. 231p. VG/dj. A10. $25.00

SIMPSON, A.W.B. *Biographical Dictionary of the Common Law.* 1984. London. Butterworths. M11. $75.00

SIMPSON, A.W.B. *Legal Theory & Legal History, Essays on Common Law.* 1987. London. Hambledon. M11. $45.00

SIMPSON, Bruce L. *Development of Metal Castings Industry.* 1948. Chicago. Am Foundry-man's Assoc. 246p. VG/torn. K3. $25.00

SIMPSON, C.T. *In Lower Florida Wilds: A Naturalist's Observations...* 1920. NY. Putnam. ils/photos/2 fld maps. 404p. pict cloth. VG. M12. $37.50

SIMPSON, Dorothy. *Suspicious Death.* 1988. Michael Joseph. 1st. VG/dj. P3. $20.00

SIMPSON, Dorothy. *Wake the Dead.* 1992. Scribner. 1st. F/F. P3. $20.00

SIMPSON, George. *Narrative of a Voyage to California Ports in 1841-42.* 1930. SF. TC Russell. facimile fld map. 232p. quarter red/navy bdg. as new. K7. $295.00

SIMPSON, George. *Narrative of a Voyage to California Ports in 1841-42.* 1988. Fairfield. Ye Galleon. rpt. 1/271p. ils/map. 270p. P4. $40.00

SIMPSON, George. *Splendid Isolation: Curious History of S Am Mammals.* 1980. New Haven. 266p. dj. A10. $25.00

SIMPSON, J. *Wild Rabbit in a New Aspect; or, Rabbit Warrens...* 1908 (1895). VG. E6. $25.00

SIMPSON, John M. *Osier Culture.* 1989. WA, DC. USDA Forestry Bulletin 19. 27p. wrp. B26. $12.50

SIMPSON, Lesley. *Enomienda in New Spain.* 1982. Berkeley. rpt. 263p. F3. $25.00

SIMPSON, Louis. *Riverside Drive.* 1962. Atheneum. 1st. sgn. assn copy. F/dj. V1. $65.00

SIMPSON, Margaret. *Sorry, Wrong Number.* 1973. Andre Deutsch. 1st. F/dj. P3. $22.00

SIMPSON, Mona. *Anywhere But Here.* 1987. Knopf. 1st. author's 1st book. F/F. H11. $75.00

SIMPSON, Mona. *Anywhere But Here.* 1987. Knopf. 1st. author's 1st book. VG/VG. L1. $50.00

SIMPSON, Mona. *Lost Father.* 1992. 1st. author's 2nd book. F/dj. A15/A24/B3. $30.00

SIMPSON, O.J. *OJ: The Education of a Rich Rookie.* 1970. Macmillan. 1st. photos. F/F. B4. $100.00

SIMS, George R. *Nelle's Prayer.* ca 1890. London. Raphael Tuck. ils J Willis Grey. pict brd. NF. T10. $65.00

SIMS, George. *End of the Web.* 1976. Gollancz. 1st. NF/dj. P3. $25.00

SINCLAIR, Andrew. *Project.* 1960. S&S. 1st. F/dj. P3. $10.00

SINCLAIR, Andrew. *Under Milk Wood.* 1972. S&S. 1st Am from Eng sheets. VG/wrp. B4. $75.00

SINCLAIR, Angus. *Development of the Locomotive Engine.* 1970. Cambridge. rpt 1907. ils. VG. B18. $25.00

SINCLAIR, Isabella. *Indigenous Flowers of the Hawaiian Islands.* 1885. London. Sampson Low. folio. 44p+44 chromolitho pl. aeg. gilt olive cloth. A22. $575.00

SINCLAIR, John L. *Death in the Claimshack.* 1947. Denver. Sage Books. 1st. Ils Harold West. F/F. B4. $100.00

SINCLAIR, Mary. *Intercessor & Other Stories.* 1932. Macmillan. 1st. VG. M2. $35.00

SINCLAIR, Michael. *Dollar Covenant.* 1973. Gollancz. 1st. VG/fair. P3. $20.00

SINCLAIR, Sally. *Muted Murder.* 1953. Arcadia. 1st. VG/dj. P3. $20.00

SINCLAIR, Upton. *American Outpost: A Book of Reminiscences.* 1932. Upton Sinclair. 1st. G. V4. $20.00

SINCLAIR, Upton. *Another Pamela.* 1950. Viking. 1st. NF/VG. M19. $25.00

SINCLAIR, Upton. *Another Pamela.* 1950. Viking. 1st. VG. P3. $10.00

SINCLAIR, Upton. *Brass Check.* nd. np. self pub. 1st. G. V4. $20.00

SINCLAIR, Upton. *Dragon Harvest.* 1945. Viking. 1st. VG. M2. $10.00

SINCLAIR, Upton. *Flivver King.* 1969. Phaedra. new ed. F/NF. B2. $35.00

SINCLAIR, Upton. *Goslings: A Study of American Schools.* 1924. Pasadena. self pub. 1st. F/fair. M23. $30.00

SINCLAIR, Upton. *Goslings: A Study of American Schools.* 1924. self pub. 1st. VG. V4. $15.00

SINCLAIR, Upton. *Jungle.* 1906. Jungle Pub. 2nd. G. V4. $20.00

SINCLAIR, Upton. *Little Steel.* 1938. NY. 1st. F/NF. B4. $125.00

SINCLAIR, Upton. *Our Lady.* 1938. Rodale. 1st. VG. M2. $25.00

SINCLAIR, Upton. *World to Win.* 1946. Viking. 1st. F/VG. M19. $25.00

SINCLAIR, Upton. *100%: The Story of a Patriot.* 1920. self pub. 1st. VG. V4. $15.00

SINCLAIR, William A. *Aftermath of Slavery.* 1905. Boston. Sm Maynard. 1st. 358p. NF. B4. $300.00

SINGER, Bant. *Don't Slip, Delaney.* 1954. Collins. 1st. VG/dj. P3. $25.00

SINGER, Charles. *From Magic to Science.* 1928. London. Ernest Benn. 1st. ils. xl. K3. $50.00

SINGER, Charles. *Short History of Scientific Ideas to 1900.* 1959. NY/London. 1st. ils. 8vo. 525p. VG/dj. K3. $30.00

SINGER, Howard. *Wake Me When It's Over.* 1959. Putnam. 1st. F/VG clip. B4. $125.00

SINGER, Isaac Bashevis. *Crown of Feathers.* 1973. FSG. 1st. 342p. F/VG. H1. $30.00

SINGER, Isaac Bashevis. *Death of Methuselah.* 1988. Franklin Lib. 1st/ltd. sgn for members. aeg. full leather. F. Q1. $100.00

SINGER, Isaac Bashevis. *Family Moskat.* 1950. NY. Knopf. 1st. F/dj. Q1. $40.00

SINGER, Isaac Bashevis. *Gifts.* 1985. Jewish Pub Soc. 1st. F/case. B35. $85.00

SINGER, Isaac Bashevis. *King of the Fields.* 1988. FSG. 1st. F/F. T12. $15.00

SINGER, Isaac Bashevis. *Naftali the Storyteller & His Horse, Sus.* 1976. FSG. 1st. ils Margot Zemach. 1st. 129p. NF/VG. P2. $35.00

SINGER, Isaac Bashevis. *Old Love.* 1979. Farrar. 1st. inscr. F/F. B2. $125.00

SINGER, Isaac Bashevis. *Penitent.* 1983. FSG. 1st. F/F. B35. $18.00

SINGER, Isaac Bashevis. *Power of Light, Eight Stories for Hanukkah.* 1983 (1980). London. Robson. ils Lieblich. F/F. C8. $25.00

SINGER, Isaac Bashevis. *Scum.* 1991. FSG. 1st. F/F. B4. $45.00

SINGER, Isaac Bashevis. *When Shlemiel Went to Warsaw.* 1968. FSG. 1st. ils Margot Zemach. beige cloth. NF/NF. D1. $50.00

SINGER, Isaac Bashevis. *Why Noah Chose the Dove.* 1974. FSG. 1st. ils Eric Carle. F/NF. P2. $65.00

SINGER, Isaac Bashevis. *Young Man in Search of Love.* 1978. Doubleday. 1/300. sgn/#d. w/ils Raphael Soyer sgn mc prt. F/F case. B2. $250.00

SINGER, Kurt. *Laughton Story.* 1954. Winston. 1st. VG/dj. P3. $15.00

SINGER, Kurt. *More Spy Stories.* 1955. WH Allen. 1st. VG/dj. P3. $25.00

SINGER, Kurt. *Spy Stories From Asia.* 1955. Winfred Funk. VG. P3. $20.00

SINGER, Kurt. *Tales From the Unknown.* 1970. London. 1st. F/dj. M2. $27.00

SINGER, Loren. *Parallax View.* 1970. Doubleday. 1st. rem mk. F/F. B4. $100.00

SINGER, Shelley. *Spit in the Ocean.* 1987. St Martin. 1st. VG/dj. P3. $15.00

SINGERMAN, Philip. *Red Adair: An American Hero.* 1989. London. Bloomsbury. 1st. sgn. VG/VG. A23. $40.00

SINKANKAS, J. *Gem Cutting: A Lapidary's Manual.* 1960. 4th prt. VG/clip. D8. $15.00

SINYARD, Neil. *Directors: The All-Time Greats.* 1985. Gallery Books. 1st. VG/dj. P3. $12.00

SIODMAK, Curt. *City in the Sky.* 1975. Barrie Jenkins. 1st. F/dj. P3. $18.00

SIODMAK, Curt. *Donovan's Brain.* 1944. Triangle. 1st. VG/dj. P3. $20.00

SIODMAK, Curt. *Third Ear.* 1971. Putnam. 1st. NF/dj. P3. $18.00

SIPLE, Paul. *90 (degrees) South: Story of American South Pole Conquest.* 1959. Putnam. 8vo. 384p. VG/dj. P4. $60.00

SIRAGUSA, Charles. *Trail of the Poppy.* 1966. Prentice Hall. 1st. inscr. F/NF. B2. $35.00

SIRINGO, Charles A. *Texas Cowboy.* 1886. Rand McNally. 3rd (from sheets of 2nd). complete. poor. M24. $250.00

SISKIND, Aaron. *Photographs.* 1959. Horizon. intro Harold Rosenberg. 108p. cloth. dj. D11. $150.00

SISKIND, Patrick. *Perfume: The Story of a Murder.* 1986. Knopf. 1st Am. F/F. B4. $75.00

SISLEY, Nick. *Deer Hunting Across North America.* 1975. Freshet. 281p. lg 8vo. VG. A17. $18.50

SISON & WERNING. *Philippine Revolution.* 1989. NY. Crane Russak. 1st. 241p. M. P1. $15.00

SITCHIN, Zecharia. *Lost Realms.* 1990. Santa Fe. Bear. 1st. 298p. dj. F3. $10.00

SITGREAVES, L. *Report of Expedition Down the Zuni & Colorado River 1851.* 1962. Chicago. facsimile 1853 Washington. 198p. VG+. F7. $65.00

SITWELL, Edith. *Canticle of the Rose: Poems 1917-1949.* 1949. Vanguard. 1st. F/F. B4. $65.00

SITWELL, Edith. *I Live Under a Black Sun.* 1938. 1st. F/NF. M19. $45.00

SITWELL, Sacheverell. *Fine Bird Books 1700-1900.* 1990. NY. Atlantic Monthly. 1st. 180p. F/dj. A17/S15. $37.50

SITWELL, Sacheverell. *Great Flower Books 1700-1900.* 1990. NY. 1st. 189p. F/dj. A17. $35.00

SJOWALI & WAHLOO. *Fire Engine That Disappeared.* 1970. Pantheon. 1st Am. F/clip. M15. $45.00

SJOWALL & WAHLOO. *Abominable Man.* nd. BC. VG/dj. P3. $8.00

SJOWALL & WAHLOO. *Laughing Policeman.* 1970. Pantheon. 1st Am. F/clip. D10. $85.00

SJOWALL & WAHLOO. *Man on the Balcony.* 1968. Pantheon. 1st Am. F/NF. M15. $35.00

SJOWALL & WAHLOO. *Terrorists.* 1976. Pantheon. 1st. VG/dj. P3. $23.00

SKAF, Robert. *Story of the Planet Candy.* 1990. Vantage. 1st. sgn. VG/dj. P3. $15.00

SKAGGS, Jimmy M. *Clipperton: A History of the Island the World Forgot.* 1989. NY. Walker. 8vo. 318p. gilt bdg. VG/dj. P4. $45.00

SKAL, David. *Antibodies.* 1988. Congdon Weed. 1st. F/F. M2. $15.00

SKAL, David. *Hollywood Gothic: Tangled Web of Dracula...* 1990. Norton. 1st. 4to. F/F. B2. $25.00

SKARMETA, Antonio. *Burning Patience.* 1987. Pantheon. 1st Am. F/F. B4. $125.00

SKAZKA. *Ivan Czarevich, the Firebird & Grey Wolf.* 1901. USSR. 1st. ils Ivan Bilibine. F. D1. $600.00

SKINNER, J.S. *Discourse on the Wants of Agriculture.* 1848. Middlesex Agric Soc. 12p. VG/wrp. A10. $25.00

SKINNER, Margaret. *Old Jim Canaan.* 1990. Algonquin. AP. NF/wrp. R13. $15.00

SKIRVING, R. Scot. *Wire Splicing.* 1953. Glasgow. Brn, Son & Ferguson. rpt. ils. half cloth. VG. P4. $20.00

SKLEPOWICH, Edward. *Death in a Serene City.* 1990. Morrow. 1st. F/F. N4. $25.00

SKUES, G.E.M. *Minor Tactics of the Chalk Stream.* 1910. London. Adam/Chas Blk. 1st. 8vo. gilt cloth. NF. T10. $300.00

SLADE, Irene. *Ring of Bells: Poems Selected for Younger Readers.* 1963. Houghton Mifflin. 1st Am. ils Ardizzone. 129p. NF/NF. D4. $45.00

SLADEK, John. *Bugs.* 1989. Macmillan. 1st. F/dj. P3. $28.00

SLADEK, John. *Reproductive System.* 1968. Gollancz. 1st. VG/dj. P3. $65.00

SLADEN, Douglas. *Younger American Poets.* 1891. NY. Cassell. 1st. gilt bl cloth. F/dj. M24. $75.00

SLATER, Leonard. *Aly: A Biography.* 1965. Random BC. 1st. 8vo. 10 pl. 207p. VG/dj. W1. $18.00

SLATER, Nigel. *Falcon.* 1979. Atheneum. 1st. F/dj. P3. $15.00

SLATER, Philip. *How I Saved the World.* 1985. Dutton. 1st. VG/dj. P3. $17.00

SLATZER, Robert F. *Life & Curious Death of Marilyn Monroe.* 1975. WH Allen. VG/dj. P3. $20.00

SLAUSON, H.W. *Everyman's Guide to Motor Efficiency.* 1920. Leslie Judge. 1st ed. 290p. limp leatherette. A17. $30.00

SLAVITT, David R. *Agent.* 1986. Doubleday. 1st. VG/dj. P3. $15.00

SLAVITT, David R. *Cold Comfort.* 1980. Methuen. 1st. VG/VG. P3. $20.00

SLESAR, Henry. *Gray Flannel Shroud.* 1959. Random. author's 1st book. G+/dj. N4. $20.00

SLETTEBAK, Arne. *Stellar Rotation.* 1970. NY. Gordon Breach. sm 4to. 355p. VG/VG. K5. $65.00

SLEVIN, Joseph R. *Log of the Schooner Academy on a Voyage...* 1931. CA Adademy of Sciences. 162p. VG/prt wrp. P4. $75.00

SLILPER, E.J. *Whales.* 1962. Basic Books. trans from Dutch. 473p. VG. S15. $30.00

SLOANE, Eric. *Age of Barns.* nd. Funk Wagnalls. 1st. VG/G. O3. $65.00

SLOANE, Eric. *Age of Barns.* 1976. NY. Natural Hist. 50p. A10. $20.00

SLOANE, Eric. *Mr Daniels & the Grange.* 1968. NY. 1st. sgn. VG/VG. B5. $40.00

SLOANE, Eric. *Museum of Early American Tools.* 1964. NY. 1st. ils. 108p. F/dj. M4. $25.00

SLOANE, Eric. *Return to Taos.* 1960. Wilfred Funk. 1st. NF/1st state. T11. $130.00

SLOANE, William. *Edge of Running Water.* nd. BC. VG/dj. P3. $10.00

SLOANE, William. *Space, Space, Space.* nd. Grosset. VG/dj. M2. $18.00

SLOBODKIN, Louis. *Gogo, the French Sea Gull.* 1960. Macmillan. 1st. lib bdg. VG/dj. T5. $30.00

SLOBODKIN, Louis. *Horse With High-Heeled Shoes.* 1954. Vanguard. 1st. 32p. NF/VG-. P2. $60.00

SLOBODKIN, Louis. *Seaweed Hat.* 1947. Macmillan. 1st. sq 8vo. VG/VG. P2. $60.00

SLOCHOWER, Harry. *No Voice Is Wholly Lost. Writers & Thinkers in War & Peace.* 1946. London. Dobson. 1st. VG/VG. B2. $30.00

SLOCHOWER, Harry. *Thomas Mann's Joseph Story: An Interpretation.* 1938. Knopf. 1st. F/VG. B4. $55.00

SLOMAN, Larry. *Reefer Madness.* 1979. Bobbs Merrill. 1st. VG/dj. p3. $20.00

SLOSSON, Elvenia. *Pioneer American Gardening.* 1951. NY. Coward. 306p. VG/dj. A10. $12.00

SLOTE, Alfred. *Air in Fact & Fancy.* 1968. Cleveland. World. 8vo. 160p. VG/dj. K5. $16.00

SLOVO, Gillian. *Death by Analysis.* 1988. Crime Club. 1st. VG/dj. P3. $15.00

SLUNG, Michele. *I Shudder at Your Touch.* 1991. Roc. 1st. F/dj. P3. $20.00

SMALL, Austin J. *Avenging Ray.* 1930. Crime Club. VG. P3. $30.00

SMALL, Austin J. *Mystery Maker.* 1930. Crime Club. 1st. G. P3. $20.00

SMALL, Austin J. *Pearls of Desire.* nd. Grosset. F/dj. M2. $15.00

SMALL, Austin J. *Vantine Diamonds.* 1930. Crime Club. 1st. G. P3. $20.00

SMALL, John K. *Monograph of the North American Species of Genus Polygonum.* 1895. Lancaster, PA. 85 pl. 183p. new gr buckram. VG. B26. $95.00

SMALLEY, George H. *My Adventures in Arizona.* 1966. Tucson. sgn. 8vo. 154p. gr wrp. F7. $30.00

SMEDLEY, Agnes. *Portraits of Chinese Women in Revolution.* 1976. Old Westbury. Feminist Pr. 1st. ils. VG+. A25. $10.00

SMILEY, Jane. *Age of Grief.* 1987. Knopf. 1st. sgn. F/F. D10. $95.00

SMILEY, Jane. *At Paradise Gate.* 1981. S&S. 1st. F/F. B4. $300.00

SMILEY, Jane. *Catskill Crafts.* 1988. Crown. 1st. F/F. M19. $25.00

SMILEY, Jane. *Catskill Crafts.* 1988. NY. Crown. 1st. sgn. author's 3rd book. F/F. B3. $45.00

SMILEY, Jane. *Duplicate Keys.* 1984. London. Cape. 1st. F/F. T12. $100.00

SMILEY, Jane. *Greenlanders.* 1988. Crown. 1st. F/F. M19. $45.00

SMILEY, Jane. *Moo.* 1995. Knopf. 1st. F/F. H11. $35.00

SMILEY, Jane. *Moo.* 1995. Knopf. 1st. sgn. F/F. A23. $40.00

SMILEY, Jane. *Ordinary Love & Good Will.* 1989. Knopf. 1st. F/F. H11. $50.00

SMILEY, jane. *Thousand Acres.* 1991. Knopf. 1st. NF/dj. R13. $45.00

SMILEY, Jane. *Thousand Acres.* 1991. Knopf. 1st. sgn. F/dj. D10. $125.00

SMISS, W.G. *Gift... for 1837.* (1836). Phil. Carey Hart. 1st. aeg. full brn morocco. M24. $125.00

SMISS, W.G. *Opal.* 1848. NY. JC Riker. 1st. hand-mc pres pl. aeg. gilt full blk morocco. VG. M24. $100.00

SMIT, Mary P. Wells. *Boy Captive of Old Deerfield.* 1929. Little Brn. 1st thus. ils Frank Schoonover. gilt blk cloth. NF. T10. $100.00

SMITH, A.C. *British Dogs.* 1947. London. Collins. 48p. VG/VG. H7. $10.00

SMITH, A.C. *Fijian Plant Studies II: Botanical Results...* 1942. Jamaica Plain. Arnold Arboretum of Harvard. 148p. gray wrp. P4. $65.00

SMITH, Alexander. *Mushroom Hunter's Field Guide.* 1967. Ann Arbor. revised/enlarged. ils. 264p. VG. B26. $15.00

SMITH, Alexander. *Veiled Species of Hebeloma in Western United States.* 1983. Ann Arbor. ils 219p. F. S15. $15.00

SMITH, Alfred E. *Campaign Addresses of Governor Alfred E Smith.* 1929. WA. Democratic Comm. 1st. 322p. cloth. F. B22. $20.00

SMITH, Alice Upham. *Trees in a Winter Landscape.* 1969. NY. Holt. 207p. dj. A10. $20.00

SMITH, Andrew. *Tomato in America.* 1994. Columbia. 224p. dj. A10. $25.00

SMITH, Anthony. *Explorers of the Amazon.* 1990. Viking. 1st. 344p. dj. F3. $20.00

SMITH, Barbara Burnett. *Writers of the Purple Sage.* 1994. St Martin. 1st. sgn. author's 1st book. VG/VG. A23. $45.00

SMITH, Ben. *Design Your Own Yacht.* 1988. London. Coles. ils/31 pl. 204p. dj. T7. $38.00

SMITH, Bernard. *European Vision & the South Pacific.* 1985. London/New Haven. Yale. 2nd. 222 ils. 370p. gilt navy cloth. P4. $85.00

SMITH, Bertha H. *Yosemite Legends.* 1904. SF. Paul Elder. ils. 64p. terra-cotta cloth. F. K7. $150.00

SMITH, Bertha Whitridge. *Only a Dog, Story of the Great War.* (1917). Dutton. 12mo. VG. C8. $17.50

SMITH, C. Fox. *There Was a Ship: Chapters From the History of Sail.* 1930. Hartford. Edwin Valentine Mitchell. ils PW Smith. F/rpr. O7. $45.00

SMITH, C. Ross. *Sinbad the Sailor.* 1972. NY. Good Book/Doubleday. 1st. 4to. ils Alain LeFoll. VG/dj. W1. $15.00

SMITH, C.H. *Ancient Costumes of Great Britain & Ireland...* 1989. London. 85 mc pl. 224p. F/dj. M4. $40.00

SMITH, Carl N. *Inside the Circle of Samuel F & Lulu J Smith Family...* 1977. private prt. 1st. ils. 151p. F/sans. B19. $75.00

SMITH, Charles. *Comprehensive History of Minnehaha County, South Dakota.* 1949. Educator Supply. 504p. VG. J2. $145.00

SMITH, Charlie. *Canaan.* 1984. S&S. 1st. NF/F. B3. $30.00

SMITH, Charlie. *Crystal River.* 1991. NY. Linden. 1st. F/F. B3. $40.00

SMITH, Charlie. *Lives of the Dead.* 1990. S&S. 1st. F/F. H11. $35.00

SMITH, Charlie. *Lives of the Dead.* 1990. S&S. 1st. F/NF. R13. $20.00

SMITH, Clark Ashton. *Strange Shadows.* 1989. Greenwood. 1st. VG/sans. M2. $40.00

SMITH, Cornelius C. *Don't Settle for Second: Life & Times of Cornelius C Smith.* 1977. Presidio. 1st. ils/chronology/bibliography. 229p. F/NF. B19. $25.00

SMITH, Cornelius C. *Emilo Kosterlitsky, Eagle of Sonora & Southwest Border.* 1970. Clark. 1st. 344p. VG. J2. $65.00

SMITH, D.A. *Rocky Mountain Mining Camps: The Urban Frontier.* 1967. IN U. 304p. VG/clip. D8. $30.00

SMITH, D.W. *Silver Spoon Murders.* 1988. Lyle Stuart. 1st. VG/dj. P3. $16.00

SMITH, Dave. *Blue Spruce.* 1981. Tamarack. 1/300. sgn. F/wrp. V1. $35.00

SMITH, Dave. *Gray Soldiers.* 1983. np. Stuart Wright. 1/75. inscr/sgn twice. F/sans. R13. $150.00

SMITH, Dave. *Mean-Rufus-Throw-Down.* 1973. Basilisk. 1/200 (of 600). sgn. VG+/wrp. V1. $35.00

SMITH, David. *Days of His Flesh.* nd. Harper. 549p. VG. B29. $6.50

SMITH, David. *Rara Arithemtica: A Catalogue of Arithmetics...* nd (1908). rpt. 1/100. ils. 532p. F. A4. $95.00

SMITH, Dennis. *Glitter & Ash.* 1980. Dutton. 1st. VG/dj. P3. $13.00

SMITH, Dodie. *Hundred & One Dalmations.* 1956. London. Heinemann. 1st. inscr/dtd 1956. ils Janet/Anne Graham-Johnstone. NF/VG. B4. $2,500.00

SMITH, E. *Official Cookbook of the Hay System.* 1947 (1934). Mt Pocono, PA. G. E6. $18.00

SMITH, E. Boyd. *Early Life of Mr Man.* 1914. Houghton Mifflin. 1st. VG. P2. $185.00

SMITH, E. Boyd. *Railroad Book: Bob & Betty's Summer on the Railroad.* 1913. Houghton Mifflin. 1st. 12 full-p mc pl. obl 4to. cloth/label. R5. $200.00

SMITH, E. Boyd. *Run in the Radio World.* 1923. Stokes. 1st. 12 full-p mc pl/b&w ils. gr cloth/label. R5. $200.00

SMITH, E.E. *Skylark of Space.* 1950. FFF. VG/dj. P3. $100.00

SMITH, E.E. *Skylark of Valeron.* 1949. Fantasy. 1st. 1/500. sgn/#d/inscr also. NF/VG. P3. $175.00

SMITH, E.E. *Skylark Three.* 1975. Garland. F. M2. $20.00

SMITH, E.E. *Spacehounds of Ipc.* 1947. Fantasy. 1st. inscr. NF/G. P3. $125.00

SMITH, E.E. *Subspace Explorers.* 1965. Canaveral. 1st. F/dj. M2/M19. $45.00

SMITH, Edgar Newbold. *American Naval Broadsides.* 1974. Clarkson Potter. 4to. 117 pl. 225p. M/dj. B24. $185.00

SMITH, Edgar W. *Profile by Gaslight: An Irregular Reader...Sherlock Holmes.* 1944. S&S. 1st. sm 8vo. 312p. red brd. G. H1. $45.00

SMITH, Edmund Ware. *One-Eyed Poacher of Privilege.* 1991. Derrydale. 187p. aeg. gilt leather. F. A17. $22.50

SMITH, Elihu Hubbard. *Diary of Elihu Hubbard Smith 1771-1798.* 1973. Phil. Am Philosophical Soc. 481p. B18. $45.00

SMITH, Emma. *Emily.* 1959. McDowell/Obolensky. 1st Am. ils Katherine Wigglesworth. 76p. F/VG+. P2. $50.00

SMITH, Ethan. *Daughters of Zion Excelling. A Sermon Preached to Ladies...* 1814. Concord, NH. George Hough. 1st. 12mo. 23p. VG/wrp. M1. $125.00

SMITH, Ethan. *View of the Hebrews; or, Tribes of Israel in America...* 1825. Smith Shute. 12mo. full contemporary calf. VG. M1. $325.00

SMITH, F.G. *Pulsars.* 1977. Cambridge. 8vo. 239p. VG/dj. K5. $30.00

SMITH, Fay Jackson. *Captain on the Phantom Presidio, a History...* 1993. Clark. 1st. 217p. as new. J2. $55.00

SMITH, Florence Pritchett. *These Entertaining People.* 1966. Macmillan. G/dj. A16. $15.00

SMITH, Francis Henney. *Introductory Lecture Read Before Corps of Cadets...1864.* 1865. Richmond. McFarlane Fergusson. 1st. VG/prt wrp. M8. $650.00

SMITH, Frank A. *Corpse in Handcuffs.* 1969. Macmillan of Canada. 1st. F/dj. P3. $15.00

SMITH, Frank A. *Dragon's Breath.* 1980. Nelson Foster/Scott General. 1st. VG/dj. P3. $18.00

SMITH, G. Geoffrey. *Gas Turbines & Jet Propulsion for Aircraft.* 1944. Aerosphere. 123p. G. A17. $17.50

SMITH, G. Royde. *History of Bradshaw.* 1939. London/Manchester. Henry Blaylock. 4to. ils. VG. K3. $25.00

SMITH, G.M. *History & Government of South Dakota.* 1904. NY/Cincinnati/Chicago. Am Book Co. A19. $15.00

SMITH, Gary. *Windsinger.* 1976. Ballantine. A19. $15.00

SMITH, George O. *Brain Machine.* 1975. Garland. 1st. F/sans. M2. $50.00

SMITH, George O. *Hellflower.* 1953. Abelard-Schuman. 1st. F/NF. P3. $60.00

SMITH, George O. *Nomad.* 1950. Prime. 1st. VG/fair. P3. $20.00

SMITH, George O. *Pattern for Conquest.* 1949. Gnome. 1st. VG/dj. P3. $30.00

SMITH, H. Allen. *Complete Practical Joker.* 1953. Garden City. 1st. VG/VG. B5. $40.00

SMITH, H. Allen. *Desert Island Decameron.* 1945. Doubleday. VG/dj. P3. $20.00

SMITH, H. Allen. *Rhubarb.* 1946. Doubleday. 1st. VG. P3. $15.00

SMITH, H. Maynard. *Inspector Frost in the City.* 1930. Doubleday. 1st. VG. P3. $28.00

SMITH, Harmon. *Nursing in Diseases of the Eye, Ear, Nose & Throat.* 1927. Phil. Saunders. 4th. ils/photos. 335p. VG. A25. $30.00

SMITH, Harris P. *Farm Machinery & Equipment.* 1937. McGraw Hill. 460p. xl. A10. $20.00

SMITH, Harris P. *Farm Machinery & Equipment.* 1948. McGraw Hill. 520p. cloth. A10. $28.00

SMITH, Helen V. *Michigan Wildflowers.* 1966. Cranbrook Inst. Bulletin 42. ils/drawings. 468p. F/dj. S15. $10.00

SMITH, Helena Huntington. *War on Powder River.* 1966. NY/London/Toronto. McGraw Hill. dj. A19. $55.00

SMITH, Hervey Garrett. *Marlinspike Sailor.* 1952. NY. Rudder Pub. 2nd enlarged. 115p. G. A17. $22.50

SMITH, Holland. *Coral & Brass: Howlin' Mad Smith's Own Story...* 1949. NY. 1st. 289p. VG. S16. $40.00

SMITH, Ingrid. *When Grandma Was a Little Girl.* nd. DSP. ils Mela Koehler-Broman. VG. M20. $20.00

SMITH, Jack. *Spend All Your Kisses, Mr Smith.* 1978. McGraw Hill. 1st. 8vo. F/dj. T10. $45.00

SMITH, James H. *History of Duchess County, New York.* 1882. Syracuse. 1st. thick 4to. 562p. VG. C6. $150.00

SMITH, Janet Adam. *Children's Illustrated Books.* 1948. London. ils. NF/VG. A4. $45.00

SMITH, Jeff. *Frugal Gourmet.* 1984. NY. Morrow. sm 4to. VG+/VG. A16. $12.00

SMITH, Jessie Wilcox. *Baby's Red Letter Days.* (1901). Syracuse, NY. Justs Food. 1st. VG/emb stiff wht wrp. D1. $160.00

SMITH, John. *Narrative of Some Sufferings, for His Christian...* 1800. Phil. Johnson. 43p. worn. V3. $85.00

SMITH, Joseph S.J. *Biblical Greek.* 1979. Reeditio. Eng ed from 4th Latin. 185p. VG. B29. $8.00

SMITH, Julie. *Axeman's Jazz.* 1991. St Martin. 1st. F/NF. D10. $35.00

SMITH, Julie. *Axeman's Jazz.* 1991. St Martin. 1st. F/VG. B3. $30.00

SMITH, Julie. *Axeman's Jazz.* 1991. St Martin. 1st. VG/VG. M22. $10.00

SMITH, Julie. *Huckleberry Fiend.* 1987. Mysterious. 1st. F/F. D10. $40.00

SMITH, Julie. *New Orleans Mourning.* 1990. St Martin. 1st. sgn. F/F. M22. $60.00

SMITH, Julie. *Tourist Trap.* 1986. Mysterious. 1st. author's 4th book. NF/F. B3. $35.00

SMITH, Julie. *True-Life Adventure.* 1985. Mysterious. 1st. sgn. F/NF. D10. $65.00

SMITH, Kenneth. *Plant Viruses.* 1974. London. Chapman. 5th. 211p. dj. VG. A10. $18.00

SMITH, L. Neil. *Crystal Empire.* 1986. Tor. 1st. F/dj. P3. $18.00

SMITH, L.A. *Catalogue of Pre-Revival Dulcimers.* 1983. MO U. photos. 128p. F/dj. M4. $40.00

SMITH, Lawrence B. *American Game Preserve Shooting.* 1933. NY. Windward. photos/drawing/200p+ pl. pict cloth. VG. M12. $20.00

SMITH, Lawrence B. *Fur or Feather: Days With Dog & Gun.* 1946. Scribner. 1st Am. sgn. ils/sgn Paul Brown. VG/VG. O3. $95.00

SMITH, Lawrence Dwight. *Mystery of the Yellow Tie.* 1939. Grosset Dunlap. 220p. cloth. VG/dj. M20. $30.00

SMITH, Lee. *Cakewalk.* 1981. Putnam. 1st. F/F. D10. $75.00

SMITH, Lee. *Family Linen.* 1985. Putnam. 1st. F/F. B3. $35.00

SMITH, Lee. *Family Linen.* 1985. Putnam. 1st. sgn. F/clip. R13. $50.00

SMITH, Lee. *Me & My Baby View the Eclipse.* 1990. Putnam. 1st. F/F. A20/B3. $25.00

SMITH, Lee. *Me & My Baby View the Eclipse.* 1990. Putnam. 1st. sgn. F/F. R13. $35.00

SMITH, LeRoi. *We Came in Peace.* 1969. Classic Pr. 4to. 77p. G. K5. $10.00

SMITH, Lucy. *Biographical Sketches of Joseph Smith, the Prophet...* 1853. London. 1st. 16mo. 297p. contemporary bdg. xl. M1. $950.00

SMITH, Mark. *Moon Lamp.* 1976. Knopf. 1st. NF/dj. M2. $15.00

SMITH, Martin Cruz. *Canto for a Gypsy.* 1972. NY. Putnam. 1st. VG/G. L3. $85.00

SMITH, Martin Cruz. *Gorky Park.* 1981. Random. 1st. 356p. F/NF. W2. $30.00

SMITH, Martin Cruz. *Nightwing.* 1977. Andre Deutsch. 1st. NF/dj. P3. $30.00

SMITH, Martin Cruz. *Polar Star.* 1989. Random. 1st trade. sgn. NF/NF. B3. $45.00

SMITH, Martin Cruz. *Stallion Gate.* 1986. 1st. NF/dj. K3. $20.00

SMITH, Martin Cruz. *Stallion Gate.* 1986. Random. 1st. F/F. A20. $25.00

SMITH, Michael L. *Pacific Visions.* 1987. Yale. ils. 243p. F/F. S15. $15.00

SMITH, Mitchell. *Daydreams.* 1987. McGraw Hill. 1st. F/F. H11. $30.00

SMITH, Mitchell. *Daydreams.* 1987. McGraw Hill. 1st. NF/dj. P3. $18.00

SMITH, Mrs. J.G. *Angels & Women.* 1924. AB Abac Co. 1st revised. VG. M2. $27.00

SMITH, Myron. *WWII at Sea: Bibliography of Sources in English.* 1976-1990. Metuchen. 4 vol. VG. S16. $95.00

SMITH, N. Gerard. *Dahlia Cultivation.* ca 1948. NY. ils. 96p. dj. B26. $10.00

SMITH, Nathan. *Case of Ovarian Dropsy, Successfully Removed...* 1822. Phil. 1st. 780p. full leather. A13. $150.00

SMITH, Perry Michael. *Last Rites.* 1971. Scribner. 1st. F/NF. B4. $85.00

SMITH, Peter C. *Design & Construction of Stables & Ancillary Buildings.* 1967. London. Allen. 1st. VG/G. O3. $40.00

SMITH, Philip. *Mineral Resources of Alaska: Report on Progress...* 1936. GPO. 8vo. gilt burgundy cloth. VG. P4. $45.00

SMITH, Philip. *New Directions in Bookbinding.* 1974. London. 1st. VG/VG. T9. $50.00

SMITH, Red. *Best of Red Smith.* 1963. WAtts. 1st. VG.VG. P8. $30.00

SMITH, Richard Gordon. *Ancient Tales & Folklore of Japan.* 1986. Mitchell. F/dj. P3. $25.00

SMITH, Richard K. *Airships Akron & Macon.* 1972. Annapolis. later prt. 228p. VG/torn. B18. $65.00

SMITH, Robert. *Illustrated History of Pro Football.* 1970. Grosset Dunlap. 1st. photos. VG/VG. P8. $8.50

SMITH, Rosamond; see Oates, Joyce Carol.

SMITH, S. Bayliss. *British Waders in Their Haunts.* 1950. London. photos. VG/VG. M17. $25.00

SMITH, Shelley. *Game of Consequences.* 1978. Macmillan. 1st. F/dj. P3. $20.00

SMITH, Steve. *Hunting Upland Gamebirds.* 1987. Stackpole. 176p. M/dj. A17. $17.50

SMITH, Surrey. *Village That Wandered.* 1960. London. 1st. F/dj. M2. $25.00

SMITH, Thorne. *Bishop's Jaegers.* 1933. Doubleday Doran. VG. P3. $12.00

SMITH, Thorne. *Dreams End.* 1927. NY. 1st. VG. B5. $65.00

SMITH, W.D.A. *Under the Influence: History of Nitrous Oxide...* 1982. London. 1st. 188p. dj. A13. $75.00

SMITH, Wallace. *Little Tigress.* 1923. Putnam. 1st. ils. 209p. decor cloth. F3. $15.00

SMITH, Wilbur. *Burning Stove.* 1985. Stoddard. VG/dj. P3. $20.00

SMITH, Wilbur. *Hungry as the Sea.* 1978. Heinemann. 1st. VG/dj. P3. $25.00

SMITH, Wilbur. *Men of Men.* 1981. Heinemann. 1st. VG/dj. P3. $20.00

SMITH, Wilbur. *Rage.* 1987. Little Brn. 1st. VG/dj. P3. $18.00

SMITH, Wilbur. *When the Lion Feeds.* 1964. Viking. 1st. NF/dj. P3. $75.00

SMITH, William Gardner. *Last of the Conquerors.* 1948. Farrar Straus. 1st. gray brd. VG. M25. $75.00

SMITH, William Gardner. *South Street.* 1954. FSY. 1st. NF/dj. M25. $60.00

SMITH, William Gardner. *Stone Face.* 1963. Farrar. 1st. NF/NF. B2. $75.00

SMITH, William Jay. *Army Brat.* 1980. NY. Persea. 1st. F/NF. B4. $45.00

SMITH, William Jay. *Ho for a Hat!* 1989. Little Brn. 1st thus. inscr. sm 4to. unp. VG+. C14. $12.00

SMITH, William. *Diary & Selected Papers of Chief Justice Wm Smith 1784-1794.* 1965. Toronto. Champlain Soc. 1/775. 8vo. 335p. red cloth. unopened. P4. $95.00

SMITH, William. *Pseudoic Majesty.* 1903. Liberty Pub. 1st Am. VG. M2. $27.00

SMITH, Winifred. *Children's Singing Games.* 1894. David Nutt. 1st. lg 8vo. M5. $65.00

SMITH & WEBER. *Field Guide to Southern Mushrooms.* 1985. Ann Arbor. 280p. VG/wrp. B1. $20.00

SMITH & WILCOX. *Farmer's Cyclopedia of Agriculture.* 1922. Orange Judd. 619p. cloth. VG. A10. $25.00

SMITS, Ted. *Game of Soccer.* 1968. Prentice Hall. 1st. photos/stats/index. G+/dj. P8. $15.00

SMOLUCHOWSKI, R. *Solar System.* 1983. Scientific Books. 174p. F/dj. D8. $12.00

SMUCKER, Samuel M. *Life of Col John Charles Fremont & His Narrative...* 1856. Miller Orton Mulligan. G+. M20. $35.00

SMYTH, Henry D. *Atomic Energy for Military Purposes.* 1945. Princeton. 1st commercial. 264p. F/dj. A17. $150.00

SMYTH, W.H. *Sailor's Word-Book.* 1867. London. Blackie. revised. 744p. T7. $110.00

SMYTHE, H. DeWolf. *Atomic Energy for Military Purposes.* 1945. Princeton. 1st hc. VG. E6. $65.00

SNAITH, J.C. *Araminta.* 1923. McLeod. 1st. VG. P3. $20.00

SNAVELY, Joseph Richard. *Intimate Story of Milton S Hershey.* 1957. self pub. sgn/dtd. photos. 549p. F. H1. $95.00

SNEDEKER, Caroline Dale. *Downright Dencey.* (1927). Doubleday. early prt ($3.95 dj). 8vo. 314p. dj. T5. $30.00

SNELGROVE, L.E. *Queen Rearing.* 1946. London. 1st. 344p. VG. B5. $25.00

SNELL, Roy J. *Eskimo Island & Penguin Land.* 1930. Chicago. Albert Whitman. later prt. school xl. P4. $35.00

SNELL, Roy J. *Mystery Stories for Boys: White Fire.* 1922. Reilly Lee. 238p. VG/dj. M20. $25.00

SNELL, Roy J. *Sign of the Green Arrow.* 1939. Reilly lee. VG/dj. P3. $30.00

SNELL, Roy J. *Sparky Ames of the Ferry Command.* 1943. Racine. Whitman. 1st. ils EL Darwin. VG/VG. A25. $22.00

SNELL, Roy J. *Whispers at Dawn.* 1934. Reilly Lee. sgn. 247p. VG/dj. M20. $35.00

SNODGRASS, W.D. *Heart's Needle.* 1959. Knopf. 1st. 1/1500. author's 1st book. F/NF. B2. $125.00

SNOW, Dorothea. *Circus Boy Under the Big Top.* 1957. Whitman. TVTI. VG. P3. $20.00

SNOW, Edward Rowe. *Fury of the Seas.* 1964. Dodd Mead. 271p. gr cloth. VG/dj. P4. $25.00

SNOW, Edward Rowe. *Tales of Terror & Tragedy.* 1979. NY. Dodd Mead. 1st. sm 8vo. 250p. VG/dj. P4. $20.00

SNOW, Jack. *Shaggy Man of Oz.* (1949). Reilly Lee. 1st/1st state. ils Frank Kramer. 32p. NF/dj. D1. $300.00

SNOWDON. *Snowdon: Personal View.* 1979. London. Weidenfeld Nicholson. 240p. cloth. dj. D2. $125.00

SNOWDEN, J. *Truth About Mormonism.* 1926. NY. 1st. ils/index. 369p. VG/VG. B5. $35.00

SNYDER, Gary. *Dimensions of a Life.* 1991. Sierra Club. 1st. NF/NF. B3. $40.00

SNYDER, T.E. *Our Enemy the Termite.* 1935. Ithaca. Comstock. ils. 196p. decor cloth. NF/VG+. M12. $45.00

SNYDER, Zilpha Keatley. *Headless Cupid.* 1972 (1971). Atheneum. 2nd. 8vo. orange cloth. NF/VG. T5. $25.00

SODERLUND, Jean R. *Quakers & Slavery.* 1988. Princeton. 220p. sc. V3. $14.00

SOGGIN, Alberto. *Introduction to the Old Testament From Its Origins...* 1980. Westminster. 508p. VG. B29. $18.00

SOHL, Jerry. *Altered Ego.* 1954. Rinehart. 1st. VG. P3. $13.00

SOHL, Jerry. *Prelude to Peril.* 1957. Rinehart. 1st. VG/dj. P3. $30.00

SOHL, Jerry. *Spun Sugar Hole.* 1951. S&S. 1st. VG/dj. P3. $15.00

SOLC, V. *Swords & Daggers of Indonesia.* 1970. London. Spring. ils/pl. gilt pict cloth/brass sword closure. VG. M12. $45.00

SOLDATI, Mario. *Malacca Cane.* 1973. NY. 1st. F/F. H11. $20.00

SOLECKI, Ralph S. *Shanidar: The First Flower People.* 1971. Knopf. 1st. 290p. NF/dj. W1. $20.00

SOLOGUB, F. *Petty Demon.* 1962. NY. 1st. trans A Field. VG/VG. T9. $25.00

SOLOGUB, F. *Sweet-Scented Name & Other Fairy Tales, Fables & Stories.* 1915. Putnam. 1st Am. 8vo. 240p. gilt blue cloth. F. T10. $50.00

SOLOMITA, Stephen. *Bad to the Bone.* 1991. Putnam. 1st. F/dj. P3. $22.00

SOLOMON, David. *LSD: The Consciousness-Expanding Drug.* 1964. Putnam. 1st. 8vo. 273p. F/G. H1. $35.00

SOLOMON, Maury. *Album of Voyager.* 1990. Franklin Watts. 4to. 64p. xl. dj. K5. $15.00

SOLOVYEV, Vladimir. *Meaning of Love.* 1947. Internat U Pr. 2nd (1946 sic). 8vo. 82p. F/VG. H1. $25.00

SOLZHENITSYN, Alexander. *Candle in the Wind.* 1973. Bodley Head/Oxford. 1st Eng. trans from Russian. F/dj. Q1. $50.00

SOLZHENITSYN, Alexander. *Lenin in Zurich.* 1976. FSG. 1st. F/F. B35. $25.00

SOLZHENITSYN, Alexander. *Stories & Prose Poems.* 1971. FSG. 1st. F/F. B35. $26.00

SOMERVILLE, Hugh. *Sceptre.* 1959. NY. Funk. ils/55 photos/charts. 185p. dj. T7. $35.00

SOMERVILLE, J. Alexander. *Man of Color, an Autobiography.* 1949. Los Angeles. Morrison. 1st. NF/VG. B4. $175.00

SOMERVILLE, Mollie. *Washington Walked Here.* 1970. Acropolis. 1st. 256p. cloth. VG/dj. M20. $25.00

SOMERVILLE & ROSS. *Irish RM Complete.* 1962. London. Faber. 1st. VG/VG. O3. $45.00

SOMERVILLE & ROSS. *Wheel-Tracks.* 1934. London. Longman Gr. VG. O3. $35.00

SOMMER, Frederick. *Frederick Sommer at Seventy-Five: A Retrospective.* 1980. Long Beach. CA State. exhibition catalog. 72p. wrp. D11. $50.00

SOMMER, Scott. *Nearing's Grace.* 1979. Taplinger. 1st. sgn. author's 1st book. F/NF. L3. $125.00

SOMMERS, Richard J. *Richmond Redeemed: Siege at Petersburg.* 1981. ils. VG/VG. M17. $27.50

SONDERN, Fredric. *Brotherhood of Evil: The Mafia.* 1959. FSC. VG. P3. $15.00

SONNICHSEN, C.L. *Billy King's Tombstone, the Private Life of AZ Boom Town.* 1942. Caxton. 1st. 233p. VG. J2. $145.00

SONNICHSEN, C.L. *I'll Die Before I'll Run.* 1951. NY. 1st. 294p. G+/torn. B18. $25.00

SONTAG, Susan. *Benefactor.* 1963. Farrar Straus. 1st. NF/VG. M19. $45.00

SONTAG, Susan. *Volcano Lover.* 1992. FSG. 1st. sgn. VG/VG. A23. $40.00

SORACCO, Sin. *Edge City.* 1992. Dutton. 1st. author's 1st novel. F/F. M22. $15.00

SORACCO, Sin. *Low Bite.* 1989. Black Lizard. 1st. VG/dj. P3. $17.00

SOREL, Charles. *Bibliotheqve Francoise.* 1664. Paris. 8vo. gilt calf. R12. $375.00

SOREL, Stefan. *Tarzan Hat Getraumt.* 1924. Vienna. Carl Stephenson. 242p. VG. M20. $250.00

SORENSON, Theodore C. *Kennedy.* 1965. Harper Row. 1st. F/dj. Q1. $40.00

SORRENTINO, Gilbert. *Darkness Surrounds Us.* 1960. Highlands. Williams. 1st. author's 1st book. F/stapled wrp/dj. R13. $75.00

SOSEKI, Muso. *Sun at Midnight. 23 Poems by...* 1985. NY. Jadja. 1st. 1/226. sgn Merwin/Frasconi. M/striped bl wrp. B24. $165.00

SOUSTELLE, Jacque. *Olmecs.* 1984. Doubleday. 1st. 214p. dj. F3. $30.00

SOUTAR, Andrew. *Kharduni.* 1934. Macauley. 1st. VG. M2. $22.00

SOUTHALL, Eliza. *Brief Memoir With Portions of Diary, Letters...* 1869. Diffusion of Knowledge. 195p. xl. V3. $18.00

SOUTHERN, Terry. *Blue Movie.* 1973. Calder Boyars. 1st. F/F. M19. $35.00

SOUTHERN, Terry. *Flash & Filigree.* 1958. Coward McCann. VG/dj. P3. $35.00

SOUTHERN, Terry. *Magic Christian.* 1960. Random. 1st. F/F. B4. $150.00

SOUTHERN, Terry. *Red-Dirt Marijuana.* 1967. NAL. 1st. NF/NF. H11. $50.00

SOUTHERN, Terry. *Red-Dirt Marijuana.* 1967. NAL. 1st. VG/dj. P3. $45.00

SOUTHWART, Elizabeth. *Password to Fairyland.* 1920. Stokes. 1st Am. ils Anderson/8 full-p pl. R5. $225.00

SOUTHWICK, L. *Dwarf Trees.* 1948. 1st. ils. VG/dj. E6. $20.00

SOUTHWORTH, J.R. *El Estado de Sinaloa, Mexico: Sus Industrias Commerciales...* 1898. SF. Southworth. Spanish/Eng text. 102p+30p ads. gilt cloth. D11. $100.00

SOWELL, Thomas. *Ethnic America: A History.* 1981. Basic. 1st. 353p. NF/NF. B4. $65.00

SOWERBY, Millicent. *Our Pets' Play Book. Mrs Strang's Play Books.* ca 1925. np. 12p. R5. $125.00

SOWERBY & SOWERBY. *Yesterday's Children.* 1908. London. 1st. 4to. gilt cloth/mc pl. VG. M5. $110.00

SOWLS, L.K. *Peccaries.* 1984. Tucson. 8vo. ils/photos. 251p. F/F. M12. $30.00

SOYER, A. *Modern Housewife; or, Menagere.* 1857 (1849). VG. E6. $125.00

SPAIGHT, J.M. *Aircraft in War.* 1914. London. 1st. 172p. xl. B18. $75.00

SPAIN, John. *Death Is Like That.* 1943. Dutton. 1st. VG. P3. $30.00

SPALDING, H. *Treasure-Trove of American Jewish Humor.* 1978 (1976). VG/VG. E6. $12.00

SPALDING, J.L. *Socialism & Labor & Other Arguments: Social, Political...* 1902. McClurg. 1st. VG/VG. V4. $20.00

SPALDING, Jesse. *War Years of Canada's Bluenose.* 1974. NY. Vantage. 61p. dj. T7. $20.00

SPALDING, W.R. *Music at Harvard: Historical Review.* 1935. ils. VG. M17. $20.00

SPARK, Muriel. *Fanfarlo & Other Verse.* 1952. Hand & Flower. 1st. F/1st issue wrp. Q1. $200.00

SPARK, Muriel. *Only Problem.* 1984. Franklin Lib. 1st. sgn. ils Vivienne Flesher. full leather. F. Q1. $40.00

SPARK & STANFORD. *Emily Bronte: Her Life & Work.* 1960. NY. London House/Maxwell. 1st. photos. 271p. VG/dj. A25. $35.00

SPARKE, Michael. *Truth Brought to Light.* 1692. London. Baldwin. 4 parts in 1. 8vo. disbound. R12. $200.00

SPARKS, H.F.D. *Synopsis of the Gospels.* 1964. Fortress. 248p. VG/dj. B29. $14.00

SPARLING, Sharon. *Glass Mountain.* 1986. London. O'Mara. 1st. F/F. T12. $20.00

SPARROW, Walter Shaw. *Angling in British Art.* 1923. London. 1st. ils/index/bibliography. 288p. buckram. B18. $225.00

SPATE, O.H.K. *Spanish Lake.* 1979. NM U. ils/maps. 372p. 372p. F/dj. O7. $50.00

SPAULDING, E.S. *Venison & Breath of Sage.* 1967. Santa Barbara. Genns. ils DR Johnson. 312p. cloth. F/VG+. M12. $45.00

SPAULDING, Karen. *Huarochiri.* 1984. Stanford. 1st. 364p. F3. $20.00

SPAULDING, Perley. *Diseases of North American Forest Trees Planted Abroad.* 1956. WA, DC. USDA Agric Handbook 100. sc. B26. $12.50

SPEAIGHT. *History of English Toy Theatre.* 1969. 2nd/revised. 4to. ils/12 mc pl. F/dj. A4. $95.00

SPEARE, Elizabeth George. *Witch of Blackird Pond.* 1958. Boston. Houghton Mifflin. 19th. 249p. VG/dj. V3. $9.50

SPEARS, John R. *Short History of the American Navy.* 1907. Scribner. 8vo. ils. 134p. P4. $55.00

SPECTOR, R.H. *After Tet, the Bloodiest Year in Vietnam.* 1993. NY. 1st. ils/photos. VG+/dj. B18. $19.50

SPECTOR, R.H. *Eagle Against the Sun: American War With Japan.* 1985. NY. 1st. ils. 589p. VG. S16. $18.50

SPEED, Nell. *Molly Brown's Freshman Days.* 1912. NY. Hurst. 1st. ils CL Wrenn. G+. A25. $8.00

SPEED, Thomas. *Guilty-Covered Clergy-Man Unveiled...* 1657. London. Giles CAlvert. sm 8vo. 79p. recent bdg. H13. $95.00

SPEER, Albert. *Spandau: Secret Diaries.* 1976. NY. photos/index. 463p. VG/VG. S16. $22.50

SPEER, William. *Oldest & Newest Empire: China & the United States.* 1870. Hartford. Scranton. thick 8vo. ils. red fabricoid. F. R3. $225.00

SPEISER & SPEISER. *Changing West.* 1975. Miles City, MT. H&T Quality Prt. $45.00

SPELTZ, Robert. *Real Runabouts II.* 1978. Lake Mills, IA. Graphic Pub. 4to. 800+ ils. 230p. dj. T7. $45.00

SPENCE, Bill. *Harpooned: Story of Whaling.* 1980. Crescent. 192p. VG/dj. P4. $20.00

SPENCE, William. *Tracts on Political Economy.* 1933. private prt (Viking). 8vo. rpt from 1822 London. paper brd. VG. T10. $75.00

SPENCER, Colin. *Anarchy of Love.* 1963. Weybright Talley. 1st. VG/dj. P3. $35.00

SPENCER, Cornelia. *Romulo Voice of Freedom.* 1953. John Day. 256p. VG+. P1. $20.00

SPENCER, Ross H. *Fedorovich File.* 1991. DIF. 1st. NF/dj. P3. $20.00

SPENCER, Ross H. *Monastery Nightmare.* 1986. Mysterious. 1st. F/dj. P3. $20.00

SPENCER, Scott. *Last Night at the Brain Thieves Ball.* 1973. Houghton Mifflin. 1st. VG/dj. P3. $25.00

SPENCER, Scott. *Preservation Hall.* 1976. Knopf. 1st. F/clip. M25. $25.00

SPENCER, William Browning. *Maybe I'll Call Anna.* 1990. Permanent Pr. 1st. F/F. M22. $15.00

SPENDER, Michael. *Island-Reefs of the Queensland Coast.* 1930. Royal Geographical Soc. ils/fld maps. wrp. P4. $45.00

SPENDER, Ramon. *Counter-Attack in Spain.* 1937. Houghton Mifflin. 1st. NF/dj. B2. $35.00

SPENDER, Stephen. *Journals 1939-1983.* 1985. London. 1/150. sgn. edit J Goldsmith. VG/case. T9. $150.00

SPENSER, Edmund. *Faerie Queene.* 1953. Oxford. LEC. 1st thus. 2 vol. 1/1500. lils/sgn Agnes Miller. F/djs/case. Q1. $250.00

SPERDUTI, Dominick R. *For You I Commit Murder.* 1956. Christoper. 1st. VG/dj. P3. $20.00

SPERRY, Armstrong. *One Day With Jambi in Sumatra.* (1934). Phil. John Winston. 1st. 8vo. VG. D1. $60.00

SPHYROERAS. *Maps & Map-Makers of the Aegean.* 1985. Athens. Olkos Ltd. 4to. ils/166 maps. 264p. VG/worn. A4. $245.00

SPICE ISLANDS HOME ECONOMICS. *Spice Islands Cookbook.* 1961. Menlo Park, CA. Lane. 1st. 8vo. 208p. cloth. NF/VG. T10. $30.00

SPICER, Edward H. *People of Pascua.* 1988. AZ U. 1st. 331p. F/F. B19. $30.00

SPIELMANN, Mrs. M.H. *Rainbow Book. Tales of Fun & Fancy.* 1909. Chatto Windus. 1st. ils Rackham. B24. $300.00

SPIELMANN. *Catalogue of Library of Miniature Books...* nd (1961). rpt. 1/150. ils. 500+ entries. 304p. F. A4. $85.00

SPIESS, Gerry. *Along Against the Atlantic.* 1981. Control Data Pub. 1st. sgn. VG/VG. B11. $25.00

SPILHAUS, Athelstan F. *Weathercraft.* 1967 (1951). Viking. 10th. xl. dj. K5. $12.00

SPILLANE, Mickey. *Bloody Sunrise.* 1965. Dutton. 1st. F/VG. M19. $45.00

SPILLANE, Mickey. *Day of Ghosts.* 1964. Dutton. 1st. F/F. M15. $50.00

SPILLANE, Mickey. *Death Dealers.* 1965. Dutton. 1st. VG/VG. M22. $20.00

SPILLANE, Mickey. *Deep.* 1961. Dutton. 1st. VG/F. M19. $45.00

SPILLANE, Mickey. *Erection Set.* 1972. WH Allen. 1st. NF/dj. P3. $30.00

SPILLANE, Mickey. *I, the Jury.* 1947. Dutton. 1st. NF/VG. B4. $450.00

SPILLANE, Mickey. *Killing Man.* 1989. Dutton. 1st. inscr. rem mk. F/F. R14. $60.00

SPILLANE, Mickey. *Killing Man.* 1989. Dutton. 1st. VG/dj. T12. $20.00

SPILLANE, Mickey. *Killing Man.* 1989. Franklin Lib. 1st. sgn. full leather. F. Q1. $60.00

SPILLER, Burton L. *More Grouse Feathers.* (1938). Derrydale. 1/950. tall 8vo. ils Lynn Bogue Hunt. NF. H7. $100.00

SPILLMAN, Louis. *So This Is South America.* 1962. VA. 1st. inscr. 140p. dj. F3. $15.00

SPINAR, Zdenek V.. *Life Before Man.* 1981. NY. Crescent. color ils. 4to. NF/VG. R16. $45.00

SPINAZZE, Libera Martina. *Index to the Argonauts of California: Chas Warren Haskins.* 1975. New Orleans. Polyanthos. 514p. prt wrp. D11. $50.00

SPINDLER, Will. *Tragedy Strikes at Wounded Knee.* 1955. Gordon Journal Pub. 1st. sgn. photos. 80p. VG/pict wrp. J2. $85.00

SPINGARN, Amy. *Humility & Pride.* 1926. Harcourt Brace. 1st. ils. NF. B4. $85.00

SPINRAD, Norman. *Agent of Chaos.* 1988. Watts. 1st. F/dj. M2. $15.00

SPINRAD, Norman. *Child of Fortune.* 1985. Bantam. 1st. VG/dj. P3. $20.00

SPINRAD, Norman. *Men in the Jungle.* 1967. Doubleday. 1st. F/dj. M2. $60.00

SPINRAD, Norman. *Songs From the Stars.* 1980. S&S. 1st. F/dj. P3. $20.00

SPIVACK & STAPLES. *Company of Camelot.* 1994. Greenwood. F. P3. $45.00

SPLIT, S. *Art of Cooking & Serving.* 1929. Proctor & Gamble. mc pl. G+. E6. $15.00

SPOCK, L.E. *Guide to the Study of Rocks.* 1953. Harper. 1st. 256p. F. D8. $15.00

SPOTA, Luis. *Wounds of Hunger.* 1957. Houghton Mifflin. 1st Am. F/F. B4. $150.00

SPOTO, Donald. *Dark Side of Genius: Life of Alf.* 1983. Little Brn. 1st. VG/dj. P3. $20.00

SPRAGUE, Marshall. *Gallery of Dudes.* 1966. Little Brn. 1st. ils. F/dj. C8/M4. $20.00

SPRAT, Thomas. *History of Royal-Society of London.* 1702. London. Scot Chiswell Chapman Sawbridge. 4to. 2 fld pl. cloth. R12. $475.00

SPRATLIN, V.B. *Juan Latino: Slave & Humanist.* 1938. NY. Spinner. 1st. 216p. F. B4. $500.00

SPRATLING, William Philip. *Epilepsy & Its Treatment.* 1904. Phil. Saunders. heavy 8vo. 522p+16p catalog. ruled olive cloth. VG. G1. $175.00

SPRATT, H. Philip. *Transatlantic Paddle Steamers.* 1951. Glasgow. Brn Ferguson. 1st. 9 pl/4 fld tables. 82p. dj. T7. $40.00

SPRING, Agnes Wright. *Caspar Collins, Life & Exploits of an Indian Fighter...* 1927. Columbia. 1st. ils. 187p. VG. J2. $185.00

SPRING, Agnes Wright. *Tales of the 04 Ranch, Recollections of Harold J Cook...* 1968. NE U. 1st. photos. 221p. VG/VG. J2. $90.00

SPRING, Agnes Wright. *70 Years in Cow Country.* 1942. Wyoming Stock Growers. 1st. photos Adams Herd. 273p. VG. J2. $175.00

SPRING, Gardiner. *Glory of Christ: Illustrated in His Character & History...* 1852. Dodd Mead. vol 2 only. 8vo. 312p. gilt stp cloth. H1. $35.00

SPRING, Howard. *Darkie & Co.* 1947 (1932). London. Oxford. rpt. 12mo. 288p. VG. T5. $26.00

SPRING, Norma. *Alaska: The Complete Travel Book.* 1970. Macmillan. xl. dj. A19. $10.00

SPRINGER, Norman. *Dark River.* 1928. Watt. 1st. VG. M2. $35.00

SPROAT, Lin. *Wodehouse at War.* 1981. Ticknor Fields. 1st. NF/dj. P3. $20.00

SPRUILL, Steven. *Paradox Planet.* 1988. Doubleday. 1st. NF/dj. P3. $18.00

SPRUNGMAN, Ormal I. *Photography Afield.* 1951. Stackpole. 1st. 449p. 4to. A17. $15.00

SPURR, J.E. *Geology Applied to Selenology III.* (1948). Rumford. 253p. xl. K5. $35.00

SPURZHEIM, Johann Gaspar. *Anatomy of the Brain With General View of Nervous System.* 1834 (1826). Boston. Marsh Capen Lyon. 1st Am. 18 pl. 244p. drab brn cloth. G. G1. $325.00

SPURZHEIM, Johann Gaspar. *Observations on Deranged Manifestations of the Mind...* 1836. Boston. Marsh Capen Lyon. 3rd Am. 272p. VG. G1. $175.00

SPYRI, Johanna. *Erick & Sally.* 1921. Boston. 3 mc pl. teg. gilt cloth. VG. M5. $55.00

SPYRI, Johanna. *Eveli the Little Singer.* nd. AL Burt. decor brd. VG. P3. $20.00

SPYRI, Johanna. *Heidi.* 1915. Grosset Dunlap. 318p. cloth. VG/dj. M20. $22.50

SPYRI, Johanna. *Heidi.* 1944. Whitman. ils Arthur Jameson. VG/dj. P3. $15.00

SQUIBB, G.D. *High Court of Chivalry, a Study of Civil Law in England.* 1959. Clarendon. M11. $85.00

SQUIRES, W.H.T. *Through Centuries Three: Short History of Virginia.* 1929. Portsmouth. 1st. sgn/#d. 605p. NF. M4. $40.00

STABLEFORD, Brian M. *Empire of Fear.* 1988. London. 1st. sgn. F/dj. M2. $35.00

STABLEFORD, Brian M. *Man in a Cage.* 1975. John Day. 1st. VG/dj. P3. $20.00

STABLEFORD, Brian M. *Paradox Game.* 1976. London. 1st. sgn. F/dj. M2. $45.00

STABLEFORD, Brian M. *Promised Land.* 1975. Dent. 1st. sgn. F/F. P3. $25.00

STABLER & STAINBACK. *Snake.* 1986. Doubleday. 1st. photos. F/dj. P8/T12. $25.00

STABLES, Gordon. *On to the Rescue: A Tale of the Indian Mutiny.* ca 1898. London. John Shaw. New Ed. 8vo. 374p. teg. gilt pict cloth. T10. $50.00

STACEY, Susannah. *Goodbye, Nanny Gray.* 1987. Summit. 1st. VG/dj. P3. $16.00

STACEY, Susannah. *Knife at the Opera.* 1988. Summit. 1st. F/VG+. N4. $15.00

STACKPOLE, Edouard A. *Voyage of the Huron & the Huntress.* 1955. Mystic. Marine Hist Assc. 86p. prt wrp. P4. $55.00

STACKPOLE, Edward J. *Chancellorsville: Lee's Greatest Battle.* 1958. Bonanza. 384p. cloth. VG/dj. M20. $20.00

STACKPOLE, H. DeVere. *Blue Lagoon.* nd. World Wide. NF/dj. M2. $25.00

STACKPOLE, H. DeVere. *City in the Sea.* 1926. London. 1st. VG. M2. $25.00

STADE, George. *Confessions of a Lady-Killer.* 1980. Muller. 1st. F/dj. P3. $18.00

STADLEY, Pat. *Autumn of a Hunter.* 1971. Collins Crime Club. 1st. VG/dj. P3. $20.00

STAFF, Frank. *Picture Postcard & Its Origin.* 1966. Praeger. 95p. cloth. VG+/dj. M20. $35.00

STAFFORD, Edward P. *Far & the Deep.* 1967. Putnam. 1st. inscr. VG/VG. B11. $65.00

STAFFORD, Jean. *Collected Stories.* 1969. FSG. 1st. F/F. B4. $125.00

STAFFORD, Muriel. *X Marks the Dot.* 1943. DSP. 1st. VG. P3. $25.00

STAFLEU, F.A. *Taxonomic Literature.* 1967. Utrecht. 8vo. 556p. VG. B1. $65.00

STAGG, D.J. *Calendar of New Forest Documents 1244-1334.* 1979. Trowbridge. Hampshire County Council. M11. $50.00

STALKER, John. *Stalker Affair: Shocking True Story of 6 Deaths...* 1988. Viking. 2nd. VG/dj. V4. $20.00

STALLINGS, Penny. *Flesh & Fantasy.* 1981. Bell. 2nd. ils/photos. NF/dj. C9. $35.00

STALLYBRASS, W.T.S. *Salmond's Law of Torts, a Treatise on English Law...* 1945. London. crimson buckram. M11. $45.00

STANDARD, Stella. *Our Daily Bread.* 1970. Bonanza. VG/dj. A16. $12.00

STANDISH, Burt L. *Frank Merriwell's School Days.* 1901 (1896). McKay. 302p. cloth. G. M20. $30.00

STANDISH, Robert. *Elephant Walk.* 1949. Macmillan. 1st. VG. T12. $25.00

STANDLEY, Paul C. *Trees & Shrubs of Mexico. Part 4 of 5.* 1924. WA. GPO. 8vo. gr buckram. xl. A22. $60.00

STANDON. *Gore Vidal: Primary & Secondary Bibliography.* 1978. 247p. VG. A4. $75.00

STANDS IN TIMBER, John. *Cheyenne Memories.* 1967. New Haven. Yale. 1st. photos/mc pl. NF/dj. L3. $85.00

STANEK, V.J. *Pictorial Encyclopedia of Insects.* 1972 (1969). Hamlyn, London. 8vo. 544p. dj. B1. $22.50

STANFORD, Alfred. *Navigator: Story of Nathaniel Bowditch.* 1927. NY. Morrow. 1st. 300p. T7. $35.00

STANFORD, Derek. *Inside the Forties, Literary Memoirs.* 1977. London. 1st. VG/VG. w/3 sgn letters. T9. $50.00

STANFORD, Ernest Elwood. *Mascot Goes Across.* 1929. NY. Century. 1st. ils. VG. K3. $20.00

STANFORD, J.K. *Last Chukker.* 1954. Devin Adair. 1st. VG/VG. O3. $25.00

STANFORTH, Deirdre. *New Orleans Restaurant Cookbook.* 1967. Doubleday. intro/index. VG. A16. $17.50

STANGER, Frank M. *South From San Francisco.* 1963. San Mateo Co Hist Assn. ils/photos. 214p. terra-cotta cloth. F. K7. $50.00

STANHOPE, Hester. *Memoirs of Lady Hester Stanhope...* 1845. ils. 3-quarter leather/marbled brd. VG+. S13. $100.00

STANLEY, Edwin. *Rambles in Wonderland; or, Up the Yellowstone...* 1878. Appleton. 1st. 179p. G. J2. $225.00

STANLEY, Henry M. *In Darkest Africa; or, Quest, Rescue & Retreat...* 1890. Scribner. 2 vol. 1st Am. 8vo. xl/missing 2 maps. VG. W1. $45.00

STANLEY, S.M. *Extinction.* 1987. Scientific. ils. 242p. F/dj. D8. $26.00

STANLEY, Wallace. *Our Week Afloat; or, How We Explored the Pequonset River.* 1890. Chicago. Belford-Clarke. 367p. VG. H7. $12.50

STANS, Maurice. *Terrors of Justice.* 1978. NY. Everest. 3rd. sgn. VG/VG. A23. $40.00

STANTON. *Truman Capote, a Primary & Secondary Bibliography.* 1980. 302p. F. A4. $65.00

STANWOOD, Brooks. *Glow.* 1979. McGraw Hill. 1st. F/dj. P3/T12. $25.00

STANWOOD, Brooks. *Seventh Child.* 1981. Linden. F/dj. P3. $18.00

STAPLEDON, Olaf. *Far Future Calling.* 1979. Oswald Train. 1st. F/dj. P3. $20.00

STAPLEDON, Olaf. *Flames.* 1947. London. 1st. VG/dj. M2. $35.00

STAPLEDON, Olaf. *Odd John.* 1935. Dutton. 1st Am. VG. M2. $50.00

STAPLEDON, R.G. *Land Now & Tomorrow.* 1934. London. Faber. 336p. fld maps. A10. $22.00

STARBUCK, Alexander. *History of the American Whale Fishery.* 1989. Secaucus. Castle. rpt. 779p. NF/dj. P4. $45.00

STARBUCK, Alexander. *History of the American Whale Fishery.* 1989 (1878). Castle. rpt. 779p. F/F. S15. $20.00

STARK, Freya. *Baghdad Sketches.* 1937. London. Murray. 1st. 8vo. 269p. VG. W1. $35.00

STARK, Freya. *Journey's Echo.* 1963. John Murray. 1st. NF/dj. M25. $35.00

STARK, Richard; see Westlake, Donald E.

STARK, Stephen. *Outskirts.* 1988. Algonquin. 1st. author's 1st book. F/F. H11. $20.00

STARKELL, Don. *Paddle to the Amazon.* 1989. CA. Prima Pub. 1st. 319p. dj. F3. $15.00

STARNES, Arthur. *Aerial Maniac.* 1938. Hammond. 1st. sgn pres. ils. 136p. G+. B5. $45.00

STARNES, Richard. *Another Mug for the Bier.* nd. Frederick Muller. 1st. VG/dj. P3. $30.00

STARNES, Richard. *Another Mug for the Bier.* 1950. Lippincott. 1st. author's 2nd book. F/F. H11. $30.00

STARR, Blaze. *Blaze Starr: My Life.* 1974. Praeger. 1st. inscr. NF/NF. B4. $250.00

STARR, Fredrick. *Physical Characters of the Indians of Southern Mexico.* 1902. Chicago. ils/photos/mc chart. 59p. wrp. F3. $75.00

STARR, Jimmy. *Three Short Biers.* 1945. Hollywood. Murray Gee. 1st. inscr. F/F. B4. $200.00

STARR, Louis M. *Bohemian Brigade Civil War Newsmen in Action.* 1987. WI U. 1st. 387p. cloth. as new. M8. $35.00

STARR, Moses Allen. *Brain Surgery.* 1991. Birmingham. facsimile. 295p. tooled purple leather. G1. $65.00

STARR, Moses Allen. *Familiar Forms of Nervous Disease...* 1890. NY. Wm Wood. heavy 8vo. 339p. G. G1. $75.00

STARRETT, Vincent. *Books Alive.* 1940. Random. 1st. 360p. VG/partial dj. K3. $25.00

STARRETT, Vincent. *Penny Wise & Book Foolish.* 1929. Covici Friede. ltd ed. inscr. 200p. G. K3. $75.00

STARRETT, Vincent. *Seaports in the Moon.* 1928. Doubleday. 1st. VG. M2. $27.00

STARRETT, William. *Nurse Blake Overseas.* 1943. NY. Gramercy. 1st. 256p. VG. A25. $10.00

STASHEFF, Christopher. *Company of Stars.* 1991. Del Rey. 1st. F/dj. P3. $20.00

STAUBACH, Roger. *Time Enough to Win.* 1980. Waco. Word. 1st. sgn. F/clip. A23. $48.00

STAUSS, Lehman. *Daniel.* 1969. Loizeaux. 384p. VG/dj. B29. $9.00

STAVELEY, Gaylord. *Broken Waters Sing.* 1971. Boston. 1st. 283p. gr/wht bdg. VG+. F7. $15.00

STAVIS, Barrie. *Man Who Never Died.* 1954. NY. Haven. 1st. sgn. F/NF. B2. $35.00

STAVROULAKIS, Nikos. *Book of Jeremiah: New Translation.* 1973. JPS. folio. ils/woodcuts. 93p. VG. S3. $45.00

STAVROULAKIS, Peter. *Distributed Parameter Systems Theory, Part 1, Control.* 1983. Stroudsburg. 1st. 396p. A17. $35.00

STAWELL, Mrs. Rodolph. *Fabre's Book of Insects.* 1937 (1921). Tudor. 6th. 271p. gilt gr cloth. M20. $40.00

STEADMAN, John. *Best (& Worst) of Steadman.* 1974. Press Box. 1st. VG/G+. P8. $25.00

STEADMAN, Ralph. *Little Red Computer.* 1969. McGraw Hill. 1st Am. 4to. VG/G+. P2. $25.00

STEADMAN, William E. *La Tierra Encantada.* 1969. private prt. ils. 159p. NF/NF. B19. $35.00

STEAM, Jess. *Sisters of the Night: Startling Story of Prostitution...* 1956. NY. Gramercy. 1st. 182p. VG/dj. A25. $18.00

STEARN, William T. *Botanical Masters.* 1990. Prentice Hall. 1st Am. 56 full-p pl. F/dj. A22. $25.00

STEARNS & STEARNS. *Jazz Dance.* 1968. Macmillan. 1st. F/F. B2. $40.00

STEBBING, E.P. *Diary of a Sportsman Naturalist in India.* 1920. London. Jonn Lane. 1st. ils/photos. 298p. G. H7. $45.00

STEBBING, G. *Beating the Record: Story of Life & Times of Geo Stephenson.* ca 1890. London. John Shaw. ils. 8vo. 383p. VG. K3. $30.00

STEBBINS, G. Ledyard. *Flowering Plants: Evolution Above Species Level.* 1974. Cambridge. Harvard. 399p. dj. A10. $30.00

STEBBINS, G. Ledyard. *Variation & Evolution in Plants.* 1963. NY. Columbia. 643p. cloth. A10. $25.00

STEEGMULLER, Francis. *Cocteau: A Biography.* 1970. Boston. 1st. 583p. F/dj. A17. $25.00

STEEL, F.A. *Voices in the Night.* 1900. London. 1st. VG. M2. $45.00

STEEL, Kurt. *Imposter.* 1945. Tower. VG/dj. P3. $15.00

STEEL, Kurt. *Murder for What?* 1936. Bobbs Merrill. 1st. F/dj. M15. $90.00

STEELE, Adison; see Lupoff, Richard.

STEELE, Danielle. *Full Circle.* 1984. Delacorte. 1st. F/NF. W2. $25.00

STEELE, Danielle. *Kaleidoscope.* 1987. Delacorte. 1st. 395p. NF/NF. W2. $25.00

STEELE, David J. *Yachtsman in Red China.* 1970. NY. DeGraff. photos. 208p. dj. T7. $22.00

STEELE, Joel Dorman. *New Descriptive Astronomy.* ca 1900. NY. Am Book Co. 326p. cloth. K5. $25.00

STEELE, Matthew Forney. *American Campaigns.* 1922. WA, DC. US Infantry Assn. maps. A19. $100.00

STEELE, Matthew Forney. *American Campaigns. Vol 1.* 1909. Bryon Adams. 1st. 731p. bl cloth. VG. H1. $58.00

STEERE, Douglas V. *On Beginning From Within.* 1943. Harper. 3rd. 149p. VG/dj. V3. $12.50

STEERE, Douglas V. *Prayer & Worship.* 1941. NY. Hazen. 2nd. 70p. VG. V3. $14.00

STEERE, Douglas V. *Time to Spare.* 1949. Harper. 1st. 187p. VG/clip. V3. $14.00

STEERE, Douglas V. *Work & Contemplation.* 1957. Harper. 1st. 148p. VG/clip. V3. $18.00

STEERS, J.A. *Applied Coastal Geomorphology.* 1971. Cambridge. MIT. ils/photos/maps. 227p. cloth. F/F. M12. $15.00

STEFAN, Verena. *Shedding.* 1978. NY. Daughters. 1st Am. trans Johanna Moore/Beth Weckmueller. 118p. VG. A25. $20.00

STEFANSSON, Vilhjalmur. *Adventure of Wrangel Island.* 1925. NY. 1st. 424p. VG. A17. $40.00

STEFANSSON, Vilhjalmur. *Adventure of Wrangel Island.* 1925. NY. Macmillan. 1st. inscr. ils/fld map. 424p. VG. K3. $60.00

STEFANSSON, Vilhjalmur. *Friendly Arctic: Story of 5 Years in Polar Regions.* 1939. NY. later prt. 784p. rear pocket map. A17. $40.00

STEFANSSON, Vilhjalmur. *Northward Course of Empire.* 1924. NY. 2nd. 274p. fld map. A17. $22.50

STEFANSSON, Vilhjalmur. *Northwest to Fortune: Search...Commercially Route Far East.* 1958. NY. 1st. 356p. F/dj. A17. $20.00

STEFANSSON & WEIGERT. *Compass of the World: A Symposium on Political Geography.* 1945. NY. 2nd. 466p. dj. A17. $16.50

STEGNER, Wallace. *All the Little Live Things.* 1967. Viking. BC. 1st. 248p. NF/dj. W2. $20.00

STEGNER, Wallace. *All the Little Live Things.* 1967. Viking. 1st. F/F. A18. $75.00

STEGNER, Wallace. *All the Little Live Things.* 1967. Viking. 1st. NF/VG+. T11. $60.00

STEGNER, Wallace. *All the Little Live Things.* 1967. Viking. 1st. sgn. VG+/dj. D10. $60.00

STEGNER, Wallace. *Angle of Repose.* 1971. 1st. VG/VG. S13. $50.00

STEGNER, Wallace. *Angle of Repose.* 1971. Garden City. 1st. sgn. F/F. B4. $650.00

STEGNER, Wallace. *Beyond the Hundreth Meridian.* 1954. Houghton Mifflin. 1st. xl. NF/VG+. T11. $195.00

STEGNER, Wallace. *Big Rock Candy Mountain.* 1943. DSP. 1st. author's 3rd novel. VG/VG. B5. $250.00

STEGNER, Wallace. *Big Rock Candy Mountain.* 1943. DSP. 1st. F/VG+ clip. B4. $850.00

STEGNER, Wallace. *Big Rock Candy Mountain.* 1978. Franklin Lib. 1st. sgn. NF/sans. T11. $200.00

STEGNER, Wallace. *City of the Living & Other Stories.* 1956. Houghton Mifflin. 1st. sgn. VG/VG clip. B4. $450.00

STEGNER, Wallace. *Collected Stories of Wallace Stegner.* 1989. Random. 1st. F/F. T11. $50.00

STEGNER, Wallace. *Collected Stories of Wallace Stegner.* 1989. Random. 1st. NF/NF. B3. $40.00

STEGNER, Wallace. *Crossing to Safety.* 1987. Franklin Lib. 1st/ltd. sgn. full leather. F. Q1. $125.00

STEGNER, Wallace. *Crossing to Safety.* 1987. Random. 1st. F/F. B3. $50.00

STEGNER, Wallace. *On a Darkling Plain.* 1940. Harcourt Brace. 1st. F. A18. $175.00

STEGNER, Wallace. *One Way to Spell Man.* 1982. Doubleday. 1st. NF/NF. B3. $75.00

STEGNER, Wallace. *Recapitulation.* 1979. Doubleday. 1st trade after Franklin Lib. NF/NF. D10. $65.00

STEGNER, Wallace. *Recapitulation.* 1979. Doubleday. 1st trade. blk cloth. F/NF. T11. $80.00

STEGNER, Wallace. *Recapitulation.* 1979. Franklin LIb. true 1st. ils Walter Rane. full leather. F. B3/T11. $95.00

STEGNER, Wallace. *Shooting Star.* 1961. Viking. 1st. F/NF. B4. $150.00

STEGNER, Wallace. *Shooting Star.* 1961. Viking. 1st. NF/dj. from $100 to $125.00

STEGNER, Wallace. *Spectator Bird.* 1976. Franklin Lib. 1st ltd. leather. F/sans. from $65 to $85.00

STEGNER, Wallace. *Where the Bluebird Sings to the Lemonade Springs.* 1992. Random. 1st. F/F. B3. $30.00

STEGNER, Wallace. *Women on the Wall.* 1950. Houghton Mifflin. 1st. NF/VG+. D10. $175.00

STEICHEN, Edward. *Life in Photography.* 1963. NY. 249 photos. dj. A17. $30.00

STEICHEN, Edward. *US Navy War Photographs.* ca 1945. US Camera. 108p. sq 4to. G/wrp. A17. $17.00

STEIG, William. *Amazing Bone.* 1976. FSG. 1st. ils. F/VG. P2. $75.00

STEIG, William. *Farmer Palmer's Wagon Ride.* 1974. FSG. 1st. VG/VG. P2. $40.00

STEIG, William. *Yellow & Pink.* 1984. FSG. 1st. wide 8vo. F/NF. C8. $35.00

STEIN, Aaron Marc. *Days of Misfortune.* 1949. Doubleday Crime Club. 1st. VG/NF. M22. $25.00

STEIN, Aaron Marc. *We Saw Him Die.* 1947. Doubleday. 1st. VG/dj. P3. $20.00

STEIN, Ben. *Croesus Conspiracy.* 1978. S&S. 1st. NF/dj. P3. $10.00

STEIN, Benjamin J. *Manhattan Gambit.* 1983. 1st. NF/dj. K3. $20.00

STEIN, David Lewis. *Living the Revolution: Yippies in Chicago.* 1969. Bobbs Merrill. 1st. F/VG+. B4. $100.00

STEIN, Gertrude. *Wars I Have Seen.* 1945. London. 1st. VG/VG. T9. $65.00

STEIN, Gertrude. *World Is Round.* 1988. Northpoint. 1st. F/F. B3. $20.00

STEIN, Leonard. *Balfour Declaration.* 1961. S&S. 1st. 8vo. 681p. xl. VG/torn. W1. $35.00

STEIN, Peter. *Character & Influence of the Roman Civil Law...* 1988. London. Hambledon. M11. $60.00

STEIN, Robert H. *Difficult Passages in the New Testament.* 1990. Baker. 392p. VG/dj. B29. $10.00

STEIN, Robert Louis. *French Slave Trade in the Eighteenth Century...* 1979. Madison, WI. dj. A19. $35.00

STEIN, Robert. *Children of Light.* 1986. Knopf. 1st. F/NF. B3. $30.00

STEIN, Robert. *Flag for Sunrise.* 1981. Knopf. 1st. VG/NF. B3. $50.00

STEIN, Sol. *Touch of Treason.* 1985. St Martin. 1st. VG/dj. P3. $15.00

STEINBECK, John. *Cannery Row.* 1945. Viking. 1st/1st issue. buff brd. NF/NF. B4. $750.00

STEINBECK, John. *Cup of Gold.* 1929. McBride. 1st/1st issue. 1/2746. inscr. VG. L3. $6,500.00

STEINBECK, John. *East of Eden.* 1952. Viking. Sears Reading Club Special. gr cloth. NF. W2. $300.00

STEINBECK, John. *Forgotten Village.* 1941. Viking. 1st. F/G. M19. $75.00

STEINBECK, John. *Grapes of Wrath.* 1939. London. Heinemann. 1st. F/VG+. A18. $300.00

STEINBECK, John. *Grapes of Wrath.* 1939. NY. 1st. VG+/dj. B5. $1,000.00

STEINBECK, John. *Log From the Sea of Cortez.* 1951. Viking. ils/photos/map ep. 282p. cloth. VG+/G+. M12. $95.00

STEINBECK, John. *Long Valley.* 1939 (1938). VG/VG. S13. $30.00

STEINBECK, John. *Moon Is Down.* 1942. Viking. 1st. inscr. G+/VG. B4. $2,250.00

STEINBECK, John. *Of Mice & Men.* 1937. Covici Friede. 1st/1st issue. 1/2500. F/F clip. B4. $1,500.00

STEINBECK, John. *Red Pony.* 1945. Viking. 1st. ils Wesley Dennis. 132p. gilt gray cloth. F/case. H3. $50.00

STEINBECK, John. *Russian Journal.* 1948. Viking. 1st. NF/G. M19. $75.00

STEINBECK, John. *Sweet Thursday.* 1954. Viking. 1st. F/VG+ clip. A24. $90.00

STEINBECK, John. *Travels With Charley.* 1962. Viking. VG. W2. $75.00

STEINBECK, John. *Winter of Our Discontent.* 1960. Viking. 1st. NF/G. A24. $45.00

STEINBECK & WALLSTEN. *Steinbeck: A Life in Letters.* 1975. Viking. 1/1000. bl cloth. F/case. w/3 facsimile letters. M25. $200.00

STEINBERG, Avraham. *Jewish Medical Law: Concise Response.* 1980. Israel. Gefen. 180p. VG/dj. S3. $26.00

STEINBERG, I.N. *In the Workshop of the Revolution.* 1953. Rinehart. 1st. G/G. V4. $20.00

STEINBERG, Noach. *Tsu Loyterkayt: Lirishe Proze.* 1931. Dezshey. Yiddish text. 109p. VG. S3. $30.00

STEINBRUNNER, Chris. *Cinema of the Fantastic.* 1972. Saturday Review. 1st. G/dj. P3. $20.00

STEINER, Mona Lisa. *Philippine Ornamental Plants & Their Care.* 1960. Manila. 2nd. 233p. VG. B26. $42.00

STEINER, Ralph. *Point of View.* 1978. Middletown. Wesleyan U. 1st. inscr/dtd. 144p. cloth. dj. D11. $200.00

STEINGRABER, Erich. *Royal Treasures.* 1968. 1st. lg 4to. photos. NF/G+. S13. $30.00

STEINMAN, David B. *Miracle Bridge at Mackinac.* 1957. Grand Rapids. Eerdmans. 2nd. sgn. 208p. G. B11. $35.00

STEKEL, Wilhelm. *Auto-Eroticism: Pyschiatric Study of Onanism & Neurosis.* 1950. Liveright. 1st Am. 289p. VG. A25. $20.00

STELL, Flora Anne. *Tales of Punjab.* 1983. Greenwich House. 1st. F/dj. P3. $15.00

STELLMAN, Louis J. *Vanished Ruin Era.* 1910. SF. Paul Elder. 52 pl. quarter natural burlap/tan sides. F. K7. $125.00

STELLMAN & STRONG. *Chinatown Photographer Louis J Stellman...* 1989. Sacramento. CA State Lib. 1/550. ils. F/gray wrp. R3. $30.00

STEMPEL, John D. *Inside the Iranian Revolution.* 1981. Bloomington, IN. 1st. sgn pres. 8vo. 336p. NF/dj. W1. $22.00

STENNING, Derrick J. *Savannah Nomads: A Study of Wodaabe Pastoral Fulain...* 1964. Oxford. 2nd. ils/fld map. 266p. VG/dj. W1. $25.00

STEPHEN, David. *Bodach the Badger.* 1983. St Martin. 1st. VG/dj. P3. $11.00

STEPHEN, James Fitzjames. *History of Criminal Law of England.* 1883. London. Macmillan. 3 vol. cloth. M11. $650.00

STEPHENS, H. *Farmer's Guide to Scientific & Practical Agriculture.* 1858. NY. 2 vol. lg 8vo. ils. E6. $125.00

STEPHENS, James. *Crock of Gold.* 1926. London. Macmillan. 1/525. sgn. 12 tipped-in pl. F. T10. $300.00

STEPHENS, James. *Crock of Gold.* 1946. Macmillan. VG. M2. $18.00

STEPHENS, John L. *Incidents of Travel in Central America, Chipas & Yucatan.* 1949. New Brunswick. Rutgers. ils Catherwood. F/dj. O7. $35.00

STEPHENSON, George. *Puritan Heritage.* 1952. Macmillan. 282p. G/torn. B29. $7.00

STEPTOE, John. *Stevie.* 1969. Harper Row. later ed. author/ils 1st book. NF/dj. M25. $45.00

STEPTOE, John. *Uptown.* 1970. Harper Row. 1st. NF/dj. M25. $60.00

STERCHI, Beat. *Cow.* 1988. NY. Pantheon. 1st Am. author's 1st novel. F/NF. R13. $20.00

STERLING, Bruce. *Crystal Express.* 1989. Arkham. 1st. F/NF. M19. $25.00

STERLING, Bruce. *Crystal Express.* 1990. Legend. 1st. F/dj. P3. $25.00

STERLING, Bryan B. *Will Rogers Scrapbook.* 1976. Bonanza. dj. A19. $30.00

STERLING, Claire. *Time of the Assassins.* 1984. HRW. 1st. VG/VG. W2. $20.00

STERLING, Dorothy. *Ahead of Her Time: Abby Kelley & Politics of Antislavery.* 1991. Norton. 1st. VG/VG. V3. $18.50

STERLING, Dorothy. *Lucretia Mott: Gentle Warrior.* 1964. Doubleday. 237p. dj. V3. $12.00

STERLING, George. *After Sunset.* 1939. SF. Howell. 1/25. 70p. D11. $75.00

STERLING, George. *Beyond the Breakers & Other Poems.* 1914. SF. Robertson. 1st. 141p. gilt cloth. D11. $50.00

STERLING, George. *Robinson Jeffers, the Man & the Artist.* 1926. NY. Knopf. 1st. blk cloth. F/dj. M24. $85.00

STERLING, George. *Rosamund: A Dramatic Poem.* 1920. SF. AM Robertston. 1/500. sgn/#d. D11. $60.00

STERLING, George. *Sonnets to Craig.* 1928. Boni. 1st. intro Upton Sinclair. 12mo. 120p. NF/dj. T10. $75.00

STERLING, George. *Wine of Wizardry & Other Poems.* 1909. SF. AM Robertson. 1st/1st issue. 137p. gilt cloth. D11. $75.00

STERLING, Gray. *Tooth of Time.* 1955. Marshall Jones. sgn. 151p. VG/dj. M20. $45.00

STERLING, Helen. *Horse That Takes the Milk Around.* 1946. NY. ils Marjorie Hartwell. VG+/dj. M5. $65.00

STERLING, Robert Thayer. *Lighthouses of the Maine Coast & the Men Who Keep Them.* 1935. Battleboro. Stephen Daye. 1st. sgn. 224p. xl. A17. $17.50

STERLING, Stewart. *Dead of Night.* 1950. Dutton. 1st. VG/dj. P3. $25.00

STERLING, W.W. *Trails & Trials of a Texas Ranger.* 1959. private prt. 1st. inscr. VG. A15. $150.00

STERN, H.J. *Rubber: Natural & Synthetic...* 1954. London. 1st. ils. 491p. dj. B18. $65.00

STERN, J. David. *Eidolon.* 1952. Messner. 1st. VG/VG. P3. $20.00

STERN, Madeleine B. *We the Women: Career Firsts of 19th-C America.* 1994. Lincoln, NE. 8vo. ils. pb. R12. $12.95

STERN, Norton B. *California Jewish History: A Descriptive Bibliography.* 1967. Glendale, CA. 1st. NF. O4. $25.00

STERN, Philip Van Doren. *Drums of Morning.* 1942. Doubleday Doran. 1st. VG/dj. P3. $20.00

STERN, Philip Van Doren. *End to Valor: Last Days of the Civil War.* 1958. Houghton Mifflin. 1st. 8vo. 428p. F/dj. H1. $25.00

STERN, Philip Van Doren. *Man Who Killed Lincoln.* 1939. 1st. 408p. O8. $12.50

STERN, Richard Martin. *Flood.* 1979. Doubleday. 1st. VG/dj. P3. $20.00

STERN, Roger. *Death & Life of Superman.* 1993. Bantam. 1st. F/dj. P3. $20.00

STERNBERG & WILSON. *Landscaping With Native Trees.* 1995. Shelburn, VT. Chapters. 288p. cloth. A10. $35.00

STEVENS, Abel. *Compendious History of American Methodism.* nd. Eaton Mains. abridged. 608p. VG. B29. $10.50

STEVENS, Abel. *History of Religious Movement of 18th C Called Methodism.* 1861. Phillips Hunt. Vol III only. 524p. G. B29. $15.00

STEVENS, Benjamin F. *Cruise on the Constitution.* 1904. NY. rpt. sgn. T7. $50.00

STEVENS, Doris. *En Prison Pour la Liberte! Comment Nous Avons Conquis...* 1936. Paris. A Pedone. 1st French. 359p. F. A25. $60.00

STEVENS, George T. *Illustrated Guide to Flowering Plants of Middle Atlantic...* 1910. NY. 1800+ ils. 749p. gilt olive cloth. VG. B26. $45.00

STEVENS, Henry. *Recollections of James Lenox...* 1951. NY Public Lib. revised. 1/1000. ils. 187p. VG. K3. $20.00

STEVENS, Isaac. *Liberators.* 1908. Dodge. 1st. VG. M2. $32.00

STEVENS, Lyla. *Birds of Australia in Color.* nd. Melbourne. 61p. NF/F. S15. $12.00

STEVENS, Orin. *Handbook of North Dakota Plants.* 1963. Fargo, ND. ND Inst Regional Studies. 3rd. 328p. VG. A10. $22.00

STEVENS, Phillips. *Stone Images of Esie, Nigeria.* 1978. Ibadan. 398p+1581 b&w photos. F/dj. A17. $25.00

STEVENS, Ruth. *Hi-Ya Neighbor.* 1947. Tupper Love. 1st. sgn. 16 photo pl. 122p. G/G. B11. $25.00

STEVENS, Shane. *Anvil Chorus.* 1985. Delacorte. VG/dj. P3. $20.00

STEVENS, Shane. *By Reason of Insanity.* 1979. S&S. 1st. NF/dj. P3. $75.00

STEVENS, Shane. *Dead City.* 1973. HRW. 1st. F/F. T2. $35.00

STEVENS, Stanford. *Plants of Sun & Sand: Desert Growth of Arizona.* 1939. Tucson. 2nd. ils/sgn Gerry Pierce. wood brd/cloth backstrip. B26. $27.50

STEVENS, Wallace. *And the Critical Schools.* 1988. AL U. 1st. F/F. V1. $15.00

STEVENS, Wallace. *Collected Poems.* 1954. NY. Knopf. 1st/1st state bdg (rust brn cloth). 1/2500. dj. M24. $3,000.00

STEVENS, William Oliver. *Charleston, Historic City of Gardens.* 1939. NY. 1st. ils. 331p. VG. B18. $15.00

STEVENSON, Adlai. *Wit & Wisdom of...* 1965. Hawthorn. 1st. ils. NF/clip. Q1. $40.00

STEVENSON, Burton E. *King in Babylon.* 1917. Sm Maynard. 1st. VG. M2. $25.00

STEVENSON, D.E. *Mrs Tim Gets a Job.* 1974. HRW. 2nd. VG/dj. P3. $18.00

STEVENSON, Janet. *Woman Aboard.* 1969. NY. Crown. 8vo. 312p. VG/dj. P4. $25.00

STEVENSON, M.C. *Zuni Indians: Their Mythology...* 1970. Rio Grande Classic. rpt. 139 pl. F. M4. $35.00

STEVENSON, Robert Louis. *Apology for Idlers.* 1932. NY. Ashlar. 1/200. 8vo. 28p. gilt brd. F. B24. $150.00

STEVENSON, Robert Louis. *Black Arrow.* 1888. Scribner. 1st (precedes Eng). yel prt wrp. M24. $375.00

STEVENSON, Robert Louis. *Child's Garden of Verses.* (1888). Scribner. early. quarter cloth/paper brd. G. M5. $42.00

STEVENSON, Robert Louis. *Child's Garden of Verses.* 1896. Bodley Head. 1st Eng. ils Charles Robinson. 8vo. aeg. gr cloth. R5. $250.00

STEVENSON, Robert Louis. *Child's Garden of Verses.* 1929. 1st. ils Eulalie. VG. S13. $18.00

STEVENSON, Robert Louis. *Child's Garden of Verses.* 1929. Saalfield. ils Clara Burd. folio. stiff sc. M5. $50.00

STEVENSON, Robert Louis. *Child's Garden of Verses.* 1947. Oxford. 1st thus. ils Tasha Tudor. 118p. F/VG-. P2. $250.00

STEVENSON, Robert Louis. *Child's Garden of Verses.* 1978. Golden. 1st. sm 4to. 45p. VG. C14. $12.00

STEVENSON, Robert Louis. *Dr Jekyll & Mr Hyde & an Inland Voyage.* 1912. Tauchnitz. F/wrp. M2. $25.00

STEVENSON, Robert Louis. *Dr Jekyll & Mr Hyde.* 1923. Everleigh Nash/Grayson. VG/fair. P3. $35.00

STEVENSON, Robert Louis. *Footnote to History. Eight Years of Trouble in Samoa.* 1892. Scribner. 1st Am. 8vo. 322p. olive gr cloth. F. B24. $75.00

STEVENSON, Robert Louis. *Kidnapped.* 1913. Scribner. 1st. ils NC Wyeth/14 mc pl. 289p. blk cloth/label. M20. $100.00

STEVENSON, Robert Louis. *Morality of the Profession of Letters.* 1899. Gouverneur, NY. Brothers of the Book. 1st separate. 1/299. gilt cloth. M24. $75.00

STEVENSON, Robert Louis. *Poems, Hitherto Unpublished.* 1921. Bibliophile Soc. 1st. 1/450. 8vo. faux vellum/cloth. F. B24. $150.00

STEVENSON, Robert Louis. *Poems From Child's Garden of Verses.* 1987. London. Orchard. 4 pop-ups. F. P2. $15.00

STEVENSON, Robert Louis. *Songs With Music From a Child's Garden of Verses.* nd. Nelson. ils Margaret Tarrant. 55p. gilt bdg. VG+. P2. $65.00

STEVENSON, Robert Louis. *St Ives, Being the Adventures of a French Prisoner in Eng...* 1898. London. Heinemann. 1st/1st issue. 8vo. 312p. B24. $100.00

STEVENSON, Robert Louis. *Stevenson Medley.* 1899. Chatto Windus. 1st. 1/300. sgn. half morocco/gilt bl cloth. M24. $200.00

STEVENSON, Robert Louis. *Travels With a Donkey.* 1957. NY. LEC. 1st thus. 1/1500. ils/sgn Roger Duvoisin. F/glassine/case. Q1. $100.00

STEVENSON, Robert Louis. *Treasure Island.* 1938. Rand McNally. decor brd. NF. P3. $20.00

STEVENSON, Robert Louis. *When the Devil Was Well.* 1921. Bibliogphile Soc. 1st. 1/450. 8vo. 127p. faux vellum/cloth. B24. $150.00

STEVENSON, W.F. *Wounds in War: Mechanism on Their Production & Treatment.* 1898. NY. 1st. ils/photos. 437p. A13. $200.00

STEVENSON, William G. *Thirteen Months in the Rebel Army.* 1959. VG/VG. M17. $20.00

STEWARD, John F. *Reaper: History of Those Who...Made Bread Cheap.* nd (1931). NY. Greenburg. 1st. 382p. gr cloth. xl. B22. $16.00

STEWART, Charles Samuel. *Visit to the South Seas in the United States Ship Vincennes.* 1833. NY. John P Haven. 2nd. rebound modern cloth. T7. $350.00

STEWART, Desmond. *Middle East. Temple of Janus.* 1971. Doubleday. 1st. 8vo. 414p. cloth. VG. W1. $12.00

STEWART, Desmond. *TE Lawrence.* 1977. Harper Row. 1st. 8vo. 352p. NF/dj. W1. $25.00

STEWART, Edgar. *Custer's Luck.* 1955. Norman, OK. 1st. 522p. VG/dj. J2. $85.00

STEWART, Elihu. *Down the Mackenzie & Up the Ukon in 1906.* 1912. London. John Lane. 2nd. fld map/30 photo pl. 270p. VG. P4. $65.00

STEWART, Fred Mustard. *Pomp & Circumstance.* 1991. Dutton. 1st. F/dj. P3. $20.00

STEWART, Fred Mustard. *Titan.* 1985. S&S. 1st. F/dj. P3. $18.00

STEWART, George R. *California Trail: Epic With Many Heroes.* 1962. McGraw Hill. 10th. F/F. O4. $15.00

STEWART, George R. *Committee of Vigilance: Revolution in San Francisco.* 1851. Houghton Mifflin. 1st. NF/VG clip. O4. $25.00

STEWART, George R. *Earth Abides.* 1949. Random. NF/dj. M2. $50.00

STEWART, George R. *Fire.* 1946. Random. 1st. inscr. F. M19. $25.00

STEWART, George R. *Man, an Autobiography.* 1948. 1st Eng. F/VG. M19. $35.00

STEWART, George R. *North-South Continental Highway Looking South.* 1957. Boston. Houghton Mifflin. 230p. dj. F3. $15.00

STEWART, George R. *Ordeal by Hunger: Story of the Donnor Party.* 1960. Houghton Mifflin. New Ed. VG/G. O4. $15.00

STEWART, George R. *Pickett's Charge: Microhistory of Final Attack Gettysburg.* 1959. Houghton Mifflin. 1st. 354p. cloth. VG/VG. M8. $65.00

STEWART, Gordon T. *Documents Relating to Greata Awakening of Nova Scotia...* 1982. Toronto. Champlain Soc. 299p. gilt red cloth. NF. P4. $95.00

STEWART, Henry. *Domestic Sheep: Its Culture & General Management.* (1900). Chicago. Am Sheep Breeder. photos. 383p. cloth. VG. M12. $25.00

STEWART, Henry. *Shepherd's Manual: A Practical Treatise on the Sheep.* 1876. Orange Judd. 12mo. 252p. cloth. K3. $40.00

STEWART, Ian. *Peking Payoff.* 1975. Macmillan. 1st. F/dj. P3. $15.00

STEWART, Jane L. *Campfire Girl's Adventure.* 1914. Saalfield. 245p. G. W2. $45.00

STEWART, Mary. *Airs Above the Ground.* 1965. Hodder Stoughton. 1st. VG/dj. P3. $35.00

STEWART, Mary. *Crystal Cave.* 1970. Morrow. 1st. NF/NF clip. H11. $30.00

STEWART, Mary. *Gabriel Hounds.* 1967. Hodder Stoughton. 1st. VG/dj. P3. $30.00

STEWART, Mary. *Hollow Hills.* 1973. Morrow. 1st. NF/F. H11. $25.00

STEWART, Mary. *Ivy Tree.* 1961. London. Hodder Stoughton. 1st Eng. NF/VG+. T11. $35.00

STEWART, Mary. *Last Enchantment.* 1979. Hodder Stoughton. 1st. F/dj. P3. $25.00

STEWART, Mary. *Thornyhold.* 1988. Hodder Stoughton. 1st. F/F. P3. $25.00

STEWART, Mary. *Wickey Day.* 1983. Morrow. 1st Am. F/F. B4. $45.00

STEWART, Michael. *Blindsight.* 1987. St Martin. 1st. F/dj. M2. $22.00

STEWART, Michael. *Far Cry.* 1984. Freundlich. 1st. VG/dj. P3. $18.00

STEWART, Michael. *Monkey Shines.* 1983. Freundlich. 1st. F/F. H11. $30.00

STEWART, P. *Winter in the Kitchen: Wine & Cookery of the West.* 1974. ils. easel stand format. VG. E6. $18.00

STEWART, R.J. *Book of Merlin.* 1987. Blanford. 1st. F/dj. P3. $25.00

STEWART, Ramona. *Possession of Joel Delaney.* nd. Little Brn. 2nd. VG/dj. P3. $13.00

STEWART, Watt. *Keith & Costa Rica.* 1964. Albuquerque. 1st. 210p. dj. F3. $25.00

STEWART & STEWART. *Adolph Sutro: A Biography.* 1962. Berkeley. 1st. NF/G+. O4. $15.00

STEYERMARK, Julian A. *Flora of Missouri.* 1963. Ames. 390 pl/line drawings/distribution maps. F/dj. B26. $100.00

STICK, David. *Graveyard of the Atlantic, Shipwrecks of NC Coast.* 1952. Chapel Hill. sgn. 8vo. 276p. VG/worn. P4. $45.00

STICK, David. *Outer Banks of North Carolina.* 1958. Chapel Hill. 1st. sgn. VG/VG. B11. $60.00

STILL, William. *Underground Railroad.* 1872. Phil. Porter Coates. 1st. 70 engravings. 780p. gilt cloth/rebacked. NF. B4. $500.00

STILLE, Charles. *Northern Interests & Southern Independence.* 1863. Phil. 1st. prt wrp. O8. $45.00

STILLMAN, Jacob D.B. *Around the Horn to California in 1849.* 1967. Lewis Osbourne. 1st. 1/1150. F/sans. O4. $25.00

STILLMAN, Jacob D.B. *Wanderings in the Southwest in 1855.* 1990. Clark. Western Frontiersmen Series XXIII. 193p. VG. J2. $65.00

STILLWELL, Norma. *Bird Songs.* 1964. NY. 194p. VG/dj. S15. $10.00

STINE, G. Harry. *ICBM.* 1994. NY. Orion. 1st. 8vo. 291p. VG/dj. K5. $22.00

STINE, G. Harry. *Rocket Power & Space Flight.* 1957. Holt. 1st. 8vo. 182p. VG/partial. K5. $32.00

STIRLING, M.W. *Native Peoples of New Guinea.* 1943. Smithsonian. 8vo. 25p. VG/prt wrp. P4. $25.00

STIRLING, Monica. *Wild Swan: Life & Times of Hans Christian Andersen.* 1965. London. Collins. 1st. 8vo. bl tweed. VG/G. T5. $45.00

STIRTON, R.A. *New Genus of Interatheres From Miocene of Colombia.* 1953. Berkeley. ils/figures/2 maps. F/wrp. M12. $25.00

STOCKING, Charles Francis. *Thou Israel.* 1921. Maestro. 1st. VG. M2. $25.00

STOCKTON, Frank R. *Great Stone of Sardis.* 1899. Harper. VG. M2. $30.00

STOCKTON, Frank R. *Great War Syndicate.* nd. Dodd Mead. VG. M2. $40.00

STOCKTON, Frank R. *Stockton's Stories, First Series. The Lady or the Tiger.* 1886. Scribner. 1st thus. 201p. teg. gr buff cloth. VG. B22. $15.00

STOCKTON, Robert F. *Sketch of Life of Com Robert F Stockton...* 1856. NY. Derby Jackson. 1st. 8vo. 131p+2p ads. gilt tan cloth/red leather. K7. $65.00

STODDARD, Charles Warren. *Island of Tranquil Delights.* 1904. Boston. Herbert Turner. 1st. gilt gr cloth. F. M24. $150.00

STODDARD, John L. *John L Stoddard's Lectures. Vol X.* 1904. Balch Bros. VG. O4. $20.00

STODDARD, John L. *John L Stoddard's Lectures. Vol 10.* 1905. Boston. Balch Bros. 8vo. 304p. VG+. F7. $35.00

STODDARD, R.H. *Anecdote Bibliographies of Thackeray & Dickens.* 1874. Scribner. 1st. gilt cream cloth. F. M24. $60.00

STODDARD, S.R. *Midnight Sun...Story of Cruise of the Ohio...1897.* 1901. Glenfalls. self pub. inscr. 200p. A17. $75.00

STODDARD, Sandol. *Doubleday Illustrated Children's Bible.* 1983. Doubleday. ils Tony Chen. 383p. F/dj. B29. $6.50

STODDARD, Theodore Lothrop. *Rising Tide of Color Against White World-Supremacy.* 1920. Scribner. 1st/2nd prt. 320p. cloth. VG. M8. $65.00

STODDART, Anna M. *Elizabeth Pease Nichol.* 1899. London. Dent. 314p. G. V3. $18.00

STOFF, Michael B. *Manhattan Project.* 1991. McGraw Hill. 1st. 298p. VG/wrp. K3. $15.00

STOFFLET. *Dr Seuss From Then to Now, a Catalog.* 1986. San Diego Mus Art. 4to. ils. 96p. F/F. A4. $45.00

STOIKO, Miahael. *Soviet Rocketry.* 1970. HRW. 8vo. 272p. G/dj. K5. $30.00

STOKER, Bram. *Annotated Dracula.* 1975. Potter. 1st. F/dj. M2. $75.00

STOKER, Bram. *Dracula's Guest.* 1937. NY. 1st. G. B5. $40.00

STOKER, Bram. *Dracula.* nd. Modern Lib. VG/fair. P3. $15.00

STOKER, Bram. *Personal Reminiscences of Henry Irving.* 1906. Macmillan. 1st. 2 vol. teg. gilt red cloth. F. M24. $150.00

STOKER, Bram. *Snake's Pass.* Authorized Facsimile (1891 Sampson Low). NF/wrp. M22. $30.00

STOKES, Donald. *Appointment With Fear.* 1950. Coward McCann. 1st. VG/G. P3. $18.00

STOKES, William. *Honduras.* 1950. Madison, WI. 1st. 315p. dj. F3. $20.00

STOKES, William. *William Stokes: His Life & Work (1804-1878).* 1989. London. Fisher Unwin. 1st. 8vo. 255p. gilt bdg. K3. $40.00

STOLBOV, Bruce. *Last Fall.* 1987. Doubleday. 1st. F/dj. M2/P3. $15.00

STOLTE, Lawrence. *Forgotten Salmon of the Merrimack.* 1981. Dept of Interior. 214p. VG. S15. $18.00

STOLZ, Mary. *Go & Catch a Flying Fish.* 1979. Harper Row. 1st. VG/VG-. P2. $25.00

STOLZ, Mary. *Leftover Elf.* 1952. Harper. probable 1st. ils Peggy Bacon. 48p. VG/G. P2. $30.00

STOLZ, Mary. *Pangur Ban.* 1988. Harper Row. 1st. ils Pamela Johnson. tan brd/brn cloth spine. F/F. T5. $20.00

STONE, Chuck. *King Strut.* 1970. Bobbs Merrill. 1st. inscr. F/VG. B4. $75.00

STONE, Ebenezer. *Digest of Militia Laws of Massachusettes.* 1851. VG. E6. $65.00

STONE, Elizabeth Arnold. *Unita County: Its Place in History.* nd. np. scarce. A19. $85.00

STONE, Hampton. *Kid Who Came Home With a Corpse.* 1972. S&S. 1st. VG/dj. P3. $15.00

STONE, I.F. *War Years 1939-1945: A Nonconformist History of Our Times.* 1988. Little Brn. 1st. VG/G. V4. $12.50

STONE, Irving. *Agony & the Ecstasy.* 1963. Doubleday. 1st ils. inscr/dtd 1965. F/case. w/MTI souvenir book. Q1. $100.00

STONE, Irving. *Depths of Glory.* 1985. Franklin Lib. 1st. sgn. leather. F. B35. $55.00

STONE, Irving. *Manana Land: Irving Stone's Southern California.* 1991. LA. Hist Soc of S CA. rpt. 8vo. M/wrp. T10. $15.00

STONE, Irving. *Passions of the Mind: Biographical Novel of Sigmund Freud.* 1971. Doubleday. 1st trade. inscr. F/NF. M25. $45.00

STONE, Josephine Rector. *Green Is for Galanx.* 1980. Atheneum. 1st. VG/dj. P3. $18.00

STONE, Julius. *Messiah Idea in Jewish History.* 1906. Phil. Jewish Pub. 1st. 347p. brn cloth. B22. $7.00

STONE, Raymond. *Tommy Tiptop & His Boy Scouts (#5).* 1914. Chas E Graham. lists 6 titles. 124p. VG. M20. $16.00

STONE, Robert. *Children of Light.* 1986. Knopf. 1st. NF/dj. A24. $25.00

STONE, Robert. *Children of Light.* 1986. Knopf. 1st. sgn. F/F. T11. $75.00

STONE, Robert. *Dog Soldiers.* 1974. Houghton Mifflin. 1st. NF/VG+. A24. $75.00

STONE, Robert. *Dog Soldiers.* 1974. Houghton Mifflin. 1st. sgn. F/F. D10. $125.00

STONE, Robert. *Flag for Sunrise.* 1981. NY. Knopf. 1st. sgn. F/NF. T11. $125.00

STONE, Robert. *Outerbridge Reach.* 1992. NY. Ticknor Fields. 1st. 1/300. sgn/#d/special bdg. F/case. Q1. $125.00

STONE, Stuart B. *Kingdom of Why, Being the Strange Story of Lucile's...* 1913. Bobbs Merrill. 1st. ils Peter Newell. blk cloth/label. VG. M24. $125.00

STONE, Ted. *13 Canadian Ghost Stories.* 1988. Prairie BOoks. 1st. F/dj. P3. $20.00

STONE, Witmer. *Bird Studies at Old Cape May.* 1965 (1937). NY. Dover. rpt. 2 vol. ils/maps. VG. S15. $27.50

STONE, Zackary. *Modigliani Scandal.* 1976. Collins Crime Club. 1st. NF/dj. P3. $25.00

STONEHOUSE, J.H. *Picaddily Notes.* 1933-1938. London. Henry Sotheran Ltd. crude bdg. A17. $45.00

STONER, Dayton. *Rodents of Iowa.* 1918. Des Moines. ils. 172p. VG. S15. $15.00

STONES, E.L.G. *FW Maitland, Letters to George Neilson.* 1976. Glasgow. 56p. sewn wrp. M11. $45.00

STOPES, Marie Carmichael. *Enduring Passion: Further New Contributions...* 1931. Putnam. 1st. 181p. VG. A25. $12.00

STOREY, David. *This Sporting Life.* 1960. Macmillan. 1st Am. author's 1st book. F/NF. B4. $100.00

STORM, Hyemeyohsts. *Seven Arrows.* (19728). Harper Row. 1st. F/dj. M25. $100.00

STORM, Hyemeyohsts. *Song of Heyoehkah.* 1981. Harper Row. 1st. VG/VG. L3. $40.00

STORR, Anthony. *Solitude: Return to the Self.* 1989. Ballantine. 216p. VG. B29. $6.50

STORRS, Les. *Santa Monica: Portrait of a City, Yesterday & Today.* 1974. Santa Monica. 68p. pict brd. D11. $50.00

STOUT, David. *Carolina Skeletons.* 1988. Mysterious. 1st. F/dj. M15. $65.00

STOUT, David. *Hell Gate.* 1990. Mysterious. 1st. VG/dj. P3. $15.00

STOUT, Gardner D. *Shorebirds of North America.* 1967. NY. 32 full-p mc pl. 270p. F/VG. S15. $150.00

STOUT, Rex. *Alphabet Hicks.* 1941. Farrar Rhinehart. 1st. VG/dj. M15. $250.00

STOUT, Rex. *Before Midnight.* 1955. Viking. 1st. F/F. M15. $200.00

STOUT, Rex. *Family Affair.* 1975. Viking. 1st. F/F. M15. $45.00

STOUT, Rex. *Final Deduction.* 1961. Viking. 1st. NF/remnant. M25. $25.00

STOUT, Rex. *Golden Remedy.* 1931. Vanguard. 1st. author's 3rd novel. VG/dj. M15. $400.00

STOUT, Rex. *In the Best of Families.* 1950. Viking. 1st. NF/dj. M25. $150.00

STOUT, Rex. *Mother Hunt.* 1963. Viking. 1st. F/NF. Q1. $125.00

STOUT, Rex. *Murder by the Book.* 1951. Viking. 1st. NF/NF. M22. $125.00

STOUT, Rex. *Please Pass the Guilt.* 1973. Viking. 1st. VG/dj. P3. $40.00

STOUT, Rex. *Prisoner's Base.* 1952. Viking. 1st. NF/dj. M15. $150.00

STOUT, Rex. *Right to Die.* 1974. Viking. 1st. F/NF. B2. $65.00

STOUT, Rex. *Second Confession.* 1973. Tom Stacey. F/dj. P3. $22.00

STOUT, Rex. *Too Many Women.* 1947. Viking. 1st. VG/G. M22. $70.00

STOUT, Rex. *Triple Jeopardy.* 1952. Viking. 1st. VG/VG. M22. $95.00

STOUT, Wesley W. *Bullets by the Billion.* 1946. Detroit, MI. Chrysler Corp. A19. $20.00

STOUT, Wesley W. *Secret.* 1947. Detroit. Chrysler Corp. ils. 67p. K3. $25.00

STOUT, William B. *Boy's Book of Mechanical Models.* 1916. Little Brn. 1st. 8vo. 257p. cloth. VG. T10. $75.00

STOWE, Harriet Beecher. *Earthly Care, a Heavenly Discipline.* 1855. Boston. JP Jewett. 1st/later prt. glazed gr pict wrp. M24. $150.00

STOWE, Harriet Beecher. *Home & Home Papers.* 1865. Ticknor Fields. 1st/A bdg (gilt bl cloth). F. M24. $100.00

STOWE, Harriet Beecher. *Men of Our Times.* 1868. Hartford. 1st/2nd state. aeg. gilt gr cloth. F. M24. $100.00

STOWE, Harriet Beecher. *My Wife & I; or, Harry Henderson's History.* 1871. NY. JB Ford. 1st. 474p. stp purple cloth. G. H1. $12.00

STOWE, Harriet Beecher. *Palmetto-Leaves.* 1873. Boston. JR Osgood. 1st. gr pict cloth (1st bdg, Osgood imp at foot). M24. $200.00

STOWE, Harriet Beecher. *Story of Topsy From Uncle Tom's Cabin.* 1908. Reilly Britton. ils JR Neill. 12mo. pict brd. R5. $150.00

STOWE, Harriet Beecher. *Uncle Tom's Cabin.* ca 1910. Ward Lock. 12mo. VG. M5. $65.00

STOWELL, Robert E. *Thoreau Gazetteer.* 1970. Princeton. 1st. thin 4to. 56p. F/dj. T10. $75.00

STRAHAN, Kay Cleaver. *Footprints.* 1929. Crime Club. 1st. G. P3. $20.00

STRAHORN, Carrie Adell. *Fifteen Thousand Miles by Stage.* 1911. ils Chas M Russell/others. G+. M17. $100.00

STRAIGHT, Susan. *Blacker Than a Thousand Midnights.* 1994. Hyperion. 1st. sgn. F/F. B3. $40.00

STRAIGHT, Susan. *I Been in Sorrow's Kitchen & Licked Out All the Pots.* 1992. NY. Hyperion. 1st. F/F. H11. $50.00

STRAIN, Frances Bruce. *New Patterns in Sex Teaching: Guide to Answering Children...* 1951. Appleton Century Crofts. revised. photos. 262p. VG. A25. $10.00

STRAND, Mark. *Late Hour.* 1978. Atheneum. 1st. assn copy. F/dj. V1. $35.00

STRAND, Mark. *Monument.* 1978. Ecco. 1st. sgn. NF/VG. R14. $275.00

STRAND, Mark. *Mr & Mrs Baby & Other Stories.* 1985. Knopf. 1st. assn copy. F/dj. V1. $25.00

STRANG, Herbert. *Lord of the Seas.* nd. London. 1st. VG. M2. $35.00

STRANGE, Ian. *Bird Man: An Autobiography.* 1976. London. ils. 182p. NF. S15. $15.00

STRANGE, John Stephen. *Night of Reckoning.* 1959. Collins Crime Club. 1st. VG. P3. $20.00

STRANGE, John Stephen. *Strangler Fig.* 1930. Crime Club. 1st. VG. P3. $30.00

STRANGER, Joyce. *Fox at Drummers' Darkness.* 1977. FSG. 1st Am. VG/VG. O3. $25.00

STRANGER, Joyce. *Running Foxes.* 1966. Viking. 1st Am. VG/VG. O3. $25.00

STRAPAROLA. *Italian Novelists.* 1909. London. Soc of Bibliophiles. 7 vol. 1/300. half red morocco. A17. $150.00

STRATEMEYER, Edward. *Colonial Series: At the Fall of Montreal.* 1903. Lee Shepard. 212p. gilt red cloth. VG. M20. $25.00

STRATEMEYER, Edward. *Lakeport Series: Boat Club Boys of Lakeport (#3).* 1908. Lee Shepard. 297p. VG. M20. $25.00

STRATEMEYER, Edward. *Old Glory Series: Under Otis in the Philippines.* 1899. Lee Shepard. 332p+ads. tan cloth. VG. M20. $22.50

STRATEMEYER, Edward. *Stratemeyer Popular Series: Oliver Bright's Search.* 1899 (1895). Lee Shepard. 245p+ads. VG+. M20. $20.00

STRATTON, R.B. *Captivity of the Oatman Girls...* 1982. Time-Life. rpt. 290p. aeg. F. M4. $25.00

STRAUB, Peter. *Floating Dragon.* 1983. London. Collins. 1st. F/dj. P3. $35.00

STRAUB, Peter. *Floating Dragon.* 1983. NY. Putnam. 1st. NF/dj. N4. $40.00

STRAUB, Peter. *Ghost Story.* 1979. CMG. 1st. VG/dj. H11/P3. $45.00

STRAUB, Peter. *Koko.* 1988. Dutton. 1st. F/F. H11. $40.00

STRAUB, Peter. *Shadow Land.* 1980. CMG. 1st. F/dj. M2. $25.00

STRAUB, Peter. *Throat.* 1993. Dutton. 1st. inscr/sgn. F/F. A23. $46.00

STRAUB, Peter. *Wild Animals.* 1984. Putnam. 1st. VG/dj. P3. $35.00

STRAUS, Rachael. *Regensburg & Augsburg.* 1939. JPS. 16mo. ils. 261p. VG+. S3. $35.00

STRAUS, Ralph. *Pengard Awake.* 1920. Appleton. 1st am. F/NF. M15. $125.00

STRAUSS, I. *Paint, Powder & Make-Up.* 1938. NY. 219p. cloth. A17. $20.00

STRAUSS, Lewis L. *Men & Decisions.* 1962. Doubleday. ils. 468p. VG. K3. $20.00

STREATFIELD, Noel. *Beyond the Vicarage.* 1971. London. Collins. 1st. 214p. VG/dj. P2. $35.00

STREATFIELD, Noel. *Vicarage Family.* 1963. London. Collins. 1st. 8vo. 246p. red tweed brd. VG. T5. $45.00

STREET, David. *Horses: A Working Tradition.* 1976. Toronto. McGraw Hill Ryerson. 1st. 4to. VG/VG. O3. $38.00

STREET, Donald M. *Ocean Sailing Yacht.* 1973. Norton. 4th. 703p. F/dj. A17. $20.00

STREET, James. *Look Away: A Dixie Notebook.* 1936. NY. 1st. VG/dj. B5. $50.00

STREET, P. *Animal Reproduction.* 1974. Taplinger. 8vo. 263p. VG/F. B1. $22.50

STREET, P. *Crab & Its Relatives.* 1966. London. Faber. photos/drawings, 167p. dj. B1. $35.00

STREETER, Daniel W. *Camels!* 1927. NY/London. Putnam. 1st. 8vo. 277p. VG. W1. $12.00

STRETE, Craig. *Bleeding Man.* 1977. Greenwillow. 1st. F/dj. M2. $45.00

STRIEBER, Whitley. *Billy.* 1990. Putnam. 1st. F/dj. P3. $20.00

STRIEBER, Whitley. *Black Magic.* 1982. Morrow. 1st. VG/VG. N4. $40.00

STRIEBER, Whitley. *Communion.* 1987. Morrow. 1st. F/dj. M2. $25.00

STRIEBER, Whitley. *Night Church.* 1983. S&S. 1st. F/dj. M2. $20.00

STRIEBER, Whitley. *Transformation.* 1988. London. Century. 1st. VG/VG. M22. $12.00

STRIEBER, Whitley. *Wolf in Shadows.* 1985. Knopf Sierra Club. 1st. VG/dj. P3. $12.00

STRIEBER, Whitley. *Wolfen.* 1978. Morrow. 1st. F/dj. M2. $65.00

STRIEBER, Whitley. *Wolfen.* 1978. Morrow. 1st. VG/dj. P3. $25.00

STRIKER, Fran. *Lone Ranger & the Code of the West (#16).* 1954. Grosset Dunlap. 180p. VG/dj (lists 18 titles). M20. $65.00

STRIMPLE, Helen. *Lindy Lou & the Green Umbrella.* 1946. Broadman. 1st. pict brd. VG. M5. $28.00

STRODE, Hudson. *Jefferson Davis: American Patriot, 1808-1861.* 1955. Harcourt Brace. 1st. 460p. VG/ragged. M20. $25.00

STRODE, Hudson. *Now in Mexico.* 1947 (1946). Harcourt. 1st. dj. F3. $15.00

STRODE, Muriel. *My Little Book of Prayer.* 1906. Open Court. 3rd. inscr/dtd 1911. teg. gilt blk cloth. M24. $475.00

STROM, Sharon Hartman. *Beyond the Typewriter: Gender, Class & Origins...* 1992. IL U. 1st. F/F. V4. $20.00

STRONG, Anna Louise. *Cash & Violence in Laos & Vietnam.* 1962. Mainstream. 1st. NF/wrp. B2. $30.00

STRONG, L.A.G. *Corporal Time.* 1934. Gollancz. VG. P3. $15.00

STRONG, Phil. *Horses & Americans.* 1939. Stokes. 1st. 333p. VG/VG. O3. $48.00

STRONG, Phil. *No-Sitch: The Hound.* 1936. Dodd Mead. 1st. ils Kurt Wiese. 80p. VG+/VG. P2. $75.00

STRONG, Phil. *25 Stories of Mystery & Imagination.* nd. Garden City. VG. P3. $25.00

STRONG, W.C. *Culture of the Grape.* 1866. Boston. Tilton. 355p. A10. $80.00

STRONG, William. *Paracas, Nazca & Tiahuanacoid Cultural Relationships...* 1957. Salt Lake City. photos/fld map. 48p. wrp. F3. $30.00

STRONGIN, Lynn. *Bones & Kim.* 1980. Argyle, NY. Spinsters Inc. 1st. 116p. sc. VG. A25. $10.00

STROOTMAN, Ralph. *History of the 363rd Infantry...* 1947. WA, DC. 1st. photos/maps/roster. 354p. VG. S16. $65.00

STROUD, Carsten. *Sniper's Moon.* 1990. Bantam. 1st. VG/dj. P3. $20.00

STROUD, D.V. *Inscribed Union Swords 1861-1865.* 1983. Kilgore. 1/1500. inscr/#d. photos. 192p. F. M4. $60.00

STROUP, Thomas B. *Religious Rite & Ceremony in Milton's Poetry.* 1968. Lexington, KY. sgn. VG/VG. B11. $18.00

STRUGATSKY & STRUGATSKY. *For Rainbow & the Second Invasion From Mars.* 1979. Macmillan. 1st. VG/dj. P3. $15.00

STRUGATSKY & STRUGATSKY. *Noon: 22nd Century.* 1978. Macmillan. 1st. VG/dj. P3. $18.00

STRUGATSKY & STRUGATSKY. *Time Wanderers.* 1986. NY. Richardson Steirman. 1st English-language ed. F/F. T2. $20.00

STRUGATSKY & STRUGATSKY. *Ugly Swans.* 1979. Macmillan. 1st. VG/dj. P3. $15.00

STRUNSKY, Simson. *King Akhnaton.* 1928. Longmans. 1st. NF/dj. M2. $15.00

STRUTHER, Jan. *Sycamore Square.* 1932. Oxford. 1st Am. ils Ernest Shepard. VG-/fair. P2. $30.00

STRYK, Lucian. *Bells of Lombardy.* 1986. IL U. 1st. inscr. F/dj. V1. $20.00

STUART, Alexander. *War Zone.* 1989. Doubleday. 1st. F/dj. M2. $17.00

STUART, Anthony. *Russian Leave.* 1981. Arbor. 1st. VG/dj. P3. $15.00

STUART, Bernard. *How to Become a Successful Engineer.* 1871. Edinburgh. 5th. 127p. VG. B14. $75.00

STUART, David. *Garden Triumphant.* 1988. Harper Row. 8vo. ils. 316p. F/dj. A22. $25.00

STUART, Dora Jessie. *Return to Thrush Green.* 1979. Houghton Mifflin. 1st Am. ils JS Goodall. 256p. VG+. A25. $8.00

STUART, Henry Logan. *Weeping Cross: Unworldly Story.* 1908. Doubleday. 1st. 497p. purple cloth. VG+. B22. $7.50

STUART & STUART. *Field Guide to the Mammals of Southern Africa.* 1988. Sanibel. Curtis. 100+ mc pl/ils/distribution maps. 272p. NF/F. M12. $20.00

STUART & STUART. *Lost Kingdoms of the Mayas.* 1993. NGS. 1st. 4to. 248p. dj. F3. $35.00

• **STUBBIER, Adrian.** *Road to Revolution in Spain: The Coal Miners of Asters...* 1987. IL U. 1st. F/F. V4. $12.50

STUBBS, Jean. *Dear Laura.* 1973. Macmillan. 1st. VG/fair. P3. $13.00

STUBBS, Jean. *Painted Face.* 1974. Macmillan. 1st. VG/dj. P3. $20.00

STUBBS, Jean. *Painted Face.* 1974. Stein Day. 1st. sgn. 240p. F/VG. W2. $25.00

STUBER, Stanley I. *Illustrated Bible & Church Handbook.* 1966. Assn. 532p. VG/dj. B29. $8.00

STUCKY & STUCKY. *Lithographs of Stow Wengenroth 1931-1972.* 1974. Boston Public Lib. 1st. VG/VG. M17. $75.00

STUEWER, Roger H. *Nuclear Physics in Retrospect.* 1979. NM U. 340p. VG. K3. $20.00

STUFF, Harry S. *Siwash, His Book. Being a Bit of Indian Philosophy...* 1908. Stuff Prt Concern. 8vo. die-cut bdg as house. F/prt tan wrp. B24. $200.00

STUFF, Olive Griffith. *Variations & Relationships in Snakes of Genus Pituophis.* 1940. Smithsonian. 225p. VG. S15. $30.00

STUPHEN, W.G. Van T. *Golficide & Other Tales.* 1898. Harper. 1st. VG. M2. $25.00

STUPKA, Arthur. *Wildflowers in Color.* 1982 (1965). NY. photos. 144p. B26. $14.00

STURGEON, Theodore. *Godbody.* 1986. DIF. 1st. VG/dj. P3. $20.00

STURTEVANT, Edgar H. *Hittite Glossary: Words of Known or Conjectured...* 1936-39. Phil. PA U. 2nd. 2 parts in 1. lg 8vo. VG/wrp. W1. $45.00

STYKES, Christopher. *Troubled Loyalty, a Biography.* 1968. London. 1st. VG/VG. T9. $35.00

STYKES, Jo. *Stubborn Mare.* 1957. Winston. 1st. VG. O3. $15.00

STYRON, William. *Confessions of Nat Turner.* 1967. Random. 1st. sgn. F/F. D10. $145.00

STYRON, William. *Darkness Visible.* 1990. Random. 1st. F/dj. Q1. $25.00

STYRON, William. *Sophie's Choice.* 1979. Random. 1st. F/F. B35. $35.00

STYRON, William. *This Quiet Dust & Other Writings.* 1982. Random. 1st. F/F. B3. $30.00

STYRON, William. *Tidewater Morning.* 1990. Helsinki. Eurographica. 1st. 1/350. sgn/#d. F/stiff wrp/dj. B4. $200.00

STYTHE, R. Margaret. *Art of Illustration 1750-1900.* 1970. London. Lib Assn. 1st. sq 4to. ils/index. T10. $45.00

SUBIK, Rudolf. *Decorative Cacti.* 1972. NY. 132p. VG/dj. B26. $9.00

SUBLETT, Jesse. *Rock Critic Murders.* 1989. Viking. 1st. author's 1st book. F/dj. M25. $35.00

SUBRAMANI. *Indo-Fijan Experience.* 1979. St Lucia. 1st. 8vo. 207p. M/dj. P4. $20.00

SUDHALTER, R. *Bix: Man & Legend.* 1974. Arlington. 1st. VG/VG. B5. $75.00

SUDWORTH, G.B. *Forest Trees of the Pacific Slope.* 1967. Dover. 8vo. 455p. B1. $18.00

SUE, Eugene. *Wandering Jew.* 1844-1845. London. 3 vol. 1st. rebound. VG. M2. $350.00

SUGDEN, John. *Sir Francis Drake.* 1991. NY. Holt. 1st. 8vo. 353p. map ep. half cloth. F/dj. P4. $30.00

SUHL, Yuri. *One Foot in America.* 1951. Macmillan. not stated 1st. author's 1st novel. 252p. F/VG. H1. $15.00

SULLIVAN, Eleanor. *Fifty Years of the Best From Ellery Queen.* 1991. Carroll Graf. VG/dj. P3. $23.00

SULLIVAN, Frank. *Pearl in Every Oyster.* 1938. Little Brn. 1st. sgn. VG. B11. $85.00

SULLIVAN, Katharine. *Girls on Parole.* 1956. Houghton Mifflin. 1st. 243p. VG/dj. A25. $38.00

SULLIVAN, Maurice. *Jedediah Smith, Trader & Trailbreaker.* 1936. Pr of Pioneers. 1st. 233p. VG/dj. J2. $225.00

SULLIVAN, May Kellogg. *Woman Who Went to Alaska.* 1910. Boston. JH Earle. photos/maps. 392p. dk olive cloth. VG. P4. $75.00

SULLIVAN, T.R. *Boston Old & New.* 1912. Houghton Mifflin. 1/785. 8vo. teg. gilt blk brd. NF. T10. $100.00

SULLIVAN, T.R. *Hand of Petrarch.* 1913. Houghton Mifflin. 1st. VG. M2. $15.00

SULLIVAN, Walter. *Assault on the Unknown.* 1961. McGraw Hill. 8vo. 460p. dj. K5. $14.00

SULLIVAN, Walter. *Landprints on the Magnificent American Landscape.* 1984. Times. 1st. 384p. NF/VG. W2. $30.00

SULLIVAN, Walter. *Long, Long Love.* 1958. Holt. 1st. F/VG. B4. $50.00

SULLIVAN, Walter. *We Are Not Alone.* 1966 (1964). McGraw Hill. revised. 8vo. 325p. VG/dj. K5. $12.00

SULLY, Langdon. *No Tears for the General, the Life of Alfred Sully...* 1879. Am West Pub. 1st. facsimile/photos. VG/VG. J2. $135.00

SULZBERGER, C.L. *Resistentialists.* 1962. Harper. 1st. F/VG+ clip. B4. $450.00

SULZBERGER, C.L. *Tooth Merchant.* 1973. Quadrangle. 1st. G/dj. P3. $10.00

SUMMER, Charles. *Selected Letters.* 1990. Boston. Northwestern. 1st. 8vo. 2 vol. gray cloth. M/djs. T10. $100.00

SUMMERFIELD. *Fantasy & Reason: Children's Literature in 18th Century.* 1985. ils. 315p. F/F. A11. $55.00

SUMMERHAYS, R.S. *Arabian Horse.* 1976. N Hollywood. Wilshire. 8vo. 103p. VG. O3. $10.00

SUMMERHAYS, R.S. *Problem Horse.* 1959. London. Allen. G/dj. A18. $20.00

SUMMERLIN, Lee B. *Skylab: Classroom in Space.* 1977. NASA. 4to. 182p. VG. K5. $40.00

SUMMERS, Ian. *Tomorrow & Beyond.* 1978. Workman. 1st. NF/dj. P3. $25.00

SUMMERS, Mongague. *Popular History of Witchcraft.* 1973. Causeway Books. VG. P3. $15.00

SUMMERS, Montague. *Witchcraft & Black Magic.* 1958. Rider. F/dj. M2. $20.00

SUMMERSELL, C.G. *Journal of George Townley Fullam, Boarding Officer...* 1973. AL U. 1/600. sgn/#d. 229p. bl cloth/leatherette spine. F. M4. $45.00

SUMMERSKILL, Mimi LaFollette. *Aegean Summer: A Family Odyssey.* 1990. Middlebury. PS Eriksson. 1st. ils. 263p. VG/dj. A25. $18.00

SUMMERSON, Henry. *Crown Pleas of the Devon Eyre of 1238.* 1985. Torquay. Devon & Cornwall Record Soc. 163p. prt sewn wrp. M11. $45.00

SUMNER, Charles. *White Slavery in the Barbary States.* 1853. Boston. Jewett. 1st. gilt brn cloth. M24. $650.00

SUMNER, Cid Rickets. *Traveler in the Wilderness.* 1957. NY. Harper. 8vo. blk cloth. NF. F7. $40.00

SUMNER, George. *Compendium of Physiological & Systematic Botany.* 1820. Hartford. 1st. 12mo. 300p. contemporary calf. M1. $150.00

SUMNER, William L. *Organ: Its Evolution, Principles of Construction & Use.* 1958. MacDonald. ils. 466p. fair. B29. $6.00

SUMPTON, Lois. *Cookies & More Cookies.* 1948. IL. Bennet Pub. G/dj. A16. $10.00

SURFACE, Bill. *Roundup at the Double Diamond.* 1974. Houghton Mifflin. 1st. 237p. cloth. VG/dj. M20. $20.00

SURTEES, R.S. *Plain or Ringlets.* 1860. London. Bradbury Evans. 1st. ils. red leather. VG. O3. $250.00

SUSKIND, Patrick. *Pigeon.* 1988. Knopf. 1st Am. F/F. T12. $25.00

SUTCLIFF, Rosemary. *Beowulf.* 1962. Dutton. 1st. 8vo. 93p. yel cloth. VG/G+. T5. $30.00

SUTCLIFF, Rosemary. *Knight's Fee.* 1960. London. Oxford. 1st. 8vo. 241p. VG/G. T5. $40.00

SUTCLIFF, Rosemary. *Road to Camlann.* 1982. Dutton. 1st. VG/VG. P3. $20.00

SUTCLIFF, Rosemary. *Sword & the Circle.* 1981. Bodley Head. 1st. F/dj. P3. $20.00

SUTHERLAND, Donald W. *Assize of Novel Disseisin.* 1973. Clarendon. M11. $75.00

SUTHERLAND. *Best in Children's Books, Children's Literature 1973-78.* 1980. 1400 entries/6 indexes. 559p. F/F. A4. $35.00

SUTHERLAND. *Best in Children's Books, University of Chicago Guide...* 1986. 1400 entries. 521p. F/F. A4. $35.00

SUTIN, Lawrence. *Divine Invasions: Life of Philip K Dick.* 1989. Harmony. 1st. NF/dj. M21. $40.00

SUTLEY, Zack T. *Last Frontier.* 1930. Macmillan. VG. A19. $75.00

SUTTER, Barton. *Cedar Home.* 1977. BOA Ed. 1/26 (of 770). sgns. w/poem card. F. V1. $75.00

SUTTON, Ada Louis. *Teddy Bears.* 1907. Saalfield. ils AJ Schaefer. VG. M5. $65.00

SUTTON, George Miksch. *Eskimo Year.* 1934. NY. 1st. 321p+photos. xl. G. A17. $15.00

SUTTON, George P. *Rocket Propulsion Elements.* 1956. John Wiley. 2nd. 8vo. 483p. xl. K5. $40.00

SUTTON, Henry. *Sacrifice.* 1978. Grosset Dunlap. 1st. F/dj. P3. $20.00

SUTTON, Margaret. *Judy Bolton: Discovery at the Dragon's Mouth (#31).* 1960. Grosset Dunlap. lists to Secret Quest. 182p. VG/dj. M2/M20. $80.00

SUTTON, Margaret. *Judy Bolton: Ghost Parade (#5).* nd. Grosset Dunlap. VG/G. P3. $12.00

SUTTON, Margaret. *Judy Bolton: Haunted Attic (#2).* 1932. Grosset Dunlap. 212p. cloth. VG/dj (lists 10 titles). M20. $50.00

SUTTON, Margaret. *Judy Bolton: Pledge of the Twin Knights (#36).* 1965. Grosset Dunlap. 1st. 172p. lists to this title. pict brd. VG. M20. $225.00

SUTTON, Margaret. *Judy Bolton: Secret of the Sand Castle (#38).* 1967. Grosset Dunlap. lists to this title. 174p. VG. scarce. M20. $325.00

SUTTON, Margaret. *Judy Bolton: Unfinished House (#11).* 1938. Grosset Dunlap. ils Pelagie Doane. F/NF. P3. $30.00

SUTTON, Margaret. *Judy Bolton: Yellow Phantom (#6).* 1933. Grosset Dunlap. lists 10 titles. 210p. VG/dj. M20. $35.00

SUTTON, Thomas. *Daniells: Artists & Travellers.* 1954. London. Theodore Brun. 1/150 deluxe. 31 pl. gilt leatherette. NF. B24. $250.00

SUTTON & SUTTON. *Wilderness World of the Grand Canyon.* 1971. Lippincott. 1st. ils/map ep. 241p. NF/VG+. B19. $25.00

SUTTON & SUTTON. *Wilderness World of the Grand Canyon.* 1971. Lippincott. 1st. 8vo. 241p. salmon cloth. F/dj. F7. $35.00

SUVIN, Darko. *Other Worlds, Other Seas.* 1970. Random. 1st. VG/dj. P3. $22.00

SUYIN, Han. *Enchantress.* 1985. Bantam. 1st. F/dj. M2. $25.00

SUYKER, Betty. *Death Scene.* 1981. St Martin. 1st. F/F. N4. $15.00

SVEND, Otto S. *Ling & the Little Devils.* 1984. London. Pelahm. 1st. 4to. unp. as new. T5. $20.00

SVENDSEN, Linda. *Marine Life.* 1992. FSG. 1st. author's 1st book. F/F. R13. $20.00

SVENSSON, Sam. *Sails Through the Centuries.* 1965. NY. Macmillan. sq 12mo. ils. 115p. dj. T7. $25.00

SWAIN, Margaret H. *Historical Needlework: A Study of Influences in Scotland...* 1970. Scribner. 1st. 140p. cloth. VG/dj. M20. $25.00

SWALLOW, Jay. *Pony Care.* 1976. St Martin. 1st. VG. O3. $10.00

SWAN, Joseph. *Demonstration of the Nerves of the Human Body.* 1934. London. 1st 4to ed. 25 pl. half leather/rebacked. A13. $900.00

SWAN, Mark. *Top O' the World.* 1908. Dutton. 1st. 8vo. VG+. M5. $75.00

SWAN, Michael. *Marches of El Dorado.* 1958. Beacon Hill. 1st. 304p. dj. F3. $20.00

SWANBERG, W.A. *Sickles the Incredible.* 1956. 1st. 433p. O8. $21.50

SWANN, Francis. *Brass Key.* 1964. S&S. 1st. VG/dj. P3. $20.00

SWANNER, Charles D. *Santa Ana: Narrative of Yesterday.* 1953. Claremont, CA. Saunder. 1st. sgn. 157p. VG/dj. M20. $40.00

SWANSON, Logan; see Matheson, Richard.

SWANSON, Neil H. *Unconquered.* 1947. Doubleday. 1st. VG/dj. P3. $15.00

SWANWICK, Michael. *In the Drift.* 1989. Legend. 1st Eng. F/F. M19. $25.00

SWARUP, Shanti. *Study of the Chinese Communist Movement 1927-1934.* 1966. Oxford. 1st. G/F. V4. $25.00

SWEELL, Helen. *Belinda the Mouse.* 1944. Oxford. 1st. VG+/VG. P2. $55.00

SWEENEY, B.M. *Rhythmic Phenomena in Plants.* 1973 (1969). London. ils/figures. mottled cloth. B26. $20.00

SWEET, Oliver E. *South Dakota Laws.* 1922. Kansas City, MO. Banker Law Pub. A19. $20.00

SWEET, William Herbert. *Not in Our Genes: Biology, Ideology & Human Nature.* 1975. Baltimore. U Park Pr. thick 8vo. 768p. gray cloth. G1. $65.00

SWEETMAN, Luke D. *Back Trailing on Open Range.* 1951. Caldwell. Caxton. A19. $75.00

SWEETSER, Kate Dickinson. *Peggy's Prize Cruise.* 1925. Barse Hopkins. 313p. red silk cloth/pict label. VG. M20. $25.00

SWIFT, Graham. *Learning to Swim & Other Stories.* 1985. Poseidon. 1st. NF/F. M23. $25.00

SWIFT, Graham. *Out of This World.* 1988. Poseidon. UP. sgn. VG/wrp. B3. $50.00

SWIFT, Hildegarde Hoyt. *North Star Shining.* 1947. NY. Morrow. 1st. 4to. blk cloth/label. dj. R5. $100.00

SWIFT, Jonathan. *Gulliver's Travels.* 1940. Whitman. ils Erwin L Hess. VG/VG. P3. $20.00

SWIFT, Jonathan. *Gulliver's Travels.* 1947. Crown. 1st thus. 358p. F/VG. H1. $25.00

SWIFT, Jonathan. *Swift's Works.* 1751-1779. London. 27 vol. some detached covers/missing spine labels. G. A15. $300.00

SWIFT, Mary A. *First Lessons on Natural Philosophy for Children.* 1875. Hartford. Wm Hamersley. new/enlarged. 12mo. 123p. cloth. R5. $150.00

SWIGART, Rob. *Little America.* 1977. Houghton Mifflin. 1st. VG/dj. P3. $20.00

SWIGART, Rob. *Time Trip.* 1979. Houghton Mifflin. 1st. F/dj. M2. $15.00

SWIHART, Thomas L. *Stellar Atmosphere Theory.* nd. Tucson. 4to. 104p. G. K5. $15.00

SWINBURNE, Algernon Charles. *Lesbia Brandon.* 1952. Falcon. 1st Eng. NF/NF. M19. $25.00

SWINBURNE, Algernon Charles. *Letters.* 1918. London. 2 vol. edit Gosse/Wise. VG/djs. T9. $60.00

SWINBURNE, Algernon Charles. *Love's Cross Currents. A Year's Letters.* 1905. London. Harper. 1st book ed. 8vo. 245p. mauve cloth. H13. $95.00

SWINDELLS, P. *Overlook Water Gardener's Handbook.* 1984. Overlook. 172p. VG/VG. B1. $26.50

SWINDOLL, Charles R. *Simple Faith: Do You Feel Confined by the Christian Life?* 1991. Word. 259p. VG/dj. B29. $8.50

SWINGER, S. *Stalking the Ice Dragon: An Alaskan Journey.* 1991. Tucson. 8vo. sgn pres. 219p. F/F. M12. $20.00

SWINGLEHURST, Edmund. *Romantic Journey. Story of Thomas Cook & Victorian Travel.* 1974. Harper Row. 1st Am. 201p. VG/dj. K3. $20.00

SWINK, Floyd. *Plants of the Chicago Region.* 1969. Morton Arboretum. sgn. 445p. VG. A22. $30.00

SWINK & WILHELM. *Plants of the Chicago Region.* 1994. Lisle. IN Academy of Sci. 4th. 921p. dj. B1. $70.00

SWINNERTON, H.H. *New Naturalist: Fossils.* 1973. London. Bloomsbury. ils/pl. 274p. F/F. M12. $20.00

SWINNERTON, Jimmy. *Hosteen Crotchetty.* 1960. Palm Desert. Best West. 1st. sgn. VG/VG. A23. $30.00

SWINTON, George. *Sculpture of the Eskimo.* 1972. Greenwich. NYGS. 255p. gray cloth. VG/clip. P4. $125.00

SWINTON, John. *Striking for Life or Labor's Side of the Labor Question...* 1894. Am Mfg & Pub. VG. V4. $75.00

SYKES, W. Stanley. *Essays on First Hundred Years of Anaesthesia.* 1982. Park Ridge, IL. 1st. 3 vol. A13. $125.00

SYLVESTER, Jerry. *Salt-Water Fishing Is Easy.* 1956. Stackpole. sgn. 208p. VG/dj. M20. $15.00

SYMONDS, John A. *Percy Bysshe Shelley.* 1879. NY. Harper. 1st/1st prt. blk cloth. F. M24. $65.00

SYMONDS, John. *Great Beast.* 1951. London. Rider. 2nd. VG/shabby. B5. $45.00

SYMONS, Julian. *Criminal Comedy.* 1985. Viking. 1st Am. F/F. M22. $15.00

SYMONS, Julian. *Plot Against Roger Rider.* 1973. Harper Row. 1st. VG/dj. P3. $18.00

SYMONS, Julian. *Portraits of the Missing.* 1991. London. Andre Deutsch. ARS. RS. F/dj. A24. $25.00

SYMONS, Julian. *Tigers of Subtopia.* 1983. Viking. 1st Am. VG+. A24. $15.00

SYMONS, Scott. *Helmet of Flesh.* 1986. Toronto. 1st. F/F. T12. $20.00

SYNTAX, Dr. see Combe, William.

SZILARD, Leo. *Genius in the Shadow.* 1994. Chicago. prt. M/wrp. K3. $20.00

SZILARD, Leo. *His Version of the Facts. Vol 2.* 1978. MIT. 1st. ils. dj. K3. $40.00

SZOLNOKI, Rose Namath. *Namath: My Son Joe.* 1975. Oxmoor. 1st. photos. VG+/dj. P8. $35.00

TABB, Warner. *Pondering Muse*. 1973. Whittet Sheperson. 17p. VG. B10. $8.00

TABER, Gladys. *Especially Dogs*. 1968. Phil. 1st ed. 191p. F/dj. A17. $15.00

TABER, Gladys. *First Book of Dogs*. 1949. Franklin Watts. ils Bob Kuhn. VG/VG. S13. $25.00

TABER, Gladys. *One Dozen & One*. 1966. Lippincott. 1st ed. sgn. 239p. cloth. VG+/dj. M20. $60.00

TABER, Gladys. *Stillmeadow Kitchen*. 1947. Macrae Smith. revised/1st prt. 311p. VG/dj. M20. $30.00

TABORI, Paul. *Private Life of Adolf Hitler...* 1949. London. 1st ed. 171p. VG. A17. $15.00

TAFF, Laurence G. *Celestial Mechanics: Computational Guide...* 19854). John Wiley. 1st prt. 8vo. 520p. VG/VG. K5. $45.00

TAFT, Robert. *Artists & Illustrators of the Old West 1850-1900*. 1953. Scribner. 1st ed. ils. map ep. VG/dj. T10. $75.00

TAIBO, Paco Ignacio II. *An Easy Time*. 1990. Viking. 1st Am ed. AN/dj. M22. $20.00

TAINE, Hippolyte Adolph. *De L'Intelligence*. 1870. Paris. Hachette. 2 vol. contemporary bdg. VG. G1. $225.00

TAINE, Hippolyte Adolph. *On Intelligence*. 1872. Holt Williams. 1st Am ed. thick 8vo. xl. G1. $85.00

TAITS, S.W. *Wildcatters: Informal History of Oil-Hunting in America*. 1946. Princeton. 218p. VG. D8. $12.00

TALBERT, Bill. *Tennis Observed*. 1967. Barre. 1st ed. sgn. VG. B5. $45.00

TALBOT-BOOTH, E.C. *Merchant Ships 1939*. 1939. London. Sampson Low Marston. G/dj. A16. $175.00

TALBOYS, W.P. *West Indian Pickles*. 1876. NY. ils. G+. B18. $22.50

TALESE, Gay. *Unto the Sons*. 1992. Knopf. 1st trade ed. F/F. B35. $20.00

TALLANT, Edith. *Girl Who Was Marge*. 1939. Lippincott. sgn. ils Dorothy Bayley. VG/dj. M20. $27.00

TAMURA, Naomi. *Japanese Bride*. 1893. NY. 1st ed. ils. 92p. VG. B14. $60.00

TAN, Amy. *Hundred Secret Senses*. 1995. Putnam. 1/175. sgn. F/case/swrp. S9. $175.00

TAN, Amy. *Hundred Secret Senses*. 1995. Putnam. 1st ed. sgn. F/F. M23. $40.00

TAN, Amy. *Hundred Secret Senses*. 1995. Putnam. 1st ed. sgn. M/M. B4. $50.00

TAN, Amy. *Joy Luck Club*. 1989. Putnam. 1st ed. author's 1st book. NF/F. H11. $160.00

TAN, Amy. *Kitchen God's Wife*. 1991. NY. 1st ed. sgn. F/F. C2. $30.00

TAN, Amy. *Kitchen God's Wife*. 1991. Putnam. 1st ed. F/F. G10. $25.00

TANGIER. *La Singulieree Zone de Tangier*. 1955. Paris. Eurafricaines. 8vo. 313p. VG/wrp. P4. $25.00

TANNER, Clara Lee. *Southwest Indian Painting: A Changing Art*. 1973. Tucson. AZ U. 2nd. lg 4to. 477p. gr cloth. F/dj. T10. $75.00

TANNER, Helen Hornbeck. *Atlas of Great Lakes Indian History*. 1987. OK U. 1st ed. 33 maps/80 ils. M/dj. O7. $85.00

TARBELL, Harlan. *Tarbell Course in Magic. Vol 4*. 1945. Louis Tannen. revised ed. inscr. 8vo. 418p. gilt gr brd. F. B11. $65.00

TARBELL, Ida. *History of the Standard Oil Company*. 1904. np. 2 vol. sgn. VG. A4. $300.00

TARG, William. *American West*. 1946. Cleveland. World. sgn. 8vo. 595p. VG. B11. $35.00

TARG, William. *Bibliophile in the Nursery*. 1957. World. 503p. cloth. VG/dj. M20. $62.00

TARG, William. *Bouillabaisse for Bibliophiles*. 1955. Cleveland. 1st ed. VG/VG. B5. $40.00

TARG, William. *10,000 Rare Books & Their Prices*. 1940. VG+. S13. $18.00

TARKENTON, Fran & RESNICOW, Herb. *Murder at the Super Bowl*. 1986. Morrow. 1st ed. F/NF. H11. $20.00

TARKENTON, Fran & RESNICOW, Herb. *Murder at the Super Bowl*. 1986. Morrow. 1st ed. VG/VG. P3. $15.00

TARKINGTON, Booth. *Beasley's Christmas Party*. 1909. Harper. 1st ed/1st state. ils RS Clements. 99p. VG. M20. $37.00

TARKINGTON, Booth. *Penrod*. 1914. Garden City. 1st ed. VG. B5. $50.00

TARKINGTON, Booth. *Seventeen*. 1916. Harper. 1st (B-Q) ed. 329p. VG. M20. $105.00

TARKINGTON, Booth. *Two Vanrevels*. 1902. 1st ed. teg. VG. w/sgn. S13. $40.00

TARN, Nathaniel. *Old Savage Young City*. 1964. London. Cape. 1st ed. inscr. F/nf. w/sgn note. V1. $65.00

TARRANT, Margaret. *Favourite Fairy Tales*. 1920s. London. Ward Lock. 1st ed. 24 pl. VG/G. P2. $120.00

TARRANT, Margaret. *Margaret Tarrant Christmas Book*. 1940. Hale Cushman Flint. lg 4to. VG. M5. $25.00

TARRANT, Margaret. *Margaret Tarrant's Christmas Garland*. 1942. Boston. 19 mtd pl. silvered red cloth. VG+. M5. $60.00

TARTT, Donna. *Secret History*. 1992. Knopf. 1st ed. author's 1st book. F/F. B35. $38.00

TARTT, Donna. *Secret History*. 1992. Knopf. 1st ed. sgn. F/F. B2. $65.00

TARVIN, A.H. *Century of Baseball*. 1938. Standard Prt. G+. P8. $45.00

TASHLIN, Frank. *Bear That Wasn't*. 1946. Dutton. 1st ed. sm 4to. NF/G. C8. $75.00

TASSIN, Ray. *Stanley Vestal: Champion of the Old West*. 1973. Glendale. 299p. F/NF. P4. $18.00

TATE, Allen. *Collected Poems 1919-1976*. 1988. LSU. 1st ed. F/wrp. V1. $15.00

TATE, Allen. *Constant Defender*. 1983. Ecco. 1st ed. F/NF. w/pub card. V1. $30.00

TATE, Allen. *Fragment of a Meditation*. 1947. Cummington. VG/hand-tied gray wrp. V1. $100.00

TATE, Allen. *Hovering Fly & Other Essays*. 1949. Cummington. 1st ed. 1/245. NF. B24. $650.00

TATE, Allen. *Man of Letters in the Modern World*. 1957. Meridian. 2nd imp. 352p. VG/VG. B10. $45.00

TATE, Allen. *Mr Pope & Other Poems*. 1928. Minton Balch. 1st ed. F/NF. B2. $600.00

TATE, Allen. *Winter Sea, a Book of Poems*. 1944. Cummington. 1st ed. 1/330. blk cloth/paper label. B24. $325.00

TATE, Florence Lee. *Random Reveries, True Incidents & Echoes*. 1942. np. 204p. VG/fair. B10. $8.00

TATNALL, Robert R. *Flora of Delaware & the Eastern Shore*. 1946. Wilmington. ils. 313p. F. B26. $55.00

TATON, R. *Reason & Chance in Scientific Discovery*. 1957. London. 171p. VG. A13. $30.00

TAUBENHAUS, J.J. *Culture & Diseases of the Sweet Pea*. 1917. NY. 232p. cloth. scarce. B26. $22.00

TAUBER, Gerald E. *Man & the Cosmos*. 1979. Greenwich. 4to. photos/diagrams. 352p. VG/VG. K5. $30.00

TAVERNIER, John Baptista. *Collection of Several Relations & Treatises...* 1680. London. Godbid Playford. 1st ed. 2 parts in 1. lg fld map/7 fld pl. full calf. C6. $2,500.00

TAVERS, P.L. *Maria Poppin AB A-Z.* 1968. Harcourt Brace. 1st ed. 12mo. trans GM Lyne. F/F. C8. $50.00

TAX, Sol. *Penny Capitalism.* 1963. Chicago. rpt of 1953 ed. VG. F3. $20.00

TAXAY, Don. *Money of the American Indians & Other Primitive Currencies.* 1970. NY. Mummus. 8vo. ils. 158p. F/dj. T10. $50.00

TAYLER, Zack; see Marshall, Mel.

TAYLOR. *Art Nouveau Book in Britain.* 1966. MIT. 176p. VG/VG. A4. $95.00

TAYLOR. *From the White House Inkwell: Am Presidential Autographs.* 1968. ils. 147p. F/NF. A4. $125.00

TAYLOR. *Introduction to Cartooning.* 1947. F/F. D2. $25.00

TAYLOR, Alan R. *Arab Balance of Power.* 1982. Syracuse. 1st ed. 8vo. map. VG/wrp. W1. $12.00

TAYLOR, Bayard. *At Home & Abroad.* 1889. NY. 12mo. 500p. red cloth. G. T3. $20.00

TAYLOR, Charles F. *Pathology & Treatment of Lateral Curvature of the Spine.* 1868. NY. 18p. prt gray wrp. B14. $125.00

TAYLOR, Charles H. *Simplified Review of the Important Laws of Bridge.* nd. NY. sm format. 22p. VG/wrp. S1. $5.00

TAYLOR, Frank J. *High Horizons.* 1962. NY. new revised ed. ils. 266p. VG/dj. B18. $12.50

TAYLOR, Henry J. *Big Man.* 1964. Random. 1st ed. inscr. 311p. VG/G+. B10. $15.00

TAYLOR, Henry. *Afternoon of Pocket Billiards.* 1978. UT U. 1st ed. F/VG. V1. $10.00

TAYLOR, Jane. *Little Ann: A Book.* nd. Warne. early prt. ils Kate Greenaway. VG+. S13. $55.00

TAYLOR, John. *All the Works of John Taylor, the Water Poet.* 1630. Menston, Yorkshire. 4to. 146p. gilt gr cloth. dj. K1. $75.00

TAYLOR, Louis. *Harper's Encyclopedia for Horsemen.* 1973. NY. Harper Row. VG/G. O3. $25.00

TAYLOR, Lucy. *Close to the Bone.* 1993. Seattle. Silver Salamander. 1st ed. sgns. F/F. T2. $35.00

TAYLOR, Meadows. *Confession of a Thug.* 1968. NY. 338p. F/worn. A17. $12.50

TAYLOR, Peter. *Conversations With Peter Taylor.* 1987. Jackson, MS. 1st ed. F/F. C2. $25.00

TAYLOR, Peter. *Summons to Memphis.* 1986. Knopf. 1st ed. F/F. B4. $75.00

TAYLOR, Peter. *Tennessee Day in St Louis: A Comedy.* 1957. Random. 1st ed. sgn. NF/NF. C2. $150.00

TAYLOR, Robert Lewis. *Niagara.* 1980. Putnam. 1st ed. F/F clip. B4. $50.00

TAYLOR, Robert Lewis. *Travels of Jaimie McPheeters.* 1958. NY. 1st ed. VG/VG. B5. $30.00

TAYLOR, Samuel W. *Line Haul.* 1959. San Francisco. 1st ed. 307p. NF. B18. $15.00

TAYLOR, Sidney. *More All-Of-A-Kind Family.* 1954. Follett. ils Mary Stevens. 149p. VG/dj. M20. $22.00

TAYLOR, Telford. *Munich: The Price of Peace.* 1979. NY. 1st ed. photos. cloth. G. A17. $14.50

TAYLOR, Thomas E. *Running the Blockade: A Personal Narrative of Adventures...* 1897. London. John Murray. 3rd. fld map. 180p. cloth. VG. M8. $150.00

TAYLOR, W. *Historic Survey of German Poetry I.* 1828-1830. London. 1st ed. later 19th-C half morocco. VG. C6. $120.00

TAYLOR, W.C. *WC Fields: His Follies & Fortunes.* 1949. Doubleday. brd. VG. D2. $10.00

TAYLOR, William H. *Yachting in North America.* 1948. Van Nostrand. VG/dj. A16. $50.00

TAYLOR, William. *California Life Illustrated.* ca 1885. NY. 12mo. ils. 404p. brn cloth. xl. VG. T3. $45.00

TAYLOR & TAYLOR. *Black Dutch.* 1991. NY. Walker. 1st ed. F/F. H11. $20.00

TAYLOR & TAYLOR. *Neon Dancers.* 1991. Walker. 1st ed. author's 3rd novel. AN/dj. M22. $15.00

TAYLOR-HALL, Mary Ann. *Come & Go, Molly Snow.* 1995. Norton. 1st ed. author's 1st book. F/F. M23. $45.00

TAZEWELL, Charles. *Littlest Angel.* 1946. Chicago. 1st ed. 50p. F/dj. A17. $16.00

TAZEWELL, William L. *Down to the Sea With Jack Woodson.* 1987. Algonquin. ils. 72p. VG/dj. T7. $40.00

TEASDALE, Sara. *Stars To-Night: Verses New & Old for Boys & Girls.* 1930. Macmillan. 1st ed. 8vo. VG/G. M5. $75.00

TEASDALE, Sara. *Strange Victory.* 1933. Macmillan. 1st ed. xl. F. V1. $25.00

TEBBEL. *American Magazine, a Compact History.* 1969. np. 287p. RS. NF/VG. A4. $45.00

TEBBEL & ZUKERMAN. *Magazine in America 1741-1990.* 1991. Oxford. 433p. F/F. A4. $35.00

TEMIANKA. *Jack Vance Lexicon, From Ahulph to Zipangote...* 1992. np. 136p. F. A4. $55.00

TEMPEST, Margaret. *Little Lamb of Bethlehem.* 1963. Medici Soc. 3rd imp. 16mo. VG. B17. $7.50

TEMPLE, Shirley. *Shirley Temple's Favorite Tales of Long Ago.* 1958. NY. Random. 1st prt. unp. NF. C14. $20.00

TENGGREN, Gustaf. *Tenggren's Story Book.* 1944. Simon Schuster. stated 1st ed. ils. VG/dj. M5. $40.00

TENISON, Robin Hansbury. *Worlds Apart: An Explorer's Life.* 1984. Boston. Little Brn. 1st Am ed. sm 4to. dj. F3. $20.00

TENNANT, Eleanor A. *ABC of Bridge.* ca 1904. Toronto. 5th. 128p. VG. S1. $6.00

TENNEY, Jack. *Red Fascism: Boring From Within...* 1947. Los Angeles. Federal Prt. 1st ed. 700+p. NF. B2. $45.00

TENNYSON, Alfred Lord. *Enoch Arden.* 1864. London. 2nd issue. VG. C6. $75.00

TENNYSON, Alfred Lord. *Idylls of the King.* 1859. London. Moxon. 1st ed. Arthur Machen's copy. 12mo. emb cloth. T10. $1,000.00

TENNYSON, Alfred Lord. *Morte d'Arthur.* 1912. Chatto Windus. 4to. sgn Alberto Sangorski. NF. T10. $100.00

TENNYSON, Alfred Lord. *Seven Poems & Two Translations.* 1902. Hammersmith. 1/325. 8vo. 55p. full limp vellum. NF. B24. $350.00

TENNYSON, Alfred Lord. *Tennyson's Guinevere & Other Poems.* 1912. Blackie. 1st ed. ils Florence Harrison. VG+. M5. $250.00

TENNYSON, Alfred Lord. *Tennyson's Poems.* 1897. Crowell. gilt red cloth. F. V1. $20.00

TEPFER, Sanford S. *Floral Anatomy & Oteogeny in Aquilegia Formosa...* 1953. Berkeley. 136p. wrp. B26. $15.00

TERENTIUS AFER, Publius. *Comoediae Sex en Recensione Frid.* 1820. London. Priestley. 2 vol. 8vo. teg. gilt gr calf. K1. $175.00

TERHUNE, Albert Payson. *Real Tales of Real Dogs.* (1955). Saalfield. ne. 4to. 92p. F/VG. C14. $20.00

TERHUNE, Albert Payson. *Real Tales of Real Dogs.* 1955. Saalfield. 1st ed. ils Diana Thorne. VG. B30. $35.00

TERHUNE & THORNE. *Dog Book.* 1932. Saalfield. 4to. ils. NF/fair. M5. $45.00

TERKEL, Studs. *Good War.* 1984. Pantheon. 1st ed. sgn. F/F. B2. $50.00

TERKEL, Studs. *Great Divide.* 1988. Pantheon. 1st ed. F/F. B2. $45.00

TESICH, Steve. *Summer Crossings.* 1982. Random. 1st ed. F/F. H11. $25.00

TESNOLIDEK, Rudolf. *Cunning Little Vixen.* 1985. FSG. 1st ed. 8vo. ils Sendak. F/F. B17. $15.00

TESSIER, Thomas. *Nightwalker.* 1980. Atheneum. 1st Am ed. F/VG. M21. $75.00

TEUKOLSKY, Roselyn. *How to Play Bridge With Your Spouse...and Survive.* 1991. NY. 192p. VG/wrp. S1. $10.00

TEVIS, Walter. *Far From Home.* 1981. Doubleday. 1st ed. NF/NF. R10. $10.00

TEVIS, Walter. *Queen's Gambit.* 1983. NY. 1st ed. VG/VG. B5. $25.00

TEVIS, Walter. *Steps of the Son.* 1983. Doubleday. 1st ed. VG/VG. M22. $15.00

THACKERAY, William Makepeace. *Doctor Birch & His Young Friends.* 1849. London. 16 pl. NF/orig pk wrp/Zaehnsdorf bdg. C6. $175.00

THACKERAY, William Makepeace. *Four Georges: Sketches of Manners, Morals, Court...* 1861. London. Smith Elder. 1st ed/1st issue. 8vo. 226p. gr cloth. F. B24. $375.00

THACKERAY, William Makepeace. *Rose & the Ring; or, History of Prince Giglio...* 1937. Macmillan. 16mo. 212p. VG. C14. $15.00

THACKERAY, William Makepeace. *Thackeray's Letters to an American Family...* 1904. Merrymount. ils. VG. A4. $45.00

THACKERAY, William Makepeace. *Thackery Alphabet.* 1930. Harper. 1st ed. ils. VG/G. P2. $25.00

THACKERAY, William Makepeace. *Works...* 1871. London. Smith Elder. 12 vol. half leather/marbled brd. NF. T10. $500.00

THACKREY, Ted. *Gambling Secrets of Nick the Greek.* 1968. 1st ed. VG/VG. K2. $12.00

THALL, Michael. *Let Sleeping Afghans Lie.* 1990. Walker. 1st ed. F/F. H11. $25.00

THANE, Edith. *Marionettes Are People.* 1948. DSP. 1st ed. VG/VG. P3. $8.50

THANE, Elswyth. *Ever After.* 1945. DSP. 2nd. 334p. VG. B10. $8.00

THARP, Louise Hall. *Baroness & the General.* 1962. Little Brn. 1st ed. ils. 458p. VG/VG. B10. $12.00

THAYER, Bert Clark. *Horses in the Blue Grass.* 1940. DSP. 2nd. photos. 78p. VG. O3. $20.00

THAYER, Bert Clark. *Thoroughbred: Pictorial Highlights...* 1964. DSP. 1st ed. VG/fair. O3. $25.00

THAYER, Emma Homan. *Wild Flowers of the Pacific Coast.* 1887. NY. Cassell. 24 chromolithographs. aeg. cloth. F. T10. $350.00

THAYER, Jane. *Part-Time Dog.* 1965. Morrow. ils Seymour Fleishman. VG/G. B17. $5.00

THAYER, Steve. *Saint Mudd.* 1992. Viking. 1st ed. author's 1st book. rem mk. F/F. H11. $30.00

THAYER, W.M. *From Tannery to White House: Life of Ulysses S Grant.* 1885. NY. 12mo. 480p. bl cloth. G. T3. $20.00

THAYER, W.M. *Marvels of the New West.* 1888. Norwich, CT. thick royal 8vo. ils/maps. 715p. gilt gr cloth. G. T3. $30.00

THAYER, William Roscoe. *Life & Letters of John Hay.* 1915. Boston. 2 vol. 10th. VG. V4. $60.00

THEINER, George. *Let's Go to the Circus.* 1963. London. Bancroft. 8vo. ils Rudolf Lukes/5 moveables. unp. T10. $150.00

THEODOR, O. *Fauna Palaestina. Insecta I: Diptera Pupipara.* 1975. Jerusalem. tall 8vo. 168p. cloth. NF. B1. $40.00

THERNSTROM, Mel. *Dead Girl.* 1990. Pocket. 1st ed. F/F. A20. $15.00

THEROUX, Alexander. *Darconville's Cat.* 1981. Doubleday. 1st ed. 704p. VG/G. B10. $20.00

THEROUX, Alexander. *Lollipop Trollops.* 1992. Dalkey Arch. 1st ed. F/wrp. V1. $10.00

THEROUX, Alexander. *Three Wogs.* 1972. Boston. 1st ed. author's 1st book. sgn. F/NF. C2. $200.00

THEROUX, Paul. *My Secret History.* 1989. Putnam. 1st ed. 8vo. F/dj. T10. $25.00

THEROUX, Paul. *O-Zone.* 1986. Putnam. 1st ed. F/VG. A20. $20.00

THEROUX, Paul. *Pillars of Hercules: Grand Tour of the Mediterranean.* 1995. Putnam. 1st ed. sgn. AN/dj. B4. $65.00

THEROUX, Peter. *Sandstorms: Days & Nights in Arabia.* 1990. Norton. 1st ed. 8vo. 281p. NF/dj. W1. $20.00

THESIGER, Wilfred. *Arabian Sands.* 1959. Dutton. 1st ed. 8vo. ils/fld map. 326p. VG. W1. $25.00

THIFFAULT, Mark. *Fisherman's Digest.* 1984. DBI Books. photos. VG. P12. $5.00

THOMAS, Alan G. *Great Books & Book Collectors.* 1988. London. Spring. rpt. 280p. F/dj. A17. $25.00

THOMAS, Alfred Barnaby. *Teodoro de Croix & the Northern Frontier of New Spain...* 1968. Norman. 2nd. 273p. red cloth. VG/dj. P4. $25.00

THOMAS, Benjamin P. *Lincoln's New Salem.* 1954. Knopf. new/revised ed. sgn. 166p. VG/dj. B18. $30.00

THOMAS, D. Gourlay. *Simple, Practical Hybridising for Beginners.* 1962. BC. 127p. F/dj. B26. $15.00

THOMAS, D.M. *Shaft.* 1973. Dalkey Arch. 1/400. ils. NF/wrp. w/promo sheet. V1. $20.00

THOMAS, Dylan. *Child's Christmas in Wales.* 1985. Holiday House. 1st ed. ils Trina Hyman. AN/dj. C8. $75.00

THOMAS, Dylan. *Conversations About Christmas.* 1954. New Directions. 1st ed. 12mo. F/wrp. B24. $200.00

THOMAS, Dylan. *Letters to Vernon Watkins.* 1957. London. 1st ed. F/VG+ clip. N3. $20.00

THOMAS, Dylan. *Twenty-Five Poems.* 1939. London. Dent. 1st ed. 1/730. gray brd. F/prt gray dj. B24. $950.00

THOMAS, Dylan. *Under Milk Wood.* 1954. New Directions. 1st Am ed. 12mo. F/VG. T10. $50.00

THOMAS, Frederick W. *Emigrant; or, Reflections While Descending the Ohio.* 1872. Cincinnati. 48p. cloth. G. B5. $45.00

THOMAS, Graham S. *Shrub Roses of Today.* 1962. London. 1st ed. ils. 241p. VG/dj. B26. $20.00

THOMAS, Ianthe. *Lordy, Aunt Hattie.* 1973. Harper. 1st ed. 8vo. AN/dj. C8. $20.00

THOMAS, Isaiah. *Diary of Isaiah Thomas 1805-1828.* 1909. Am Antiquarian Soc. 2 vol. portrait. F. A4. $185.00

THOMAS, John. *British Railways, Steamers of the Clyde.* 1948. London. Ian Allan Ltd. G/wrp. A16. $25.00

THOMAS, Joseph. *Hounds & Hunting Through the Ages.* 1937. Garden City. rpt. G+. O3. $35.00

THOMAS, L. *Lives of a Cell.* 1974. Viking. 5th. 12mo. 153p. half cloth. clip dj. B1. $15.00

THOMAS, Leslie. *Some Lovely Islands.* 1969. Coward McCann. 1st Am ed. F/NF. B4. $65.00

THOMAS, Lewis. *Long Line of Cells: Collected Essays.* 1990. NY. 361p. VG. A13. $20.00

THOMAS, Lowell. *Count Luckner, the Sea Devil.* 1927. Garden City. ils. 308p. G+. P12. $20.00

THOMAS, Lowell. *Seeing Canada With Lowell Thomas.* 1936. Akron. 1st ed. photos. 108p. pict brd. VG. A17. $12.50

THOMAS, Lowell. *Wreck of the Dumaru.* 1930. Doubleday Doran. 1st ed. sgn by survivor. 8vo. 271p. VG. B11. $75.00

THOMAS, Norman. *Conscientious Objector in America.* 1923. NY. Huebsch. 1st ed. F/NF. B2. $125.00

THOMAS, Patricia. *There Are Rocks in My Socks!* 1979. Lee Shepard. 1st ed. ils Mordicai Gerstein. unp. G+/dj. T5. $24.00

THOMAS, R.S. *Old Brick Church Near Smithfield Virginia Built in 1632.* (1892). VHS. rpt. hc. 37p. VG. B10. $15.00

THOMAS, Ross. *Briarpatch.* 1984. Simon Schuster. 1st ed. rem mk. NF/NF. H11. $20.00

THOMAS, Ross. *Eighth Dwarf.* 1979. Simon Schuster. 1st ed. F/F. T2. $35.00

THOMAS, Ross. *Mordida Man.* 1981. Simon Schuster. 1st ed. F/F. T2. $35.00

THOMAS, Ross. *No Questions Asked.* 1976. Morrow. 1st ed. F/NF. T2. $130.00

THOMAS, Ross. *Procane Chronicle.* 1972. Morrow. 1st ed. 3rd novel as Oliver Beeck. F/NF. B4. $150.00

THOMAS, Ross. *Thumbsuckers, Etc.* 1989. Northridge, CA. Lord John. 1st ed. 1/300. sgn/#d. F/sans. A11. $75.00

THOMAS, Ross. *Twilight at Mac's Place.* 1990. Mysterious. 1st ed. rem mk. F/F. N4. $15.00

THOMAS, Ross. *Voodoo, Ltd.* 1992. Mysterious. ARC. NF/wrp. M22. $20.00

THOMAS, Ross. *Voodoo, Ltd.* 1992. Mysterious. 1st ed. AN/dj. N4. $20.00

THOMAS, Witts. *Enola Gay.* 1977. np. 1st ed. NF/VG. w/mtd photo sgn by Tibbets & Caron. S13. $40.00

THOMAS & THOMAS. *Nature, a Quote by John Muir.* 1996. Santa Cruz. brn morocco w/inset onlay flower. miniature. M. B24. $300.00

THOMAS & THOMAS. *Our Flight to Adventure.* 1956. Doubleday. 1st ed. sgn Lowell Thomas Jr. 8vo. 318p. F/clip. B11. $45.00

THOMAS & WITTS. *San Francisco Earthquake.* 1971. Stein Day. 316p. F/dj. D8. $10.00

THOMAS. *History of Printing in America.* 1970. rpt. F/F. D2. $45.00

THOMAS. *With Bleeding Footsteps: Mary Baker Eddy's Path...* 1994. np. 363p. F/F. A4. $25.00

THOMASON, John W. *Fix Bayonets!* 1926. NY. later prt. 245p. G+. B18. $22.50

THOMASON, John W. *Gone to Texas.* 1937. 1st ed. VG/fair. S13. $75.00

THOMASON, John W. *Jeb Stuart.* 1934. Scribner. early prt. 512p. cloth. VG/dj. M8. $35.00

THOMLINSON, H.M. *Norman Douglas.* 1931. Harper. 1st ed. 77p. VG/VG. B18. $22.50

THOMPSON, Blanche Jennings. *All the Silver Pennies.* 1967. NY. 1st ed. VG/VG. B5. $30.00

THOMPSON, Blanche Jennings. *Silver Pennies: A Collection of Modern Poems...* 1925. Macmillan. 1st ed. sm 8vo. bl pict cloth. VG. M5. $95.00

THOMPSON, Dorothy. *I Saw Hitler!* 1932. NY. 1st ed. inscr. NF/VG. B4. $250.00

THOMPSON, Dunstan. *Poems.* 1943. Simon Schuster. 1st ed. F/NF. V1. $55.00

THOMPSON, Edgar T. *Perspectives on the South: Agenda for Research.* 1967. Duke. 231p. VG/G. B10. $12.00

THOMPSON, Edmund. *Maps of Connecticut Before the Year 1800.* 1940. Hawthorn. 1/250. sgn. 4 maps. F. O7. $325.00

THOMPSON, Fresco. *Every Diamond Doesn't Sparkle.* 1964. McKay. later prt. VG/VG. P8. $30.00

THOMPSON, G.A. *Geographical & Historical Dictionary of America...* 1970. Burt Franklin. 5 vol. 4to. F3. $250.00

THOMPSON, H.T. *Ousting the Carpetbagger From South Carolina.* 1926. Columbia. 1st ed. ils. 182p. VG. B5. $75.00

THOMPSON, Hunter S. *Fear & Loathing in Las Vegas.* 1971. Random. 1st ed. F/F. B4. $300.00

THOMPSON, Hunter S. *Fear & Loathing in Las Vegas.* 1971. Random. 1st ed. NF/dj. S9. $275.00

THOMPSON, Hunter S. *Fear & Loathing on the Campaign Trail.* 1963. San Francisco. 1st ed. F/F. B5. $60.00

THOMPSON, Hunter S. *Generation of Swine.* 1988. Summit. 1st ed. 304p. NF/dj. M20. $37.00

THOMPSON, Hunter S. *Generation of Swine.* 1988. Summit. 1st ed. 304p. VG/dj. M20. $18.00

THOMPSON, Hunter S. *Great Shark Hunt.* 1979. Summit. 1st ed. F/NF. B4. $85.00

THOMPSON, Hunter S. *Great Shark Hunt. Gonzo Papers, Vol 1.* 1979. NY. Summit. 1st ed. 8vo. 600+p. VG/dj. S9. $40.00

THOMPSON, J. Eric. *Thomas Gage's Travels in the New World.* 1958. OK U. 1st ed. 8vo. 379p. gr cloth. VG. T10. $50.00

THOMPSON, Jim. *Black Box Thrillers: 4 Novels by Jim Thompson.* 1983. London. Zomba. 1st hc ed. F/F. T2. $35.00

THOMPSON, Jim. *End of the Book.* 1937. Viking. 1st ed. NF/VG+. A11. $300.00

THOMPSON, Jim. *More Hardcore.* 1986. NY. Donald Fine. 1st ed. F/F. B4. $65.00

THOMPSON, Jim. *Mourn the Hangman.* 1952. Hasbrouck Hts, NJ. F. A11. $40.00

THOMPSON, Jim. *Now & on Earth.* 1986. Bellen, NM. Dennis McMillan. 1/400. F/F. A11. $95.00

THOMPSON, Josiah. *Six Seconds in Dallas.* 1967. NY. 1st ed. VG/VG. B5. $55.00

THOMPSON, Kay. *Eloise.* nd. Simon Schuster. 22nd. VG/VG. B17. $8.50

THOMPSON, Kay. *Eloise at Christmastime.* 1958. NY. Random. 1st prt. 4to. VG/VG+. C8. $150.00

THOMPSON, Kay. *Eloise in Moscow.* 1959. NY. 1st ed. VG/fair. B5. $95.00

THOMPSON, Kay. *Eloise in Moscow.* 1959. Simon Schuster. 1st ed. ils Hilary Knight. orange cloth. VG/dj. D1. $200.00

THOMPSON, Kay. *Eloise in Moscow.* 1959. Simon Schuster. 1st ed. ils/sgn Hilary Knight. F/VG. P2. $225.00

THOMPSON, Kay. *Eloise in Moscow.* 1960. Max Reinhardt Ltd. 1st ed. ils Hilary Knight. unp. gr cloth. VG/dj. M20. $125.00

THOMPSON, Kay. *Eloise in Paris.* 1957. Simon Schuster. 1st ed. 4to. G. M5. $45.00

THOMPSON, Kay. *Kay Thompson's Miss Pooky Peckinpaugh.* 1970. Harper Row. 1st ed. 4to. F/VG. B17. $20.00

THOMPSON, L.M. *Soils & Soil Fertility.* 1957. McGraw Hill. 2nd. 451p. VG. D8. $15.00

THOMPSON, Lawrence. *Essays in Hispanic Bibliography.* 1970. Shoe String. 1st ed. 117p. F3. $25.00

THOMPSON, Lawrence. *New Sabin.* 1974-1975. 4 vol. describes 5802 items. xl. VG. A4. $125.00

THOMPSON, Mark L. *Steamboats & Sailors of the Great Lakes.* 1991. Detroit. Wayne State. AN. A16. $27.50

THOMPSON, Morton. *Joe, the Wounded Tennis Player.* 1945. Garden City. 1st ed. VG/VG. B5. $25.00

THOMPSON, Ruth Plumley. *Giant Horse of Oz.* 1928. Reilly Lee. 1st ed/1st state. F/G+. P2. $600.00

THOMPSON, Ruth Plumley. *Grampa in Oz.* 1924. Reilly Lee. 1st ed. ils JR Neill. VG/tattered. D1. $300.00

THOMPSON, Ruth Plumley. *Kabumpo in Oz.* nd. Reilly Lee. 1st ed/later state. ils JR Neill. pict bl cloth. G. D1. $285.00

THOMPSON, Ruth Plumley. *Royal Book of Oz.* 1921. Reilly Lee. 1st ed. ils JR Neill. VG. D1. $275.00

THOMPSON, Ruth Plumley. *Speedy in Oz.* 1934. Reilly Lee. 1st ed. ils J Neill. orange stp blk cloth. VG. D1. $375.00

THOMPSON, Silvanus P. *Elementary Lessons in Electricity & Magnetism.* 1888. Chicago. Thompson Thomas. 43rd thousand. 456p. cloth. VG. M20. $40.00

THOMPSON, Silvanus P. *Light Visibile & Invisible.* 1897. London. 1st. 294p. xl. bl cloth. VG. B14. $375.00

THOMPSON, Silvanus P. *Pied Piper of Hamelin.* 1905. London. 1/199. inscr. 40p. F/prt gray wrp. B14. $200.00

THOMPSON & THOMPSON. *Science Fiction & Fantasy Collectibles Price Guide.* 1989. 482p. F. M13. $30.00

THOMSON, Basil. *Case of the Dead Diplomat.* 1935. Crime Club. 1st. xl. VG/dj. P3. $20.00

THOMSON, Christine Campbell. *Not at Night Omnibus.* 1937. London. 1st. G. M2. $35.00

THOMSON, D. *Pair Trawling & Pair Seining...* 1978. Fishery News. ils/tables. 167p. pict brd. VG+. M12. $15.00

THOMSON, David. *Shining Mountains.* 1979. Knopf. A19. $25.00

THOMSON, David. *Showman: Life of David O Selznick.* 1992. NY. 1st. 793p. F/dj. A17. $15.00

THOMSON, H. Douglas. *Great Book of Thrillers.* 1937. Odhams. G. P3. $20.00

THOMSON, J.E. *Grenville Problem: Royal Society of Canada Special Pub 1.* 1956. Toronto. 119p. cloth. NF. D8. $24.00

THOMSON, James. *Seasons, With the Castle of Indolence.* 1814. Georgetown. Richards Mallory/Wm Fry. full calf. B18. $250.00

THOMSON, James. *Seasons.* 1927. London. 1/1500. 8vo. ils Jacquier. Riviere bdg. F/case. B24. $750.00

THOMSON, Origen. *Crossing the Plains.* 1983. Ye Galleon. 1st thus. ils. M/sans. A18. $17.50

THOMSON, Richard. *Antique American Clocks & Watches.* 1968. NY. Galahad Books. ils/photos. 192p. brd. dj. D2. $30.00

THOMSON, Samuel. *New Guide to Health; or, Botanic Family Physician...* 1829. Clairsville, OH. Horton Howard. 12mo. 115p. contemporary calf. M1. $375.00

THOMSON, William. *Practical Treatise on Cultivation of Grape Vine.* 1865. London. Blackwood. 77p. cloth. VG. A10. $78.00

THON, Melanie Rae. *Girls in the Grass.* 1991. Random. 1st. F/dj. A24. $50.00

THON, Melanie Rae. *Iona Moon.* 1993. Poseidon. 1st ed. F/F. A20. $15.00

THON, Melanie Rae. *Meteors in August.* 1990. Random. 1st. author's 1st book. F/dj. A24. $60.00

THON, Melanie Rae. *Meteors in August.* 1990. Random. 1st. sgn. F/F. D10. $75.00

THORBURN, Archibald. *British Birds.* 1925-26. Longman Gr. 4 vol. 192 mc pl. red cloth. djs. T10. $400.00

THORBURN, Grant. *Forty Years' Residence in America...* 1834. Boston. Russell. 264p. rebound. A10. $28.00

THOREAU, Henry David. *Excursions.* 1863. Boston. 1st ed. NF. A9. $450.00

THOREAU, Henry David. *Henry David Thoreau.* 1967. Viking. 1st. ils James Daugherty. sm 4to. F/F. P2. $25.00

THOREAU, Henry David. *Journal of...* 1984. Salt Lake. GM Smith. 15 vol. F. M12. $125.00

THOREAU, Henry David. *Letters to Various Persons.* 1965. Boston. 1st ed. 1st issue. NF. C2. $400.00

THOREAU, Henry David. *Summer: From the Journal of Henry David Thoreau.* 1884. Boston. 1st ed. cloth. VG. C2. $200.00

THOREAU, Henry David. *Walking.* 1914. Riverside. 1st separate. 1/550. quarter linen. uncut/box. M24. $125.00

THOREAU, Henry David. *Yankee in Canada.* 1866. Boston. Ticknor Fields. 1st/1st prt/1st bdg. gilt gr cloth. NF. M24. $125.00

THORN, John. *Treasures of the Baseball Hall of Fame.* 1998. NY. Villard. 1st. 4to. color pict 238 p. F/F. R16. $65.00

THORNBURG, Newton. *Black Angus.* 1978. Little Brn. 1st. VG/dj. P3. $23.00

THORNBURG, Newton. *Lion at the Door.* 1990. Morrow. 1st. F/VG. P3. $20.00

THORNBURY, W.D. *Principles of Geomorphology.* 1969. John Wiley. 2nd. 594p. pict brd. VG. D8. $17.00

THORNDYKE, Helen. *Honey Bunch: Her First Visit to the City.* 1923. Grosset Dunlap. ils. 182p. VG. T5. $15.00

THORNDYKE, Helen. *Honey Bunch: Her First Visit to the Seashore.* 1924. Grosset Dunlap. ils. 180p. VG. T5. $15.00

THORNE, Anthony. *She Takes a Lover.* 1932. Macmillan. 1st Am. F/F. B4. $85.00

THORNE, Diana. *Diane Thorne's Dogs: Album of Drawings.* 1944. Messner. 1st. sbdg. VG/dj. M20. $75.00

THORNE, Guy. *When It Was Dark.* 1904. Putnam. 1st. VG. P3. $25.00

THORNE, John. *Simple Cooking.* 1987. Viking. 2nd. sgn. 290p. VG/VG. B10. $12.00

THORNE, Paul. *Murder in the Fog.* 1929. Penn. 1st. VG. P3. $40.00

THORNE, S.E. *Discourse Upon Exposicion & Understandinge of Statuetes...* 1942. San Marino. Huntington Lib. M11. $85.00

THORNE, S.E. *Essays in English Legal History.* 1985. London. Hambledon. M11. $50.00

THORNE-THOMSEN, Kathleen. *Why the Cake Won't Rise & the Jelly Won't Set.* 1979. NY. A&W Pub. G/dj. A16. $8.00

THORNTON, A.G. *Astronomer at Large.* 1924. Putnam. 1st. VG. P3. $25.00

THORNTON, B.M. *Steelhead: Supreme Trophy Trout.* 1978. Seattle. Hancock. ils/photos. 159p. VG+/VG. M12. $25.00

THORNTON, J. Quinn. *California Tragedy.* 1945. Biobooks. 1/1500. 4to. F/F. O4. $30.00

THORP, Raymond. *WF Carver, Spirit Gun of the West.* 1957. Clark. 1st. ils. 266p. VG/dj. J2. $185.00

THORP, Roderick. *Detective.* 1966. Dial. 1st ed. F/F. B4. $150.00

THORP, Roderick. *Nothing Lasts Forever.* 1979. Norton. 1st ed. F/rem mk sticker. B4. $250.00

THORP, W. *Southern Reader.* 1955. VG/VG. M17. $25.00

THRAPP, Dan L. *Al Sieber, Chief of Scouts.* 1964. Norman, OK. 1st. 432p. VG. J2. $195.00

THRAPP, Dan L. *Juh: An Incredible Indian.* 1973. TX W Pr. 1st. 44p. F/wrp. B19. $25.00

THROM, Edward L. *Boy Engineer.* 1959. Golden. 4to. 248p. G. K5. $18.00

THROWER, Norman J.W. *Three Voyages of Edmund Halley in the Paramore 1698-1701.* 1981. London. 2 vol. ils/pl/maps. as issued. K3. $65.00

THRUM, Thomas G. *Hawaiian Folk Tales.* 1907. Chicago. McClurg. 1st. ils/glossary/ads. 284p. VG. P4. $185.00

THUNBERG, Carl Peter. *Flora Japonica.* 1975. NY. Oriole. 8vo. 418p. F/VG. A22. $45.00

THURBER, James. *Beast in Me & Other Animals.* 1948. NY. 1st ed. VG/VG. B5. $45.00

THURBER, James. *Great Quillow.* 1944. NY. 1st ed. VG/VG. B5. $75.00

THURBER, James. *Further Fables of Our Time.* 1956. S&S. 1st. 174p. brd/cloth spine. NF/NF. B22. $12.00

THURBER, James. *Lanterns & Lances.* 1961. Harper. 1st. NF/VG. M19. $25.00

THURBER, James. *Let Your Mind Alone...* 1937. NY. Armed Services ed. 256p. wrp. B18. $17.50

THURBER, James. *Middle-Aged Man on the Flying Trapeze.* 1935. NY. Armed Services ed. 282p. G+. B18. $17.50

THURBER, James. *Thurber Album.* 1952. S&S. 1st. sgn. xl. G. W2. $75.00

THURBER, James. *White Deer.* 1945. Harcourt Brace. 1st. NF/VG+. C8. $50.00

THURBER, James. *Wonderful O.* 1957. Simon Schuster. 1st ed. 72p. VG/dj. M20. $32.00

THURMAN, Howard. *Growing Edge.* 1956. NY. Harper. 1st. 131p. G+/dj. V3. $15.00

THURMAN, Howard. *Jesus & the Disinherited.* 1949. NY. Abingdon-Cokesbury. 112p. VG/dj. V3. $9.00

THURMAN, Howard. *Negro Spiritual Speaks of Life & Death.* 1947. Harper. VG/VG. B4. $25.00

THURMAN, Sue Bailey. *Pioneers of Negro Origin in California.* ca 1952. SF. Acme. 1st. 70p. sbdg. B4. $150.00

THURSTON, P.C. *Geology of Ontario.* 1991. Toronto. 711p. B1. $85.00

THURSTON, Robert. *Alicia II.* 1978. Putnam. 1st. F/dj. P3. $20.00

THWAITE, Mary. *From Primer to Pleasure in Reading: An Introduction...* 1972. Boston. Horn Book. 1st Am. ils. 4to. 350p. F/F. A4. $45.00

THWING, Eugene. *World's Best 100 Detective Stories 1.* 1929. Funk Wagnalls. VG. P3. $15.00

TIBBETS, Paul. *Mission: Hiroshima.* 1985. Stein Day. VG/wrp. K3. $15.00

TIBBETS, Paul W. *Tibbets Story.* 1978. NY. 1st ed. ils. 316p. VG/VG. B5. $50.00

TIBURZI, Bonnie. *Take Off! The Story of America's First Woman Pilot...* 1984. NY. 1st ed. ils. 299p. VG/dj. B18. $25.00

TICE, George A. *Artie Van Blarcum.* 1977. Addison. 1st ed. inscr/dtd 1979. VG/wrp. S9. $45.00

TICKNER, John. *Tickner's Dogs.* 1988. London. Sportsman's Pr. VG. O3. $18.00

TICKNER, John. *Tickner's Hunting Field.* 1970. London. Putnam. 1st ed. VG/VG. O3. $25.00

TIDYMAN, Ernest. *Line of Duty.* 1974. Little Brn. 1st. VG/dj. P3. $20.00

TIDYMAN, Ernest. *Shaft.* 1973. 1st ed. inscr. MTI. author's 1st book. NF/VG+. S13. $40.00

TIEDE, Tom. *Coward.* 1968. NY. Trident. 1st ed. F/NF. B4. $85.00

TIEMANN & TIEMANN. *Boy Named John.* 1948. Platt Munk. 4to. VG. B17. $6.50

TIERNANN, Terence. *Adventures of Michael & the Pirates.* 1939. Little Brn. 1st ed. ils. cloth. G. M5. $15.00

TIGER, John; see Wager, Walter.

TILDEN, W.T. *Art of Lawn Tennis.* 1922. Garden City. rpt/enlarged/expanded. G/G. P8. $20.00

TILLICH, Paul. *History of Christian Thought.* 1956. Tillich. edit Peter John. 309p. G/wrp. B29. $11.00

TILLICH, Paul. *Theology of Paul Tillich.* 1952. Macmllan. edit Kegley/Bretall. 370p. VG/dj. B29. $14.00

TILLMAN, Barrett. *Hellcat: The F6F in WWII.* 1979. Annapolis. photos/notes/biblio/index. 265p. VG/VG. S16. $21.50

TILMAN, H.W. *Ice With Everything.* 1974. Sidney. Gray's Pub. 142p. VG/dj. P4. $25.00

TILMAN, H.W. *Mostly Mischief.* 1967. London. Adventurers Club. later prt. 8vo. 191p. P4. $35.00

TILNEY, Frederick. *Form & Function of the Nervous System.* 1921. NY. Hoeber. heavy 4to. 1019p. ruled bl cloth. xl. G1. $50.00

TILTON, Theodore. *True Church. Ils From Designs by Granville Perkins.* 1883. Phil. Claxton. 8vo. gilt pub cloth. F. B24. $125.00

TIMBERLAKE, R.E. *Somewhere in Time. Paintings & Commentary by Bob Timberlake.* 1989. Raleigh, NC. 1st ed. photos/pl. 159p. cloth/leather spine. D2. $225.00

TIMBERLAKE, R.E. *World of Bob Timberlake.* 1979. Oxmoor. pres. ils/137 pl. 141p. dj. D2. $200.00

TIME-LIFE EDITORS. *Old West: The Soldiers.* 1973. NY. 4to. 239p. emb simulated leather. F. T3. $17.00

TIME-LIFE EDITORS. *Spanish West.* 1979. Alexandria, VA. 2nd. leather. A19. $20.00

TIMMIS, R.S. *Modern Horse Management.* nd. London. Cassell. 4to. VG. O3. $25.00

TIMPERLEY, Rosemary. *Child in the Dark.* 1956. Crowell. 1st. VG/dj. P3. $35.00

TIMPERLEY, Rosemary. *Eighth Ghost Book.* 1972. Barrie Jenkins. 1st. xl. VG/dj. P3. $15.00

TINGLEY, Katherine. *Wine of Life: Compilation From Extemporaneous Address...* 1925. Point Loma. Womans Internat Theosophical League. ils. 332p. D11. $50.00

TINKER, F.G. *Some Still Live.* 1937. Funk Wagnalls. 1st. VG/dj. M2. $17.00

TINKHAM, George H. *History of Stockton.* 1880. SF. WM Hinton. A19. $45.00

TINKLE, Lon. *J Frank Dobie, Makings of an Ample Mind.* 1968. Encino. 1st. 1/850. sgn. 57p. VG/box. J2. $140.00

TINSLEY, Jim Bob. *He Was Singin' This Song.* 1981. Orlando. inscr. fwd Gene Autry/S Omar Baker. 255p. F/VG. B11. $75.00

TIONGSON, Nicanor G. *Pilipinas Circa 1907: Production Score for Piano & Voice.* 1985. Quezon City. Philippine Edu Theater Assn. 266p. F/VG. P1. $15.00

TIPPETT, James S. *Crickety Cricket!* 1973. Harper Row. 1st. ils Mary Chalmers. 83p. reinforced cloth. F/F. D4. $35.00

TIPPETT, James S. *Picnic.* 1936. NY. Grosset Dunlap. ils Samuel J Brown. NF. C8. $125.00

TIPPETT, Tom. *When Southern Labor Stirs.* 1931. NY. Cape Smith. 1st ed. 2nd tan bdg. NF/NF. B2. $40.00

TIPPING, H. Avray. *English Gardens.* 1925. London. folio. 600 ils/photos. 366p. aeg. B26. $200.00

TIPPING, H. Avray. *Gardens Old & New: Country House & Its Garden Environment.* 1900. London. Country Life. 295p. folio. A10. $95.00

TISSOT, V. *Unknown Switzerland.* nd. NY. 19 tipped-in photos. 2-tone cloth. VG+. A15. $225.00

TITCOMBE, Marianne F. *Bookbinding Career or Rachel McMasters Miller Hunt.* 1974. Pittsburgh. ils. 63p. marbled cover. VG. B26. $12.00

TITIEV, Mischa. *Araucanian Culture in Transition.* 1951. Ann Arbor. 164p. wrp. F3. $25.00

TITLEY, Norah M. *Persian Miniature Painting & Its Influence on Art...* 1984. TX U. 1st ed. ils/pl. NF/dj. W1. $35.00

TITOV, Gherman. *I Am Eagle!* 1962. Bobbs Merrill. 8vo. photos. 212p. Vg/dj. K5. $30.00

TOBE, John H. *Proven Herbal Remedies.* 1969. Provoker. 304p. VG/VG. M20. $15.00

TOBEY, James A. *Medical Department of the Army: Its History, Activities...* 1927. Johns Hopkins. 161p. bl buckram. F. B14. $75.00

TOBIAS, Thomas J. *Hebrew Benevolent Society of Charleston, SC, Founded 1784.* 1965. The Society. 62p. B10. $45.00

TOBIN, Brian. *Missing Person.* 1994. St Martin. 1st ed. author's 2nd novel. AN/dj. M22. $25.00

TODD, Barbara. *Earthy Mangold & Worzel Gummidge.* 1954. London. Hollis Carter. 1st. ils JJ Crockford. 200p. NF/VG-. P2. $25.00

TODD, Edwin. *Neuroanatomy of Leonardo da Vinci.* 1983. Santa Barbara. 1st. 189p. A13. $75.00

TODD, Frank Morton. *Eradicating Plague From San Francisco.* 1908. Citizen Health Comm. 1st/only. 313p. maroon cloth. F. K7. $95.00

TODD, John M. *Luther: A Life.* 1982. Crossroad. 396p. VG/dj. B29. $10.00

TODD, Mabel Loomis. *Cycle of Sunsets.* 1910. Boston. Sm Maynard. 1st. teg. gilt gr cloth. VG. M24. $165.00

TODD, Ruthven. *Mantlepiece of Shells.* 1954. Bonacio Saul/Grove. 1st ed. sgn. NF/VG+. V1. $35.00

TODD, Walter E. *Gathered Treasures.* 1912. WA, DC. Murray. 1st. F. B4. $250.00

TODD, William B. *Suppressed Commentaries on Wiseian Forgeries.* 1969. Austin. 1st. 1/750. fld pl. 50p. VG. K3. $60.00

TODER, C.P. *Delaware Canal Journal.* 1972. Bethlehem, PA. 1st. ils/charts. 287p. VG+/dj. B18. $45.00

TOEPPERWEIN & TOEPPERWEIN. *Unkle Kris & His Pets.* 1948. Boeme, TX. Higland. 1/200. sgn/#d. VG/VG. B11. $40.00

TOLAND, John. *Ships of the Sky.* 1957. NY. 1st ed. ils. 352p. VG/dj. B18. $37.50

TOKLAS, Alice B. *Alice B Toklas Cookbook.* 1984 (1954). Harper. 1st thus. 8vo. F/F. C8. $25.00

TOKLAS, Alice B. *Aromas & Flavors of Past & Present.* 1958. Harper. 1st. F/clip. B35. $70.00

TOKLAS, Alice B. *What Is Remembered.* 1963. Holt. 1st. F/NF. B2. $45.00

TOLAND, John. *Battle: Story of the Bulge.* 1959. NY. maps/photos/index. 400p. VG/G. S16. $27.50

TOLAND, John. *Last 100 Days: Tumultuous & Controversial Story...* 1966. NY. 622p. VG/G. S16. $23.50

TOLBER, John. *Who's Who in Rock & Roll.* 1991. Mitchell. NF/dj. P3. $20.00

TOLKIEN, Christopher. *Pictures by JRR Tolkien.* 1992. Houghton Mifflin. 1st. unp. cloth. VG+/dj. M20. $50.00

TOLKIEN, J.R.R. *Adventures of Tom Bombadil & Other Verses...* 1962. London. Allen Unwin. 2nd prt. 8vo. NF/NF. C8. $25.00

TOLKIEN, J.R.R. *Devil's Coach-Horses.* 1925. London. 1st ed. VG/wrp. C6. $275.00

TOLKIEN, J.R.R. *Father Christmas Letters.* 1976. Houghton Mifflin. 1st ed. ils. F/VG. P2. $75.00

TOLKIEN, J.R.R. *Hobbit.* 1984. 1st thus. 4to. ils Michael Hague. F/F. A4. $45.00

TOLKIEN, J.R.R. *Letters of JRR Tolkien.* 1981. Houghton Mifflin. 1st. VG/VG. P3. $20.00

TOLKIEN, J.R.R. *Lord of the Rings Part One, the Film Book of...* 1978. Ballantine. 1st thus. ils. obl sm 4to. NF/NF. C8. $45.00

TOLKIEN, J.R.R. *Lord of the Rings.* 1967. Houghton Mifflin. 2nd Am. 3 vol. F/F. B4. $350.00

TOLKIEN, J.R.R. *Return of the Shadow.* 1988. Houghton Mifflin. 1st. VG/dj. P3. $20.00

TOLKIEN, J.R.R. *Middle English Losenger.* 1953. Paris. 1st ed. 14p. F/wrp. C6. $200.00

TOLKIEN, J.R.R. *Pictures by JRR Tolkien.* 1978. Houghton Mifflin. 1st Am ed. F/case. G10. $100.00

TOLKIEN, J.R.R. *Poems & Stories.* 1994. Houghton Mifflin. 8vo. 342p. AN/dj. T10. $20.00

TOLKIEN, J.R.R. *Road Goes Ever On.* 1967. Houghton Mifflin. 1st ed. NF/dj. M21. $75.00

TOLKIEN, J.R.R. *Road Goes Ever On.* 1967. Houghton Mifflin. 1st. lg 8vo. VG+. M21. $40.00

TOLKIEN, J.R.R. *Silmarillion.* 1977. London. Allen Unwin. 1st. F/F. T12. $30.00

TOLKIEN, J.R.R. *Sir Gawain & the Green Knight, Pearl, Sir Orfeo.* 1975. Houghton Mifflin. 1st Am. 149p. F/dj. H1. $32.00

TOLKIEN, J.R.R. *Smith of Wooten Major.* 1967. Houghton Mifflin. 1st. F/VG. M19. $45.00

TOLKIEN, J.R.R. *Unfinished Tales.* 1980. BC. F/dj. M2. $10.00

TOLKIEN, J.R.R. *Unfinished Tales.* 1980. Houghton Mifflin. 1st. VG/dj. P3. $25.00

TOLKIN, Michael. *Player.* 1988. Atlantic. 1st. author's 1st book. F/F. H11/M22. $40.00

TOLKOWSKY, Samuel. *They Took to the Sea.* 1964. NY. Yoseloff. ils. 316p. dj. T7. $20.00

TOLLES, Frederick B. *George Logan of Philadelphia.* 1953. Oxford. VG+/VG+. H4. $25.00

TOLLES, Frederick B. *Meeting House & Counting House: Quaker Merchants...* 1948. Chapel Hill. 1st. 292p. VG/worn. V3. $18.00

TOLMAN, Richard C. *Relativity, Thermodynamics & Cosmology.* 1962. Clarendon. 6th. 8vo. 501p. G. K5. $60.00

TOLSON, Berneita. *Beer Cookbook.* 1968. Hawthorn. G/dj. A16. $15.00

TOLSON, M.B. *Harlem Gallery.* (1965). Twayne. 1st. VG/dj. M25. $65.00

TOLSON, M.B. *Libretto for the Republic of Liberia.* 1953. Twayne. 1st. VG/dj. M25. $60.00

TOLSTOY, Leo. *Anna Karenina.* 1886. NY. Thomas Crowell. 1st Am. gilt bl cloth. NF. M24. $400.00

TOLSTOY, Leo. *Childhood, Boyhood, Youth.* (1886). NY. Crowell. 1st Am. author's 1st book. gilt brn cloth. F. M24. $225.00

TOLSTOY, Leo. *Ivan Ilyitch & Other Stories.* (1887). Crowell. 1st Am (311p instead of 219p). gilt gr cloth. F. M24. $200.00

TOLSTOY, Leo. *Kreutzer Sonata & Other Stories.* 1890. NY. Ogilvie. 1st Am. VG/bl pict cloth. M24. $100.00

TOLSTOY, Leo. *Letters.* 1978. NY. 1st. 2 vol. VG/VG. T9. $30.00

TOLSTOY, Leo. *War & Peace.* 1889. NY. Crowell. 1st from Russian. 4 vol in 2 (as issued). gilt bl bdg. M24. $450.00

TOLSTOY, Nikolai. *Coming of the King.* 1989. Bantam. 1st. NF/dj. M2. $15.00

TOMALIN, Claire. *Katherine Mansfield: A Secret Life.* 1988. NY. 1st ed. 282p. F/dj. A17. $10.00

TOMKINS, William. *Universal Indian Sign Language.* 1929. San Diego. self pub. A19. $30.00

TOMLINSON, Everett T. *Washington's Young Aids, a Story of American Revolution.* 1897. Boston. 1st. ils Charles Copeland. 391p. VG. B14. $75.00

TOMLINSON, P.B. *Botany of Mangroves.* 1986. Cambridge, Eng. Cambridge Tropical Biology series. ils. 413p. F/dj. B26. $70.00

TOMMAY, Pat. *Crunch.* 1975. Norton. 1st. photos. VG+/VG. P8. $25.00

TOMPKINS, Peter. *Secrets of the Great Pyramids.* 1971. Harper Row. 1st ed. NF/NF. G10. $20.00

TOMPKINS, Stuart Ramsay. *Triumph of Bolshevism-Revolution or Reaction?* 1967. OK U. 1st. xl. VG/dj. V4. $7.50

TOMPKINS, Walter A. *Little Giant of Signal Hill.* 1964. Englewood Cliffs. 1st. NF/NF. O4. $15.00

TONNESSEN, Johnsen. *History of Modern Whaling.* 1982. Berkeley. thick 8vo. 798p. NF/dj. P4. $65.00

TOOKER, Elva. *Nathan Trotter: Philadelphia Merchant, 1787-1853.* 1955. Cambridge. 1st. 276p. G/tattered. V3. $16.50

TOOKER, L. Frank. *Joys & Tribulations of an Editor.* 1924. Century. 1st. VG. M2. $25.00

TOOLE, John K. *Neon Bible.* 1989. Grove. 1st. F/F. A20. $15.00

TOOLEY, R.V. *Maps & Map-Makers.* 1990. NY. Dorsett. later prt. 140p. M/dj. P4. $40.00

TOOMAY, Pat. *On Any Given Sunday.* 1984. Donald Fine. 1st ed. F/F. B35. $20.00

TOOR, Frances. *Guide to Mexico.* 1940. McBridge. revised/enlarged. 270p. F3. $15.00

TOPSELL, Edward. *Fowles of Heaven; or, History of Birds.* 1972. Austin. ils. 332p. VG/VG. S15. $30.00

TORGOVNICK, Marianna. *Gone Primitive.* 1990. Chicago. 1st. F/dj. P3. $25.00

TORME, Mel. *It Wasn't All Velvet.* 1988. Viking. 1st ed. sgn. F/F. B2. $50.00

TORME, Mel. *Wynner.* 1978. Stein Day. 1st. NF/VG+. A20. $25.00

TORREY, Julia Whitemore. *Old Sheffield Plate.* 1918. ils. VG. M17. $35.00

TOSCHES, Nick. *Cut Numbers.* 1988. Harmony. 1st ed. F/F. B4. $65.00

TOSKI, Bob. *How to Become a Complete Golfer.* 1984. S&S. revised/later prt. inscr. F/NF. B4. $45.00

TOULOUSE, Julian Harrison. *Fruit Jars.* 1969. Thomas Nelson/Everybodys. tall 8vo. 542p. F/dj. H1. $65.00

TOURGEE, Albion W. *Appeal to Caesar.* 1884. NY. 422p. O8. $12.50

TOURGEE, Albion W. *Bricks Without Straw.* 1880. Howard Hulbert. 1st prt. 16mo. 521p. emb brn cloth. G+. O8. $12.50

TOURNIER, Michel. *Golden Droplet.* 1987. Doubleday. 1st. F/NF. B35. $16.00

TOUSEY, Sanford. *Jerry & the Pony Express.* 1936. Doubleday. stated 1st. ils. F/fair. M5. $45.00

TOUSEY, Sanford. *Trouble in the Gulch.* 1944. Whitman. 12mo. VG. B17. $12.50

TOUSEY, Thomas G. *Military History of Carlisle & Carlisle Barracks.* 1939. Richmond, VA. Dietz. 1st. tall 8vo. 447p. VG. H1. $36.00

TOWNE, Robert D. *Teddy Bears at the Circus.* 1907. Reilly Britton. 1st thus. ils JR Bray. 12mo. mc pict brd. R5. $150.00

TOWNSEND, C.W. *Along the Labrador Coast.* 1907. Boston. 1st. ils/fld map. 289p. VG. B5. $35.00

TOWNSEND, G.W. *Memorial Life of William McKinley.* 1901. np. sm 4to. 520p. emb gilt bdg. VG. H1. $28.00

TOWNSEND, George A. *Rustics in Rebellion.* 1950. 1st/2nd state. 292p. O8. $14.50

TOWNSEND, John Rowe. *Tom Tiddler's Ground.* 1986. Lippincott. 1st Am. 8vo. 170p. rem mk. NF/NF. T5. $20.00

TOWNSEND, John T. *Code of Procedure, of the State of New York. Fifth Edition.* 1857. NY. Voorhies. modern quarter calf. M11. $150.00

TOWNSEND, William H. *Lincoln the Litigant.* 1925. Boston. 1st ed. 1/1050. 116p. brd. VG. B18. $25.00

TOWNSEND. *Written for Children: Outline of English Language...* 1983. 2nd revised/1st prt. ils. 384p. F/F. A4. $35.00

TOXOPEUS, Klaas. *Flying Storm.* 1954. Dodd Mead. ils. 246p. T7. $20.00

TOYNBEE, Arnold. *Lectures on the Industrial Revolution in England.* 1884. London. Rivington. 1st. 8vo. 256p. gilt gr cloth. VG. T10. $75.00

TOZZER, Alfred M. *Maya Grammar With Bibliography & Appraisement of Works...* 1921. Cambridge. 301p. F3. $40.00

TRACHSEL, Herman H. *Government & Administration of...Wyoming.* 1956. NY. Crowell. A19. $20.00

TRACHTMAN, Paula. *Disturb Not the Dream.* 1981. Crown. 1st. F/dj. M2. $12.00

TRACY, David F. *Psychologist at Bat.* 1951. Sterling. 1st ed. VG/G. P8. $50.00

TRACY, Edward B. *Great Horse of the Plains.* 1954. Dodd Mead. 1st ed. inscr/sgn. F/fair. M5. $18.00

TRACY, Louis. *American Emperor.* 1918. Putnam. decor brd. VG. P3. $75.00

TRACY, Louis. *Man With the Sixth Sense.* nd. Hodder Stoughton. G/dj. P3. $25.00

TRACY, Louis. *Pillar of Light.* 1904. Clode. 1st. VG. M2. $15.00

TRAIN, Arthur. *Mr Tutt Comes Home.* 1941. Scribner. 1st. VG/dj. Q1. $60.00

TRAIN, Arthur. *Mr Tutt's Case Book.* 1945. Scribner. VG. P3. $25.00

TRAIN, Arthur. *Old Man Tutt.* 1938. Scribner. 1st. VG/dj. Q1. $60.00

TRALL, R.T. *Digestion & Dyspepsia: A Complete Explanation...* 1873. NY. SR Wells. ils. 160p. xl. VG. K3. $20.00

TRAUB, Charles. *Beach.* 1978. NY. Horizon. photos. 60p. wrp. D11. $30.00

TRAUBEL, Horace L. *Camden's Compliment to Walt Whitman.* 1889. Phil. McKay. 1st. teg. gilt maroon cloth. NF. M24. $250.00

TRAUSCH, William. *Grab Bag.* 1939. Pegasus. 1st. 156p. dj. A17. $20.00

TRAVEN, B. *Rebellion of the Hanged.* 1952. Knopf. 1st Am. NF/dj. M25. $200.00

TRAVER, Robert. *Laughing Whitefish.* 1965. McGraw Hill. 1st. VG/dj. P3. $25.00

TRAVER, Robert. *Jealous Mistress.* 1967. Boston. 1st ed. F/NF. A17. $35.00

TRAVER, Robert. *Trout Madness.* 1960. St Martin. 1st ed. 178p. VG/clip. M20. $35.00

TRAVERS, Hugh. *Madame Aubry Dines With Death.* 1967. Harper Row. 1st. VG/dj. P3. $10.00

TRAVERS, Louise A. *Romance of Shells in Nature & Art.* 1962. NY. Barrows. 1/400. sgn. F/F case. B11. $18.00

TRAVERS, P.L. *Friend Monkey.* 1971. HBJ. 1st/2nd prt. inscr. ils Mary Shepard. 122p. VG. T5. $25.00

TRAVERS, P.L. *Mary Poppins Comes Back.* 1935. Reynal Hitchcock. 1st ed. ils Mary Shepard. G+. M5. $55.00

TRAVERS, P.L. *Mary Poppins From A-Z.* 1962. Harcourt. stated 1st. 8vo. F/VG. M5. $55.00

TRAVERS, P.L. *Mary Poppins in Cherry Tree Lane.* 1982. London. Collins. 1st. ils Mary Shepard. VG+. C8. $15.00

TRAVERS, P.L. *Mary Poppins in the Kitchen.* 1975. HBJ. 1st/B prt. 122p. mauve brd. VG/VG. T5. $45.00

TRAVERS, P.L. *Mary Poppins in the Park.* 1952. Harcourt. stated 1st. ils Mary Shepard. VG+/dj. M5. $60.00

TRAVERS, P.L. *Mary Poppins Opens the Door.* 193. Reynal Hitchcock. 3rd. 8vo. 239p. G+. T5. $20.00

TREASE, Geoffrey. *So Wild the Heart.* 1959. Vanguard. 1st. VG/fair. P3. $12.00

TREAT, Lawrence. *H as in Hangman.* 1944. Books Inc. VG/dj. P3. $20.00

TREAT, Mary. *Injurious Insects of the Farm & Garden.* 1887. Orange Judd. 296p. VG. A10. $35.00

TREATT, Stella Court. *Cape to Cairo. Record of a Historic Motor Journey.* 1927. Little Brn. 1st. 8vo. 251p. xl. G. W1. $12.00

TREATT, Stella Court. *Cape to Cairo. Record of a Historic Motor Journey.* 1927. London. Harrap. 1st. ils. VG. K3. $25.00

TREECE, Henry. *Amber Princess.* 1963. Random. 1st. NF/dj. P3. $25.00

TREECE, Henry. *Crusades.* 1963. Random. 1st Am ed. 334p. VG. W1. $18.00

TREECE, Henry. *New Romantic Anthology.* 1949. London. Gray Walls. 1st ed. VG/VG. V1. $20.00

TREGANOWAN & WEEKS. *Rugs & Carpets of Europe & the Western World.* 1969. Chilton. ils/bibliography/index. cloth. dj. D2. $40.00

TREGARTHEN, Enys. *White Ring.* 1949. harcourt Brace. 1st. ils Nora Unwin. sq 8vo. 65p. VG/VG-. P2. $40.00

TREGASKIS, Richard. *Guadalcanal Diary.* 1943. NY. photos/maps. 263p. VG. S16. $17.50

TREITEL, Jonathan. *Red Cabbage Cafe.* 1990. Pantheon. 1st. author's 1st book. F/F. H11. $25.00

TRELEASE, William. *Winter Botany.* 1918. Urbana. self pub. 1st. 394p. VG. A10. $24.00

TRENHAILE, John. *Mah-Jongg Spies.* 1986. Dutton. 1st. F/NF. H11. $25.00

TRENHAILE, John. *Nocturne for the General.* 1985. Congdon Weed. 1st. VG/dj. P3. $15.00

TRENHOLM, Virginia Cole. *Footprints on the Fontier.* 1945. np. 1st. 284p. VG/dj. J2. $385.00

TRENTO, Joseph J. *Prescription for Disaster.* 1987. NY. Crown. 8vo. 312p. VG/dj. K5. $20.00

TRESSELT, Alvin. *Beaver Pond.* 1970. Lee Shepard. 1st. ils Roger Duvoisin. 4to. VG+/VG. P2. $40.00

TREUTLEIN, Theodore E. *San Francisco Bay, Discovery & Colonization 1769-1776.* 1968. CA Hist Soc. 1st. 4 facsimile maps. quarter bl cloth/gr sides. dj. K7/O4. $25.00

TREVANIAN. *Eiger Sanction.* 1972. Crown. 1st. author's 1st book. F/NF. M25. $100.00

TREVANIAN. *Summer of Katya.* 1983. Crown. 1st. F/F. N4. $25.00

TREVANIAN. *Summer of Katya.* 1983. Granada. 1st. NF/dj. P3. $18.00

TREVER, John C. *Scrolls From Qumran Cave I: Great Isaiah Scroll...* 1972. Jerusalem. Allbright Inst Archaeological Research. 163p. VG+. S3. $75.00

TREVINO, Lee. *Snake in the Sandtrap.* 1985. HRW. 1st. sgn. F/F. A23. $50.00

TREVOR, Elleston. *Blaze or Roses.* 1952. Harper. 1st. 249p. VG/dj. M20. $12.00

TREVOR, William. *News From Ireland & Other Stories.* 1986. Viking. 1st Am. F/F. D10. $45.00

TREVOR, William. *Old Boys.* 1964. NY. Viking. 1st. F/NF. L3. $125.00

TREW, Antony. *Ultimatum.* 1976. St Martin. 1st. VG/VG. M22. $15.00

TREW, Cecil. *Accoutrements of the Riding Horse.* (1951). London. Seeley. 1st ed. ils. VG. O3. $85.00

TRIBUTSCH, H. *When the Snakes Awake.* 1982. Cambridge. MIT. 248p. dj. B1. $25.00

TRIER, Walter. *10 Little Negroes: A New Version.* 1944. London. Sylvan. 1st. obl 8vo. pict brd. R5. $275.00

TRIGG, Emma Gray. *After Eden: Poems.* 1937. Putnam. 1st ed. 110p. VG/VG. B10. $15.00

TRIGG, Emma Gray. *Paulownia Tree.* 1969. Golden Quill. inscr. 80p. VG/VG. B10. $8.00

TRIGG, Roberta. *Haworth Idyll: A Fantasy.* 1946. Whittet Shepperson. sgn. 88p. VG. B10. $12.00

TRIGGS, J.H. *History of Cheyenne & North Wyoming Embracing Gold Fields...* 1955. Laramie, WY. Powder River Pub. 2 vol. boxed. A19. $45.00

TRIMBLE, Barbara Margaret. *Fifth Rapunzel.* 1991. Hodder Stoughton. 1st. VG/dj. P3. $20.00

TRIMBLE, Marshall. *Arizona.* 1977. Garden City. dj. A19. $20.00

TRIMBLE, Michael R. *Post-Traumatic Neurosis: From Railway Spine to Whiplash.* 1981. Chichester, Eng. Wiley. 3rd. 8vo. 156p. navy cloth. F/dj. G1. $40.00

TRIMBLE, Vance H. *Sam Walton.* 1990. Dutton. 1st. F/F. W2. $30.00

TRIMBLE, William F. *High Frontier: History of Aeronautics in Pennsylvania.* 1982. Pittsburgh. 344p. VG+/wrp. B18. $17.50

TRIMMER, Eric. *Rejuvenation: The History of an Idea.* 1970. NY. 189p. dj. A13. $40.00

TRIPP, Miles. *Death of a Man-Tamer.* 1987. St Martin. 1st. VG/dj. P3. $15.00

TRIPP, Miles. *Fifth Point of the Compass.* 1967. Macmillan. 1st. VG/dj. P3. $23.00

TRIPP, Wallace. *Great Big Ugly Man Came Up & Tied His Horse to Me.* 1973. Little Brn. 1st ed. ils. VG+/VG. P2. $30.00

TRIPP, Wallace. *Sir Toby Jingle's Beastly Journey.* 1976. CMG. 1st. ils. VG-/G. P2. $20.00

TRIPTREE, James Jr. *Her Smoke Rose Up Forever.* 1990. Arkham. 1st. VG/dj. M22. $30.00

TROLLOPE, A. *Claverings.* 1866. NY. 1st Am ed. VG+. A15. $200.00

TROLLOPE, Anthony. *Barchester Towers.* 1958. NY. LEC. 1st thus. 1/1500. ils/sgn Fritz Kredel. F/case. Q1. $100.00

TROLLOPE, Anthony. *La Vendee: Historical Romance.* June 1874. London. Chapman Hall. rpt. gilt brn cloth. NF. M24. $1,250.00

TROLLOPE, Anthony. *Orley Farm.* 1862. London. Chapman Hall. 2 vol. 1st. lg 8vo. Bumpus bdg. H13. $495.00

TROLLOPE, Anthony. *Rachel Ray, a Novel.* 1868. London. Chapman Hall. so-called 10th. tall 8vo. 347p. Victorian bdg. H13. $195.00

TROLLOPE, Anthony. *Travelling Sketches.* 1866. London. Chapman Hall. 1st. gilt red cloth. entirely unopened. M24. $500.00

TROLLOPE, Anthony. *Warden.* 1955. NY. LEC. 1st thus. 1/1500. ils/sgn Fritz Kredel. F/glassine/case. Q1. $100.00

TROLLOPE, Mrs. Frances. *Domestic Manners of the Americans.* 1949. edit D Smalley. VG/VG. M17. $25.00

TROLLOPE, Thomas Adolphus. *Decade of Italian Women.* 1859. London. Chapman Hall. 2 vol. 1st. 8vo. teg. 3-quarter crushed morocco. F. H13. $295.00

TROSCLAIR. *Cajun Night Before Christmas.* 1976. Gretna. 1st ed. VG/VG. B5. $25.00

TROTTER, I. Lilias. *Between the Desert & the Sea.* ca 1920. Marshall Morgan Scott. 1st ed. ils. 63p. VG/dj. W1. $75.00

TROUT, Kilgore; see Farmer, Philip Jose.

TROWBRIDGE, J.T. *South: A Tour of Its Battle-Fields & Ruined Cities.* 1866. 1st. ils. 590p. O8. $55.00

TROWBRIDGE, W.R.H. *Court Beauties of Old Whitehall.* 1906. Scribner. 1st. F. M19. $65.00

TROY, Simon. *Drunkard's End.* 1961. Walker. 1st. VG/dj. P3. $15.00

TRUAX, Rhoda. *Doctors Warren of Boston: First Family of Surgery.* 1968. Boston. 1st. 369p. A13. $20.00

TRUAX, Rhoda. *Joseph Lister: Father of Modern Surgery.* 1944. Indianapolis. 1st. 287p. A13. $30.00

TRUDEAU, Gary. *Doonesbury Deluxe.* 1987. Holt. sc. F. M13. $19.00

TRUE, Frederick W. *Whalebone Whales of the Western North Atlantic...* 1983. Smithsonian. rpt. 50 pl. 332p. gr cloth. F. P4. $75.00

TRUEBLOOD, Elton. *Abraham Lincoln: Theologian of American Anguish.* 1973. NY. Harper Row. 1st. 149p. VG/dj. V3. $16.00

TRUEBLOOD, Elton. *Company of the Committed.* 1961. Harper. 1st. 113p. VG/dj. V3. $12.00

TRUEBLOOD, Elton. *Doctor Johnson's Prayers.* 1947. Harper. 1st. 66p. VG/G+. V3. $12.00

TRUEBLOOD, Elton. *Lord's Prayers.* 1965. Harper Row. 1st. 128p. VG/dj. V3. $12.00

TRUEBLOOD, Elton. *Signs of Hope in a Century of Despair.* 1950. Harper. 324p. dj. V3. $12.00

TRUEBLOOD, Elton. *Validity of the Christian Mission.* 1972. Harper Row. 1st. 113p. VG/dj. V3. $12.00

TRUEBLOOD, Elton. *While It Is Day: An Autobiography.* 1974. Harper Row. sgn. 170p. VG/dj. V3. $17.50

TRUEBLOOD, Ernest V.; see Faulkner, William.

TRUEBLOOD, Ted. *Ted Trueblood Hunting Treasury.* 1978. McKay. 1st ed. photos. NF/VG. P12. $15.00

TRUESDELL, S.R. *Rifle: Its Development for Big Game Hunting.* 1947. Harrisburg. 1st ed. photos. 274p. VG. B5. $80.00

TRUMAN, Margaret. *Murder at the Kennedy Center.* 1989. Random. 1st ed. F/F. A20. $10.00

TRUMBALL, Charles G. *Taking Men Alive.* 1915. Assoc. 199p. G. B29. $6.00

TRUMBO, Dalton. *Harry Bridges.* 1941. League Am Writers. 1st ed. F/wrp. B2. $45.00

TRUMBO, Dalton. *Night of the Aurochs.* 1979. Viking. 1st. F/F. A20. $30.00

TRUMBULL, Robert. *Nine Who Survived Hiroshima & Nagasaki.* 1965. Dutton. 5th. VG/dj. K3. $25.00

TRUMP, Donald J. *Art of the Deal.* 1987. Random. 1st. F/F. W2. $30.00

TRUMP, Ivana. *For Love Alone.* 1992. Pocket. 1st. F/F. W2. $35.00

TRUMPS. *American Hoyle/Hoyle's Games.* 1907. NY. 18th. 532p. VG. S1. $15.00

TRUSS, Seldon. *Doctor Was a Dame.* 1953. Crime Club. 1st. VG/dj. P3. $20.00

TRUSSLER, D.J. *Early Commercial Vehicles.* 1968. London. 1st. 10 full-p mc pl. 45p. F. M4. $35.00

TRYON, Thomas. *Harvest Home.* 1973. Knopf. 1st. F/F. H11. $40.00

TRYON, Thomas. *Other.* 1971. Knopf. 1st ed. author's 1st book. NF/VG. H11. $35.00

TRYON, Thomas. *Wings of the Morning.* 1990. Franklin Lib. 1st. sgn. full leather. F. Q1. $40.00

TSCHIRKY, O. *Cook Book by Oscar of the Waldorf.* 1896. 4to. 907p. VG. E6. $95.00

TSE-TUNG, Mao. *Poems.* 1976. Foreign Language Pr. 1st. F/dj. V1. $25.00

TSUNA, Masuda. *Kodo Zuroku.* 1983. Norwalk, CT. Burndy Lib. ils. wrp. K3. $25.00

TUCHMAN, Barbara. *Distant Mirror.* 1978. NY. Knopf. 11th. 677p. map ep. VG/dj. P4. $20.00

TUCHMAN, Barbara. *First Salute.* 1988. BC. 347p. M/dj. P4. $10.00

TUCHMAN, Barbara. *Stillwell & the American Experience in China 1911-45.* 1971. BC. dj. A17. $10.00

TUCHMAN, Barbara. *Zimmerman Telegram.* 1958. NY. 1st ed. 244p. VG/dj. B18. $22.50

TUCKER, G.C. *Taxonomy of Cyperus (Cyperaceae) in Costa Rica & Panama.* 1983. Ann Arbor. 8vo. 85p. stiff wrp. B1. $22.00

TUCKER, Glenn. *Zeb Vance: Champion of Personal Freedom.* 1965. Bobbs Merrill. 1st ed. 564p. NF/NF. M8. $75.00

TUCKER, George Fox. *Quaker Home.* 1891. Boston. George Reed. 426p. G. V3. $12.00

TUCKER, Jerry. *Bermuda's Story.* 1970. Bermuda Bookstores. rpt. sgn. 8vo. 213p. F/VG. B11. $35.00

TUCKER, Kerry. *Still Waters.* 1991. Harper Collins. 1st ed. inscr. F/F clip. H11. $40.00

TUCKER, Sarah. *Memoirs of Life & Religious Experience.* 1848. Moore Choate. 204p. G. V3. $16.00

TUCKER, St. George. *Devoted Bride; or, Faith & Fidelity, a Love Story.* 1878. Peterson. 370p. fair. B10. $25.00

TUCKER, St. George. *Hansford: A Tale of Bacon's Rebellion.* 1857. GM West. 356p. fair. B10. $35.00

TUCKER, William. *Family Dyer & Scourer...Arts of Dyeing & Cleaning...* 1831. Phil. 2nd. 12mo. woodcut. 123p. cloth/lacks label. M1. $250.00

TUCKER, Wilson. *Ice & Iron.* 1974. Doubleday. 1st. NF/dj. M2. $30.00

TUCKER, Wilson. *Ice & Iron.* 1974. Doubleday. 1st. VG/dj. P3. $25.00

TUCKER, Wilson. *Procession of the Damned.* 1965. Crime Club. 1st. VG/dj. P3. $25.00

TUCKERMAN, Edward. *Synopsis of Lichens of New England...* 1848. Cambridge. inscr. 93p. VG. B26. $60.00

TUDOR, Tasha. *Corgiville Fair.* 1971. NY. 2nd. VG/VG. B5. $50.00

TUDOR, Tasha. *Dorcas Porkus.* 1942. Oxford. not 1st ed. lists to A Tale for Easter. polka-dot brd. VG. M5. $150.00

TUDOR, Tasha. *First Delights, a Book About the Five Senses.* 1966. Platt Munk. early prt. 8vo. unp. NF. T5. $35.00

TUDOR, Tasha. *First Poems of Childhood.* 1967. Platt Munk. ils. 8vo. 45p. pict ep. gray brd. VG. T5. $30.00

TUDOR, Tasha. *Mother Goose.* 1989. Random. 16mo. Caldecott Honor. F/F. B17. $11.00

TUDOR, Tasha. *Pumpkin Moonshine.* 1993. Jenny Wren. 55th Aniversary ed. sgn. F/F. B17. $35.00

TUDOR, Tasha. *Springs of Joy.* 1979. Rand McNally. 1st ed. 4to. VG. B17. $30.00

TUDOR, Tasha. *Take Joy.* 1966. Cleveland. 1st ed. VG/G. B5. $50.00

TUDOR, Tasha. *Tale for Easter.* 1989. Random. 16mo. rem mk. F/sans. B17. $7.00

TUDOR, Tasha. *Tasha Tudor Book of Fairy Tales.* 1969. Platt Munk. folio. VG. B17. $15.00

TUDOR, Tasha. *Tasha Tudor's Bedtime Book.* 1977. Platt Munk. folio. VG. B17. $14.00

– U –

UBELAKER, Douglas. *Ayalan Cementary*. 1981. Smithsonian. 175p. xl. wrp. F3. $10.00

UBELAKER, Douglas. *Bones: A Forensic Detective's Casebook*. 1992. Burlinghame. later prt. F/F. N4. $15.00

UDRY, Janice May. *Tree Is Nice*. 1956. Harper. possible 1st ed. ils. VG. M5. $18.00

UKERS, William. *Trip to Brazil*. 1935. Tea & Coffee Trade Journal Co. 37p. wrp. F3. $15.00

ULANOV, Barry. *Incredible Crosby*. 1948. NY. 1st ed. VG/VG. B5. $30.00

ULPH, Owen. *Leather Throne*. 1984. Dream Garden. 1st ed. sgn. F/dj. A18. $25.00

UMBLE, John. *Ohio Mennonite Sunday Schools: Studies in Anabaptist...* 1941. Goshen College. 522p. dj. A17. $17.50

UNDERHILL, Ruth. *Here Come the Navaho!* 1953. Lawrence, KS. 4to. 285p. NF/pict wrp. N3. $30.00

UNDERWOOD, Adin B. *Three Years' Service of the 33rd MA Infantry Regiment...* 1881. Boston. xl. w/record. B18. $95.00

UNDERWOOD, F.H. *Quabbin: Story of a Small Town*. 1893. Boston. VG. M17. $40.00

UNDERWOOD, J.L. *Women of the Confederacy*. 1906. Neale. 1st ed. 313p. VG. B10. $175.00

UNDERWOOD, Tom. *Thoroughbred Racing & Breeding*. nd. NY. Coward McCann. VG. O3. $25.00

UNGER, Douglas. *Leaving the Land*. 1984. Harper Row. 1st ed. F/F. A20. $30.00

UNGERER, Tomi. *Christmas Eve at the Mellops*. 1960. Harper. ils. VG. P2. $25.00

UNGERER, Tomi. *Emile*. 1960. Harper. BC. orange brd. VG/G. B17. $7.50

UNGERER, Tomi. *Hat*. nd. Parents Magazine. possible 1st ed. 4to. unp. VG+. C14. $10.00

UNGNAD, Arthur. *Babylonish-Assyrische Grammatik*. 1926. Munich. Beck'sche. 2nd. 184p. VG/torn. W1. $20.00

UNNERSTAD, Edith. *Pysen*. 1955. Macmillan. 1st ed. ils Louis Slobodkin. 172p. VG/G. P2. $18.00

UNRUH, John D. *Plains Across*. 1979. Urbana. 3rd. ils/index. 565p. NF/VG. T10. $45.00

UNSWORTH, Barry. *Hide*. 1970. London. Gollancz. 1st ed. NF/VG. B4. $250.00

UNSWORTH, Barry. *Sacred Hunger*. 1992. Doubleday. 1st ed. F/F. M23. $30.00

UNTERMEYER, Jean Starr. *Love & Need: Collected Poems*. 1940. Viking. 1st ed. VG/G. V1. $15.00

UNTERMEYER, Louis. *More Poems From the Golden Treasury of Poetry*. (1959). Golden. 12mo. 80p. VG. C14. $8.00

UPDEGRAFF, Allan. *Native Soil*. 1930. NY. 1st ed. dj. A17. $7.50

UPDIKE, John. *Bech Is Back*. 1982. Knopf. 1st ed. NF/VG. B35. $32.00

UPDIKE, John. *Bech: A Book*. 1970. NY. 1st ed. 1/500. sgn. F/F/case. C2. $75.00

UPDIKE, John. *Bottom's Dream*. 1969. Knopf. 1st ed. F/NF. B2. $85.00

UPDIKE, John. *Brazil*. 1994. Knopf. 1st trade ed. as issued. A20. $28.00

UPDIKE, John. *Buchanan Dying*. 1974. NY. 1st ed. F/F. C6. $40.00

UPDIKE, John. *Carpentered Hen & Other Tame Creatures*. 1958. Harper. 1st ed. author's 1st book. NF/NF clip 1st state dj. C6. $500.00

UPDIKE, John. *Carpentered Hen*. 1982. Knopf. 1st ed thus. assn copy. F/VG+. V1. $20.00

UPDIKE, John. *Collected Poems 1953-1993*. 1993. Knopf. 1st ed. F/F. V1. $25.00

UPDIKE, John. *Coup*. 1978. Knopf. 1st ed. F/F. B35. $24.00

UPDIKE, John. *In the Beauty of the Lilies*. London. 1st ed. VG/VG. C4. $60.00

UPDIKE, John. *In the Cemetery High Above Shillington*. 1995. 1st ed. 1/100. sgn. ils/sgn Barry Moser. VG/VG. C4. $175.00

UPDIKE, John. *Just Looking*. 1989. NY. AP. 4to. F/wrp. C2. $60.00

UPDIKE, John. *Marry Me*. 1976. Knopf. 1st ed. F/F. H11. $40.00

UPDIKE, John. *Memories of the Ford Administration*. 1992. KNopf. 1st trade ed. rem mk. F/F. B35. $24.00

UPDIKE, John. *Midpoint & Other Poems*. 1969. Knopf. 1st ed. F/NF. H11. $65.00

UPDIKE, John. *Poorhouse Fair*. 1959. Knopf. 1st ed. F/NF. B4. $450.00

UPDIKE, John. *Rabbit at Rest*. 1990. Knopf. 1st ed. F/F. B35. $28.00

UPDIKE, John. *Rabbit Is Rich*. 1981. Knopf. 1st ed. F/F. B35/H11. $35.00

UPDIKE, John. *Rabbit Redux*. 1971. Knopf. 1st ed. NF/NF. B35. $45.00

UPDIKE, John. *Roger's Version*. 1986. Franklin Lib. 1st ed. sgn. leather. F. C2. $40.00

UPDIKE, John. *Roger's Version*. 1986. Knopf. 1st trade ed. F/F. B35. $28.00

UPDIKE, John. *Roger's Version*. 1986. NY. 1st ed. 1/350. sgn. quarter calf. F/case. C2. $75.00

UPDIKE, John. *Telephone Poles & Other Poems*. 1963. NY. 1st ed. F/F. C6. $65.00

UPDIKE, John. *Trust Me*. 1987. Knopf. 1st ed. F/F. H11. $40.00

UPDIKE, John. *Witches of Eastwick*. 1984. Knopf. 1st ed. F/F. H11. $30.00

UPDYKE, James; see Burnett, W.R.

UPHAM, C.W. *Life, Explorations & Public Services of John Chas Fremont*. 1856. Boston. 12mo. 356p. G. T3. $42.00

UPHAM, Thomas C. *Elements of Mental Philosophy Embracing Two Departments...* 1828. Portland, ME. Shirley Hyde. 2nd. 576p. contemporary calf. G1. $125.00

UPHAM, Thomas C. *Outlines of Imperfect & Disordered Mental Action*. 1840. harper. 16mo. 400p. pub pebbled dk brn cloth. G1. $85.00

URDANG, Constance. *Only the World*. 1983. Pittsburgh U. 1st ed. F/wrp. V1. $10.00

URE, James M. *Benedictine Office: Old English Text*. 1957. Edinburgh. 8vo. 141p. gilt maroon cloth. NF. T10. $45.00

URIS, Leon. *Exodus*. 1958. Garden City. Doubleday. 1st ed. 8vo. 2 maps. 626p. VG/torn. W1. $18.00

URIS, Leon. *Mila 18*. 1961. Doubleday. 1st ed. F/NF clip. H11. $40.00

URIS, Leon. *Milta Pass*. 1988. Doubleday. 1st ed. w/sgn leaf. F/F. B2. $40.00

URIS, Leon. *Topaz*. 1967. McGraw Hill. 1st ed. NF/VG. M22. $30.00

URNER, Clarence H. *Thrush*. 1927. Henkel. 88p. VG-. B10. $25.00

UTLEY, Robert M. *Four Fighters of Lincoln County*. 1986. NM U. 1st ed. 8vo. 3 maps. 116p. NF/dj. T10. $35.00

UTTLEY, Alison. *Traveller in Time*. 1973 (1939). London. Faber. ils Phyllis Bray. 331p. gr brd. NF/NF. T5. $30.00

UZANNE, Octave. *Chronique, Scandaleuse*. 1879. Paris. Quantin. ils/index. 325p. half red cloth/marbled brd. K1. $150.00

– V –

VACHSS, Andrew. *Batman the Ultimate Evil.* 1995. Warner. 1st. F/dj. P3. $20.00

VACHSS, Andrew. *Blossom.* 1990. Knopf. 1st. NF/NF. N4. $25.00

VACHSS, Andrew. *Blue Belle.* 1988. Knopf. 1st ed. author's 3rd novel. NF/NF. M22. $20.00

VACHSS, Andrew. *Flood.* 1985. Donald Fine. 1st ed. author's 1st book. F/NF. M23. $30.00

VACHSS, Andrew. *Hard Candy.* 1989. Knopf. 1st ed. sgn. F/NF. M23. $20.00

VACHSS, Andrew. *Strega.* 1987. Knopf. 1st ed. F/F. A20. $33.00

VAETH, J. Gordon. *Blimps & U-Boats: US Navy Airships in Battle of Atlantic.* 1992. Annapolis. 1st ed. ils. 205p. VG/dj. B18. $22.50

VAGTS, Alfred. *Hitler's Second Army.* 1943. 1st. F/F. E6. $18.00

VAGO, Bela. *Shadow of the Swastika: Rise of Fascism...* 1975. London. Inst for Jewish Affairs. 1st ed. 431p. dj. A17. $25.00

VAILLANT, George C. *Aztecs of Mexico: Origin, Rise & Fall of Aztec Nation.* 1950. Doubleday. 8vo. 340p. tan cloth. M/F. K7. $35.00

VAINSTEIN, Yaacov. *Cycle of the Jewish Year: Study of Festivals...* 1953. Jerusalem. WZO. Eng/Hebrew text. 152p. G+/poor. S3. $24.00

VALE, R.B. *Wings, Fur & Shot.* 1936. Harrisburg. 1st ed. VG. B5. $32.50

VALENTINE, Benjamin Bachelder. *Old Marster & Other Verses.* 1921. Whittet Shepperson. 117p. VG. B10. $25.00

VALENTINE, Jean. *Pilgrims.* 1969. FSG. 1st ed. F/NF. V1. $30.00

VALENTINE, Laura. *Aunt Louisa's London Gift Book.* ca 1880. London. Warne. chromolithographs. pict cloth. T10. $75.00

VALENTINE, Laura. *Aunt Louisa's Sunday Book.* ca 1871. London. Warne. ils Kroheim. gilt/red decor gr cloth. VG. T10. $215.00

VALENTINE. *Noah's Ark.* nd. Dundee. Valentine. shaped book. 23p. VG. D1. $95.00

VALLEJO, Doris. *Boy Who Saved the Stars.* 1978. NY. O'Quinn Studios. 1st ed. ils Boris Vallejo. NF/VG. B4. $85.00

VALLIER, Dora. *Henri Rousseau.* 1962. Abrams. ils. 382p. yel stp gr cloth. dj. K1. $100.00

VALIN, Jonathan. *Day of Wrath.* 1982. Congdon Lattes. 1st. VG/dj. P3. $25.00

VALIN, Jonathan. *Dead Letter.* 1981. Dodd Mead. 1st. VG/dj. P3. $30.00

VALIN, Jonathan. *Extenuating Circumstances.* 1989. Delacorte. 1st. F/dj. P3. $25.00

VALIN, Jonathan. *Life's Work.* 1986. Delacorte. 1st. sgn. F/dj. P3. $30.00

VALIN, Jonathan. *Second Chance.* 1987. Harper Row. 1st. F/dj. P3. $20.00

VAN ALLSBURG, C. *Ben's Dream.* nd. Houghton Mifflin. 1st ed. ils Van allsburg. VG/dj. D1. $150.00

VAN ALLSBURG, C. *Jumanji.* 1981. Houghton Mifflin. 1st ed. ils. unp. F/F. D1. $225.00

VAN ALLSBURG, Chris. *Just a Dream.* 1990. Houghton Mifflin. 1st. 4to. F/VG. P2. $45.00

VAN ALLSBURG, C. *Mysteries of Harry Burdick.* 1984. Houghton Mifflin. 1st ed. ils. unp. F/F. D1. $135.00

VAN ALLSBURG, C. *Stranger.* 1986. Houghton Mifflin. 1st ed. ils. NF/NF. D1. $85.00

VAN ALLSBURG, C. *Z Was Zapped.* 1987. Houghton Mifflin. 1st ed. ils. unp. F/F. D1. $85.00

VAN ANDEL, T.H. *New Views on an Old Planet.* 1990. Cambridge. 324p. F/dj. D8. $30.00

VAN ANTWERP, William C. *Collectors' Comment on His First Editions...Walter Scott.* 1932. San Francisco. Gelber. Lilienthan. 1st ed. 1/400. sgn. NF. T10. $125.00

VAN ARSDALE, G.D. *Hydrometallurgy of Base Metals.* 1953. McGraw Hill. 1st ed. 370p. F. D8. $25.00

VAN ASH, Clay. *Fires of Fu Manchu.* 1987942. Harper Row. 1st ed. F/F. H11. $30.00

VAN ASH, Clay. *Ten Years Beyond Baker Street.* 1984. Harper Row. 1st ed. author's 1st novel. F/F clip. H11. $40.00

VAN BEEK, Gus W. *Hajar Bin Humeid.* 1969. Johns Hopkins. 1st ed. 4to. 69 pl. 421p. VG/dj. W1. $45.00

VAN CAENEGEM, R.C. *Birth of the English Common Law.* 1973. Cambridge. M11. $65.00

VAN CAENEGEM, R.C. *Law, History, the Low Countries, Europe...* 1994. London. Hambledon. 14 collected essays. M11. $50.00

VAN DE POLL, Willem. *Surinam.* 1951. Hague, Netherlands. 1st. 199p. F3. $15.00

VAN DE WATER, F. *Lake Champlain-Lake George.* 1946. Indianapolis. 1st ed. VG/VG. B5. $40.00

VAN DE WETERING, Janwillem. *Blond Baboon.* 1978. Houghton Mifflin. 1st ed. sgn. F/NF. T2. $45.00

VAN DE WETERING, Janwillem. *Hard Rain.* 1986. Pantheon. 1st ed. sgn. F/NF. B2. $40.00

VAN DE WETERING, Janwillem. *Inspector Saito's Small Satori.* 1985. Putnam. 1st ed. F/F. H11. $25.00

VAN DE WETERING, Janwillem. *Inspector Salto's Small Satori.* 1985. NY. Putnam. 1st ed. sgn. F/F. T2. $40.00

VAN DE WETERING, Janwillem. *Just a Corpse at Twilight.* 1994. Soho. 1st ed. F/F. T2. $25.00

VAN DE WETERING, Janwillem. *Rattle-Rat.* 1985. Pantheon. 1st ed. sgn. F/NF. B2. $45.00

VAN DE WETERING, Janwillem. *Sergeant's Cat & Other Stories.* 1987. Pantheon. 1st ed. sgn. F/F. T2. $40.00

VAN DE WIELE, Annie. *West in My Eyes.* 1956. Dodd Mead. 4 plans/9 maps. VG/dj. T7. $24.00

VAN DEN KEER, Pieter. *Germania Inferior.* 1966. Amsterdam. Theatrvm Orbis Terrarvm. facsimile. AN/dj. O7. $175.00

VAN DER LINDEN, Peter. *Great Lakes Ships We Remember. Vol I.* 1992. Freshwater. rpt of 1979 ed. AN/dj. A16. $27.00

VAN DER LINDEN, Peter. *Great Lakes Ships We Remember. Vol III.* 1994. Freshwater. AN. A16. $35.00

VAN DER MEULEN, D. *Aden to the Hadhramaut.* 1947. London. Murray. 2nd. xl. VG. W1. $65.00

VAN DER POST, Laurens. *Lost World of the Kalahari.* 1958. Morrow. 1st ed. map. 279p. VG/torn. W1. $14.00

VAN DERVEER, Helen. *Little Sallie Mandy Story Book.* 1935. Platt Munk. 4to. red brd. VG+. M5. $55.00

VAN DINE, S.S. *Benson Murder Case.* 1928. Scribner. VG. P3. $20.00

VAN DINE, S.S. *Canary Murder Case.* 1927. Scribner. 1st. VG/dj. M25. $25.00

VAN DINE, S.S. *Garden Murder Case.* 1935. Scribner. 1st. VG/dj. P3. $50.00

VAN DOREN, Carl. *Benjamin Franklin.* 1938. Viking. 1/625. 1st ed. 3 vol set. sgn. 8vo. VG/case. B11. $75.00

VAN DOREN, Carl. *James Branch Cabell.* 1932. np. revised. ils. 95p. VG. A4. $25.00

VAN DOREN, Carl. *Mutiny in January.* 1943. Viking. 1st. 288p. VG/dj. M20. $30.00

VAN DOREN, Carl. *Secret History of American Revolution.* 1941. Viking. 1st trade. sgn. 534p. VG/dj. M20. $45.00

VAN DOREN, Mark. *Henry David Thoreau: A Critical Study.* 1916. Boston/NY. 1st ed. author's 1st book. VG. C6. $95.00

VAN DOREN, Mark. *Noble Voice: Study of Ten Great Poems.* 1946. 1st ed. VG+/VG. S13. $14.00

VAN DUYN, Mona. *Merciful Disguises.* 1973. Atheneum. 1st ed. assn copy. sgn. F/NF. V1. $45.00

VAN DUYN, Mona. *Near Changes.* 1990. Knopf. 1st ed. F/NF. V1. $10.00

VAN DYKE, Henry. *Blue Fowler.* 1902. 1st. ils Howard Pyle. VG. B15. $75.00

VAN DYKE, Henry. *First Christmas Tree.* 1897. Scribner. 1st. ils Howard Pyle. teg. VG+. B15. $175.00

VAN DYKE, Henry. *White Bees & Other Poems.* 1909. Scribner. 1st. sm 8vo. 105p. gilt gr cloth. F. H1. $22.50

VAN GIESON, Judith. *Lies That Bind.* 1993. Harper Collins. 1st. sgn. F/F. A20. $30.00

VAN GIESON, Judith. *Other Side of Death.* 1991. Harper Collins. 1st. sgn. author's 3rd book. F/dj. A24. $75.00

VAN GIESON, Judith. *Raptor.* 1990. Harper Row. 1st. author's 2nd book. F/F. H11. $100.00

VAN GULIK, Robert. *Chinese Bell Murders.* 1958. Harper. 1st Am ed. 8vo. NF/dj. T10. $200.00

VAN GULIK, Robert. *Poets & Murder.* 1968. Scribner. 1st ed. NF/NF. N4. $65.00

VAN GULIK, Robert. *Red Pavilion.* 1968. Scribner. 1st Am ed. F/NF. T2. $45.00

VAN HINTE, J.E. *Proceedings of Second West African Micropaleontological...* 1966. Leiden. EJ Brill. 294p. F/dj. D8. $30.00

VAN HOESEN, Henry. *Brown University Library 1767-1782.* 1938. Providence. private prt. brn brd/wht label. F. B14. $45.00

VAN INGEN, Phillip. *New York Academy of Medicine: Its First Hundred Years.* 1949. NY. 1st ed. 573p. A13. $40.00

VAN LAREN, A.J. *Succulents Other Than Cacti.* 1934. Los Angeles. sgn John Thomas Howell. ils/woodcut. NF. B26. $125.00

VAN LAREN, A.J. *Vetplanten.* 1932. Zaandam. Dutch text. ils. 4to. VG+. B26. $60.00

VAN LOON, Gerard. *Story of Hendrick Willem Van Loon.* 1972. np. ils. 410p. F/F. A4. $45.00

VAN LUSTBADER, Eric. *Angel Eyes.* 1991. Fawcett. 1st ed. F/F. N4. $25.00

VAN LUSTBADER, Eric. *Black Heart.* 1983. NY. Evans. 1st ed. NF/NF. H11. $20.00

VAN LUSTBADER, Eric. *Dai-San.* 1978. Doubleday. 1st ed. NF/NF. P3. $25.00

VAN LUSTBADER, Eric. *Miko.* 1984. Villard. 1st ed. NF/NF. P3. $30.00

VAN LUSTBADER, Eric. *Sirens.* 1981. Evans. 1st ed. VG/VG. P3. $15.00

VAN LUSTBADER, Eric. *Zero.* 1988. Random. 1st ed. VG/VG. P3. $20.00

VAN METRE, T.W. *Tramps & Liners.* 1931. Doubleday Doran. 1st ed. 8vo. 324p. gr cloth. NF. T10. $75.00

VAN PAASSEN, Pierre. *Forgotten Ally.* 1943. Dial. 1st ed. 8vo. 343p. map ep. VG/torn. W1. $12.00

VAN RIPER, Guernsey. *Mighty Macs.* 1972. Garrard. 1st ed. photos. F/VG. P8. $17.50

VAN RJNDT, Philippe. *Blueprint.* 1977. Putnam. 1st. VG/dj. P3. $18.00

VAN RJNDT, Philippe. *Tetramachus Collection.* 1976. Lester Orpen. 1st. VG/dj. P3. $20.00

VAN ROOTEN, Luis d'Antin. *Floriculturist's Vade-Mecum of Exotic & Recondite Plants...* 1973. NY. 126p. dj. B26. $15.00

VAN STOCKUM, Hilda. *Mitchells.* 1945. Viking. ils. 246p. VG/G+. P2. $25.00

VAN THAL, Herbert. *James Agate: An Anthology.* 1961. Hill Wang. 1st. VG/G. P3. $25.00

VAN THIENEN, F. *Great Age of Holland 1600-1660.* 1951. London. Harrap. VG/G. D2. $15.00

VAN TRAMP, John C. *Prairie & Rocky Mountain Adventures; or, Life in the West.* 1869 (1867). Segner Condit. 775p. leather. VG. M20. $87.00

VAN URK, J. Blan. *Horse, the Valley & the Chagrin Valley Hunt.* 1947. NY. Richard Ellis. 1/700. F/dj/worn case. O3. $225.00

VAN URK, J. Blan. *Little Charlie the Fox.* 1977. Wilmington. Serendipity. 1/1000. VG/VG. O3. $300.00

VAN VOGT, A.E. *Book of Ptath.* 1947. Fantasy. 1st. sgn/#d. F/VG. P3. $250.00

VAN VOGT, A.E. *Book of Ptath.* 1975. Garland. F. M2. $20.00

VAN VOGT, A.E. *Destination: Universe.* 1952. Pelligrini Cudahy. 1st. F/NF. P3. $45.00

VAN VOGT, A.E. *Empire of the Atom.* 1957. SFBC. F/dj. M2. $35.00

VAN VOGT, A.E. *Weapon Shops of Isher.* 1951. Greenberg. 1st. F/dj. M2. $50.00

VAN VOGT, A.E. *World of Null-A.* 1948. S&S. 1st. NF/dj. M2. $50.00

VAN WATERS, George. *Illustrated Poetical Geography.* 1864. NY. 96p. fair. B18. $20.00

VAN WORMER, Joe. *World of the Black Bear.* nd. NY Times. 442p. F/dj. B22. $5.00

VAN ZANDT, J. Parker. *Geography of World Air Transport.* 1944. Brookings Inst. 67p. G/tape rpr. B18. $19.50

VANCE, Eleanor. *Tall Book of Fairy Tales.* 1947. VG. K2. $18.00

VANCE, Jack. *Blue World.* 1979. Underwood Miller. 1st hc ed. 1/700. F/F. T2. $35.00

VANCE, Jack. *Five Gold Bands.* 1993. Underwood Miller. rpt of The Space Pirate. F/NF. G10. $15.00

VANCE, Jack. *Palace of Love.* 1968. Dobson. 1st. VG/dj. P3. $40.00

VANCE, Louis Joseph. *Street of Strange Faces.* 1939. Caxton. 1st. VG. P3. $30.00

VANCE, Marguerite. *Martha, Daughter of Virginia: Story of Martha Washington.* 1947. Dutton. 1st ed. ils Nedda Walker. 190p. G+. B10. $8.00

VANCOUVER, G. *Voyage of Discovery to the North Pacific Ocean...* 1984. London. 4 vol. 46 pl/10 maps. F/dj. M4. $85.00

VANDENBELD, J. *Nature of Australia.* 1988. NY. Facts on File. 8vo. photos. brd. dj. B1. $28.00

VANDENBURG, Arthur H. *Private Papers of Senator Vandenburg.* 1952. Boston. 599p. A17. $10.00

VANDENBUSCHE, Duane. *Gunnison Country.* 1980. Gunnison. B&B Prt. 3rd. 4to. 472p. F. S9. $75.00

VANDERBILT, Cornelius Jr. *Ranches & Ranch Life in America.* 1968. Crown. dj. A19. $35.00

VANDERBILT, Harold S. *Club Convention System of Bidding at Contract Bridge.* 1964. NY. inscr. 186p. VG. S1. $20.00

VANDERDECKEN, William Cooper. *Yachts & Yachting.* 1979 (1873). London. facsimile. 47 pl. 391p. dj. T7. $65.00

VANDERHAEGE, Guy. *Homesick.* 1989. Toronto. 1st Canadian. sgn. F/NF. B3. $60.00

VANDERHAEGE, Guy. *Homesick.* 1990. Ticknor Fields. 1st. F/F. A20. $20.00

VANDERHAEGE, Guy. *My Present Age.* 1985. Ticknor Fields. 1st. F/F. A20. $25.00

VARDRE, Leslie. *Nameless Ones.* 1967. John Long. VG/dj. P3. $15.00

VARLEY, John. *Steel Beach.* 1992. Ace/Putnam. 1st. NF/dj. P3. $23.00

VARLEY, John. *Titan.* 1979. Berkeley. 1st. NF/dj. M2. $40.00

VARMA, Devendra P. *Voices From the Vaults.* 1987. Key Porter. 1st. F/dj. P3. $25.00

VARNER & VARNER. *Dogs of the Conquest.* 1983. OK U. 1st. ils. 238p. F/dj. M4. $25.00

VASEY, George. *Grasses of the Pacific Slope.* 1893. GPO. xl. A10. $75.00

VASILOFF, Mary Jean. *Alone With Your Horse.* 1978. Harper Row. 1st ed. sgn. VG/G. O3. $25.00

VASSILTCHIKOV, Marie. *Berlin Diaries 1940-1945.* 1991. London. Folio Soc. 1st ed. 8vo. 3 maps. 296p. full red buckram. F/case. T10. $40.00

VASSOS, Ruth. *Ultimo.* 1930. NY. 1st ed. F/VG. H7. $60.00

VATIKIOTIS, P.J. *Modern History of Egypt.* 1969. Praeger. 1st ed. 8vo. 16 pl. 512p. VG. W1. $25.00

VAUGHAN, Beatrice. *Old Cook's Almanac.* 1966. NY. Gramercy. G/dj. A16. $17.50

VAUGHAN, Matthew. *Discretion of Dominick Ayres.* 1980. Linden. 1st. VG/dj. P3. $15.00

VAUGHAN, Norman D. *With Byrd at the Bottom of the World.* 1990. Harrisburg. Stackpole. later prt. ils/map. 196p. M/dj. P4. $40.00

VAUGHN, Agnes. *Akka, Dwarf of Syracuse.* 1940. Longman. 1st. VG. M2. $12.00

VAUGHN, Elizabeth Dewberry. *Break the Heart of Me.* 1994. Doubleday. 1st ed. sgn. F/F. M23. $50.00

VAUGHN, Elizabeth Dewberry. *Many Things Have Happened Since He Died.* 1990. Doubleday. 1st ed. sgn. author's 1st book. F/F. H11. $45.00

VAUX, W.S.W. *Ancient History From the Monuments.* ca 1876. London. 1st ed. 12mo. 190p. VG. W1. $20.00

VAVRA, Robert. *Tiger Flower.* 1968. London. Collins. 1st ed. 4to. olive cloth. VG+/VG. T5. $45.00

VAVRA, Robert. *Vavra's Horses.* 1989. Morrow. 1st prt. F/F. O3. $45.00

VECESY, George. *Joy in Mudville.* 1970. McCall. 1st ed. VG+/G+. P8. $20.00

VECSEY, George. *Year in the Sun.* 1989. Times. 1st. F/F. P8. $10.00

VECESY, George. *One Sunset a Week. Story of a Coal Miner.* 1974. NY. Saturday Review. 2nd. NF/NF. B2. $25.00

VEECK, Bill. *Hustler's Handbook.* 1965. NY. 1st. VG/VG. B5. $20.00

VEECK, Bill. *Thirty Tons a Day.* 1972. Viking. 1st. VG/VG. P8. $25.00

VELIMIROVIC, Nicholas. *Servia in Light & Darkness.* 1916. Longman Gr. 1st ed. 20 pl. 147p. VG. W1. $20.00

VENABLE, Charles L. *American Furniture in the Bybee Collection.* 1989. Austin. 1st ed. 80+ pl. 192p. F/dj. A17. $25.00

VENABLES, Bernard. *Baleia! Baleia! Whale Hunters of the Azores.* 1969. NY. Knopf. 16 pl/drawings. 204p. dj. T7. $25.00

VENABLES, Hubert. *Frankenstein Diaries.* 1980. Viking. 1st. VG/dj. P3. $20.00

VENKUS, Robert E. *Raid on Qaddafi: The Untold Story...* 1992. NY. 1st ed. 197p. VG+/dj. B18. $25.00

VENNING, Frank D. *Cacti.* 1974. NY. ils. 12mo. red buckram. F. B26. $12.50

VENNING, Hugh. *End.* 1948. Desmond & Stapleton. 1st. F/dj. M2. $25.00

VENTURA, Piero. *Magic Well.* 1976. Random. 1st ed. 4to. unp. gray cloth/bl spine. NF/G+. T5. $20.00

VENZI, G. *Little Angel With the Pink Wings.* (1963). Boston. Daughters of St Paul. 12mo. 21p. VG. C14. $6.00

VER BECK, Frank. *Donkey Child.* 1917. Oxford. 1st ed. 12mo. ils. VG+/pict wrp. C8. $65.00

VER WEIBE, W.A. *Oil Fields in the United States.* 1930. McGraw Hill. 1st ed/2nd imp. sgn. VG. D8. $30.00

VERBRUGGE, Frank. *Whither Thou Goest.* 1979. Minneapolis. private prt. sgn. 8vo. photos. 120p. gr cloth. F. B11. $30.00

VERDELLE, A.J. *Good Negress.* 1995. Algonquin. 1st ed. author's 1st book. F/F. M23. $40.00

VERDERY, Katherine. *Little Dixie Captain.* 1930. Bobbs Merrill. stated 1st ed. ils Winifred Bromhall. VG+/dj. M5. $85.00

VERKLER & ZEMPEL. *Book Prices: Used & Rare.* 1993. 4to. 613p. F. A4. $60.00

VERLAINE, Paul. *Forty Poems.* 1948. London. 1st ed. F/dj. A17. $15.00

VERMEULE, Emily. *Greece in the Bronze Age...* 1966. Chicago. 2nd. 406p. NF/dj. W1. $30.00

VERNE, Jules. *Adventures in the Land of the Behemoth.* 1874. Sheperd. VG. M2. $200.00

VERNE, Jules. *Captain Antifer.* 1895. Fenno. VG. M2. $125.00

VERNE, Jules. *Desert of Ice.* 1874. Phil. Porter Coates. A19. $65.00

VERNE, Jules. *From the Earth to the Moon.* 1918. Scribner. 4 pl. F. A17. $35.00

VERNE, Jules. *Fur Country.* 1876. Montreal. 1st Canadian ed. ils Ferat. VG. C6. $60.00

VERNE, Jules. *Mysterious Island.* 1924. Scribner. ils NC Wyeth. VG. B17. $40.00

VERNE, Jules. *20,000 Leagues Under the Sea.* 1993. Annapolis. Naval Inst. 1st ed thus. F/F. M23. $50.00

VERNE, Jules. *Wreck of the Chancellor.* 1875. Boston. Osgood. 1st. NF. M24. $125.00

VERNER, Elizabeth O'Neill. *Stonewall Ladies.* 1963. Tradd Street. 2nd. 144p. VG/VG. B10. $12.00

VERNON, Bowen. *Lazy Beaver.* 1948. McKay. early ed. VG/VG. B17. $14.00

VERRILL, A. Hyatt. *Boy's Book of Buccaneers.* 1927. Dodd Mead. G. P3. $12.00

VERRILL, A. Hyatt. *Bridge of Light.* 1950. Fantasy. 1st. sgn/#d. F/NF. P3. $100.00

VERRILL, A. Hyatt. *Golden City.* 1916. Duffield. 1st. VG. M2. $50.00

VERRILL, A. Hyatt. *Old Civilizations of the New World.* 1942. Home Lib. F/dj. M2. $35.00

VERRILL, A. Hyatt. *Romantic & Historical Virginia.* 1935. Dodd Mead. 1st ed. ils/map ep. VG/G. B10. $25.00

VERSCHAFFELT, Alexandre. *New Iconography of the Camellias.* 1945. Avery Island, LA. trans EA McIhenny. gilt maroon cloth. VG. B26. $45.00

VERTREGT, M. *Principles of Astronautics.* 1960. Amsterdam. Elsevier. 8vo. 221p. VG/dj. K5. $20.00

VERY, Jones. *Essays & Poems.* 1839. Little Brn. 1st. brn cloth/label. VG. M24. $350.00

VERY, Lydia. *Poems.* 1856. Andover. WF Draper. 1st. 12mo. 22p. cloth. M1. $150.00

VESALIUS, Andreas. *Epitome of Andreas Vesalius.* 1949. NY. 1st Eng trans. trans LR Lind. 103p. A13. $75.00

VESALIUS, Andreas. *Icones Anatomicae.* 1934. Bremer Presse. NY Adacemy Medicine/Lib of U of Munich. F/dj/box. B24. $6,800.00

VICKER, Ray. *Kingdom of Oil. The Middle East: Its People & Its Power.* 1974. Scribner. 1st ed. 8vo. 264p. VG/dj. W1. $22.00

VICKERS, Roy. *Best Police Stories.* 1966. Faber. 1st. VG. P3. $15.00

VICKERS, Roy. *Some Like Them Dead*. 1960. Hodder Stoughton. 1st. sgn by contributors. F/NF. M15. $350.00

VICTOR, Orville J. *History of American Conspiracies: A Record of Treason...* 1863. NY. James D Torrey. 1st. VG. B2. $250.00

VICTORIA, R.I. (Queen). *More Leaves From the Journal of a Life in the Highlands.* 1884. London. 404p. ils cloth. G. B18. $25.00

VIDAL, Gore. *Creation.* 1981. NY. Random. 1st ed. F/F. M23. $25.00

VIDAL, Gore. *Empire.* 1987. Random. 1st. NF/VG. P3. $25.00

VIDAL, Gore. *Evening With Richard Nixon.* 1972. Random. 1st ed. F/F. B35. $28.00

VIDAL, Gore. *Hollywood.* 1990. Random. 1st ed. 1/200. sgn. F/case. B35. $70.00

VIDAL, Gore. *Kalki.* 1978. Random. 1st. VG/dj. P3. $22.00

VIDAL, Gore. *Live From Golgotha.* Random. F/F. B35. $18.00

VIDAL, Gore. *Second American Revolution.* 1982. Random. 1st ed. rem mk. F/F. B35. $20.00

VIDAL, Gore. *Two Sisters.* 1970. Little Brn. 1st. VG/dj. P3. $30.00

VIERECK, Leslie. *Alaska Trees & Shrubs.* 1972. GPO. USDA Handbook 40. 265p. w/map. VG. S15. $12.00

VIERECK, Peter. *Archer in the Marrow.* 1987. np. 1st ed. F/VG+. V1. $15.00

VIERECK, Peter. *First Morning.* 1952. Scribner. 1st ed. F/G. V1. $15.00

VIERECK, Peter. *New & Selected Poems.* 1967. Bobbs Merrill. ARC. sgn assn copy. F/NF. V1. $25.00

VIERECK, Peter. *Tree Witch.* 1961. Scribner. 1st ed. F/VG+. V1. $20.00

VIETS, Henry. *Brief History of Medicine in Massachusetts.* 1930. Boston. 194p. VG. A13. $50.00

VIETZEN, Raymond. *Ancient Man in Northern Ohio.* 1941. Lorain, OH. 1st. sgn 159p. VG. B5. $35.00

VILLA, Jose Garcia. *Have Come Am Here.* 1942. Viking. 1st ed. VG+/VG. V1. $35.00

VILLARD, Henry Serrano. *Contact! Story of the Early Birds.* 1968. NY. 1st ed. ils. 263p. VG/torn. B18. $22.50

VILLIERS, Alan. *Men, Ships & the Sea.* 1973. NGS. G/torn. A16. $10.00

VILLIERS, Alan. *Men, Ships & the Sea.* 1973. NGS. ils. 434p. VG/G+. P12. $12.00

VILLIERS, Alan. *Sons of Sinbad: An Account of Sailing With the Arabs...* 1940. Scribner. 1st ed. ils/maps. 429p. xl. VG. W1. $50.00

VILLIERS, Alan. *Whalers of the Midnight Sun.* 1934. Scribner. 1st ed. ils. 285p. VG. T7. $30.00

VINCENT, Leon H. *Bibliotaph & Other People.* 1898. Boston. Houghton Mifflin. 1st ed. 8vo. 233p. teg. F. T10. $75.00

VINCENT, Thomas MacCurdy. *Abraham Lincoln & Edwin M Stanton.* 1892. WA, DC. 1st ed. 35p. NF/prt wrp. M8. $37.50

VINCENT, William. *Voyage de Nearque...* 1799. Paris. Imprimerie Republique. folio. contemporary bdg. VG. W1. $650.00

VINE, Barbara; see Rendell, Ruth.

VINE, Peter. *Jewels of the Kingdom.* 1987. London. Immel. 1st ed. folio. ils. 159p. xl. F/dj. W1. $28.00

VINGE, Joan. *Psion.* 1982. Delacorte. 1st ed. F/NF. G10. $25.00

VINGE, Joan D. *Fireship.* 1978. SFBC. 1st. F/dj. M2. $10.00

VINGE, Joan D. *Phoenix in the Ashes.* 1985. Bluejay. 1st. VG/dj. P3. $20.00

VINGE, Joan D. *Return of the Jedi Storybook.* 1983. St Michael. MTI. VG. P3. $15.00

VINGE, Joan D. *Summer Queen.* 1991. Warner. 1st. Nf/dj. P3. $22.00

VINGE, Joan D. *World's End.* 1984. Bluejay. 1st. VG/dj. P3. $20.00

VINGE, Venor. *Fire Upon the Deep.* 1992. Tor. 1st ed. F/F. G10. $50.00

VIOLA, Herman J. *After Columbus.* 1990. Orion. 1st. F/dj. P3. $45.00

VIOLA, Herman J. *Exploring the West.* 1987. Smithsonian. 4to. 256p. brn cloth. F/F. F7. $35.00

VIORST, Milton. *Sandcastles: The Arabs in Search of the Modern World.* 1994. Knopf. ARC. RS. F/F. B35. $22.00

VIPONT, Elfrida. *Pavilion.* 1970 (1969). HRW. 1st Am ed. 8vo. 218p. pk brd. G+/G. T5. $25.00

VIRAMONTES, Helena Maria. *Under the Feet of Jesus.* 1995. Dutton. 1st. sgn. F/F. B3. $40.00

VISINTIN, Luigi. *Atlante Geografico Metodico.* 1935. Novarra. Istituto Geografico de Agostini. 69 maps. F. O7. $85.00

VIZCAYNO, Sebastian. *Jornada Principal des Las Californias.* 1963. Liberia Anticuaria. 1/300. full red leather/raised bands. miniature. T10. $125.00

VIZENOR, Gerald. *Darkness in Saint Louis Bearheart.* 1978. St Paul. Truck Pr. 1st ed. NF/wrp. B4. $85.00

VLIET, R.G. *Events & Celebrations.* 1966. Viking. 1st ed. assn copy. F/VG. V1. $15.00

VOEGELIN, C.F. *Shawnee Stems & Jacob P Dunn Miami Dictionary.* 1940. Indianapolis. IN Hist Soc. 478p. VG/wrp. B18. $12.50

VOGEL, Ilse-Margret. *Willy, Willy, Don't Be Silly.* 1965. Atheneum. 1st ed. 8vo. unp. G+. T5. $20.00

VOGEL, John. *This Happened in the Hills of Kentucky.* 1952. Zondervan. 382p. VG. B10. $15.00

VOIGHT, Ellen Bryant. *Two-Trees.* 1992. Norton. 1st ed. F/NF. V1. $15.00

VOIGHT, Cynthia. *Dicey's Song.* 1983. Atheneum. 2nd. 8vo. 196p. brn cloth. G. T5. $20.00

VOIGT, Cynthia. *Solitary Blue.* 1984. Atheneum. 3rd prt. 8vo. Newberry Honor. VG/VG. B17. $6.50

VOINOVICH, Vladimir. *Pretender to the Throne.* 1981. FSG. UP. F. B35. $26.00

VOLLMANN, William T. *Father & Crows.* 1992. Viking. 1st. F/F. D10. $45.00

VOLLMANN, William T. *Ice-Shirt.* 1990. Viking. 1st. F/F. T11. $40.00

VOLLMANN, William T. *Rainbow Stories.* 1989. Atheneum. ARC/1st Am. sgn. author's 2nd book. F/F. D10. $125.00

VOLLMANN, William T. *Whores for Gloria.* 1991. Pantheon. 1st. sgn. F/F. B3. $45.00

VOLLMANN, William T. *You Bright & Risen Angels.* 1987. Atheneum. 1st Am. author's 1st book. F/F. from $100 to $135.00

VOLNEY, Constantin F. *View of the Climate & Soil of the USA...* 1804. London. missing 1 fld map. 504p. full calf. B18. $125.00

VOLTAIRE. *An Epistle...Upon His Arrival at His Estate...1755.* 1755. London. Dodsley. 1st Eng. 4to. cloth/brd. R12. $225.00

VOLTAIRE. *History of Charles the Twelfth, King of Sweeden.* 1831. Hartford. leather. G+. M17. $50.00

VOLTAIRE. *History of Zadig; or, Destiny.* 1952. Paris. LEC. 1st thus. 1st thus. 1/1500. F/case. Q1. $150.00

VOLTAIRE. *Jeannot et Colin.* 1895. Paris. 1/50 in red on Japon. F/wrp/chemise/case. B24. $200.00

VOLTAIRE. *Virgin of Orleans; or, Joan of Arc.* 1965. Alan Swallow. trans Howard Nelson. F/clip. B35. $55.00

VOLTAIRE. *Voltaire Recueil des Particularites Curieuses...* 1781. Porrentruy. Goetschy. 8vo. calf/brd. R12. $225.00

VON ALENITCH, Victor. *Dressage.* 1982. Chicago. Adams. 1st ed. sgn. 205p. VG. O3. $15.00

VON DANIKEN, Erich. *According to the Evidence.* 1977. Souvenir. 1st. VG. P3. $20.00

VON DANIKEN, Erich. *Gods & Their Grand Design.* 1982. Putnam. 1st. F/dj. M2. $12.00

VON DOBSCHUTZ, Ernst. *Influence of the Bible on Civilization.* 1914. NY. 1st. xl Harvard Divinity School. B14. $30.00

VON ECKARDT, Hans. *Russia.* 1932. Knopf. 1st ed. VG+. B2. $40.00

VON ELSNER, Don. *Cruise Bridge.* 1980. Hawthorne, CA. 187p. VG/wrp. S1. $5.00

VON FOERSTER, Heinz. *Cybernetics: Circular Causal & Feedback Mechanisms...* 1951. NY. Josiah Macy Jr Foundation. 252p. prt gr cloth. VG/dj. G1. $40.00

VON GASSNER, Paul. *Figure & Dance Skating.* 1949. A&S Pub. 1st. ils/photos. VG. P8. $12.50

VON GOETHE, Johann Wolfgang. *Gedichte.* 1906. Venice. S Rosen. 78x56mm. 267p. F/prt wrp. B24. $75.00

VON GOETHE, Johann Wolfgang. *Story of Reynard the Fox.* 1954. LEC. 1/1500. ils/sgn Fritz Eichenberg. F/NF case. T10. $75.00

VON HAGEN, Victor Wolfgang. *Frederick Catherwood, Architect.* 1950. NY. 1st ed. ils. 177p. gilt bl cloth. F/VG. H3. $75.00

VON KARMAN, Theodore. *Wind & Beyond: Theodore Von Karman.* 1967. Boston. Little Brn. 1st. inscr. VG/dj. K3. $20.00

VON KRIES, Johannes. *Allgemeine Sinnesphysiologie.* 1923. Leipzig. Vogel. 300p. emb mauve cloth. VG. G1. $40.00

VON KRUSENTSTERN, Adam J. *Atlas of the Voyage Round the World.* 1974 (1813). Amsterdam/NY. Israel/DaCapo. 104 pl. ribbon ties. M. O7. $475.00

VON LISINGEN, F.W.B. *Pressure Gauge Murder.* 1930. Dutton. VG. P3. $25.00

VON MATT, Leonard. *Ancient Crete.* 1968. Praeger. 1st ed. 4to. ils. 238p. VG/dj. W1. $65.00

VON SAVIGNY, Frederick C. *Of the Vocation of Our Age for Legislation & Jurisprudence.* 1986. Birmingham. facsimile of 1831 London ed. modern leather. M11. $65.00

VON TRAPP, Maria. *Creation House.* 1972. Carol Stream, IL. 1st. 16 pl. 203p. as new/F. H1. $25.00

VON TRAPP, Maria. *Maria.* 1972. Carol Stream. Creation. 1st ed. sgn. F/NF. H11. $30.00

VON WOLFF, Christian. *Psychologia Rationalis...* 1734. Veronae. Typis Dionyssi Ramanzini Bibliopolae. 2nd. 397p. G1. $500.00

VONNEGUT, Kurt. *Bluebird.* 1987. Delacorte. 1st ed. F/F. H11. $30.00

VONNEGUT, Kurt. *Breakfast of Champions.* 1973. Delacorte. 1st. F/clip. B35. $32.00

VONNEGUT, Kurt. *Deadeye Dick.* 1982. Delacorte. 1st ed. F/NF. H11. $30.00

VONNEGUT, Kurt. *Galapagos.* 1985. Delacorte. 1st trade after Franklin Lib. sgn. NF/F. D10. $65.00

VONNEGUT, Kurt. *Galapagos.* 1985. Delacorte. 1st. F/NF. H11. $30.00

VONNEGUT, Kurt. *Galapagos.* 1985. Delacorte. 1st. sgn. VG/VG. A23. $50.00

VONNEGUT, Kurt. *God Bless You, Mr Rosewater.* 1965. London. Cape. 1st Eng. NF/dj. Q1. $200.00

VONNEGUT, Kurt. *Hocus Pocus.* 1990. Putnam. 1st. VG/dj. P3. $22.00

VONNEGUT, Kurt. *Jailbird.* 1979. Delacorte. 1st ed. NF/VG clip. B35. $25.00

VONNEGUT, Kurt. *Palm Sunday.* 1981. Delacorte. 1st. F/dj. P3. $30.00

VONNEGUT, Kurt. *Slapstick; or, Lonesome No More.* 1976. Delacorte. 1st ed. F/NF. H11. $30.00

VONNEGUT, Kurt. *Slaughterhouse-Five; or, Children's Crusade.* 1969. Delacorte. 2nd. NF/NF. B35. $40.00

VONNEGUT, Kurt. *Slaughterhouse Five; or, Children's Crusade.* 1969. Lawrence/Delacorte. 1st ed. sgn bookplate. NF/F. M22. $275.00

VONNEGUT, Kurt. *Sun Moon Star.* 1980. Harper. 1st. NF/NF. C8. $55.00

VONNEGUT, Kurt. *Wampeters, Foma & Granfalloons.* 1974. Delacorte. 1st. VG/dj. M2/P3. $30.00

VONNEGUT, Kurt. *Welcome to the Monkey House.* 1968. Delacorte. 1st. NF. M21. $50.00

VOOUS, K.H. *Atlas of European Birds.* 1960. London. Nelson. 284p. xl. B1. $22.00

VORHEES, Oscar. *History of Phi Beta Kappa.* 1945. NY. 372p. A13. $30.00

VORRES, I. *Last Grand Duchess.* 1965. NY. 1st ed. VG/VG. B5. $45.00

VORSE, M.H. *Time & the Town.* 1942. NY. 1st ed. VG/VG. B5. $35.00

VOTH, H.R. *Oraibi Powamu Ceremony.* 1901. Chicago. Field Columbian Mus. 8vo. 37 pl. 158p. limp morocco. VG. K7. $245.00

VOZNESENSKY, Andrei. *Nostalgia for the Present.* 1978. Doubleday. 1st ed. inscr. NF/NF. V1. $45.00

VRIENDS, Matthew M. *Parakeets of the World.* 1979. TFH. photos. 384p. F. S15. $10.00

VULLIAMY, C.E. *Cakes for Your Birthday.* 1959. British Book Centre. 1st. VG/dj. P3. $25.00

VYSE, Michael. *Overworld.* 1957. Macmillan. 1st. NF/dj. P3. $23.00

– W –

WAAGENAAR, Sam. *Woman of Israel.* 1961. Schocken Books. 1st. 112 pl. 47p. F/dj. H1. $12.00

WACE, Robert. *Notice Sur la Vie et les Escrits.* 1824. French text. marbled ep. VG. S13. $20.00

WACHOLDER, Ben Zion. *Eupolemus: Study of Judaeo-Greek Literature.* 1974. HUC. 332p. VG/VG. S3. $35.00

WACHTEL, Curt. *Idea of Psychosomatic Medicine.* 1951-27. NY. 239p. dj. A13. $45.00

WACK, Henry Wellington. *Story of the Congo Free State.* 1905. NY/London. Putnam. 1st. 8vo. ils/maps. 634p. teg. xl. W1. $35.00

WADDELL, Helen. *Peter Abelard.* 1947. NY. 1st ils ed. 277p. F/F. A17. $10.00

WADDELL, Helen. *Stories From the Holy Writ.* 1949. Macmillan. 1st ed. 244p. gray cloth. F/dj. B22. $4.50

WADE, Blanche Elizabeth. *Ant Ventures.* 1924. Rand McNally. 1st ed. 12mo. VG/tattered. M5. $110.00

WADE, Brent. *Company Man.* 1992. Algonquin. 1st. author's 1st book. F/F. H11. $30.00

WADE, David. *Pattern in Islamic Art.* 1976. Woodstock. Overlook. 1st ed. ils. 144p. VG/dj. W1. $45.00

WADE, Henry. *Litmore Snatch.* 1957. Macmillan. 1st. NF/dj. P3. $23.00

WADE, J.L. *What You Should Know About the Purple Martin.* 1963. Griggsville, IL. ils. 223p. NF. S15. $10.00

WADE, Jonathan. *Back to Life.* 1961. Pantheon. F/dj. P3. $13.00

WADE, Mary Hazelton. *Our Little Jewish Cousin.* 1904. Boston. Page. 1st. ils LJ Bridgman. 12mo. pict cloth. R5. $100.00

WADE, Wyn Craig. *Titanic: End of a Dream.* 1979. Rawson Wade. BC. ils. 366p. VG/G. P12. $5.00

WADE-EVANS, A.W. *Welsh Medieval Law, Being a Text of the Laws of Howel...* 1909. Oxford. Clarendon. gilt gr cloth. M11. $125.00

WADSWORTH, Beula. *Design Motifs of the Pueblo Indians.* 1957. Naylor. A19. $35.00

WADSWORTH, H.A. *Quarter-Centennial History of Lawrence, MA.* 1878. Lawrence. Hammon Reed. 180p. gilt/blk stp brn cloth. K1. $50.00

WADSWORTH, W. Austin. *Hunting Diaries of...* 1984. Genesee Valley Hunt. 1/950. F. O3. $45.00

WADSWORTH, Wallace. *Peter Rabbit.* 1960 (1953). Rand McNally. ils Anne Sellers Leaf. folio. F. M5. $20.00

WADSWORTH, William P. *Riding to the Hounds in America.* 1976. Berryville, VA. 8vo. 47p. VG. O3. $12.00

WAFER, Lionel. *New Voyage & Description of Isthmus of America.* 1970. Burt Franklin. rpt. 8vo. 212p. bl cloth. NF. P4. $45.00

WAGENKNECHT, Edward. *Fireside Book of Ghost Stories.* 1947. Bobbs Merrill. 1st. VG. M2. $20.00

WAGENKNECHT, Edward. *Six Novels of the Supernatural.* 1944. Viking. 1st. VG. P3. $35.00

WAGENKNECHT, Edward. *William Dean Howells: The Friendly Eye.* 1969. NY. 1st. 340p. dj. A17. $12.50

WAGER, Walter. *Blue Leader.* 1979. Arbor. VG/dj. P3. $15.00

WAGER, Walter. *Designated Hitter.* 1982. NY. Arbor. 1st. F/F. H11. $20.00

WAGER, Walter. *Swap.* 1972. Macmillan. 1st. VG/dj. P3. $25.00

WAGER, Walter. *Time of Reckoning.* 1977. Playboy. 1st. VG/dj. P3. $18.00

WAGER, Walter. *Viper Three.* 1971. Macmillan. 1st. F/F. H11. $25.00

WAGER, Walter. *58 Minutes.* 1987. Macmillan. 1st. VG/dj. P3. $25.00

WAGERIN, Walter Jr. *Book of Sorrows.* 1985. Harper Row. 1st. F/dj. P3. $16.00

WAGERIN, Walter Jr. *Book of the Dun Cow.* 1980. Allen Lane. F/dj. P3. $25.00

WAGERIN, William. *Book of the Dun Cow.* 1978. Harper Row. 1st ed. NF/VG. N4. $15.00

WAGGONER, Diana. *Hills of Faraway.* 1978. Atheneum. 1st. ils. VG/dj. K3. $10.00

WAGLEY, Charles. *Amazon Town: Study of Man in the Tropics.* 1953. Macmillan. 1st ed. 305p. dj. F3. $20.00

WAGLEY, Charles. *Social & Religious Life of a Guatemalan Village.* 1949. Am Anthro Assoc. 3 pl. 150p. wrp. F3. $25.00

WAGNER, Betty Jane. *Limericks.* 1973. Houghton Mifflin. 1st. ils Gorey. F/wrp. A11. $75.00

WAGNER, Frederick. *Robert Morris.* 1976. Dodd Mead. 1st. NF/NF. W2. $20.00

WAGNER, Henry R. *California Voyages 1539-1541.* 1925. San Francisco. John Howell. 8 full-p maps. F. O7. $250.00

WAGNER, Henry R. *Collecting, Especially Books.* 1968. Ward Ritchie. 1/400. ils. 25p. F. K3. $85.00

WAGNER, Henry R. *Ernest Hemingway: A Reference Guide.* 1977. 382p. VG. A4. $125.00

WAGNER, Henry R. *One Rare Book.* 1956. Los Angeles. Zamorano Club. 1/250. F/wrp. A4. $125.00

WAGNER, Henry R. *Plains & the Rockies: Bibliography of Original Narratives...* 1921. SF. John Howell. 2nd. 40 tipped-in photostats of title p. 193p. D11. $400.00

WAGNER, Henry R. *Sir Francis Drake's Voyage Around the World.* 1926. SF. John Howell. 1st. 543p. bl cloth. P4. $250.00

WAGNER, Henry R. *Spanish Southwest 1542-1794, an Annotated Bibliography.* nd. 2 vol in 1. 1/150. F. A4. $150.00

WAGNER, Jack R. *Gold Mines of California.* 1980. San Diego. 259p. F/dj. A17. $25.00

WAGNER, Jack R. *Gold Mines of Newmont: A 50-Year History.* 1973. NY. 1st. 344p. F/dj. A17. $12.50

WAGNER, Jon. *Sex Roles in Contemporary American Communes.* 1982. Bloomington, IN. IU. 1st. 242p. VG/dj. A25. $12.00

WAGNER, Karl. *Echoes of Valor II.* 1989. Tor. 1st. F/dj. M2. $25.00

WAGNER, Philip M. *Wine-Grower's Guide.* 1973. Knopf. 2nd. VG/dj. W2. $20.00

WAGNER, Richard. *Parsifal.* 1918. Vienna. Munch. ils Willy Pogany. F/pict wrp. B24. $575.00

WAGNER, Richard. *Ring of the Niblung.* 1939. NY. ils Arthur Rackham. VG. A17. $35.00

WAGONER, David. *Baby, Come on Inside.* 1968. FSG. 1st ed. sgn. F/VG+. V1. $25.00

WAGONER, David. *Hanging Garden.* 1980. Little Brn. ARC. sgn. RS. F/NF. V1. $25.00

WAGONER, David. *Rock.* 1958. Viking. 1st ed. F/NF. V1. $25.00

WAGONER, David. *Staying Alive.* 1966. IN. 1st ed. RS. F/F. V1. $30.00

WAGONER, David. *Travelling Light.* 1976. Graywolf. 1/150. sgn. F/F. V1. $40.00

WAGONER, Don M. *Conditioning to Win.* 1974. Grapevine. VG. O3. $25.00

WAGONER, Don M. *Feeding to Win.* 1973. Grapevine. VG. O3. $25.00

WAGONER, Don M. *Quine Genetics & Selection Procedures.* 1978. Tyler. VG. O3. $35.00

WAHL, Jan. *Christmas in the Forest.* 1967. Macmillan. 1st. lg 8vo. NF/VG+. C8. $40.00

WAHL, Jan. *Grandpa's Indian Summer.* 1976. Prentice Hall. 1st. ils Joanne Scribner. obl 8vo. F/F. C8. $20.00

WAHL, Jan. *Little Blind Goat.* 1981. Stemmer. 1st. ils Antonio Frasconi. 32p. VG+/NF. P2. $40.00

WAHL, Jan. *Pleasant Field Mouse.* 1964. Harper Row. 1st. ils Sendak. 66p. NF/dj. P2. $350.00

WAHLOO, Peter. *Assignment.* 1977. Knopf. 1st. VG/dj. P3. $25.00

WAHLOO, Peter. *Generals.* 1974. Pantheon. 1st Am. F/dj. M25. $15.00

WAHLOO, Peter. *Murder on the 31st Floor.* 1966. Michael Joseph. 1st Eng language. F/dj. M25. $25.00

WAHLOO, Peter. *Necessary Action.* 1968. Pantheon. 1st. VG/dj. P3. $20.00

WAHLROOS, Sven. *Mutiny & Romance in the South Seas.* 1989. Topsfield. Salem. 497p. VG/dj. P4. $40.00

WAHLSTEDT, Viola. *Travel Alone, Eva.* 1949. HRW. 1st. 158p. VG/dj. A25. $12.00

WAHLSTRUM, E. *Optical Crystallography.* 1969. John Wiley. 4th. VG. D8. $20.00

WAHRHAFT, Mordecai. *Blue Box the Bold.* ca 1940. Jerusalem. Rubin Mass. 8vo. 22p. F/ils wrp. B24. $250.00

WAIN, Louis. *Cat Alphabet & Picture-Book for Little Folk.* 1913. NY. Dodge. 8vo. brd/label. R5. $1,400.00

WAINER, Cord; see Dewey, Thomas B.

WAINWRIGHT, John. *All Through the Night.* 1985. St Martin. 1st Am. VG+/dj. N4. $15.00

WAINWRIGHT, John. *Bastard.* 1976. St Martin. 1st. NF/dj. P3. $22.00

WAINWRIGHT, John. *Brainwash.* 1979. Macmillan. 1st. NF/dj. P3. $18.00

WAINWRIGHT, John. *Man Who Wasn't There.* 1989. St Martin. 1st. VG/dj. P3. $18.00

WAINWRIGHT, John. *Who Goes Next?* 1976. St Martin. 1st. VG/dj. P3. $18.00

WAITE, Arthur Edward. *Belle & the Dragon: An Elfin Comedy.* 1894. London. ils. VG-. M17. $100.00

WAITE, Frederick C. *History of the New England Female Medical College 1848-74.* 1950. Boston. ils. 132p. red cloth. VG. B14. $55.00

WAITE, Terry. *Taken on Trust.* 1993. Harcourt Brace. 1st ed. 8vo. 16 pl. 370p. NF/dj. W1. $18.00

WAKEFIELD, Bob. *Jean Dehaven's Trail of the Jackasses.* 1968. Aberdeen, SD. A19. $20.00

WAKEFIELD, H.R. *Strayers From Sheol.* 1961. Arkham. 1st. F/VG. Q1. $50.00

WAKEFIELD, Ruth. *Ruth Wakefield's Toll House Tried & True Recipes.* 1945. NY. Barrows. G. A16. $10.00

WAKELEY, Cecil. *Great Teachers of Surgery in the Past.* 1969. Bristol. 147p. A13. $40.00

WAKEMAN, Edgar. *Log of an Ancient Mariner.* 1878. SF. Bancroft. 378p. emb cloth. P4. $150.00

WAKEMAN, Frederic. *Shore Leave.* 1944. NY. Farrar Rhinehart. 1st. author's 1st book. F/F. B4. $150.00

WALCOTT, Charles D. *Forest Reserves.* 1900. WA. Dept Interior. 712p. cloth. D11. $500.00

WALCOTT, Derek. *Arkansas Testament.* 1987. FSG. 1st. inscr/dtd 1993. F/F. R14. $75.00

WALCOTT, Derek. *Sea Grapes.* 1976. FSG. 1st Am. sgn/dtd 1994. F/F. R14. $100.00

WALDA, A. *Sequential Analysis.* 1947. John Wiley. 1st. 212p. F/dj. D8. $10.00

WALDEN, Amelia Elizabeth. *Girl Called Hank.* (1951). Morrow. BC. 8vo. 192p. G+/dj. T5. $12.00

WALDEN, Hillary. *Ice Cream.* 1985. S&S. G/dj. A16. $10.00

WALDEN, Howard T. *Native Inheritance.* 1966. NY. 1st ed. 199p. F/VG. B18. $17.50

WALDMAN, Carl. *Who Was Who in Native American History.* 1990. Facts on File. 410p. F/dj. A17. $25.00

WALDMAN, Frank. *Famous American Athletes of Today.* 1949. Page. 1st. photos. VG. P8. $25.00

WALDO, F. *Grenfell: Knight Errant of the North.* 1924. photos. VG. M17. $25.00

WALDO, Myra. *Seven Wonders of the Cooking World.* 1971. Dodd Mead. VG/dj. A16. $10.00

WALDORF, John Taylor. *Kid on the Comstock.* 1970. Palo Alto. Am West. 198p. gr cloth. VG+/dj. P4. $25.00

WALDRON, Charles. *Practical Hints for Better Navigation & Guidance...* 1826. London. Norie. ils. 104p. rebound modern cloth. T7. $250.00

WALDROP, Howard. *Night of the Cooters.* 1990. KS City, MO. Ursus. 1/374p. sgn. ils sgns. F/dj/case. M21. $45.00

WALDROP, Howard. *Them Bones.* 1989. Ziesing. 1st. 1/350. sgn/#d. F/dj. P3. $50.00

WALDROP, Keith. *Poems From Memory.* 1975. Providence. 1st ed. 1/500. wrp. A17. $15.00

WALDROP, Keith. *Windmill Near Calvary.* 1968. MI U. 1st ed. NF/NF. V1. $15.00

WALDROP, R. *Peculiar Motions.* 1990. Kelsey. 1st ed. inscr/sgn. F/wrp. V1. $20.00

WALDROP, R. *Reproduction of Profiles.* 1987. New Directions. 1st ed. inscr. F/wrp. V1. $15.00

WALDROP & WALDROP. *Since Volume.* 1975. Burning Deck. 1/500. sgn. NF. V1. $20.00

WALES, George C. *Etchings & Lithographs of American Ships.* 1927. Boston. Goodspeed. 1/500. 4to. 125p. F/VG. C6. $200.00

WALES, Hubert. *Brocklebank Riddle.* 1914. Century. 1st. VG. M2. $28.00

WALFORD, Frank. *Ghost & Albert.* 1945. London. VG/frayed. M2. $25.00

WALFORD, Lionel. *Marine Game Fishes of the Pacific Coast From Alaska...* 1937. CA U. 1st. 70 pl. 205p. bl cloth. VG. S15. $70.00

WALKER, Alice. *Color Purple.* 1982. NY. HBJ. 1st. F/NF clip. B4. $550.00

WALKER, Alice. *Finding the Greenstone.* 1991. HBJ. 1st. ils Catherine Deeter. F/F. B3. $50.00

WALKER, Alice. *Good Night Willie Lee, I'll See You in the Morning.* 1979. NY. Dial. 1st. lg 12mo. VG+. C8. $35.00

WALKER, Alice. *Her Blue Body Everything We Know.* 1991. Harcourt Brace. 1st. sgn. F/F. A23. $40.00

WALKER, Alice. *Her Blue Body Everything We Know.* 1991. San Diego. HBJ. 1st. F/F. R13. $30.00

WALKER, Alice. *In Search of Our Mothers' Gardens.* 1983. HBJ. 1st. NF/VG. A24. $45.00

WALKER, Alice. *Living by the Word.* 1988. HBJ. 1st. sgn. F/dj. A24. $60.00

WALKER, Alice. *Meridian.* 1976. HBJ. 1st ed. B stp on edges. VG/VG. H11. $140.00

WALKER, Alice. *Once.* 1968. HBW. 1st. author's 1st book. F/F. L3. $850.00

WALKER, Alice. *Possessing the Secret of Joy.* 1992. London. Cape. 1st. sgn. F/dj. Q1. $75.00

WALKER, Alice. *Temple of My Familiar.* 1989. HBJ. 1st. sgn. F/F. A23. $45.00

WALKER, Alice. *Third Life of Grange Copeland.* 1970. HBJ. 1st. author's 2nd book. F/F. L3. $400.00

WALKER, Alice. *You Can't Keep a Good Woman Down.* 1981. HBJ. 1st ed. F/F. B4. $275.00

WALKER, Anne. *Once Long Ago.* 1989. Paris. self pub. 12mo. sgn/dtd. AN/box. B24. $475.00

WALKER, Barbara M. *Little House Cookbook, Frontier Foods From LI Wilder...* 1979. ils. 240p. F/VG. A4. $35.00

WALKER, Danton. *Spooks Deluxe.* 1956. Watts. 1st. VG. M2. $25.00

WALKER, David. *Devil's Plunge.* 1968. Collins. 1st. NF/dj. P3. $22.00

WALKER, David. *Lord's Pink Ocean.* 1972. Collins. 1st. VG/dj. P3. $18.00

WALKER, David. *Lord's Pink Ocean.* 1972. Houghton Mifflin. 1st. F/dj. M2. $20.00

WALKER, David. *Moving Out.* 1976. VA U. 1st ed. F/dj. V1. $25.00

WALKER, David. *Oxford Companion to Law.* 1980. Clarendon. M11. $65.00

WALKER, David. *Winter of Madness.* 1964. Collins. 1st. VG/dj. P3. $30.00

WALKER, Dugald Stewart. *Six Who Were Left in a Shoe.* 1923. Volland. 1st. 8vo. mc pict brd. R5. $150.00

WALKER, Elizabeth. *In the Mist & Other Uncanny Encounters.* 1979. Arkham. 1st ed. 1/4053. F/F. T2. $12.00

WALKER, Eric A. *History of South Africa.* 1940. London/NY/Toronto. Longman Gr. 2nd. 13 maps. 7190p. xl. VG. W1. $20.00

WALKER, Franklin. *Seacost of Bohemia, Account of Early Camel.* 1973. Peregrine Smith. new/enlarged. 30 photos/5 cartoons. 127p. VG/dj. K7. $35.00

WALKER, Fred. *Destination Unknown.* 1935. Lippincott. 1st. 285p. dj. F3. $15.00

WALKER, Ira. *Man in the Driver's Seat.* 1964. Abelard Schuman. 1st. VG/dj. P3. $15.00

WALKER, Irma. *Inherit the Earth.* 1981. Atheneum. 1st. F/dj. M2. $17.00

WALKER, J. Bernard. *America Fallen!* 1915. Dodd Mead. 1st. VG. M2. $75.00

WALKER, Jeanie Mort. *Life of Capt Joseph Fry, the Cuban Martyr...* 1875. Hartford. JB Burr. 1st ed. 589p. cloth. VG-. M8. $85.00

WALKER, Jerry. *Mission Accomplished.* 1947. Cosmos. F/dj. M2. $22.00

WALKER, Joseph A. *River Niger.* 1973. Hill Wang. ARC. RS. NF/dj. M25. $60.00

WALKER, M. *Curlews Cry.* 1955. NY. 1st ed. VG/VG. B5. $25.00

WALKER, Margaret. *For My People.* 1942. New Haven. 1st. author's 1st book. VG/torn. A15. $150.00

WALKER, Marian C. *Dahlias for Every Garden.* 1954. Barrows. 8vo. 128p. VG/torn. A22. $15.00

WALKER, Martin. *Daily Sketches: A Cartoon History of 20th-C Britain.* 1978. Frederick Muller. 1st ed. ils. NF/VG. P12. $10.00

WALKER, Mary Willis. *Red Scream.* 1994. Doubleday. 1st ed. sgn. F/F. T2. $60.00

WALKER, Mary Willis. *Under the Beetle's Cellar.* 1995. Doubleday. 1st. sgn. F/F. A23. $45.00

WALKER, Mildred. *Southwest Corner.* 1951. Harcourt Brace. probable rpt. inscr to author Samuel Hopkins. F/VG. B4. $75.00

WALKER, Nancy A. *Very Serious Thing: Women's Humor & American Culture.* 1988. MN U. 1st. as new. V4. $12.50

WALKER, Nigel. *Crime & Insanity in England... Historical Perspective.* 1968. Edinburgh. M11. $65.00

WALKER, Robert Harris. *Cincinnati & the Big Red Machine.* 1988. IN U. 1st ed. sgn. VG/wrp. P8. $12.50

WALKER, Sam. *Up the Slot (307th Bomb Group).* 1984. OK City. photos/map/index. 292p. F. S16. $60.00

WALKER, Walter. *Immediate Prospect of Being Hanged.* 1989. Viking. 1st. VG/dj. P3. $20.00

WALKER, Walter. *Rules of the Knife Fight.* 1986. Harper Row. 1st. F/dj. P3. $20.00

WALKER, William J. *Essay on the Treatment of Compound & Complicated Fractures.* 1845. Boston. 46p. wrp. B14. $175.00

WALKOWITZ, Judith. *Prostitution & Victorian Society: Women, Class & the State.* 1980. Cambridge. 1st ed. 347p. A13. $40.00

WALL, Bernhardt. *Following Abraham Lincoln, 1809-1865.* 1943. NY. ils. 415p. VG/dj. B18. $35.00

WALL, Dorothy. *Blinky Bill: The Quaint Little Australian.* 1933. Angus Robertson. 1st. sm 4to. VG. M5. $75.00

WALL, Mervyn. *Return of Fursey.* 1948. London. 1st. VG. M2. $20.00

WALL, Roy. *Contemplative Angler.* 1948. NY. 215p. NF. A17. $12.50

WALLACE, Alexander. *Heather in Lore, Lyric & Lay.* 1903. NY. DeLaMare. 245p. VG. A10. $50.00

WALLACE, Alexander. *Heather in Lore, Lyric & Lay.* 1903. NY. DeLaMare. 245p. cloth. VG. A10. $75.00

WALLACE, Alfred R. *Wonderful Century.* 1898. Toronto. Morang. ils/fld chart. 400p. cloth. VG. M12. $60.00

WALLACE, Andrew. *Grand Canyon.* 1972. Time Life. 1st. ils/index. 184p. NF/VG. B19. $15.00

WALLACE, Anthony F.C. *Death & Rebirth of the Seneca.* 1970. Knopf. 1st. tall 8vo. 384p. F/F. H1/M4. $28.00

WALLACE, Anthony F.C. *King of the Delawares: Teedyudcung 1700-1763.* 1949. PA U. 1st. 8vo. 305p. F/F. H1. $40.00

WALLACE, Archer. *Adventures in the Air.* 1932. Ryerson. sgn. VG. P3. $20.00

WALLACE, Brenton. *Patton & His Third Army.* 1951. Harrisburg. maps/photos/chronology. 232p. VG/VG. S16. $45.00

WALLACE, Cornelia. *O'Nelia.* 1976. Holman. 1st. inscr. full-p photos. 240p. VG/VG. B11. $25.00

WALLACE, David Foster. *Broom of the System.* 1987. Viking. 1st ed. author's 1st book. F/NF. B2. $200.00

WALLACE, David Foster. *Girl With Curious Hair.* 1989. Norton. 1st ed. sgn. F/F. B2. $75.00

WALLACE, David Rains. *Turquoise Dragon.* 1985. Sierra Club. 1st. F/F. M19. $25.00

WALLACE, David Rains. *Wilder Shores.* 1984. SF. Sierra Club. 1/300 for sale. photos M Baer. 162p. loth. F/case. M12. $175.00

WALLACE, Dillon. *Lure of the Labrador Wild.* 1905. NY. Revell. photos/fld map. 339p. VG. T7. $60.00

WALLACE, Edgar. *Again the Three Just Men.* nd. Hodder Stoughton. VG/dj. P3. $25.00

WALLACE, Edgar. *Avenger.* nd. Leisure Lib. VG/dj. P3. $18.00

WALLACE, Edgar. *Day of Uniting.* 1930. Mystery League. 1st. VG/fair. P3. $25.00

WALLACE, Edgar. *Edgar Wallace Reader of Mystery.* 1943. Tower. VG. P3. $15.00

WALLACE, Edgar. *Feathered Serpent.* 1928. Crime Club. 1st. G. P3. $20.00

WALLACE, Edgar. *Flying Squad.* 1929. Crime Club. 1st. VG. P3. $18.00

WALLACE, Edgar. *Four Just Men.* 1905. Tallis. xl. VG. P3. $75.00

WALLACE, Edgar. *Fourth Plague.* 1928. Ward Lock. VG. P3. $20.00

WALLACE, Edgar. *Fourth Plague.* 1930. Doubleday Crime Club. 1st Am. NF/dj. M15. $100.00

WALLACE, Edgar. *Frightened Lady.* 1933. Musson. 1t. VG. P3. $20.00

WALLACE, Edgar. *Governor of Chi-Foo.* 1933. World Syndicate. 1st. VG. P3. $60.00

WALLACE, Edgar. *Green Archer.* 1924. Sm Maynard. 1st. NF/F later dj. M19. $35.00

WALLACE, Edgar. *Green Rust.* 1919. Ward Lock. 1st Eng. VG/VG. M19. $35.00

WALLACE, Edgar. *Gunman's Bluff.* 1929. Crime Club. 1st. VG. P3. $30.00

WALLACE, Edgar. *Mr Commissioner Sanders.* 1930. Garden City. 1st. VG/VG. B5. $35.00

WALLACE, Edgar. *White Face.* 1932. Musson. 1st. VG. P3. $20.00

WALLACE, F.L. *Address: Centauri.* 1955. Gnome. 1st. NF/dj. P3. $30.00

WALLACE, George C. *Stand Up for America.* 1976. Doubleday. 1st ed. photos. 183p. F/VG. B10. $8.00

WALLACE, George Selden. *Charters of Blenheim: A Genealogy...* 1955. self pub. 1/300. 139p. VG. B10. $50.00

WALLACE, Ian. *Deathstar Voyage.* 1972. Dobson. 1st. F/dj. P3. $13.00

WALLACE, Ian. *Pan Sagittarius.* 1973. Putnam. NF/dj. P3. $15.00

WALLACE, Ian. *Purloined Prince.* 1971. McCall. 1st. NF/dj. P3. $25.00

WALLACE, Irving. *Mexico Today.* 1936. Boston. Meador. 1st. ils. 364p. map ep. F3. $20.00

WALLACE, Irving. *Pigeon Project.* 1979. S&S. 1st. F/dj. P3. $15.00

WALLACE, Irving. *R Document.* 1976. S&S. 1st. F/dj. P3. $18.00

WALLACE, Irving. *Twenty-Seventh Wife.* 1971. S&S. 1st. 443p. VG/dj. M20. $20.00

WALLACE, Ivy L. *Pookie at the Seaside.* 1940s?. Collins. ils. VG. B17. $20.00

WALLACE, Kathleen. *Without a Stair.* 1933. Doubleday Doran. 1st. F/VG+. B4. $85.00

WALLACE, Lew. *Ben-Hur, a Tale of the Christ.* 1880. NY. Harper. 1st/1st prt. lt bl pict cloth (1st bdg). VG. M24. $250.00

WALLACE, Lew. *Fair God; or, Last of the 'Tzins. A Tale of Conquest Mexico.* 1873 (1873). Boston. Osgood. 1st thus. G+. B22. $15.00

WALLACE, Lew. *Fair God; or, Last of the 'Tzins. A Tale of Conquest Mexico.* 1894 (1873). Houghton Mifflin. 586p. gilt cloth. VG. F3. $20.00

WALLACE, Lew. *Prince of India.* 1893. Harper. 1st/1st issue (no dedication). 2 vol. VG. H1. $45.00

WALLACE, Marcia. *Barefoot in the Kitchen.* 1971. St Martin. G/dj. A16. $10.00

WALLACE, Michele. *Black Macho & the Myth of the Superwoman.* 1979. Dial. 2nd. 182p. F/F. B4. $35.00

WALLACE, P.B. *Colonial Ironwork in Old Philadelphia.* 1930. NY. Architectural Pub. 1st ed. VG/VG. B5. $70.00

WALLACE, Paul A.W. *Muhlengers of Pennsylvania.* 1950. PA U. 1st. tall 8vo. 358p. F/VG. H1. $25.00

WALLACE, Paul A.W. *Thirty Thousand Miles With John Heckewelder.* 1958. Pittsburgh. 1st. 2 fld maps. 474p. F/VG. H1. $35.00

WALLACE, Philip B. *Colonial Ironwork in Old Philadelphia.* ca 1965. NY. Bonanza. 147p. dj. A10. $35.00

WALLACE, Philip B. *Colonial Ironwork in Old Philadelphia...* 1970. Dover. rpt. VG. M17. $25.00

WALLACE, Robert. *Seven Men Are Murdered.* 1930. Fiction League. VG. P3. $25.00

WALLACE, Robert. *Ungainly Things.* 1968. Dutton. 1st ed. NF/NF. V1. $20.00

WALLACE, Robert. *World of Leonardo 1452-1519.* 1967. Time Life. NF/case. H4. $15.00

WALLACE, W.M. *Traitorous Hero: Life & Fortunes of Benedict Arnold.* 1954. VG/VG. M17. $25.00

WALLACE, Willard M. *East to Gagaduce.* 1963. Chicago. Regnery. 1st. inscr/dtd 1963. NF/VG+. T11. $35.00

WALLACE, Willard M. *Raiders.* 1970. Little Brn. 1st. NF/VG+ clip. T11. $35.00

WALLACE, William N. *Frank Figgord: The Golden Year, 1956.* 1956. Prentice Hall. 1st. photos. VG+/dj. P8. $25.00

WALLACE, Wolf. *Hive.* 1966. NY. Softcover Lib. 1st. 156p. VG. A25. $18.00

WALLACE-DUNLOP. *Fairies, Elves & Flower-Babies.* 1899. Duckworth. 1st. obl 4to. gray cloth. R5. $300.00

WALLACH, Anne Tolstoi. *Women's Work.* 1981. NAL. 1st Canadian. F/VG. T12. $15.00

WALLACH, Carla. *Reluctant Weekend Gardener.* 1973. Macmillan. 1st. inscr. 214p. VG/dj. A25. $12.00

WALLENIUS, K.M. *Men's Sea.* 1955. Staples. 1st. trans from Finnish. 262p. dj. A17. $20.00

WALLER, Effie. *Rhumes From the Cumberland.* 1909. NY. Broadway. 1st. VG. B4. $850.00

WALLER, George. *Saratoga: Sage of an Impious Era.* 1966. Prentice Hall. 1st. 392p. cloth. VG/dj. M20. $30.00

WALLER, Leslie. *Change in the Wind.* 1969. Bernard Geis. 1st. VG/dj. P3. $20.00

WALLER, Robert James. *Bridges of Madison County.* (1992). later prt. sgn. NF/dj. A15. $30.00

WALLER, Robert James. *Bridges of Madison County.* 1992. Warner. 1st. F/F. D10. $150.00

WALLER, Robert James. *Bridges of Madison County: The Film.* 1995. Warner. 1st thus. F/dj. Q1. $30.00

WALLER, Robert James. *Old Songs in a New Cafe.* 1994. Warner. 1st. F/F. A23. $45.00

WALLER, Robert James. *Slow Waltz in Cedar Bend.* 1993. Warner. 1st. sgn. F/F. A23. $45.00

WALLIN, Homer N. *Pearl Harbor: Why, How, Fleet Salvage & Final Appraisal.* 1968. WA. 377p. G+. B18. $25.00

WALLING, R.A.J. *Corpse With the Eerie Eye.* 1944. Books Inc. VG/G. P3. $12.00

WALLING, R.A.J. *Fatal 5 Minutes.* 1943. Tower. 2nd. VG/dj. P3. $15.00

WALLING, William. *World I Left Behind Me.* 1979. St Martin. 1st. F/dj. M2. $10.00

WALLIS, Dave. *Only Lovers Left Alive.* 1964. Dutton. 1st. VG/dj. P3. $20.00

WALLIS, George A. *Cattle Kings of the Staked Plains.* 1964. Denver Co. dj. A19. $25.00

WALLIS, Helen. *Discovery of the World: Maps of the Earth & the Cosmos...* 1985. Montreal. 66 maps. F. O7. $65.00

WALLIS, Helen. *Historians' Guide to Early British Maps...* 1994. London. Royal Hist Soc. 465p. VG. A4. $125.00

WALLIS, Helen. *Voyage of Sir Francis Drake Mapped in Silver & Gold.* 1979. Friends of Bancroft Lib. 29p. gray wrp. P4. $40.00

WALLIS, M. *Oil Man: Story of Frank Phillips...* 1988. Doubleday. 480p. F/torn. D8. $30.00

WALLMANN, Jeffrey M. *Judas Cross.* 1974. Random. 1st. F/dj. P3. $16.00

WALLS, Ian. *Tomato Growing Today.* 1977. Newton Abbot. 239p. VG/dj. A10. $24.00

WALMSLEY, Lee. *Light Sister, Dark Sister.* 1994. Random. 1st ed. author's 1st book. F/F. H11. $25.00

WALPOLE, Hugh. *All Soul's Night.* 1933. London. Macmillan. 1st. F/NF. M2. $150.00

WALPOLE, Hugh. *Bright Pavilions.* 1940. London. 1st. VG. T9. $10.00

WALPOLE, Hugh. *Captain Nicholas.* 1934. London. 1/275. sgn. VG. T9. $35.00

WALPOLE, Hugh. *Jeremy.* (1919). Grosset Dunlap. rpt. VG/dj. T5. $15.00

WALPOLE, Hugh. *Portrait of a Man With Red Hair.* 1925. Doran. 1st. VG. M2. $25.00

WALSH, Chad. *From Utopia to Nightmare.* 1962. London. 1st. F/dj. M2. $25.00

WALSH, Chad. *Literary Legacy of CS Lewis.* 1979. Harcourt. 1st. F/dj. M2. $25.00

WALSH, James J. *What Civilization Owes to Italy.* 1923. Boston. 8vo. 432p. red cloth. VG. B14. $35.00

WALSH, James Morgan. *Spies Are Abroad.* 1936. Collins. 6th. VG/dj. P3. $20.00

WALSH, James Morgan. *Vandals of the Void.* 1976 (1931). Hyperion. rpt. F. M2. $30.00

WALSH, Jill Paton. *Dawnstone.* 1977 (1973). London. Hamish Hamilton. rpt. ils. VG. T5. $20.00

WALSH, John Evangelist. *Hidden Life of Emily Dickinson.* 1971. S&S. 1st. 286p. VG/dj. A25. $18.00

WALSH, John Evangelist. *Poe the Detective: Curious Circumstances Behind Mystery...* 1968. Rutgers. 1st. VG+/VG. N4. $30.00

WALSH, M.M.B. *Four-Colored Hoop.* 1976. Putnam. 1st. F/dj. P3. $13.00

WALSH, Thomas. *Action of the Tiger.* 1967. S&S. 1st. xl. VG/dj. P3. $5.00

WALSTROM, E.E. *Ingenious Minerals & Rocks.* March 1947. John Wiley. 4th prt. VG. D8. $25.00

WALTARI, Mika. *Egyptian.* 1949. Putnam. 1st Am. F/NF. B4. $125.00

WALTER, Elizabeth. *Dead Woman.* 1975. St Martin. 1st. F/dj. M2. $25.00

WALTER, Gerard. *Paris Under the Occupation.* 1960. Orion. 1st. 208p. VG/dj. M20. $12.00

WALTER, L. Edna. *Mother Goose's Nursery Tales.* 1923. London. Blk. 1st. ils Folkard/Hartley. pict cloth. R5. $285.00

WALTER, Leibrecht. *Religion & Culture: Essays in Honor of Paul Tillich.* 1959. Harper. 399p. VG. B29. $13.00

WALTER, Richard. *Anson's Voyage Round the World.* 1928. London. Hopkinson. 1/1500. ils/4 charts. teg. T7. $120.00

WALTERS, Frank. *Colorado.* 1946. Rinehart. 1st ed. 8vo. 400p. VG/partially separated. H4. $25.00

WALTERS, L. *Year's at the Spring.* 1920. Brentano. 1st Am ed. ils Henry Clarke. VG/G. P2. $300.00

WALTERS, L.D'O. *Year's at the Spring: An Anthology of Recent Poetry.* 1920. Brentano. Prt Great Britain. 1st Am. 12 mc pl/other ils. 128p. VG. D4. $120.00

WALTERS, Minette. *Scold's Bridle.* 1994. London. Macmillan. 1st. sgn. F/F. D10. $85.00

WALTERS, Minette. *Scold's Bridle.* 1994. St Martin. 1st. F/dj. P3. $22.00

WALTERS, Minette. *Sculptress.* 1993. St Martin. 1st Am. sgn. author's 2nd novel. NF/dj. A24. $50.00

WALTERS, Rachel. *Mountain Bouquet. Wildflowers of Southern Highlands.* 1971. Cullowhee, NC. Greenstone. 71x67mm. ils Benoit. unbound as issued. B24. $385.00

WALTHER, Edvard. *Geographische Charakterbilder.* 1891. Esslingen. JF Schreiber. 4to. 48p. 24 double-p pl. NF. B24. $650.00

WALTON, Alan Hull. *Open Grave.* 1971. Taplinger. VG. P3. $20.00

WALTON, Evangeline. *Cross & the Sword.* 1956. Ryerson. VG/G. P3. $25.00

WALTON, Frank L. *Tomahawks to Textiles.* 1953. Appleton Century Crofts. 1st. 177p. VG/ragged. M20. $25.00

WALTON, Isaak. *Compleat Angler.* nd. Phil. McKay. 1st Am trade. ils Rackham/12 mc pl. 223p. VG+. M20. $160.00

WALTON, John. *Brain's Diseases of the Nervous System.* 1985. Oxford. 9th revised/1st prt. ils. prt bl cloth. G1. $50.00

WAMBAUGH, Joseph. *Black Marble.* 1978. Delacorte. 1st. F/F. A20. $35.00

WAMBAUGH, Joseph. *Black Marble.* 1978. Delacorte. 1st. VG/dj. P3. $20.00

WAMBAUGH, Joseph. *Blooding.* 1989. Morrow. 1st. F/F. A20/W2. $20.00

WAMBAUGH, Joseph. *Echoes in the Darkness.* 1987. Morrow. 1st. F/F. N4. $25.00

WAMBAUGH, Joseph. *Finnegan's Week.* 1993. Morrow. 1st ed. F/NF. N4. $20.00

WAMBAUGH, Joseph. *Fugitive Nights.* 1992. Morrow. 1st. F/F. W2. $30.00

WAMBAUGH, Joseph. *Golden Orange.* 1990. Perigord/Morrow. 1st. VG/dj. P3. $20.00

WAMBAUGH, Joseph. *New Centurions.* 1970. Atlantic/Little Brn. 1st. author's 1st book. F/NF. N4. $40.00

WAMBAUGH, Joseph. *Onion Field.* 1973. Delacorte. 1st. sgn. F/VG+ clip. A24. $60.00

WAMBAUGH, Joseph. *Secrets of Harry Bright.* 1985. Morrow. 1st. VG+/NF. A20. $20.00

WANDREI, Donald. *Donald Wandrei: Collected Poems.* 1988. W Warwick. Necronomicon. 1st ed. ils Howard Wandrei. F/pict wrp. T2. $20.00

WANDREI, Donald. *Web of Easter Island.* 1948. Arkham. 1st. 1/3068. F/dj. P3. $45.00

WANDREI, Howard. *Time Burial: Collected Fantasy Tales of...* 1995. Minneapolis. Fedogan Bremer. 1st ed. ils. F/F. T2. $30.00

WANEFSKY, David. *Prophets Speak to Us Anew.* 1952. Philosophical Lib. 232p. xl. G. B29. $7.00

WANGERIN, Walter. *Thistle.* 1983. Harper Row. 1st. sgn. ils Marcia Sewall. VG+/dj. M20. $25.00

WAPLES. D. *Organic Geochemisty for Exploration Geologists.* 1981. Burgess Pub. 151p. xl. F. D8. $35.00

WARBASSE, James. *Medical Sociology: A Series of Observations...* 1909. NY. 1st ed. 355p. A13. $100.00

WARBURG, Fredric. *All Authors Are Equal.* 1973. London. 1st ed. 310p. dj. A17. $10.00

WARD, A. *Grocer's Handbook & Directory for 1883.* 1882. ils. VG. E6. $35.00

WARD, A.C. *Bernard Shaw.* 1951. Longman Gr. ne. VG/dj. V4. $20.00

WARD, Adolphus William. *Dickens.* 1882. London. Macmillan. 1st. blk stp red cloth. M24. $100.00

WARD, Andrew. *Blood Seed.* 1985. Viking. 1st. sgn. F/F. B11. $35.00

WARD, Anne G. *Quest for Theseus.* 1970. Praeger. 1st ed. ils. 281p. VG. W1. $45.00

WARD, Arch. *Green Bay Packers: Records 1919-1945.* 1946. Putnam. 1st ed. photos. 240p. VG/VG. B5. $30.00

WARD, Barbara. *Urban Planet?* 1971. Phil. Girard Bank. 1st. ils Howard Watson. 53p. VG+/case. A25. $10.00

WARD, C.L. *Delaware Continentals 1776-1783.* 1941. Delaware. battle maps. 620p. F. M4. $45.00

WARD, Fay E. *Cowboy at Work.* 1958. Hastings. A19. $35.00

WARD, Fay E. *Cowboy at Work.* 1987. Norman/London. A19. $20.00

WARD, Geoffrey C. *Tiger-Wallahs.* 1993. NY. ils. 175p. F/NF. S15. $27.50

WARD, Geoffrey and Burns, Ken. *Baseball: An Illustrated History.* 1994. NY. Knopf. 1st. 486p. color pict. 4to. F/F. $85.00

WARD, James M. *Deites & Demigods.* 1980. Tsr Advanced D&D. VG. P3. $15.00

WARD, Jonas (some); see Block, Lawrence.

WARD, Josiah. *Come With Me to Babylon.* 1902. Stokes. 1st. VG. M2. $27.00

WARD, Lynd. *God's Man.* 1933. NY. Peter Smith. 6th. VG/fair. B5. $75.00

WARD, Lynd. *Silver Pony.* 1973. Houghton Mifflin. 1st. ils. 176p. NF/VG. P2. $85.00

WARD, Maisie. *Robert Browning & His World: Private Face 1821-1861, Vol 1.* 1967. HRW. 1st. tall 8vo. 335p. as new/dj. H1. $17.50

WARD, Margaret. *Testimony of Mrs George R Ward Before US Committee...1883.* 1965. Birmingham, AL. 1st. cloth. NF. M8. $250.00

WARD, R. Gerald. *American Activities in the Central Pacific 1790-1870...* 1966. Ridgewood, NJ. Gregg. 8 vol. fld maps. whit cloth. NF. P4. $295.00

WARDE, Beatrice. *Stanley Morison, Man of Letters.* nd. Wakefield. Fleece. 1/240. 66x49mm. yel striped cloth/prt label. F. B24. $85.00

WARDEN, Florence. *Mystery of the Thames.* 1913. Ward Lock. G. P3. $25.00

WARDLAW, C.W. *Morphogenesis in Plants: A Contemporary Study.* 1968. London. ils. 451p. VG/dj. B26. $27.50

WARE, Evelyn Woodford. *Islanders. A Romance of Martha's Vineyard.* 1892. Boston. Alfred Mudge. 1st. 12mo. 153p. prt wrp. M1. $125.00

WARE, Wallace. *Charka Memorial.* 1954. Crime Club. VG/dj. P3. $15.00

WARGA, Wayne. *Fatal Impressions.* 1989. Arbor/Morrow. 1st ed. F/F. T2. $20.00

WARGA, Wayne. *Hardcover.* 1985. Arbor. 1st. sgn. 8vo. F/dj. T10. $50.00

WARHOL, Andy. *A.* 1968. Grove. 1st. NF/G. M19. $85.00

WARHOL, Andy. *Philosophy of Andy Warhol: From A to B & Back Again.* 1975. HBJ. later prt. inscr w/drawing. F/F. M25. $300.00

WARHOL, Andy. *Philosophy of Andy Warhol: From A to B & Back Again.* 1975. HBJ. 1st. inscr. NF/F. T12. $100.00

WARING, G. *Draining for Profit & Health.* 1887 (1886). VG. E6. $40.00

WARING, Holburt. *Surgical Management of Malignant Disease.* 1928. London. 1st. 667p. A13. $75.00

WARING, Robert Lewis. *As We See It.* 1918. WA, DC. Sudwarth. 1st. fair. B4. $275.00

WARINGTON, R. *Chemistry of the Farm.* 1881. London. Bradbury. 128p. xl. VG. A10. $25.00

WARK, Robert R. *Drawings From the Turner Shakespeare.* 1973. San Marino. sgn. 89p. D2. $25.00

WARLOCK, Peter. *English Ayre.* 1926. London. 1st. VG/dj. T9. $45.00

WARMAN, Eric. *Preview Film Album 1963.* 1962. Golden Pleasure. VG. P3. $30.00

WARMINGTON, G.R. *King of Dreams.* 1926. Doran. 1st. F/dj. M2. $75.00

WARNER, C. *My Summer in a Garden.* 1878 (1870). VG. E6. $25.00

WARNER, Charles. *Roundabout Journey.* 1891. Houghton Mifflin. 5th. 8vo. cloth. VG. W1. $20.00

WARNER, Charles Dudley. *Being a Boy.* 1878 (1877). Houghton Osgood. 244p. cloth. VG. M20. $25.00

WARNER, Deborah Jean. *Alvan Clark & Sons.* 1968. Smithsonian. 1st. 8vo. 120p. VG. K5. $100.00

WARNER, E.J. *Generals in Blue: Lives of Union Commanders.* 1989. LSU. lg 8vo. 680p. F/dj. T3. $25.00

WARNER, E.J. *Generals in Gray: Lives of Confederate Commanders.* 1991. LSU. lg 8vo. ils. 420p. F/dj. T3. $25.00

WARNER, Ezra J. *General's in Blue.* 1993. 680p. O8. $27.50

WARNER, Francis. *Physical Expression: Its Modes & Principles.* 1886. NY. Appleton. 1st Am. 12mo. red cloth. G1. $75.00

WARNER, Frank A. *Bobby Blake in Frozen North; or, Old Eskimo's Last Message.* 1923. NY. Barse. 250p. P4. $35.00

WARNER, Ken. *Gun Digest.* 1984. DBI Books. sc. P12. $5.00

WARNER, Matt. *Last of the Bandit Riders.* 1940. Caxton. 1st. photos. 337p. VG. J2. $475.00

WARNER, Oliver. *Crown Jewels.* 1951. King Penguin. 1st. VG/dj. P3. $20.00

WARNER, Oliver. *Nelson.* 1975. Chicago. Follett. 20 mc pl/100 halftones. 231p. dj. T7. $25.00

WARNER, Oliver. *Victory: Life of Lord Nelson.* 1958. ils. VG/VG. M17. $20.00

WARNER, Sylvia Townsend. *Kingdoms of Elfin.* 1977. Viking. 1st. VG/dj. M2. $20.00

WARNER, Sylvia Townsend. *Lolly Willowes.* 1926. Viking. VG. M2. $10.00

WARNER, Sylvia Townsend. *Mr Fortune's Maggot.* 1927. Viking. 1st. VG. M2. $20.00

WARNER. *From the Beast to the Blonde: On Fairy Tales...* 1994. London. Chatto Windus. 458p. NF/NF. A4. $65.00

WARREN, B.S. *Health Insurance: Its Relation to the Public Health.* 1916. WA. 1st ed. 76p. wrp. A13. $75.00

WARREN, J. Mason. *Cases of Occlusion of the Vagina...* 1853. Boston. offprint. 28p. F/prt wrp. B14. $150.00

WARREN, J. Mason. *Lithotrity & Lithotomy, With Use of Ether...* 1849. Boston. 15p. bl prt wrp. NF. B14. $475.00

WARREN, James. *Disappearing Corpse.* 1958. Washburn. 1st. VG/dj. P3. $20.00

WARREN, Patricia Nell. *Beauty Queen.* 1978. Morrow. 1st. F/dj. M25. $35.00

WARREN, Patricia Nell. *Fancy Dancer.* 1976. Morrow. 1st. F/dj. M25. $45.00

WARREN, Robert Penn. *All the King's Men.* 1953. Random. 2nd. revised intro. 464p. NF. W2. $50.00

WARREN, Robert Penn. *Band of Angels.* 1955. Random. 1st ed. VG/VG. V1. $20.00

WARREN, Robert Penn. *Cave.* 1959. Putnam. 1st ed. F/NF. H11. $40.00

WARREN, Robert Penn. *Chief Joseph of the Nez Perce.* 1983. Random. 1st ed. F/VG+. V1. $25.00

WARREN, Robert Penn. *Homage to Theodore Dreiser.* 1971. Random. 1st. 1/5000. inscr/dtd 1986. F/NF. R14. $90.00

WARREN, Robert Penn. *Legacy of the Civil War Meditations on the Centennial.* 1961. NY. Random. 1st. 190p. cloth. NF/NF. M8. $85.00

WARREN, Robert Penn. *New & Selected Poems 1923-1985.* 1985. Franklin Center. 1st. sgn. full leather. F. Q1. $60.00

WARREN, Robert Penn. *Or Else. Poem/Poems 1968-1974.* 1974. Random. 1st. sgn/dtd 1981. F/clip. D10. $110.00

WARREN, Robert Penn. *Place to Come to.* 1977. Random. 1st ed. F/F. H11. $40.00

WARREN, Robert Penn. *Rumor Verified.* 1981. Random. 1st ed. F/NF. V1. $25.00

WARREN, Robert Penn. *Segregation: The Inner Conflict in the South.* 1957. Eyre Spottiswoode. 1st Eng. F/dj. Q1. $75.00

WARREN, Robert Penn. *Selected Poems, New & Old 1923-1966.* 1966. Random. 1st. NF/dj. B35. $28.00

WARREN, Rosanna. *Stained Glass.* 1993. Norton. 1st ed. F/F. V1. $10.00

WARREN, W.L. *Henry II. Third Printing.* 1991. Berkeley. 693p. prt wrp. M11. $17.50

WARWICK, Sidney. *Silver Basilisk.* nd. Hodder Stoughton. VG/fair. P3. $10.00

WASHBURN, Cephas. *Reminiscences of the Indians With a Biography...* 1955. Van Buren. 1/990. ils. 192p. F. M4. $40.00

WASHBURN, Cephas. *Reminiscences of the Indians...* (1869). Richmond. Presbyterian Comm of Pub. 1st. 236p. cloth. D11. $250.00

WASHBURN, Mark. *Mars at Last!* 1977. Putnam. 8vo. 291p. VG/dj. K5. $15.00

WASHINGTON, Booker T. *Character Building.* 1902. Toronto. Wm Briggs. 1st Canadian ed. xl. VG. B2. $50.00

WASHINGTON, Booker T. *Future of the American Negro.* 1899. Boston. Sm Maynard. 1st. inscr. 244p. F. B4. $1,500.00

WASHINGTON, Booker T. *Tuskegee: Its People...* 1906. Appleton. 3rd. ils. 354p. G+. B18. $45.00

WASHINGTON, Booker T. *Up From Slavery.* 1901. Doubleday Page. 1st. G/VG. B5. $55.00

WASHINGTON, George. *Official Letters to Honorable American Congress...* 1795. London. 2 vol. 1st ed. VG. M8. $350.00

WASHINGTON, George. *Washington's Farewell Address to the People...* 1922. San Francisco. 1/50 (of 175). sgn Grabhorn/others. F. B24. $375.00

WASHINGTON NATIONAL GALLERY. *Mary Cassatt 1844-1926.* 1970. WA. ils/pl. 119p. stiff wrp. D2. $40.00

WASON, Betty. *Encyclopedia of Cheese & Cheese Cookery.* 1966. NY. Galahad. G/dj. A16. $10.00

WASTELL, W.L.F. *Barnet Book of Photography.* 1922. Barnet Herts. new ed. 270p. pict cloth. A17. $20.00

WATERFIELD, Margaret. *Garden Colour.* 1907. London. Dent. 4th. 196p. cloth. VG. A10. $35.00

WATERLOO, Stanley. *Story of AB.* 1914. Doubleday. G+. M2. $20.00

WATERMAN, Charles F. *Fisherman's World.* 1971. NY. 1st. 250p. F/dj. A17. $18.50

WATERS, Alice. *Fanny at Chez Panisse, a Child's Restaurant Adventure...* 1992. Harper. 1st. ils Ann Arnold. F/NF. C8. $25.00

WATERS, D.W. *Elizabethan Navy & Armada of Spain.* 1975. London. Nat Maritime Mus. Maritime Monograph/Reports 17. 4to. NF/wrp. O7. $35.00

WATERS, Ethel. *To Me It's Wonderful.* 1972. NY. Harper. 1st. sgn. NF/VG. B4. $45.00

WATERS, Frank. *Colorado.* 1946. 1st. Rivers of Am series. NF/dj. A15. $75.00

WATERS, Frank. *Earp Brothers of Tombstone, Story of Mrs Virgil Earp.* 1931. Neville Spearman. 1st Eng. 520p. VG. J2. $75.00

WATERS, Frank. *Masked Gods: Navajo & Pueblo Ceremonialism.* 1950. Sage Books. 2nd. tall 8vo. gray bdg. NF. F7. $40.00

WATERS, Frank. *Mexico Mystique.* 1975. Chicago. Swallow. 1st. F/F clip. L3. $125.00

WATERS, Frank. *People of the Valley.* 1941. NY. 1st ed. VG/VG. B5. $50.00

WATERS, Frank. *Pike's Peak.* 1971. Chicago. Sage. 1st. NF/NF. T11. $65.00

WATERS, J.M. Jr. *Bloody Winter.* 1967. Princeton. ils/charts. 279p. VG/VG. S16. $20.00

WATERS, John. *Shock Value.* 1985. Delta. 5th. sgn. photos. VG+. C9. $50.00

WATERS, Ralph. *Chloroform: Study After 100 Years.* 1951. Madison. 1st. 138p. VG. A13. $30.00

WATERTON, Charles. *Wanderings in South America.* 1909. NY. Sturgis Walton. 1st. 16 pl. F3. $45.00

WATKINS, Ivor. *Demon.* 1983. MacDonald. 1st. VG/fair. P3. $13.00

WATKINS, John V. *ABC of Orchid Growing.* 1971. Prentice Hall. 3rd/5th prt. 190p. clip. B1. $18.50

WATKINS, John V. *Florida Landscape Plants: Native & Exotic.* 1975. Gainsville. revised. 420p. dj. B26. $24.00

WATKINS, John V. *Gardens of Antilles.* 1952. Gainesville. ils. 244p. VG. B26. $25.00

WATKINS, Lura Woodside. *American Glass & Glassmaking.* 1950. Chanticleer. 1st. 104p. cloth. VG/dj. M20. $40.00

WATKINS, Lura Woodside. *Cambridge Glass 1818 to 1888.* 1930. Bramhall. ils. 199p. F/G. H1. $30.00

WATKINS, Lura Woodside. *Cambridge Glass.* 1930. Marshall Jones. 1st. 199p. cloth/pict label. VG/tattered. M20. $50.00

WATKINS, Paul. *Calm at Sunset, Calm at Dawn.* nd. London. Hutchinson. 1st. sgn. author's 2nd book. F/dj. A24. $75.00

WATKINS, Paul. *Calm at Sunset, Calm at Dawn.* 1989. Houghton Mifflin. 1st. author's 2nd book. F/F. H11. $60.00

WATKINS, Paul. *In the Blue Light of African Dreams.* 1990. Houghton Mifflin. 1st Am. author's 3rd book. F/dj. A24/H11. $40.00

WATKINS, Paul. *Night Over Day Over Night.* 1988. Knopf. 1st Am. author's 1st book. F/dj. A24. $85.00

WATKINS, Paul. *Promise of Light.* 1992. London. Faber. 1st. author's 4th book. F/NF. B3. $50.00

WATKINS, T.H. *Mark Twain's Mississippi.* 1974. Palo Alto. Am West Pub. ils/halftone. 221p. dj. T7. $22.00

WATKINS, T.H. *On the Shore of the Sundown Sea.* 1973. SF. Sierra Club. 1st. F/NF. O4. $20.00

WATKINS, William Jon. *God Machine.* 1973. Doubleday. 1st. VG/dj. P3. $20.00

WATKINS, Vernon. *Affinities.* 1963. New Directions. 1st ed. assn copy. F/VG. V1. $20.00

WATKINS-PITCHFORD, Denys. *Little Grey Men.* 1949. Jr Literary Guild. 1st/A ed. 8vo. VG/worn. B17. $30.00

WATSON, Aldren. *Village Blacksmith.* 1968. NY. Crowell. 1st ed. VG/VG. O3. $45.00

WATSON, Alan. *Daube Noster, Essays in Legal History of David Daube.* 1974. Edinburgh. Scottish Academic Pr. M11. $65.00

WATSON, Clarissa. *Runaway.* 1985. Atheneum. 1st. F/dj. P3. $20.00

WATSON, Clyde. *Tom Fox & the Apple Pie.* 1972. Crowell. 1st. 8vo. unp. VG. T5. $20.00

WATSON, Colin. *Bump in the Night.* 1961. Walker. 1st. NF/dj. P3. $25.00

WATSON, Edward James. *Pleas of the Crown for the Hundred Swineshead...* 1902. Bristol. W Crofton Hemmons. pres copy. M11. $85.00

WATSON, Frederick. *Hunting Pie: Whole Art & Craft of Foxhunting.* 1931. Derrydale. 1/750. VG. O3. $125.00

WATSON, George E. *Birds of the Antarctic & the Sub-Antarctic.* 1975. WA. ils. 350p. F/VG. S15. $17.00

WATSON, Ian. *Embedding.* 1973. Scribner. 1st. F/dj. M2. $45.00

WATSON, Ian. *Evil Water.* 1987. Gollancz. 1st. F/dj. P3. $22.00

WATSON, Ian. *Fire Storm.* 1988. Gollancz. 1st. sgn. F/F. B11. $35.00

WATSON, Ian. *Queenmagic, Kingmagic.* 1986. Gollancz. 1st. sgn. F/dj. P3. $30.00

WATSON, Ian. *Slow Birds & Other Stories.* 1985. Gollancz. 1st. sgn. F/dj. P3. $30.00

WATSON, Ian. *Stalin's Teardrops.* 1991. Gollancz. 1st. F/dj. P3. $25.00

WATSON, J.N.P. *World of Polo.* 1986. Topsfield. Salem House. 1st Am. VG/VG. O3. $45.00

WATSON, James B. *Tairora Culture: Contingency & Pragmatism.* 1983. Seattle/London. 6 maps/15 tables/figures. 346p. red cloth. P4. $25.00

WATSON, Lyall. *Heavens' Breath.* 1984. Morrow. 1st. 8vo. 384p. dj. K5. $22.00

WATSON, Margaret G. *Silver Theatre, Amusements of the Mining Frontier...* 1964. Clark. 1st. ils. 387p. VG/VG. J2. $80.00

WATSON, Virginia. *Manhattan Acres.* 1934. Dutton. 1st. B4. $100.00

WATSON, William. *Cactus Culture for Amateurs.* 1920s. London. 4th revised. ils/pl/woodcuts. binding copy. B26. $15.00

WATT, Lauchlan Maclean. *Advocate's Wig.* 1932. Herbert Jenkins. 1st. VG. P3. $30.00

WATT, Leilani. *Caught in the Conflict.* 1984. Harvest. 1st ed. sgn. 191p. VG/VG. B11. $8.50

WATTERS, Pat. *Down to Now!* 1971. Pantheon. 1st ed. 426p. NF/NF. R11. $18.00

WATTERS, Pat. *Fifty Years of Pleasure.* 1980. Lakeland. Publix. inscr. F/VG. B11. $30.00

WATTERSON, Henry. *Marse Henry.* 1919. 2 vol. 1st. O8. $23.50

WATTS, Alan W. *Cloud-Hidden, Whereabouts Unknown: A Mountain Journal.* 1973. Pantheon. 1st. F/clip. M25. $35.00

WATTS, Alan W. *Reading the Weather.* (1987). Dodd Mead. 4to. 208p. VG. K5. $12.00

WATTS, Alan W. *Two Hands of God: Myths of Polarity.* 1963. Braziller. 1st. NF/clip. M25. $35.00

WATTS, Mabel. *Dozens of Cousins.* 1950. Whittlesey. 1st. ils Roger Duvoisin. VG/G+. M5. $32.00

WATTS, Mabel. *Story of Zachary Zween.* nd (1967). Parents Magazine. sm 4to. ils. NF. C14. $12.00

WATTS, Peter. *Dictionary of the Old West.* 1977. Knopf. 1st. 399p. VG/VG. J2. $65.00

WAUGH, Alec. *Hot Countries.* 1930. ils Lynd Ward. VG. M17. $15.00

WAUGH, Alec. *In Praise of Wine & Certain Noble Spirits.* 1960 (1959). Sloane. 2nd. VG/VG. B10. $12.00

WAUGH, Evelyn. *Brideshead Revisited.* 1946. Little Brn. 1st Am trade ed. NF/NF. B4. $450.00

WAUGH, Evelyn. *Edmund Campion.* 1946. Little Brn. 1st Am ed. F/NF clip. B4. $175.00

WAUGH, Evelyn. *Helena.* 1950. Little Brn. 1st. VG/VG. M19. $25.00

WAUGH, Evelyn. *Men at Arms.* 1952. Little Brn. 1st. NF/G. M19. $45.00

WAUGH, Evelyn. *Men at Arms.* 1952. London. Chapman Hall. 1st. F/NF. B2. $85.00

WAUGH, Evelyn. *Officers & Gentlemen.* 1955. Little Brn. 1st. F/VG. M19. $45.00

WAUGH, Evelyn. *Scott-King's Modern Europe.* 1947. London. 1st ed. F/NF. B4. $85.00

WAUGH, Evelyn. *They Were Still Dancing.* 1931. Cape Smith. 1st Am ed. F/NF. C2. $450.00

WAUGH, Evelyn. *When the Going Was Good.* 1947. Little Brn. 1st. F/VG. M19. $65.00

WAUGH, Hillary. *Death in a Town.* 1990. Dodd Mead. 2nd. VG/dj. P3. $17.00

WAUGH, Hillary. *Death in a Town.* 1989. Carroll Graf. 1st ed. inscr. F/F. B11. $25.00

WAUGH, Hillary. *Murder on Safari.* 1987. Dodd Mead. 1st. VG/dj. P3. $16.00

WAUGH, Julia. *Silver Cradle.* 1955. Austin, TX. 1st. 160p. dj. F3. $15.00

WAUMETT, Victor. *Teardown.* 1990. St Martin. 1st. F/dj. P3. $17.00

WAUTERS, A.J. *Stanley's Emin Pasha Expedition.* 1890. NY. Alden. 1st. 8vo. 210p. cloth. VG. W1. $22.00

WAXELL, Sven. *American Expedition.* 1952. London. 1st Eng. 8vo. map ep. bl/gr cloth. VG/dj. P4. $60.00

WAXMAN, Mordecai. *Tradition & Change: Development of Conservative Movement.* 1958. Burning Bush. 34 essays. 477p. VG/poor. S3. $29.00

WAY, Frederick. *Way's Pocket Directory, 1848-1983.* 1983. Athens, OH. ils/over 5000 entries. VG+/dj. B18. $35.00

WAY, F. *Log of the Betsy Ann.* 1933. NY. 1st ed. sgn. VG/VG. B5. $55.00

WAY, F. *Pilotin' Comes Natural.* 1943. Farrar Rinehart. 1st ed. ils John Cosgrove. G/G. A16. $65.00

WAY, Peter. *Belshazzar's Feast.* 1982. Atheneum. 1st. F/dj. M2. $20.00

WAYLAND, John W. *Hopewell Friends History, 1734-1934...Virginia.* 1936. Strasburg, VA. Shenandoah Pub. 1st. 671p. V3. $85.00

WAYNE, Joseph. *By Gun & a Spur.* 1952. Dutton. 1st. VG. P3. $10.00

WEATHERHEAD, Leslie D. *Psychology, Religion & Healing.* 1952. Hodder Stoughton. 544p. G. B29. $6.50

WEATHERLY, F.E. *Punch & Judy & Some of Their Friends.* 1987. Sidney, Australia. View Productions. 1st ed thus. F/VG. B17. $8.50

WEATHERLY, Fred J. *Holly Boughs.* ca 1885. NY. EP Dutton. ils ME Edwards/Staples. pict brd/cloth spine. VG. T10. $75.00

WEATHERWAX, Clara. *Marching! Marching!* 1935. John Day. 1st. F/NF. B4. $125.00

WEAVER, D. *Account of Principle Difficulties & Embarrassments...* 1872. Nashville, TN. 1st. 8vo. 37p. prt wrp. M1. $200.00

WEAVER, J.E. *Native Vegetation of Nebraska.* 1965. Lincoln. 1st. 8vo. cloth. F/clip. A22. $17.00

WEAVER, Michael D. *Mercedes Nights.* 1987. St Martin. 1st. F/dj. P3. $17.00

WEAVER, Paul E. *Charlie Dye.* 1981. Los Angeles. dj. A19. $45.00

WEAVER, W.G. *Yankee Doodle Went to Town.* 1959. Ann Arbor. Edwards Bros. 1st. inscr. VG. A23. $40.00

WEBB, Alexander S. *Peninsula.* 1881. NY. 1st. 219p. O8. $21.50

WEBB, Charles. *Graduate.* 1963. NY. NAL. 1st ed. F/VG clip. B4. $150.00

WEBB, Jack. *Deadly Sex.* 1959. Rinehart. 1st. xl. VG/dj. P3. $10.00

WEBB, Jack. *Make My Bed Soon.* 1963. HRW. 1st. F/NF. T12. $25.00

WEBB, Jack. *One for My Dame.* 1961. HRW. 2nd. VG/G. P3. $12.00

WEBB, James. *Fields of Fire.* 1978. Prentice Hall. 1st. author's 1st book. 344p. NF/dj. M19/W2. $45.00

WEBB, James. *Spence of Honor.* 1981. Prentice Hall. 1st. F/NF. M19. $25.00

WEBB, Joe. *Care & Training of the Tennessee Walking Horse.* 1962. Searcy. 1st ed. VG/VG. O3. $48.00

WEBB, Marion St. John. *Forest Faries.* 1932. London. Medici Soc. 4th imp. ils Tarrant. 16mo. gr brd. dj. R5. $100.00

WEBB, Marion St. John. *Littlest One Again.* 1923. Harrap. 1st. ils Margaret Tarrant. VG+/VG. M5. $85.00

WEBB, Marion St. John. *Littlest One.* 1919. Harrap. ils Margaret Tarrant. sm 8vo. NF. M5. $65.00

WEBB, Roy. *Riverman: Story of Bus Hatch.* 1990. Labyrinth. 2nd. 8vo. G+/stiff bl wrp. F7. $12.50

WEBB, Sharon. *Half Life.* 1989. Tor. VG/VG. P3. $18.00

WEBB & WEBB. *Decay of Capitalist Civilization.* 1923. Harcourt. 1st. NF/VG. B2. $45.00

WEBB & WEBB. *Littlest Fairy.* 1910. Dodge. 1st. ils Ruth Clements. 4to. decor brd/pict label. R5. $250.00

WEBBER, Alexander. *Wine: A Series of Notes on This Valuable Product...* nd. London. Simpkins Marshall. aeg. G+. B10. $150.00

WEBBER, C.W. *Wild Scenes & Song-Birds.* 1855. NY. Tiker Thorne. 2nd. 8vo. 347p. pub rose cloth. B24. $225.00

WEBER, Elizabeth Anne. *Duk-Duks.* 1929. Chicago. 1st. 8vo. 142p. F/dj. T10. $75.00

WEBER, Francis J. *California Mission Poetry.* Hong Kong. Libra Pr w/Los Angeles 1978 imp. 1/350. 8vo. NF/wrp. O4. $25.00

WEBER, Francis J. *History of San Buenaventura Mission.* 1977. San Buenaventura. 1st. inscr. NF/F. O4. $25.00

WEBER, Francis J. *Rose: America's Flower.* 1988. San Fernando. Junipero Serra. 1/200. aeg. red leather. miniature. T10. $50.00

WEBER, Francis J. *San Xavier del Bac.* 1975. San Fernando. Junipero Serra. 1/300. aeg. gray leather. miniature. T10. $50.00

WEBER, R.L. *Random Walk in Science.* 1973. NY. Crane Russak. ils. VG/dj. K3. $25.00

WEBER, William A. *Handbook of Plants of the Colorado Front Range.* 1953. Boulder. 8vo. 232p. G+. A22. $20.00

WEBER, William A. *Rocky Mountain Flora.* 1976. Boulder, CO. 5th revised. 12mo. 16 mc pl. 479p. VG. B1. $18.00

WEBERS, G.F. *Geology & Paleontology of Ellsworth Mountains...* 1992. Boulder. Geological Soc of Am. ils/charts. 459p. NF/dj. P4. $125.00

WEBSTER, A.D. *Tree Wounds & Diseases.* 1916. London. Williams Norgate. 1st. 8vo. 215p. A22. $30.00

WEBSTER, D.K. *Myth & Maneater: Story of the Shark.* 1963. Norton. ils/photos/drawings. 223p. cloth. F/VG+. M12. $17.50

WEBSTER, Frank V. *Two Boys of the Battleship.* 1915. Cupples Leon. 208p. VG/dj. M20. $20.00

WEBSTER, Frank. *Results in Taxidermy, Illustrated by 140 Half-Tone...* (1905). Boston. Marsh. 1st. tall 8vo. ils. unp. VG. H7. $20.00

WEBSTER, H.T. *Best of HT Webster.* 1953. S&S. 1st. VG/dj. P3. $35.00

WEBSTER, H.T. *Webster's Bridge.* 1924. NY. VG. S1. $15.00

WEBSTER, H.T. *Who Dealt This Mess?* 1948. Garden City. 1st. bridge cartoons. VG/VG. B5. $25.00

WEBSTER, Noah. *Compendious Dictionary of English Language, a Facsimile...* 1970. np. intro Philip Gove. 446p. NF/VG. A4. $45.00

WEBSTER, Noah. *Webster's Biographical Dictionary.* 1943. np. 8vo. 1697p. brn cloth. VG. T3. $15.00

WECHSBERG, Joseph. *Lost World of the Great Spas.* 1979. Harper Row. 1st Am. 208p. cloth. VG/dj. M20. $30.00

WEDDLE, A.E. *Techniques of Landscape Architecture.* 1969. NY. Elsevier. 2nd. dj. A10. $30.00

WEDECK, Harry. *Treasury of Witchcraft.* 1961. Philosophical Lib. 1st. F/dj. M2. $18.00

WEEDEN, Robert B. *Alaska: Promises to Keep.* 1978. Boston. Houghton Mifflin. 1st prt. 8vo. 254p. NF/dj. P4. $25.00

WEEKES, R.K. *Convict B 14.* 1920. Brentano. VG. P3. $20.00

WEEKLEY, Robert S. *House in Ruins.* 1958. Random. 1st. F/VG+. B4. $85.00

WEEKS, Edward. *Lowells & Their Institute.* 1966. Atlantic Little Brn. 1st ed. 4-line inscr. 202p. F. B14. $55.00

WEEKS, Herbert. *Mystery of Cedar Bluff.* 1928. Colonial. 1st. VG. P3. $30.00

WEEKS, Jim. *Sooners.* 1974. STrode. 1st. photos. F/VG+. P8. $30.00

WEEKS, Morris. *Complete Boating Encyclopedia.* 1964. NY. 560p+500 photos. dj. A17. $15.00

WEEMS, John Edward. *If You Don't Like the Weather...* 1986. TX Monthly. ils. 121p. VG/dj. K5. $14.00

WEEMS, John Edward. *Race for the North Pole.* 1961. NY/London. ils. 240p. dj. T7. $20.00

WEES, Frances Shelley. *Country of Strangers.* 1960. Doubleday. 1st. VG/dj. P3. $20.00

WEESNER, Theodore. *Children's Hearts.* 1992. Summit. 1st. F/F. A20. $15.00

WEHR, Julian. *Animated Animals.* 1943. Saalfield. 4 moveables. VG/dj. D1. $150.00

WEHR, Julian. *Animated Circus Book.* 1943. Grosset Dunlap. 4 moveables. sbdg. VG/dj. D1. $300.00

WEHR, Julian. *Raggedy Ann & Andy.* 1944. Saalfield. ils Gruelle. 8vo. pict brd/sbdg. R5. $175.00

WEHR, Julian. *Puss in Boots.* 1944. Dunewald. 1st ed thus. 6 moveables. VG/VG. D1. $200.00

WEHR, Julian. *Snow White.* 1949. Duenewald. 4 moveables. sbdg. VG. D1. $150.00

WEHR, Julian. *Snow White.* 1949. Duenewald. 4 moveables. 8vo. pict brd/sbdg. NF. T10. $75.00

WEHRLE, Joe. *Cauliflower Catnip.* 1981. Teacup. F. M2. $20.00

WEIDEMAN, Polly. *Polly's Kaleidoscope.* nd. Rapid City, SD. Blk Hills Power & Light/KOTA. A19. $35.00

WEIDMAN, Jerome. *Praying for Rain.* 1986. Harper. 1st. F/F. B4. $35.00

WEIGALL, Arthur. *Tutankamen & Other Essays.* 1923. Thornton Butterworth. 1st. VG. P3. $45.00

WEIGL, Bruce. *Song of Napalm.* 1988. NY. Atlantic Monthly. 1st. inscr. NF/dj. R13. $30.00

WEIGLEY, Russell F. *Eisenhower's Lieutenants.* 1981. IN U. 1st. sm 4to. 800p. bl cloth. as new/dj. H1. $25.00

WEIL, Lisl. *Pandora's Box.* 1986. Atheneum. 1st. lg 8vo. F/NF. C8. $30.00

WEILEN, Helen. *Mein Grosses Teddy Buch.* 1961. Vienna. ils Anny Hoffmann. VG+. M5. $110.00

WEILL, Gus. *Bonnet Man.* 1978. Macmillan. 1st. F/dj. M2. $20.00

WEINBAUM, Stanley G. *Black Flame.* 1948. Fantasy. 1st/ltd. F/NF. P3. $175.00

WEINBAUM, Stanley G. *Martian Odyssey.* nd. Fantasy. ltd/#d. F/VG. P3. $150.00

WEINBAUM, Stanley G. *Red Peri.* 1952. Fantasy. ltd. F/NF. P3. $175.00

WEINBERG, George. *Numberland.* 1987. St Martin. 1st. F/dj. P3. $10.00

WEINBERG, Robert. *Biographical Dictionary Science Fiction & Fantasy Artists.* 1988. Greenwood. 1st. sgn. P3. $75.00

WEINBERG, Robert. *Far Below & Other Horrors.* 1974. Fax. 1st. inscr. F/dj. P3. $45.00

WEINBURG, Steven. *Discovery of Subatomic Particles.* 1983. Scientific Am Lib. 1st. 206p. cloth. VG+/dj. M20. $28.00

WEINBURG, Steven. *First Three Minutes.* 1977. Basic. 1st. F/dj. M2. $10.00

WEINER, Andrew. *Station Gehenna.* 1987. Congdon Weed. 1st. F/dj. M2. $15.00

WEINER, Jonathan. *Planet Earth.* 1986. Bantam. F/dj. M2. $17.00

WEINER, Shirley. *Happy Dieter.* 1974. Regional Ent. 152p. photos. sbdg. B10. $10.00

WEINSTEIN, Frida Scheps. *Hidden Childhood.* 1985. Hill Wang. 151p. F/VG+. S3. $24.00

WEINTRAUB, Stanley. *Last Great Cause, Intellectuals & Spanish Civil War.* 1968. NY. 1st. VG/dj. T9. $18.00

WEINTRAUB, Stanley. *Savoy: Nineties Experiment.* 1966. PA State. 1st. 294p. VG+/dj. M20. $70.00

WEIR & WEIR. *Hostage Bound, Hostage Freed.* 1987. Phil. Westminster. 1st. sgns. VG/VG. B11. $25.00

WEISBACH, Werner. *Die Kunst Des Barock in Italien, Frankreich, Deutschland...* 1924. Berlin. 44 pl. 596p. modern half leather. A17. $40.00

WEISBORD, Albert. *Conquest of Power.* 1937. Covici Friede. 2 vol. NF/NF. B2. $125.00

WEISGARD, Leonard. *Family Mother Goose: Father Goose/Little Goose/Mother Goose.* 1951. Harper. early ed. lg 12mo. VG+/VG. C8. $45.00

WEISHAUPT, C.G. *Vascular Plants of Ohio.* 1971. Dubuque. Kendall/Hunt. 3rd. 293p. B1. $22.00

WEISS, Diane. *Raven.* nd. Mill Valley. Figment. 1/60. 74x74mm. ils/prt/bdg/inscr Diane Weiss. F. B24. $135.00

WELCH, Adam C. *Jeremiah: His Time & His Work.* 1928. London. Oxford. index. 263p. G+/fair. S3. $25.00

WELCH, James. *Death of Jim Loney.* 1979. Harper Row. 1st. author's 2nd novel. F/VG. B3. $40.00

WELCH, James. *Fools Crow.* 1986. Viking. 1st. F/F. T11. $40.00

WELCH, James. *Riding the Earthboy 40.* 1971. NY. World. 1st. author's 1st book. F/F. L3. $150.00

WELCH, James. *Winter in the Blood.* 1974. NY. Harper Row. 1st trade. F/F. L3. $150.00

WELCH, William H. *Pathology & Preventive Medicine.* 1920. Baltimore. 1st. 678p. xl. A13. $100.00

WELCOME, H.S. *Story of Metlakahtla.* 1887. London. 1st. ils. 483p. M4. $50.00

WELCOME, John. *Reasons of Hate.* 1990. Collins Crime Club. 1st. F/dj. P3. $20.00

WELDON, Fay. *...And the Wife Ran Away.* 1968. McKay. 1st Am. author's 1st novel. VG/dj. M25. $60.00

WELDON, Fay. *Heart of the Country.* 1988. Viking. 1st Am. sgn. F/dj. A24. $35.00

WELDON, Fay. *Life Force.* 1992. London. Harper Collins. 1st. F/dj. A24. $25.00

WELDON, Fay. *Life & Loves of a She-Devil.* 1983. Pantheon. 1st ed. F/NF. H11. $30.00

WELDON, Fay. *Remember He.* 1976. Hodder Stoughton. 1st. sgn. F/dj. A24. $60.00

WELFARE, Simon. *Arthur C Clarke's Mysterious World.* 1980. A&W. 1st. VG/dj. P3. $20.00

WELLARD, James. *Lost Worlds of Africa.* 1967. Dutton. 1st. ils/maps. 214p. VG/dj. W1. $12.00

WELLER, J.M. *Course of Evolution.* 1969. McGraw Hill. ils. 696p. NF. D8. $35.00

WELLER, Philip. *Life & Times of Sherlock Holmes.* 1992. Crescent. F/dj. P3. $20.00

WELLES, Patricia. *Babyhip.* 1967. Dutton. 1st. F/F. B4. $85.00

WELLES, Patricia. *Switch.* 1971. Michael Joseph. 1st. NF/dj. P3. $20.00

WELLMAN, Manly Wade. *After Dark.* 1980. Doubleday. 1st. VG/dj. P3. $25.00

WELLMAN, Manly Wade. *Brave Horse: Story of Janus.* 1968. Colonial Williamsburg. ils Peter Burchard. VG. P3. $15.00

WELLMAN, Manly Wade. *Old Gods Waken.* 1979. Doubleday. 1st. VG/dj. P3. $25.00

WELLMAN, Manly Wade. *School of Darkness.* 1985. Doubleday. 1st ed. F/F. G10. $15.00

WELLMAN, Manly Wade. *Worse Things Waiting.* 1973. Carosa. 1st. sgn. F/dj. P3. $150.00

WELLMAN, Paul I. *Death on Horseback.* 1947. Phil. ils. 484p. G. B18. $22.50

WELLS, Anna Mary. *Talent for Murder.* 1942. Knopf. 1st. VG. P3. $25.00

WELLS, Carolyn. *Affair at Flower Acres.* nd. Doubleday Doran. VG. P3. $15.00

WELLS, Carolyn. *All at Sea.* 1927. Lippincott. 1st. VG+. N4. $25.00

WELLS, Carolyn. *Book of American Limericks.* 1925. 1st ed. VG/G. w/sgn. S13. $45.00

WELLS, Carolyn. *Curved Blades.* 1916. Lippincott. 1st. VG. M2. $12.00

WELLS, Carolyn. *Furthest Fury.* 1924. Lippincott. 1st. 320p. VG+/dj. M20. $75.00

WELLS, Carolyn. *Mother Goose's Menagerie.* 1901. Noyes Platt. 1st. ils Peter Newell/12 mc pl. G. C8. $175.00

WELLS, Carolyn. *Patty's Romance.* 1924 (1915). Dodd Mead. 8vo. 303p. VG. T5. $20.00

WELLS, Carolyn. *Prillilgirl.* 1924. Lippincott. 1st ed. VG. M22. $15.00

WELLS, Carolyn. *Ptomaine Street.* 1921. Lippincott. 1st. VG. M20. $20.00

WELLS, Carveth. *Bermuda in Three Colors.* 1938. NY. McBride. 100+photos/map. 271p. cloth. VG+/VG. M12. $17.50

WELLS, Carveth. *Panmexico!* 1937. National Travel Club. 1st. photos/map ep. dj. F3. $15.00

WELLS, David A. *Natural Philosophy for Use of Schools, Academies...* 1865. NY. Iveson Phinney Blakeman. 15th. 375 engravings. xl. K3. $40.00

WELLS, H.G. *Adventures of Tommy.* 1929. NY. Stokes. 1st Am. lg 4to. red cloth/label. pict dj. R5. $225.00

WELLS, H.G. *Anatomy of Frustration.* 1936. Macmillan. 1st. VG. P3. $30.00

WELLS, H.G. *Croquet Player.* 1937. Viking. 1st ed. 8vo. VG/dj. S9. $30.00

WELLS, H.G. *Crux Ansata: Indictment of the Roman Catholic Church.* 1953. NY. Freethought. 1st ed. VG/wrp. B14. $35.00

WELLS, H.G. *Dream.* 1924. London. Cape. true 1st. F/clip. D10. $265.00

WELLS, H.G. *Experiment in Autobiography.* 1934. Canada. Macmillan. 1st. VG. P3. $35.00

WELLS, H.G. *Food of the Gods.* 1924. Scribner. F. M2. $35.00

WELLS, H.G. *Future in America.* nd. copyright ed. NF. M2. $30.00

WELLS, H.G. *Joan & Peter.* 1918. Macmillan. 1st. G. P3. $12.00

WELLS, H.G. *Mr Britling Sees It Through.* 1916. Macmillan. 1st. VG. P3. $40.00

WELLS, H.G. *Outline of History.* 1949. Garden City. VG. P3. $20.00

WELLS, H.G. *Passionate Friends.* 1913. London. 1st. VG. T9. $18.00

WELLS, H.G. *Research Magnificent.* 1915. Macmillan. 1st. G. M2. $22.00

WELLS, H.G. *Seven Famous Novels by...* 1934. Knopf. 1st. VG. P3. $30.00

WELLS, H.G. *Seven Science Fiction Novels of...* nd. Dover. F/dj. M2. $13.00

WELLS, H.G. *Shape of Things to Come.* 1933. London. 1st. VG. M2. $50.00

WELLS, H.G. *Star-Begotten.* 1937. Viking. 1st. VG/dj. M2. $50.00

WELLS, H.G. *Time Machine.* 1931. Random. 1st thus. VG. M2. $12.00

WELLS, H.G. *Tono-Bungay.* 1960. NY. LEC. 1st thus. 1/1500. ils Lynton Lamb. F/case. Q1. $100.00

WELLS, H.G. *War in the Air.* 1908. Macmillan. VG. M2. $75.00

WELLS, H.G. *War of the Worlds.* 1898. Harper. 1st Am ed. NF. H4. $650.00

WELLS, H.G. *When the Sleeper Awakes.* 1899. NY. 1st Am. 15 pl. 328p. decor gr cloth. B18. $175.00

WELLS, H.G. *World of William Crissold Vol II.* 1926. Doran. VG. P3. $25.00

WELLS, H.G. *World Set Free.* 1914. Dutton. 1st Am. G. M2. $12.00

WELLS, H.P. *American Salmon Fisherman.* 1886. NY. 1st ed. G. B5. $50.00

WELLS, Helen. *Cherry Ames' Book of First Aid & Home Nursing.* 1959. Grosset Dunlap. 250p. VG+/dj. M20. $35.00

WELLS, Helen. *Cherry Ames: Camp Nurse (#19).* 1957. Grosset Dunlap. 182p. VG/dj (lists to #21). M20. $20.00

WELLS, Helen. *Vicki Barr: Secret of Magnolia Manor (#4).* 1949. Grosset Dunlap. 1st. 213p. cloth. VG/dj (lists to this title). M20. $20.00

WELLS, Henry P. *Fly-Rods & Fly Tackle, Suggestions as to Their Manufacture.* 1885. Harper. 1st. 364p. NF. H7. $125.00

WELLS, Henry W. *Introduction to Emily Dickinson.* 1947. Packard. 286p. F/dj. H1. $18.00

WELLS, James M. *Chisolm Massacre.* 1878. WA, DC. 331p. decor cloth. G. B18. $35.00

WELLS, Joel. *Grim Fairy Tales for Adults.* 1967. Macmillan. 1st. VG/dj. P3. $25.00

WELLS, Louisa Susannah. *Journal of a Voyage From Charlestown, SC to London.* 1906. NY Hist Soc. 1/200. 121p. teg. gilt bdg. VG. B18. $225.00

WELLS, Peter. *Pirate's Apprentice.* 1943. Winston. 1st. sm 4to. unp. VG/VG. T5. $35.00

WELLS, Stuart W. *Science Fiction & Fantasy Author Index.* 1978. Purple Union. 1st. F. P3. $25.00

WELLS, Tobias. *How to Kill a Man.* 1972. Crime Club. 1st. VG/dj. P3. $15.00

WELLS, Tobias. *Matter of Love & Death.* 1966. Crime Club. 1st. VG/dj. P3. $18.00

WELSH, Doris. *History of Miniature Books.* 1987. ils. 160p. F. A4. $135.00

WELSH, Frank. *Building the Trireme.* 1988. London. Constable. ils. 231p. dj. T7. $30.00

WELTNER, Charles Longstreet. *Southerner.* 1966. Lippincott. 1st ed. VG/G. B10. $10.00

WELTY, Eudora. *Acrobats in a Park.* 1980. Lord John. 1/100. sgn. F. B4. $350.00

WELTY, Eudora. *Collected Stories of Eudora Welty.* 1980. Franklin Lib. 1st. aeg/ribbon marker. gilt red leather. F. B2. $50.00

WELTY, Eudora. *Conversations With Eudora Welty.* 1984. Jackson, MS. 1st. 1/2000. inscr. F/F. R14. $125.00

WELTY, Eudora. *Fairy Tale of the Natchez Trace.* 1975. MS Hist Soc. 1/1000. brd. F. M24. $125.00

WELTY, Eudora. *Losing Battles.* 1970. Random. 1st. author's 8th book. NF/dj. D10. $45.00

WELTY, Eudora. *One Writer's Beginnings.* 1984. Harvard. 1st trade. F/dj. M24. $65.00

WELTY, Eudora. *Optimist's Daughter.* 1972. Random. 1st. author's 10th book. NF/clip. D10. $70.00

WENDT, Emil. *Buch der Rathsel. Ein Festgeschenk fur die Jugend.* 1842. Leipzig. Dorffling. 12mo. 60p. gr pebbled cloth. NF. B24. $350.00

WENGER, Stephen R. *Flowers of Mesa Verde National Park.* 1976. Mesa Verde Nat Park. photos. 47p. sc. B26. $7.50

WENHAM, Edward. *Old Clocks for Modern Use.* 1951. London. Bell. ils. 174p. VG/dj. K3. $25.00

WENIGER, Del. *Cacti of Texas & Neighboring States.* 1984. Austin. 187 photos. sc. M. B26. $23.00

WENIGER, Del. *Cacti of the Southwest.* ca 1970. Austin. ils/184 mc photos. 249p. VG+/dj. B26. $87.50

WENTWORTH, Lady. *Swift Runner.* 1957. London. Allen Unwin. 1st ed. VG. W1. $45.00

WENTWORTH, Lady. *Swift Runner: Racing Speed Through the Ages.* 1957. London. Allen Unwin. 1st. sm 4to. VG. O3. $65.00

WENTWORTH, Patricia. *Dead or Alive.* 1936. Lippincott. 1st Am. F/dj. M15. $85.00

WENTWORTH, Patricia. *Gazebo.* 1956. Lippincott. 1st ed. VG/VG. M22. $40.00

WENTWORTH, Patricia. *Hue & Cry.* 1927. Lippincott. 1st. VG/dj. P3. $75.00

WENTWORTH, Patricia. *Ivory Dagger.* 1951. Lippincott. 1st. VG. P3. $20.00

WENTWORTH, Patricia. *Miss Silver Comes to Stay.* 1949. Lippincott. 1st. VG. P3. $20.00

WENTWORTH, Patricia. *Red Shadow.* 1932. Lippincott. 1st. VG. N4. $35.00

WENTWORTH, Patricia. *Wicked Uncle.* 1947. Lippincott. 1st. VG. P3. $35.00

WERFEL, Franz. *Song of Bernadette.* 1942. Viking. 1st. VG. M2. $12.00

WERNER, Eliza Jane. *Patrick.* 1946. Whitman. Fuzzy Wuzzy Book. pict brd. VG/dj. M20. $25.00

WERNER, Helmut. *From the Aratus Globe to the Zeiss Planet Arium.* 1957. Stuttgart. revised/enlarged. 204p. K5. $80.00

WERNER, Jane. *Giant Golden Book of Elves & Fairies.* 1951. S&S. 1st. folio. VG. M5. $165.00

WERT, J. Howard. *Poems of Camp & Hearth.* 1887. Harrisburg. 176p. VG. B10. $15.00

WERTMULLER, Lina. *Head of Alvise.* 1982. Morrow. 1st ed. sgn. F/F. B11. $20.00

WESCHCKE, Carl. *Growing Nuts in the North.* 1954. St Paul. Webb. 124p. VG/dj. A10. $32.00

WESCHER, Paul. *Time in the Wastebasket: Poems, Collages, Parables...* 1975. Santa Monica. Mary Wescher. private prt. photos. D2. $50.00

WESCOTT, Cynthia. *Gardener's Bug Book.* 1946. Doubleday. 1st. 590p. G/dj. H1. $18.00

WESCOTT, Cynthia. *Westcott's Plant Disease Handbook.* 1979. Van Nostrand. 4th. 8vo. VG/dj. A22. $25.00

WESLEY, Mary. *Harnessing Peacocks.* 1985. London. Macmillan. 1st. VG/NF. B3. $50.00

WEST, Anthony. *Aspects of a Life.* 1984. London. 1st. VG/dj. T9. $25.00

WEST, Charles E. *Prison-Ship Martyrs.* 1895. Brooklyn. 20p. VG/prt wrp. B11. $35.00

WEST, Edwin; see Westlake, Donald E.

WEST, Herbert Faulkner. *Mind on the Wing.* 1947. Coward McCann. 1st. 308p. VG/dj. M20. $25.00

WEST, Jessamyn. *Crimson Ramblers of the World, Farewell.* 1970. HBJ. 1st ed. sgn. F/F. B4. $125.00

WEST, Jessamyn. *Friendly Persuasion.* 1945. NY. 1st ed. F/VG. H7. $75.00

WEST, Jessamyn. *Except for Me & Thee.* 1969. 1st. sgn. NF/NF. M19. $45.00

WEST, Morris L. *Cassidy.* 1986. Doubleday. 1st. VG/dj. P3. $15.00

WEST, Morris L. *Proteus.* 1979. Collins. 1st. F/dj. P3. $20.00

WEST, Morris L. *Tower of Babel.* 1968. Morrow. VG/G. P3. $15.00

WEST, Morris L. *World Is Made of Glass.* 1981. Morrow. 1st. NF/NF. W2. $30.00

WEST, Owen; see Koontz, Dean R.

WEST, Patrick C. *Resident Peoples & National Parks: Social Dilemmas...* 1991. AZ U. 1st. as new/dj. V4. $22.50

WEST, Ray. *Kingdom of the Saints, Story of Brigham Young & the Mormons.* 1957. Viking. 1st. 389p. VG/VG. J2. $75.00

WEST, Rebecca. *Thinking Reed.* 1936. Viking. 1st. red cloth. F/dj. Q1. $75.00

WEST, Richard. *Gideon Welles: Lincoln's Navy Department.* 1943. 1st. 379p. O8. $23.50

WEST, Richard. *Mr Lincoln's Navy.* 1957. 1st. 328p. O8. $14.50

WEST, Wallace. *Bird of Time.* 1959. Gnome. 1st. VG/dj. P3. $25.00

WESTALL, Robert. *Rachel & the Angel.* 1986. Greenwillow. VG/dj. P3. $18.00

WESTBROOK, Robert. *Nostalgia Kills.* 1988. Crown. 1st. F/dj. P3. $18.00

WESTCOTT, Jan. *Hepburn.* 1950. Crown. 1st. VG/dj. P3. $15.00

WESTERHOFF. *McGuffey & His Readers: Piety, Morality & Education...* 1978. 206p. xl. VG/VG. A4. $45.00

WESTERMAN, Percy F. *Captain Cain.* 1939. Musson. G. P3. $10.00

WESTERMAN, Percy F. *White Arab.* nd. Blackie. ils Henry Coller. VG/dj. P3. $30.00

WESTERMANN, Diedrich. *Shilluk People, Their Language & Folklore.* 1970 (1912). Negro U. rpt. 312p. VG. W1. $35.00

WESTERMEIER, Clifford. *Man, Beast, Dust: The Story of Rodeo.* 1947. World. 1st. 450p. VG/VG. J2. $135.00

WESTERMEYER, Arthur J. *Udara, Prince of Bidur.* 1913. Dillingham. 1st. NF. M2. $35.00

WESTHEIMER, David. *Von Ryan's Express.* 1964. Doubleday. 1st. F/F. B4. $150.00

WESTHEIMER, David. *Von Ryan's Return.* 1980. London. Michael Joseph. 1st. inscr. A23. $45.00

WESTING, Fred. *Locomotives That Baldwin Built.* 1966. Bonanza. 191p. cloth. VG/dj. M20. $18.00

WESTLAKE, Donald. *Busy Body.* 1966. Broadman. 1st Eng ed. F/VG. M19. $75.00

WESTLAKE, Donald E. *Damsel.* 1967. Macmillan. 1st. VG/dj. P3. $75.00

WESTLAKE, Donald E. *Gangway!* 1986. Mysterious. 1st. NF/dj. P3. $18.00

WESTLAKE, Donald E. *High Adventure.* 1982. Mysterious. 1/250. sgn/#d. F/F. B11. $35.00

WESTLAKE, Donald E. *High Adventure.* 1985. Mysterious. 1st. NF/dj. P3. $20.00

WESTLAKE, Donald E. *I Know a Trick Worth Two of That.* 1986. Tor. 1st. F/F. T12. $20.00

WESTLAKE, Donald E. *Killy.* 1963. Random. 1st. VG/dj. P3. $75.00

WESTLAKE, Donald E. *Levine.* 1984. Mysterious. 1st. VG/dj. P3. $13.00

WESTLAKE, Donald E. *Point Blank.* 1984. Allison Busby. 1st. F/dj. P3. $25.00

WESTLAKE, Donald E. *Sacred Monster.* 1989. Mysterious. 1st. NF/dj. P3. $18.00

WESTLAKE, Donald E. *Score.* 1985. Allison Busby. 1st. NF/dj. P3. $20.00

WESTLAKE, Donald. *Slayground.* 1971. Random. ARC. inscr w/both names. F/VG. M19. $100.00

WESTLAKE, Donald E. *Somebody Owes Me Money.* 1969. Random. 1st. sgn. F/NF. M15. $45.00

WESTLAKE, Donald. *Split.* 1985. London. Allison Busby. 1st hc ed. AN/dj. M22. $25.00

WESTLAKE, Donald E. *Trust Me on This.* 1988. Mysterious. 1st. VG/dj. P3. $17.00

WESTLAKE, Donald E. *Up Your Banners.* 1969. Macmillan. 1st. F/dj. M15. $75.00

WESTON, Carolyn. *Rouse the Demon.* nd. Random. 2nd. VG/dj. P3. $8.00

WESTON, Edward. *Photographer: From a Motion Picture About Edward Weston.* ca 1946. Monterey. WT Lee Co. photos. 12p. wrp. D11. $200.00

WESTON, Garnett. *Hidden Portal.* 1946. Crime Club. 1st. VG/dj. P3. $20.00

WESTON, George. *His First Million Women.* 1934. Farrar. 1st. VG. M2. $30.00

WESTON, Jack. *Real American Cowboy.* 1985. New Amsterdam. 8vo. 267p. rem mk. F/wrp. T10. $12.00

WESTON & WILSON. *Cats of Wildcat Hill.* 1947. 1st. photos. VG/VG. M17. $100.00

WETMORE, Alexander. *Observations on the Birds of Northern Venezuela.* 1939. Smithsonian. 88p. VG. S15. $12.00

WETMORE, Claude. *Queen Magi's Little People.* 1913. St Louis. Curran. 1st. 8vo. tan cloth. R5. $75.00

WETMORE, Helen Cody. *Last of the Great Scouts: Buffalo Bill.* 1918. Grosset Dunlap. VG/dj. A19. $45.00

WEVERKA, Robert. *One Minute to Eternity.* 1968. Morrow. VG/VG. P3. $13.00

WEYER, Diane. *Assassin & the Deer.* 1989. Norton. 1st. F/F. H11. $30.00

WEYER, Edward. *Primitive Peoples Today.* 1958. Doubleday. 4to. 288p. F3. $20.00

WEYGOLDT, P. *Biology of Pseudoscorpions.* 1969. Harvard. ils. 145p. cloth. F/NF. M12. $25.00

WEYMOUTH, Richard F. *New Testament in Modern Speech.* 1929. Harper. 5th. 711p. G. B29. $9.00

WHALEN, Philip. *Memoirs of an Interglacial Age.* 1960. SF. Auehahn. 1st. F/wrp. B2. $45.00

WHALEN, Richard E. *Neural Control of Behavior.* 1970. NY. Academic. 301p. gr cloth. VG/dj. G1. $25.00

WHALEY, Gould. *William D Witliff & the Encino Press.* (1989). Dallas. Stillpoint. 1st. 1/500. quarter cloth/gilt label. M24. $75.00

WHALLEY, Joyce. *Cobwebs to Catch Flies: Illustrated Books for Nursery...* 1975. Berkeley. ils. 163p. F/F. A4. $65.00

WHALLEY, Joyce. *Cobwebs to Catch Flies: Illustrated Books for Nursery...* 1975. Berkeley. 1st. 8vo. 163p. bl cloth. NF/NF. D1. $60.00

WHALLEY, Peter. *Mortician's Birthday Party.* 1988. Walker. F/dj. P3. $20.00

WHALLEY, Peter. *Robbers.* 1986. Walker. 1st. F/dj. P3. $20.00

WHALLEY, Peter. *Rogues.* 1986. Walker. 1st. F/dj. P3. $20.00

WHARTON, Edith. *Certain People.* 1930. Appleton. 1st ed. 8vo. gilt bl cloth. VG. S9. $25.00

WHARTON, Edith. *Children.* 1928. Appleton. 1st ed. 346p. VG/dj. M20. $82.00

WHARTON, Edith. *Ethan Frome.* 1911. Scribner. 1st/1st prt/2nd bdg. teg. gilt red cloth. M24. $200.00

WHARTON, Edith. *Ghost Stories of...* 1973. Scribner. 1st. F/dj. M2. $35.00

WHARTON, Edith. *French Ways & Their Meaning.* 1919. London. Macmillan. 1st ed. F. B4. $45.00

WHARTON, Edith. *Gods Arrive.* 1932. NY. Appleton. 1st/1st prt/A bdg. gilt bl cloth. F/NF. M24. $200.00

WHARTON, Edith. *Hudson River Bracketed.* 1930. Appleton. 1st. F/dj. B4. $600.00

WHARTON, Edith. *Italian Villas & Their Gardens.* 1904. Bodley Head. 1st Eng ed. ils Parrish. A bdg (gr cloth). VG. B4. $750.00

WHARTON, Edith. *Madame de Treymes.* 1907. NY. 1st ed. NF. C6. $60.00

WHARTON, Edith. *Mother's Recompense.* 1925. Appleton. 1st ed. VG. B4. $125.00

WHARTON, Edith. *Touchstone.* 1900. Scribner. 1st/1st prt. teg. uncut. M24. $300.00

WHARTON, Edith. *Valley of Decision.* 1902. Scribner. 1st/2nd state. 2 vol. teg. cloth. NF. M24. $125.00

WHARTON, Edith. *Xingu.* 1916. Scribner. 1st. VG. Q1. $150.00

WHARTON, William. *Birdy.* 1979. Knopf. 1st. sgn. author's 1st book. F/NF. L3. $250.00

WHARTON, William. *Dad.* 1981. Knopf. 1st. author's 2nd book. F/NF. H11. $30.00

WHARTON, William. *Dad.* 1981. NY. 1st ed. F/clip. A17. $8.50

WHARTON, William. *Midnight Clear.* 1982. Knopf. 1st. F/NF. W2. $40.00

WHEATLEY, Dennis. *Bill for the Use of a Body.* 1964. Hutchinson. 1st. G/G. P3. $15.00

WHEATLEY, Dennis. *Dangerous Inheritance.* 1965. London. 1st. VG. M2. $12.00

WHEATLEY, Dennis. *Dark Secret of Josephine.* 1955. Hutchinson. 1st. VG/dj. P3. $30.00

WHEATLEY, Dennis. *Desperate Measures.* 1974. London. 1st. F/dj. M2. $25.00

WHEATLEY, Dennis. *Devil & All His Works.* 1971. ils. VG/VG. M17. $25.00

WHEATLEY, Dennis. *Gunmen, Gallants & Ghosts.* 1955. London. VG/dj. M2. $17.00

WHEATLEY, Dennis. *Malinsay Massacre.* 1986. Magnolia. F. P3. $15.00

WHEATLEY, Dennis. *Man Who Killed the King.* 1965. NY. 1st Am ed. dj. A17. $7.50

WHEATLEY, Dennis. *Shadow of Tyburn Tree.* 1953. London. VG. M2. $10.00

WHEATLEY, Dennis. *Strange Conflict.* 1952. Hutchinson. VG/dj. P3. $25.00

WHEATLEY, Dennis. *Sultan's Daughter.* 1963. Hutchinson. 1st. VG/dj. P3. $25.00

WHEATLEY, Dennis. *Uncharted Seas.* 1938. London. 1st. VG. M2. $30.00

WHEATLEY, Dennis. *Vendetta in Spain.* 1961. Hutchinson. 1st. VG/dj. P3. $15.00

WHEATLEY, Dennis. *Worlds Far From Here.* 1952. London. 1st. F/dj. M2. $30.00

WHEELER, Francis Rolt. *Boy With the US Survey.* 1909. Lee Shepard. 1st. 8vo. 2-tone cloth. G+. F7. $40.00

WHEELER, George M. *Report Upon US Geographical Surveys West of 100th Meridian.* 1787. GPO. Vol VI. 4to. cloth. A22. $150.00

WHEELER, Harold F. *Story of the British Navy.* 1922. London. Harrap. 1st. 8vo. 384p. gilt bl cloth. P4. $40.00

WHEELER, Harold F. *War in the Underseas.* 1919. London. Harrap. ils 319p. T7. $45.00

WHEELER, Kate. *Not Where I Started From.* 1993. Houghton Mifflin. 1st. sgn. author's 1st book. F/F. D10. $50.00

WHEELER, Keith. *Pacific Is My Beat.* 1943. NY. 1st. 383p. VG/poor. S16. $24.50

WHEELER, Opal. *Sing in Praise.* 1946. Dutton. 1st. ils Marjorie Torrey. Caldecott Honor. VG/dj. P2. $60.00

WHEELER, Richard. *Dodging Red Cloud: An Evans Novel of the West.* 1987. Evans. 1st ed. 12mo. F/F. T10. $10.00

WHEELER, Richard S. *Pagans in the Pulpit.* 1974. Arlington. 137p. VG/dj. B29. $6.50

WHEELER, William Morton. *Ants: Their Structure, Development & Behavior.* 1926 (1910). Columbia. 663p. cloth. VG+. M20. $50.00

WHELAN & WHELAN. *Making Sense Out of Sex: A New Look At Being a Man.* 1975. McGraw Hill. 1st. 178p. VG/dj. A25. $8.00

WHELEN, Townsend. *Why Not Load Your Own.* 1949. WA. 1st. ils. 216p. VG. B5. $30.00

WHELESS, Joseph. *Is It God's Word? An Exposition of Fables & Mythology...* 1926. Knopf. 474p. VG. S3. $30.00

WHELTON, Paul. *Angels Are Painted Fair.* 1947. Lippincott. 1st. NF/VG. M19. $25.00

WHELTON, Paul. *Women Are Skin Deep.* 1948. Lippincott. 1st. NF/VG. M19. $25.00

WHERRY, Edgar. *Southern Fern Guide.* 1964. Doubleday. 349p. dj. A10. $20.00

WHERRY, Joseph. *Indian Masks & Myths of the West.* 1969. NY. 1st ed. VG/VG. V4. $35.00

WHIDDEN, John D. *Ocean Life in the Old Sailing Ship Days.* 1908. Little Brn. 1st. sgn. 314p. bl cloth. G. B11. $45.00

WHIFFEN, Erwin Thomas. *Outing Lore.* 1928. NY. 1st. 185p. VG. A17. $20.00

WHIGHTMAN, W.P.D. *Growth of Scientific Ideas.* 1953. New Haven. 495p. A13. $15.00

WHIPPLE, Allen. *Evolution of Surgery in the United States.* 1963. Springfield. 1st. 180p. A13. $75.00

WHISTLER, W.A. *Ethnobotany of Tonga: Plants, Their Tongan Names & Uses.* 1991. Honolulu. Bishop Mus. 155p. F/wrp. B1. $35.00

WHISTON, Willima. *Life & Works of Flavius Josephus.* 1957. Winston. 1055p. G/partial. B29. $9.00

WHITAKER, Herman. *West Winds: California's Book of Fiction.* 1914. SF. Paul Elder. 1st. ils. G. O4. $45.00

WHITAKER, Muriel. *Stories From the Canadian North.* 1980. Edmonton. Hurtig. 191p. VG/dj. P4. $35.00

WHITALL, Henry. *Moveable Planisphere of the Heavens at Every Month.* 1871. Phillipsburg. 6th. M1. $275.00

WHITCOMB, Carrie Niles. *Reminiscences of the Springfield Women's Club 1884-1924.* ca 1925. Springfield, MA. 1st. ils. 218p. VG. A25. $25.00

WHITCOMB, Jon. *Coco, the Far-Out Poodle.* 1963. Random. 1st prt. VG/VG. B17. $10.00

WHITCOMBE, Rick Trader. *Savage Cinema.* nd. Bounty. F/dj. P3. $10.00

WHITE, A. *Come Next Spring.* 1990. Clarion. 1st ed. 8vo. 170p. NF/G+. T5. $20.00

WHITE, A. *Golden Sunbeams for the Young People.* 1956. Zarephath. 6th. 135p. VG. A17. $8.50

WHITE, A. *Stapelieae.* 1937. Pasadena. 3 vol. 2nd. 39 mc pl/1233 photos/drawings. VG. B26. $375.00

WHITE, A.R. *Succulent Euphorbieae.* 1941. Pasadena. 2 vol. photos/pl/drawings. new buckram. F. B26. $425.00

WHITE, Alma. *Story of My Life. Vol 1.* 1919. Pillar of Fire. 392p. G. B29. $16.00

WHITE, Anne Terry. *George Washington Carver, Story of a Great American.* 1953. Random. 2nd. sm 8vo. F/NF. C8. $17.50

WHITE, Barbara. *Growing Up Female.* 1985. lists 275 novels. 273p. F/F. A4. $35.00

WHITE, Barbara. *Lady Leatherneck.* 1945. NY. 180p. VG. S16. $28.50

WHITE, Charles. *Life & Times of Little Richard.* 1984. Harmony. dj. A19. $18.00

WHITE, Colin. *World of the Nursery.* 1984. 4to. ils. 224p. F/F. A4. $55.00

WHITE, David. *Flora of the Hermit Shale, Grand Canyon, Arizona.* 1929. Carnegie Inst. 8vo. 221p. stiff tan wrp. F7. $75.00

WHITE, E.B. *Annotated Charlotte's Web.* 1994. Harper Collins. AP. 8vo. NF/wrp. S9. $25.00

WHITE, E.B. *Charlotte's Web.* 1952. Harper Row. 1st. ils Garth William. G+/VG-. M17. $150.00

WHITE, E.B. *Chrlotte's Web.* 1952. NY. Harper. 1st. F/VG. B4. $675.00

WHITE, E.B. *Essays of EB White.* 1977. Harper. 1st. inscr/dtd 1979. F/VG. B4. $600.00

WHITE, E.B. *Letters of EB White.* 1976. Harper. 1st. sgn tipped-in leaf. F/NF. B2. $45.00

WHITE, E.B. *One Man's Meat.* 1942. NY. 1st. VG/VG. B5. $35.00

WHITE, E.B. *Stuart Little.* 1945. Harper. 1st. ils Garth Williams. VG/G. M22. $125.00

WHITE, Edmund. *Beautiful Room Is Empty.* 1988. Knopf. 1st. VG/dj. P3. $18.00

WHITE, Edmund. *Genet: A Biography.* 1993. Knopf. 1st ed. AN/dj. C2. $35.00

WHITE, Eliza Orne. *Patty Makes a Visit.* 1939. Houghton Mifflin. 1st. ils Helen Blair. 133p. F/VG-. P2. $25.00

WHITE, Eliza Orne. *When Esther Was a Little Girl.* 1944. Houghton Mifflin. 1st ed. inscr. 141p. VG/G+. P2. $40.00

WHITE, Ethel Lina. *Step in the Dark.* 1946. Books Inc. VG. P3. $13.00

WHITE, Ethel Lina. *Wax.* 1935. Doubleday Crime Club. 1st ed. NF/VG+. B4. $200.00

WHITE, F. *Panorama of the Tabernacle & Its Service.* nd. London. 12 chromos. G+. E6. $75.00

WHITE, Frank. *Overview Effect.* 1987. Houghton Mifflin. lg 8vo. 318p. Vg/dj. K5. $20.00

WHITE, Gleason. *English Illustration. The Sixties: 1855-70.* 1897. London. Constable. 4to. ils/5 pl. teg. gilt bdg. VG. B24. $125.00

WHITE, Harvey Elliott. *Intro to Atomic Spectra.* 1934. NY. 457p. A17. $10.00

WHITE, Henry A. *Robert E Lee & the Southern Confederacy.* 1911. NY. ils/index/ads. 467p. G. B5. $50.00

WHITE, J. Samuel. *Shipbuilding.* nd. London. Albion. folio. ils. rebacked. T7. $125.00

WHITE, J.F. *Study of the Earth.* 1962. Prentice Hall. 2nd. 408p. F/dj. D8. $15.00

WHITE, J.E. Grant. *Designing a Garden Today.* 1966. NY. 1st Am. ils/pl. 184p. VG+/dj. B26. $22.00

WHITE, James. *Genocidal Healer.* nd. BC. F/dj. P3. $8.00

WHITE, James. *Life Span & Reminiscences of Railway Mail Service.* 1973. Bl Letter. facsimile of 1904 ed. 1/500. F. A17. $30.00

WHITE, James. *Watch Below.* 1966. Walker. 1st. VG/dj. P3. $40.00

WHITE, John. *United States Marines in North China.* 1974. Millbrae. 1st. sgn. ils/map. 217p. VG/VG. S16. $50.00

WHITE, Joseph J. *Cranberry Culture.* 1909. Orange Judd. new/enlarged. ils. 12mo. 131p. cloth. K3. $30.00

WHITE, Joseph J. *Cranberry Culture.* 1916. Orange Judd. 131p. F. A10. $32.00

WHITE, Lionel. *To Find a Killer.* 1954. Dutton. 1st. VG/dj. P3. $40.00

WHITE, Margaret Bourke. *For the World to See: The Life of...* 1983. Viking. 1st. F/dj. Q1. $40.00

WHITE, Margaret Bourke. *Portrait of Myself.* 1963. NY. 1st ed. sgn. F/NF. A17. $100.00

WHITE, Margaret Bourke. *They Called It Purple Heart Valley.* 1944. NY. 1st ed. VG/VG. B5. $40.00

WHITE, Randall. *Salute to the Marines.* 1943. NY. 210p. VG. S16. $22.50

WHITE, Randy Wayne. *Batfishing in the Rainforest.* 1991. NY. Burford. 1st. sgn. F/F. B3. $175.00

WHITE, Randy Wayne. *Heat Islands.* 1992. St Martin. 1st. sgn. author's 3rd book. F/F. M15. $100.00

WHITE, Randy Wayne. *Sanibel Flats.* 1990. St Martin. 1st. VG+/VG+. M22. $425.00

WHITE, Richard G. *New Gospel of Peace According to St Benjamin.* 1863-1864. NY. 4 parts in 1. NF. M8. $350.00

WHITE, Steve. *Privileged Information.* 1991. Viking. 1st. author's 1st novel. F/F. M22. $20.00

WHITE, Stewart Edward. *African Camp Fires.* 1913. Doubleday Page. 1st ed. 8vo. VG. T10. $50.00

WHITE, Stewart Edward. *Arizona Nights.* nd. Grosset Dunlap. G. P3. $10.00

WHITE, Stewart Edward. *Conjuror's House.* 1903. McClure Phillips. A19. $30.00

WHITE, Stewart Edward. *Daniel Boone: Wilderness Scout.* (1922). Garden City. later prt. 274p. NF. C14. $10.00

WHITE, Stewart Edward. *Folded Hills.* 1934. Doubleday Doran. A19. $20.00

WHITE, Stewart Edward. *Land of Footprints.* ca 1920. Thomas Nelson. ils/photos. 462p. gilt brn cloth. VG. T10. $50.00

WHITE, Stewart Edward. *Leopard Woman.* 1916. Doubleday. 1st. VG. M2. $25.00

WHITE, Stewart Edward. *On Tiptoe.* 1922. Doran. A19. $25.00

WHITE, Stewart Edward. *Riverman.* 1908. NY. McClure. ils NC Wyeth. A19. $35.00

WHITE, Stewart Edward. *Rules of the Game.* 1911. Thomas Nelson. A19. $15.00

WHITE, T.H. *America in Search of Itself.* 1982. Harper Row. 1st. 465p. VG. W2. $30.00

WHITE, T.H. *Book of Merlyn.* 1977. TX U. 1st. F/dj. M2. $30.00

WHITE, T.H. *Mistress Masham's Repose.* 1946. Putnam. VG/dj. M2. $15.00

WHITE, T.H. *Once & Future King.* 1958. Putnam. 1st Am. F/NF. T12. $200.00

WHITE, T.H. *Verses.* 1962. London. Alderney. 1st. 1/100. inscr. Japanese vellum/cloth. NF/sans. B4. $850.00

WHITE, T.H. *Witch in the Wood.* 1939. Putnam. 1st. VG/dj. M2. $50.00

WHITE, Ted. *Trouble on Project Ceres.* 1971. Westminster. 1st. xl. VG/dj. P3. $8.00

WHITE, Teri. *Bleeding Hearts.* 1984. Mysterious. 1st. NF/NF. P3. $20.00

WHITE, Teri. *Thursday's Child.* 1991. Mysterious. 1st. NF/dj. P3. $20.00

WHITE, Walter. *Man Called White.* 1948. Viking. 1st. VG. M25. $15.00

WHITE, William. *Pale Blonde of Sands Street.* 1946. Viking. 1st. VG/dj. M2. $20.00

WHITEHEAD, Don. *Journey Into Crime.* 1960. Random. 1st ed. VG/VG. M22. $12.00

WHITEHEAD, Hal. *Voyage to the Whales.* 1990. Post Mills. Chelsea Gr. 195p. 8vo. F/dj. P4. $35.00

WHITEHEAD, Jessup. *Steward's Handbook & Guide to Party Catering in 5 Parts.* 1889. 1st. lg 8vo. 500 double-column p. VG. E6. $65.00

WHITEHEAD, John. *Religious Apartheid: Separation of Religion...* 1994. Moody. sgn. 318p. F. B29. $7.00

WHITEHEAD, John. *Solemn Mockery: Art of Literary Forgery.* 1973. London. Arlington. 1st. ils. 177p. F/VG. K3. $50.00

WHITEHEAD, Paul. *Manners: A Satire.* 1739. London. Dodsley. 1st. sm folio. 20p. recent marbled wrp. H13. $265.00

WHITELEY, George. *Northern Seas, Hardy Sailors.* 1982. NY. Norton. 1st. 8vo. 270p. half cloth. VG/dj. P4. $35.00

WHITELOCK, Dorothy. *Anglo-Saxon Wills.* 1930. Cambridge. gilt olive cloth. M11. $150.00

WHITFIELD, Nella. *Kitchen Encyclopedia.* nd. London. Spring Books. G/torn. A16. $25.00

WHITFIELD, Raoul. *Wings of Gold.* 1930. Phil. Penn. 1st. F/VG. B4. $1,250.00

WHITFORD, David. *Extra Innings.* 1991. Burlinghame. 1st ed. F/F. P8. $20.00

WHITFORD, Genevieve Smith. *Sound of the Harp.* 1987. Harp Pr. sgn. 8vo. 52p. F/VG. B11. $10.00

WHITFORD, William. *Art Stories for Young Children. Book Two.* (1934). Reilly Lee. 1st ed thus. 168p. VG. B22. $5.50

WHITLEY, M.J. *German Coastal Fores of World War Two.* 1992. London. Ams/Armour. 191p. dj. T7. $40.00

WHITLOCK, V.H. *Cowboy Life on the Llano Estacado.* 1970. Norman, OK. 1st. photos. 278p. VG/VG. J2. $135.00

WHITMAN, Royal. *Treatise on Orthopaedic Surgery.* 1901. Phil. 1st. 650p. A13. $100.00

WHITMAN, Ruth. *Marriage Wig.* 1968. HBW. 1st ed. F/NF. V1. $10.00

WHITMAN, S.E. *Troopers.* 1962. Hastings. dj. A19. $35.00

WHITMAN, Walt. *Complete Prose Works.* 1892. McKay. 1st. VG. B4. $125.00

WHITMAN, Walt. *Franklin Evans; or, The Inebriate: A Tale of the Times.* 1929. Random. 1st hc ed. author's 1st book/only novel. 1/700. NF. B4. $200.00

WHITMAN, Walt. *Half-Breed & Other Stories.* 1927. NY. Columbia. 1st ed/A prt. 1/155. ils Allen Lewis. B18. $195.00

WHITMAN, Walt. *Leaves of Grass.* 1881-1882. Boston. Osgood. 1st prt (of 3). mustard cloth. F. M23. $500.00

WHITMAN, Walt. *Leaves of Grass.* 1913. NY/London. Dutton/Dent. folio. ils Margaret Cook. gr brd. NF. M23. $225.00

WHITMAN, Walt. *Leaves of Grass.* 1920 (1855). Grollier. facsimile (2nd issue). 1/500. gilt gr cloth. M24. $200.00

WHITMAN, Walt. *Poems.* 1868. London. John Camden Hotten. 1st. bl cloth (primary bdg). M24. $450.00

WHITMORE, Charles. *Winter's Daughter.* 1984. Timescape. 1st. VG/dj. P3. $15.00

WHITNEY, Alec. *Armstrong.* 1977. Crime Club. F/dj. P3. $13.00

WHITNEY, C.S. *Bridges: Study in Their Art, Science & Evolution.* 1929. NY. 400 pl. 363p. NF/frayed. M4. $65.00

WHITNEY, Harry. *Hunting With the Eskimos: Unique Record of Sportsman's Year.* 1910. NY. Century. 1st. photos. 453p. teg. VG. H7. $120.00

WHITNEY, J.P. *Silver Mining Regions of Colorado.* 1865. Van Nostrand. 1st. 12mo. 107p. prt wrp. M1. $1,050.00

WHITNEY, Leon F. *How to Breed Dogs.* 1937. NY. 1st ed. ils. 338p. bl cloth. VG. B14. $45.00

WHITNEY, Milton. *Field Operations of the Bureau of Soils.* 1910. WA. USDA. 1772p. G. A17. $35.00

WHITRIDGE, Arnold. *No Compromise!* 1960. FSC. 1st. 212p. VG/dj. M20. $35.00

WHITTAKER, Frederick W. *Samuel Harris, American Theologian.* 1982. Vintage. 268p. VG/dj. B29. $10.00

WHITTEMORE, Edward. *Jericho Mosaic.* 1987. Norton. 1st. NF/dj. M25. $25.00

WHITTEN, Leslie H. *Moon of the Wolf.* 1967. Doubleday Crime Club. 1st. Harlan Ellison's copy. F/F. M15. $100.00

WHITTIER, John Greenleaf. *At Sundown.* 1892. Houghton Mifflin. VG. M19. $25.00

WHITTIER, John Greenleaf. *Declaration of Sentiments of American Anti-Slavery Society.* 1844. NY. Wm S Dorr. early leaflet prt. F. M24. $200.00

WHITTIER, John Greenleaf. *Early Poems of...* 1885. Boston. Houghton Mifflin. 1st ed. gilt navy cloth. NF. V1. $20.00

WHITTIER, John Greenleaf. *History of Pennsylvania Hall.* 1838. Phil. Merrihew Gunn. 1st/1st issue. ES. M24. $450.00

WHITTIER, John Greenleaf. *In War Time & Other Poems.* 1864. Ticknor Fields. 1st ed/1st state. teg. NF. T10. $200.00

WHITTIER, John Greenleaf. *Literary Recreations & Miscellanies.* 1854. Ticknor Fields. 1st/1st catalogue. 1/1500. gilt brn cloth. F. M24. $85.00

WHITTIER, John Greenleaf. *Pennsylvania Pilgrim.* 1872. 1st/1st state. F. M19. $65.00

WHITTIER, John Greenleaf. *Tent on the Beach & Other Poems.* 1867. Ticknor Fields. 1st/earliest state (N on p172). 12mo. gilt gr cloth. VG. H1. $145.00

WHITTINGHAM, C.P. *Mechanism of Photosynthesis.* 1974. London. Arnold. 125p. stiff wrp. B1. $18.50

WHITTINGTON, Harry. *Bonanza: Treachery Trail.* 1968. Whitman. TVTI. VG. P3. $20.00

WHITTLE, Frank. *Jet: The Story of a Pioneer.* 1953. London. Frederick Muller. 1st. ils. 8vo. 32p. K3. $15.00

WHITTMAN, George. *Matter of Intelligence.* 1975. Macmillan. 1st. F/dj. P3. $15.00

WHITTON, Blair. *Paper Toys of the World.* 1986. Hobby House. obl 4to. 240p. T10. $25.00

WHYMPER, Edward. *Scrambles Amongst the Alps.* 1986. Salt Lake City. 262p. F/dj. A17. $20.00

WHYTE, Frederic. *William Heinemann, a Memoir.* 1929. Doubleday Doran. 326p. G. B18. $17.50

WIATER, Stanley. *After the Darkness.* 1993. Maclay. 1st ed. 1/750. sgn all 18 contributors. F/case. G10. $40.00

WIBBERLEY, Leonard. *Hound of the Sea.* 1969. NY. Washburn. 152p. dj. T7. $20.00

WIBERLEY, Leonard. *Young Man From the Piedmont.* 1965 (1963). FSG/Ariel. 3rd. 8vo. 184p. xl. VG. T5. $18.00

WICKENDEN, L. *Make Friends With Your Land.* 1949. Devin Adair. 132p. cloth. VG. A10. $20.00

WICKERSHAM, James. *Old Yukon Tales, Trails, Trials.* 1973. St Paul. 514p. F. A17. $30.00

WIDDEMER, Mabel Cleland. *Aleck Bell, Ingenious Boy.* 1947. Bobbs Merrill. 1st. 8vo. orange prt cloth. T10. $50.00

WIDEMAN, John Edgar. *Fever.* 1989. NY. Holt. 1st. F/dj. A24/B3. $25.00

WIDEMAN, John Edgar. *Reuben.* 1987. Henry Holt. 1st. sgn. F/F. D10. $50.00

WIDEMAN, John Edgar. *Reuben.* 1987. Holt. 1st. F/F. T11. $30.00

WIDEMAN, John Edgar. *Sent for You Yesterday.* 1984. Allison Busby. 1st. author's 3rd book. F/NF. B3. $25.00

WIDTSOE, J. *Dry Farming: A System of Agriculture for Countries...* 1912 (1911). ils. VG. E6. $25.00

WIEDERSHEIM, Robert. *Elements of Comparative Anatomy of Vertebrates.* 1897. London. 2nd. 488p. A13. $65.00

WIEGAND, Wayne A. *History of a Hoax: Edmund Lester Pearson...* 1979. Pittsburgh. Beta Phi Mu. 1st. ils. 8vo. 75p. F. K3. $25.00

WIEGERT, W.J. *Lords of the Leaf.* 1988. NY. Carlton. 1st ed. author's 1st book. F/F. H11. $25.00

WIENER, Leo. *Commentary to the Germanic Laws & Medieval Documents.* 1915. Cambridge. M11. $85.00

WIENER, Norbert. *Ex-Prodigy: My Childhood & Youth.* 1953. S&S. 2nd. ils. 309p. VG/dj. K3. $15.00

WIENER, Willard. *Two Hundred Thousand Flyers.* 1945. WA. Infantry Journal. 1st. 196p. VG/dj. B18. $37.50

WIER, Ester. *What Every Air Force Wife Should Know.* 1963. Stackpole. 2nd. 227p. VG/VG. A25. $20.00

WIESE, C. *Expedition in East-Central Africa 1888-91.* 1983. OK U. 1st. photos/maps. 383p. F/dj. M4. $30.00

WIESEL, Elie. *Beggar in Jerusalem.* 1970. Random. 1st. F/F. B35. $18.00

WIESEL, Elie. *Golem.* 1983. Summit. 1st ed. F/F. B35. $35.00

WIESEL, Elie. *Testament.* 1981. Summit. 1st ed. NF/F. B35. $30.00

WIESS, John. *Trail Cooking.* 1981. Van Nostrand Reinhold. 323p. VG/VG. B10. $10.00

WIGGIN, Kate Douglas. *Affair at the Inn.* Sept 1904. Houghton Mifflin. 1st. 220p. VG. H1. $22.50

WIGGIN, Kate Douglas. *Bird's Christmas Carol.* 1912. Houghton Mifflin. 1st ed thus. ils Katharine Wireman. gr cloth. VG/VG. D1. $125.00

WIGGIN, Kate Douglas. *Bluebeard, a Humorous Musical Fantasy.* 1914. Harper. 1st ed. 16mo. NF/G. C8. $200.00

WIGGIN, Kate Douglas. *Cathedral Courtship.* 1893. 1st. ils Carleton. VG. M19. $35.00

WIGGIN, Kate Douglas. *Diary of a Goose Girl.* 1902. Houghton Mifflin/Riverside. 1st. ils Claude Shepperson. B15. $55.00

WIGGIN, Kate Douglas. *Pinafore Palace: Book of Rhymes for the Nursery.* 1907. McClure. edit Sara Smith. VG. B15. $70.00

WIGGIN, Kate Douglas. *Rebecca of Sunnybrook Farm.* 1903. Houghton Mifflin. 1st ed. F. M19. $175.00

WIGGINS, Marianne. *Gone South.* 1980. Delacorte. 1st. F/F. B4. $175.00

WIJNGAARDS, John. *Handbook to the Gospels.* 1979. Servant Books. 301p. F/dj. B29. $7.50

WILBUR, Richard. *Bestiary.* 1983 (1955). rpt. ils Alexander Calder. VG/VG. M17. $20.00

WILBUR, Richard. *Ceremony & Other Poems.* 1950. NY. 1st ed. VG/VG. B5. $90.00

WILBUR, Richard. *Tartuffe.* 1964. London. Faber. trans/sgn Wilbur. F/NF. V1. $50.00

WILBUR, Richard. *Walking to Sleep.* 1969. Harcourt Brace. 1st ed. sgn. F/NF. V1. $45.00

WILCOX, Collin. *Bernhardt's Edge.* 1988. Tor. 1st. NF/dj. P3. $18.00

WILCOX, Collin. *Disappearance.* 1970. Random. 1st. sgn. VG/VG. M19. $25.00

WILCOX, James. *Modern Baptists.* 1983. Dial. 1st ed. F/F. B4. $100.00

WILCOX, Sylvia. *For Every Hero: Novel of Waves in World War II.* 1961. NY. McKay. 1st. 346p. VG/dj. A25. $22.00

WILCOX. *Japan's Secret War.* 1985. 1st. dj. K3. $25.00

WILD, Peter. *Pioneer Conservationists of Western America.* 1979. Missoula. 246p. dj. A10. $22.00

WILDE, Oscar. *Ballad of Reading Gaol.* 1905. Portland, ME. Mosher. 12mo. 34p+16p end blanks. VG. K7. $95.00

WILDE, Oscar. *Birthday of the Infanta.* 1929. Macmillan. 1st. ils Pamela Bianco. 58p. gray cloth. VG/dj. D1. $85.00

WILDE, Oscar. *Fisherman & His Soul & Other Fairy Tales.* 1929. Farrar Rhinehart. 8vo. 212p. bl cloth. VG. K7. $60.00

WILDE, Oscar. *Happy Prince & Other Tales.* 1940. Winston. 1st ed thus. 148p. VG/G. P2. $38.00

WILDE, Oscar. *House of Pomegranates.* 1926. Dodd Mead. 1st thus. 180p. VG+. K7. $60.00

WILDE, Oscar. *Picture of Doran Gray.* 1957. LEC. 1st thus. 1/1500. ils/sgn Lucille Corcos. F/remnant glassine/case. Q1. $200.00

WILDE, Oscar. *Picture of Dorian Gray.* 1945. Tower. 4th. VG/dj. P3. $20.00

WILDE, Oscar. *Poems.* 1881. Boston. Roberts Bros. 1st Am/1st bdg (cherub). gilt brn cloth. M24. $250.00

WILDE, Oscar. *Poems.* 1881. London. David Bogue. 1st. gilt full vegetable vellum. M24. $850.00

WILDE, Oscar. *Portrait of Mr WH.* 1921. NY. Mitchell Kennerley. 1/1000. sm 8vo. 133p. M/NF case. K7. $125.00

WILDE, Oscar. *Salome: A Tragedy in One Act.* 1907. Boston. John W Luce. early pirated ed. 36p. gilt blk cloth. K7. $125.00

WILDE, Oscar. *Salome: A Tragedy in One Act.* 1930. Dutton. new ed. 17 ils. bl cloth. VG. K7. $65.00

WILDE, Oscar. *Selfish Giant.* 1980. Issaquah, WA. Archive. 1/135. sgn at colophon. unp. w/prospectus. as new/wrp. K7. $95.00

WILDE, Oscar. *Selfish Giant.* 1986. S&S. 1st Am thus. 8vo. unp. F/NF. C14. $15.00

WILDE, Percival. *P Moran, Operative.* 1947. Random. 1st. F/F. M15. $45.00

WILDER, Billy. *Apartment & the Fortune Cookie: Two Screenplays.* 1971. 1st. NF/NF. S13. $20.00

WILDER, Gerrit Parmile. *Fruits of the Hawaiian Islands.* 1911 (1906). Honolulu. revised ed. 247p. tan buckram/red leather label. B26. $75.00

WILDER, Laura Ingalls. *Farmer Boy.* (1933). Harper. not 1st. ils Helen Sewell. VG. M5. $75.00

WILDER, Laura Ingalls. *Farmer Boy.* (1933). Harper. 10th. ils Helen Sewell. VG. C8. $30.00

WILDER, Laura Ingalls. *Little House in the Big Woods.* 1953. Harper. 1st ed thus. ils Garth Williams. VG/G. M5. $40.00

WILDER, Laura Ingalls. *Little House on the Prairie.* (1935). Eau Claire, WI. EM Hale. rpt. lg 12mo. ils Helen Sewell. G. C8. $45.00

WILDER, Laura Ingalls. *Little Town on the Prairie.* (1941). Harper. 7th. ils Helen Sewell. VG/VG. C8. $45.00

WILDER, Laura Ingalls. *On the Banks of Plum Creek.* 1937. Harper. 1st. ils Sewell/Boyle. 8vo. 239p. tan cloth. R5. $250.00

WILDER, Louise Beebe. *Adventures in My Garden & Rock Garden.* 1925 (1923). Garden City. ils/pl/halftones. 355p. VG. B26. $35.00

WILDER, Louise Beebe. *Colour in My Garden.* 1927. NY. sgn. pl. VG. M17. $25.00

WILDER, Louise B. *Garden in Color.* 1937. NY. 327p. cloth. B26. $27.50

WILDER, Louise B. *My Garden.* 1916. Garden City. 1st ed. 308p. decor cloth. B26. $27.50

WILDER, Thornton. *Bridge of San Luis Rey.* 1927. London. Longman. 1st. 8vo. bl brd. G. M23. $30.00

WILDER, Thornton. *Bridge of San Luis Rey.* 1927. NY. Boni. 1st. 8vo. cloth. NF. M23. $65.00

WILDER, Thornton. *Eighth Day.* 1967. Harper Row. 1st. NF/VG. B35. $16.00

WILDER, Thornton. *Ides of March.* 1948. Harper. 1st. F/VG. M19. $35.00

WILDER, Thornton. *Theophilus North.* 1973. Harper Row. 1/275. sgn/#d. F/dj/case. M25. $100.00

WILDER, Thornton. *Woman of Andros.* 1930. Boni. 1st ed. F/VG. M19. $75.00

WILDES, Harry Emerson. *Voice of the Lord: Biography of George Fox.* 1965. Phil. 1st. 473p. VG/dj. V3. $20.00

WILDING, Philip. *Spaceflight Venus.* 1955. Philosophical Lib. 1st. xl. VG. P3. $10.00

WILDSMITH, Brian. *Birds.* 1967. London. Oxford. 1st. obl sm 4to. NF/NF. C8. $25.00

WILDSMITH, Brian. *Hare & the Tortoise.* 1966. London. Oxford. 1st. sm 4to. VG+/NF. C8. $35.00

WILDSMITH, Brian. *Maurice Maeterlinck's Blue Bird.* 1976. Franklin Watts. 1st. ils Wildsmith. 37p. VG/dj. M20. $30.00

WILDSMITH, Brian. *Owl & the Woodpecker.* 1971. Oxford. 1st. ils. 4to. NF/F. P2. $50.00

WILDSMITH, Brian. *Python's Party.* 1974. London. Oxford. 1st. ils. 4to. NF/VG+. P2. $60.00

WILEY, Bell Irvin. *Embattled Confederates.* 1964. Bonanza. VG/dj. A19. $45.00

WILEY, Bell Irvin. *Embattled Confederates.* 1964. Bonanza. 290p. VG. O8. $14.50

WILEY, Hugh. *Manchu Blood.* 1927. Knopf. 1st. F/VG. B4. $100.00

WILEY, John L. *History of Monrovia.* 1927. Pasadena. Star-News. ils. 291p. cloth. D11. $100.00

WILEY, Richard. *Festival for Three Thousand Maidens.* 1991. Dutton. 1st. F/F. B4. $65.00

WILEY, Richard. *Fool's Gold.* 1988. Knopf. 1st. F/F. B4. $50.00

WILHELM, Kate. *Clewiston Test.* 1976. FSG. 1st. VG/dj. P3. $15.00

WILHELM, Kate. *Hamlet Trap.* 1987. St Martin. 1st. NF/dj. P3. $16.00

WILHELM, Kate. *Huysman's Pets.* 1986. Bluejay. 1st. F/dj. M2. $20.00

WILHELM, Kate. *Juniper Time.* 1979. Harper Row. 1st. VG/dj. P3. $20.00

WILHELM, Kate. *More Bitter Than Death.* 1963. S&S. 1st. NF/dj. M2. $65.00

WILHELM, Kate. *Somerset Dreams.* 1978. Harper Row. 1st. F/dj. P3. $20.00

WILHELM, Kate. *Welcome, Chaos.* 1983. Houghton Mifflin. 1st. F/dj. P3. $15.00

WILK, Max. *And Did You Once See Sidney Plain?* 1986. NY. Norton. 1st. F/F. B4. $45.00

WILKES, Charles. *Narrative of the United States Exploring Expedition Vol IV.* 1845. Phil. Lee Blanchard. ils/maps. half leather. worn. K3. $80.00

WILKINS, Cary. *Treasury of Fantasy.* 1981. Avenel. 1st. F/dj. M2/P3. $15.00

WILKINS, Harold. *Mysteries of Ancient South America.* 1956. Citadel. 1st Am. photos/drawings. 216p. dj. F3. $25.00

WILKINS, Mary E. *Jerome: A Poor Man.* 1897. Harper. 1st. 506p. gilt bl cloth. VG. M20. $20.00

WILKINS, W.G. *Charles Dickens in America.* 1911. Scribner. 1st. gilt lavender cloth. uncut. M24. $100.00

WILKINSON, Bud. *Oklahoma Split Football.* 1952. Prentice Hall. 1st. sgn. photos. VG. P8. $45.00

WILKINSON, Doug. *Land of the Long Day.* 1956. London/Toronto. Harrap/Clarke Irwin. 8vo. 261p. map ep. NF/dj. P4. $40.00

WILKINSON, Frederick. *Collecting Military Antiques.* 1984. London. 208p. VG+/dj. B18. $25.00

WILKINSON, Helen Hunscher. *Gates Mills & a History of Its Village Church.* 1955. Gates Mills. 1st ed. sgn. ils. 123p. VG/dj. B18. $22.50

WILKINSON, Henry C. *Adventures of Bermuda: A History of Island...* 1958. 2nd. ils/fld pocket map. VG/G+. M17. $25.00

WILKINSON, Roderick. *Murder Belongs to Me!* 1956. Museum Pr. 1st. VG/dj. P3. $20.00

WILLARD, Barbara. *Surprise Land.* 1966. Meredith. 1st ed. 8vo. 110p. xl. VG. T5. $12.00

WILLARD, Barbara. *Three & One to Carry.* 1965 (1964). HBW. 1st Am. 8vo. 197p. VG/G+. T5. $25.00

WILLARD, Nancy. *Ballad of Biddy Early.* 1987. Knopf. 1st. 4to. unp. NF/VG. T5. $35.00

WILLARD, Nancy. *Ballad of Biddy Early.* 1989. Knopf. 1st. ils/sgn Barry Moser. F/F. B3. $45.00

WILLARD, Nancy. *Childhood of the Magician.* 1973. Liveright. 1st. author's 1st book. F/NF. B3. $75.00

WILLARD, Nancy. *East of the Sun & West of the Moon.* 1989. HBJ. 1st. ils Barry Moser. F/F. B3. $30.00

WILLARD, Nancy. *East of the Sun & West of the Moon.* 1989. HBJ. 1st. 64p. VG+/VG. M20. $25.00

WILLARD, Nancy. *Visit to William Blake's Inn.* nd (1982). Methuen Children's Books. possible 1st. 45p. NF/VG. C14. $25.00

WILLARD, Wyeth. *Leathernecks Come Through.* 1944. NY. 224p. VG. S16. $25.00

WILLARD, X.A. *Practical Butter Book: A Complete Treatise.* 1875. NY. Rural. 171p. VG. A10. $45.00

WILLCOX, William B. *Portrait of a General: Sir Henry Clinton...* 1964. Knopf. 1st. 526p. VG/clip. M20. $40.00

WILLEFORD, Charles. *Burnt Orange Heresy.* 1971. Crown. 2nd. 2nd. NF/clip. P3. $45.00

WILLEFORD, Charles. *Cockfighter Journal.* 1989. Neville. 1st. 1/300. sgn/#d. F/sans. M15. $100.00

WILLEFORD, Charles. *Miami Blues.* 1984. St Martin. 1st. F/F. D10. $175.00

WILLEFORD, Charles. *Myth of Shakespeare.* 1928. Oxford. 1st. NF. B4. $200.00

WILLEFORD, Charles. *Off the Wall.* 1980. Montclair. Pegasus Rex. 1st. F/F. M15. $200.00

WILLEFORD, Charles. *Shark-Infested Custard.* 1993. Underwood Miller. 1st ed. F/F. T2. $25.00

WILLEFORD, Charles. *Way We Die Now.* 1988. Hastings-On-Hudson. Ultramarine. 1st. 1/99 special bdg. sgn. F/sans. M15. $150.00

WILLEFORD, Charles. *Way We Die Now.* 1989. London. Gollancz. 1st. F/dj. P3. $25.00

WILLENS, Doris. *Lonesome Traveler: Life of Lee Hays.* 1988. Norton. 1st. VG/VG. V4. $15.00

WILLET, B. *Blood River: Passionate History of South Africa.* 1982. NY. 1st. photos. 255p. F/dj. M4. $15.00

WILLETS, Gilson. *First Law.* 1911. Dillingham. 1st. VG. M2. $22.00

WILLETS, William. *Chinese Art.* 1958. Braziller. 2 vol. 12mo. F/VG case. H1. $35.00

WILLETT, George. *Birds of the Pacific Slope of Southern California.* 1912. Cooper Ornithological Club. 122p. S15. $12.00

WILLETT, John. *Art & Politics in the Weimar Period: New Sobriety...1933.* 1978. Pantheon. 1st Am. 272p. dj. A17. $25.00

WILLIAMS, Alan. *Presence.* 1983. Knopf. 1st ed. F/NF. V1. $10.00

WILLIAMS, Alan. *Shah-Mak.* 1976. CMG. 1st. F/dj. P3. $18.00

WILLIAMS, Alan. *Snake Water.* 1965. London. Anthony Blond. 1st. F/F. M15. $45.00

WILLIAMS, Barbara. *Whatever Happened to Beverly Bigler's Birthday?* 1979. Harcourt Brace. 1st. 8vo. VG. C8. $17.50

WILLIAMS, Ben Ames. *Happy End.* 1991. Derrydale. 1/2500. gilt leather. F. A17. $22.50

WILLIAMS, Ben Ames. *House Divided.* 1947. Houghton Mifflin. 1st. F/NF. H11. $25.00

WILLIAMS, Ben Ames. *Pirate's Purchase.* 1931. NY. 1st ed. NF/dj. A17. $15.00

WILLIAMS, Beryl. *Young Faces in Fashion.* 1956. Phil. Lippincott. VG. D2. $15.00

WILLIAMS, C.K. *Flesh & Blood.* 1987. FSG. F/dj. V1. $35.00

WILLIAMS, C.K. *Lies.* 1969. Houghton Mifflin. 1st. poet's 1st book. wrp. V1. $100.00

WILLIAMS, Charles. *Aground.* 1960. Viking. 1st. F/NF. M19. $75.00

WILLIAMS, Charles. *Descent Into Hell.* 1949. Payson Clarke. 1st. VG/dj. M2. $30.00

WILLIAMS, Charles. *Greater Trumps.* 1950. Payson Clarke. 1st. VG/dj. M2. $35.00

WILLIAMS, Charles. *Man on a Leash.* 1973. Putnam. 1st. F/F. M15. $55.00

WILLIAMS, Charles. *Big Bite.* 1956. Dell. 1st ed. NF. B4. $85.00

WILLIAMS, Charles. *Place of the Lion.* 1952. London. Faber. 1st ed/2nd prt. 12mo. gilt red cloth. F/NF. T10. $125.00

WILLIAMS, Charles. *Sailcloth Shroud.* 1960. Viking. 2nd. VG/dj. P3. $25.00

WILLIAMS, Charles. *Shadows of Ectasy.* 1948. Faber. VG/dj. P3. $30.00

WILLIAMS, D.R. *United States & the Philippines.* 1925. Doubleday Page. 335p. VG. P1. $15.00

WILLIAMS, David. *Copper, Gold & Treasure.* 1982. St Martin. 1st. VG/dj. P3. $10.00

WILLIAMS, David. *Murder in Advent.* 1985. St Martin. 1st. NF/dj. P3. $15.00

WILLIAMS, David. *Treasure by Degrees.* 1977. Collins Crime Club. 1st. NF/dj. P3. $20.00

WILLIAMS, Dorian. *Pancho: Story of a Horse.* 1967. Walker. 1st Am. VG. O3. $15.00

WILLIAMS, Emily Wildington. *Homing Pigeon.* 1927. NY. Macaulay. 1st. F/VG+. B4. $100.00

WILLIAMS, Eugenia. *Invitation to Cryptograms.* 1959. NY. 1st. 126p. VG/dj. S1. $15.00

WILLIAMS, Geoffrey J. *Bibliography of Sierra Leone 1925-1967.* 1971. London/Munich. Africana Pub. 209p. xl. VG. W1. $35.00

WILLIAMS, Gordon. *Hazell Plays Solomon.* 1975. Walker. 1st. NF/dj. P3. $13.00

WILLIAMS, Gordon. *Pomeroy.* 1982. Arbor. 1st. VG/dj. P3. $15.00

WILLIAMS, Harold. *One Whaling Family.* 1964. Houghton Mifflin. 401p. G+/dj. V3. $18.00

WILLIAMS, Hawley. *Rover Boys: At College (#14).* 1910. Grosset Dunlap. 292p. cloth. VG/dj (lists 19 titles). M20. $40.00

WILLIAMS, Henry Lionel. *Country Furniture of Early America.* 1966. NY/London. 3rd. ils. VG/VG. M17. $25.00

WILLIAMS, J.R. *Redrawn by Request.* 1955. NY. 1st. VG/VG. B5. $45.00

WILLIAMS, J.R. *Bull of the Woods.* 1944. NY. VG/VG. B5. $40.00

WILLIAMS, J.R. *Cowboys Out Our Way.* 1951. NY. 1st ed. VG/VG. B5. $85.00

WILLIAMS, J.R. *Out Our Way.* 1943. NY. 1st ed. cartoons. F/VG. w/sgn card. H3. $150.00

WILLIAMS, Jay. *Practical Princess.* 1969. Parents Magazine Pr. ils Friso Henstra. VG. B15. $45.00

WILLIAMS, Jay. *Time of the Kraken.* 1978. Gollancz. NF/dj. P3. $20.00

WILLIAMS, Jerome. *Tin Box: Story of Texas Cattle & Oil.* 1958. Vantage. 1st. sgn. VG/VG. A23. $34.00

WILLIAMS, Jett. *Ain't Nothin' as Sweet as My Baby.* 1990. Harcourt Brace. 1st. sgn. VG/VG. A23. $30.00

WILLIAMS, John A. *Man Who Cried I Am.* 1967. Little Brn. 1st. NF/dj. M25. $60.00

WILLIAMS, John A. *This Is My Country Too.* 1965. NAL. 1st. NF/dj. M25. $75.00

WILLIAMS, John. *Apology for the Pulpits, Being in Answer to a Late Book...* 1688. London. Dorman Newman. 1st. sm 4to. H13. $195.00

WILLIAMS, John. *King God Didn't Save.* 1970. NY. 1st. VG/VG. B5. $20.00

WILLIAMS, Joy. *Taking Care.* 1982. Random. 1st ed. F/F. M23. $20.00

WILLIAMS, Kenneth P. *Lincoln Finds a General.* Macmillan. 5 vol. 1st. F. O8. $125.00

WILLIAMS, M. *Velveteen Rabbit.* 1983. Holt. 13th. ils Michael Hague. F/VG. B17. $9.00

WILLIAMS, Martin. *Jazz Panorama.* 1962. Crowell Collier. 1st ed. NF/NF. B2. $65.00

WILLIAMS, Mona. *Voices in the Dark.* 1968. Doubleday. 1st ed. F/NF. V1. $15.00

WILLIAMS, Nigel. *Black Magic.* 1988. Hutchinson. 1st. F/dj. P3. $12.00

WILLIAMS, Paul. *New Homes for Today.* 1946. Murray Gee. 1st. 4to. 96p. tan cloth. VG. A8. $25.00

WILLIAMS, R. James. *Pussy-Cats ABC.* ca 1920. London. Deans Rag Book. 12mo. cloth/sewn bdg. R5. $75.00

WILLIAMS, Robert Chadwell. *Klaus Fuchs: Atom Spy.* 1987. Cambridge. Harvard. 1st. ils. VG/dj. K3. $18.00

WILLIAMS, Samuel H. *Voodoo Roads.* 1939. Vienna. Jugend Volk. Eng text. F/NF. B2. $50.00

WILLIAMS, Sherley Anne. *Some One Sweet Angel Chile.* 1982. Morrow. 1st. F/F. B4. $85.00

WILLIAMS, Stanley T. *Life of Washington Irving.* 1935. Oxford. 1st. 2 vol. F/dj. H1. $45.00

WILLIAMS, Tad. *Stone of Farewell.* 1990. Doran. 1st. sgn. F/F. M19. $25.00

WILLIAMS, Tennessee. *Baby Doll.* 1957. London. Secker Warburg. 1st Eng/photoplay. F/F. B4. $150.00

WILLIAMS, Tennessee. *Collected Stories.* 1985. New Directions. 1st. intro Gore Vidal. F/dj. Q1. $40.00

WILLIAMS, Tennessee. *One Arm & Other Stories.* 1954. New Directions. 1st trade. NF/VG. M25. $25.00

WILLIAMS, Tennessee. *Milk Train Doesn't Stop Here Anymore.* 1951. Norfolk. 1st ed. F/F. C2. $275.00

WILLIAMS, Tennessee. *Roman Spring of Mrs Stone.* 1950. New Directions. 1st ed. author's 1st novel. inscr. F/rpr dj. B24. $375.00

WILLIAMS, Tennessee. *Steps Must Be Gentle.* 1980. NY. 1/350. sgn. F/F. C2. $200.00

WILLIAMS, Thomas Harry. *Hayes of the 23rd, the Civil War Volunteer Officer.* 1965. Knopf. 1st. 325p. cloth. NF/dj. M8. $45.00

WILLIAMS, Thomas. *Ceremony of Love.* 1955. Bobbs Merrill. 1st. author's 1st book. F/NF. L3. $150.00

WILLIAMS, Valentine. *Crouching Beast.* nd. Grosset Dunlap. VG/dj. P3. $30.00

WILLIAMS, Violet M. *Sambo's Party.* ca 1930s. London. Dean. 8vo. pict stiff paper wrp. R5. $150.00

WILLIAMS, W.C. *Pink Church.* 1949. Golden Goose. 1st. 1/400. sgn. uncut. bl prt wrp. M24. $250.00

WILLIAMS, Walter Jon. *Aristoi.* 1992. NY. Tor. 1st ed. F/F. T2. $20.00

WILLIAMS, Walter Jon. *Facets.* 1990. NY. Tor. 1st ed. sgn. F/F. T2. $25.00

WILLIAMS, Walter Jon. *Hardwired.* 1986. NY. Tor. 1st ed. sgn. F/F. T2. $35.00

WILLIAMS, Walter Jon. *Voice of the Whirlwind.* 1987. NY. Tor. 1st ed. sgn. F/F. T2. $30.00

WILLIAMS, William Carlos. *Collected Later Poems.* 1950. New Directions. 1st. NF/NF. w/supplement The Rose. D10. $75.00

WILLIAMS, William Carlos. *Pictures From Brueghel.* 1962. New Directions. 1st. F/wrp. Q1. $75.00

WILLIAMS, William Carlos. *Selected Letters.* 1957. McDowell Obolensky. 1st. F/NF. M25. $35.00

WILLIAMS, William Carlos. *Selected Poems.* 1949. New Directions. 1st/1st imp (tan ep). intro Jarrell. F/NF. A4. $125.00

WILLIAMS, William Carlos. *Something to Say.* 1985. New Directions. 1st. F/dj. Q1. $40.00

WILLIAMS, William. *Mr Penrose, the Journal of Penrose, Seaman.* 1969. IU. 1st. 8vo. F/NF. T10. $50.00

WILLIAMSON, Chilton Jr. *Roughnecking It, a Brillant Portrait of Life...* 1982. S&S. 1st. 288p. VG/VG. J2. $45.00

WILLIAMSON, Harold E. *American Petroleum Industry: Age of Energy 1899-1959.* 1963. Northwestern. sm 4to. 928p. F/G. H1. $20.00

WILLIAMSON, Hugh Pritchard. *Overland Diary of James A Pritchard.* 1959. San Francisco. Old West Pub. A19. $125.00

WILLIAMSON, J. Bruce. *History of the Temple, London, From the Institution...* 1924. London. gr cloth. M11. $125.00

WILLIAMSON, J.N. *How to Write Horror Fantasy & Science Fiction.* 1987. Writers Digest. F/dj. P3. $18.00

WILLIAMSON, J.N. *Masques II.* 1987. Maclay. 1st. NF. P3. $25.00

WILLIAMSON, Jack. *Brother to Demons, Brother to Gods.* 1979. Bobbs Merrill. 1st. F/dj. P3. $18.00

WILLIAMSON, Jack. *Cometeers.* 1950. Fantasy. 1st. inscr/sgn/#d. NF/VG. P3. $150.00

WILLIAMSON, Jack. *Darker Than You Think.* 1948. Fantasy. 1st. inscr/sgn/#d. F/NF. P3. $300.00

WILLIAMSON, Jack. *Humanoid Touch.* 1989. Holt. 1st. sgn. F/dj. M2. $40.00

WILLIAMSON, Jack. *Humanoids.* 1949. S&S. 1st. VG/dj. P3. $40.00

WILLIAMSON, Jack. *Legion of Time.* 1952. Fantasy. 1st. inscr/sgn/#d. F/NF. P3. $200.00

WILLIAMSON, Jack. *Lifeburst.* 1984. Del Rey. 1st. F/dj. M2. $20.00

WILLIAMSON, Jack. *Manseed.* 1982. Del REy. 1st. F/F. M19. $25.00

WILLIAMSON, Jack. *Seetee Ship.* 1951. Gnome. 1st. VG/dj. P3. $60.00

WILLIAMSON, James A. *Maritime Enterprise, 1485-1588.* 1972. NY. Octagon. rpt. 15 ils/maps. F. O7. $50.00

WILLIAMSON, James J. *Mosby's Rangers...Forty-Third Battalion Virginia Cavalry.* 1982. Time Life. facsimile of 1896 ed. 511p. aeg. F. A17. $25.00

WILLIAMSON, Julia. *Stars Through Magic Casements.* 1931 (1930). Appleton. ils Edna Reindel. 246p. G. K5. $25.00

WILLIAMSON, Robert W. *Essays in Polynesian Ethnology.* 1975. Cooper Sq. facsimile of 1939 ed. 10 pl/2 maps. red cloth. F. T10. $50.00

WILLIAMSON, Thames. *Lobster War.* 1935. Lee Shepard. 1st. VG/VG+. B4. $85.00

WILLIS, Chester. *Roaring Camp.* 1973. Collins. VG/VG. P3. $12.00

WILLIS, John. *Screen World 1967 Film Annual.* 1967. Crown. VG/G. P3. $20.00

WILLIS, Stephen. *Weed Control in Farm & Garden.* 1960. London. Garden BC. 184p. VG/dj. A10. $24.00

WILLISTON, S.W. *University Geological Survey of Kansas Vol IV. Paleontology.* 1898. 594p. cloth. G. D8. $40.00

WILLISTON, Teresa Pierce. *Japanese Fairy Tales.* 1923 (1904). Rand McNally. ils Sanchi O Gawa. VG-. M5. $20.00

WILLMINGTON, Harold L. *Willmington's Complete Guide to Bible Knowledge: NT People.* 1990. Tyndale. 255p. as new/dj. B29. $13.00

WILLMOTT, H.P. *Barrier & the Javelin: Japanese & Allied Pacific Strategies.* 1942. Annapolis. ils. 596p. VG/VG. S16. $22.50

WILLOCKS, Tim. *Green River Rising.* 1994. Morrow. 1st. author's 1st book. F/dj. Q1. $40.00

WILLS, W. David. *Barns Experiment.* 1947. London. Allen Unwin. 2nd. 148p. VG/worn. V3. $20.00

WILLSON, M.W. *Garden Memories.* 1920. poem anthology/pl. G+. M17. $20.00

WILMOT, A. *Monomotapa (Rhodesia): Its Monuments, History...* 1969 (1896). Negro U. rpt. 16mo. ils/fld map. VG. W1. $25.00

WILMOT, Robert Patrick. *Death Rides a Painted Horse.* 1954. Lippincott. 1st. VG/dj. P3. $30.00

WILSIE, Carroll. *Crop Adaptation & Distribution.* 1962. SF. Freeman. 448p. cloth. A10. $22.00

WILSON, A.N. *Laird of Abbotsford, a Side View of Sir Walter Scott.* 1980. Oxford. 1st. VG/VG. T9. $25.00

WILSON, Alan. *Story of the Potato Through Ils Varieties.* 1995 (1993). London. Wilson. 120p. pb. M. A10. $28.00

WILSON, Albert. *How Does Your Garden Grow.* 1955 (1949). Menlo Park. 2nd. photos. 500+p. VG+/dj. B26. $17.50

WILSON, Angus. *Hemlock & After.* 1952. London. 1st. VG/rpr. w/sgn Christmas greeting. T9. $40.00

WILSON, Angus. *No Laughing Matter.* 1967. Viking. 1st. F/dj. Q1. $35.00

WILSON, Barbara M. *Ontario & the First World War, 1914-18. A Collection...* 1977. Toronto. Champlain Soc. 201p. NF. P4. $100.00

WILSON, C.P.H. *Bush Peaches.* 1958. London. Collingridge. 140p. VG/dj. A10. $25.00

WILSON, Carl. *Botany.* 1950. Dryden. 483p. cloth. VG. A10. $12.00

WILSON, Carol Green. *Chinatown Quest: Life Adventures of Donaldina Cameron.* 1931. Stanford. 1st. sgn. stp gr cloth. F/dj. R3. $45.00

WILSON, Carol Green. *Gump's Treasure Trade: Story of San Francisco.* 1965. Crowell. expanded (1st thus). NF/VG. O4. $15.00

WILSON, Charles. *Middle America.* 1944. Norton. 1st. ils/map. 317p. F3. $15.00

WILSON, Charles L. *World of Terrariums.* 1975. Middle Village. ils/photos. VG/torn. B26. $15.00

WILSON, Charles William. *Picturesque Palestine, Sinai & Egypt.* 1881-1883. Appleton. 1st ed. 480p. aeg. VG/dj. W1. $65.00

WILSON, Colin. *Adrift in Soho.* 1961. Houghton Mifflin. 1st Am ed. F/VG+. B4. $75.00

WILSON, Colin. *Dark Dimensions.* 1977. Everest House. 1st. VG/dj. P3. $15.00

WILSON, Colin. *Lingard.* 1970. Crown. 1st. NF/dj. M2. $60.00

WILSON, Colin. *Outsider.* 1950s. Houghton Mifflin. 1st Am. VG/G+. R10. $15.00

WILSON, Colin. *Philosopher's Stone.* 1971. Crown. 1st Am. VG/dj. M2. $45.00

WILSON, Colin. *Ritual in the Dark.* 1960. Gollancz. 2nd. VG/G. P3. $35.00

WILSON, Colin. *Schoolgirl Murder Case.* 1975. Hart Davis. 2nd. VG/dj. P3. $15.00

WILSON, Colin. *Strength to Dream: Literature & the Imagination.* 1962. Houghton Mifflin. 1st Am ed. xl. reading copy. R10. $8.00

WILSON, D. *Henrietta Robinson.* 1855. NY/Auburn. Miller Orton Mulligan. 1st. 12mo. cloth. M1. $125.00

WILSON, Derek. *Circumnavigators.* 1989. NY. Evans. 1st Am. 345p. half cloth. NF/dj. P4. $35.00

WILSON, Dorothy Clarke. *Bright Eyes: Story of Susette LaFlesche, an Omaha Indian.* 1974. McGraw Hill. 1st. ils. 396p. VG/dj. A25. $8.00

WILSON, E. Raymond. *Thus Far on My Journey.* 1976. IN. Friends United Pr. 308p. G/dj. V3. $12.00

WILSON, E. Raymond. *Uphill for Peace: Quaker Impact on Congress.* 1975. Richmond, IN. Friends United Pr. 432p. VG/dj. V3. $18.00

WILSON, Earl. *Betio Beachhead: US Marines' Own Story of Battle of Tarawa.* 1945. NY. photos/maps. 160p. VG. S16. $30.00

WILSON, Edmund. *Forties.* 1983. FSG. 1st. F/F. B35. $25.00

WILSON, Edmund. *O Canada: An American's Notes on Canadian Culture.* 1966. FSG. 1st. NF/dj. D10. $45.00

WILSON, Edmund. *Piece of My Mind.* 1956. FSC. 1st. 12mo. 239p. gray cloth. F/dj. H1. $20.00

WILSON, Ella Grant. *Famous Old Euclid Avenue of Cleveland.* 1937. np. ils/index. 265p. G. B18. $45.00

WILSON, Erica. *Erica Wilson's Embroidery Book.* 1973. Scribner. sgn. 374p. VG/VG. B11. $25.00

WILSON, Ernest H. *Aristocrats of the Trees.* 1930. Boston. 66 halftones. 279p. teg. xl. new buckram. B26. $100.00

WILSON, Everett B. *Fifty Early American Towns.* 1966. AS Barnes. 353p. VG/dj. M20. $20.00

WILSON, F. Paul. *Black Wind.* 1988. Tor. 1st. NF/NF. P3. $30.00

WILSON, F. Paul. *Healer.* 1976. Doubleday. 1st. F/dj. M2. $30.00

WILSON, F. Paul. *Keep.* 1981. Morrow. 1st. NF/dj. M2. $60.00

WILSON, F.W. *Kansas Landscapes: A Geologic Diary.* 1978. KS Geological Survey. 50p. VG. D8. $5.00

WILSON, Frazier Ells. *Advancing the Ohio Frontier.* 1937. Blanchester, OH. 1st ed. 124p. xl. VG. B18. $17.50

WILSON, Gahan. *Eddy Deco's Last Caper.* 1981. Timescape. 1st. F/dj. M2. $15.00

WILSON, Jeremy. *TE Lawrence.* 1988. London. 1st. VG/VG. T9. $75.00

WILSON, John Fleming. *Master Key.* nd. Grosset Dunlap. VG. P3. $20.00

WILSON, John. *Cruise of the Gypsy...1838-1843.* 1991. Fairfield. Ye Galleon. rpt. 404p. M/sans. P4. $45.00

WILSON, John. *Somewhere at Sea.* 1924. Dutton. VG. M2. $12.00

WILSON, L.M. *Clothing of the Ancient Romans.* 1938. Baltimore. 95 pl. NF. M4. $20.00

WILSON, Laura. *Good Morning Mexico.* 1937. NY. Suttonhouse. 1st. 75p. F3. $10.00

WILSON, Louis. *Bromeliads for Modern Living.* 1977. Kalamazoo. photos. sc. F. B26. $7.50

WILSON, Margaret. *Kenworthys.* 1925. Harper. 1st ed. author's 2nd novel. F/VG. B4. $125.00

WILSON, Marjorie. *Children's Rhymes of Travel.* 1924. Boston/NY. Houghton Mifflin. possible 1st ed. 56p. VG/VG. C14. $20.00

WILSON, Merzie. *Nealities: Doc Genius & Henry the Stud.* 1980. Vantage. 1st. F/dj. M2. $10.00

WILSON, Mitchell. *American Science & Invention.* 1954. NY. 437p. dj. A17. $20.00

WILSON, Richard. *Girls From Planet 5.* 1955. Ballantine. 1st. VG/dj. P3. $60.00

WILSON, Robert C. *Crooked Tree.* 1980. Putnam. 1st. VG/dj. P3. $15.00

WILSON, Ruth. *Here Is Hati.* 1957. Philosophical Lib. 1st. 204p. dj. F3. $20.00

WILSON, Sloan. *Man in the Gray Flannel Suit II.* 1984. NY. Arbor. 1st. sgn. VG/VG. B11. $40.00

WILSON, Steve. *Dealer's Wheels.* 1982. St Martin. F/dj. P3. $15.00

WILSON, Thomas. *Arrowheads, Spears & Knives of Pre-Historic Times.* nd. US National Mus. ils/photos. blk cloth/gr spine. VG. K7. $60.00

WILSON, Thomas. *Brief Journal of Life, Travels & Labors of Love...* 1991. Phil. Friends Bookstore. 124p. VG. V3. $14.00

WILSON, Violet. *Coaching Era.* nd. Dutton. 1st Am ed. VG. O3. $58.00

WILSON, Warren. *Rediscovery of Jerusalem.* 1872. Appleton. 8vo. 435p. xl. G. W1. $45.00

WILSTACH, Paul. *Tidewater Maryland.* 1931. Bobbs Merrill. 1st. 39 ils. 383p. T7. $45.00

WILTZ, Chris. *Diamond Before You Die.* 1987. Mysterious. 1st. VG/dj. P3. $16.00

WIND, Herbert Warren. *Story of American Golf.* 1956. S&S. revised/1st prt. VG+/dj. P8. $40.00

WIND, Herbert Warren. *World of PG Wodehouse.* 1972. Praeger. NF/dj. P3. $20.00

WINDLE, Ernest. *Windle's History of Santa Catalina Island.* 1931. Avalon. Catalina Islander. 1st. fld linen-backed map. 159p. D11. $150.00

WINEGARDNER, Mark. *Prophet of the Sandlots.* 1990. Atlantic Monthly. 1st ed. F/clip. M23. $20.00

WINEGARDNER, Mark. *Prophet of the Sandlots.* 1990. Atlantic Monthly. 1st ed. F/F. P8. $25.00

WINFIELD, Arthur M. *Rover Boys in the Jungle (#3).* 1899. Grosset Dunlap. 234p. gr pict cloth. VG/2-color dj. M20. $30.00

WINFIELD, Arthur M. *Rover Boys in the Land of Luck.* 1921. Grosset Dunlap. 1st/4th format. 310p. G/dj. H1. $18.00

WINFIELD, Dave. *Winfield: A Player's Life.* 1988. Norton. 1st. F/F. P8/T12. $35.00

WINFIELD, P.H. *Cases on the Law of Tort.* 1941. London. gilt bl cloth. M11. $50.00

WINFIELD, P.H. *Chief Sources of English Legal History.* 1925. Cambridge. bl cloth. M11. $125.00

WINFIELD, P.H. *Select Legal Essays.* 1952. London. Sweet & Maxwell. M11. $75.00

WINFIELD, P.H. *Text-Book of the Law of Tort. Second Edition.* 1943. London. Sweet & Maxwell. M11. $65.00

WINGROVE, David. *Broken Wheel.* 1991. Delacorte. 1st. F/F. H11. $25.00

WINGROVE, David. *Chung Kuo.* 1990. Delacorte. 1st. F/NF. H11. $30.00

WINKS, Robin W. *Modus Operandi.* 1982. Godine. 1st. NF/dj. M25. $35.00

WINN, Dilys. *Murder Ink.* 1977. Workman. 1st. VG/dj. M2. $25.00

WINN, Patrick. *Colour of Murder.* 1965. Robert Hale. 1st. VG/dj. P3. $15.00

WINSLOW, Charles Frederick. *Force & Nature: Attraction & Repulsion.* 1869. Lippincott. 1st. 8vo. 492p. G+. K3. $35.00

WINSLOW, Don. *Cool Breeze on the Underground.* 1991. St Martin. 1st. sgn. author's 1st book. F/F. B3. $175.00

WINSLOW, Pauline. *Copper Gold.* 1978. St Martin. 1st. VG/dj. P3. $15.00

WINSLOW, Richard. *General John Sedgwick.* 1982. 204p. O8. $12.50

WINSOR, Kathleen. *Forever Amber.* 1944. London. MacDonald. 1st Eng. NF/VG. B4. $150.00

WINSTER, Owen. *Journey in Search of Christmas.* 1904. Harper. ils Frederic Remington. 93p. red cloth. VG. K7. $55.00

WINSTON, Joan. *Making of Star Trek Conventions.* 1977. Doubleday. 1st. F/dj. M2. $35.00

WINSTON, Robert W. *Robert E Lee, a Biography.* 1934. Morrow. 1st. 428p. cloth. NF. M8. $45.00

WINTER, Douglas E. *Prime Evil.* 1988. NAL. 1st. F/VG+. N4. $25.00

WINTER, Douglas E. *Stephen King: Art of Darkness.* 1984. NAL. 1st. F/dj. P3. $20.00

WINTER, John Strange. *Magic Wheel.* 1901. Lippincott. 1st. G+. M2. $22.00

WINTER, Milo. *Arabian Nights Entertainments.* 1914. Rand McNally. Windermere series. sm 4to. 12 mc pl. 293p. cloth. W1. $25.00

WINTERBOTHAM, F.W. *Nazi Connection.* 1978. Harper Row. 1st. VG/dj. P3. $15.00

WINTERBOTHAM, Russ. *Joyce of the Secret Squadron.* 1942. Whitman. VG. P3. $12.00

WINTERICH, John T. *Primer of Book Collecting.* 1935. Greenberg. revised/enlarged. 8vo. 265p. VG. K3. $22.00

WINTERICH, John T. *Three Lantern Slides.* 1949. Urgana. IL U. 1st. 8vo. 109p. VG. K3. $20.00

WINTERS, Roy Lutz. *Francis Lambert of Avignon (1487-1530).* 1938. United Lutheren Pub House. 1st ed. sgn. F. B35. $30.00

WINTERS, Yvor. *Anatomy of Nonsense.* 1943. New Directions. 1st ed. 8vo. VG/dj. s9. $25.00

WINTERS, Yvor. *In Defense of Reason.* 1947. New Directions. 1st ed. NF/dj. V1. $20.00

WINTERSON, Jeanette. *Written on the Body.* 1993. Knopf. 1st Am. F/dj. A24. $25.00

WINTHER, Oscar Osburn. *Transportation Frontier Trans-Mississippi West.* 1964. HRW. A19. $15.00

WINWARD, Walter. *Fives Wild.* 1976. Atheneum. 1st. VG/dj. P3. $15.00

WINWARD, Walter. *Seven Minutes Past Midnight.* 1980. S&S. 1st. VG/dj. P3. $15.00

WIRT, Mildred A. *Brownie Scouts at Silver Beach.* 1952. Cupples Leon. 1st. ils. VG+/VG. A25. $20.00

WIRT, Mildred A. *Courageous Wings.* 1937. Penn. 217p. red cloth. VG+. M20. $50.00

WIRT, Mildred A. *Courageous Wings.* 1940 (1937). Books Inc. 217p. bl cloth. NF/dj. M20. $50.00

WIRT, Mildred A. *Madge Sterling: Deserted Yacht (#2).* 1932. Goldsmith. 123p. VG/dj. M20. $10.00

WIRT, Mildred A. *Painted Shield.* ca 1950s. World. Jr Lib ed. 207p+ad. M20. $25.00

WIRT, Mildred A. *Penny Parker: Behind the Green Door (#4).* 1940. Cupples Leon. 211p. VG/dj. M20. $20.00

WIRT, Mildred A. *Penny Parker: Danger at the Drawbridge (#3).* 1950 (1940). Cupples Leon. 211p. VG/dj. M20. $25.00

WIRT, Mildred A. *Penny Parker: Saboteurs on the River (#9).* 1943. Cupples Leon. lists 10 titles. 211p. red cloth. VG/dj. M20. $30.00

WIRT, Mildred A. *Penny Parker: Wishing Well (#8).* 1942. Cupples Leon. 1st ed. 206p. VG/dj. M20. $52.00

WIRT, Mildred A. *Sky Racers.* 1940. Books Inc. 224p. VG+/dj. M20. $40.00

WISE, Arthur. *Who Killed Enoch Powell?* 1971. Harper Row. 1st. VG/dj. P3. $20.00

WISE, David Burgess. *Illustrated Encyclopedia of World's Automobiles.* 1979. A&W. 1st. 352p. cloth. VG+/dj. M20. $30.00

WISE, Herbert A. *Great Tales of Terror & the Supernatural.* 1944. Modern Lib. VG. P3. $20.00

WISEMAN, Thomas. *Czar.* 1965. London. correct 1st. inscr assoc copy. F/F. A11. $85.00

WISTER, Owen. *Lady Baltimore.* 1906. Macmillan. 1st. sm 8vo. 406p. gr cloth. G. H1. $7.50

WISTER, Owen. *Seven Ages of Washington.* 1907. Grosset Dunlap. VG. A19. $25.00

WISTER, Owen. *Virginian.* (1902). Macmillan. 1st. 12mo. VG. C8. $45.00

WITHERS, E.L. *Birthday.* 1962. Crime Club. 1st. VG/dj. P3. $18.00

WITHEY, Lynne. *Dearest Friend: Life of Abigail Adams.* 1981. Free Pr (Macmillan). 1st. 369p. blk cloth. as new/dj. B22. $6.50

WITHEY, Lynne. *Voyages of Discovery: Captain Cook & Exploration of Pacific.* 1987. Morrow. 1st. 512p. map ep. P4. $35.00

WITHGOLL, Coleen K. *Webster's Legal Secretaries' Handbook.* 1981. Meriam-Webster. 1st. F/NF. W2. $50.00

WITKIN, Joel-Peter. *Gods of Earth & Heaven.* 1989. Twelvetrees. 4to. 52 duotone pl. w/sgn letter. F/case. S9. $500.00

WITKIN, Lee D. *Photograph Collector's Guide.* 1979. Boston. 4to. 438p. red cloth. G. T3. $22.00

WITKOWSKI, Walt. *Civil War Trivia.* 1987. Boston. 12mo. 184p. VG. T3. $10.00

WITNEY, K.P. *Jutish Forest, a Study of Weald of Kent From 450 to 1380AD.* 1976. London. Athlone. M11. $75.00

WITTEN, Barbara Yager. *Isle of Fire Murder.* 1987. Walker. 1st. F/F. N4. $15.00

WITWER, H.C. *Fighting Back.* nd. Grosset Dunlap. VG. P3. $18.00

WLLIS, A.B. *Land of Fetish.* 1970 (1883). Negro U. rpt. 316p. VG. W1. $25.00

WODEHOUSE, P.G. *Angel Cake.* 1952. Doubleday. 1st ed. 8vo. F/VG. T10. $100.00

WODEHOUSE, P.G. *Big Money.* 1931. McClelland Stewart. 1st. VG. P3. $60.00

WODEHOUSE, P.G. *Bring on the Girls.* 1953. S&S. 1st. G. P3. $40.00

WODEHOUSE, P.G. *Catnappers.* 1974. S&S. 1st. 190p. cloth. VG/dj. M20. $25.00

WODEHOUSE, P.G. *Eggs, Beans & Crumpets.* 1940. Doubleday. 1st Am. F/VG. B4. $250.00

WODEHOUSE, P.G. *Full Moon.* 1947. Doubleday. 1st. VG. P3. $40.00

WODEHOUSE, P.G. *Girl in Blue.* 1971. Simon Schuster. 1st ed. VG+/dj. M21. $40.00

WODEHOUSE, P.G. *Heavy Weather.* 1933. McClelland Stewart. 1st Canadian. VG. P3. $60.00

WODEHOUSE, P.G. *Laughing Gas.* 1936. Doubleday Doran. 1st Am. orange brd. VG. M25. $50.00

WODEHOUSE, P.G. *Little Nugget.* 1941. NY. 1st Am ed. NF. C6. $225.00

WODEHOUSE, P.G. *Luck of the Bodkis.* 1935. McClelland Stewart. 1st Canadian. VG/dj. P3. $75.00

WODEHOUSE, P.G. *Mike at Wrykn.* 1953. Meredith. 1st. VG. P3. $25.00

WODEHOUSE, P.G. *Mr Mulliner Speaking.* 1929. McClelland Stewart. 1st Canadian. VG. P3. $50.00

WODEHOUSE, P.G. *Mulliner Nights.* 1933. Herbert Jenkins. 1st. NF. P3. $60.00

WODEHOUSE, P.G. *Nothing But Wodehouse.* nd. NY. edit Ogden Nash. 1200p. G. A17. $12.50

WODEHOUSE, P.G. *Pigs Have Wings.* 1952. Doubleday. 1st. F/dj. B24. $150.00

WODEHOUSE, P.G. *Plot That Thickened.* 1973. S&S. 1st. VG/dj. P3. $25.00

WODEHOUSE, P.G. *Plum Pie.* 1967. 1st Am. F/torn. A15. $50.00

WODEHOUSE, P.G. *Psmith Jouralist.* nd. Leipzig. Tauchnitz. 1st. 16mo. 270p. F/buff prt wrp. H3. $200.00

WODEHOUSE, P.G. *Spring Fever.* 1948. Doubleday. 1st Am. F/VG. B4. $100.00

WODEHOUSE, P.G. *Stiff Upper Lip, Jeeves.* 1963. S&S. 1st. F/dj. B24. $100.00

WODEHOUSE, P.G. *Uncle Fred in the Springtime.* 1939. Doubleday. 1st. F/NF. B4. $350.00

WODEHOUSE, P.G. *Uncle Fred in the Springtime.* 1939. Herbert Jenkins. 1st. VG. P3. $60.00

WODEHOUSE, P.G. *Very Good, Jeeves.* 1930. McClelland Stewart. 1st Canadian. VG. P3. $60.00

WODEHOUSE, P.G. *Wodehouse Nuggets.* 1983. Hutchinson. 1st. F/dj. P3. $18.00

WOELFEL, Barry. *Through a Glass, Darkly.* 1984. Beaufort. 1st. NF/dj. P3. $20.00

WOIWODE, Larry. *Born Brothers.* 1988. FSG. 1st ed. F/VG. A20. $24.00

WOIWODE, Larry. *What I'm Going to Do, I Think.* 1969. FSG. 1st. inscr. author's 1st novel. F/NF. L3. $225.00

WOLCOTT, Imogene. *New England Yankee Cookbook.* 1939. Coward McCann. ils. VG. A16. $10.00

WOLF, Betty Hartman. *Journey Through the Holy Land.* 1967. Doubleday. 1st. 8vo. 267p. NF/dj. W1. $10.00

WOLF, Blue. *Dwifa's Curse: A Tale of the Stone Age.* 1921. Robert Scott. NF. P3. $60.00

WOLF, Gary. *Generation Removed.* 1977. Doubleday. 1st. NF/dj. M2. $15.00

WOLF, George D. *William Warren Scranton: Pennsylvania Statesman.* 1981. PA State. 1st. 220p. F/dj. H1. $22.50

WOLF, Leonard. *False Messiah.* 1982. Houghton Mifflin. 1st. F/dj. M2. $12.00

WOLF, Leonard. *Wolf's Complete Book of Terror.* 1979. Clarkson Potter. VG/dj. P3. $10.00

WOLFE, Aaron; see Koontz, Dean R.

WOLFE, Alfred. *In Alaskan Waters.* 1943. Caxton. ils. 196p. dj. T7. $28.00

WOLFE, Bernard. *Deep.* 1957. Knopf. 1st. F/NF. B4. $100.00

WOLFE, Bernard. *Limbo.* 1952. Random. 1st. VG/dj. M2. $75.00

WOLFE, Bertram. *Fabulous Life of Diego Rivera.* 1963. NY. 1st. ils. 457p. VG/dj. B5. $47.50

WOLFE, Gene. *Book of the New Sun.* 1981-1983. S&S/Timescape. 1st. 4 vol. F/dj. M2. $260.00

WOLFE, Gene. *Castle of the Otter.* 1982. Willimantic, CT. Ziesing. 1st. 1/100. sgn. il/sgn SE Fabian. F/F. T2. $400.00

WOLFE, Gene. *Castleview.* 1990. Tor. 1st. F/dj. P3. $25.00

WOLFE, Gene. *Claw of the Conciliator.* 1981. Timescape. 1st. F/dj. P3. $50.00

WOLFE, Gene. *Endangered Species.* 1989. NY. Tor. 1st. sgn. F/F. T2. $35.00

WOLFE, Gene. *Fifth Head of Cerberus.* 1972. Scribner. 1st. F/dj. P3. $35.00

WOLFE, Gene. *Fifth Head of Cerberus.* 1972. Scribner. 1st. VG/dj. M2. $20.00

WOLFE, Gene. *Sword of Lictor.* 1981. Timescape. 1st. VG/dj. M2. $35.00

WOLFE, Gene. *There Are Doors.* 1988. Tor. 1st. F/dj. M2. $22.00

WOLFE, Gene. *Urth of the New Sun.* 1987. NY. Tor. 1st Am. inscr. F/F. T2. $25.00

WOLFE, Gene. *Urth of the New Sun.* 1987. Tor. 1st. F/dj. P3. $20.00

WOLFE, Theodore F. *Literary Haunts & Homes.* 1899. Phil. Lippincott. 1st. teg. gilt tan cloth. NF. M24. $65.00

WOLFE, Thomas. *Mannerhouse.* 1948. Harper. 1st. VG/G. M19. $35.00

WOLFE, Thomas. *Of Time & the River.* 1935. NY. 1st. VG/fair. B5. $60.00

WOLFE, Thomas. *Stone, a Leaf, a Door.* 1945. NY. 1st ed. VG/VG. B5. $50.00

WOLFE, Thomas. *Web & the Rock.* 1939. Harper. 1st ed. 695p. VG. B10. $35.00

WOLFE, Thomas. *Welcome to Our City.* 1983. LSU. 1st ed. F/F. B4. $85.00

WOLFE, Thomas. *You Can't Go Home Again.* 1940. Harper. 1st ed. bl cloth. F. B24. $150.00

WOLFE, Tom. *Bonfire of the Vanities.* 1987. FSG. 1st. NF/NF. N4. $35.00

WOLFE, Tom. *Electric Kool-Aid Acid Test.* 1968. FSG. 1st. NF/dj. Q1. $200.00

WOLFE, Tom. *Mauve Gloves & Madmen, Clutter & Vine.* 1976. FSG. 1st ed. F/F. H11. $50.00

WOLFE, Tom. *Painted Word.* 1975. NY. 1st ed. inscr. NF/NF. C6. $100.00

WOLFE, Tom. *Right Stuff.* 1979. FSG. 1st. F/F. M25. $45.00

WOLFERT, Ira. *Battle for the Solomons: October-November 1942.* 1943. MA. 200p. VG/G. S16. $23.50

WOLFF, Geoffrey. *Bad Debts.* 1969. S&S. 1st. sgn. NF/clip. R14. $85.00

WOLFF, Geoffrey. *Black Sun.* 1976. Random. 1st. inscr. F/F. T11. $45.00

WOLFF, Geoffrey. *Final Club.* 1990. Knopf. 1st. inscr. F/F. T11. $45.00

WOLFF, Geoffrey. *Inklings.* 1978. Random. 1st. F/F. B35. $25.00

WOLFF, Paul. *Skikamerad Toni.* 1936. Frankfurt. 93p+76 full-p b&w photos. sq 4to. cloth. A17. $35.00

WOLFF, Robert Lee. *Strange Stories: Explorations in Victorian Fiction.* 1971. Gambit. 1st. VG/dj. P3. $25.00

WOLFF, Theodore. *Eve of 1914.* 1936. Knopf. 1st Am. 655p. bl silk-type cloth. VG. B22. $9.50

WOLFF, Tobias. *Barracks Thief.* 1984. NY. Ecco. 1st. inscr. F/F. R14. $100.00

WOLFF, Tobias. *In the Garden of the North American Martyrs.* 1981. Ecco. 1st. inscr. F/clip. D10. $135.00

WOLFF, Tobias. *This Boy's Life.* 1989. Atlantic Monthly. 1st. sgn/dtd. F/F. D10. $95.00

WOLFSON, Theresa. *Woman Worker & the Trade Union.* 1926. NY. Internat'l. 1st. F. B2. $75.00

WOLLASTON, Nicholas. *Red Rumba.* 1964. London. Readers Union. 192p. dj. F3. $15.00

WOLLHEIM, Donald A. *Mike Mars Flies the X-15.* 1961. Doubleday. 1st. VG. P3. $10.00

WOLO. *Sir Archibald.* 1944. Morrow. 1st. 41p. VG/G. T5. $35.00

WOLPOLE, Horace. *Castle of Otranto.* 1950940s. London. Grey Walls. 8vo. 137p. F/dj. B24. $100.00

WOLTHUYS, J.J. Verbeek. *Het Cactusboex.* 1928. Utrecht. Dutch text. ils/photos. 168p. sc. B26. $40.00

WOMACK, Bob. *Echo of Horsebeats.* 1973. Walking Horse Pub. 1st. VG/VG. O3. $165.00

WOMACK, Jack. *Ambient.* 1987. Weidenfeld Nicholson. 1st. NF/NF. N4. $25.00

WOMACK, Jack. *Heathern.* 1990. Tor. 1st. F/dj. P3. $17.00

WOMEN OF ST. JAMES CHURCH. *300 Favorite Recipes.* nd. NYC. 138p. sbdg. B10. $12.00

WOOD, Bari. *Tribe.* 1981. NAL. 1st. VG/dj. P3. $15.00

WOOD, Charles Erskine Scott. *Poet in the Desert.* 1915. Portland, OR. 1/1000. inscr. 124p. natural linen/tan brd. VG. K7. $35.00

WOOD, Christine. *Safari South America.* 1973. NY. 224p. NF/VG. S15. $12.00

WOOD, Oliver. *West Point Scrapbook, a Collection of Stories, Songs...* 1874 (1871). lg 8vo. ils. 339p. VG. E6. $175.00

WOOD, R.G. *Stephen Harriman Long 1784-1864.* 1966. Clark. ils/map. 292p. F. M4. $25.00

WOOD, Robert L. *Men, Mules & Mountains.* 1976. Seattle, WA. Mountaineers. dj. A19. $35.00

WOOD, Robert W. *Physical Optics.* 1934. Macmillan. 3rd. 8vo. 846p. G. K5. $30.00

WOOD, Robert. *Day Trips to Archaeological Mexico.* 1991. Hastings. revised. 174p. wrp. F3. $10.00

WOOD, S. *Over the Range to the Golden Gate.* 1891. Chicago. 8vo. ils. 351p. brn cloth. G. T3. $39.99

WOOD, Stanley. *Over the Range to the Golden Gate.* 1889. Chicago. RR Donnelley. 1st. ils. 351p+29p ads. gilt bl cloth. G. K7. $50.00

WOOD, Theodore. *Natural History for Young People.* late 1800s. London/NY. 12 chromolithographs/ils. VG. M17. $60.00

WOOD, Wallace. *Wizard King.* 1978. Wood. 1st. F/dj. M2. $30.00

WOOD, Winifred. *We Were Wasps.* 1945. Glade House. 1st. ils Dorothy Swain. 196p. VG. A25. $35.00

WOODARD, Charles L. *Ancestral Voice.* 1989. Lincoln, NE. NE U. 1st. F/F. L3. $35.00

WOODARD, Charles L. *Ancestral Voice: Conversations With N Scott Momaday.* 1989. NE U. 1st. ils/sgn NS Momaday. F/F. D10. $60.00

WOODARD, Lt., M.D.; see Silverberg, Robert.

WOODBERRY, George. *Edgar Allan Poe.* 1885. Houghton Mifflin. 1st. teg. gilt maroon cloth. M24. $50.00

WOODBINE, George E. *Four Thirteenth Century Law Tracts.* 1910. New Haven. Yale. cloth. M11. $125.00

WOODBURNE, Lloyd S. *Neural Basis of Behavior.* 1967. Columbus, OH. Merrill. 378p. beige cloth. VG/dj. G1. $25.00

WOODCOCK, Louise. *Guess Who Lives Here.* (1949). S&S. 2nd/B prt. sq 8vo. unp. G+. T5. $22.00

WOODCOTT, Keith; see Brunner, John.

WOODHOUSE, Barbara. *Barbara's World of Horses & Ponies.* 1984. NY. Summit. 1st Am. VG. O3. $12.00

WOODHOUSE, James. *Young Chemist's Pocket Companion.* 1797. Phil. 56p. marbled wrp. B14. $600.00

WOODING, F.H. *Angler's Book of Canadian Fishes.* 1959. Ontario. 1st. 303 p. F/G. A17. $20.00

WOODLEY, Richard. *Dealer.* 1971. Holt. 1st. F/F. H11. $25.00

WOODMAN, Charles M. *Quakers Find a Way.* 1950. Bobbs Merrill. 1st. 280p. VG/dj. V3. $10.00

WOODRELL, Daniel. *Muscle for the Wing.* 1988. Holt. 1st. F/F. M15. $45.00

WOODRELL, Daniel. *Under the Bright Lights.* 1986. Holt. 1st. author's 1st mystery. F/F. L3. $100.00

WOODRESS, James. *Willa Cather: A Literary Life.* 1987. U NE. VG/dj. P3. $35.00

WOODRUFF, Philip. *Call the Next Witness.* 1945. Jonathan Cape. 1st. VG. P3. $30.00

WOODS, Jo. *Bridge Teacher's Manual: Basic Course.* nd. np. lg format sbdg pb. VG. S1. $12.00

WOODS, Lawrence M. *British Gentlemen in the Wild West...* 1989. NY. Free Pr. 1st ed. 245p. F/dj. T10. $30.00

WOODS, Robert Archey. *English Social Movements.* 1891. Scribner. 1st ed. inscr. F. B2. $85.00

WOODS, Sara. *Enter Certain Murderers.* 1966. 1st ed. F/F. M19. $17.50

WOODS, Sara. *Error of the Moon.* 1963. Collins Crime Club. 1st. VG. P3. $20.00

WOODS, Sara. *Weep for Her.* 1980. Macmillan. 1st. F/dj. P3. $20.00

WOODS, Stuart. *Blue Water, Green Skipper.* 1977. Norton. 1st. F/NF. B4. $200.00

WOODS, Stuart. *Grass Roots.* 1989. S&S. 1st. VG/dj. P3. $20.00

WOODS, Stuart. *LA Times.* 1993. Harper Collins. 1st ed. F/F. H11. $20.00

WOODS, Stuart. *Palindrome.* 1991. Harper Collins. 1st. VG/dj. P3. $20.00

WOODSON, Carter. *Negro Orators & Their Orations.* 1925. WA. Assoc Pub. 1st. G. B4. $125.00

WOODWARD, Arthur. *Lances at San Pasqual.* 1948. SF. CA Hist Soc. 84p. gilt cloth. D11. $150.00

WOODWARD, Ian. *Werewolf Delusion.* 1979. Paddington. 1st. VG/dj. P3. $20.00

WOODWARD, W.E. *Meet General Grant.* 1928. 1st. xl. O8. $12.50

WOODWARD, W.E. *Meet General Grant.* 1928. NY. 1st. 512p. F. O8. $18.50

WOODWARD & WOODWARD. *Woodward's Graperies & Horticultural Buildings.* 1865. NY. Woodward. 1st. 139p. A10. $86.00

WOOLCOCK, Helen R. *Rights of Passage. Emigration to Australia...* 1986. London/NY. Tavistock. 8vo. 337p. M/dj. P4. $30.00

WOOLF, Virginia. *Common Reader: Second Series.* 1932. London. Hogarth. 1st ed. gr cloth. F/dj. B24. $375.00

WOOLF, Virginia. *Letter to a Young Poet.* 1932. London. Hogarth. 1st. 1/5500. F/wrp. Q1. $100.00

WOOLF, Virginia. *London Scene: Five Essays.* 1975. NY. Frank Hallman. 1st/ltd. F/F. B2. $40.00

WOOLF, Virginia. *Night & Day.* 1920. Doran. 1st Am. gr cloth. F. M24. $125.00

WOOLF, Virginia. *Waves.* (1931). Harcourt Brace. 1st Am. gilt bl cloth. M24. $35.00

WOOLF, Virginia. *Widow & the Parrot.* 1988. London. Hogarth. 1st. lg 8vo. F/F. C8. $37.50

WOOLF, Virginia. *Writer's Diary.* 1954. Harcourt Brace. 1st Am ed. 356p. VG/clip. M20. $52.00

WOOLLCOTT, Alexander. *While Rome Burns.* 1934. Viking. 1st. sgn. VG. B11. $75.00

WOOLLCOTT, Alexander. *Woollcott Reader.* 1935. Viking. 1st. VG/dj. P3. $30.00

WOOLLEY, Catherine. *Ginnie & the Mystery House.* 1957. Morrow. 1st. 191p. cloth. VG/dj. M20. $22.00

WOOLLEY, Lazelle T. *Just Alike Twins.* 1912. Dutton. 265p. G. M20. $20.00

WOOLMAN, John. *Journal of John Woolman.* 1871. Boston. Osgood. 1st. gilt terra-cotta cloth. NF. M24. $85.00

WOOLMAN, John. *Journal of Life, Gospel Labours & Christian Experiences...* 1776. Dublin. R Jackson. 1st Irish ed. 434p. worn leather. V3. $185.00

WOOLMAN, John. *Some Considerations on Keeping of Negroes.* 1976. Grossman. 85p. VG/VG. V3. $22.00

WOOLRICH, Cornell. *Deadline at Dawn.* 1946. Tower Books. MTI. F/NF. M25. $25.00

WOOLRICH, Cornell. *Nightwebs.* 1971. Harper Row. 1st. F/NF. M15. $85.00

WOOLRICH, Cornell. *Phantom Lady.* 1944. Tower. MTI. VG/VG. P3. $25.00

WOOLRICH, Cornell. *Ten Faces of Cornell Woolrich.* 1965. S&S. 1st. VG/dj. P3. $45.00

WORCESTER, Hugh M. *Hunting the Lawless.* 1955. Berkeley. Am Wildlife Assn. inscr. dj. A19. $25.00

WORKMAN, Benjamin. *Gauging Epitomized.* 1788. Phil. Young. 1st. 8vo. 120p. contemporary bdg. M1. $375.00

WORM, Piet. *Three Little Horses at the King's Palace.* (1962). Random. 4to. unp. G. T5. $20.00

WORMALD, H. *Diseases of Fruits & Hops.* 1945. London. Lockwood. 294p. cloth. A10. $22.00

WORMSER, Richard. *Trem McRea & the Golden Cinders.* 190. McKay. VG/dj. P3. $15.00

WORNUM, R.N. *Characteristics of Styles: Introduction to Study of History.* 1969. London. ils. VG. M17. $60.00

WORTH, C. Brooke. *Naturalist in Trinidad.* 1967. Lippincott. 1st. ils Don Edkelberry. 291p. F/VG. S15. $20.00

WORTS, George F. *Red Darkness.* 1928. Allen. 1st. VG. M2. $25.00

WOUK, Herman. *Caine Mutiny Court-Martial.* 1954. Doubleday. 1st ed in play form. F/NF. B24. $110.00

WOUK, Herman. *Caine Mutiny.* 1952. Doubleday. 1st ils ed. sgn. NF. w/2 facsimile letters. B4. $150.00

WOUK, Herman. *War & Remembrance.* 1978. Little Brn. 4th. F/NF. W2. $30.00

WOUK, Herman. *Winds of War.* 1971. London. Collins. 1st ed. 806p. gray cloth. NF. B22. $7.00

WPA WRITERS PROGRAM. *Copper Camp: Stories of the World's Greatest Mining Town...* 1943. NY. 1st. ils. 308p. G. B18. $22.50

WPA WRITERS PROGRAM. *Death Valley, a Guide.* 1939. Houghton Mifflin. ils. VG/G. O4. $25.00

WPA WRITERS PROGRAM. *Okalahoma.* 1941. Norman. VG/VG. B5. $85.00

WPA WRITERS PROGRAM. *Pennsylvania Cavalcade.* 1942. PA U. 1st. 8vo. VG/dj. H1. $28.00

WPA WRITERS PROGRAM. *San Francisco: The Bay & Its Cities.* 1947. Hastings. Am Guide series. ils. 531p. VG/dj. K7. $25.00

WPA WRITERS PROGRAM. *University of Louisville History.* 1939. Louisville. 1st. ils/index. 301p. G+. B5. $50.00

WPA WRITERS PROGRAM. *Urbana & Champaign County.* 1942. Urbana. 1st. VG/VG. B5. $85.00

WREDE, Patricia C. *Snow White & Rose Red.* 1989. Tor. 1st. 273p. VG?dj. M20. $20.00

WREN, M.K. *Seasons of Death.* 1984. Firecrest. VG/dj. P3. $18.00

WREN, P.C. *Action & Passion.* 1933. Stokes. 1st. VG. M2. $13.00

WREN, P.C. *Bubble Reputation.* 1936. Longman. 1st. VG. P3. $40.00

WREN, R.C. *Potter's Cyclopaedia of Botanical Drugs & Preparations.* 1950. Potter Clarke. 6th. 12mo. VG. A22. $30.00

WRIGHT, A.J. *Red Demon.* 1933. Putnam. 1st. VG. M2. $20.00

WRIGHT, Anna Rose. *Whirligig House.* 1951. Houghton Mifflin. 1st. ils Joshua Tolford. 280p. VG-/dj. P2. $25.00

WRIGHT, Bart. *Largent.* 1990. D&C Incorp. 1st. photos. VG+. P8. $40.00

WRIGHT, Bruce. *Black Robes.* 1987. Secaucus, NJ. Lyle Stuart. 1st. 214p. F/F. B4. $45.00

WRIGHT, D. Macer. *Gardening With Strawberries.* 1973. NY. Drake. 207p. VG/dj. A10. $20.00

WRIGHT, Dare. *Edith & Midnight.* 1978. Doubleday. stated 1st. lg 4to. VG/dj. M5. $85.00

WRIGHT, Dare. *Lonely Doll.* 1957. Doubleday. 1st. VG+/dj. M5. $115.00

WRIGHT, Dare. *Look at the Gull.* 1967. Random. photos. unp. VG. T5. $25.00

WRIGHT, Dudley. *Book of Vampires.* 1973. Causeway. 1st. VG. P3. $20.00

WRIGHT, Edmond. *Fire of Liberty.* 1983. London. Folio Soc. 1st thus. 8vo. 256p. F/case. T10. $45.00

WRIGHT, Edmond. *History of the World.* 1985. Bonanza. dj. A19. $45.00

WRIGHT, Eric. *Body Surrounded by Water.* 1987. Collins Crime Club. 1st. VG/dj. P3. $15.00

WRIGHT, Eric. *Death in the Old Country.* 1985. Collins Crime Club. 1st. VG/dj. P3. $18.00

WRIGHT, Eric. *Question of Murder.* 1988. Collins Crime Club. 1st. VG/dj. P3. $20.00

WRIGHT, Eric. *Sensitive Case.* 1990. Doubleday. 1st Canadian. NF/dj. P3. $23.00

WRIGHT, Eugene. *Great Horn Spoon.* 1928. Garden City. 2nd. 8vo. 4 pl. 320p. VG. W1. $12.00

WRIGHT, Frank Lloyd. *American Architecture.* 1955. Horizon. 1st ed. VG. B5. $55.00

WRIGHT, Frank Lloyd. *Future of Architecture.* 1953. NY. 1st ed. VG/VG. B5. $70.00

WRIGHT, Frank Lloyd. *Natural House.* 1954. Horizon. 2nd. 223p. new ep. F/NF. A17. $27.50

WRIGHT, Gene. *Horror Shows.* 1986. Facts on File. 1st. VG/dj. P3. $25.00

WRIGHT, Gordon. *Between the Guillotine & Liberty, Two Centuries of Crime...* 1983. NY. Oxford. M11. $45.00

WRIGHT, Grahame. *Jog Rummage.* 1974. Random. 1st. F/dj. P3. $10.00

WRIGHT, Harold Bell. *Devil's Highway.* 1932. Appleton. VG. M2. $40.00

WRIGHT, Harold Bell. *Eyes of the World.* 1914. 1st. VG/G. M19. $35.00

WRIGHT, Harold Bell. *Mine With the Iron Door.* 1923. Appleton. 1st ed. 338p. VG/dj. M20. $62.00

WRIGHT, Harold Bell. *Winning of Barbara Worth.* 1911. AL Burt. photoplay ed. 511p. VG/dj. M20. $12.50

WRIGHT, Helen. *James Lick's Monument.* 1987. Cambridge. 8vo. 231p. VG/VG. K5. $75.00

WRIGHT, James W.A. *Cement Hunters: Lost Gold Mine of High Sierra.* 1950. Los Angeles. Dawson. 1/200. ils Margaret Atkinson. 52p. as new. K7. $65.00

WRIGHT, John H. *Compendium of the Confederacy: Annotated Biography.* 1989. Broadfoot. 1326p. 4to. F. A17. $150.00

WRIGHT, L. *Practical Poultry Keeper.* 1857. 5th. VG. E6. $25.00

WRIGHT, L.R. *Among Friends.* 1984. Doubleday. 1st Am. NF/dj. M25. $45.00

WRIGHT, L.R. *Sleep While I Sing.* 1986. Doubleday. 1st Canadian. F/dj. P3. $20.00

WRIGHT, L.R. *Suspect.* 1985. Viking. 1st Am. F/dj. M25. $60.00

WRIGHT, Louis B. *Louis B Wright, a Bibliography & an Appreciation.* 1968. Charlottesville. 1st. VG. w/dinner menu. VG. K3. $15.00

WRIGHT, M. *Candy-Making at Home: 200 Ways.* 1924 (1915). Phil. VG. E6. $20.00

WRIGHT, Mabel Osgood. *Flowers & Ferns in Their Haunts.* 1901. Macmillan. 1st. 358p. VG. M20. $25.00

WRIGHT, Madison. *Plant Adaptation to Mineral Stress in Problem Soils.* 1976. Cornell/USDA. 420p. pb. A10. $20.00

WRIGHT, Mark R. *Heat.* 1893. Longman Gr. ils. 8vo. 336p. G+. K3. $25.00

WRIGHT, Olgivanna. *Shining Brow.* 1960. NY. 1st ed. VG/VG. B5. $50.00

WRIGHT, Olgivanna. *Struggle Within.* 1955. NY. 1st ed. VG/VG. B5. $55.00

WRIGHT, R.C.M. *Roses.* 1961 (1957). London. ils. 160p. F/dj. B26. $17.50

WRIGHT, Richard. *American Hunger.* 1977. Harper Row. 1st. F/VG. M19. $35.00

WRIGHT, Richard. *Black Boy.* 1945. Harper. 1st. NF/G. M19. $125.00

WRIGHT, Richard. *Black Power.* 1954. NY. 1st. 358p. F/NF. B4. $150.00

WRIGHT, Richard. *Bright & Morning Star.* (1941). Internat Pub. 1st thus. VG/yel & blk wrp. M25. $75.00

WRIGHT, Richard. *Outsider.* 1945. 1st Eng. VG/VG. M19. $100.00

WRIGHT, Richard. *Native Son.* 1940. Harper. 1st ed. NF/NF later dj. M19. $100.00

WRIGHT, S. Fowler. *Deluge.* 1928. Cosmopolitan. 1st Am. NF/dj. M2. $50.00

WRIGHT, S. Fowler. *Throne of Saturn.* 1951. London. 1st. F/NF. M2. $35.00

WRIGHT, S. Fowler. *World Below.* 1976 (1930). Hyperion. rpt. F. M2. $25.00

WRIGHT, T.M. *Place.* 1989. Tor. 1st. NF/dj. P3. $18.00

WRIGHT, T.M. *Strange Seed.* 1978. Everest House. 1st. VG/dj. P3. $20.00

WRIGHT, Walter P. *Ils Encyclopedia of Gardening.* nd. London. Dent Dutton. 16mo. 323p. gilt cloth. NF. A22. $15.00

WRIGHT, William. *Von Bulow Affair.* 1983. Delacorte. 1st. sgn. F/dj. T10. $50.00

WRIGHTSON, Patricia. *Ice Is Coming.* 1978. Hutchinson. 2nd. NF/dj. P3. $15.00

WRIGHTSON, Patricia. *Nargun & the Stars.* 1974. Hutchinson. 2nd. VG/dj. P3. $7.00

WU, William F. *Hong on the Range.* 1989. Walker. 1st. F/dj. P3. $18.00

WUEST, Kenneth S. *New Testament: Expanded Translation.* 1962. Eerdmans. 624p. G. B29. $8.50

WUL, Stefan. *Temple of the Past.* 1973. Seabury. 1st. G/dj. P3. $15.00

WYATT, George. *Brains Benton: Case of the Robing Rolls (#4).* 1961. Whitman. VG. P3. $8.00

WYE, Deborah. *Louise Bourgeois.* 1983. NY. MOMA. 124p. stiff wrp. D2. $55.00

WYCKOFF, Nicholas E. *Braintree Mission.* nd. BC. VG/dj. P3. $8.00

WYETH, N.C. *Great Stories of the Sea & Ships.* 1986. Galahad. VG/dj. P3. $15.00

WYETH, N.C. *Robinson Crusoe.* 1920. Cosmopolitan. 1st ed. VG/VG. B5. $135.00

WYETH, N.C. *Scottish Chiefs.* 1923 (1921). Scribner. 9 pl. blk cloth. VG+. M5. $70.00

WYETH, N.C. *Wyeths: Intimate Correspondence of NC Wyeth 1901-1945.* 1971. np. 1st ed. VG/VG. M17. $75.00

WYKES, Alan. *Pen-Friend.* 1950. Duckworth. 1st. VG/dj. P3. $30.00

WYLIE, Elinor. *Angels & Earthly Creatures.* 1929. Knopf. 1st. 8vo. NF/NF. M23. $50.00

WYLIE, Elinor. *Mr Hodge & Mr Hazard.* 1928. Knopf. 1st. 1/145. sgn. F/F/NF case. B4. $250.00

WYLIE, Francis E. *Tides & the Pull of the Moon.* 1979. Brattleboro, VT. Stephen Greene. 2nd. 246p. VG/dj. K5. $25.00

WYLIE, Philip. *Answer.* 1955. Rhinehart. 1st. VG/dj. M2. $20.00

WYLIE, Philip. *Best of Crunch & Des.* 1954. NY. 1st ed. F/F. B5. $40.00

WYLIE, Philip. *Other Horseman.* 1942. Farrar Rinehart. 1st. xl. VG/dj. P3. $20.00

WYLIE, Philip. *Sons & Daughters of Mom.* 1971. Doubleday. 1st. VG/dj. P3. $20.00

WYLIE, Philip. *Tomorrow!* 1954. Rinehart. 1st. VG. P3. $20.00

WYLIE, Philip. *Triumph.* 1963. Doubleday. 1st. F/dj. M2. $25.00

WYLLIE, John. *Pocket Full of Dead.* 1978. Crime Club. 1st. VG/fair. P3. $13.00

WYMAN, Barry. *Behind the Mask of Tutankhamen.* 1972. Souvenir. 1st Eng. 8vo. 203p. NF/dj. W1. $10.00

WYMAN, L.P. *Golden Boys Along the River Allagash (#7).* 1923. AL Burt. 247p. VG/dj. M20. $30.00

WYMAN, L.P. *Lakewood Boys in Montana (#6).* 1927. AL Burt. lists 7 titles. 241p. cloth. VG/ragged. M20. $20.00

WYND, Oswald. *Black Fountains.* 1947. Doubleday. 1st. VG/dj. P3. $40.00

WYNDHAM, John. *Jizzle.* 1954. London. Dennis Dobson. 1st/Currey A ed. VG/1st state dj. M21. $75.00

WYNDHAM, John. *Midwich Cuckoos.* 1957. London. 1st. F/dj. M2. $85.00

WYNDHAM. *Writing for Children & Teen-Agers.* 1972. revised. 267p. F/VG. A4. $40.00

WYNMALEN, Henry. *Horse Breeding & Stud Management.* 1966. London. Country Life. VG/VG. O3. $20.00

WYNNE, Anthony. *Fourth Finger.* 1929. Lippincott. 1st Am ed. VG/VG. B4. $75.00

WYNNTON, Pattrick. *Third Messenger.* 1927. Doran. 1st ed. NF/NF. B4. $85.00

WYRICK, E.L. *Strange & Bitter Crop.* 1994. St Martin. 1st ed. author's 1st book. sgn. NF/VG+. P10. $25.00

When we are collecting books, we are collecting happiness.

Vincent Starrett
1886 – 1974

– X –

XAVIER, Paul. *Anarchist Papers.* 1969. Berkeley. Undermine. 1/1000. F/wrp. B2. $25.00

XENOPHON. *Art of Horsemanship.* 1987. London. Allen. rpt. 12mo. VG/VG. O3. $15.00

XENOPHON. *Art of Riding.* 1968. NY. Vantage. 1st ed thus. VG/VG. O3. $15.00

XERXES SOCIETY. *Butterfly Gardening.* 1990. San Francisco. 192p. sc. AN. B26. $16.00

XILINAS, Elephteri M. *Le Nil, Son Limon et la Terre Egyptienne...* 1936. Cairo. Noury. 1st. 8vo. 192p. lib buckram. xl. W1. $10.00

XOLSON, Charles. *Body.* 1992. World. 455p. VG/dj. B29. $10.50

– Y –

YABES, Leopoldo Y. *University of the Philippnes & Graduate Education Goals.* 1973. Quezon City. sgn. 66p. P1. $6.00

YADEUN, Juan. *Towina.* 1993. Mexico/Madrid. ils/map. 158p. F3. $75.00

YADIN, Yigael. *Bar-Kokhba.* 1971. Random. 1st Am. 271p. VG/G+. S3. $30.00

YADIN, Yigael. *Art of Warfare in Biblical Lands.* 1963. np. 2 vol. photos. VG/VG case. M17. $45.00

YAFFE, Alan. *Magic Meatball.* 1979. Dial. 1st. ils KB Andersen. VG/dj. M20. $15.00

YAGODA, Ben. *Will Rogers.* 1993. Knopf. ARC/1st ed. RS. F/dj. S9. $35.00

YALE, William. *Near East: Modern History.* 1958. Ann Arbor. 1st ed. 8vo. 486p. VG/dj. W1. $22.00

YAN, Mo. *Red Sorghum.* 1993. London. Heinemann. AP. 8vo. F/wrp. S9. $75.00

YANCEY, Lewis A. *Aerial Navigation & Meteorology.* 1927. self pub. 8vo. 68p. G. K5. $16.00

YANDELL, Elizabeth. *Henry.* 1976. St Martin. 1st Am ed. 8vo. 136p. NF/VG. C14. $12.00

YANG, Hongxun. *Classical Gardens of China.* 1982. NY. photos. F/dj. B26. $25.00

YARBRO, Chelsea Quinn. *Locadio's Apprentice.* 1984. Harper Row. 1st. F/dj. P3. $15.00

YARBRO, Chelsea Quinn. *Messages From Michael.* 1979. Playboy. 1st. inscr. VG/dj. M2. $35.00

YARBRO, Chelsea Quinn. *Tempting Fate.* 1982. St Martin. 1st. VG/dj. M2. $30.00

YARBROUGH, Camille. *Cornrows.* 1979. Coward McCann. 1st ed. sgn. AN/dj. C8. $60.00

YARBROUGH, Steve. *Family Men.* 1990. Baton Rouge. LSU. 1st. author's 1st book. F/dj. A24. $35.00

YARBWOOD, Edmund. *Vselod Garshin.* 1981. Boston. Twayne. 1st prt. 147p. xl. VG. A17. $7.50

YARDLEY, H. *Education of Poker Player.* 1957. NY. 1st ed. VG/VG. B5. $25.00

YARROW, C.H. Mike. *Quaker Experiences in International Conciliation.* 1978. Yale. 1st. 308p. VG/VG. V3. $14.00

YATES, Dornford. *Blind Corner.* 1927. Hodder Stoughton. 3rd. VG. P3. $20.00

YATES, Elizabeth. *Amos Fortune, Free Man.* 1962 (1950). Dutton. 13th. inscr. 8vo. 182p. VG/G. T5. $35.00

YATES, Elizabeth. *Carolina's Courage.* 1964. Dutton. 1st ed. sgn. ils/sgn NS Unwin. 96p. VG+/dj. C14. $45.00

YATES, Elizabeth. *Christmas Story.* 1949. Aladdin. 1st ed. ils Nora S Unwin. VG/G. B17. $12.50

YATES, Elizabeth. *Once in the Year.* 1947. sgn. ils/sgn Nora Unwin. VG/VG. M17. $25.00

YATES, George Worthing. *Body That Wasn't Uncle.* 1941. Triangle. 2nd. VG/dj. P3. $15.00

YATES, Richard. *Revolutionary Road.* 1961. Little Brn. 1st trade. F/NF. L3. $125.00

YAUGHAM, Clark. *Addictive Drinking: Road to Recovery...* 1982. Viking. 313p. VG/dj. B29. $5.50

YAVA, Albert. *Big Falling Snow.* 1978. NY. Crown. 1st. F/VG. L3. $45.00

YASTRZEMSKI, Carl. *Play Ball.* 1969. Grow Ahead. 1st ed. VG+/wrp. P8. $15.00

YASTRZEMSKI, Carl. *Yaz, Baseball, the Wall & Me.* 1990. Doubleday. 1st ed. photos. F/F. P8. $20.00

YASTRZEMSKI, Carl. *Yaz.* 1968. Viking. 1st ed. sgn. VG+/F. P8. $75.00

YEAGER, Chuck. *Press On.* 1988. Bantam. 1st. F/F. T12. $20.00

YEAGER, Chuck. *Yeager: An Autobiography.* 1985. Bantam. 1st. F/F. W2. $35.00

YEAKLEY & YEAKLEY. *Heisey Glass in Color.* 1973. self pub. 2nd. 8vo. cbdg. G. H1. $18.00

YEARNS, W. Buck. *Confederate Governors.* 1985. 295p. O8. $12.50

YEATS, William Butler. *Discoveries: A Volume of Essays.* 1903. Dundrum. 1/200. rpt. F/NF. V1. $20.00

YEATS, William Butler. *Full Moon in March.* 1935. London. Macmillan. 1st ed. F. C2. $50.00

YEATS, William Butler. *Green Helmet & Other Poems.* 1912. NY. 1st. VG. M17. $85.00

YEATS, William Butler. *Ideas of Good & Evil.* 1903. NY. 1st. VG-. M17. $100.00

YEATS, William Butler. *Memoirs: Original Previously Unpublished Text...* 1972. edit D Donoghue. VG/VG. M17. $25.00

YEATS, William Butler. *Packet for Ezra Pound.* 1929. Cuala. 1st ed. 1/425. F. C2. $200.00

YEATS, William Butler. *Permanence of Yeats.* 1950. Macmillan. 1st ed. assn copy. NF/VG. V1. $20.00

YEATS, William Butler. *Poems.* 1901. London. Fisher Unwin. 3rd/1st prt. dk bl cloth. M24. $200.00

YEATS, William Butler. *Stone Cottage.* 1988. Oxford. 1st ed. F/F. V1. $15.00

YEE, Chiang. *Silent Traveler in Boston.* 1959. Norton. 1st. 275p. tan cloth. VG/dj. B22. $7.00

YEE, Chiang. *Silent Traveler in San Francisco.* 1946. Norton. inscr/ils author. 8vo. bl stp gray cloth. F/dj. R3. $25.00

YEFREMOV, Ivan. *Andromeda.* 1959. Foreign Language Pub. 1st. VG/dj. P3. $30.00

YENNE, Bill. *All Aboard!: The Golden Age of American Rail Travel.* 1990. Greenwich. rpt. 192p. F/dj. A17. $17.50

YENNE, Bill. *Encyclopedia of US Spacecraft.* 1985. NY. Exeter. 4to. 192p. VG/VG. K5. $25.00

YEP, Laurence. *Child of the Owl.* 1977. Harper Row. VG/G. P3. $15.00

YEP, Laurence. *Seademons.* 1977. Harper Row. 1st. VG/dj. P3. $13.00

YERBY, Frank. *Bride of Liberty.* 1954. Doubleday. 1st. VG/dj. P3. $20.00

YERBY, Frank. *Woman Called Fancy.* 1951. Dial. 1st. F/VG. M19. $25.00

YERUSHALMI, Yosef Hayim. *Haggadah & History: Panorama in Facsimile...* 1975. JPS. 2nd. ils. 494p. VG/dj. S3. $150.00

YEVTUSHENKO, Yevgeny. *Almost at the End.* 1987. Holt. 1st ed. F/F. B35. $22.00

YEVTUSHENKO, Yevgeny. *From Desire to Desire.* 1976. Doubleday. 1st ed. F/VG+. V1. $20.00

YEVTUSHENKO, Yevgeny. *Precocious Autobiography.* 1963. Dutton. 1st ed. F/F clip. B35. $45.00

YEVTUSHENKO, Yevgeny. *Selected Poems.* 1962. Dutton. ARC. author's 1st book in Eng. F/NF. V1. $35.00

YEVTUSHENKO, Yevgeny. *Stolen Apples.* 1971. Doubleday. 1/250. sgn/#d. F/case. M25. $150.00

YEVTUSHENKO, Yevgeny. *Wild Berries.* 1981. Morrow. 1st. F/F. B35. $18.00

YGLESIAS, Jose. *Home Again.* 1987. Arbor. 1st ed. sgn. F/F. B11. $30.00

YGLESIAS, Jose. *Truth About Them.* 1971. World. 1st. NF/NF. B4. $125.00

YGLESIAS, Rafael. *Fearless.* 1993. Warner. 1st ed. rem mk. F/F. H11. $35.00

YOKOI, Yuho. *Zen Master Dogen.* 1976 (1920). Weatherhill. 1st. 217p. F/F. W3. $48.00

YOLEN, Jane. *All Those Secrets of the World.* 1991. Little Brn. 1st. sm 4to. F/F. C8. $30.00

YOLEN, Jane. *Books of Great Alta.* nd. BC. VG/dj. P3. $10.00

YOLEN, Jane. *Dove Isabeau.* 1989. HBJ. B prt. ils Dennis Nolan. F/F. B17. $7.50

YOLEN, Jane. *Dragon's Blood.* 1982. Julia MacRae. F/dj. P3. $20.00

YOLEN, Jane. *Girl Who Cried Flowers & Other Tales.* 1974. Crowell. 1st ed. 55p. xl. VG+/G+. T5. $18.00

YOLEN, Jane. *Inway Investigators.* 1969. Seabury. 1st ed. ils. 80p. F/VG. P2. $30.00

YOLEN, Jane. *Owl Moon.* 1987. Philomel. 1st ed. F/F. C8. $50.00

YOLEN, Jane. *Piggins.* 1987. HBJ. 1st. unp. cloth. VG/dj. M20. $22.00

YOLEN, Jane. *Sister Light, Sister Dark.* 1988. Tor. 1st ed. NF/NF. G10. $10.00

YOLEN, Jane. *Sleeping Beauty.* 1st. ils/sgn Ruth Sanderson. VG/VG. M17. $20.00

YOLEN, Jane. *Stone Silenus.* 1984. Philomel. 1st. VG/dj. P3. $15.00

YOLEN, Jane. *Sultan's Perfect Tree.* 1977. Parents Magazine. probable 1st ed. ils Barbara Garrison. G+. T5. $15.00

YOLEN, Jane. *Tam Lin.* 1990. HBJ. 1st. ils Charles Mikolaycak. F/NF. B3. $15.00

YOLEN, Jane. *Touch Magic.* 1981. NY. Philomel. 1st. 8vo. ils. 96p. VG/VG. T5. $30.00

YOLEN, Jane. *Transfigured Heart.* 1975. Crowell. 1st. VG/VG. P2. $25.00

YOLEN, Jane. *White Jenna.* 1989. Tor. 1st ed. F/F. G10. $25.00

YOLEN, Jane. *Wizard Islands.* 1973. Crowell. 1st ed. ils Robert Quackenbush. 115p. VG/G. P2. $25.00

YOLEN, Jane. *Wizard of Washington Square.* 1969. Cleveland. World. 1st. 8vo. 126p. VG/G+. T5. $25.00

YOLEN, Jane. *World on a String, the Story of Kites.* 1968. Cleveland. World. 1st ed. 8vo. 143p. F/NF. T5. $25.00

YONGE, C.M. *Sea Shore.* 1990 (1949). London. New Naturalist series. ils. 311p. F/dj. S15. $14.00

YONGE, Charlotte. *Chaplet of Pearls.* 1898. London. Macmillan. sgn. 12mo. gilt bl cloth. G. B11. $65.00

YORK, Andrew. *Tallant for Disaster.* 1978. Crime Club. 1st. VG/dj. P3. $12.00

YORK, Herbert F. *Advisors: Oppenheimer, Teller & the Bomb.* 1989. Stanford. rpt. M/wrp. K3. $10.00

YORK, Jeremy; see Creasey, John.

YORKE, Margaret. *Come-On.* 1979. Harper Row. 1st. NF/dj. P3. $15.00

YORKE, Margaret. *Hand of Death.* 1981. St Martin. 1st. VG/dj. P3. $13.00

YORKE, Margaret. *Silent Witness.* 1975. Walker. 1st. VG/dj. P3. $18.00

YORKE, Margaret. *Small Deceit.* 1991. Hutchinson. 1st. F/dj. P3. $25.00

YOSHIMOTO, Banana. *Kitchen.* 1993. Grove. 1st Am. F/F. B4. $75.00

YOST, Nellie Snyder. *Call of the Range, Nebraska, History of Its Cattle Industry.* 1966. Sage Books. 1st. ils/photos. 437p. VG/VG. J2. $85.00

YOUATT, William. *History, Treatment & Diseases of the Horse.* 1883. Lippincott. rpt. 470p. VG. A10. $45.00

YOUATT, William. *Horse: A New Edition...Together With a General History...* 1843. Phil. Lea Blanchard. 1st Am. leather. G. O3. $85.00

YOUNG, A.S. *Black Champions of the Gridiron.* 1969. HBW. 1st. photos. VG+. P8. $12.50

YOUNG, A.S. *Great Negro Baseball Stars.* 1953. Barnes/ 1st ed. sgn. G+. P8. $145.00

YOUNG, A.S. *Mets From Mobile.* 1970. HBW. 1st ed. VG/VG. P8. $30.00

YOUNG, Agatha. *Blaze of Glory.* 1950. Random. 1st ed. NF/NF. B35. $20.00

YOUNG, Al. *Geography of the Near Past.* 1976. HRW. 1st ed. assn copy. F/VG. V1. $15.00

YOUNG, Andrew. *Retrospect of Flowers.* 1950. London. Cape. 1st. 176p. VG/dj. A10. $28.00

YOUNG, Andrew W. *First Lessons in Civil Government.* 1846. Cleveland. MC Younglove. 224p. full calf. B18. $25.00

YOUNG, Art. *Art Young's Inferno.* 1934. NY. Delphic Studios. 1st. F. B2. $85.00

YOUNG, Arthur. *Travels During Years 1787-1789...the Kingdom of France.* 1793. Dublin. Cross. 2 vol. rebound. xl. A10. $150.00

YOUNG, Charles A. *Lessons in Astronomy.* 1895 (1890). Boston. Ginn. 357p. G. K5. $15.00

YOUNG, Charles R. *Royal Forest of Medieval England.* 1979. Leicester. M11. $50.00

YOUNG, Clarence. *Jack Ranger's Gun Club (#5).* 1910. Cupples Leon. lists 6 titles. 288p. VG+/dj. M20. $50.00

YOUNG, Clarence. *Jack Ranger's School Victories (#1).* 1908. Cupples Leon. lists 6 titles. 286p. VG/dj. M20. $45.00

YOUNG, Clarence. *Jack Ranger's Treasure Box (#6).* June 1926. Cupples Leon. 303p. VG. M20. $20.00

YOUNG, Clarence. *Jack Ranger's Western Trip (#2).* 1908. Cupples Leon. lists 6 titles. 302p. VG/ragged. M20. $45.00

YOUNG, Clarence. *Motor Boys Afloat (#5).* 1908. Cupples Leon. lists 22 titles. 244p. VG/dj. M20. $50.00

YOUNG, Clarence. *Motor Boys Bound for Home (#21).* 1920. Cupples Leon. 246p. G+. M20. $30.00

YOUNG, Clarence. *Motor Boys on the Pacific (#8).* 1909. Cupples Leon. lists 12 titles. VG/dj. M20. $17.50

YOUNG, Clarence. *Motor Boys Overland (#2).* 1906. Cupples Leon. lists 22 titles. 228p. VG/dj. M20. $50.00

YOUNG, Clarence. *Motor Boys: Ned, Bob & Jerry on the Firing Line.* 1919. Cupples Leon. lists to this title. 250p+ads. VG. M20. $25.00

YOUNG, Collier; see Bloch, Robert.

YOUNG, D. *Rommel: Desert Fox.* 1950. NY. ils/maps. 264p. VG/VG. S16. $22.50

YOUNG, David L. *Millions Want To.* 1963. Tucson. Three Flags. 1st. inscr. F/NF. O4. $25.00

YOUNG, Edward. *Brothers, a Tragedy...* 1777. London. John Bell. sm 8vo. recent marbled wrp. H13. $175.00

YOUNG, Edward. *Complaint; or, Night Thoughts.* 1817. London. aeg. gilt stp bdg. VG. V4. $75.00

YOUNG, Everild. *Rogues & Raiders of the Caribbean & the South Sea.* 1959. Jarrolds. 1st ed. VG/dj. M20. $25.00

YOUNG, Everild. *Rogues & Raiders of the Caribbean & the South Sea.* 1959. London. Jarrolds. 1st ed. inscr. photos. 240p. VG/VG. B11. $45.00

YOUNG, Francis Brett. *Century of Boys' Stories.* nd. Hutchinson. VG. P3. $30.00

YOUNG, G.O. *Alaskan-Yukon Trophies, Won & Lost.* (1947). Huntington. Standard. 2nd. ils/photos/map ep. 273p. VG. M12. $175.00

YOUNG, G.O. *Alaskan-Yukon Trophies, Won & Lost.* 1947. Huntington. 1st. VG. B5. $145.00

YOUNG, Gordon. *Days of '49.* 1939. Caxton. NF/dj. M2. $15.00

YOUNG, Gordon. *Devil's Passport.* 1942. Triangle. VG/fair. P3. $20.00

YOUNG, Hugh Hampton. *Genital Abnormalities, Hermaphroditism & Related...* 1937. Williams Wilkins. 1st. 649p. G. A17. $18.50

YOUNG, Ian. *Private Life of Islam. Young Doctor's Harrowing Account...* 1974. Liveright. 1st. 8vo. 308p. NF/dj. W1. $18.00

YOUNG, J.P. *Seventh Tennesse Calvary.* 1976. Dayton. NF. V4. $25.00

YOUNG, J.Z. *Life of Vertebrates.* 1958 (1950). Oxford. ils. 767p. VG. S15. $24.50

YOUNG, James. *What Price Sex in Hollywood?* 1932. NY. 1st ed. F/dj. A17. $12.50

YOUNG, James C. *Harvey S Firestone, 1868-1938.* nd. np. 82p. teg. quarter leather. VG. B18. $22.50

YOUNG, James C. *Roosevelt Revealed.* 1936. NY. 1st. VG+/VG+. A20. $30.00

YOUNG, James C. *School Days & Schoolmates of Harvey S Firestone.* 1929. np. 48p. VG. B18. $48.00

YOUNG, John Richard. *Schooling for Young Riders.* 1985. Norman. ils Randy Steffen. VG/G. O3. $20.00

YOUNG, John V. *Ghost Towns of the Santa Cruz Mountains.* nd. Santa Cruz. Paper Vision Pr. rpt. F/F. O4. $20.00

YOUNG, John Zachary. *Model of the Brain. Being William Withering Lectures...* 1964. Oxford. Clarendon. 348p. bl cloth. xl. G1. $50.00

YOUNG, Margaret B. *First Book of American Negroes.* 1966. Franklin Watts. 1st ed. photos. NF. B2. $35.00

YOUNG, Marguerite. *Moderate Fable.* 1944. NY. 1st ed. assn copy. NF/dj. V1. $40.00

YOUNG, Martha. *Plantation Bird Tales.* 1902. Russell. 1st ed. J Conde. 249p. VG. P2. $125.00

YOUNG, Miriam. *Bear Named George.* 1969. NY. Crown. ils Harold Berson. 8vo. unp. VG. T5. $18.00

YOUNG, Miriam. *If I Drove a Tractor.* 1973. Lee Shepard. 1st possible. lg 8vo. F/VG. C8. $30.00

YOUNG, O.E. *Black Powder & Hand Steel: Miners & Machines...* 1976. OK U. 1st. ils. 196p. F/dj. M4. $20.00

YOUNG, Otis. *West of Philip St George Cooke, 1809-1895.* 1955. Clark. 1st. 393p. VG. J2. $325.00

YOUNG, P. *Revolutionary Ladies.* 1977. NY. 1st. F/dj. M4. $20.00

YOUNG, Paul H. *Making & Using the Dry Fly.* 1934. Birmingham. VG. B5. $95.00

YOUNG, Percy. *Ding Dong Bell: A First Book of Nursery Songs.* 1957. London. Dobson. 1st. 143p. VG/dj. D4. $85.00

YOUNG, Peter. *Illustrated World War II Encyclopedia.* 1978. Great Britain. 24 vol. ils/maps/photos. VG. S16. $200.00

YOUNG, Ralph W. *Grizzlies Don't Come Easy! My Life as Alaskan Bear Hunter.* (1981). Tulsa. Winchester. 1st. 168p. NF/F. H7. $17.50

YOUNG, Richard S. *Life Beyond Earth.* 1969. Little Brn. 107p. G. K5. $10.00

YOUNG, S. *Practical Pointer Training: Hints on Training...* 1974. NY. ils/photos. 178p. cloth. F/NF. M12. $37.50

YOUNG, Scott. *Boy on Defense.* nd. Little Brn. 12th. F/VG. P3. $10.00

YOUNG, Scott. *Murder in Cold Climate.* 1988. Canada. Macmillan. 1st. F/dj. M25. $35.00

YOUNG, Thomas Daniel. *John Crow Ransom: An Annotated Bibliography.* 1982. Garland. ARC. VG/VG. B10. $25.00

YOUNG, Thomas. *Bakerian Lecture. Experiments & Calculations...* 1803. London. Bulmer. 190p. rare. G1. $350.00

YOUNGBLOOD, Charles L. *Mighty Hunter.* 1890. Chicago. 2nd. 362p. gilt cloth. B18. $150.00

YOUNGER, Edward. *John A Kasson.* 1955. State Hist Soc IA. A19. $25.00

YOUNT, John. *Hardcastle.* 1980. NY. Marek. 1st. F/F. B2. $35.00

YOUNT, John. *Trapper's Last Shot.* 1973. Random. 1st. NF/NF. B2. $30.00

YOUNT, John. *Wolf at the Door.* 1967. Random. 1st. author's 1st book. NF/NF. L3. $125.00

YOURCENAR, Marguerite. *Abyss.* 1976. FSG. 1st. F/NF. D10. $35.00

YOURCENAR, Marguerite. *Coup de Grace.* 1957. FSC. 1st. F/clip. D10. $75.00

YOUSSEF BEY, Amine. *Independent Egypt.* 1940. London. Murray. 1st. 8vo. ils. 272p. VG. W1. $20.00

YUILL, P.B.; see Williams, Gordon.

YUNGBLUT, John R. *Rediscovering Prayer.* 1972. NY. Seabury. 180p. xl. V3. $7.50

YUNGJOHANN, John. *White Gold.* 1989. AZ. Synergetic. 1st. 103p. wrp. F3. $15.00

YURDIN, Betty. *Tiger in the Teapot.* 1968. HRW. 1st. VG+/VG. P2. $35.00

YURICK, Sol. *Warriors.* 1965. HRW. 1st. author's 1st novel. F/dj. L3. $100.00

YURICK, Sol. *Warriors.* 1965. HRW. 1st. VG/dj. P3. $35.00

ZABEL. *Frigoli Detective.* 1947. Paris. Bias. 4to. ils Andre Jourcin. 2 moveable wheels. prt brd. NF. B24. $265.00

ZABRISKIE, Geroge A. *Bon Vivant's Companion; or, How to Mix Drinks...* 1948. Ormond Beach. Doldrums. 1/1200. 97p. B10. $45.00

ZACKEL, Fred. *Cocaine & Blue Eyes.* 1978. CMG. 1st. VG/dj. P3. $20.00

ZAEHNSDORF, Joseph W. *Art of Bookbinding: A Practical Treatise.* 1914. London. Bell. 8th. 12mo. Zaehnsdorf bdg. NF. T10. $400.00

ZAFFO, George J. *Your Police.* 1956. 1st ed. VG. K2. $15.00

ZAFFO, George. *Tommy on the Train.* 1946. Akron. Saalfield. mechanical. sbdg. NF. C8. $125.00

ZAGAT, Arthur Leo. *Seven Out of Time.* 1949. Fantasy. 1st/ltd. F/NF. P3. $75.00

ZAHM, Albert F. *Aerial Navigation.* 1911. NY/London. 1st. ils. 496p. VG. B18. $150.00

ZAHN, Timothy. *Cascade Point & Other Stories.* 1986. Bluejay. 1st. F/dj. M2. $20.00

ZAHN, Timothy. *Heir to the Empire.* 1991. Bantam. 2nd. F/dj. M2. $16.00

ZAHN, Timothy. *Star Wars III: The Last Command.* 1993. Bantam. 1st. F/F. B3. $15.00

ZAISER, Marion. *Beneficent Blaze.* 1960. NY. Pageant. 1st. sgn. 347p. VG/VG. B11. $40.00

ZALBEN, Jane Breskin. *Cecilia's Older Brother.* 1973. Macmillan. 1st. 12mo. unp. NF/G. T5. $35.00

ZALBEN, Jane Breskin. *Oliver & Alison's Week.* 1980. FSG. 1st. 4to. 40p. VG. T5. $20.00

ZAMORANO, Agustin V. *Copybook From the Hand of...* 1974. Los Angeles. Zamorano Club. 1/250. unp. blk cloth. F. K7. $95.00

ZANELLI, Dario. *Fellini's Satyricon.* 1970. Ballantine. ils. trans Walter/Matthews. NF/lg wrp. C9. $50.00

ZANGER, Jack. *Brooks Robinson Story.* 1967. Messner. 1st ed. xl. G/G. P8. $15.00

ZANGER, Jack. *Ken Boyer.* 1965. Nelson. 1st ed. VG+. P8. $40.00

ZANGWILL, Israel. *Dreamers of the Ghetto.* 1898. 1st. VG. E6. $30.00

ZANGWILL, Israel. *Italian Fantasies.* 1921. Am Jewish Book Co. 408p. VG. S3. $18.00

ZANGWILL, Israel. *Principle of Nationalities.* 1917. Macmillan. 16mo. 116p. G. S3. $20.00

ZAPPLER, Lisabeth. *Natural History of the Nose.* 1976. Doubleday. 1st. lg 8vo. F/NF. C8. $17.50

ZAR, Rubin. *Four Generations.* 1979. CA. self pub. inscr. 87p. VG. S3. $16.00

ZAUGG, Hans. *Decorative Trees & Shrubs.* 1960. NY. lg 4to. ils Schwarzenbach/60 mc pl. F/dj. B26. $32.00

ZAWODNY, J.K. *Death in the Forest: Story of the Katyn Forest Massacre.* 1972. Notre Dame. photos/notes/biblio/index. 235p. VG/torn. S16. $21.50

ZDINAK, Paul. *Bessie's House.* 1976. Carlton. ils/photos. 143p. red cloth. F/dj. H1. $18.00

ZEBROWSKI, George. *Macrolife.* 1990. Easton. sgn. leather. F. M2. $45.00

ZEBROWSKI, George. *Stars Will Speak.* 1985. Harper Row. 1st. sgn. F/F. B11. $45.00

ZEBROWSKI, George. *Sunspacer.* 1978. Harper Row. 1st. F/dj. P3. $15.00

ZEEMANN, P. *Progress Recents en Magneto-Optique.* 1907. Fevrier. ils. VG/wrp. K3. $35.00

ZEHREN, Erich. *Crescent & the Bull.* 1962. NY. Hawthorn. 1st ed. 366p. VG. W1. $24.00

ZEIER, Franz. *Books, Boxes & Portfolios; Binding, Construction & Design...* 1983. np. ils. 304p. F/NF. A4. $65.00

ZEIGLER, Wilbur G. *Story of the Earthquake & Fire.* 1906. SF. Leon C Osteyee. 1st. 100 half-tone ils. VG/archival case. O4. $20.00

ZEITLIN, Joseph. *Disciples of the Wise: Religious & Social Opinions...* 1947. Columbia Teachers College. 2nd. 233p. VG+/G+. S3. $25.00

ZELAZNY, Roger. *Blood of Amber.* 1986. Arbor. 1st. F/dj. P3. $20.00

ZELAZNY, Roger. *Chronicles of Amber.* nd. BC. 2 vol. VG/dj. P3. $15.00

ZELAZNY, Roger. *Courts of Chaos.* 1978. Doubleday. 1st. F/dj. P3. $35.00

ZELAZNY, Roger. *Doorways in the Sand.* 1977. WH Allen. 1st. F/dj. P3. $20.00

ZELAZNY, Roger. *Eye of Cat.* 1982. Timescape. 1st. NF/dj. P3. $20.00

ZELAZNY, Roger. *Four for Tomorrow.* 1975. Garland. 1st Am. F/sans. M2. $35.00

ZELAZNY, Roger. *Guns of Avalon.* 1974. Faber. NF/dj. P3. $50.00

ZELAZNY, Roger. *Hand of Oberon.* 1978. Faber. 1st. NF/dj. P3. $45.00

ZELAZNY, Roger. *Illustrated Roger Zelazny.* 1978. Baronet. 1st. sgn. F/sans. P3. $60.00

ZELAZNY, Roger. *Last Defender of Camelot.* 1980. SFBC. F/dj. M2. $12.00

ZELAZNY, Roger. *Roadmarks.* 1979. Del Rey. 1st. F/dj. P3. $25.00

ZELAZNY, Roger. *Sign of Chaos.* 1987. Arbor. 1st. F/dj. P3. $16.00

ZELAZNY, Roger. *To Die in Italbar.* 1973. SFBC. F/dj. M2. $12.00

ZELAZNY, Roger. *Trumps of Doom.* 1985. Arbor. 1st. F/NF. R14. $25.00

ZELAZNY, Roger. *Wilderness.* 1994. NY. Forge. 1st. sgn. F/dj. A24. $50.00

ZELIKOFF, M. *Threshold of Space.* 1957. NY. Pergamon. 4to. 342p. G. K5. $25.00

ZELLERS, Parker. *Tony Pastor, Dean of the Vaudeville Stage.* 1971. Ypsilanti, MI. Eastern U. dj. A19. $25.00

ZEMACH, Harve. *Awake & Dreaming.* 1970. FSG. 1st. ils. F/F. D1. $45.00

ZEMACH, Harve. *Mommy, Buy Me a China Doll.* (1966). Chicago. Follett. 2nd. obl 8vo. 32p. G+. T5. $150.00

ZEMACH, Harve. *Salt, a Russian Tale.* 1977 (1965). 1st thus. ils Margot Zemach. as new/F. C8. $25.00

ZEMACH, Margot. *It Could Always Be Worse.* 1976. FSG. 1st. obl sm 4to. F/VG+. C8. $75.00

ZEMPEL, Edward N. *First Editions: A Guide to Identification.* 1985. Spoon River. 2nd. F/dj. P3. $25.00

ZERNER, Henri. *School of Fontainebleau: Etchings & Engravings.* 1969. NY. Abrams. ils/23p fld-out in back. ES. cloth. dj. D2. $175.00

ZETTERLING, Mai. *Night Games.* 1966. Coward McCann. 1st Am ed. NF/VG+. B4. $75.00

ZETTERLUND. *Bibliografiska Anteckningar om August Strindberg.* 1968. rpt of 1913 Stockholm ed. VG. A4. $85.00

ZEVIN, Israel. *Parables of the Preacher of Doubno.* 1925. NY. Tashrak. Yiddish text. 318p. S3. $19.00

ZHADIN, V.I. *Fauna & Flora of the Rivers, Lakes & Reservoirs of USSR.* 1963. Jerusalem. IPST. ils. 626p. VG+/wrp. M12. $37.50

ZHDANOV, Aleksandr I. *Shadow of Peril.* 1963. Doubleday. 1st. VG/dj. P3. $25.00

ZHUKOV, G. *Marshall Zhukov's Greatest Battles.* 1969. 1st. F/F. E6. $15.00

ZIADEH, Nicola A. *Syria & Lebanon.* 1957. London. Benn. 1st ed. 8vo. 312p. VG/dj. W1. $32.00

ZIEFERT, Harriet. *Measure Me.* 1991. Harper Collins. ils Susan Baum. unp. NF. T5. $22.00

ZIEGLER, Mel. *Amen: Diary of Rabbi Martin Siegel.* 1971. World. 276p. VG/G. S3. $17.00

ZIEGLER, Tom. *Zen of Base & Ball.* 1964. Simon Schuster. 1st ed. VG+/VG. P8. $35.00

ZIEMANN, H. *White House Cookbook.* 1919 (1887). sm 4to. 619p. VG. E6. $50.00

ZIEMANN, Hans Heinrich. *Accident.* 1979. St Martin. 1st. F/dj. P3. $15.00

ZIETLOW, E.R. *Country for Old Men.* 1977. Hermosa, SD. Lame Johnny Pr. A19. $10.00

ZIGMOND, M.L. *Kawaiisu Ethnobotany.* 1981. Salt Lake City. 102p. F/wrp. B1. $37.00

ZIGROSSER, C. *Ars Medica: Collection of Medical Prints...* 1959. Phil Mus Art. ils. 91p. F. M4. $30.00

ZILESKI, George. *Prince in Space.* 1986. Vantage. 1st. F/dj. M2. $25.00

ZILLER, Wolf G. *Tree Rusts of Western Canada.* 1974. Victoria, BC. ils/botanical keys/descriptions/photos. 272p. VG/dj. B26. $22.50

ZIMBALIST, Andrew. *Baseball & Billions.* 1992. Basic. 1st ed. F/F. P8. $12.50

ZIMEN, E. *Wolf: His Place in the Natural World.* 1981. London. Souvenir. ils. 373p. F/F. M12. $37.50

ZIMILES & ZIMILES. *Early American Mills.* 1973. NY. ils. F/dj. M4. $35.00

ZIMMER, Heinrich. *Celtic Church in Britain & Ireland.* 1902. London. David Nutt. 8vo. 131p. gilt bl cloth. VG. T10. $75.00

ZIMMER, Heinrich. *Philosophies of India.* nd. Princeton. Bollingen series. 687p. F/VG. W3. $86.00

ZIMMER, Joseph. *History of the 43rd Infantry Division.* 1946. Baton Rouge. 1st. maps/photos. 96p. VG. S16. $95.00

ZIMMERMAN, Arthur. *Francisco De Toledo.* 1938. Caxton. 1st. 307p. map ep. F3. $15.00

ZIMMERMAN, Bruce. *Crimson Green.* 1994. Harper Collins. 1st. F/dj. P3. $20.00

ZIMMERMAN, Heinrich. *Third Voyage of Captain Cook.* 1988. Fairfield. 1/500. 128p. gilt bl cloth. P4. $45.00

ZIMMERMAN, John. *Guadalcanal Campaign.* 1990. Nashville. maps/photos. 189p. VG/VG. S16. $32.50

ZIMMERMAN, Paul. *Year the Mets Lost Last Place.* 1969. World. 1st ed. F/G+. P8. $20.00

ZIMMERMAN, R.D. *Midscream.* 1989. DIF. VG/dj. P3. $25.00

ZIMMERMAN, Tom. *Working at the Stadium.* 1989. Pacific Tides. 1st ed. F. P8. $10.00

ZIMMERMANN, A. *Die Morphologie und Physiologie des Pflanzlichen Zellkernes.* 1896. Jena. ils. 188p. detached wrp. B26. $10.00

ZINDEL, Paul. *When Darkness Falls.* 1984. Bantam. VG/G. P3. $13.00

ZINN, Howard. *Southern Mystique.* 1964. Knopf. 1st ed. VG/VG. B10. $10.00

ZINNES, Harriet. *Book of Ten.* 1981. Bellevue. ltd ed. 1/350. F/wrp. V1. $15.00

ZINSSER, William. *Spring Training.* 1989. Harper Row. 1st ed. F/F. P8. $20.00

ZIPES, Jack. *Spells of Enchantment.* nd. BC. VG/dj. P3. $15.00

ZIPSER & ZIPSER. *Fire & Grace: Life of Rose Pastor Stokes.* 1989. Athens, GA. 1st. F/F. B2. $25.00

ZITKALSA. *Old Indian Legends.* 1901. Boston. Ginn. 1st. author's 1st book. xl. G. L3. $675.00

ZIVANOVIC, S. *Ancient Diseases: Elements of Palaeopathology.* 1982. London. 1st Eng trans. 285p. dj. A13. $40.00

ZLOTOWITZ, Bernard M. *Septuagint Translation of the Hebrew Terms...* 1981. Ktav. inscr. biblio/index. 196p. VG. S3. $27.00

ZOCHERT, Donald. *Laura: Life of Laura Ingalls Wilder.* 1976. Regnery. 1st. 260p. cloth. VG/dj. M20. $25.00

ZOCHERT, Donald. *Man of Glass.* 1981. HRW. 1st. VG/dj. P3. $13.00

ZOGNER, Lothar. *Karten in Bibliotheken: Festgabe fur Heinrich Kramm...* 1971. Bonn-Bad Godesberg. Institut fur Landeskunde. 8 maps. F/wrp. O7. $75.00

ZOLBROD, Paul G. *Dine Bhane: Navajo Creation Story.* 1985. VG/VG. M17. $20.00

ZOLLERS, George D. *Thrilling Incidents on Sea & Land.* 1892. Mt Morris, IL. rebound. V4. $200.00

ZOLOTKOFF, Leon. *From Vilna to Hollywood.* 1932. NY. Bloch. 1st. yel brd. NF. M25. $45.00

ZOLOTOW, Charlotte. *Everything Glistens & Everything Sings.* 1987. Harcourt Brace. 1st/1st prt. sm 8vo. F/F. C8. $27.50

ZOLOTOW, Charlotte. *My Grandson Lew.* 1974. Harper Row. probable 1st ed. 8vo. unp. VG/G+. T5. $25.00

ZOLOTOW, Charlotte. *Sky Was Blue.* 1963. Harper Row. 1st ed. ils/sgn Garth Williams. unp. G+. T5. $95.00

ZOLOTOW, Charlotte. *Someone New.* 1978. Harper Row. 1st. 32p. VG. T5. $25.00

ZOLOTOW, Charlotte. *Tiger Called Thomas.* (1963). Lee Shepard. 1st. sm 4to. unp. VG/VG. T5. $25.00

ZOLOTOW, M. *Marilyn Monroe.* 1960. NY. 1st ed. VG/VG. B5. $40.00

ZOLTAN, Janos. *Die Anwendung des Spalthautlappens in der Chirurgie.* 1962. Jena. 1st. ils. 391p. A13. $125.00

ZOMBECK, Martin V. *Handbook of Space Astronomy & Astrophysics.* 1982. Cambridge. 8vo. 326p. VG. K5. $25.00

ZON, Raphael. *Chestnut in Southern Maryland.* 1904. WA, DC. 5 pl. 31p. NF/wrp. B26. $150.00

ZOSS, Joel. *Greatest Moments in Baseball.* 1987. Bison Books. 1st. VG/dj. P3. $10.00

ZOSS, Joel and Bowman, John. *History of Major Leauge Baseball.* 1992. NY. Crescent. 1st. 4to. color pict. 392p. NF/NF. R16. $75.00

ZUBRO, Mark Richard. *Echo of Death.* 1994. St Martin. 1st. sgn. F/F. M15. $35.00

ZUBRO, Mark Richard. *Simple Suburban Murder.* 1989. St Martin. 1st. inscr. F/NF. N4. $40.00

ZUCKER, Harvey. *Sports Films: A Complete Reference.* 1987. McFarland. 1st ed. F/sans. P8. $27.50

ZUCKERKANDL, E. *Atlas der Topographischen Anatomie des Menschen.* 1904. Vienna. 1st. 2 vol. 834p. A13. $150.00

ZUCKERKANDL, Otto. *Atlas & Epitome of Operative Surgery.* 1898. Phil. 1st Eng trans. 395p. A13. $100.00

ZUELKE, Ruth. *Horse in Art.* 1964. Minneapolis. Lerner. ils. 64p. VG. O3. $25.00

ZUKOFSKY, Louis. *Barely & Widely.* 1958. NY. CZ. 1st ed. 1/300. sgn. F/wrp. B24. $225.00

ZUKOFSKY, Louis. *Little.* 1970. NY. Grossman. 1st ed. author's 1st novel. F/NF. V1. $25.00

ZUKOFSKY, Louis. *Test of Poetry.* 1948. Objectivist. 1st ed pres. NF/dj. B24. $300.00

ZUKOR, Adolph. *Public Is Never Wrong: My 50 Years in Motion Pictures.* 1953. Putnam. 1st ed. F/F. B4. $200.00

ZUG, G.R. *Lizards of Fiji: Natural History & Systematics.* 1991. Honolulu. Bishop Mus. 8vo. ils/maps/references. 136p. wrp. B1. $36.00

ZUMBERGE, J.H. *Elements of Geology.* 1959. John Wiley. 1st ed/2nd prt. VG/dj. D8. $12.50

ZUROY, Michael. *Second Death.* 1992. Walker. 1st. F/dj. P3. $20.00

ZWANZIGER. *Animal Kingdom Fully Illustrated in Colors.* ca 1920. Saalfield. ils/27 double-p lithos. cloth. NF. M12. $95.00

ZWEIG, Arnold. *Education Before Verdun.* 1936. Viking. 447p. VG. S3. $22.00

ZWEIG, Stefan. *Old-Book Peddler & Other Tales for Bibliophiles.* 1938. Evanston, IL. Chas Deering Lib/Northwestern. 2nd. trans Koch. NF. B4. $100.00

ZWEIG, Stefan. *Royal Game & Other Stories.* 1981. Harmony. 1st ed. F/NF. H11. $35.00

ZWEIG, Stefan. *Royal Game With Amok & the Letter From an Unknown Woman.* 1944. Viking. 1st ed. F/F. B4. $125.00

ZWEMER, Samuel M. *Moslem World.* 1908. NY. Young People's Missionary Movement. 2nd. ils. VG. W1. $25.00

ZWINGER, Ann. *Aspen Blazon of the High Country.* 1991. Salt Lake City. Gibbs Smith. 1st. sgn. F/wrp. B3. $25.00

ZWINGER, Ann. *Desert Country Near the Sea.* 1983. NY. 1st ils. 399p. VG/dj. B26. $25.00

ZWINGER, Ann. *John Xantus: The Fort Tejon Letters 1857-1859.* 1986. Tucson. 1st. sgn. F/F. B3. $45.00

ZWINGER, Ann. *Wind in the Rock.* 1978. NY. 1st. ils. 258p. F/dj. M4. $20.00

> In the tight little cosmos of the fisher of books just one form of collecting is wholly admirable and understandable, namely, the acquisition of rare books and manuscripts. The book collector has known many stamp and coin collectors, old furniture men, old glass and old pewter men who turned to books, but he has never known a first-grade bookman who got down off his hobby before the undertaker was sent for.
>
> Barton W. Currie
> 1878 – 1962

Glossary of Terms

4to, 8vo, 12mo, etc. — the number of pages into which a single printed sheet has been folded in the production of a book. Although this is not strictly speaking an indication of size, the fewer the folds, the larger the book is likely to be.

a.e.g. — all edges gilt, gilt applied to top edge, bottom edge & fore edge of the volume.

ABAA — Antiquarian Booksellers Association of America.

ABPC — American Book Prices Current, an annual compilation of book, autograph & manuscript auction records.

ADS — Autograph document signed ads, advts., adverts. advertisements.

advance copy — a copy of a book usually sent to reviewers prior to publication, may be in a different format and may or may not be bound.

advance sheets — the unbound sheets of a new book, often galleys, distributed prior to publication.

advertisements — many books & pamphlets, especially of the 19th century contained ads, especially ones advertising others books by the same publisher, often located at the back of the volume, following the text pages.

all published — the book or set is complete as is, and any additional parts or volumes were never published.

ALS — autograph letter signed, letter handwritten by the person signing the letter as opposed to LS, which is a manuscript letter written by someone other than the signer.

ANS — autograph note signed.

antiquarian (book) — antiquarian books should refer to an old and rare book, preferably 100 years old or more, similar to an antique, but with common usage the term has come to mean any book that is out of print, old, rare, scarce; virtually any book that is not new or in print.

ARC — advanced reading copy, typically sent out by a publisher to solicit reviews or to promote sales of a book prior to its publication. ARCs are sometimes but not always in the form of bound proofs; a message from the publisher may be laid in or tipped in.

association copy — a copy with extraordinary associations, usually because it demonstrably belonged to a notable person, or has a presentation inscription by its author.

b/w — black & white.

BAL — The Bibliography of American Literature (nine volumes, but now also available on CD-ROM), the standard source for definitive descriptions of the different printings and editions of the works of many leading American authors, and as such, an invaluable tool for the proper.

bc, bce — see book club edition, BCE.

bdg. — binding.

binding — the method of holding pages or sheets together; may be simply stapled or sewn, or sewn and enclosed in wrappers, but most often refers to a "hard" binding or covers. This type of binding may be covered with cloth, various leathers, paper over boards, or other more exotic materials. The binding can be done by hand or by machine as in a publisher's "trade binding."

binding copy — a book lacking the original binding or with a binding in poor condition, i.e., a book in need of a new binding.

blindstamp — embossed design or text on binding or pages: "blind" because uncolored.

BM or BMC — British Museum or British Museum Catalog.

boards — the covers of a hardbound book; the boards are the stiff cardboard or paperboard which is usually covered with cloth or leather; and when covered with paper, the covers are properly referred to as "boards." Many pre-1850 books were issued by the publishers bound in boards (paper-covered), allowing for an inexpensive binding which could later be replaced with leather by a hand bookbinder. Early (medieval) manuscript volumes were often bound between two oak boards, hence the probable origin of this term. Often abbreviated "bds."

BOMC — Book-of-the-Month Club.

book club edition, BCE — usually an inexpensive reprint utilizing poor quality paper and binding and sold by subscription to members of a book club; in gener-

al, of little interest to book collectors and of low monetary value.

book format — the traditional terms in use for describing book format are derived from early printing methodology and the size of early handmade sheets of paper. When two leaves (four pages when printed on both sides) were printed on a sheet so that it could be folded once, collated with other folded sheets and bound, the size of the volume was a "folio." When four leaves (eight pages) were printed on the same size sheet, which would later be folded twice, the size of the resultant volume was a "quarto" (four leaves). The term "octavo" relates to the sheet having eight leaves printed on it. Today some booksellers are providing the height of a book in inches or centimeters rather than using these early terms which do not relate directly to the sheet size or process used for printing today. There are smaller and larger books, i.e., many miniatures are 64mo, and most hardbound books are either octavo or duodecimo in size.

book jacket — the paper, often with illustrations and information about the book and author, used as a protective covering over the book; usually referred to as a "dust jacket" or "dj," sometimes called a "dust wrapper." Dust jacket art work is used to promote and sell the book.

book sizes — see book format

bookworm — any of a number of moth or fly larvae which tunnel through the pages of books leaving behind small channels, holes in individual leaves. Very early books often have some evidence of bookworm damage.

broadside — a printing, often an official announcement, poem, or music, which occurs on a single sheet of paper and only on one side; the verso (other side) is blank. When printed on both sides, the sheet becomes a "broadsheet."

brodart — plastic cover which protects a book's dust jacket or binding.

buckram — a stiff, coarsely woven, filled cloth used for less expensive, but stronger wearing, cloth bookbinding material; often used for library books.

bumped — dented (usually on edge of boards).

calf — book binding leather from a calf

hide or cattle hide; a commonly used material for leather binding.

CBEL — Cambridge Bibliography of English Literature.

chipped — small tears or excisions along the edge of pages or dust jacket.

cl — cloth (covering the boards of a book's binding).

clamshell — hinged box (board covered in paper, cloth or leather, or a combination of these), usually custom-made, to hold a book for its protection. On a shelf, the clamshell box may look like a book, with a title on its spine.

cloth — book binding material woven from cotton, linen, wool or synthetic fibers.

cocked — twisted.

collation — used in descriptive bibliography as the term which describes the nonbinding portion of the book, verifying the proper sequence and completeness of pages & their gatherings (signatures).

colophon — a statement occurring at the rear of a volume following the text, relating information about the printing history and physical aspects of the book; often includes name of printer, type of paper, typeface, size of edition, date of printing, etc. Early books often had a colophon instead of a title page imprint and modern private press or other examples of fine printing often use a colophon.

conjugate leaves — leaves which are physically attached, part of the same sheet.

covers — the binding of a book; i.e., cloth, calf, morocco, boards, wrappers, etc.

cut edges — the most common type of book edges, trimmed even with a large binders knife prior to finishing the binding process.

DAB — Dictionary of American Biography, a useful 20 volume reference, especially when collecting manuscripts and autographs and attempting to learn about the authors.

damp stain — stain often of a shade of tan or gray resulting from water or other liquid damage to a volume; tolerated by collectors when it is minimal and occurs in very old, scarce volumes; its presence does lower the monetary value.

dec., decor — decorated, often to refer to a binding.

deckle edge — natural or sometimes artificial rough edge of page.

disbound — a book or pamphlet or ephemera which has been removed from its binding.

DNB — (British) Dictionary of National Biography.

duodecimo — see definition under book format.

dust jacket — the paper, often with illustrations and information about the book, used as a protective covering over the book; sometimes called a book jacket (dj) or a dust wrapper (dw). Collectors of literary first editions usually insist on having a fine copy of the original dust jacket with the book.

dust wrapper — see dust jacket.

ed — edition.

edition — the copies of a book or other printed material which originate from the same plates or setting of type.

edition & printing — the copies of a book or other printed material which originate from the same plates or setting of type. If 500 copies of a book are printed on Oct. 5 and 300 copies are printed from the same substantially unchanged plates on Dec. 10, all 800 copies are part of the same edition.

printing — the copies of a book or other printed material which originate from the same press run or from the same plates or setting of type at one time. In the example given for "edition" above, the 500 copies would be the first printing and the 300 copies comprise the second printing. In the 19th century some publishers labelled later printings as if they were later editions, i.e., a second printing would be called a "second edition" on the copyright page.

endpaper — paper, often of coated stock or marbled paper or otherwise "fancy" paper, with one half pasted to the cover; used primarily to give a finished appearance to the binding. Abreviated "ep."

ex-library — legitimately removed (discarded/deaccessioned) from an institutional library, such as a public library, university library, historical society, etc. Often has catalog numbers inked or painted on the spine, library bookplates, embossed or rubber-stamped identification on the title page and plates, library card pockets and often shows considerable wear and/or rebinding in a plain buckram. Referred to as "ex-lib" and of considerably lower monetary value than the respective book which has never been the property of an institutional library.

ex-libris — a Latin phrase meaning "from the books" or to paraphrase, "from the library or collection of"; the phrase is frequently used on bookplates.

exlib, ex-lib — book from a library, usually with library markings.

extra-illustrated — usually a volume made into a unique copy with additional illustrations, autographs, or manuscripts added by carefully glueing or tipping-in this extra material.

f, ff, or fol — folio(s); leaves of a book or a size of a book.

ffee, or ffep — front free endpaper (i.e., the blank that is not pasted down onto the boards).

fine — defining a book's description is not an exact science, but probably all would agree that a book in "fine" condition is a mint copy, in the same condition as when it was sent out by the printer or binder.

first appearances — could be one of three concepts: first time author appears in print, first time a specific writing of an author appears in print, or the first time a specific subject is treated in book form.

first books — the first book appearance by an author (usually refers to a book entirely written by the author, not merely a part of anthology). Frequently these are not widely known, even of well-established authors.

first edition — often, but not always, more valuable than later editions (though of course most books don't get beyond a first edition or even a first printing!).

first thus — first thus indicates the volume in question contains some new feature. It does not indicate that this is the first edition of the title, but rather that it is the first published in this particular format, be it with a new illustrator, publisher, binding, or introduction.

flyleaf — a blank leaf (or leaves) inserted during the binding process between the free endpaper and the beginning or end of the printed pages.

folio — see book format.

foxing — rust colored spots which occur on paper resulting from oxidation processes apparently caused by certain mold fungi; there is no visible evidence of mold, only brown to rusty brown spots on the paper.

frontispiece — an illustration or plate inserted immediately in front of the title page, with the illustration facing the title page, often abbreviated as "frontis."

full binding — volume is entirely encased in leather (calf, sheep, morocco, etc.).

gathering — a folded printed sheet of leaves prior to binding; referred to as a signature after binding.

gilt — indicates the pages of a book have been trimmed and the outside edges covered in gilt, or gold. The abbreviation g.e. or gilt edges is sometimes used.

gutter — the inner margin of the leaves of a bound book; adjacent inner margins of facing pages when book is open.

half binding — the spine and corner leather occupy only approx. one half of top edge.

half-title — page before title page, usually only with the book's title printed on it.

hinge — the inside portion of the flexible area where book cover meets the book spine; often used interchangeably with the term joint, which should be used to designate the outside or exterior portion of the "hinge." A volume which has received heavy or rough use often has cracked or broken hinges.

illum. — (illuminated) usually as in illuminated manuscript, referring to polychromeillustrations.

imprint — when used as a noun refers to the publication data located at the base of a title page, usually includes the city of publication, name of the publisher (sometimes the printer), and the year of publication. Sometimes this information is located in a colophon at the back of a book. Imprint can also be used to refer to a printed piece from a certain location or period of time, i.e., the university has a collection of 18th century Massachusetts imprints.

incunable — anything printed during the 15th century, the first century of printing with "moveable type"; from the Latin, meaning "from the cradle"; can also be used in a relative sense to refer to other early printings, i.e., incunables from the Pacific islands.

incunabulum — a book published before 1501, while publishing was still "in the cradle." Incunabula fetch high prices even though most of them are indescribably dull theological works.

inscribed — a book, or other printed piece, with a handwritten and signed statement usually written for a specific named person(s) and often located on the endpaper or title page; when "inscribed" is used to describe a book, unless otherwise stated, it is implied that the author has written the inscription. When used to designate the recipients of a book as a gift from the author (or publisher), it is called a "presentation inscription."

issue — a portion of an edition printed or published deliberately by the printer or publisher in a distinct form differing from the rest of the printing relative to paper, binding, format, etc. The distinction between "issue" and "state" is that the former relates to changes done on purpose by the publisher or printer and intentionally treated as a separate unit, i.e., a large paper issue or an issue in publisher's leather.

issue — usually refers to a change within a single printing which occurs after some copies of that printing have already been released from the publisher and are in circulation.

joint — the exterior flexible "hinge" where book cover meets book spine; "hinge" is usually used to designate the equivalent inside or interior flexible area. The joint is often an area that splits or cracks or otherwise shows wear in an older cloth or leather volume.

laid in — sometimes, loosely laid in; a letter or other sheet(s) inserted but not glued into a book.

large paper copy — a special edition printed with the pages reconfigured to result in larger leaves with very wide page margins; the text of the individual pages remaining the same as the normal edition; usually large paper copies are printed in small, limited editions.

leaf (leaves) — refers to the smallest, standard physical unit of paper in a printed piece; in the case of books and pamphlets, usually with a printed page on each side of a leaf; a broadside is printed on a single side of a single leaf.

LOC — Library of Congress.

lp — large-paper edition.

ltd., limited ed. — an edition limited to a specified number of copies.

marbled edges — usually the top, bottom and fore edge of a book with a multicolored, swirled-design, somewhat resembling the coloration pattern of marble stone.

marbled paper — paper decorated with a multicolored, swirled-design or pattern; often used for endpapers or for paper-covered boards, especially with ¾ or ½ leather bindings.

mint — unread, or as new.

mo — a suffix as in 12mo, 16mo, etc., used for the size of a book.

morocco — leather binding made from goat hides; usually used in high quality or fine bindings for the interesting texture of the leather; originally tanned with sumac in the country of Morocco.

ms, mss — manuscript, manuscripts.

n.d. — this abbreviation means "no date" provided in the imprint.

n.p. — "no place" of publication provided in the imprint.

nd — no date given for publication.

nf — near-fine condition.

np — no place, publisher, or printer.

NUC — National Union Catalogue; when used in antiquarian book descriptions, usually refers to the pre-1956 imprints NUC which lists Library of Congress holdings plus the holdings of all reporting libraries in the U.S. When a catalog desciption states "Not in NUC," the item described is usually rare (in terms of U.S. library holdings).

OCLC — online combined catalog of most large US libraries and in some other countries. Has about 50 million records, most with invaluable bibliographic information. Accessed only by fee-paying subscribers, but can be used by readers in some libraries.

octavo, 8vo — book in which the sheet has been folded to make 8 pages; like other such designations (4to, folio, etc.), this is not strictly speaking an indication of size. Generally, however, the fewer the folds, the larger the book is likely to be.

offsetting — the process which causes a reversed image inadvertently to appear on the page facing the original impression.

orig. — original (as in original cloth binding).

out-of-print — no longer available from the publisher; abreviated o.p. or op.

pastedown — page which is pasted onto the front or inside board of a book.

PBO — paperback original.

pc, or price clipped — usually a small triangle cut from the front inside corner of a dust jacket to remove the indication of a book's price. Dust jackets with clipped prices are generally considered inferior to ones that are intact.

plate — an illustration(s) printed on a separate sheet of paper (usually heavy and better quality than the text pages) and added to the book during the binding process.

poi — previous owner inscription.

ppr — paperback.

presentation copy — a copy of a printed item inscribed and signed by the author (or publisher) and provided as a gift; see "inscribed."

printing — the copies of a book or other printed material which originate from the same press run or from the same plates or setting of type at one time.

pub — publisher or published.

quarter binding — usually lacks leather corners and leather of the spine occupies only approx. ¼ of the top edge.

quarto, 4to — book in which the sheet has been folded to make 4 pages; like other such designations (octavo, folio, etc.), this is not strictly speaking an indication of size. Generally, however, the fewer the folds, the larger the book is likely to be. See our book size chart for precise details.

reading copy — well-worn, usually abused copy of a book, often in need of rebinding; i.e., suitable for reading, but unlikely to be included in a book collection unless rebound; sometimes refers to a copy that can be read, but is not of a quality worth rebinding.

rebacked — the spine or backstrip has been replaced with new material, in some cases the original worn backstrip is saved and glued over the new material.

rebound — copy of a book which has had the original binding removed and a new binding attached; when there is no need to resew or trim the book, the term "recased" is sometimes used to indicate that a new binding and new endpapers have been added.

recto — the front side of a leaf or in the case of an open book the page on the right, with the page on the left being the verso.

rem or rm — remainder. A copy sold by a publisher after withdrawing the book from publication. Often slightly disfigured, either with a rubber stamp or with a black line crudely drawn across one of the edges.

rubbed — indicates that the outer layer of the material used on the binding has been rubbed off.

sc — soft cover (paperback or similar).

self-wrappers — the wrappers of a pamphlet consist of the first leaf of the first signature and the final leaf of the last signature; i.e., no special or distinct paper wrappers have been added; often government pamphlets and almanacs have self-wrappers.

sewn-as-issued — a pamphlet which has been sewn together and exists in its original state relative to binding; normally a pamphlet with self-wrappers.

shaken — indicates that sections (signatures) of a book or pamphlet are becoming quite loose, but remain attached to the binding. Used to speak of a book that is no longer firm in its covers (typically, publisher's cloth) because of deteriorating inner hinges (should not be used of a book that is in but detached from its covers).

sheep — a common leather binding material from sheep hides; used like calf for a less expensive binding than morocco, appears to have been frequently used for textbooks and law books in the 19th century.

shelfback — another term for spine or backstrip.

signature — a group or gathering of leaves printed together on a sheet of paper which is folded, bound with other signatures and trimmed to form a book or pamphlet; i.e., a section or grouping of pages in a book resulting from printing and binding methodology; also refers to a person's self-handwritten name (autograph signature).

signed — refers to a printed item on which the author (or illustrator or publisher) has written their name, usually on the endpapers, title page, or in the case of pamphlets, on the wrappers.

slipcase — container/box with one open side (made of board covered in paper, cloth or leather, or a combination of these) into which a book may be "slipped" for its protection; Publishers often issue a slipcase with two and three volume sets.

solander case — a box in which a book is stored for protection which has one end (often leather) which resembles the spine or backstrip of a book.

spine — bound outer edge; the back portion of a book's binding which is visible when a book is shelved in a bookcase; the portion which is attached at the joints to the front and rear covers.

started — indicates that one or more signatures of a book are protruding beyond the rest of the fore edge, i.e., beginning to pull away from the binding to which they are still attached; not as loosened as the term "shaken" indicates.

state — usually refers to a change made within a single printing prior to any circulation of copies of the printing.

teg — top edge gilt.

three-quarter binding — volume has leather spine and corners which occupy approx. ¾ of the space along top edge of board (cover). The remainder of the board is covered with marbled paper, plain paper, cloth, different leather, etc.

tipped in — a sheet or sheets which were not part of the original bound book, but are now. Pages are tipped in by dabbing minute amounts of glue onto the edge which is to be inserted into the book.

TLS — typed letter signed, as opposed to ALS, a handwritten letter signed by the writer.

tp — title page.

trade edition — usually, "first trade edition" (as distinct from limited editions, often signed or with special paper or bindings, which appear before the full commercial publication of a book).

ts — typescript.

unbound — indicates that the item has never been bound, i.e., unbound sheets; not the same as disbound which indicates that the binding has been removed

uncut — refers to the edges of a book in an untrimmed state, edges are somewhat uneven, also see "deckle edge."

unopened — a book with signatures which have never been cut as opposed to untrimmed and uneven (see "uncut"); unopened books retain the folds of the original gathering and contain many pages which cannot be read without first opening the pages with a knife. Some collectors prefer an unopened book because it indicates that the book has never been read; other collectors who read their books would rather not have the task of cutting open pages and risking tears and jagged leaf edges.

variants — refers to the differences in bindings or endpapers, such as different colors of stamping.

vellum — true vellum is a thin specially treated untanned "leather" from calf skin, also known as parchment (high quality parchment from calf skin is called vellum; general quality parchment is made from calf, goat or sheep skin); used for documents and for book bindings; many early books (of the sixteenth and seventeenth centuries) have vellum bindings; paper makers have produced parchment and/or vellum papers also used for book bindings.

verso — the reverse or opposite or left-hand side, especially used in reference to a leaf which has a recto and verso side; in a open book the recto is the right hand page and the verso is the left hand page; in the case of a broadside only the recto is printed and the verso is blank.

VG — very good condition.

VG/VG — or some variant (e.g., NF/VG) describes the condition of the binding (sometimes of both the binding and interior) and dust-jacket of a book, respectively.

vol. — volume.

w.a.f. — with all faults; indicates a book or other item which is being offered without careful delineation of its condition or without careful collation; usually indicates a less than "very good" copy, which probably does have faults, often including excessive wear or missing leaves, plates, or maps.

wrappers, wrp — abbreviated as "wraps," wrappers are the paper covers of a pamphlet, often of a paper of heavier weight than the text paper; when you see "wrappers," you know the item is not a hardbound book, but is instead a pamphlet or magazine with paper covers; usually not used to refer to 20th century paperback books which are called "soft bound" (with paper covers).

One book at a time, or a very few at a time – there's the ideal way! Bargain a bit, grouse a bit: go home and consult the oracles of bibliography and the auction records; then go back with the gleam of the hunter in your eye and bring down your bird. There is no other method. You must have the urge to rummage about. You must learn to love the fell of old books; the smell of them must be unto you a delicious aroma. But at first confine your prowling – if you can – to times when your pocketbook is lean. Your resistance is apt to be very low when the exchequer overflows. You will find it much easier to stick to a one-book or one-author plan if you buy when you are comparatively hard up.

Barton W. Currie
1878 – 1962

Pseudonyms

Edward S. Aarons
Paul Ayres
Edward Ronns

Marvin H. Albert
Albert Conroy
Stuart Jason
Nick Quarry
Anthony Rome

William (Thomas) Ard
Ben Kerr
Jonas Ward (some)
Thomas Willis

Paul Auster
Paul Benjamin

Mike Avallone
Nick Carter (a few)
Troy Conway (a few)
Priscilla Dalton
Stuart Jason
Edwina Noone
Sidney Stuart
Max Walker

W. T. Ballard
D'Allard Hunter
Neil MacNeil
John Shepherd

Bill Ballinger
B.X. Sanborn

Robert Barnard
Bernard Bastable

Julian Barnes
Dan Kavanagh
Basil Seal

Charles Beaumont
Keith Grantland

Robert Beck
Slim Iceberg

H. Bedford-Jones
Paul Feval
Lucien Pemjean
L. Pemjion

Roger Blake
Mark Sade

Lurton Blassingame
Peter Duncan

James Blish
William Atheling

Robert Bloch
Collier Young

Lawrence Block
William Ard
Jill Emerson
Chip Harrison
Sheldon Lord
Benjamin Morse, M.D.
Andrew Shaw

Marion Zimmer Bradley
Lee Chapman
John Dexter (some)
Miriam Gardner
Valerie Graves
Morgan Ives

John Brunner
Keith Woodcott

Kenneth Bulmer
Adam Hardy
Manning Norvil
Dray Prescot

W.R. Burnett
John Monachan
James Updyke

William S. Burroughs
William Lee

Stuart Byrne
John Bloodstone

Paul Cain
George Sims

Ramsey Campbell
Carl Dreadstone
Jay Ramsay

John Dickson Carr
Carter Dickson
Roger Fairbairn

Basil Cooper
Lee Falk

Clarence Cooper
Robert Chestnut

John Creasey
Gordon Ashe
Harry Carmichael
Norman Deane
Robert Caine Frazier
Patrick Gill
Michael Holliday
Brian Hope
Colin Hughes
Kyle Hunt
J.J. Marric
Jeremy York

Michael Crichton
John Lange

David Cross
George B. Chesbro

Norman Daniels
Dorothy Daniels
David Wade

Avram Davidson
Ellery Queen
(about 2 titles only)

August Derleth
Stephen Grendon

Thomas B. Dewey
Tom Brandt
Cord Wainer

Thomas Disch
Thomas Demijohn
Knye Cassandra (both with John
Sladek)

James Duffy
Haughton Murphy

Peter Beresford Ellis
Peter Tremayne

Harlan Ellison
Paul Merchant

Dennis Etchison
Jack Martin

Paul Fairman
F.W. Paul

Lionel Fanthorpe
John E. Muller

Philip Jose Farmer
William Norfolk
Kilgore Trout

Frederick S. Faust
Max Brand
George Owen Baxter

John Russell Fearn
Aston Del Martia

Alan Dean Foster
George Lucas

Gardner F. Fox
Glen Chase
Jefferson Cooper
Jeffrey Gardner
Matt Gardner
James Kendricks Gray
Dean Jennings
Simon Majors
Kevin Matthews
John Medford Morgan
Rod Morgan
Bart Summers

Erle Stanley Gardner
A.A. Fair
Carleton Kendrake
Charles Kinney

Randall Garrett
Walter Bupp
David Gordon
½ of Mark Phillips and
Robert Randall

Richard Geis
Robert Owen
Peggy Swenson

Theodor Seuss Geisel
Dr. Seuss

Walter B. Gibson
Douglas Brown
Maxwell Grant

Ron Goulart
Lee Falk
Josephine Kains
Julian Kearney
Kenneth Robeson
Frank S. Shaw(n)
Joseph Silva

Charles L. Grant
Felicia Andrew
Deborah Lewis

Ben Haas
Richard Meade

Joe Haldeman
Robert Graham

Oakley Hall
O.M. Hall

Brett Halliday
Mike Shayne

Joseph Hansen
Rose Brock
James Colton

Terry Harknett
Joseph Hedges
Thomas H. Stone

Timothy Harris
Harris Hyde

Carolyn G. Heilbrun
Amanda Cross

Eleanor Alice Burford Hibbert
Philippa Carr
Victoria Holt
Jean Plaidy

Jamake Highwater
J. Marks
J. Marks-Highwater

Hochstein, Peter
Jack Short

C. Hodder-Williams
James Brogan

John Robert Holt
Elizabeth Giles
Raymond Giles

Cornell Hoppley-Woolrich
George Hopley
William Irish
Cornell Woolrich

E. Howard Hunt
David St. John

Evan Hunter
Curt Cannon
Hunt Collins
Ezra Hannon
Richard Marsten
Ed McBain

Oliver Jacks
Kenneth R. Gandley

J. Denis Jackson
Julian Moreau

John Jakes
William Ard
Alan Payne
Jay Scotland
J.X. Williams

Will F. Jenkins
Murray Leinster

Frank Kane
Frank Boyd

Henry Kane
Anthony McCall

Hal Kent
Ron Davis

Stephen King
Richard Bachman

Philip K. Klass
William Tenn

Andrew Klavan
Keith Peterson

William Knowles
Clyde Allison
Clyde Ames

Dean R. Koontz
David Axton
Brian Coffey
Deanna Dwyer
K.R. Dwyer
John Hill
Leigh Nichols
Anthony North
Richard Paige
Owen West
Aaron Wolfe

Cyril Kornbluth
Simon Eisner
Jordan Park

Jerzy Kosinski
Joseph Novak
Jane Somers

P. Kubis
Casey Scott

Michael Kurland
Jennifer Plum

Louis L'Amour
Tex Burns
Jim Mayo

Lawrence Lariar
Adam Knight

Keith Laumer
Anthony LeBaron

Milton Lesser
Stephen Marlowe

Doris Lessing
Jane Somers

Alfred Henry Lewis
Dan Quinn

Paul Linebarger
Cordwainer Smith

Frank Belknap Long
Lyda Belknap Long

Peter Lovesey
Peter Lear

Mark Lucas
Drew Palmer

Robert Ludlum
Jonathan Ryder
Michael Shepherd

Richard Lupoff
Adison Steele

Dennis Lynds
Michael Collins
John Crowe
Maxwell Grant (some)
Mark Sadler

Barry Malzberg
Mike Berry
Claudine Dumas
Mel Johnson
M.L. Johnson
Barrett O'Donnell
K.M. O'Donnell

Frederick Manfred
Feike Feikema

Mel Marshall
Zack Tayler

Robert Martin
Lee Roberts

Van Wyck Mason
Geoffrey Coffin

Graham Masterton
Thomas Luke

Richard Matheson
Swanson, Logan

Dudley McGaughy
Dean Owen

Marijane Meaker
Ann Aldrich
Vin Packer

H.L. Menken
Owen Hatteras

Barbara Gross Mertz
Barbara Michael
Elizabeth Peters

Kenneth Millar
Ross MacDonald
John Ross MacDonald

Michael Moorcock
Bill Barclay
Edward P. Bradbury

Brian Moore
Bernard Mara
Bryan Michael

James Morris
Jan Morris (after sex change)

Petroleum Nasby
David R. Locke

Andre Alice Norton
Andrew North
Alice Norton
Andre Norton

Alan E. Nourse
Doctor X

Charles Nuetzel
Albert Jr. Augustus
John Davidson
Charles English
Alec Rivere

Joyce Carol Oates
Rosamond Smith

Andrew Offutt
John Cleve
Baxter Giles
J.X. Williams (some)

Edith Mary Pargeter
Ellis Peter

Henry Patterson
Martin Fallon
James Graham
Jack Higgins
Harry Patterson
Hugh Marlowe

Dennis Phillips
Peter Chambers
Peter Chester

James Atlee Philips
Philip Atlee

Judson Phillips
Hugh Pentecost

Richard Posner
Iris Foster
Beatrice Murray
Paul Todd

Richard Prather
David Knight
Douglas Ring

Bill Pronzini
Jack Foxx

Peter Rabe
J. T. MacCargo

R. L. Radford
Ford, Marcia

Clayton Rawson
Stuart Towne

Ruth Rendell
Barbara Vine

Mack Reynolds
Bob Belmont
Todd Harding
Maxine Reynolds

Anne Rice
Anne Rampling
A.N. Roquelaure

Robert Rosenblum
Robert Maxxe

W.E.D. Ross
Rose Dana
Jan Daniels
Clarissa Ross
Dan Ross
Dana Ross
Marilyn Ross

Jean-Baptiste Rossi
Sebastien Japrisot

John Sandford
John Camp

Sandra Scoppetone
Jack Early

Con Sellers
Della Bannion

Alice Bradley Sheldon
Alice Bradley
Raccoona Sheldon
James Tiptree

Robert Silverberg
Loren Beauchamp
W.R. Burnett (some only)
Walter Drummond
Don Elliott (some)
Hilary Ford
Franklin Hamilton
Calvin Knox
Lt. Woodard, M.D.

George H. Smith
J.M. Deer
Jan Hudson
Jerry Jason
M.E. Knerr
Diana Summers

David Stacton
Bud Clifton

Theodore Sturgeon
Frederick R. Ewing
Ellery Queen (1 book only)

Ross Thomas
Oliver Bleeck

Don Tracy
Roger Fuller

Bob Tralins
Keith Miles
Sean O'Shea

E.C. Tubb
Gregory Kern

Jack Vance
Peter Held
Ellery Queen (some/few)

Luther Vidal
Edgar Box
Cameron Kay
Gore Vidal

Walter Wager
John Tiger
Max Walker

Harold Ward
Zorro

Jack Webb
John Farr

Joe Weiss
Ray Anatole
Claude Dauphine
Ken Mirbeau

Donald E. Westlake
John B. Allan
Curt Clark
Timothy Culver
J. Morgan Cunningham
Samuel Holt
Alan Marshall
Richard Stark
Edwin West

Harry Whittington
Whit Harrison
Shep Shepherd

Gordon Williams
P.B Yuill

Jack Williamson
Will Stewart

Don Wollheim
David Grinnell

George F. Worts
Loring Brent

Bookbuyers

In this section of the book we have listed buyers of books and related material. When you correspond with these dealers, be sure to enclose a self-addressed stamped envelope if you want a reply. Do not send lists of books for appraisal. If you wish to sell your books, quote the price you want or send a list and ask if there are any on the list they might be interested in and the price they would be willing to pay. If you want the list back, be sure to send a SASE large enough for the listing to be returned. When you list your books, do so by author, full title, publisher and place, date, edition, and condition, noting any defects on cover or contents.

Adventure

Ken Hebenstreit, Bookseller
813 N Washington Ave.
Royal Oak, MI 48067
phone/fax 248-548-5460
kenhebenstreit@home.com
www.khbooks.com

The Silver Door
P.O. Box 3208
Redondo Beach, CA 90277
310-379-6005

African-American

Beasley Books
Paul & Beth Garon
1533 W Oakdale, 2nd Floor
Chicago, IL 60657
773-472-4528
fax 773-472-7857
beasley@mcs.com

Children's Book Adoption Agency
P.O. Box 643
Kensington, MD 20895-0643
310-565-2834
 fax 301-585-3091
KIDS_BKS@interloc.com

Fran's Bookhouse
6601 Greene St.
Philadelphia, PA 19119
215-438-2729
fax 215-438-8997

Ken Hebenstreit, Bookseller
813 N Washington Ave.
Royal Oak, MI 48067
phone/fax 248-548-5460
kenhebenstreit@home.com
www.khbooks.com

Monroe Stahr Books
5112 Van Noord Ave.
Sherman Oaks, CA 91423
818-501-3419
fax 818-995-0966
MStahrBks@aol.com

Recollection Books
4519 University Way NE
Seattle, WA 98105
206-548-1346

Alaska

Artis Books
201 N Second Ave.
P.O. Box 822
Alpena, MI 49707
517-354-3401
artis@freeway.net

Albania

W.B. O'Neill-Old & Rare Books
11609 Hunters Green Ct.
Reston, VA 20191
703-860-0782
fax 703-620-0153
nyc1918@aol.com

Alcoholics Anonymous

The Book Baron
1236 S Magnolia Ave.
Anaheim, CA 92804
714-527-7022
fax 714-527-5634
bkbaron1@pacbell.net or
bkbaron3@qte.net

American Southwest

Arizona, Northern & New Mexcico
Books West Southwest
W. David Laird
Box 6149, University Station
Irvine, CA 92616-6149
714-509-7670
fax 714-854-5102
bkswest@ix.netcom.com

Americana

Amaranth Books
P.O. Box 421
Wilmette, IL 60091-0421
708-328-2939

Aplan Antiques & Art
James & Peg Aplan
21424 Clover Pl.
Piedmont, SD 57769-9403
605-347-5016
fax 605-347-9336
aplanpeg@rapidnet.com

The Bookseller, Inc.
174 W Exchange St.
Akron, OH 44302
330-762-3101
fax 330-762-4413
booklein@apk.net

The Captain's Bookshelf, Inc.
31 Page Ave.
Asheville, NC 28801
828-253-6631
fax 828-253-4917
captsbooks@aol.com

Chapel Hill Rare Books
P.O. Box 456
Carrboro, NC 27510
919-929-8351
rarebooks@mindspring.com

Terry Harper, Bookseller
P.O. Box 312
Vergennes, VT 05491-0312
802-877-9262
bookvend@together.net

Susan Heller, Pages for Sages
22611 Halburton Rd.
Beachwood, OH 44122-3939
216-283-2665
hellersu@cyberdrive.net

Jim Hodgson Books
908 S Manlius St.
Fayetteville, NY 13066
315-637-6264
jimhbooks@aol.com

M & S Rare Books, Inc.
P.O. Box 2594, E Side Sta.
Providence, RI 02906
401-421-1050
fax 401-272-0831
(attention M & S)
dsiegel@msrarebooks.com

Parmer Books
7644 Forrestal Rd.
San Diego, CA 92120-2203
619-287-0693
fax 619-287-6135
ParmerBook@aol.com

Randall House
Pia Oliver
835 Laguna St.
Santa Barbara, CA 93101
805-963-1909
fax 805-963-1650
pia@piasworld.com
www.piasworld.com/randall

Thorn Books
P.O. Box 1244
Moorpark, CA 93020
805-529-3647
fax 805-529-0022
thornbooks@earthlink.net

Yesterday's Books
229 Riverview Dr.
Parchment, MI 49004
616-345-1011
yesbooks@aol.com

Anarchism
Beasley Books
Paul & Beth Garon
1533 W Oakdale, 2nd Floor
Chicago, IL 60657
773-472-4528
fax 773-472-7857
beasley@mcs.com

Nutmeg Books
354 New Litchfield St. (Rte. 202)
Torrington, CT 06790
203-482-9696
nutmeg@compsol.net

Angling
Book & Tackle Shop
29 Old Colony Rd.
P.O. Box 114
Chestnut Hill, MA 02467
phone/fax 617-965-0459
bktack@ibm.net

Anthropology
The King's Market Bookshops
P.O. Box 709
Boulder, CO 80306-0709
303-232-3321

Anthologies
Cartoonists from 1890 – 1960
Craig Ehlenberger
Abalone Cove Rare Books
7 Fruit Tree Rd.
Portuguese Bend, CA 90275

Antiquarian
A.B.A.C.U.S.®
Phillip E. Miller
343 S Chesterfield St.
Aiken, SC 29801
803-648-4632

Fine, hard-to-find books
Arnold's of Michigan
Judith A. Herba
218 South Water St.
Marine City, MI 48039-1688
810-765-1350 or 800-276-3092
fax 810-765-7914
arnoldbk@ees.eesc.com

The Book Baron
1236 S Magnolia Ave.
Anaheim, CA 92804
714-527-7022
fax 714-527-5634
bkbaron1@pacbell.net or
bkbaron3@qte.net

Children's Book Adoption Agency
P.O. Box 643
Kensington, MD 20895-0643
310-565-2834
fax 301-585-3091
KIDS_BKS@interloc.com

James Tait Goodrich
Antiquarian Books & Manuscripts
135 Tweed Blvd.
Grandview-on-Hudson, NY 10960
914-359-0242
fax 914-359-0142
jtg.jamestgoodrich.com

Terry Harper, Bookseller
P.O. Box 312
Vergennes, VT 05491-0312
802-877-9262
bookvend@together.net

Murray Hudson
Antiquarian Books & Maps
109 S. Church St.
P.O. Box 163
Halls, TN 38040
901-836-9057 or 800-748-9946
fax 901-836-9017
mapman@usit.net

The Old Map Gallery
Paul F. Mahoney
1746 Blake St.
Denver, CO 80202
303-296-7725
fax 303-296-7936
oldmapgallery@denver.net

Jeffrey Lee Pressman, Bookseller
3246 Ettie St.
Oakland, CA 94608
510-652-6232

Robert Mueller Rare Books
8124 W 26th St.
N Riverside, IL 60546
708-447-6441

Scribe Company
Attn: Bonnie Smith
427 Hidden Forest S
Longview, TX 75605
903-663-6873

Also Agriculture, Biographies, Law, Travel,
Turn-of-the-Century Fiction & Philosophy
David R. Smith
30 Nelson Circle
Jaffrey, NH 03452
603-532-8666
Bookinc@Cheshire.net

Antiques, Collectibles & Reference
Antique & Collectors Reproduction News
Mark Chervenka, Editor
Box 12130-OB
Des Moines, IA 50312-9403
515-270-8994
fax 515-255-4530

Collector's Companion
Perry Franks
P.O. Box 24333
Richmond, VA 23224

Galerie De Boicourt
Eva M Boicourt
6136 Westbrooke Dr.
W. Bloomfield, MI 48322
248-788-9253

Henry H. Hain III
Antiques, Collectibles & Books
2623 N Second St.
Harrisburg, PA 17110-1109
717-238-0534
antcolbks@ezonline.com

Appraisals
J. Sampson Antiques & Books
107 S Main
Harrodsburg, KY 40330
606-734-7829

Lee Barnett Temares
50 Heights Rd.
Plandome, NY 11030
516-627-8688
fax 516-627-7822
tembooks@aol.com

Arabian Horses
Worldwide Antiquarian
P.O. Box 410391
Cambridge, MA 02141-0004
617-876-6220
fax 617-876-0839
mbalwan@aol.com

Arabian Nights
Worldwide Antiquarian
P.O. Box 410391

Cambridge, MA 02141-0004
617-876-6220
fax 617-876-0839
mbalwan@aol.com

Archaelogy
Flo Silver Books
8442 Oakwood Ct. N
Indianapolis, IN 46260
phone/fax 317-255-5118
Flosilver@aol.com

Architecture
Cover to Cover
Mark Shuman
P.O. Box 687
Chapel Hill, NC 27514
919-967-1032

Arctic
Artis Books
201 N Second Ave.
P.O. Box 822
Alpena, MI 49707
517-354-3401
artis@freeway.net

Parmer Books
7644 Forrestal Rd.
San Diego, CA 92120-2203
619-287-0693
fax 619-287-6135
ParmerBook@aol.com

Armenia
W.B. O'Neill
Old & Rare Books
11609 Hunters Green Ct.
Reston, VA 20191
703-860-0782
fax 703-620-0153
nyc1918@aol.com

Art
AL-PAC
Lamar Kelley Antiquarian Books
2625 E Southern Ave., C-120
Tempe, AZ 85282
480-831-3121
fax 480-831-3193
alpac2625@aol.com

Book & Tackle Shop
Bernard L. Gordon
29 Old Colony Rd.
P.O. Box 114
Chestnut Hill, MA 02467
phone/fax 617-965-0459 (winter)
bktack@ibm.net

Books West Southwest
W. David Laird
Box 6149, University Station

Irvine, CA 92616-6149
714-509-7670
fax 714-854-5102
bkswest@ix.netcom.com

The Captain's Bookshelf, Inc.
Chandler W. Gordon
31 Page Ave.
Asheville, NC 28801
828-253-6631
fax 828-253-4917
captsbooks@aol.com

Fine, applied
L. Clarice Davis Art Books
P.O. Box 56054
Sherman Oaks, CA 91413-1054
818-787-1322
fax 818-780-3281
davislc@earthlink.net
www.abcbooks.com/home/LCALART

Galerie De Boicourt
Eva M. Boicourt
6136 Westbrooke Dr.
W. Bloomfield, MI 48322
248-788-9253

Edison Hall Books
5 Ventnor Dr.
Edison, NJ 08820
908-548-4455

Heritage Book Shop, Inc.
8540 Melrose Ave.
Los Angeles, CA 90069
310-659-3674
fax 310-659-4872
HBSINCLA@aol.com

David Holloway, Bookseller
7430 Grace St.
Springfield, VA 22150
703-659-1798

Significant Books
3053 Madison Rd.
P.O. Box 9248
Cincinnati, OH 45209
513-321-7567 or 800-750-1153
signbook@iac.net

Lee Barnett Temares
50 Heights Rd.
Plandome, NY 11030
516-627-8688
fax 516-627-7822
tembooks@aol.com

Xanadu Records, Ltd.
3242 Irwin Ave.
Kingsbridge, NY 10463
718-549-3655

Arthurian
Camelot Books
Charles E. Wyatt
P.O. Box 2883
Vista, CA 92083
619-940-9472

Astronomy
Knollwood Books
Lee & Peggy Price
P.O. Box 197
Oregon, WI 53575-0197
608-835-8861
fax 608-835-8421
books@tdsnet.com

Atlases
Murray Hudson
Antiquarian Books & Maps
109 S Church St.
P.O. Box 163
Halls, TN 38040
901-836-9057 or 800-748-9946
fax 901-836-9017
mapman@usit.net

The Old Map Gallery
Paul F. Mahoney
1746 Blake St.
Denver, CO 80202
303-296-7725
fax 303-296-7936
oldmapgallery@denver.net

Atomic Bomb
Key Books
P.O. Box 58097
St. Petersburg, FL 33715-8097
813-867-2931

Autobiographies
Herb Sauermann
21660 School Rd.
Manton, CA 96059

Warren's Collector Books
For Sale Now
Warren Gillespie, Jr.
112 Royal Ct.
Friendswood, TX 77546
281-482-7947

Wellerdt's Books
3700 S Osprey Ave. #214
Sarasota, FL 34239
813-365-1318

Autographs
Ads Autographs
P.O. Box 8006
Webster, NY 14580-8006
716-671-2651
fax 716-671-5727

The American Dust Co.
47 Park Ct.
Staten Island, NY 10301
phone/fax 718-442-8253

Michael Gerlicher
1375 Rest Point Rd.
Orono, MN 55364

Susan Heller, Pages for Sages
22611 Halburton Rd.
Beachwood, OH 44122-3939
216-283-2665
hellersu@cyberdrive.net

Heritage Book Shop, Inc.
8540 Melrose Ave.
Los Angeles, CA 90069
310-659-3674
fax 310-659-4872
HBSINCLA@aol.com

Key Books
P.O. Box 58097
St. Petersburg, FL 33715-8097
813-867-2931

McGowan Book Co.
P.O. Box 4226
Chapel Hill, NC 27515-4226
919-968-1121 or 800-449-8406
fax 919-968-1644
mcgowanbooks@mindspring.com
www.mcgowanbooks.com

Randall House
Pia Oliver
835 Laguna St.
Santa Barbara, CA 93101
805-963-1909
fax 805-963-1650
pia@piasworld.com
www.piasworld.com/randall

Aviation
The Book Corner
Michael Tennaro
728 W Lumsden Rd.
Brandon, FL 33511
813-684-1133
bookcrnr@worldnet.att.net
www.abebooks.com/home/bookcrnr

The Bookseller, Inc.
174 W Exchange St.
Akron, OH 44302
330-762-3101
fax 330-762-4413
booklein@apk.net

Cover to Cover
Mark Shuman
P.O. Box 687
Chapel Hill, NC 27514
919-967-1032

Baedeker Handbooks
W.B. O'Neill
Old & Rare Books
11609 Hunters Green Ct.
Reston, VA 20191
703-860-0782
fax 703-620-0153
nyc1918@aol.com

Barbie
Glo's Books & Collectibles
Gloria Stobbes
906 Shadywood
Southlake, TX 76092
817-481-1438

Baseball
The American Dust Co.
47 Park Ct.
Staten Island, NY 10301
phone/fax 718-442-8253

R. Plapinger, Baseball Books
P.O. Box 1062
Ashland, OR 97520
541-488-1220

Rising Stars
Don Carnahan
P.O. Box 2991
Yuma, AZ 85366
phone/fax 520-329-6054

L. Frank Baum
Alcott Books
Barbara Ruppert
5909 Darnell
Houston, TX 77074-7719
713-774-2202

Beat Generation
Twice Read Books & Comics
42 S Main St.
Chambersburg, PA 17201
717-261-8449

Bibliographies
About Books
6 Sand Hill Ct.
P.O. Box 5717
Parsippany, NJ 07054
973-515-4591

Books West Southwest
W. David Laird
Box 6149, University Station
Irvine, CA 92616-6149
714-509-7670
fax 714-854-5102
bkswest@ix.netcom.com

Oak Knoll Books
310 Delaware St.
New Castle, DE 19720

800-996-2556 or 302-328-7232
fax 302-328-7274
oakknoll@oakknoll.com
www.oakkknoll.com

Big Little Books
Jay's House of Collectibles
75 Pky. Dr.
Syosset, NY 11791

Biographies
Herb Sauermann
21660 School Rd.
Manton, CA 96059

Third Time Around Books
Norman Todd
R.R. #1
Mar., Ontario
Canada N0H 1XO
519-534-1382

Warren's Collector Books
For Sale Now
112 Royal Ct.
Friendswood, TX 77546
281-482-7947

Black Americana
Especially Little Black Sambo
Glo's Books & Collectibles
Gloria Stobbes
906 Shadywood
Southlake, TX 76092
817-481-1438

History & literature; general literature
Thomas L. Coffman
TLC Books
9 N College Ave.
Salem, VA 24153
540-389-3555

History & literature
David Holloway, Bookseller
7430 Grace St.
Springfield, VA 22150
703-569-1798

Mason's Bookstore, Rare Books
    & Record Albums East
115 S Main St.
Chambersburg, PA 17201
717-261-0541

Black Fiction & Literature
Almark & Co.-Booksellers
P.O. Box 7
Thornhill, Ontario
Canada L3T 3N1
905-764-2665
fax 905-764-5771
al@almarkco.com or
mark@almarkco.com

The American Dust Co.
47 Park Ct.
Staten Island, NY 10301
phone/fax 718-442-8253

Ken Hebenstreit, Bookseller
813 N Washington Ave.
Royal Oak, MI 48067
phone/fax 248-548-5460
kenhebenstreit@home.com
www.khbooks.com

Black Studies
Recollection Books
4519 University Way NE
Seattle, WA 98105
206-548-1346

Black Hills
James F. Taylor
515 Sixth St.
Rapid City, SD 57701
605-341-3224

Blues
Beasley Books
Paul & Beth Garon
1533 W Oakdale, 2nd Floor
Chicago, IL 60657
773-472-4528
fax 773-472-7857
beasley@mcs.com

Book Search Service
Authors of the West
191 Dogwood Dr.
Dundee, OR 97115
503-538-8132
Lnash@georgefox.edu

Ackley Books & Collectibles
Bryant & Suzanne Pitner
912 Hidden Cove Way
Suisun City, CA 94585-3511
707-421-9032
fax 978-285-6554
www.ackleybooks.com
(mail order only)

Avonlea Books Search Service
P.O. Box 74, Main Station
White Plains, NY 10602-0074
914-946-5923
fax 914-761-3119
avonlea@bushkin.com

Bookingham Palace
Rosan Van Wagenen & Eileen Layman
52 North 2500 East
Teton, ID 83451
209-458-4431

Heritage Book Shop, Inc.
8540 Melrose Ave.
Los Angeles, CA 90069

310-659-3674
fax 310-659-4872
HBSINCLA@aol.com

Hilda's Book Search
Hilda Gruskin
199 Rollins Ave.
Rockville, MD 20852
301-948-3181

Lost n' Found Books
Linda Lengerich
3214 Columbine Ct.
Indianapolis, IN 46224
phone/fax 317-298-9077

Passaic Book Center
594 Main Ave.
Passaic, NJ 07055
201-778-6646
fax 201-778-6738

Recollection Books
4519 University Way NE
Seattle, WA 98105
206-548-1346

The Silver Door
P.O. Box 3208
Redondo Beach, CA 90277
310-379-6005

Especially children's out-of-print books
Treasures from the Castle
Connie Castle
1277 Candlestick Lane
Rochester, MI 48306
248-651-7317
treasure23@juno.com
www.abebooks.com/home/treasure

Book Sets
AL-PAC
Lamar Kelley Antiquarian Books
2625 E Southern Ave., C-120
Tempe, AZ 85282
480-831-3121
fax 480-831-3193
alpac2625@aol.com

Books About Books
About Books
6 Sand Hill Ct.
P.O. Box 5717
Parsippany, NJ 07054
973-515-4591

Books West Southwest
W. David Laird
Box 6149, University Station
Irvine, CA 92616-6149
714-509-7670
fax 714-854-5102
bkswest@ix.netcom.com

First Folio
Dennis R. Melhouse
1206 Brentwood
Paris, TN 38242
phone/fax 910-944-9940
firstfol@aeneas.net

Susan Heller, Pages for Sages
22611 Halburton Rd.
Beachwood, OH 44122-3939
216-283-2665
hellersu@cyberdrive.net

Key Books
P.O. Box 58097
St. Petersburg, FL 33715-8097
813-867-2931

Oak Knoll Books
310 Delaware St.
New Castle, DE 19720
800-996-2556 or 302-328-7232
fax 302-328-7274
oakknoll@oakknoll.com
www.oakknoll.com

Randall House
Pia Oliver
835 Laguna St.
Santa Barbara, CA 93101
805-963-1909
fax 805-963-1650
pia@piasworld.com
www.piasworld.com/randall

George H. Tweney
16660 Marine View Dr. SW
Seattle, WA 98166
206-243-8243

Botany
Brooks Books
Phil & Marty Nesty
P.O. Box 91
Clayton, CA 94517
925-672-4566
fax 925-672-3338
brooksbk@netvista.net

Charles Bukowski
Ed Smith Books
20 Paget Rd.
Madison, WI 53704-5929
608-241-3707
ed@edsbooks.com
www.edsbooks.com

Edgar Rice Burroughs
W. J. Leveridge
W & L Trading Company
2301 Carova Rd.
Carova Beach, Corolla, NC 27927
252-453-3408

C.S. Lewis & Friends
Aslan Books
191 Dogwood Dr.
Dundee, OR 97115
503-538-8132
Lnash@georgefox.edu

California
Books West Southwest
W. David Laird
Box 6149, University Station
Irvine, CA 92616-6149
714-509-7670
fax 714-854-5102
bkswest@ix.netcom.com

Thorn Books
P.O. Box 1244
Moorpark, CA 93020
805-529-3647
fax 805-529-0022
thornbooks@earthlink.net

Canadiana
David Armstrong, Bookseller
Box 551
Lethbridge, Alberta
Canada T1J 3Z4
403-381-3270
dabooks@telusplanet.net
www.telusplanet.net/public/dabooks

Third Time Around Books
Norman Todd
R.R. #1
Mar., Ontario
Canada N0H 1XO
519-534-1382

Cartography
Overlee Farm Books
P.O. Box 1155
Stockbridge, MA 01262
413-637-2277

Cartoon Art
Jay's House of Collectibles
75 Pky. Dr.
Syosset, NY 11791

Catalogs
Antiques or other collectibles
Antique & Collectors Reproduction News
Mark Chervenka, Editor
Box 12130-OB
Des Moines, IA 50312-9403
515-270-8994
fax 515-255-4530

Hillcrest Books
961 Deep Draw Rd.
Crossville, TN 38555-9547
phone/fax 931-484-7680
hillcrst@usit.net
www.oldcatalogues.com

Farming/Tractors
Henry Lindeman
8723 Clarklake Rd.
Clarklake, MI 49234

Glass, pottery, furniture, doll, toy, jewelry, general merchandise, fishing tackle
Bill Schroeder
5801 Kentucky Dam Rd
Paducah, KY 42003

Celtic
Camelot Books
Charles E. Wyatt
P.O. Box 2883
Vista, CA 92083
619-940-9472

Central America
Flo Silver Books
8442 Oakwood Ct. N
Indianapolis, IN 46260
phone/fax 317-255-5118
Flosilver@aol.com

Marc Chagall
Paul Melzer Fine & Rare Books
12 E Vine St.
P.O. Box 1143
Redlands, CA 92373
909-792-7299
fax 909-792-7218
pmbooks@eee.org

Children's Illustrated
Noreen Abbot Books
2666 44th Ave.
San Francisco, CA 94116-2635
415-664-9464

Alcott Books
Barbara Ruppert
5909 Darnell
Houston, TX 77074-7719
713-774-2202

Book & Tackle Shop
Bernard L. Gordon
29 Old Colony Rd.
P.O. Box 114
Chestnut Hill, MA 02467
phone/fax 617-965-0459 (winter)
bktack@ibm.net

Books of the Ages
Gary J. Overmann
Maple Ridge Manor
4764 Silverwood Dr.
Batavia, OH 45103-9740
phone/fax 513-732-3456

Including Dick & Jane readers, Little Golden Books, older Weekly Reader
Bookcase Books
P. Gayle Hendrington

R.R. 1 Box 242
Newport, NH 03773
603-863-9517
books@bookcasebooks.com
www.bookcasebooks.com

Bromer Booksellers
607 Boylston St.
Boston, MA 02116
617-247-2818
fax 617-247-2975
books@bromer.com
www.bromer.com

Non-series or published after 1925
Cattermole
20th Century Children's Books
9880 Fairmount Rd.
Newbury, OH 44065
440-338-3253
fax 440-338-1675
books@cattermole.com
www.cattermole.com

19th & 20th Century
Children's Book Adoption Agency
P.O. Box 643
Kensington, MD 20895-0643
301-565-2834
fax 301-585-3091
KIDS_BKS@interloc.com

Free search service
Steven Cieluch
15 Walbridge St., Suite #10
Allston, MA 02134-3808
617-734-7778
scieluch@channel1.com

Ursula Davidson
Children's & Illustrated Books
134 Linden Ln.
San Rafael, CA 94901
414-454-3939
fax 415-454-1087
davidson_u@compuserve.com
www.abebooks.com/home/uschi

Drusilla's Books
817 N Howard St.
Baltimore, MD 21201-4696
410-225-0277
fax 410-321-4955
Tues-Sat: 12 noon to 5 p.m.
or by appointment
drusilla@mindspring.com

Edison Hall Books
5 Ventnor Dr.
Edison, NJ 08820
908-548-4455

Circa 1850s through 1970s
Encino Books
Diane Yaspan

5063 Gaviota Ave
Encino, CA 91436
818-905-711
fax 818-501-7711

First Folio
Dennis R. Melhouse
1206 Brentwood
Paris, TN 38242-3804
phone/fax 901-944-9940
firstfol@aeneas.net

Fran's Bookhouse
6601 Greene St.
Philadelphia, PA 19119
215-438-2729
fax 215-438-8997

Madeline, Eloise, Raggedy Ann & Andy, Uncle
Wiggly, Wizard of Oz
Glo's Books & Collectibles
Gloria Stobbes
906 Shadywood
Southlake, TX 76092
817-481-1438

Susan Heller, Pages for Sages
22611 Halburton Rd.
Beachwood, OH 44122-3939
216-283-2665
hellersu@cyberdrive.net

Ilene Kayne
1308 S Charles St.
Baltimore, MD 21230-4219
410-347-7570
kayne@clark.net

Bob Lakin Books
P.O. Box 186
Chatfield, TX 75105
972-247-3291

Marvelous Books
Dorothy (Dede) Kenn
P.O. Box 1510
Ballwin, MO 63022
314-458-3301
fax 314-273-5452
marvbooks@aol.com

Much Ado
Seven Pleasant St.
Marblehead, MA 01945
781-639-0400
fax 781-639-0840
muchado@shore.net

Nerman's Books
Gary Nerman
233 Dunkirk Drive
Winnipeg, Manitoba
Canada R2M 3X1
nerman@escape.ca

Margaret E. Page
Page Books
HCR 65, Box 233
Kingston, AR 72742
870-861-5831
pagebook@eritter.net

Jo Ann Reisler, Ltd.
360 Glyndon St., NE
Vienna, VA 22180
703-938-2967
fax 703-938-9057
reisler@clark.net
www.clark.net/pub/reisler

Scribe Company
Attn: Bonnie Smith
427 Hidden Forest S
Longview, TX 75605
903-663-6873

Barbara Smith Books
P.O. Box 1185
Northampton, MA 01061
413-586-1453

Treasures from the Castle
Connie Castle
1277 Candlestick Lane
Rochester, MI 48306
248-651-7317
treasure23@juno.com
www.abebooks.com/home/treasure

Yesterday's Books
229 Riverview Dr.
Parchment, MI 49004
616-345-1011
yesbooks@aol.com

Children's Series
Children's Book Adoption Agency
P.O. Box 643
Kensington, MD 20895-0643
301-565-2834
fax 301-585-3091
KIDS_BKS@interloc.com

Circa 1900s through 1970s
Encino Books
Diane Yaspan
5063 Gaviota Ave
Encino, CA 91436
818-905-711
fax 818-501-7711

Judy Bolton, Nancy Drew, Rick Brant, Cherry
Ames, etc.; also Dick & Jane
Glo's Books & Collectibles
Gloria Stobbes
906 Shadywood
Southlake, TX 76092
817-481-1438

Ilene Kayne
1308 S Charles St.
Baltimore, MD 21230-4219
410-347-7570
kayne@clark.net

Bob Lakin Books
P.O. Box 186
Chatfield, TX 75105
972-247-3291

Nerman's Books
Gary Nerman
233 Dunkirk Drive
Winnipeg, Manitoba
Canada R2M 3X1
nerman@escape.ca

Scribe Company
Attn: Bonnie Smith
427 Hidden Forest S
Longview, TX 75605
903-663-6873

Lee Barnett Temares
50 Heights Rd.
Plandome, NY 11030
516-627-8688
fax 516-627-7822
tembooks@aol.com

Yesterday's Books
229 Riverview Dr.
Parchment, MI 49004
616-345-1011
yesbooks@aol.com

Christian Faith
Books Now & Then
Dennis & Jan Patrick
P.O. Box 337
Stanley, ND 58784
phone/fax 701-628-2084
bnt@stanley.ndak.net
www.ourchurch.com/member/b/
booksnow-then

Christmas
Especially illustrated antiquarian
Drusilla's Books
817 N Howard St.
Baltimore, MD 21201-4696
410-225-0277
fax 410-321-4955
Tues-Sat: 12 noon to 5p.m.
or by appointment
drusilla@mindspring.com

Sir W.S. Churchill
Chartwell Booksellers
55 E 52nd St.
New York, NY 10055
212-308-0643

Robert L. Merriam
Rare, Used & Old Books
39 Newhall Rd.
Conway, MA 01341-9709
413-369-4052
rmerriam@valinet.com

Cinema, Theatre & Films
The American Dust Co.
47 Park Ct.
Staten Island, NY 10301
phone/fax 718-442-8253

Cinemage Books
105 W 27th St.
New York, NY 10001
212-243-4919
irajoel@aol.com

Xanadu Records, Ltd.
3242 Irwin Ave.
Kingsbridge, NY 10463
718-549-3655

Civil War
Chapel Hill Rare Books
Douglas & Maureen O'Dell
P.O. Box 456
Carrboro, NC 27510
919-929-8351
rarebooks@mindspring.com

Stan Clark Military Books
915 Fairview Ave.
Gettysburg, PA 17325
717-337-0581

Also the South
Elder's Book Store
2115 Elliston Pl.
Nashville, TN 37203
615-327-1867

Rick Harmon
Military Books & Relics
910 Sullivan Dr.
Belvidere, IL 61008
815-547-7580

Jim Hodgson Books
908 S Manlius St.
Fayetteville, NY 13066
315-637-6264
jimhbooks@aol.com

Mason's Bookstore, Rare Books
 & Record Albums East
115 S Main St.
Chambersburg, PA 17201
717-261-0541

K.C. & Jean Owings
Box 389

Whitman, MA 02382
781-447-7850
fax 781-447-3435

Irvin S. Cobb
*Always paying $3.00 each plus shipping. Send
 for immediate payment:*
Bill Schroeder
5801 Kentucky Dam Rd.
Paducah, KY 42003

Collectibles, Antiques & Reference
Antique & Collectors Reproduction News
Mark Chervenka, Editor
Box 12130-OB
Des Moines, IA 50312-9403
515-270-8994
fax 515-255-4530

Galerie De Boicourt
Eva M. Boicourt
6136 Westbrooke Dr.
W. Bloomfield, MI 48322
248-788-9253

Henry H. Hain III
Antiques, Collectibles & Books
2623 N Second St.
Harrisburg, PA 17110-1109
717-238-0534
antcolbks@ezonline.com

Color Plate Books
Drusilla's Books
817 N Howard St.
Baltimore, MD 21201-4696
410-225-0277
fax 410-321-4955
Tues – Sat: 12 noon to 5 p.m.
or by appointment
drusilla@mindspring.com

Worldwide Antiquarian
P.O. Box 410391
Cambridge, MA 02141-0004
617-876-6220
fax 617-876-0839
mbalwan@aol.com

Comics
Passaic Book Center
594 Main Ave.
Passaic, NJ 07055
201-778-6646
fax 201-778-6738

Communism
Beasley Books
Paul & Beth Garon
1533 W Oakdale, 2nd Floor
Chicago, IL 60657
773-472-4528
fax 773-472-7857
beasley@mcs.com

Cookery & Cookbooks
Arnold's of Michigan
Judith A. Herba
218 South Water St.
Marine City, MI 48039-1688
810-765-1350 or 800-276-3092
fax 810-765-7914
arnoldbk@ees.eesc.com

Book & Tackle Shop
Bernard L. Gordon
29 Old Colony Rd.
P.O. Box 114
Chestnut Hill, MA 02467
phone/fax 617-965-0459 (winter)
bktack@ibm.net

Book Broker
114 Bollingwood Rd.
Charlottesville, VA 22902
804-296-2194
fax 804-296-1566
bookbrk@cfw.com
mail order or appointment only

RAC Books
P.O. Box 296 RD 2
Seven Valleys, PA 17360
717-428-3776
racbooks@cyberia.com

Barbara Smith Books
P.O. Box 1185
Northampton, MA 01061
413-586-1453

Warren's Collector Books
 For Sale Now
Warren Gillespie, Jr.
112 Royal Ct.
Friendswood, TX 77546
281-482-7947

Crime
Ken Hebenstreit, Bookseller
813 N Washington Ave.
Royal Oak, MI 48067
phone/fax 248-548-5460
kenhebenstreit@home.com
www.khbooks.com

The Silver Door
P.O. Box 3208
Redondo Beach, CA 90277
310-379-6005

Cuba & Panama
The Book Corner
Mike Tennaro
728 W Lumsden Rd.
Brandon, FL 33511
813-684-1133
bookcrnr@worldnet.att.net
www.abebooks.com/home/bookcrnr

Cyprus

W.B. O'Neill
Old & Rare Books
11609 Hunters Green Ct.
Reston, VA 20191
703-860-0782
fax 703-620-0153
nyc1918@aol.com

Decorative Arts

Robert L. Merriam
Rare, Used & Old Books
39 Newhall Rd.
Conway, MA 01341-9709
413-369-4052
rmerriam@valinet.com

Detective

First editions
Karl M. Armens
740 Juniper Dr.
Iowa City, IA 52245
319-337-7755

Ken Hebenstreit, Bookseller
813 N Washington Ave.
Royal Oak, MI 48067
phone/fax 248-548-5460
kenhebenstreit@home.com
www.khbooks.com

Monroe Stahr Books
5112 Van Noord Ave.
Sherman Oaks, CA 91423
818-501-3419
fax 818-995-0966
MStahrBks@aol.com

Mordida Books
P.O. Box 79322
Houston, TX 77279
713-467-4280
fax 713-467-4182
mordida@swbell.net
www.mordida.com

The Silver Door
P.O. Box 3208
Redondo Beach, CA 90277
310-379-6005

Thomas Books
P.O. Box 14036
Phoenix, AZ 85063
623-247-9289
fax 623-945-1023
sales@thomasbooks.com
www.thomasbooks.com

Disney

Cohen Books & Collectibles
Joel J. Cohen
P.O. Box 810310

Boca Raton, FL 33481-0310
561-487-7888
fax 561-487-3117
cohendisney@prodigy.net
www.cohendisney.com

Jay's House of Collectibles
75 Pky. Dr.
Syosset, NY 11791

Documents

McGowan Book Co.
P.O. Box 4226
Chapel Hill, NC 27515-4226
919-968-1121 or 800-449-8406
fax 919-968-1644
mcgowanbooks@mindspring.com
www.mcgowanbook.com

Dogs

Kathleen Rais & Co.
Rais Place Cottage
211 Carolina Ave.
Phoenixville, PA 19460
610-933-1388

Emily Dickinson

Robert F. Lucas
Antiquarian Books
P.O. Box 63
Blandford, MA 01008
413-848-2061
books@lucasbooks.com
www.lucasbooks.com

Robert L. Merriam
Rare, Used & Old Books
39 Newhall Rd.
Conway, MA 01341-9709
413-369-4052
rmerriam@valinet.com

Thomas Edison

Edison Hall Books
5 Ventnor Dr.
Edison, NJ 08820
908-548-4455

Ephemera

Antique valentines
Kingsbury Productions
Katherine & David Kreider
4555 N Pershing Ave., Suite 33-138
Stockton, CA 95207
209-467-8438

The Mulberry Cat
Yvonne Davis
Jan Davis Martel
P.O. Box 3573
Boone, NC 28607
704-963-7693

Equestrine

Books, antiques, art
Artiques, Ltd.
Veronica Jochens
P.O. Box 67
Lonedell, MO 60360
phone/fax 314-629-1374
veronica@nightowl.net

Espionage

Ken Hebenstreit, Bookseller
813 N Washington Ave.
Royal Oak, MI 48067
phone/fax 248-548-5460
kenhebenstreit@home.com
www.khbooks.com

The Silver Door
P.O. Box 3208
Redondo Beach, CA 92077
310-379-6005

Estate Libraries

The Book Collector
2347 University Blvd.
Houston, TX 77005
713-661-2665

Exhibition Catalogs

L. Clarice Davis Fine & Applied Art Books
P.O. Box 56054
Sherman Oaks, CA 91413-1054
818-787-1322
fax 818-780-3281
davislc@earthlink.net
www.abebooks.com/home/LCALART

Exploration

Western
Terry Harper, Bookseller
P.O. Box 312
Vergennes, VT 05491-0312
802-877-9262
bookvend@together.net

Heritage Book Shop, Inc.
8540 Melrose Ave.
Los Angeles, CA 90069
310-659-3674
fax 310-659-4872
HBSINCLA@aol.com

Key Books
P.O. Box 58097
St. Petersburg, FL 33715-8095
813-867-2931

Flo Silver Books
8442 Oakwood Ct. N
Indianapolis, IN 46260
phone/fax 317-255-5118
Flosilver@aol.com

Fantasy

The Book Baron
1236 S Magnolia Ave.
Anaheim, CA 92804
714-527-7022
fax 714-527-5634
bkbaron1@pacbell.net or
bkbaron3@qte.net

Camelot Books
Charles E. Wyatt
P.O. Box 2883
Vista, CA 92083
619-940-9472

Ken Hebenstreit, Bookseller
813 N Washington Ave.
Royal Oak, MI 48067
phone/fax 248-548-5460
kenhebenstreit@home.com
www.khbooks.com

Science fiction, horror or supernatural
Xanadu Records Ltd.
3242 Irwin Ave.
Kingsbridge, NY 10463
718-549-3655

Farming

First editions
Karl M. Armens
740 Juniper Dr.
Iowa City, IA 52245
319-337-7755

Also gardening
Hurley Books/Celtic Cross Books
1753 Rt. 12
Westmoreland, NH 03467-4742
603-399-4342
fax 603-399-8326
hurleybook@adam.cheshire.net

Henry Lindeman
8723 Clarklake Rd.
Clarklake, MI 49234

Fiction

American, European, detective or crime
The American Dust Co.
47 Park Ct.
Staten Island, NY 10301
phone/fax 718-442-8253

McGee's First Varieties
330 Franklin Rd., Suite 135A
Brentwood, TN 37027
615-373-5318
TMcGee@BellSouth.net
www.mcgees1st.com

Southern
Ken Hebenstreit, Bookseller
813 N Washington Ave.

Royal Oak, MI 48067
phone/fax 248-548-5460
kenhebenstreit@home.com
www.khbooks.com

Alice Robbins, Bookseller
3002 Round Hill Rd.
Greensboro, NC 27408
910-282-1964

Third Time Around Books
Norman Todd
R.R. #1
Mar., Ontario
Canada N0H 1XO
519-534-1382

Warren's Collector Books
   For Sale Now
Warren Gillespie, Jr.
112 Royal Ct.
Friendswood, TX 77546
281-482-7947

American, European, detective or crime
Ace Zerblonski Books
Malcolm McCollum, Proprietor
1419 North Royer
Colorado Springs, CO 80907
719-634-3941

Bob Lakin Books
P.O. Box 186
Chatfield, TX 75105
972-247-3291

19th & 20th-C American
Mason's Bookstore, Rare Books
   & Record Albums East
115 S Main St.
Chambersburg, PA 17201
717-261-0541

Filipiniana

Pacific Rim Books
Michael Onorato
P.O. Box 30575
Bellingham, WA 98228-2575
206-676-0256
pacrimbks@aol.com

Financial

Warren's Collector Books
   For Sale Now
Warren Gillespie Jr.
112 Royal Ct.
Friendswood, TX 77546
281-482-7947

Fine Bindings & Books

The Book Collector
2347 University Blvd.
Houston, TX 77005
713-661-2665

Bromer Booksellers
607 Boylston St.
Boston, MA 02116
617-247-2818
fax 617-247-2975
books@bromer.com
www.bromer.com

Dad's Old Bookstore
Green Hills Ct.
4004 Hillsboro Rd.
Nashville, TN 37215
615-298-5880

Terry Harper, Bookseller
P.O. Box 312
Vergennes, VT 05491-0312
802-877-9262
bookvend@together.net

Heritage Book Shop, Inc.
8540 Melrose Ave.
Los Angeles, CA 90069
310-659-3674
fax 310-659-4872
HBSINCLA@aol.com

George Robert Kane Fine Books
252 Third Ave.
Santa Cruz, CA 95062
phone/fax 408-426-4133
gkanebks@cruzio.com

Kenneth Karmiole, Bookseller, Inc.
509 Wilshire Blvd.
Santa Monica, CA 90401
310-451-4342
fax 310-458-5930
karmbooks@aol.com

Mason's Bookstore, Rare Books
   & Record Albums East
115 S Main St.
Chambersburg, PA 17201
717-261-0541

Paul Melzer Fine & Rare Books
12 E Vine St.
P.O. Box 1143
Redlands, CA 92373
909-792-7299
fax 909-792-7218
pmbooks@eee.org

Also sets
Randall House
Pia Oliver
835 Laguna St.
Santa Barbara, CA 93101
805-963-1909
fax 805-963-1650
pia@piasworld.com
www.piasworld.com/randall

David R. Smith
30 Nelson Circle
Jaffrey, NH 03452
603-532-8666
Bookinc@Cheshire.net

Fine Press
Susan Heller, Pages for Sages
22611 Halburton Rd.
Beachwood, OH 44122-3939
216-283-2665
hellersu@cyberdrive.net

Heritage Book Shop, Inc.
8540 Melrose Ave.
Los Angeles, CA 90069
310-659-3674
fax 310-659-4872
HBSINCLA@aol.com

Randall House
Pia Oliver
835 Laguna St.
Santa Barbara, CA 93101
805-963-1909
fax 805-963-1650
pia@piasworld.com
www.piasworld.com/randall

Firearms
Melvin Marcher, Bookseller
6204 N Vermont
Oklahoma City, OK 73112
405-946-6270
(12 noon to 7 p.m. *only*)

First Editions
A Tale of Two Sisters
1401 Emerald Circle
Southlake, TX 76092
817-329-0988
tts.mcc@ix.netcom.com

Ken Hebenstreit, Bookseller
813 N Washington Ave.
Royal Oak, MI 48067
phone/fax 248-548-5460
kenhebenstreit@home.com
www.khbooks.com

After 1937
A.B.A.C.U.S.®
Phillip E. Miller
343 S Chesterfield St.
Aiken, SC 29801
803-648-4632

Hyper-modern
Almark & Co.-Booksellers
P.O. Box 7
Thornhill, Ontario
Canada L3T 3N1
905-764-2665

fax 905-764-5771
al@almarkco.com or
mark@almarkco.com

Modern or signed
AL-PAC
Lamar Kelley Antiquarian Books
2625 E Southern Ave., C-120
Tempe, AZ 85282
480-831-3121
fax 480-831-3193
alpac2625@aol.com

Modern or signed
Alcott Books
Barbara Ruppert
5909 Darnell
Houston, TX 77074-7719
713-774-2202

Amaranth Books
P.O. Box 421
Wilmette, IL 60091-0421
708-328-2939

Modern or signed
The American Dust Co.
47 Park Ct.
Staten Island, NY 10301
phone/fax 718-442-8253

Karl M. Armens
740 Juniper Dr.
Iowa City, IA 52245
319-337-7755

Modern
Beasley Books
Paul & Beth Garon
1533 W. Oakdale, 2nd floor
Chicago, IL, 60657
773-472-4528
fax 773-472-7857
beasley@mcs.com

Bella Luna Books
4697 Stone Canyon Ranch Rd.
Castle Rock, CO 80104
800-497-4717
fax 303-663-2113
Bellalun@aol.com

Between the Covers
35 W Maple Ave.
Merchantville, NJ 08109
609-665-2284
fax 609-665-3639
mail@betweenthecovers.com
www.betweenthecovers.com

The Book Baron
1236 S Magnolia Ave.
Anaheim, CA 92804

714-527-7022
fax 714-527-5634
bkbaron1@pacbell.net or
bkbaron3@qte.net

Modern or signed
Burke's Bookstore
1719 Poplar Ave.
Memphis, TN 38104-6447
901-278-7484
fax 901-272-2340
burkes@netten.net

Modern
Chapel Hill Rare Books
Douglas & Maureen O'Dell
P.O. Box 456
Carrboro, NC 27510
919-929-8351
rarebooks@mindspring.com

Modern
Tom Davidson, Bookseller
3703 Ave. L
Brooklyn, NY 11210
718-338-8428
fax 718-338-8430
tdbooks@att.net

Modern
The Early West/Whodunit Books
P.O. Box 9292
College Station, TX 77842
409-775-6047
fax 409-764-7758
EarlyWest@aol.com

Edison Hall Books
5 Ventnor Dr.
Edison, NJ 08820
908-548-4455

Modern
Bernard E. Goodman, Bookseller
7421 SW 147 Ct.
Miami, FL 33193-1116
305-385-8526
bgbooks@bellsouth.net
www.abebooks.com/home/bgbookman

Ruth Heindel Associates
First Editions, Rare & Used Books
660 Boas St., Suite 1618
Harrisburg, PA 17110
717-213-9010

Modern
Susan Heller, Pages for Sages
22611 Halburton Rd.
Beachwood, OH 44122-3939
216-283-2665
hellersu@cyberdrive.net

Heritage Book Shop, Inc.
8540 Melrose Ave.
Los Angeles, CA 90069
310-659-3674
fax 310-659-4872
HBSINCLA@aol.com

Modern
David Holloway, Bookseller
7430 Grace St.
Springfield, VA 22150
703-569-1798

Modern
Ken Lopez, Bookseller
51 Huntington Rd.
Hadley, MA 01035
413-584-4827
fax 413-584-2045
mail@lopezbooks.com
www.lopezbooks.com

Modern
McGee's First Varieties
330 Franklin Rd., Suite 135A
Brentwood, TN 37027
615-373-5318
TMcGee@BellSouth.net
www.mcgees1st.com

Monroe Stahr Books
5112 Van Noord Ave.
Sherman Oaks, CA 91423
818-501-3419
fax 818-995-0966
MStahrBks@aol.com

Much Ado
Seven Pleasant St.
Marblehead, MA 01945
781-639-0400
fax 781-639-0840
muchado@shore.net

Robert Mueller Rare Books
8124 W 26th St.
N Riverside, IL 60546
708-447-6441

Jeffrey Lee Pressman, Bookseller
3246 Ettie St.
Oakland, CA 94608
510-652-6232

American & British
Quill & Brush
Patricia & Allen Alearn
1137 Sugarloaf Mtn. Rd.
Dickerson, MD 20842
301-874-3200
fax 301-874-0824
Firsts@qbbooks.com
www.qbbooks.com

Alice Robbins, Bookseller
3002 Round Hill Rd.
Greensboro, NC 27408
910-282-1964

Scribe Company
Attn: Bonnie Smith
427 Hidden Forest S
Longview, TX 75605
903-663-6873

*Especially fiction, cookery, children's, business,
    sports & illustrated*
Eileen Serxner
Box 2544
Bala Cynwyd, PA 19004
610-664-7960
fax 610-664-1940
serxner@erols.com
www.abebooks.com/home/serxnerbooks

Modern
Ed Smith Books
20 Paget Rd.
Madison, WI 53704-5929
608-241-3707
ed@edsbooks.com
www.edsbooks.com

Spellbound Books
M. Tyree
3818 Vickie Ct. #B
Prescott Valley, AZ 86314
520-759-2625

*20th-century authors of nature, natural
    history, 20th-century Americana, historical
    & nautical fiction*
Town's End Books
John D. & Judy A. Townsend
132 Hemlock Dr.
Deep River, CT 06417
860-526-3896 or 888-732-2668
john@townsendbooks.com
www.townsendbooks.com

*Modern; especially British & European
    literature*
The Typographeum Bookshop
246 Bennington Rd.
Francestown, NH 03043
603-547-2425

Harrison Fisher
Parnassus Books
218 N 9th St.
Boise, ID 83702

Fishing
Artis Books
201 N Second Ave.
P.O. Box 822
Alpena, MI 49707-0822
517-354-3401
artis@freeway.net

Edison Hall Books
5 Ventnor Dr.
Edison, NJ 08820
908-548-4455

Jim Hodgson Books
908 S Manlius St.
Fayetteville, NY 13066
315-637-6264
jimhbooks@aol.com

Melvin Marcher, Bookseller
6204 N Vermont
Oklahoma City, OK 73112
405-946-6270
(12 noon to 7 p.m. *only*)

Mason's Bookstore, Rare Books
    & Record Albums East
115 S Main
Chambersburg, PA 17201
717-261-0541

Yesterday's Books
229 Riverview Dr.
Parchment, MI 49004
616-345-1011
yesbooks@aol.com

Florida
The Book Corner
Michael Tennaro
728 W Lumsden Rd.
Brandon, FL 33511
813-684-1133
bookcrnr@worldnet.att.net
www.abebooks.com/home/bookcrnr

Fore-Edge Painted Books
Susan Heller, Pages for Sages
22611 Halburton Rd.
Beachwood, OH 44122-3939
216-283-2665
hellersu@cyberdrive.net

George Robert Kane Fine Books
252 Third Ave.
Santa Cruz, CA 95062
phone/fax 408-426-4133
gkanebks@cruzio.com

Freemasonry
Mason's Bookstore, Rare Books
    & Record Albums East
115 S Main St.
Chambersburg, PA 17201
717-261-0541

Gambling & Gaming
Gambler's Book Shop
630 S Eleventh St.
Las Vegas, NV 89101
800-634-6243

Games

Card or board; Whist & Bridge
Bill & Mimi Sachen
927 Grand Ave.
Waukegan, IL 60085-3709
847-662-7204
FutileWill@aol.com

Gardening

The American Botanist
P.O. Box 532
Chillicothe, IL 61523
309-274-5254
fax 309-274-6143
www.amerbot.com

Brooks Books
Phil & Marty Nesty
P.O. Box 91
Clayton, CA 94517
925-672-4566
fax 925-672-3338
brooksbk@netvista.net

The Captain's Bookshelf, Inc.
Chandler W. Gordon
31 Page Ave.
Asheville, NC 22801
828-253-6631
fax 828-253-4917
captsbooks@aol.com

Gazetteers

Murray Hudson
Antiquarian Books & Maps
109 S Church St.
P.O. Box 163
Halls, TN 38040
901-836-9057 or 800-748-9946
fax 901-836-9017
mapman@usit.net

Genealogy

Elder's Book Store
2115 Elliston Pl.
Nashville, TN 37203
615-327-1867

General Out-of-Print

Best-Read Books
332 Thompson Rd.
Sedro-Woolley, WA 98284-9555

Bicentennial Book Shop
820 S Westnedge Ave.
Kalamazoo, MI 49008
616-345-5987

The Book Baron
1236 S Magnolia Ave.
Anaheim, CA 92804
714-527-7022
fax 714-527-5634
bkbaron1@pacbell.net or
bkbaron3@qte.net

Book Den South
Nancy Costello
2249 First St.
Ft. Myers, FL 33901-2943
813-332-2333

Pulp fiction & modern first editions
Bookcase Books
P. Gayle Hendrington
R.R. 1 Box 242
Newport, NH 03773
603-863-9517
books@bookcasebooks.com
www.bookcasebooks.com

The Bookseller, Inc.
174 W Exchange St.
Akron, OH 44302
330-762-3101
fax 330-762-4413
booklein@apk.com

Cinemage Books
105 W 27th St.
New York, NY 10001
212-243-4919
irajoel@aol.com

Antiquarian
Eastside Books & Paper
P.O. Box 1581, Gracie Station
New York, NY 10028-0013
212-759-6299

Edison Hall Books
5 Ventnor Dr.
Edison, NJ 08820
908-548-4455

Fran's Bookhouse
6601 Greene St.
Philadelphia, PA 19119
215-438-2729
fax 215-438-8997

Grave Matters
P.O. Box 32192
Cincinnati, OH 45232-0192
513-242-7527
fax 513-242-5115
books@gravematters.com
www.gravematters.com

George Robert Kane Fine Books
252 Third Ave.
Santa Cruz, CA 95062
phone/fax 408-426-4133
gkanebks@cruzio.com

Ken Hebenstreit, Bookseller
813 N Washington Ave.
Royal Oak, MI 48067
phone/fax 248-548-5460
kenhebenstreit@home.com
www.khbooks.com

McGowan Book Co.
P.O. Box 4226
Chapel Hill, NC 27515-4226
919-968-1121 or 800-449-8406
fax 919-968-1644
mcgowanbooks@mindspring.com
www.mcgowanbooks.com

Robert L. Merriam
Rare, Used & Old Books
39 Newhall Rd.
Conway, MA 01341-9709
413-369-4052
rmerriam@valinet.com

The Mulberry Cat
Yvonne Davis
Jan Davis Martel
P.O. Box 3573
Boone, NC 28607
704-963-7693

Passaic Book Center
594 Main Ave.
Passaic, NJ 07055
201-778-6646
fax 201-778-6738

RAC Books
P.O. Box 296 RD 2
Seven Valleys, PA 17360
717-428-3776
racbooks@cyberia.com

J. Sampson Antiques & Books
107 S Main
Harrodsburg, KY 40330
606-734-7829

Significant Books
3053 Madison Rd.
P.O. Box 9248
Cincinnati, OH 45209
800-750-1153 or 513-321-7567
signbook@iac.net

A.A. Vespa
P.O. Box 637
Park Ridge, IL 60068
708-692-4210

Genetics

The King's Market Bookshops
P.O. Box 709
Boulder, CO 80306-0709
303-232-3321

Geographies

Murray Hudson
Antiquarian Books & Maps
109 S Church St.
P.O. Box 163
Halls, TN 38040

901-836-9057 or 800-748-9946
fax 901-836-9017
mapman@usit.net

The Old Map Gallery
Paul F. Mahoney
1746 Blake St.
Denver, CO 80202
303-296-7725
fax 303-296-7936
oldmapgallery@denver.net

Overlee Farm Books
P.O. Box 1155
Stockbridge, MA 01262
413-637-2277

Sue Grafton
Glo's Books & Collectibles
Gloria Stobbes
906 Shadywood
Southlake, TX 76092
817-481-1438

Thomas Books
P.O. Box 14036
Phoenix, AZ 85063
623-247-9289
fax 480-945-1023
sales@thomasbooks.com
www.thomasbooks.com

Grand Canyon & Colorado River
Five Quail Books — West
P.O. Box 9870
Phoenix, AZ 85068-9870
602-861-0548
fax 602-861-1113
5quail@grandcanyonbooks.com
www.grandcanyonbooks.com

The Great Lakes
Artis Books
201 N Second Ave.
P.O. Box 822
Alpena, MI 49707-0822
517-354-3401
artis@freeway.net

Greece
W.B. O'Neill
Old & Rare Books
11609 Hunters Green Ct.
Reston, VA 20191
703-860-0782
fax 703-620-0153
nyc1918@aol.com

Zane Grey
British Stamp Exchange
12 Fairlawn Ave.
N Weymouth, MA 02191
871-335-3075

Health
Warren's Collector Books
   For Sale Now
Warren Gillespie, Jr.
112 Royal Court
Friendship, TX 77546
281-482-7947

Herbals
The American Botanist
P.O. Box 532
Chillicothe, IL 61523
309-274-5254
fax 309-274-6143
www.amerbot.com

Brooks Books
Phil & Marty Nesty
P.O. Box 91
Clayton, CA 94517
925-672-4566
fax 925-672-3338
brooksbk@netvista.net

Heritage Press
Lee Barnett Temares
50 Heights Rd.
Plandome, NY 11030
516-627-8688
fax 516-627-7822
tembooks@aol.com

History
American & natural
Ace Zerblonski Books
Malcolm McCollum, Proprietor
1419 North Royer
Colorado Springs, CO 80907
719-634-3941

Science & medicine
Amaranth Books
P.O. Box 421
Wilmette, IL 60091-0421
708-328-2939

*Especially US military, US Marine Corps &
   American Civil War*
Stan Clark Military Books
915 Fairview Ave.
Gettysburg, PA 17325
717-337-0581

Camelot Books
Charles E. Wyatt
P.O. Box 2883
Vista, CA 92083
619-940-9472

Postal & postal artifacts
McGowan Book Co.
P.O. Box 4226
Chapel Hill, NC 27515-4226

919-968-1121 or 800-449-8406
fax 919-968-1644
mcgowanbooks@mindspring.com
www.mcgowanbooks.com

Local & regional
Significant Books
3053 Madison Rd.
P.O. Box 9248
Cincinnati, OH 45209
800-750-1153 or 513-321-7567
signbook@iac.net

General, Civil & Revolutionary Wars
David R. Smith
30 Nelson Circle
Jaffrey, NH 03452
603-532-8666
Bookinc@Cheshire.net

Twice Read Books & Comics
42 S Main St.
Chambersburg, PA 17201
717-261-8449

Hollywood
Cinemage Books
105 W 27th St.
New York, NY 10001
212-243-4919
irajoel@aol.com

Novels
Monroe Stahr Books
5112 Van Noord Ave.
Sheramn Oaks, CA 91423
818-501-3419
fax 818-995-0966
MStahrBks@aol.com

Horror
The Book Baron
1236 S Magnolia Ave.
Anaheim, CA 92804
714-527-7022
fax 714-527-5634
bkbaron1@pacbell.net or
bkbaron3@qte.net

Ken Hebenstreit, Bookseller
813 N Washington Ave.
Royal Oak, MI 48067
phone/fax 248-548-5460
kenhebenstreit@home.com
www.khbooks.com

Kai Nygaard
19421 Eighth Pl.
Escondido, CA 92029
619-749-9039

Pandora's Books, Ltd.
P.O. Box 54

Neche, ND 58265
204-324-8548
fax 204-324-1628
jgthiess@MTS.Net

Horse Books
October Farm
2609 Branch Rd.
Raleigh, NC 27610
919-772-0482
fax 919-779-6265
octoberfarm@bellsouth.net
www.octoberfarm.com

Horticulture
The American Botanist
P.O. Box 532
Chillicothe, IL 61523
309-274-5254
fax 309-274-6143
www.amerbot.com

Ornamental
Brooks Books
Phil & Marty Nesty
P.O. Box 91
Clayton, CA 94517
925-672-4566
fax 925-672-3338
brooksbk@netvista.net

L. Ron Hubbard
AL-PAC
Lamar Kelley Antiquarian Books
2625 E Southern Ave., C-120
Tempe, AZ 85282
480-831-3121
fax 480-831-3193
alpac2625@aol.com

Hunting
Artis Books
201 N Second Ave.
P.O. Box 822
Alpena, MI 49707-0822
517-354-3401
artis@freeway.net

Edison Hall Books
5 Ventnor Dr.
Edison, NJ 08820
908-548-4455

Jim Hodgson Books
908 S Manlius St.
Fayetteville, NY 13066
315-637-6264
jimhbooks@aol.com

Melvin Marcher, Bookseller
6204 N Vermont
Oklahoma City, OK 73112
405-946-6270
(12 noon to 7 p.m. *only*)

Yesterday's Books
229 Riverview Dr.
Parchment, MI 49004
616-345-1011
yesbooks@aol.com

Idaho
Parnassus Books
218 N 9th St.
Boise, ID 83702

Illustrated
Noreen Abbot Books
2666 44th Ave.
San Francisco, CA 94116-2635
415-664-9464

The American Dust Co.
47 Park Ct.
Staten Island, NY 10301
phone/fax 718-442-8253

Books of the Ages
Gary J. Overmann
Maple Ridge Manor
4764 Silverwood Dr.
Batavia, OH 45103-9740
phone/fax 513-732-3456

Bromer Booksellers
607 Boylston St.
Boston, MA 02116
617-247-2818
fax 617-247-2975
books@bromer.com
www.bromer.com

George Robert Kane Fine Books
252 Third Ave.
Santa Cruz, CA 95062
phone/fax 408-426-4133
gkanebks@cruzio.com

Randall House
Pia Oliver
835 Laguna St.
Santa Barbara, CA 93101
805-963-1909
fax 805-963-1650
pia@piasworld.com
www.piasworld.com/randall

Barbara Smith Books
P.O. Box 1185
Northampton, MA 01061
413-586-1453

Gary R. Smith
517 Laurel Ave.
Modesto, CA 95351

Indians
Wars
K.C. & Jean C. Owings

Box 389
Whitman, MA 02382
781-447-7850
fax 781-447-3435

Plains, Black Hills, etc.
Flo Silver Books
8442 Oakwood Ct. N.
Indianapolis, IN 46260
phone/fax 317-255-5118
Flosilver@aol.com

Iowa
Karl M. Armens
740 Juniper Dr.
Iowa City, IA 52245
319-337-7755

Will James
British Stamp Exchange
12 Fairlawn Ave.
N Weymouth, MA 02191
871-335-3075

Jazz
Beasley Books
Paul & Beth Garon
1533 W Oakdale, 2nd Floor
Chicago, IL 60657
773-472-4528
fax 773-472-7857
beasley@mcs.com

Chartwell Booksellers
55 E 52nd St.
New York, NY 10055
212-308-0643

John Deere
Henry Lindeman
8723 Clarklake Rd.
Clarklake, MI 49234

Judaica
Stanley Schwartz
1934 Pentuckett Ave.
San Diego, CA 92104-5732
619-232-5888
fax 619-233-5833
Schwartz@cts.com

Juvenile
Cover to Cover
Mark Shuman
P.O. Box 687
Chapel Hill, NC 27514
919-967-1032

Edison Hall Books
5 Ventnor Dr.
Edison, NJ 08820
908-548-4455

Susan Heller, Pages for Sages
22611 Halburton Rd.
Beachwood, OH 44122-3939
216-283-2665
hellersu@cyberdrive.net

Margaret E. Page
Page Books
HRC 65, Box 233
Kingston, AR 72742
870-861-5831
pagebook@eritter.net

Jo Ann Reisler, Ltd.
360 Glyndon St., NE
Vienna, VA 22180
703-938-2967
fax 703-938-9057
reisler@clark.net
www.clark.net/pub/reisler

Lee Barnett Temares
50 Heights Rd.
Plandome, NY 11030
516-627-8688
fax 516-627-7822
tembooks@aol.com

John F. Kennedy
British Stamp Exchange
12 Fairlawn Ave.
N Weymouth, MA 02191
871-335-3075

Kentucky Authors
Bill Schroeder
5801 Kentucky Dam Rd.
Paducah, KY 42003

Kentucky History
Bill Schroeder
5801 Kentucky Dam Rd.
Paducah, KY 42003

King Arthur
Also early Britain
Thorn Books
P.O. Box 1244
Moorpark, CA 93020
805-529-3647
fax 805-529-0022
thornbooks@earthlink.net

Stephen King
Fostoria Trading Post
B. L. Foley III
P.O. Box 142
Fostoria, IA 51340
712-262-5936
books@ncn.net
www.ncn.net/~books

Labor
A\K\A Fine Used Books
4124 Brooklyn Ave. NE
Seattle, WA 98107

Volume I Books
One Union St.
Hillsdale, MI 49242
517-437-2228
fax 517-437-7923
volume1book@dmci.net

Lakeside Classics
Linda Holycross
109 N Sterling Ave.
Veedersburg, IN 47987
fax 765-793-2249

Landscape Architecture
The American Botanist
P.O. Box 532
Chillicothe, IL 61523
309-274-5254
fax 309-274-6143
www.amerbot.com

Brooks Books
Phil & Marty Nesty
P.O. Box 91
Clayton, CA 94517
925-672-4566
fax 925-672-3338
brooksbk@netvista.net

Latin American Literature
Almark & Co.-Booksellers
P.O. Box 7
Thornhill, Ontario
Canada L3T 3N1
905-764-2665
fax 905-764-5771
al@almarkco.com or
mark@almarkco.com

Flo Silver Books
8442 Oakwood Ct. N
Indianapolis, IN 46260
phone/fax 317-255-5118
Flosilver@aol.com

Law & Crime
Meyer Boswell Books, Inc.
2141 Mission St.
San Francisco, CA 94110
415-255-6400
fax 415-255-6499
rarelaw@meyerbos.com

T. E. Lawrence/Lawrence of Arabia
Denis McDonnell, Bookseller
653 Park St.
Honesdale, PA 18431-1445
570-253-6706

fax 570-253-6786
dmd@ptd.net
www.denismcd.com

Lebanon
W. B. O'Neill
Old & Rare Books
11609 Hunters Green Ct.
Reston, VA 20191
703-860-0782
fax 703-620-0153
nyc1918@aol.com

Lewis & Clark Expedition
George H. Tweney
16660 Marine View Dr. SW
Seattle, WA 98166
206-243-8243

Literature
Amaranth Books
P.O. Box 421
Wilmette, IL 60091-0421
708-328-2939

In translation
Almark & Co.-Booksellers
P.O. Box 7
Thornhill, Ontario
Canada L3T 3N1
905-764-2665
fax 905-764-5771
al@almarkco.com or
mark@almarkco.com

First editions
Karl M. Armens
740 Juniper Dr.
Iowa City, IA 52245
319-337-7755

Bromer Booksellers
607 Boylston St.
Boston, MA 02116
617-247-2818
fax 617-247-2975
books@bromer.com
www.bromer.com

18th & 19th-C English
The Book Collector
2347 University Blvd.
Houston, TX 77005
713-661-2665

African-American
Between the Covers
35 W Maple Ave.
Merchantville, NJ 08109
609-665-2284
fax 609-665-3639
mail@betweenthecovers.com
www.betweenthecovers.com

The Captain's Bookshelf, Inc.
Chandler W. Gordon
31 Page Ave.
Asheville, NC 22801
828-253-6631
fax 828-253-4917
captsbooks@aol.com

Chapel Hill Rare Books
Douglas & Maureen O'Dell
P.O. Box 456
Carrboro, NC 27510
919-929-8351
rarebooks@mindspring.com

Southern
Elder's Book Store
2115 Elliston Pl.
Nashville, TN 37203
615-327-1867

18th century
Hartfield Rare Books
Ruth Inglehart
117 Dixboro Rd.
Ann Arbor, MI 48105
phone/fax 313-662-6035

Susan Heller, Pages for Sages
22611 Halburton Rd.
Beachwood, OH 44122-3939
216-283-2665
hellersu@cyberdrive.net

Ken Hebenstreit, Bookseller
813 N Washington Ave.
Royal Oak, MI 48067
phone/fax 248-548-5460
kenhebenstreit@home.com
www.khbooks.com

Ken Lopez, Bookseller
51 Huntington Rd.
Hadley, MA 01035
413-584-4827
fax 413-584-2045
mail@lopezbooks.com
www.lopezbooks.com

Mason's Bookstore, Rare Books
    & Record Albums East
115 S Main St.
Chambersburg, PA 17201
717-261-0541

Much Ado
Seven Pleasant St.
Marblehead, MA 01945
781-639-0400
fax 781-639-0840
muchado@shore.net

Also records and out-of-print comics
Twice Read Books & Comics
42 S Main St.

Chambersburg, PA 17201
717-261-8449

Magazines
Mystery only
Grave Matters
P.O. Box 32192
Cincinnati, OH 45232-0192
513-242-7527
fax 513-242-5115
books@gravematters.com
www.gravematters.com

Robert A. Madle
4406 Bestor Dr.
Rockville, MD 20853
301-460-4712

Relating to decorative arts
Mordida Books
P.O. Box 79322
Houston, TX 77279
713-467-4280
fax 713-467-4182
mordida@swbell.net
www.mordida.com

Passaic Book Center
594 Main Ave.
Passaic, NJ 07055
201-778-6646
fax 201-778-6738

Manuscripts
Susan Heller, Pages for Sages
22611 Halburton Rd.
Beachwood, OH 44122-3939
216-283-2665
hellersu@cyberdrive.net

Heritage Book Shop, Inc.
8540 Melrose Ave.
Los Angeles, CA 90069
310-659-3674
fax 310-659-4872
HBSINCLA@aol.com

Key Books
P.O. Box 58097
St. Petersburg, FL 33715-8097
813-867-2931

Asiatic languages
Worldwide Antiquarian
P.O. Box 410391
Cambridge, MA 02141-0004
617-876-6220
fax 617-876-0839
mbalwan@aol.com

Randall House
Pia Oliver
835 Laguna St.

Santa Barbara, CA 93101
805-963-1909
fax 805-963-1650
pia@piasworld.com
www.piasworld.com/randall

Maps
State, pocket-type, ca 1800s
The Bookseller, Inc.
174 W Exchange St.
Akron, OH 44302
330-762-3101
fax 330-762-4413
booklein@apk.com

Elegant Book & Map Company
815 Harrison Ave.
Cambridge, OH 43725
614-432-4068

Maritime
Including pirates, treasure, shipwrecks, the Caribbean, Cuba & Panama
The Book Corner
Michael Tennaro
728 W Lumsden Rd.
Brandon, FL 33511
813-684-1133
bookcrnr@worldnet.att.net
www.abebooks.com/home/bookcrnr

Book & Tackle Shop
Bernard L. Gordon
29 Old Colony Rd.
P.O. Box 114
Chestnut Hill, MA 02467
phone/fax 617-965-0459 (winter)
bktack@ibm.net

Overlee Farm Books
P.O. Box 1155
Stockbridge, MA 01262
413-637-2277

J. Tuttle Maritime Books
1806 Laurel Crest
Madison, WI 53705
608-238-SAIL (7245)
fax 608-238-7249

Martial Arts
Nutmeg Books
354 New Litchfield St. (Rte. 202)
Torrington, CT 06790
203-482-9696
nutmeg@compsol.net

Masonic History
Mason's Bookstore, Rare Books
    & Record Albums East
115 S Main St.
Chambersburg, PA 17201
717-261-0541

Mathematics
Significant Books
3053 Madison Rd.
P.O. Box 9248
Cincinnati, OH 45209
800-750-1153 or 513-321-7567
signbook@iac.net

Cormac McCarthy
Alice Robbins, Bookseller
3002 Round Hill Rd.
Greensboro, NC 27408
910-282-1964

Medicine
Amaranth Books
P.O. Box 421
Wilmette, IL 60091-0421
708-328-2939

Antiquarian
Book & Tackle
Bernard L. Gordon
29 Old Colony Rd.
P.O. Box 114
Chestnut Hill, MA 02467
phone/fax 617-965-0459 (winter)
bktack@ibm.net

W. Bruce Fye
1607 N Wood Ave.
Marshfield, WI 54449-1298
715-384-8128
fax 715-389-2990
byfe@tznet.com

Procedures before 1915
Ron Gibson, The Bookshop
110 Windsor Cir.
Burlington, IA 52601-1477
319-752-4588

Key Books
P.O. Box 58097
St. Petersburg, FL 33715-8097
813-867-2931

M&S Rare Books, Inc.
P.O. Box 2594, E Side Station
Providence, RI 02906
401-421-1050
fax 401-272-0831 (attention M & S)
dsiegel@msrarebooks.com

Medieval
Camelot Books
Charles E. Wyatt
P.O. Box 2883
Vista, CA 92083
619-940-9472

Metaphysics
AL-PAC
Lamar Kelley Antiquarian Books

2625 E Southern Ave., C-120
Tempe, AZ 85282
480-831-3121
fax 480-831-3193
alpac2625@aol.com

Meteorology
Knollwood Books
Lee & Peggy Price
P.O. Box 197
Oregon, WI 53575-0197
608-835-8861
fax 608-835-8421
books@tdsnet.com

Mexico
Flo Silver Books
8442 Oakwood Ct. N
Indianapolis, IN 46260
phone/fax 317-255-5118
Flosilver@aol.com

Michigan
Artis Books
201 N Second Ave.
P.O. Box 822
Alpena, MI 49707-0822
517-354-3401
artis@freeway.net

Yesterday's Books
229 Riverview Dr.
Parchment, MI 49004
616-345-1011
yesbooks@aol.com

Middle Eastern Countries
Denis McDonnell, Bookseller
653 Park St.
Honesdale, PA 18431-1445
570-253-6706
fax 570-253-6786
dmd@ptd.net
www.denismcd.com

Levant countries: travel, archaeology,
*   history; Byzantine studies*
Quest Books
Peter & Veronica Burridge
Harmer Hill
Millington
York YO42 1TX UK
Quesbks@aol.com

Worldwide Antiquarian
P.O. Box 410391
Cambridge, MA 02141-0004
617-876-6220
fax 617-876-0839
mbalwan@aol.com

Militaria
The Bookseller, Inc.

174 W Exchange St.
Akron, OH 44302
330-762-3101
fax 330-762-4413
booklein@apk.com

Edison Hall Books
5 Ventnor Dr.
Edison, NJ 08820
908-548-4455

Rick Harmon
Military Books & Relics
910 Sullivan Dr.
Belvidere, IL 61008
815-547-7580

Robert L. Merriam
Rare, Used & Old Books
39 Newhall Rd.
Conway, MA 01341-9709
413-369-4052
rmerriam@valinet.com

Significant Books
3053 Madison Rd.
P.O Box 9248
Cincinnati, OH 45209
800-750-1153 or 513-321-7567
signbook@iac.net

Histories Before 1900
Tryon County Bookshop
2071 State Hwy. 29
Johnstown, NY 12905
518-762-1060

Volume I Books
One Union St.
Hillsdale, MI 49242
517-437-2228
fax 517-437-7923
volume1book@dmci.net

Miniature Books
Bromer Booksellers
607 Boylston St.
Boston, MA 02116
617-247-2818
fax 617-247-2975
books@bromer.com
www.bromer.com

Foreign atlases
Murray Hudson
Antiquarian Books & Maps
109 S Church St.
P.O. Box 163
Halls, TN 38040
901-836-9057 or 800-748-9946
fax 901-836-9017
mapman@usit.net

Hurley Books/Celtic Cross Books
1753 Rt. 12
Westmoreland, NH 03467-4724
603-399-4342
fax 603-399-8326
hurleybook@adam.cheshire.net

Gary R. Smith
517 Laurel Ave.
Modesto, CA 95351

Movies
The American Dust Co.
47 Park Ct.
Staten Island, NY 10301
phone/fax 718-442-8253

Cinemage Books
105 W 27th St.
New York, NY 10001
212-243-4919
irajoel@aol.com

Mysteries
Alcott Books
Barbara Ruppert
5909 Darnell
Houston, TX 77074-7719
713-774-2202

The American Dust Co.
47 Park Ct.
Staten Island, NY 10301
phone/fax 718-442-8253

Karl M. Armens
740 Juniper Dr.
Iowa City, IA 52245
319-337-7755

Ken Hebenstreit, Bookseller
813 N Washington Ave.
Royal Oak, MI 48067
phone/fax 248-548-5460
kenhebenstreit@home.com
www.khbooks.com

First editions
Island Books
P.O. Box 19
Old Westbury, NY 11568
516-759-0233

W.J. Leveridge
W & L Trading Company
2301 Carova Rd.
Carova Beach, Corolla, NC 27927
252-453-3408

McGee's First Varieties
330 Franklin Rd., Suite 135A
Brentwood, TN 37027
615-373-5318
TMcGee@BellSouth.net
www.mcgees1st.com

Mordida Books
P.O. Box 79322
Houston, TX 77279
713-467-4280
fax 713-467-4182
mordida@swbell.net
www.mordida.com

mail order; primarily first editions
Norris Books
Charles Chavdarian, owner
2491 San Ramon Vly. Blvd.
Suite 1 PMB 201
San Ramon, CA 94583
online at abebooks and bibliofind
phone/fax 925-867-1218
norrisbooks@slip.net

Pandora's Books, Ltd.
P.O. Box 54
Neche, ND 58265
204-324-8548
fax 204-324-1628
jgthiess@MTS.Net

RAC Books
P.O. Box 296 RD 2
Seven Valleys, PA 17360
717-428-3776
racbooks@cyberia.com

The Silver Door
P.O. Box 3208
Redondo Beach, CA 90277
310-379-6005

Napoleonic Memorabilia
The Book Collector
2347 University Blvd.
Houston, TX 7005
713-661-2665

Narcotics
Nutmeg Books
354 New Litchfield St. (Rte. 202)
Torrington, CT 06790
203-482-9696
nutmeg@compsol.net

Natural History
Thomas C. Bayer
85 Reading Ave.
Hillsdale, MI 49242-1941
517-439-4134
fax 517-439-5661
bayerbooks@dmci.net

Noriko I. Ciochon
Natural History Books
1025 Keokut St.
Iowa City, IA 52240-3303
319-354-9088
fax 319-354-0844
nathist@avalon.net
www.avalon.net/~nathist

Melvin Marcher, Bookseller
6204 N Vermont
Oklahoma City, OK 73112
405-946-6270
(12 noon to 7 p.m. *only*)

Snowy Egret Books
1237 Carroll Ave.
St. Paul, MN 55104
612-641-0917
snowy@mr.net

Nautical
Much Ado
Seven Pleasant St.
Marblehead, MA 01945
781-639-0400
fax 781-639-0840
muchado@shore.net

Overlee Farm Books
P.O. Box 1155
Stockbridge, MA 01262
413-637-2277

Needlework
Galerie De Boicourt
Eva M. Boicourt
6136 Westbrooke Dr.
W. Bloomfield, MI 48322
248-788-9253

Stanley Schwartz
1934 Pentuckett Ave.
San Diego, CA 92104-5732
619-232-5888
fax 619-233-5833
Schwartz@cts.com

Neuroscience
John Gach Fine & Rare Books
10514 Marriottsville Rd.
Randallstown, MD 21133
410-465-9023
fax 410-465-0649
inquiry@gach.com
www.gach.com

New England
Book & Tackle
Bernard L. Gordon
29 Old Colony Rd.
P.O. Box 114
Chestnut Hill, MA 02467
phone/fax 617-965-0459 (winter)
bktack@ibm.net

Newspapers & Periodicals
Significant & unusual American
Periodyssey
151 Crescent St.
Northampton, MA 01060
413-527-1900
fax 413-527-1930

Randall House
Pia Oliver
835 Laguna St.
Santa Barbara, CA 93101
805-963-1909
fax 805-963-1650
pia@piasworld.com
www.piasworld.com/randall

Thorn Books
P.O. Box 1244
Moorpark, CA 93020
805-529-3647
fax 805-529-0022
thornbooks@earthlink.net

Wellerdt's Books
3700 S Osprey Ave. #214
Sarasota, FL 34239
813-365-1318

Xanadu Records, Ltd.
3242 Irwin Ave.
Kingsbridge, NY 10463
718-549-3655

Nonfiction
Warren's Collector Books
   For Sale Now
Warren Gillespie, Jr.
112 Royal Court
Friendship, TX 77546
281-482-7947

Novels
Ken Hebenstreit, Bookseller
813 N Washington Ave.
Royal Oak, MI 48067
phone/fax 248-548-5460
kenhebenstreit@home.com
www.khbooks.com

The Silver Door
P.O. Box 3208
Redondo Beach, CA 90277
310-379-6005

Occult & Mystics
AL-PAC
Lamar Kelley Antiquarian Books
2625 E Southern Ave., C-120
Tempe, AZ 85282
480-831-3121
fax 480-831-3193
alpac2625@aol.com

British Stamp Exchange
12 Fairlawn Ave.
N Weymouth, MA 02191
871-335-3075

Ohio
The Bookseller, Inc.
174 W Exchange St.
Akron, OH 44302

330-762-3101
fax 330-762-4413
booklein@apk.com

Omar Khayyam
Worldwide Antiquarian
P.O. Box 410391
Cambridge, MA 02141-0004
617-876-6220
fax 617-876-0839
mbalwan@aol.com

Oriental Books & Art
Ruth Woods Oriental Books & Art
6 Hillside Ave.
Daren, CT 06820-5010

Original Art
By children's illustrators
Kendra Krienke
230 Central Park West
New York, NY 10024
201-930-9709 or 201-930-9765

Paperbacks
Michael Gerlicher
1375 Rest Point Rd.
Orono, MN 55364

Bernard E. Goodman, Bookseller
7421 SW 147 Ct.
Miami, FL 33193-1116
305-385-8526
bgbooks@bellsouth.net
www.abebooks.com/home/bgbookman

Vintage
Grave Matters
P.O. Box 32192
Cincinnati, OH 45232-0192
513-242-7527
fax 513-242-5115
books@gravematters.com
www.gravematters.com

Also pulp magazines
Modern Age Books
Jeff Canja
P.O. Box 325
East Lansing, MI 48826
517-487-9313

Originals
Mordida Books
P.O. Box 79322
Houston, TX 77279
713-467-4280
fax 713-467-4182
mordida@swbell.net
www.mordida.com

Olde Current Books
Daniel P. Shay

356 Putnam Ave.
Ormond Beach, FL 32174
904-672-8998
peakmyster@aol.com

Pandora's Books, Ltd.
P.O. Box 54
Neche, ND 58265
204-324-8548
fax 204-324-1628
jgthiess@MTS.Net

Also trades; want lists welcomed
Roger Reus
9412 Huron Ave.
Richmond, VA 23294
(mail order only)

Andrew Zimmerli
5001 General Branch Ct.
Sharpsburg, MD 21781
301-432-7476

Robert B. Parker
Thomas Books
P.O. Box 14036
Phoenix, AZ 85063
623-247-9289
fax 480-945-1023
sales@thomasbooks.com
www.thomasbooks.com

Pennsylvania
Mason's Bookstore, Rare Books
   & Record Albums East
115 S Main
Chambersburg, PA 17201
717-261-0541

Philosophy
John Gach Books
10514 Marriottsville Rd.
Randallstown, MD 21133
410-465-9023
fax 410-465-0649
inquiry@gach.com
www.gach.com

Photography
The Captain's Bookshelf, Inc.
Chandler W. Gordon
31 Page Ave.
Asheville, NC 22801
828-253-6631
fax 828-253-4917
captsbooks@aol.com

Significant Books
3053 Madison Rd.
P.O. Box 9248
Cincinnati, OH 45209
800-750-1153 or 513-321-7567
signbook@iac.net

19th-C Middle & Far East Countries
Worldwide Antiquarian
P.O. Box 410391
Cambridge, MA 02141-0004
617-876-6220
fax 617-876-0839
mbalwan@aol.com

Xanadu Records, Ltd.
3242 Irwin Ave.
Kingsbridge, NY 10463
718-549-3655

Playing Cards
Bill & Mimi Sachen
927 Grand Ave.
Waukegan, IL 60085-3709
847-662-7204
FutileWill@aol.com

Poetry
The American Dust Co.
47 Park Ct.
Staten Island, NY 10301
phone/fax 718-442-8253

Edison Hall Books
5 Ventnor Dr.
Edison, NJ 08820
908-548-4455

Ed Smith Books
20 Paget Rd.
Madison, WI 53704-5929
608-241-3707
ed@edsbooks.com
www.edsbooks.com

David R. Smith
30 Nelson Circle
Jaffrey, NH 03452
603-532-8666
Bookinc@Cheshire.net

VERSEtility Books
P.O. Box 1133
Farmington, CT 06034-1133
860-677-0606
versebks@tiac.net

Polar Explorations & Ephemera
Alaskan Heritage Bookshop
174 S Franklin, P.O. 22165
Juneau, AK 99802

Parmer Books
7644 Forrestal Rd.
San Diego, CA 92120-2203
619-287-0693
fax 619-287-6135
ParmerBook@aol.com

Political
Realm of Colorado

P.O. Box 24
Parker, CO 80134

Radical
Volume I Books
One Union St.
Hillsdale, MI 49242
517-437-2228
fax 517-437-7923
volume1book@dmci.net

Postcards
Book & Tackle Shop
Bernard L. Gordon
29 Old Colony Rd.
P.O. Box 114
Chestnut Hill, MA 02467
phone/fax 617-965-0459
bktack@ibm.net

Posters
The Mulberry Cat
Yvonne Davis
Jan Davis Martel
P.O. Box 3573
Boone, NC 28607
704-963-7693

Pre-Colombian Art
Flo Silver Books
8442 Oakwood Ct. N.
Indianapolis, IN 46260
phone/fax 317-255-5118
Flosilver@aol.com

Press Books
Heritage Book Shop, Inc.
8540 Melrose Ave.
Los Angeles, CA 90069
310-659-3674
fax 310-659-4872
HBSINCLA@aol.com

Randall House
Pia Oliver
835 Laguna St.
Santa Barbara, CA 93101
805-963-1909
fax 805-963-1650
pia@piasworld.com
www.piasworld.com/randall

Prints
The Mulberry Cat
Yvonne Davis
Jan Davis Martel
P.O. Box 3573
Boone, NC 28607
704-963-7693

Private Presses
First Folio
Dennis R. Melhouse

1206 Brentwood
Paris, TN 34842-3804
phone/fax 910-944-9940
firstfol@aeneas.net

Susan Heller, Pages for Sages
22611 Halburton Rd.
Beachwood, OH 44122-3939
216-283-2665
hellersu@cyberdrive.net

**Promoters of Paper, Ephemera &
Book Fairs**
Kingsbury Productions
Katherine and David Kreider
4555 N Pershing Ave., Suite 33-138
Stockton, CA 95207
209-467-8438

Psychedelia
Nutmeg Books
354 New Litchfield St. (Rte. 202)
Torrington, CT 06790
203-482-9696
nutmeg@compsol.net

Psychiatry
Beasley Books
Paul & Beth Garon
1533 W Oakdale, 2nd Floor
Chicago, IL 60657
773-472-4528
fax 773-472-7857
beasley@mcs.com

John Gach Fine & Rare Books
10514 Marriottsville Rd.
Randallstown, MD 21133
410-465-9023
fax 410-465-0649
inquiry@gach.com
www.gach.com

Psychoanalysis
Beasley Books
Paul & Beth Garon
1533 W Oakdale, 2nd Floor
Chicago, IL 60657
773-472-4528
fax 773-472-7857
beasley@mcs.com

Also related subjects
John Gach Fine & Rare Books
10514 Marriottsville Rd.
Randallstown, MD 21133
410-465-9023
fax 410-465-0649
inquiry@gach.com
www.gach.com

Psychology
Beasley Books

Paul & Beth Garon
1533 W Oakdale, 2nd Floor
Chicago, IL 60657
773-472-4528
fax 773-472-7857
beasley@mcs.com

John Gach Fine & Rare Books
10514 Marriottsville Rd.
Randallstown, MD 21133
410-465-9023
fax 410-465-0649
inquiry@gach.com
www.gach.com

The King's Market Bookshops
P.O. Box 709
Boulder, CO 80306-0709
303-232-3321

Pulps
Science fiction & fantasy before 1945
Robert A. Madle
4406 Bestor Dr.
Rockville, MD 20853
301-460-4712

Quaker
Vintage Books
Nancy & David Haines
181 Hayden Rowe St.
Hopkinton, MA 01748
508-435-3499
vintage@gis.net

Quilt Books
Bill Schroeder
5801 Kentucky Dam Rd.
Paducah, Kentucky 42003

Galerie De Boicourt
Eva M. Boicourt
6136 Westbrooke Dr.
W. Bloomfield, MI 48322
248-788-9253

R.R. Donnelley Christmas Books
Linda Holycross
109 N Sterling Ave.
Veedersburg, IN 47987
fax 765-793-2249

Arthur Rackham
Books of the Ages
Gary J. Overmann
Maple Ridge Manor
4764 Silverwood Dr.
Batavia, OH 45103-9740
phone/fax 513-732-3456

Radical
Beasley Books
Paul & Beth Garon

1533 W Oakdale, 2nd Floor
Chicago, IL 60657
773-472-4528
fax 773-472-7857
beasley@mcs.com

Railroading
Mason's Bookstore, Rare Books
    & Record Albums
115 S Main St.
Chambersburg, PA 17201
717-261-0541

Rare & Unusual Books
Chapel Hill Rare Books
P.O. Box 456
Carrboro, NC 27510
919-929-8351
rarebooks@mindspring.com

First Folio
Dennis R. Melhouse
1206 Brentwood
Paris, TN 38242-3804
phone/fax 910-944-9940
firstfol@aeneas.net

Terry Harper, Bookseller
P.O. Box 312
Vergennes, VT 05491-0312
802-877-9262
bookvend@together.net

Susan Heller, Pages for Sages
22611 Halburton Rd.
Beachwood, OH 44122-3939
216-283-2665
hellersu@cyberdrive.net

Heritage Book Shop, Inc.
8540 Melrose Ave.
Los Angeles, CA 90069
310-659-3674
fax 310-659-4872
HBSINCLA@aol.com

Kenneth Karmiole, Bookseller, Inc.
509 Wilshire Blvd.
Santa Monica, CA 90401
310-451-4342 or 310-458-5930
karmbooks@aol.com

M & S Rare Books, Inc.
P.O. Box 2594, E Side Station
Providence, RI 02906
401-421-1050
fax 401-272-0831 (attention M & S)
dsiegel@msrarebooks.com

Paul Melzer Fine & Rare Books
12 E Vine St.
P.O. Box 1143
Redlands, CA 92373

909-792-7299
fax 909-792-7218
pmbooks@eee.org

The Old London Bookshop
Michael & Marlys Schon
P.O. Box 922
Bellingham, WA 98227-0922
360-733-7273
fax 360-647-8946
OldLondon@aol.com

Richard C. Ramer
Old & Rare Books
225 E 70th St.
New York, NY 10021
212-737-0222 or 212-737-0223
fax 212-288-4169
5222386@mcimail.com

Revere Books
P.O. Box 420
Revere, PA 18953-0420
610-847-2709
fax 610-847-1910

Leona Rostenberg
    & Madeleine Stern
Rare Books
40 East 88th St.
New York, NY 10128-1176
212-831-6628
fax 212-831-1961

Thorn Books
P.O. Box 1244
Moorpark, CA 93020
805-529-3647
fax 805-529-0022
thornbooks@earthlink.net

Reference
About Books
6 Sand Hill Ct.
P.O. Box 5717
Parsippany, NY 07054
973-515-4591

Religion
Books Now & Then
Dennis & Jan Patrick
P.O. Box 337
Stanley, ND 58784
phone/fax 701-628-2084
bnt@stanley.ndak.net
www.ourchurch.com/member/b/
booksnow-then

Chimney Sweep Books
Lillian Smith Kaiser
P.O. Box 24649
San Jose, CA 95154-4649
chimney@cruzio.com

David R. Smith
30 Nelson Circle
Jaffrey, NH 03452
603-532-8666
Bookinc@Cheshire.net

Reptiles
Mason's Bookstore, Rare Books
    & Record Albums East
115 S Main St.
Chambersburg, PA 17201
717-261-0541

Revolutionary War
K.C. & Jean Owings
Box 389
Whitman, MA 02382
781-447-7850
fax 781-447-3435

Science & Technology
Thomas C. Bayer
85 Reading Ave.
Hillsdale, MI 49242-1941
517-439-4134
fax 517-439-5661
bayerbooks@dmci.net

Book & Tackle Shop
Bernard L. Gordon
29 Old Colony Rd.
P.O. Box 114
Chestnut Hill, MA 02467
phone/fax 617-965-0459
bktack@ibm.net

Thomas L. Coffman
TLC Books
9 N College Ave.
Salem, VA 24153
540-389-3555

Key Books
P.O. Box 58097
St. Petersburg, FL 33715-8097
813-867-2931

M & S Rare Books, Inc.
P.O. Box 2594, E Side Station
Providence, RI 02906
401-270-0831
fax 401-272-0831 (attention M & S)
dsiegel@msrarebooks.com

Science Fiction
AL-PAC
Lamar Kelley Antiquarian Books
2625 E Southern Ave., C-120
Tempe, AZ 85282
480-831-3121
fax 480-831-3193
alpac2625@aol.com

Also Fantasy
Ackley Books & Collectibles
Bryant & Suzanne Pitner
912 Hidden Cove Way
Suisun City, CA 94585-3511
707-421-9032
fax 978-285-6554
www.ackleybooks.com
(mail order only)

The American Dust Co.
47 Park Ct.
Staten Island, NY 10301
phone/fax 718-442-8253

Karl M. Armens
740 Juniper Dr.
Iowa City, IA 52245
319-337-7755

Bernard E. Goodman, Bookseller
7421 SW 147 Ct.
Miami, FL 33193-1116
305-385-8526
bgbooks@bellsouth.net
www.abebooks.com/home/bgbookman

Ken Hebenstreit, Bookseller
813 N Washington Ave.
Royal Oak, MI 48067
phone/fax 248-548-5460
kenhebenstreit@home.com
www.khbooks.com

First editions
Island Books
P.O. Box 19
Old Westbury, NY 11568
516-759-0233

Horror & Occult
Bob Lakin Books
P.O. Box 186
Chatfield, TX 75105
972-247-3291

Robert A. Madle
4406 Bestor Dr.
Rockville, MD 20853
301-460-4712

McGee's First Varieties
330 Franklin Rd., Suite 135A
Brentwood, TN 37027
615-373-5318
TMcGee@BellSouth.net
www.mcgees1st.com

Also fantasy
Kai Nygaard
19421 Eighth Pl.
Escondido, CA 92029
619-749-9039

Pandora's Books, Ltd.
P.O. Box 54
Neche, ND 58265
204-324-8548
fax 204-324-1628
jgthiess@MTS.Net

Also fantasy
Xanadu Records, Ltd.
3242 Irwin Ave.
Kingsbridge, NY 10463
718-549-3655

Sciences
Cover to Cover
Mark Shuman
P.O. Box 687
Chapel Hill, NC 27514
919-967-1032

Significant Books
3053 Madison Rd.
P.O. Box 9248
Cincinnati, OH 45209
800-750-1153 or 513-321-7567
signbook@iac.net

Series Books
Glo's Books & Collectibles
Gloria Stobbes
906 Shadywood
Southlake, TX 76092
817-481-1438

Set Editions
AL-PAC
Lamar Kelley Antiquarian Books
2625 E Southern Ave., C-120
Tempe, AZ 85282
480-831-3121
fax 480-831-3193
alpac2625@aol.com

Sherlockiana
The Silver Door
P.O. Box 3208
Redondo Beach, CA 90277
310-379-6005

Ships & Sea
Book & Tackle Shop
Bernard L. Gordon
29 Old Colony Rd.
P.O. Box 114
Chestnut Hill, MA 02467
phone/fax 617-965-0459 (winter)
bktack@ibm.net

Parmer Books
7644 Forrestal Rd.
San Diego, CA 92120-2203
619-287-0693
fax 619-287-6135
ParmerBook@aol.com

J. Tuttle Maritme Books
1806 Laurel Crest
Madison, WI 53705
608-238-SAIL (7245)
fax 608-238-7249

Signed Editions
Chapel Hill Rare Books
P.O. Box 456
Carrboro, NC 27510
919-929-8351
rarebooks@mindspring.com

Ken Hebenstreit, Bookseller
813 N Washington Ave.
Royal Oak, MI 48067
phone/fax 248-548-5460
kenhebenstreit@home.com
www.khbooks.com

Dan Simmons
Thomas Books
P.O. Box 14036
Phoenix, AZ 85063
623-247-9289
fax 480-945-1023
sales@thomasbooks.com
www.thomasbooks.com

Socialism
Beasley Books
Paul & Beth Garon
1533 W Oakdale, 2nd Floor
Chicago, IL 60657
773-472-4528
fax 773-472-7857
beasley@mcs.com

Volume I Books
One Union St.
Hillsdale, MI 49242
517-437-2228
fax 517-437-7923
volume1book@dmci.net

South America
Flo Silver Books
8442 Oakwood Ct. N
Indianapolis, IN 46260
phone/fax 317-255-5118
Flosilver@aol.com

South Dakota
Also any pre-1970 Western-related books
James F. Taylor
515 Sixth St.
Rapid City, SD 57701
605-341-3224

Space Exploration
Knollwood Books
Lee & Peggy Price
P.O. Box 197

Oregon, WI 53575-0197
608-835-8861
fax 608-835-8421
books@tdsnet.com

Speciality Publishers
Arkham House, Gnome, Fantasy, etc.
Robert A. Madle
4406 Bestor Dr.
Rockville, MD 20853
301-460-4712

Spiritual Literature
Monroe Stahr Books
5112 Van Noord Ave.
Sherman Oaks, CA 91423
818-501-3419
fax 818-995-0966
MStahrBks@aol.com

Sports
Baseball or boxing
Ace Zerblonski Books
Malcolm McCollum, Proprietor
1419 North Royer
Colorado Springs, CO 80907
719-634-3941

Adelson Sports
13610 N Scottsdale Rd. #10
Scottsdale, AZ 85254
480-596-1913
fax 480-598-1914
www.adelsonsports.com

Thomas L. Coffman, Bookseller
TLC Books
9 N College Ave.
Salem, VA 24153
540-389-3555

Rare & out-of-print baseball; general
R. Plapinger, Baseball Books
P.O. Box 1062
Ashland, OR 97520
541-488-1220

Randall House
Pia Oliver
835 Laguna St.
Santa Barbara, CA 93101
805-963-1909
fax 805-963-1650
pia@piasworld.com
www.piasworld.com/randall

Rising Stars
Don Carnahan
P.O. Box 2991
Yuma, AZ 85366
phone/fax 520-329-6054

Statue of Liberty
Mike Brooks

7335 Skyline
Oakland, CA 94611

Surfing
Monroe Stahr Books
5112 Van Noord Ave.
Sherman Oaks, CA 91423
818-501-3419
fax 818-995-0966
MStahrBks@aol.com

Surveying
Also tools, instruments & ephemera
David & Nancy Garcelon
10 Hastings Ave.
Millbury, MA 01527-4314
508-754-2667

Technology
Thomas C. Bayer
85 Reading Ave.
Hillsdale, MI 49242-1941
517-439-4134
fax 517-439-5661
bayerbooks@dmci.net

Cover to Cover
Mark Shuman
P.O. Box 687
Chapel Hill, NC 27514
919-967-1032

Significant Books
3053 Madison Rd.
P.O. Box 9248
Cincinnati, OH 45209
800-750-1153 or 513-321-7567
signbook@iac.net

Tennessee History
Elder's Book Store
2115 Elliston Pl.
Nashville, TN 37203
615-327-1867

Texana Fiction & Authors
Alcott Books
Barbara Ruppert
5909 Darnell
Houston, TX 77074-7719
713-774-2202

Bob Lakin Books
P.O. Box 186
Chatfield, TX 75105
972-247-3291

Textiles
Galerie De Boicourt
Eva M. Boicourt
6136 Westbrooke Dr.
W. Bloomfield, MI 48322
248-788-9253

Stanley Schwartz
1934 Pentuckett Ave.
San Diego, CA 92104-5732
619-232-5888
fax 619-233-5833
Schwartz@cts.com

Theology
Books Now & Then
Dennis & Jan Patrick
P.O. Box 337
Stanley, ND 58784
phone/fax 701-628-2084
bnt@stanley.ndak.net
www.ourchurch.com/member/b/
booksnow-then

Chimney Sweep Books
Lillian Smith Kaiser
P.O. Box 24649
San Jose, CA 95154-4649
chimney@cruzio.com

Hurley Books/Celtic Cross Books
1753 Rt. 12
Westmoreland, NH 03467-4724
603-399-4342
fax 603-399-8326
hurleybook@adam.cheshire.net

Trade Catalogs
Eastside Books & Paper
P.O. Box 1581, Gracie Station
New York, NY 10028-0013
212-759-6299

Trades & Crafts
19th Century
Cover to Cover
Mark Shuman
P.O. Box 687
Chapel Hill, NC 27514
919-967-1032

Hillcrest Books
961 Deep Draw Rd.
Crossville, TN 38555-9547
phone/fax 931-484-7680
hillcrst@usit.net
www.oldcatalogues.com

Travel
19th-century travel & adventure
The Book Corner
Michael Tennaro
728 W Lumsden Rd.
Brandon, FL 33511
813-684-1133
bookcrnr@worldnet.att.net
www.abebooks.com/home/bookcrnr

Also exploration
Terry Harper, Bookseller

P.O. Box 312
Vergennes, VT 05491-0312
802-877-9262
bookvend@together.net

Heritage Book Shop, Inc.
8540 Melrose Ave.
Los Angeles, CA 90069
310-659-3674
fax 310-659-4872
HBSINCLA@aol.com

Jim Hodgson Books
908 S Manlius St.
Fayetteville, NY 13066
315-637-6264
jimhbooks@aol.com

Flo Silver Books
8442 Oakwood Ct. N
Indianapolis, IN 46260
phone/fax 317-255-5118
Flosilver@aol.com

Tasha Tudor
Books of the Ages
Gary J. Overmann
Maple Ridge Manor
4764 Silverwood Dr.
Batavia, OH 45103-9740
phone/fax 513-732-3456

Turkey
W.B. O'Neill
Old & Rare Books
11609 Hunters Green Ct.
Reston, VA 20191
703-860-0782
fax 703-620-0153
nyc1918@aol.com

UFO
AL-PAC
Lamar Kelley Antiquarian Books
2625 E Southern Ave., C-120
Tempe, AZ 85282
480-831-3121
fax 480-831-3193
alpac2625@aol.com

Vargas
Parnassus Books
218 N 9th St.
Boise, ID 83702

Vietnam War
A\K\A Fine Used Books
4124 Brooklyn Ave. NE
Seattle, WA 98107
206-632-5870

Thomas L. Coffman, Bookseller
TLC Books

9 N College Ave.
Salem, VA 24153
540-389-3555

Rick Harmon
Military Books & Relics
910 Sullivan Dr.
Belvidere, IL 61008
815-547-7580

Voyages, Exploration & Travel
Chapel Hill Rare Books
Douglas & Maureen O'Dell
P.O. Box 456
Carrboro, NC 27510
919-929-8351
rarebooks@mindspring.com

Terry Harper, Bookseller
P.O. Box 312
Vergennes, VT 05491-0312
802-877-9262
bookvend@together.net

Heritage Book Shop, Inc.
8540 Melrose Ave.
Los Angeles, CA 90069
310-659-3674
fax 310-659-4872
HBSINCLA@aol.com

Jim Hodgson Books
908 S Manlius St.
Fayetteville, NY 13066
315-637-6264
jimhbooks@aol.com

Key Books
P.O. Box 58097
St. Petersburg, FL 33715-8097
813-867-2931

Overlee Farm Books
P.O. Box 1155
Stockbridge, MA 01262
413-627-2277

George H. Tweney
16660 Marine View Dr. SW
Seattle, WA 98166
206-243-8243

Weapons
All edged types
Knife Readables
115 Longfellow Blvd.
Lakeland, FL 33810
813-666-1133

Western Americana
Dawson's Book Shop
535 N Larchmont Blvd.
Los Angeles, CA 90004

323-469-2186
fax 323-469-9553
dawsonbk@ix.netcom.com
www.dawsonbooks.com

Nonfiction 19th-C outlaws, lawmen, etc.
The Early West/Whodunit Books
P.O. Box 9292
College Station, TX 77842
409-775-6047
fax 409-764-7758
EarlyWest@aol.com

Terry Harper, Bookseller
P.O. Box 312
Vergennes, VT 05491-0312
802-877-9262
bookvend@together.net

Rare & historical ephemera
Jordon Book Gallery
1349 Sheridan Ave.
Cody, WY 82414
307-587-6689
fax 307-527-4944
jjordon@trib.com

K.C. & Jean Owings
Box 389
Whitman, MA 02382
781-447-7850
fax 781-447-3435

Thorn Books
P.O. Box 1244

Moorpark, CA 93020
805-529-3647
fax 805-529-0022
thornbooks@earthlink.net

George H. Tweney
16660 Marine View Dr. SW
Seattle, WA 98166
206-243-8243

Wine
Second Harvest Books
Warren R. Johnson
P.O. Box 3306
Florence, OR 97439-3306
phone/fax 541-902-0215
2harvest@presys.com
www.abebooks.com/home/47002

Warren's Collector Books
    For Sale Now
Warren Gillespie, Jr.
112 Royal Ct.
Friendswood, TX 77546
281-482-7947

Women Authors
Ken Hebenstreit, Bookseller
813 N Washington Ave.
Royal Oak, MI 48067
phone/fax 248-548-5460
kenhebenstreit@home.com
www.khbooks.com
Alice Robbins, Bookseller
3002 Round Hill Rd.

Greensboro, NC 27408
910-282-1964

Women's History
Also related areas of everyday life
An Uncommon Vision
1425 Greywall Ln.
Wynnewood, PA 19096-3811
610-658-0953
fax 610-658-0961
Uncommvisn@aol.com

Volume I Books
One Union St.
Hillsdale, MI 49242
517-437-2228
fax 517-437-7923
volume1book@dmci.net

World War I
Denis McDonnell, Bookseller
653 Park St.
Honesdale, PA 18431-1445
570-253-6706
fax 570-253-6786
dmd@ptd.net
www.denismed.com

World War II
Cover to Cover
Mark Shuman
P.O. Box 687
Chapel Hill, NC 27514
919-967-1032

Booksellers

This section of the book lists names and addresses of used book dealers who have contributed the retail listings contained in this edition of *Huxford's Old Book Value Guide*. The code (A1, S7, etc.) located before the price in our listings refers to the dealer offering that particular book for sale. (When more than one dealer has the same book listing codes are given alphabetically before the price.) Given below are the dealer names and their codes.

Many bookdealers issue printed catalogs, list catalogs on the internet, have open shops, are mail order only, or may be a combination of these forms of business. When seeking a book from a particular dealer, it would be best to first write (enclose SASE), e-mail, or call to see what type of business is operated (open shop or mail order).

A1
A-Book-A-Brac Shop
6760 Collins Ave.
Miami Beach, FL 33141
305-865-0092

A2
Aard Books
31 Russell Ave.
Troy, NH 03465
603-242-3638
aardbooks@cheshire.net

A3
Noreen Abbot Books
2666 44th Ave.
San Francisco, CA 94116-2635
415-664-9464

A4
About Books
6 Sand Hill Ct.
P.O. Box 5717
Parsippany, NJ 07054
973-515-4591

A5
Adelson Sports
13610 N Scottsdale Rd. #10
Scottsdale, AZ 85254
480-596-1913
fax 480-596-1914
www.adelsonsports.com

A6
Ads Autographs
P.O. Box 8006
Webster, NY 14580-8006
716-671-2651
fax 716-671-5727

A7
Avonlea Books Search Service
P.O. Box 74, Main Station
White Plains, NY 10602-0074
914-946-5923
fax 914-761-3119
avonlea@bushkin.com

A8
AL-PAC
Lamar Kelley Antiquarian Books
2625 E Southern Ave., C-120
Tempe, AZ 85282
480-831-3121
fax 480-831-3193
alpac2625@aol.com

A9
Amaranth Books
P.O. Box 421
Wilmette, IL 60091-0421
708-328-2939

A10
The American Botanist
P.O. Box 532
Chillicothe, IL 61523
309-274-5254
fax 309-274-6143
www.amerbot.com

A11
The American Dust Co.
47 Park Ct.
Staten Island, NY 10301
phone/fax 718-442-8253

A13
Antiquarian Medical Books
W. Bruce Fye
1607 N Wood Ave.
Marshfield, WI 54449-1298
715-384-8128
fax 715-389-2990
bfye@tznet.com

A14
Almark & Co.-Booksellers
P.O. Box 7
Thornhill, Ontario
Canada L3T 3N1
905-764-2665
fax 905-764-5771
al@almarkco.com or
mark@almarkco.com

A15
Karl M. Armens
740 Juniper Dr.
Iowa City, IA 52245
319-337-7755

A16
Arnold's of Michigan
Judith A. Herba
218 South Water St.
Marine City, MI 48039 -1688
810-765-1350
800-276-3092
fax 810-765-7914
arnoldbk@ees.eesc.com

A17
Artis Books
201 N Second Ave.
P.O. Box 822
Alpena, MI 49707-0822
517-354-3401
artis@freeway.net

A18
Authors of the West
191 Dogwood Dr.
Dundee, OR 97115
503-538-8132
Lnash@georgefox.edu

A19
Aplan Antiques & Art
James & Peg Aplan
21424 Clover Pl.
Piedmont, SD 57769-9403
605-347-5016
fax 605-347-9336
alpanpeg@rapidnet.com

A20
Ace Zerblonski Books
Malcolm McCollum, Proprietor
1419 North Royer
Colorado Springs, CO 80907
719-634-3941

A21
Artiques Ltd.
Veronica Jochens
P.O. Box 67
Lonedell, MO 60360
phone/fax 314-629-1374
veronica@nightowl.net

A23
Alcott Books
Barbara Ruppert
5909 Darnell
Houston, TX 77074-7719
713-774-2202

A24
A Tale of Two Sisters
1401 Emerald Circle
Southlake, TX 76092
817-329-0988
tts.mcc@ix.netcom.com

A25
An Uncommon Vision
1425 Greywall Ln.
Wynnewood, PA 19096-3811
610-658-0953
fax 610-658-0961
Uncommvisn@aol.com

A26
David Armstrong, Bookseller
Box 551
Lethbridge, Alberta
Canada T1J 3Z4
403-381-3270
dabooks@telusplanet.net
www.telusplanet.net/public/dabooks

A27
Aslan Books
191 Dogwood Dr.
Dundee, OR 97115
503-538-8132
Lnash@georgefox.edu

A28
Ackley Books & Collectibles
Bryant & Suzanne Pitner
912 Hidden Cove Way
Suisun City, CA 94585-3511
707-421-9032
fax 978-285-6554
www.ackleybooks.com
(mail order only)

B1
Thomas C. Bayer
85 Reading Ave.
Hillsdale, MI 49242-1941
517-439-4134
fax 517-439-5661
bayerbooks@dmci.net

B2
Beasley Books
Paul & Beth Garon
1533 W Oakdale, 2nd Floor
Chicago, IL 60657
773-472-4528
fax 773-472-7857
beasley@mcs.com

B3
Bella Luna Books
4697 Stone Canyon Ranch Rd
Castle Rock, CO 80104
800-497-4717
fax 303-663-2113
Bellalun@aol.com

B4
Between the Covers
35 W Maple Ave.
Merchantville, NJ 08109
609-665-2284
fax 609-665-3639
mail@betweenthecovers.com
www.betweenthecovers.com

B5
Bicentennial Book Shop
820 S Westnedge Ave.
Kalamazoo, MI 49008
616-345-5987

B6
Bibliography of the Dog
The New House
216 Covey Hill Rd.
Havelock, Quebec
Canada J0S 2C0
514-827-2717
fax 514-827-2091

B7
Best-Read Books
332 Thompson Rd.
Sedro-Woolley, WA 98284-9555

B9
The Book Baron
1236 S Magnolia Ave.
Anaheim, CA 92804
714-527-7022
fax 714-527-5634
bkbaron1@pacbell.net or
bkbaron3@qte.net

B10
Book Broker
114 Bollingwood Rd.
Charlottesville, VA 22902
804-296-2194
fax 804-296-1566
bookbrk@cfw.com
mail order or appointment only

B11 The Book Corner
Michael Tennaro
728 W Lumsden Rd.
Brandon, FL 33511
813-684-1133
bookcrnr@worldnet.att.net
www.abebooks.com/home/bookcrnr

B14
Book & Tackle Shop
Bernard L. Gordon
29 Old Colony Rd.
P.O. Box 114
Chestnut Hill, MA 02467
phone/fax 617-965-0459 (winter)
bktack@ibm.net

B15
Book Treasures
P.O. Box 121
E Norwich, NY 11732

B16
The Book Den South
Nancy Costello
2249 First St.
Ft. Myers, FL 33901-2943
813-332-2333

B17
Books of the Ages
Gary J. Overmann
Maple Ridge Manor
4764 Silverwood Dr.
Batavia, OH 45103-9740
phone/fax 513-732-3456

B18
The Bookseller, Inc.
174 W Exchange St.
Akron, OH 44302
330-762-3101
fax 330-762-4413
booklein@apk.net

B19
Books West Southwest
W. David Laird
Box 6149, University Station
Irvine, CA 92616-6149
714-509-7670
fax 714-854-5102
bkswest@ix.netcom.com

B22
Bridgman Books
906 Roosevelt Ave.
Rome, NY 13440
315-337-7252

B23
British Stamp Exchange
12 Fairlawn Ave.
N Weymouth, MA 02191
871-335-3075

B24
Bromer Booksellers
607 Boylston St.
Boston, MA 02116
617-247-2818
fax 617-247-2975
books@bromer.com
www.bromer.com

B25
Mike Brooks
7335 Skyline
Oakland, CA 94611

B26
Brooks Books
Phil & Marty Nesty
P.O. Box 91
Clayton, CA 94517
925-672-4566
fax 925-672-3338
brooksbk@netvista.net

B27
The Bookstall
570 Sutter St.
San Francisco, CA 94102
fax 415-362-1503
bstallsf@best.com

B29
Books Now & Then
Dennis & Jan Patrick
P.O. Box 337
Stanley, ND 58784
phone/fax 701-628-2084
bnt@stanley.ndak.net
www.ourchurch.com/member/b/
books-now-then

B30
Burke's Bookstore
1719 Poplar Ave.
Memphis, TN 38104-6447
901-278-7484
fax 901-272-2340
burkes@netten.net

B36
Bookcase Books
P. Gayle Hendrington
R.R. 1 Box 242
Newport, NH 03773
603-863-9517
books@bookcasebooks.com
www.bookcasebooks.com

C1
Camelot Books
Charles E. Wyatt
P.O. Box 2883
Vista, CA 92083
619-940-9472

C2
The Captain's Bookshelf, Inc.
Chandler W. Gordon
31 Page Ave.
Asheville, NC 22801
828-253-6631
fax 828-253-4917
captsbooks@aol.com

C3
Cattermole
20th Century Children's Books
9880 Fairmount Rd.
Newbury, OH 44065
440-338-3253
fax 440-338-1675
books@cattermole.com

C4
Bev Chaney, Jr. Books
73 Croton Ave.
Ossining, NY 10562
914-941-1002

C5
Chimney Sweep Books
Lillian Smith Kaiser
P.O. Box 24649
San Jose, CA 95154-4649
chimney@cruzio.com

C6
Chapel Hill Rare Books
Douglas & Maureen O'Dell
P.O. Box 456
Carrboro, NC 27510
919-929-8351
rarebooks@mindspring.com

C7
Chartwell Booksellers
55 E 52nd St.
New York, NY 10055
212-308-0643

C8
Children's Book Adoption Agency
P.O. Box 643
Kensington, MD 20895-0643
301-565-2834
fax 301-585-3091
KIDS_BKS@interloc.com

C9
Cinemage Books
105 W 27th St.
New York, NY 10001
212-243-4919
irajoel@aol.com

C10
Cohen Books & Collectibles
Joel J. Cohen

P.O. Box 810310
Boca Raton, FL 33481-0310
561-487-7888
fax 561-487-3117
cohendisney@prodigy.net
www.cohendisney.com

C11
Cover to Cover
Mark Shuman
P.O. Box 687
Chapel Hill, NC 27514
919-967-1032

C12
Noriko I. Ciochon
Natural History Books
1025 Keokut St.
Iowa City, IA 52240-3303
319-354-9088
fax 319-354-0844
nathist@avalon.net
www.avalon.net/~nathist

C14
Steven Cieluch
15 Walbridge St. Ste. #10
Allston, MA 02134-3808
617-734-7778
scieluch@channel1.com

C15
Thomas L. Coffman
TLC Books
9 N College Ave.
Salem, VA 24153
540-389-3555

C16
Cover to Cover
Meta Fouts
5499 Belfast Rd.
Batavia, OH 45103
513-625-2628
fax 513-625-2683
METAFOUTS@aol.com

D1
Ursula Davidson
Children's & Illustrated Books
134 Linden Ln.
San Rafael, CA 94901
415-454-3939
fax 415-454-1087
davidson_u@compuserve.com
www.abebooks.com/home/uschi

D2
L. Clarice Davis
Fine & Applied Art Books
P.O. Box 56054
Sherman Oaks, CA 91413-1054
818-787-1322

fax 818-780-3281
davislc@earthlink.net
www.abebooks.com/home/LCALART

D4
Carol Docheff, Bookseller
1390 Reliez Valley Rd.
Lafayette, CA 94549-2647
925-935-9595
fax 925-256-8569
docheffc@inreach.com
www.abebooks.com/home/docheff

D5
Dover Publications
Dept. A 214
E Second St.
Mineola, NY 11501

D6
Drusilla's Books
817 N Howard St.
Baltimore, MD 21201-4696
410-225-0277
fax 410-321-4955
Tues-Sat: 12 to 5; or by appointment
drusilla@mindspring.com

D9
Dad's Old Bookstore
Green Hills Ct.
4004 Hillsboro Rd.
Nashville, TN 37215
615-298-5880

D10
Tom Davidson, Bookseller
3703 Ave. L
Brooklyn, NY 11210
718-338-8428
fax 718-338-8430
tdbooks@att.net

D11
Dawson's Book Shop
535 N Larchmont Blvd.
Los Angeles, CA 90004
323-469-2186
fax 323-469-9553
dawsonbk@ix.netcom.com
www.dawsonbooks.com

E1
The Early West/Whodunit Books
P.O. Box 9292
College Station, TX 77842
409-775-6047
fax 409-764-7758
EarlyWest@aol.com

E2
Edison Hall Books

5 Ventnor Dr.
Edison, NJ 08820
908-548-4455

E4
Elder's Book Store
2115 Elliston Pl.
Nashville, TN 37203
615-327-1867

E5
Elegant Book & Map Company
815 Harrison Ave.
Cambridge, OH 43725
614-432-4068

E6
Eastside Books & Paper
P.O. Box 1581, Gracie Station
New York, NY 10028-0013
212-759-6299

F1
First Folio
Dennis R. Melhouse
1206 Brentwood
Paris, TN 38242-3804
phone/fax 910-944-9940
firstfol@aeneas.net

F2
Fisher Books & Antiques
345 Pine St.
Williamsport, PA 17701

F3
Flo Silver Books
8442 Oakwood Ct. N
Indianapolis, IN 46260
phone/fax 317-255-5118
Flosilver@aol.com

F5
Fran's Bookhouse
6601 Greene St.
Philadelphia, PA 19119
215-438-2729
fax 215-438-8997

F6
Fostoria Trading Post
B.L.Foley III
P.O. Box 142
Fostoria, IA 51340
712-262-5936
books@ncn.net
www.ncn.net/~books

F7
Five Quail Books — West
P.O. Box 9870
Phoenix, AZ 85068-9870

602-861-0548
fax 602-861-1113
5quail@grandcanyonbooks.com
www.grandcanyonbooks.com

G1
John Gach Fine & Rare Books
10514 Marriottsville Rd.
Randallstown, MD 21133
410-465-9023
fax 410-465-0649
inquiry@gach.com
www.gach.com

G2
Galerie De Boicourt
Eva M. Boicourt
6136 Westbrooke Dr.
W. Bloomfield, MI 48322
248-788-9253

G3
Gambler's Book Shop
630 S Eleventh St.
Las Vegas, NV 89101
800-634-6243

G4
David & Nancy Garcelon
10 Hastings Ave.
Millbury, MA 01527-4314
508-754-2667

G5
Michael Gerlicher
1375 Rest Point Rd.
Orono, MN 55364

G6
Glo's Books & Collectibles
Gloria Stobbes
906 Shadywood
Southlake, TX 76092
817-481-1438

G7
James Tait Goodrich
Antiquarian Books & Manuscripts
135 Tweed Blvd.
Grandview-on-Hudson, NY 10960-4913
914-359-0242
fax 914-359-0142
jtg.jamestgoodrich.com

G8
Grave Matters
P.O. Box 32192
Cincinnati, OH 45232-0192
513-242-7527
fax 513-242-5115
books@gravematters.com
www.gravematters.com

G10
Bernard E. Goodman, Bookseller
7421 SW 147 Ct.
Miami, FL 33193-1116
305-385-8526
bgbooks@bellsouth.net
www.abebooks.com/home/bgbookman

G11
Ron Gibson, The Bookshop
110 Windsor Cir.
Burlington, IA 52601-1477
319-752-4588

H1
Henry F. Hain III
Antiques, Collectibles & Books
2623 N Second St.
Harrisburg, PA 17110-1109
717-238-0534
antcolbks@ezonline.com

H2
Rick Harmon
Military Books & Relics
910 Sullivan Dr.
Belvidere, IL 61008
815-547-7580

H3
Terry Harper, Bookseller
P.O. Box 312
Vergennes, VT 05491-0312
802-877-9262
bookvend@together.net

H4
Susan Heller, Pages for Sages
22611 Halburton Rd.
Beachwood, OH 44122-3939
216-283-2665
hellersu@cyberdrive.net

H5
Heritage Book Shop, Inc.
8540 Melrose Ave.
Los Angeles, CA 90069
310-659-3674
fax 310-659-4872
HBSINCLA@aol.com

H6
Hillcrest Books
961 Deep Draw Rd.
Crossville, TN 38555-9547
phone/fax 931-484-7680
hillcrst@usit.net
www.oldcatalogues.com

H7
Jim Hodgson Books
908 S Manlius St.
Fayetteville, NY 13066
315-637-6264
jimhbooks@aol.com

H9
Murray Hudson
Antiquarian Books & Maps
109 S Church St.
P.O. Box 163
Halls, TN 38040
901-836-9057 or 800-748-9946
fax 901-836-9017
mapman@usit.net

H10
Hurley Books/Celtic Cross Books
1753 Rt. 12
Westmoreland, NH 03467-4742
603-399-4342
fax 603-399-8326
hurleybook@adam.cheshire.net

H11
Ken Hebenstreit, Bookseller
813 N Washington Ave.
Royal Oak, MI 48067
phone/fax 248-548-5460
kenhebenstreit@home.com
www.khbooks.com

H13
Hartfield Rare Books
Ruth Inglehart
117 Dixboro Rd.
Ann Arbor, MI 48105
phone/fax 313-662-6035

H14
Ruth Heindel Associates
First Editions, Rare & Used Books
660 Boas St., Suite 1618
Harrisburg, PA 17110
717-213-9010

I1
Island Books
P.O. Box 19
Old Westbury, NY 11586
516-759-0233

J1
Jay's House of Collectibles
75 Pky. Dr.
Syosset, NY 11791

J2
Jordan Book Gallery
1349 Sheridan Ave.
Cody, WY 82414
307-587-6689
fax 307-527-4944
jjordan@trib.com

J3
Pricilla Juvelis, Inc.
1166 Massachusetts Ave.
Cambridge, MA 02138

617-497-7570
fax 617-497-9343
pjbooks@tiac.com

K1
Kenneth Karmiole, Bookseller, Inc.
509 Wilshire Blvd.
Santa Monica, CA 90401
310-451-4342
fax 310-458-5930
karmbooks@aol.com

K2
Ilene Kayne
1308 S Charles St.
Baltimore, MD 21230-4219
410-347-7570
kayne@clark.net

K3
Key Books
P.O. Box 58097
St. Petersburg, FL 33715-8097
813-867-2931

K4
The King's Market Bookshop
P.O. Box 709
Boulder, CO 80306-0709
303-232-3321

K5
Knollwood Books
Lee & Peggy Price
P.O. Box 197
Oregon, WI 53575-0197
608-835-8861
fax 608-835-8421
books@tdsnet.com

K6
Kendra Krienke
230 Central Park West
New York, NY 10024
201-930-9709 or 201-930-9765

K7
George Robert Kane Fine Books
252 Third Ave.
Santa Cruz, CA 95062
phone/fax 408-426-4133
gkanebks@cruzio.com

L1
Bob Lakin Books
P.O. Box 186
Chatfield, TX 75105
972-247-3291

L2
Henry Lindeman
8723 Clarklake Rd.
Clarklake, MI 49234

L3
Ken Lopez, Bookseller
51 Huntington Rd.
Hadley, MA 01035
413-584-4827
fax 413-584-2045
mail@lopezbooks.com
www.lopezbooks.com

L4
W.J. Leveridge
W & L Trading Company
2301 Carova Rd.
Carova Beach, Corolla, NC 27927
252-453-3408

L5
Robert F. Lucas Antiquarian Books
P.O. Box 63
Blandford, MA 01008
413-848-2061
books@lucasbooks.com
www.lucasbooks.com

M1
M & S Rare Books, Inc.
P.O. Box 2594, E Side Station
Providence, RI 02906
401-421-1050
fax 401-272-0831 (attention M & S)
dsiegel@msrarebooks.com

M2
Robert A. Madle
4406 Bestor Dr.
Rockville, MD 20853
301-460-4712

M4
Melvin Marcher, Bookseller
6204 N Vermont
Oklahoma City, OK 73112
405-946-6270
(12 pm to 7 pm **only**)

M5
Marvelous Books
Dorothy (Dede) Kern
P.O. Box 1510
Ballwin, MO 63022
314-458-3301
fax 314-273-5452
marvbooks@aol.com

M6
Mason's Bookstore, Rare Books
   & Record Albums East
115 S Main St.
Chambersburg, PA 17201
717-261-0541

M7
Denis McDonnell, Bookseller

653 Park St.
Honesdale, PA 18431-1445
570-253-6706
fax 570-253-6786
dmd@ptd.net
www.denismcd.com

M8
McGowan Book Co.
P.O. Box 4226
Chapel Hill, NC 27515-4226
919-968-1121 or 800-449-8406
fax 919-968-1644
mcgowanbooks@mindspring.com
www.mcgowanbooks.com

M9
Paul Melzer Fine & Rare Books
12 E Vine St.
P.O. Box 1143
Redlands, CA 92373
909-792-7299
fax 909-792-7218
pmbooks@eee.org

M10
Robert L. Merriam
Rare, Used & Old Books
39 Newhall Rd.
Conway, MA 01341-9709
413-369-4052
rmerriam@valinet.com

M11
Meyer Boswell Books, Inc.
2141 Mission St.
San Francisco, CA 94110
415-255-6400
fax 415-255-6499
rarelaw@meyerbos.com
www.meyerbos.com

M12
Frank Mikesh
1356 Walden Rd.
Walnut Creek, CA 94596
925-934-9243
fax 925-947-6113

M13
Ken Mitchell
710 Conacher Dr.
Willowdale, Ontario
Canada M2M 3N6
416-222-5808

M14
Modern Age Books
Jeff Canja
P.O. Box 325
East Lansing, MI 48826
517-487-9313

M15
Mordida Books
P.O. Box 79322
Houston, TX 77279
713-467-4280
fax 713-467-4182
mordida@swbell.net
www.mordida.com

M16
The Mulberry Cat
Yvonne Davis
Jan Davis Martel
P.O. Box 3573
Boone, NC 28607
704-963-7693

M17
Much Ado
Seven Pleasant St.
Marblehead, MA 01945
781-639-0400
fax 781-639-0840
muchado@shore.net

M19
My Book Heaven
2212 Broadway
Oakland, CA 94612
510-893-7273 or 510-521-1683
MBHR@ix.netcom.com

M20
My Bookhouse
27 S Sandusky St.
Tiffin, OH 44883
419-447-9842
mybooks@bright.net

M21
Brian McMillan, Books
1429 L Ave.
Traer, IA 50675
319-478-2360
(Mon – Sat: 9 am to 9pm)
Brianbks@netins.net

M22
M/S Books
53 Curtiss Rd.
New Preston, CT 06777
860-868-0627
fax 860-868-0504

M23
McGee's First Varieties
330 Franklin Rd., Suite 135A
Brentwood, TN 37027
615-373-5318
TMcGee@BellSouth.net
www.mcgees1st.com

M25
Monroe Stahr Books
5112 Van Noord Ave.
Sherman Oaks, CA 91423
818-501-3419
fax 818-995-0966
MStahrBks@aol.com

N1
Nerman's Books
Gary Nerman
233 Dunkirk Drive
Winnipeg, Manitoba
CanadaR2M 3X1
nerman@escape.ca

N2
Nutmeg Books
354 New Litchfield St. (Rte. 202)
Torrington, CT 06790
203-482-9696
nutmeg@compsol.net

N3
Kai Nygaard
19421 Eighth Pl.
Escondido, CA 92029
619-749-9039

N4
Norris Books
Charles Chavdarian, Owner
2491 San Ramon Vly. Blvd.
Suite 1, PMB 201
San Ramon, CA 94583
online at abebooks and bibliofind
phone/fax 925-867-1218
norrisbooks@slip.net

O1
David L. O'Neal, Antiquarian
    Bookseller
234 Clarendon St.
Boston, MA 02116
617-266-5790
fax 617-266-1089
staff@onealbooks.com

O2
W.B. O'Neill
Old & Rare Books
11609 Hunters Green Ct.
Reston, VA 20191
703-860-0782
fax 703-620-0153
nyc1918@aol.com

O3
October Farm
2609 Branch Rd.
Raleigh, NC 27610
919-772-0482
fax 919-779-6265

octoberfarm@bellsouth.net
www.octoberfarm.com

O4
The Old London Bookshop
Michael & Marlys Schon
P.O. Box 922
Bellingham, WA 98227-0922
360-733-7273
fax 360-647-8946
OldLondon@aol.com

O5
The Old Map Gallery
Paul F. Mahoney
1746 Blake St.
Denver, CO 80202
303-296-7725
fax 303-296-7936
oldmapgallery@denver.net

O6
Old Paint Lick School Antique Mall
Raymond P. Mixon
11000 Hwy. 52 West
Paint Lick, KY 40461
606-925-3000 or 606-792-3000

O7
Overlee Farm Books
P.O. Box 1155
Stockbridge, MA 01262
413-637-2277

O8
K.C. & Jean C. Owings
Box 389
Whitman, MA 02382
781-447-7850
fax 781-447-3435

O9
Olde Current Books
Daniel P. Shay
356 Putnam Ave.
Ormond Beach, FL 32174
904-672-8998
peakmyster@aol.com

O10
Oak Knoll Books
310 Delaware St.
New Castle, DE 19720
800-996-2556 or 302-328-7232
fax 302-328-7274
oakknoll@oakknoll.com
www.oakknoll.com

O11
Orpheus Books
Don Stutheit/Barbara Wight
11522 NE 20th St.
Bellevue, WA 98004-3005
425-451-8343
orpheusbooks@earthlink.net

P1
Pacific Rim Books
Michael Onorato
P.O. Box 30575
Bellingham, WA 98228-2575
206-676-0256
pacrimbks@aol.com

P2
Margaret E. Page
Page Books
HCR 65, Box 233
Kingston, AR 72742
870-861-5831
pagebook@eritter.net

P3
Pandora's Books Ltd.
P.O. Box 54
Neche, ND 58265
204-324-8548
fax 204-324-1628
jgthiess@MTS.Net

P4
Parmer Books
7644 Forrestal Rd.
San Diego, CA 92120-2203
619-287-0693
fax 619-287-6135
ParmerBook@aol.com

P5
Parnassus Books
218 N 9th St.
Boise, ID 83702

P6
Passaic Book Center
594 Main Ave.
Passaic, NJ 07055
201-778-6646
fax 201-778-6738

P7
Pauper's Books
206 N Main St.
Bowling Green, OH 43402-2420
419-352-2163

P8
R. Plapinger, Baseball Books
P.O. Box 1062
Ashland, OR 97520
541-488-1220

P9
Prometheus Books
59 John Glenn Dr.
Buffalo, NY 14228-2197
716-691-0133
fax 716-691-0137

P11
Pelanor Books
7 Gaskill Ave.
Albany, NY 12203

P12
Popek's Pages Past
Pete & Connie Popek
3870 S Hwy 23
Oneonta, NY 13820
607-432-0836
popeks@magnum.wpe.com

P13
Periodyssey
151 Crescent St.
Northampton, MA 01060
413-527-1900
fax 413-527-1930

Q1
Quill & Brush
Patricia & Allen Ahearn
1137 Sugarloaf Mtn. Rd.
Dickerson, MD 20842
301-874-3200
fax 301-874-0824
Firsts@qbbooks.com
www.qbbooks.com

Q2
Quest Books
Peter & Veronica Burridge
Harmer Hill
Millington
York YO42 1TX UK
Quesbks@aol.com

R1
Raintree Books
432 N Eustis St.
Eustis, FL 32726
904-357-7145

R2
Kathleen Rais & Co.
Rais Place Cottage
211 Carolina Ave.
Phoenixville, PA 19460
610-933-1388

R3
Randall House
Pia Oliver
835 Laguna St.
Santa Barbara, CA 93101
805-963-1909
fax 805-963-1650
pia@piasworld.com
www.piasworld.com/randall

R5
Jo Ann Reisler, Ltd.
360 Glyndon St., NE

Vienna, VA 22180
703-938-2967
fax 703-938-9057
reisler@clark.net
www.clark.net/pub/reisler

R6
Wallace Robinson Books
RD #6, Box 574
Meadville, PA 16335
800-653-3280 or 813-823-3280
814-724-7670 or 814-333-9652

R8
RAC Books
P.O. Box 296 RD 2
Seven Valleys, PA 17360
717-428-3776
racbooks@cyberia.com

R9
Realm of Colorado
P.O. Box 24
Parker, CO 80134

R10
Roger Reus
9412 Huron Ave.
Richmond, VA 23294
(mail order only)

R11
Recollection Books
4519 University Way NE
Seattle, WA 98105
206-548-1346

R12
Leona Rostenberg
    & Madeleine Stern
Rare Books
40 East 88th St.
New York, NY 10128-1176
212-831-6628
fax 212-831-1961

R13
Alice Robbins, Bookseller
3002 Round Hill Rd.
Greensboro, NC 27408
910-282-1964

R14
Revere Books
P.O. Box 420
Revere, PA 18953-0420
610-847-2709
fax 610-847-1910

R15
Richard C. Ramer
Old & Rare Books
225 E 70th St.

New York, NY 10021
212-737-0222 or 212-737-0223
fax 212-288-4169
5222386@mcimail.com

R16
Rising Stars
Don Carnahan
P.O. Box 2991
Yuma, AZ 85366
phone/fax 520-329-6054

S1
Bill & Mimi Sachen
927 Grand Ave.
Waukegan, IL 60085-3709
847-662-7204
FutileWill@aol.com

S2
J. Sampson Antiques & Books
107 S Main
Harrodsburg, KY 40330
606-734-7829

S3
Stanley Schwartz
1934 Pentuckett Ave.
San Diego, CA 92104-5732
619-232-5888
fax 619-233-5833
Schwartz@cts.com

S4
Scribe Company
Attn: Bonnie Smith
427 Hidden Forest S
Longview, TX 75605
903-663-6873

S5
Significant Books
3053 Madison Rd.
P.O. Box 9248
Cincinnati, OH 45209
800-750-1153
513-321-7567
signbook@iac.net

S6
The Silver Door
P.O. Box 3208
Redondo Beach, CA 90277
310-379-6005

S7
K.B. Slocum Books
P.O. Box 10998 #620
Austin, TX 78766
800-521-4451
fax 512-258-8041

S8
Barbara Smith Books
P.O. Box 1185
Northampton, MA 01061
413-586-1453

S9
Ed Smith Books
20 Paget Rd.
Madision, WI 53704-5929
608-241-3707
ed@edsbooks.com
www.edsbooks.com

S13
Eileen Serxner
Box 2544
Bala Cynwyd, PA 19004
610-664-7960
fax 610-664-1940
serxner@erols.com
www.abebooks.com/home/
serxnerbooks/

S14
Second Harvest Books
Warren R. Johnson
P.O. Box 3306
Florence, OR 97439-3306
phone/fax 541-902-0215
2harvest@presys.com
www.abebooks.com/home/47002

S15
Snowy Egret Books
1237 Carroll Ave.
St. Paul, MN 55104
612-641-0917
snowy@mr.net

S16
Stan Clark Military Books
915 Fairview Ave.
Gettysburg, PA 17325
717-337-0581

S17
David R. Smith
30 Nelson Circle
Jaffrey, NH 03452
603-532-8666
Bookinc@Cheshire.net

S18
Spellbound Books
M. Tyree
3818 Vickie Ct. #B
Prescott Valley, AZ 86314
520-759-2625

S19
Vera L. Scheer
408 S. Main St.

Salem, IA 52649
319-258-7641
beeba@lisco.com

T1
Lee Barnett Temares
50 Heights Rd.
Plandome, NY 11030
516-627-8688
fax 516-627-7822
tembooks@aol.com

T2
Thomas Books
P.O. Box 14036
Phoenix, AZ 85063
623-247-9289
fax 623-945-1023
sales@thomasbooks.com
www.thomasbooks.com

T4
Trackside Books
8819 Mobud Dr.
Houston, TX 77036
713-772-8107

T5
Treasures From the Castle
Connie Castle
1277 Candlestick Lane
Rochester, MI 48306
248-651-7317
treasure23@juno.com
www.abebooks.com/home/treasure

T7
J. Tuttle Maritime Books
1806 Laurel Crest
Madison, WI 53705
608-238-SAIL (7245)
fax 608-238-7249

T8
George H. Tweney
16660 Marine View Dr. SW
Seattle, WA 98166
206-243-8243

T9
Typographeum Bookshop
246 Bennington Rd.
Francestown, NH 03043
603-547-2425

T10
Thorn Books
P.O. Box 1244
Moorpark, CA 93020
805-529-3647
fax 805-529-0022
thornbooks@earthlink.net

T11
Town's End Books
John D. & Judy A. Townsend
132 Hemlock Dr.
Deep River, CT 06417
860-526-3896 or 888-732-2668
john@townsendbooks.com
www.townsendbooks.com

T12
Third Time Around Books
Norman Todd
R.R. #1
Mar., Ontario
Canada N0H 1XO
519-534-1382

T13
Twice Read Books & Comics
42 S Main St.
Chambersburg, PA 17201
717-261-8449

V1
VERSEtility Books
P.O. Box 1133
Farmington, CT 06034-1133
860-677-0606
versebks@tiac.net

V2
A.A. Vespa
P.O. Box 637
Park Ridge, IL 60068
708-692-4210

V3
Vintage Books
Nancy & David Haines
181 Hayden Rowe St.
Hopkinton, MA 01748
508-435-3499
vintage@gis.net

V4
Volume I Books
One Union St.
Hillsdale, MI 49242
517-437-2228
fax 517-437-7923
volume1book@dmci.net

W1
Worldwide Antiquarian
P.O. Box 410391
Cambridge, MA 02141-0004
617-876-6220
fax 617-876-0839
mbalwan@aol.com

W2
Warren's Collector Books
For Sale Now

Warren Gillespie, Jr.
112 Royal Ct.
Friendswood, TX 77546
281-482-7947

W3
Ruth Woods Oriental Books & Art
6 Hillside Ave.
Darien, CT 06820-5010

W4
Glenn Wiese
5078 Lynwood Ave.
Blasdell, NY 14219
716-821-0972

W5
Gary Warinner
P.O. Box 155
Boyers, PA 16020
724-735-2369

X1
Xanadu Records, Ltd.
3242 Irwin Ave.
Kingsbridge, NY 10463
718-549-3655

Y1
Yesterday's Books
229 Riverview Dr.
Parchment, MI 49004
616-345-1011
yesbooks@aol.com

Reach **Thousands** with Your **Free Listing** in Our Next Edition!

☞ **Booksellers!** If you publish lists or catalogs of books for sale, take advantage of this free offer. Put us on your mailing list right away so that we can include you in our next edition. We'll not only list you in our directory under the genre that best represents your special interests (please specify these when you contact us), but each book description we choose to include from your catalog will contain a special dealer code that will identify you as the book dealer to contact in order to buy that book. Please send your information and catalogs or lists right away, since we're working on a first-come, first-served basis. Be sure to include your current address, just as you'd like it to be published. You may also include a fax number or an e-mail address. Our dealers tell us that this service has been very successful for them, both in buying and selling.

Send your listings to:

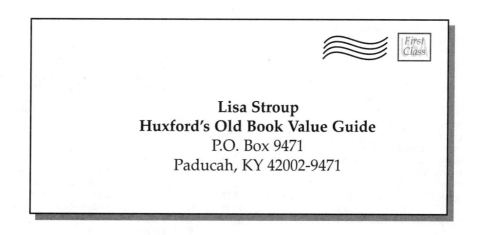

Lisa Stroup
Huxford's Old Book Value Guide
P.O. Box 9471
Paducah, KY 42002-9471

COLLECTOR BOOKS

Informing Today's Collector

For over two decades we have been keeping collectors informed on trends and values in all fields of antiques and collectibles.

DOLLS, FIGURES & TEDDY BEARS

4707	A Decade of **Barbie Dolls** & Collectibles, 1981–1991, Summers	$19.95
4631	**Barbie Doll** Boom, 1986–1995, Augustyniak	$18.95
2079	**Barbie Doll** Fashion, Volume I, Eames	$24.95
4846	**Barbie Doll** Fashion, Volume II, Eames	$24.95
3957	**Barbie** Exclusives, Rana	$18.95
4632	**Barbie** Exclusives, Book II, Rana	$18.95
5672	The **Barbie Doll** Years, 4th Ed., Olds	$19.95
3810	**Chatty Cathy** Dolls, Lewis	$15.95
5352	Collector's Ency. of **Barbie** Doll Exclusives & More, 2nd Ed.,Augustyniak	$24.95
2211	Collector's Encyclopedia of **Madame Alexander** Dolls, Smith	$24.95
4863	Collector's Encyclopedia of **Vogue Dolls**, Izen/Stover	$29.95
5821	**Doll Values**, Antique to Modern, 5th Ed., Moyer	$12.95
5829	**Madame Alexander** Collector's Dolls Price Guide #26, Crowsey	$12.95
5833	**Modern Collectible Dolls**, Volume V, Moyer	$24.95
5689	**Nippon Dolls** & Playthings, Van Patten/Lau	$29.95
5365	**Peanuts Collectibles**, Podley/Bang	$24.95
5253	Story of **Barbie**, 2nd Ed., Westenhouser	$24.95
5277	**Talking Toys** of the 20th Century, Lewis	$15.95
1513	**Teddy Bears & Steiff** Animals, Mandel	$9.95
1817	**Teddy Bears & Steiff** Animals, 2nd Series, Mandel	$19.95
2084	**Teddy Bears, Annalee's & Steiff** Animals, 3rd Series, Mandel	$19.95
5371	**Teddy Bear** Treasury, Yenke	$19.95
1808	Wonder of **Barbie**, Manos	$9.95
1430	World of **Barbie** Dolls, Manos	$9.95
4880	World of **Raggedy Ann** Collectibles, Avery	$24.95

TOYS, MARBLES & CHRISTMAS COLLECTIBLES

2333	Antique & Collectible **Marbles**, 3rd Ed., Grist	$9.95
5353	**Breyer Animal** Collector's Guide, 2nd Ed., Browell	$19.95
4976	**Christmas Ornaments**, Lights & Decorations, Johnson	$24.95
4737	**Christmas Ornaments**, Lights & Decorations, Vol. II, Johnson	$24.95
4739	**Christmas Ornaments**, Lights & Decorations, Vol. III, Johnson	$24.95
4559	Collectible **Action Figures**, 2nd Ed., Manos	$17.95
2338	Collector's Encyclopedia of **Disneyana**, Longest, Stern	$24.95
5038	Collector's Guide to **Diecast Toys** & Scale Models, 2nd Ed., Johnson	$19.95
4651	Collector's Guide to **Tinker Toys**, Strange	$18.95
4566	Collector's Guide to **Tootsietoys**, 2nd Ed., Richter	$19.95
5169	Collector's Guide to **TV Toys** & Memorabilia, 2nd Ed., Davis/Morgan	$24.95
5360	**Fisher-Price Toys**, Cassity	$19.95
4720	The Golden Age of **Automotive Toys**, 1925–1941, Hutchison/Johnson	$24.95
5593	Grist's Big Book of **Marbles**, 2nd Ed.	$24.95
3970	Grist's Machine-Made & Contemporary **Marbles**, 2nd Ed.	$9.95
5267	**Matchbox Toys**, 1947 to 1998, 3rd Ed., Johnson	$19.95
5830	**McDonald's** Collectibles, 2nd Edition, Henriques/DuVall	$24.95
5673	Modern **Candy Containers** & Novelties, Brush/Miller	$19.95
1540	Modern **Toys** 1930–1980, Baker	$19.95
3888	**Motorcycle Toys**, Antique & Contemporary, Gentry/Downs	$18.95
5693	**Schroeder's Collectible Toys**, Antique to Modern Price Guide, 7th Ed.	$17.95

FURNITURE

1457	American **Oak** Furniture, McNerney	$9.95
3716	American **Oak** Furniture, Book II, McNerney	$12.95
1118	Antique **Oak** Furniture, Hill	$7.95
2271	Collector's Encyclopedia of **American** Furniture, Vol. II, Swedberg	$24.95
3720	Collector's Encyclopedia of **American** Furniture, Vol. III, Swedberg	$24.95
5359	Early **American** Furniture, Obbard	$12.95
1755	Furniture of the **Depression Era**, Swedberg	$19.95
3906	**Heywood-Wakefield** Modern Furniture, Rouland	$18.95
1885	**Victorian** Furniture, Our American Heritage, McNerney	$9.95
3829	**Victorian** Furniture, Our American Heritage, Book II, McNerney	$9.95

JEWELRY, HATPINS, WATCHES & PURSES

1712	Antique & Collectible **Thimbles** & Accessories, Mathis	$19.95
1748	Antique **Purses**, Revised Second Ed., Holiner	$19.95
1278	Art Nouveau & Art Deco **Jewelry**, Baker	$9.95
4850	Collectible **Costume Jewelry**, Simonds	$24.95
5675	Collectible **Silver Jewelry**, Rezazadeh	$24.95
3722	Collector's Ency. of **Compacts**, Carryalls & Face Powder Boxes, Mueller	$24.95
4940	**Costume Jewelry**, A Practical Handbook & Value Guide, Rezazadeh	$24.95
1716	Fifty Years of Collectible **Fashion Jewelry**, 1925–1975, Baker	$19.95
1424	**Hatpins** & Hatpin Holders, Baker	$9.95
5695	**Ladies' Vintage Accessories**, Bruton	$24.95
1181	100 Years of Collectible **Jewelry**, 1850–1950, Baker	$9.95
4729	**Sewing Tools** & Trinkets, Thompson	$24.95
5620	Unsigned Beauties of **Costume Jewelry**, Brown	$24.95
4878	Vintage & Contemporary **Purse Accessories**, Gerson	$24.95
5696	Vintage & Vogue Ladies' **Compacts**, 2nd Edition, Gerson	$29.95

INDIANS, GUNS, KNIVES, TOOLS, PRIMITIVES

1868	Antique **Tools**, Our American Heritage, McNerney	$9.95
5616	Big Book of **Pocket Knives**, Stewart	$19.95
4943	Field Guide to Flint **Arrowheads** & **Knives** of the North American Indian	$9.95
2279	**Indian Artifacts** of the Midwest, Book I, Hothem	$14.95
3885	**Indian Artifacts** of the Midwest, Book II, Hothem	$16.95
4870	**Indian Artifacts** of the Midwest, Book III, Hothem	$18.95
5685	**Indian Artifacts** of the Midwest, Book IV, Hothem	$19.95
5687	**Modern Guns**, Identification & Values, 13th Ed., Quertermous	$14.95
2164	**Primitives**, Our American Heritage, McNerney	$9.95
1759	**Primitives**, Our American Heritage, 2nd Series, McNerney	$14.95
4730	Standard **Knife** Collector's Guide, 3rd Ed., Ritchie & Stewart	$12.95

PAPER COLLECTIBLES & BOOKS

4633	**Big Little Books**, Jacobs	$18.95
4710	Collector's Guide to **Children's Books**, 1850 to 1950, Volume I, Jones	$18.95
5153	Collector's Guide to **Children's Books**, 1850 to 1950, Volume II, Jones	$19.95
5596	Collector's Guide to **Children's Books**, 1950 to 1975, Volume III, Jones	$19.95
1441	Collector's Guide to **Post Cards**, Wood	$9.95
2081	Guide to Collecting **Cookbooks**, Allen	$14.95
5825	Huxford's **Old Book** Value Guide, 13th Ed.	$19.95
2080	Price Guide to **Cookbooks** & Recipe Leaflets, Dickinson	$9.95
3973	**Sheet Music** Reference & Price Guide, 2nd Ed., Pafik & Guiheen	$19.95
4654	**Victorian Trade Cards**, Historical Reference & Value Guide, Cheadle	$19.95
4733	**Whitman Juvenile Books**, Brown	$17.95

GLASSWARE

5602	Anchor Hocking's **Fire-King** & More, 2nd Ed.	$24.95
4561	Collectible **Drinking Glasses**, Chase & Kelly	$17.95
5823	Collectible **Glass Shoes**, 2nd Edition, Wheatley	$24.95
5357	Coll. **Glassware** from the 40s, 50s & 60s, 5th Ed., Florence	$19.95
1810	Collector's Encyclopedia of **American Art Glass**, Shuman	$29.95
5358	Collector's Encyclopedia of **Depression Glass**, 14th Ed., Florence	$19.95
1961	Collector's Encyclopedia of **Fry Glassware**, Fry Glass Society	$24.95
1664	Collector's Encyclopedia of **Heisey Glass**, 1925–1938, Bredehoft	$24.95
3905	Collector's Encyclopedia of **Milk Glass**, Newbound	$24.95
4936	Collector's Guide to **Candy Containers**, Dezso/Poirier	$19.95
4564	**Crackle Glass**, Weitman	$19.95
4941	**Crackle Glass**, Book II, Weitman	$19.95
4714	**Czechoslovakian Glass** and Collectibles, Book II, Barta/Rose	$16.95
5528	Early American **Pattern Glass**, Metz	$17.95
5682	**Elegant Glassware** of the Depression Era, 9th Ed., Florence	$19.95
5614	Field Guide to **Pattern Glass**, McCain	$17.95
3981	Evers' Standard **Cut Glass** Value Guide	$12.95
4659	**Fenton Art Glass**, 1907–1939, Whitmyer	$24.95
5615	Florence's **Glassware Pattern Identification** Guide, Vol. II	$19.95

4719	**Fostoria**, Etched, Carved & Cut Designs, Vol. II, Kerr	$24.95
3883	**Fostoria Stemware**, The Crystal for America, Long/Seate	$24.95
5261	**Fostoria Tableware**, 1924 – 1943, Long/Seate	$24.95
5361	**Fostoria Tableware**, 1944 – 1986, Long/Seate	$24.95
5604	**Fostoria**, Useful & Ornamental, Long/Seate	$29.95
4644	**Imperial Carnival Glass**, Burns	$18.95
5827	**Kitchen Glassware** of the Depression Years, 6th Ed., Florence	$24.95
5600	Much More Early American **Pattern Glass**, Metz	$17.95
5690	Pocket Guide to **Depression Glass**, 12th Ed., Florence	$9.95
5594	Standard Encyclopedia of **Carnival Glass**, 7th Ed., Edwards/Carwile	$29.95
5595	Standard **Carnival Glass** Price Guide, 12th Ed., Edwards/Carwile	$9.95
5272	Standard Encyclopedia of **Opalescent Glass**, 3rd Ed., Edwards/Carwile	$24.95
5617	Standard Encyclopedia of **Pressed Glass**, 2nd Ed., Edwards/Carwile	$29.95
4731	**Stemware Identification**, Featuring Cordials with Values, Florence	$24.95
4732	**Very Rare Glassware** of the Depression Years, 5th Series, Florence	$24.95
4656	**Westmoreland Glass**, Wilson	$24.95

POTTERY

4927	**ABC Plates & Mugs**, Lindsay	$24.95
4929	**American Art Pottery**, Sigafoose	$24.95
4630	**American Limoges**, Limoges	$24.95
1312	**Blue & White Stoneware**, McNerney	$9.95
1958	So. Potteries **Blue Ridge Dinnerware**, 3rd Ed., Newbound	$14.95
1959	**Blue Willow**, 2nd Ed., Gaston	$14.95
4851	Collectible **Cups & Saucers**, Harran	$18.95
1373	Collector's Encyclopedia of **American Dinnerware**, Cunningham	$24.95
4931	Collector's Encyclopedia of **Bauer Pottery**, Chipman	$24.95
4932	Collector's Encyclopedia of **Blue Ridge Dinnerware**, Vol. II, Newbound	$24.95
4658	Collector's Encyclopedia of **Brush-McCoy Pottery**, Huxford	$24.95
5034	Collector's Encyclopedia of **California Pottery**, 2nd Ed., Chipman	$24.95
2133	Collector's Encyclopedia of **Cookie Jars**, Roerig	$24.95
3723	Collector's Encyclopedia of **Cookie Jars**, Book II, Roerig	$24.95
4939	Collector's Encyclopedia of **Cookie Jars**, Book III, Roerig	$24.95
5748	Collector's Encyclopedia of **Fiesta**, 9th Ed., Huxford	$24.95
4718	Collector's Encyclopedia of **Figural Planters & Vases**, Newbound	$19.95
3961	Collector's Encyclopedia of **Early Noritake**, Alden	$24.95
1439	Collector's Encyclopedia of **Flow Blue China**, Gaston	$19.95
3812	Collector's Encyclopedia of **Flow Blue China**, 2nd Ed., Gaston	$24.95
3431	Collector's Encyclopedia of **Homer Laughlin China**, Jasper	$24.95
1276	Collector's Encyclopedia of **Hull Pottery**, Roberts	$19.95
3962	Collector's Encyclopedia of **Lefton China**, DeLozier	$19.95
4855	Collector's Encyclopedia of **Lefton China**, Book II, DeLozier	$19.95
5609	Collector's Encyclopedia of **Limoges Porcelain**, 3rd Ed., Gaston	$29.95
2334	Collector's Encyclopedia of **Majolica Pottery**, Katz-Marks	$19.95
1358	Collector's Encyclopedia of **McCoy Pottery**, Huxford	$19.95
5677	Collector's Encyclopedia of **Niloak**, 2nd Edition, Gifford	$29.95
3837	Collector's Encyclopedia of **Nippon Porcelain**, Van Patten	$24.95
1665	Collector's Ency. of **Nippon Porcelain**, 3rd Series, Van Patten	$24.95
4712	Collector's Ency. of **Nippon Porcelain**, 4th Series, Van Patten	$24.95
5053	Collector's Ency. of **Nippon Porcelain**, 5th Series, Van Patten	$24.95
5678	Collector's Ency. of **Nippon Porcelain**, 6th Series, Van Patten	$29.95
1447	Collector's Encyclopedia of **Noritake**, Van Patten	$19.95
1038	Collector's Encyclopedia of **Occupied Japan**, 2nd Series, Florence	$14.95
4951	Collector's Encyclopedia of **Old Ivory China**, Hillman	$24.95
5564	Collector's Encyclopedia of **Pickard China**, Reed	$29.95
3877	Collector's Encyclopedia of **R.S. Prussia**, 4th Series, Gaston	$24.95
5679	Collector's Encyclopedia of **Red Wing Art Pottery**, Dollen	$24.95
5618	Collector's Encyclopedia of **Rosemeade Pottery**, Dommel	$24.95
5841	Collector's Encyclopedia of **Roseville Pottery**, Revised, Huxford/Nickel	$24.95
5842	Collector's Encyclopedia of **Roseville Pottery**, 2nd Series, Huxford/Nickel	$24.95
4713	Collector's Encyclopedia of **Salt Glaze Stoneware**, Taylor/Lowrance	$24.95
3314	Collector's Encyclopedia of **Van Briggle Art Pottery**, Sasicki	$24.95
4563	Collector's Encyclopedia of **Wall Pockets**, Newbound	$19.95
2111	Collector's Encyclopedia of **Weller Pottery**, Huxford	$29.95
5680	Collector's Guide to **Feather Edge Ware**, McAllister	$19.95
3876	Collector's Guide to **Lu-Ray Pastels**, Meehan	$18.95

3814	Collector's Guide to **Made in Japan Ceramics**, White	$18.95
4646	Collector's Guide to **Made in Japan Ceramics**, Book II, White	$18.95
2339	Collector's Guide to **Shawnee Pottery**, Vanderbilt	$19.95
1425	**Cookie Jars**, Westfall	$9.95
3440	**Cookie Jars**, Book II, Westfall	$19.95
4924	Figural & Novelty **Salt & Pepper Shakers**, 2nd Series, Davern	$24.95
2379	Lehner's Ency. of **U.S. Marks** on Pottery, Porcelain & China	$24.95
4722	**McCoy Pottery**, Collector's Reference & Value Guide, Hanson/Nissen	$19.95
5691	**Post86 Fiesta**, Identification & Value Guide, Racheter	$19.95
1670	**Red Wing Collectibles**, DePasquale	$9.95
1440	**Red Wing Stoneware**, DePasquale	$9.95
1632	**Salt & Pepper Shakers**, Guarnaccia	$9.95
5091	**Salt & Pepper Shakers** II, Guarnaccia	$18.95
3443	**Salt & Pepper Shakers** IV, Guarnaccia	$18.95
3738	**Shawnee Pottery**, Mangus	$24.95
4629	Turn of the Century **American Dinnerware**, 1880s–1920s, Jasper	$24.95
3327	**Watt Pottery** – Identification & Value Guide, Morris	$19.95

OTHER COLLECTIBLES

5838	Advertising **Thermometers**, Merritt	$16.95
4704	Antique & Collectible **Buttons**, Wisniewski	$19.95
2269	Antique **Brass & Copper** Collectibles, Gaston	$16.95
1880	Antique **Iron**, McNerney	$9.95
3872	Antique **Tins**, Dodge	$24.95
4845	Antique **Typewriters & Office Collectibles**, Rehr	$19.95
5607	Antiquing and Collecting on the **Internet**, Parry	$12.95
1128	**Bottle** Pricing Guide, 3rd Ed., Cleveland	$7.95
3718	Collectible **Aluminum**, Grist	$16.95
4560	Collectible **Cats**, An Identification & Value Guide, Book II, Fyke	$19.95
5060	Collectible **Souvenir Spoons**, Bednersh	$19.95
5676	Collectible **Souvenir Spoons**, Book II, Bednersh	$29.95
5666	Collector's Encyclopedia of **Granite Ware**, Book 2, Greguire	$29.95
5836	Collector's Guide to **Antique Radios**, 5th Ed., Bunis	$19.95
5608	Collector's Gde. to Buying, Selling & Trading on the **Internet**, 2nd Ed., Hix	$12.95
4637	Collector's Guide to **Cigarette Lighters**, Book II, Flanagan	$17.95
3966	Collector's Guide to **Inkwells**, Identification & Values, Badders	$18.95
4947	Collector's Guide to **Inkwells**, Book II, Badders	$19.95
5681	Collector's Guide to **Lunchboxes**, White	$19.95
5621	Collector's Guide to **Online Auctions**, Hix	$12.95
4862	Collector's Guide to **Toasters** & Accessories, Greguire	$19.95
4652	Collector's Guide to **Transistor Radios**, 2nd Ed., Bunis	$16.95
4864	Collector's Guide to **Wallace Nutting Pictures**, Ivankovich	$18.95
1629	**Doorstops**, Identification & Values, Bertoia	$9.95
5683	**Fishing Lure** Collectibles, 2nd Ed., Murphy/Edmisten	$29.95
5259	**Flea Market Trader**, 12th Ed., Huxford	$9.95
4945	**G-Men and FBI Toys** and Collectibles, Whitworth	$18.95
5605	**Garage Sale & Flea Market Annual**, 8th Ed.	$19.95
3819	**General Store** Collectibles, Wilson	$24.95
5159	Huxford's Collectible **Advertising**, 4th Ed.	$24.95
2216	**Kitchen Antiques**, 1790–1940, McNerney	$14.95
5686	**Lighting Fixtures** of the Depression Era, Book I, Thomas	$24.95
4950	The **Lone Ranger**, Collector's Reference & Value Guide, Felbinger	$18.95
2026	**Railroad** Collectibles, 4th Ed., Baker	$14.95
5619	**Roy Rogers and Dale Evans** Toys & Memorabilia, Coyle	$24.95
5692	**Schroeder's Antiques Price Guide**, 19th Ed., Huxford	$14.95
5007	**Silverplated Flatware**, Revised 4th Edition, Hagan	$18.95
5694	**Summers' Guide to Coca-Cola**, 3rd Ed.	$24.95
5356	**Summers' Pocket Guide to Coca-Cola**, 2nd Ed.	$9.95
3892	**Toy & Miniature Sewing Machines**, Thomas	$18.95
4876	**Toy & Miniature Sewing Machines**, Book II, Thomas	$24.95
5144	Value Guide to **Advertising Memorabilia**, 2nd Ed., Summers	$19.95
3977	Value Guide to **Gas Station Memorabilia**, Summers & Priddy	$24.95
4877	Vintage **Bar Ware**, Visakay	$24.95
4935	The W.F. Cody **Buffalo Bill** Collector's Guide with Values	$24.95
5281	**Wanted to Buy**, 7th Edition	$9.95

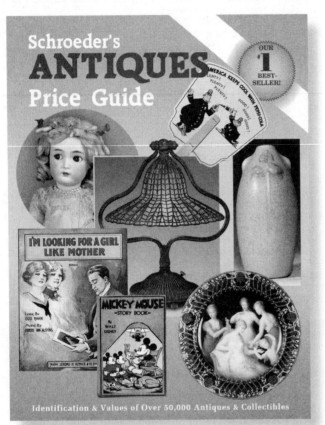